CRITICAL AND EXEGETICAL

HAND-BOOK

TO

THE GOSPEL OF JOHN.

BY

HEINRICH AUGUST WILHELM MEYER, Th.D.,

OBERCONSISTORIALRATH, HANNOVER.

TRANSLATED FROM THE FIFTH EDITION OF THE GERMAN BY
Rev. WILLIAM URWICK, M.A.

THE TRANSLATION REVISED AND EDITED BY
FREDERICK CROMBIE, D.D.,
PROFESSOR OF BIBLICAL CRITICISM, ST. MARY'S COLLEGE, ST. ANDREWS.

WITH A PREFACE AND SUPPLEMENTARY NOTES TO THE AMERICAN EDITION BY
A. C. KENDRICK, D.D.,
GREEK PROFESSOR IN THE UNIVERSITY OF ROCHESTER.

ALPHA PUBLICATIONS
P. O. BOX 655
WINONA LAKE, IN   46950

Reprinted 1980

First English edition T & T. Clark 1883
Funk & Wagnalls 1884
Alpha Publications 1979

Last printed in 1906. This 1979 edition by ALPHA
PUBLICATIONS is an exact reprint of the 6th edition of
1884.

Published by ALPHA PUBLICATIONS.

H. A. W. Meyer's COMMENTARY ON THE NEW
TESTAMENT is a part of THE ALPHA GREEK LIBRARY.

Printed in the United States of America.

PREFACE

TO THE AMERICAN EDITION.

THE Gospel of John stands pre-eminent among the Gospels, as does Paul's Epistle to the Romans among the New Testament Epistles. It is, indeed, except in the identity of their fundamental principles, as unlike it as possible. It does not forge, link by link, a chain of impassioned argument, and construct a reasoned system of Christian doctrine, but, in simplest and half-fragmentary utterances, brings out those sublime truths in which the entire doctrinal system finds its centre and foundation. Its eagle flight springs directly to the skies, and it exhibits the sublime Being who is its subject, not springing amidst the changes of time and the weaknesses of humanity, but having His home in the bosom of the Father and the deeps of eternity. Beyond either of its fellows it opens to our vision the spiritual world, and portrays the kingdom of heaven, not in its more earthly guise and human manifestations, but in its origin in the counsels of eternal love, and in the heavenly truths which originate and underlie it. Its unique and marvellous opening condenses within its compass a whole system of Theology, in the person of Him who to a world of sin and error comes with grace and truth, and to a world of death and darkness, with life and light. And the entire work is in keeping with the Prologue. It is throughout, like the seamless robe of the crucified Lord, consistent and harmonious. There is in its plan and purpose no momentary wavering. All its topics are so selected and treated as to subserve the unfolding of the grand truths proclaimed in its introduction, to show us the very heavens opened, and the Son of God and the Son of Man, in the paradoxical harmony of this twofold nature, re-establishing the suspended intercourse between earth and heaven.

The unerring instinct of infidelity has discerned in this Gospel the real battle-ground of Christian Apologetics, and has felt that if the authenticity and authority of this production could be discredited the whole evangelical system shares its discomfiture, and the battle of unbelief is virtually won. Hence it has labored, with equal zeal, learning,

and acuteness, to find evidence of its later origin or mythical character, and establish the radical unlikeness of the Jesus of the Fourth
Gospel to Him who is delineated by the Synoptists, and make out between them irreconcilable contradictions.

And there seems at first view much to sustain these assumptions.
The Jesus of our Gospel is indeed ushered to our view in a very different manner, and presents in His character some striking diversities of
feature and coloring. Yet a deeper penetration and a longer survey dis-
solve the apparent contradictions : the inconsistencies disappear ; the
difference of situations accounts for the difference in the subjects and
mode of treatment, and the many-sided, or rather myriad-sided, character
of the Lord, answering to the myriad lights in which its varied relations
present it, appears rounded into symmetry and completeness, not a
single feature but harmonizing with, and at last appearing logically demanded by, every other feature of the wondrous portraiture. The character, as it rises under the handling of its different portrayers, appears in
perfect harmony with itself, all that is unfolded in John being poten-
tially and in germ contained in its sister Gospels, and all that is unfolded at length by the Synoptists being really presupposed in John as its
logical consequence or condition, while the whole together forms a
character drawn with the utmost freedom and independence, with fear-
lessness of any slight and seemingly discrepant deviations, and exhibiting
a personality and a life to which the annals of the world furnish no parallel, which no human imagination could possibly have created, and
whose *existence* on the historic canvas proves its reality and its divinity.

The instinct of the Church too, no less keen than that of infidelity, has
settled the question of the substantial accordance of this Gospel with its
fellows. Had they been really contradictory, either this or the others
would have been long ago discredited. They would not have been suffered
for all these centuries to repose side by side in loving fellowship, the Gospel of the beloved disciple crowning and completing the others, and
putting on their work its grand climax : they constituting, as it were,
the body, this " the heart of Christ ;" they conducting us *about* Mount
Zion, this leading us into its inner temple ; each contributing its separate
share to the marvellous individuality ; but finally the fourth, latest in time,
unique in character, simple with the simplicity of a child, but sublime
with seraphic sublimity, breathing the spirit of the disciple who had lain
upon his Master's bosom, and sharing the very fulness of those spiritual
influences which it so fully promises as the gift of the glorified Messiah.

In Meyer our Gospel finds a fitting commentator. The great
merits of Meyer as a Biblical expositor are too universally known to
need dwelling upon here, and for the work of expounding this Gos-

pel he has some very special qualifications. To his wide learning, his philological exactness, his exegetical tact and acuteness, his independence and candour, he adds a hearty and loving sympathy with his author that is among the surest aids to a right understanding of him. With a hearty interest in Biblical truth generally, an interest which evidently grew by what it fed on, Meyer has an especial love for the Gospel of John. He has a thorough conviction of its authenticity and its complete apostolic authority, such a sympathy both with the Beloved Disciple and his Master, as it would seem could only have grown out of deep communion with that Master's person and discourses. The miraculous works and the theanthropic nature of the Lord he fully recognizes, and constantly discerns, under different forms of conception, the essential agreement of the Johannean and Pauline Christology.

To the historical statements of our Gospel, Meyer awards his fullest confidence. Indeed, it may be questioned whether he is not unduly partial towards our Gospel, and willing sometimes to yield to it an honour which places the others at comparative disadvantage. Believing as does the present writer firmly in the substantial inspiration and historical reliableness of all the Gospel records, it is not pleasant to see any of them, even confessedly the most spiritual, unduly exalted over its fellows, and awarded, at their expense, the palm of historical credibility. Meyer partakes the loose notions of inspiration so prevalent in Germany, and carrying out his views allows himself to draw distinctions between the Gospels which are not justified by the evidence. To those who have carefully weighed all the evidence, and surveyed the phenomena in their totality, it would seem that even independently of the question of inspiration, *all* the Gospels have proved their claim to credibility as faithful records of the life of Jesus, and that we both have a right, and are logically bound, in judging them, to proceed upon the assumption that their confessedly fragmentary notices are equally faithful ; are in themselves fairly reconcilable, and that where we cannot unite them into a harmonious whole, the fault must be in our lack of information rather than in the truthfulness of records. The Gospels are all clearly in a sense fragmentary. None of them pretends to give a complete account of the Lord's ministry ; each of them manifestly passes over large sections both of the time and field of His labours ; and none attempts to show where and why the deficiencies occur. In these cases it is both our duty and our privilege, on the one hand, to read each record by itself, and get its full legitimate individual impression, and on the other to bring them into close and constant comparison, fill out as far as we can their respective vacancies, and take for granted that where we cannot, the reason does not lie in any real lack of harmony. The "harmonistic presuppositions," which Meyer occasionally mentions not very respectfully, seem to me, while they of course are to be applied always cautiously and with judgment, to be yet among the indispensable qualifications of a complete interpreter of the Gospels. It must be both his pleasure and his duty to blend the fourfold narrative into the harmony which the totality of the evidence shows *must* belong to it.

In aiding to bring this Commentary of Meyer in a new form before the American public, the editor will state briefly what he has, at the request of the publishers, attempted. First, he has transferred to the bottom of the page most of its numerous references to the classics and other illustrative works, so as, without lessening its scholarly value, to present a more continuous and readable text. Secondly, he has appended to the several chapters a few notes, partly such as might counteract for the general reader the unfortunate influence of Meyer's free notions of inspiration, and his too great readiness to find discrepancies between John and his fellow-Evangelists. He could, however, by no means call special attention to all such cases, and in those which he has noticed he has in no instance denied a discrepancy where in his opinion the *evidence* did not warrant the denial. On various other points also the editor has added notes, generally, though not exclusively, where he dissented from Meyer's views. The limits of some twenty to twenty-five pages to which he was restricted necessarily precluded, even were there no other hindrances, his commenting upon very many of the almost numberless topics of interest comprised in this Gospel. The points of discussion have been partly such as he was specially interested in, and partly selected somewhat at random, while many on which the editor would have been glad to remark have been necessarily passed in silence. He cannot but hope that, such as they are, they will not be wholly void of interest and profit to the students of this Gospel.

Most readers of John are doubtless aware that this along with some other volumes of Meyer has been recently edited in Germany, with great freedom and ability, by Dr. Bernhard Weiss. As the publishers proposed to reprint Meyer without alteration, only occasional use could be made of Weiss's labours. The editor has, however, had by him Weiss's work, and considering his great ability and eminence as a Biblical critic and theologian, deemed it proper, as often as convenient, to give Weiss's view, sometimes of assent, more frequently of dissent from those of his author. On occasional points in which Weiss agrees with Meyer, the editor has ventured to differ from them both. In all cases he would differ from such eminent men with modesty, but in most he has the comfort of reflecting that other equally eminent names can be cited in support of his opinions. In his own notes he has not cited many names or authorities. Such authorities are now very generally accessible, and the editor would not encumber his pages with unnecessary citations. In his extended note on the time of the Last Supper—on which he entertains very decided convictions—while he has read various recent discussions, he acknowledges special indebtedness to the articles on this subject of Dr. Edward Robinson in his N. T. Harmony and the Bib. Sacra, vol. ii. 1845. He is glad to learn that Dr. Ezra Abbot, whose recent lamented death has deprived our American Biblical scholarship of one of its brightest ornaments, takes the same view with that eminent scholar of this alleged disagreement in the Gospels. It is also pleasant to reflect that one of the latest efforts of Dr. Abbot's distinguished pen was directed to setting forth the external evidences of the authenticity of the Fourth Gospel, on which subject his researches shed some important light. He had it in his purpose, I believe, to devote another essay to the internal branch of the inquiry.

The translation here given is not quite an exact reprint of the English original. That work, though done with conscientious fidelity, has been subjected to considerable revision, both for the removal of occasional errors and for greater smoothness and sometimes perspicuity of style. Still, the editor is but partially responsible either for the defects or the excellences of the translation. Meyer's numerous references he believes to be given with great accuracy. The references to Winer's N. T. Grammar have been made to conform in this edition to Thayer's translation. Those made to Buttmann's N. T. Grammar conform in the English work to the American edition.

The Topical Index at the end of the volume has been prepared by the Rev. G. F. Behringer, of Brooklyn, N. Y., who has kindly exercised a general supervision of the work while passing through the press.

In conclusion, while expressing his hope and prayer that this Commentary in its new form may subserve the interests of Biblical truth, and aid to the deeper study of this thrice-precious portion of the Sacred Word, the editor takes the liberty to borrow from Rev. Dr. Schaff's Introduction to his edition of Lange's Commentary on this Gospel the following beautiful Latin characterization of its human author, by Adam of St. Victor, with its English translation by Dr. Washburn :

> Volat avis sine meta,
> Quo nec vates nec propheta
> Evolavit altius ;
> Tam implenda, quam impleta,
> Nunquam vidit tot secreta
> Purus homo purius.

Bird of God ! with boundless flight,
Soaring far beyond the height
    Of the bard or prophet old ;
Truth fulfilled and truth to be,
Never purer mystery
    Did a purer tongue unfold.

A. C. KENDRICK.

ROCHESTER, *May*, 1884.

PREFACE.

The Gospel of John, on which I now for the fifth time present the result of my labours, still at the present day continues to be the subject —recently, indeed, brought once more into the very foreground—of so much doubt and dissension, and to some extent, of such passionate party controversy, as to increase the grave sense of responsibility, which already attaches to the task of an unprejudiced and thorough exposition of so sublime a production. The strong tendency now prevalent towards explaining on natural grounds the history of our Lord, ever calling forth new efforts, and pressing into its service all the aids of modern erudition, with an analytic power as acute as it is bold in its free-thinking, meets with an impassable barrier in this Gospel, if it really proceeds from that disciple whom the Lord loved, and consequently is the only one that is entirely and fully apostolic. For it is now an admitted fact, and a significant proof of the advances which have been gradually achieved by exegesis, that the pervading supranaturalism—clearly stamped on it in all the simplicity of truth—cannot be set aside by any artifices of exposition. This, however, does not prevent the work of a criticism, which obeys the conviction that it is *able*, and for the sake of the right knowledge of the Gospel history *ought*, to establish the non-apostolic origin of the fourth Gospel. Accordingly, in pursuance of the programme which was traced for it fifty years ago by Bretschneider, and of the ampler investigations subsequently added by the criticism of Baur, unwearied efforts have been made with augmented and more penetrating powers, and to some extent also with a cordial appreciation of the lofty ideas which the Gospel presents, to carry out this project to completion. Such critical labour submits itself to be tried by the judgment of scholars, and has its scientific warrant. Nay, should it succeed in demonstrating that the declaration of the Gospel's apostolic birth, as written by all the Christian centuries, is erroneous, we would have to do honour to the truth, which in this case also, though painful at first, could not fail to approve itself that which maketh free. There is, however, adequate reason to entertain very grave doubts of the attainment of this result, and to refuse assent to the prognostication of universal victory, which has been too hastily associated with these efforts of criticism. Whoever is acquainted with the most recent investigations, will, indeed, gladly leave to themselves the clumsy attempts to establish a parallelism between the Gospel of John and ancient fabrications concocted with a special aim, which carry their own impress on their face ; but he will still be unable to avoid the immediate and general duty of considering whether those modern investigators who deny that it is the work of the apostle have at least discovered a *time* in which—putting aside in the meanwhile all the substantive elements of their proof—the origin of the writing would be historically conceivable. For it is a remarkable circumstance in itself, that of the two most recent controversialists, who have treated the subject with the greatest scientific independence, the one assumes the latest, the other the earliest possible, date. If now, with the first, I place its composition not sooner than from 150 to 160, I see myself driven to the bold assertion of Volkmar, who makes the evangelist sit at the feet of Justin—a piece of daring which lands me in a historical absurdity. If I rightly shrink from so preposterous a view, and prefer to follow the thoughtful Keim in his more judicious estimate of the ecclesiastical testimonies and the relations of the time, then I obtain the very beginning of the second century as the period in which the work sprang up on the fruitful soil of the church of Asia Minor, as a plant Johannine indeed in spirit, but post-Johannine in origin. But from this position also I feel myself at once irresistibly driven. For I am now brought into such immediate contact with the days in which the aged apostolic pillar was still amongst the living, and see myself transported so entirely into the living presence of his numerous Asiatic disciples and admirers, that it cannot but appear to me an absolutely insoluble enigma how precisely *then* and *there* a non-Johannine work—one, moreover, so great and so divergent from the older Gospels—could have been issued and have passed into circulation under the name of the highly honoured apostle. Those disciples and admirers, amongst whom he, as the high priest, had worn the πέταλον, could not but know whether he had written a Gospel, and if so, of what kind ; and with the sure tact of sympathy and of knowledge, based upon experience, they could not but have rejected what was not a genuine legacy from their apostle. Keim, indeed, ventures upon the bold attempt of calling altogether in question the fact that John had his sphere of labour in Asia Minor ; but is not this denial, in face of the traditions of the church, in fact an impossibility ? It is, and must remain so, as long as the truth of historical facts is determined by the criterion of historical testimony. Turning, then, from Volkmar to Keim, I see before my eyes the fate indicated by the old proverb : τὸν καπνὸν φεύγοντα εἰς τὸ πῦρ ἐκπίπτειν.

The necessary references have been made in the Introduction to the substantive grounds on which in recent years the assaults have been renewed against the authenticity of the Gospel, and there also the most recent apologetic literature upon the subject has been noticed. After all that has been said for and against up to the present time, I can have no hesitation in once more expressing my delight in the testimony of Luther —quoted now and again with an ironical smile—that "*John's Gospel is the only tender, right, chief Gospel, and is to be far preferred before the other three, and to be more highly esteemed.*"[1] In order to make the confession one's own, it is not necessary to be either a servile follower of Luther or a special adherent of the immortal Schleiermacher. I am neither the one nor the other, and in particular I do not share the individual, peculiar motive, as such, which underlies the judgment of the former.

Since the publication of the fourth edition of my Commentary (1862), many expository works upon John and his system of doctrine, and among these several of marked importance, have seen the light, along with many other writings and disquisitions,[2] which serve, directly or indirectly, the purpose of exposition. I may venture to hope that the consideration which I have bestowed throughout upon these literary accessions, in which the one aim is followed with very varying gifts and powers, has not been without profit for the further development of my

[1] So Luther, in that section of his Preface to the New Testament containing the superscription, "Which are the right and noblest books of the New Testament?" This section, however, is wanting in the editions of the New Testament subsequent to 1539, as also in the edition of the whole Bible of 1534.

[2] The essay of Riggenbach, "*Johannes der Apostel und der Presbyter*," in the *Jahrb. f. D. Theologie*, 1868, p. 319 ff., came too late for me to be able to notice it. It will never be possible, I believe, to establish the identity of the apostle with the presbyter, and I entertain no doubt that Eusebius quite correctly understood the fragment of Papias in reference to this point.—To my regret, I was unable, also, to take into consideration Wittichen's work, *Ueber den geschichtlichen Charakter des Evang. Joh.* The same remark applies to the third edition of Ebrard's *Kritik der evangel Geschichte*, which appeared in 1868, and in which I regret to observe a renewed display of the old vehemence of passion. Renan's *Life of Jesus*, even as it has now appeared in its thirteenth edition, I have, as formerly, left out of consideration.—The first part of Holtzmann's dissertation upon "The Literary Relation of John to the Synoptics" (Hilgenfeld's *Zeitschrift*, 1869, p. 62 ff.) has just been published, and the conclusion is still to follow. Of course, before the latter appears, no well-founded judgment can be passed upon this essay of this acute theologian ; but I have doubts whether it will ever be successfully shown that in the case of the fourth Gospel there is any dependence of a literary kind upon the Synoptics, especially upon the Gospel of Luke.

work, probably more by way of antagonism (especially towards Hengstenberg and Godet) than of agreement of opinion. In our like conscientious efforts after truth we learn from each other, even when our ways
diverge.

The statement of the readings of Tischendorf's text I was obliged to
borrow from the second edition of his *Synopsis*, for the reasons already
mentioned in the preface to the fifth edition of my Commentary on
Mark and Luke. The latest part of his *editio octava*, now in course of
appearance, was published last September, and extends only to John vi.
23, while the printing of my book had already advanced far beyond that
point. I may add that the deviations in the text of this *editio octava*
from that of the *Synopsis* in reference to the various readings noticed
in my critical annotations down to vi. 23, are not numerous, and scarcely
any of them are of importance exegetically. Of such a nature are those,
in particular, in which this highly meritorious critic had in his *Synopsis*
too hastily abandoned the Recepta,[1] and has now returned to it. I
would fain think that this may also be the case in future with many
other of the readings which he has now adopted, where apparently the
Cod. Sinait. has possessed for him too great a power of attraction.[2]

In conclusion, I have to ask for this renewed labour of mine the goodwill of my readers,—I mean such a disposition and tone in judging of
it as shall not prejudice the rights of critical truth, but shall yet with
kind consideration weigh the difficulties which are connected with the
solution of the task, either in itself, or amidst the rugged antagonisms of
a time so vexed with controversy as the present. So long as God shall
preserve to me in my old age the necessary measure of strength, I shall
continue my quiet co-operation, however small it may be, in the service
of biblical exegesis. This science has in fact, amid the dark tempests
of our theological and ecclesiastical crisis, in face of all agitations and
extravagances to the right and left, the clear and lofty vocation gradually,

---

[1] I. 18, where the *Synopsis* has μονογενὴς θεός, the *editio octava* has restored
ὁ μονογενὴς υἱός : iii. 13, where ὁ ὢν ἐν τῷ οὐρανῷ was deleted in the *Synopsis*, these words have again been received into the text.

[2] *E.g.* with the reading θαυμάζετε in v. 20 ; in the same way with φεύγει,
which is found *only* in א of all the Codd. In the great predominance of testimonies against it, I regard the former as the error of an ancient copyist, while
the latter appears to me as a marginal gloss, quite inappropriate to the strain
of tender feeling in which John speaks of Jesus, which perhaps originated in a
similar manner, as Chrysostom, while reading in the text ἀνεχώρησεν, says
by way of explanation, ὁ δὲ Χριστὸς φεύγει. Had φεύγει been the original reading, and had it been desired to replace it by a more becoming expression, then
probably ἐξένευσεν from v. 13, or ἀνῆλθεν in vi. 3, to which passage πάλιν in
ver. 15 points back, would have most naturally suggested themselves.

by means of its results,—which can be reached with certainty only through a purely historical method, and can be settled by no human confession of faith,—to make such contributions to the tumult of strife as must determine the course of a sound development, and finally form the standard of its settlement and the regulative basis of peace. And what writing of the New Testament can in such a relation stand higher, or be destined to produce a more effective union of spirits, than the wondrous Gospel of John, with its fulness of grace, truth, peace, light, and life? Our Lutheran Church, which was born with a declaration of war and had its confession completed amid controversy from without and within, has raised itself far too little to the serene height and tranquil perfection of this Gospel.

DR. MEYER.

Hanover, 1st December, 1868.

LIST OF COMMENTARIES

UPON

THE GOSPEL OF ST. JOHN.

[It has not been deemed necessary to include in the following list more than a *selection* from the works of those who have published commentaries upon St. John's Gospel. For full details upon the literature of the controversy regarding the authenticity and genuineness, the reader is referred, in addition to Meyer's own Introduction, vol. i., to the very copious account appended by Mr. Gregory to his translation of Luthardt's work on the authorship of the Gospel, recently published by the Messrs. Clark.]

ABBOT (Ezra) : Authorship of the Fourth Gospel : External Evidences.
Boston, 1880.
ALFORD (Henry) : Greek Testament with critically revised text and Commentary. 4 vols. London, 4th ed. 1859.
AGRICOLA (Francis) : Commentarius in Evangelium Ioannis. Coloniae, 1599.
ALESIUS (Alexander) : Commentarius in Evangelium Ioannis. Basileae, 1553.
AMYRALDUS (Moses) : Paraphrase sur l'évangile selon Saint Jean. Salmuri, 1651.
AQUINAS (Thomas) : Aurea Catena in Lucae et Ioannis Evangelia.
Venetiae, 1775. English translation, Oxford, 1841–45.
ARETIUS (Benedictus) : Commentarius in Evangelium Ioannis.
Lausannae, 1578.
ASTIE (S. J.) : Explication de l'évangile selon Saint Jean, avec une traduction nouvelle. Genève, 1864.
AUGUSTINE : Tractatus 124 in Ioannem. Ed. 1690, iii. p. 2. 290–826.
English translation, 2 vols. (T. & T. Clark, Edinburgh). 1873–74.

BAEUMLEIN (W.) : Commentar über das Evangelium Johannis. Stuttgart, 1863.
BAUMGARTEN (Crusius) : Theologische Auslegung der Johanneischen Schriften. 2 vols. Jena, 1844–45.
BAUMGARTEN (S. J.) : Auslegung des Evangelii Johannis, cum Jo. Salomonis Semleri praefatione. Halae, 1762.
BEZA (Theodore) : Commentarius in Novum Testamentum.
Geneva, 1556 ; ed. quinta, 1665.
BENGEL (J. A.) : Gnomon Novi Testamenti. Latest ed., London, 1862. English translation, 5 vols. and 3 vols. (T. & T. Clark). 1874.
BISPING (A.) : Exegetisches Handbuch zu den Evangelien, etc. Erklärung des Evangelium nach Johannes. Münster, 1869.
BROWN (Rev. David, D.D.) : Commentary on St. John (in his Commentary upon the Four Gospels). Glasgow, 1863.
BUCER (Martin) : Enarrationes in Ioannem. Argentorati, 1528.
BULLINGER (Henry) : Commentariorum in Evangelium Ioannis libri Septem.
Tiguri, 1543.

CALVIN (John) : Commentarius in Evangelium secundum Ioannem. Genevae, 1553, 1555 ; ed. Tholuck, 1833. Translated into English by Rev. W. Pringle. 1847.

CHRYSOSTOM : Homilies on the Gospel of St. John, translated with Notes and
    Indices. Library of the Fathers.   Oxford, 1848-52
CHYTRAEUS (Dav.) : Scholia in Evangelium Ioannis.
                                              Francofurti ad Moenum, 1588.
COOK (F. C.) : Holy Bible, with Explanatory and Critical Commentary by Clergy
    of the Anglican Church. 9 vols. The Gospel of John, with Introduc-
    tion and Notes, by B. F. Westcott.   Am. ed., New York, 1880.
CRUCIGER (Caspar) : Enarratio in Evangelium Ioannis.
                              Witembergae, 1540. Argentorati, 1546.
CYRILLUS (Alexandrinus) : Commentarii in Sancti Ioannis Evangelium. English
    translation by Dr. Pusey.   Oxford, 1875.

DANAEUS (Lamb.) : Commentarius in Ioannis Evangelium.   Genevae, 1585.
DE WETTE (W. M. L.) : Kurzgefasstes Exegetisches Handbuch zum Neuen Testa-
    ment. Kurze Erklärung des Evangeliums und der Briefe Johannes.
    Fünfte Ausgabe von B. Brückner.   Leipzig, 1863.
DUNWELL (Rev. F. H.) : Commentary on the authorized English version of the
    Gospel according to St. John.   London, 1872.

EBRARD (J. H. A.) : Das Evangelium Johannis und die neueste Hypothese
    über seine Entsehung.   Zürich, 1845.
ELLICOTT (C. J.) : New Testament Commentary for English Readers. Gospel
    according to John by H. W. Watkins. 3 vols.   New York.
EUTHYMIUS ZIGABENUS : Commentarius in IV. Evangelia, graece et latine, ed.
    Matthaei. 4 vols.   Berolini, 1845.
EWALD (H.) : Die Johanneischen Schriften übersetzt und erklärt. 2 vols.
                                                         Göttingen, 1862.

FERUS (J.) : In sacro sanctum Iesu Christi Evangelium secundum Joannem piae
    et eruditae juxta Catholicam doctrinam enarrationes. Numerous edi-
    tions.   Moguntiae, 1536. Romae, 1517.
FORD (J.) : The Gospel of John, illustrated from ancient and modern authors.
                                                         London, 1852.
FROMMANN (K.) : Der Johanneische Lehrbegriff in seinem Verhältnisse zur ge-
    sammten biblisch-christlichen Lehre dargestellt.   Leipzig, 1839.

GODET (F.) : Commentaire sur l'évangile de Saint Jean. 2 vols.
                                      Paris, 1863. [New ed. preparing.]
GROTIUS (H.) : Annotationes in Novum Testamentum. 9 vols.
                                                         Gröningen, 1826-34.

HEINSIUS (Dan.) : Aristarchus Sacer, sive ad Nonni in Joannem Metaphrasin
    exercitationes : accedit Nonni et sancti Evangelistae contextus.
                                           Lugduni Batavorum, 1627.
HEMMINGIUS (Nicol.) : Commentarius in Evangelium Joannis.   Basileae, 1591.
HENGSTENBERG (E. W.) : Commentar zum Evangelium Johannes. 2 vols.
    English translation (T. & T. Clark).   1865.
HEUBNER (H. L.) : Praktische Erklärung des Neuen Testaments. 2 vols.
    Evangelien des Lucas und Johannes 2d ed.   Potsdam, 1860.
HILGENFELD (A.) : Das Evangelium und die Briefe Johannis nach ihrem Lehr-
    begriff.   Halle, 1849.
HUNNIUS (Aegidius) : Commentarius in Iesu Christi Evangelium secundum
    Joannem.   Francofurti, 1585, 1591, 1595.
HUTCHINSON (G.) : Exposition of the Gospel of Jesus Christ according to John.
                                                         London, 1657.

JANSONUS (Jac.) : Commentarius in Joannis Evangelium.   Louanii, 1630.

KLEE (H.) : Commentar über das Evangelium nach Johannes.   Mainz, 1829.
KLOFUTAR (L) : Commentarius in Evangelium Joannis.   Viennae, 1862.
KÖSTLIN (C. R.) : Lehrbegriffe des Evangelium und der Briefe Johannis.
                                                         Berlin, 1843.
KUINOEL (Ch. G.) : Commentarius in Novi Testamenti libros Historicos. 4 vols.
                                                         Leipzig, 1825-43.

LAMPE (F. A.) : Commentarius analytico exegeticus, tam litteralis, quam realis
      Evangelii secundum Joannem.   III Tomi.
                        Amstelodami, 1724, 1726.   Basileae, 1725, 1726, 1727.
LANGE (T. G.) : Das Evangelium Johannis übersetzt und erklärt.
                                                          Weimar, 1797.
LANGE (J. P.) : Theolg : Homiletisch : Bibel Werk. Das Evangelium nach
      Johannis, 1860.   English translation, greatly enlarged.
                        Ed. Philip Schaff, London and Edinburgh, 1872–75.
LAPIDE (Cornel. à) : Commentaria in Scripturam Sacram.   10 vols.
                                                 (last ed.) Lugduni, 1865.
LASSUS (Gbr.) : Commentaire Philosophique sur l'évangile St. Jean.
                                                          Paris, 1838.
LÜCKE (G. Ch. F.) : Commentar über die Schriften Johannis.   4 vols.
                                                          Bonn, 1840–56.
LUTHARDT (Ch. E.) : Das Johanneische Evangelium nach seinen Eigenthüm-
      lichkeiten geschildert und erklärt. 2 vols. Nurnberg, 1852–53.   New
      ed. Part 1st, 1875.   (English translation preparing.)
LUTHARDT (C. E.) : St. John the author of the Fourth Gospel.   Translated by
      C. R. Gregory.   Edinburgh, 1875.

MAIER (Adal.) : Commentar zum Evangelium Johannis.   2 vols.
                                            Carlsruhe and Freiburg, 1843.
MALDONATUS : Commentarii in IV. Evangelia curavit Sauser.
                                                 Latest ed.   Mainz, 1840.
MATTHAEI (J.) : Auslegung des Evangelium Johannis zur Reform der Auslegung
      desselben.   Gothingen, 1837.
MELANCHTHON (Phil.) : Enarrationes in Evangelium Joannis.
                                                      Wittenbergae, 1523.
MORUS (S. F. N.) : Recitationes in Evangelium Joannis.   ed. G. J. Dindorf.
                                                          Leipzig, 1796.
MUNTER (J.) : Symbolae ad interpretandum Evangelium Johannis ex marmori-
      bus et nummis maxime graecis.   Kopenhagen, 1826.
MUSCULUS (Wolf G.) : Commentarii in Evangelium Joannis in tres Heptadas
      digesti.   Basileae, 1552, 1564, 1580, 1618.
MYLIUS (G.) : Commentarius in Evangelium Johannis absolutissimus.
                                                       Francofurti, 1624.

NONNUS : Metaphrasis Evangelii Johannis. red. Passow.   Leipzig, 1834.

OECOLAMPADIUS (I.) : Annotationes in Evangelium Johannis.   Basileae, 1532.
OLSHAUSEN (H.) : Biblischer Commentar über d. Neue Testament fortgesetzt
      von Ebrard und Wiesinger.   Evangelium des Johannes.   1862.
      English translation (T. & T. Clark).   1855.
ORIGEN : Commentarii in Evangelium Joannis.   ed. 1759, vol. iv. 1–460.

PARITIUS (F. H.) : In Joannem Commentarius.   Romae, 1863.
PAULUS (H. E. G.) : Philologisch-Kritischer und Historischer Commentar über
      das Evangelium des Johannes.   Leipzig, 1812.
PELARGUS (Christ.) : Commentarius in Joannem per quaesita et responsa, ex
      antiquitate orthodoxa magnam partem erutus.   Francofurti, 1559.

ROLLOCK (Rob.) : Commentarius in Evangelium Joannis.
                                                 Genevae, 1599, 1608.
ROSENMÜLLER (J. G.) : Scholia in Novum Testamentum.   5 vols.
                                                      Leipzig, 1815–31.

SARCERIUS (Erasm.) : In Johannis Evangelium Scholia justa ad perpetuae tex-
      tus cohaerentiae filum.   Basileae, 1540.
SCHAFF (Philip) : Popular Commentary on the New Testament. 4 vols.   The
      Gospel of John, by W. Milligan and W. F. Moulton.   New York, 1880.
SCHMID (Sebast.) : Resolutio brevis cum paraphrasi verborum Evangelii Joannis
      Apostoli.   Argentorati, 1685, 1699.

SCHLTEN (J. H.) : Het Evangelie naar Johannes.
    Leyden, 1865. Supplement 1866. French translation by Albert
    Reville in *Revue de Théologie*. Strasburg, 1864, 1866. German trans-
    lation by H. Lang, Berlin, 1867.
SCHWEIZER (Alb.) : Das Evangelium Johannis kritisch untersucht.
                                                          Leipzig, 1841.
SEMLER (J. Sal.) : Paraphrasis Evangelii Joannis, cum notis et Cantabrigiensis
    Codicis Latino textu.   Halae, 1771.

TARNOVIUS (Paul.) : In Sancti Johannis Evangelium Commentarius.
                                                         Rostochii, 1629.
THEODORE (of Mopsuestia) : In novum Testamentum Commentaria. Ed.
    Fritzsche.   Turici, 1847.
THOLUCK (A.) : Commentar zum Evangelium Johannis.
              7th ed. 1857. English translation (T. & T. Clark), 1860.
TITTMANN (K. Ch.) : Meletemata Sacra, sive Commentarius critico-exegeticus-
    dogmaticus in Evangelium Johannis.   Leipzig, 1816.
    (English translation in Biblical Cabinet, T. & T. Clark.)
TOLETUS (Franc.) : Commentarii et Annotationes in Evangelium Joannis.
          Romae, 1588, 1590 ; Lugduni, 1589, 1614 ; Venetii, 1587.

THE GOSPEL OF JOHN.

INTRODUCTION.

SEC. I.—BIOGRAPHICAL NOTICE OF JOHN.

THE parents of John were Zebedee, a fisherman on the Sea of Galilee, probably not of the poorer class (Mark i. 20 ; Luke v. 10), and Salome (Mark xv. 40 ; comp. Matt. xxvii. 56). To his father the evangelists ascribe no special religious character or personal participation in the events of the Gospel history ; but his mother was one of the women who followed Jesus even up to His crucifixion (comp. on xix. 25). To her piety, therefore, it is justly attributable that John's deeply receptive spirit was early fostered and trained to surrender itself to the sacredly cherished, and at that time vividly excited expectation of the Messiah, with its moral claims, so far as such a result might be produced by a training which was certainly not of a learned character. (Acts iv. 13.) If, too, as we may infer from xix. 25, Salome was a sister of the mother of Jesus, his near relationship to Jesus would enable us better to understand the close fellowship of spirit between them, though the evangelists are silent as to any early intimacy between the families ; and in any case, higher inward sympathy was the essential source out of which that fellowship of spirit unfolded itself. The entrance of the Baptist on his public ministry—to whom John had attached himself, and whose prophetical character and labours he has described most clearly and fully—was the occasion of his becoming one of the followers of Jesus, of whom he and Andrew were the first disciples (i. 35 f.). Among these, again, he and Peter, and his own brother James the elder, brought by himself to Jesus (see on i. 42), formed the select company of the Lord's more intimate friends ; he himself being the most trusted of all,[1] the one whom Jesus pre-eminently loved, and to whose filial care He on the cross entrusted Mary (xix. 26). Hence the ardent, impetuous disposition, which led the Lord Himself to give to him and his brother the name *Boanerges*, and which he

---

[1] On account of his devoted love to the person of the Lord, on which Grotius finely remarks : "Quod olim Alexandrum de amicis suis dixisse memorant, alium esse φιλα-λέξανδρον, alium φιλοβασιλέα, putem ad duos Domini Jesu apostolos posse aptari, ut Pe-trum dicamus maxime φιλόχριστον, Johannem maxime φιλοιησοῦν, . . . quod et Dominus respiciens, illi quidem *ecclesiam* praecipuo quodam modo, huic autem *ma-trem* commendavit."

exhibited on more than one occasion (Mark iii. 17, ix. 38 ff. ; Luke ix.
49 f., 54),—connected even though it was with an ambition which his
mother had fostered by her sensuous Messianic notions (Matt. xx. 20 ff. ;
Mark x. 35 ff.),—is by no means of such a character as to be incapable of
gradually subjecting itself to the mind of Jesus, and becoming serviceable
to his highest aims. After the ascension he abode, save perhaps when
engaged on some minor apostolical journey (such as that to Samaria, Acts
viii. 14), at Jerusalem, where Paul met with him as one of the three pillars
of the Christian church (Gal. ii. 1 ff.). How long he remained in this city
cannot, amid the uncertainty of tradition, be determined ; and, indeed, it is
not even certain whether he had already left the city when Paul was last
there. He is indeed not mentioned in Acts xxi. 18, but neither is he in
Acts xv., though we know from Gal. ii. 1 ff. that he nevertheless was
present ; and therefore, as on the occasion of Gal. i. 19, so on that of
Acts xxi., he may have been temporarily absent. In after years he took up
his abode at Ephesus,[1] probably only after the destruction of Jerusalem ;
not by any means, however, before Paul had laboured in Ephesus (Rom.
xv. 20 ; 2 Cor. x. 16 ; Gal. ii. 7 f.), although it cannot be maintained with
certainty that he could not have been there when Paul wrote his letter to
the Ephesians : for, in the enigmatic silence of this epistle as to all personal
references, such a conclusion from the non-mention of his name is doubtful.

The distinguished official authority with which he was invested at
Ephesus, the spiritual elevation and sanctity ascribed to him, cannot be
better indicated than by the fact that Polycrates (Euseb. iii. 31, v. 24) not
only reckons him among the μεγάλα στοιχεῖα (great fundamental elements of
the church ; comp. Gal. ii. 9), but also calls him ἱερεὺς τὸ πέταλον [2] πεφορηκώς.
Of his subsequent fortunes we have only untrustworthy and sometimes manifestly false traditions, amongst the latter of which is one based on Rev. i.
9,[3] but unknown even to Hegesippus (ap. Euseb. iii. 20), of his banishment

---

[1] Iren. *Haer.* iii. 3. 4 ; Euseb. iii. 1. 23. It
is no argument against this, that Ignat.
ad Ephes. 12 mentions Paul, but not John ;
for Paul is mentioned there as the *founder*
of the church at Ephesus, and as *martyr*,
—neither of which holds good of John.
Besides, this silence is far outweighed by
the testimonies of Polycarp in Irenaeus,
Polycrates in Euseb., Irenaeus, Clement of
Alexandria, Origen, Eusebius, etc. To account for these, as Keim in particular now
attempts to do (*Gesch. J.* I. p. 161 ff.), by
supposing some confusion of John the
Presbyter with the *Apostle* John, is in my
opinion futile, simply because the silence
of Papias as to the apostle's residence in
Asia proves nothing (he does not mention
the residence of *any* of the Lord's apostles
and disciples, to whom he makes reference), and because it seems scarcely conceivable that Irenaeus should have so misinterpreted what Polycarp said to him in

his youth regarding his intimacy with John,
as to suppose he spoke of the *Apostle*, when
in fact he only spoke of the *Presbyter* of that
name. It is pure caprice to assume that
Eusebius "*lacked the courage*" to correct
Irenaeus. Why so? See, on the other hand,
Steitz in the *Studien u. Kritiken*, 1868, p.
502 ff.

[2] The plate of gold worn by the high
priest on his forehead. See Ewald, *Alterth.*
p. 393 f., ed. 3; Knobel on Ex. xxviii. 36.
The phrase used by Polycrates is not to be
taken as signifying relationship to a priestly
family (xviii. 15 ; Luke i. 36), but as *symbolic*
of high *spiritual* position in the *church*, just
as it is also used of James the Lord's
brother in Epiphanius, *Haer.* xxix. 4. Compare now also Ewald, *Johann. Schriften*, II.
p. 401 f.

[3] See especially Düsterdieck on the *Revelation, Introduction*, p. 92 ff.

to Patmos under Domitian (first mentioned by Irenæus and Clem. Alex.), —an event said to have been preceded by others of a marvellous kind, such as his drinking poison at Rome without injury (see especially the Acta Johannis in Tischendorf's *Acta Apocr.* p. 266 ff.), and his being thrown into boiling oil, from which, however, he came out "nihil passus" (Tertullian), nay, even "purior et vegetior" (Jerome). The legend is also untrustworthy of his encounter with Cerinthus in a bath, the falling in of which he is said to have foreseen and avoided in time (Iren. *Haer.* iii. 3. 28 ; Euseb. iii. 28, iv. 14) ; it is only indirectly traceable to Polycarp, and betrays a purpose of glorifying the apostle at the expense of the heretic, however unfounded may be the assumption that it is only what we should expect from the author of the Apocalypse (Baur, *Kanon. Evang.* p. 371). The great age to which John attained, which is variously stated,—according to Irenæus, Eusebius, and others, about a hundred years, reaching down to Trajan's time,—gave some countenance to the saying (xxi. 23) that he should not see death ; and this again led to the report that his death, which at last took place at Ephesus, was only a slumber, his breath still moving the earth on his grave (Augustine). In harmony, however, with a true idea of his character, though historically uncertain, and first vouched for by Jerome on Gal. vi. 10,[1] is the statement that, in the weakness of old age, he used merely to say in the Christian assemblies, *Filioli, diligite alterutrum.* For *love* was the most potent element of his nature, which was sustained by the truest, deepest, and most affectionate communion in heart and life with Christ. In this communion John, nurtured on the heart of Jesus, discloses, as no other evangelist, the Lord's *innermost* life, in a contemplative but yet practical manner, with a profound idealizing mysticism, though far removed from all mere fiction and visionary enthusiasm ; like a bright mirror, faithfully reflecting the most delicate features of the full glory of the Incarnate One (i. 14 ; 1 John i. 1) ; tender and humble, without sentimentalism, and with all the resolute earnestness of apostolical energy. In the centre of the church life of Asia he shone with the splendour of a spiritual highpriesthood, the representative of all true Christian Gnosis, and personally a very παρθένιος ("virgo mente et corpore," Augustine) in all moral purity. From the starting-point of an apostle of the Jews, on which he stands in contrast (Gal. ii. 9) with the apostle of the Gentiles, he rose to the purest universalism, such as we meet with only in Paul, but with a clear, calm elevation above strife and conflict ; as the last of the apostles, going beyond not only Judaism, but even Paul himself, and interpreting most completely out of his own lengthened, pure, and rich experience, the life and the light made manifest in Christ. He it is who most fully

---

[1] Earlier attested (Clemens, *Quis. div. salv.* 42) is the equally characteristic legend (Clement calls it μῦθον οὐ μῦθον, ἀλλὰ ὄντα λόγον) of a young man, formerly converted by the apostle's labours, who lapsed and became a leader of robbers, by whose band John, after his return from Patmos, voluntarily allowed himself to be taken prisoner in order to bring their captain back to Christ, which he succeeded in doing by the mere power of his presence. The robber chief, as Clement says, was baptized a second time by his tears of penitence. Comp. Herder's legend "*der gerettete Jüngling*" in his *Werke z. schön. Lit.* vi. p. 31, ed. 1827.

connects Christianity with the person of Christ,—a legacy to the church for all time, of peace, union, and ever advancing moral perfection ; among the apostles the true gnostic, in opposition to all false Gnosticism of the age ; the prophet among the evangelists, although not the seer of the Apocalypse. "The personality of John," says Thiersch,[1] "has left far deeper traces of itself in the church than that of any other of Christ's disciples. Paul laboured more than they all, but John stamped his image most deeply upon her ;" the former in the mighty *struggle* for the victory, which *overcometh* the world ; the latter in the sublime and, for the whole future of the gospel, decisive celebration of the victory which *has overcome* it.

SEC. II.—GENUINENESS OF THE GOSPEL.

With regard to the *external testimonies*, we remark the following :—

1. Chap. xxi. could only serve as a testimony, if it proceeded altogether from another hand, or if the obviously spurious conclusion should be made to include ver. 24. See, however, on chap. xxi.—2 Pet. i. 14 also, and the Gospel of Mark, cannot be adduced as testimonies ; since the former passage cannot be shown to refer to John xxi. 18 f., while the second Gospel was certainly written much earlier than the fourth.

2. In the apostolical Fathers[2] we meet with no express quotation from, or sure trace of any use of, the Gospel. Barnabas 5, 6, 12 (comp. John iii. 14), and other echoes of John in this confused anti-Judaizing epistle, to which too great importance is attached by Keim, as well as Herm. *Past. Simil.* 9, 12 (comp. John x. 7, 9, xiv. 6), Ignat. *ad Philad.* (comp. John iii. 8) 9 (comp. John x. 9), *ad Trall.* 8 (comp. John vi. 51), *ad Magnes.* 8 (comp. John x. 30, xii. 49, xiv. 11), *ad Rom.* 7 (John vi. 32 ff., vii. 38 f.), are so adequately explained by tradition, and the common types of view and terminology of the apostolical age, that it is very unsafe to attribute them to some definite written source. Nor does what is said in Ignat. *ad Rom.* 7, and *ad Trall.* 8, of Christ's flesh and blood, furnish any valid exception to this view, since the *origin* of the mystical conception of the σάρξ of Christ is not necessarily due to its dissemination through this Gospel, although it does not occur in the Synoptics.[3] Hence the question as to the

---

[1] *Die Kirche im apostol. Zeitalt.* p. 273.

[2] It is true that Barnabas, 4, quotes, with the formula *sicut scriptum est* (which is confirmed, against Credner, by the Greek text of the Codex Sinaiticus), a passage from Matthew (xx. 16, xxii. 14; not 2 Esdr. viii. 3, as Volkmar maintains). To find, however, in this alone canonical confirmation of the *fourth* Gospel (Tischendorf) is too rash a conclusion, since the close joint relation of the four, as composing one fourfold Gospel, cannot be proved so early as the apostolical Fathers ; nor do even Justin's citations exhibit any *such* corpus evangel-

icum. Besides, that very remarkable ὡς γέγραπται makes it probable that the passage in Matthew may have erroneously appeared to the writer of the epistle as taken from the *Old Testament.*—Again, it is incorrect to say (with Volkmar) that the citation in Barnabas 5 of Ps. xxii. 21 tells *against* our Gospel, since that citation has no bearing on the spear-thrust spoken of in xix. 34, but simply refers to death on the *cross* as such, in contrast with death by the *sword.*

[3] In opposition to Rothe, *Anfänge d. Chr. Kirch.* p. 715 ff. ; Huther, in *Illgen's Zeitschr.*

genuineness of the several epistles of Ignatius, and their texts, may here be altogether left out of consideration. Just as little from the testimony of Irenaeus *ad Florin.* (ap. Eus. v. 20) to Polycarp, that in all which the latter has spoken of Christ he has spoken σύμφωνα ταῖς γραφαῖς, may we infer any use of our Gospel on Polycarp's part, considering the generality of this expression, which, moreover, merely sets forth Irenaeus' opinion, and does not necessarily mean *New Testament* writings. When, again, Irenaeus[1] quotes an interpretation given by the "*presbyteri apostolorum discipuli*" of the saying in John xiv. 2 ("*In my Father's house*," etc.), it must remain doubtful whether these *presbyteri* knew that saying from our Gospel or from apostolical tradition, since Irenaeus quotes their opinion simply with the general words : καὶ διὰ τοῦτο εἰρηκέναι τὸν κύριον.

3. Of indirect but decided importance, on the other hand,—assuming, that is, what in spite of the doubts still raised by Scholten must be regarded as certain, that the Gospel and First Epistle of John are from one author, —is the use which, according to Euseb. iii. 39, Papias[2] made of the First Epistle. That in the fragment of Papias no mention is made of our *Gospel*, should not be still continually urged (Baur, Zeller, Hilgenf., Volkmar, Scholten) as a proof, either that he did not know it, or at least did not acknowledge its authority (see below, No. 8). Decisive stress may also be laid on Polycarp, *ad Phil.* 7 (πᾶς γὰρ ὃς ἂν μὴ ὁμολογῇ Ἰησοῦν Χριστὸν ἐν σαρκὶ ἐληλυθέναι ἀντίχριστός ἐστι), as a quotation from 1 John iv. 3 ; Polycarp's chapter containing it being unquestionably genuine, and free from the interpolations occurring elsewhere in the Epistle. It is true that it may be said, "What can such general sentences, which may have circulated anonymously, prove ?"[3] but it may be answered that that characteristic type of this fundamental article of the Christian system, which in the above form is quite peculiar to the First Epistle of John, points to the evangelist in the case of no one more naturally than of Polycarp, who was for so many years his disciple.[4] It is nothing less than an unhistorical inversion of the relations between them, when some (Bretschneider, and again Volkmar) represent John's Epistle as dependent on Polycarp's, while Scholten tries to make out a difference in the application and sense of the respective passages.

4. It is true that Justin Martyr, in his citations from the ἀπομνημονεύματα τῶν ἀποστόλων ("ἃ καλεῖται εὐαγγέλια," *Apol.* I. 66), which also served as church lessons,[5] has not used *exclusively* our canonical Gospels (the older

---

1841, iv. p. 1 ff. ; Ebrard, *Evang. Joh.* p. 102 ; *Kritik d. evang. Gesch.* ed. 2, p. 840 ff. ; Tischend. Ewald *Jahrb.* V. p. 188, etc.

[1] *Hær.* v. 36. 1 f.

[2] A disciple of the *Presbyter* John. From the fragments of Papias in Eusebius, it is abundantly clear that he mentions *two different* disciples of the Lord called John,— John the *Apostle*, and John the *Presbyter*, who was not one of the twelve, but simply a disciple, like Aristion. The attempt to make the Presbyter, in the quotation from Papias, no other than the Apostle, leads

only to useless controversy. See especially Overbeck in Hilgenfeld's *Zeitschr.* 1867, p. 35 ff. ; Steitz in the *Stud. u. Krit.* 1868, p. 63 ff., in opposition to Zahn in the *Stud. u. Krit.* 1866, pp. 649 ff.

[3] Baur, *Kanon. Evangel.* p. 350.

[4] Comp. Ewald, *Johann. Schriften*, II. p. 395.

[5] For the course of the discussions upon Justin's quotations, and the literature of the subject, see Volkmar, *Ueb. Justin d. M. u. s. Verh. z. uns. Evangelien*, 1853 ; Hilgenfeld, *Evangelien*, 1855 ; Volkmar, *Urspr. d.*

view, and still substantially held by Bindemann [1] and Semisch ; [2] also by Luthardt, Tischendorf, and Riggenbach); but neither has he used *merely* an "uncanonical" Gospel (Schwegler), or *chiefly* such a one (Credner, Volkmar, Hilgenfeld), as was " a special recension of that Gospel to the Hebrews which assumed so many forms" (Credner, *Gesch. d. Kanon*, p. 9). For he used *alike* our canonical Gospels, and in addition other evangelic writings *now lost*, which—rightly or wrongly—he must have looked upon as proceeding from the apostles, or from disciples of theirs (comp. *Tryph.* 103 : ἐν γὰρ τοῖς ἀπομνημονεύμασιν, ἅ φημι ὑπὸ τῶν ἀποστόλων αὐτοῦ καὶ τῶν ἐκείνοις παρακολουθησάντων συντετάχθαι); in which his deviations from our canonical Gospels hardly agree more than once or twice with the Clementines. His *Apologies* certainly belong (see *Apol.* i. 46) to somewhere about the middle of the second century. [3] His citations, even when they can be referred to our canonical Gospels, are generally free, so that it is often doubtful where he got them. [4] From Matthew and Luke only five are verbally exact. He has also borrowed from John, [5] and indeed so evidently, that those who would deny this are in consistency obliged, with Volkmar, to represent John as making use of Justin, which is an absurdity.

Evang. 1866, p. 92 ff. See also in particular, Luthardt, *Justin d. M. u. d. Joh. Evang.*, in the *Erlanger Zeitschr. f. Protest. u. K.* 1856, xxxi. parts 4–6, xxxii. parts 1 and 2 ; Ewald, *Jahrb.* VI. 59 ff. ; Riggenbach, *Zeugn. f. d. Ev. Joh.* p. 139 ff.

[1] *Stud. u. Krit.* 1842, p. 355 ff.

[2] *D. apost. Denkw. Justins*, 1848.

[3] The controversy as to the date of the first Apology (Semisch, A.D. 138–139 ; Volkmar, about 147 ; Keim, 155–160) need not here be discussed, since in any case our Gospel is in the same position as the Synoptics, so far as Justin's use and estimate of it are concerned.

[4] See Credner, *Beitr*, I. p. 151 ff. ; Frank, in the *Würtemb. Stud.* XVIII. p. 61 ff. ; Hilgenf. *Krit. Untersuch. üb. die Evang. Justins*, etc., 1850 ; Volkmar *ueber Justin*.

[5] He has made most use of Matthew, and then of the Pauline Luke, but also of Mark. That he has taken very little comparatively from John, seems to be due to the same reason as his silence in respect of Paul, which is not tantamount to an exclusion of the apostle of the Gentiles ; for he is rich in Pauline ideas, and there can be no mistake as to his knowledge of Paul's epistles (Semisch, p. 123 ff.). It is probably to be explained by prudential consideration for the antagonism of the Jewish Christians to Paul's (and John's) anti-Judaism. In the obvious possibility of this circumstance, it is too rash to conclude that this Gospel had not yet won the high authority which it could not have failed to have, *had it really*

been *a work of the apostle* (Weisse, *d. Evangelienfr.* p. 129) ; or even, that "had Justin known the fourth Gospel, he would have made, not only repeated and ready, but even preferential use of it. To assume, therefore, the use of only one passage from it on Justin's part, is really to concede the point" (Volkmar, *üb. Justin*, p. 50 f. ; Zeller, p. 650). The Clementine Homilies (see hereafter under 5) furnish an analogous phenomenon, in that they certainly knew and used our Gospel, while yet borrowing very little from it. The synoptic evangelic literature was the older and more widely diffused ; it had already become familiar to the most diverse Christian circles (comp. Luke i. 1), when John's Gospel, which was so very dissimilar and peculiar, and if not *esoteric* (Weizsäcker), certainly *antichiliastic* (Keim), made its appearance. How conceivable that the latter, though the work of an apostle, should only very gradually have obtained general recognition and equal authority with the Synoptics among the Jewish Christians! how conceivable, therefore, also, that a man like Justin, though no Judaizer, should have hesitated to quote from it in the same degree as he did from the Synoptics, and the other writings connected with the Synoptic cycle of narratives ! The assumption that *he had no occasion* to refer frequently and expressly to John (Luthardt, *op. cit.* p. 398) is inadmissible. He might often enough, where he has other quotations, have quoted quite as appropriately from John.

See Keim, *Gesch. J.* I. p. 137 ff. It is true that some have found in too many passages references to this Gospel, or quotations from it ;[1] still we may assume it as certain, that as, in general, Justin's whole style of thought and expression implies the existence of John's writings,[2] so, in the same way, must the mass of *those* passages in particular be estimated, which, in spite of all variations arising from his Alexandrine recasting of the dogma, correspond with *John's doctrine of the Logos.*[3] For Justin was conscious that his doctrine, especially that of the Logos, which was the central point in his Christology, had an *apostolic* basis,[4] just as the ancient church in general, either expressly or as a matter of course, traced the origin of its doctrine of the Logos to John. It is therefore unhistorical, in the special case of Justin, merely to point to an acquaintance with Philo, and to the Logos-speculations and Gnostic ideas of the age generally (against Zeller, Baur, Hilgenf., Scholten, and many others), or to satisfy oneself possibly with the assumption that Paul furnished him with the premisses for his doctrine (Grimm in the *Stud. u. Krit.* 1851, p. 687 ff.), or even to make the fourth evangelist a pupil of Justin (Volkmar). It seems, moreover, certain that *Apol.* i. 61, καὶ γὰρ Χριστὸς εἶπεν· ἂν μὴ ἀναγεννηθῆτε, οὐ μὴ εἰσέλθητε εἰς τὴν βασιλείαν τῶν οὐρανῶν. Ὅτι δὲ καὶ ἀδίνατον εἰς τὰς μήτρας τῶν τεκουσῶν τοὺς ἅπαξ γεννωμένους ἐμβῆναι, φανερὸν πᾶσίν ἐστι, is derived from John iii. 3–5. See especially Semisch, p. 189 ff. ; Luthardt, *l.c.* XXXII. p. 93 ff. ; Riggenb. p. 166 ff. It is true, some have assigned this quotation through the medium of Matt. xviii. 3, to the Gospel to the Hebrews, or some other uncanonical evangelic writing (Credner, Schwegler, Baur, Zeller, Hilgenfeld, Volkmar, Scholten), or have treated it as a more original form of the mere oral tradition (see Baur, against Luthardt, in the *Theol. Jahrb.* 1857, p. 232). But in the face of Justin's free mode of citation, to which we must at-

---

[1] See against this, Zeller, *Theol. Jahrb.* 1845, p. 600 ff.

[2] Comp. Ewald, *Jahrb.* V. p. 186 f.

[3] See Duncker, *d. Logoslehre Justins d. M.*, Göttingen 1848, and Luthardt as above, xxxii. pp. 69 ff., 75 ff. ; Weizsäcker in the *Jahrb. f. D. Theol.* 1862, p. 703 ff. ; Tischendorf, *wann wurden uns. Ev. verf.* p. 31 ff., ed. 4 ; Weizsäcker, *d. Theol. d. M. Just.*, in the *Jahrb. f. D. Theol.* 1867, p. 78 ff. Great weight is due to Justin's doctrine of the *incarnation* of the Logos (*Apol.* i. 32, 66 ; *c. Tryph.* 100), which is foreign to the system of Philo, etc., and is specially Johannean.

[4] Hence his frequent reference to the ἀπομνημονεύματα τῶν ἀποστόλων. On one occasion led to do so casually, because he is speaking directly of Peter, he refers definitely to the ἀπομνημονεύματα τοῦ Πέτρου (*c. Tryph.* 106 : μετανομακέναι αὐτὸν Πέτρον ἕνα τῶν ἀποστόλων καὶ γεγράφθαι ἐν τοῖς ἀπομνημονεύμασιν αὐτοῦ, κ.τ.λ. Here Credner (*Beitr.* I. p. 132 ; *Gesch. d. Kanon*, p. 17) quite correctly referred αὐτοῦ to Πέτρον (Lücke conjectures that αὐτοῦ is spurious, or that τῶν ἀποστόλων is to be inserted, so that αὐτοῦ would refer to Jesus), but he understood these ἀπομν. to be the apocryphal Gospel of Peter, — the more groundlessly, that the substance of Justin's quotation is from Mark iii. 17. Justin understood by ἀπομνη. τοῦ Πέτρου the *Gospel of Mark*. So also Luthardt, *op. cit.* xxxi. p. 316 ff. ; Weiss, in the *Stud. u. Krit.* 1861, p. 677 ; Riggenb. and others ; comp. Volkmar, *Urspr. d. Evang.* p. 154. According to Tertullian, *c. Marc.* iv. 5, "Marcus quod edidit evangelium, *Petri* adfirmatur, cujus interpres Marcus." Comp. Irenaeus also, iii. 10. 6, iii. 1. 1. According to this, compared with what Papias says of Mark, Justin might have expressed himself exactly as he has done. With respect to the controversy on the subject, see Hilgenfeld, *Krit. Unters.* p. 23 ff., and Luthardt, *l.c.*; comp. on Mark, Introduction. Notice also how unfavourable the passage seems to the notion that Justin's *Memorials* are a *compilation* (Ewald and others).

tribute the ἀναγενν. instead of γενν. ἀ ν ω θ ε ν,—ἀνωθεν being taken, according to the common ancient view, in the sense of *denuo* (comp. also Clem. Recogn. vi. 9),—this is most arbitrary, especially when Justin himself gives prominence to the impossibility of a second natural birth.   Moreover, in the second half of the quotation (οὐ μὴ εἰσέλθ. εἰς τ. βασιλ. τ ῶ ν ο ὐ ρ.), some reminiscence of Matt. xviii. 3 might easily occur ; just as, in fact, several very ancient witnesses (among the Codices, ℵ*) read in John *l.c.* βασιλείαν τ ῶ ν ο ὐ ρ α ν ῶ ν, but the Pseudo-Clemens (*Homil.* xi. 26) by quoting the second half exactly in this way, and in the first half adding after ἀναγενν. the words ὕδατι ζῶντι εἰς ὄνομα πατρὸς, υἱοῦ, ἁγίου πνεύματος, exhibits a free combination of Matt. xxviii. 19 and xviii. 3.   Other passages of Justin, which some have regarded as allusions to or quotations from John, may just as fitly be derived from evangelic tradition to be found elsewhere, and from Christian views generally ; and this must even be conceded of such passages as *c. Tryph.* 88 (John i. 20 ff.), *de res.* 9 (John v. 27), *Apol.* I. 6 (John iv. 24), *Apol.* I. 22 and *c. Tryph.* 69 (John ix. 1), *c. Tryph.* 17 (John i. 4).   However, it is most natural, when once we have been obliged to assume in Justin's case the knowledge and use of our Gospel, to attribute to it other expressions also which exhibit Johannean peculiarities, and not to stop at *Apol.* I. 61 merely (against Frank).   On the other hand, the remarkable resemblance of the quotation from Zech. xii. 10 in John xix. 37 and *Apol.* I. 52, leaves it doubtful whether Justin derived it from John's Gospel (Semisch, Luthardt, Tisch., Riggenb.), or from one of the variations of the LXX. already existing at that time (Grimm, *l.c.* p. 692 f.), or again, as is most probable, from the original Hebrew, as is the case in Rev. i. 7.   It is true that the Epistle to Diognetus, which, though not composed by Justin, was certainly contemporary with and probably even prior to him, implies the existence of John's Gospel in certain passages of the concluding portion, which very distinctly re-echo John's Logos-doctrine (see especially Zeller, *l.c.* p. 618, and Credner, *Gesch. d. neut. Kanon*, p. 58 ff.) ; but this conclusion (chapp. 11, 12) is a later appendix, probably belonging to the third century at the earliest.   Other references to our Gospel in the Epistle are uncertain.

5. To the testimonies of the second century within the church, the *Clavis* of Melito of Sardis certainly does not belong (in Pitra, *Spicileg. Solesmense*, Paris 1852), since this pretended κλεὶς, in which the passages John xv. 5. vi. 54, xii. 24, are quoted as contained " *in Evangelio*," is a much later compilation ;[1] but they include the *Epistle of the Churches at Vienne and Lyons* (Eus. v. 1), where John xvi. 2 is quoted as a saying of the Lord's, and the Spirit is designated as the Paraclete : Tatian, Justin's disciple, *ad Graec.* 13, where John i. 5 is cited as τὸ εἰρημένον ; chap. 19, where we have indications of an acquaintance with John's prologue (comp. chap. 5) ; and chap. 4, πνεῦμα ὁ θεός, compared with John iv. 24 ; also the *Diatessaron* of this Tatian,[2] which

---

[1] See Steitz, *Stud. u. Krit.* 1857, p. 584 ff.

[2] According to Theodoret (*Haeret. fab.* i. 20), who from his account must have known it accurately, and who removed it

from his diocese as dangerous, it was nothing else than a brief summary by way of extract of our four Gospels, in which the genealogies, and all that referred to

is based on the canon of the four Gospels, certainly including that of John : Athenagoras, *Leg. pro Christ.* 10, which is based upon a knowledge of John's prologue and of xvii. 21–22 : Apollinaris, Bishop of Hierapolis, in a Fragment in the *Paschal Chronicle*, ed. Dindorf, p. 14 (ὁ τὴν ἁγίαν πλευρὰν ἐκκεντηθεὶς ὁ ἐκχέας ἐκ τῆς πλευρᾶς αὐτοῦ τὰ δύο πάλιν καθάρσια ὕδωρ καὶ αἷμα· λόγον κ. πνεῦμα, comp. John xix. 34), where Baur, of course, takes refuge in a tradition older than our Gospel ; also in another Fragment in the same work ὅθεν ἀσυμφώνως τὲ νόμῳ ἡ νόησις αὐτῶν καὶ στασιάζειν δοκεῖ κατ' αὐτοὺς τὰ εὐαγγέλια), where, if we rightly interpret it,[1] John's Gospel is meant to be included

Christ as a descendant of the seed of David, were left out. This account must (see also Semisch, *Tatiani Diatess.*, Vratisl. 1856) prevail against modern views of an opposite kind ; it agrees also with what is said by Euseb. iv. 29, who, however, did not himself exactly know the peculiar *way in which* Tatian had combined the four. The statement of Epiphanius, *Haer.* xlvi. 1, "Many called it καθ᾽ Ἑβραίους," is, on the other hand, simply an historical remark, which decides nothing as to the fact itself. According to the Jacobite bishop of the thirteenth century, Dionysius Bar-Salibi in Assemanni (*Bibl. Orient.* i. p. 57 f., ii. p. 159), the Diatessaron of Tatian, who therefore must have laid chief stress on John, began with the words, *In the beginning was the Word;* he also reports that Ephraem Syrus wrote a commentary on the Diatessaron. Credner (*Beitr.* I. p. 446 ff. ; *Gesch. d. neut. Kanon*, p. 19 ff.), whom Scholten follows, combats these statements by showing that the Syrians had confounded Tatian and Ammonius and their writings with one another. But Bar-Salibi certainly keeps them strictly apart. Further, the orthodox Ephraem could write a commentary on Tatian's Diatessaron the more fitly, if it was a grouping together of the *canonical* Gospels. Lastly, the statement that it began with John i. 1 agrees thoroughly with Theodoret's account of the rejection of the genealogies and the descent from David, whereas the work of Ammonius cannot have begun with John i. 1, since, according to Eusebius (see Wetstein, *Proleg.* p. 68), its basis was the Gospel of Matthew, by the side of which Ammonius placed the parallel sections of the other evangelists in the form of a synopsis. The testimony of Bar-Salibi above quoted ought not to have been surrendered by Lücke, de Wette, and various others, on the ground of Credner's opposition. What Credner quotes in his *Gesch. d. neut. Kanon*, p. 20, from Ebed-Jesu (in Maii *Script. vet. nova collect.* x. p. 191), rests merely on a confusion of Ta

tian with Ammonius on the part of the Syrians ; which confusion, however, is not to be charged upon Dionysius Bar-Salibi. Further, there is the less ground for excluding the fourth Gospel from the Diatessaron, seeing that Tatian has made use of it in his *Oratio ad Graecos*.

[1] The correct explanation is the usual one, adopted by Wieseler, Ebrard, Weitzel, Schneider, Luthardt, Bleek, Weizsäcker, Riggenbach, and many others, also by Hilgenfeld, Volkmar, Scholten : "*and the Gospels, according to them* (in consequence of their asserting that Jesus, according to Matthew, died on the 15th Nisan), *appear to be at variance*" (namely, with one another). This ground of refutation rests on the assumption (which, however, is really erroneous) that there could be no disagreement among the Gospels as to the day when Jesus died, while there would be such a disagreement if it were correct that, according to Matthew, Jesus died on the 15th Nisan. Now it is true that Matthew really has this statement ; only Apollinaris does not admit it, but assumes that both the Synoptics and John record the 14th Nisan as the day of Christ's death, so that on this point harmony reigns among the Gospels, as in fact, generally, the real disagreement among them had not come to be consciously observed. Comp. Clem. Al. in the *Chron. Pasch.:* ταύτῃ τῶν ἡμερῶν τῇ ἀκριβείᾳ . . . καὶ τὰ εὐαγγέλια συνῳδά. According to Schwegler (*Montanism*, p. 194 f.), Baur, Zeller, the sense must be : " According to their view, the Gospels are in conflict *with the Law*." This, however, is incorrect, because, after having given prominence to the irreconcilability with the Law, a *new* point is introduced with στασιάζειν, bearing on the necessary *harmony of the Gospels*. Moreover, there is no need whatever, in the case of στασιάζειν, of some such addition as ἐν ἑαυτοῖς or the like, since τὰ εὐαγγέλια represents a collective totality supposed to be well known. Comp. Xen.

among the εὐαγγέλια : Polycrates of Ephesus, in Euseb. v. 24, where, with a
reference to John xiii. 23 f., xxi. 20, he designates the Apostle John as ὁ ἐπὶ
τὸ στῆθος τοῦ κυρίου ἀναπεσών. The Clementine Homilies[1] contain in xix. 22
an undeniable quotation from John ix. 2, 3 ;[2] as also, in iii. 52, a citation
occurs from John x. 9, 27,[3] and after these undoubted quotations, there is no
longer any reason to question a reference also in xi. 26 (compare above,
under 4) to John iii. 3. On the other hand, no great stress must be laid on
the citations in the *Recognitiones*, since this work is to be placed (in opposition to Hilgenfeld, Merx, Volkmar) somewhat later, though still in the second
century, and now only exists in the obviously free Latin translation of
Rufinus.[4] The first Father who quotes our Gospel *by name* is Theophilus, *ad
Autolyc.* ii. 31 (ii. 22) : Ὅθεν διδάσκουσι ἡμᾶς αἱ ἅγιαι γραφαὶ καὶ πάντες οἱ πνευ-
ματοφόροι, ἐξ ὧν Ἰωάννης λέγει· ἐν ἀρχῇ ἦν ὁ λόγος, κ.τ.λ. Be-
sides this, according to Jerome (*Ep.* 151, *ad Aglas.*), he composed a work
comparing the four Gospels together, which, like Tatian's Diatessaron, implies the recognition of John by the church. Of importance also here is the
testimony of Irenaeus, *Haer.* iii. 1 (ἔπειτα Ἰωάννης ὁ μαθητὴς τοῦ κυρίου, ὁ καὶ ἐπὶ
τὸ στῆθος αὐτοῦ ἀναπεσών, καὶ αὐτὸς ἐξέδωκε τὸ εὐαγγέλιον, ἐν Ἐφέσῳ τῆς Ἀσίας δια-
τρίβων), comp. iii. 11. 1, 7, 8, 9, v. 10. 3, and especially ap. Eus. v 8 ; partly
because in his youth Polycarp was his teacher, and partly because he was an
opponent of Gnosticism, which, however, could easily find, and did actually
find, nutriment in this very Gospel. Hence the assumption is all the more
natural, that the Gospel so emphatically acknowledged and frequently quoted
by Irenaeus had Polycarp's communications in its favour, either *directly*, in
that Polycarp made Irenaeus acquainted with John's Gospel, or at any rate
indirectly, in that he found confirmed by that Gospel what had been delivered to him by Polycarp as coming from the apostle's own mouth respecting
the words and works of Jesus, and which had remained vividly impressed
on his recollection.[5]—Finally, here belong, because we may take it for granted
they are not later than the second century, the Canon of Muratori,[6] and the

Cyrop. viii. 8. 2, ἐπεὶ μέντοι Κῦρος ἐτελεύτησεν,
εὐθὺς μὲν αὐτοῦ οἱ παῖδες ἐστασίαζον. Often so
in Greek ; comp. also Hilgenfeld, *Paschastreit*, p. 258.

[1] Ed. Dressel, Götting. 1853.

[2] See Uhlhorn in the *Gött. gel. Anz.* 1853,
p. 1810; Volkmar, *ein neu entdeckt. Zeugn.
über d. Joh. Evang.*, in the *theol. Jahrb.* 1854,
p. 446 ff. In spite of this clear testimony,
however, Volkmar places the date of
John's Gospel and of the Homilies so near
each other (150-160 A.D.), that the former
must have been used by the author of the
Homilies directly after its origination " as
an interesting but *unapostolic Novum*"
(*Urspr. d. Evang.* p. 63). This use manifestly implies dissemination and admitted
apostolic authority such as Matthew and
Luke, and a Gospel of Peter, possibly used
by him, must have possessed in the opinion of the author. Comp. **Luthardt** as

above, XXXI. p. 368 ff. This also tells
against Baur, who, in the *Theol. Jahrb.* 1857,
p. 240, strangely enough thinks to weaken
this testimony as a " casual and external"
use of the Gospel ; while Scholten (*die älte-
sten Zeug.* p. 60 ff.), in a precarious and artificial fashion, raises doubts as to the use
itself.

[3] See, against Zeller and Hilgenf., especially Uhlhorn, *d. Homil.'u. Recogn. des Clem.*
p. 223.

[4] *Recogn.* vi. 9, comp. John iii. 3-5 ; *Recogn.*
ii. 48, comp. John v. 23 ; *Recogn.* v. 12, comp.
John viii. 34.

[5] *Epist ad Florin.* in Eus. v. 20.

[6] Credner erroneously maintains in the
Theol. Jahrb. 1857, p. 297, and *Gesch. d. neut.
Kanon*, p. 158 f., that the Canon Murat.
distinguishes John the Evangelist as a
simple *discipulus* Christi from the *Apostle*.
See, on the other hand, Ewald, *Jahrb.* IX.

Canon of the Syrian church in the Peshito, and in the Fragments of the Curetonian text. The Itala also, if its origin really falls within the second century,[1] may be quoted among the testimonies of this century.

6. Among the heretics of the second century, besides the Tatian already referred to, we must name Marcion as a witness for our Gospel. He rejected, according to Tertullian (*c. Marc.* iv. 3), Matthew and John, and, according to the same writer, *de carne Christi* 3, John,—a fact which implies their apostolic authority, and that Marcion knew them to be apostolic,[2] although Hilgenfeld, Volkmar, and Scholten, following Zeller and Schwegler, assume the contrary. But he rejected the non-Pauline Gospels, not on critical grounds, but as a one-sided adherent of Paul, and, as such, in Tertullian's judgment ("*videtur*") chose Luke's Gospel, in order to shape it anew for the purpose of restoring the pure Gospel of Christ, and in such a way, in fact, that he now " evangelio scilicet suo nullum adscribit auctorem," Tertull. *c. Marc.* iv. 2, by which he deprived Luke of his canonical position (" *Lucam videtur elegisse, quem caederet*"). To question Tertullian's credibility in the above passages,[3] though he too frequently judged with the hostility of a partisan those whom he opposed, is yet without sufficient warrant, since he states particularly (*c. Marc.* iv. 3) how Marcion came to reject the other canonical Gospels ; striving, namely, on the ground of the Epistle to the Galatians (chap. ii.), to subvert the position of those Gospels —" quae propria et sub *apostolorum* nomine eduntur vel etiam *apostolicorum*, ut scilicet fidem, quam illis adimit, suo conferat." Comp. Weizsäcker, p. 230 ff. (who, however, misunderstands *videtur* in the above passage), and Riggenb. p. 130 ff. Marcion, therefore, must in consistency have renounced the gain to Gnosticism with which John could have furnished him. The opposite course would have been inconsistent with his Paulinism. Again, that Tertullian understood, by the " Gospels peculiarly and specially apostolical," those of Matthew and John (against Zeller, who, with Volkmar, understands the apocryphal Gospels of the Jewish Christians), is clear from *c. Marc.* iv. 2 : " Nobis fidem ex apostolis *Johannes* et *Matthaeus* insinuant, ex apostolicis Lucas et Marcus." Further, the Valentinians used our Gospel fully and in many ways, in support of their fine-spun fancies (Iren. *Haer.* iii. 11. 7). Heracleon, who is not to be brought down in time into a contemporary of Origen,[4] wrote a commentary on it (see the Fragments of Origen in Grabe, *Spicil. Patr.* ii. p. 85 ff.). Ptolemaeus (in Epiphan. *Haer.* xxxiii. 3 ff.) cites John i. 3 as an apostolical utterance, and according to Irenaeus, i. 8. 5, expressly described John's prologue as proceeding from the apostle ; and Theodotus also (according to the extracts from his writings appended to the works of Clem. Alex.) often quotes the Gospel of

p. 96; Weiss in the *Stud. u. Krit.* 1863, p. 597.

[1] Lachmann, *N. T. Praef.* p. x. f.

[2] Which certainly can be least of all doubted in the case of John's Gospel, of which *Asia* was the native country. The rejection of John as one of the *twelve* apos-

tles is easily enough explained by Marcion's anti-Judaizing temper.

[3] Zeller, Baur, Volkmar.

[4] Origen himself (in *Joann.* ii. c. 8) alleges that Heracleon was esteemed a trusty disciple (γνώριμος) of Valentinus.

John.   Whether *Valentinus himself* used it, is a question on which also, apart from other less evident proofs, we are not without very distinct testimony since the publication of the *Philosophumena Origenis*, which were probably composed by Hippolytus ; for in the *Philos.* vi. 35, among the proof-texts used by Valentinus, John x. 8 is cited : so that the subterfuge, " *The author likes to transfer the doctrines of the disciple to the Master*" (Zeller, Hilgenfeld, Volkmar, comp. Scholten), can be of no avail here, where we have an instance to the contrary lying clearly before us.[1]   When, therefore, Tertullian says, *Praescr. Haer.* 38, "Valentinus integro instrumento uti *videtur,*" we may find this *videtur* in respect of John's Gospel simply confirmed by the *Philosophumena.*[2] — That, again, also Basilides, who is not, however, to be looked upon as a disciple of the Apostle Matthias (Hofstede de Groot), used our Gospel,—a point which Baur even, with unsatisfactory opposition on the part of Hilgenfeld, Volkmar, and others, concedes,—and that he has employed as proof-texts in particular John i. 9, ii. 4, is likewise proved by the *Phil. Orig.* vii. 22, 27, with which many of the author's errors in *other* things are quite unconnected.—The Gospel also was in use among the *Naassenes* (*Philos. Or.* v. 6 ff.) and *Peratae* (v. 12 ff.), who belong to the close of the second century.—It is true that Montanism had not its original root in the Gospel of John, but in the doctrine of the Parousia ; still, in its entire relation to the church and its doctrine (see especially Ritschl, *Altkathol. Kirche*, p. 477 ff.), and particularly in its ideas of prophecy, its asceticism, and its eschatology, it had no occasion to *reject* our Gospel, though some have erroneously found some evidence to this effect in Irenaeus,[3] though at the same time *dependence* on this Gospel

---

[1] See Jacobi in the *Deutsch. Zeitschrift*, 1851, No. 28 f., 1853, No. 24 f. ; Ewald, *Jahrb.* V. p. 200 f.

[2] When Baur and Zeller, on the other hand, lay stress on the fact that among the texts adduced by the Valentinians in proof of their doctrine of the Aeons, none occur from John, and hence conclude that the Valentinian system which Irenaeus there describes does not imply the existence of our Gospel at that time, it is still adverse to their view that Irenaeus immediately, i. 8. 5, adduces quotations from John out of Ptolemaeus, and in iii. 11. 7 testifies to the most ample use of our Gospel ("*plenissime utentes*") on the part of the Valentinians. So, also, the fact that Irenaeus, i. 20. 2, cites among the proof-texts of the Marcosians none from John, cannot serve to prove that the "Valentinian system originally stood in no connection with the fourth Gospel." Zeller, 1845, p. 635. Assuredly the whole theosophy of Valentinus was intertwined with, and grew upon, the ground and soil of John's distinctive theology. " Valentinus . . . *non ad materiam scripturas* (as Marcion), *sed materiam ad scripturas excogitavit*, et

tamen plus abstulit et plus adjecit, auferens proprietates singulorum quoque verborum et adjiciens dispositiones non comparentium rerum." Tertullian, *de praescr. haer.* 38. The Valentinian Gnosis, with its Aeons, Syzygies, and so on, stands related to John's prologue as a product of art and fancy to what is simple and creative. Attempts to weaken the testimonies of the *Philosoph. Orig.* as to a use of John's Gospel on the part of Valentinus and Basilides, have been very unsuccessfully made : Zeller, in the *Theol. Jahrb.* 1853, p. 144 ff. ; Volkmar, *ibidem*, 1854, p. 125 f. ; Baur, *ib.* p. 269 f. ; Hilgenf. in his *Zeitschrift*, 1862, p. 452 ff. ; Scholten, *d. alt. Zeug.* p. 67 ff. ; and Volkmar, *Urspr. uns. Evang.* p. 70 ff. See further, Bleek, *Beitr.* I. p. 214 ff. ; Schneider, p. 27 ff. ; Luthardt, *l.c.* p. 100 ff. ; Tisch. *l.c.* p. 45 ff. ; Riggenbach, p. 118 ff.

[3] This is in answer to Bretschneider, *Probab.* p. 210 ff. The passage in Irenaeus, iii. 2. 9, reads thus : " Alii vero, ut donum Spiritus frustrentur, quod in novissimis temporibus secundum placitum patris effusum est in humanum genus, illam speciem non admittunt, quae est secundum Johannis evan-

cannot in its case be proved.   There was a rejection of the Gospel on the
part of the Alogi, consequently on that of the *opponents* of Montanism (Epiph.
Haer. li. 3 f.), in the interests, indeed, of *dogmatic* Antimontanism, though
they also adduced harmonistic reasons ; but by this very rejection they furnish an indirect testimony to the recognition in their day of our Gospel as
an *apostolic* work, both in the church and among the Montanists.   They
ascribed it to Cerinthus, who was yet a contemporary of John,—a proof
how ancient they thought it, in spite of their rejection of it.

7. Celsus, whom we must certainly not assign, with Volkmar, to so late a
date as the third century, has been cited as a witness of the second century
standing *outside* the church,—all the more important, indeed, because her
enemy,—and, from the Fragments of his work as cited in Origen, we may
certainly infer that he was to some extent acquainted with the evangelic
tradition and the evangelic writings, for he even alludes to the designation
of the Logos and other peculiar points which are found in John, especially
c. Cels. ii. 36, comp. John xx. 27 ; *c. Cels*. i. 67, comp. John ii. 18.   He
assures us that he drew his objections chiefly from the writings of the Christians (*c. Cels*. ii. 74).   But it is highly probable that the Gospel of John
was also among them, since he (*c. Cels*. ii. 13) expressly distinguishes the
writings of the *disciples* of Jesus from *other* works treating of Him, which
he proposes to pass over.—A weighty testimony from the oldest *apocryphal*
literature might be furnished by the *Acta Pilati*, which are quoted even by
Justin and Tertullian (see Tischendorf, *Evang. apocr. Prolegg*. p. liv. ff.),
if their original form were satisfactorily determined, which, however, cannot be successfully done.   Just as little do other apocryphal Gospels furnish anything which we may lay hold of as certain.   The labour expended
by Tischendorf therefore leads to no results.

8. By the end of the second century, and from the beginning of the third,
tradition in the church testifies so clearly and uniformly in favour of the
Gospel, that we need cite no additional vouchers.[1]   Euseb. iii. 25 places it
among the Homologumena.

---

gelium, in qua Paracletum se missurum
Dominus promisit ; sed simul et evangelium
et prophaeticum repellunt Spiritum, infelices
vere, qui pseudoprophetae quidem esse
volunt, prophetiae vero gratiam ab ecclesia
repellunt." He is here speaking of the *opponents* of Montanism, who for a polemical
purpose did not acknowledge the characteristic Johannean nature of this Gospel, rec-
ognizable by the promise of the Paraclete ;
by which course Irenaeus thinks they reject
equally both the Gospel (of John) and the
prophetical Spirit also (who, in fact, was to
be sent precisely as the *Paraclete*),—" truly
unhappy men, who indeed ascribe it (the
Gospel) to a false prophet, while they are
repelling the grace of prophecy from the
church." — The passage is not to be regarded, with Neander, as a Montanist inter-

polation ; nor must we admit in the last
words the conjecture "*pseudoprophetas*" (so
Merkel, *Aufklärung d. Streitigk. der Aloger*,
p. 13 ; also Gieseler, *Kirchengesch*. I. i. p. 200,
and Tischendorf), or *pseudoprophetae* esse
nolunt (so Lücke), or *pseudoprophetas* esse
nolunt (so Ritschl).   Rather is *pseudoprophetae* to be taken as genitive : that "*it is
the work of a false prophet*."   Accordingly
the "*pseudoprophetae esse volunt*" answers to
the preceding "*evangelium . . . repellunt*,"
while the "*prophetiae vero gratiam*" answers
to the "*propheticum repellunt Spiritum*."
Hence also we must decline Volkmar's conjecture, that in Greek ψευδῶς προφῆται stood
instead of ψευδοπροφῆται.

[1] Clem. Al., Tertull., Hippolyt., Orig.,
Dionys. Al., etc.

From this examination of witnesses, it is clear [1] that our Gospel was not
merely in use in the church, and recognized by her as apostolical, from about
170 A.D. (Hilgenfeld, A.D. 150), and composed somewhere about 150 A.D.
(Hilgenfeld, 120–140), but that the continuity of the attestations to it, and
their growing extent in connection with the literature of the church, are as
evident as we ever can and do require for the external confirmation of any
New Testament writing. The continuity in particular goes back from Irenaeus through Polycarp, and from Papias, so far as he is credited with the
use of John's first *Epistle*, although not directly (Iren., Hieron.), yet indirectly (Euseb., Dionys.),—that is, through the *Presbyter* John,—to the *Apostle
himself*. That the *Fragment of Papias* in Euseb. iii. 39 does not mention
John's *Gospel*, cannot be of any consequence, since it does not quote any
written sources at all from which the author drew his accounts, but rather
describes his procedure as that of an inquirer after sayings of the apostles
and other of the Lord's disciples (such as Aristion and John the Presbyter),
and expressly enunciates the principle : οὐ γὰρ τὰ ἐκ τῶν βιβλίων τοσοῦτόν με
ὠφελεῖν ὑπελάμβανον, ὅσον τὰ παρὰ ζώσης φωνῆς καὶ μενούσης. Papias here throws
together the then existing evangelic writings (τῶν βιβλίων), of which there
was a multitude (Luke i. 1), all without distinction, not probably some
merely apocryphal ones (Tischendorf ; Riggenbach, p. 115) ; and as he included among them the Gospel of Matthew and that of Mark, both of which
he specially mentions subsequently, so he also may have intended to include
the Gospel of John among τῶν βιβλίων, since he manifestly does not indicate
that he has any conception of *canonical* Gospels as such (comp. Credner,
Beitr. I. p. 25), and has no occasion to note the distinction. When, further
on, Eusebius quotes two statements of Papias on the Gospels of Matthew
and Mark, this does not indicate that our Gospel did not exist in his day
(Baur), or was at any rate not recognized by him (Hilgen., Credner, and
Volkmar) ; but these two statements are simply made prominent, because they
contain something specially noteworthy as to the *origin* [2] of those Gospels,
just as Eusebius refers to it as specially worthy of remark that Papias makes
use of proofs from two *epistolary* writings [3] (1 John and 1 Peter), and has a

---

[1] Comp. the acknowledgment of Keim,
Gesch. J. i. p. 137 : " It is used in the extant
literature as early as the Synoptics." In
opposition both to the usual determination
of the date, which fixes on the last quarter
of the first century, and to the criticism of
Baur, Hilgenfeld, and Volkmar, Keim (pp.
146, 155) assigns the *origin* of the Gospel to
Trajan's time, between A.D. 100 and 117.
The difficulty here is, that, according to
Keim, the Epistle of Barnabas necessarily
implies the use of our Gospel in its time.
This epistle, however, he places in Hadrian's
day, about 120 A.D. In this case, the interval during which the Gospel had to become
known and recognized is much too narrow ;
and besides, the date assigned to Barnabas is by no means so certain as Keim is

disposed to infer from chap. 4 and 16. Hilgenfeld places it under Nerva ; Ewald and
Weizsäcker even in the time of Vespasian.
The question is, in any case, still uncertain.
[2] When, in this statement, Papias intimates in regard to Mark : οὔτε γὰρ ἤκουσε τοῦ
κυρίου οὔτε παρηκολούθησεν αὐτῷ, we may observe here a contrast to *other* evangelists
who *had* heard the Lord and followed Him ;
which was not the case with Mark, whose
credibility depended rather on Peter. Such
other evangelists were Matthew and John.
[3] *Why* Eusebius makes this prominent,
we cannot tell, since we do not know on
what occasions Papias used these epistolary testimonies. We can hardly connect
this prominent reference with the question
of the genuineness of the epistles, to which

narrative which occurs in the Gospel to the Hebrews.[1] Further, in opposition to the weighty testimony of Justin Martyr, it is incorrectly urged that, if he had known of John as *evangelist*, he would not have referred to him as the author of the Apocalypse, with the bare words (*c. Tryph.* 81), ἀνήρ τις, ᾧ ὄνομα Ἰωάννης, εἰς τῶν ἀποστόλων τοῦ Χριστοῦ. Justin had, in fact, no *occasion* at all, in the context of this passage, to describe John as evangelist, and all the less that to him it was self-evident that in εἰς τῶν ἀποστόλων were included the authors of the ἀπομνημονεύματα τῶν ἀποστόλων.

A *historical* argument specially adduced by some against our Gospel is derived from the history of the *Easter Controversy.* See, on the one side, Bretschneider, *Prob.* 109 f. ; Schwegler, *Montanism*, p. 191 f. ; Baur, p. 343 ff., and in the *Theol. Jahrb.* 1844, p. 638 ff., 1847, p. 89 ff., 1848, p. 264 ff. On the opposite side, Weitzel, *d. christl. Passafeier der drei ersten Jahrb.*, Pforzheim 1848, and in the *Theol. Stud. u. Krit.* 1848, p. 806 ;—in answer to which, again, Hilgenfeld, in the *Theol. Jahrb.* 1849, p. 209 ff., and in his *Galaterbrief*, p. 78 f. ; Baur, *d. Christenth. d. drei ersten Jahrb.* p. 141 ff. ; Scholten, *d. Evang. nach Joh. krit. hist. Untersuch.* p. 385 ff. ; and *d. altest. Zeugnisse*, p. 139 ff. See further, *for* the genuineness of John : Ewald, *Jahrb.* V. p. 203 ff. ; Schneider, p. 43 ff. ; Bleek, *Beitr.* p. 156 ff., and *Einl.* p. 187 ff. ; Steitz, in the *Stud. u. Krit.* 1856, p. 721 ff., 1857, p. 741 ff., 1859, p. 717 ff., and in the *Jahrb. f. Deutsche Theologie*, 1861, p. 102 ff. ;— against whom, Baur, in the *Theol. Jahrb.* 1857, p. 242 ff., and in Hilgenfeld's *Zeitschr.* 1858, p. 298 ; Hilgenf. *Theol. Jahrb.* 1857, p. 523 ff., and in his *Zeitschr.* 1858, p. 151 ff., 1862, p. 285 ff., 1867, p. 187 ff. On the whole course of the investigations, Hilgef., *d. Paschastreit d. alt. Kirche*, 1860, p. 29 ff. ; *Kanon u. Krit. d. N. T.* 1863, p. 220 ff. Comp. also the apologetic discussion by Riggenbach, *d. Zeugnisse f. d. Ev. Joh.* p. 50 ff. The reasons derived from the Easter controversy against the genuineness of the Gospel are obviated, not by forcing the fourth Gospel into agreement with the Synoptics in their statements as to the day on which Jesus died (see on xviii. 28), which is not possible, but by a correct apprehension of the point of view from which the Catholic Quartodecimani in Asia Minor, who appealed for their observance of their festival on the 14th Nisan to apostolic custom,

the subsequent mention of the Gospel to the Hebrews would not be at all appropriate. Probably Eusebius mentions the reference to the two epistles only as an *exceptional* procedure on the part of Papias, who elsewhere dispenses with the citation of *written* testimonies. Comp. the passage previously adduced from the Fragment.—Scholten (*a. ältest. Zeugn.* p. 17) very arbitrarily, and without any reason, doubts whether Papias held the epistle to be a work of the apostle.

[1] Besides, it is not to be overlooked that Papias may *somewhere else* in his book have mentioned the fourth Gospel, which he does not name in the Fragment in Eusebius. We do not know, since the book is lost. See also Steitz, in the *Stud. u. Krit.* 1868, p. 493.

It is true, a Latin Codex of the ninth century, in the Vatican, expressly testifies to such a mention (see Aberle in the *Tüb. Quartalschr.* 1864, p. 1 ff. ; Tisch. as above, p. 118 f. ; Zahn, in the *Stud. u. Krit.* 1867, p. 539 ff.) ; but less importance is to be attached to it, since the testimony is connected with the statement that Papias *put together* what was *dictated* by the apostle,— a late and worthless legend (occurring also in Corder. *Caten. Prooem.*), which might easily enough have originated from Irenaeus' speaking of Papias as Ἰωάννου ἀκουστής. See, moreover, Hilgenf. in his *Zeitschr.* 1865, p. 75 ff. ; Overbeck, *ibidem*, 1867, p. 63 ff.

and especially to the example of John (Polycarp in Eusebius v. 24 ; and Polycrates, *ibidem*), regarded the observance of this particular day of the month.   The opponents of the Gospel, it is true, say, If the custom of those in Asia Minor to celebrate the Lord's last supper on the 14th Nisan, contemporaneously with the Jewish passover, mainly originated with and proceeded from the Apostle John, then this apostle could not have written the fourth Gospel, because that custom agrees exactly with the Synoptic account of the last supper and the day of Jesus' death, while the fourth Gospel states the exact opposite,—namely, that Jesus kept His last supper, and therefore no true passover, on the 13th Nisan, and was crucified on the 14th Nisan. But the men of Asia Minor celebrated the 14th Nisan,—and that, too, by terminating the fast kept upon this day in remembrance of Christ's passion, down to the hour of His death, and by a joyous celebration of the Lord's supper immediately after, in gratitude for the accomplishment of His work of redemption,—not because Jesus ate the *passover* on that day, but because He *died* on that day, and by His death became the *real* and *true* Paschal Lamb of whom the Mosaic paschal lamb was the *type* (1 Cor. v. 7 ; John xix. 36); comp. also Ritschl, *Altkath. Kirche*, p. 269.   Accordingly, they might justly maintain (see Polycrates in Euseb. *l.c.*) that their festival on the 14th Nisan was κατὰ τὸ εὐαγγέλιον (for any disagreement in the Gospels in reference to the day of Jesus' death was not yet perceived, and the passover meal of Jesus in the Synoptics was looked upon as an anticipation), and κατὰ τὸν κανόνα τῆς πίστεως,—this latter, namely, because Jesus, by the observance of the passover on another day, would not have appeared as the antitype of the slaughtered paschal lamb.   Also πᾶσα ἁγία γραφή might be rightly quoted in proof by Polycrates, since in no part of the Old Testament does any other day occur as that on which the paschal lamb was slaughtered, except the 14th Nisan, and Jesus was in fact the true Paschal Lamb.   It is self-evident that John's example, which the Catholics of Asia Minor urged in favour of their "Quartodecima," perfectly agrees with the account of the fourth Gospel, and that the κατὰ τὸ εὐαγγέλιον of Polycrates, though by it no single Gospel, but the written evangelic history collectively, is meant, does not exclude, but includes John's Gospel, since its existence and recognition at that time is perfectly clear from other proofs.   True, there was also a party of Quartodecimans in Asia Minor [1] who formed their judgments from a Judaistic (Ebionite) standpoint, whose celebration of the 14th Nisan did not rest on the assumption that Jesus, as the

---

[1] Characteristically referred to thus by Apollinaris in the *Chron. Pasch.* p. 14 : ἔνιοι τοίνυν οἳ δι' ἄγνοιαν φιλονεικοῦσι περὶ τούτων, συγγνωστὸν πρᾶγμα πεπονθότες· ἄγνοια γὰρ οὐ κατηγορίαν ἀναδέχεται, ἀλλὰ διδαχῆς προσδεῖται. Comp. Hippolyt. *ibid.* p. 13 : ὁρῶ μὲν οὖν, ὅτι φιλονεικίας τὸ ἔργον, κ.τ.λ. With the mild description of these people in Apollinaris agrees also *Philos. Orig.* viii. 18, where they are simply distinguished as ἕτεροί τινες, and indeed as φιλόνεικοι τὴν φύσιν and ἰδιῶται τὴν γνῶσιν, while it is said of them that in other points they agree with the doctrine of the apostles. Against Baur and Hilgenfeld, by whom the distinction between Catholic and Judaic Quartodecimani is alleged to be pure fancy, see Steitz, 1856, p. 782 ff., 1857, p. 764; also in Herzog's *Encyclop.* xi. p. 156 ff.   Even the ἔνιοι of Apollinaris and the ἕτεροί τινες of Hippolytus should have precluded them from thinking of the Asiatic church.   On the other hand, Hilgenfeld, in his *Paschastreit*, pp. 256, 282, 404, is evasive.

true Paschal Lamb, died on this day, but on the legal injunction that the passover was to be eaten on this day, and on the assumption that Jesus Himself ate it on the very same day, and did not suffer till the 15th Nisan.[1] These[2] men stirred up the so-called *Laodicean* controversy, and had as opponents, first Melito of Sardis and Apollinaris of Hierapolis, and afterwards Irenaeus, Hippolytus, Clement, and others (Eus. iv. 26. 3). They were attacked partly by their own weapon —*the law*— according to which Christ could not have been put to death, that is, slain as the true Paschal Lamb, on the first day of the feast ; partly by an appeal to the *Gospels*, in respect of which it was assumed that they agree in reporting the 14th Nisan as the day of Jesus' death (Apollinaris, in the *Chron. Pasch.* p. 14 : ἀσυμφώνως τε νόμῳ ἡ νόησις αὐτῶν καὶ στασιάζειν δοκεῖ κατ' αὐτοὺς τ ὰ ε ὐ α γ γ έ λ ι α . See above, under 5, the note on this passage). Moreover, it was urged by some who appealed to Matthew (Apollinaris, *l.c.*, διηγοῦνται Ματθαῖον οὕτω λέγειν), that according to the words of Jesus, οὐκέτι φάγομαι τὸ πάσχα (comp. Luke xxii. 16), He did not eat of the legal passover, but died as the perfect Paschal Lamb on this day, and indeed before the time of eating the meal appointed by the law. See Hippolytus, in the *Chron. Pasch.* p. 13 : ὁ πάλαι προειπὼν, ὅτι οὐκέτι φάγομαι τὸ πάσχα, εἰκότως τὸ μὲν δεῖπνον ἐδείπνησεν πρὸ τοῦ πάσχα, τὸ δὲ πάσχα οὐκ ἔφαγεν, ἀλλ' ἔπαθεν, οὐδὲ γὰρ καιρὸς ἦν τῆς βρώσεως αὐτοῦ (*i.e.* "*because the legal period for eating the passover had not even come,*"—it only came several hours after the death of Jesus) ; and just before : πεπλάνηται μὴ γινώσκων, ὅτι ᾧ καιρῷ ἔπασχεν ὁ Χριστός, οὐκ ἔφαγε τὸ κατὰ νόμον πάσχα, οὗτος γὰρ ἦν τὸ πάσχα τὸ προκεκηρυγμένον καὶ τὸ τελειούμενον τῇ ὡρισμένῃ ἡμέρᾳ (on the 14th Nisan). That, however, Justin Martyr himself regarded the first day of the feast as the day on which Jesus died (so Baur and Hilgenfeld), is an erroneous assumption. For when he says (*c. Tryth.* 111, p. 338), καὶ ὅτι ἐν ἡμέρᾳ τοῦ πάσχα συνελάβετε αὐτὸν καὶ ὁμοίως ἐν τῷ πάσχα ἐσταυρώσατε, γέγραπται, he plainly means by ἐν ἡμέρᾳ τοῦ πάσχα, and by ἐν τῷ πάσχα, the day on which the paschal lamb was eaten—the 14th Nisan ; since he shows immediately before that Christ was the true Paschal Lamb, and immediately after continues : ὡς δὲ τοὺς ἐν Αἰγύπτῳ ἔσωσε τὸ αἷμα τοῦ πάσχα, οὕτως καὶ τοὺς πιστεύσαντας ῥύσεται ἐκ θανάτου τὸ αἷμα τοῦ Χριστοῦ. Comp. chap. 40, p. 259. He *might* therefore have regarded Christ not as dying on the 15th Nisan, but simply on the 14th, as this is expressed in the second fragment of Apollinaris,[3] without our needing to understand "ἐν ἡμέρᾳ τῇ τοῦ πάσχα" of the 15th Nisan.[4] Thus it is also said in the *Chron.*

---

[1] Comp. Steitz, 1856, p. 776 ff.

[2] Whose observance is not to be regarded as a mere Jewish simultaneous celebration of the passover, which John assented to, as a custom which he found in existence in Ephesus (Bleek, De Wette, following Lücke). See, on the other hand, Hilgenfeld, *Kanon u. Krit. d. N. T.* p. 224 ff. The difference rests on a fundamental opposition. Comp. Ritschl, *Altkath. Kirche*, pp. 123 f., 269 f.

[3] To the same effect is p. 14 : ἡ ιδ ' τὸ ἀληθινὸν τοῦ κυρίου πάσχα, ἡ θυσία ἡ μεγάλη,

ὁ ἀντὶ τοῦ ἀμνοῦ παῖς θεοῦ, ὁ δηθεὶς, ὁ δήσας τὸν ἰσχυρόν, καὶ ὁ κριθεὶς κριτὴς ζώντων καὶ νεκρῶν, καὶ ὁ παραδοθεὶς εἰς χεῖρας ἁμαρτωλῶν, ἵνα σταυρωθῇ, ὁ ὑψωθεὶς ἐπὶ κεράτων μονοκέρωτος, καὶ ὁ τὴν ἁγίαν πλευρὰν ἐκκεντηθεὶς . . . καὶ ὁ ταφεὶς ἐν ἡμέρᾳ τῇ τοῦ πάσχα, ἐπιτεθέντος τῷ μνήματι τοῦ λίθου.

[4] Recently Steitz also (in Herzog's *Encyklop.* xi. 1859, p. 151), who formerly agreed with Baur, has admitted that Justin, agreeing with the other Fathers of the second and third centuries, did not in the above passage, *c. Tr.* p. 338, mean the 15th, but

Pasch. p. 12 : ἐν αὐτῇ δὲ τῇ τοῦ πάσχα ἡμέρᾳ, ἤτοι τῇ ιδ' τοῦ πρώτου μηνὸς, παράσκευῆς οὔσης ἐσταύρωσαν τὸν κύριον οἱ Ἰουδαῖοι, καὶ τότε τὸ πάσχα ἔφαγον. Comp. p. 415 : ἐν ἡμέρᾳ δὲ παρασκευῇ σταυρωθῆναι τὸν κύριον διδάσκουσιν τὰ θεόπνευστα λόγια, ἐν τῇ τοῦ πάσχα ἑορτῇ. On this fourteenth day the passover was celebrated according to the practice prevailing in Asia Minor, because on that day the true Paschal Lamb, Christ, was slain. Thus had Philip, John, Polycarp, and other μεγάλα στοιχεῖα, whom Polycrates mentions, already acted, and so John's example in this particular agrees with his own Gospel.

If some have also argued [1] against the early existence of our Gospel, from the antiquity and fixedness of the tradition which limited the ministry of Jesus to a single *year* (see *Homil. Clem.* xvii. 19), it is decisive against this that this tradition occurs in many writers who recognized the Gospel as the genuine work of John ;[2] whence it is clear that it does not imply the non-existence of the Gospel, but seemed just as reconcilable with John as with the Synoptics. It may have originated from the Synoptic history (see on Luke iv. 19) ; but the counter statement of John, although it actually existed, did not disturb it. It is the same also with the antiquity and fixedness of the tradition of the 14th Nisan as the day of Jesus' death, which nevertheless does not imply non-acquaintance with the synoptic Gospels. — If, further, the reasons which are alleged for a Johannean origin of the *Apocalypse* are likewise urged, especially by the Tübingen critics, as evidence against a similar origin for the *Gospel*, yet a reverse procedure is equally justifiable ; and, apart from the utter futility of those reasons in other respects, the testimonies for the Apocalypse (which was excluded even from the Peshito), do not attain to any such general recognition as those for this Gospel. The attribution by the unanimous judgment (and that too, erroneous) of the church, of this work to the Apostle, would, granting its origin in the first half of the second century, be, as it were, the magical result of a few decenniums; and would be historically the more enigmatical, in proportion as in contents and character it diverged from the other Gospels on the one hand, and from the much earlier and apostolically accredited Apocalypse on the other. For we have in this book no spiritualized Apocalypse, but simply an independent Gospel, marked by profound spiritual perfection, whose linguistic and other characteristics, and whose doctrinal contents, spirit, and aim, are, on the whole, so specifically different from those of the Apocalypse, in spite of various Christological points of connection, as to point to a totally different author (against Hengst., Godet, Riggenb., and others). The Gnostic tendency of the time, in which some have sought for the solution of that incomprehensible enigma, does not solve it, since the

the 14th Nisan. Comp. Lev. xxiii. 5, 6 ; Num. xxviii. 16 f. ; Ezek. xlv. 21. The 15th Nisan is called *postridie paschatis*, Num. xxxiii. 3, Josh. v. 11. Hilgenfeld's objection (*d. Paschastr. d. alten Kirche*, p. 206), that the *arrest* mentioned by Justin as taking place likewise on the ἡμέρα τοῦ πάσχα does not suit the 14th *Nisan*, is altogether futile.

Justin correctly includes the arrest in the day of crucifixion, as, *c. Tryph.* 99, the agony in Gethsemane is already put by him τῇ ἡμέρᾳ, ᾗπερ ἔμελλε σταυροῦσθαι.

[1] See Hilgenfeld, Baur, Volkmar.
[2] Clem. Al., Orig., Ptolemaeus ; and see generally Semisch, *Denkw. Justin's*, p. 199 f.

strong reaction in the church against Gnosticism would rather have condemned a Gospel furnishing the Gnostics with so much apparent support, and with materials so liable to be misused, than left to opponents so rich a mine, to be worked out for their designs, if its apostolic origin had not been known and acknowledged.

SEC. III.—GENUINENESS CONTINUED.

As an *internal testimony* to its apostolic origin, we have, above all, the whole grand ideal peculiarity of the book, wherein the πνευματικὸν εὐαγγέλιον (Clem. Al.) is delineated with so much character and spirit, with such simplicity, vividness, depth, and truth, that a later fabricator or composer—who, moreover, could have occupied no other standing-point than that of his own time—becomes an impossibility, when we compare with it any production of Christian authorship of the second century. The Gospel of John, especially through the unity and completeness of its *Christological idea*, is no artificial antithesis (Keim, *Gesch. J.* p. 129), but the completion of the previous evangelic literature, to which the Pauline Christology appears as the historical middle term. But such a creation, which constitutes such a completion, without imitating the older Gospels, is not the work of some later forger, but of an immediate eye-witness and recipient.[1] In it there beats the *heart* of Christ,—as the book itself has been justly named (Ernesti). But, say some (Lützel., Baur and his school), it is precisely this tender, fervent, harmonious, spiritual character of the Gospel, which is as little in keeping with those traits of the *Apostle John himself* exhibited in the other Gospels[2] as the testimony borne to his anti-Pauline Judaism (Gal. ii.) is to the ideal universalism which pervades his Gospel (see especially iv. 24, x. 16, xii. 20). Yet the Judaizing partisanship which is said to be chargeable

[1] In order to make the unique peculiarities of the Gospel agree with a non-apostolic author, neither the Epistle to the Hebrews nor the Apostle Paul ought to be brought into comparison. Both of them belong to the apostolic age, and the latter was called in an extraordinary manner by Christ, as a true apostle, and furnished with a revelation. To suppose that the author of this Gospel also received a revelation in *a similar way*, and yet to make him compose his Gospel no earlier than the second century, is unhistorical ; and to attribute to any one deemed worthy of such a revelation the design of passing off his work as John's, is unpsychological, and morally opposed to the spirit of truth which pervades and underlies it. The originating creative energy of the Spirit had no longer, in the second century, its season ordained by God, as is clearly shown by the entire literature of that later period, not excepting even the most distinguished (such as the Epistle to Diognetus). And the assumption of the apostolic guise would have been, in the case of that creative energy, as unworthy as unnecessary. The pseudonymous post-apostolic literature of the early church may be sufficiently accounted for by the custom—excusable, considering the defective conception at that time of literary property—of assuming the name of any one according to whose ideas one intended to write (see Köstlin in the *Theol. Jahrb.* 1851, p. 149 ff.) ; but the deliberate purpose on which this custom was founded, would, in the case especially of a book so sublime, and in an intellectual point of view, so thoroughly independent as our Gospel, have been *utterly incongruous*—a paradox of the Holy Ghost.

[2] Mark iii. 17 ; Luke ix. 49, 54 ; Mark ix. 38, x. 35.

on John, is simply *imported* into Gal. ii., and cannot without utter arbitrariness be inferred from the conflicts with Judaism in Paul's subsequent
epistles. And as to the destination of an apostle of the Jews, a position
which John certainly, in common with Peter and James, still held at the
time of the Apostolical Council, might it not afterwards (though even Keim
discovers in this assumption a mockery of history and psychology) expand
gradually into that universalism which appears in the Gospel ? Might not,
in particular, the fuller insight into Paul's work which John attained (Gal.
ii.), and the bond of fellowship which he formed with that apostle (Gal. ii.),
as well as his entrance subsequently into the sphere of Paul's labours in Asia
Minor, have contributed powerfully to that expansion and transformation
which went beyond that of Paul himself ; for the perfecting of which, down
to the time when our Gospel[1] was composed, so long a period of church
history and of personal experience had been vouchsafed ? Moreover, like
Paul, he still retained his Israelitish theocratic consciousness as an inalienable inheritance (iv. 22 ; his use of the Old Test.). With regard to the
traits of character indicated in the Synoptics, is not the holy fervour of spirit
which everywhere pervades his Gospel, and still marks his First Epistle, to
be conceived as the glorified transfiguration of his former fiery zeal ? And
as to this transfiguration itself,[2] who may define the limits in the sphere of
what is morally possible to man, beyond which, in a life and labours so long
continued, the development of the new birth could not extend under influences so mighty as the apostles experienced through the Spirit's training in
the school of the holiest calling ? What purification and growth did Peter,
for example, experience between his smiting with the sword and denial, and
his martyrdom ! Both his labours and his Epistle bear witness on this
point. Similarly must we judge of the objection, that the higher, nay, philosophical (or rather Christian speculative) Hellenistic culture of the evangelist,
especially his doctrine of the Logos, cannot be made to suit[3] the Galilean
fisherman John,[4] for whom the fathomless hardihood of modern criticism
has substituted some highly cultured *Gentile* Christian,[5] who, wishing to
lead *heathen* readers (xix. 35, xx. 31) to Christian faith, exhibited the
remarkable phenomenon "of historical evangelic authorship turning away

[1] The well-known words of Polycrates, τὸ πέταλον πεφορηκώς, ought not to have been used as a proof that, in his later ministry in Asia, John was still the representative of Judaism, for they describe high-priestly dignity (see sec. 1) in a Christian, *spiritual* sense. Again, the words which John is said to have uttered, according to Irenaeus, iii. 3, when he encountered Cerinthus at the bath : φύγωμεν μὴ καὶ τὸ βαλανεῖον συμπέσῃ ἔνδον ὄντος Κηρίνθου, τοῦ τῆς ἀληθείας ἐχθροῦ, are alleged to be inappropriate to our evangelist. Why so? The very designation of Cerinthus as τῆς ἀληθείας ἐχθροῦ in the legend points to the evangelist, with whom ἀλήθεια was one of the great fundamental conceptions, whereas the author of

the Apocalypse never once uses the word. The allegation that the latter, again, in Rev. xxi. 14, compared with ii. 4, testifies to the anti-Pauline sentiments of the Twelve, and hence of the Apostle John also, is simply foisted into the passage by a criticism on the look-out for it.

[2] Keim (p. 160) says, inappositely, of Mark and Luke : "Since they clearly imply the death of the apostles (of all ?), they have not even allowed a *possibility* of further developments." Neither Mark nor Luke undertook to write in their Gospels a history of the *apostles*, but of *Jesus*.

[3] Bretschneider, Baur, and others.
[4] Comp. also Acts iv. 13.
[5] So also Schenkel.

from the existing Christian communities, for whom there were already Gospels enough in existence, to appeal to the educated conscience of the heathen world." [1] Even the fact that John was, according to xviii. 15, an acquaintance of the high priest, is said to be unsuited to the circumstances of the Galilean fisherman, [2]—a statement wholly without adequate ground.

It is true the author does not give his *name*, just as the other historical works of the N. T. do not designate their authors. But he shows himself to have been an eye-witness in the plainest possible way, both at i. 14 (comp. John i. 1, iv. 14) and at xix. 35 (comp. xxi. 24); while the vividness and directness of so many descriptions and individual details, in which no other Gospel equals ours, as well as its necessarily conscious variation from the synoptic representation as a whole and in particular points of great importance, can only confirm the truth of that personal testimony, which is not to be set aside either by interpreting ἐθεασάμεθα, i. 14, of the Christian consciousness in general, or by the pretext that ἐκεῖνος in xix. 35 distinguishes the evangelist from such as were eye-witnesses. [3] See the exegetical remarks on those passages. And as a proof that the eye-witness was, in fact, no other than John, the significant *concealment of the name John* is rightly urged against Bretschneider, Baur, and others. Though allowed to be one of the most intimate friends of Jesus, and though the Gospel describes so many of his peculiar and delicate traits of character, this disciple is never referred to by name, but only in a certain masked, sometimes very delicate and thoughtful way, so that the nameless author betrays himself at once as the individual who modestly suppresses his name in i. 35 ff. The true feeling of the church, too, has always perceived this ; while it was reserved only for a criticism which handles delicate points so roughly, [4] to lend to the circumstance this explanation : " The author speaks of his identity with the apostle, as one, simply, to whom the point was of no consequence : his Gospel is to be regarded as Johannean, without bearing the apostle's name on its front ; at least the author will himself not mention the name in order to make it his own, but the reader is merely to be led to make this combination, so as to place the Apostle John's name in the closest and most direct connection with a Gospel written in his spirit" (Baur, p. 379). In fact, a fraud so deliberately planned, and, in spite of its attempting no imitation of the Apocalypse, so unexampled in its success, a striving after apparent self-renunciation so crafty, that the lofty, true, transparent, and holy spirit of which the whole bears the impress, would stand in the most marked contradiction to it ! Moreover, the instances of other non-apostolic works which were intended to go forth as apostolic, and therefore do not at all conceal the lofty names of their pretended authors, would be opposed to it. On the

---

[1] Hilgenfeld, *d. Evangelien*, p. 349.

[2] See Scholten, p. 379.

[3] Köstlin, Hilgenfeld, Keim, and several others.

[4] See, besides the Tübingen critics and Scholten, also Weisse, *d. Evangelienfr.* p. 61, according to whom, if John could have designated himself the disciple beloved by Christ, there would be in this an offensive and impudent self-exaltation : comp. also Keim, *Gesch. J.* i. p. 157 f. See for the opposite and correct view, Ewald, *Johann. Schrif.* i. p. 48 ff.

other hand, the universal recognition which this *nameless* author as the
Apostle John obtained in the church is the more striking, since a later production of *this* kind, which had been anticipated by so well-known a work
of a *totally different* character, passing for Johannean,—that is, the Apocalypse,—in contrast to the latter recognized as apostolic, while not once
mentioning the name of that disciple, would be an historical phenomenon
hardly conceivable. At least it is far more intelligible that the Apocalypse,
bearing John's name on its very face, and solemnly repeating it to the end
more than once, should, in an uncritical age, make good its claim to be an
apostolic work, though not permanently.[1] [See Note I. p. 39.] Further,
the circumstance that in our Gospel John the *Baptist* is always mentioned
simply as Ἰωάννης, never as ὁ βαπτιστής, is not *so* weighty (in opposition to
Credner, Bleek, Ebrard) as to prove that the writer was the *apostle*, who,
as its author, has found no occasion to point out the other John distinctly
by that appellation : for the name ὁ βαπτιστής was by no means designed to
mark any such distinction. But we may doubtless be of opinion that a
writer who had simply to appropriate the evangelic materials in the Gospels
already existing, and develop them in a peculiar way, would hardly have
failed to employ the surname of the Baptist so commonly and formally used
in the Gospels. But it is conceivable that our apostle, having been a
personal disciple of the Baptist, and having a *lively recollection* of his former
close relation to him, mentions him by his bare name, as he had been wont
to do when he was his disciple, and not with the designation ὁ βαπτιστής,
which had come down to him through the medium of *history*.

In the extended *discourses* of Jesus, in the chronological *arrangement* of
the historical materials, in the prominence given to the Lord's *extra-Galilean* ministry, in the *significant* and *peculiar narratives* omitted by the Synoptics (among which the most noteworthy is that of the raising of Lazarus),
in the *important variations from the Synoptics* in parallel narratives (the chief
of which are in the history of the last supper, and in the date of the day
when Jesus died), in the noticeable *omissions* of evangelic matter (the most
remarkable being the silence as to the institution of the supper, and the
agony in Gethsemane) which our Gospel exhibits, we recognize just so many
indications of an *independence*, which renders the general *recognition* of its
apostolic authorship in the church only explicable on the ground of the indubitable *certainty* of the fact. It was this certainty, and the high general
reputation of the beloved disciple, which far outweighed all variations from
the form and contents of the older Gospels, nay, even subordinated the
credit and independence of the Synoptics (as in the history of the last supper,
which in them was placed on the 13th Nisan). All these points of difference have therefore been wrongly urged against the apostolic authorship :
they make the external attestation all the stronger, far too strong to be
traceable to the aims and fictions of a writer of the second century.[2] With
regard especially to the *discourses and conversations* of Jesus (which, accord-

---

[1] Comp. Ewald, *Jahrb.* v. p. 182 f.; Düsterd. *on the Apocalypse*, Introduction.

[2] Comp. Bleek, *Beitr.* p. 66 ff.; Brückner on de Wette, p. xxviii. f.

ing to Baur's school, are wanting in appropriateness of exposition and nat-
uralness of circumstances, are connected with unhistorical facts, and intended to form an explication of the Logos-Idea), they certainly imply [1] a
free reproduction and combination on the part of an intelligent writer, who
draws out what is historically given beyond its first concrete and immediate
form, by further developing and explaining it. Often the originality is certainly not that of purely objective *history*, but savours of *John's* spirit (compare the First Epistle of John), which was most closely related with that of
Jesus. This *Johannean* method was such that, in its undoubted right to
reproduce and to clothe in a new dress, which it exercised many decenniums
after, it could not carry the mingling of the objective and subjective, una-
voidable as it was to the author's idiosyncrasy, so far as to merge what constituted its original essence in the mere view of the individual. Thus the
λόγος, especially in the distinct *form* which it assumes in the *prologue*, does
not reappear in the *discourses* [2] of Jesus, however frequently the λόγος of God
or of Christ, as the verbum *vocale* (not *essentiale* [3]), occurs in them. All the
less, therefore, in these discourses can the form be externally separated from
the matter to such an exent as to treat the one as the subjective, the other
as the objective[4]—a view which is inconceivable, especially when we consider
the intellectual Johannean unity of mould, unless the substance of the matter
is to be assigned to the sphere of the subjective along with the form. The
Jesus of John, indeed, appears in His discourses as in general more sublime,
more solemn, frequently more hard to understand, nay, more enigmatical,
more mysterious, and, upon the whole, more ideal, than the Jesus of the
Synoptics, especially as the latter is seen in His pithy proverbs and parables.
Still, we must bear in mind that the manifestation of Jesus as the divine
human life was intrinsically too rich, grand, and manifold, not to be represented variously, according to the varying individualities by which its rays
were caught, and according to the more or less ideal points of view from
which those rays were reflected,—variously, amid all that resemblance of

[1] It cannot be shown that he records the
experiences of the later apostolic age, and
makes Jesus speak accordingly (see Weizsäcker, p. 285 f.). The passages adduced in
proof (xvii. 20, xx. 29, xiv. 22, xvii. 9, xvii. 3,
iii. 13, vi. 57, 62 f., iv. 36-38) are fully explained exegetically without the assumption of any such ὕστερον πρῶτον.

[2] Although the *essential conception of the
Logos*, as regards its *substance*, is everywhere
with John a prominent feature in the consciousness of Jesus, and is re-echoed
throughout the Gospel. (Comp. iii. 11, 13, 31,
vi. 33 ff., vi. 62, vii. 29, viii. 12, 23, 58, xvi. 28,
xvii. 5, 24, and other places.) To deny that
John exhibits Jesus as having this superhuman self-consciousness, is exegetically
baseless, and would imply that (in his prologue) the evangelist had, from the public
life of the Lord, and from His words and
works, formed an abstract idea as to His

nature, which was not sustained, but rather
refuted, by his own representation of the
history,—a thing inconceivable. This, in
general, against Weizsäcker in *d. Jahrb. f.
Deutsche Theologie*, 1857, p. 154 ff., 1862, p. 634
ff. ; Weiss, *Lehrbegr.* p. 244. See my com-
ments on the particular passages (also
against Beyschlag).—The idea of the Logos,
moreover, is related to that of the ζωή, not
as something accidental, but in such a way
that the Logos is conceived as the original
and personally conscious substratum of the
latter. Thus was it *given* to the author by
the history itself, and by his profoundly
vivid realization of that history through
communion with Him in whom the ζωή
dwells. The Logos is the same fundamental
conception (only in a more definite speculative form) as the υἱὸς τοῦ θεοῦ.

[3] Comp. Weizsäck. *Evangel. Gesch.* p. 257.
[4] Reuss in the *Strassb. Denkschr.* p. 37 ff.

essential character, and peculiar fundamental type, in which it allowed itself to be recognized by manifold receptivities, and under dissimilar circumstances. It was on the soul of this very apostle that the image of that wonderful life, with which his inspired recollections were connected, was, without a single discordant feature, most *perfectly* delineated, and in all the deep fulness of its nature : it *lives* in him ; and his own thinking and feeling, with its profound contemplativeness, is so thoroughly intertwined with and transfigured by this life and the ideal it contains, that each *individual* recollection and representation becomes the more easily blended by him into harmony with the *whole*. His very language must needs ever retain that inalienable stamp which he once involuntarily received from the heart and living word of Christ, and appropriated and preserved in all its depth and transparency in the profoundly spiritual laboratory of his own long regenerate life.[1] Some have assigned to the Gospel the honour rather of a well-devised work of art, than of a truly earnest and real history.[2] It is both, in the inseparable unity and truth of the art of the Holy Ghost.—If, again, some have urged that the author of the fourth Gospel appears as one *standing apart* from any personal participation in the history he was writing, and from Judaism,[3] still we should bear in mind, that if John wrote his Gospel at a later time, and among a community moulded by Hellenistic culture, after the liberation of his Christian nature from the Judaism by which it had long been penetrated, and when he had long been familiar with the purest spiritual Christianity and its universalism, as well as raised through the medium of speculation to a higher standpoint in his view of the Gospel history, he certainly did stand much further apart than the earlier evangelists, not indeed from his history strictly speaking, but from its former surroundings and from Judaism. This, however, does not warrant the substitution in his place of a non-Jewish author, who out of elements but slightly historical and correlative myths wove a semblance of history. On the contrary, many peculiar traits marked by the greatest vividness and originality, revealing a personal participation in the history,[4] rise up in proof, to bridge over the gulf between the remoteness of the author and the proximity of a former eye-witness, in whose view the history throughout is not developed from the doctrine, but the doctrine from the history.[5] Hence, also, he it is who, while he rose much higher above Judaism than Paul, yet, like Matthew in his Gospel, though with more individuality and independence,

[1] Comp. Ewald, *Jahrb.* III. p. 163, X. p. 90 f., and his *Johann. Schriften*, I. p. 32 ff. ; also Brückner on de Wette, p. 25 ff.

[2] Keim, *Gesch. J.* 1. p. 123.

[3] Compare the frequent οἱ Ἰουδαῖοι, v. 16, vii. 1, 19, 25, viii. 17, x. 34, etc. See Fischer in the *Tüb. Zeitschr.* 1840, II. p. 96 ff. ; Baur, *Neut. Theol.* p. 390 f. : Scholten and others. On the other side, Bleek, p. 246 ff. ; Luthardt, I. p. 143 ff. Compare notes on i. 19, viii. 17 ; also Ewald, *Johann. Schriften*, I. p. 10 f.

[4] See i. 35 ff., v. 10 ff., vii. 1 ff. ; chap. ix. 11, 12, xiii. 22 ff., xviii. 15 ff., xix. 4 ff., xxi.

[5] Compare Weizsäcker in the *Jahrb. f. D. Th.* 1859, p. 690 ff. See the opposite view in Keim, p. 127. Scholten comes even to the melancholy conclusion : " The contents of the fourth Gospel cannot be of use as historical authority in any single point." The author threw into the form of an *historical drama* what was subjective truth to himself, unconcerned as to its historical accuracy.

took pains to exhibit the connection between the events of the Gospel history and Old Testament prophecy. In this way, as well as by the explanations of Jewish facts, views, appellations, and so on, which are interspersed, he shows himself to belong to the ancient people of God, as far as his spiritual renewal was, and necessarily must have been, compatible with this connection.[1] Lastly, the historical *contradictions* with the Synoptics are either only apparent (for instance, a ministration on several occasions at Jerusalem is implied, Matt. xxiii. 37, Luke xiii. 34), or such as cannot fairly lead to the conclusion of a non-apostolic authorship, since we do not possess Matthew in its original form, and therefore are not prevented by the counterweight of equally apostolic evidence from assigning to John a preponderating authority, which especially must be done in regard to such very striking variations as the date of the day on which Jesus died, and the account of the last supper. Besides, if what was erroneous and unhistorical might, after the lapse of so long a time, have affected even the memory of an apostle, yet matters of this sort, wherever found in particular passages of our Gospel, are rather chargeable on commentators than on the author, especially in the exceptions taken to the names of such places as Bethany, i. 28, and Sychar, iv. 5. On the whole, the work is a phenomenon so sublime and unique among productions of the Christian spirit,[2] that if it were the creation of an unknown author of the second century, it would be beyond the range of all that is historically conceivable. In its contents and tone, as well as in its style, which is unlike that of the earlier Gospels, it is so entirely without any internal connection with the development and literary conditions of that age, that had the church, instead of *witnessing* to its apostolic origin, raised a *doubt* on that point, historical criticism would see assigned to it the inevitable task of proving and vindicating such an origin from the book itself. In this case, to violate the authority of the church *in favor* of the Gospel, would necessarily have a more happily and permanently successful result than can follow from *opposing* the Gospel. After having stood the critical tests originated by Bretschneider and Baur, this Gospel will continue to shine with its own calm inner superiority and undisturbed transparency, issuing forth victorious from never-ceasing conflicts ; the last star, as it were, of evangelic history and teaching, yet beaming with the purest and highest light, which could never have arisen amid the scorching heat of Gnosticism, or have emerged from the fermentation of some catholicizing process, but which rose rather on the horizon of the

---

[1] Comp. Weizsäcker, *Evang. Gesch.* p. 263.

[2] Gfrörer, of course, makes it a product of dotage and fancy. Origen, on the other hand, calls it τῶν εὐαγγελίων ἀπαρχήν, and says of it, οὗ τὸν νοῦν οὐδεὶς δύναται λαβεῖν μὴ ἀναπεσὼν ἐπὶ τὸ στῆθος Ἰησου, and, τηλικοῦτον δὲ γενέσθαι δεῖ τὸν ἐσόμενον ἄλλον Ἰωάννην, ὥστε οἰονεὶ τὸν Ἰωάννην δειχθῆναι ὄντα Ἰησοῦν ἀπὸ Ἰησοῦ. Hence, also, we can understand the constant recurrence, so as to make them regulate the presentation of the history, both of the ideas lying at the basis of Christ's whole work, and of the fundamental views which John, beyond any other evangelist, had derived from the history itself, in which he had borne a part on the breast of Jesus. Thus, with him, the grand simple theme of his book is through all its variations in harmonious and necessary concord, a living monotone of the one spirit, not a "leaden" one. (Keim, *Gesch. J.* p. 117.)

apostolic age, from the spirit of the disciple most intimate with his Lord, and which is destined never again to set,[1]—the guide to a true catholicity, differing wholly from the ecclesiastical development of the second century,[2] and still remaining as the unattained goal of the future.

Nor can the attempt be successful to treat only a certain *nucleus* of our Gospel as genuinely apostolical, and to assign the rest to disciples of John or other later hands. The reasons for this procedure are inadequate, while it is itself so destitute of all historical evidence and warrant, and runs so entirely into caprice and diversity of subjective judgment, and hence also presents such a variety of results in the several attempts which have been made, that it would be in any case critically more becoming to leave still unsolved the difficulties in the matter and connection of particular passages, than to get rid of them by striking them out according to an arbitrary standard. This remark applies not merely to some of the older attempts of this kind by Eckermann, Vogel, Ammon,[3] and Paulus, but also to Rettig's opinion (*Ephemer. exeg.* I. p. 83 ff.) : ''Compositum esse et digestum a seriori Christiano, Johannis auditore forsitan gnosticae dedito philosophiae, qui, quum in ecclesiae Ephesinae scriniis ecclesiasticis vel alio loco privato plura Jesu vitae capita per Johannem descripta reperisset, vel a Johanne ipso accepisset, iis compositis et ordinatis suam de λόγῳ philosophiam praefixit ;"—and even to the more thorough attempts made by Weisse,[4] and Alex. Schweizer.[5] According to Weisse (compare, however, his partial retraction in his *Philos. Dogmat.* 1855, I. p. 153), John, for the purpose of setting forth his own idea of Christ and the doctrinal system in discourses of Jesus, selected such discourses, adding those of the Baptist and the prologue. After his death, one of his adherents and disciples (xix. 35), by further adding what he had learnt from the apostle's own mouth, and from the evangelic tradition, but without any knowledge of the Synoptics, worked up these ''*Johannean Studies*" into a Gospel history, the plan of which was, of course, very imperfect ; so that the apostle's communications consequently form only the *groundwork* of the Gospel, though among them must be reckoned all the strictly didactic and contemplative portions, in determining which the First Epistle of John serves as a test. According to Schweizer (comp. also Schenkel, previously in the *Stud. u. Krit.* 1840, p. 753 ff., who resolves the apostolical portion into two sets of discourses), such sections are to be excluded from the apostle's original work, as ''are quite disconnected and abrupt, interwoven with no discourses, are altogether without any impor-

---

[1] If the apostle, in composing his work, employed an amanuensis, which is not improbable, judging from similar cases in the New Testament Epp. (see especially Ewald, *Jahrb.* X. p. 87 ff.), though it is not proved by xix. 35, still the writer must be regarded only as simply drawing up what the apostle *dictated,*—a conclusion arising out of the peculiar character, tenderness, and profundity of the book, and its entire resemblance to the First Epistle of John.

[2] Comp. Holtzm. *Judenth. u. Christenth.* 1867, p. 713.

[3] Progr. quo docetur, Johannem evang. *auctorem* ab *editore* huj. libri fuisse diversum, 1811.

[4] Both in his *Evang. Gesch.* I. p. 96 ff., II. p. 184 ff., 486 ff., 520 ff. ; as also in his *Evangelienfrage*, 1856, p. 111 ff.

[5] d. *Ev. Joh. nach s. innern Werthe kritisch untersucht*, 1841.

tant word of Jesus, permeated by an essentially different estimate and idea of miracle, without vividness of narration, and moreover are divergent in style, and agree, besides, in recounting Galilean incidents." These excluded sections, along with which especially fall to the ground the turning of the water into wine at Cana, the healing of the nobleman's son, the miraculous feeding (ii. 1 ff., iv. 44 ff., vi. 1 ff.), are said to have originated with the author of chap. xxi., who also, according to Scholten, must have added a cycle of interpolated remarks, such as ii. 21 f., vii. 39, xii. 33, xviii. 32. All such attempts at critical dismemberment, especially in the case of a work so thoroughly of one mould, must undoubtedly fail. Even Weizsäcker's view,[1] that our Gospel was derived from the apostle's own communications, though not composed by his own hands, but by those of his trusted disciples in Ephesus, is based on insufficient grounds, which are set aside by an unprejudiced exegesis.[2] This hypothesis is all the more doubtful, if the Gospel (with the exception of chap. xxi.) be allowed to have been composed while the apostle was still living ; it is not supported by the testimony of Clem. Alex. and the Canon of Muratori,[3] and in fact antiquity furnishes no evidence in its favour.

Literature :—(1) *Against the Genuineness :* Evanson, *Dissonance of the Four — — Evangelists,* Ipswich 1792. (Vogel), *d. Evangelist Joh. u. s. Ausleger vor d. jüngsten Gericht,* I. Lpz. 1801, II. 1804. Horst, in Henke's *Mus.* I. 1, pp. 20 ff., 17 ff., 1803. Cludius, *Uransichten des Christenth.,* Altona 1808, p. 40 ff. Ballenstedt, *Philo. u. Joh.,* Gött. 1812. The most important among the older works : Bretschneider, *Probabilia de evangelii et epistolarum Joh. apost. indole et origine,* Lpz. 1820, who makes the Gospel originate in the first half of the second century, in the interest of Christ's divinity. Later opponents : Rettig, *Ephem. exeg.* I. p. 62 ff. Strauss, *Leben Jesu,* despite a half retractation in the third edition (1838), the more decidedly against in the fourth (1840). Weisse, *Evang. Gesch.* 1838, and *d. Evangelienfrage,* 1856. Lützelberger, *die kirchliche Tradition üb. d. Apostel Joh.* 1840. B. Bauer, *Krit. d. evang. Gesch. d. Joh.* 1840, and *Kritik d. Evangelien,* I. 1850. Schwegler, *Montanism,* 1841, and *nachapost. Zeitalter,* 1846. Baur,[4]

---

[1] *Untersuch. üb. d. evang. Gesch.* 1864, p. 298 ff.

[2] See also Ewald, *Jahrb.* XII. p. 212 ff.

[3] Clement of Alexandria, in Euseb. vi. 14, says John composed the spiritual Gospel προτραπέντα ὑπὸ τῶν γνωρίμων πνεύματι θεοφορηθέντα. How different is this statement from the above view ! Just as much at variance with it is the similar testimony of Muratori's Fragment, which lays special stress upon the composition by the apostle himself, and indeed supports it by 1 John i. 1-4. Moreover, see on xviii. 15, xix. 35, xxi. 23 f.

[4] According to Baur's school, the Gospel, the existence of which is only conceivable at the time of the church's transition into Catholicism, originated about the middle of the second century (according to Volkmar, only towards 150-160 ; according to Hilgenfeld, as soon as 120-140, contemporaneously with the second Jewish war, or soon after). The author, who, it is said, appropriated to himself the authority of the Apostle John, the author of the Apocalypse, transfigured in a higher unity into the Christian Gnosis the interests of Jewish and Pauline Christianity, while going beyond both, so that the historical materials taken from the Synoptics, and wrought up according to the ideas of the prologue, form merely the basis of the dogmatic portions, and are the reflex of the idea. To bring the new form of the Christian consciousness to a genuine apostolic expression, the author, whose Gospel stands upon the boundary line of Gnosticism, and "now and then goes beyond the limits," made an ingenious and

Krit. Untersuchungen üb. d. kanonischen Evang., Tüb. 1847, p. 79 ff. (previously in the *Theol. Jahrb.* 1844). Zeller, in the *Theol. Jahrb.* 1845, p. 579 ff., and 1847, p. 136 ff. Baur, *ibidem*, 1848, p. 264 ff., 1854, p. 196 ff., 1857, p. 209 ff. ; and in his *Christenth. d. drei ersten Jahrb.* p. 131 ff. ; also in his controversial work, *An Herrn Dr. Karl Hase*, Tüb. 1855 ; and in his treatise, *" die Tübinger Schule,"* 1859. Hilgenfeld, *d. Evang. u. die Briefe Joh. nach ihrem Lehrbegr. dargestellt*, Halle 1849, and in the *Theol. Jahrb.* 1849, p. 209 ff.; also in his works, *die Evangelien nach ihrer Entstehung u. s. w.*, Lpz. 1854, p. 227 ff.; and in his controversial treatise, *das Urchristenth. in d. Hauptwendepunkten seines Entwickelungsganges*, Jena 1855 ; also in the *Theol. Jahrb.* 1857, p. 498 ff., and in the *Zeitschr. f. wissenschaft Theol.* 1859, p. 281 ff., 383 ff.; similarly in the *Kanon u. Krit. d. N. T.* 1863, p. 218 ff., and in his *Zeitschr.* 1863, 1 and 2, 1867, p. 180 ff. Köstlin, in the *Theol. Jahrb.* 1851, p. 183 ff. Tobler, *die Evangelienfrage*, Zürich 1858 (anonymously), and in the *Zeitschr. f. wiss. Theol.* 1860, p. 169 ff. Schenkel[1] in his *Charakterbild Jesu*, chap. 2. Volkmar, most recently in his work against Tischendorf, *" d. Ursprung uns. Evangel."* 1866. Scholten, *d. ältest. Zeug. betr. d. Schriften d. N. T.*, translated from the Dutch by Manchot, 1867 (compare his *Evang. according to John*, translated by Lang). Keim, *Geschichte Jesu*, 1867, I. p. 103 ff.   (2)

artistic use of the relative points of connection with the Apocalypse, in order to spiritualize the Apocalypse into a Gospel. The relation of the Gospel to the parties of the time (whose exciting questions it touches), especially to Gnosticism, Montanism, Ebionism, the Easter controversy, is indeed very variously defined by Baur's school, yet always in such a way that the historical character of the contents is given up. In exchange for this loss, the consolation is offered us, that " the Christianity thus fashioned into a perfect theory was simply a development of that which, according to its most primitive and credible representation, the religious consciousness of Jesus contained in creative fulness,"—Hilgenfeld (*d. Evangelien*, p. 349), who even makes John's theology stand in the same relation to the religious consciousness of Jesus, " as, according to the promise in John xvi. 12, the work of the Paraclete, as the Spirit leading the church into all truth, was to stand to the teachings of its Founder." The most extravagant judgment is that of Volkmar: the Evangelist *" starts from the Gospel of the dualistic anti-Judaical Gnosis of Marcion, and overcomes it by the help of Justin's doctrine of the Logos with its monism."*—Tobler, though attributing the first Epistle to the apostle, makes the author of our Gospel to be *Apollos*, whom he also regards as the author of the Epistle to the Hebrews, and of First and Second John. See against this error, which makes the Gospel to have been intended for the Corinthians, Hilgenf. in the *Zeitschr. f. wiss. Theol.* 1859, p. 411 ff. Moreover, what Tobler has subsequently advanced in the *Zeitschr. f. wiss. Theol.* 1860, p. 169 ff., cannot support his hypothesis.

[1] According to this modern notion of Schenkel, our Gospel originated about 110–120 A.D., under the influence of the Christian doctrine of wisdom prevailing in Asia Minor. The author, he says, certainly did not write a work of fiction or fancy, but separated a cycle of evangelic traditions from their historical framework, and forced them up into the region of eternal thought, etc. Thus, Jesus was such as the author depicts Him, not always in *reality*, but in truth. At this result Keim also substantially arrives : he attributes the Gospel to a Jewish Christian of liberal opinions and friendly to the Gentiles, probably one of the Diaspora in Asia Minor about the beginning of the second century, who published it under the name of the Apostle John. He wrote with the just conviction that the apostles and John would have so written, had they been living in his time, and did not aim at establishing an external history, but at exhibiting the spirit which sits enthroned in every history of the life of Jesus. According to Scholten, the Gospel was written about 150 A.D., by a philosophically enlightened Gentile Christian, assuming the guise of an ideal apostle, setting aside what was untrue in the various tendencies of the day (Gnosticism, Antinomianism, Montanism, Quartodecimanism, but recognizing the correlated truths, and expressing them in appropriate forms, though it was recognized as apostolic only towards the close of the second century.

For the Genuineness, and especially against Bretschneider (comp. the latter's later confession in his *Dogmat*. ed. 3, I. p. 268 : "The design which my *Probabilia* had—namely, to raise a fresh and further investigation into the authenticity of John's writings—has been attained, and the doubts raised may perhaps be now regarded as removed") : Stein, *Authentia ev. Joh. contra Bretschn. dubia vindicat.*, Brandenb. 1822. Calmberg, *Diss. de antiquiss. patrum pro ev. Joh. authentia testim.*, Hamb. 1822. Hemsen, *die Authent. der Schriften des Ev. Joh.*, Schleswig 1823. Usteri, *Comment. crit., in qua ev. Joh. genuinum esse ex comparatis quatuor evangelior. narrationib. de coena ultima et passione J. Ch.*, ostenditur, Turici 1823. Crome, *Probabilia haud probabilia*, or *Widerlegung der von Dr. Bretschneider gegen die Aechtheit des Ev. u. d. Briefe Joh. erhobenen Zweifel*, Lpz. 1824. Rettberg, *an Joh. in exhibenda Jesu natura reliquis canonicis scriptis ver repugnet*, Gött. 1826. Hauff, *die Authent. u. der hohe Werth des Ev. Joh.*, Nürnberg 1831.—Against Weisse ; Frommann, in the *Stud. u. Krit.* 1840, p. 853 ff. ; Hilgenfeld, in the *Zeitschr. f. wiss. Theol.* 1859, p. 397 ff.—Against Schweizer : Luthardt, i. p. 6 ff.—Against Baur and his school : Merz, in the *Würtemb. Stud.* 1844, ii. Ebrard, *d. Ev. Joh. u. die neueste Hypothese üb. s. Entstehung*, Zürich 1845 ; and in his *Kritik d. evang. Gesch.* ed. 2, 1850, p. 874 ff. Hauff, in the *Stud. u. Krit.* 1846, p. 550 ff. Bleek, *Beiträge z. Ev. Krit.* 1846, p. 92 ff., u. *Einl.* p. 177 ff. Weitzel, in the *Stud. u. Krit.* 1848, p. 806 ff., 1849, p. 578 ; also de Wette, *Einl.*, whose final judgment, however (§ 110 g.), only declares against the view which would deny to the apostle *any* share in the composition of the Gospel. See, besides, Niermeyer, *Verhandeling over de echtheid d. Johanneischen Schriften*, s' Gravenhage 1852. Mayer (Catholic), *Aechtheit d. Ev. nach Joh.*, Schaffh. 1854. Schneider, *Aechth. des Joh. Ev. nach den äusseren Zeugen*, Berl. 1854. Kahnis, *Dogmat.* I. p .416 ff. Ritschl, *Altkath. K.* p. 48. Tischendorf, *wann wurden uns. Ev. verfasst?* 1865 ; 4th enlarged edition, 1866. Riggenbach, *d. Zeug. f. d. Ev. Joh. neu unters.* 1866. Dr. Pressensé, *Jes. Christus, son Temps*, etc., 1866. Oosterzee, *d. Johannes-evang., vier Vorträge*, 1867 [Eng. trans.] ; also Hofstede de Groot (against also the previously mentioned work of Scholten), *Basilides als erster Zeuge für Alter und Auctorit. neutest. Schr.* German edition, 1868. Jonker, *het evang. v. Joh.* 1867. Compare generally, besides the Commentaries, Ewald, *Jahrb.* III. p. 146 ff., V. p. 178 ff., X. p. 83 ff., XII. p. 212 ff. Grimm, in the *Hall. Encykl.* ii. 22, p. 5 ff.

SEC. IV.—DESIGN OF THE GOSPEL.

John himself, xx. 31, tells us very distinctly the purpose of the Gospel which he wrote for the Christians of his own day. It was nothing else than to impart the conviction that Jesus was the Messiah, by describing the history of His appearance and of His work ; and through faith in this, to communicate the Messianic life which was revealed in Jesus when on earth. While it has this general purpose in common with the other Gospels, it has as its special and definite task to exhibit in Jesus the Messiah, as *in the highest sense the Son of God*, that is, *the Incarnate Divine Logos ;* and hence John places the section on the Logos at the very beginning as his distinctive programme, therewith furnishing the key for the understanding of the whole. In the existing name and conception of the Logos, he recognizes a perfectly

befitting expression for his own sublime view of Christ, the humanly manifested divine source of life ; and accordingly, he has delineated the human
manifestation and the historical life of the divine in Christ with creative
spirit and vividness, in order that the eternal and highest power of life,
which had thus entered bodily into the world, might be appropriated by
faith. Even the Gospel of Matthew (and of Luke) grasps the idea of the
Son of God metaphysically, and explains it by the divine generation. John,
however, apprehends and explains it by raising it into the premundane and
eternal relation of the Son to the Father, who sent the Son ; just as Paul
also earnestly teaches this pre-existence, though he does not conceive of it
under the form of the Logos, and therefore has nothing about a beginning
of divine Sonship by a divine generation in time. John therefore occupies
a far higher standing-point than Matthew ; but, like the other evangelists,
he develops his proof *historically*, not sacrificing historic reality and tradition to idealism (against Baur and his school), but partly selecting from the
materials furnished by the extant tradition and already presented in the
older evangelic writings, partly leaving these, and carefully selecting solely
from the rich stores of his own memory and experience. In this way, it is
quite obvious how important the discourses of Jesus, especially upon His
divine Messianic dignity in opposition to the unbelief of the Jews, were as
elements of John's plan ; and further, how necessary it was that the testimonies of the Baptist, the prophetical predictions, and the select miraculous
proofs,—the latter forming at the same time the bases of the more important discourses,—should co-operate towards his purpose. The general similarity of his aim with that of the current Galilean tradition on the one hand,
and on the other hand its special distinctiveness, which is due to his own
more sublime and spiritual intuition and his purpose to delineate Jesus as
the Incarnate Logos, the possessor and imparter of divine and eternal life, as
well as his independence in both these respects, as a most intimate eye and
ear witness, of all the previous labours of others, and his original peculiar
arrangement and reproduction of the doctrines of Jesus as from a centre,
determining every detail and binding them into one,—this, and the primary
destination of the work for readers who must have been acquainted with
Graeco-Judaic speculations, gave the book the characteristic form which it
possesses. The intellectual unity, which thus runs through it, is the reflection of the author's peculiar view of the whole, which was not formed *à
priori*, but as the result of experience,[1] the fruit of a long life in Christ, and
of a fulness and depth of recollection such as he only, among the living,
could possess. Written after the destruction of Jerusalem, and by *that* disciple who had long advanced beyond Jewish Christianity, and in the centre
of Asiatic culture was still labouring amidst the highest esteem, as probably
the only aged apostle remaining, this Gospel could not have an eye to Palestinian readers,[2] as had been formerly the case with Matthew's Collection
of Logia, and the Gospel which originated from it. It was very naturally

[1] i. 14 ; comp. Hauff, in the *Stud. u. Krit.*
1846, p. 574 ff.

[2] Hence the interpretations and explanations which presuppose the readers to be
non-Palestinian, i. 38, 41 f., iv. 25, v. 2, *al.*

destined, first of all, for those Christian circles among which the apostle lived and laboured, consequently for readers belonging to churches originally founded by Paul, and who had grown up out of Jewish and Gentile Christian elements, and had been carried on by John himself to that higher unity for which Paul could work only amidst continual conflict with yet unconquered Judaism. The Gospel of John, therefore, is not a Pauline one, but one more transfigured and spiritual, rising with more absolute elevation above Judaism than Paul, more tender and thoughtful than his, and also more original, but agreeing as to its main ideas with the doctrine dialectically wrought out by Paul, though exhibiting these ideas in a tranquil height above the strife of opposing principles, and in harmony with the full perfection of fundamental Christian doctrine ; and thus communicating for all time the essence, light, and life of the eminently *catholic* tendency and destination of Christianity. It represents the true and pure Christian Gnosis, though by this we are not to suppose any *polemical purpose against the heretical Gnostics,* as even Irenaeus in his day (iii. 11. 1) indicates the errors of *Cerinthus* and of the *Nicolaitans* as those controverted by John, to which Epiphanius[1] and Jerome[2] added also those of the *Ebionites,* while modern writers also have thought that it controverted more or less directly and definitely the Gnostic doctrine, especially of Cerinthus.[3] It is decisive against the assumption of any such polemical purpose, that, in general, John nowhere in his Gospel allows any direct reference to the perverted tendencies of his day to appear ; while to search for indirect and hidden allusions of the kind, as if they were intentional, would be as arbitrary as it would be repugnant to the decided character of the apostolic standpoint which he took when in conscious opposition to heresies. [See Note II. p. 40.] In his First *Epistle* the apostle controverts the vagaries of Gnosticism, and it is improbable that these came in his way only after he had already written his Gospel (as Ewald, *Jahrb.* III. p. 157, assumes) ; but the task of meeting this opposition, to which the apostle set himself in his Epistle, cannot have been the task of his Gospel, which in its whole character keeps far *above* such controversies. At any rate, we see from his Epistle how John would have carried on a controversy, had he *wished* to do so in his Gospel. The development of Gnosticism, as it was in itself a movement which could not have failed to appear, lay brooding then, and for some time previously, in the whole atmosphere of that age and place ; it appears in John pure, and in sententious simplicity and clearness, but ran off, in the heresies of the partly contemporaneous and partly later formed Gnosticism, into all its varied aberrations, amid which it seemed even to derive support by what it drew from John. That it has been possible to explain many passages as *opposed* to the Gnostics, as little justifies the assumption of a set purpose of this kind, as the interpretation *favourable* to Gnosticism, which is possible in other passages, would justify the inference of an *irenical* purpose (Lücke) in respect of this heresy, since any *express* and *precise indication* of such tenden-

---

[1] *Haer.* li. 12, lxix. 23.
[2] *De vir. illustr.*
[3] Erasmus, Melanchthon, Grotius, Michae-lis, Storr, Hug, Kleucker, Schneckenburger, Ebrard, Hengstenberg, and several others.

cies does not appear. Similarly must we judge the assumption of a polemical purpose against the *Docetae*,[1] for which some have adduced i. 14, xix. 34, xx. 20, 27 ; or an opposition to *Ebionism* and *Judaism ;*[2] or to the plots of Jews who had been restored after the destruction of Jerusalem.[3] At the same time, it seems quite arbitrary, nay, injurious to John's historical fidelity and truth, to set down his omissions of evangelic circumstances to the account of a polemical purpose ; as, for example, Schneckenburger, *Beitr.* p. 60 ff., who regards the omission of the agony as based on an anti-Gnostic, and the silence as to the transfiguration on the mount on an anti-Docetic interest. A controversial reference to the *disciples of John*[4] is not supported by such passages as i. 6–8, 15, 19–41, iii. 22 ff., v. 33–36, x. 40 f., since the unique sublimity of Jesus, even when contrasted with *John* who was sent by God, must have been vindicated by the apostle in the necessary course of his history and of his work ; but in these passages no such *special* purpose can be proved, and we must assume that, with any such tendency, expressions like that in Matt. xi. 11 would not have been overlooked. Besides, those disciples of John who *rejected* Christ,[5] and the *Zabaeans* or *Mendeans*,[6] who became known in the seventeenth century, were of later origin, while those who appear in Acts xviii. 25, xix. 1 ff., were simply not yet accurately acquainted with Christ, and therefore as regards them we should have to think only of a tendency to gain these over ;[7] but we cannot assume even this, considering the utter want of any more precise reference to them in our Gospel.

Moreover, in general, as to the development of heresy, so far as it was conspicuous in that age, and especially in Asia (comp. the Epistles to the Galatians and Colossians), we must assume as an internal necessity that John, in opposition to its errors, especially those of a Gnostic and Judaizing character (according to Hengstenberg, to the inundation of *Gentile* errors into the church), must have been conscious that his Gospel ought to set forth the original *truth*, unobscured by those errors. We must therefore admit indeed in general, that the influence of the existing forms of opposition to the truth, for which he had to testify, practically contributed to determine the shape of his treatise, but only to the extent that, while abiding solely by his thesis, he provided therein, by its very simplicity, the weightiest counterpoise against errors,[8] without stooping to *combat* them, or even undertaking the *defence* of the Gospel against them,[9] his task being elevated far *above* the then existing conflicts of opinion.[10] This must be

[1] Semler, Bertholdt, Eckermann ; Niemeyer, *de Docetis*, Hal. 1823 ; Schneckenburger, Schott, Ebrard.

[2] Jerome, Grotius ; Lange, *die Judenchristen, Ebioniten und Nikolaiten d. apost. Zeit.* Lpz. 1828 ; Ebrard, and many others.

[3] Aberle in the *Tüb. Quartalschr.* 1864, p. 1 ff.

[4] Grotius, Schlichting, Wolzogen ; Overbeck, *über d. Ev. Joh.* 1784 ; Michael., Storr, Lützelberger, and others, also Ewald.

[5] *Recogn. Clem.* i. 54, 60.

[6] Gieseler, *Kirchengesch.* I. i, p. 76, Eng.

trans. vol. I. p. 58.

[7] Herder, *vom Sohne Gottes*, p. 24 ; also de Wette.

[8] Comp. Reuss, *Denkschr.* p. 27.

[9] Seyffarth, *Specialcharakterist.* p. 39 f. ; Schott, *Isag.* § 40 ; de Wette, Hengstenberg, and many others.

[10] Even Baur, p. 373, acknowledges that "John's Gospel stands amid all the oppositions of the age, without anywhere exhibiting the definite colour of a temporary or local opposition." But this is really only conceivable if the Gospel belongs to the apos-

maintained, lest on the one hand we degrade the Gospel, in the face of its whole character, into a controversial treatise, or on the other hand withdraw it, as a product of mere speculation, from its necessary and concrete relations to the historical development of the church of that age.

Seeing that our Gospel serves in manifold ways not only to *confirm*, but moreover, on a large scale (as especially by relating the extra-Galilean journeys, acts, discourses) as well as in particulars, to *complete* the synoptic accounts, nay, even sometimes (as in determining the day of the crucifixion) in important places to *correct* them, it has been assumed very often, from Jerome (comp. already Euseb. iii. 24) downwards, and with various modifications even at the present day (Ebrard, Ewald, Weizsäcker, Godet, and many others), that this relation to the Synoptics *was the designed object of the work*. Such a view, however, cannot be supported ; for there is not the slightest hint in the Gospel itself of any such purpose ; and further, there would thus be attributed to it an historico-critical character totally at variance with its real nature and its design, as expressly stated, xx. 30, 31, and which even as a collateral purpose would be quite foreign to the high spiritual tone, sublime unity, and unbroken compactness of the book. Moreover, in the repetition of synoptical passages which John gives, there are not always any material additions or corrections leading us to suppose a confirmatory design, in view of the non-repetition of a great many other and more important synoptical narrations. Again, where John diverges from parallel synoptical accounts, in the absence of contradictory references (in iii. 24 only does there occur a passing note of *time* of this kind), his independence of the Galilean tradition fully suffices to explain the divergence. Finally, in very much that John has not borrowed from the synoptical history, and against the truth of which no well-founded doubt can be urged, to suppose in such passages any intentional though silent purpose on his part to correct, would be equivalent to his rejection of the statements. In short, had the design in question exercised any determining influence upon the apostle in the planning and composition of his work, he would have accomplished his task in a very strange, thoroughly imperfect, and illogical manner. We may, on the contrary, take it for granted that he was well acquainted with the Galilean tradition,[1] and that the written accounts drawn from the cycle of that tradition, numbers of which were already in circulation, and which were especially represented in our Synoptics, were likewise sufficiently known to him ; for he presupposes as known the historical existence of this tradition in all its essential parts.[2] But it is precisely his per-

tolic age, and its author stands upon an apostolic elevation ; it is inconceivable if it originated in the second century, when those oppositions were developing, and had already developed into open and deep-seated divisions, and where the conditions necessary for the production of *such* a Formula Concordiae were utterly wanting in the bosom of the time.

[1] According to Ewald, John only compared and made use of what is assumed by Ewald to be the "oldest Gospel," "the collection of discourses," and "the original Mark." But a limitation to these three books, considering the number already existing (Luke i. 1), is in itself improbable, and is all the less demonstrable, that the first and third treatises named by Ewald have themselves only a very problematical existence.

[2] See Weizsäcker in the *Jahrb. fur Deutsche Theol.* 1859, p. 691 ff. He goes, how-

fect independence of this tradition and its records—keeping in view his aim to bring fully out the higher Messianic proof, and the abundant material from which his own recollection could so fully draw—which enables us to understand the partial coincidence, and still greater divergence, between him and the Synoptics, and his entire relation to them generally, which is not determined by any special design on his part ; so that the confirmation, correction, and enlargement of their narratives often appear as a *result* of which he is conscious, but never as the *object* which he had sought to accomplish in his treatise. As to any design, so understood, of *correcting* the Synoptics, the *silence* of John upon many portions of the cycle of synoptic narrative is undoubtedly very significant, in so far as the historical truth of these in their traditional form would have been of special value for the apostle's purpose. This holds true particularly of the account of the temptation, the transfiguration, and the ascension as actual occurrences, as well as of the cure of demoniacs as such. As criticism, however, is here pledged to special caution, so the opposite conclusion—viz. that facts which would have been of great importance even for the synoptical Messianic proof, but which are recorded only in John, cannot be regarded as originally historical in the form in which he gives them—is everywhere inadmissible, especially where he speaks as an eye-witness, in which capacity he must be ranked above Matthew : for Matthew did indeed compose the collection of discourses which is worked up into the Gospel that bears his name, but not the Gospel itself as it lies before us in its gradually settled canonical form. If, while taking all into account, the complete, unbiassed independence of John in relation to the Synoptics, above whom he stands distinguished by his exact determination of the succession of time, must be preserved intact ; we must at the same time bear in mind that, as the last evangelist and apostle, he had to satisfy the higher needs of Christian knowledge, called forth by the development of the church in this later stage, and thus had boldly to go beyond the range of the whole previous Gospel literature.[1] This higher need had reference to that deeper and uniform insight into the peculiar eternal essence of Christianity and its Founder, which John, as no other of his contemporaries, by his richly stored experience was fitted and called to impart. He had thus, indeed, as a matter of fact, supplemented and partly corrected the earlier evangelists, though not to such an extent as to warrant the supposition that this was his deliberate object. For, by giving to the entire written history its *fullest completion*, he took rank far above all who had worked before him ; not doctrinally making an advance from πίστις to γνῶσις (Lücke), but, in common with the Synoptics, pursuing the same goal of πίστις (xx. 31), yet bringing the subject-matter of this common faith to a higher, more uniform, and universal stage of the original γνῶσις of its essence than was possible in the earlier Gospel histories, composed under diverse relations, which had now passed

ever, too far, when (*Evang. Gesch.* p. 270) he calls the fourth Gospel, without enlargement from other sources, " a misty picture without reality." Taken *all in all*, it contains

even more concrete history than the Gospels whose range is limited to Galilee.

[1] Comp. Keim, *Gesch. Jesu*, p. 106 f.

away, and with different and (measured by the standard of John's fellowship with Jesus) very inferior resources.

John prosecutes his design, which is to prove that Jesus is the Messiah in the sense of the incarnate Logos, by first of all stating this leading idea in the prologue, and then exhibiting in well-selected[1] historical facts its historical realization in Jesus. This idea, which belongs to the very highest Christological view of the world, guided his choice and treatment of facts, and brought out more clearly the opposition—which the author had constantly in view—with unbelieving and hostile Judaism ; but so far from detracting from the historical character of the Gospel, it appears rather only to be derived from the actual experience of the history, and is in turn confirmed thereby. To defend the Gospel against the suspicion of being a free compilation from synoptical materials in subservience to some main idea, is, on the one hand, as unnecessary for him who recognizes it as of necessity apostolic, and as a phenomenon explicable *only* upon this supposition ; as, on the other hand, in the face of the man who can transfer to the second century, and ascribe to so late a period so great a creative power of Christian thought, such defence, under the altered conditions of the problem, has been proved by experience to be impossible.

SEC. V.— SOURCES, TIME AND PLACE OF WRITING.

The main source is John himself (1 John i. 1 f.), his own inalienable recollection, his experience, his life of fellowship with Christ, continued, increased, and preserved in its freshness by the Spirit of truth, together with the constant impulse to preach and otherwise orally communicate that sublime view of the nature and life of Jesus, which determined the essential contents of his work, as a whole and in details. Accordingly, the credibility of the work asserts itself as being relatively the highest of all, so that it ought to have the deciding voice in case of discrepancies in all essential portions, where the author speaks as an eye and ear witness. This also applies to the discourses of Jesus, in so far as their truthfulness is to be recognized, not indeed to all their details and form,—for they were freely reproduced and resuscitated by his after recollection, and under the influence of a definite and determining point of view, after the Lord's thoughts and ex-

---

[1] In connection with this, the selection made of the *miracles* of Jesus is specially noteworthy. Only one of each kind is chosen, viz. one of transformation, ii. 1 ff. ; one fever cure, iv. 47 ff. ; one cure of lameness, v. 1 ff. ; one feeding, vi. 4 ff. ; one walking on the sea, vi. 16 ff. ; one opening the eyes of the blind, ix. 1 ff. ; one raising from the dead, xi. 1 ff. The number seven is hardly accidental, nor yet the exclusion of any instance of the casting out of demons. That a paragraph containing an account of an instance of casting out has fallen out after chap. v. (Ewald), finds no support in the connection of chap. v. and vi. or elsewhere, and has left no trace appreciable by criticism in evidence of its existence ; while that completed number seven, to which an eighth miracle would thus be added, is against it. This number seven is evidently based upon 3 + 3 + 1,—viz. three miracles of *nature*, three of *healing*, and one of *raising* the dead. An eighth miracle was only added in the appendix, chap. xxi., after the book was finished.

pressions had by a lengthened process of elaboration been blended with his own, which thus underwent a transfiguration,—but as to the subject-matter and its characteristic clothing and thoughtful changes and variations, in all their simplicity and dignity. Their truthfulness is, I say, all the more to be recognized, the more inwardly and vividly the apostle in particular stood in harmony with his Lord's mind and heart. So familiar was he with the character and nature of Christ's discourses, and so imbued with His spirit, that even the reflections of his own which he intertwines, as well as his Epistle, nay, even the discourses of the Baptist, bear one and the same stamp ; a fact, however, which only places the essential originality of the Johannean discourses so much the more above suspicion.[1]

In those portions in which we have no vouchers for personal testimony, the omission is sufficiently supplied, by the author's connection with Christ and his fellow-apostles (as well as with Mary), and by the investigations which we may assume he made, because of his profound interest in the subject ; and by the living, harmonious, and comprehensive view of Christ's life and work with which he was inspired, and which of itself must have led to the exclusion of any strange and interpolated features.

The supposition that in his own behoof he made use of *notes taken by himself* (so Bertholdt, Wegscheider, Schott, and others), does not, indeed, contradict the requirements of a living apostolic call, but must be subordinated so as to be compatible with the unity of spirit and mould of the whole work ; a unity which is the gradually ripened and perfected fruit of a long life of recollection, blending all particulars in one true and bright collective picture, under the guidance of the Divine Spirit as promised by Christ Himself (xiv. 26).

The synoptical tradition was known to John, and his Gospel presupposes it. He was also certainly acquainted with the evangelic writings which embodied it—those at least that were already widely spread and held in esteem ; but all this was not his *source* properly so called : his book itself is proof enough that, in writing it, he was independent of this, and stood *above* all the then existing written and traditional authorities. He has preserved this independence even in the face of Matthew's collection of discourses and Mark's Gospel, both of which doubtless he had read, and which may have suggested to him, unintentionally and unsought for on his part, many expressions in his own independent narrative, but which can in no way interfere with its apostolic originality.[2] We cannot determine whether he likewise knew the somewhat more recent Gospel of *Luke* (Keim and others) ;

---

[1] Ewald, *Jahrb.* III. p. 163 f. : "As, under the Old Covenant, it is precisely the earliest prophets who are the strictest and purest interpreters of Him who, though never visible in bodily form, yet moves, lives, and speaks in them as if He were ; so at the very close of the New Testament a similar phenomenon reappears, when the Logos comes on the scene in bright and clear manifestation. The Spirit of the historical Christ was concentrated in His former familiar disciple in the most compact strength and transparent clearness, and now streams forth from him over this later world, which had never yet so understood Him. The mouth of John is for this world the mouth of the glorified Christ, and the full historical resuscitation of that Logos who will not reappear till the end of all things."

[2] Comp. Ewald, *Gesch. Christi*, p. 127 ff.

for the points of contact between the two are conceivable upon the supposition of their writing independently side by side, especially as Luke had a rich range of sources, which are to us for the most part unknown. That John likewise knew the *Gospel of the Hebrews* is not made probable by the saying which he records concerning " the birth from above." The combination, on that account, of this saying with the corresponding quotation made by Justin and the Clementines (see above, sec. ii.) rests upon the very precarious premiss that both of these cite from the Gospel of the Hebrews.

As to the question whence John derived his representation of the divine element in Christ as the *Logos*, see on chap. i. 1.

As to the PLACE where the gospel, which was certainly written in Greek, not in Aramaic (against Salmasius, Bolten, and partly Bertholdt), was composed, the earliest tradition [1] distinctly names *Ephesus ;* and the original document is said to have been preserved there to a late period, and to have been the object of believing veneration (*Chron. Pasch.* p. xi. 411, ed. Dind.). By this decision as to the place we must abide, because the Gospel itself bears upon its very face proofs of its author's remoteness from Palestine, and from the circle of Jewish life, along with references to cultured Greek readers ; and because the life of the apostle himself, as attested by the history of the church, speaks decidedly for Ephesus. The tradition that he wrote at *Patmos* (Pseudo-Hippolytus, Theophylact, and many others, also Hug) is a later one, and owes its origin to the statement that the Apocalypse was written on that island. With this, the tradition which tries to reconcile the two, by supposing that John dictated his Gospel in Patmos and published it at Ephesus (Pseudo-Athanasius, Dorotheus), loses all its value.—The assumption that a long time elapsed before it gained any wide circulation, and that it remained within the circle of the apostle's friends in Ephesus, at whose request a very ancient tradition (Canon Muratori, Clement of Alexandria, in Euseb. vi. 14) makes him to have written it, is not indeed sanctioned by the silence of Papias concerning it (Credner), but receives confirmation by the fact that the appendix, chap. xxi., is found in all the oldest testimonies,—leading us to conclude that its publication in more distant circles, and dissemination through multiplication of copies, did not take place till after this addition.

As to the TIME of its composition, the earliest testimonies (Irenaeus, Clement of Alex., Origen) go to prove that John wrote subsequently to the Synoptics, and (Irenaeus) not till after the deaths of Peter and Paul. A later and more precise determination of the time,[2] in the advanced old

---

[1] Already in Iren. iii. 1, Clement of Alex., Origen, Eusebius, etc.

[2] Epiphanius, *Haer.* li. 12. Διὸ ὕστερον ἀναγκάζει τὸ ἅγιον πνεῦμα τὸν Ἰωάννην παραιτούμενον εὐαγγελίσασθαι δι' εὐλάβειαν καὶ ταπεινοφροσύνην, ἐπὶ τῇ γηραλέᾳ αὐτοῦ ἡλικίᾳ, μετὰ ἔτη ἐνενήκοντα τῆς ἑαυτοῦ ζωῆς, μετὰ τὴν αὐτοῦ ἀπὸ τῆς Πάτμου ἐπάνοδον τὴν ἐπὶ Κλαυδίου γενομένην Καίσαρος, καὶ μετὰ ἱκανὰ ἔτη τοῦ διατρίψαι αὐτὸν ἀπὸ τῆς

Ἀσίας ἀναγκάζεται ἐκθέσθαι τὸ εὐαγγέλιον. These last words are not corrupt, nor is ἀπὸ τῆς Ἀσίας to be joined with ἀναγκάζεται as if it meant *ab Asiae episcopis* (Lücke) ; but we must render them, " and many years after he had lived away from Asia, he was obliged," etc.,—thus taking the words in their essential sense, " many years after his extra-Asiatic sojourn," many years after his return from

age of the apostle, is connected with the desire to ascribe to the Gospel an anti-heretical design, and therefore loses its critical weight. The following points may perhaps be regarded as certain, resulting as they do from a comparison of this tradition with historical circumstances and with the Gospel itself. As John certainly did not settle in Ephesus until after St. Paul's removal from his Asiatic sphere of labour, nor indeed, doubtless, until after the destruction of Jerusalem, where until then John resided: as, further, the estrangement from Palestinian conditions, so evident in the Gospel, implies an already prolonged residence away from Palestine ; as the elaborate view of the Logos is a post-Pauline phase of the apprehension and exposition of Christ's higher nature, and suggests a longer familiarity with philosophical influences ; as the entire character and nature of the book, its clearness and depth, its calmness and completeness, most probably indicate the matured culture and clarifying influence of riper years, without, however, in the least degree suggesting to us the weakness of old age,—we must put the composition not *before* the destruction of Jerusalem (Lampe, Wegscheider), but a considerable time *after ;* for if that catastrophe had been still fresh in the recollection of the writer, in the depths of its first impression, it could hardly, on psychological grounds, have escaped express mention in the book. No such express reference to it occurs ; but if, notwithstanding, Jerusalem and its environs are to be regarded, and that rightly, as in ruins, and in the distant background of the apostle's view, the $\tilde{\eta}\nu$ in xi. 18, xviii. 1, xix. 41, reads more naturally than if accounted for from the mere context of historical narration, while on the other hand the ἐστι in v. 2 may retain its full appropriateness. If a *year* is to be definitely named, A.D. 80 [1] may be suggested as neither too far preceding or following it.[2]

Note.—As to PLAN, the Gospel divides itself into the following sections :— After the prologue, i. 1–18, which at once sets before the reader the lofty point of view of the most sacred history, the revelation of the glory of the only-begotten Son of the Father (which constitutes the theme of the Gospel, i. 14) begins, first through John the Baptist, and its manifestation onwards to the

Patmos. The genitive τοῦ διατρίψαι αὐτὸν ἀπὸ τ. 'Ασίας, denotes the dwelling away, etc., as the point of departure from which the ἱκανὰ ἔτη begin to run. See Kühner, II. pp. 164, 514. Comp. Bernhardy, p. 138.

[1] There therefore lies between the Apocalypse and the Gospel a space of from ten to twelve years. Considering the maturity of mind which the apostle, who was already aged in the year 70, must have attained, this space was too short to effect such a change of view and of language as we must suppose if the apocalyptist was also the evangelist. This also against Tholuck, p. 11.

[2] It is evident from the distinctive and internal characteristics of the Gospel, and especially from the form of its ideas, that it was written after the downfall of the Jewish state and the labours of St. Paul ; but

we cannot go so far as to find reflected in it precisely the beginning of the second century (*i.e.* a time only 20 or 30 years later), nor to argue *therefrom* the non-apostolic origin of the Gospel (and of the Epistle). The interval is too short, and our knowledge of church movements, especially of Gnosticism, so far as they might be said to belong, at least in their stages of impulse and development, to the beginning only of the new century, and not to the two or three preceding decades of years, is not sufficiently special and precise. This tells, at the same time, against Keim, *Gesch. J.* I. p. 147 ff. How can it be said, on any reliable grounds, that the Gospel discloses the state of the church about the year 100, but not the state of the church about the year 80 ?

first miracle, and as yet without any opposition of unbelief, down to ii. 11. Then (2) this self-revelation passes on to publicity, and progresses in action and teaching amid the contrast of belief and unbelief, on to another and greater miracle, ii. 12–iv. 54. Further, (3) new miracles of the Lord's in Judea and Galilee, with the discourses occasioned thereby, heighten that contrast, causing among the Jews a desire to persecute and even kill Him, and among His disciples many to fall away, v.–vi. 71. After this, (4) unbelief shows itself even among the brothers of Jesus ; the self-revelation of the Only-begotten of the Father advances in words and deeds to the greatest miracle of all, that of the raising of the dead, by which, however, while many believe upon Him, the hostility of unbelief is urged on to the decisive determination to put Him to death, vii.–ix. 57. There ensues, (5) in and upon the carrying out of this determination, the highest self-revelation of Christ's divine glory, which finally gains its completed victory in the resurrection, xii.–xx. Chap. xxi. is an appendix. Many other attempts have been made to exhibit the plan of the book ; on which see Luthardt, I. p. 255 ff., who (comp. also his treatise, *De composit. ev. Joh.*, Norimb. 1852 ; before this Köstlin, in the *Theol. Jahrb.* 1851, p. 194 ff., and afterwards Keim, *Gesch. J.* I. p. 115 f.) endeavours on his part to carry out a *threefold* division of the whole and of the several parts ; and in Godet, *Comment.* I. p. 111. The arrangement which approaches most nearly to the above is that of Ewald, *Jahrb.* III. p. 168, comp. VIII. 109, and *Johann. Schr.* I. p. 18 ff. In every mode of division, the opposition of the world's ever-increasing unbelief and hatred to the revelation of the divine glory in Christ, and to faith in Him, must ever be held fast, as the thread which runs systematically through the whole. Comp. Godet,[1] as before.

NOTES BY AMERICAN EDITOR.

I. *The Apocalypse.* Page 22.

This is of course no place for controverting at length Meyer's very positive view of the non-Johannean authorship of the Apocalypse. I may adduce two or three suggestions, remarking that his view is rejected by many of the ablest scholars, who maintain the identity in authorship of the two works. As to outward evidence, the thread of direct testimony in the early church is nearly unbroken, including Justin Martyr, Irenaeus, Clement of Alexandria, and the Muratorian Fragment ; and indirect testimony is by no means wanting. The difference in the style is explicable from the difference in the subject matter and in the two classes of composition. The account of a succession of vivid symbolical scenes, drawing in all the agencies of nature, and shifting rapidly between earth and heaven, in the midst of which the author stands, could scarcely fail to differ widely in style from the narration of a series of quiet historical

---

[1] Who (p. 121) gives what he calls the "*photographie de l'histoire*" as follows : " La foi nait, i.–iv. ; l'incrédulité domine, v.–xii. ; la foi atteint sa perfection relative, xiii.–xvii. ; l'incrédulité se consomme, xviii., xix. ; la foi triomphe, xx. (xxi.)" Such special abstract designations of place give too varied play to the subjectivities, still more so the subdivision of the several main parts, as by Ewald especially, and Keim, with different degrees of skill ; but the latter considers that his threefold division and subdivision of the two halves (i.–xii, xiii.–xx.) "has its root in the *absolute ground of the divine mystery* of the number three,"—a *lusus ingenii*.

events long past by. As to grammatical construction, the very excitement of
the grand dramatic scene would naturally lead, in one not a native to the language, to the merging of grammatical niceties in forcible, if inaccurate, diction.
The book itself furnishes abundant evidence that, as to style, the writer "knew"
better than he "builded ;" that his errors are not errors of ignorance of the
usages which he sometimes so daringly violates (as witness the ἀπὸ ὁ ὢν, καὶ ὁ
ἦν, καὶ ὁ ἐρχόμενος). On grounds of intrinsic fitness, too, it would seem eminently
natural that the beloved disciple who had witnessed personally one prefigured
coming of his Master in His kingdom, and been half promised that he should
wait to behold yet another coming of the Lord, should be selected to give to the
church this magnificent outline of the pivotal epochs of its history and revealing of its final glory.   While much in the book is mysterious and as yet unrav-
elled, enough has yielded itself to the labors of devout exegesis to assure us that
the whole is one of the richest products of inspiration, worthy alike of its
author, its medium, and its destination.   The "Conquering Hero" of the
Apocalypse (xix. 11–16), the " WORD of God " is that "Word " of the opening
of the Gospel, who " was in the beginning with God."

Weiss, Meyer's German editor, also dissents from his conclusions regarding
the relation of the Gospel to the Apocalypse.   He holds that, especially through
Justin Martyr and Papias, the attestations to the apostolic origin of the Apocalypse are earlier and more direct in the church than to that of the Gospel.   He
thinks the absence of the Apocalypse from the Peshito may be due rather to
other reasons (as dislike of its chiliasm) than doubts of its apostolic origin.
He holds that the fundamental diversity of the two writings in tendency and
contents allows but a limited comparison between them ; that they are separated by an interval of twenty years, in which the author was removed from
Palestine to Asia Minor, from the sphere of Jewish to that of Gentile Christianity, with the intervening shock of the destruction of Jerusalem, with its
many and far-reaching changes ; and that finally, in spite of all differences, there
exist such remarkable coincidences in essential and fundamental thoughts, as
well as in individual forms of doctrine, images, expressions, and linguistic peculiarities, as, while not proving identity of authorship, allow the apostolical authorship of each to be discussed and maintained without prejudice to the claims
of the other.

II. *Anti-Gnostic purpose in the Gospel.*   Page 31.

" Meyer declares himself against any anti-Gnostic polemical purpose in the
Gospel, since it nowhere discloses any direct design to combat perverted sectarian developments, and to look for indirect and concealed references, as
intended, were alike arbitrary and opposed to the decided character of the
apostolic position in its known hostility to heresies. But when he concedes that
the Apostle in his first Epistle assails Gnostic perversions, and that these have
not first come within his sphere of action after the composition of his Gospel
(as Ewald, *Jahrb.* iii. p. 157, assumes),it is exceedingly probable that his purpose,
by his *historical* portraiture to establish and confirm the true knowledge of
Christ's deepest nature, is partly conditioned by the threatening aspect in this
direction of the germinating Gnosis. For that the antagonism to this Gnosis
should not come out in the same way in the Gospel as in the Epistle, lies in
the very character of the Gospel narrative, if it would not blend fictitious
elements with its narratives and discourses."—Weiss.

Εὐαγγέλιον κατὰ Ἰωάννην.

B. **ℵ**. have merely κατὰ Ἰωάνν. Others : τὸ κατὰ Ἰωάνν. (ἅγιον) εὐαγγ. Others : ἐκ τοῦ κ. Ἰωάνν. Others : εὐαγγ. ἐκ τοῦ κατὰ Ἰωάνν. See on Matthew.

CHAPTER I.

Ver. 4. ζωὴ ἦν] D. **ℵ**. Codd. in Origen and Augustine, It. (Germ. Foss. excepted), Sahidic, Syr.ᶜᵘ Clem. Valentt. in Ir. Hilary, Ambrose, Vigil. : ζωή ἐστιν. So Lachm. and Tisch. Generalization in connection with the words : ὁ γέγ. ἐν αὐτῷ, ζωὴ ἦν, and perhaps in comparison with 1 John v. 11. — Ver. 16. καὶ ἐκ] B. C.* D. L. X. **ℵ**. 33. Copt. Aeth. Arm. Ver. Verc. Corb. Or. and many Fathers and Schol. : ὅτι ἐκ. So Griesb., Lachm., Tisch. ; ὅτι is to be preferred on account of the preponderating evidence in its favour, and because ver. 16 was very early (Heracl. and Origen) regarded as a continuation of the Baptist's discourse, and the directly continuous καὶ naturally suggested itself, and was inserted instead of the less simple ὅτι. — Ver. 18. υἱός] B. C.* L. **ℵ**. 33. Copt. Syr. Aeth. and many Fathers : θεός. Dogmatic gloss in imitation of ver. 1 whereby not only υἱός, but the article before μονογ. (which Tisch. deletes), was also (in the Codd. named) suppressed. The omission of υἱός (Origen, *Opp.* IV. 102 ; Ambrose, *ep.* 10) is not sufficiently supported, and might easily have been occasioned by ver. 14. — Ver. 19. After ἀπέστειλαν, B. C.* Min. Chrys. and Verss. have πρὸς αὐτόν. So Lachm., an addition which other Codd. and Verss. insert after Λευίτας. — Ver. 20. οὐκ εἰμὶ ἐγώ] A. B. C.* L. X. Δ. **ℵ**. 33. Verss. and Fathers have : ἐγὼ οὐκ εἰμι. So Lachm., Tisch. Rightly, on account of the preponderating evidence. Comp. iii. 28, where οὐκ εἰμὶ ἐγώ is attested by decisive evidence. — Ver. 22. The οὖν after εἶπον (Lachm. Tisch. read εἶπαν) is deleted by Lachm., following B. C. Syr. ᶜᵘ,—testimonies which are all the less adequate, considering how easily the οὖν, which is not in itself necessary, might have been overlooked after the final syllable of εἶπον.[1] — Ver. 24. The article before ἀπεσταλμ. is wanting in A.* B. C.* L. **ℵ**.* Origen (once), Nonn. Perhaps a mere omission on the part of the transcriber, if ἀπεστ. ἦσαν were taken together ; but perhaps intentional, for some (Origen and Nonn.) have here supposed a second deputation. The omission is therefore doubly suspicious, though Tisch. also now omits the art. — Ver. 25. Instead of the repeated οὔτε, we must, with Lachm., Tisch., following A. B. C. L. X. **ℵ**. Min. Origen, read οὐδέ. — Ver. 26. δέ after μέσος must, with Tisch., on weighty testimony (B. C. L. **ℵ**. etc.), be deleted, having been added as a connecting

---

[1] Matthaei, ed. min. ad x. 39, well says : "in nullo libro scribae ita vexarunt particulas καί, δέ, οὖν, πάλιν . . . quam in hoc evangelio. Modo temere inculcarunt, modo permutarunt, modo omiserunt, modo transposuerunt. Accedunt interpretes, qui cum demum locum aliquem tractant, illas particulas in principio modo addunt, modo omittunt."

particle. — Ver. 27. Against the words αὐτός ἐστιν (for which G. Min. Chrys. read οὗτός ἐστιν) and ὃς ἐμπροσθέν μου γέγονεν the testimonies are so ancient, important, and unanimous, that they must be rejected together. Lachm. has bracketed them, Tisch. deletes them. αὐτός ἐστιν is an unnecessary aid to the construction, and ὃς ἐμπρ. μου γέγονεν (though defended by Ewald) is a completion borrowed from vv. 15, 30. — Ver. 28. Βηθανίᾳ] Elz.: Βηθαβαρᾷ (adopted of late by Hengstenberg), against conclusive testimony, but following Syr.ᶜᵘ and Origen (Opp. II. 130), who himself avows that σχεδὸν ἐν πᾶσι τοῖς ἀντιγράφοις is found Βηθανίᾳ, yet upon geographical grounds decides in favour of Βηθαβαρᾷ,— a consideration by which criticism cannot be bound. See the exegetical notes. — Ver. 29. After βλέπει Elz. has ὁ Ἰωάνν., against the best testimonies. Beginning of a church lesson. — Ver. 32. ὡς] Elz. : ὡσεί, against the oldest and most numerous Codd. See Matt. iii. 16 ; Luke iii. 22. — Ver. 37. ἤκουσ. αὐτοῦ] Tisch., following B. ℵ., puts αὐτοῦ after μαθητ. ; C.* L. X. T.ᵇ have it after δύο. The Verss. also have this variation of position, which must, however, be regarded as the removal of the αὐτοῦ, made more or less mechanically, in imitation of ver. 35. — Ver. 40. ἴδετε] B. C.* L. T.ᵇ Min. Syr. utr. Origen, Tisch.: ὄψεσθε. Correctly ; the words which immediately follow and ver. 47 (comp. xi. 34) make it much more likely that the transcriber would write ἴδετε for ὄψεσθε than vice versa. After ὥρα Elz. has δέ, against which are the weightiest witnesses, and which has been interpolated as a connecting link. — Ver. 43. Ἰωνᾶ] Lachm. : Ἰωανου, after B.; the same variation in xxi. 15–17. We must, with Tisch., after B.* L. ℵ. 33, read Ἰωάννου. Comp. Nonnus : υἱὸς Ἰωάνναο. The Textus Receptus has arisen from Matt. xvi. 17. — Ver. 44. After ἠθέλησεν Elz. has ὁ Ἰησοῦς, which the best authorities place after αὐτῷ. Beginning of a church lesson. — Ver. 52. ἀπάρτι] wanting in B. L. ℵ. Copt. Aeth. Arm. Vulg. It. and some Fathers, also in Origen. Deleted by Lachm. Tisch. Omitted, because it seemed inappropriate to the following words, which were taken to refer to actual angelic appearances.

Ver. 1. Ἐν ἀρχῇ] John makes the beginning of his Gospel parallel with that of Genesis ;[1] but he rises above the historical conception of בְּרֵאשִׁית, which (Gen. i. 1) includes the beginning of time itself, to the absolute conception of *anteriority to time:* the creation is something subsequent, ver. 3. Prov. viii. 23, ἐν ἀρχῇ πρὸ τοῦ τὴν γῆν ποιῆσαι, is parallel ; likewise, πρὸ τοῦ τὸν κόσμον εἶναι, John xvii. 5 ; πρὸ καταβολῆς κόσμου, Eph. i. 4. Comp. Nezach Israel, f. 48, 1 : *Messias erat* כיפני תוהו (*ante Tohu*). The same idea we find already in the book of Enoch, xlviii. 3 f., 6 f., lxii. 7,—a book which (against Hingenfeld and others) dates back into the second century B.C. (Dilm., Ewald, and others). The notion, in itself *negative,* of anteriority to time (ἄχρονος ἦν, ἀκίχητος, ἐν ἀρρήτῳ λόγος ἀρχῇ, Nonnus), is in a popular way *affirmatively* designated by the ἐν ἀρχῇ as "*primeval ;*" the more exact dogmatic definition of the ἀρχή as "*eternity*"[2] is a correct development of John's meaning, but not strictly what he himself says. Comp. 1 John i. 1 ; Rev. iii. 14. The *Valentinian* notion, that ἀρχή was a *divine*

---

[1] See Hoelemann, *de evangelii Joh. introitu introitus Geneseos augustiore effigie,* Leipsic 1855, p. 26 ff.

[2] Theodor. Mopsuest., Euthym. Zig.; comp. Theophylact.

Hypostasis distinct from the Father and the λόγος (Iren. Haer. i. 8. 5), and
the Patristic view, that it was the divine σοφία (Origen) or the everlasting
Father (Cyril. Al.), rest upon speculations altogether unjustified by correct exegesis.[1] — ἦν] *was, existed.* John writes *historically*, looking *back*
from the later time of the incarnation of the λόγος (ver. 14). But he does
not say, "In the beginning the λόγος *came into existence,*" for he does not
conceive the generation (comp. μονογενής) according to the Arian view of
creation, but according to that of Paul, Col. i. 15. — ὁ λόγος] *the Word;*
for the reference to the history of the creation leaves room for no other
meaning (therefore not *Reason*). John assumes that his readers understand the term, and, notwithstanding its great importance, regards every
additional explanation of it as superfluous. Hence those interpretations
fall of themselves to the ground, which are unhistorical, and imply any sort
of a substitution, such as (1) that ὁ λόγος is the same as ὁ λεγόμενος, "*the
promised one*;"[2] (2) that it stands for ὁ λέγων, "*the speaker*" (Storr, Eckerm.,
Justi, and others). Not less incorrect (3) is Hofmann's interpretation (*Schriftbeweis*, I. 1, p. 109 f.) : "ὁ λόγος is the word of God, the *Gospel*, the personal subject of which however, namely *Christ*, is here meant :" against which
view it is decisive, first, that neither in Rev. xix. 13, nor elsewhere in the
N. T., is Christ called ὁ λόγος merely as the *subject-matter of the word;* secondly, that in John, ὁ λόγος, without some additional definition, never once
occurs as the designation of the *Gospel*, though it is often so used by Mark
(ii. 2, iv. 14, *al.*), Luke (i. 2 ; Acts xi. 19, *al.*), and Paul (Gal. vi. 6 ; 1 Thess.
i. 6) ; thirdly, that in the context, neither here (see especially ver. 14) nor
in 1 John i. 1 (see especially ὁ ἑωράκαμεν . . . καὶ αἱ χεῖρες ἡμῶν ἐψηλάφησαν)
does it seem allowable to depart in ὁ λόγος from the *immediate* designation
of the *personal* subject,[3] while this immediate designation, *i.e.* of the creative
Word, is in our passage, from the obvious parallelism with the history of the
creation, as clear and definite as it was appropriate it should be at the very
commencement of the work. These reasons also tell substantially against
the turn which Luthardt has given to Hofmann's explanation : "ὁ λόγος is
the *word of God, which in Christ*, Heb. i. 1, *has gone forth into the world, and
the substance of which was His own person.*"[4] The investigation of the Logos
idea can lead to a true result only when pursued by the path of *history*.
But here, above all, history points us to the O. T.,[5] and most directly to
Gen. i., where the act of creation is effected by *God speaking.* The reality
contained in this representation, anthropomorphic as to its form, of the revelation of Himself made in creation by God, who is in His own nature hidden, became the root of the Logos idea. The Word as creative, and em-

---

[1] Quite opposed to correct exegesis,
although in a totally different direction, is
the rendering of the Socinians (see *Catech.
Racov.* p. 135, ed. Oeder), that ἐν ἀρχῇ signifies in *initio evangelii.*

[2] Valla, Beza, Ernesti, Tittm., etc.

[3] See, with reference to 1 John i. 1 (in opposition to Beyschlag's impersonal interpretation), besides Düsterdieck and Huther,

Johansson, *de aeterna Christi praeexist. sec.
ev. Joh.*, Lundae 1866, p. 29 f.

[4] See, on the other hand, Baur in the
Theol. Jahrb. 1854, p. 206 ff. ; Lechler, *apost.
u. nachapost. Zeit.* p. 215 ; Gess, *v. d. Person
Chr.* p. 116 ; Kahnis, *Dogmat.* I. p. 466.

[5] See Röhricht in the *Stud. u. Krit.* 1868,
p. 299 ff.

44 THE GOSPEL OF JOHN.

bodying generally the divine will, is *personified* in Hebrew poetry (Ps. xxxiii. 6, cvii. 20, cxlvii. 15 ; Isa. lv. 10, 11) ; and consequent upon this concrete and independent representation, divine attributes are predicated of it (Ps. xxxiv. 4 ; Isa. xl. 8 ; Ps. cxix. 105), so far as it was at the same time the continuous revelation of God in law and prophecy. A way was thus paved for the *hypostatizing* of the λόγος as a further step in the knowledge of the relations in the divine essence ; but this advance took place gradually, and only after the captivity, so that probably the oriental doctrine of emanations, and subsequently the Pythagoreanized Platonism, were not without influence upon what was already given in germ in Gen. i. Another *form* of the conception, however, appears,—not the original one of the *Word*, but one which was connected with the advanced development of ethical and teleological reflection and the needs of the Theodicy,—that of *wisdom* (חָכְמָה), of which the creative word was an expression, and which in the book of Job (xxviii. 12 ff.) and Proverbs (viii., ix.), in Eccles. i. 1–10, xxiv. 8, and Baruch iii. 37–iv. 4, is still set forth and depicted under the form of a *personification*, yet to such a degree that the portrayal more closely approaches that of the *Hypostasis*, and all the more closely as it ceases to maintain the elevation and boldness of the ancient poesy. The actual transition of the σοφία into the Hypostasis occurs in the book of Wisdom vii. 7–xi., where wisdom (manifestly under the influence of the idea of the Platonic soul of the world, perhaps also of the Stoic conception of an all-pervading world-spirit) appears as a being of light proceeding essentially from God,—the true image of God, co-occupant of the divine throne,—a real and independent principle revealing God in the world (especially in Israel), and mediating between it and Him, after it has, as His organ, created the world, in association with a spirit among whose many predicates μονογενές[1] also is named, vii. 22. The divine λόγος also appears again in the book of Wisdom, ix. 1, comp. ver. 2, but only in the O. T. sense of a poetically personified declaration of God's will, either in blessing (xvi. 12, comp. Ps. cvii. 20) or in punishing (xviii. 15).[2] While, then, in the Apocrypha the Logos representation retires before the development of the idea of wisdom,[3] it makes itself the more distinctly prominent in the *Chaldee Paraphrasts*, especially Onkelos.[4] The Targums, the peculiarities of which rest on older traditions, exhibit the Word of God, מֵימְרָא or דִּבּוּרָא, as the divinely revealing Hypostasis, identical with the שְׁכִינָה which was to be revealed in the Messiah. Comp. Schoettg. *Hor.* II. p. 5 ; Bertholdt, *Christol.* p. 121. Thus there runs through entire Judaism under various forms of conception (comp. es-

---

[1] Comp. vii. 25, where it is said of wisdom, ἀπόρροια τῆς τοῦ παντοκράτορος δόξης εἰλικρινής. Μονογενές should not have been rendered *single* (Bauerm., Lücke, Bruch, after the early writers), which it neither is nor is required to be by the merely *formal contrast* to πολυμερές. This idea *single*, as answering to the following πολυμερές, would have been expressed by μονομερές (Luc. *Calumn.* 6). Also Grimm (*exeget. Handb.* p. 152) has now rightly abandoned this interpretation.

[2] See especially Grimm, *in loc.* ; Bruch, *Weisheitslehre d. Hebr.* p. 347 ff. Comp. also Eccles. xliii. 46.

[3] *Wisdom* as appearing in *Christ* is mentioned in N. T. also, in Luke xi. 49, comp. Matt. xi. 19.

[4] See Gfrörer, *Gesch. d. Urchristenth.* I. 1, p. 301 ff. ; Winer, *De Onkel.* p. 44 f. ; Anger, *De Onkel.* II. 1846.

pecially the מַלְאַךְ יְהוָֹה in the O. T. from Gen. xvi., Ex. xxiii. downwards, frequently named, especially in Hosea, Zechariah, and Malachi, as the representative of the self-revealing God), the idea that God never reveals Himself directly, but mediately, that is, does not reveal His hidden invisible essence, but only a manifestation of Himself (comp. especially Ex. xxxiii. 12–23) : and this idea, modified however by Greek, and particularly Platonic and Stoic speculation, became a main feature in the Judaeo-Alexandrine philosophy, as set forth in PHILO, an older contemporary of Jesus.[1] According to the intellectual development, so rich in its results, which Philo gave to the transmitted Jewish doctrine of Wisdom, the Logos is the comprehension or sum-total of all the divine energies, so far as these are either hidden in the Godhead itself, or have come forth and been disseminated in the world (λόγος σπερματικός). As immanent in God, containing within itself the archetypal world, which is conceived as the real world-ideal (νοητὸς κόσμος), it is, while not yet outwardly existing, like the immanent reason in men, the λόγος ἐνδιάθετος ; but when in creating the world it has issued forth from God, it answers to the λόγος προφορικός, as with man the word when spoken is the manifestation of thought. Now the λόγος προφορικός is the comprehension or sum-total of God's active relations to the world ; so that creation, providence, the communication of all physical and moral power and gifts, of all life, light, and wisdom from God, are its work, not being essentially different in its attributes and workings from the σοφια and the Divine Spirit itself. Hence it is the image of the Godhead, the eldest and first-begotten (πρεσβύτατος, πρωτόγονος) Son of God, the possessor of the entire divine fulness, the Mediator between God and the world, the λόγος τομεύς, δημιουργός, ἀρχιερεύς, ἱκέτης, πρεσβευτής, the ἀρχάγγελος, the δεύτερος θεός, the substratum of all Theophanies, also the Messiah, though ideally apprehended only as a Theophany, *not as a concrete incarnate personality ;* for an incarnation of the Logos is foreign to Philo's system.[2] There is no doubt that Philo has often designated and described the Logos as a *Person,* although, where he views it rather as immanent in God, he applies himself more to describe a power, and to present it as an attribute. There is, however, no real ground for inferring, with some (Keferst., Zeller), from this variation in his representation, that Philo's opinion wavered between personality and impersonality ; rather, as regards the question of subsistence in its bearing upon Philo's Logos,[3] we must attribute to him no separation between the subsistence of God and the Logos, as if there came forth a Person

---

[1] See especially Gfrörer, I. 243 ff. ; Dähne, *Jüdisch-Alex. Religionsphil.* I. 114 ff. ; Grossmann, *Quaestion. Philon.*, Lpz. 1829 ; Scheffer, *Quaest. Phil. Marb.* 1829, 1831 ; Keferstein, *Philo's Lehre von dem göttl. Mittelwesen,* Lpz. 1846 ; Ritter, *Gesch. d. Philos.* IV. 418 ff. ; Zeller, *Philos. d. Griechen,* III. 2 ; Lutterb. *neut. Lehrbegr.* I. 418 ff. ; Müller in *Herzog's Encykl.* XI. 484 ; Ewald, *apost. Zeit.* 257 ; Delitzsch *in d. Luther. Zeitschr.* 1863, ii. 219 ; Riehm, *Hebr. Brief,* p. 249 ; Keim, *Gesch.*

J. I. 212. Comp. also Langen, *d. Judenth. z. Zeit. Christi,* 1867 ; Röhricht as formerly quoted.

[2] See Ewald, p. 284 ff. ; Dorner, *Entwickelungsgesch.* I. 50.

[3] See especially Dorner, *Entwickelungsgesch.* I. 21 ; Niedner, *de subsistentia τῷ θείῳ λόγῳ apud Philon. tributa,* in the *Zeitsch. f. histor. Theol.* 1849, p. 337 ff. ; and Hölemann, *de evang. Joh. in roitu, etc.,* p. 39 ff.

distinct from God, whenever the Logos is described as a Person ; but, "ea duo, in quibus cernitur τοῦ ὄντος καὶ ζῶντος θεοῦ essentia s. deitas plenum esse per suam ipsius essentiam et implere cuncta hac sua essentia, primo diserte *uni substantiae tribuuntur*, deinde *distribuuntur*, sed tantum inter *essentiam* et hujus *actionem*, quemadmodum nomina τοῦ θεοῦ et τοῦ λόγου hujus ipsius dei" (Niedner).   Accordingly, Philo's conception of the Logos resolves itself into the sum-total and full exercise of the divine energies ; so that God, so far as He reveals Himself, is called Logos, while the Logos, so far as he reveals God, is called God.   That John owed his doctrine of the Logos— in which he represents the divine Messianic being as pre-existent, and entering into humanity in a human form—*solely* to the Alexandrine philosophy, is an assertion utterly arbitrary, especially considering the difference between Philo's doctrine and that of John, not only in general (comp. also Godet, I. 233), but also in respect to the subsistence of the Logos in particular.[1]   The form which John gave to his doctrine is understood much more naturally and historically thus, without by any means excluding the influence of the Alexandrine Gnosis upon the apostle ;—that while the ancient popular wisdom of the Word of God, which (as shown above) carries us back to Gen. i. 1, is acknowledged to be that through which the idea of the Logos, as manifested in human form in Christ, was immediately suggested to him, and to which he appended and unfolded his own peculiar development of this idea with all clearness and spiritual depth, according to the measure of those personal testimonies of his Lord which his memory vividly retained, he at the same time allowed the widespread Alexandrine speculations, so similar in their origin and theme, to have due influence upon him, and used [2] them in an independent manner to assist his exposition of the nature and working of the divine in Christ, fully conscious of their points of difference (among which must be reckoned the cosmological dualism of Philo, which excluded any real incarnation, and made God to have created the world out of the ὕλη).   Whether he first adopted these speculations while dwelling in Asia Minor, need not be determined, although it is in itself very conceivable that the longer he lived in Asia, the more deeply did he penetrate into the Alexandrine theologoumenon which prevailed there, without requiring for this any intermediate agency of Apollos (Tobler). The doctrine is not, however, on account of this connection with speculations lying outside of Christianity, by any means to be traced back to a

---

[1] It tells also against it, that in John the name λόγος is undoubtedly derived from the divine *speaking* (*Word*) ; in Philo, on the other hand, from the divine *thinking* (*Reason*). See Hoelemann as before, p. 43 ff.

[2] Comp. Delitzsch, *l.c.*, and *Psychol.* p. 178 [E. T. pp. 210, 211] ; Beyschlag, *Christol. d. N. T.* p. 156; Keim, *Gesch. J.* I. p. 112 ff. If some attempt to deny the influence of the Judaeo-Alexandrine Gnosis on the Logos doctrine of John (Hoelemann, Weiss, J. Köstlin, Hengstenberg), they at the same time sever, though in the interests of apostolic dignity, its historical credibility from its connection with the circumstances of the time, as well as the necessary presumption of its intelligibility on the part of the readers of the Gospel. But it is exactly the noble simplicity and clearness of the Prologue which shows with what truly apostolic certainty John had *experienced* the influence of the speculations of his day, and was *master* of them, modifying, correcting, and utilizing them according to his own ideas. This is also in answer to Luthardt, p. 200, and Röhricht *l.c.*

mere fancy of the day. The main truth in it (the idea of the Son of God and His incarnation) had, long before he gave it this peculiar form, been in John's mind the sole foundation of his faith, and the highest object of his knowledge ; and this was no less the case with Paul and all the other apostles, though they did not *formally* adopt the Logos doctrine, from their different idiosyncrasies and the different conditions of their after development. That main truth in it is to be referred absolutely to Christ Himself, whose communications to His disciples, and direct influence upon them (i. 14), as well as His further revelations and leadings by means of the Spirit of truth, furnished them with the material which was afterwards made use of in their various modes of representation. This procedure is specially apparent also in John, whose doctrine of the divine and pre-existent nature of Christ, far removed from the influences of later Gnosticism, breaks away in essential points from the Alexandrine type of doctrine, and moulds itself in a different shape, especially rejecting decidedly all dualistic and docetic elements, and in general treating the form once chosen with apostolic independence. That idea of God's essential self-revelation, which took its rise from Gen. i., which lived and grew under various forms and names among the Hebrews and later Jews, but was moulded in a peculiar fashion by the Alexandrine philosophy, was adopted by John for the purpose of setting forth the abstract divinity of the Son,—thus bringing to light the reality which lies at the foundation of the Logos idea. Hence, according to John,[1] by ὁ λόγος, which is throughout viewed by him (as is clear from the entire Prologue down to ver. 18)[2] under the conception of a *personal*[3] subsistence, we must understand nothing else than *the self-revelation of the divine essence, before all time immanent in God* (comp. Paul, Col. i. 15 ff.), *but for the accomplishment of the act of creation proceeding hypostatically from Him, and ever after operating also in the spiritual world as a creating, quickening, and illuminating personal principle, equal to God Himself in nature and glory* (comp. Paul, Phil. ii. 6) ; *which divine self-revelation appeared bodily in the man Jesus, and accomplished the work of the redemption of the world.* John fashions and determines his Gospel from beginning to end with this highest christological idea in his eye ; this it is which constitutes the distinctive character of its doctrine.[4] The Synoptics contain the fragments

---

[1] In the Apocalypse also, chap. xix. 13, Christ is called the λόγος, but (not so in the Gospel) ὁ λόγος τοῦ θεοῦ. The writer of the Apocalypse speaks of the whole Person of the God-man in a different way from the evangelist,—in fact, as in his state of exaltation. (See Düsterdieck, z. Apok. Einl. p. 75 ff.) But the passage is important against all interpretations which depart from the metaphysical view of the Logos above referred to. Comp. Gess, v. d. Person Chr. p. 115 ff.

[2] Comp. Wörner, d. Verhältn. d. Geistes zum Sohne Gottes, 1862, p. 24 ; also Baur, neutest. Theol. 352 ; Godet, l.c.

[3] That is, the subsistence as a conscious intelligent Ego, endued with volition. Against the denial of this *personal* transcendency in John (de Wette, Beyschlag, and others), see in particular Köstlin, Lehrbegr. 90 ; Brückn. 7 f. ; Liebner, Christol. 155 f. ; Weiss, Lehrbegr. 242 f. When Dorner (Gesch. d. prot. Theol. 875 ff.) claims for the Son, indeed, a special divine mode of existence as His eternal characteristic, but at the same time denies Him any direct participation in the absolute divine personality, his limitation is exegetically opposed to the view of John and of the Apostle Paul.

[4] Comp. Weizsäcker, üb. d. evang. Gesch.

and materials, the organic combination and ideal formation of which into one complete whole is the pre-eminent excellence of this last and highest Gospel. Paul has the Logos, only not in name. — The second and third ἦν is the *copula ;* but καὶ ὁ λόγος, as the repetition of the great subject, has a *solemn* emphasis. — πρὸς τὸν θεόν] not simply equivalent to παρὰ τῷ θεῷ, xvii. 5, but expressing, as in 1 John i. 2, the *existence* of the Logos in God in respect of *intercourse* (Bernhardy, p. 265). So also in all other passages where it appears to mean simply *with*, Mark vi. 3, ix. 19 ; Matt. xiii. 56, xxvi. 55 ; 1 Cor. xvi. 6, 7 ; Gal. i. 18, iv. 18 ; and in the texts cited in Fritzsche, *ad Marc.* p. 202.[1] Upon the thing itself, comp. concerning Wisdom, Prov. viii. 30, Wisd. ix. 4. The *moral* essence of this essential fellowship is *love* (xvii. 24 ; Col. i. 13), with which, at the same time, any merely *modalistic* conception is excluded. — καὶ θεὸς ἦν ὁ λόγος] *and the Logos was God.* This θεός can only be the *predicate*, not the subject (as Röhricht takes it), which would contradict the preceding ἦν πρὸς τὸν θεόν, because the conception of the λόγος would be only a periphrasis for God. The predicate is *placed before* the subject emphatically (comp. iv. 24), because the progress of the thought, "He was *with* God, and (not at all a Person of an inferior nature, but) possessed of a *divine nature*," makes this latter—the new added element —the naturally and logically *emphasized* member of the new clause, on account of its relation to πρὸς τὸν θεόν.[2] The *omission of the article* was necessary, because ὁ θεός after the preceding πρὸς τὸν θεόν would have assigned to the Logos identity of *Person* (as, in fact, Beyschlag, p. 162, construes θεός without the art.). But so long as the question of God's self-mediation objectively remains out of consideration, ὁ θεός would have been out of place here, after πρὸς τὸν θεόν had laid down the *distinction* of Person ; whereas θεός *without* the article makes the unity of *essence* and *nature* to follow the distinction of Person.[3] As, therefore, by θεός without the article, John neither indicates, on the one hand, identity of Person with the Father ; nor yet, on the other, any lower nature than that of God Himself : so his doctrine of the Logos is definitely distinguished from that of Philo, which predicates θεός without the article of the Logos as subordinate in nature, nay, as he himself says, ἐν καταχρήσει (I. 655, ed. Mang.) ; see Hoelemann, I. 1, p. 34. Moreover, the name ὁ δεύτερος θεός, which Philo gives to the Logos, must, according to II. 625 (Euseb. *praep. ev.* vii. 13), expressly designate an intermediate nature between God and man, after whose image God created man. *This* subordinationism, according to which the Logos is indeed μεθόριός τις

---

pp. 241 ff., 297 ; also his *Abh. über d. Joh. Logoslehre*, in *d. Jahrb. f. D. Th.* 1862, pp. 619 ff., 701 f.

[1] The expressions, in the language of the common people, in many districts are quite analogous : "he was with me," "he stays with you" (bei mich, bei dich), and the like. Comp. for the Greek, Krüger, § 68. 39. 4.—As against all impersonal conceptions of the Logos, observe it is never said ἐν τῷ θεῷ. Röhricht (p 312), however, arrives at the meaning ἐν τῷ θεῷ, and by unwarrantably

comparing the very different usage of πρός, takes exception to our explanation of πρὸς τὸν θεόν.

[2] There is something *majestic* in the way in which the description of the Logos, in the three brief but great propositions of ver. 1, is unfolded with *increasing* fulness.

[3] "The last clause, *the Word was God*, is against Arius ; the other, *the Word was with God*, against Sabellius."—LUTHER. See also Thomasius, *Chr. Pers. u. Werk*, I. 83 ff.

θεοῦ φύσις, but τοῦ μὲν ἐλάττων, ἀνθρώπου δὲ κρείττων (I. 683), is not that of the N. T., which rather assumes (comp. Phil. ii. 6, Col. i. 15, 16) the eternal unity of being of the Father and the Son, and places the subordination of the latter in His dependence on the Father, as it does the subordination of the Spirit in His dependence on the Father and the Son. Θεός, therefore, is not to be explained from Philo, nor converted into a general qualitative idea —"*divine*," "*God-like*" (B. Crusius),—which deprives the expression of the precision demanded for it by the strict monotheism of the N. T. (in John, see in particular xvii. 3), through the conception of the divine *essence* of the personal Logos. Comp. Schmid, *bibl. Theol.* II. 370. On Sam. Crell's conjecture (*Artemonii initium ev. Joh. ex. antiquitate eccl. restitut.* 1726) that θ ε ο ῦ is an idle antitrinitarian invention, see Bengel, *Appar. crit.* p. 214 ff.

Ver. 2 again emphatically combines the first and second clauses of ver. 1, in order to connect with them the work of creation, which was wrought by the λόγος.[1] In this way, however, the subject also of the *third* clause of ver. 1 is included in and expressed by ο ὗ τ ο ς. On this ο ὗ τ ο ς—to which πάντα standing at the beginning of ver. 3 significantly corresponds—lies the emphasis in the continued discourse. In ver. 2 is given the necessary premiss to ver. 3 ; for if it was *this same Logos*, and no *other* than He, who *Himself was* God, who lived in the beginning in fellowship with God, and consequently when creation began, the *whole* creation, *nothing excepted*, must have come into existence *through Him*. Thus it is assumed, as a self-evident middle term, that God created the world not immediately, but, according to Gen. i., through the medium of the Word.

Ver. 3. Π ά ν τ α] "grande verbum, quo *mundus, i.e.* universitas rerum factarum denotatur, ver. 10," Bengel. Comp. Gen. i. ; Col. i. 16 ; Heb. i. 2. Quite opposed to the context is the Socinian view : "the *moral* creation is meant." Comp. rather Philo, *de Cherub.* I. 162, where the λόγος appears as the ὄργανον δι' οὗ (comp. 1 Cor. viii. 6) κατεσκευάσθη (ὁ κόσμος). The further speculations of Philo concerning the relation of the λόγος to the creation, which however are not to be imputed to John, see in Hoelemann, *l.c.* p. 36 ff. John *might* have written τὰ πάντα (with the article), as in 1 Cor. viii. 6 and Col. i. 16, but was not *obliged* to do so. Comp. Col. i. 17, John iii. 35. For his thought is "*all*" (unlimited), whereas τὰ πάντα would express "the whole of what actually exists." — κ α ὶ χ ω ρ ὶ ς α ὐ τ ο ῦ, κ.τ.λ.] an emphatic *parallelismus antitheticus*, often occurring in the classics.[2] This negative reference does not exclude (so Lücke, Olshausen, de Wette, Frommann, Maier, Baeumlein) the doctrine of a ὕλη having an extra-temporal existence (Philo, *l.c.*), because ἐγένετο and γέγονεν describe that which exists only *since the creation*, as *having come* into existence, and therefore ὕλη would not be included in the conception. John neither holds nor opposes the idea of the ὕλη ; the antithesis has no polemical design—not even of an anti-gnostic kind—to point out that the Logos is raised above the series of Aeons (Tholuck) ; for though the world of spirits is certainly included in the πάντα and the οὐδὲ

---

[1] Who accordingly now worked as λόγος προφορικός.

[2] Dissen. *ad. Dem. de Cor.* p. 228 ; Maetz-

ner, *ad Antiph.* p. 157 ; in the N. T. through-out, and especially in John (ver. 20, x. 28 ; 1 John ii. 4, 27, *al.*).

ἐν, it is not specially designated (comp. Col. i. 16). How the Valentinians had already referred it to the *Aeons*, see in Iren. *Haer.* i. 8. 5 ; Hilgenfeld, *d. Ev. u. d. Briefe Joh.* p. 32 ff. — ο ὐ δ ὲ ἐ ν] *ne unum quidem, i.e. prorsus nihil*, more emphatic than οὐδέν.[1] — ὃ γ έ γ ο ν ε ν] Perfect : *which has come into being, and now is.* Comp. ἔκτισται, Col. i. 16. This belongs to the emphatic *fulness* of the statement (Bornemann, *Schol. in Luc.* p. xxxvii.), and connects itself with what *precedes.* The very ancient connection of it with what *follows*,[2] by putting the comma after either γέγ. or αὐτῷ (so already the Valentinians),[3] is to be rejected, although it would harmonize with John's mode of linking the members of his discourse, whereby "ex proximo membro sumitur gradus sequentis" (Erasmus) ; but in fine would still be Johannean only if the comma were placed after γέγ. (so also Lachm.). The ground of rejection lies not in the ambiguity of ζωή, which cannot surprise us in John, but in this, that the *perfect* γέγονεν, as implying continuance, would have logically required ἐστί instead of ἦν after ζωή ; to ἦν not γέγονεν, but ἐγένετο, would have been appropriate, so that the sense would have been : "what came into existence had in Him its ground or source of life."

Ver. 4. An advance to the nature of the Logos[4] as *life*, and thereby as *light.* — ἐ ν α ὐ τ ῷ ζ ω ὴ ἦ ν] *in Him was life*, He was πηγὴ ζωῆς (Philo). *Life* was that which existed in Him, of which He was full. This must be taken in the most comprehensive sense, nothing that is life being excluded, *physical, moral, eternal* life (so already Chrysostom),—all life was contained in the Logos, as in its principle and source. No limitation of the conception, especially as ζωή is without the article (comp. v. 26), has any warrant from the context ; hence it is not to be understood either merely of *physical* life, so far as it is the sustaining power,[5] or of *spiritual* and *eternal* life,—of the Johannean ζωὴ αἰώνιος,[6] where Hengstenberg drags in the negative notion that the creature was excluded from life until Christ was manifested in the flesh, and that down to the time of His incarnation He had only been virtually life and light. — κ α ὶ ἡ ζ ω ὴ κ.τ.λ.] *and the life*, of which the Logos was

---

[1] Comp. 1 Cor. vi. 5; see Stallbaum, *ad Plat. Sympos.* p. 214 D ; Kühner, *ad Xen. Mem.* i. 6. 2. As to the thing itself, comp. Philo, II. p. 225: δι' οὗ σ ύ μ π α ς ὁ κόσμος ἐδημιουργεῖτο.

[2] C. D. L. Verss., Clem. Al., Origen, and other Greeks, Heracleon, Ptolemaeus, *Philos. Orig.* v. 8, Latin Fathers, also Augustine, Wetst., Lachm., Weisse.

[3] " *Whatever originated in Him* (self) *is life.*" The latter is said to be the Zoë, which with the Logos formed one Syzygy. Hilgenfeld regards this view as correct, in connection with the assumption of the later Gnostic origin of the Gospel. But the construction is false as regards the *words*, because neither ἐστί nor ἐγένετο stands in the passage ; and false also as regards the *thought*, because, according to vv. 1-3, a

principle of life cannot have first *originated* in the Logos, but must *have existed* from the very beginning. Also Bunsen (*Hypol.* II. 291, 357) erroneously preferred the punctuation of the Alexandrines and Gnostics.

[4] The Logos must necessarily be taken as in vv. 1-3, but not from ver. 4 onwards in Hofmann's sense, as no longer a person but a thing, viz. the Gospel, as Röhricht (p. 315) maintains, as if the *verbum vocale* were now a designation of Christ, who is the bearer of it. No such change of meaning is indicated in the text, and it only brings confusion into the clear advance of the thought.

[5] B. Crusius, comp. Chrysostom, Euthymius Zigabenus, Calvin.

[6] Origen, Maldonatus, Lampe, Kuinoel, Köstlin, Hengstenberg, Weiss.

the possessor, *was the light of men*.   The exposition thus passes over from the universal to the relation of the Logos to *mankind ;* for, being Himself the universal source of *life* to the world made by Him, He could as such least of all remain inactive with respect to men, but must show Himself as operating upon them conformably to their rational and moral nature, especially as *the light*, according to the necessary connection of life and light in opposition to death and darkness.   (Comp. viii. 12 ; Ps. xxxvi. 10 ; Eph. v. 14 ; Luke i. 78, 79).   The *light* is *truth pure and divine*, theoretical and moral (both *combined* by an inner necessity, and not simply the former, as Weiss maintains), the reception and appropriation of which *enlightens* the man ($vi\grave{o}\varsigma\ \phi\omega\tau\acute{o}\varsigma$, xii. 36), whose non-appropriation and non-reception into the consciousness determines the condition of *darkness*.   The Life *was* the Light of men, because in its working upon them it was the necessary *determining power of their illumination*.   Comp. such expressions as those in xi. 25, xiv. 6, xvii. 3.   Nothing as yet is said of the working of the Logos *after His incarnation* (xiv. 6), but (observe the $\mathring{\eta}\nu$) that the divine truth in that primeval time came to man from the Logos as the source of life ; the life in Him was for mankind the actively communicating principle of the divine $\mathring{a}\lambda\acute{\eta}\theta\epsilon\iota a$, in the possession of which they lived in that fair morning of creation, before through sin darkness had broken in upon them.   This reference to the time when man, created after God's image, remained in a state of innocency, is necessarily required by the $\mathring{\eta}\nu$, which, like the preceding $\mathring{\eta}\nu$, must refer to the creation-period indicated in ver. 3.   But we are thus at the same time debarred from understanding, as here belonging to the enlightening action of the Logos, God's revelations to the Hebrews and later Jews (comp. Isa. ii. 5), by the prophets, etc. (Ewald), or even the elements of moral and religious truth found in heathendom ($\lambda\acute{o}\gamma o\varsigma\ \sigma\pi\epsilon\rho\mu a\tau\iota\kappa\acute{o}\varsigma$).   In that fresh, untroubled primeval age, when the Logos as the source of *life* was the *Light* of men, the contrast of light and darkness did not yet exist ; but this tragic contrast, as John's readers knew, originated with the fall, and had continued ever after.   There follows, therefore, after a fond recalling of that fair bygone time (ver. 4), the sad and mournful declaration of the later and still enduring relation (ver. 5), where the light still *shines* indeed, but in *darkness*,—a darkness which has not received it.   But if that closely to be observed reference of $\mathring{\eta}\nu$ to the time of the creation, and this view of the progress of the thought be correct, it cannot embrace also the *continuous* (ver. 17) creative activity of the Logos, through which a consciousness and recognition of the highest truth have been developed among men (de Wette) ; and just as little may we find in $\tau\grave{o}\ \phi\tilde{\omega}\varsigma\ \tau.\ \mathring{a}\nu\theta\rho.$ what *belongs to the Logos in His essence only*, in which case the reading $\mathring{e}\sigma\tau\acute{\iota}$ would (against Brückner) be more appropriate ; comp. $\phi\omega\tau\acute{\iota}\zeta\epsilon\iota$, ver. 9.   As in $\mathring{e}\nu\ a\mathring{v}\tau\tilde{\varphi}\ \zeta\omega\grave{\eta}\ \mathring{\eta}\nu$, so also by $\mathring{\eta}\nu\ \tau\grave{o}\ \phi\tilde{\omega}\varsigma\ \tau.\ \mathring{a}\nu\theta\rho.$ must be expressed what the Logos was in His *historical activity*, and not merely what He was *virtually* (Hengstenberg). Comp. Godet, who, however, without any hint from the text, or any historical appropriateness whatever, finds in " *life* and *light* " a reminiscence of the trees of life and of knowledge in Paradise.

Ver. 5. Relation of the light to the darkness. — $\kappa a\grave{\iota}\ \tau\grave{o}\ \phi\tilde{\omega}\varsigma$] *and the light* shineth ;¹ not *"and thus, as the light,* 'the Logos shineth" (Lücke). The discourse steadily progresses link by link, so that the preceding predicate becomes the subject. — φαίνει] Present, *i.e.* uninterruptedly *from the beginning until now ;* it embraces, therefore, the illuminating activity of the λόγος ἄσαρκος² and ἔνσαρκος. As it is arbitrary to supply the idea of *" still present "* (Weiss), so also is its limitation to the revelations through the *prophets of the O. T.,* which would make φαίνει merely the descriptive *praesens historicum* (de Wette). For the assumption of this in connection with pure preterites there is no warrant ; comp. rather φωτίζει, ver. 9. According to Ewald,³ φαίνει represents as present the time in which the Light, which since the creation had enlightened men only from afar, has come suddenly into the world which without it is darkness, and is shining from the midst of this darkness. An antithetic relation is thus assumed (*" only from afar,—suddenly in the midst "*) which has no support in the present tense alone, without some more distinct intimation in the text. The stress, moreover, is not on φαίνει, but rests with tragic force on the emphatically placed ἐν τῇ σκοτίᾳ. It is the continuation of the discourse, ver. 7 ff., which first leads *specially* to the action of the *Incarnate One* (this also against Hengst.). — The σκοτία is the negation and opposite of the φῶς, the state of things in which man possesses not the divine ἀλήθεια, but has become the prey of folly, falsehood, and sin, as a godless ruling power, with all its misery. Here the abstract term " darkness," as the *element in which* the light shines, denotes not the *individual subject* of darkness (Eph. v. 8), but, as the context requires, the totality previously described by τῶν ἀνθρώπων, thus *mankind in general, in so far as* in and for themselves they since the fall have been destitute of divine truth, and become corrupt in understanding and will. Melanchthon well says, " genus humanum oppressum peccato vocat tenebras." Frommann is altogether mistaken in holding that σκοτία differs in the two clauses, and means (1) humanity so far as it yet lay *beyond* the influence of the light, and (2) humanity so far as it was *opposed* thereto. But Hilgenfeld is likewise in error, when, out of a different circle of ideas, he imports the notion that " light and darkness are *primeval* opposites, which did not originate with the fall ;" see on viii. 44. — οὐ κατέλαβεν] *apprehended it not, took not possession of it ;* it was not *appropriated* by the darkness, so that the latter might become light, instead of remaining aloof and alien to it. Comp. Phil. iii. 12, 13, 1 Cor. ix. 24, and especially Rom. ix. 30 ; also expressions like καταλαμβ. σοφίαν, Ecclus. xv. 1, 7. The explanation *comprehended, i.e.* ἔγνω, ver. 10,⁴ is on one

---

¹ φαίνει, *lucet,* not to be confounded with φαίνεται, which means *apparet.* See on Phil. ii. 15. Godet's criticism of the distinction is erroneous.

² Godet thinks that the *law written in the h art, the light of conscience,* is meant (Rom. ii. 14,) which the Logos makes use of ; and that this His relation to all mankind is essential and permanent. But this would be utterly inadequate to the fulness of meaning expressed by φῶς, especially in its an-

tithesis to σκοτία. The φῶς shines as *divine* light *before* Christ (by revelation and prophecy), and *after* Him. It is *supernatural, heavenly.* Comp. 1 John ii. 8. There is no mention here of the λόγος σπερματικός.

³ *Jahrb.* V. 194 (see his *Johann. Schr.* I. 121).

⁴ Eph. iii. 18 ; Acts x. 34, iv. 13 ; Plato, *Phaedr.*, p. 250 D ; Phil. p. 16 D ; Polyb. viii. 4. 6.

side arbitrarily narrowing, on another anticipatory, since for the σκοτία, which is conceived as a *realm*, it substitutes the *subjects*. Erroneously Origen, Chrysostom, Theophylact, Euthymius Zigabenus, Bos, Schulthess, Hoelemann, p. 60, and Lange interpret : " The darkness did not hem it in, repress it ; it was invincible before it." Linguistically this is allowable,[1] but it nowhere so occurs in the N. T., and is here opposed to the parallels, vv. 10, 11. — Observe that οὐ κατέλαβεν, which presupposes no Gnostic absolutism, but freedom of moral self-determination (comp. vv. 11, 12), reflects the phenomenon *as a whole*, and as it presented itself to John in *history* and *experience ;* hence the *aorist*. Comp. iii. 19.

Ver. 6. In the painful antithesis of ver. 5 which pervades the entire Gospel, was included the relation of the Logos to mankind, not only before, but *after His incarnation* (see on φαίνει). This latter is now *more minutely unfolded* as far as ver. 11. To strengthen the antithesis John adduces first the *testimony of the Baptist* (vv. 6–8) to the Light, on the ground of which he then designates the Logos *as the true light* (ver. 9) ; and finally makes the *antithesis*, thus prefaced (vv. 10, 11), follow with all the more tragic effect. The *mention of John's testimony* here in the Prologue is not therefore a mere confirmation of the reality of the appearance of the Logos (Brückner), which the statements of vv. 9, 10 did not require. Still less is it a pressing forwards of the thought to the beginning of the Gospel history (de Wette), or an intimation of the first step in the reconcilement of the contrasted light and darkness (Baur), or " an illustrious exception" (Ewald) to the preceding ἡ σκοτία, κ.τ.λ. Introducing a new paragraph, and hence without a connecting particle, it forms a historical *preparation*, answering to the fact, for that *non-recognition and rejection* (vv. 10, 11), which, in spite of that testimony of the Baptist, the light shining in the darkness had experienced. Ver. 15 stands to ver. 7 in the relation of a particular definite statement to the general testimony of which it is a part. — ἐ γ έ ν ε τ ο] not *there was* (ἦν, iii. 1), but *there appeared*, denoting the historical *manifestation*. See on Mark i. 4 ; Luke i. 5 ; Phil. ii. 7. Hence not with Chrys.: ἐ γ έ ν ε τ ο ἀ π ε σ τ α λ μ έ ν ο ς ἀντὶ τοῦ ἀ π ε σ τ ά λ η ; which Hengstenberg repeats. — Observe in what follows the noble simplicity of the narrative : we need not look out for any antithetical reference (ἐγένετο—ἄνθρωπος—ἀπεστ. π. θεοῦ) to ver. 1 (B. Crusius, Luthardt, and older expositors). With ἀ π ε σ τ α λ μ. π. θ ε ο ῦ, comp. iii. 28 ; Mal. iii. 1, 23. Description of the true *prophet ;* comp. also Luke iii. 2, 3.

Ver. 7. Ε ἰ ς μ α ρ τ υ ρ ί α ν] *to bear witness ;* for John *testified* what had been prophetically *made known* to him by divine revelation respecting the Light which had come in human form. Comp. ver. 33. — ἵ ν α π ά ν τ ε ς, κ.τ.λ.] Purpose of the μαρτυρήσῃ, final end of the ἦλθεν. — π ι σ τ ε ύ σ.] *i.e.* in the light ; comp. vv. 8, 9, xii. 36. — δ ι' α υ τ ο ῦ] by means of *John*, as he by his witness-bearing *was the medium of producing* faith : "and thus John is a *servant* and *guide* to the Light, which is Christ" (Luther) ; not by means of *the light* (Grotius, Lampe, Semler), for here it is not faith in *God* (1 Pet. i. 21) that is spoken of.

---

[1] See Schweighäuser, *Lex. Herod.* II. p. 18.

Ver. 8. ἦν is *emphatic*, and is therefore placed in the front : he *was* not the Light, but he was to *bear witness* of the Light ; and hence, in the second clause, μ α ρ τ υ ρ ή σ η emphatically takes the lead. The object of making this antithesis prominent is not controversy, or at least with any reference to the disciples of John (see the Introduction), but to point out[1] the true position of the Baptist in face of the historical fact, that when he first appeared, men took him for the Messiah Himself (comp. ver. 20 ; Luke iii. 15), so that his witness shall appear in its proper *historical* aspect.   Comp. Cyril. — ἀ λ λ᾽ ἵ ν α , κ.τ.λ.] Before ἵνα we must from the preceding supply ἦλθεν ; a rapid hastening on to the main thought ;[2] not taken imperatively (*sent to bear witness*) (de Wette), nor dependent upon ἦν (Lücke, Lange, Godet) : not the latter, because εἶναι ἵνα (for εἰς τό), even if it were linguistically possible, is here forbidden by the emphasis on the ἦν ; while to take ἦν in the sense of *aderat*, as again understood before ἵνα (Godet), would be more forced and arbitrary than to supply ἦλθεν from ver. 7.

Ver. 9. For the correct apprehension of this verse, we must observe, (1) that ἦν has the main emphasis, and stands therefore at the beginning : (2) that τὸ φῶς τὸ ἀληθ. cannot be the predicate, but must be the subject, because in ver. 8 another was the subject ; consequently without a τοῦτο, or some such word, there are no grounds for supposing a subject not expressed : (3) that ἐρχόμ. εἰς τὸν κόσμον[3] can only be connected with πάντα ἄνθρωπον, not with ἦν ; because when John was bearing witness the Logos *was* already in the world (ver. 26), not simply then *came* into the world, or was *about* to come, or *had* to come. We should thus be obliged arbitrarily to restrict ἐρχ. εἰς τ. κόσμ. to His *entrance upon His public ministry*, as Grotius already did (from whom Calovius differs), and because the order of the words does not suggest the connecting of ἦν with ἐρχόμ ; rather would the prominence given to ἦν, and its wide separation from ἐρχόμ., be without any reason. Hence the connection by the early church of ἐρχόμ. with π. ἄνθρ. is by no means (with Hilgenfeld) to be regarded as obsolete, but is to be retained,— and explained thus : "*There was present the true Light, which lighteth every man that cometh into the world.*" [See Note III. p. 95.] This, with the following ἐν τῷ κόσμῳ ἦν onward to ἐγένετο, serves to prepare for and strengthen the portentous and melancholy antithesis, καὶ ὁ κόσμ. αὐτὸν οὐκ ἔγνω. The usual objection that ἐρχόμ. εἰς τ. κ., when referred to πάντα ἄνθρ., is a superfluous by-clause, is inept. There is such a thing as a *solemn* redundance, and that we have here, an *epic fulness of words*. Hence we must reject (1) the usual interpretation by the older writers (before Grotius), with whom also Kaeuffer sides : "*He* (or even *that*, namely τὸ φῶς) *was the true Light which lighteth all*

---

[1] Not to bring more fully to light the greatness of Christ, through the subordination to Him of the greatest men and prophets, as Hengstenb. asserts. In this case John ought to have been described according to his own greatness and rank, and not simply as in ver. 6.

[2] Comp. ix. 3, xiii. 18, xv. 25 ; 1 John ii. 19 ; Fritzsche, *ad Matt.* 840 f. ; Winer, p. 297

[E. T. p. 458].

[3] With Origen, Syr., Copt., Euseb., Chrys., Cyril., Epiph., Nonnus, Theophyl., Euth. Zig., It., Vulg., Augustine, Erasmus, Luther, Beza, Calvin, Aret., and most of the early expositors. So of late Paulus also, and Klee, Kaeuffer in the *Sächs. Stud.* 1844, p. 116, Hoelemann, and Godet.

men who come into this world" (Luther), against which we have already re-marked under (1) and (2) above ; again, (2) the construction of ἐρχόμ. with φῶς as an accompanying definition : [1] " He was the true Light, *which was at that time to come into the world ;*"[2] also, (3) the connecting of ἦν with ἐρχόμενον, either in a sense purely historical, " *He came* " (Bleek, Köstlin, B. Crusius, Lange, Hengstenberg, with reference to Mal. iii. 1 ; and so already Bengel); or relatively, as de Wette, Lücke : " when John had appeared to bear wit-ness of Him, *even then* came the true Light into the world ; "[3] or as future, of Him who was soon to appear : *venturum erat* (Rinck, Tholuck), according to Luthardt (comp. Baeuml.) : " it had been *determined* of God that He should come ;" or more exactly, of an unfulfilled state of things, still present at that present time : " *It was coming*" (Hilgenfeld, *Lehrbegr.* p. 51) ; [4] and after Ewald, who attaches it to vv. 4, 5 : " It *was at that time always coming into the world,* so that every human being, if he had so wished, might have let himself be guided by it ;" comp. Keim: " He was *continually coming* into the world." As to details, we have further to remark : ἦν] *aderat,* as in vii. 39 and often ; its more minute definition follows in ver. 10 : ἐν τῷ κόσμῳ ἦν. The Light *was* already *there* (in Jesus) when John bore witness of Him, ver. 26. The reference of vv. 9–13 to the preincarnate agency of the Logos [5] entirely breaks down before vv. 11–13, as well as before the comparison of the Baptist with the Logos, which presupposes the personal manifestation of the latter (comp. also ver. 15) ; and therefore Baur erroneously denies any distinction in the Prologue between the preincarnate and the postincar-nate agency of the Logos.[6] — τ ὸ ἀ λ η θ ι ν ό ν [Because it was neither John nor any other, but the *true, genuine,* archetypal Light, corresponding to the idea—*the idea* of the light *realized.*[7] Comp. iv. 23, 37, vi. 32, vii. 28, xv. 1. See, generally, Schott, *Opusc.* I. p. 7 ff. ; Frommann, *Lehr-begr.* p. 130 ff. ; Kluge in the *Jahrb. f. D. Th.* 1866, p. 333 ff. ; also Hoelemann, *l.c.* p. 63, who, however, supposes an antithesis, which is without any support from the connection, to the *cosmic* light (Gen. i.). — ὁ φ ω τ ί ζ ε ι π ά ν τ α ἄ ν θ ρ.] a characteristic of the true light ;

---

[1] So probably Theod. Mopsu. ; some in Augustine, *de pecc. mer. et rem.* i. 25 ; Cas-talio, Vatablus, Grotius ; Schott, *Opusc.* I. p. 14 ; Maier.

[2] The interpretation of Schoettgen, Sem-ler, Morus, Rosenmüller, as if instead of ἐρχόμ. we had ἦλθεν, is quite erroneous. Luther's explanation down to 1527 was better: " through His advent into this world."

[3] Comp. Hauff in the *Stud. u. Krit.* 1846, p. 575.

[4] That is, during the time before His bap-tism ; the man Jesus (according to the Val-entinian Gnosis) did not become the organ of the Logos until His baptism, and accord-ingly through that rite the Logos first came into the world. The birth of Jesus was only introductory to that coming. Brück-

ner, while rejecting this importation of Gnosticism, agrees in other respects with Hilgenfeld.—Philippi (*der Eingang d. Joh. Ev.* p. 89) : " He was to come, *according to the promises of the O. T. ;*" and ver. 10 : " These promises had now received their fulfilment."

[5] Tholuck, Olshausen, Baur, also Lange, *Leben J.* III. p. 1806 ff.

[6] Comp. Bleek in the *Stud. u. Krit.* 1833, p. 414 ff.

[7] In the classics, see Plato, *Pol.* i. p. 347 D (τῷ ὄντι ἀληθινός), vi. p. 499 C ; Xen. *Anab.* i. 9. 17 ; *Oec.* x. 3 ; Dem. 113. 27, 1248. 22 ; Theo-crit. 16 (*Anthol.*) ; Pindar, *Ol.* ii. 201 ; Polyb. i. 6. 6, *et al.* Rück., *Abendm.* p. 266, errone-ously says, " the word *seldom* occurs in the classics." It is especially common in Plato, and among later writers in Polybius.

it illumines *every one.* This remains true, even though, as a matter of fact, the illumination is not received by many (see on Rom. ii. 4), so that every one does not really *become* what he *could* become, a child of light, φῶς ἐν κυρίῳ, Eph. v. 8. The relation, as a *matter of experience,* resolves itself into this : " quisquis illuminatur, ab hac luce illuminatur," Bengel ; comp. Luthardt. It is not this, however, that is expressed, but the *essential* relation as it exists on the part of the Logos.[1] Bengel well says : " numerus *singularis* magnam hic vim habet." Comp. Col. i. 15 ; Rom. iii. 4. — ἐρχό-μενον εἰς τ. κόσμον] every man *coming into the world ;* rightly without the article ; comp. 2 John 7. The addition of the predicative clause gives emphatic prominence to the conception of πάντα. There is no need to compare it with the Rabbinic בָּא בְעוֹלָם (see Lightfoot and Schoettgen). Comp. xvi. 21, and see on xviii. 37.

Ver. 10. What here follows is linked to the preceding by ἐν τῷ κόσμῳ ἦν, following upon εἰς τ. κόσμ. This is a fuller defining of the emphatic ἦν of ver. 9 : " *It was in the world,*" viz. in the person of Jesus, when John was bearing witness. There is no mention here of its *continual* presence in humanity (B. Crusius, Lange), nor of the "lumière innée" (Godet) of every man ; see on ver. 5. The triple *repetition* of κόσμος, which in its last occurrence has the narrower sense of the world of *mankind, gives prominence* to the mournful antithesis ; Buttm. *neut. Gr.* p. 341 [E. T. p. 398]. — ἦν] not pluperfect (" It had been already always in the world, but was not recognized by it"), as Herder, Tholuck, Olshausen, and Klee maintain, but like ἦν in ver. 9. — καὶ ὁ κόσμος δι' αὐτοῦ ἐγέν.] Further preparation, by way of climax, for the antithesis, with reference to ver. 3. If the Light was *in the world,* and the world was *made* by it, all the more could and ought the world to have recognized it : it *could,* because it needed only not to close the inner eye against the Light, and to follow the impulse of its original necessary moral affinity with the creative Light ; it *ought,* because the Light, shining within the world, and having even given existence to the world, could demand that recognition, the non-bestowal of which was ingratitude, originating in culpable delusion and moral obduracy. Comp. Rom. i. 19 ff. We need not attach to the καί, which is simply conjunctive, either the signification *although* (Kuinoel, Schott), or the force of the relative (*which* was made by it, Bleek). — αὐτόν] *the Logos,* identified with the Light, and spoken of as its possessor, according to vv. 4 ff. ; αὐτοῦ was still *neuter,* but the antithesis passes over into the *masculine,* because the object which was not recognized was this very *personal manifestation* of the Logos.—With regard to the last καί, observe : " cum vi pronuntiandum est, ut saepe in sententiis oppositionem continentibus, ubi frustra fuere qui καίτοι requirerent."[2] Very often in John.

Ver. 11. More particular statement of the contrast. Observe the gradual advance to greater definiteness : ἦν, ver. 9 ; ἐν τῷ κόσμῳ ἦν, ver. 10 ; εἰς

---

[1] Luther : " Of what avail is it that the clear sun shines and lightens, if I shut my eyes and will not see his light, or creep away from it beneath the earth?" Comp.

also Delitzsch, *Psychol.* p. 348 [E. T. p. 410].

[2] Stallbaum, *ad Plat. Apol.* p. 29 B. Comp. Hartung, *Partikell.* p. 147.

τὰ ἴδια ἦλθε, ver. 11.— ε ἰ ς τ ὰ ἴ δ ι α] *to His own possession*, [See Note IV. p. 95.]
is [1] to be explained of the *Jewish people* as specially belonging to the *Messiah*
(Ecclus. xxiv. 7 ff.), as they are called in Ex. xix. 5, Deut. vii. 6, Ps. cxxxv.
4, Isa. xxxi. 9, *Jehovah's* possession ; from Israel salvation was to spread
over all the world (iv. 22 ; Matt. viii. 12 ; Rom. i. 16). This interpretation is required by the *progress* of the discourse, which by the use of ἦλθε
excludes any reference to the *world*,[2] as was proposed alongside of this by
Chrysostom, Ammonius, Theophylact, Euth. Zig., and conjoined with it
by Augustine and many others. "He *was* in the *world ;*" and now
follows His *historical advent*, "He *came* to His *own possession*." Therefore
the sympathy of God's people, who were *His own* people, should have
led them to reach out the hand to Him. — ο ἱ ἴ δ ι ο ι] the *Jews*. — π α ρ έ -
λ α β ο ν] *They received Him not*, *i.e.* not as Him to whom they peculiarly belonged.[3] Observe that the special guilt of Israel appears still greater (οὐ
παρέλαβον, they despised Him) than the general guilt of mankind (οὐκ
ἔγνω). Comp. the οὐκ ἠθελήσατε of Matt. xxiii. 37 ; Rom. x. 21. In the
negative form of expression (vv. 10, 11) we trace a deeply elegiac and
mournful strain.

Ver. 12. The mass of the Jews rejected Him, but still *not all* of them.
Hence, in this fuller description of the relation of the manifested Logos to
the world, the refreshing light is now (it is otherwise in ver. 5) joyfully recognized and placed over against the shadow. — ἔ λ α β ο ν] He *came*, they *received* Him, did not reject Him.[4]—The nominative ὅσοι stands with emphasis
independent of the construction that follows. See on Matt. vii. 24, x. 14,
xiii. 12, xxiii. 16 ; Acts vii. 40. — ἐ ξ ο υ σ ί α ν] not *dignity* or *pre-eminence*
(Erasmus, Beza, Flacius, Rosenmüller, Semler, Kuinoel, Schott), nor *possibility* (de Wette, Tholuck), nor *capability* (Hengstenberg, Brückner), which
does not reach the force of the word,[5] but *He gave them full power* (comp. v.
27, xvii. 2). The rejection of the Logos when He came in person, excluded
from the attainment of that sacred condition of fitness—received through
Him—for entering into the relationship of children of God, and they only
who received Him in faith obtained through Him this *warrant*, this *title*
(ἐπιτροπὴ νόμου, Plato, *Defin.* p. 415 B). It is, however, an arrangement *in
the gracious decree of God ;* neither a claim of right on man's part, nor any
internal ability (Lücke, who compares 1 John v. 20 ; also Lange),—a meaning which is not in the word itself, nor in the connection, since the commencement of the filial relationship, which is the consummation of that
highest theocratic ἐξουσία, is conceived as a *being born*, ver. 13, and therefore
as passive (against B. Crusius). — τ έ κ ν α θ ε ο ῦ] Christ alone *is* the Son of
God, manifested as such *from His birth*, the μονογενής. Believers, from their
knowledge of God in Christ (xvii. 3), *become* children of God, by being *born*

<hr/>

[1] With Erasmus, Luther, Beza, Calvin,
Bengel, Lampe, and many expositors, also
Lücke, Tholuck, Bleek, Olshausen, de Wet-
te, B. Crusius, Maier, Frommann, Köstlin,
Hilgenfeld, Luthardt, Ewald, Hengsten-
berg, Godet, and most interpreters.

[2] Corn. à Lapide, Kuinoel, Schott, Reuss,
Keim.

[3] Comp. Matt. i. 20, xxiv. 40, 41 ; Herod. i.
154, vii. 106 ; Plato, *Soph.* p. 218 B.

[4] Comp. v. 43 ; Soph. *Phil.* 667, ἰδών τε καὶ
λαβὼν φίλον.

[5] Comp. Godet : " il les a *mis en position*."

of God (comp. iii. 3 ; 1 John iii. 9), *i.e.* through the moral transformation and renewal of their entire spiritual nature by the Holy Ghost ; so that now the divine element of life rules in them, excludes all that is ungodly, and permanently determines the development of this moral fellowship of nature with God, onwards to its future glorious consummation (1 John iii. 2 ; John xvii. 24). See also 1 John iii. 9 and 1 Pet. i. 23. It is thus that *John* represents the idea of filial relationship to God, for which he *always* uses τέκνα from the point of view of a *spiritual genesis ;* [1] while *Paul* apprehends it from the *legal* side (as adoption, Rom. viii. 15 ; Gal. iv. 5), regarding the spiritual renewal connected therewith (regeneration), the καινότης ζωῆς (Rom. vi. 4), as a new creation (2 Cor. v. 17 ; Gal. vi. 15), a moral resurrection (Rom. vi.), and the like ; while the *Synoptics* (comp. also Rom. viii. 23) make the υἱοθεσία appear as first commencing with the kingdom of the Messiah (see on Matt. v. 9, 45 ; Luke vi. 35), as conditioned, however, by the moral character. There is no difference as to the thing itself, only in the manner of apprehending its various sides and stages. — τ ο ῖ ς π ι σ τ ε ύ ο υ σ ι ν , κ.τ.λ.] *quippe qui credunt*, is conceived as *assigning the reason ;* for it is as believers that they have fulfilled the subjective *condition* of arriving at sonship, not only negatively, since they are no longer under the wrath of God and the condemnation of the law (iii. 36, 16, 17, v. 45), but also positively, inasmuch as they now possess a capacity and susceptibility for the operation of the Spirit (vii. 38, 39). John does not say πιστεύσασιν, but π ι σ τ ε ύ ο υ σ ι ν , for the faith, the *entrance* of which brought about the ἔλαβον, is thenceforth their *enduring habitus*. — ε ἰ ς τ ὸ ὄ ν ο μ α α ὐ τ ο ῦ] not essentially different from εἰς αὐτόν, but characterizing it more fully ; for the entire *subject-matter* of faith lies in the *name* of the person on whom we believe ; the *uttered* name contains the whole *confession* of faith. Comp. ii. 23, iii. 18, 1 John iii. 23, v. 13. The name itself, moreover, is no other than that of the historically manifested Logos—*Jesus Christ*, as is self-evident to the consciousness of the reader. Comp. ver. 17 ; 1 John v. 1, ii. 22.

Ver. 13. Oἵ] refers to τέκνα θεοῦ (the *masculine* in the well-known *constructio* κατὰ σύνεσιν, 2 John 1, Philem. 10, Gal. iv. 19),[2] not to τοῖς πιστεύουσιν, because the latter, according to ver. 12, are said to *become* God's children, so that ἐγεννήθησαν would not be appropriate. The conception *"children of God"* is more precisely defined as denoting those who came into existence not after the manner of natural human generation, but who were begotten of God.

---

[1] Hilgenfeld, indeed, will have it that those spoken of are already regarded as *originally* τέκνα θεοῦ (comp. iii. 6, viii. 44, xi. 52), and attempts to escape the dilemma into which γενέσθαι brings him, by help of the interpretation: "the power by which the man who is born of God realizes this, and actually *becomes* what he is *in himself* according to his nature !" Thus we should have here the Gnostic *semen arcanum electorum et spiritualium*. See Hilgenfeld, *Evangelien*, p. 233. The reproach of tautology which he also brings against the ordinary

explanation (in his *Zeitschr.* 1863, p. 110) is quite futile. The great conception of the τέκνα θεοῦ, which appears here for the first time, was in John's eye important enough to be accompanied by a more detailed elucidation. Generally, against the anthropological dualism discovered in John by Hilgenfeld (also by Scholten), see Weiss, *Lehrbegr.* p. 128 ff. ; also Weizsäcker in the *Jahrb. f. D. Th.* 1862, p. 680 f. ; and even Baur, *neutest. Theol.* p. 359 ff.

[2] Comp. Eurip. *Suppl.* 12, *Androm.* 571.

CHAP. I., 13.   59

The negative statement exhibits them as those in whose coming into existence human generation (and consequently also Abrahamic descent) has no
part whatever. *This latter* brings about no *divine* sonship, iii. 6. — ο ὐ κ ἐ ξ
α ἱ μ ά τ ω ν] *not of blood,* the blood being regarded as the seat and basis of
the physical life (comp. on Acts xv. 20), which is transmitted by generation.[1]
The plural is not to be explained of the commingling of the *two sexes* ("ex
sanguinibus enim homines nascuntur maris et feminae," Augustine ; comp.
Ewald), because what follows (ἀνδρός and the corresponding ἐκ θεοῦ) points
simply to generation on the *man's* side ; nor of the *multiplicity of the children
of God* (B. Crusius), to which there is no reference in what follows ; quite
as little does it refer to the *continuos propagationum ordines* from Adam, and
afterwards from Abraham downwards (Hoelemann, p. 70), which must necessarily have been more distinctly indicated.   Rather is the plural used in a
sense not different from the singular, and founded only on this, that the
material blood is represented as the sum-total of all its parts.[2]—The negation of human origination is so important to John (comp. iii. 6), that he
adds *two further parallel definitions* of it by οὐδέ—οὐδέ (which he arranges co-
ordinately) ; *nor—nor,* where σ α ρ κ ό ς designates the flesh as the substratum of the *generative impulse,* not "*the woman*" (Augustine, Theophylact,
Rupertus, Zeger, Schott, Olshausen),—an interpretation which is most
inappropriately supported by a reference to Gen. ii. 22, Eph. v. 28, 29, Jude
7, while it is excluded by the context (ἀνδρός, and what follows).   The
man's generative will is meant, and this is more exactly, *i.e.* personally,
defined by ἐκ θελ. ἀνδρός, to which the contrasted ἐκ θεοῦ is correlative ; and
hence ἀνήρ must not be generalized and taken as equivalent to ἄνθρωπος
(Lücke), which never occurs—even in in the Homeric πατὴρ ἀνδρῶν τε θεῶν τε
only *apparently*—but here least of all, because the act of *generation* is the
very thing spoken of.   The following are merely arbitrary glosses upon the
points which are here only rhetorically accumulated to produce an ever-increasing distinctness of description ; *e.g.* Baumgarten Crusius : "There is
an advance here from the most sensual to the most noble" (nature, inclination, will—in spite of the twice repeated θελήματος !) ; Lange (*L. J.* III. p.
558) : "There is a progress from natural generation to that which is caused
by the will, and then to that consummated in theocratic faith ;" Hoelemann :
"σάρξ, meant of both sexes, stands midway between the universalis humani
generis propagatio (αἵματα) and the proprius singularis propagationis auctor
(ἀνήρ)."   Even Delitzsch refines upon the words, finding in θελήμ. σαρκός the
unholy side of generation, though John has only in view the antithesis between the *human* and the *divine* viewed in and by themselves. — ἐ κ   θ ε ο ῦ

---

[1] ὡς τοῦ σπέρματος ὕλην τοῦ αἵματος ἔχοντος,
Eustath. *ad Hom. Il.* , vi. 211. Comp. Delitzsch, *Pyschol.* p. 246 [E. T. p. 290, and note].
Comp. Acts xvii. 26 ; Hom. *Il.* vi. 211, xx.
241 ; Soph. *Aj.* 1284, *El.* 1114 ; Plato, *Soph.* p.
268 D ; Liv. xxxviii. 28. Kypke and Loesner
on the passage, *Interpp. ad. Virg. Aen.* vi.
836 ; Horace, *Od.* ii. 20. 6 ; Tib. i. 6. 66.
[2] Kühner, II. p. 28. Comp. Eur. *Ion.* 705,

ἄλλων τραφεὶς ἀφ' αἱμάτων ; Soph. *Ant.* 121,
and many places in the tragedians where
αἵματα is used in the sense of *murder.* Aesch.
Eum. 163, 248 ; Eur. *El.* 137 ; *Or.* 1547, *al.* ;
Monk, ad Eur. *Alc.* 512 ; Blomf. *Gloss. Choeph.*
60. Comp. Ecclus. xxii. 22, xxxi. 21 ; 2 Macc.
xiv. 18 ; also Plato, *Legg.* x. p. 887 D, ἔτι ἐν
γάλαξι τρεφόμενοι.

ἐ γ ε ν ν ή θ .] *were begotten of God*, containing the *real* relation of sonship to God, and *thus explaining* the former τέκνα θεοῦ, in so far as these were begotten by no human being, but by God, who through the Holy Spirit has restored their moral being and life, iii. 5.   Hence ἐκ θεοῦ ἐγενν. is not tautological.   'Ἐκ indicates the issuing forth from God as cause, where the relation of immediateness (in the first and last points) and of mediateness (in the second and third) lies in the very *thing*, and is self-evident without being distinctively indicated in the simple representation of John.

    Ver. 14. Κ α ί] *and ;* not *assigning a reason* for the sonship just mentioned (Chrys., Theophyl., Jansen, Grotius, Lampe, and several others); nor = οὖν (Bleek), nor in the sense of *namely* (Frommann), nor *yea* (Godet), but simply *carrying forward the discourse*, like *every* καί in the Prologue ; and not therefore pointing back to ver. 4 (Maldonatus) or to ver. 9 (de Wette), nor joining on to ver. 11 (Lücke : " The Logos came not only to His own possession, but appeared *visibly ;*" so, substantially, also Baur and Hilgenfeld), which would be a merely *apparent* advance in the exposition, because the visible manifestation is already intimated by φαίνει in ver. 5 and in vv. 9-13. No ; after having in vv. 4-13 spoken of the Logos as the light, of the melancholy contrast of the darkness of unbelief to that true light divinely attested by the Baptist, and of the exceedingly blessed agency which He has exercised on believers through the bestowal of the gift of sonship, the evangelist, on arriving at this last point, which expresses his own deepest and most blessed experience, can no longer delay formally and solemnly again to proclaim *the great event by which the visible manifestation* of the Logos— previously so frequently presupposed and referred to—had, with all its saving power, been brought about ; and thus by an outpouring of speech, which, prompted by the holiest recollections, soars involuntarily upwards until it reaches the loftiest height, to set forth and celebrate the *mode* of that manifestation of the Logos which was attended with such blessed results (vv. 12, 13), and which he had himself experienced.   The *transition*, therefore, is from what is said in vv. 12, 13 of the agency of the manifested Logos, to the *nature and mode of that manifestation itself*, *i.e.* consequently to the *incarnation*, as a result of which He, as Jesus Christ, exhibited the glory of the Only-begotten, and imparted the fulness of grace and truth,—that *incarnation* which historically determined what is recorded of Him in vv. 12, 13. Accordingly καί is not definitive, "under such circumstances, with such consequences" (Brückner, who inappropriately compares Heb. iii. 19, where καί connects the answer with the question as in continuous narration), but it *carries onward the discourse*, leading up to the highest summit, which even from ver. 5 shows itself as in. the distance. We must interpret it : *and*—to advance now to the most momentous fact in the work of redemption, namely, *how* He who had come and wrought so much blessing was manifested and was able to accomplish such a work—*the Word became flesh,* etc. — ὁ λόγος] John does not simply say καὶ σὰρξ ἐγένετο, but he *names* the great subject as he had done in ver. 1, to complete the solemnity of the weighty statement, which he now felt himself constrained still to subjoin and to carry onward, as in joyful triumph, to the close of the Prologue.—

σ ά ρ ξ ἐ γ έ ν ε τ ο] The word σ ά ρ ξ is *carefully chosen*, not as against *the divine idea of humanity*, which is here not in question,[1] but as opposed to the *purely divine*, and hence also to the *purely immaterial nature*[2] of the Logos,[3] whose transition, however, into this other form of existence necessarily presupposes that He is conceived of as a *personality*, not as a *principle* (Beyschlag, *Christol.* p. 169); as is, besides, required by the whole Prologue. The incarnation of a principle would be for John an unrealizable notion. Just as decidedly is ὁ λόγος σὰρξ ἐγένετο opposed to the idea that the Logos became *more and more completely* σάρξ (Beyschlag) during the whole *unfolding* of His *earthly life*. The ὁ λόγος σὰρξ ἐγένετο is a definite *act* in the consummation of His history. He became *flesh*, *i.e.* a corporeal material being, visible and tangible (1 John i. 2), which He was not before,[4] and by which evidently was intended the human mode of existence in which He appeared, and which was known to the reader in the person of *Jesus*. Ἐν σαρκὶ ἐλήλυθεν (1 John iv. 2 ; 2 John 7 ; comp. 1 Tim. iii. 16) is, in fact, the same thing, though expressed from the point of view of that *modality* of His *coming* which is conditioned by the σὰρξ ἐγένετο. As, however, ἐγένετο points out that He *became* what He *was* not before, the incarnation cannot be a mere *accident* of His substantial being (against Baur), but is the assumption of another real existence, whereby out of the purely divine Logos-Person, whose specific nature at the same time remained unaltered, and in order to accomplish the work of redemption,[5] a really corporeal personality, *i.e.* the God-man Jesus Christ (ver. 17), came into existence.[6] Since σάρξ necessarily carries with it the idea only of the ψυχή,[7] it might seem as if John held the Apollinarian notion, that in Christ there was no human νοῦς, but that the λόγος took its place.[8] But it is not really so,[9] because the human ψυχή does not exist by itself, but in necessary connection with the πνεῦμα,[10] and because the N. T. (comp. viii. 40)

---

[1] Against Beyschlag in the *Stud. u. Krit.* 1860, p. 459.

[2] Hence also σ ά ρ ξ is selected for the purpose of expressing the full antithesis, and not σῶμα, because there might be a σῶμα without σάρξ (1 Cor. xv. 40, 44) ; and besides, the expression ὁ λόγος σῶμα ἐγένετο would not necessarily include the possession of a human soul. John might also have written ἄ ν θ ρ ω π ο ς ἐγένετο (v. 27, viii. 40), but σάρξ presented the antithesis of the two forms of existence most sharply and strikingly, and yet at the same time unquestionably designates the human personality (xvii. 2). According to Baur, indeed, it is said to be *impossible* to understand by the incarnation any proper assumption of humanity.

[3] Clem. *ad Cor.* II. 9, ὧν μὲν τὸ πρῶτον πνεῦμα ἐγένετο σάρξ ; comp. Hahn, *Theol. d. N. T.* I. 197.

[4] Comp. the well known " *Sum quod eram, nec eram quod sum, nunc dicor utrumque.*" In Jesus Christ we have the absolute synthesis of the divine and the human.

[5] Chap. vi. ; Rom. viii. 3 ; Heb. ii. 14, 15.

[6] Comp. on the point, 1 John iv. 2 ; Phil. ii. 7 ; 1 Tim. iii. 16 ; Heb. ii. 14, v. 7.

[7] See Schulz, *Abendm.* p. 94 ff. ; Weiss, *Lehrbegr.* p. 256.

[8] Of late, Zeller in particular (in the *Theol. Jahrb.* 1842, I. 74) has limited the Johannean doctrine of the human element in the person of Jesus simply to His *corporeity*, excluding any special human *anima rationalis*. Comp. also Köstlin, p. 148 ff., and Baur, *neutest. Theol.* p. 362. That σάρξ was the merely *formal* non-personal *clothing* of the Logos-subject (Pfleiderer, in Hilgenfeld's *Zeitschr.* 1866, p. 260), does not correspond with the conception of ἄνθρωπος, under which Christ represents Himself (viii. 40). This is also in answer to Scholten, who in like manner comes to the conclusion that, in John's view, Jesus was man as to His body only, but the Logos as to His spirit.

[9] See, on the other side, Mau, *Progr. de Christolog. N. T.*, Kiel 1843, p. 13 ff.

[10] Beck, *bibl. Seelenl.* § 13 ; Hahn, *Theol. d. N. T.* I. § 154.

knows Jesus only as *perfect* man.[1]   In fact, John in particular expressly speaks of the ψυχή (xii. 27) and π ν ε ῦ μ α of Christ (xi. 33, xiii. 21, xix. 30), which he does not identify with the Logos, but designates as the substratum of the human self-consciousness (xi. 38).[2]   The *transcendental* character, however, of this self-consciousness, as necessarily given in the incarnation of the Logos, Weizsäcker has not succeeded, in his interpretation of the passages referred to, in explaining away by anything Jesus Himself says in this Gospel.   The conception of *weakness and susceptibility of suffering*,[3] which Luther, Melanchthon, Calvin, Olshausen, Tholuck, Hengstenberg, Philippi, and others find in σάρξ, is quite remote from this verse (comp. 1 John iv. 2), where the point in question is simply that change in the divine mode of existence in which the σάρξ bears the δόξα ; and so also is any anti-Docetic reference, such as Frommann and others, and even de Wette and Lechler, imagine. — The *supernatural generation* of Jesus is neither presupposed nor included (as also Godet maintains), nor excluded,[4] in the ὁ λόγος σὰρξ ἐγένετο, for the expression contains nothing as to the *manner* of the incarnation ; it is an *addition* to the primitive apostolical Christology, of which we have no certain trace either in the oldest Gospel (Mark), or in the only one which is fully apostolic (John), or anywhere in Paul : see on Matt. i. 18 ; comp. John v. 27, Rom. i. 3, 4. — κ α ὶ ἐ σ κ ή ν ω σ ε ν ἐ ν ἡ μ ῖ ν) *and tabernacled, i.e. took up His abode, among us* : ἐ σ κ ή ν ω σ ε ν here is *chosen* merely to draw our attention to the manifestation of the incarnate Logos, whose holy σκήνωμα (2 Pet. i. 13) was in fact His human substance,[5] as the fulfilment of the promise of God's dwelling with His people,[6] and therefore as the *Shekinah* which formerly revealed itself in the tabernacle and in the temple (see on Rom. ix. 4) ; an assumption which the context justifies by the words : ἐθεασ. τ. δόξαν αὐτοῦ.   The Targums, in like manner, represent the Word

---

[1] So John in particular. See Hilgenfeld, *Lehrbegr.* p. 234 ff., who, however, explains the σὰρξ ἐγένετο from the Valentinian system, and attributes to the evangelist the notion of a corporeity, real indeed, but not fettered by the limitation of a material body, appealing to vi. 16 ff., vii. 10, 15, viii. 59, ii. 19 ff. Baur's view is similar, though he does not go so far. Baur, p. 367.

[2] Rightly has the church held firmly to the *perfection* (perfectio) of the divine and human natures in Christ in the Athanasian sense. No change and no defect of nature on the one side or the other can be justified on exegetical grounds, and especially no such doctrine as that of Gess, that by the incarnation the Logos became a human soul or a human spirit (comp. also Hahn, *Theol. d. N. T.* I. 198 f.). *This* modification, which some apply to the κένωσις, is unscriptural, and is particularly opposed to John's. testimony throughout his Gospel and First Epistle. How little does Gess succeed in reconciling his view with John v. 26, for example,—a passage which is always an

obstacle in his way ! Further, according to Wörner, *Verhältn. d. Geistes zum Sohne Gott.* p. 27, the Logos became a *soul*. Against Hahn, see Dorner in the *Jahrb. f. d. Theol.* 1856, p. 393 ff.

[3] See on Acts ii. 17.

[4] For assuredly the same subject, which in His divine essence was *pre-existent* as the eternal Logos, may as a temporal human manifestation *come into existence* and begin to be, so that in and by itself the manner of this origination, natural or supernatural, makes no difference in the conceivableness of the fact (against Baur in the *Theol. Jahrb.* 1854, p. 222).

[5] In this He tabernacled among us not merely as a divine *principle* (Beyschlag), but as πᾶν τὸ πλήρωμα τῆς θεότητος (Col. ii. 9), *i.e.* exactly what He *was* as the personal *Logos.* Thus His *body* was the *temple* of God (ii. 19), the true special dwelling of God's gracious presence.

[6] Ex. xxv. 8, xix. 45 ; Lev. xxvi. 11 ; Joel iii. 21 ; Ezek. xxxvii. 27 ; Hagg. ii. 8 : comp. Ecclus. xxiv. 8 ; Rev. xxi. 3.

(מימרא) as the שכינה, and the Messiah as the manifestation of this. — ἐ ν
ἡ μ ῖ ν] refers to the ὅσοι ἔλαβον αὐτόν, vv. 12, 13, to whom John belongs, not
simply to the Twelve (Tholuck), nor to the Christian consciousness (Hilgenfeld), nor to mankind generally ; comp. ver. 16. The *believers* whom
Jesus found are the *fellowship* who, as the holy people, surrounded the incarnate Word, and by whom His glory was beheld (comp. 1 John i. 1). —
κ α ὶ ἐ θ ε α σ ά μ ε θ α, κ.τ.λ.] We must not (as most expositors, even Lücke,
Frommann, Maier, de Wette) take this clause as far as πατρός to be a lively
insertion, interrupting the narrative ; for the having beheld the δόξα is the
essential element in the progress of the discourse. [See Note V. p. 96.]
It is an *independent part in the connection ;* so that πλήρης χάρ. κ. ἀλ., which
is usually joined grammatically with ὁ λόγος, is to be referred to αὐτοῦ in an
irregular combination of cases, determined by the logical subject (B.
Crusius, Brückner, Weiss, comp. Grotius), by which the nominative instead
of the dependent case (Augustine *read* πλήρους) sets forth the statement
more emphatically without any governing word.[1] — τ ὴ ν δ ό ξ α ν α ὐ τ ο ῦ]
the Majesty (כבור) of the Logos, *i.e.* of necessity the *divine* glory (in the
O. T. symbolically revealing itself as the brilliant light which surrounded
the manifestation of Deity, Ex. xxiv. 17, xl. 34 ff. ; Acts vii. 2), so far as
the Logos from His nature (see what follows) essentially participated therein, and possessed it in and from His pre-existent state.[2] It presented itself
to the recognition of believers as a reality, in the entire manifestation,
work, and history of Him who became man ; so that they (not unbelievers)
beheld it [3] (*intuebantur*), because its rays shone forth, so as to be recognized
by them, through the veil of the manhood, and thus it revealed itself visibly
to them (1 John i. 1 ; comp. chap. ii. 11). The idea of an *inner* contemplation is opposed to the context (against Baur). The δόξα τοῦ λόγου, which
before the incarnation could be represented to the prophet's eye alone (xii.
41), but which otherwise was, in its essence, incapable of being beheld by
man, became by means of the incarnation an object of external observation by
the eye-witnesses (Luke i. 2 ; 1 John iv. 14) of His actual self-manifestation.
We must, however, bear in mind that the manifestation of this divine glory
of the Logos in His human state is conceived of *relatively*, though revealing
beyond doubt the divine nature of the Logos, and nothing else than that, yet
as limited and conditioned on the one hand by the imperfection of human intuition and knowledge, and on the other by the state of humiliation (Phil. ii.
6 ff.) which was entered upon with the " becoming flesh." For the absolute
glory, which as such is also the adequate " form of God," was *possessed* by the
Incarnate One—the Logos, who entered into our human life—only in His
pre-existent state (xvii. 5), and was *resumed* only after His exaltation (xii. 41,
xvii. 5, xxii. 24) ; while during His earthly life His δόξα as the manifestation of the ἴσα εἶναι θεῷ was not the *absolutely divine*, but that of the *God-man*.[4]

---

[1] See especially Bernhardy, p. 68 ; Heind. *ad Plat. Theaet.* 89, *Soph.* 7 ; Winer, p. 524 [E. T. p. 564].

[2] Comp. Gess, *Person Chr.* p. 123.

[3] All limitations to individual points, as

e.g. to the miracles, or even specially to the history of the transfiguration (Luke ix. 32 ; Wetstein. Tittmann), are arbitrary.

[4] Which indeed, even after His exaltation, is and ever continues to be that of the *God-*

See on Phil. ii. 8, note, and chap. xvii. 5. No distinction is hereby made between the divine and the theanthropic δόξα (as objected by Weiss) ; the difference is simply in the degrees of manifestation and appearance. Still Weiss is right in denying, as against Köstlin and Reuss, that there is in John no idea whatever of humiliation (comp. xii. 32, 34, xvii. 5). — δ ό ξ α ν] more animated without δέ.[1]— ὡ ς μ ο ν ο γ ε ν ο ῦ ς] as of an only-begotten, i.e. as belongs to such an one,[2] corresponds to the nature of one who is μονογενὴς παρὰ πατρός; Chrysostom : οἶαν ἔπρεπε καὶ εἰκὸς ἔχειν μονογενῆ καὶ γνήσιον υἱὸν ὄντα, κ.τ.λ. The idea of reality [3] (ὄντως) lies as little in ὡς as in the erroneously so called ? veritatis (against Olshausen, Klee, and earlier writers) ; it involves rather the idea of comparison, approaching the meaning of quippe.[4]— μ ο - ν ο γ ε ν ή ς] of Christ, and regarded, indeed, in His divine nature, is Johannean, expressing the apostle's own idea of Christ's unique relationship as the son of God, i. 18, iii. 16, 18, 1 John iv. 9, though it is put into the mouth of Christ Himself in iii. 16, 18. Comp. the Pauline πρωτότοκος, Col. i. 15, Heb. i.6, which as to the thing corresponds with the Johannean μονογ-ενής, but presents the idea in the relation of time to the creation, and in Rom. viii. 29 to Christianity. Μονογ. designates the Logos as the only Son (Luke vii. 12, viii. 42, ix. 38 ; Heb. xi. 17 ; Tob. viii. 17 ; Herod. vii. 221 ; Plato, Legg. III. p. 691 D ; Aesch. Ag. 898 ; Hes. ἔργ. 378), besides whom the Father has none, who did not, like the τέκνα θεοῦ (vv. 12, 13), become such by moral generation, nor by adoption, but by the intrinsic relation inhering in the divine essence, whereby He was in the beginning with God, being Himself divine in nature and person, vv. 1, 2. He did not become this by His incarnation, but is this before all time as the Logos, and manifests Himself as the μονογ. by means of the incarnation, so that consequently the μονογ. υἱός is not identical (Beyschlag, p. 151 ff.) with the historical person Jesus Christ, but presents Himself in that person to believers ; and therefore we are not to think of any interchange of the predicates of the Logos and the Son, "who may be also conceived of retrospectively." [5] Finally, the designation corresponds to human relations, and is anthropomorphic, as is υἱὸς θεοῦ itself,—a circumstance which necessarily limits its applicability as an expression of the metaphysical relation, which of course excludes the idea of birth as involving the maternal function. Origen well remarks : τὸ δὲ ὡς μονογ. παρὰ πατρ. νοεῖν ὑποβάλλει, ἐ κ τ ῆ ς ο ὐ σ ί α ς τοῦ πατρὸς εἶναι τὸν υἱὸν . . . εἰ γὰρ καὶ ἄλλα παρὰ πατρὸς ἔχει τὴν ὕπαρξιν, ματαίως ἡ τοῦ μονογενοῦς ἔκειτο φωνή. — π α τ ρ ό ς] without the article.[6] Παρὰ πατρ. must be joined to μονογ., to which it adds the definite idea of having gone forth, i.e. of having come from the Father

man, though without limitation and perfect. —According to Weiss (Lehrbegr. p. 261), the δόξα of the Logos cannot be that of the originally divine essence itself, but one vouchsafed to Christ for the purpose of His works. This, however, is contrary to the express meaning of the word here, where by the τὴν δόξ. αὐτοῦ, κ.τ.λ., we can only understand His proper glory brought with Him by the Logos into His incarnate life. As to xvii. 22, see on that passage.

[1] Comp. Hom. Od. a, 22 f. ; Dem. de. cor. 143 (p. 275, Reisk.) : πόλεμον εἰς τ. Ἀττικὴν εἰσάγεις . . . πόλεμον Ἀμφικτυονικόν. See Krüger, § 59, 1. 3, 4.

[2] Therefore μονογ. is without the article. The expression is qualitative.

[3] Euthymius Zigabenus : ὄντως.

[4] Ellendt, Lex. Soph. II. p. 1002 ; see Kühner, § 330. 5.

[5] Weizsäcker, 1862, p. 699.

[6] Winer. p. 116 [E. T. p. 122].

(vi. 46, vii. 29, xvi. 27). [See Note VI. p. 96.] Correlative with this is ver. 18, ὁ ὢν εἰς τ. κόλπον τοῦ πατρός, where the only-begotten Son who *came forth* from the Father is viewed as having again *returned* to the Father. The conception of *having been begotten*, and thus of *essential origin*, would be expressed by the simple genitive (πατρός) ; or by the dative, or by ἐκ or ἀπό, but lies in the word μονογενοῦς itself ; since this expresses the very *generation*, and therefore the ἐκ τῆς οὐσίας τοῦ πατρὸς εἶναι (Origen). Its connection with δόξαν (Erasmus, Grotius, Hofmann, *Schriftbew.* I. 120, Weiss ; already Theophyl.?) is in itself grammatically admissible (Plut. *Agis*, 2 ; Plato, *Phaedr.* p. 232 A ; Acts xxvi. 12), but is favoured here neither by the position of the words nor by the connection, which has no concern with the *origin* of the δόξα, but only with the designation of its *nature ;* moreover, the anarthrous μονογ. requires a more precise definition, which is exactly what it has in παρὰ πατρός. — π λ ή ρ η ς χ ά ρ κ . ἀ λ η θ .] To be referred to αὐτοῦ as its subject, though this stands in the genitive. See above. It explains *how* the Logos, having become incarnate, manifested Himself to those who beheld His glory. *Grace* and *truth* [1] are the two efficaciously saving and inseparable factors of His whole manifestation and ministry, not *constituting* His δόξα (Luthardt),—a notion opposed to ii. 11 and xvii.,—but displaying it and making it known to those who beheld that glory. Through God's *grace* to sinful man He became man ; and by His whole work on earth up to the time of His return to His Father, He has been the instrument of obtaining for believers the blessing of becoming the children of God. *Truth*, again, was what revealed itself in His entire work, especially by His preaching, the theme of which was furnished by His intuition of God (ver. 18), and which therefore must necessarily reveal in an adequate manner God's nature and counsel, and be the opposite of *darkness* and *falsehood.* Comp. Matt. xi. 27. The truth (ἀλήθεια) corresponds formally to the nature of the Logos as light (φῶς) ; the grace (χάρις), which bestows everlasting life (iii. 15), to His nature as life (ζωή), vv. 4, 5. That the χάρις κ. ἀλήθεια with which He was filled are *divine* grace and truth, of which He was the possessor and bearer, so that in Him they attained their complete manifestation (comp. xiv. 6), is self-evident from what has preceded, but is not specially indicated, as would necessarily have been done by the use of the article, which would have expressed the grace and truth (simply) κατ' ἐξοχήν. Ver. 16 f. is decisive against the construction of πλήρης with what follows (Erasmus, Paulus). Whether John, moreover, used the words πλήρ. χάριτος κ. ἀληθ. with any reference to Ex. xxxiv. 6 (Hengstenberg) is very doubtful, for אֱמֶת in that passage has a different meaning (truthfulness, fidelity). John is speaking independently, from his own full experience and authority as a witness. Through a profound living experience, he had come to feel, and here declares his conviction, that all salvation depends on the *incarnation* of the Logos.

[1] Where, according to Hilgenfeld, the author must have had in view the female Aeons of the two first Syzygies of the Valentinian system. John undoubtedly has the word χάρις only in the Prologue, but Matthew and Mark also do not use it ; while Luke does not employ it in the sense of saving Christian grace, in which sense it first occurs in the Acts and in Paul.

Ver. 15. [See Note VII. p. 96.] It is to this great fact of salvation to which the Baptist bears testimony, and his testimony was confirmed by the gracious experience of us all (ver. 16). — μαρτυρεῖ] Represents it as present, as if the testimony were still sounding forth. — κέκραγε] "clamat Joh. cum fiducia et gaudio, uti magnum praeconem decet," Bengel. He *crieth*, comp. vii. 28, 37, xii. 44 ; Rom. ix. 27. The *Perfect* in the usual classical sense as a present.[1] Not so elsewhere in the N. T. Observe, too, the *solemn circumstantial* manner in which the testimony is introduced : "*John bears witness of Him, and cries while he says.*" — οὗτος ἦν] ἦν is used, because John is conceived as speaking *at the present time*, and therefore as pointing back to a testimony *historically past :* "This was He whom I meant at the time when I said." With εἰπεῖν τινα, "*to speak of any one,*" comp. x. 36.[2] See on viii. 27. — ὁ ὀπίσω μου ἐρχόμ. ἔμπροσθέν μου γέγονεν] "*He who cometh after me is here before me ;*"—in how far is stated in the clause ὅτι πρῶτός μου ἦν, which assigns the reason. The meaning of the sentence and the point of the expression depend upon this,—namely, that Christ in His human manifestation appeared *after* John, but yet, as the pre-mundane Logos, *preceded* him, because He existed before John. On γίνεσθαι with an adverb, especially of place, in the sense of *coming* as in vi. 25.[3] Both are adverbs of *place*, yet under the local image representing *time* and not *rank* (ἐντιμότερός μού ἐστι, Chrysostom ; so most critics, with Lücke, Tholuck, Olshausen, Maier, de Wette),[4] which would involve a diverse mode of construing the two particles (the first being taken *temporally*), and the sentence then becomes trivial, and loses its enigmatical character, since there is no reason why later comers should stand lower in dignity. Origen long ago rightly understood both clauses as relating to time, though the second is not therefore to be rendered "He was before me" (Luther and many, also Brückner, Baeumlein), since ἦν is not the word ;[5] nor : "He *came into being* before me," which would not be referable "to the O. T. advent of Christ" (Lange), but, in harmony with the idea of μονογενής, to His having come forth from God prior to all time. It is decisive against both, that ὅτι πρῶτός μου ἦν would be tautological,—an argument which is not to be set aside by any fanciful rendering of πρῶτος (see below). Nonnus well remarks : πρῶτος ἐμεῖο βέβηκεν, ὀπίστερος ὅστις ἱκάνει. Comp. Godet and Hengst. ; also in his *Christol.* III. 1, p. 675, "my successor is my predecessor," where, however, his assumption of a reference to Mal. iii. 1 is without any hint to that effect in the words. According to Luthardt (comp. Hofmann, *Weissag. u. Erf.* II. 256), what is meant to be said is : "He who at first walked behind me, as if he were my *disciple*, has taken precedence of

---

[1] Βοῶν ... καὶ κεκραγώς, Dem. 271, 11 ; Soph. *Aj.* 1136 ; Arist. *Plut.* 722, *Vesp.* 415.

[2] Xen. *Cyr.* vii. 3. 5 ; Plato, *Crat.* p. 432 C ; Hom. *Il.* ζ. 479.

[3] See Krüger on Xen. *Anab.* i. 2. 7 ; Kühner, II. p. 39 ; Nägelsbach, note on *Iliad*, ed. 3, p. 295. Comp. Xen. *Cyrop.* vii. 1. 22, ἐγένετο ὄπισθεν τῶν ἁρμαμαξῶν ; *Anab.* vii. 1. 10 ; i. 8. 24.

[4] This rendering is not ungrammatical (in opposition to Hengstenberg), if only we maintain that, while adopting it, the local meaning of ἔμπροσθεν is not changed. (Comp. Gen. xlviii. 20 ; Baruch ii. 5.)

[5] So, too, in Matt. xix. 8 and John xx. 27, γίνεσθαι does not mean *esse*, but *fieri* (against Baeumlein) ; so also in passages such as Luke i. 5, 2 Pet. ii. 1.

me, *i.e.* He has become my *master.*" But the enigma of the sentence lies just in this, that ὁ ὀπίσω μου ἐρχόμ. expresses something still *future*, as this also answers to the customary ἔρχεσθαι of the Messiah's advent. Hofmann's view, therefore, is more correct, *Schriftbew.* II. 1, p. 10 ff.,—namely, that the meaning of the Baptist is, "*while Jesus is coming after him, he is already before Him.*" But even thus ἔμπρ. μου γέγ. amounts to a figurative designation of *rank*, which is not appropriate to the clause ὅτι πρῶτός μου ἦν, which assigns the reason, and manifestly refers to time. — ὅ τ ι   π ρ ῶ τ ό ς   μ ο υ   ἦ ν] is a direct portion of the Baptist's testimony which has just been adduced,[1] as ver. 30 shows, presenting the key to the preceding oxymoron : *for before me He was in existence.* The reference to *rank*,[2] requiring our construing, " *He was more than I*," is overthrown by ἦν, for which we should have had ἐστίν. Comp. Matt. iii. 11. Only a rendering which refers to *time* (*i.e.* only the pre-existence of the Logos) solves the apparent opposition between subject and predicate in the preceding declaration. — πρῶτος in the sense of πρότερος, answering to the representation, "*first in comparison with me.*"[3] We must not, with Winer and Baur, force in the idea of *absolute* priority.[4] This also against Ewald ("*far* earlier"), Hengstenberg, Brückner, Godet ("the principle of my existence"). To refuse to the Baptist all *idea of the pre-existence of the Messiah*, and to represent his statement merely as one put into his mouth by the evangelist,[5] is the more baseless, the more pointed and peculiar is the testimony ; the greater the weight the evangelist attaches to it, the less can it be questioned that deep-seeing men were able, by means of such O. T. passages as Mal. iii. 1, Isa. vi. 1 ff., Dan. vii. 13 ff., to attain to that idea, which has also Rabbinical testimony in its support,[6] and the more decidedly the harbinger of the Messiah, under the influence of divine revelation, took his stand as the last of the prophets, the Elijah who had come.

Ver. 16. Not the language of the Baptist,[7] against which ἡμεῖς πάντες is decisive, but that of the *evangelist* continued. — ὅ τ ι (see critical notes) introduces *the personal and superabounding gracious experience of believers*, with a retrospective reference indeed to the πλήρ. χάριτος κ. ἀληθ., ver. 14, and in the form of a *confirmation of John's testimony* in ver. 15 : this testimony is justified by what was imparted to us all out of the fulness of Him who was borne witness to. — ἐ κ   τ ο ῦ   π λ η ρ ώ μ. α ὐ τ ο ῦ] *out of that whereof He was full*, ver. 14 ; πλήρωμα in a *passive* sense ; see on Col. i. 19. The phrase and idea were here so naturally furnished by the immediate context, that it is quite far-fetched to find their source in Gnosticism, especially in that of the

---

[1] Against Hengstenberg.

[2] Chrysostom, Erasmus, Beza, Calvin, Grotius, and most comm., also B. Crusius and Hofmann.

[3] Comp. the genitive relation in πρωτότοκος πάσης κτίσεως, Col. i. 15. See Herm. *ad Viger.* p. 718; Dorvill. *ad Charit.* p. 478; Bernhardy, *Eratosth.* 42, p. 122.

[4] Philippi, *d. Eingang d. Joh. Ev.*, p. 179 : "He is the *unconditioned first* (*i.e.* the eter-

nal), in relation to me." The comparison of A and Ω in the Revelation is inapplicable here, because we have not the absolute ὁ πρῶτος, but πρῶτός μου. Comp. xv. 18 ; and Buttmann, *neut. Gr.* p. 74 [E. T. p. 84].

[5] Strauss, Weisse, B. Bauer, de Wette, Scholten, and many others.

[6] Bertholdt, *Christol.* p. 131.

[7] Heracleon, Origen, Rupertus, **Erasmus**, Luther, Melanchthon, Lange.

68   THE GOSPEL OF JOHN.

Valentinians.[1] — ἡ μ ε ῖ ς] *we on our part*, giving prominence to the personal experience of the believers (which had remained unknown to unbelievers), vv. 10, 11. — π ά ν τ ε ς] None has gone empty away. *Inexhaustibleness* of the πλήρωμα. — ἐ λ ά β ο μ ε ν] absolute : *we have received.* — κ α ί] *and indeed.*[2] — χ ά ρ ι ν ἀ ν τ ὶ χ ά ρ ι τ ο ς] *grace for grace*, is not to be explained,[3] *N. T. instead of O. T. grace,*[4] or instead of the *original* grace lost in Adam (see especially Calovius), since in ver. 17 ὁ νόμος and ἡ χάρις are opposed to each other, and since in the N. T. generally χάρις is the distinctive essence of *Christian* salvation (comp. especially Rom. vi. 14, 15) ; but with Beza and most modern expositors,[5] " *so that ever and anon fresh grace appears in place of that already received.*" " Proximam quamque gratiam satis quidem magnam gratia subsequens cumulo et plenitudine sua quasi obruit," Bengel. So superabundant was the λαμβάνειν ! This rendering is justified linguistically by Theogn. *Sent.* 344, ἀντ' ἀνιῶν ἀνίας ; Philo, *de poster. Caini*, I. p. 254 ; Chrys. *de sac.* vi. 13,—as in general by the primary meaning of ἀντί (grace interchanging with grace) ; it corresponds, in the context, with the idea of the πλήρωμα, from which it is derived, and is supported further by the increasingly blessed condition of those individually experiencing it (justification, peace with God, consolation, joy, illumination, love, hope, etc. : see on Rom. v. 1 ff. ; Gal. v. 22 ; Eph. v. 9). John might have written χάριν ἐπὶ χάριτι or χάριν ἐπὶ χάριν (Phil. ii. 27), but his *conception* of it was different. Still, any special reference to the fulness of the *special* χ α ρ ί σ μ α τ α , 1 Cor. xii.–xiv. (Ewald), lies remote from the context here (ver. 17) ; though these, as in general *any* spiritual blessing (Eph. i. 3), wherewith God in Christ has blessed believers, are not *excluded.*

Ver. 17. Antithetical confirmation of χάριν ἀντὶ χάριτος ; " for how high above what was formerly given by Moses, does that stand which came through Jesus Christ !" Comp. Rom. iv. 15, x. 4 ; Gal. iii. 10 ff., *al.* The former is the *law*, viewed by Paul as the *antithesis* of grace (Rom. vi. 14, vii. 3 ; Gal. iv. 4, and many other passages), in so far as it only lays us under obligation, condemns us, and in fact arouses and intensifies the need of grace, but does not bestow peace, which latter gift has been realized for us through Christ. The antithesis without μὲν—δέ has rhetorical force (iv. 22, vi. 63).[6] — ἡ χ ά ρ ι ς] in the *definite* and *formal* sense of redemption, *saving grace, i.e.* the grace of the *Father* in the *Son.* Hence also καὶ ἡ ἀλήθεια is added with a pragmatical reference to ver. 14 ; this, like all Christ's gifts of grace, was included in the universal χάριν ἀντὶ χάριτος of ver. 16. Moreover, the ἀ λ ή θ ε ι α was not given in the law, in so far as its substance, which was not indeed untrue, but an outflow of the divine will for salvation (Rom.

---

[1] Schwegler, Hilgenfeld.

[2] See Winer, p. 407 [E. T. p. 437] ; Hartung, *Partikell.* I. 145.

[3] With Chrysostom, Cyril, Severus, Nonnus, Theophylact, Erasmus, Beza, Aretius, Calovius, Jansen, Wolf, Lampe, and many others, even Paulus.

[4] Euthymius Zigabenus: τὴν καινὴν διαθήκην ἀντὶ τῆς παλαιᾶς.

[5] Among whom, however, Godet regards the phrase with ἀντί as a *play upon words,* referring to the O. T. law of retaliation, according to which " *chaque grâce était la récompense d'un mérite acquis.*" But such an allusion would be inappropriate, since χάρις in ἀντὶ χάριτος is not something human, but divine.

[6] Buttm. *N. T. Gk.* p. 344 (E. T. p. 364).

vii. 10 sqq. ; Acts vii. 38), was related only as type and preparation to the absolute revelation of truth in Christ and hence through its very fulfilment (Matt. v. 17) had come to be done away.¹ Comp. Gal. iii. 24. *Grace* was still wanting to the law, and with it *truth* also in the *full* meaning of the word. See also 2 Cor. iii. 13 ff. — ἐγένετο] The non-repetition of ἐδόθη is not to point out the *independent* work of the Logos,² with which διά is inconsistent, or of God (Origen), whose work the law also was. It comes from a change of thought (not recognized by Lücke), in that each clause sets forth the historical phenomenon *as it actually occurred*. In the case of the law, this took place in the historical form of *being given*, whereas grace and truth *originated, came into being*, not absolutely, but in relation to mankind, for whom they had not before existed as a matter of experience, but which now, in the manifestation and work of Christ, unfolded their historical origin. Comp. 1 Cor. i. 30.—Observe how appropriately, in harmony with the creative skilful plan of the Prologue, after the incarnation of the Logos, and the revelation of His glory which was therewith connected, have been set forth with glowing animation, there is now first announced the great historical NAME, *Jesus Christ*, which designates the incarnate Logos as the complete concrete embodiment of His manifestation. Comp. 1 John i. 1–3. Only now is the Prologue so fully developed, that Jesus Christ, the historical person of the λόγος ἔνσαρκος (hence all the less, with Hofmann and Luthardt, to be understood immediately from the beginning under the Logos), comes before the eye of the reader, who now, however, knows how to gather up in this name his full theanthropic glory.

Ver. 18 furnishes an explanation of what had just been said, that ἡ ἀλήθεια διὰ 'I. X. ἐγένετο, ;³ for this there was required immediate knowledge of God, the result of experience, which His only-begotten Son alone possessed. — οὐδείς] no man, not even Moses. "Besides is no doctor, master, or preacher, than the only Teacher, Christ, who is in the Godhead inwardly," Luther ; comp. Matt. xi. 27. — ἑώρακε] *has seen, beheld* (comp. iii. 11), of the beholding of God's *essence* (Ex. xxxiii. 20), to the exclusion of visions, theophanies, and the like.⁴ Agreeably to the context, the reference is to the direct vision of God's essential glory, which no man could have (Ex. *l.c.*), but which Christ possessed in His pre-existent condition as λόγος (comp. vi. 46), and possesses again since His exaltation. — ὁ ὢν εἰς τὸν κόλπ. τοῦ πατρός] As ἐξήγησ. refers to the state *on earth* of the Only-begotten, ὢν consequently, taken as an imperfect, cannot refer to the *pre-human* state ;⁵ yet it cannot coincide with ἐξήγη. in respect of time (Beyschlag), because the εἶναι εἰς τὸν κόλ. τ. π. was not true of Christ during His earthly life (comp. especially i. 52).⁶ The right explanation therefore is, that John, when he wrote

---

¹ Rom. x. 4; Col. ii. 14; Heb. x. 1 ff., vii. 18.

² Clemens, *Paedag.* i. 7.

³ Not including any explanation of ἡ χάρις also (Luthardt), because ἑώρακε and ἐξηγή-σατο answer only to the conception of the *truth* in which the vision of God is interpreted.

⁴ Comp. 1 John iv. 12 ; also Rom. i. 20 ; Col. i. 15 ; 1 Tim. i. 17.

⁵ Against Luthardt, Gess, pp. 123, 236, and others.

⁶ Hence we must not say, with Brückner, comp. Tholuck and Hengstenberg, that a relation of the μονογενής is portrayed which was neither interrupted nor modified by

ὁ ὢν εἰς τ. κ. τ. π., expressed himself from *his own* present standing-point, and conceived of Christ as in His state of *exaltation*, as having returned to the bosom of the Father, and therefore into the state of the εἶναι πρὸς τὸν θεόν.[1] Thus also must we explain the statement of direction towards, ε ἰ ς τ ὸ ν κόλπ., which would be otherwise without any explanation (Mark ii. 1, xiii. 16 ; Luke xi. 7) ; so that we recognize in εἰς as the prominent element the idea of *having arrived at*,[2] not the notion of *leaning upon*,[3] nor of *moving towards*, which is warranted neither by the simple ὢν (in favour of which such analogies as *in aurem dormire* are inappropriate) nor by εἰς, instead of which πρός[4] or ἐπί with the accusative ought rather to be expected.[5] This forced interpretation of εἰς would never have been attempted, had not ὢν been construed as a *timeless* Present, expressing an *inherent* relation, and in this sense applied[6] also to the earthly condition of the Son ; comp. Beyschlag, pp. 100, 150. So far as the *thing* itself is concerned, the εἶναι εἰς τὸν κόλπ· does not differ from the εἶναι πρὸς τὸν θεόν of ver. 1 ; only it expresses the fullest fellowship with God, not before the incarnation, but after the exaltation, and at the same time exhibits the relation of *love* under a sensuous form (κόλπον) ; not derived, however, from the custom (xiii. 23) of reclining at table (thus usually, but not appropriately in respect of fellowship with *God*), but rather from the analogy of a father's embrace (Luke vi. 22). In its *pragmatic* bearing, ὁ ὢν is the historical *seal* of the ἐξηγήσατο ; but we must not explain it, with Hilgenfeld, from the Gnostic idea of the πλήρωμα. [See Note VIII. p. 97.] — ἐ κ ε ῖ ν ο ς] strongly emphatic, and pointing heavenwards.[7] — ἐ ξ η γ ή σ α τ ο] namely, the substance of His intuition of God ; comp. viii. 38. The word is the usual one for denoting the *exposition*, interpretation of *divine* things, and intuitions.[8] It does not occur elsewhere in

the incarnation. The communion of the Incarnate One with God remained, He in God, and God in Him, but not in the same manner metaphysically as before His incarnation and after his exaltation. He while on earth was still *in heaven* (iii. 13), yet not *de facto*, but *de jure*, because heaven was His home, His ancestral seat.

[1] So Hofmann, *Schriftbew.* I. 120, II. 23 ; Weiss, *Lehrbegr.* 239.

[2] Ellendt, *Lex. Soph.* I. p. 537 ; Jacobs, *ad Anthol.* XIII. p. 71 ; Buttm. *N. T. Gr.* p. 286 ; [E. T. p. 333].

[3] Godet, after Winer, Lücke, Tholuck, Maier, Gess, and most others.

[4] Hom. *Il.* vi. 467.

[5] Philippi's objections (*Glaubensl.* IV. 1, p. 409 f.) to my rendering are quite baseless. For an explanation of the ὢν εἰς τὸν κόλπ. which occurs to every unprejudiced expositor as coming directly from the words themselves cannot be "arbitrary." And it is not *contrary to the connection*, as both Godet and Beyschlag hold, because what the words, as usually interpreted, say, is already contained in the ὁ μονογενὴς υἱός,

whereupon ὁ ὢν, κ.τ.λ. sets forth the exaltation of the Only-begotten—just as in ὁ μονογ· υἱός were given the *ground* and *source* of the ἐξηγήσατο—as its infallible *confirmation*. This also against Gess, p. 124. My interpretation is quite as compatible with *earnest treatment of the deity of Christ* (Hengstenberg) as the usual one, while both are open to abuse. Besides, we have nothing at all to do here with the *earnestness* referred to, but simply with the *correctness* or *incorrectness* of the interpretation. Further, I have not through fear of spiritualism (as Beyschlag imagines) deviated from the usual meaning, which would quite agree with iii. 13.

[6] Lücke, Tholuck, de Wette, Lange, Brückner, Hengstenberg, Philippi, and most expositors.

[7] As with Homer (see Nitzsch, p. 37, note 1), so in the N. T. John pre-eminently requires not merely to be *read*, but to be *spoken*. His work is the epic among the Gospels.

[8] Plato, *Pol.* iv. p. 427 C ; Schneid. *Theag.* p. 131 ; Xen. *Cyr.* viii. 3. 11 ; Soph. *El.* 417 ;

John, and hence a *special* reference in its *selection* here is all the more to be presumed, the more strikingly appropriate it is to the context (against Lücke, Maier, Godet). Comp. LXX. Lev. xiv. 57. [See Note IX. p. 71].

Note.—The Prologue, which we must not with Reuss restrict to vv. 1–5, is not "*A History of the Logos,*" describing Him down to ver. 13 as He was *before* His incarnation, and from ver. 14 ff. as *incarnate* (Olshausen). Against this it is decisive that vv. 6–13 already refer to the period of His *human* existence, and that, in particular, the sonship of believers, vv. 12, 13, cannot be understood in any other than a specifically *Christian* sense. For this reason, too, we must not adopt the division of Ewald : (1) The pre-mundane history of the Logos, vv. 1–3 ; (2) the history of His first purely spiritual agency up to the time of His incarnation, vv. 4–13 ; (3) the history of His human manifestation and ministry, vv. 14–18. John is intent rather on securing, in grand and condensed outline, a profound *comprehensive view of the nature and work* of the Logos ; which latter, the work, was in respect of the world *creative*, in respect of mankind *illuminative* (the *Light*). As this working of the Logos was historical, the *description* must necessarily also bear an historical character ; not in such a way, however, as to give a formal history, first of the λόγος ἄσαρκος (which *could* not have been given), and then of the λόγος ἔνσαρκος (which forms the substance of the *Gospel itself*), but in such a way that the whole forms a *historical picture*, in which we see, in the world which came into existence by the creative power of the Logos, His *light* shining before, after, and through His incarnation. This at the same time tells against Hilgenfeld, p. 60 ff., according to whom, in the Prologue, "the Gnosis of the absolute religion, from its immediate foundation to its highest perfection, runs through the series of its historical interventions." According to Köstlin, p. 102 ff., there is a brief triple description of all Christianity from the beginning onwards to the present ; and this, too, (1) from the standing-point of God and His relation to the world, vv. 1–8 ; then (2) from the relations of the Logos to mankind, vv. 9–13 ; and lastly, (3) in the individual, vv. 14–18, by which the end returns to the beginning, ver. 1. But a triple beginning (which Kaeuffer too assumes in the *Sächs. Stud.* 1844, p. 103 ff.) is neither formally hinted at nor really made : for, in ver. 9, ὁ λόγος is not the subject to ἦν, and this ἦν must, agreeably to the context, refer to the time of the Baptist, while Köstlin's construction and explanation of ἦν—ἐρχόμενον is quite untenable ; and because in the last part, from ver. 14 onwards, the antithesis between receiving and not receiving, so essential in the first two parts, does not at all recur again. The simple explanation, in harmony with the text, is as follows : The Prologue consists of three parts,—namely, (1) a description (*a*) of the primeval *existence* of the Logos, vv. 1, 2, and (*b*) of His *creative* work, ver. 3 (with the addition of the first part of ver. 4, which is the transition to what follows). Next, (2) a representation of Him in whom was life as the *Light of mankind*, ver. 4 ff., and this indeed (*a*) as He once had been, when still without the contrast of darkness, ver. 4, and (*b*) as He was in this contrast, ver. 5. This shining in the darkness is continuous (hence φαίνει, ver. 5), and the tragic opposition occasioned thereby now unfolds itself before our eyes onwards to ver. 13, in the following manner : "Though

comp. the ἐξηγηταί in Athens: Ruhnken, *ad Tim.* p. 109 ff. ; Hermann, *gottesd. Alterth.* § 1, 12.

John came forward and testified of the Light, not being himself the Light, but a witness of the Light (vv. 6–8,—though He, the true Light, was already *exist-ing* (ver. 9),—though He was *in the world*, and the world was made by Him, still men acknowledged Him not ; though He came to *His own*, His own received Him not (vv. 10, 11) ; whereas those who did receive Him obtained from Him power to become the spiritual sons of God (vv. 12, 13.'' Lastly, (3) this blessedness of believers, due to the Logos who had historically come, now constrains the apostle to make still more prominent the *mode* and *fashion* in which *He was manifested in history* (His *incarnation*), and *had revealed His glory*, vv. 14–18. Thus the Prologue certainly does not (against Baur) *lift* the histori-cal *out of* its own proper soil, and transfer it to the sphere of metaphysics, but rather unveils its metaphysical side, which was essentially contained in and connected with it, as existing prior to its manifestation, and in the light of this its metaphysical connection sums it up according to its *essence* and *antithe-sis*, its actual development and the proof of its historical truth being furnished by the subsequent detailed narrative in the Gospel. We may distinguish the three parts thus : (1) The *premundane existence* and *creative work of the Logos*, vv. 1–4*a* ; (2) *His work as the Light of men*, and the opposition to this, vv. 4–13 ; (3) The *revelation of His glory which took place through the incarnation*, vv. 14–18. Or, in the briefest way : the Logos (1) as the *creator ;* (2) as the *source of light ;* (3) as *the manifestation of the God-man*. This third part shows us the Incarnate One again, ver. 18, where as ἄσαρκος He was in the beginning—ὁ ὢν εἰς τ. κόλπ. τοῦ πατρός ; and the cycle is complete.

Vv. 19, 20. The *historical narrative*, properly so called, now begins, and quite in the style of the primitive Gospels (comp. Mark i. ; Acts x. 36, 37, xiii. 23–25), with the testimony of the Baptist. — κ α ί] *and*, now first of all to narrate the testimony already mentioned in ver. 15 ; for *this*, and not another borne before the baptism, is meant ; see note foll. ver. 18. — α ὔ τ η] '' The following is the testimony of John, which he bore when,'' etc.[1] In-stead of ὅτι, the evangelist puts ὅτε, because the idea of time was with him the predominant one.[2] Had he written ὅτι, his thought would have been : '' Herein did his testimony consist, that the Jews sent to him, and he con-fessed,'' etc. — ο ἱ Ἰ ο υ δ α ῖ ο ι] means, even in such passages as this, where it is no merely indifferent designation of the people (as in ii. 6, 13, iii. 1, iv. 22, v. 1, xviii. 33 ff., and often), nothing else than *the Jews ;* yet John, writing when he had long severed himself from Judaism, makes *the body of the Jews*, as the old religious community from which the Christian Church had already completely separated itself, thus constantly appear in a *hostile* sense in face of the Lord and His work, as the ancient theocratic people in corporate opposition to the new community of God (which had entered into their promised inheritance) and to its Head. How little may be de-duced from this as ground of argument against the age and genuineness of the Gospel, see my *Introd.* § 3. For the rest, in individual passages, the

---

[1] Following Origen and Cyril, Paulus and B. Crusius suppose that ὅτε begins a new sentence, of which καὶ ὡμολόγησε, etc., is to be taken as the apodosis—contrary to the

simplicity of John's style.

[2] Comp. Pflugk, *ad Hec.* 107 ; Ellendt, *Lex. Soph.* II. p. 393.

context must always show *who*, considered more minutely as matter of history, the persons in question were by whom the Jews are represented, as in this place, where it was plainly the *Sanhedrim* [1] who represented the people of the old religion. Comp. v. 15, ix. 22, xviii. 12, 31, etc. — καὶ Λευίτας] priests, consequently, with their *subordinates*, who had, however, a position as teachers, and aspired to priestly authority (see Ewald and Hengstenberg). The mention of these together is a trait illustrative of John's *precision of statement*, differing from the manner of the Synoptics, but for that very reason, so far from raising doubts as to the genuineness, attesting rather the independence and originality of John (against Weisse), who no longer uses the phrase so often repeated in the Synoptics, "the *scribes* and *elders*," because it had to him already become strange and out of date. — σὺ τίς εἶ] for John *baptized* (ver. 25), and this baptism had reference to Messiah's kingdom (Ezek. xxxvi. 25, 26, xxxiii. 23 ; Zech. xiii. 1). He had, generally, made a great sensation as a prophet, and had even given rise to the opinion that he was the Messiah (Luke iii. 15 ; comp. Acts xiii. 25) ; hence the question of the supreme spiritual court was *justified*, Deut. xviii. 21, 22, Matt. xxi. 23. The question itself is not at all framed in a captious spirit. We must not, with Chrysostom and most others, regard it as prompted by any *malicious* motive, but must explain it by the authoritative position of the supreme court. Nevertheless it implies the assumption that John regarded himself as the Messiah ; and hence his answer in ver. 20, hence also the emphatic precedence given to the σύ ; comp. viii. 25. Luthardt too hastily concludes from the form of the question, that the main thing with them was the *person*, not the call and purpose of God. But they would have inferred the call and purpose of God from the *person*, as the question which they ask in ver. 25 shows. — ἐξ 'Ιεροσ.] belongs to ἀπέστειλαν. — καὶ ὡμολόγ.] still dependent on the ὅτε. — ὡμολ. καὶ οὐκ ἠρνήσ.] emphatic prominence given to his straightforward confession ; ὡς ἀληθὴς καὶ στερρός, Euthymius Zigabenus. [2] — καὶ ὡμολ.] The first κ. ὡμολ. was absolute ; [3] this second has for subject the following sentence (ὅτι recitative). Moreover, "vehementer auditorem commovet ejusdem redintegratio verbi," *ad Herenn.* iv. 28. There is, however, no side glance here at the disciples of John (comp. the Introd.). To the evangelist, who had himself been the pupil of the Baptist, the testimony of the latter was weighty enough in itself to lead him to give it emphatic prominence. — According to the right order of the words (see crit. notes), ἐγὼ οὐκ εἰμὶ ὁ Χ., the emphasis lies upon ἐγώ ; *I on my part*, which implies that he knew *another* who was the Messiah.

Ver. 21. In consequence of this denial, the next point was to inquire whether he was the *Elijah* who, according to Mal. iv. 5, was expected (back from heaven) as the immediate *forerunner* of the Messiah. — τί οὖν] not, *quid ergo es* (Beza *et al.*), but as τίς does not again occur (vv. 19, 22) :

[1] Comp. 'Αχαιοί in Homer, which often means the *proceres* of the Greeks.

[2] Comp. Eur. *El.* 1057 : Φημὶ καὶ οὐκ ἀπαρνοῦμαι; Soph. *Ant.* 443 ; Dem. *de Chers.* 108.

73 : λέξω πρὸς ὑμᾶς καὶ οὐκ ἀποκρύψομαι. See Bremi *in loc. :* Valcken. *Schol. ad Act.* xiii. 11.

[3] *Add. ad Esth.* i. 15, and in the classics.

what then is the case, if thou art not the Messiah ? what is the real state of the matter ? — *Art thou Elijah?* So put, the question assumes it as certain that John must give himself out to be *Elijah,* after he had denied that he was the Messiah. — οὐκ εἰμί] He *could* give this answer, notwithstanding what is said in Luke i. 17, Matt. xi. 14, xvii. 10 (against Hilgenfeld), since he could only suppose his interrogators were thinking of the *literal,* not of the *antitypical* Elijah. Bengel well says : "omnia a se amolitur, ut Christum confiteatur et ad Christum redigat quaerentes." He was conscious, nevertheless, according to ver. 23, in what sense he was *Elijah;* but taking the question as *literally* meant, there was no occasion for him to go beyond that meaning, and to ascribe to himself in a special manner the character of an antitypical Elijah, which would have been neither prudent nor profitable. The οὐκ εἰμί is too *definite* an answer to the definite question, to be taken as a denial in general of *every externally defined position* (Brückner) ; he would have had to answer evasively. — ὁ προφήτης εἶ σύ;] The absence of any connecting link in the narrative shows the rapid, hasty manner of the interrogation. ὁ προφήτης is marked out by the article as the *well-known promised* prophet, and considering the previous question 'Ηλίας εἶ σύ, can only be a *nameless* one, and therefore not *Jeremiah,* according to Matt. xvi. 14,[1] but the one *intended* in *Deut.* xviii. 15, the reference of whom to the Messiah Himself (Acts iii. 22, vii. 37 ; John i. 46, vi. 14) was at least not universal (comp. vii. 40), and was not adopted by the interrogators here. Judging from the descending climax of the questions, they must rather have thought of some one inferior to Elijah, or, in general, of an individual undefined, owing to the fluctuation of view regarding Him who was expected as "*the prophet.*"[2] Nonnus well expresses the namelessness and yet eminence of this ὁ προφήτης : μὴ σύ μοί, ὃν καλέουσι, θεηγόρος ἐσσὶ προφήτης, ἀγγελος ἐσσομένων ; Observe how the rigid denials become shortened at last to the bare οὔ. *Here* also we have a *no* on the Baptist's lips, because in his view *Jesus* was the prophet of Deut. xviii.

Vv. 22, 23. Now comes the question which *cannot* be met by a bare negative ; ἵνα as in ix. 36. — The *positive* answer to this is from Isa. xl. 3 according to the LXX., with the variation εὐθύνατε instead of ἑτοιμάσατε, in unison with the second half of the words in the LXX. For the rest, see on Matt. iii. 3. The designation of himself, the herald of the coming Messiah calling men to repentance, as a *voice,* was *given* in the words of the prophet, and the accompanying βοῶντος ἐν τῇ ἐρήμῳ excludes the idea which Baur entertains, that John here intended to *divest* himself, as it were, of every *personal* characteristic. According to Hilgenfeld,[3] the evangelist has put the passage of Scripture *applied* to the Baptist by the Synoptics (who, however, have not *this* account at all) "at last into the Baptist's own mouth."

---

[1] Grotius, Kuinoel, Olshausen, Klee, Lange.

[2] Luthardt thinks of the prophet in the second portion of Isaiah. Comp. Hofmann, *Weissag. u. Erf.* II. p. 69. It would agree with this, that John immediately **gives** an answer taken from Isa. xl. But if his interrogators had had in mind Isa. xl. ff., they would probably have designated him whom they meant more characteristically, viz. as the *servant of Jehovah.*

[3] *Evang.* p. 236.

Ver. 24 ff. The inquiry, which proceeds still further, finds a pragmatic issue in *pharisaic* style (for the Sanhedrim had chosen their deputies from this learned, orthodox, and crafty party). From their strict scholastic standing-point, they could allow (οὖν) so thoroughly reformatory an innovation as that of baptism (see on Matt. iii. 5), considering its connection with Messiah's kingdom, only to the definite personalities of the Messiah, Elijah, or the promised prophet, and not to a man with so vague a call as that which the Baptist from Isa. xl. 3 ascribed to himself,—a passage which the Pharisees had not thought of explaining in a Messianic sense, and were not accustomed so to apply in their schools. Hence the parenthetical remark here inserted : " *And they that were sent belonged to the Pharisees,*"—a statement, therefore, which points *forward*, and does not serve as a *supplementary* explanation of the hostile spirit of the question (Euthymius Zigabenus, Lücke, and most others). — The *reply* corresponds to what the Baptist had said of himself in ver. 23, that he was appointed to *prepare* the way for the Messiah. *His* baptism, consequently, was not the baptism of the Spirit, which was reserved for the *Messiah* (ver. 33), but a *baptism* of water, as yet without the *elementum coeleste ;* there was already standing, however, in their midst the far greater One, to whom this preparatory baptism pointed. The *first* clause of the verse, ἐγὼ βαπτ. ἐν ὕδατι, implies, therefore, that by *his* baptism he does not lay claim to anything that belongs to the *Messiah* (the baptism of the *Spirit*) ; and this portion refers to the εἰ σὺ οὐκ εἶ ὁ Χριστός of ver. 25. The *second* clause, however, μέσος, etc., implies that this preliminary baptism of his had now the justification, owing to his relation to the Messiah, of a divinely ordained necessity (ver. 23) ; since the Messiah, unknown indeed to them, already stood in their midst, and consequently what they allowed to Elijah, or the prophet, must not be left unperformed on his part ; and this part of his answer refers to the οὐδὲ Ἠλίας οὐδὲ ὁ προφήτης in ver. 25. Thus the question τί οὖν βαπτίζεις is answered by a *twofold* reason. There is much that is inappropriate in the remarks of expositors, who have not sufficiently attended to the connection : *e.g.*, de Wette overlooks the appropriateness of the answer to the Elijah question ; Tholuck contents himself with an appeal to the "laconic-*comma* style" of the Baptist ; and Brückner thinks that " John wished to give no definite answer, but yet to indicate his relation to the Messiah, and the fact of his pointing to Him ;" while Baeumlein holds that the antithetical clause, ὃς βαπτίσει ἐν πνεύμ. ἁγ., intended to be here inserted, was *forgotten*, owing to the intervening sentences ; and finally, Hilgenfeld, from comparison of Matthew and Luke, deduces the unhistorical character of the narrative. Heracleon already held that John did not answer according to the question asked of him, but as he αὐτὸς ἐβούλετο. In answer to him, Origen. — ἐ γ ώ] has the emphasis of an *antithesis* to the high Baptizer (μέσος δὲ, etc.), not to ὑμεῖς (Godet). Next to this, the stress lies on ἐ ν ὕ δ α τ ι. This is the *element* (see on Matt. iii. 11) in which his baptism was performed. This otherwise superfluous addition has a *limiting* force, and hence is *important*. — μ έ σ ο ς] without the spurious δέ is all the more emphatic ; see on ver. 17. The emphasizing of the *antithesis*, however, brings this μέσος to the front, because it was *the manifestation of the Messiah*, already taking place *in the very midst of the Jews*, which justified John in baptizing. Had the Messiah been still far off, that baptism would have lacked its divine necessity ; He was, however, standing in their midst, *i.e.* ἀναμεμιγμένος τότε τῷ λαῷ (Euthymius Zigabenus). — ὃν ὑμεῖς οὐκ οἴδατε] reveals the reason why they could question as they had done in ver. 25. The emphasis is on ὑμεῖς, as always (against Tholuck) ; here in contrast with the knowledge which he himself had (see on ver. 28, note) of the manifested Messiah : *you on your part, you people,* have the Messiah among you, and know Him not (that is, as the Messiah). In ver. 27, after rejecting the words αὐτός ἐστιν and ὃς ἔμπροσ. μου γέγονεν (see the critical notes), there remains only ὁ ὀπίσω μου ἐρχόμενος (ver. 15), and that in fact as the subject of μέσος ἔστηκεν, which subject then receives the designation of its superiority over the Baptist in the οὗ ἐγὼ οὐκ εἰμὶ ἄξιος, κ.τ.λ. Concerning this designation, see on Matt. iii. 11. — ἐγώ] *I for my part.* — ἄξιος ἵνα] *worthy that I should loose ;* ἵνα introduces the *purpose* of the ἀξιότης. Comp. ἱκανὸς ἵνα, Matt. viii. 8, Luke vii. 6. — αὐτοῦ] placed *first* for emphasis, and corresponding to the ἐγώ.[1] Τούτου would have been still more emphatic.

Ver. 28. On account of the importance of His public appearance, a definite statement of its locality is again given. — A place so exactly described by John himself (xi. 18), according to its situation, as *Bethany on the Mount of Olives,* cannot be meant here ; there must also have been another Bethany situated in Peraea, probably only a village, of which nothing further is known from history. Origen, investigating both the locality and the text, did not find indeed any Bethany, but a Bethabara instead [2] (comp. Judg. vii. 24 ?), which the legends of his day described as the place of baptism ; the legend, however, misled him. For Bethany in Peraea could not have been situated at all in the same latitude with Jericho, as the tradition represents, but must have lain much 'farther north : for Jesus occupied about three days in travelling thence to the Judaean Bethany for the raising of Lazarus (see on xi. 17). Yet Paulus (following Bolten) understood the place to be Bethany on the Mount of Olives, and puts a period after ἐγένετο, in spite of the facts that τῇ ἐπαύριον (comp. ver. 35) must begin the new narration, and that ὅπου ἦν Ἰωάνν. βαπτ. must clearly refer to ver. 25 ff. Baur, however, makes the name, which according to Schenkel must be attributed to an error of a non-Jewish author, to have been *invented,* in order to represent Jesus (?) as *beginning* His public ministry at a *Bethany,* seeing that He came out of a *Bethany* at its close. Against the objection still taken to this name even by Weizsäcker (a name which a third person was certainly least of all likely to venture to insert, seeing that Bethany on the Mount of

---

[1] On αὐτοῦ after οὗ, see Winer, p. 140 [E. T. p. 155].

[2] To suppose, with Possinus, *Spicil. Evang.* p. 32 (in the Catena in Marc. p. 382 f.), that both names have the same signification (בֵּית עֲבָרָה, *domus transitus,* ford-house ; בֵּית אֳנִיָה, *domus navis,* ferry-house),—a view to which also Lange inclines, *L. J.* II. 431,—is the more untenable, as this etymol-

ogy is not at all appropriate to the position of Bethany on the Mount of Olives. Origen himself explains the name Bethabara with an evident intention to allegorize : οἶκος κατασκευῆς (ברא). The derivation of the name Bethany (Lightfoot : בֵּי הִינֵי, house of dates ; Simon : בֵּית עֲנִיָה *locus depressionis ;* others : בֵּית עַנְיָא, *domus miseri*) is doubtful.

Olives was so well known), see Ewald, *Jahrb.* XII. p. 214 ff. As to the *historic truth of the whole account* in vv. 19–28, which, especially by the reality of the situation, by the idiosyncrasy of the questions and answers, and their appropriateness to the characters and circumstances of the time, as well as by their connection with the subsequent designations of the day, reveals the recollections and interest of an eye-witness, see Schweizer, p. 100 ff.; Bleek, *Beitr.* p. 256. — ὅπου ἦν Ἰωάνν. βαπτ.] where John was employed in baptizing.

Note. — (1) Since, according to vv. 26, 27 (comp. especially ὃν ὑμεῖς οὐκ οἴδατε, which implies his own personal acquaintance), the Baptist already knows the Messiah, while according to vv. 31–33 he first recognized Him at His baptism through a divine σημεῖον, it follows that the occurrences related in vv. 19–28 took place *after the baptism of Jesus;* and consequently this baptism could not have occurred on the same or the following day (Hengst.), nor in the time between vv. 31 and 32 (Ewald). Wieseler, Ebrard, Luthardt, Godet, and most expositors, as already Lücke, Tholuck, de Wette, following the older expositors, rightly regard the events of ver. 19 ff. as *subsequent to* the baptism. It is futile to appeal, as against this (Brückner), to the "*indefiniteness*" of the words ὃν ὑμεῖς οὐκ οἴδατε, for there is really no indefiniteness in them ; while to refer them to a merely preliminary knowledge, in opposition to the *definite* acquaintance which began at the baptism, is (against Hengst.) a mere subterfuge. That even after the baptism, which had already taken place, John could say, "Ye know Him not," is sufficiently conceivable, if we adhere to the purely historical account of the baptism, as given in vv. 31–34. See on Matt. p. 111 ff. (2) Although, according to Matt. iii. 14, John already knows Jesus as the Messiah when He came to be baptized of him, there is in this only an apparent discrepancy between the two evangelists ; see on ver. 31. (3) Mark i. 7, 8, and Luke iii. 16 ff., are not at variance with John ; for those passages only speak of the Messiah as being Himself near at hand, and do not presuppose any personal acquaintance with Jesus as the Messiah. (4) The testimonies borne by the Baptist, as recorded in the Synoptics, are, both as to time (*before* the baptism) and occasion, very different from that recorded in John i. 19 ff., which was given before a deputation from the high court ; and therefore the historic truth of both accounts is to be retained side by side,[1] though in details John (against Weisse, who attributes the narrative in John to another hand ; so Baur and others) must be taken as the standard. (5) To deny any reference in ver. 19 ff. to the baptism of Jesus (Baur), is irreconcilable with vv. 31 and 33 ; for the evangelist could not but take it for granted that the baptism of Jesus (which indeed Weisse, upon the whole, questions) was a well-known fact. (6) Definite as is the reference to the baptism of Jesus, there is to be found no allusion whatever in John's account to the history of the temptation with its forty days, which can be brought in only before ver. 19, and even then involving a contradiction

---

[1] Keim, *Gesch. J.* I. p. 522, sees in John's account *not so much an historical narrative,* as rather (?) a "very *significant* literary *introduction* to the Baptist, who to *a certain extent* (?) is officially declaring himself. According to Scholten, the Baptist, during his ministry, did not at all recognize Jesus as Messiah, and Matt. iii. 14, 15 is said to be an addition to the text of Mark ;" while the fourth Gospel does not relate the baptism of Jesus, but only mentions the revelation from heaven then made, because to narrate the former would not be appropriate to the Gnosis of the Logos.

with the Synoptics. [See Note X. p. 98.] The total absence of any mention of this—important as it would have been in connection with the baptism, and with John's design generally in view of his idea of the Logos (against B. Crusius)—does not certainly favour the reality of its historic truth as an actual and outward event. Comp. Schleiermacher, *L. J.* p. 154. If the baptism of Jesus be placed between the two testimonies of ver. 19 ff. and ver. 29 ff. (so Hilgenfeld and Brückner, following Olshausen, B. Crusius, and others), which would oblige us still to place it on the day of the first testimony (see Brückner), though Baeumlein (in the *Stud. u. Krit.* 1846, p. 389) would leave this uncertain ; then the history of the temptation is as good as *expressly* excluded by John, because it must find its place (Mark i. 12 ; Matt. iv. 1 ; Luke iv. 1) immediately after the baptism. In opposition to this view, Hengstenberg puts it in the period after iii. 22, which is only an unavailing makeshift.

Ver. 29. Τ $\tilde{\eta}$ ἐπαύριον] *on the following day*, the next after the events narrated in vv. 19–28. Comp. vv. 35, 44 (ii. 1), vi. 22, xii. 12. — ἐρχόμ. πρὸς αὐτ.] *coming towards him*, not *coming to him*, *i.e.* only so near that he could *point to* Him (Baur). He came, however, neither to take leave of the Baptist before His temptation (Kuinoel, against which is ver. 35), nor to be baptized of him (Ewald, Hengstenberg ; see the foregoing note) ; but with a purpose not more fully known to us, which John has not stated, because his concern here was only with the *testimony of the Baptist*. If we were to take into account the narrative of the temptation,—which we are not,—Jesus might be regarded as here *returning* from the temptation.[1]— ἴδε ὁ ἀμνὸς τοῦ θεοῦ, κ.τ.λ.] These words are not addressed to Jesus, but to those who are around the Baptist, and are suggested by the sight of Jesus ; comp. ver. 36. As to the use of the singular ἴδε, when several are addressed, see on Matt. x. 16. The *article* denotes the *appointed* Lamb of God, which, according to the prophetic utterance presupposed as well known, was *expected* in the *person* of the Messiah. This characteristic form of Messianic expectation is based upon Isa. liii. 7. Comp. Matt. viii. 17 ; Luke xxii. 37 ; Acts viii. 32 ; 1 Pet. ii. 22 ff. ; and the ἀρνίον in the Apocalypse.[2] The *genitive* is that of possession, that which *belongs to God, i.e.* the lamb appointed as a sacrifice by God Himself. This interpretation follows from the entire contents of Isa. liii., and from the idea of *sacrifice* which is contained in ὁ αἴρων, κ.τ.λ. We must not therefore render : " the Lamb *given* by God " (Hofmann, Luthardt). But while, according to this view, the lamb, designated and appointed by God, is meant,—the lamb spoken of in holy prophecies of old, whose fulfilment in Jesus was already recognized by the Baptist,—it is erroneous to assume any reference to the *paschal* lamb.[3] Such an assumption derives no support from the more precise definition in ὁ αἴρων, κ.τ.λ., and would produce a ὕστερον πρότερον ; for the view which regarded Christ as the *paschal* lamb first arose *ex eventu*, because He was crucified upon the same day on which the paschal lamb was slain (see

---

[1] See Euthymius Zigabenus, Lücke, Luthardt, Riggenbach, Godet.

[2] On the force of the article, see ver. 21, ὁ προφήτης ; also ἡ ῥίζα τοῦ Ἰεσσαί, Rom. xv.

12 ; ὁ λέων ὁ ἐκ τῆς φυλῆς Ἰούδα, Rev. v. 5.

[3] Luther, Grotius, Bengel, Lampe, Olshausen, Maier, Reuss, Luthardt, Hofmann, Hengstenberg ; comp. Godet.

on xviii. 28 ; 1 Cor. v. 7). He certainly thus became the antitype of the paschal lamb, but, according to the whole tenor of the passage in Isaiah, He was not regarded by the Baptist in this *special* aspect, nor could He be so conceived of by his hearers. The *conception of sacrifice* which, according to the prophecy in Isaiah and the immediate connection in John, is contained in ὁ ἀμνὸς τοῦ θεοῦ, is that of the trespass-offering, אָשָׁם, Isa. liii. 10 ; [1] 1 John ii. 2, iv. 10, i. 7. It by no means militates against this, that, according to the law, lambs were not as a rule employed for trespass-offerings (Lev. xiv. 2, Num. vi. 12, relate to exceptional cases only ; and the daily morning and evening sacrifices, Ex. xxix. 38 ff., Num. xxviii., which Wetstein here introduces, were prayer- and thank-offerings), but for sacrifices of purification (Lev. v. 1–6, xiv. 12 ; Num. vi. 12) : [2] for in Isaiah the Servant of Jehovah, who *makes atonement* for the people by His vicarious sufferings, is represented as a lamb ; and it is this *prophetic* view, not the *legal* prescription, which is the ruling thought here. Christ was, as the Baptist here prophetically recognizes Him, the antitype of the O. T. sacrifices : He must therefore, as such, be represented in the form of some animal appointed for sacrifice ; and the appropriate figure was given not in the law, but by the *prophet*, who, contemplating Him in His gentleness and meekness, represents Him as a sacrificial *lamb*, and from this was derived the form which came to be the *normal* one in the Christian manner of view. The apostolic church consequently could apprehend Him as the Christian *Passover ;* though legally the passover lamb, as a trespass-offering, which it certainly was, differed from the ordinary trespass-offerings. [3] This Christian method of view accordingly had a *prophetical*, and not a legal foundation. To exclude the idea of sacrifice altogether, and to find in the expression Lamb of God the representation merely of a divinely consecrated, innocent, and gentle *sufferer*, [4] is opposed to the context both in Isaiah and in John, as well as to the view of the work of redemption which pervades the whole of the N. T. Weiss, *Lehrbegr.* p. 159 ff. — ὁ αἰρων τ. ἁμαρτ. τ. κόσμου] may either signify, " who *takes away* the sin of the world," or, " who *takes upon himself*," etc., *i.e.* in order to bear it. Both renderings (which Flacius, Melanchthon, and most others, even Baeumlein, combine) must, according to Isa. liii., express the idea of *atonement ;* so that in the first the cancelling of the guilt is conceived of as a *removing*, a doing away with sin (an abolition of it) ; in the second, as a *bearing* (an expiation) of it. The latter interpretation is *usually* preferred, [5] because in Isa. liii. the idea is certainly that of *bearing* by way of expiation (נָשָׂא : LXX. φέρει, ἀνένεγκε, ἀνοίσει). But since the LXX. never use αἰρειν to express the *bearing* of sin, but always φέρειν etc.,

---

[1] As to the distinction between trespass or guilt and sin offerings, הַטָּאת, see Ewald, *Alterth.* p. 76 ff.; and for the various opinions on this distinction, especially Keil, *Arch.* I. § 46 ; Oehler in Herzog's *Encykl.* X. p. 462 ff.; Saalschütz, *M. R.* p. 321 ff.

[2] Concerning אָשָׁם, Lev. v. 6, see Knobel *in loc.*

[3] Ewald, *Alterth.* p. 467 f.; Hengstenberg

takes a different view, *Opfer. d. h. Schr.* p. 24 ff.

[4] Gabler, *Melet. in Joh.* i. 29, Jen. 1808–1811, in his *Opusc.* p. 514 ff. ; Paulus, Kuinoel.

[5] So Lücke, B. Crusius, de Wette, Hengstenberg, Brückner, Ewald, Weber, *v. Zorne Gottes*, p. 250.

while on the other hand they express the *taking away* of sin by αἴρειν;[1] and as the context of 1 John iii. 5, in like manner, requires us to take τὰς ἁμαρτίας ἡμῶν ἄρῃ, there used to denote the act of expiation (comp. ii. 2), as signifying the *taking away* of sins ; so ὁ αἴρων, etc., here is to be explained in this sense,—not, indeed, that the Baptist expresses an idea different from Isa. liii., but the expiation there described as a *bearing* of sins is represented, according to its necessary and immediate result, as the *abolition* of sins by virtue of the vicarious sacrificial suffering and death of the victim, as the ἀθέτησις ἁμαρτίας, Heb. ix. 26.[2] John himself expresses this idea in 1 John i. 7, when referring to the sin-cleansing power of Christ's blood, which operates also on those who are already regenerate,[3] by καθαρίζει ἡμᾶς ἀπὸ πάσης ἁμαρτίας. The taking away of sins by the Lamb presupposes His taking them upon Himself. The interpretation "*to take away*," in itself correct, is (after Grotius) misused by Kuinoel : "*removebit* peccata hominum, *i.e. pravitatem e terra ;*"[4] and Gabler has misinterpreted the rendering "to *bear :*" "qui pravitatem hominum . . . *i.e. mala sibi inflicta*, patienti et mansueto animo *sustinebit.*" Both are opposed to the necessary relation of the word to ὁ ἀμνὸς τ. θεοῦ, as well as to the real meaning of Isa. liii. ; although even Gabler's explanation would not in itself be linguistically erroneous, but would have to be referred back to the signification, to *take upon oneself, to take over.*[5] — The *Present* ὁ αἴρων arises from the fact that the Baptist prophetically views the act of atonement accomplished by the Lamb of God as *present.* This act is *ever-enduring*, not in itself, but in its *effects* (against Hengstenberg). Luthardt holds that the words are not to be understood of the future, and that the Baptist had not Christ's death in view, but only regarded and designated Him in a general way, as one who was manifested in a body of weakness, and with liability to suffering, in order to the salvation of men. But this is far too general for the concrete representation of Christ as the *Lamb* of God, and for the express reference herein made to *sin*, especially from the lips of a man belonging to the old theocracy, who was himself the son of a sacrificing priest, a Nazarite and a prophet. — τ ὴ ν ἁ μ α ρ τ ί α ν] the sins of the world conceived of as a collective unity ; "una pestis, quæ omnes corripuit," Bengel. Comp. Rom. v. 20. — τ ο ῦ κ ό σ μ ο υ] an extension of the earlier prophetic representation of atonement for the *people,* Isa. liii., to all *mankind,* the reconciliation of whom has been *objectively* accomplished by the ἱλαστήριον of the Lamb of God, but is accomplished *subjectively* in all who believe (iii. 15, 16). Comp. Rom. v. 18.

Note.—That the Baptist describes Jesus as the Messiah, who by His *sufferings* makes *expiation* for the world's sin, is to be explained by considering his apoc-

---

[1] Sam. xv. 25, xxv. 28 ; Aq. Ps. xxxi. 5, where Symm. has ἀφέλῃς and the LXX. ἀφῆκας.

[2] Comp. already Cyril: ἵνα τοῦ κόσμου τὴν ἁμαρτίαν ἀνέλῃ ; Vulgate : qui *tollit ;* Goth. : *afnimith.*

[3] See Düsterdieck *in loc.*, p. 99 ff.

[4] Comp. Baur, *N. T. Theol.* p. 396 : "In a general sense, He bears away and removes sin by His personal manifestation and ministry throughout." This is connected with the error that we do not find in John the same significance attached to Christ's death which we find in Paul.

[5] Æsch. *Pers.* 544 ; Soph. *Tr.* 70 ; Xen. *Mem.* iv. 4. 14 ; 1 Macc. xiii. 17 ; Matt. xi. 29, *al.*

alyptic position, by which his prophecies, that had immediate reference to the person and work of Jesus, were conditioned ; comp. vv. 31 ff. It was not from a sudden glimpse of light obtained in a natural manner (Hofmann, Schweizer, Lange), or from a growing presentiment (de Wette), or from a certitude arrived at by reason and deep reflection (Ewald) ; but from a *revelation* (comp. ver. 33). This was necessary in order to announce the idea of a suffering Messiah with such decision and distinctness, even according to its historical realization in Jesus ;—an idea which, though it had been discovered by a few deep-seeing minds through prophetic hints or divine enlightenment (Luke ii. 25, 34, 35), nevertheless undoubtedly encountered in general expectations of a kind dia-metrically opposite (xii. 34 ; Luke xxiv. 26),—and in order likewise to give to that idea the impress of world-embracing universality, although the way was already prepared for this by the promise made to Abraham. The more foreign the idea of a suffering Messiah was to the people in general ; the more disin-clined the disciples of Jesus showed themselves to accept such a view (Matt. xvi. 21 ; Luke xxiv. 25) ; the more certain that its unfolding was on the path of historical development, while even thus remaining a constant σκάνδαλον to the Jews ; at once the more necessary and justifiable does it appear to suppose a special divine revelation, with which the expression borrowed from Isa. liii. may very well be consistent. And the more certain it is that the Baptist really was the subject of divine revelations as the forerunner of the Messiah (comp. Matt. iii. 14), all the more unhistorical is the assumption that the evangelist divests the idea of the Messiah of its historical form (Keim) by putting *his own* knowledge into the Baptist's mouth (Strauss, Weisse, Baur, Hilgenfeld, Schol-ten ; comp. de Wette's doubt, but against this latter, Brückner). This view receives no support from the subsequent vacillation of the Baptist (Matt. xi. 3), because the revelation which he had received, as well as that made to him at the baptism ver. 32), would not exclude a subsequent and temporary falling in-to error, and because this was not caused by any sufferings which Jesus under-went, but by his own sufferings in the face of the Messianic works of Jesus, whereby the divine light previously received was dimmed through human weakness and impatience. It is only by surrendering the true interpretation (see ὁ αἴρων above) that Luthardt avoids such a supposition as this. The notion of a spiritualizing legend (Schenkel) is of itself excluded by the genuineness of the Gospel, whose author had been a disciple of the Baptist. Moreover, Jesus Himself, according also to the testimony of the Synoptics (Mark ii. 20 ; Matt. xii. 39, etc.), was sufficiently acquainted from the very first with the certainty of His final sufferings.

Ver. 30 does not refer to vv. 26, 27, where John bears his witness before the deputies from the Sanhedrim, but to an earlier testimony borne by him before his disciples and hearers, and in this definite enigmatic form, to which ver. 15 likewise refers. So essential is this characteristic form, that of itself it excludes the reference to vv. 26, 27.[1] The *general* testimony which John had previously borne to the *coming Messiah*, here receives its definite application to the *concrete personality* there standing before him, *i.e.* to *Jesus*. — ἐ σ τ ί] not ἦν again, as in ver. 15, for Jesus is now *present*. — ἐ γ ώ] possesses the emphasis of a certain inward feeling of prophetic certitude. —

---

[1] De Wette, Hengst., Ewald, Godet, and others.

ἀνήρ] as coming from the Baptist, more reverential and honourable than ἄνθρωπος.[1]

Ver. 31. Κἀγώ] not *I also*, like all others, but *and I*, resuming and carrying forward the ἐγώ of ver. 30. Though the Baptist had borne witness in a general way concerning the Messiah, as ver. 30 affirms, Jesus was, at the time when he bare that witness, still unknown to him as in His own person the historic Messiah. [See Note XI. p. 99.] Ver. 34 shows that καί in κἀγώ is the simple *and;* for the thrice repeated κἀγώ, vv. 31–34, can only be arbitrarily interpreted in different senses. The emphasis of the ἐγώ, however (*I on my part*), consists in his ignorance of the special individuality, in the face of the divine revelation which he had received. — οὐκ ᾔδειν αὐτόν] that is, *as the Messiah*, see ver. 33 ; not "as the manifestation of a pre-existent personality" (Hilgenfeld); still not denying, in general, every kind of previous acquaintance with Jesus (Lücke, Godet), which the following ἵνα φανερωθῇ and ὃν ὑμεῖς οὐκ οἴδατε in ver. 26 forbid. This οὐκ ᾔδειν leaves it quite uncertain whether the Baptist had any personal acquaintance *generally* with Jesus (and this is by no means placed beyond doubt by the legendary prefatory history in Luke i. 36 ff., which is quite irreconcilable with the text before us). *That Jesus was the Messiah* became known to the Baptist only at the baptism itself, by the sign of the descending dove ; and this sign was immediately preceded only by the prophetic presentiment of which Matt. iii. 14 is the impress (see on that passage). Accordingly, we are not to assume any contradiction between our text and Matt. *l.c.*,[2] nor leave the οὐκ ᾔδειν with its meaning unexplained ;[3] nor, again, are we to interpret it only comparatively as a denial of *clear* and *certain* knowledge.[4] — ἀλλ' ἵνα φανερωθῇ, κ.τ.λ.] emphatically beginning the clause, and stating the purpose of the Baptist's manifestation as referring to Messiah, and as still applying notwithstanding the κἀγὼ οὐκ ᾔδειν, and being thus independent of his own intention and choice, and purely a matter of *divine* ordination. — ἵνα φανερωθῇ] This *special* purpose, in the expression of which, moreover, no reference can be traced to Isa. xl. 5 (against Hengstenberg), does not exclude the more generally and equally divine ordinance in ver. 23, but is included in it. Comp. the tradition in Justin, *c. Tryph.* 8, according to which the Messiah remained unknown to Himself and others, until Elijah anointed Him and made Him manifest to all (φανερὸν πᾶσι ποιήσῃ). — ἐν τῷ ὕδατι βαπτίζων] a humble description of his own baptism as compared with that of Him who baptizes with the Spirit, ver. 33 ; comp. ver. 26. Hence also the ἐγώ, *I* on my part. For the rest, we must understand ἐν τ. ὑδ. βαπτ. of John's call to baptize *in general;* in which was also *included the conception* of the baptizing of *Jesus*, to which ver. 32 refers.[5]

Ver. 32. What John had said in ver. 31, viz. that though Jesus was un-

---

[1] Acts xvii. 31 ; Zech. vi. 12 ; Dem. 426. 6 ; Herod. vii. 210 ; Xen. *Hier.* vii. 3.

[2] Strauss, Baur, and most others.

[3] Brückner.

[4] Neander, Maier, Riggenbach, Hengstenberg, Ewald.

[5] For ἐν τῷ ὕδατι, Lachmann (now also Tischendorf), following B. C. G. L. P. A. ℵ., cursives, and some of the Fathers, reads ἐν ὕδατι ; but the article after ver. 26, comp. ver. 33, would be more easily omitted than inserted. It is *demonstrative*, for John as he speaks is standing by the *Jordan*.

known to him as the Messiah, yet his commission was to make him known to the people, needed *explanation ;* and that as *to the way in which he himself had come to recognize Him as the Messiah.* This was, indeed, a necessary condition before he could make the *manifestation* to the people. This explanation he now gives in the following testimony (not first spoken upon another occasion, Ewald) concerning the divine *sign, which he beheld.* And the evangelist considers this testimony so weighty, that he does not simply continue the words of the Baptist, but solemnly and emphatically introduces the testimony as such : καὶ ἐμαρτύρησεν, κ.τ.λ., words which are not therefore parenthetical (Bengel, Lücke, and most), but form an impressive part of the record : "And a testimony did John bear, when he said." The following ὅτι is simply *recitative.* — τεθέαμαι] *I have seen ;* Perfect, like ἑώρακα in ver. 34, which see. The phenomenon itself took place at the baptism, which is assumed as known through the Gospel tradition, and is referred to in ver. 33 by ὁ πέμψας με βαπτίζειν ἐν ὕδατι, which implies that the sign was to take place at the *baptism* of the person spoken of. This is in answer to Baur, p. 104 ff., according to whom there is no room here for the supposition that Jesus was baptized by John,—an assertion all the more groundless, because for inserting the baptism of Jesus before ver. 19, and with this for the narration of a fact which is assumed as universally known, there is no place in the plan of this Gospel.—The *sight itself* here spoken of was no mere product of the imagination, but a *real vision ;* it indicates an actual *event* divinely brought about, which was traditionally worked up by the Synoptics into a visible occurrence more or less objective (most unhesitatingly by Luke) but which can be the subject of *testimony* only by virtue of a θεωρία νοητική (Origen). See on Matt. iii. 17, note. — ὡς περιστεράν] *i.e. shaped like a dove :* ἀντίτυπον μίμημα πελειάδος, Nonnus. See on Matt. iii. 16. According to Ewald, "the sudden downward flight of a bird, coming near to Him at the moment, confirmed the Baptist's presentiment," etc. Conjectures of this kind are additions quite alien to the prophetic mode of view. — καὶ ἔμεινεν ἐπ' αὐτόν] The transition here to the finite verb is owing to the importance of the fact stated.[1] ἐπ' αὐτόν, however, is not synonymous with ἐπ' αὐτοῦ (xix. 31); the idea is, "*it remained* ('fluttered not away,' Luther) *directed towards Him.*" We are to suppose the appearance of a dove coming down, and poising itself for a considerable time over the head of the person. See on ἐπί with the accusative (iii. 36 ; 1 Pet. iv. 14), seemingly on the question "where ?"[2]

Ver. 33. John's recognition of Jesus as the Messiah (whom he had not before known as such) rested upon a revelation previously made to him with this intent ; and this he now states, solemnly repeating, however, the declaration of his own ignorance (κἀγὼ οὐκ ᾔδειν αὐτόν). — ἐκεῖνος] in emphatic contrast with his own reflection. — εἶπεν] *i.e. by express revelation.* We cannot tell the precise *time* or *manner* of this prior revelation. By it John was referred to some outwardly visible σημεῖον (ἴδῃς) of the Spirit, in a

---

[1] Bernhardy, p. 473 ; Buttmann, *N. T. Gk.* p. 327 [E. T. p. 382]

[2] Schaef. *ad Long.* p. 427 ; Matthiae, p. 1375 ; Kühner, *ad Xen. Anab.* i. 2. 2.

general way, without *any defining of its form.* He was to *see* it descending, and this descent *took place* in the form of a *dove*, and after that divine intimation there was no room for doubt. Comp. on Matt. iii. 17, note. — ἐ φ' ὃ ν ἀ ν ἰ δ η ς] that is, when thou baptizest Him with water. This is not expressly *stated* in the divine declaration, but John could not fail so to understand it, because, being sent to *baptize,* he would naturally expect the appearance of the promised sign *while fulfilling His mission ;* comp. ver. 31. He therefore describes the giver of the revelation as ὁ πέμψας με, κ.τ.λ., and the evangelist puts the statement in the conditional form : ἐφ' ὃν ἂν, κ.τ.λ., *i.e.*, according to the connection of the narrative : " *When, in the fulfilment of this your mission, you shall see the Spirit descending upon one of those whom thou baptizest, this is He,*" etc. — ἐ ν π ν ε ύ μ . ἁ γ ί ῳ] by communicating it to those who believe upon Him. See on Matt. iii. 11. The designation of this communication as a *baptism* very naturally arose from its close relation to the work of the Baptist's mission,[1] because the gift of the Spirit, according to the prophetic figure (Joel iii. 1 ; Isa. xliv. 3), had been promised under the form of an *outpouring* (comp. Acts ii. 33). The contrast itself distinctly sets before us the difference between the two baptisms : the one was a preparation for the Messianic salvation by *repentance ;* the other, an introduction thereto by the divine principle of life and salvation, the communication of which presupposes the forgiveness of sins (see on Mark i. 4).

Ver. 34. A still more distinct and emphatic conclusion of what John had to adduce from ver. 31 onwards, in explanation of the οὗτός ἐστιν mentioned in ver. 30. — κ ἀ γ ώ] *and I* on my part, answering triumphantly to the double κἀγώ in vv. 31, 33. — ἑ ώ ρ α κ α] *i.e.* as the divine declaration in ver. 33 had promised (ἴδης). This *having seen* is to the speaker, as he makes the declaration, an accomplished fact. Hence the *Perfect*, like τεθέαμαι in ver. 32. Nor can the μ ε μ α ρ τ ύ ρ η κ α be differently understood unless by some arbitrary rendering : it does not mean : " *I shall have borne witness*" (de Wette, Tholuck, Maier), as in the classics the aorist is used (see on vi. 36) ; or, " *I have borne witness, and do so still*" (Grotius, Lücke), or "*testis sum factus*" (Bengel, comp. Bernhardy, p. 378 ff.) ; but, *I have borne witness*, that is, since I saw that sight ; so that, accordingly, John, *immediately after the baptism of Jesus,* uttered the testimony which he here refers to as an accomplished fact, and by referring to which he ratifies and confirms what he *now* has testified (ver. 30).[2] — ὅ τ ι ο ὗ τ ο ς, κ.τ.λ.] the subject-matter of the μεμαρτ. — ὁ υ ἱ ὸ ς τ ο ῦ θ ε ο ῦ] *the Messiah,* whose divine Sonship, however, had already been apprehended by the Baptist in the *metaphysical sense* (against Beyschlag, p. 67), agreeably to the testimony borne to His pre-existence in vv. 30, 15.[3] The heavenly voice in Matt. iii. 17, in the synoptic account of the baptism, corresponds to this testimony. All the less on this account are the statements of the Baptist concerning Jesus to be regarded as unhistorical, and only as an echo of the position assigned to the former in the Prologue (Weizsäcker). The position of the Baptist

---

[1] Comp. Matt. iii. 11 ; Mark i. 8 ; Luke iii. 16 ; Acts i. 5, xi. 16.

[2] Comp. also Winer, p. 256 [Th. T. p. 273].

[3] ὅττι θεοῦ γόνος οὗτος, ἀειζώοιο τοκῆος, Nonnus.

in the Prologue is the result of the history itself. That the meaning attaching to υἱὸς τ. θεοῦ in the fourth Gospel generally is quite different from that which it has in the Synoptics (Baur), is a view which the passages Matt. xi. 27, xxviii. 19, should have prevented from being entertained.

Note.—On vv. 32–34 we may observe in general : (1) The λόγος and the πνεῦμα ἅγιον are not to be regarded as identical in John's view,[1] against which the ὁ λόγος σὰρξ ἐγένετο in ver. 14 is itself conclusive, in view of which the πνεῦμα in our passage appears as an hypostasis distinct from the λόγος, an hypostasis of which the σὰρξ ἐγένετο could not have been predicated. The λόγος was the substratum of the divine side in Christ, which having become incarnate, entered upon a human development, in which the theanthropic subject needed the power and incitement of the πνεῦμα. (2) He was of necessity under this influence of the Spirit from the very outset of the development of His theanthropic consciousness (comp. Luke ii. 40, 52, and the visit when twelve years old to the temple), and long before the moment of His baptism, so that the πνεῦμα was the awakening and mediating principle of the consciousness which Jesus possessed of His oneness with God ; see on x. 36. Accordingly, we are not to suppose that the Holy Ghost was given to Him now for the first time, and was added consciously to His divine-human life as a new and third element ; the text speaks not of a *receiving*, but of a *manifestation* of the Spirit, as seen by John, which in this form visibly came down and remained over Him, in order to point Him out to the Baptist as the Messiah who, according to O. T. prophecy (Isa. xi. 2, xlii. 1), was to possess the fulness of the Spirit. The purpose of this divine σημεῖον was not, therefore (as Matthew and Mark indeed represent it), to *impart* the Spirit to Jesus (which is not implied even in iii. 34), but simply for the sake of the Baptist, to divinely *indicate* to him who was to make Him known in Israel, that individuality who, as the incarnate Logos, must long before then have possessed the powers of the Spirit in all their fulness (comp. iii. 34). The πνεῦμα in the symbolic form of a dove hovered over Jesus, remained over Him for a while, and then again vanished (comp. Schleiermacher, *L. J.* p. 150). This the Baptist saw ; and he now knows, through a previously received revelation made to him for the purpose, *who* it is that he has to make known as the Messiah who baptizes with the Spirit. To find in this passage a special stimulus imparted through the Spirit to Jesus Himself, and perceived by the Baptist, tending to the development or opening up of His divine-human consciousness and life,[2] or the equipment of the Logos for a coming forth from his state of *immanence* (Frommann), or the communication of *official* power,[3] as the principle of which the Spirit was now given in order to render the σαρξ fit to become the instrument of His self-manifestation,[4] —as in a similar way B. Crusius already explained the communication of the Spirit as if the πνεῦμα (in distinction from the λόγος) were now received by Jesus, as that which was to be further *communicated to mankind ;*—these and all

[1] Against Baur, *bibl. Theol. d. N. T.* II. 268; J. E. Chr. Schmidt, in *d. Bibl. f. Krit. u. Exeg.* I. 3, p. 361 ff.; Eichhorn, *Einl.* II-158 ff.; Winzer, *Progr.*, Lps. 1819.

[2] Lücke, Neander, Tholuck, Osiander, Ebrard, de Wette, Riggenbach, and others ; comp. Lange and Beyschlag, p. 103.

[3] Gess, *Pers. Chr.* p. 374 ; comp. Wörner, *Verhältn. d. Geistes*, p. 44.

[4] Luthardt, after Kahnis, *vom heiligen Geiste*, p. 44 ; comp. also Hofmann, *Schriftbew.* I. 191, II. 1, 166 ; Godet ; and Weisse, *Lehrbegr.* p. 268, who connects with ver. 52.

such theories find no justification from our Gospel at least, which simply records a *manifestation* made to the *Baptist*, not a communication to *Jesus ;* and to it must be accorded decisive weight when brought face to face with those other diverging accounts. Thus, at the same time, the whole phenomenon must not be regarded as an empty, objectless play of the imagination (Lücke) : it was an objective and real *sign* divinely presented to the Baptist's spiritual vision, the design of which (*ἵνα φανερωθῇ τῷ Ἰσραήλ*, ver. 31, that is, through the Baptist's testimony) was sufficiently important as the *γνώρισμα* of the Messiah,[1] and the result of which (ver. 34) corresponded to its design ; whereas, the supposition that we have here a record of the *receiving* of the Spirit imports into the exposition something quite foreign to the text. Discarding this supposition, we deprive of all support the opinion that the descent of the Spirit upon Jesus at His baptism is a mythical inference of Ebionitism (Strauss), as well as the assertion that here too our Gospel stands upon the verge of Gnosticism (Baur) ; while the still bolder view which (in spite of the *βαπτίζων ἐν πνεύματι ἁγίῳ*) takes the *πνεῦμα* to be, not the Holy Spirit, but the *Logos* (in spite of i. 14), which as a heavenly Aeon was for the first time united at the baptism with Jesus the earthly man (so Hilgenfeld, following the Valentinian Gnosis), does not even retain its claim to be considered a later historical analogy. There remains, however, in any case, the great fact of which the Baptist witnesses—"*the true birth-hour of Christendom*" (Ewald) : for, on the one hand, the divinely sent forerunner of the Messiah now received the divinely revealed certainty as to *whom* his work as Elijah pointed ; and, on the other hand, by the divinely assured testimony which he now bore to Jesus before the people, the Messianic consciousness of Jesus Himself received not only the consecration of a heavenly ratification, but the warrant of the Father's will, that now *the hour was come for the holy beginning* of His ministry in word and work. It was not the formation of the Messiah's *purpose*, but rather His *entrance* on its realization (comp. Acts xiii. 23) which was the event of world-historical significance that marked this hour, when the fulness of time was come for the accomplishment of the counsel of God.

Vv. 35, 36. Πάλιν εἰστήκει] pointing back to ver. 29. —δύο] One was Andrew, ver. 41. The other ? Certainly *John* himself,[2] partly on account of that peculiarity of his which leads him to refrain from naming himself, and partly on account of the special vividness of the details in the following account, which had remained indelibly impressed upon his memory ever since this first and decisive meeting with his Lord. — ἐμβλέψας] denoting *fixed attention.*[3] The profoundest interest led him to fix his gaze upon Him. — ἴδε ὁ ἀμνὸς τ. θεοῦ] These few words were quite sufficient

---

[1] Justin. *c. Tryph.* 88.

[2] Already Chrysostom (according to Corderius, *Cat.;* Theodore of Mopsuestia) mentions the same view, but along with it the other : ὅτι ἐκεῖνος οὐχὶ τῶν ἐπισήμων ἦν, which he seems to approve of.—But if *John* is here already (and see on ver. 42) indicated though not by name, and afterwards (ver. 46) *Bartholomew* under the name *Nathanael ;* if, again, ver. 42 implies that *James* is brought to Jesus by his brother John, and

that he therefore has his place *after* John ; then we certainly cannot say, with Steitz (in the *Stud. u. Krit.* 1868, p. 497) : "The order in which Papias, in Euseb. iii. 39, quotes the six apostles, Andrew, Peter, Philip, Thomas, James, John, exactly corresponds with that in which these names occur in succession in the fourth Gospel."

[3] Comp. ver. 43; Mark x. 21, 27, xiv. 67 ; Luke xx. 17, xxii. 61.

to direct the undivided attention of both to Him who was passing that way ; for, beyond a doubt (against de Wette, Ewald,—because the fact that nothing is now added to the ὁ ἀμνὸς τ. θεοῦ gives the words quite a *retrospective* character), they had been witnesses the day before of what is recorded in vv. 29–34. The assumption of a further conversation not here recorded [1] is unnecessary, overlooks the emphasis of the one short yet weighty word on which hangs their recollection of all that occurred the day before, and moreover is not required by ver. 37. — We need not even ask why Jesus, who was now walking along (περιπατ.) in the same place, was with John, because the text says nothing about it. Answers have been devised ; *e.g.* Bengel : "Jesus had sufficiently humbled Himself by once joining Himself with John ;" Lampe : "He wished to avoid the suspicion of any private understanding with the Baptist." Equally without warrant in the text, B. Crusius and Luthardt : "Jesus had already separated Himself from the Baptist to begin His own proper ministry, while the Baptist desired indirectly to command his disciples to join themselves with Jesus ;" as Hengstenberg also supposes, judging from the result, and because he at the same time regards the two as representatives of all John's disciples.

Vv. 37–40. *And the two disciples heard (observed) him speak.* For he had not addressed the words ἴδε ὁ ἀμνὸς τ. θεοῦ directly *to them*, but in general (comp. ver. 29) to those round about him. — ἠκολούθησαν] not the following of discipleship, nor in a " sens profondément symbolique" (Godet), but simply : "*they went after Him*" (ὀπίστεροι ἦλθον ὁδῖται Χριστοῦ νεισσομένοιο, Nonnus), in order to know Him more intimately.[2] Nevertheless Bengel rightly says : *primae origines ecclesiae Christianae.* — στραφείς] for He heard the footsteps of those following Him. — τί ζητεῖτε] *what do you desire?* He anticipates them by engaging in conversation with them, not exactly because they were shy and timid (Euthymius Zigabenus). But no doubt the significant θεασάμενος, κ.τ.λ. (*intuitus*), was accompanied by a glance into their hearts, ii. 25. — ποῦ μένεις] correlative to the περιπατοῦντι, ver. 36 ; therefore : "*where dost thou sojourn ?*"[3] They regarded Him as a travelling Rabbi, who was lodging in the neighbourhood at the house of some friend. — ἔρχεσθε κ. ὄψεσθε] *come and ye will see* (see the critical notes) ; a friendly invitation to accompany Him at once.[4] They had sought only to know where the place was, so that they might afterwards seek Him out, and converse with Him undisturbed. We have not here the Rabbinical form of calling attention, בא וראה,[5] nor an imitation of Rev. vi. 1 (Weisse), nor yet an allusion to Ps. lxvi. 5, 9, and a gentle reference on the part of Jesus to His Godhead (Hengstenberg), for which there was no occasion, and which He could not expect to be understood. — ἦλθον, κ.τ.λ.] marks the simplicity of the narrative. — μένει] insertion of the direct address, common in dependent clauses. Kühner, II. 594 ; Winer, p. 251

[1] Kuinoel, Lücke, and most.
[2] πεῖραν λαβεῖν αὐτοῦ, Euthymius Zigabenus.
[3] Polyb. xxx. 4. 10 ; Strabo, iii. p. 147.
[4] There is nothing to indicate whether the place where He was lodging was near or remote, although Ewald would infer the latter from the reading ὄψεσθε.
[5] Buxt. *Lex. Talm.* p. 248 ; Lightfoot, p. 968.

[E. T. p. 268]. — τ ὴ ν ἡ μ έ ρ. ὲ κ.] *i.e.* the remaining part of that day, not at once from that day onwards (Credner, against whom is Ebrard). — δ ε κ ά τ η] that is, at the beginning of their stay with Him. We have no reason to suppose in John, as Rettig,[1] Tholuck, Ebrard, Ewald, the *Roman* mode of counting the hours (from midnight to midnight, therefore ten o'clock in the morning) instead of the *Jewish*, which is followed elsewhere in the N. T. and by Josephus (*Vit.* 54), *i.e.* four o'clock in the afternoon ; because there is time enough from 4 P.M. till late in the evening to justify the popular expression τὴν ἡμέρ. ὲκ. ; because, moreover, in xi. 9 it is plainly the Jewish method which is followed ; which also in iv. 6 best suits the context, and is not excluded in iv. 52, while in xix. 14 it is with a harmonistic view that the Roman reckoning is resorted to. The Romans themselves, moreover, frequently measured the day after the Babylonian computation of the hours, according to the twelve hours from sunrise to sunset ; and the *tenth* hour especially is often named, as in our text, as the hour of return from walking, and mention of it occurs as a *late* hour in the day, when *e.g.* the soldiers were allowed to rest,[2] or when they went to table,[3] etc. See Wetstein. — The great significance of this hour for John (it was *the first of his Christian life*) had indelibly impressed it on his grateful recollection, and hence the express mention of it here. This consideration forbids our giving, with Hilgenfeld and Lichtenstein, to the statement of time an onward reference to the incident next mentioned, the finding by Andrew of his brother Simon. Brückner, too, imports a foreign element into this statement of time, when he says that it indicates, in connection with ver. 41 ff., how rapidly faith developed itself in these disciples.

Vv. 41–43. Still on the same day (not on the following, as, after the early expositors, de Wette, Baur, Luthardt, Ewald, and most others suppose ; see, on the contrary, the ὲπαύριον which again appears, but not till ver. 44), Andrew first meets his brother Simon. — π ρ ῶ τ ο ς] We must understand the matter thus : Both disciples go out from the lodging-place (at the same time, or perhaps Andrew first), still in the first fresh glow of joy at having found the Messiah,[4] that each of them may seek his own brother (we must assume that both brothers were known to be in the neighbourhood), in order to inform him of the new joy, and to bring him to Christ. Andrew is *the first*[5] who finds his brother. John does not say that he also sought *his* brother *James*, found him, and brought him to Jesus ; and this is in keeping with the delicate reserve which prevents him from naming either himself or those belonging to him (even the name of James does not occur in the Gospel). Still this may be clearly seen from the πρῶτος, and is con-

---

[1] *Stud. u. Krit.* 1830, p. 106.

[2] Liv. ix. 37.

[3] Martial, vii. 1.

[4] John's use here and in iv. 25 of τὸν Μεσσίαν (מָשִׁיחַ) is accounted for by the depicting of the scene exactly as it occurred whereas in i. 20, 25, when he simply writes historically, he uses the ordinary translation Χριστός. The *genre* picture is spe-cially minute ; so here. According to Baur, *N. T. Theol.* p. 393, the author has given an *antiquarian* notice, as it were, of this Hebrew name, which occurs nowhere else in the N. T.

[5] πρῶτος, not πρῶτον, an inelegant change adopted by Lachmann, after A. B. M. X. אּ**.

firmed by the narrative of the Synoptics, in so far that both James and John are represented as being called at the same time by Jesus (Mark i. 19 and parallels). Bengel, Tholuck, de Wette, Hengstenberg, wrongly say that Andrew and John *both* sought out *Simon.* The τὸν ἴδιον is against this ; as it neither here nor elsewhere (comp. v. 18) occurs as a mere possessive (against Lücke, Maier, de Wette, and others), but in opposition to that which is foreign. Any antithetic relation to the *spiritual* brotherhood in which John as well as Andrew stood to Simon (Hengstenberg), is quite remote from the passage. — ε ὑ ρ ή κ α μ ε ν] emphatically beginning the clause, and presupposing the feeling of *anxious desire* excited by the Baptist. The *plural* is used because Andrew had in mind the other disciple also. — ἐ μ β λ έ - ψ α ς, κ.τ.λ.] This fixed look (ver. 36) on the countenance of Simon pierces his inner soul. Jesus, as the Searcher of hearts,[1] sees in him one who should hereafter be called ,to be the *rock* of the church, and calls him by the *name* which he was henceforth to bear as His disciple (not first in Matt. xvi. 18, as Luthardt thinks). A *rock* is the emblem of firmness as early as Homer (*Od.* xvii. 463) ; comp. Ezek. iii. 9. There is no contradiction here with Matt. xvi. 18 (it is otherwise with Mark iii. 16), as if John transferred the giving of the name to this place (Hilgenfeld, comp. Baur and Scholten), for in Matt. xvi. 18 the earlier giving of the name is really *presupposed, confirmed,* and *applied.* See on Matt. — σ ὺ ε ἰ Σ ί μ ω ν, κ.τ.λ.] This belongs to the circumstantiality of the solemn ceremony of the name-giving ; it is first said *who he is,* and what in future he should be *called.*[2] Σὺ εἰ Σίμων is not, as Ewald thinks, a question ; and there is no ground for supposing that Jesus *immediately* recognized him,[3] for Andrew introduced his brother to Jesus. Grotius and Paulus[4] give arbitrary explanations of the reading Ἰωνᾶ, but see the critical notes. For the rest, we must not say, with Hilgenfeld, "Peter here *loses* the pre-eminence of the first called disciple ;" but : Peter is first *given* this pre-eminence in the synoptical accounts (Matt. iv. 18 and parallels) ; but the personal recollection of John must take precedence of these. See especially the note following ver. 52.

Vv. 44, 45. Τ ῇ ἐ π α ύ ρ.] *i.e.* after the last-mentioned day, ver. 39, which is the same with the τῇ ἐπαύρ. of ver. 35, consequently the *fourth* day from i. 19. — ἠ θ έ λ η σ ε ν, κ.τ.λ.] He *just willed to go forth, and findeth,* etc. ; therefore still at the lodging-place, ver. 40, for ἐξελθεῖν refers to the stay there (μένει, ver. 40). — ε ὑ ρ ί σ κ ε ι] as if accidentally, but see xvii. 5 ff. — The statement, instead of being hypotactic in form ("*when he would go out, he findeth*"), is *paratactic,* as often in Greek from Homer downwards.[5] We

---

[1] ii. 25 ; Weiss, *Lehrbegr.* p. 263.

[2] Comp. Gen. xxxii. 28, xxxv. 10, xvii. 5.

[3] Cyril, Chrysostom, Augustine, Aretius, Maldonatus, Cornelius à Lapide, Bengel, Luthardt, and many, comp Strauss.

[4] The fantastic play upon the words in Lange's *L. J.* II. 469, is of this sort. He renders : "Now thou art the son of the timid dove of the rock ; in future shalt thou be called the sheltering rock of the dove

(the church)." According to the true read ing of the passage, the name of Peter's father contained in Βαριωνά which occurs in Matthew, must be regarded as an abbreviation for *John,* and has nothing whatever to do with *dove.* See on Matt. xvi. 17.

[5] Nägelsbach, *z. Ilias,* p. 65, ed. 3 ; Kühner, II. p. 416, and in the N. T.; Buttmann, *N. T. Gr.* p. 249 [E. T. p. 196].

must place the scene at the *commencement* of the journey homeward, not *on the road* during the journey (Lücke). — ἀ κ ο λ . μ ο ι] of following *as disciples*. Comp. Matt. iv. 19, 20, ix. 9 ; see also ver. 46, ii. 2. The invitation to do this (not merely to go with Him) is explained by ver. 45, as brought about by the communications of Andrew and Peter, though certainly the heart-piercing look of Jesus Himself, and the impression produced by His whole bearing, must be regarded as the causes which mainly led Philip to come to a decision. John does not record the further conversations which of course ensued upon the ἀκολ. μοι, and the obedience which followed, because his aim was to narrate the *call*. — ἐ κ τ . π ό λ ε ω ς , κ.τ.λ.] see on Matt. viii. 14.

Ver. 46. Εὑ ρ ί σ κ ε ι] *when* and *where* in the course of the journey we are not told, — perhaps at some distance from the road, so that Philip, observing him, quitted the road, and went towards him. According to Ewald, " not till after their arrival in the village of Cana, which nevertheless is named for the first time in ii. 1, and to which Nathanael belonged " (xxi. 2). The supposition that Nathanael was on his way to John's baptism (Godet) is quite groundless. — N α θ α ν α ή λ , נְתַנְאֵל, *i.e.* *Theodorus* (Num. i. 8 ; 1 Chron. ii. 14), is identical with Bartholomaeus. For, according to this passage, in the midst of calls to the *apostleship*, comp. xxi. 2, he appears as one of the twelve ; while in the lists of the apostles,[1] where his name is wanting, we find *Bartholomaeus*, and placed, moreover, side by side with Philip (only in Acts i. 13 with Matthew ;[2] comp. *Constitt. Apol.* vi. 14. 1). This identity is all the more probable, because *Bartholomew* is only a patronymic, and must have become the ordinary name of the individual, and that in most frequent use ; and thus it came to pass that his own distinctive name does not appear in the synoptic narrative. — ὃ ν ἔ γ ρ α ψ ε] *of whom*, etc. See on Rom. x. 5. — Μ ω ϋ σ ῆ ς] Deut. xviii. 15, and generally in his Messianic reference and types. See on ver. 46. — τ ὸ ν ἀ π ὸ Ν α ζ α - ρ έ τ] for *Nazareth*, where Jesus has *lived* with His parents from infancy upwards, passed for His birthplace. Philip may have obtained his knowledge from Andrew and Peter, or even from Jesus Himself, who had no occasion at this time to state more fully and minutely his relation to Nazareth ; while the τὸν υἱὸν τοῦ Ἰωσήφ, which must rest upon a communication from Jesus, leaves His divine Sonship undisturbed. To attribute to Philip knowledge of the facts with regard to both points (Hengstenberg) is in

---

[1] Matt. x. 3; Luke vi. 14 ; Mark i. 18; Acts i. 13.

[2] Hilgenfeld regarded him as identical with *Matthew ;* but how much opposed is this view to the history of Matthew's call ! though the *meaning* of his name is not different from that of Matthew's. Very recently, however, Hilgenfeld has supposed that the name answers to the Matthias who was appointed in the place of Judas (*N. T. extra canon.* IV. p. 105). Schleiermacher, *L. J.* p.368,considers it very doubtful whether Nathanael belonged to the twelve at all. Chrys- ostom, Augustine, and others, long ago denied that he did, but this is already assumed in the " *duae viae* "(Hilgenfeld, *N. T. extra canon.* IV.). According to Spaeth, in Hilgenfeld's *Zeitschrift*, 1868, p. 168 ff., Nathanael is to be taken as a *symbolical* name, invented by the writer, under which the *Apostle John himself* is said to be represented. The author of the Appendix, chap. xxi. 2, where Nathanael is expressly *distinguished* from the sons of Zebedee, is said to have made a *mistake*.

itself improbable, and is not in keeping with the simplicity of his words. But it is a groundless assumption to suppose that *John knew* nothing of the birth at Bethlehem ; for it is *Philip's own* words that he records (against Strauss, de Wette). See on vii. 41.

Ver. 47. *Can anything good come out of Nazareth ?* A question of astonishment that the Messiah should come *out of Nazareth.* But Nathanael asks thus doubtingly, not because Nazareth lay in *Galilee,* vii. 52,[1] nor because of its *smallness,* as too *insignificant* to be the birthplace of the Messiah,[2] nor from both reasons together (Hengstenberg); nor, again, because the prophecy did not speak of Nazareth as the Messiah's birthplace (Godet); but, as the general expression τὶ ἀγαθόν proves (it is not the more special ὁ Χριστός), because Nathanael, and probably public opinion likewise, looked upon the little town as morally degenerate : it must have been so regarded at least in the narrow circle of the surrounding villages (Nathanael belonged to Cana). We have no historical proof that this was so ; outside the `N. T.` the place is not mentioned, not even in Josephus ; nevertheless Mark vi. 6, and the occurrence recorded Luke iv. 15 ff., well correspond with Nathanael's judgment as to its disrepute in a moral point of view. — ἀ γ α θ ό ν] which must be pre-eminently the case if the Messiah were to come therefrom,—He whose coming must be a signally holy and sublime manifestation. — ἔ ρ χ ο υ κ . ἴ δ ε] "*optimum remedium contra opiniones praeconceptas,*" Bengel.

Ver. 48. Π ε ρ ὶ α ὐ τ ο ῦ] to those, therefore, journeying with Him, but so that the approaching Nathanael hears it, ver. 49. — ἀ λ η θ ῶ ς] *truly* an Israelite, not merely in outward descent and appearance, but in the moral nature which really corresponds to that of an upright Israelite. Comp. Rom. ix. 6, ii. 29. Ἐν ᾧ δόλος οὐκ ἐστι tells *by what means* he is so. Thus sincere and honest, thus inwardly true, *should* every Israelite be (not simply free from self-righteousness, but possessing what essentially belongs to truth) ; and Nathanael *was* all this. This virtue of guilelessness, as the characteristic of the true Israelite, is not named as belonging generally to the ancient *ideal* of the nation (Lücke, de Wette ; this view arbitrarily passes by the reference to the nation *historically* which lay much nearer) ; but in view of the venerable and honourable testimonies which had been uttered concerning the people of Israel (*e.g.* Num. xxiii. 10), whose father was himself already designated תָּם אִישׁ, LXX. ἄπλαστος,[3] Gen. xxv. 27 ; Aq. ἀπλοῦς,[4] Symm. ἄμωμος. — Jesus here also, as in vv. 43, 44, appears as the *searcher of hearts.*

Ver. 49. The approaching Nathanael heard the testimony of Jesus, and does not decline His commendation,—itself a proof of his guileless honesty ; but he asks in amazement *how Jesus knew him.* — ὄ ν τ α ὑ π ὸ τ . σ υ κ ῆ ν] belongs, as ver. 51 shows, not to φωνῆσαι, but to εἰδόν σε. Thus, before

---

[1] The Fathers, Luther, Melanchthon, Ebrard, and many.

[2] Lücke, de Wette, Hug, Krabbe, Ewald, Lange, Brückner, and others.

[3] Comp. Plato, *Legg.* I. p. 642 D : ἀ λ η θ ῶ ς

καὶ οὔτι πλαστῶς εἰσὶν ἀγαθοί. Soph. 216 C : οἱ μὴ π λ α σ τ ῶ ς, ἀλλ' ὄ ν τ ω ς φιλόσοφοι.

[4] Comp. Aristoph. *Plut.* 1159 : οὐ γὰρ δ ό λ ο ν νῦν ἔργον, ἀλλ' ἁ π λ ῶ ν τρόπων.

Philip, vv. 46, 47, met and called him (φωνῆσαι, comp. ii. 9, iv. 16, xi. 28, xviii. 33), Nathanael had been under a fig-tree ; whether the fig-tree of his own *house* (Mic. iv. 4 ; Zech. iii. 10), whether *meditating* (perchance upon the Messianic hope of the nation), praying, reading,—which employments, according to Rabbinical statements (see in Lightfoot, Schoettgen, Wetstein), took place beneath such trees,—we are not informed. He had just come from the tree to the place where Philip met him.[1]— ε ἰ δ ό ν   σ ε] is usually taken as referring to *a glance into the depth of his soul*,[2] but contrary to the simple meaning of the words, which affirm nothing else than : *I saw thee*, not *I knew* (ἔγνων) *thee*, or the like. Comp. also Hengst. The miraculous element in the εἰδόν σε, which made it a σημεῖον to Nathanael, and which led to his confession which follows in ver. 50, must have consisted in the fact that the fig-tree either stood out of sight of the place, or so far off that no ordinary power of vision could have discerned a person under it. Εἰδόν σε thus simply interpreted gives the true *solution* to Nathanael's question, because there could not have been this *rapport* of miraculous *far-seeing* on the part of Jesus, unless brought about by the immediate *recognition* of the true Israelite when he was at that distance. This spiritual elective affinity was the *medium* of the supernatural εἰδόν σε. Nonnus well says : ὄμμασι καὶ πραπίδεσσι τὸν οὐ παρεόντα δοκεύων. Jesus would not have seen an *ordinary* Jew, who, as being without this spiritual affinity, was beyond the limits of sight. ἦ π ὸ   τ ὴ ν   σ υ κ.] with the article : " under that *well-known* fig-tree, beneath which you were," or, if the tree was within the range of vision, *pointing towards it*. De Wette also rightly abides by the simple meaning, *I saw thee*, but thinks that what caused the astonishment of Nathanael was the fact that Jesus saw him *when he believed himself to be unobserved* (though *John* regarded this seeing as supernatural). But this gives no adequate psychological motive for the confession of ver. 50 ; and we must then further assume, with Ewald, that the words of Jesus reminded Nathanael of the deep and weighty thoughts which he was revolving when alone under the fig-tree, and he thus perceived that the depths of his soul were laid open before the spiritual eye of Jesus—which, however, is not indicated in the text.

Ver. 50. The double designation is uttered in the excitement of joyful certainty. The simple faith in the Messiah, expressed in ver. 41, is here intensified, not as to its subject-matter, but in its outward expression. Comp. Luthardt, p. 344. The second designation is the more definite of the two ; and therefore the first, in the sense in which Nathanael used it, is not as yet to be apprehended metaphysically (against Hengstenberg) in John's sense, but is simply theocratic, presupposing the national view (Ps. ii. 7 ; John xi. 27) of the promised and expected theocratic King,[2] without perhaps implying the teaching of the Baptist (Olshausen). The early occurrence of such con-

---

[1] The reference of the εἰδόν σε to the same place where Philip called him (so, after the Greek Fathers, B. Crusius) must be rejected, because neither the πρὸ τοῦ— φωνῆσαι nor the ὄντα ὑπὸ τὴν συκὴν would thus have any essential significance.

[2] Where it is imagined, though without the slightest hint to that effect in the text, that Jesus had a short time before *passed by the fig-tree unobserved*.

[3] Comp. Riehm in the *Stud. u. Krit.* 1865, p. 63 ff.

fessions therefore by no means conflicts with that later one of Peter (Matt. xvi. 3), in which is recognized the higher import of the words (against Strauss).

Ver. 51. Πιστεύεις is, with Chrysostom and most others (also Lachmann and Tischendorf, not Godet), to be taken *interrogatively ;* see on xx. 29.[1] But the question is not one of *censure,* which would only mar the fresh bloom of this first meeting (Theophylact : "he has not yet rightly believed in Christ's Godhead "); nor the expression of slight disapproval of a faith not yet based upon adequate grounds (de Wette, comp. Ewald); but rather of the *surprise* with which Jesus joyfully *acknowledges* the faith, hardly thus early to be looked for, of Nathanael. And to this faith, so surprisingly *ready* in its beginning, He promises something *greater* (ἐς ἐλπίδα φέρτερον ἔλκων, Nonnus) by way of further *confirmation.* — τ ο ύ τ ω ν] Plural of the category : "*than this* which you now have met with, and which has become the ground of your faith." — κ α ὶ λ έ γ ε ι α ὐ τ ῷ] specially introduces the further *explanation* of the *μείζω τούτων as a most significant word.* — ἀ μ ὴ ν ἀ μ ὴ ν λ έ γ ω ὑ μ ῖ ν] The double ἀμήν does not occur in other parts of the N. T., but we find it twenty-five times in John, and only in the mouth of Jesus,—therefore the more certainly original. — ὑ μ ῖ ν] to thee and Andrew, John, Peter (James, see in ver. 42), and Philip. — ἀ π ά ρ τ ι] *from now onwards,* for Jesus was about to begin His Messianic work. See chap. ii. Thus, in this weighty word He furnishes His disciples with the key for the only correct understanding of that work. — ὄ ψ ε σ θ ε , κ.τ.λ.] The "opened heaven" has no literal and independent significance, but is conformed to the imagery of the metaphor which follows. [See Note XII. p. 99.] Observe here the *perfect* participle : *heaven stands open ;* comp. Acts vii. 56. The *ascending and descending angels* are, according to Gen. xxviii. 12, a symbolical representation of the *uninterrupted and living intercourse between the Messiah and God,*—an intercommunion which the disciples would *clearly* and vividly recognize, or, according to the symbolic form of the thought, would *see* as matter of experience throughout the subsequent ministry of Jesus.[2] The "angels" are not therefore personified divine *powers* (Olshausen, de Wette, and several), or personal energies of God's Spirit (Luthardt and Hofmann), but as always, God's *messengers,* who bring to the Messiah God's commands, or execute them on Him,[3] and return again to God (ἀναβαίνοντας), while others descend with new commissions (καταβαίν.). We are not told whether, and to what extent, Nathanael and his companions already perceived the *symbolic* meaning of the declaration. It certainly does not refer to the *actual appearances of angels* in the course of the Gospel history,[4] against which ἀπάρτι is con-

[1] As to the *paratactic protasis,* which may be read interrogatively or not according to the character of the discourse, see C. F. Hermann, *Progr.* 1849, p. 18 ; Scheibe in Schneidew. *Philolog.* 1850, p. 362 ff. Comp. also Nägelsbach's note on the *Iliad,* p. 350, ed. 3.

[2] This expression tells us nothing concerning the origin of Christ's knowledge of God, which ver. 18 clearly declares, and

which cannot therefore be attributed to a series of progressive revelations (Weizsäcker); the expression rather presupposes that origin. Comp. also Weiss, *Lehrbegr.* p. 286 ff.

[3] Comp. Matt. iv. 11, xxvi. 53 ; Luke xxii. 43.

[4] Chrysostom, Cyril., Euthymius Zigabenus, and most of the early expositors.

clusive ; nor merely to *the working of miracles* (Storr, Godet), which accords neither with the expression itself, nor with that reference to the Messiah's ministry *as a whole* which is implied in ἀπάρτι ὄψεσθε, etc. — ἀ ν α β α ί ν .] is placed *first*, in remembrance of Gen. xxviii. 12, without any special purpose, but not inappropriately, because when the ὄψεσθε takes place, the intercourse between heaven and earth is already going on. We may supply ἀπὸ τοῦ υἱοῦ τοῦ ἀνϑρ. after ἀναβαίν from the analogy of what follows.[1] — Concerning ὁ υ ἱ ὸ ς τ ο ῦ ἀ ν ϑ ρ ., see on Matt. viii. 20 ; Mark ii. 8, note. In John likewise it is Jesus' standing Messianic designation of Himself ; here, where angelic powers are represented as waiting upon Him who bears the Messianic authority, it corresponds rather with the prophetic vision of the Son of Man (Dan. vii. 14), and forms the impressive conclusion of the whole section, confirming and ratifying the joyous faith and confession of the first disciples, as the first solemn self-avowal on the part of Jesus in their presence. It *thus* retained a deep and indelible hold upon the recollection of John, and therefore stands as the utterance of the clear Messianic consciousness of Jesus unveiled before us at the outset of His work. It is precisely in John that the Messiahship of Jesus comes out with the greatest definiteness, not as consequence and result, but already, from the beginning, the subject-matter of our Lord's self-consciousness.[2]

Note.—[See Note XIII. p. 99.] The synoptical account of the call of the two pairs of brothers, Matt. iv. 18 ff. and parallels, is utterly *irreconcilable* with that of John as to place, time, and circumstances ; and the usual explanations resorted to—that what is here recorded was only a *preliminary* call,[3] or only a *social union* with Christ (Luther, Lücke, Ebrard, Tholuck ; comp. also Ewald and Godet), or only the *gathering together of the first believers* (Luthardt), but not their call—fall to the ground at once when we see how the narrative proceeds ; for according to it the μαϑηταί, ii. 2, are with Jesus, and remain with Him. See on Matt. iv. 19, 20. The harmony of the two accounts consists in this simply, that the two pairs of brothers are the earliest apostles. To recognize in John's account not an actual history, but a picture of the author's own, drawn for the sake of illustrating his idea (Baur, Hilgenfeld, Schenkel),—that, viz., the knowledge of the disciples and that of Jesus Himself as to His Messianic destination should appear perfect from the outset,—is only one of the numerous self-deceptions in criticism which form the premisses of the unhistorical conclusion that the fourth Gospel is not the work of the apostle, but of some writer of much later date, who has moulded the history into the form of his own ideal. On the contrary, we must here specially observe that the author, if he wished to antedate the time and place of the call, certainly did not need to invent a totally different *situation* from that which was before his eyes in the

[1] See Kühner, II. p. 603.

[2] The historic accuracy of this relation, as testified by John, stands with the apostolic origin of the Gospel, against which also the objections of Holtzmann in his historically excellent investigation (*Jahrb. f. D. Theol.* 1867, p. 389), can have no effect.

[3] So, most recently, Märcker, *Ueberein-* *stimm. der Evang. d. Matt. u. Joh.*, Meiningen 1868, p. 10 ff. The τὸν λεγόμενον Πέτρον, Matt. iv. 18, furnishes no proof, as is plain from the parallel in Mark i. 16, which is the source of Matthew's account, but has not those words. They are simply a personal notice added from the standing-point of the writer, as in Matt. x. 2.

Synoptics. Besides this, the assumption that, by previously receiving John's baptism, Jesus renounced any independent action (Schenkel), is pure imagination. Weizsäcker (p. 404) reduces John's account to this : "The first acquaintance between Jesus and these followers of His was brought about by His meeting with the Baptist ; and on that occasion, amid the excitement which the Baptist created, Messianic hopes, however transitory, were kindled in this circle of friends." But this rests upon a treatment of the fourth Gospel, which refuses to it the authority of an independent witness, and finds in its author merely the poet of a thoughtful Idyll. And when Keim (I. p. 553) finds here only the invention of an age that could no longer endure the humble and human beginnings of Jesus, but would transfer to His first appearance the glory which, as a matter of history, distinguished His departure and exaltation, his procedure is all the more daring, the more close he himself brings the origin of the Gospel to the lifetime of the apostle, and into contact therefore with the most vivid recollections of His disciples.

NOTES BY AMERICAN EDITOR.

III. ἦν τὸ φῶς τὸ ἀληθινόν.—" *There was the genuine light.*" Ver. 9.

It is difficult to give to ἦν the meaning of *aderat* (as if παρῆν), *was present*, assigned to it by Meyer, but hardly supported by the analogy of vii. 39. It seems better, with Weiss, to construct it with ἐρχόμενον, but regard it as placed emphatically in advance. "There *was*" (as against the preceding οὐκ ἦν) "the *genuine* light" (in contrast with John, the *supposed* but not the *real* light ; the λύχνος ; not the φῶς) " which lighteth every man, coming into the world.'' Thus ἦν ἐρχόμενον forms a periphrastic imperfect : not equivalent to ἦλθεν, *came*, but marking *impendency*—what was just on the point of being. Or ἦν may be taken independently, as the verb of existence, "there *was*, as against the supposed and mere secondary light, the *genuine* Light, which, coming into the world," etc. The one of these constructions the Revised Version has placed in its text, the other in the margin. In either case Weiss seems right, against Meyer, in constructing ἐρχόμενον with φῶς and not with ἄνθρωπον. The latter construction seems idle in thought and un-Johannean in diction. There is scarcely a phrase more characteristic of John than that which designates Christ as " coming into the world," while he never distinctively so designates human birth.

IV. εἰς τὰ ἴδια ἦλθεν. Ver. 11.

This is among the expressions which try the capacities of a foreign tongue, to reproduce the flexible and delicate Greek. The rendering of the Common Ver., "He came unto his own, and his own," etc., is very defective, and that of the Revision, "He came unto his own (marg. *his own things*)," is scarcely better. Meyer's rendering, " to his own possession," is much preferable, yet inferior, I think, to that suggested by Frederick Field (Otium. Norv. vol. ii., p. iii.), " He came to his own *home*, and his own *people*," or without the italics : "his own home, and his own people." The meaning of ἴδια would perhaps be adequately given without the " own." He came unto his *home*. See John ix. 27, " From that hour the disciple took her εἰς τὰ ἴδια ;" Acts xxi. 6, ὑπέστρεψαν εἰς τὰ ἴδια ; Esth. v. 10.

The verse is of striking significance.   A single brief. phrase binds into one
the Old and the New Testament, identifying the Jesus of the New Covenant with
the Jehovah of the Old.   Its climactic character is also striking.   He who had
made the world was in it, and it did not recognize Him ; He came to what had
been His special inheritance, His chosen *home*, and they of His household did
not receive Him—the Evangelist's euphemism for hate, rejection, persecution,
and murder.

V. " And we beheld His glory." Ver. 14.

It is, I think, much better and simpler to regard, with most editors and interpreters (against Meyer and Weiss), καὶ ἐθεασάμεθα—πατρός, as parenthetical,
and rather momentarily interrupting the course of thought than following in
its main drift.   It is rather the essential nature of the Word : " full of grace
and truth," that is for the time being in the writer's mind.   He turns aside
for a moment to his and his companions' vision of His glory, but immediately
resumes with πλήρης the suspended thought and construction.   The assumption of the violent change by which πλήρης is attached ungrammatically to the
sentence as an incidental member, is unnecessary and unnatural.   The " grace
and the truth" dwelling in the Word is the main idea (ver. 15 being also parenthetical) from ver. 14 to ver. 17.

The ἐθεασάμεθα δόξαν, as aor. (not ἐθεώμεθα, *used to behold*) may not improbably
refer specifically to the extraordinary display of glory on the Mount of Transfiguration, which must have made and *did* make (2 Pet. i. 16–19) a most powerful impression on those who witnessed it.

VI. Παρὰ πατρός, *from the Father*.   Ver. 14.

The more natural construction of παρὰ πατρός is, I think, rather with δόξαν
(*a glory from the Father*) than with μονογενοῦς.   Granting that παρὰ πατρός admits
the explanation " An only-begotten (sent) from the Father," still it seems less
natural than " a glory from the Father," which is explained by the interjected
ὡς μονογενοῦς, *as of an* (not *the*) *Only-begotten*.   With this construction παρὰ
is easier ; the construction is more forcible and elegant, and it suggests the
instances in which the Father bestows direct honour upon the Son.   Matt. iii.
17 ; xvii. 5 ; John xii. 28.   "He received from God the Father honour and
glory." And this testimony directly from the Father John seems repeatedly to
have heard.

VII. " John beareth witness." Ver. 15.

Vv. 14, 15, 16, should, I think, be constructed as follows.   14. And the word
became flesh and tabernacled among us (and we beheld [gazed upon] his glory,
a glory, as of an Only-begotten, from the Father) full of grace and truth ; (15.
John testifieth concerning him, and crieth, saying, He who cometh after me
hath taken place in advance of me ; because he was before me) ; 16. and out
of his fulness did all we receive, and grace for grace.

The mind of the Evangelist is so impregnated with the testimony of the
Baptist in its fulness and great significance, that he breaks the main thread of
his thought to introduce it at ver. 15, anticipating here the testimony which
was historically borne at vv. 26, 30.   It seems to me also that the words ὁ ἐρχόμενος ὀπίσω μου do not here refer to "something still future," to an advent of
the Messiah yet to come (which indeed *formally* it actually was), but expresses

the *economical* relation of the two personages ; John being the predicted and recognized predecessor of Jesus ; Jesus in the order of time, his follower.— *Hath taken place in advance of me.* Although he cometh and came after and behind me, yet he has already taken precedence of me, and this on account of his intrinsic and essential superiority. Jesus has not yet been made manifest to Israel, but the Baptist recognizes him as already present, and as having already taken that place of transcendent superiority which belongs to his nature, and will very soon publicly display itself.

VIII. ὁ ὢν εἰς τὸν κόλπον τοῦ πατρός. Ver. 17.

Three constructions of ὁ ὢν are grammatically possible. One would make it strictly an imperfect participle, relative to ἐξηγήσατο, the *being* being contemporaneous with the *unfolding*. This view would have few advocates. The second and more common construction takes it as a *timeless* present, expressing the eternal relation of the Son to the Father, irrespective of the incarnation. Meyer and Weiss both reject this, and refer it to the *existing historical* relation of the Son since His exaltation. They explain by this the Prep. εἰς (marking His *re-entrance* into this relation), for which otherwise we should have ἐν. In either case we must ask after the logical import and relation of the participial clause to the entire sentence. If it refer to the Son's essential and eternal relation to the Father, it would then account for His *capacity* and fitness to unfold God : He fathoms and discloses the depths of the Being in whose bosom He dwells. If it refer to His post-incarnate relation, this idea would be irrelevant, and the clause would naturally express the relation of *affection* in which He stands to the Father, not indeed as a table-companion, reclining upon His bosom, but as enfolded in the arms of His love. This harmonizes, it is true, with the frequent language of the Gospels ("my beloved Son"), yet seems scarcely to meet the logical demands of the passage. I cannot but think the prevalent interpretation, which makes it express Christ's inherent and essential relation to the Deity, as here more probable, while still the εἰς, instead of ἐν, may be determined by the fact, present so naturally to the mind of the writer, of the Son's recent resumption of the apparently suspended relation.

IX. Vv. 1–18. *Analysis.*

Of this pre-eminently profound and wonderful passage—without its rival in human literature—it may not be inadmissible to endeavour to aid the understanding by a brief additional analysis. It falls, I think, naturally into three main divisions.

I. The Pre-incarnate and Eternal Word in His *essential character* and relations, vv. 1–5.

II. *Preparation*, through His harbinger John, for His entrance into the world, with anticipatory glance at His actual coming and its consequences, vv. 6–13.

III. Resumption from ver. 9 (or ver. 5). *Incarnation* of the Word, as imparter to men of essential grace and truth.

I. The Word, in His relation to God of distinction and identity (1, 2) ; as medium of creation (3) ; as possessing inherently life and light, and their source to men (4) ; and the rejection of the light by men (5).

II. Preparation for the coming of the Word into the world by the sending

of His harbinger, as His witness (6, 7) ; not the light, but the lamp ; not the
original, but the reflected light ; emphatically, for testimony (8).   In contrast
with this secondary light, the genuine, archetypal light, the universal enlightener, was then coming into the world (9).   Under the prompting of this
contrast of the coming of the real (as against the supposed) light, the writer
anticipates and beholds Him actually *in* the world which he had made, but unknown by it (10), coming to His own home-people, but rejected by them (11) ;
yet to all who received Him by faith, bringing sonship with God (12) through a
supernatural and divine birth (13).

III. Resumption from ver. 9 (or ver. 5), taking up the next great stage in
the Word's history, His *becoming incarnate*, tabernacling among men (revealing to
us His glory) full of grace and truth (15).   (Interjected parenthetical testimony
of John by anticipation, regarding Him as subsequent in appearance, but taking
place in advance of and above him, 15).   Universal communication of this
fulness of truth and grace (16) ; the Law being given through Moses, but essential grace and truth through Christ (17) ; ·through whom finally—(the
grand and solemn climax and sum of all),—as the only-begotten Son, the invisible God has been unfolded to men.

X. *The Temptation.*   Ver. 28, Note.

Meyer summarily rules out the Synoptic account of the Temptation as unhistorical.   It cannot come into the narrative of John (he holds) before the deputation from Jerusalem (ver. 19), without being in contradiction with the Synoptists. · If the baptism be placed between vv. 19 and 25, then of course John's
narrative leaves no place for it until ch. iii. vv. 22–36, where Hengstenberg
places it, and which Meyer calls "an unavailing makeshift."   But remembering,
in the first place, that there are broad gaps to fill up alike in Matthew and in
John, and that it is often a matter of judgment, and of somewhat difficult decision, to determine just where the *lacunae* are ; and then observing that in Matt.
the Temptation, while on the one hand it immediately follows the baptism,
yet on the other immediately precedes that return to Galilee which is probably
to be identified with that of John iv. 1-3, it does not seem by any means impossible to place it during that period of our Lord's sojourn on the Jordan
which John· describes in chap. iii. 22 ff.   True, the connecting particles of
Matt. and Mark (τότε *then* and εὐθύς *straightway*) are somewhat against this, yet
(considering the elasticity of the connecting particles in the Gospels) I think
not insuperably.   That this is its only possible or its most probable location, I
would not maintain. · It certainly cannot be affirmed without hazard that it
cannot find a place in the Synoptics without contradiction to John ; for it and
the baptism *may* have come in before the Jewish deputation, and αὔριον *he next
day* of John i. 19 may be the day of Jesus' return from the wilderness.   The
historical accounts are so obviously and intentionally incomplete, that contradiction here between John and the Synoptists can be affirmed only by those
who deny in general the historical validity of the Gospels, or who know a good
deal more about the details of the history which they outline than did their
writers.   Hengstenberg's view is not here "an unavailing makeshift."   It is
simply an alternative—possibly not the most probable one,—between different
modes of filling out the brief and fragmentary notices of the Gospels.

XI. "*I knew him not.*" Ver. 31.

That John first became aware at the baptism that Jesus was the Messiah is by no means certain, though perhaps not improbable. The "*I knew him not*" does not, as Weiss justly remarks, refer necessarily to the time of the baptism, but more probably to the time when the Baptist entered on his ministry. Besides, the decided emphasis in the above phrase on the ἐγώ, as if he had said, "It was not *I* that knew him," makes it doubtful if the Baptist does not mean simply to affirm that his cognizance of the Messiahship of Him whom he was announcing was not a thing *self-derived*, but he was indebted for his *knowledge* to the same Divine source whence he received his commission. It really has nothing to do with the nature or degree of his previous personal acquaintance with Jesus. The careful and exact narrative of Luke i. 36 ff., which Meyer stigmatizes as "legendary," is therefore by no means "irreconcilable with the text before us." The narrative of Luke neither affirms nor necessarily implies any such acquaintance of the Baptist with Jesus as to make certain his previous knowledge of the Lord's Messiahship ; and if it did, it would still be true that he knew him not from his *own* knowledge (κἀγὼ οὐκ ᾔδειν αὐτόν), but from the heavenly revelation. And whatever his previous knowledge, the testimony at the baptism sealed and confirmed it.

XII. "*Heaven standing open.*" Ver. 51.

So Meyer gives exactly the force of the part. ἀνεῳγότα. It does not denote the *process of* opening (ἀνοιγόμενον : see σχιζομένους, Mark i. 10), or the mere fact of being momentarily opened (ἀνοιχθέντα, ἀνεῴχθησαν, Mark iii. 16), or being open as *sequel* to the act of opening (ἀνεῳγμένον, διηνοιγμένους, Acts vii. 56). Both the common Eng. Ver. (*open*) and that of the Rev. Ver. (*opened*) are inaccurate or ambiguous, failing of the precise force of the Greek (*standing open*), which denotes simply the *permanent condition* of mutual intercommunion between earth and heaven.

XIII. Ver. 51, Note.

It seems entirely gratuitous in Meyer thus to assume the utter irreconcilableness of John's account of the calling of the two pairs of brothers with that of the Synoptists. The facts of the call must have been matter of such complete notoriety in the apostolic circle, that *ignorance* on the part of either of the Evangelists seems out of the question ; and we are certainly not to assume contradiction between them in so simple and plain a matter without strong necessity. We are bound to suppose that the interstices existing in the Gospel records — confessedly fragmentary — would here, as elsewhere, if filled up, render them a coherent and consistent narrative. And in point of fact there is here scarce even the semblance of contradiction. John informs us that Peter, Andrew, and himself (John) formed the acquaintance of Jesus at the Jordan, with the Baptist, but gives no intimation that they were then called by Him to permanent discipleship. The Synoptists inform us that these three, along with James the brother of John, were called by Jesus later on the Sea of Galilee into His permanent intimacy, but gives no hint that they had not seen and known Him earlier. On the contrary, the promptness with which they then obeyed His call and abandoned their vocation and home renders probable precisely the preparation of some such previous acquaintance. The two accounts, in fact, mutually supplement and explain each other. The call in the Synoptists is the natural sequel to the seemingly incidental meeting in John. The meeting in John explains the otherwise unexplained and seemingly accidental occurrence in the Synoptists. True, we have disciples now accompanying Jesus into Galilee, attending with Him the marriage feast, visiting with Him Capernaum, and going with Him up to Jerusalem. But precisely who and how many these were we have no word of information ; probably among them were, during much of the time, most of those mentioned in the first chapter of this Gospel. But these were undoubtedly not the only ones, nor is it probable that at this time they were constantly the same. With our Lord's increasing notoriety, the number of His adherents was doubtless enlarging and fluctuating, and it is extremely probable that the *first* whom He called to His *abiding* intimacy were the two pairs of brothers (one of whom, James, we have, indeed, no *assurance* to have been with Him at the Jordan) from their employment on the Lake of Galilee. At what time Jesus had dismissed them to their callings before He finally recalled them we do not and need not know. Our Lord had had them with Him long enough to try their fitness for their destined work, and they had been with Him long enough to enable them, when the hour arrived, to make an intelligent decision. Nothing is more natural than that Jesus, before requiring the final decision, should send them for a season to their homes and pursuits, and let them there review the extraordinary scenes through which they had passed. That Meyer, de Wette, and Brückner should find here a certain contradiction in the Gospels is extraordinary indeed, and fittingly has his latest German editor, Weiss (with Lücke, Thol. Ew. Lüth. Hengst. God.), held to their entire agreement.

CHAPTER II.

Ver. 10. τότε is wanting in B. L. א.* Min. Verss. ; deleted by Tisch. But how easily might it, in itself superfluous, have been passed over before τὸν ! — Ver. 11. The τήν before ἀρχήν we must delete, with Lachm. and Tisch., following A. B. L. Λ. Min., Origen, and other Fathers. — Ver. 12. ἔ μ ε ι ν α ν . A. F. G. Λ. Min. Copt. Arm. Pers. p. Ver. Nonn. : ἔμεινεν. In keeping with the preceding κατέβη and the following ἀνέβη. — Ver. 15. For τ ὸ κ έ ρ μ α , B. L. Tᵇ. X. 33. Copt. Arm. Ver. Origen : τὰ κέρματα (explanatory). — Ver. 17. δέ is wanting in B. L. X. א. Copt. ; bracketed by Lachm., deleted by Tisch. Added for the connection. For κ α τ α φ ά γ ε τ α ι Elz. has κατέφαγε, against all the Uncials, from the LXX. — Ver. 22. After ἔλεγε Elz. has αὐτοῖς, an addition feebly supported.

Ver. 1. T ρ ί τ η] is, with Origen, c. Cels. vi. 30, to be reckoned from the last-named day, i. 44, not from the coming to Cana (Ewald), which has not yet been alluded to. Thus we have in all *six* days from i. 19, not *seven* (see on i. 41), in which number Luthardt would find this symbolic meaning : "It is a Sabbath, as it were, which Jesus here is keeping." — By τ ῆ ς Γ α λ ι - λ α ί α ς the village of Cana (now not *Kafar kenna*, as Hengstenberg and Godet still think, but *Kana el-Jelîl ;* see Robinson, III. p. 443 ; Ritter, XVI. 753 ff.), about three hours N.W. from Nazareth, is distinguished from *another* Cana ; for in ver. 11, iv. 46, xxi. 2, τῆς Γαλιλαίας is also added, and hence it must be taken as a *standing* descriptive addition, as if belonging to the name (like our "Freiburg im Breisgau" and the like), and not here as a mere allusion to the *arrival* in Galilee (B. Crusius). The *other* Cana lay in the tribe of *Asher*, Josh. xix. 28 (S.E. from Tyre ; comp. Robinson, III. 657), and though also to be considered as belonging to Galilee, was yet so near to *Phoenicia*, that the designation of our Cana as κ. τῆς Γαλιλαίας, in distinction from the other, is justified on geographical grounds. Ewald distinguishes our Cana from the Kanath lying east of the river district, but the name (קְנָת, Num. xxxii. 42, 1 Chron. ii. 23 ; and Bertheau on the word ; Καναθ LXX., Κανάθα Josephus) does not correspond. — κ α ὶ ἦ ν ἡ μ ή τ η ρ , κ.τ.λ.] Mary was already there when Jesus and His disciples arrived in Cana, no doubt arranging and helping (see vv. 3, 5) in the friend's house where the wedding was to take place. That shortly before the baptism of Jesus she had *come to live* at Cana (Ewald), but soon after removed thence to Capernaum (ii. 12), disregards the specific intimation both here and in iv. 46. That Joseph was not there with her, is in keeping with his entire and unexplained disappearance from the Gospel narrative after Luke ii.41 ff. It is usually, though without special proof (see vi. 42), assumed that he was already *dead.*

Ver. 2. *Jesus also and His disciples* (those won in chap. i.) *were invited, i.e.*
when, in the meanwhile, He had come to Cana.[1] To take ἐκλήθη as *pluperfect* is objectionable both in itself (see on xviii. 24), and also because the
disciples had been first won by Jesus on the way. But there is nothing
against the supposition that Jesus had journeyed not to Nazareth, but to
Cana, on account of the wedding ; for He may have known (through
Nathanael, Godet thinks) that His mother was there, and because, considering the friendly relations with the family, He did not need a *previous* invitation. This is in answer at once to Weisse, II. 203, who finds an invitation
inconceivable ; to Lange, who holds that Jesus found the invitation awaiting Him at Nazareth (?) ; and to Schleiermacher, who makes the invitation
to have preceded even His baptism. Of the disciples, Nathanael, moreover,
was himself a native of Cana (xxi. 2). But apart from this, the friendly
invitation of the disciples along with Jesus by no means implies a previous
extended ministry of Jesus in Galilee (Schenkel), or even such a ministry at
all before His baptism (Schleiermacher). — As to the sing. ἐκλήθη, see
Kühner, § 433, 1 ; Buttmann, *N. T. Gk.* 110 [E. T. p. 126 ff.].

Ver. 3. Ὑστερήσ. οἴνου] *when a scarcity of wine had occurred,*—on
what day of the marriage feast (it usually lasted seven, Gen. xxix. 27 ;
Judg. xiv. 14 ; Tob. ix. 12, x. 1) we are not told.[2] The expression ὑστερεῖ
τι, *something fails* or *runs short*, belongs to later Greek (Mark x. 21 ; Isa. li.
14 ; Neh. ix. 21 ; Diosc. v. 86).—οἴνου οὐκ ἔχουσι] *they are short of
wine, they, i.e.* the family of the bridegroom, who provided the feast. [See
Note XIV. p. 117.] They might be *disgraced* by the failure of the wine. The
words, however, are not only an expression of interest, which was the more
reasonable, as the deficiency was accelerated by the invitation of her Son
and His disciples ; but they also contain, as Jesus Himself understood
(ver. 4), an indirect *appeal for help*, as is confirmed by ver. 5, prompted by
thoughtful consideration for the credit of the house providing the feast.
Some find herein a call to *work a miracle*. But this would imply either that
Mary had inferred from the conception, birth, etc., of her Son, His power
of working miracles, which she now expected Him to display, or that Jesus
had already, on some previous occasion, though in a narrower circle,
wrought wonderful works (the former hypothesis in Chrysostom, Theophylact, Euthymius Zigabenus, Baumgarten, Maier, Godet, Hengstenberg, and
many more ; the latter in Lücke and others),—assumptions which are
equally incapable of proof. Nor would the supply of *this* want of itself
suggest the need of a miracle, and the thought of so disproportionate a
means occurring to Mary's mind without any adequate reason, even by the
recollection of such traits as are related in Luke ii. 49 ff. (Brückner), or by

[1] Schenkel inconsiderately says, that," according to our Gospel, Jesus was to all
appearance transported to Cana by a
miracle of almighty power."

[2] The text does not say that it lasted only
one day, as Hengstenberg finds expressed
in ver. 1, where we are simply told that the
marriage *began* on the third day,—which

has nothing to do with its *duration*. Nor is
there any hint in the text of "*poor circumstances,*" for it speaks of the master of the
feast and of servants. Least of all does
the inviting of Jesus' *disciples* along with
Himself imply poverty. This also in answer
to Godet.

the miracle at His baptism, or by the call of the disciples, or by the declaration of i. 52, of which she would be informed at the marriage (Godet), is quite inexplicable, even supposing that she had observed more clearly than any others the change which had taken place in her Son, and had therefore with fuller expectation looked up to Him as the Messiah (Ewald's view, comp. Tholuck). Rather did she wish to prompt Jesus in *a general way* to render help ; and this she would suppose He would do in the most natural manner (by furnishing wine), a method as obvious as that of miracle was the reverse. But Jesus, in the feeling of His divine call (ver. 4), *intended* to render help in a special and *miraculous* manner ; and with this design of His *own* in view, returns the answer contained in ver. 4. In this way the *obscurity* of the words is removed (which Lampe and de Wette dwell upon), and at the same time the objection raised from ver. 11 (by Strauss, B. Bauer, Schweizer, Scholten) against the entire narrative, upon the assumption that Mary (from the Logos standing-point of the evangelist, it is supposed !) expected a miracle. Lastly, it is purely gratuitous to suppose that Mary wished to *give a hint* to Jesus and His disciples *to go away* (Bengel, Paulus); yet Ebrard (on Olshausen) has again preferred this view, explaining afterwards "mine hour" of the time of His death, when Jesus would have to leave the marriage-feast (which thus symbolizes the period of His earthly ministry). This is not profundity, but a mere playing with exegesis.

Ver. 4. Jesus understands His mother's wish, but has in mind a method of help altogether *different* from what she meant. He therefore repels her interference, in the consciousness of the call which here is given Him to begin His Messianic ministry of miracles, and holds out the prospect of rendering help at a *later* period. — τ ί ἐμοὶ καὶ σοί;] a rejection of fellowship (מַה-לִּ֥י וָלָךְ, Josh. xxii. 24 ; Judg. xi. 12, *al. ;* Matt. viii. 29 ; xxvii. 19 ; Mark i. 24 ; Luke viii. 28 ; also in the classics ; see Bernhardy, p. 98), here with reference to the help to be rendered, which He Himself, without His mother's assistance, and independently of her, would accomplish, according to His own divinely determined call and will, and in a miraculous manner. Godet well says : "Sa devise sera desormais: *mon père et moi.*" [1] The appellation γύναι added to the τί — σοί (which Hofmann thinks should be joined to what· follows ; but why ?) does not contain anything unfriendly ("*duriter respondet,*" Melanchthon), as is clear already from xix. 21 ; see also Wetstein. Comp. xx. 15. But His not saying μῆτερ followed involuntarily from the consciousness of His higher wonder-working capacity and will, by virtue of which, as an ἀμήτωρ, He rejects the interference of feminine weakness, such as was presented here before Him in His mother. The remark of Euthymius Zigabenus is not happy (comp. Augustine) : "He spoke thus *as God ;*" that of Epiphanius, Beza, Calvin, and many others, is singular : "His aim was to oppose that future *Mariolatry* which He foresaw." Still, the passage tells against that worship. Schenkel says erroneously, quoting Mark iii. 21, "He was at *variance* with the members of His family." — ἡ ὥρα μου] can only mean, *the requisite time for me to*

[1] Comp. Dorner, *Jesu sündlose Vollkommenh.* p. 11.

help.[1] So also Hengstenberg, in accordance with the context. Jesus, conscious of His close communion with the Father, sees clearly that this His first manifestation of Himself as Messiah in the working of miracles stands, even with reference to its time of beginning, in connection with the divine appointment ; and He feels that the moment (ἡ ὥρα = ὁ καιρός, as in xvi. 21, and often in the N. T. and the classics) for this first Messianic display of power is not yet present when His mother refers to the want of wine. *How* He was conscious of the exact *horas et moras* for working, cannot be more precisely determined. Euthymius Zigabenus is substantially right : ἡ τοῦ θαυματουργῆσαι ; and Ewald : "the hour of full Messianic sense of power." Strangely attributing to Mary thoughts of that kind, Baumgarten Crusius remarks, "the moment of my *public appearance* as Messiah ;" and Godet : "l'heure de l'avénement *royal.*" Anticipating ver. 11, Lücke, Tholuck, Brückner, Maier, Baur, Baumgarten render : "the moment of the *revelation of my glory.*" Comp. Luthardt : "This miracle, as the figurative *prolepsis* of Christ's subsequent full relation of Himself before the eyes of men, was of significance only for that narrow circle, and was intended to lead Jesus on from it into public life,"—of which, however, the text contains no hint either in ver. 5 or elsewhere.

Ver. 5. The words of Jesus last spoken implied that He intended to help, though not immediately. Hence Mary's direction to the servants, whose service she supposed Jesus would require (perhaps to go and fetch wine). Any allusion to Gen. xli. 55 (Hengstenberg) is remote from the text. Ebrard reads *into* the passage, that Jesus, after He had spoken, ver. 4, rose and turned towards the servants.

Ver. 6. Ἐκεῖ] Whether in the feast chamber, or perhaps in the vestibule, we are not told. — ὑδρίαι] *water-pitchers* for carrying water, iv. 28.[2] — ἐξ] Not stated as explanatory of the Jewish *custom*, but as vividly describing the exact circumstances, yet not with any symbolic signficance (six, Lange thinks, was the number of poverty and labour). — κείμεναι] *positae, set down, placed there.* Comp. xix.29 ; Jer. xxiv. 1 ; Xen. *Oec.* viii. 19 : χύτρας . . . εὐκρινῶς κείμεναι. — κατὰ τὸν καθαρ. τῶν Ἰουδ.] *i.e. for the sake of cleansing* (the hands and vessels, Matt. xv. 2 ; Mark vii. 3 ff. ; Luke xi. 39 ; Lightfoot, p. 974), which *the Jews* practised before and after meals. On κατά, in which, as in 2 Tim. i. 1, "notio *secundum* facile transit in notionem *propter.*"[3] — μετρητάς] In conformity with his Hellenic tendency, John gives the *Attic* measure, which, however, is equal to the Hebrew בת

---

[1] It is an error to suppose that ἡ ὥρα μου in John always signifies *the hour of Christ's death.* Its reference depends entirely upon the *context,* as in vii. 30, viii. 20, where it means the hour of Christ's seizure ; and xiii. 1, where the more precise definition is expressly given. Already τινές in Chrysostom, Ebrard, and many, take it here as meaning the hour of Christ's death. Hilgenfeld understands it of the hour of the *g'crification* of Jesus, the culminating point of which was certainly the crucifixion ; and that Jesus, according to John, gives expression to the full consciousness of the Logos, and its superhuman independence of all human counsel.

[2] Often in the LXX. ; Dem. 1155. 6 ; Arist. *Vesp.* 926 ; *Lysistr.* 327, 358 ; Lucian, *Dem. enc.* 29.

[3] Kühner, *ad Xen. Mem.* i. 3. 12. Comp. Winer, p. 376 [E. T. p. 398].

(Josephus, *Antt.* viii. 2. 9). The Attic *metretes* contained 12 χόες or 144 κοτύλαι, 1½ Roman *amphorae*, *i.e.* about 21 Würtemburg measures (seeWurm, *de ponderum etc. rationib.* 126), and about 33 Berlin quarts, in weight eighty pounds of water [about 8⅔ gallons] (Bertheau, *Gesch. d. Israel*, p. 77).[1] *Each* pitcher contained two or three *metretae* (which are not, with Ammon, after Syr. to be referred to a smaller measure, nor with Ebrard, to that of an *amphora*) ; for as a row of *six* pitchers is named, ἀνά can, consistently with the context, only be taken in a *distributive* sense, not in the signification— which is, besides, linguistically untenable (see Winer, p. 372 [E. T. p. 398])—of *circiter*, according to which all six must have held only about two or three *metretae* (Paulus, Hug). The *great* quantity of water thus turned into wine (252–378 Würtemburg measures, 106–160 gallons) seems out of proportion, and is used by Strauss and Schweizer to impugn the historic character of the narrative ; but the *beneficent* purpose of the miracle makes it conceivable (compare the miraculous Feedings), and we are to suppose that what was left over may have been intended by Jesus as a present for the married pair, while the possible abuse of it during the feast itself was prevented by the presence of the Giver. We must also bear in mind that the quantity was suggested to Him by the six pitchers standing there ; and therefore, if the beneficent Wonder-worker has not in general to measure the exact *need*, He had occasion all the more not to fall below this quantity suggested by the circumstances, by transforming the contents of but one or two pitchers, and omitting the rest. The blessing conferred by the Wonder-worker has also, considering the circumstances, its appropriateness and *decorum*, in keeping with which He was not to act in a spirit of calculation, but rather to give plentifully, if the abundance was suggested by the number of the vessels.

Vv. 7, 8. The transformation is accomplished in the time between ver. 7 and ver. 8.[2] — αὐτοῖς] the servants, who obeyed Him according to the direction of Mary, ver. 5 ; not, as Lange's imagination suggests, "under the influence of a miraculously excited feeling pervading the household."— γεμίσατε] The most natural supposition from this and ver. 6 is that the pitchers were *empty*, the water in them having been used up before the feast began, and were to be filled afresh for use after meat. Observe, moreover, that Christ does not proceed *creatively* in His miracles, either here or in the feedings. — ἕως ἄνω] This is stated for no other purpose than to give prominence to the *quantity* of the wine which Jesus miraculously produced. — ἀντλήσατε] Altogether general, without specifying any particular pitcher, —showing that as *all* were filled, the water in *all* was turned into wine (in answer to Selmer and Olshausen). From the nature of the case, *no object* is appended, and we therefore can only understand the general word *it*. The

[1] Comp. Böckh, *Staatshaush.* I. 127 ; Hermann, *Privatalterth.* § 46. 10.
[2] The commencement of the transformation might indeed be placed after the drawing out, and consequently after ver. 8. so that only that portion of water which was drawn was converted into wine. But the minute statement of the number and large size of the vessels in ver. 6, by which it is manifestly intended to draw attention to the greatness in a quantitative point of view of the miracle of transformation, presupposes rather that *all* the water in the pitchers was converted into wine.

106 THE GOSPEL OF JOHN.

drawing out was done by means of a vessel, a tankard,[1] out of which the
master of the feast would fill the cups upon the table.[2] — The ἀ ρ χ ι τ ρ ί -
κ λ ι ν ο ς, *table-master*,[3] is the chief of the waiters at table, upon whom devolved
the charge of the meats and drinks, and the entire arrangement of the repast.
See Walch, *De architriclino*, Jena 1753. Comp. Fritzsche on Ecclus. xxxv.
1, where he is designated as ἡγούμενος. He was at the same time the taster
of the meats and drinks, and is not to be confounded with the συμποσίαρχος,
modimperator, arbiter bibendi, who was chosen by the guests themselves from
among their own number.[4]

Vv. 9, 10. The parenthesis, usually made to begin with κ. οὐκ ᾔδει, must
be limited to ο ἱ δ ὲ δ ι ά κ ο ν ο ι — ὕ δ ω ρ, because the καὶ οὐκ ᾔδει not only continues the construction, but assigns a reason for the φωνεῖ τὸν νυμφίον, κ.τ.λ.,
which follows ; for had the man known whence the new wine had come,
he would not in surprise have called the bridegroom, etc. — τ ὸ ὕ δ ω ρ ο ἶ ν .
γ ε γ ε ν .] not *the wine which had been water* (Luther), but *the water after having
become wine* (and now *being* wine : observe the force of the perfect). Had
the τ ό been repeated, this water, as that which had been made wine, would
have been distinguished from *other* water (*aquam, eam dico quae*, etc.).[5] The
τό not being repeated, the ὕδωρ οἶν. γεγεν. is united into *one conception*. —
π ό θ ε ν ἐ σ τ ί ν] *whence it came*, i.e. that it had been drawn out of the water-
pitchers. This is evident from the following οἱ ἠντληκότες τὸ ὕδωρ. The
table-master, therefore, cannot have been present at the drawing out of the
water, ver. 8. Concerning the present ἐστίν, see i. 40. — The insertion of
the words οἱ δὲ διάκονοι, κ.τ.λ., serves to give prominence *to the reality of the
miracle.* — ᾔ δ ε ι σ α ν] i.e. πόθεν ἐστίν, but they did not know that it was *wine*
which they brought. — φ ω ν ε ῖ] *He called him to him* (comp. i. 49), and said
to him. Whether the bridegroom was just outside at the time (as Nonnus
represents), or was reclining at the table, or is to be supposed as employed
in the chamber, does not appear. — ὁ ἀ ρ χ ι τ ρ ί κ λ .] an unneeded repetition,
but occasioned by the parenthesis, as often in Greek. — π ᾶ ς ἄ ν θ ρ ω π ο ς ,
κ.τ.λ.] spoken under the impression that the bridegroom had kept the good
wine in reserve, and had not allowed it to be put forth (τίθησι), but now
was regaling them with it. We may suppose the words to have been spoken
jocularly, in joyous surprise after tasting the wine. The general custom,
however, to which the table-master refers, is not elsewhere with any certainty confirmed (the proof in Wetstein is doubtful) ; nor, indeed, considering the playful way in which it was spoken, does it need any voucher. —
ὅ τ α ν μ ε θ υ σ θ ῶ σ ι] *when they have become intoxicated*, so that they can no
longer appreciate the goodness of the wine. The word does not mean anything else ; not *when they have well drunk*,[6] because *intoxication* is the essential though relative conception (see also Gen. xliii. 34 ; Hag. i. 6 ; Rev.
xvii. 2). The man says only in joke, as if it were a *general experience*, what

[1] πρόχοος, Hom. *Od.* xviii. 397.
[2] Comp. Nitzsch on Hom. *Od.* η. 183.
[3] Heliod. vii. 27, in Petron. 27 *triclinar-
ches*, elsewhere also called τραπεζοποιός
(Athen. iv. p. 170 D E·′ Beck. *Char.* II. 252).

[4] Xen. *Anab.* vi. 1. 30 ; Herm. *Privatalterth.*
§ 28, 29 ; Mitscherlich, *ad Hor. Od.* i. 4. 18.
[5] See Kühner, *ad Xen. Anab.* iv. 6. 1.
[6] Tholuck, de Wette, and several, *e.g.*
Beza, Cornelius à Lapide, and others.

he certainly may often have observed, and no inference can be drawn from his words that the guests at Cana were already intoxicated ; especially as ἕως ἄρτι simply means *till now*, after they have been drinking so long at the table, in antithesis with the πρῶτον.

Ver. 11. The τήν before ἀρχήν being spurious (see critical notes), we must translate : *This, as a beginning of His miracles, did Jesus at Cana.* See on iv. 54.[1] From this it is clear that it is the first miracle *in general*, and not merely the first of those that were wrought in *Cana* (iv. 46 sqq.), that is meant (so already τινές in Chrysostom and Paulus). This concluding remark of John's simply serves to express, with the very first of them, the *teleological* nature of the miracles of Jesus generally. — τὴν δόξαν αὐτοῦ] not "His excellent humanity" (Paulus), but *His divine Messianic majesty*, as in i. 14. The miracles of Jesus, as He Himself testified, had for their object not only the δόξα of the *Father*, but also *His own*, xi. 4 (in opposition to Weizsäcker, *Jahrb. f. Deutsche Theol.* 1857, p. 165). The former is in fact the latter, and the latter the former. Observe how in John (as well as in the Synoptics) Jesus begins His Messianic ministry in *Galilee*, even in this His first miracle. — καὶ ἐπίστευσαν, κ.τ.λ.] *and His disciples became believers in Him.* The faith which they already had (i. 35–52) was only introductory, belonging to the commencement of their connection with Jesus; now, upon the basis of this manifestation of His glory (i. 14), came the more advanced and fuller decision, a new epoch in their faith, which, moreover, still continued susceptible of and requiring fresh additions even to the end (xi. 15, xiv. 11). There is no hint here of any contrast with the unbelief afterwards manifested by the people (Brückner), nor can this be inferred from ver. 12 ff. Comp. Weiss, *Lehrbegriff*, p. 102.

Note.—This turning of the water into wine must be regarded as an *actual miracle:* for John as an eye-witness (see on i. 41, 42), in the most simple and definite manner (comp. iv. 46), represents it as such, and as the first manifestation of the divine glory dwelling in Christ in the direction of miraculous working (not as portraying beforehand the heavenly marriage supper, Rev. xix. 8, Matt. xxvi. 29, as Hofmann, *Schriftbeweis*, II. 2, p. 407, and Baumgarten, p. 99, take it). Every exposition which explains away the miraculous element contradicts the words and the purpose of St. John, infringes on his credibility and capacity for simple observation, and places even the character of Jesus in an ambiguous light. The *physical inconceivability*, which nevertheless is not identical with absolute impossibility (against Scholten, p. 215), pertains to this work in common only with every miracle ;[2] and hence the appeal made to a supposed *accelerated process of nature* (Olshausen, comp. already Augustine and Chrysostom), which must have been at the same time an artificial process, is only a superfluous crutch on which the representation is made to lean, inapplicable to the other miracles, and as arbitrary as it is (in the ab-

---

[1] Bernhardy, p. 319 ; Stallbaum, *ad Plat. Gorg.* p. 510 D.

[2] It does not become more conceivable by Lange's fiction (*L. J.* II. p. 479), which is quite unsupported by the text, viz. that the company were elevated to a higher tone of feeling, as the disciples were at a later time upon the mount of transfiguration, and that Christ, from the full spring of His highest life-power, made them drink creatively "in the element of this higher feeling."

sence of a vine) inadequate. Its *inconceivableness* in a *telic* point of view John
himself removes in ver. 11 ; and remembering its design as there stated, the
miracle was not an act of luxury (de Wette), but of abounding human kindness in
blessing (see on ver. 6). To suppose another design, viz. that Jesus wished to
show how opposed He was to the strict asceticism of the Baptist (Flatt, Olshausen), is pure and arbitrary invention, in opposition to ver. 11. The fact
that the *Synoptics* have not the narrative amounts to nothing, because John
selected and wrote independently of the synoptical series of narrations ; and
as they have not the first, so neither have they the last and greatest miracle.
We must, after all, abide by the simple statement that there was *a change of
substance* (ver. 9), effected by the power of Jesus over the sphere of nature, in
conformity with a higher law of causation. Granting this power, which the
whole range of the Gospel miracles demands, there is no ground whatever for
resting (against ver. 9) in the assumption of a mere *change of attributes* in the
water, whereby (after the analogy of mineral waters) it may have received the
colour and taste of wine (Neander). It is levity equally objectionable, and a
wronging of a writer so serious as John, to explain what occurred as a *wedding
joke*, as Paulus (Jesus had a quantity of wine brought into the house, and had
it mixed with water out of the pitchers and put upon the tables, ver. 4 having
been spoken jestingly) and Gfrörer (Mary brought the wine with her as a wedding present, and during the feast, at the right moment, she gave her son a
sign to bring out and distribute the gift) unite in doing. Thus, instead of the
transmutation of the water, we have a frivolous transmutation of the history.[1]
Lastly, the *mythical* explanation contradicts the trustworthiness and genuineness of the Gospel. According to it, *fact* is resolved into *legend*—a legend derived from the analogies of the histories of Moses (Ex. xv. 23 sqq.) and Elisha
(2 Kings ii. 19), as Strauss will have it, or from a misunderstood parable, as
Weisse thinks ; while de Wette—without, however, adopting the mythical
view, but not fully recognizing the historic character of the narrative—regards
the dispensing of the wine as a counterpart to the dispensing of the bread,
and both as answering to the bread and wine in the Lord's Supper ; an explanation all the more inept, as there is not the least hint of it in the narrative, and as the Lord's Supper is not even mentioned in John. Schweizer
and Weisse reckon the paragraph among the interpolations which have been
added to the genuine Johannean nucleus,—an arbitrary assertion ; while Baur,
whose criticism rejects the whole Gospel, transforms the narrative into an allegory, wherein water is the symbol of the Baptist, wine of the Messiah's dignity (*i.e.* the bridegroom's), and the transformation typifies the transition
from the preparatory stage of the Baptist to the epoch of Messianic activity
and glory (comp. Baumgarten Crusius, p. 82) ; and Hilgenfeld (*Evang.* p.
248) looks upon the turning of the water into wine as a counterpart to the
synoptical narrative of the temptation, and illustrating the elevation of Jesus
above all narrow asceticism. Thus, too, some of the Fathers (Cyril, Augustine, and many others) allegorize the miracle, without, however, surrendering
its objective and historical character as a fact ; whereas Ewald, while re-

[1] Ammon also, *L. J.* I., falls back upon an erroneous idea and representation on the part of John: "What took place in the intervening time, when the water pitchers were empty, and soon after were filled to the brim, is unknown to us." The miracle is thus reduced into a natural event behind the scenes. Schenkel simply enough removes every miraculous element from the history, as being legendary adornments.

nouncing any investigation into the historic probability of the narrative, regards it as the gilding of the idea of the beneficent power of the Messianic
spirit, whereby even now water should everywhere become wine. Luthardt
holds, indeed, the objective historical reality, but regards the manifestation of
the δόξα to have been *in contrast with that given in the O. T.*,—the gift of God
occupying the place of the command, and the higher life, which Jesus the
bridegroom makes known in this miracle, the place of outward purification.
Similarly Scholten, p. 164. But while the representation of Christ as bridegroom is quite remote from the narrative, John gives no support or sanction to
the idea that the miracle was symbolical, either in the remark of ver. 6 (κατὰ τ.
καθαρ. τ. 'Ιουδ.) or in that of ver. 11 (ἐφανέρ. τ. δόξ. αὐτοῦ). — The miracle at Cana
is, finally, the only one to which the Synoptics have *no* one that corresponds.
But all the less are the miracles in John to be used in support of the assertion
that, in John, Christ, after the manner of the Gnostics, announces another
and higher God than the God of the O. T.[1] According to Keim, the marriage
in Cana, the first great beaming forth of the divine glory, stands in John as
" a loving portrait" of Christ, and designedly in place of the painful temptation in the wilderness. But this glory beamed forth still more grandly, and
more significantly in its bearing upon the Saviour's whole ministry, in his
threefold triumph over Satan.

Ver. 12. Μετὰ τοῦτο κατέβη, κ.τ.λ.] Direct from Cana? or from
Nazareth (i. 46), whither Mary, Jesus, and the disciples had returned? The
latter must be assumed as the correct view, because the *brothers* of Jesus
(His brothers *literally*, not His *cousins*, as Hengstenberg again maintains:
see vii. 3, 5, and on Matt. i. 25, xii. 46, 1 Cor. ix. 5) had not been with
Him at the wedding. It is quite arbitrary to suggest that they were accidentally omitted to be mentioned in ver. 2 (Baumgarten Crusius, following
earlier commentators). — κατέβη] *down*, for Καφαρναούμ (to be written
thus, with Lachmann and Tischendorf, in John likewise) lay on the shore
of the *lake of Tiberias.* — αὐτὸς κ. ἡ μήτηρ, κ.τ.λ.] A common ἐπανόρθω-
σις (correction).[2] John does not tell us *why* they went down to Capernaum[3]
(Matt. iv. 13 is in a totally different connection). The *settlement* of the
family at Capernaum is left uncertain by John ; the fact had but little interest for the Judaistic standing-point of his history, and is neither *recorded* here,
as Ewald maintains (the κ. ἐκεῖ ἔμειναν οὐ πολλ. ἡμ. which follows is against
this), nor even *presupposed* (Wieseler, de Wette, Tholuck), for the mention of
the brothers who were not with Him at the marriage forbids this. Nor is
the settlement attested either by iv. 3, 43, or by vi. 17, 59. — οὐ πολλὰς
ἡμέρας] because the Passover was at hand, ver. 13, which Jesus (and the
disciples, iii. 22) attended ; not, therefore, on account of misconstruction
and hostility (Ewald).

---

[1] Hilgenfeld, *Lehrbegr.* 281.

[2] See Fritzsche, *Conject.* p. 25; *ad Matt.*
p. 420 ; *ad Marc.* p. 70 ; Stallbaum, *ad Plat.*
Crit. p. 50 E.

[3] Hengstenberg supposes that John mentions this only from a feeling of personal
interest ; that he himself had belonged to
Capernaum, and Jesus had stayed at his
father's house. An utterly groundless
conjecture, made for the sake of harmonizing (i. 45 ; comp. Luke iv. 38, Mark i. 29),
which would require us to regard Bethsaida
as a suburb of Capernaum ; see, on the
contrary, Matt. xi. 21, 23.

Vv. 13–16. Καί] Simply the continuative *and*, *i.e.* during this short stay at Capernaum. — For vv. 14–16, see on Matt. xxi. 12, 13. — πάντας] refer not to the *persons*, but to the *animals* named immediately afterwards with the τὲ—καί, *i.e. not only*, *but also*.[1] Thus the unseemliness which some have found in the *use* of the scourge,—certainly intimated by the connection of ποιήσας and ἐξέβαλεν,—and along with it every *typical* explanation of the scourge (Grotius, Godet, and others regard it as the symbol of God's wrath), disappear. [See Note XVI. p. 118.] —᾿Εξέχεε] uncontracted form, to be taken as *aor.*[2] — τὸ κέρμα] *coin*, especially small coin. Mostly in the plural in Greek. The singular here is *collective.* — καὶ τοῖς τὰς περισε-ράς, κ.τ.λ.] He *could* not of course *drive out* the doves like the other animals, and He therefore says to those who sold them, ἄρατε ταῦτα ἐντεῦθεν. John is here more *minute* than the Synoptics ; but we must not regard the words as indicating greater *mildness* towards the sellers of the doves, because these were used by the *poor* (Rupertius, de Wette). The command μὴ ποιεῖτε, κ.τ.λ., addressed to *them* applied to *all.* — τοῦ πατρός μου] *Admiranda auctoritas*, Bengel ; the full *consciousness of the Son* manifested itself already (as in Luke ii. 49) in the temple. — οἶκ. ἐμπορίου] *a house of*, a place of, *merchandise.* The holy temple *house* had, in the Lord's view, become this, while the temple *court* had been made a place of buying and marketing.[3] Possibly Zech. xiv. 21 was in His thoughts.

Ver. 17. ᾿Εμνήσθησαν] At the very time of the occurrence, and not (as Olshausen) after the resurrection, which, as in ver. 22 (comp. xii. 16), would have had to be *stated.* — The text quoted is Ps. lxix. 10 ; the theocratic sufferer in this psalm, a psalm written during the exile, is a *type of the Messiah ;* see xv. 25, xix. 28 ff. Comp. Rom. xv. 3, xi. 9 ; Acts i. 20. — καταφάγεταί με] *will devour or consume me*, is to be understood of a power which wears one out *internally*, Ps. cxix. 139, not to be referred to the *death* of Jesus,[4] for the disciples could at that time have thought of anything but His death ; comp. ver. 22. In this wrathful zeal, which they saw had taken hold of Jesus, they thought they saw the Messianic fulfilment of that word in the psalm, wherein the speaker declares his great zeal for God's house, which was yet to wear him out. The fulfilment relates to the ὁ ζῆλος τοῦ οἴκου σου, of which the καταφάγεται indicates only the violence and permanence ; and there is therefore no ground for imagining already any gloomy forebodings on the part of the disciples (Lange).[5] As to the *future* φάγομαι, which belongs to the LXX. and Apocrypha, see Lobeck, *ad Phryn.* p. 327 ; like the classical ἔδομαι, it never stands as present (against Tholuck, Hengstenberg, Godet, and others).

Note.—[See Note XV. p. 117.] If there was but *one* cleansing of the temple, then either John or the Synoptics have given an erroneous narrative. But if it hap-

---

[1] See Baeuml. *in loc.*, and *Partik.* 225.

[2] Lobeck, *ad Phryn.* p. 222.

[3] ᾿Εμπόριον, Thuc. i. 13. 3 ; Dem. 957, 27 ; Xen. *de red.* iii. 3 ; Herodian. viii. 2. 6 ; Ezek. xxvii. 3 ; Isa. xxiii. 17, not the same as ἐμπορία.

[4] Bengel, Olshausen, Hofmann, *Weissag. u. Erf.* p. 111 ; Luthardt, comp. Brückner.

[5] For ἐσθίειν and ἔδειν, used of consuming emotions (as in Aristophanes, *Vesp.* 287), see Jacobs, *ad Anthol.* VI. 280 ; *Del. epigr.* p. 257.

pened *twice*,[1] first at the beginning, and then at the end of the Messianic ministry of Jesus,—a supposition which in itself corresponds too well to the significance of the act (in so far as its repetition was occasioned by the state of disorder remaining unchanged after so long an interval had elapsed) to be inconceivable (as has been asserted by some), or even merely to pass the limits of probability,—it is then, on the one hand, conceivable that the Synoptics do not contain the first cleansing, because Christ's early labours in Jerusalem do not belong to the range of events which they generally narrate ; and, on the other hand, that John passes over the second cleansing, because he had already recorded the Messianic σημεῖον of the same kind. We are not therefore to suppose that the one account is true, and the other false, but to assume that the act was *repeated*. See on Matt. xxi. 12, 13. So the Fathers and most subsequent writers ; also Schleiermacher, Tholuck, Olshausen, B. Crusius, Maier, Ebrard, Luthardt, Riggenbach, Lange, Baumgarten, Hengstenberg, Godet, etc. *Others*, on the contrary, *admitting* only one temple-cleansing, decide in favour, some of the synoptical account,[2] and some of John's.[3] The latter would be the correct view, because John was an eye-witness ; although we are not to suppose, as Baur, in accordance with his view of the fourth Gospel, thinks that John derived the facts from the Synoptics, but fixed the time of the transaction independently, in consistency with his idea of the reformatory procedure. See also Hilgenfeld, who traces here the "peculiarity of John," who, with reference at least to the knowledge of the disciples and the relations of Jesus to the Jews, begins where the Synoptics leave off ; and thus his narrative is merely a peculiar development of synoptical materials. Finally, upon the supposition of two distinct cleansings of the temple, any essential difference between the two acts themselves is not to be discovered. Luthardt, indeed, following Hofmann (comp. Lichtenstein, p. 156), thinks that, in the synoptical account, Jesus as prophet protects the place of *divine worship*, but that in John's He as Son exercises His *authority over the house ;* but the ὁ οἶκός μου of the Synoptics, as the declaration of God, exactly corresponds with τὸν οἶκον τοῦ πατρός μου in John as the word of Christ. The distinction, moreover, that the first cleansing was the announcement of *reformation*, and the second of *judgment* (Hengst.), cannot be made good, separates what is clearly connected, and attaches too much importance to collateral minutiae. This remark in answer to Godet, who regards the first cleansing as "*un appel*," the second as "*une protestation*." The essential element of difference in John's account lies in the very striking declaration of Jesus about the temple of His body, ver. 19, of which the Synoptics have not a word, and which possesses great prophetic significance as uttered at the outset of His Messianic ministry, but has no special fitness at the end of it. Jesus accordingly did not utter it again at the second cleansing, but only at the first, though upon that second cleansing also, occasion was given for so doing (Matt. xxi. 23). It is this very declaration, however, which marks unmistakably from the beginning the *Messianic* character of the appearance of Jesus in Jerusalem (against Weizsäcker, *Evang. Gesch.* p. 260). Chap. vii. 3 is not the first place which has to do with the Messianic appearance.

---

[1] "Whether it took place before or after, once or twice, it takes nothing from our faith."—LUTHER.

[2] Strauss, Weisse, Baur, Hilgenfeld, Scholten, Schenkel. Comp. also Luther : "It seems to me that John here *skips over* the three first years."

[3] Lücke, de Wette, Ammon, Krabbe, Brückner, Ewald, Weizsäcker, and many others ; Baeumlein hesitatingly.

Vv. 18, 19. The same question as in Matt. xxi. 23, but how totally different an *answer!* It cannot therefore be used to confirm the supposed *identity* of the two events. — ἀπεκρίθ.] As in Matt. xi. 25 (which see), and often, denoting what is said *upon occasion of* Christ's act, and *with reference thereto.* — τί σημεῖον] If what He had done was to be recognized as appropriate to Him, it must be based upon a really *prophetic* ἐξουσία, and consequently upon divine authorization ; in proof of this, they desired a special *miraculous sign or act, accrediting Him as a divine messenger,* and which was to be wrought by Him before their eyes, אוֹת, σημεῖον τῆς αὐθεντίας, Euthymius Zigabenus ; comp. vi. 30. — δεικνύεις] *dost thou bring before us,* lettest us see.[1] — ὅτι] εἰς ἐκεῖνο, ὅτι, ix. 17, xi. 51, xvi. 9 ; Mark xvi. 14 ; 2 Cor. i. 18, xi. 10.[2] Consequently in the sense of *quatenus.*[3] — ποιεῖς] The *present* denotes the act just performed, but which is still *regarded as present.* —Ver. 19. λύσατε τὸν ναὸν τοῦτον, κ.τ.λ.] refers, according to the apostle's explanation in ver. 21, to the *death and resurrection of Jesus,* so that he consequently means His body as the dwelling-place of God, who was *in* Christ (x. 38, xiv. 10, 11, 20, xvii. 21, i. 14), *i.e.* as the antitype of the temple,[4] and, in conformity with this, His violent death as *the pulling down,* and His resurrection as the *rebuilding* of it. We must therefore, according to John, suppose that Jesus, with the temple structure before Him, to which He points (*this temple here*), sees in it the sacred type of His body, and with the directness of ancient prophecy (as often, *e.g.*, in Isaiah), substitutes the image for the object represented, so that these sharp, vivid strokes, dashed down without explanation, contain, as in a pictorial riddle, a symbolico-prophetic announcement of His resurrection,[5] as in Matt. xii. 39, xvi. 4, and in harmony with what we are to assume throughout, that He never in express terms foretold His resurrection, but only obscurely and by figure. The thought accordingly, divested of this figurative envelope, is, according to John, no other than this : *kill me, and within three days*[6] *I will rise again.* The *imperative* in the protasis is not *permissive* merely, which weakens the emotion, but *contains a challenge ;* it springs from painfully ex-

---

[1] Comp. Hom. *Il. v.* 244 : Κρονίων—δεικνὺς σῆμα Βροτοῖσιν. *Od.* γ. 174.

[2] See Fritzsche *ad Matt.* p. 248.

[3] See Ast, *Lex. Plat.* II. 485.

[4] Considering the oft-recurring representation of the indwelling of God in Christ, it is very far-fetched to derive the temple comparison here from the Valentinian Christology concerning a higher body of the Messiah appropriate for union with the Logos (in answer to Hilgenfeld, *Lehrbegr.* 247). Seeing, further, that Christ (ver. 16) calls the literal temple "*His Father's* house," how can the *Demiurge* be conceived of as the God of the Jews ? How can we reconcile with that expression even " a milder Gnosticism" (Hilgenfeld, in the *Theol. Jahrb.* 1857, p. 516)? Simply to admit that " a weak reference to the supreme God was not wanting even in Judaism," is both incorrect in itself, and altogether unsuited to solve the palpable contradiction.

[5] It is assumed (with Bengel) still in my 4th edition, that Jesus indicated the reference to his body " *nutu gestuve,*" but that the Jews did not notice it. This is inadmissible, because thus the τοῦτον would have no reference whatever to the temple of stone, whereas the entire scene in the temple court shows that this reference is contained in it. Besides, such a gesture would be inappropriate to the use of an *enigmatical* word, for it would at once give the key to its solution. The intellectual *point* would be quite lost.

[6] Ἐν, see Bernhardy, p. 209 ; Winer, p. 361 [E. T. p. 385].

cited feeling, as He looks with heart-searching gaze upon that implacable opposition which already shows itself, and will be satisfied only with His death. Comp. πληρώατσε, Matt. xxiii. 32. *John's* explanation is adopted by the ancients, and among modern expositors by Kuinoel, Tholuck, Hilde-brand,[1] Kling,[2] Krabbe, Klee, Olshausen (at least as to their *inner* meaning, while the words, he thinks, were *apparently* simply a repelling paradox), Maier, Hasert,[3] Hauff,[4] Brückner (against de Wette), Laurillard,[5] Baum-garten, Maier, Baeumlein, Godet, also Luthardt (though introducing a double meaning ; by putting Jesus to death, Israel destroyed itself as the house of God, while the resurrection was the setting up of God's spiritual house ;[6] similarly Baur, p. 137 ff., who, however (and with him Hilgenfeld), traces the expression to synoptic elements much later in point of time. But John's explanation is abandoned, since the time of Herder (*vom Sohne Gottes*) and Henke,[7] by Eckermann, Paulus, Lücke, Schweizer, Bleek, B. Crusius, Ammon, Strauss, Gfrörer, de Wette, Ewald, Weizsäcker, Schenkel, Scholten, and many others, who, with various modifications, explain the pulling down of the temple of the *decay of the old temple religion*, and the setting up in three days of *the new spiritual theocracy* so soon to be established ; thus the imperative is taken by some as a challenge (as above) (Herder, Henke, Ewald), by some again as a concession (Schen-kel), and by some as an hypothesis (Lücke, B. Crusius, de Wette : " Granted that ye destroy")—according to de Wette, with allusion perhaps to the late partial demolition of the temple by Herod. But (1) before we can assume that John of all men, who elsewhere was so deeply im-bued with the mind of Jesus, wholly misunderstood Him, and that too at the time when he wrote his Gospel, when the old degenerate religion had been long since overthrown, and the new spiritual sanctuary long since set up,—we must have the most decisive evidence of such a misunderstanding. Otherwise, we are to seek the *true* interpretation of any saying of Jesus from *him*, and especially *in this case*, where he distinctly *opposes* his own explanation to the misconception of the Jews, and gives it not only as *his own*, but also as that of *the rest of the disciples*. (2) The accusation in Matt. xxvi. 61, Mark xiv. 58 (comp. Acts vi. 13) is no argument in favour of the modern in-terpretation, for it is based only upon the Jewish misunderstanding of the saying. (3) The place and occasion alike suggested the temple as an *illus-tration*, but they determined nothing as to the *subject-matter* of the compari-son ; a *sign* in general was asked for, not one *bearing specially upon the temple*. (4) The setting up of the spiritual temple was an event not at all dependent upon a *previous destroying* of the old economy ; on the contrary, a be-ginning had already been made, the further development of which was not the effect but the cause (the fermenting element) of the dissolution of the

---

[1] In Hüffell's *Zeitschr.* II. 1.

[2] In *d. Stud. u. Krit.* 1836, p. 127.

[3] *Ueb. d. Vorhersagungen Jesu von seinem Tode*, Berlin 1839, p. 81.

[4] *Stud. u. Krit.* 1849, p. 106 ff.

[5] *De locis ev. Joh. in quibus ipse auctor* verba *J. interpretat. est*, Lugd. B. 1853, p. 1 ff.

[6] Comp. Ebrard, Lange, Riggenbach, Hengstenberg.

[7] *Programm* 1798, in Pott, *Sylloge*, I. p. 8 ff.

old theocracy : hence the relation of the protasis to the apodosis of the
sentence would be neither logically nor historically correct. (5) This spiritual building up was so far from being a momentary act, and was to so
great a degree a gradual development, that neither the conception of a
sign in general, nor the words *in three days*, which belong essentially
to this conception, have any corresponding relation thereto ; the latter
expression, even if taken in a proverbial sense, [1] could only mean "*in a
few days*," and therefore would be quite unsuited to the comparison, and
would even have the appearance of grandiloquence. Moreover, as the
three days joined to the ἐγερῶ (*raising up*) were the *fixed* correlative of Christ's
resurrection, this should itself exclude the modern explanation. (6) A
new temple would of necessity have been spoken of as *another* (comp.
Mark xiv. 58), but ἐγερῶ αὐτόν can only mean the *same ;* and thus the Jews
as well as John rightly understood it, for Jesus did not say ἐγερῶ ἄλλον or
ἕτερον, or the like. [2] (7) It is only a seeming objection to John's explanation, that according to N. T. theology Christ did not raise Himself from the
dead, but was raised by the Father. [3] Any such contradiction to the Christian mode of view, if real, must have prevented John himself above every
one from referring the words to the resurrection. But the objection disappears if we simply give due weight to the figurative nature of the expression, which rests upon that visible contemplation of the *resurrection*,
according to which the *Subject* that arises, whose resurrection is described as
the re-erecting of the destroyed temple, must also be the Subject that erects
the temple,—without affecting the further doctrine, which, moreover, does
not come under consideration, that the *causa efficiens, i.e.* the actual revivify-
ing power, is the Father. Christ receiving His life again from the Father
(x. 17) and rising again, Himself raises up by His very resurrection the
destroyed temple. [4] — For ἐγείρειν of erecting buildings, see Ecclus.
xlix. 11 ; 3 Esdras v. 44, viii. 81 ; Ael. *V. H.* 12, 23 ; Herodianus, 3, 15,
6 ; Jacobs, *ad Anthol.* XII. p. 75.

Note.—It cannot perplex us in John's explanation, that the answer which
Jesus gave was rightly understood at the time neither by the Jews nor by the
disciples. It was the manner of Jesus, as especially appears in John, to throw
out seeds of thought for the *future* which could not take root *at the time.* Comp.
Chrysostom : πολλὰ τοιαῦτα φθέγγεται τοῖς μὲν τότε ἀκούουσιν οὐκ ὄντα δῆλα, τοῖς
δὲ μετὰ ταῦτα ἐσόμενα. Τίνος δὲ ἕνεκεν τοῦτο ποιεῖ ; ἵνα δειχθῇ προειδὼς ἄνωθεν τὰ
μετὰ ταῦτα, ὅταν ἐξέλθῃ καὶ τῆς προρρήσεως τὸ τέλος ὃ δὴ καὶ ἐπὶ τῆς προφητείας ταύτης
γέγονεν. And that in its very first appearance He foresaw the development of
the opposition of this seemingly guileless party, onward to its goal in the de-

---

[1] Hos. vi. 2, not Luke xiii. 32; but see
Dissen *ad Dem. de cor.* p. 362.

[2] Appeal is wrongly made to Matt. x. 39,
where ψυχήν denotes *earthly* life merely,
and then αὐτήν life *eternal.* ψυχήν as well
as αὐτήν there means nothing but the *soul ;*
and the enigma of the expression lies not
in a different sense being applied to these
two words, but in a different temporal rela-

tion of εὑρών and ἀπολέσει.

[3] Comp. ver. 22 ; Acts ii. 24, 31 ff., iii. 15,
iv. 10, v. 30, *al. ;* Rom. iv. 24, viii. 11 ; 1 Cor.
vi 14 ; 2 Cor. iv. 14 ; Gal. i. 1 ; Eph. i. 21 ;
Col. ii. 12 ; 1 Thess. i. 10 ; 1 Pet. i. 21.

[4] See, moreover, Brückner, p. 57, and
Godet. Comp. Ignat. *Smyrn.* 2 : ἀληθῶς
ἀνέστησεν ἑαυτόν.

struction of the temple of His body, can be regarded as an unhistorical presupposition of the Logos doctrine only by one who, on the one hand, can by critical doubts [1] get rid of the early references of Jesus to His death which are contained in the Synoptics (*e.g.* Matt. x. 38, xii. 39, x. 23), and, on the other hand, does not sufficiently estimate Christ's higher knowledge, as shown in John, and especially that acquaintance with the heart by virtue of which He apprehends the full intent (vi. 64) of this in itself justifiable requirement of a sign.

Ver. 20. An intended *deductio ad absurdum*. Τεσσαράκ. κ. ἐξ ἔτεσιν] length of time named without ἐν.[2] The great *number* of years stands emphatically first. — ᾠκοδομήθη] *i.e.* so far as it was already complete. The proposed enlargement and renewal of the temple of Zerubbabel was begun in the 18th year of Herod the Great's reign,[3] and was first completed, according to Josephus,[4] under Herod Agrippa II., A.D. 64. How the 46 years named here prove that the passover then being held was that of the year 782 (A.D. 29), corresponding with the year of the Baptist's appearance according to Luke iii. 1 (August 781–2), see on Acts, Introd. § 4. Wieseler, p. 166, reckoning onwards from Nisan 735, places the end of the 46th year exactly in Nisan 781.[5]

Vv. 21, 22. Τοῦ σώματος][6] Genitive of apposition ; see Winer, p. 494 [E. T. p. 531]. — Ver. 22. οὖν] represents the recollection as answering to the true meaning of that declaration. — ἐμνήσθησαν] *they became mindful of*, ver. 17, xii. 16. The saying came afresh to their remembrance when it was explained as a fact by the resurrection ; previously, because not understood, it had been forgotten. With ἠγέρθη comp. ἐγερῶ, ver. 19. — καὶ ἐπίστευσαν, κ.τ.λ.] As the result of this recollection, *they believed the Scripture* (felt convinced of the truth of its statements),—observing the harmony of its prophecies concerning the resurrection of Jesus [7] with that saying of Christ's,—*and the word which Jesus had* (then, ver. 19) *spoken*, which now, as fulfilled in the resurrection, presented itself to them in its full prophetic truth. Upon πιστεύειν τινί in St. John, comp. Weiss, *Lehrbegr.* p. 20. — Schweizer (whom Scholten follows) regards vv. 21, 22 as spurious, quite groundlessly. The statement is the exact outcome of St. John's inmost personal experience.

[1] Comp. Keim, *Geschichtl. Christus*, pp. 35, 36, ed. 3.

[2] Bernhardy, p. 81 ; Winer, p. 205 [E. T. p. 218].

[3] Autumn of 734-5; see Joseph. *Antt.* xv. 11. 1.

[4] *Antt.* xx. 9. 7.

[5] Ewald reckons from B.C. 20 to A.D. 28, and, counting only the *full* intervening years, he gets the 46, thus omitting B.C. 20, the year in which the rebuilding began, and A.D. 28, the year of the passover named in our text.—For the rest, it must be remembered (in opposition to Keim's doubts in his *Gesch. J.* I. p. 615) that the statement in the text does not necessarily oblige us to suppose an οἰκοδομεῖσθαι *without any*

interruptions. The building had been going on now for 46 years. Comp. also Wieseler in Herzog's *Encykl.* XXI. 546.

[6] John explains the saying so *simply* and definitely, that there is no room for the double meaning which Luthardt, Hengstenberg, and others import into it. With equal simplicity and definiteness does he represent the meaning given as that of *Jesus Himself* (against Weizsäcker, p. 266). In like manner vii. 38, xii. 32, xxi. 19. In none of these passages is any distinction drawn between the explanation and the meaning intended by Jesus Himself.

[7] Ps. xvi. 10 ; Isa. liii. ; cf. Luke xxiv. 26 ; Acts xiii. 33 ff. ; 1 Cor. xv. 4 ; Matt. xii. 40.

Ver. 23. Δ έ] introducing a characteristic summary statement (to ver. 25) regarding this stay of Jesus at the feast, in order next to give prominence to a special scene, the story of Nicodemus in iii. 1 ff. — ἐ ν. τ. Ἱ ε ρ ο σ. ἐ ν τ. π ά σ χ α ἐ ν τ ῇ ἑ ο ρ τ ῇ] The latter clause is not added as an *explanation* for Greek readers (that should have been done at ver. 13), but " He was *at Jerusalem during the passover in the feast* (engaged in celebrating the feast) ;" thus the first ἐν is local, the second temporal, and the third joins on with ἦν, and expresses the surroundings, that in which a person is engaged (*versari in aliqua re*).[1] — θ ε ω ρ ο ῦ ν τ ε ς, κ.τ.λ.] *while they beheld His miracles,* etc.[2] Euthymius Zigabenus rightly says : ἐκεῖνοι γὰρ ἀκριβέστερον ἐπίστευον, ὅσοι μὴ διὰ τὰ σημεῖα μόνον, ἀλλὰ καὶ διὰ τὴν διδασκαλίαν αὐτοῦ ἐπίστευον. Their faith in His name (as that of the Messiah) did not yet amount to any decision of their inner life for Jesus, but was only an opinion, produced by the sight of His miracles, that He was the Messiah ; comp. viii. 30, vi. 26. Luther calls it " *milk faith.*" Comp. Matt. xiii. 20. On τ ὰ σ η μ ε ῖ α, comp. iii. 2. None of the miracles of this period has been recorded ; xx. 30, comp. iv. 45. Consequently, not only the Synoptics, but John also speaks summarily of *multitudes* of miracles, without relating any of them individually (against Schleiermacher, *L. J.* p. 201).

Vv. 24, 25. Α ὐ τ ὸ ς δ ὲ, κ.τ.λ.] *But He on His part,* though they on their part, on account of His miracles, believed on Him. — ο ὐ κ ἐ π ί σ τ. ἑ α υ τ ό ν] an intentional antithesis to the preceding ἐπίστ. εἰς τὸ ὄνομα αὐτοῦ. Observe the emphatic ἑαυτόν : it must not be taken as meaning " He kept back *His doctrine* from them" (Chrysostom, Kuinoel, and many), or " *His work*" (Ebrard) ; but He did not trust *Himself, i.e. His own person,* to them ; He refrained from any closer personal intercourse with them. Without any such reserve, rather with confident self-surrender, had He given Himself to His intimate Galilean friends. Towards the Jews in Jerusalem, on whom, from His knowledge of the human heart, He could not bestow this self-devotion, because they lacked the inward moral conditions necessary thereto, His bearing was more strange and distant. Observe the *imperfects* ἐπίστευεν and ἐγίνωσκε. — δ ι ὰ τ ὸ α ὐ τ ὸ ν γ ι ν ώ σ κ. π ά ν τ.] *because He Himself* (as in the following αὐτός) *knew all men,* universal. Respecting *none* did His personal knowledge fail Him with regard to the state of his moral feeling. — κ α ὶ ὅ τ ι, κ.τ.λ.] negative expression of the same thought in the popular form of a still *further* reason. — ἵ ν α] not instead of the infinitive construction (Matt. iii. 14 *al.*), but the object of the need is conceived of in the form of a *purpose* which the person needing guidance entertains. Comp. xvi. 30 ; 1 John ii. 27. —π ε ρ ὶ τ ο ῦ ἀ ν θ ρ.] does not apply to Jesus Himself ("concerning Him as man," Ewald), but concerning any man with whom He had at any time to do.[3] —α ὐ τ ό ς] *of Himself, i.e.* αὐτοδίδακτος, Nonnus.[4] — τ ί ἦ ν ἐ ν τ ῷ ἀ ν θ ρ.] the inward, though not outwardly indicated

---

[1] See, concerning εἶναι ἐν here, Bernhardy, p. 210 ; Ast, *Lex. Plat.* I. 623.

[2] On αὐτοῦ, comp. *Lycurg.* 28 : ταῦτα ἐμοῦ ἐθεωρήσατε, and Kühner, § 528, *ad Xen. Mem.* i. 1. 11.

[3] See Bernhardy, p. 315 ; Winer, p. 109 [E. T. p. 115].

[4] See Herm. *ad Viger.* p. 733 ; Krüger, *Anab.* ii. 3. 7 ; comp. *Clementine Homil.* iii. 13 : ἀπείρῳ ψυχῆς ὀφθαλμῷ.

capacity, character, disposition, and so on ; τὸ κρυπτὸν τοῦ νοῦς, Origen. Comp. Nonnus : ὅσα φρενὸς ἔνδοθεν ἀνὴρ εἶχεν ἀκηρύκτῳ κεκαλυμμένα φάρεϊ σιγῆς. To this supernatural and *immediate discernment*, as possessed by Jesus, special prominence is often given by John.[1] Like His working of miracles, it is the life expression of His *divine* essence.[2]

NOTES BY AMERICAN EDITOR.

XIV. " *They have no wine.*" Ver. 3.

Weiss follows Meyer in the opinion that the mother's declaration to her Son, "they have no wine" did not contemplate a miracle, but only some general, indefinite mode of meeting the want, such as possibly His varied resources might devise. But the more generally received explanation of the words seems far more probable, which finds in them an intimation to her Son that He should take the present occasion for at once supplying a want and exhibiting His miraculous powers. The long residence of Jesus in the bosom of His family had indeed produced no such miraculous displays as she had once perhaps eagerly anticipated. But the circumstances have now materially changed. He has left his home for that wonderful baptism, with its divine attestations, of which Mary cannot have been ignorant, and she cannot fail to have followed His course up to the present festival, in which He appears surrounded by a train of disciples all glowing with the ardor of the discovery of the long-looked-for Messiah, and with the enthusiastic recognition of the "Son of God and the King of Israel." All this cannot fail to have been poured by these glad disciples into the ears of the eager mother. Familiar now as was early Jewish history with miracles, and numerous and striking as were those that had clustered around the infancy of Jesus, it would seem that Mary could scarcely avoid looking for some corresponding miracles to signalize His entrance on that public career which was apparently opening.—And that her language to her Son now indicates her desire for the performance of a miracle would seem almost certain from His reply. Meyer and Weiss hold that His reply repels the idea of maternal interference with His non-Messianic functions ; but it is precisely *such* interference that His reply does not indicate. It could scarcely be an infringement of their relations that she should appeal to Him for some natural and merely human aid in the emergency, and it is far more conceivable that she should make an unwarranted appeal to His miraculous powers than that He should rebuke, ever so gently, an interposition which she had not attempted. That a half-unconscious maternal pride in her Son, and a desire before these many guests to have a display of His extraordinary powers, is not indeed intimated, but may be deemed probable.

XV. *The cleansing of the Temple.* Vv. 13–22.

Weiss in his edition of Meyer takes ground against Meyer (as well as against a large portion of the Fathers and later commentators), denying the repetition (as recorded Mark xi. 15–18) of the miraculous cleansing of the Temple. Re-

---

[1] Comp. i. 49, 50, iv. 19, 29, vi. 61, 64, xi. 4, 15, xiii. 11, xvi. 19, xxi. 17.   [2] Ps. vii. 10, cxxxix. 2 ; Acts xv. 8.

jecting one of the accounts, and assuming that that of Mark sprung from the Synoptic Gospels˄ knowing but one visit of Jesus to the Passover, he gives the preference to the record of John, and regards it as far more probable that Jesus signalized His opening ministry by this symbolic act of purification. It was thus and then, he holds, altogether appropriate; while, on the contrary, at His last visit, when His contest with the Jewish hierarchy was reaching its climax, and He had already abandoned the nation, and foretold the destruction both of the city and the Temple, it seems but an objectless and almost wanton act of provocation to His enemies.   To many, however, the matter would appear quite otherwise.   While they recognize the fittingness of the cleansing to the opening of Christ's ministry, it would seem to them equally appropriate to His final, but first strictly Messianic and kingly entrance into Jerusalem, that He should unite with His first *formal* appearance as Messianic King another symbolical assertion of the purity of His kingdom.   The miracle seems equally fitting to the opening and the close of His career.

XVI. " *Making a scourge.*"   Ver. 15.

The scourge, I cannot but think, was made by Jesus, and held in His hands, simply as a *symbol* of force.   That He actually *used* it, either on the men or the animals, we may not indeed positively deny, but can just as little positively affirm.   With neither could the use of it be *necessary*, and there is in it a certain unseemliness, something which detracts from the dignity of the Lord, and that equally in the case of the irrational and of the rational offender.   Alike in the case of the men and the brutes, the Lord's volition must have sufficed.

CHAPTER III.

Ver. 2. Instead of α ὐ τ ό ν, the Elzevir has τὸν Ἰησοῦν, in the face of decisive testimonies. The beginning of a new section and of a church lesson. — Ver. 2. The position of δύναται immediately after γάρ (Lachm. Tisch.) is supported by preponderating testimony. — Ver. 5. For τ. θ ε ο ῦ Tisch. reads τῶν οὐρανῶν, upon ancient but yet inadequate testimony (א* Inst. Hippol. etc.). — Ver. 13, ὁ ὢ ν ἐ ν τ. ο ὐ ρ .] wanting in B. L. Tᵇ. א. 33. Eus. Naz. Origen ; deleted by Tisch. But these mysterious words may easily have been regarded as objectionable or superfluous, because not understood or misunderstood ; and there was nothing to suggest the addition of them. — Ver. 15. μ ὴ ἀ π ό λ η τ α ι, ἀ λ λ ʼ] is deleted by Tisch. after B. L. Tᵇ. א. Min. Verss. Fathers. Rightly so ; it is an addition borrowed from ver. 16. — The readings ἐπ' αὐτόν (Lachm.), ἐπ' αὐτῷ and ἐν αὐτῷ (Tisch.). have indeed less support than the received ε ἰ ς α ὐ τ ό ν, but this latter forced itself in as the most current form of expression, and ἐν αὐτῷ is, following B. Tᵇ. Codd., It., to be preferred. — Ver. 19. The order α ὐ τ ῶ ν π ο ν η ρ ά has preponderating evidence in its favour. — Ver. 25. The Elzevir has Ἰ ο υ δ α ί ω ν, instead of Ἰ ο υ δ α ί ο υ, in the face of decisive testimony. The plural evidently was inserted mechanically. — Ver. 31 f. The second ἐ π ά ν ω π ά ν τ ω ν ἐ σ τ ί has against it very weak testimony, viz. D. א. Min. and some Verss. and Fathers. But the following κ α ί (bracketed by Lachm., deleted by Tisch.) is omitted not only by the same testimonies, but also by B. L. Min. Copt. Pers., and must be regarded as an interpolation, the absence of which originally led more easily to the omission of ἐπάνω π. ἐ. — Ver. 34. ὁ θ ε ό ς after δίδωσιν is wanting in B. C.* L. Tᵇ. א. Min. Ver. Brix. Cyr.; bracketed by Lachm., deleted by Tisch. A supplying of the subject, which seemed uncertain.

Vv. 1, 2. Prominence is now given to a specially important narrative, connected by the continuative δέ and belonging to that first sojourn in Jerusalem,—viz. *the conversation with Nicodemus*, wherein Jesus more fully explains His person and work. No intimation is given of any inner connection with what precedes (Lücke : "now comes an instance of that higher knowledge possessed by Jesus ;" de Wette, Lange, Hengstenberg : "an illustration of the entire statement in ii. 23–25 ;" Tholuck : "an instance of the beginnings of faith just named ;" Luthardt : "from the *people* collectively, to whom Jesus had addressed Himself, a transition is now made to His dealing with an *individual* ;" Ewald : "Nicodemus appears desirous to make an *exception* to the general standing aloof of men of weight in Jerusalem"). — ἀ ν θ ρ ω π ο ς] in its most ordinary use, simply equivalent to τὶς ; not "un exemplaire de ce type humain que Jésus connaissait si bien" (Godet). It is quite independent of ii. 25, introducing a *new* narrative. — Ν ι κ ό δ η μ ο ς , a frequent name as well among the Greeks [1] as among the Jews.[2] We know

---

[1] Demosth. 549. 23, and later writers.

[2] נַקְדֵּם or נַקְרִימוֹן, see Lightfoot and Wetstein.

nothing certain of this man beyond the statements concerning him in St. John (comp. vii. 50, xix. 39).[1] The Nicodemus of the Talmud was also called *Bunai*, must have survived the destruction of Jerusalem, and was known under this latter name as a disciple of Jesus.[2] The identity of the two is possible, but uncertain. The so-called *Evangelium Nicodemi* embraces, though in a doubtful form, two different treatises, viz. the *Acta Pilati* and the *Descensus Christi ad inferos.*[3] — ἄ ρ χ ω ν] He was a member of the Sanhedrim, vii. 50 ; Luke xxiii. 13, xxiv. 20. — He came to Jesus *by night,*[4] being still undecided, in order to avoid the suspicion and hostility of his colleagues. He was not a *hypocrite* (as Koppe in Pott[5] holds), who pretended to be simple in order to elicit from Jesus some ground of accusation ; a circumstance which, if true, John would not have failed to state, especially considering what he says of him in vii. 50 and xix. 39 : he was, on the contrary, though of a somewhat slow temperament, a man of *honourable* character, who, together with others (οἴδαμεν, comp. ὑμᾶς, ver. 7), was in a general way convinced by the miracles of Jesus that He must be a divinely commissioned and divinely supported Teacher, and he therefore sought, by a confidential interview, to determine more exactly his to that extent half-believing judgment, and especially to find out whether Jesus perhaps was the very Messiah. His position as a Pharisee and a member of the Sanhedrim shows how strongly and honestly he must have felt this need. Comp. xii. 42.[6] — That the disciples, and John in particular, were with Jesus during the interview, has nothing against it (as de Wette and most others think), for Nicodemus came to Jesus by night only through fear of the *Jews ;* and the vivid and peculiar features, with the harmonious characteristics of the narrative, even if touched up by the pen of John, confirm the supposition that he was a witness. If not, he must have received what he relates from the Lord Himself, as it impressed itself deeply and indelibly upon his recollection. As to the *result* of the interview, nothing historically to be relied upon has come down to us, simply because there was no immediate effect apparent in Nicodemus. But see vii. 50, xix. 39. — ὅ τ ι ἀ π ὸ θ ε ο ῦ ἐ λ ή λ. δ ι δ ά σ κ α λ ο ς] *that thou*

---

[1] According to Baur, p. 173, he is a *typical* person, representing the believing and yet really unbelieving Judaism, just as the Samaritan woman (chap.iv.) represents believing heathendom ; thus leaving it uncertain how far the narrative is to be taken as fact. According to Strauss, the whole owes its origin to the reproach that Christianity made way only among the common people (notwithstanding 1 Cor. i. 26, 27). Weisse rejects at least the truth of the *account*, which de Wette designates "a poetical, free, and highly spiritualized reproduction." See on the other hand Brückner. According to Hilgenfeld, the whole conversation cannot be understood "unless we view it from the evangelist's standpoint ;" in which the design is simply and solely to explain how Christianity essentially distinguished itself from Judaism.

According to Scholten, we have here set forth the power of Christianity triumphing over the slowness of heart and prejudices of the learned,—this merely, without any historical basis of fact in the story.

[2] See Delitzsch in the *Zeitschr. f. Luther. Theol.* 1854, p. 643.

[3] See Tischendorf, *Evang. Apocr.* p. 203 ff.

[4] A symbolical reference to "*the still benighted mind*" must not be attributed to this simple historical statement (against Hengstenberg).

[5] *Sylloge*, IV. p. 31 ff.

[6] For the entire section see Knapp, *Scripta var. arg.* I. 183 ; Fabricius, *Commentat. Gott.* 1825 ; Scholl in Klaiber's *Studien*, V. 1, p. 71 ; Jacobi in the *Stud. u. Krit.* 1835, 1 ; Hengstenberg in the *Evang. K. Z.* 1860, 49; Steinfass in the *Meklenb. Zeitschr.* 1864, p. 913.

art come from God as teacher. The expression implies the thought of one divinely *sent*, but not the *idea of the Logos* (as Bretschneider holds). — ταῦτα τὰ σημεῖα] emphatic, *haecce tanta signa.* — ἐὰν μὴ ᾖ ὁ θεὸς μετ' αὐτοῦ] ὅτι οὐκ ἐξ οἰκείας δυνάμεως ταῦτα ποιεῖ, ἀλλ' ἐκ τῆς τοῦ θεοῦ, Euthymius Zigabenus. From the miracles (ii. 23) Nicodemus thus infers the *assistance* of God, and from this again that the worker of them is one *sent* from God.

Ver. 3. In ver. 2 Nicodemus had only uttered the preface to what he had it in his mind to ask ; the question itself was to have followed. But Jesus interrupts him, and gives him the answer by anticipation. This question, which was not (as Lange thinks, in contradiction of the procedure of Nicodemus on other occasions) kept back with remarkable prudence and caution, is to be inferred solely from the answer of Jesus ; and it was accordingly no other than the general inquiry, " *What must a man do in order to enter the Messiah's kingdom?*" not the special one, "Is the baptism of John sufficient for this ?" (Baeumlein), for there is no mention of John the Baptist in what follows ; comp. rather Matt. xix. 16. The first is the question which the Lord *reads* in the heart of Nicodemus, and to which He gives an *answer*,—an answer in which He at once lays hold of the anxiety of the questioner in its deepest foundation, and overturns all Pharisaic, Judaistic, and merely human patchwork and pretence. To suppose that *part of the conversation* is here omitted (Maldonatus, Kuinoel, and others), is as arbitrary as to refer the answer of Jesus to the *words* of Nicodemus. Such a reference must be rejected, because Jesus had not given him time to tell the purpose of his coming. We must not therefore assume, either that Jesus wished to lead him on from *faith in His miracles* to that faith which effects a moral transformation ;[1] or that "He wished to convince Nicodemus, who imagined he had made a *great* confession in his first words, that he had not yet so much as made his way into the porticoes of true knowledge" (Chrysostom); or that "He wished to intimate that He had not come merely as a *Teacher*, but in order to the moral renewal of the world,"[2] or, "Videris tibi, O Nicodeme, *videre* aliquod signum apparentis jam regni coelorum in hisce miraculis, quae ego edo ; amen dico tibi : nemo potest *videre* regnum Dei, *sicut oportet*, si non, etc." (Lightfoot, approved by Lücke, and substantially by Godet also). — ἐὰν μή τις γενν. ἄνωθεν] *except a man be born from above, i.e.* except a man be transformed by God into a new moral life. See on i. 13. What is here required answers to the μετανοεῖτε, etc., with which Jesus usually began His preaching, Mark i. 15. ἄνωθεν, the opposite of κάτωθεν, may be taken with reference *to place* (here equivalent to ἐκ τοῦ οὐρανοῦ ;[3] or with reference to *time* (equivalent to ἐξ ἀρχῆς); Chrysostom gives both renderings. The latter is the ordinary interpretation[4]—because Nicodemus himself (ver. 4) thus understood it. Accordingly, ἄνωθεν would be equivalent to *iterum*,

---

[1] Augustine, de Wette, comp. also Luthardt and Ebrard.

[2] Baumgarten Crusius, comp. already Cyril, and Theophylact.

[3] Comp. Xen. *Mem.* iv. 3. 14; *Symp.* vi. 7 ; Thuc. iv. 75. 3; Soph. *El.* 1047 ; Eur. *Cycl.*

322 ; Baruch vi. 63 ; James i. 17, iii. 15.

[4] Syriac, Augustine, Vulgate, Nonnus, Luther, Castalio, Calvin, Beza, Maldonatus, etc. (so likewise Tholuck, Olshausen, Neander, and substantially Luthardt, Hengstenberg, Godet.

again, *anew*, as Grimm (on Wisd. xix. 6) also thinks. But this is unjustifiable even on linguistic grounds, because ἄνωθεν when used of time signifies not *iterum* or *denuo*, but *throughout, from the beginning onwards* [1] (and so Ewald and Weiss interpret it),[2] and the *local* rendering is required alike by the meaning of the word (ver. 31, xix. 11, 23), and the usage of the Evangelist, who uniformly conceives regeneration not as a *new* or *second*, but as a *heavenly* or *divine*, birth ; see i. 13 ; 1 John ii. 29, iii. 9, iv. 7, v. 1. The representation of it as a *repeated*, a *renewed* birth is *Pauline* (Tit. iii. 5, comp. Rom. xii. 2 ; Gal. vi. 15 ; Eph. iv. 23, 24 ; Col. iii. 9) and *Petrine* (1 Pet. iii. 23). ᾽Ανωθεν, therefore, is rightly taken as equivalent to ἐκ θεοῦ by Origen, Gothic Vers. (*iupathró*), Cyril, Theophylact, Aretas, Bengel, etc. ; also Lücke, B. Crusius, Maier, de Wette, Baur, Lange, Hilgenfeld, Baeumlein, Weizsäcker (who, however, adopts a double sense), Steinfass. — ἰδεῖν] *i.e.* as a *partaker* thereof. Comp. εἰσελθεῖν, ver. 5, and see ver. 36, also ἰδεῖν θάνατον (Luke ii. 26 ; Heb. xi. 5), διαφθοράν (Acts ii. 27), ἡμέρας ἀγαθάς (1 Pet. iii. 10), πένθος (Rev. xviii. 7).[3] Not therefore : "simply *to see*, to say nothing of entering," Lange ; comp. Ewald on ver. 5. It is to be observed that the expression βασ. τοῦ θεοῦ does not occur in John, save here and in ver. 5 ;[4] and this is a proof of the accuracy with which he had recorded this weighty utterance of the Lord in its original shape. In xviii. 36 Christ, on an extraordinary occasion, speaks of *His* kingdom." The *conception* of "the kingdom" in John does not differ from its meaning elsewhere in the N. T. (see on Matt. iii. 2). Moreover, its necessary correlative, the Parousia, is not wanting in John (see on xiv. 3).

Ver. 4. The question does not mean : "If the repetition of a corporeal birth is so utterly impossible, how am I to understand this ἄνωθεν γεννηθῆναι?" (Lücke); nor : "How can this ἄνωθεν γεvv. take place, save by a second corporeal birth ?" as if Nicodemus could not conceive of the beginning of a new personal life without a recommencement of natural life (Luthardt, comp. Hofmann); nor : "How comes it that a Jew must be born anew like a proselyte ?" (Knapp, Neander, comp. Wetstein ; for the Rabbins liken proselytes to new-born babes, *Jevamoth*, f. 62. 1; 92. 1); nor again : "This requirement is as impossible in the case of a man already old as for one to

---

[1] This, and not " again from the beginning," as Hofmann (*Schriftbeweis*, II. 11) arbitrarily renders it, is the meaning of ἄνωθεν. It is self-evident that the conception *from the beginning* does not harmonize with that of being *born*. Nor, indeed, would "again from the beginning," but simply "again," be appropriate. *Again from the beginning* would be πάλιν ἄνωθεν, as in Wisd. xix. 6 ; Gal. iv. 9. The passage, moreover, from Josephus, *Antt.* i. 18. 3, which Hofmann and Godet (following Krebs and others) quote as sanctioning their rendering, is inconclusive. For there we read φιλίαν ἄνωθεν ποιεῖται : " he makes friendship *from the beginning onwards*," not implying the continuance of a friendship before un-

used, nor an entering again upon it. Artemidorus also, *Oneirocr.* i. 14, p. 18 (cited by Tholuck after Wetstein), where mention is made of a dream of a *corporeal* birth, uses ἄνωθεν in the sense not of *again*, but as equivalent to *coelitus* with the idea of a divine agency in the dream (Herm. *Gottesd. Alterth.* § 37. 7. 19).

[2] Luke i. 3 ; Acts xxvi. 5 ; Gal. iv. 9 ; Wisd. xix. 6 ; Dem. 539, 22. 1082, 7. 13 ; Plat. *Phil.* 44 D.

[3] From the classics, see Jacobs *ad Del. epigr.* p. 387 ff. ; Ellendt, *Lex. Soph.* II. 343.

[4] The expression, moreover, βασ. τῶν οὐρανῶν (comp. the Critical Notes) is not found in John.

enter again, etc." [1] These meanings are not in the words, they are simply *imported* into them. But the opinion that Nicodemus wished to "*entangle Jesus in His words*" (Luther), or, under excited feelings, intentionally took the requirement literally in order to reduce it *ad absurdum* (Riggenbach), or "by a stroke of Rabbinical cleverness in argumentation" to declare it to be too strongly put (Lange, *Life of Jesus*, p. 495), is opposed to the honourable bearing of this straightforward man. According to the text, what Nicodemus really asks is *something preposterous*. And this is of such a nature, that it is only reconcilable with even the scanty culture of a Jewish theologian (ver. 10), who could not, however, be ignorant of the O. T. ideas of circumcision of heart (Deut. xxx. 6 ; Jer. iv. 4), of a new heart and a new spirit (Ex. xi. 19, 20, xxxvi. 26, 27 ; Ps. li. 12, lxxxvi. 4 ff.), as well as of the outpouring of the Spirit in the time of the Messiah (Joel ii. ; Jer. xxxi.), upon the assumption that, being a somewhat narrow-minded man, and somewhat entangled by his faith in the miracles, he was taken aback, confused and really *perplexed*, partly by the powerful impression which Jesus produced upon him generally, partly by the feeling of surprise at seeing his thoughts known to Him, partly by the unexpected and incomprehensible ἀνωθεν γεννηθῆναι, in which, however, he has an anticipation that something miraculous is contained. In this his *perplexity*, and not "in an *ironical humour*" (as Godet thinks, although out of keeping with the entire phenomenon), he asks this foolish question, as if Jesus had spoken of a *corporeal* birth, and not of a birth of one's *moral* personality. Still less can there be a suspicion of this question being an *invention*, as if John merely wished to represent Nicodemus as a very foolish man (Strauss ; comp. de Wette and Reuss),—a notion which, even on the supposition of a desire to spin out the conversation by misapprehensions on the part of the hearers, would be too clumsy to be entertained. — γ έ ρ ω ν ὤ ν] *when he is an old man ;* Nicodemus added this to represent the impossibility *with reference to himself* in a stronger light. — δ ε ύ τ ε ρ ο ν] with reference to *being for a time* in the mother's womb *before birth*. He did not take the ἀνωθεν to mean δεύτερον, he simply *did not understand it at all*.

Ver. 5. Jesus now explains more fully the ἀνωθεν γεννηθῆναι onwards to ver. 8. — ἐ ξ ὕ δ α τ ο ς κ . π ν ε ύ μ α τ ο ς] *water*, inasmuch as the man is *baptized* therewith (1 John v. 7, 8 ; Eph. v. 26) for the forgiveness of sins (Acts ii. 33, xxii. 16 ; 2 Cor. vi. 11), and *spirit*, inasmuch as the *Holy* Ghost is given to the person baptized in order to his spiritual renewal and sanctification ; both *together* [2]—the former as *causa medians*, the latter as causa *efficiens*—constitute the objective and causative *element, out of which* (comp. i. 13) the birth from above is produced (ἐκ), and therefore baptism is the λουτρὸν παλιγγενεσίας (Tit. iii. 5 ; comp. Tertullian *c. Marc.* i. 28). But that *Christian*

---

[1] Schweizer, B. Crusius, Tholuck, comp. Baumgarten and Hengstenberg.

[2] Weisse, who does not regard the rite of baptism by water as having originated in the institution of Christ, but considers that it arose from a misapplication of His words concerning the baptism of the Spirit, greatly errs when he declares that to make regeneration depend upon baptism by water "*is little better than blasphemy*" (*Evangelienfrage*, p. 194).

baptism (ver. 22, iv. 2), and not that *of John*,[1] is to be thought of in ὕδατος, is clear from the κ. πνεύματος joined with it, and from the fact that He who had already appeared as Messiah could no longer make the baptism of His forerunner the condition, not even the preparatory condition, of His Messianic grace ; for in that case He must have said οὐκ ἐξ ὕδατος μόνον, ἀλλὰ καί. If Nicodemus was not yet able to understand ὕδατος as having this definite reference, but simply took the word in general as a symbolical designation of Messianic expiation of sin and of purification, according to O. T. allusions,[2] and to what he knew of John's baptism, still it remained for him to look for more definite knowledge, to the *immediate* future, when the true explanation could not escape him (iv. 2, iii. 22).   We are not therefore to conclude from this reference to baptism, that the narrative is "a *proleptic fiction*" (Strauss, Bruno Bauer), and, besides Matt. xviii. 3, to suppose in Justin and the Clementines uncanonical developments (Hilgenfeld and others ; see Introduction, § 2).   Neither must we explain it as if Jesus were referring Nicodemus not to baptism as such, but only by way of allusion to the *symbolic import* of the water in baptism (Lücke ; Neander, p. 910).   [See Note XVII. p. 144.]   This latter view does not satisfy the definite γεννηθῇ ἐξ, upon which, on the other side, Theodore of Mopsuestia and others, in modern times Olshausen in particular, lay undue stress, taking the water to be the *female* principle in regeneration (the Spirit as the *male*)—water being, according to Olshausen, "the element of the soul purified by true repentance."   All explanations, moreover, must be rejected which, in order to do away with the reference to baptism,[3] adopt the principle of an ἓν διὰ δυοῖν, for water and Spirit are two quite separate conceptions.   This is especially in answer to Calvin, who says : "of water, *which is the Spirit*," and Grotius : "*spiritus aqueus*, i.e. *aquae instar emundans*."   It is further to be observed, (1) that both the words being without the article, they must be taken *generically*, so far as the water of baptism and the Holy Spirit are included in the general categories of *water* and *Spirit ;* not till we reach ver. 6 is the concrete term used ;—(2) that ὕδατος is put first, because the gift of the Spirit as a rule (Acts ii. 38) *followed* upon baptism (Acts x. 47 is an exceptional case) ;—(3) that believing in Jesus as the Messiah is presupposed as the condition of baptism (Mark xvi. 16) ;—(4) that the necessity of baptism in order to participation in the Messianic kingdom (a doctrine against which Calvin in particular, and other expositors of the Reformed Church, contend) has certainly its basis in this passage, but with reference to the convert to Christianity, and not extending in the same way to the children of Christians, for these by virtue of their Christian parentage are already ἅγιοι (see on 1 Cor. vii. 14).   Attempts to explain away this necessity—*e.g.* by the comparative rendering : "*not only* by water, *but also* by the Spirit" (B. Crusius ; comp. Schweizer, who refers to the baptism of proselytes, and Ewald)—are meanings *imported into* the words.

[1] B. Crusius ; Hofmann, *Schriftbeweis*, II. 2. 12; Lange, who, however, generalizes ideally ; and earlier comm.

[2] Ezek. xxxvi. 25 ; Isa. i. 16 ; Mal. iii. 3 ; Zech. xiii. 1 ; Jer. xxxiii. 8.

[3] Krummacher, recently, in the *Stud. u. Krit.* 1859, p. 509, understands by the water the working of the Holy Spirit. How untenable ! for the *Spirit* is named as a *distinct* factor *side by side* with *water*.

Ver. 6. A more minute antithetic defining of this birth, in order further to elucidate it. — We have not in what follows two originally different *classes* of persons designated (Hilgenfeld), for the new birth is needed by *all*,[1] but two different and successive *epochs of life.* — τὸ γεγεννημ.] *neuter,* though designating persons, to give prominence to the statement as *general and categorical.* See Winer, p. 167 [E. T. p. 178]. — ἐκ τῆς σαρκός] The σάρξ is that *human nature,* consisting of body and soul, which is alien and hostile to the divine, influenced morally by impulses springing from the power of sin, whose seat it is, living and operating with the principle of sensible life, the ψυχή. See on Rom. iv. 1. " *What is born of human nature thus sinfully constituted* (and, therefore, not in the way of spiritual birth *from God*), *is a being of the same sinfully conditioned nature,*[2] without the higher spiritual moral life which springs only from the working of the divine Spirit. Comp. i. 12, 13. Destitute of this divine working, man is merely *fleshly, animal* (1 Cor. ii. 14), πεπραμένος ὑπὸ τὴν ἁμαρτίαν (Rom. vii. 14), and, despite his natural moral consciousness and will in the νοῦς, is wholly under the sway of the sinful power that is in the σάρξ (Rom. vii. 14–25). The *flesh,* as the moral antithesis of the *spirit,* stands in the same relation to the *human spirit* with the *mind,* as the prevailingly sinful and morally powerless life of our lower nature does to the higher moral principle of life (Matt. xxvi. 41) with the will converted to God ; while it stands in the same relation to the *divine spirit,* as that which is determinately opposed to God stands to that which determines the new life in obedience to God (Rom. viii. 1–3). In both relations, *flesh* and *spirit* are *antitheses* to each other, Matt. xxvi. 41 ; Gal. v. 17 ff. ; accordingly in the unregenerate we have the *lucta carnis et* MENTIS (Rom. vii. 14 ff.), in the regenerate we have the *lucta carnis et* SPIRITUS (Gal. v. 17). — ἐκ τοῦ πνεύματος] *that which is born of the Spirit, i.e.* that whose moral nature and life have proceeded from the operation of the Holy Spirit,[3] *is a being of a spiritual nature,* free from the dominion of the σάρξ, and entirely filled and governed by a spiritual principle, namely by the Holy Spirit (Rom. viii. 2 ff.), walking ἐν καινότητι πνεύματος (Rom. vii. 6). — The universality of the statement forbids its limitation to the *Jews* as natural descendants of Abraham (Kuinoel and others), but they are of course included in the general declaration ; comp. ver. 7, ὑμᾶς. — In the apodoses the substantives σάρξ and πνεῦμα represent, with stronger emphasis (comp. vi. 63, xi. 25, xii. 50 ; 1 John iv. 8 ; Rom. viii. 10), the adjectives σαρκικός and πνευματικός, and are to be taken *qualitatively.*

Vv. 7, 8. To allay still more the astonishment of Nicodemus (ver. 4) at

[1] See ver. 7 ; comp. also Weiss. *Lehrbegriff,* p. 128.
[2] The *sinful* constitution of the σάρξ in itself implies the *necessity* of a being born of the Spirit (vv. 3, 7) ; comp. 1 John ii. 16. The above exposition cannot therefore be considered as attributing to John a Pauline view which is strange to him. This is in answer to Weiss, according to whom Jesus here merely says, " as the corporeal birth only produces the corporeal sensual part." Similarly J. Müller *on Sin,* vol. I. p. 449, II. 382. See on the other hand, Luthardt, *v. freien Willen,* p. 393.

[3] The ἐκ τοῦ ὕδατος, implying the ἐκ τοῦ πνεύματος (after ver. 5), and the meaning of which is clear in itself, is not repeated by Jesus, because His aim now is simply to let the contrast between the σάρξ and the πνεῦμα stand out clearly.

the requirement of ver. 3, Jesus subjoins an analogy drawn from *nature*, illustrating the operation of the Holy Spirit of which He is speaking. The man is seized by the humanly indefinable Spirit, but knows not whence He cometh to him, and whither He leadeth him. — $\dot{v}\,\mu\,\ddot{a}\,\varsigma$] individualizing the general statement : "*te et eos, quorum nomine locutus es,*" Bengel. Jesus could not have expressed Himself in the *first* person. — $\tau\dot{o}\ \pi\nu\varepsilon\ddot{v}\mu\,a$] This, as is evident from πνεῖ, means *the wind*,[1] not the *Spirit* (Steinfass). It is the double sense of the word (comp. רוּחַ) which gave rise to *this* very analogy from nature. A similar comparison has been made between the *human* soul, so far as it participates in the divine nature, and the well-known but inexplicable agency of wind.[2] On the expression τὸ πνεῦμα πνεῖ, see Lobeck, *Paral.* 503. — $\ddot{o}\,\pi\,o\,v\ \vartheta\,\acute{e}\,\lambda\,\varepsilon\,\iota$] The wind blowing now here, now there, is *personified* as a free agent, in keeping with the comparison of the personal Holy Spirit (1 Cor. xii. 2).[3] — $\pi\,o\,\ddot{v}$] with a verb of motion.[4] Expressing by anticipation the state of rest following upon the movement. Often in the N. T. as in John (vii. 35, viii. 14, xii. 35) and Heb. xi. 8. — $o\,\ddot{v}\,\tau\,\omega\,\varsigma\ \dot{e}\,\sigma\,\tau\,\dot{\iota}\ \pi\,\ddot{a}\,\varsigma$, κ.τ.λ.] A popular and concrete mode of expression (Matt. xiii. 19, etc.); *so is it, i.e.* with reference experimentally to the course of his higher birth, *with every one who has been born* (perfect) *of the Spirit.* The points of resemblance summed up in the οὕτως are : (1) *the free self-determining action* of the Holy Spirit,[5] not merely the greatness of this power, Tholuck ; (2) *the felt experience* of His operations by the subject of them (τὴν φωνὴν αὐτοῦ ἀκ.) ; and (3) yet their *incomprehensibleness* as to their origin and their end (ἀλλ᾽ οὐκ οἶδας, κ.τ.λ.), the latter pertaining to the moral sphere and reaching unto eternal life, the former proceeding from God, and requiring, in order to understand it, the previously experienced workings of divine grace, and faith ensuing thereupon. The man feels the working of grace within, coming to him as a birth from above, but he knows not whence it comes ; he feels its attraction, but he knows not whither it leads. These several elements in the delineation are so distinctly indicated by Jesus, that we cannot be satisfied with the mere general point of incomprehensibleness in the comparison (Hengstenberg), upon the basis of Eccles. xi. 5.

Vv. 9, 10. The entire nature of this birth from above (ταῦτα) is still a puzzle to Nicodemus as regards its *possibility* (the emphasis being on $\delta\,\acute{v}\,v\,a\,$- $\tau\,a\,\iota$) ; which we can easily understand in a learned Pharisee bound to the mere form and letter. He asks the question in this state of *ignorance* (*haesitantis est*, Grotius), not in *pride* (Olshausen). Still, as one acquainted with the Scriptures, he *might* and *ought* to have recognized the possibility ; for the power of the divine Spirit, the need of renewal in heart and mind, and the fact that this renewal is a divine work, are often mentioned in the O. T. Jesus therefore might well ask in wonder : *Art thou the teacher,*

---

[1] Gen. viii. 1 ; Job xxx. 15; Wisd. xiii. 2 ; Heb. i. 7 ; often in the classics.

[2] Xen. *Mem.* 4. 3. 14. Comp. also Eccles. xi. 5; Ps. cxxxv. 7.

[3] Concerning the personality of the Holy Spirit as taught in John, see especially xiv.-xvi.

[4] Comp. Hom. *Il.* 13. 219 ; Soph. *Trach.* 40 : κεῖνος δ᾽ ὅπου βέβηκεν, οὐδεὶς οἶδε ; and see Lobeck *ad Phryn.* 45 ; Mätzn. *ad Antiph.* 169, § 8.

[5] ὅπου θέλει, comp. 1 Cor. xii. 11 ; John v. 21.

etc. ? The article ὁ διδάσκ. and the τοῦ Ἰσρ. following designate the man not merely in an *official* capacity (Ewald), which would not distinguish the *individual*, but as *the well-known* and *acknowledged* teacher of the people.[1] Hengstenberg puts it too strongly : " the concrete embodiment of the *ideal* teacher of Israel ;" comp. Godet. But Nicodemus must have held a position of influence as a teacher quite inconsistent with this proved ignorance ; there is in the *article* a touch of *irony*, as in the question a certain degree of *indignation*.[2]

Ver. 11. Jesus now discloses to the henceforth silent Nicodemus, in growing excitement of feeling, the *source* of his ignorance, namely, his *unbelief* in what He testifies, and which yet is derived from His own knowledge and intuition. — The plurals *we know*, etc., are, as is clear from the singulars immediately following in ver. 12, simply rhetorical (plurals of *category*,[3] and refer only to Jesus Himself. [See Note XVIII. p. 144.] Comp. iv. 38, and its frequent use by St. Paul when he speaks of himself in the plural. To include the disciples (Hengst. Godet), or to explain them as referring to *general Christian consciousness* as contrasted with the *Jewish* (Hilgenfeld), would be quite inappropriate to the language (see especially ὃ ἑωράκ. μαρτ.). To understand them as including *John the Baptist*,[4] or *him along with the prophets*,[5] or even *God*,[6] or the *Holy Ghost* (Bengel), is arbitrary, and without a trace of support in the text, nay, on account of the *have seen*, opposed to it, for the Baptist especially did not by i. 34 occupy the same stage of ἑωρακέναι with Christ. It is, moreover, quite against the context when B. Crusius says : "*men generally* are the subjects of the verbs οἴδαμεν and ἑωράκ.," so that *human things*—what one sees and knows (τὰ ἐπίγεια, ver. 12)—are meant.—Observe the gradual *ascent* in the parallelism, in which ἑ ω ρ ά κ α μ ε ν, refers not to the knowledge attained in this earthly life (Weizsäcker), but to Christ's vision of God in His pre-existent state. Comp. ver. 32, i. 18, vi. 46, viii. 38, xvii. 5. — ο ὐ λ α μ β ά ν ε τ ε] ye Jews : comp. τοῦ Ἰσραήλ, ver. 10 ; and for the fact itself, i. 11, 12. The reproach, like the οὐ πιστεύετε of ver. 12, refers to the nation as a whole, with a reference also to Nicodemus himself. To render this as a *question* (Ewald) only *weakens* the tragic relation of the second half of the verse to the first.

Ver. 12. How grievous the prospect which your unbelief regarding the instructions I have already given opens up as to the future ! — τ ὰ ἐ π ί γ ε ι α] *what is on earth*, things which take place on earth (not in heaven). We must strictly adhere to this meaning of the word in this as in all other passages.[7] To the *category* of these *earthly things* belonged also the birth from above (against Baeumlein), because, though wrought by a power from heaven, *it is accomplished on earth ;* and because, proceeding in repentance and faith, it is a change taking place on earth within the earthly

---

[1] See Bernhardy, p. 315; Winer, p. 110 [E. T. p. 115].

[2] Nägelsbach *on the Iliad*, ed. 3, p. 424.

[3] Sauppe and Kühner *ad. Xen. Mem.* 1. 2. 46.

[4] Knapp, Hofmann, Luthardt, Weizsäcker, Weiss, Steinfass.

[5] Luther, Beza, Calvin, Tholuck.

[6] Chrysostom, Euthymius Zigabenus, Rupertus, Calovius, etc.

[7] 1 Cor. xv. 40 ; 2 Cor. v. 1 ; Phil. ii. 10, iii. 19 ; Jas. iii. 15. Comp. Wisd. ix. 16, and Grimm, *Handbuch*, p. 189.

realm of our moral life ; and because it is historically certain that Christ
everywhere began His work with this very preaching of *repentance*. But the
Lord has in His mind not *only* the doctrine of regeneration just declared to
Nicodemus, but, as the plural shows, *all* which thus far He had taught the
Jews (εἶπον ὑμῖν) ; and this had been hitherto only ἐπίγεια, and not ἐπουράνια,
of which He still designs to speak.[1] It is therefore wrong to refer the expression to the comparison of the *wind* (Beza) or of corporeal *birth* (Grotius),
as prefiguring higher doctrine ; for the relation to the faith spoken of did
not lie in these symbols, but in the truths they symbolized. The meaning
of the words is quite altered, moreover, if we change the word ἐπίγεια into
"*human* and *moral*" (B. Crusius), or confine its meaning to what is stated in
the *immediate context* (Lücke), or, with de Wette, make the point of difference to be nothing more than the antithesis between man's susceptibility of
regeneration as a work within him and his susceptibility of merely *believing*.
—The counterpart of the ἐπίγεια are the ἐ π ο υ ρ ά ν ι a, of which Jesus intends
to speak to them in future, *i.e. things which are in heaven* (so in all places,
Matt. xviii. 35 ; 1 Cor. xv. 40, 48, 49 ; Eph. i. 3 ; Phil. ii. 10, etc.). To
this category belong especially the *Messianic mysteries, i.e.* the *divine decrees
for man's redemption and final blessedness*. These are *heavenly things*, because
they have their foundation (Wisd. ix. 16, 17) in *the divine will*, though their
realization commences in the present *world*, through the entire work, and
in particular through the death of Jesus and the faith of mankind ; but while
still unaccomplished, belongs to the divine counsel, and shall be consummated and fully revealed by the exalted Christ in the kingdom of the
Messiah, when the ζωὴ αἰώνιος will reveal itself as the goal of perfection (Col.
iii. 4), and "it will appear what we shall be." To the ἐπουρανίοις, therefore,
does not first belong what is to be said of His exaltation, Matt. xxvi. 64
(Steinfass) ; but as the first and main thing, that which Jesus immediately
utters in ver. 14 ff., wherein the *heavenly* element, *i.e. what is in the counsels
of God* (vv. 15, 16), is clearly contained. In the connection, that which is
heavenly *is difficult to be understood ;* but this difficulty has nothing to do
with the word itself, as Lücke holds.

    Ver. 13. "And no other than I can reveal to you heavenly things." *This*
is what Jesus means, if we rightly take His words, not an assertion of His
divinity as the first of the heavenly things (Hengstenberg), which would
make the negative form of expression quite inexplicable. Comp. i. 18, vi.
46. — The κ a ί is simply *continuative*, not *antithetic*,[2] nor *furnishing a basis*, or
assigning the motive.[3] — ο ὐ δ ε ὶ ς ἀ ν α β έ β η κ ε ν, κ.τ.λ.] which, on account of
the perfect tense, obviously cannot refer[4] to the actual *ascension of Christ*[5]

<hr/>

[1] εἶπον is *dixi*, not *dixerunt*, as Ewald
thinks, who regards the *ancients* in the O. T.
as the subject, and upon too feeble evidence
reads ἐπιστεύσατε instead of πιστεύετε. This
new subject must have been expressed, and
an ἐγώ should have stood over against it in
the apodosis. Comp. Matt. v. 21, 22. The
earthly might be appropriate to the *law*
(following Col. ii. 17 ; Heb. ix. 5, x. 1), but
not to the prophets.

[2] Knapp, Olshausen.
[3] Beza, Tholuck ; Luke, Lange.
[4] Against Augustine, Beza, Theophylact,
Rupertus, Calovius, Bengel, etc.
[5] So also Weizsäcker, who assumes that
we have here an experience belonging to
the apostolic age, carried back and placed
in the mouth of Christ. An anachronism
which would amount to literary carelessness.

nor gives support to the unscriptural *raptus in coelum* of the Socinians ;[1]
nor is to be explained by the *unio hypostatica* of Christ's *human* nature
with the *divine*, by virtue of which the former may be said to have entered
into heaven (Calovius, Maldonatus, Steinfass, and others). It is *usually*
taken *figuratively* of a *spiritual elevation to God* in order to a knowledge of
divine things, and a coming to the perception of divine mysteries, which
thus were brought down, as it were, by Christ from heaven (see of late
especially Beyschlag) ; to support which, reference is made to Deut. xxx.
12, Prov. xxx. 4, Baruch iii. 29, Rom. x. 6, 7.   But Christ brought with
Him out of His *pre-existent state* His immediate knowledge of divine things
(ver. 11, i. 18, viii. 26, *al.*), and possesses it in uninterrupted fellowship
with the Father.   To represent Him, therefore, as, *during His earthly
life*, bringing it down by a figurative and spiritual exaltation to heaven, is
wholly inappropriate.   Ὁ ἐκ τοῦ οὐρ. καταβ. also must be taken literally, of
an *actual* descent ; and there is therefore nothing in the context to warrant
our taking ἀναβ. εἰς τ. οὐρ. *symbolically*.   Hengstenberg rightly renders the
words literally, but at the end of the verse would *complete* the sense by adding, "*who will ascend up into heaven.*"   An addition arbitrary in itself and
by no means to be looked for in John : out of harmony with the connection, and certainly not readily intelligible to one like Nicodemus, though it
were the point of the declaration : hence not properly suppressed, and least
of all as a saying concerning the *future*.   Godet does not get beyond the
explanation of essential communion with God on the part of Jesus *from the
time of His birth*.   The only rendering true to the words is simply this :
Instead of saying, " No one has *been* in heaven except," etc., Jesus says, as
this could only have happened to any other by his *ascending* thither, " No
one *has ascended* into heaven except," etc. ; and thus the εἰ μή refers to an
actual existence in heaven, which is implied in the ἀναβέβηκεν.   And thus
Jansenius rightly renders : Nullus hominum in coelo fuit, quod ascendendo
fieri solet, ut ibi coelestia contemplaretur, nisi, etc. ; and of late Fritzsche
the elder in his *Novis opusc.* p. 230 ; and now also Tholuck, and likewise
Holtzmann in Hilgenfeld's *Zeitschr.* 1865, p. 222. — ὁ ἐκ τοῦ οὐρ. κατα-
βάς] which took place through the *incarnation*.   These words, like ὁ ὢν
ἐν τ. οὐρ., are *argumentative*, for they necessarily imply *existence in heaven ;*
but ὁ ὤν, which must be taken as an attributive of ὁ υἱὸς τ. ἀνθρ., and not as
belonging to καταβάς, and therefore has the article, cannot be equivalent to
ὃς ἦν (Luthardt ; Hofmann, I. 134 ; Weiss, etc.), as if ποτέ, τὸ πρότερον or
the like were there, but is equivalent to ὃς ἐστι, *whose existence is in heaven*,
who has there His proper abode, His home.[2] — ὁ υἱὸς τοῦ ἀνθρ.] a
Messianic designation which Christ applies to Himself, in harmony with the
fulfilment of the prophetic representation in Dan. vii. 13, which began with
the καταβάς (comp. on i. 52).   *Nicodemus* could understand this only through
a fuller development of faith and knowledge.

---

[1] See Oeder *ad Catech. Racov.* p. 348 ff.

[2] Nonnus : ἀστερόεντι μελάθρῳ πάτριον οὖδας ἔχων.—IX. 25 is similar : τυφλὸς ὤν : blind from one's birth. Schleiermacher refers the coming down from heaven to the conception of His *mission*, and the being in heaven to the *continuity of His God-consciousness*. See *e.g.* his *Leben Jesu*, p. 287 ff.

Note.—According to Beyschlag, p. 99 ff., this verse is utterly opposed to the derivation of Christ's higher knowledge from the recollection of a pre-existent life in heaven. But we must bear in mind, (1) that the idea of an *ascent* to God to attain a knowledge of His mysteries (which Beyschlag considers the only right explanation) never occurs in the N. T. with reference to Jesus—a circumstance which would surprise us, especially in John, if it had been uttered by Jesus Himself. But it was *not* uttered by Him, because He *has* it not, but knows His knowledge to be the gift of His Father which accompanied Him in His mission (x. 36). (2) He could not have claimed such an ascent to heaven for Himself *alone*, for a like ascent, though not in equal degree, must belong to other men of God. He must, therefore, at least have expressed Himself *comparatively:* οὐδεὶς ο ὗ τ ω ς ἀναβέβηκεν ἐ. τ. οὐρ. ὡς ὁ, κ.τ.λ. Even the church now sings :

> " Rise, rise, my soul, and stretch Thy wings
>   Towards heaven, Thy native place."

But something distinct and *more* than this was the case with Christ, viz. as to the past, that He had His existence in heaven, and had *come down* therefrom ; and as to His earthly present, that He *is* in heaven.

Vv. 14, 15. Jesus, having in ver. 13 stated the *ground* of faith in Him, now proceeds to show the *blessedness* of the believer—which is the design of His redemptive work—in order the more to incite those whom He is addressing to fulfil the fundamental condition, contained in faith, of participating in His kingdom. That this is the logical advance in the discourse, is clear from the fact that in what follows it is the *blessedness* of faith which is *dwelt upon ;* see vv. 15, 16, 18. We have not here a transition from the *possibility* to the *necessity* of communicating heavenly things, ver. 13 (Lücke) ; nor from the *ideal* unveilings of divine things to the *chief mystery* of the doctrine of salvation which was manifested in historical reality (de Wette, comp. Tholuck and Brückner) ; nor from the first of divine things, Christ's *divinity*, to the second, the *atonement* which He was to establish (Hengstenberg, comp. Godet) ; nor from the *Word* to His *manifestation* (Olshausen) ; nor from the work of *enlightenment* to that of *blessing* (Scholl) ; nor from the present *want* of faith to its future *rise* (Jacobi : " faith will first begin to spring up when my ὕψωσις is begun") ; nor from Christ's *work* to His *person* (B. Crusius) ; nor from His *person* to His *work* (Lange). The event recorded in Num. xxi. 8 is made use of by Jesus as a type of the divinely appointed manner and efficacy of His coming death,[1] to confirm a prophecy still enigmatical to Nicodemus, by attaching it to a well-known historical illustration. The points of comparison are : (1) *the being lifted up* (the well-known brazen serpent on the pole, and Jesus on the cross) ; (2) *the being saved* (restored to health by looking at the serpent, to eternal ζωή by believing on the crucified One).[2] Any further drawing out of the illustration is arbitrary, as, for instance, that of Bengel : " ut serpens ille fuit serpens sine veneno

---

[1] Which, consequently, He had clearly foreseen not for the first time in vi. 51 (Weizsäcker) ; comp. on ii. 19.

[2] Comp. Wisd. xvi. 6, and, in the earliest Christian literature, *Epist. of Barnabas, c.* 12 ; Ignatius *ad Smyrn.* 2, *interpol.;* Justin, *Apol.* 1. 60, *Dial. c. Tr.* 94.

contra serpentes venenatos, sic Christus homo sine peccato contra serpentem antiquum," comp. Luther and others, approved by Lechler.[1] Lange goes furthest in this direction ; comp. Ebrard on Olshausen, p. 104. There is, further, no typical element in the fact that the brazen serpent of Moses was a *dead representative* ("as the sign of its conquering through the healing power of the Lord," Hengstenberg). For, apart from the fact that Christ was lifted up *alive* upon the cross, the circumstance of the brazen serpent being a *lifeless* thing is not made prominent either in Num. xxi. or here. — ὑ ψ ω θ ῆ ν α ι] not *glorified*, acknowledged in His exaltation (Paulus), which, following ὑψωσε, would be opposed to the context, but (comp. viii. 28, xii. 32, 33) *shall be lifted up*, that is, *on the cross*,[2]—answering to the Aramaean זְקַף,[3] a word used of the hanging up of the malefactor upon the beam.[4] The express comparison with the raising up of the brazen serpent, a story which must have been well known to Nicodemus, does not allow of our explaining ὑψωθῆσ. as = רוּם, of the exaltation of Jesus to glory,[5] or as *including* this, so that the cross is the stepping-stone to glory (Lechler, Godet); or of referring it to the *near coming of the kingdom*, by which God will show Him in His greatness (Weizsäcker) ; or of our abiding simply by the idea of an *exhibition*,[6] which Christ underwent in His public sufferings and death ; or of leaving wholly out of account the *form* of the exaltation (which was certainly accomplished on the cross and then in heaven), (Luthardt), and conceiving of an exaltation for the purpose of being visible to all men (Holtzmann), as Schleiermacher also held ;[7] or of assuming, as the meaning intelligible for Nicodemus, only that of *removing*, while Jesus still had in mind His being lifted up on the cross and up to God.[8] —δεῖ] according to the divine decree, Matt. xvi. 21, Luke xxiv. 26, does not refer to the type, but only to the antitype (against Olshausen), especially as between the *person* of Christ and the brazen serpent *as such* no typical relation could exist. — Lastly, that Jesus should make a thus early, though at the time enigmatic, allusion to His death by crucifixion, is conceivable both on the ground of the doctrinal peculiarity of the event, and of the extraordinary importance of His death as the fact of redemption. See on ii. 19. And in the case of Nicodemus, the enigmatic germ then sown bore fruit, xix. 39. — Adopting the reading ἐ ν α ὐ τ ῷ (see Critical Notes), we cannot refer it to πιστεύων, but, as μὴ ἀπόληται, ἀλλ᾽ is spurious (see Critical Notes), to ἔχῃ : "every believer shall *in Him* (i.e. resting upon Him as the cause) have eternal life." Comp. xx. 31, v. 39, xvi. 33, xiii. 31. — ζ ω ὴ ν α ἰ ώ -

---

[1] *Stud. u. Krit.* 1854, p. 826.

[2] The higher significance imparted to Christ's person and work by His death (Baur, *Neutest. Theol.* 379) is not implied in the word ὑψωθῆναι, but in the comparison with the *serpent*, and in the sentence following, which expresses the *object of* the lifting up. This passage (comp. i. 29) should have prevented Baur from asserting (p. 400) that the Pauline doctrine concerning such a significance in Christ's death is wholly wanting in St. John's doctrinal view. See also vi.

51, 53, 54.

[3] Comp. the Heb. זָקַף, Ps. cxlv. 14, cxlvi. 8.

[4] See Ezra vi. 11 ; Gesenius, *Thes.* I. 428 ; Heydenreich in Hüffell's *Zeitschr.* II. 1, p. 72 ff.; Brückner, 68, 69. Comp. *Test. XII. patr.* p. 739 : κύριος ὑβρισθήσεται καὶ ἐπὶ ξύλου ὑψωθήσεται.

[5] Bleek, *Beitr.* 231.

[6] Hofmann, *Weissag. u. Erf.* II. 143.

[7] *Leben Jesu*, 345.

[8] Hofmann, *Schriftbew.* II. 1, 301.

ν ι ο ν] eternal *Messianic life*, which, however, the believer already has (ἐχῃ) as an eternal possession in αἰὼν οὗτος, viz. the present self-conscious development of the only true moral and blissful ζωή, which is independent of death, and whose consummation and full glory begin with the second advent.[1]

Ver. 16. *Continuation of the address of Jesus to Nicodemus*, onwards to ver. 21,[2] not, with Erasmus, Rosenmüller, Kuinoel, Paulus, Neander, Tholuck, Olshausen, Maier (see also Baeumlein), an explanatory meditation of the evangelist's own ; an assumption justified neither by anything in the text nor by the word μονογενής, a word which must have been transferred from the language of John to the mouth of Jesus (not *vice versa*, as Hengstenberg thinks), for it is never elsewhere used by Christ, often as He speaks of His divine sonship. See on i. 14. The reflective character of the following discourse harmonizes with the didactic purpose of Christ, and the preterites ἠγάπησαν and ἦν need not be explained from the standing-point of a later time : there seems, therefore, no sufficient basis for the *intermediate* view (of Lücke, de Wette, Brückner), that in this continued account of the discourse of Jesus, .vv. 16 ff., John inserts more explanations and reflections of his own than in the preceding part, though such a supposition would scarcely (as Kling and Hengstenberg think) militate against the trustworthiness of John, who, in recording the longer discourses, has precisely in his own living recollection the abundant guarantee of *substantial certainty*. — ο ὕ τ ω] *so much ;* see on Gal. iii. 3. — γ ά ρ] reason of the purpose stated in ver. 15. — ἠ γ ά π η σ ε ν] *loved*, with reference to the time of the ἔδωκεν. — τ ὸ ν κ ό σ μ ο ν] *i.e. mankind at large*,[3] comp. πᾶς, ver. 15, xvii. 2 ; 1 John ii. 2. — τ ὸ ν μ ο ν ο γ .] to make the proof of His love the *stronger*, 1 John iv. 9 ; Heb. xi. 17 ; Rom. viii. 32.—ἐ δ ω κ ε ν] He did not reserve Him for Himself, but *gave* Him, *i.e. to the world*. The word means more than ἀπέστειλεν (ver. 17), which expresses [4] the manner of the ἔδωκεν, though it does not specially denote the giving up to *death*, but the state of humiliation as a whole, upon which God caused His Son to enter when He left His pre-existent glory (xvii. 5), and the final act of which *was to be* His death (1 John iv. 10). The indicative following, ὥστε, describes the act objectively as something actually done. See on Gal. ii. 13 ; and Klotz *ad Devar*. 772. — μ ὴ ἀ π ό λ η τ α ι, κ.τ.λ.] On the subjunctive, as marking present time, see Winer, 271 [E. T. p. 287]. Note the change from the Aorist to the Present, making destruction (by banishment

---

[1] Comp. vi. 40, 44, 45, 54, xiv. 3, xvii. 24 ; 1 John iii. 14, iv. 9.

[2] Luther rightly praised " the majesty, simplicity, clearness, expressiveness, truth, charm" of this discourse. He " exceedingly and beyond measure loved " this text.

[3] This declaration is the rock upon which the absolute. predestination doctrine goes to pieces, and the supposed (by Baur and Hilgenfeld) metaphysical dualism of the anthropology of St. John. Calovius well unfolds our text thus : (1) *salutis principium* (ἠγάπ.) ; (2) *dilectionis objectum* (the κόσμος, not the *electi*) : (3) *donum amplissimum* (His

only-begotten Son) ; (4) *pactum gratiosissimum* (faith, not works) ; (5) *finem missionis Christi saluberrimum*.

[4] Weizsäcker in the *Zeitschr. f. Deutsche Theol*. 1857, p. 176, erroneously finds wanting in John an intimation on the part of Christ that He is the Logos who came *voluntarily* to the world. He is, however, the Logos *sent* of God, who undertook this mission in the feeling of obedience. Thus the matter is presented throughout the N. T., and the thought that Christ came αὐτοθελής is quite foreign thereto.

to hell in the Messianic judgment) appear as an act accomplished ; while the possession of the Messianic *life* is described as now already existing (commencing with regeneration), and as abiding forever. Comp. on ver. 15.

Ver. 17. Confirmation of ver. 16, in which ἀπέστειλεν answers to the ἔδωκεν, κρίνῃ to the ἀπόληται, and σωθῇ to the ἔχῃ ζωὴν αἰώνιον of ver. 16. Considering this exact correspondence, it is arbitrary with modern critics (also Lücke, B. Crusius) to understand the second τὸν κόσμον differently from the first, and from the τ. κόσμον of ver. 16, as denoting in the narrow Jewish sense the *Gentile* world, for whose judgment, *i.e.* condemnation, the Messiah, according to the Jewish doctrine, was to come.[1] Throughout the whole context it is to be uniformly understood of the *world of mankind as a whole.* Of *it* Jesus says, that He was not sent to judge it,—a judgment which, as all have sinned, must have been a judgment of *condemnation*,—but to procure for it by His work of redemption the Messianic *salvation.* " Deus saepe ultor describitur in veteri pagina ; itaque conscii peccatorum merito expectare poterant, filium venire ad poenas patris nomine exigendas," Grotius. It is to be remembered that He speaks of His coming in the state of humiliation, in which He was not to accomplish judgment, but was to be the medium of obtaining the σώζεσθαι through His work and His death. Judgment upon the finally unbelieving was reserved to Him upon His Second Advent (comp. v. 22, 27), but the κρίμα which was to accompany His works upon earth is different from this (see on ix. 39). — The thrice-repeated κόσμος has in it a tone of solemnity. Comp. i. 10, xv. 19.

Ver. 18. More exact explanation of the negative part of ver. 17. Mankind are either *believing*, and are thus delivered from condemnation (comp. v. 24), because if the Messiah had come to judge the world, He would only have had to condemn sin ; but sin is forgiven to the believer, and he already has everlasting ζωή ; —or they are *unbelieving*, so that condemnation has already been passed upon them in idea (as an internal fact),[2] because they reject the Only-begotten of God, and there is no need of a special act of judgment to be passed on them on the part of the Messiah ; their own unbelief has already passed upon them the sentence of condemnation.   " He who does not believe, already has hell on his neck," Luther ; he is αὐτοκατάκριτος, Tit. iii. 11. Ver. 18 does not speak of the *last* judgment which shall be the solemn and ultimate completion of this temporal judgment,[3] but

---

[1] See Bertholdt, *Christol.* pp. 203, 223.

[2] Hence it is clear that the signification of κρίνειν as meaning *condemnatory* judgment is correct, and not the explanation of Weiss, *Lehrbegriff*, p. 184, according to whom the " judgment" here means in general only a decision either for life or death. In that case, not οὐ κρίνεται, but ἤδη κέκριται, must apply also to the *believer.* But this very distinction, the οὐ κρίνεται used of the believer and the ἤδη κέκριται of the unbeliever, places the explanation of a *condemnatory* κρίνειν beyond doubt. This is also against Godet, who with reference to the

believer hits upon the expedient of supposing that the Lord here *anticipates* the judgment (viz. the " constater l'état moral"). But according to the words of Jesus, this suggestion would apply rather to the case of the *unbeliever.*

[3] This *temporal* judgment of the world is the word's history, the conclusion of which is the *last* judgment (v. 27), which, however, must not (as Schleiermacher, *L. J.* 355) be dissipated by means of this text into a merely natural issue of the mission of Jesus. See on v. 28. See also Groos in the *Stud. u. Krit.* 1868, p. 251.

it does not call it *in question*, in opposition to the Jewish **Messianic** belief
(Hilgenfeld). See on v. 28–30, xii. 31.   Well says Euthymius Zigabenus :
ἡ ἀπιστία κατέκρινε πρὸ τῆς κατακρίσεως.   Comp. ver. 36. — π ε π ί σ τ ε υ κ ε ν] *has
become a believer* (and remains so) ; the *subjective* negation in the causal clause
(contrary to the older classical usage), as often in Lucian, etc., denoting the
relation as one *presupposed* in the view of the speaker. [1]   Otherwise in 1 John
v. 10. — τ ο ῦ μ ο ν ο γ. υ ἱ ο ῦ τ . θ ε ο ῦ] very impressively throwing light
upon the ἤδη κέκριται, because bringing clearly into view *the greatness of the
guilt.*

Ver. 19. The ἤδη κέκριται is now more minutely set forth, and this in
its moral character, as rejection of the light, *i.e.* of God's saving truth,—
the possessor and bringer in of which was Christ, who had come into the
world,—and as love of darkness.   "*But herein consists the condemnation* (as
an inner moral fact which, according to ver. 18, had already occurred),
that," etc.   ἡ κρίσις is the judgment in question, to be understood here also,
agreeably to the whole connection, of *condemnatory* judgment.   But in αὕτη
. . . ὅτι (comp. 1 John v. 11) we have not the *reason* (Chrysostom and his
followers), but the characteristic *nature* of the judgment stated. — ὅ τ ι τ ὸ
φ ῶ ς, etc., κ α ὶ ἠ γ ά π η σ α ν] The first clause is not expressed in the dependent form (ὅτι ὅτε τὸ φῶς, etc., or with Gen. abs.), but as an independent
statement, in order to give emphatic prominence to the contrast setting forth
the guilt. [2] — ἠ γ ά π η σ α ν] after it had come. Jesus could *now* thus speak
already from experience regarding His relations to mankind *as a whole ;* the
Aor. does not presuppose the consciousness of a later time. See ii. 23, 24.
Ἠγάπ. is put first with tragic emphasis, which object is also served by the
simple καί (not *and yet*). The expression itself : *they loved the darkness rather*
(*potius*, not *magis*, comp. xii. 43 ; 2 Tim. iii. 4) *than the light,*— μᾶλλον belonging not to the verb, but to the noun, and ἤ comparing the two *conceptions,* [3]—is a mournful *meiosis ;* for they did not love the light at all, but
hated it, ver. 20. The ground of this hatred, however, does not lie (comp.
ver. 6, i. 12) in a metaphysical opposition of principles, [4] but in the light-
shunning demoralization into which men had sunk through their own free
act (for they might also have done the ἀλήθεια, ver. 21). The source of unbelief is immorality. — ἦν γ ὰ ρ α ὐ τ ῶ ν, κ.τ.λ.] The *reason* why "they loved
the darkness rather," etc. (see on i. 5), was *their immoral manner of life*, in
consequence of which they must shun the light, nay, even hate it (ver. 20).
Observe the growing emphasis from αὐτῶν onwards to πονηρά, *for the works
which they* (in opposition to the individual lovers of the light) *did were evil ;*
which πονηρά does not in popular usage denote a higher degree of evil than
φαῦλα, ver. 20 (Bengel), but answers to this as *evil* does to *bad* (*worthless*). [5]

Ver. 20. Γ ά ρ] The previous γάρ laid the historical *basis* for the statement ἠγάπησαν οἱ ἄνθρωποι, κ.τ.λ. : this second γάρ is related to the same state-

[1] See Herm. *ad Viger.* p. 806 ; Winer, p.
442 [E. T. p. 474].
[2] See Kühner, II. 416 ; Winer, p. 585 [E. T.
p. 630].
[3] Ellendt, *Lex. Soph.* II. p. 51 ; Bäuml.

Partik. p. 136.
[4] Baur, Hilgenfeld, Colani.
[5] Fritzsche *ad Rom.* p. 297. Comp. v. 29 ;
Rom. ix. 11 ; 2 Cor. v. 10 ; Jas. iii. 16 ; φαῦλα
ἔργα in Plat. *Crat.* p. 429 A; 3 Macc. iii. 22.

ment as *explanatory* (see on Matt. vi. 32, xviii. 11 ; Rom. viii. 6), introducing a general elucidation, and this from the psychological and perfectly
natural relation of evil-doers to the light which was manifested (in Christ)
(τὸ φῶς not different from ver. 19), which they hated as the principle opposed to them, and to which they would not come, because they wished to
avoid the ἔλεγχος which they must experience from it. This "*coming* to
the light" is the believing adherence to Jesus, which, however, would have
to be brought about through the μετάνοια.[1] — ἵ ν α μ ὴ ἐ λ ε γ χ θ ῇ] Intention. This ἔλεγχος is the *chastening censure*, which they shunned both on
account of their being put to shame before the world, and the threatening
feeling of repentance and sorrow in their self-consciousness.[2] This dread
is both moral pride and moral effeminacy. Luthardt [3] refers the *chastening*
only to the psychological fact of an *inner* condemnation. But against this
is the parallel φανερωθῇ, ver. 21. — Observe, on the one hand, the participle *present* (for the πράξας might turn to the light), and, on the other, the
distinction between π ρ ά σ σ ω ν (he who *strives after, agit,* pursues as the goal
of his activity) and ποιῶν, ver. 21 (he who *does, facit,* realizes as a fact).

Ver. 21. 'Ο δ ὲ π ο ι ῶ ν τ ὴ ν ἀ λ ή θ.] The opposite of ὁ φαῦλα πράσσων,
ver. 20, and therefore ἀλήθεια is to be taken in the *ethical* sense : he who
does what *is morally true,* so that his conduct is in harmony with the divine
moral standard.[5] Moral truth was *revealed* before Christ, not only in the
law (Weiss), but also (see Matt. v. 17) in the prophets, and, outside Scripture, in creation and in conscience (Rom. i. 19 ff., ii. 14 ff.).[6] — ἵ ν α φ α ν ε ρ .
α ὐ τ ο ῦ τ ὰ ἐ ρ γ α] φανερ. is the opposite of the μὴ ἐλεγχθῇ of ver. 20. While
the wicked wishes his actions not to be reproved, but to remain in darkness, the good man wishes *his* actions *to come to the light and to be made manifest,* and he *therefore comes* πρὸς τὸ φῶς ; for Christ, as the personally manifested *Light,* the bearer of divine truth, cannot fail through His working
to make these good deeds be recognized in their true nature. The manifestation of true morality through Christ must necessarily throw the true
light on the moral conduct of those who come to Him, and make it manifest
and show it forth in its true nature and form. The purpose ἵνα φανερ.,
κ.τ.λ., does not spring from self-seeking, but arises from the need, originating in a moral necessity, of moral satisfaction in itself, and of the triumph
of good over the world. — α ὐ τ ο ῦ] thus put before, for emphasis, in
opposition to the evil-doer, who has altogether a different purpose in his
acts. — ὅ τ ι ἐ ν θ ε ῷ , κ.τ.λ.] the reason of the before-named purpose. How
should he not cherish this purpose, and desire the φανέρωσις, seeing that his
works are wrought *in God!* Thus, so far from *shunning,* he has really to
strive after the manifestation of them, as the revelation of all that is divine.

---

[1] In opposition to Colani, who finds a
circle in the reasoning of vv. 19, 20. See
Godet.

[2] Comp. Luke iii. 19 ; John viii. 8 ; Eph.
v. 11, 13. "Gravis malae conscientiae lux
est," Senec. *ep.* 122. 14.

[3] Comp. B. Crusius.

[4] Comp. Xen. *Mem.* iii. 9. 4 : ἐπισταμένους

μὲν ἃ δεῖ πράττειν, ποιοῦντας δὲ τἀναντία, also
iv. 5. 4, *al. ;* Rom. i. 31, ii. 3, vii. 15, xiii. 4.
See generally, Franke, *ad Dem. Ol.* iii. 15.

[5] Comp. Isa. xxvi. 10 ; Ps. cxix. 30 ; Neh.
ix. 33 ; Job iv. 6, xiii. 6 ; 1 John i. 6 ; 1 Cor.
v. 8 ; Eph. v. 9 ; Phil. iv. 8.

[6] Comp. Groos, p. 255.

We must take this ἐν θεῷ, like the frequent ἐν Χριστῷ, as denoting the *element* in which the ἐργάζεσθαι moves ; not without and apart from God, but living and moving in Him, has the good man acted.   Thus the κατὰ τὸ θέλημα τοῦ θεοῦ, 1 John v. 14, and the κατὰ θεόν, Rom. viii. 27, 2 Cor. vii. 10, also the εἰς θεόν, Luke xii. 21, constitute the necessary *character* of the ἐν θεῷ, but are not the ἐν θεῷ *itself.* — ἔ ρ γ α ε ἰ ρ γ α σ μ έ ν α] as in vi. 28, ix. 4, Matt. xxvi. 10, *et. al.*, and often in the classics.—Observe from ver. 21, that Christ, who here expresses Himself generally, yet conformably to experience, encountered, at the time of His entering upon His ministry of enlightenment, not only the φαῦλα πράσσοντες, but also those who practised what is right, and who were living in God.   To this class belonged a Nathanael, and the disciples generally, certainly also many who repented at the preaching of the Baptist, together with other O. T. saints, and perhaps Nicodemus himself.   They were drawn by the Father to come to Christ, and were given to Him (vi. 37) ; they were of God, and had ears to hear His word (viii. 47, comp. xviii. 37) ; they were desirous to do the Father's will (vii. 17) ; they were *His* (xvii. 6).   But according to ver. 19, these were exceptions amid the multitude of the opposite kind, and even their piety needed purifying and transfiguring into true *righteousness*, which could be attained only by fellowship with Christ ; and hence even in their case the way of Christian penitence, by the *manifestation* of their works wrought in God, brought about by the light of Christ, was not excluded, but was exhibited, and its commencement brought about, because, in view of this complete and highest light, the sincere Old Testament saint must first rightly feel the need of that repentance, and of the lack of moral satisfaction.   Consequently the statement of vv. 3, 5 still holds true.

Vv. 22, 23. After this interview with Nicodemus [1] (μετὰ ταῦτα) Jesus betook Himself with His disciples from the capital into the *country* of Judea, in a north-easterly direction towards Jordan.   ʼ Ι ο υ δ α ί α ν is [2] an *adjective.* — ἐ β ά π τ ι ζ ε ν] during His stay there (*Imperf.*), not Himself, however, but through His disciples, iv. 2.   Baur, indeed, thinks that the writer had a definite purpose in view in this mode of expression ; that he wished to bring Jesus and the Baptist as closely as possible together in the same work.   But if so, the remark of iv. 2 would be strangely illogical ; see also Schweizer, p. 194.   The baptism of Jesus was certainly indeed a continuation of that of John, and did not yet possess the new characteristic of Matt. xxviii. 19 (for see vii. 39); but that it already included that higher element, which John's baptism did not possess (comp. Acts xix. 2, 3),— namely, the operation of the Spirit, of which Christ was the bearer (ver. 34), for the accomplishment of the birth from above,—is manifest from ver. 5, a statement which cannot be a prolepsis or a prophecy merely. — ἦ ν δ ὲ κ α ὶ ʼ Ι ω ά ν ν., κ.τ.λ.] *and John was also employed in baptizing*, namely *in Aenon*, etc.   This name, usually taken as the intensive or adjectival form

---

[1] To interpose a longer interval, *e.g.* a return to and sojourn in Galilee, is quite gratuitous.   Not before iv. 3 does Jesus return to Galilee.

[2] As in Mark i. 5, Acts xvi. 1, 1 Macc. ii 23, xiv. 33, 37, 2 Macc. v. 23, 3 Esr. v. 47, *Anthol.* vii. 645.

of רֹעֵֽין, is rather = עַֽין יוֹן, *dove spring ;* the place itself is otherwise unknown, as is also the situation of Salim, though placed by Eusebius and Jerome eight Roman miles south of Scythopolis. This is all the more uncertain, because Aenon, according to the mention of it here (comp. iv. 3), must have been in Judaea, and not in Samaria, and *could not* therefore have been the Ainun discovered by Robinson.[1] Ewald thinks of the two places שְׁלֹחִים וְעֵין in Josh. xv. 32. So also Wieseler, p. 247. In no case could the towns have been situated on the Jordan, which would have been inconsistent with the ὅτι ὕδατα πολλά. Comp. Hengstenberg, who likewise refers to Josh. xv. 32, while Pressel[2] prefers the statement of Eusebius and Jerome. For the rest, the narrative of the temptation, which Hengstenberg places in the period after ver. 22, has nothing to do with the locality of our passage : it is wholly foreign to it. — The question why John, after the public appearance of Jesus, still *continued to baptize,* without baptizing *in His name,* is answered simply by the fact,[3] that Jesus *had not yet come forth as* John expected that the Messiah would, and that consequently the Baptist could not suppose that his work in preparing the way for the Messiah's kingdom by his baptism of repentance was already accomplished, but had to await for this the divine decision. This perseverance of John, therefore, in his baptismal vocation, was by no means in conflict with his divinely received certainty of the Messiahship of Jesus,[4] and the parallel ministry of the two must not be looked upon as improbable, as " in itself a splitting in sunder of the Messianic movement" (Keim).

Ver. 24 corrects, in passing, the synoptic tradition[5] [See Note XIX. p. 145], which John knew as being widely spread, and the discrepancy in which is not to be explained either by placing the imprisonment between John iv. 2 and 3, and taking the journey of Jesus to Galilee there related as the same with that mentioned in Matt. iv. 12,[6] or by making the journey of Matt. iv. 12 to coincide with that named in John vi. 1 (Wieseler). See on Matt. iv. 12. Apart from that purpose of correction, which (in spite of the subtleties of Ebrard) is specially apparent if we compare Matt. iv. 17, the remark, which was quite intelligible of itself, would be, to say the least, superfluous,—unnecessary even to gain space for bringing Jesus and the Baptist again alongside each other (Keim), even if we were to venture the suggestion, of which the text says nothing, that Jesus felt Himself obliged, as the time of the Baptist was not yet expired, to bring the kingdom of God near, in keeping with the form which the Baptist had adopted (Luthardt, p. 79).

Vv. 25, 26. Οὖν] in consequence of the narration of ver. 23 (ver. 24 being a parenthetical remark). Nothing is known more particularly as to this question (ζήτησις) which arose among John's disciples.[7] Its theme was

---

[1] *Later Explorations,* p. 400.

[2] In Herzog's *Encykl.* XIII. 326.

[3] Against Bretschneider, Weisse, Baur.

[4] As Weizsäcker, p. 320, thinks.

[5] It is supposed, indeed, that John simply wishes to intimate that what he records, vv. 22-36, must be placed *before* Matt. iv. 12

(Hengstenberg). But in the connection of Matthew, there is no place for it before iv. 12.

[6] Lücke, Tholuck, Olshausen, B. Crusius, Ebrard, Hengstenberg, and many others.

[7] ἐγένετο ἐκ τῶν μαθ. Ἰωάνν., comp. Lucian. *Alex.* 40 ; Herod. v. 21.

"*purification*" (περὶ καθαρισμοῦ), and, according to the context, did not refer in general to the usual prescriptions and customs (Weizsäcker), but more immediately to the baptism of John and Jesus, and was discussed *with a Jew*, who probably regarded the baptism of Jesus as higher and more efficacious in its power of purifying (from the guilt of sin) than that of John. Comp. ver. 26.   Possibly the prophetic idea of a purifying consecration preceding the Messiah's kingdom [1] was spoken of.   Who the Ἰουδαῖος was (Hofmann, Tholuck, a Pharisee) cannot be determined.   A Jewish *Christian* [2] would have been more exactly designated.   According to Luthardt, it was an *unfriendly* Jew who declared that the baptism of John might now be dispensed with, and wished thus to beguile the Baptist to become unfaithful to his calling, that he might the better work against Jesus.   An artificial combination unsupported by the text, as also by ᾧ σὺ μεμαρτύ- ρηκας, ver. 26.   For that this indicated a *perplexity on the part of the disciples as to the calling of their master* finds no support in the words of the Baptist which follow.   There is rather expressed in that ᾧ σὺ μεμαρτ., and in all that John's·disciples advance,—who therefore do not name Jesus, but only indicate Him,—a *jealous irritation* on the point, that a man, who himself had just gone forth from the fellowship of the Baptist, and who owed his standing to the Baptist's testimony in his favour (ᾧ), should have opened such a competition with him as to throw him into the shade.   Through the statements of the Jew, with whom they had been discussing the question of purification, there was awakened in them a certain feeling of envy that Jesus, the former pupil (as they thought), the receiver of a testimony at the hand of their master, should now presume to put himself forward as his superior rival.   They saw in this a usurpation, which they could not reconcile with the previous relation of Jesus to the Baptist.   But he, on the contrary, vindicates Jesus, ver. 27, and in ver. 28 brings into view His far higher position, which excluded all jealousy. — ὃς ἦν μετὰ σοῦ, κ.τ.λ.] i. 28, 29. — ἴδε and οὗτος have the emphasis of something unexpected ; namely, that this very person should (according to their view) interfere with their master in his vocation, and with such results ! — καὶ πάντες, an exaggeration of excited feeling. Comp. xii. 19. Not : "all who submit to be baptized by Him" (Hengstenberg).

Vv. 27, 28. The Baptist at first answers them, putting his reply in the form of a general truth, *that the greater activity and success of Jesus was given Him of God*, and next reminds them of *the subordinate position* which he held in relation to Jesus.   The reference of the general affirmation to *the Baptist himself* [See Note XX. p. 145], who would mean by it : "non possum mihi arrogare et rapere, quae Deus non dedit," Wetstein, [3] is not in keeping with the context ; for the petty, jealous complaint of the disciples, ver. 26, has merely prepared the way for a vindication of *Jesus* on the part of the Baptist ; and as in what follows with *this* intent, the comparison

[1] Ezek. xxxvi. 25 ; Zech. xiii. 1 ; Hofm. *Weissag. u. Erf.* II. 87.
[2] Chrysostom, Euthymius Zigabenus, Ewald.

[3] So Cyril, Rupertus, Beza, Clarius, Jansen, Bengel, Lücke, Maier, Hengstenberg, Godet, and others.

between the two, as they, in vv. 27, 28, according to our interpretation, stand face to face with each other, is thoroughly carried out ; see vv. 29, 30, 31 ; so that Jesus is always *first* characterized, and *then* John. We must not therefore take ver. 27 as referring to *both*.[1] — οὐ δύναται] relatively, *i.e.* according to divine ordination. — ἄνθρωπος] quite general, *a man*, any one ; not as Hengstenberg, referring it to John, renders it : *"because I am merely a man."* — λαμβάνειν] not *arrogate to himself* (ἑαυτῷ λαμβ., Heb. v. 4), but simply to *receive*, answering to *be given.* — αὐτοὶ ὑμεῖς] though you are so irritated about him. — μαρτυρ.] Indic : *ye are yourselves my witnesses*, see i. 19–28, the substance of which John sums up in the words οὐκ εἰμί, etc. They had themselves appealed (ver. 26) to his μαρτυρία concerning Jesus, but he περιτρέπει ταύτην καθ' αὐτῶν, Euthymius Zigabenus. — ἀλλ' ὅτι] Transition to dependent speech.[2] — ἐκείνου] referring not to the appellative ὁ Χριστός, but to *Jesus* as the Χριστός.

Vv. 29, 30. Symbolical setting forth of his subordinate relation to Jesus. The bridegroom is Jesus, John is the friend who waits upon Him ; the bride is the community of the Messianic kingdom ; the wedding is the setting up of that kingdom, now nigh at hand, as represented in the picture which the Baptist draws (comp. Matt. ix. 15, xxv. 1 ff.). The O. T. figure of God's union with His people as a marriage[3] forms the basis of this comparison. It may reasonably be doubted whether Solomon's Song (especially v. 1, 6) was in the Baptist's thoughts when employing this illustration ;[4] for no quotation is made from that book in the N. T., and therefore any allegorical interpretation of this Song with Messianic references cannot with certainty be presupposed in the N. T. Comp. Luke xiii. 31, note.—*He to whom the bride* (the bride-elect of the marriage feast) *belongs is the bridegroom*,— therefore it is not I.—*The friend* of the bridegroom (κατ' ἐξοχήν : the appointed friend, who serves at the wedding) is the παρανύμφιος, who is also, Sanhedr. f. 27, 2, called אוהב, but usually שושבן.[5] — ὁ ἑστηκὼς κ. ἀκούων αὐτοῦ] *who standeth* (tanquam apparitor, Bengel) *and attentively heareth him*, *i.e.* in order to do his bidding.[6] Contrary to the construction (καί), and far-fetched, is the rendering of B. Crusius : who is waiting for him (ἑστηκ.), and *when he hears him*, viz. the voice of the *approaching* bridegroom. (?)" Tholuck also, following Chrysostom, *adds* to the text in rendering : " who standeth,

---

[1] Kuinoel, Tholuck, Lange, Brückner, Ewald, Luthardt, who, in keeping with his view of ver. 26, takes ver. 27 to mean : " The work of both of us is divinely ordained, and therefore I, for my own part, am justified in continuing my work after the appearance of Jesus, so long at least as the self-witness of Jesus is not believed."

[2] Winér, p. 539 [E. T. p. 577 f.].

[3] Isa. liv. 5 ; Hos. ii. 18, 19 ; Eph. v. 32 ; Rev. xix. 7, xxi. 2, 9.

[4] Bengel, Luthardt, Hengstenberg.

[5] Lightfoot, p. 980 ; Buxtorf, *Lex. Talm. s. v.* ; Schoettgen, p. 335 ff. ; and see on 2 Cor. xi. 2.

[6] The working of Jesus was so *mani-*

fest, and now so *near* to the Baptist, that this feature of the comparison is fully explained by it. Neither in this place nor elsewhere is there any answer to the question, whether and what personal intercourse the Baptist had already had with Him (Hengstenberg thinks "through intermediate persons, especially through the Apostle John "). In particular, the assumption that the interview with Nicodemus became known to the Baptist (through the disciples of Jesus who had previously been the Baptist's disciples) is quite unnecessary for the understanding of the words which here follow (against Godet).

having finished his work as forerunner." The Baptist had still to continue
and still continued working. The ἕστηκ. must be regarded as taking place
at the marriage feast, not previously during the bridal procession (Ewald,
who refers to the frequent stoppages which took place in it); but it does
not mean standing *at the door of the wedding chamber*, nor ἀκ. αὐτοῦ the audible *pleasure of the newly married pair*. An indelicate sensualizing (still
found in Kuinoel) unwarranted by the text. — χαρᾷ χαίρει] *he rejoiceth
greatly*.[1] Comp. 1 Thess. iii. 9, where, in like manner, διά stands instead
of the classical ἐπί, ἐν, or the dative. — διὰ τὴν φωνὴν τοῦ νυμφ.] Not
to be understood of his loud caresses and protestations of love,[2] nor of
the command of the bridegroom to take away the cloth with the signum
virginitatis (thus debasing the beautiful figure),[3] nor of the conversing
of the bridegroom with the bride[4] — all unwarranted by the general
φωνήν, which refers merely to the *conversation and joy of the bridegroom amid
the marriage mirth*.[5] The explanation, also, which makes it the voice of
the *approaching* bridegroom who calls the bride *to fetch her home*, would
need to be more precisely indicated,[6] and is not in keeping with ὁ ἑστηκώς;[7]
the ministry of Jesus, moreover, was already *more* than a call to that bringing home, which might have symbolized His *first* appearing. Comp. Matt.
ix. 15. — Note, finally, how the ardent expression of *joy* stands contrasted
with the envious feelings of John's disciples. — αὕτη οὖν ἡ χαρὰ, κ.τ.λ.]
οὖν infers the αὕτη from the application of the figure : *this* joy, therefore,
which is mine, viz. at the bridegroom's voice. — πεπλήρωται] *has been
fulfilled* completely, so that nothing more is wanting to it. The Baptist,
with prophetic anticipation, sees, in the successful activity of Jesus, and in
the flocking of the people to Him, the already rising dawn of the Messiah's
kingdom (the beginning of the marriage). On πεπλήρ. comp. xv. 11, xvi.
24, xvii. 13 ; 1 John i. 4. — δεῖ] as in ver. 14. This noble self-renunciation
was based upon his clear assurance of the *divine purpose*. — αὐξάνειν] in
influence and efficiency. — ἐλαττοῦσθαι] the counterpart of increase : *to
become less*.[8]

Vv. 31, 32, down to ver. 35, is not the comment of the *evangelist*.[9] Ver.
32, comp. with vv. 29, 30, seems to sanction the notion that it is ; but as no
intimation to this effect is given in the text, and as the thread of discourse
proceeds uninterruptedly, and nothing in the subject-matter is opposed to
it, we may regard it as the *continued discourse of the Baptist*, though elabo-
rated in its whole style and colouring by John,—not, however, to such an

[1] See Lobeck, *Paralip.* p. 524 ; Winer, p.
424 [E. T. p. 466].

[2] Grotius, Olshausen, Lange.

[3] Michaelis, Paulus.

[4] Tholuck and older expositors.

[5] Comp Jer. vii. 34, xvi. 9, xxv. 10.

[6] Against B. Crusius and Luthardt.

[7] For the παρανύμφιος does not stand there
waiting for the bridegroom, but accom-
panies him on his way to the bride's house.
The standing and waiting pertain to the

female attendants on the bride, Matt. xxv.
1 ff.

[8] Jer. xxx. 16; Symm. ; 2 Sam. iii. 1;
Ecclus. xxxv. 23, *al. ;* Thuc. ii. 62. 4 ; Theophr. *H. pl.* vi. 8. 5 ; Josephus, *Antt.* vii. 1. 5.
Comp. Plat. *Leg.* iii. p. 681 A : αὐξανομένων
ἐκ τῶν ἐλαττόνων.

[9] So Wetstein, Bengel, Kuinoel, Paulus,
Olshausen, Tholuck, Klee, Maier, Baum-
lein.

extent that the evangelist's record passes almost entirely *into a comment of his own.*[1] We perceive how the Baptist, as with the mind of Jesus Himself, unveils before his disciples, in whose narrower circle he speaks, with the growing inspiration of the last prophet, the full majesty of Jesus ; and with this, as his swanlike song, *completes* his testimony before he vanishes from the history.[2] Even the subsequent momentary perplexity (Matt. xi.) is psychologically not irreconcilable with this (see on i. 29), simply because John was ἐκ τῆς γῆς. But the Baptist, notwithstanding his witness concerning Jesus, has not gone over to Him, because the calling of *forerunner* had been once divinely committed to him, and he felt that he must continue to fulfil it so long as the Messianic kingdom was not yet established. These remarks tell, at the same time, against the proof drawn from this passage that the entire scene is unhistorical (Strauss, Weisse, Reuss, Scholten, following Bretschneider).— ὁ ἄνωθεν ἐρχόμ.] *He who cometh from above, i.e. Christ* (comp. ver. 13, viii. 23), whose *coming, i.e.* whose coming forth from the divine glory in human form as Messiah, is here regarded as still in the process of manifestation (cf. viii. 14), and hence as a *present* phenomenon, and not ended until it has been consummated in the establishment of the kingdom. — πάντων] *Masc.* John means the category as a whole to which Jesus belonged—*all interpreters of God,* as is clear from what follows, vv. 31, 32. — ὁ ὢν ἐκ τῆς γῆς] *i.e.* the Baptist, who, as an ordinary man, springs from earth, not heaven. — ἐκ τῆς γῆς ἐστι] as predicate denotes the *nature* conditioned by such an origin. He is of no other kind or nature than that of one who springs from earth ; though withal his divine mission (i. 6), in common with all prophets, and specially his divinely conferred baptismal vocation (Matt. xxi. 25, 26), remain intact. — καὶ ἐκ τ. γῆς λαλεῖ] *and he speaketh from the earth.* His speech has not heaven as its point of departure, like that of the Messiah, who declares what He has seen in heaven (see ver. 32) ; but it proceeds from the earth, so that he utters what has come to his knowledge upon earth, and therefore under the limitation of earthly conditions,—a limitation, however, which as little excluded the reception of a revelation (i. 33 ; Luke iii. 2), as it did in the case of the saints of the O.T., who likewise were of earthly origin, nature, and speech, and afterwards *e.g.* in that of the Apostle Paul.[3] The *contents* of the discourse need not therefore relate merely to τὰ ἐπίγεια (iii. 12), as Weisse thinks, but may also have reference to ἐπουράνια, the knowledge and promulgation of which, however, do not get beyond the ἐκ μέρους (1 Cor. xiii. 9 ff.). The expression ἐκ τῆς γῆς λαλ. must not be confounded with ἐκ τοῦ κόσμου λαλεῖν, 1 John iv. 5. — ὁ ἐκ τοῦ οὐρ. ἐρχ., κ.τ.λ.] A solemn repetition of the first clause, linking on what follows, viz. the antithesis still to be brought out, of the ἐκ τῆς γῆς λαλεῖ. — ὁ ἑώρακε, καὶ ἤκουσε] *i.e.* during His pre-existence with God,

---

[1] Lücke, de Wette, Comp. also Ewald.

[2] It is self-evident, that all that is said in ver. 31 f. was intended to incite the disciples of John to believe in Jesus, and to frighten them from unbelief.

[3] The Fathers rightly perceived the *rela-*

tire character of this self-assertion. Euthymius Zigabenus : πρὸς σύγκρισιν τῶν ὑπερφυῶν λόγων τοῦ Χριστοῦ. Hofmann, *Schriftbew.* II. 1, p. 14, misapprehends this, supposing that this ver. 31 has no reference to the Baptist.

i. 15, 18, iii. 11.   From it He possesses *immediate knowledge* of divine truth,[1] whose *witness* (μαρτυρεῖ) He accordingly is.   Note the *interchange of tenses*.[2] —τοῦτο] this and nothing else. — κ. τ. μαρτ. αὐτοῦ οὐδεὶς λαμβ.] tragically related to what precedes, and introduced all the more strikingly by the bare καί.   Comp. i. 10, iii. 11.   The expression οὐδεὶς λαμβ. is the hyperbole of deep sorrow on account of the *small number* of those—small in comparison of the vast multitude of unbelievers—who receive His witness, and whose fellowship thus constitutes the bride of the marriage.   John himself limits the οὐδείς by the following ὁ λαβὼν, κ.τ.λ.   Comp. i. 10, 11, 12.   The concourse of hearers who came to Jesus (ver. 26), and the Baptist's joy on account of his progress (vv. 29, 30), could not dim his deep insight into the world's unbelief.   Hence his joy (ver. 29) and grief (ver. 32), both forming a noble contrast to the jealousy of his disciples (ver. 26).

Ver. 33.   Αὐτοῦ] placed before for emphasis : *His* witness, correlative with the following ὁ θεός. — ἐσφράγισεν] has, by this receiving, *sealed, i.e. confirmed, ratified* as an act.   For this figurative usage, see vi. 27 ; Rom. iv. 11, xv. 28 ; 1 Cor. ix. 2 ; 2 Cor. i. 22 ; Eph. i. 13.[3] — ὅτι ὁ θεὸς ἀληθ. ἐστιν] In the reception of the witness of *Jesus* there is manifested on man's part the practical ratification of the truthfulness of *God*, the human "*yea verily*" in answer to the proposition " God is true," because Jesus (see ver. 34) is the ambassador and interpreter of God.   The non-reception of that witness, whereby it is declared untrue, would be a rejection of the *divine* truthfulness, the "*nay*" to that proposition.   Comp. 1 John v. 10.   Reference to O. T. *promises* (Luthardt) is remote from the context.

Ver. 34.   The first γάρ serves to state the reason for the ἐσφράγισεν, ὅτι, etc. ; the second, for the τὰ ῥήματα τ. θεοῦ λαλεῖ, so far, that is, as it would be doubtful, if God gave the Spirit ἐκ μέτρου, whether what God's ambassador spoke was a divine revelation or not ; it might in this case be wholly or in part the word of man. — ὃν γὰρ ἀπέστ. ὁ θεός] not a general statement merely, appropriate to every prophet, but, following ver. 31, to be taken as more precisely defining a *heavenly* (ἄνωθεν, ἐκ τοῦ οὐρανοῦ) *mission*, and referring strictly to *Jesus*.   This the context demands.   But the following οὐ γὰρ ἐκ μέτρου, κ.τ.λ., must be taken as *a general statement*, because there is no αὐτῷ.   *Commentators* would quite arbitrarily supply αὐτῷ,[4] so as to render it, not by measure or limitation, *but without measure and in complete fulness, God gives the Holy Spirit to Christ*.   This supplement, unsuitable in itself, should have been excluded by the present δίδωσιν, because we must regard Christ as *possessing* the Spirit *long before*.   The meaning of this *general statement* is rather : " *He does not give the Spirit according to measure*" (as if it consequently were out of His power, or He were unwilling to give the Spirit beyond a certain quantitative degree, determined by a definite measure) ;

---

[1] Decisive against Beyschlag, p. 96, who understands the words only of a *prophetic* sight and hearing through the Spirit, is the antithesis with the Baptist (who was yet himself a prophet), running through the whole context, as also the ἐπάνω πάντων ἐστίν, which ranks Jesus *above* the prophets.

Comp. also Heb. xii. 25.

[2] Kühner, II. p. 75.

[3] Jacobs, *ad Anthol.* ix. pp. 22, 144, 172.

[4] The subterfuge of Hengstenberg is no better : " we must supply, *in the case before us*." See also Lange.

He proceeds herein *independently of any* μ έ τ ρ ο ν, confined and limited by no restricting standard. The way in which this is to be *applied* to *Jesus thus* becomes plain, viz. that God must have endowed Him [1] when He sent Him from heaven (ver. 31), in keeping with His nature and destination, with the richest spiritual gifts, namely, *with the entire fulness of the Spirit* (πᾶν τὸ πλήρωμα, Col. i. 19), more richly, therefore, than prophets or any others ;— which He could not have done had He been fettered *by a measure* in the giving of the Spirit. [2]— ἐκ μέτρου] ἐκ used of the *rule*.[3] Finally, the οὐ γὰρ ἐκ μέτρου must not be regarded as presenting a different view from ver. 32 (comp. Weiss, p. 269) ; for the Spirit was in Christ the principle whereby He *communicated* (the λαλεῖν) to men that which He had beheld with God. See on vi. 63, 64 ; Acts i. 2.

Ver. 35. A further description of the dignity of Christ. The Father hath given *unlimited power* to His beloved Son. —ἀ γ α π .] the ground of the δέδωκ. —π ά ν τ a] neut. and without limitation. Falsely Kuinoel : *omnes doctrinae suae partes* (comp. Grotius : "omnia mysteria regni ") ! Nothing is exempted from the Messianic ἐξουσία by virtue of which Christ is κεφαλὴ ὑπὲρ πάντα, Eph. i. 22, and πάντων κύριος, Acts x. 36 ; comp. xiii. 3, xvii. 2 ; Matt. xi. 27 ; 1 Cor. xv. 27 ; Heb. ii. 8. —ἐν τ ῇ χ ε ι ρ ὶ α ὐ τ ο ῦ] Result of the direction of the gift, a well-known *constructio praegnans*.[4]

Ver. 36. All the more weighty in their results are faith in the Son and unbelief ! Genuine prophetic conclusion to life or death. — ἔ χ ε ι ζ. a ι.] " he has eternal life," *i.e.* the Messianic ζωή, which, in its temporal development, is already a *present* possession of the believer ; see on vv. 15, 16. At the Second Advent it will be completed and glorified ; and therefore the antithesis οὐ κ ὄ ψ ε τ α ι ζ ω ή ν, referring to the future αἰών, is justified, because it presupposes the οὐκ ἔχει ζ. —ἀ π ε ι θ ῶ ν] not : " he who does *not believe* on the Son" (Luther and the Fathers), but : " he who *is disobedient* to the Son ;" yet, according to the context, so far as the Son *requires faith*.[5] Contrasted with this is the ὑπακοὴ πίστεως, Rom. i. 5. — ἡ ὀ ρ γ ή] not *punishment*, but *wrath*, as the necessary emotion of holiness ; see on Rom. i. 18 ; Eph. ii. 3 ; Matt. iii. 7. —μ έ ν ε ι] because unreconciled inasmuch as the faith which appropriates reconciliation (iii. 16), is rejected, comp. ix. 41. This μένει (the term is not ἔρχεται) implies that the person who rejects faith is still

---

[1] οὐ γὰρ μέτρα λόγοιο [or rather πνεύματος] φέρει λόγος.—Nonnus.

[2] Hitzig, in Hilgenfeld's *Zeitschr.* 1859, p. 152 ff., taking the first half of the verse as a general statement, applicable to every prophet, would read the relative οὗ instead of οὐ, " *according to the measure, that is, in which He gives the Spirit.*" Considering the γάρ, this rendering is impossible.—Ewald and Brückner come nearest to our interpretation. B. Crusius and Ebrard (on Olshausen) erroneously make ὅν ἀπέστ. κ.τ.λ. the subject of δίδωσιν (ὁ θεός is spurious, see the critical notes ; but this yields a thought neither true in itself, nor in keep-

ing with the context. Godet puts an antithetical but purely imported emphasis upon δίδωσιν : to other messengers of God the Spirit is not *given*, but only *lent* by a " visite momentanée ;" but when God *gives* the Spirit, He does so without measure, and this took place on the first occasion at the baptism of Jesus. This is exegetical poetizing.

[3] See Bernhardy, p. 230 ; comp. on 1 Cor. xii. 27.

[4] Winer, p. 385 [E. T. p. 414.]

[5] Comp. Acts xiv. 2, xix. 9 ; Rom. xi. 30; Fritzsche, *ad Rom.* I. p. 17.

in a moral condition which is subject to the divine wrath,—a state of subjection to wrath, which, instead of being removed by faith, *abides* upon him through his unbelief.   The wrath, therefore, is not originated by the refusal to believe (Ritschl, *de ira Dei*, pp. 18, 19 ; Godet), but already exists, and through that refusal remains.[1]   Whether or not this wrath rests upon the man *from his birth*,[2] this text gives no information.   See on Eph. ii. 3. — That *the Baptist* could already speak after this manner, is evident from chap. i. 29. — ἐπ' αὐτόν] as in i. 32, 33.

NOTES BY AMERICAN EDITOR.

XVII. *" From water and spirit."* Ver. 5.

Weiss says, " Meyer says justly that the absence of the article from ὕδατος and πνεύματος indicates that they are taken generically, but overlooks the fact that with this every direct reference to John's baptism, or even to Christian baptism, is excluded . . . The two factors are simply co-ordinated, the water conceived in its essence as a purifying factor (but not from the guilt of sin, as Meyer and others, but from sin itself), the spirit as the efficient creative principle of the new life (comp. the union of the two in Ezek. xxxvi. 25-27) ; and the thought is that without the doing away of the old sinful nature, and the creation of an entirely new nature from an efficient principle, the new birth does not exist. . . . It is historically inconceivable that Jesus should have spoken to Nicodemus of Christian baptism."

And yet in the widespread excitement which John's baptism had recently produced and was now producing, and in the near prospect of His own about to be instituted baptism, it seems scarcely possible that Jesus should not have had them both, and Nicodemus one of them, in mind.

XVIII. Οἴδαμεν, *" We know."* Ver. 11.

"To take this and the following plurals purely rhetorically as plurals of *category*, and refer them barely to Jesus Himself, is against all analogy in the discourses of Jesus, against the immediately following sing. (ver. 12), and finds support neither in the totally diverse plur. iv. 38, nor in the plur. of the Pauline Epp. Of course it cannot include *God* or the *Holy Spirit*. To make it include the disciples, or explain it from the general Christian consciousness, as against the Jewish consciousness, is forbidden by the language itself (espec. ὁ ἑωράκ. μαρτ.). Jesus rather unites himself with the *messengers of God*, whose word, if it come to that test, must be accepted as credible, while in the actual *historical situation* the one properly referred to is John the Baptist, who by his proclamation of water baptism, and of spiritual baptism through the Messiah, had already, like Christ Himself (ver. 5), pointed to the necessity of a new birth from water and spirit" (Weiss).

---

[1] Augustine ; Thomasius, *Chr. Pers. u. Werk*, I. p. 289.
[2] This is also against Hengstenberg. But certainly the μένει must, according to the context, be an *eternal* abiding, if the ὑπακοὴ πίστεως never occurs.

XIX. *The Synoptic tradition.* Ver. 24.

It is by no means certain that the Synoptic tradition needs any such correction. The conversations and events here recorded (ch. ii. 1–iii. 36) are not contained at all in the Synoptists, and their natural place—the only place *allowed* by Matt. and Mark—is before Matt. iv. 12, and thus is in no contradiction with the Synoptical account. It is clear, however, that the Baptist's imprisonment must have followed closely upon the events of ch. iii., in all probability before those of iv. 1, and that hence a tradition might have arisen somewhat antedating the imprisonment ; or that John, aware how close was the impending imprisonment upon the conversation and events here recorded, might deem it proper to inform his readers that that event, so close at hand, had not as yet taken place. That it did occur very soon after may be inferred from this very intimation of the Evangelist, and becomes nearly certain from John iv. 1, 2, which records the return of Jesus to Galilee, and must be identical, it would seem, with that, recorded, Matt. iv. 12, which follows upon Jesus' hearing of the imprisonment of the Baptist. If the two journeys do not coincide, then that recorded in John must have preceded the one related by Matt., and the Lord must have gone into Galilee and returned before the imprisonment, which seems greatly to crowd events and is altogether unlikely. Every difficulty is obviated by placing the imprisonment between chs. iii. and iv. of our Gospel, where from the very remark of the Evangelist (ver. 24) it very probably belongs. It is true that the Evangelist does not expressly mention it here, but neither does he again mention it *anywhere ;* and it is as easy to assume its occurring here as at any later period. The interval between the close of ch. iii. and the opening of ch. iv. is undoubtedly not long, but it is *indefinite,* and the οὖν which opens ch. iv. is too familiar and vague a connective with John to forbid a sufficient interval for the Baptist's imprisonment to have occurred. If, then, Meyer alleges that the returns of Jesus to Galilee in John and Matthew are identified for *harmonistic* reasons, we may reply that it is as reasonable, in dealing with credible historians, to assume their agreement when nothing forbids it, as to assume their disagreement when nothing requires it. It is not necessary to suppose, in John iv. 1, that John was *still* baptizing. The ellipsis may be as easily supplied by *had baptized* as by *was baptizing.*

XX. *" A man can receive nothing,"* etc. Ver. 27.

I think Meyer (followed by Weiss) is certainly wrong in referring the "man" here to Jesus. Nothing in the connection requires, or more than superficially suggests it. The disciples were complaining, in jealous irritation probably, of the altered relations between their Master and his late *protégé.* John does not need to defend, and does not defend Jesus. He only needs to defend himself, or rather *explain* his position, and show that the present state of things lay precisely in the line of the divine purposes, and that he had never anticipated or claimed a different result. "A man can receive nothing except it be given him from above"; he cannot transcend the sphere and destiny assigned him; and you yourselves bear me witness that I never professed to be the Messiah, but only His servant and harbinger; never the Bridegroom, but only His friend and attendant. The thought is thus most natural, and the *language* introducing the reply more appropriate to what John would use of himself than of Jesus. He would scarcely, with this exalted personage directly in mind, have naturally designated Him as an ἀνθρωπος, and referred to Him in His character of limitation and dependence. Of *himself* he would be likely to say, " A man can receive nothing except it have been given him from above ; he cannot transcend the divine limitations. Of Jesus he would have been likely to speak in a different language, implying that a being such as He must necessarily arise to the position required by His origin and nature. He who had been originally " before him" must take His place in advance of him (must " become before him"). The Baptist's statement therefore *may,* indeed (with Thol., Lange, Ewald, Luthardt, etc.) be a general statement, but having an indirect reference to himself—a view not essentially differing from that which applies it to himself primarily and specifically (as Lücke, Hengst., Godet, etc.) ; but it *cannot* be spoken with Jesus directly in mind, as the Baptist would not thus have included Him with common men. He would scarcely within a few sentences have spoken of the same person as a " man" (ἀνθρωπος) who " could receive nothing that was not given him from above," and as " He that cometh from above" and " is above all." Though the *sentiment* was strictly as true of Jesus as of John, yet it seems eminently unnatural that *regarding Jesus* John should precisely here and in this manner have uttered it.

CHAPTER IV.

Ver. 3. πάλιν] wanting in A. and many other Uncials and Cursives, Syr. p.
Pers. p. Or. Chrys. It is found, indeed, in B. (in the margin) C. D. L. M. Tᵛ. א.,
but was probably added to denote the *return.* — Ver. 5. οὖ] Elz. Tisch. ὅ, against
C.* D. L. M. S. Curss. Chrys., an inelegant correction. — Ver. 6. ὡσεί] Lach.
Tisch. read ὡς, for which the testimonies are decisive. — Vv. 7–10. For πιεῖν,
Tisch. foll. B.* C.* D. א.* reads πεῖν, for which also πῖν occurs. πεῖν is to be
adopted on account of the preponderating testimony. — Ver. 14. The words οὐ
μὴ—δώσω αὐτῷ are wanting in C.* Curss. and some Verss. and Fathers, even
Cᵣ. ; bracketed by Lach. The testimonies are too weak to warrant our striking
them out, and how easily might their omission have occurred through ὁμοιοτε-
λεύτ. ! — For διψήσῃ Lach. and Tisch. read διψήσει, following preponderating
evidence. But the Future seems to be connected with an early omission of μή
(which we still find in D.). — Ver. 15. ἔρχωμαι] the *Indicative* ἔρχομαι or διέρχο-
μαι (so Tisch.) is bad Gk., and has witnesses enough against it (A. C. D. U. V. Δ. ;
even א.*, which has διέρχωμαι) to be regarded as a transcriber's error ; comp.
xvii. 3. — Ver. 16. ὁ Ἰησοῦς is wanting in B. C.* Heracl. Or. ; an addition. The
position σου τὸν ἄνδρα (Tisch.) is too weakly attested by B. Curss. Or. (three
times) Chrys. — Ver. 21. γύναι, πίστευσόν μοι] Lach. : γ. πίστευέ μ. ; Tisch. :
πίστευέ μ. γ. Amid manifold diversities of testimony the last must be adopted
as the best authenticated, by B. C.* L. א. Ver. Sahid. Heracl. Or. Ath. Cyr.
Chrys. Hilar. — Ver. 27. For ἐθαύμαζον Elz. has ἐθαύμασαν, against decisive testimony. — Ver. 30. After ἐξῆλθον Elz. has οὖν, against decisive testimony.
Added for the purpose of connection, instead of which δέ also occurs, and C.
D. Verss. have καί before ἐξῆλθον, and accordingly Lachm. puts this καί in
brackets. — Ver. 34. ποιῶ] B. C. D. K. L. Tᵇ. Π. Cursives, Clem. Heracl. Or.
Cyr. Chrys. : ποιήσω ; recommended by Griesb., adopted by Lachm. ; a co-ordi-
nation with what follows. — Ver. 35. For τετράμηνος Elz. has τετράμηνον,
against almost all the Uncials. A clumsy emendation. Comp. Heb. xi. 23. —
Ver. 36. Before ὁ θερίζ. Elz. has καί (bracketed by Lachm., deleted by Tisch.),
condemned by B. C.* D. L. Tᵇ. א. Cursives, Verss. and Fathers. Through the
very ancient variation, which joins ἤδη either with what follows (A. C. D. Cyr.)
or with what precedes (Or.), the insertion of καί is the result of the latter mode
of connection. If καί were genuine, neither of the two constructions would
have prompted its omission. — Ver. 42. After κόσμου Elz. has ὁ Χριστός, which
Lachm. Tisch., following important witnesses, have deleted as an exegetical
addition. — Ver. 43. καί ἀπῆλθεν] wanting in B. C. D. Tᵇ. א. Cursives, Codd. It.
Copt. Or. Cyr. Bracketed by Lachm., deleted by Tisch. ; supplementing addition after ver. 3, not in keeping with John's mode of expression. — Ver. 45.
Instead of ἅ we must adopt ὅσα, with Lachm. Tisch., following A. B. C. L.
Cursives, Or. Cyr. Chrys. As the conception expressed by ὅσα is already in
πάντα, ἅ would seem more appropriate, which therefore we find in vv. 29, 39,
in Codd. — Ver. 46. After οὖν Elz. has ὁ Ἰησοῦς, which is altogether wanting in

important witnesses, and in others stands after πάλιν (so Scholz). A common addition. — Ver. 47. αὐτόν after ἦρ. is wanting in B. C. D. L. T^b. ℵ. Cursives, Verss. Or. Aug. Bracketed by Lachm., deleted by Tisch. Supplementary. — Ver. 50. ᾧ] Lachm. Tisch., following A. B. C. L. ℵ**, read ὄν. An unskilful emendation. — Ver. 51. ἀπήντησαν] B. C. D. K. L. ℵ. Cursives : ὑπήντησαν. So Lachm. and Tisch. ; rightly, for John elsewhere always has ὑπαντ. (xi. 20, 30, xii. 18). — ὁ παῖς σου] Lachm. Tisch. : ὁ π. αὐτοῦ, upon such weighty evidence that the received reading must be regarded as a mechanical alteration in imitation of ver. 50. — Ver. 52. Instead of χθές, we must, with Lachm. and Tisch., following the majority of Codd., adopt ἐχθές.

Vv. 1–3. Ὡς οὖν ἔγνω, κ.τ.λ.] οὖν, *igitur*, namely, in consequence of the concourse of people who flocked to Him, and which had been previously mentioned. Considering this concourse, He could not fail to come to know (ἔγνω, not supernatural knowledge, but comp. ver. 53, v. 6, xi. 57, xii. 9) that it had reached the ears of the Pharisees, how He, etc. This prompted Him, however, to withdraw to Galilee, *where their hostility would not be so directly aroused and cherished* as in Judea, the headquarters of the hierarchy. To surrender Himself to them before the time, before His hour arrived, and the vocation of which He was conscious had been fulfilled, was opposed to His consciousness of the divine arrangements, and the object of His mission. He *contented himself, therefore, for the present* with the interest which He had already excited in Judea on behalf of His work, and withdrew, for the time being, to His own less esteemed country.[1] As to the date of this return, see ver. 35 ; it is an arbitrary invention to say,[2] that upon leaving Judea *He gave up baptizing* because John's imprisonment (?) brought a ban of uncleanness upon Israel (515 sq.). The performance of baptism must be supposed as taking place subsequent to this, when conversions are spoken of (*e.g.* ver. 53), comp. iii. 5 ; and Matt. xxviii. 19 does not contain a wholly *new* command to baptize, but its completion and extension to all times and nations. — οἱ Φαρισ.] It is only *this* party, the most powerful and most dangerous of the Jewish sects, that is still named by John, the evangelist who had become furthest removed from Judaism. — ὅτι Ἰησοῦς, κ.τ.λ.] a

---

[1] According to Hofmann, *Schriftbew.* II. 1, p. 168 f., whom Lichtenstein follows, Jesus withdrew, because He was apprehensive lest what had come to the Pharisees' ears should be made use of by them to throw *suspicion on the Baptist.* But this is all the less credible, when we remember that Jesus certainly, as well as John himself (iii. 30), knew it to be a divine necessity that He should increase and the Baptist decrease, and therefore would hardly determine his movements by considerations of the kind supposed. He could more effectually have met any such suspicions, by testifying on behalf of the noble Baptist in the neighbourhood where he was, than by withdrawing from the scene. No ; Jesus went out of the way of the danger that threatened Himself,

and to which He knew it was not yet time for Him to expose Himself ; comp. vii. 1, x. 40, xi. 54. Nonnus : φεύγων λύσσαν ἄπιστον ἀκηλήτων Φαρισαίων. Still, however, we must not, with Hengstenberg and most others, suppose that this retirement to Galilee arose from the fact that John *had already fallen a prey to Pharisaic persecution*, and that Jesus had all the more reason to apprehend this persecution. There is no hint whatever of the supposed fact that the *Pharisees* had delivered John over to Herod. This explanation is based merely upon an attempt at harmonizing, in order to make this journey back to Galilee the same with that named in Matt. iv. 12. See on iii. 24.

[2] Lange, *L.J.* II. p. 515.

verbatim repetition of the report ; hence the *name* (1 Cor. xi. 23), and the *present tenses.* Comp. Gal. i. 23. — ἢ Ἰωάννης] whom they had less to fear, on account of his legal standpoint, and his declarations in i. 19 ff., than Jesus, who with at once so reforming, wonder-working, and effective an agency, and so weightily attested by John, had appeared in Jerusalem.— Ver. 2 is not to be put in a parenthesis, for the construction is not interrupted. [See Note XII. p. 99]. — καίτοι γε] *quanquam quidem*, although.[1] The thing is thus expressed, because "semper is dicitur facere, cui praeministratur," Tertullian. A pretext for this lay in the fact that *John* did himself baptize. *But why did not Jesus Himself baptize?* Not that He might give Himself only to preaching (1 Cor. i. 17) ; for that a *principle* underlay His non-baptizing is shown by John's unconditional statement of it ;[2] nor again, because He *would then have necessarily baptized unto Himself*,[3] for *He* could have done this ; nor again for the clear maintenance of the truth "that He is down to the present day the universal baptizer" (Hengstenberg), an arbitrarily invented abstraction, and even foreign to the N. T. Nonnus points to the true reason : οὐ γὰρ ἄναξ βάπτιζεν ἐν ὕδατι. Bengel well says : "baptizare actio *ministralis*, Acts x. 48, 1 Cor. i. 17 ; Johannes minister sua manu baptizavit, discipuli ejus ut videtur neminem, *at* Christus baptizat *Spiritu sancto*," which the disciples had not power to do until afterwards (vii. 39). Comp. Ewald *b*. For the rest, ver. 2 does not contain a correction of himself by the evangelist (Hengstenberg and early expositors),—as to whom we cannot see why he should not *at once* have expressed himself correctly,—but rather a correction of *the form of the rumour* mentioned in ver. 1. Comp. iii. 26. Nonnus : ἐτήτυμος οὐ πέλε φήμη. In this consists the historical interest of the observation,[4] which we are not to regard as an unhistorical consequence of transporting Christian baptism back to the time of Jesus.

Vv. 4, 5. Ἐδει] *from the geographical position ;* and hence the usual way for Galilean travellers lay through Samaria (Josephus, *Antt.* xx. 6. 1), unless one chose to pass through Perea to avoid the hated land, which Jesus has at present no occasion to do. Comp. Luke ix. 52. — εἰς πόλιν] *to or towards a city* (not *into*, ver. 28 ff.). Comp. Matt. xxi. 1 ; see Fritzsche, *ad Marc.* p. 81. — Συχάρ] (not Σιχάρ, as Elz. has, against the best authorities) is, according to the usual opinion,—though, indeed, the λεγομένην, comp. xi. 54, pointing to an unknown place, does not tally with it,—the same town as that called שְׁכֶם (LXX. Συχέμ, comp. Acts vii. 16 ; also Σίκιμα, comp. Josephus) in Gen. xxxiii. 18, Josh. xx. 7, Judg. ix. 7, *et. al. ;* after the time of Christ, however, called *Neapolis*,[5] and now *Nablus*.[6] Upon the remnant of the Samaritans still in this town, see Rogers on the *Modern Samaritans*, London 1855 ; Barges, *les Samaritains de Naplouse*, Paris 1855. The name

---

[1] See Baeumlein, *Partik.* p. 245 ff.; Klotz, *ad Devar.* p. 654 f.

[2] Against Thomas, Lyra, Maldonatus, and most.

[3] So already Tertullian *de bapt.* 11.

[4] Against Baur and Hilgenfeld.

[5] Joseph. *Bell.* iv. 8. 1.

[6] See Crome, *Beschreib. von Pal.* I. p. 102 ff.; Robinson, III. 336 ; Rosen, in the *Zeitschr. d. morgenl. Gesellsch.* 1860, p. 634 ff.

Συχάρ[1] (which Credner arbitrarily refers to a mere error in transcription) would be thus a *corruption* of the old name, perhaps *intentional*, though it had come into ordinary use, and signifying *drunken town* (according to Isa. xxviii. 1), or *town of lies*, or *heathen town*, after Hab. iii. 18 (שֶׁקֶר). Reland takes the former view, Lightfoot and Hengstenberg the latter, Hengstenberg supposing that *John himself* made the alteration in order to describe the *lying character of the Samaritans*—quite against the simplicity of the narrative in general, and the express λεγομένην in particular. This λεγομ., and the difference in the name, as well as the following πλησίον, etc., and ver. 7, suggest the opinion that Sychar was a *distinct* town in the *neighbourhood* of Sychem.[2] The name may still be discovered in the modern *al Askar*, east of Nablus. Schenkel still sees also here an error of a Gentile-Christian author. — The χωρίον belonged to Sychem (Gen. xxxiii. 19, xlviii. 22, LXX. Josh. xxiv. 32),[3] but must have lain *in the direction of* Sychar. — πλησίον] the town lay *in the neighbourhood* of the field, etc. Here only in the N. T., very often in the classics, a *simple* adverb.

Ver. 6. Πηγὴ τοῦ Ἰακώβ] a *spring-well* (ver. 11), the making of which tradition ascribed to *Jacob*. It is still in existence, and regarded with reverence, though there is no spring-water in it.[4] The ancient sacredness of the spot made it the more worthy of being specially noted by John. — οὕτως] *thus, without further ado, just as He was*, without any ceremony or preparation, "ut locus se obtulerat," Grotius ; ἁπλῶς ὡς ἔτυχε, Chrysostom.[5] The rendering "*tired as He was*" (Erasmus, Beza, Winer, Hengstenberg), so that the preceding participle is repeated in meaning,[6] would require the οὕτως to be *placed before*, as in Acts xxvii. 17, xx. 11. — ἐπὶ τῇ πηγῇ] *at the well*, denoting immediate proximity to it, ver. 2 ; Mark xiii. 29 ; Ex. ii. 15.[7] — ὥρα . . . ἕκτη] *noon, mid-day ;* δίχιος ὥρη, Nonnus. Here again we have not the Roman reckoning (see on i. 40), though the evening[8] was the more usual time for drawing water. Still we must not suppose that the unwonted time was intended to indicate to Jesus "that the woman was given Him of the Father" (Luthardt, p. 80). Jesus knew this, independently of the hour. But *John* could *never forget* the hour, so important in its issues, of this first preaching to the Samaritan woman, and therefore names it. Comp. i. 40.

Vv. 7–9. Γυνὴ ἐκ τ. Σαμαρ.] to be taken as one designation, *a Samaritan-woman.* John gives prominence to the country to which she belonged, to

---

[1] Concerning the Talmudic name סוכר, see Wieseler, *Synopse*, p. 256 ff.

[2] Hug, Luthardt, Lichtenstein, Ewald, Brückner, Baeumlein. See especially Delitzsch, in Guericke's *Luth. Zeitschr.* 1856, p. 244 ff.; Ewald, *Jahrb.* VIII. 255 ff., and in his *Johann Schr.* I. 181.

[3] The LXX. in Gen. xlviii. 22 render שְׁכֶם by Σίκιμα, the error being that they took the Hebrew word directly as a *name*, whereas it is only an *allusion* to the town Sichem.

[4] See Robinson, III. p. 330; Ritter, XVI. 634.

[5] See Ast, *Lex. Plat.* II. p. 495 ; Nägels-bach, *z. Ilias*, p. 63, ed. 3.

[6] See Bornemann in *Rosenmüller's Rep.* II. p. 246 ff., Ast, *l.c. ;* Stallbaum, *ad Plat. Protag.* p. 314 C.

[7] See Bernhardy, p. 249 ; Reisig, *ad Oed. Col.* 281 ; Ellendt, *Lex. Soph.* I. 541.

[8] If it had been six o'clock in the evening (as also Isenberg in the *Luther. Zeitschr.* 1868, p. 454 ff. maintains, for the sake of xix. 14), how much too short would the remainder of the day be for all that follows down to ver. 40! We must allow a much longer time, in particular, for vv. 28–30, and yet ver. 35 still presupposes bright daylight.

prepare the way for the characteristic features of the following interview. It is not the *town* two miles distant (*Sebaste*) that is meant, but the *country*. — ἀντλῆσαι ὕδωρ] The modern Nablus lies half an hour distant from the southern well, and has many wells of its own close by.[1] It is therefore probable that Sychar, out of which the woman came,[2] was a separate town.[3] It is in itself an arbitrary supposition to imagine, with Hengstenberg, that this " Give me to drink " has underlying it " a spiritual sense" (" Give me the spiritual refreshment of thy conversion)," and is opposed to ver. 8, which by no means assigns the reason why Jesus entered into conversation with the woman ; for He might have done this in the apostles' presence, though, according to Hengstenberg, He must have sent them away (all excepting John),[4] on purpose to have an undisturbed interview with the woman. All this is mere imagination. — Ver. 8. γάρ] The reason why He asked the services *of the woman ;* the *disciples*, whose services He would otherwise have claimed, were absent. — ἵνα τροφὰς ἀγορ.] According to later tradition (" Samaritanis panem comedere aut vinum bibere prohibitum est," Raschi, *ad Sota,* 515), this would not have been allowed. But the separation could not have been so distinctly marked at that time, especially as to commercial dealings and intercourse with the Galileans, since their road lay through Samaria. Jesus, moreover, was raised above these hostile divisions which existed among the people (Luke ix. 52). — Ver. 9. The woman recognized that Jesus was a *Jew* by His *language*, and not by His *accent* merely. — πῶς] *qui fit ut.* The words of the woman indicate the pert feminine *caprice* of national feeling. There is no ground for supposing (Hengst.) that the woman had at this stage any presentiment that He who addressed her was other than an ordinary Jew. — οὐ γὰρ, κ.τ.λ.] not a parenthesis, but the words of the *evangelist.* — *Jews* with *Samaritans*, without the article.

Ver. 10. Jesus certainly recognized at once the *susceptibility* of the woman ; allowing, therefore, His own need to stand in abeyance, He began the conversation, which was sufficiently striking to excite at once the full interest of her sanguine temperament, though at the outset this interest was nothing but feminine curiosity. — τὴν δωρ. τ. θεοῦ] *the gift of God,* which you may now partake of by conversation with me. Not certainly the person of *Jesus Himself* (the Greek Fathers, Erasmus, Beza, and others, also Hengst. and Godet), to which he refers only as the discourse advances with the καί of closer definition. — σὺ ἂν ᾔτησας] *thou wouldest have prayed Him (i.e.* to give thee to drink), *and He would have,* etc. Observe the emphatic σύ (the request would have come from *thee*). — ὕδωρ ζῶν] The woman takes this to mean *spring-water,* חַיִּים מַיִם, Gen. xxvi. 19, Lev. xiv. 5, Jer. ii. 13, as op-

---

[1] See Robinson, III. 333.

[2] That, considering the *sacred character* of the water, she did not hesitate about the distance of the well from Sychem (Hengstenberg), is without any hint in the text.

[3] As to the forms πεῖν and πῖν (so Jacobs, *Del. epigr.* vi. 78), see Herm. *Herodian.* § 47 ; Buttmann, *N. T. Gr.* p. 58 [E. T. p. 66], who prefers πῖν, though this is regarded by

Fritzsche (*de conform. Lachm.* p. 27) as the mistake of a copyist. As to the phrase δίδωμι πιεῖν, without any object expressed, see Krüger, § 55. 3. 21.

[4] Who must, according to Godet also, have remained with Him. A gratuitous addition, made for the purpose of securing a guarantee for the accuracy of the narrative.

posed to water in a cistern.   Comp. *vivi fontes* and the like among the Romans ; see Wetstein.   Christ does indeed mean *spring-water*, but, as in vii. 38, in a *spiritual* sense (comp. ver. 14), namely, *God's grace and truth* (i. 14), which He, who is the possessor of them, communicates by His word out of His fulness, and which in its living, regenerating, and, for the satisfying of spiritual need, ever freshly efficacious power, is typified by water from the spring.[1] He does not mean *Himself*, His own life (Olshausen, Godet, following Epiphanius and most others), in the same manner as He speaks of Himself as the bread of life, vi. 35, for this is not indicated in any part of the present colloquy ; nor does He mean *faith* (iii. 15), as Lücke thinks, nor the *Spirit*,[2] the gift of which *follows* the communication of the living water.   Any reference to *baptism*[3] is quite remote from the text.   Calvin is substantially right when he sees typified *totam renovationis gratiam*.

Vv. 11, 12.   "Thou canst not mean the spring-water here in this well ; thou couldest not give this to me, for thou hast no bucket,[4] which is needed on account of the depth of the well ; *whence hast thou, therefore, the spring-water thou speakest of?*" — κύριε] The τίς ἐστιν ὁ λέγων σοι, etc., ver. 10, has given the woman a momentary feeling of *respect*, not unmixed with irony. — οὔτε followed by καί is rare, 3 John 10.[5] — μὴ σὺ μείζων, κ.τ.λ.] Notice the emphatic σύ coming first : "*thou* surely art not greater," etc. ; "*thou* dost not look like that !" Comp. viii. 53. — μείζων] *i.e. more able*, in a position to give what is better.   By *him* was the well given us, and for *him* it was good enough for him and his to drink from ; yet thou speakest as if thou hadst another and a better spring of water ! The woman dwells upon the enigmatical word of Christ at first, just as Nicodemus did, iii. 4, but with more cleverness and vivacity, at the same time more boldly, and with feminine loquacity. — τοῦ πατρὸς ἡμῶν] for the Samaritans traced their descent back to *Joseph*.[6] They certainly were not of purely heathen origin (Hengstenberg).[7] — ὃς ἔδωκεν, κ.τ.λ.] a Samaritan tradition, not derived from the O. T. — καὶ αὐτὸς, κ.τ.λ.] καί is simply *and*, neither for καὶ ὅς, nor, *and indeed*.   The θρέμματα are the *cattle*,[8] not *servants* (Majus, Kypke),[9] whom there was no need specially to name ; the mention of the *herds* completes the picture of their *nomadic* progenitor. — τὸ ὕδωρ τὸ ζῶν] which thou hast to give ; ver. 10.

---

[1] Comp. analogous passages, Ecclus. xv. 3, xxiv. 21 ; Baruch iii. 12 ; Buxtorf, *Lex. Talm.* p. 2298.

[2] Calovius, Baumgarten Crusius, Luthardt, Hofmann.

[3] Justin, Cyprian, Ambrose, and most others.

[4] ἄντλημα, elsewhere *the drawing of water*, is used in the sense of *haustrum*. Nonnus explains it κάδον ἐλκυστῆρα (*a bucket to draw water*).—The woman had with her a ὑδρία, ver. 28 (comp. ii. 6), but she must also have had an ἄντλημα, provided with a long handle or rope to draw the water *up*, or at least some contrivance for letting down the ὑδρία itself.

[5] See Winer, p. 460 [E. T. p. 494] ; Baeumlein, *Partik.* p. 222 ; Klotz, *ad Devar.* 714.

[6] Josephus, *Antt.* vii. 7. 3, viii. 14. 3, xi. 8. 6.

[7] See Keil on 2 Kings xvii. 24 ; Petermann in *Herzog's Encykl.* XIII. 367.

[8] Plato, *Polit.* p. 261 A ; Xen. *Oec.* xx. 23 ; *Ages.* ix. 6 ; Herodian. iii. 9. 17 ; Josephus, *Antt.* vii. 7. 3.

[9] The word, the general meaning of which is *quicquid enutritur*, is found on inscriptions as applied to *slaves ;* it is used of *children* likewise in the classics (Valck. *Diatr.* p. 249), as in Soph. *Phil.* 243 ; comp. *Oed. Rex*, 1143.   It does not occur in the LXX. or Apocrypha.

Vv. 13, 14. Not an explanation, but (comp. iii. 5) a carrying out of the metaphor, to lead the woman nearer to its higher import. — τούτου] referring to the well. — οὐ μὴ διψ. εἰς τ. αἰῶνα] "*will certainly not thirst for ever*," antithesis to fleeting bodily refreshment, ver. 13.   Comp. vi. 34. *That heavenly grace and truth which Christ communicates, when received by faith into the inner life, for ever supplies what we need in order to salvation*, so that the lack of this satisfaction is never felt, because the supply is always there.   Bengel admirably remarks : " Sane aqua illa, quantum in se est, perennem habet virtutem ; et ubi sitis recurrit, hominis non aquae defectus est."   The expression in Ecclus. xxiv. 20 : οἱ πίνοντές με (Wisdom) ἔτι διψήσουσι, rests upon a different view of the continuity of enjoyment, namely, that of the individual moments passing in the continual alternation of desire and satisfaction, and not of the unity which they make up, and of their condition as a whole. — γενήσεται ἐν αὐτῷ, κ.τ.λ.] the *positive* effect following the negative (and hence τὸ ὕδωρ ὃ δώσω αὐτῷ is emphatically repeated) : *divine grace and truth appropriated by faith will so energetically develop their life in him in inexhaustible fulness, that its full impelling power endures unto eternal Messianic life.* Upon his entrance into the Messiah's kingdom (comp. iii. 3, 5), the man takes along with him this inner living power of divine χάρις καὶ ἀλήθεια, vi. 27. — ἄλλεσθαι εἰς. *to spring up into*, often also in the classics,[1] but with reference to *water* here only.   A Greek would say προρεῖν εἰς ; yet the word in the text is stronger and more vivid.   The ζωὴ αἰών. is conceived of *locally*, under the imagery of a widespreading spring ; to render εἰς " *reaching* to everlasting life*,*"[2] arbitrarily lets go the concrete comparison, one of the main features in which is endless power of springing up.   This description of the well *springing up* into everlasting life is the *finishing touch* of the picture.   On εἰς ζ. αἰ., see ver. 36.

Vv. 15, 16. The woman as yet having no apprehension of the higher meaning of the water spoken of (against B. Crusius, Lange), yet being in some degree perplexed, asks, not in irony, as Lightfoot and Tholuck think, but sincerely, for this wonderful water, which at any rate must be of great use to her.—Jesus breaks off suddenly, and commences, by a seemingly unimportant request, " Call thy husband," to lay hold of the woman *in her inner life, so that the beginnings of her faith in Him might be connected with His supernatural knowledge of her peculiar moral relations.*   This process must be accompanied with the *awakening* in her of a *sense of guilt* (see ver. 29), and thus pave the way for *repentance ;* and who dare deny that, besides the *immediate* object, this may have been included in the *purpose* of Jesus ? though He does not directly rebuke, but leaves the feeling to operate of itself (against Strauss and most others). — φώνησ. τ. ἄνδρα σου] We are not to ask here what the husband *was to do* (Chrysostom, Euthymius Zigabenus : " that he might partake with her of the gift of salvation that was before her ;" so also Lücke) ; because the command was only an *apparent* one, not *seriously* intended, for Jesus *knew* the relations of the woman, and did not merely find His próphetic gift awakened by the answer she gave, as Lücke and

---

[1] Hom. *Il. a.* 537 ; Xen. *Mem.* i. 3. 9.   [2] B. Crusius, Luthardt, Brückner, **Ewald.**

Godet gratuitously assume.   The τ. ἄνδρα σου was the *sore spot* where the healing was to begin.   According to Lange,[1] it would have been unseemly if Jesus, now that the woman showed a willingness to become His disciple (?), had continued to converse longer with her in her husband's absence ; His desire, therefore, was in keeping " with the highest and finest sense of social propriety."   But the husband was nothing more than a *paramour !* — ἐλθέ] in the sense of *come back*, as the context shows.[2]

Ver. 17, 18.   The woman is *taken aback ;* her light, naive, bantering manner is now completely gone, and she quickly seeks to shun the sensitive point with the answer, true only in words, οὐκ ἔχω ἄνδρα ; but Jesus goes deeper still. — καλῶς] *rightly, truly ;* viii. 48 ; Matt. xv. 7 ; Luke xx. 39.   *How far* truly, what follows shows,—namely, only relatively, and therefore the approval is only apparent, and in some degree ironical. — ἄνδρα οὐκ ἔχω] "*a husband* I have not ;" as it is the *conception* of ἀνήρ which Jesus has to emphasize, it stands first. — πέντε γὰρ, κ.τ.λ.] It is doubtful whether she *really* had five successive husbands, from whom she had been separated either by death or by divorce, or whether Jesus included *paramours*, using ἄνδρας in a varying sense according to the varying subjects ; or whether, again, He meant that *all five* were *scortatores* (Chrysostom, Maldonatus, and most others). The first supposition is to be adopted, because the *present* man, who is not her *husband*, stands in *contrast* with the former husbands.   She had been therefore five times married (*such* a history had already seared her conscience, ver. 29 ; how, is not stated), and now she was either a widow or a divorced wife, and had a paramour (νόθον ἀκοίτην, Nonnus), who lived with her as a husband, but really *was not* her husband (hence the οὐκ ἔστι is emphatically put first).   To interpret the story of the five husbands as a whole as a *symbolical history of the Samaritan nation*,[3] either as a divinely intended coincidence (Hengst. Köstlin, comp. Baumgarten and Scholten), or as a type in the mind of the evangelist (Weizsäcker, p. 387), so that the symbolic meaning excludes any actual fact (Keim, *Gesch. J.* p. 116), or again as fiction (B. Bauer), whose mythical basis was that history (Strauss), is totally destitute of any historical warrant.   For the man whom the woman *now* had must, symbolically understood, represent Jehovah ; and He had been the God of the Samaritans before the introduction of false gods, and therefore it would have been more correct to speak of *six* husbands (Heracleon actually read ἐξ).   But how incredible that Jesus would represent Jehovah under the similitude of a *paramour* (for the woman was now living in *concubinage*), and the "fivefold heathenism" of the nation under the type of *real* marriages !— For the rest, the Lord's *knowledge* of the woman's circumstances was *immediate* and *supernatural*.   To assume that He had ascertained her history from others (Paulus, Ammon), is opposed to the Johannean view ; while the notion that the disciples introduced into the history what they afterwards discovered,[4] is psychologically groundless, if once we admit that

---

[1] *L. J.* II. p. 530 f.

[2] See Hom. *Od.* a. 408, β. 30 ; Xen. *Anab.* ii. 1. 1, v. 1. 4 ; Baruch iv. 37 ; Tobit i. 18 ; Heind. *ad Plat. Prot.* p. 310 C.   Comp. xiv. 18 ; Luke xix. 13.

[3] According to 2 Kings xvii. 24 ff.; Josephus, *Antt.* ix. 14. 3 : πέντε ἔθνη . . . ἕκαστον ἴδιον θεὸν εἰς Σαμαρ. κομίσαντες.

[4] Schweizer, p. 139.

Jesus possessed a knowledge of the moral state of others (and here we have not merely a knowledge of outward circumstances,—against de Wette) beyond that attainable by ordinary means.[1] Lange invents the strange and unnecessary (ii. 24. f.) addition, that " the psychical effects produced by the five husbands upon the woman were traceable in her manner and mien, and these were recognized by Jesus." — ἀληθές] as something true.[2]

Vv. 19, 20. The woman now discerns in Jesus the man of God endowed with higher knowledge, a *prophet*,[3] and puts to Him accordingly—perhaps also to leave no further room for the unpleasant mention of the circumstances of her life which had been thus unveiled—the national religious question ever in dispute ; a question which does not, indeed, imply a presentiment of the superiority of the Jews' religion (Ewald), but one, the decision of which might be expected from such a *prophet* as she now deemed Him to be. The great *national* interest in this question,[4] is sufficient to remove any apparent improbability attaching to it as coming from the lips of this morally frivolous woman.[5] Luthardt thinks that she now wished to go in prayer for the forgiveness of her sins to the holy place appointed, and only desires to know where ; on Gerizim or in Jerusalem. But she has not yet arrived at this stage ; she gives no intimation of this ; she does not call the place a place of *expiation* (this also against Lange) ; and Jesus, in His answer, gives no hint to that effect. Her seeking after religious information is still theoretical merely, attaching itself to a matter of popular controversy, naive, without depth of personal anxiety, as also without thought of fundamental differences, which Hengstenberg attributes to her as a representative of the Samaritans, who would first remove the national stumbling-block ; see ver. 25. — θεωρῶ] περισκοπεῖται καὶ θαυμάζει, Chrysostom. — οἱ πατέρες ἡμ.] Since ὑμεῖς stands in contrast, we are not to go back to *Abraham* and *Jacob* (according to a tradition based upon Gen. xii. 6 ff., xiii. 4, xxxiii. 20) ;[6] we must simply take the reference to be to the ancestors of the *Samaritans* as far back as the building of the temple on Mount Gerizim in the time of Nehemiah. —In this mountain] pointing to Gerizim, between which and Ebal the town of Sychem (and Sychar) lay. The temple there had already been destroyed by *John Hyrcanus ;* but the site itself, which Moses had already fixed as that wherein the blessings of the law were to be spoken (Deut. xi. 29, xxvii. 12, 13), was still held sacred by the people,[7] especially also on account of Deut. xxvii. 4 (where the Samaritan text has גריזים instead of עיבל), and is so even at the present day.[8] Concerning the *ruins* on the top of the mountain, see especially Bargès, as before, p. 107 ff.

[1] We must not therefore suppose with Ewald that Jesus named simply a *round* number of husbands, which in a wonderful manner turned out to be right.

[2] See Winer, p. 433 [E. T. p. 464]. Comp. Plato, *Gorg.* p. 493 D: τοῦτ' ἀληθέστερον εἴρηκας ; Soph. *Phil.* 909 ; Lucian, *D. M.* vi. 3 ; *Tim.* 20.

[3] Comp. 1 Sam. ix. 9 ; in Greek and Latin writers : Hom. *Il.* i. 70 ; Hesiod, *Theog.* 38 ; Virgil, *Georg.* iv. 392 ; Macrobius, *Sat.* i. 20. 5.

[4] See Josephus, *Antt.* xiii. 3. 4.

[5] Against Strauss, B. Bauer.

[6] Chrysostom, Euthymius Zigabenus, and many others, also Kuinöel and Baumgarten Crusius.

[7] Comp. Josephus, *Antt.* xviii. 4. 1 ; *Bell.* iii. 7. 32.

[8] See Robinson, III. p. 319 ff. ; Ritter, *Erdk.* XVI. p. 638 ff. ; Abulfathi, *Annab. Samar. arab. ed.*, ed. Vilmar, 1865, Proleg. 4.

Ver. 21. Jesus decides neither for the one place nor for the other ; nor does He pronounce both wrong (B. Crusius) ; but as His aim is to give her the living water, divine grace and truth, He rises to the *higher point of view of the future*, whence both the local centres and limitations of God's true worship *disappear;* and the question itself no longer arises, because with the triumph of His work all outward localizing of God's worship comes to an end, not indeed absolutely, but as fettering the freedom of the outward service. — προσκυνήσ.] As spoken to the woman, this refers not to mankind generally (Godet), nor to the Israelites of *both* forms of religion (Hilgenfeld, comp. Hengst.), but to the future conversion of the *Samaritans*, who thus would be freed from the ritual on Mount Gerizim (which is therefore named *first*), but were not to be brought to the ritual in Jerusalem, and therefore ἐν Ἱεροσολ. has its warrant with reference to the Samaritans.[1] The divine ordainment of the temple service was *educational*. Christ was its *aim* and end, its πλήρωσις ; the modern doctrine of the re-establishing of Jerusalem in its grandeur is a chiliastic dream (see Rom. xi. 27, note). — τῷ πατρί] spoken from the standing-point of the future converts, to whom God, through their faith in the Reconciler, would be *Father* : "Tacite novi foederis suavitatem innuit," Grotius.

Ver. 22. Jesus has answered the question as to the *where* of worship ; He now turns, unasked, to the *object* of worship, and in this He pronounces in favour of the Jews. The chain of thought is not : "as matters *now* stand," and so on (Lücke and most others) ; such a change of *time* must have been *indicated*. — ὃ οὐκ οἴδατε] *ye worship what ye know not.* *God* is meant, who is named not personally, but by the neuter, according to His essence and character, not as *He* who is worshipped, but as *that* which is worshipped (comp. the neuter, Acts xvii. 23, according to the more correct reading) ; and this is simply *God Himself*, not τὰ τοῦ θεοῦ or τὰ πρὸς τὸν θεόν (Lücke), which would not be in keeping with the conception expressed in προσκυνεῖν; for what is worshipped is not what *pertains to God*, but *God* (comp. vv. 21, 23, 24). The οὐκ οἴδατε is to be understood *relatively ;* comp. vii. 28. As the Samaritans received the Pentateuch only, they were without the developed revelation of God contained in the subsequent books of the O. T., particularly in the Prophets, especially the stedfast, pure, and living development of Messianic hope, which the Jews possessed, and had also lost, with the temple and its sacred shrines, the abiding presence of the Deity.[2] Jesus, therefore, might well speak of their knowledge of God, *in comparison with that of the Jews* (ἡμεῖς), who possessed the full revelation and promise, *as ignorance ;* and He could regard this great superiority of the Jews as unaffected by the monotheism, however spiritual, of the Samaritans. According to de Wette, whom Ebrard follows, the meaning is : "ye worship, and *in so doing, ye do* what ye know not,"—which is said to refer to the arbitrary and unhistorical manner in which the Samaritan worship originated. According to this, the ὃ must be taken as in ὃ δὲ νῦν ζῶ, Gal. ii. 20 (comp. Bengel), and

[1] Against Hilgenfeld in the *Theol. Jahrb.* 1857, p. 517 ; and in his *Zeitschr.* 1863,   p. 103.
[2] Rom. iii. 2, ix. 4, 5.

would denote the προσκύνησις itself, which is accomplished in the προσκυνεῖν.[1] But in that case it would have been more logical to write ὃ ὑμεῖς προσκυνεῖτε, οὐκ οἴδατε. Tittmann, Morus, Kuinoel, also erroneously say that ὃ stands for καθ' ὅ, *pro vestra ignorantia*. It is the accusative of the object, in which is included the dative, or even the accusative of the demonstrative, for προσκύν. is construed in both ways.[2] — ἡμεῖς] *i.e.* Jews, without a conjunction, and hence all the more emphatic. According to the whole connection, it must mean *we Jews*, not *Christians*, as if ἡμεῖς were intended in the Gnostic sense to denote, as something altogether new, the distinctively Christian conscious ness, as contrasted with the unconscious worship of the Israelitish race in its Samaritan and Jewish branches.[3] That Jesus, being Himself a Jew (Gal. iv. 4 ; John i. 11), should reckon Himself among the Jews, cannot be thought strange in the antithesis of such a passage as this. But in what follows, the Lord rises so high above this antithesis between Samaritan and Jew, that in the future which He opens up to view (vv. 23, 24), this national distinctiveness ceases to have any significance. Still, in answer to the woman's question, He could simply and definitely assign to the Jews that superiority which historically belonged to them before the manifestation of that higher future ; but He could not intend " to set her free from the un reality of her national existence" (Luthardt), but rather, considering the oc casion which presented itself, could make no concession that would preju dice His Messianic patriotism, based as this was upon historical fact and upon the divine purpose (Rom. i. 16). — ὅτι ἡ σωτ., κ.τ.λ.] *because salva tion* (of course, not without the *Saviour*, though this is not *named*) proceeds from the Jews (not from the Samaritans),—a general doctrinal statement, incontestably true, based upon the promise to Abraham, Gen. xii.,[4] concern ing the salvation of the Messiah's kingdom, whose *future* establishment is *rep resented as present*, as is natural in such an axiomatic statement of historic fact. As *salvation* is of the *Jews*, this design of their existence in the econ omy of grace constitutes the reason (ὅτι) why *they*, as a nation, possessed the true and pure revelation of God, whose highest culmination and con summation is that very salvation ; comp. Rom. ix. 4, 5 It must not, indeed, be overlooked that ἡμεῖς . . . οἴδαμεν was not true of every *individual* of the ἡμεῖς (not of those who rejected the salvation), but refers to the nation as a whole in its ideal existence as the *people of God*, whose prerogative as such could not be destroyed by empirical exceptions. Thus the invisible church is hidden in the visible.

Vv. 23, 24. But [5] this antithesis will also disappear (comp. ver. 21) by the *worship* of the true (*i.e.* answering to the ideal of such, comp. i. 19) wor shippers of God, whose time is coming, yea, already is present (inasmuch as Jesus had already gathered round Him a small band of such worshippers).

[1] See Bernhardy, p. 106.
[2] See Lobeck, *ad Phryn.* p. 463.
[3] Hilgenfeld, comp. his *Zeitschr.* 1863, p. 213 ff.
[4] Comp. Isa. ii. 3 ; Mic. iv. 2.
[5] ἀ λ λ ά, *yet*, as contrasted, not with the ἡ σωτηρία ἐκ τ. Ἰουδαίων ἐστίν (Hilgenfeld, as

if μὲν . . . δέ were there), but, as is clear from what follows (the true προσκυνεῖν), with the ὑμεῖς . . . οἴδαμεν. Baeumlein re gards it as an intensified addition to ver. 21, " *yea, the hour is coming.*" But thus ver. 22 would be arbitrarily overleaped.

He could *not* add καὶ νῦν ἐστιν to the ἐρχ. ὥρα of ver. 21. — ἐν πνεύματι κ. ἀληθ.]
expresses the *element wherein* the worship is carried on in its two closely
connected parts, viz. : (1) *In spirit ; i.e.* the worship does not consist in outward acts, gestures, ceremonies, limitations of time and place, or in anything pertaining to the sphere of sense ; it has to do with that higher
spiritual nature in man which is the substratum of his moral self-consciousness, and the seat of his true moral life, manifesting itself in thoughts,
feelings, efforts of will, moods of elevation, excitements, etc. ; otherwise
the worship would belong to the sphere of the *flesh* merely, which
is the opposite of true worship.   Comp. Rom. i. 9 : ᾧ λατρεύω ἐν τῷ πνεύματί
μου.   It is *spirit*-evident, from both the O. T. and N. T. view, that the
πνεῦμα in which this takes place is influenced by the divine Spirit (comp.
Rom. viii. 14–16, 26) ; but we must not take ἐν πνεύματι (ver. 24) to
denote objectively the Divine Spirit (Luthardt, Brückner, Baeumlein, following the early expositors).   The προσκίνσιςη ἐν πνεύμ. is rational, Rom.
xii. 1 ; it does not in itself. exclude the *ritus externos*, but it does exclude all
mechanical ritualism, and all *opus operatum.*   (2) *In truth,* not "in sincerity,
honesty," which would be greatly too weak a meaning after οἱ ἀληθινοί, but,
so that the worship harmonizes with its object, not contradicting, but corresponding with, God's nature and attributes.   Otherwise it belongs to the
sphere of the ψεῦδος, either conscious or unconscious ; *this* ψεῦδος, and not
σκιά or τύποι, is the antithesis of ἀλήθεια. — προσκυνητής, save only in Eusta-
thius and Hesychius, occurs only in *Inscript. Chandl.* p. 91. — καὶ γάρ, κ.τ.λ.]
for the Father also, etc.   The καί denotes that what the προσκυνηταί do *on their
part* is *also what the Father Himself* desires.   Luther, B. Crusius, Tholuck,
Hengstenberg, and most others, erroneously render as if it were καὶ γὰρ
τοιούτους or καὶ γὰρ ζητεῖ.   The emphasis given by καί in καὶ γάρ always rests
upon the word immediately following (even in 1 Cor. xiv. 8).[1]   It does not
elsewhere occur in John.   Usually the καί has been overlooked ; but the
Vulgate rightly renders : nam *et pater."* — ζητεῖ] *He seeks after, desires.*[2]
τοιούτους is with marked emphasis put first : *of this character* He desires His
worshippers to be. — πνεῦμα ὁ θεός, κ.τ.λ.]   The predicate emphatically stands
first (comp. i. 1 : θεὸς ἦν ὁ λόγος) : *a Spirit is God,* etc.   Here to God's *will* is
added His *nature* (ver. 23), as a further motive for true worship,[3] to which
the nature and manner of the worship on man's part must correspond.
How utterly *heterogeneous* would be a carnal and spurious worship with the
perfectly pure and holy nature of God, completely raised above every limit

---

[1] Stallbaum, *ad Plat. Gorg.* p. 467 B.

[2] Comp. Herod. i. 94 ; John i. 39, iv. 27, *al.*

[3] Πνεῦμα ὁ θεός is not to be conjoined with
the assumption of a *corporeity* belonging to
God (in answer to the concessions of Ham-
berger in the *Jahrb. f. D. Th.* 1867, p. 421).
Jesus might *take it for granted* that *every
one* who belonged to the O. T. monotheism
understood that God is a Spirit, according
to Ex. xx. 4, Jer. xxxi. 3 ; and it is by no
means necessary to refer to the traces of
Samaritan spiritualism, in order to make

the expression more intelligible as addressed to the woman (Gesenius, *de Theol.
Sam.* p. 12 ; *de Pentat. Sam. orig.* p. 58 ff.).
Πνεῦμα must not be regarded as indicating
something *new* in comparison with the
O. T. (Lutz, *bibl. Dogm.* p. 45 ; Köstlin, *Lehrbegr.* p. 79), but as something known, and
emphasized with corresponding impressiveness on account of its importance.   Comp.
Hofmann, *Schriftbew.* I. 68 ff. ; Weiss, *Lehrbegr.* p. 54, 55.

of sense, of place, of particularism, of all need and dependence, simply because He is *Spirit!* while a spiritual and true worship is θεοπρεπὴς κ. κατάλληλος,[1] and is *homogeneous* with the idea of God as Spirit.

Vv. 25, 26. The woman is *struck* by Christ's answer, but she does not yet *understand* it, and she *appeals to the Messiah ;* Χριστῷ Χριστὸν ἔλεξεν, Nonnus. Well says Chrysostom : εἰλιγγίασεν ἡ γυνὴ (she grew dizzy) πρὸς τὰ λεχθέντα, καὶ ἀπηγόρευσε πρὸς τὸ ὕψος τῶν εἰρημένων, καὶ καμοῦσα ἄκουσον τί φησιν, κ.τ.λ. The presentiment that Jesus Himself was the Messiah is not to be recognized in her words (against Luthardt) ; yet these are neither evasive nor abrupt (Lücke, de Wette), but express the need of the manifestation of the Messiah, which was deeply felt in this moment of profound impression,—a need which Jesus perceived, and immediately satisfied by the declaration that followed. The Samaritans, sharing the national hope of the Jews, and taking their stand upon the Messianic passages in the Pentateuch (such as Gen. xv., xlix. 10, Num. xxiv., and especially Deut. xviii. 15), were expecting the Messiah,[2] whom they called הַשָּׁהֵב or הַתְּהֵב,[3] whose mission they apprehended less in a political aspect, though also as the restoration of the kingdom of Israel, and the re-establishment of the Gerizim-worship, yet merely as the result of human working.[4] Against B. Bauer's unhistorical assertion, that at that time the Samaritans had no Messianic belief,[5] see B. Crusius. Μεσ-σίας (without the article, as in i. 42) is uttered by the woman as a *proper name*, and thus she adopted the Jewish title, which was doubtless well known in Samaria, and the use of which might be so closely connected with a feeling of respect for the highly gifted Jew with whom she was conversing, that there is no adequate ground for the assumption that the evangelist puts the word into her mouth (Ammon). — πάντα] used in a popular indefinite sense.— ἐγώ εἰμι] *I am He, i.e.* the Messiah, ver. 25, the simple usual Greek expression, and not in imitation of Deut. xxxii. 39. Observe the plain and direct avowal, in answer to the *guilelessness of the Samaritan woman, whose faith was now ready to acknowledge Him* (comp. Chrysostom). The consideration of the special circumstances, and of the fact that here there was no danger of a political abuse of the avowal (vi. 15), obviates the seeming contradiction between this early confession and Matt. viii. 4, xvi. 20.

Ver. 27. Ἐπὶ τούτῳ] *Hereupon*, while this was going on.[6] Often in Plato. — ἐθαύμαζον] the descriptive imperfect alternates with the simply narrative Aor.[7] — μετὰ γυναικός] *with a woman ;* for they had yet to learn the fact that Jesus rose above the Rabbinical precepts, teaching that it was beneath the dignity of man to hold converse with women, and the directions of the law upon the subject (see Lightfoot, Schoettgen, and Wetstein). —

---

[1] Euthym. Zigab.

[2] The Samaritan name הַשָּׁהֵב or התהב is by some rendered *the converter* (so Gesenius and Ewald), and by others the *returning one* (Moses), as Sacy, Juynboll (*Commentar. in hist. gentis Sam. L. B.* 1846), Hengstenberg. Both are linguistically admissible ; the latter, considering Deut. xviii. 15, is the more probable.

[3] Now *el Muhdy;* see Robinson, III. 320.

[4] See Gesen. *de theol. Sam.* p. 41 ff., and *ad carmina Sam.* p. 75 f. ; Bargès, *passim ;* Vilmar, *passim.*

[5] *Evang. Gesch. Joh. Beil.* p. 415 ff.

[6] See Bernhardy, p. 250 ; Winer, p. 367 [E. T. p. 392].

[7] See Kühner, II. 74.

οὐδεὶς μέντοι, κ.τ.λ.] reverential fear. — τί ζητεῖς] *what desirest thou ?* *i.e.* what has led thee to this surprising conversation ? (i. 39). There is no warrant for referring μετ᾿ αὐτῆς by ζεῦγμα (παρ᾿ αὐτῆς) also to ζητεῖς (Lücke, de Wette); and just as little for rendering ζητεῖν by the unwonted meaning *contend*, as if the disciples thought there was a discussion prompted by national hostility going on (Ewald). — ἤ] *or*, *i.e.* if thou *desirest* nothing.

Vv. 28–30. Οὖν] in consequence of the disciples' coming, which interrupted the interview with Jesus. — ἀφῆκεν, κ.τ.λ.] οὕτως ἀνήφθη τῷ πυρὶ τῶν πνευματικῶν ναμάτων, ὡς καὶ τὸ ἄγγος ἀφεῖναι καὶ τὴν χρείαν, δι᾿ ἣν παρεγένετο, Euthymius Zigabenus. How great the power of the decisive awakening of the new life in this woman ! — πάντα ὅσα] often thus used together in the classics.[1] — ἐποίησα] thus from *a sense of guilt* she described what Jesus had said to her. His words were the summary of her moral history. — μήτι οὖτος, κ.τ.λ.] not *must he not be really the Messiah?* as if the question implied an *affirmation.* So Lücke, but against the constant use of the interrogative μήτι, which implies, *this is not perhaps the Messiah, is it ?* requiring, indeed, a negative answer, yet to be explained psychologically from fear and bashful surprise over the fact too great for belief. The woman believes it ; but startled at the greatness of the discovery, she does not trust herself, and ventures modestly only to ask as one in doubt.[2] Observe in ver. 30 the change from ἐξῆλθον to the vividly descriptive ἤρχοντο (see on ver. 27, xx. 3). In the latter word the reader *sees* the crowd coming. Comp. ver. 40, where they arrive.

Vv. 31–34. Ἐν τῷ μεταξύ] *in the meantime,*[3] after the woman had gone, and before the Samaritans came.—Ver. 32. Jesus, making the sensuous the clothing of the supersensuous (the *pastus animi*), speaks from a feeling of inner quickening and satisfaction, which He had just experienced from the change He had wrought in the Samaritan woman,—a feeling which He was to experience still more strongly throughout His divinely appointed work onwards until its completion. This inner satisfaction now prompts Him to refuse bodily sustenance. Observe the emphatic antithesis of ἐγώ and ὑμεῖς. — As to βρῶσις, and βρῶμα, ver. 34, see on Col. ii. 16. — Ver. 33. In the question μήτις, κ.τ.λ., prompted by a misunderstanding of His words, the emphasis is upon ἤνεγκεν, '' surely no one has *brought* Him,'' etc. — Ver. 34. ἐμὸν βρῶμα] *i.e.* without a figure, '' *what gives me satisfaction and enjoyment is this:* I have to do what God desires of me, and to accomplish *that* work of redemption which He (αὐτοῦ placed emphatically first) has committed to me'' (xvii. 4). Observe (1) that ἵνα is not the same as ὅτι, which would express objectively the actual subject-matter of ἐμὸν βρ. ; it rather indicates the nature of the βρῶμα viewed as to its *end*, and points to the *aim* and *purpose* which Jesus pursues,—a very frequent use of it in John. (2) The present ποιῶ denotes *continuous* action, the Aor. τελειώσω the *act of completion*, the future goal of the ποιῶ. Comp. xvii. 4.

Ver. 35. The approaching townspeople now showed how greatly already

---

[1] Xen. *Anab.* ii. 1. 2 ; Soph. *El.* 370, 880, 884; Bornem. *ad Anab.* i. 10. 3.
[2] See on Matt. xii. 23 ; Baeumlein, *Partik.*
302.
[3] Xen. *Symp.* i. 14 ; Lucian, *V. H.* i. 22, *D. D.* x. 1.

the ἵνα ποιῶ was in process of accomplishment. They were coming through the corn-field, now tinged with green ; and thus they make the fields, which for four months would not yield the harvest, in a higher sense already white harvest-fields. Jesus directs the attention of His disciples to this ; and with the beautiful picture thus presented in nature, He connects further appropriate instructions, onwards to ver. 38. — Do not ye say], that is, at the present season of the year (ἔτι). The ὑμεῖς stands contrasted with *what Jesus* means to say, though the antithesis is not indicated in what follows by ἐγώ, because the antithesis of *time* comes into the foreground.[1] The supposition that the disciples had, during their walk, made an observation of this kind to each other (and this in a spiritual sense with reference to the needed hoping and waiting), as Hengstenberg suggests, is neither hinted at, nor is in harmony with the *Praesens* λέγετε. — ὅτι ἔτι . . . ἔρχεται] Harvest began in the middle of Nisan (Lightfoot, v. 101), *i.e.* in April. The words, therefore, must have been spoken in December, when Jesus, as the seed-time fell in Marchesvan (the beginning of November), might be already surrounded by springing corn-fields, the harvest of which, however, could not be expected for four months to come. We render therefore : *there are still four months* and (we wait, *until*) *the harvest comes.* As to the paratactic expression with καί instead of a particle of time, see Stallbaum, *ad Plat. Symp.* p. 220 C ; Ellendt, *Lex. Soph.* I. 881. On the chronological importance of the passage, see Wieseler, *Synopse,* p. 214 ff. The taking of the words as *proverbial,*[2] as if the saying were a *general* one : "*from seed-time to harvest is four months*" (seed-time would thus be made to extend into December ; comp. *Bava Mezia,* f. 106, 2), is forbidden, not only by the fact that such a proverb occurs nowhere else, but by the fact that seed-time is not here mentioned, so that ἔτι (comp. the following ἤδη) does not refer to a point of time to be understood, but to the time then present, and by the fact, likewise, that the emphasized ὑμεῖς would be inexplicable in an ordinary proverb (comp. rather Matt. xvi. 2).[3] It is worth while to notice *how long* Jesus had been in Judea (since April). — τετράμηνος *sc.* χρόνος.[4] — τὰς χώρας] *regiones.* They had just been sown, and the young seed was now springing up, and yet in another sense *they were white for being reaped ;* for, by the spectacle of the townspeople who were now coming out to Christ across these fields, it appeared in concrete manifestation before the eyes of the disciples (hence ἐπάρατε τοὺς ὀφθαλμούς, κ.τ.λ.), that now for men the time of conversion (of ripeness) was come in the near establishment of the Messiah's kingdom, into which, like the harvest produce, they might be gathered (comp. Matt. iii. 12). Jesus, therefore, here gives a prophetic view, not only of the near conversion of the *Samaritans* (Acts viii. 5 ff.) ; but, rising above the concrete fact now before them, from the

[1] The versatility of thought often in Greek changes the things contrasted as the sentence proceeds. See Dissen, *ad Dem. de cor.* 163 ; Schaef. *ad Timocr.* p. 763, 13.

[2] Lightfoot, Grotius, Tittmann, etc., also Lücke, Tholuck, de Wette, Krafft, *Chronol.* p. 73.

[3] This also is in answer to Hilgenfeld, who takes ἔτι with reference to the present, and not the future, and interprets it : four months are *not yet gone,* and yet the harvest is *already here.* This strange rendering derives no support whatever from xi. 39.

[4] See Lobeck, *ad Phryn.* p. 549.

people of Sychar who were flocking through the fields of springing green, His prophetic eye takes in *all mankind*, whose conversion, begun by Him, would be accomplished by His disciples. See especially ver. 38. Godet wrongly denies this wider prophetic reference, and confines the words to the immediate occurrence, as an improvised harvest feast. Such an explanation does not suffice for what follows, vv. 36–38, which was suggested, indeed, by the phenomenon before them, but embraces the whole range of service on the part of Christ's disciples in their relation to their Lord. If we do not allow this wider reference, ver. 38 especially will be of very strange import. — ὅτι] not *because*, but according to common *attraction*,[1] *that* they are, etc. — ἤδη] *even now, at this moment*, and not after four months ; put at the end for emphasis.[2] Not, therefore, to be joined with what follows,[3] which would make the correlation with ἔτι inappropriate. For the rest, comp. Ovid, *Fast.* v. 357 : "maturis albescit messis aristis."

Ver. 36. This harvest—*how full of recompense for the reapers* (*i.e.* for you, my disciples) ! The *wages* for the reaper's labour consist in this, that (καί *explicative*) he *gathers fruit into life eternal* (this is spoken *locally*, as denoting the granary, as is clear from συνάγει, against Luthardt, who takes εἰς to denote the result) ; comp. ver. 14, without any figure : "He converts men, and thus secures for them an entrance into the Messiah's kingdom." *Thereupon, alike the sower* (Christ) *and the reaper rejoice together*, according to God's ordinance (ἵνα). Chrysostom and many others wrongly take σπείρων to denote the *prophets*. For ὁμοῦ, with one verb in the singular and two subjects, comp. Hom, *Il. ὰ.* 61 : εἰ δὴ ὁμοῦ πόλεμός τε δαμᾷ καὶ λοιμὸς Ἀχαιούς ; Soph. *Aj.* 1058. Here, however, it certainly signifies the *simultaneousness* of the joy, not simply joy *in common* (B. Crusius, Luthardt) ; for it is the *joy of harvest*, which *the sower also* shares in time of harvest, on account of the blessing with which His toil in sowing is now crowned.

Vv. 37, 38. "Alike the sower and the reaper, I say, for in this case they *are different persons.*" — ἐν γὰρ τούτῳ, κ.τ.λ.] *for herein*, in *this* relation of sowing and reaping, *the saying* (the proverb of ordinary life, τὸ λεγόμενον)[4] has *its essential truth*, *i.e.* its proper realization, setting forth its idea.[5] The reference of the λόγος to the words of the servant, Matt. xxv. 24, which Weizsäcker considers probable,[6] would be very far-fetched ; the rendering of ἀληθινός, however, as equivalent to ἀληθής, 2 Pet. ii. 22 (de Wette and many others), is quite opposed to the peculiar usage of John (so xix. 35). The *article* before ἀληθ., which through want of attention might easily have

[1] Winer, p. 581 [E. T. p. 626 f.].

[2] Stallbaum, *ad Plat. Phaedr.* p. 256 E ; *ad Menex.* p. 235 A). Comp. 1 John iv. 3 ; Kühner, *ad Xen. Anab.* i. 8. 16.

[3] A. C.* D. E. L. ℵ. Codd. It. *al.*, Schulz, Tisch., Ewald, Ebrard, Godet.

[4] Plato, *Gorg.* p. 447 A ; *Phaed.* p. 101 D ; *Pol.* x. p. 621 C ; comp. ὁ παλαιὸς λόγος, *Phaed.* p. 240 C ; *Gorg.* p. 499 C ; Soph. *Trach.* i.

[5] Comp. Plat. *Tim.* p. 26 E : μὴ πλασθέντα

μῦθον, ἀλλ᾽ ἀληθινὸν (*i.e.* a real) λόγον

[6] Weizsäcker, in his harmony of the words of John with those of the Synoptics, in which the latter are dealt with very freely (p. 282 ff.), brings in general much that is far-fetched into parallelisms which cannot be demonstrated. The intellectual independence of personal recollection and reproduction in John raises him above any such search after supposed borrowings.

been omitted,[1] marks off the predicate with exclusive definiteness.[2] With respect to other relations (not ἐν τούτῳ), the proverb does not express its proper idea.—As to the proverb itself, and its various applications, see Wetstein. The ἀληθινόν of it is explained in ver. 38. — ἐγώ] with emphasis : *I*, consequently the *sower* in the proverb. — The *preterites* ἀπέστειλα and εἰσελήλ. are not *prophetic* (de.Wette, Tholuck), but the mission and calling of the disciples were already practically involved in their reception into the apostolate.[3] Comp. xvii. 8.—ἄλλοι and αὐτῶν refer to *Jesus* (whom Ols-hausen, indeed, according to Matt. xxiii. 34, even excludes !), not to the *prophets* and *the Baptist*, nor to them together with Christ (so the *Fathers* and most of the *early* writers, also Lange, Luthardt, Ewald, and most others), nor in a general way to all who were instrumental in advancing the preparatory economy (Tholuck). They are plurals of *category* (see on Matt. ii. 20 ; John iii. 11), representing the work of Christ, into which the disciples entered, as not *theirs*, but *others'* work, *i.e.* a distinct and *different* labour. But the fact that *Jesus* was the labourer, while self-evident from the connection, is not directly expressed, but with intentional self-renuncia-tion, half concealed beneath the plural ἄλλοι. He it was who introduced the conversion of mankind ; the disciples were to complete it. He prepared and sowed the field ; they were called upon to do what was still further necessary, and to reap. The great toil of the apostles in fulfilling their call is not denied ; but, when compared with the work of Jesus Himself, it was the easier, because it was only the carrying on of that work, and was *encour-agingly* represented under the cheerful image of harvesting (comp. Isa. ix. 3 ; Ps. cxxvi. 6). If ἄλλοι is to be taken as referring to Philip's work in converting the Samaritans, Acts viii. 52, upon which Peter and John entered (Baur), or to Paul's labour among the heathen, the fruit of which has fallen to the earlier apostles (Hilgenfeld), *any* and *every* exegetical im-possibility may be with equal right allowed by a ὕστερον πρότερον of critical arbitrariness.

Ver. 39 ff. Resumption of the historical narrative of ver. 30, which here receives its elucidation, to which then the continuation of the history attaches itself, vv. 40–42.[4] — ὅτι εἶπέ μοι πάντα, κ.τ.λ.] Indication of *conscience* ratifying ver. 18. — διὰ τὸν λόγον αὐτοῦ] *on account of His word* (teaching). No mention is made of *miracles*, but we must not infer from this that there was no need of miracles among the Samaritans ; see, on the other hand, Acts viii. 6 ff. Jesus found that in this case His *word* sufficed, and there-

---

[1] B. C.* K. L. T.ᵇ Δ. Or.

[2] Comp. Bernhardy, p. 322 ; Kühner, II., 140.

[3] According to Godet, ἀπέστ. is to be taken as referring to a summons, discovered by him in ver. 36, to the work of reaping among the aproaching Sycharites. He then takes ἄλλοι κεκοπ. to refer to the labour of Jesus in His interview with the woman. The latter words are said to have been spoken to the disciples, who thought He had been resting during their absence, with a

"finesse qu'on oserait presque appeler légèrement malicieuse," and with an "aim-able sourire." Such weighty thoughts as ἀποστολή and κόπος represent are utterly incompatible with such side hints and pass-ing references. And it is a pure invention to find in ver. 36 an "invitation à prendre la faucille."

[4] As to the position of the words π ο λ λ ο ὶ ἐπ. εἰς αὐτ. τ ῶ ν Σ α μ., see Buttmann, *N. T. Gr.* p. 332 [E. T. p. 388].

fore upon principle (see ver. 48) He forbore to work miracles, and His mighty word was all the mightier among the unprejudiced people. — διὰ τὴν σὴν λαλιάν] *on account of thy talk.* So λαλιά invariably in classical Greek. The term is *purposely chosen*, as from the standing-point of the *speaker ;* whereas John, as an impartial *narrator*, with equal appropriateness, writes τὸν λόγον in ver. 39. As to λαλιά in viii. 43, where Jesus thus designates *His own* discourse, see *in loc.* Observe, besides, the emphatic σήν as contrasted with the λόγος of Jesus which they themselves (αὐτοί) have now heard. — ἀκηκόαμεν] the following ὅτι refers to both verbs. They have *heard* that Jesus was the Messiah, for this became *evident* to them from His words. — ὁ σωτὴρ τοῦ κόσμου] not due to the *individuality of John* (1 John iv. 14), and put into the mouths of the people, as Lücke and Tholuck are inclined to suppose, but a confession quite conceivable as the result of the two days' ministry of Jesus ; universalism, moreover, being more akin to the Messianic faith of the Samaritans (see Gesenius, *de Samar. theol.* p. 41 ff.) than to that of the Jews, with their definite and energetic feeling of nationality.

Note.—The prohibition in Matt. x. 5 militates neither against this narrative of John iv. in general, nor in particular against the promise of ver. 35 ff. It had merely a *temporary* force, and was abrogated again by Matt. xxviii. 19, 20, and Acts i. 8 ; and, moreover, it presented no insuperable barrier to restrict Jesus in *His* work (for He did not wholly exclude even Gentiles from His teaching). Acts viii. 5 ff. is no proof whatever that this history in John is of mythical origin ; it is, on the contrary, the fulfilment of the promise given here. Its several features are so original, and so psychologically true, and the words of Jesus (see especially vv. 21-24) come so directly from the living depths of His soul, that the exceptions taken against certain particulars (as, for instance, against the misunderstandings on the part of the woman ; against the words concerning the food, ver. 32 ; against the command of Jesus, " Go, call thy husband ;" against the woman's question concerning the place of worship ; against the faith of the Samaritans, which is said to contradict Luke ix. 53) are of no real weight, and are explicable only by the very authenticity of the narrative, not by the supposition of an intentional poetizing. This is in answer to Strauss, B. Bauer, and partly Weisse ; also to Scholten, who considers that the author's object was to describe in a non-historical picture the *spirit* which actuated Jesus even towards the Samaritans. As a full guarantee for that part of the narrative, which the disciples, being absent, could not have witnessed, we may, considering the vivid impress of genuineness which marks it, fairly assume that Jesus Himself communicated it to the evangelist, and there is no need for the unfounded supposition that (ver. 8) John was left behind with Jesus (Hengstenberg, Godet). When, finally, Baur (p. 145 ff. ; comp. also Hilgenfeld) resolves our history into a *typus,*—"the Samaritan woman being a figure of *heathendom,* susceptible, readily opening itself to faith, and presenting a wide harvest field," a contrast to Nicodemus, the type of unsusceptible Judaism,—with all this arbitrariness on the part of the inventor, it is passing strange, if this were his object, that he did not bring Jesus into contact with a real *heathen* woman, for this would have been quite as easy to invent ; and that he should keep the words of the woman so free from the least tinge of anything of a *heathen* nature (ver. 20 ff.), and have put into her mouth so clear an expression of Messianic hope (vv. 25, 42),—this bungling is quite out of character on the part of such an inventor.

Vv. 43, 44.[1] Τὰς δύο ἡμέρας] The article is to be explained by ver. 40. — αὐτός] ipse, not merely others with reference to Him, but "He Himself did not hesitate to testify," etc. As to the fact itself, see Matt. xiii. 57 ; Mark vi. 4 ; Luke iv. 24. Schenkel's inference from προφήτης that Jesus did not yet regard Himself as the Messiah, involves a misuse of the general term within the category of which the conception of Messiah is embraced. — ἐμαρτύρ.] not in the sense of the Pluperfect (Tholuck, Godet ; see on xviii. 24), but then, when He returned to Galilee. [See Note XXII. p. 170.] — γάρ is the ordinary for; and πατρίδι is not the native town, but, as is clear from Γαλιλαίαν, vv. 43, 45, the native country. So also usually in Greek writers, from Homer downwards. The words give the reason why He did not hesitate to return to Galilee. The gist of the reason lies in the antithetical reference of ἐν τῇ ἰδίᾳ πατρίδι. If, as Jesus Himself testified, a prophet had no honour in his own country, he must seek it abroad. And this Jesus had done. Abroad, in Jerusalem, He had by His mighty works inspired the Galileans who were there with that respect which they were accustomed to deny to a prophet at home. Thus He brought the prophet's honour with Him from abroad.[2] Accordingly (ver. 45) He found a reception among the Galileans also, because they had seen His miracles in Jerusalem (ii. 23). It is therefore obviously incorrect to understand Γαλιλαίαν specially of Upper Galilee, as distinct from Lower Galilee, where Nazareth was situated. So Lange, in spite of the fact that Γαλιλ. here must be the universal and popular name for the whole province, as distinct from Samaria (ἐκεῖθεν), whether we retain καὶ ἀπῆλθεν as in the Elzevir or not. It is further incorrect, and an utterly arbitrary gloss, to interpret πατρίς as meaning Nazareth, and γάρ as referring to the fact that He went, indeed, to Galilee, but not to Nazareth (Chrysostom and Euthymius Zigabenus : to Capernaum).[3] It is also opposed alike to the context, and the universal (including the Johannean) view which regards Galilee as Christ's home (i. 46, ii. 1, vii. 3, 41, 52), to take πατρίς as denoting Judea, and γάρ as stating the reason (in the face of the quite different reason already given, vv. 1-3) why Jesus had left Judea ;[4]

---

[1] See Ewald, Jahrb. X. 1860, p. 108 ff. He agrees for the most part with my rendering ; comp. also his Johann. Schr. I. p. 194; in like manner Godet, who, however, without the slightest hint of it in the text, supposes a purpose on the writer's part, in connection with iii. 24, to correct the synoptical tradition. John wishes "constater l'intervalle considérable qui sépara du baptême de Jésus son retour définitif et son établissement permanent en Galilée." In iii. 24 he states the fact, and here he gives the motive. Scholten puts the emphasis which prompts the following γάρ upon ἐκεῖθεν, a word which is quite unessential, and might just as well have been omitted.

[2] Baeumlein urges, against my explanation : "We cannot believe that, after the words 'He betook himself to Galilee,' there should follow the reason why He had before left Galilee." This, however, is not the logical connection at all.

[3] So Cyril, Nonnus, Erasmus, Beza, Calvin, Aretius, Grotius, Jansen, Bengel, and many ; also Kypke, Rosenmüller, Olshausen, Klee, Gemberg in Stud. u. Krit. 1845, I. ; Hengstenberg, Baeumlein.

[4] Origen, Maldonatus, B. Bauer, Schwegler, Wieseler, B. Crusius, Schweizer, Köstlin, Baur, Hilgenfeld, and formerly Ebrard.

whence some, *e.g.* Origen and Baur, take πατρίς in a higher sense, as signifying the native land of the *prophets*,[1] and therefore of the Messiah also, and most, like Hilgenfeld, as having reference to the *birth at Bethlehem*. Lücke has rightly, in his 3d ed., abandoned this interpretation ; but, on the other hand, takes γάρ as equivalent to *namely*, and refers it not to what precedes, but *to what follows*,[2] so that ver. 44 gives an explanation in passing on the point : "that the Galileans on this occasion received Jesus well, but only on account of the miracles which they had seen in Jerusalem" (de Wette). But though in the classics γάρ explicative often precedes the sentence to be explained,[3] especially in parenthesis,[4] this usage is without precedent in the N. T. (Rom. xiv. 10, Heb. ii. 8, are not instances in point), and especially foreign to John's simple style of narration ; moreover, the " *indeed,—but only*," thus put into ver. 45, is obtruded on the words, which have neither μέν after ἐδέξ., nor afterwards a μόνον δέ, or any similar expression.[5] According to Brückner, Jesus came to Galilee *because* (but see vv. 1–3) He supposed that He should find no honour there, and consequently with the intention of *undertaking the conflict* for the recognition of His person and dignity. According to Luthardt, whom Ebrard now follows,[6] the words imply the hope entertained by Jesus of *being able to remain in rest and silence in Galilee* more easily than anywhere else. But both explanations are incompatible with the following ὅτε οὖν, κ.τ.λ., which certainly means that the Galileans received Him with honour, as He was called immediately thereafter to perform a miracle. We should at least expect δέ or ἀλλά (comp. Nonnus) to introduce the statement, and not οὖν. In what follows, moreover, regarding the residence in Galilee, we are told neither about conflict nor about the repose of Jesus, but simply of the healing of the nobleman's son. Lastly,

---

[1] So also B. Crusius, who compares vii. 52. Quite erroneously, when the general and proverbial character of the statement is considered. After iv. 3, however, the reader can expect no further explanation of the reason why Jesus did not remain in Judea. Schwegler and B. Bauer suppose that here Judea is meant as the native land of Jesus, and make use of this as an argument against the genuineness and historical truth of the Gospel. Comp. also Köstlin in the *Theol. Jahrb.* 1851, p. 186. Hilgenfeld, *Evang.* p. 266 : " a remarkable inversion of the synoptical statement, wherein the Gospel appears as a free compilation by a post-apostolic author" (*Zeitschr.* 1862, p. 17). Schweizer also finds it such a stumbling-block, that he regards it as proving the following narrative to be a Galilean interpolation. Gfrörer, *heil. Sage*, II. 289, rightly indeed understands the words as referring to *Galilee*, but considers that we should supply the following : "*but very slowly and reluctantly, for*," etc.

[2] So substantially also Tholuck, Olshausen, Maier, de Wette.

[3] See Hartung, *Partikell.* I. p. 467 ; Baeumlein, *Partik.* p. 75 ff.

[4] See Bremi, *ad Lys.* p. 66 ; Ellendt, *Lex. Soph.* I. 338.

[5] Weizsäcker also, in the *Jahrb. f. Deutsche Theol.* 1859, p. 695, regards γάρ not as introducing a reason, but as demonstrative. John intimates that he will not narrate much of Christ's ministry in Galilee ; he refers to that saying as if shrinking from unpleasant recollections. But this is not in the text, nor is it compatible with the connection in ver. 45, and the history that follows. Weizsäcker, indeed, thinks (comp. his *Unters. üb. d. ev. Gesch.* p. 276) that in this synoptic saying John refers to the *synoptic* account of that Galilean ministry, *which he would not himself describe*. Who ever could imagine that ? especially when John at once goes on to narrate the *good reception* given to Jesus in Galilee, and His *miracle of blessing* there. Did the Lord betake Himself to " *a voluntary obscurity*," concerning which John wishes *to be silent ?*

[6] Comp. Hofmann, *Weissag. u. Erf.* II. 88, also *Schriftbew.* II. 1, p. 171.

it is contrary to the words (because ὅτε οὖν ἧλθεν in ver. 45 directly resumes the εἰς τ. Γαλ. of ver. 43, and admits of no interval), to make, with Hauff,[1] the train of thought terminate with ver. 44, and take ver. 44 itself as a general description of the result of Christ's Galilean ministry. Thus ἐδέξαντο is said to indicate *that He did and taught much there ;* which is clearly a gloss *foisted* into the text.

Vv. 45, 46. Ἐδέξαντο αὐτόν] The *reception* which He found among them was one *of faith*, for He now brought with him *from Jerusalem* the honour which the prophet had not in his own country ; hence πάντα ἑωρακότες, κ.τ.λ., *because they had seen*, etc., and in this we have the key to the right understanding of ver. 44. -- Ver. 46. οὖν] in consequence of this reception, which encouraged Him to go farther into the country. He goes, however, again straight to *Cana*, because here He had relatives, and might hope in consequence of His first miracle to find the soil prepared for his further labours. — κ. ἦν τις βασιλικός, κ.τ.λ.] ἐν Καφαρναούμ should be joined to ἦν. Βασιλικός, a *royal person*, is, according to the frequent usage of Josephus (see Krebs, p. 144) and other writers,[2] not a *relation* of the king,[3] but one in the *service* of the king (Herod Antipas) ; whether military man (thus often in Josephus ; Nonnus : ἰθύνων στρατιήν), civilian, court retainer, is uncertain. — ὁ υἱός] according to ver. 49, still young. The *article* indicates, perhaps, that he was the only one.

Vv. 47, 48. Ἀπῆλθε πρὸς αὐτόν] from Capernaum to Cana.— ἵνα] the subject of the request is its *purpose*. — ἠμελλε] *in eo erat, ut*.[4] The man's prayer is conceivable partly from the first miracle at Cana, and partly from the fame of Jesus which had followed Him from Jerusalem. — " *Unless ye see signs and wonders, ye will certainly not believe*," is spoken in displeasure against *the Galileans generally* (ver. 45), but *including the suppliant ;* Jesus foreseeing that the healing of his son would make him believe, but at the same time that his faith would not be brought about without a miracle. The Lord's *teaching* was in His own view the weightiest ground of faith, especially according to John (comp. ver. 41), though faith based on *miracles* was not rejected, but under certain circumstances even required by Him (x. 38, xiv. 11, xv. 24), though not as of *highest*, but *secondary* rank. according to their purpose as a divine attestation of the teaching. It is incorrect to put the emphasis upon ἴδητε, unless ye see *with your own eyes*, etc., condemning the entreaty to accompany him. In this case should both ἴδητε have been put first (against Bengel and Storr), and τοῖς ὀφθαλμοῖς or the like been added ; and in truth the man *saw* the miracle, and a greater one than if Jesus had gone with him. — σημεῖα καὶ τέρατα] see on Matt. xxiv. 24 ; Rom. xv. 19. As to the reproach itself, comp. 1 Cor. i. 22.

Vv. 49, 50. Then follows a still more urgent entreaty of the father's love, tried by the answer of Jesus ; the τὸ παιδίον μου, *my child*, marking the father's tender affection. Comp. Mark v. 23. — Jesus rewards his confidence with the short answer, *Go thy way, thy son liveth ;* thus an-

---

[1] *Stud. u. Krit.* 1849, p. 117 ff.
[2] Plutarch, Polyb., etc. ; see Wetstein.
[3] So Baronius, Bos, and many, also al-

lowed by Chrysostom.
[4] Comp. Luke vii. 2 ; Hemsterhuis, *ad Lucian. D. M.* II. p. 546.

nouncing *the deliverance from death* accomplished at that very moment by *an act of His will* through miraculous power operating at a distance (not by *magnetic healing power*, against Olshausen, Krabbe, Kern, thus resorting to a sphere as foreign to the miracles of healing as it is inadequate as an explanation). As little can Christ's word be regarded as a *medical prognosticon*,[1] nor is any trace found in the text of an effect resulting from faith in general, and the spiritual movement of the masses (Weizsäcker).—According to the text, Jesus speaks from a conscious knowledge of the crisis of the sickness, effected that moment at a distance by Himself : " *Thy son* is not dead, but *liveth !* " — ἐπιστ. τῷ λόγῳ] Thus he now overleaps the limit of faith which supposed Christ's presence necessary to the working of the cure ; *he believed the word, i.e.* had confidence in its realization.

Vv. 51–54. Αὐτοῦ καταβ . . . αὐτῷ] see Buttmann, *N. T. Gr.* p. 270 [E. T. p. 315]. — ἤδη] belongs to καταβ., not to ὑπήντ. (B. Crusius) : *when he was already going down*, and now was no longer in Cana, but upon his journey back. — οἱ δοῦλοι, κ.τ.λ.] to reassure the father, and prevent the now unnecessary coming of Jesus. — ζῇ] he is not dead, but the sickness has the opposite issue : *he lives !* — κομψότερον] *finer, prettier*, as in common life we are wont to say, "he is pretty well." [2] Here it is an "amoenum verbum" (Bengel) of the father's heart, which apprehends its good fortune still with feelings of tenderness and anxiety. — ἐχθές] see Lobeck, *ad Phryn.* p. 323. — ὥραν ἑβδόμην] He had therefore been on the way since one o'clock the day before, because we must suppose from ver. 50 that he set out immediately after the assurance of Jesus. This surprises us, even apart from the distance from Cana to Capernaum, not exactly known to us indeed, but hardly three geographical miles. That in his firm faith he travelled " *non festinans* " (Lampe) is unnaturally assumed against the impulse of parental love which would hurry him home ; as also that somewhere on the way, or even at Cana (Ewald assumes the latter, making the seventh hour seven in the evening, according to the Roman reckoning) *he spent the night*. We may suppose some delay not named, on the journey back, or (with Hengstenberg, Brückner, and others) take the *to-day* in the mind of the Jewish servants as denoting the day which began at six P.M. (sunset). According to Baur and Hilgenfeld, this noting of the time is to be attributed, not to the genuineness and originality of the account, but to the subjective aim of the writer, which was to make the miracle as great and pointed as possible (comp. ver. 54, note). — ἐν ἐκ. τ. ὥρᾳ] *sc.* ἀφῆκεν αὐτὸν ὁ πυρετός. Observe, with reference to ἐκεῖνος, that it does not mean *idem*, but is the simple relative *ille*. — κ. ἐπίστευσεν, κ.τ.λ.] upon Jesus as the Messiah.[3] Observe how faith here attains its realization as to its object, and further, the importance of this καὶ ἡ οἰκία αὐτοῦ (the first *household*), which now occurs for the first time. Comp. Acts xvi. 14, 15, 34, xviii. 8. — τοῦτο πάλιν δεύτερον, κ.τ.λ.] Referring back to ii. 11. Literally inaccurate, yet true as to

---

[1] Paulus, comp. Ammon.

[2] Exactly so in Arrian. *Epict.* iii. 10 of the sick : κομψῶς ἔχεις, and its opposite κακῶς ἔχεις. Comp. the Latin *belle habere*.

[3] Καλῶς οὖν καθήψατο αὐτοῦ ὁ τὴν καρδίαν αὐτοῦ γινώσκων Χριστὸς, εἰπών· ὅτι ἐὰν μὴ σημεῖα, κ.τ.λ., Euthymius Zigabenus.

its import, is the rendering of Luther : " *This is the second miracle that Jesus did ;*" τοῦτο stands by itself, and the following δεύτ. σημ. supplies the place of the predicate (*this Jesus did as the second miracle*), hence no article follows τοῦτο.[1] Πάλιν, however, must not be overlooked, nor is it to be joined with δεύτερον (so *usually*) as a current pleonasm,[2] for δεύτερον is not an adverb, but an adjective. It rather belongs to ἐποίησεν, thus affirming that Jesus *now again* did this as a *second* miracle (comp. Beza) *upon his return from Judea to Galilee* (as in ii. 1). Thus the idea of the repeatedly recurring miracle upon His coming out of Judea into Galilee is certainly *doubly* expressed,—once *adverbially* with the verb (πάλιν ἐποίησεν), and then *adjectivally* with the noun (δεύτερον σημ.) ; both are more definitely determined by ἐλθών, κ.τ.λ. Schweizer (p. 78) quite arbitrarily considers the reference to the first miracle at Cana unjohannean.

Note.—The βασιλικός is not the same with the *Centurion* of Matt. viii. 5 ff.; comp. Luke vii. 2 ff. (Origen, Chrysostom, Theophylact, Euthymius Zigabenus, and most others). On the assumption of their *identity*,[3] which attributes the greater originality with some to Matthew and Luke,[4] with others to John,[5] and to the latter an *adjusting* purpose,[6] the discrepancies as to place, time, and even as to the sick person, constitute less difficulties than the entirely different character in which the suppliant appears in John and in the two Synoptics. In these latter he is still a heathen, which, according to John, he cannot be ;[7] see ver. 48, which associates him with the Galileans, and thus with Jews ; and thus alone establishes the diversity of the two miracles, apart from the fact that there is no more objection against the supposition of two healings wrought at a distance than against one. This is at the same time against Schweizer's view, that the section in John is an interpolation. Indeed, a single example of healing at a distance, the historical truth of which, moreover, even Ewald maintains, might more easily be resolved by the arbitrariness of criticism into a *myth* borrowed from the history of Naaman, 2 Kings ix. 5, 9 ff. (Strauss), or explained away as a misunderstanding of a *parable* (Weisse), or dissolved into a *subjective transposition and development of the synoptical materials* on John's part for his own purpose, which would make the belief in miracles pass absolutely beyond the Jewish range of view (Hilgenfeld), and appear in its highest form as a πιστεύειν διὰ τόν λόγον (Baur, p. 152) ;[8] although πιστεύειν τῷ λόγῳ, ver. 41, is something quite different from πιστεύειν διὰ τὸν λόγον, and the ἐπίστευσεν in ver. 53 took place, not διὰ τὸν λόγον, but διὰ τὸ σημεῖον.

---

[1] See on ii. 11, and Bremi, *ad. Lys. Exc.* II. p. 436 f.; Ast, *Lex. Plat.* II. 406 ; Stallbaum, *ad Plat. Apol.* pp. 18 A, 24 B.

[2] See on Matt. xxvi. 42 ; comp. John xxi. 15, Acts x. 15.

[3] Irenaeus, Eusebius, Semler, Seyffarth, Strauss, Weisse, B. Bauer, Gfrörer, Schweizer, Ammon, Baumgarten Crusius, Baur, Hilgenfeld, Ewald, Weizsäcker.

[4] Strauss, B. Bauer, Weiss, Baur, Hilgenfeld.

[5] Gfrörer, Ewald.

[6] Weizsäcker.

[7] Against Cyril, Jerome, Baur, and Ewald.

[8] If John had really derived his matter from the Synoptics, it would be quite inconconceivable how, according to the design attributed to him by Baur, he could have left unused the statement of Matt. viii. 10, especially if the βασιλικός is taken to be a Gentile. See Hase, *Tübingen Schule*, pp. 32, 33.

NOTES BY AMERICAN EDITOR.

XXI. "*Although Jesus Himself*," etc.   Ver. 2.

Although, etc. It seems to me that the construction *is* interrupted, and requires a parenthesis.

As to Meyer's statement that "ver. 2 does not contain a correction of himself by the Evangelist," Weiss properly suggests that the Evangelist might be correcting or rather making definite his own previous vague and general statement (ch. iii. 22, "He remained with them and baptized"), as well as *the form of the rumour* that had reached the Pharisees (ver. 1).

XXII. "*For Jesus Himself testified.*"   Ver. 43.

The difficulty of this verse lies in its assigning a reason for Christ's return to Galilee, which would seem to be of precisely opposite tendency. It is among the perplexing passages in John, and the solutions have been very various. *Four*, which distinguish Galilee from "His own country (πα-τρίδι, fatherland)," making the latter respectively either *Judea*, or *Lower Galilee*, or *Nazareth*, or even *Capernaum*, may, I think, be readily dismissed. According to this view Jesus in going into Galilee *avoided* His "own country." *Three* find in the lack of esteem for the Lord in Galilee the actual reason for His return to it : 1. That He might find, in the neglect and disesteem which awaited Him, the desired rest and seclusion. 2. That He might, amidst an incredulous and stubborn people, prosecute the struggle for prophetic and Messianic recognition. 3. Akin to this, that in this pre-eminently *missionary* field, in the ungrateful soil of His peculiarly prejudiced and unbelieving countrymen, He might sow the seed and reap the harvest which He had so successfully sown and reaped in Judea and Samaria (Weiss).

Others find in the verse an anticipative reference to what follows. By a familiar Greek use of γάρ explicative, the sentence *precedes* the thought which it would naturally follow, as if the writer had said, "He came into Galilee. When therefore He arrived in Galilee the Galileans received Him, having seen, i.e. *because* they had seen His miracles in Judea ; for Jesus Himself testified," etc. This explanation, like that of Meyer, seems harsh and unnatural, nor do I think that given by Weiss can be deemed satisfactory. Is not perhaps the simplest solution one which assumes before the γάρ some such ellipsis as, "He came into Galilee [contrary to what might naturally be expected ; or, though He might look for an unfavorable reception] ; for Jesus Himself testified," etc., the γάρ with its suppressed ellipsis thus answering nearly to our *although*? The verse becomes thus a merely incidental remark, as to Christ's *probable* reception in Galilee, suggested partly by what He actually *did* subsequently experience in His peculiarly "own country," Nazareth (L. N. 16–29), and the fact that He there bore in substance precisely this testimony (ver. 23). Ver. 45 then has no connection with ver. 44, but goes back and resumes the narrative of ver. 43, suspended by the parenthetical quotation of ver. 44. Indeed so Weiss constructs it, and, though contrary to the demands of his exegesis, also Meyer. The ellipsis thus assumed with γάρ is not especially harsh ; for there is no other particle whose elliptical uses the Greeks treat with the same freedom.—As to αὐτός, Weiss obsẻrves that it refers to Jesus not in contrast with "others" testifying of Him, but to Jesus "Himself" testifying, and thus authorizing the *Evangelist* in saying what he would not have ventured to say without the Lord's example.—ἐμαρτύρησε, says Meyer, "*then* when He returned to Galilee." Probably afterwards at Nazareth (L. iv. 23), and an incidental confirmation of the Synoptical narrative.

CHAPTER V.

Ver. 1. ἑορτή] C. E. F. H. L. M. Δ. Π. א. Cursives, Copt. Sahid. Cyr. Theophyl.: ἡ ἑορτή. So Tisch. But the witnesses *against* the article are still stronger (A. B. D. etc. Or.) ; and how easily might the insertion have occurred through the ancient explanation of the feast as that of Easter ! — Ver. 2. ἐπὶ τῇ προβατικῇ] ἐν τ. πρ. is more weakly attested (though sanctioned by A. D. G. L. א.**). Only א.* Cursives, some Verss. and Fathers have simply προβατική. A change following another construction (*sheep-pool*). Unnecessary, and unsupported on critical grounds, is the conjecture of Gersdorf : ἡ προβατικὴ κολυμβήθρα ἡ λεγομένη 'Εβρ. Βηθ. Tisch. following א.* has τὸ λεγόμενον instead of ἡ ἐπιλεγομένη.— Ver. 3. πολύ] wanting in B. C. D. L. א. Cursives, and some verss. Bracketed by Lachmann, deleted by Tisch. A strengthening addition that might easily present itself.—The words ἐκδεχου. τὴν τοῦ ὕδατος κίνησιν, together with the whole of ver. 4, are wanting in B. C.* D. א. 157, 314, Copt. Ms. Sahid. Syr^cu· Those words are wanting only in A. L. 18 ; the fourth verse only in D. 33, Arm. Mss. Codd. It. Aug., Nonnus (who describes *the stirring*, but does not mention *the angel*), and is marked as doubtful in other witnesses by an obelus or asterisks. There is, moreover, great variation in particular words. For κατέβαινεν, A. K. Verss. have even ἐλούετο, which Grotius approves. The entire passage from ἐκδεχομ. to the end of ver. 4, though recognized by Tertullian (Origen is silent), is a legendary addition (so also Lücke, Olshausen, Baeumlein, and now even Brückner, reject it), though left in the text by Lachmann in conformity with his principles, but deleted by Tisch. ; by de Wette not decidedly rejected ; vindicated on various grounds by B. Crusius, Hahn, *Theol. N. T.* I. 303, Lange, Reuss, and Hengstenberg ; left doubtful by Luthardt. Had the passage been genuine, its contents would have led more easily to its being retained than omitted ; moreover, the comparatively numerous ἅπαξ λεγόμενα in it make it suspicious, viz. κίνησιν, ταραχή, δήποτε (instead of ᾧ δήποτε Lachmann has οἰῳδηποτοῦν), νόσημα. When it is judged (de Wette) that John would hardly have ended the sentence with ξηρῶν, and then have immediately proceeded with ἦν δέ τις, etc., this is really arbitrary, for we should miss nothing if nothing had been there ; ὅταν ταραχθῇ τὸ ὕδωρ, ver. 7, by no means makes a preceding explanation " almost necessary,'' but probably states the original form of the popular belief, out of which the legend soon developed itself and found its way into the text. This also against Hofmann, *Schriftbeweis*, I. 327 f., whose vindication of ver. 4 is approved by Hilgenfeld, *Evang.* p. 268. Ewald (so also Tholuck and Godet) rejects ver. 4, but defends the words ἐκδεχομένων . . . κίνησιν in ver. 3 for the sake of ver. 7 ; Hofmann, *in loc.*, follows an opposite course. But the critical witnesses do not sanction such a separation. — Ver. 5. καί is wanting in the Elz., and is bracketed by Lachmann, but adopted by Tisch., and this upon preponderating evidence. — ἀσθεν.] B. C.* D. L. א. Cursives, Codd. It. Vulg. Copt. Sahid. Arm. Cyr. Chrys. append αὐτοῦ, which Lachmann puts in brackets, and Tisch. receives. Rightly ; between ἀσθενειΑ and ΤΟΥτον the superfluous ΑΥΤΟΥ might easily escape notice. — Ver. 7. For βάλῃ Elz. has βάλλῃ, against decisive evidence. — Ver. 8. ἔγειρε] Elz. : ἔγειραι, against the best Codd. See the critical notes on Mark ii. 2. — Ver. 12. τὸν κράββ. σου is wanting in B. C.* L. א. Sahid. An addition from vv. 8, 11. Deleted by Tisch. — Ver. 13. ἰαθείς] Tisch., following D. and Codd. of the It., reads ἀσθενῶν, apparently original, but inappropri ate after τῷ τεθεραπευμένῳ in ver. 10 ; to be regarded as a subject added to ver. 7, and besides this too weakly supported. — Ver. 15. ἀνήγγειλε] C. L. א. Syr. Syr^cu· Copt. Cyr. read εἶπεν ; D. K. U. D. Cursives, Chrys. : ἀπήγγ. The latter reading might easily arise by joining ἀνήγγ. with ἀπῆλθεν ; but this makes the testimonies against εἶπεν, which Tisch. adopts, still stronger. — Ver. 16. After Ἰουδαῖοι, Elz. Scholz (bracketed by Lachmann), read καὶ ἐζήτουν αὐτὸν ἀποκτεῖναι, against decisive witnesses. A supplement borrowed from ver. 18. — Ver. 20. Tisch. : θαυμάζετε, which is far too weakly supported by L. א. — Ver. 25. ζήσονται] Lachmann and Tisch. : ζήσουσιν, following B. D. L. א. Cursives, Chrys. Rightly ; the more usual form crept in — Ver. 30. After με Elz. has πατρός, an addition opposed by decisive witnesses. — Ver. 32. οἶδα] Tisch. οἴδατε, following only D. א. Codd. It. Syr^cu· Arm. — Ver. 35. The form ἀγαλλιαθῆναι (Elz., following B.: ἀγαλλιασθῆναι) has preponderating evidence in its favour.

Ver. 1. Μετὰ ταῦτα] after this stay of Jesus in Galilee ; an approximate statement of time, within the range of which the harmonist has to bring much that is contained in the Synoptics. The distinction made by Lücke between this and μετὰ τοῦτο, which makes the former denote *indirect*, and the latter *immediate* sequence, is incapable of proof : μετὰ ταῦτα is the more usual in John ; comp. ver. 14, iii. 22, vi. 1, vii. 1. — ἑορτὴ τῶν Ἰουδαίων] *a feast of the Jews ;* John does not describe it more definitely. But *what* feast is meant appears with certainty from iv. 35 ; comp. vi. 4. For in iv. 35 Jesus spoke in *December*, and it is clear from vi. 4 that the Passover was still *approaching ;* it must therefore [1] be a feast occurring in the interval between December *and the Passover*, and this is no other than the *feast of Purim,*[2] *the feast of lots*, celebrated on the 14th and 15th of Adar (Esth. ix. 21), consequently in March, in commemoration of the nation's deliverance from the bloody designs of Haman. So Keppler, d'Outrein, Hug, Olshausen, Wieseler, Krabbe, Anger, Lange, Maier, Baeumlein, Godet, and most others. So also Holtzmann [3] and Märcker.[4] In favour of this interpretation is the fact that, as this feast was by no means a great one, but of less importance and less known to Hellenistic readers, the indefinite mention of it on John's part is thoroughly appropriate ; while he *names* the greater and well-known feasts,—not only the Passover, but the σκηνοπηγία in vii. 2, and the ἐγκαίνια in x. 22. To suppose, in explanation of the omission of the name, that he

[1] If *this feast itself* is taken to be the Passover, we are obliged, with the most glaring arbitrariness, to put a *spatium vacuum* of a year between it and the Passover of vi. 4, of which, however, John (vi. 1–4) has not given the slightest hint. On the contrary, he lets his narrative present the most uninterrupted sequence. Hengstenberg judges, indeed, that the gap can appear strange only to those who do not rightly discern the relation in which John stands to the Synoptics. But this is nothing more than the dictum of harmonistic presuppositions.

[2] יְמֵי הַפּוּרִים, Esth. ix. 24 ff., iii. 7.

[3] *Judenth. u. Christenth.* p. 374.

[4] *Uebereinst. d. Matth. u. Joh.* 1868, p. 11.

had forgotten what feast it was (Schweizer), is compatible neither with the accuracy of his recollection in other things, nor with the importance of the miracle wrought at this feast.   It is arbitrary, however, to suppose that John did not wish to lay stress upon the *name* of the feast, but upon the fact that Jesus did not go up to Jerusalem *save on occasion of a feast* (Luthardt, Lichtenstein) ; indeed, the giving of the name *after* 'Ιουδαίων (comp. vii. 2) would in no way have interfered with that imaginary design.   It is objected that the feast of *Purim*, which was not a temple feast, required no journey to Jerusalem ;[1] and the high esteem in which it is held in *Gem. Hier. Megill.* i. 8 cannot be shown to refer to the time of Jesus.   But might not Jesus, even without any legal obligation, have availed Himself of this feast for His further labours in Jerusalem ?   And are we to suppose that the character of the feast—a feast for eating and drinking merely—should *hinder Him from going* to Jerusalem ?   The *Sabbath* (ver. 9), on which apparently (but see Wieseler, p. 219) the feast could never occur, may have been before or after it ;   and, lastly, what is related of Jesus (vi. 1 ff.) between this festival and the Passover, only a month afterwards, may easily have occurred within the space of that month.   In fine, it can neither have been the *Passover*,[2] nor *Pentecost*,[3] nor *the feast of Tabernacles*,[4] nor *the feast of the Dedication* (a possible surmise of Keppler and Petavius) ; nor can we acquiesce in leaving the feast *undeterminable*.[5] Baumgarten Crusius hesitates between Purim and the Passover, yet inclines to the latter.

Vv. 2, 3. Ἐστι] is the less opposed to the composition of the Gospel *after* the destruction of Jerusalem, as what is mentioned is a *bath*, whose surroundings might very naturally be *represented* as still existing.   According to Ewald, the charitable uses which the building served might have *saved it* from destruction.   Comp. Tobler, *Denkblätt.* p. 53 ff., who says that the porches were still pointed out in the fifth century. — ἐπὶ τῇ προβατικῇ] is *usually* explained by πύλη supplied : *hard by the sheep-gate* ; see on iv. 6.   Concerning the שַׁעַר הַצֹּאן, Neh. iii. 1, 32, xii. 39, so called perhaps because sheep for sacrifice were sold there, or brought in there at the Passover, nothing further is known.   It lay north-east of the city, and near the temple. Still the word supplied, "gate," cannot be shown to have been in use ; nor could it have been self-evident, especially to Gentile Christian readers, not minutely acquainted with the localities.   I prefer, therefore, following Theodore of Mopsuestia, Ammonius, Nonnus, to join κολυμβ. with προβατικῇ, and, with Elz. 1633 and Wetstein, to read κολυμβήθρα as a dative (comp. already Castalio): " *Now there is in Jerusalem, at the sheep-pool,* [a place called] *Bethesda, so called in the Hebrew tongue.*" According to Ammonius, the sheep used for sacrifice were washed in the sheep-pool.— ἐπιλεγ.] " *this ad-*

---

[1] See especially Hengstenberg, *Christol.* III. p. 187 f., Lücke, de Wette, Brückner.
[2] Cod. Λ., Irenaeus, Eusebius' *Chron.*, Rupertus, Luther, Calovius, Grotius, Jansen, Scaliger, Cornelius à Lapide, Lightfoot, Lampe, Paulus, Kuinoel, Süsskind, Klee, Neander, Ammon, Hengstenberg.

[3] Cyril, Chrysostom, Theophylact, Euthymius Zigabenus, Erasmus, Melanchthon, Beza, Calvin, Maldonatus, Bengel.
[4] Cod. 131, Cocceius, Ebrard, Ewald, Hilgenfeld, Lichtenstein, Krafft, Riggenback.
[5] Lücke, de Wette, Luthardt, Tholuck, Brückner.

ditional name being given to it."[1] The pool was called *Bethesda*, a characteristic *surname* which had supplanted some other original name. — Βηθεσδά] בֵּית חִסְדָּא, *locus benignitatis*, variously written in Codd.,[2] not occurring elsewhere, not even in Josephus ; not *house of pillars,*" as Delitzsch supposes. It is impossible to decide with certainty which of the present pools[3] may have been that of Bethesda.[4] To derive, with Eusebius, the healing virtue of the, according to him, red-coloured water, which perhaps was *mineral*, from the blood of the sacrifices flowing down from the temple, and the name from אֶשְׁדָּא, *effusio*[5] is unwarranted, and contrary to ver. 7. The *five porches* served as a shelter for the sick, who are *specially* described as τυφλῶν, etc., and those afflicted with diseases of the nerves and muscles. On ξηρῶν, " persons with withered and emaciated limbs," comp. Matt. xii. 10 ; Mark iii. 1 ; Luke vi. 6, 8. Whether the sick man of ver. 5 was one of them or of the χωλοῖς is not stated.

Ver. 5. Τριάκοντα, κ.τ.λ.] i.e. "*having passed thirty-eight years in his sickness,*" so that ἔχων belongs to τρ. κ. ὀκτὼ ἔτη,[6] and ἐν τ. ἀσθ. αὐτ. denotes the state in which he spent the thirty-eight years. Against the connection of ἔχων with ἐν τ. ἀσθ. ἀ. (*being in his sickness* thirty-eight years ; so Kuinoel and most others) ver. 6 is decisive, as also against the perversion of Paulus, who puts a comma after ἔχων (" thirty-eight years *old* "). The *duration* of the sickness makes the miracle all the more striking ; comp. Luke viii. 43. There is no intimation of any reference to the sentence of death pronounced upon Israel in the wilderness (Baumgarten, p. 139 f. ; comp. Hengstenberg).

Ver. 6, 7. Τοῦτον. . . . ἔχει] two points which excited the compassion of Jesus, where γνούς, however (as in iv. 1), does not denote a *supernatural* knowledge of this external (otherwise in ver. 14) and easily known or ascertained fact (against Godet and the early expositors). — ἔχει] i.e. ἐν ἀσθενείᾳ, ver. 5. — θέλεις, κ.τ.λ.] *Wilt thou become whole?* The *self-evident* nature of this desire made the question an appropriate one to rouse the sufferer's *attention* and *expectation*, and this was the object Jesus had in view in order to

___

[1] On ἐπιλέγειν, elsewhere usually in the sense of selecting, see Plat. *Legg.* iii. p. 700 B.

[2] Tisch., following א. 33, Βεθζαθά.

[3] *Probably* it was the present ebbing and flowing " *Fountain of the Virgin Mary,*" an intermittent spring called by the inhabitants " *Mother of Steps.*" See Robinson, II. 148 f. According to Wieseler, *Synopse*, p. 260, it may have been the pool Ἀμύγδαλον mentioned in Josephus, *Antt.* v. 11. 4, as was already supposed by Lampe and several others, to which, however, the difference of name is an objection ; it has no claim to be received on the ground of etymology, but only of similarity of sound. Ritter, *Erdk.* XVI. pp. 329, 443 ff., describes the pool as now choked up, while Krafft, in his *Topogr.* p. 176, thinks it was the *Struthion* of Josephus. It certainly

was not the ditch, now pointed out by tradition as Bethesda, at the north of the temple wall. See also Tobler as before, who doubts the possibility of discovering the pool. As to the *meaning* of the name (*House of Mercy*), it is possible that the arrangement for the purposes of a bath together with the porches was intended as *a charitable foundation* (Olshausen, Ewald), or that the divine favour, whose effects were here manifested, gave rise to the name. This latter is the more probable, and perhaps gave occasion to the legend of the Angel in the Received Text.

[4] See Robinson, II. 136 f., 158 f.

[5] Calvin, Aretius, Bochart, Michaelis.

[6] viii. 57, xi. 17 ; Josephus, *Arch.* vii. 11. 1 ; Krebs, p. 150.

the commencement of His miraculous work. *This* question was inappropriate for the purpose of merely *beginning a conversation upon the subject* (de Wette). Paulus falsely supposes that the man might have been a dishonest beggar, *feigning* sickness, and that Jesus asks him with reproving emphasis, "*Wilt* thou be made whole? *art thou in earnest?*" So, too, Ammon; while Lange regards him as simply *languid in will*, and that Christ again roused his *dormant* will; but there is nothing of this in the text, and just as little of Luthardt's notion, that the question was meant for all the people of whom the sick man is supposed to be the type. *This* miracle alone furnishes an example of an *unsolicited interrogation* upon Christ's part (a feature which Weisse urges against it); but in the case of the man born blind, chap. ix., we have also an unsolicited *healing.— ἄνθρωπον οὐκ ἔχω*] *ad morbum accedebat inopia*, Grotius; *ἄνθρ.* emphatically takes the lead; the *ἔρχομαι ἐγώ* that follows answers to it. — *ὅταν ταραχθῇ τὸ ὕδωρ*] The occasional and intermittent disturbance of the water is not to be understood as a *regular* occurrence, but as something *sudden* and *quickly passing away*. Hence the man's waiting and complaint. — *βάλῃ*] *throw*, denoting a *hasty* conveyance before the momentary bubbling was over. — *ἔρχομαι*] he therefore was obliged to help himself along, but slowly. — *ἄλλος πρὸ ἐμοῦ*] so that the place where the bubbling appeared was occupied by another. Observe the *sing.;* the short bubbling is to be regarded as occurring only in *one fixed springing-point* in the pool, so that *one* person only could secure its influence. The apocryphal ver. 4 has perverted this circumstance, in conformity with a popular superstition, which probably reaches as far back as the time of Christ.

Vv. 8, 9. Comp. Matt. ix. 6; Mark ii. 9, 11. — *περιπάτει*] *walk, go;* hitherto he had lain down there, ver. 6. The command implies the man's *faith*, which had been recognized by Christ. — *καὶ ἦρε*] simply and emphatically told in the very words which Jesus had spoken.—Some (Strauss) quite arbitrarily regard this story as a legendary exaggeration of the healing of the paralytic in the Synoptics (Matt. ix.; Mark ii.); time, place, circumstances, and what ensues, especially its essential connection with the healing on the Sabbath-day, are all original and independent, as is also the whole account, so full of life and psychologically true, and very different from that in the Synoptics. Notwithstanding, Baur again (p. 243 ff.) would make the story in John a composition out of synoptical materials, appealing especially to Mark ii. 9, 10; and Hilgenfeld, *Evang.* 269 f., adopts the same course, finding the "inner peculiarity" of the narrative in the idea that the omnipotence of the Logos cannot be controlled by any earthly law or human custom; whilst Weisse (*Evangelienfr.* 268) sees in the man's lameness the helplessness of one *morally* sick, and attributes the origin of the entire narrative to what was originally a *parable*. Thus they *themselves* complete the fiction, and then pass it off on the *evangelist*, while the simplest as well as the most distinctive and characteristic historical features are now interwoven into his supposed plans. See, on the contrary, Brückner, *in loc.*

Vv. 10–13. *Οἱ Ἰουδαῖοι*] The *Sanhedrim* are here meant; see vv. 15, 33. They never once mention the *healing;* with hostile coldness they only watch for their point of attack; "Quaerunt non quod mirentur, sed quod calumnientur," Grotius. — ὁ ποιήσας, etc., and ἐκεῖνος are, in the mouth of the man who was healed, an appeal to the *authority* which, as a matter of fact, his Deliverer must possess ; there is something *defiant* in the words, so natural in the first realization of his wonderful cure. — ὁ ἄνθρωπος] contemptuous.[1] — ἐξένευσεν] *He withdrew*,[2] *i.e.* when this encounter with the Jews began. As He wished to avoid the scene which would occur with the crowd who were in the place, He conveyed Himself away (not *pluperfect*).

Vv. 14, 15. Μετὰ ταῦτα] whether on the same day does not appear. But it is psychologically probable that the new feeling of restored health led the man at once into the sanctuary. — μηκέτι ἁμάρτ.] Jesus therefore knew (by direct intuition) that the sickness of this sufferer had been brought about (see on Matt. ix. 2, 3) by special *sin* (of what *kind* does not appear); and this *particular* form of sin is what He refers to, not generally to the universal connection between sin and physical evil (Neander, following the early expositors), or between sin and sickness (Hengstenberg), which would not be in keeping with the character of this private interview, that sought the good of the man's soul. The man's own *conscience* would necessarily give an *individual* application to the μεκέτι ἁμάρτ. Comp. viii. 11. — χεῖρον] to be left indefinite ; for if the ἁμαρτάνειν recurred, it might bring with it a worse sickness (so Nonnus), and other divine punishment, even the loss of eternal salvation. See generally Matt. xii. 45 ; 2 Pet. ii. 20. — Ver. 15. ἀνήγγειλε, κ.τ.λ.] The motive was neither *malice*,[3] nor *gratitude*, to bring Jesus into notice and recognition among the Jews,[4] nor *obedience to the rulers*,[5] under the influence of stupidity (Tholuck) or fear (Lange), but, in keeping with ver. 11, and the designation ὁ ποιήσας αὐτὸν ὑγιῆ (comp. ver. 11) : the *supplementary vindication of the authority* in obedience to which he had acted, though it was the Sabbath (vv. 9, 10), and which he was bound to name to the Jews. This authority is with him decidedly higher than that of the Sanhedrim ; and he not only employs it for his own acquittal, but even *defies* them with it. Comp. the man born blind, ix. 17, 31 ff. Yet for this purpose how easily could he ascertain the *name* of Jesus !

Vv. 16, 17. Διὰ τοῦτο] on account of this notice referring to Jesus, and then ὅτι, because *He* that is. See on x. 17. — ἐδίωκ.] not *judicially*, through the law,[6] of which the sequel says nothing, but in a *general* way : they made Him the object of their persecutions. — ταῦτα] *these things*, such as the healing of the paralytic. — ἐποίει] *he was doing*, not ἐποίησεν. — ἀπεκρίνατο] In reply to the διώκειν of the Jews, whether this then showed itself in accusations, reproaches, machinations, or otherwise in overt acts of hostility. *This Aorist* occurs in John only here, ver. 19, and xii. 23. — ὁ πατήρ μου, κ.τ.λ.] *My Father is working up to this moment ; I also work.* This expression is not borrowed from *Philo* (Strauss) ; Jesus alludes to the unresting activity of God for human salvation[7] since the creation was finished, notwith-

---

[1] Ast, *Lex. Plat.* I. p. 178.

[2] See Dorvill. *ad Char.* p. 273 ; Schleusner, *Thes.* II. 293.

[3] Schleiermacher, Paulus, comp. Ammon.

[4] Cyril, Chrysostom, Theophylact, Euthy-mius Zigabenus, Grotius, and many early writers ; also Maier and Hengstenberg.

[5] Bengel, Lücke, de Wette, Luthardt.

[6] Lampe, Rosenmüller, Kuinoel.

[7] Jesus accordingly does not deny that

standing the divine rest of the Sabbath (Gen. ii. 1–3) after the six days' work. This distinct reference (not generally " to the sustaining and government of the world ") is presented in the activity of Christ answering to that of God the Father. As the *Father*, says Jesus, has not ceased from the beginning to work for the world's salvation, but ever works on even to the present moment,[1] so of necessity and right, notwithstanding the law of the Sabbath, does He also, *the Son*, who as such (by virtue of His essentially divine relationship of equality with the Father) cannot in this His activity be subject to the sabbatical law, but is *Lord* of the Sabbath (comp. Matt. xii. 8 ; Mark ii. 28).   Olshausen and de Wette import into the words : "As in God rest and action are united, so in Christ are contemplation and activity." There is no mention whatever of rest and contemplation.   According to Godet, Jesus says, " *Jusqu'à chaque dernier moment où* mon père agit, j'agis aussi ;" the Son can only cease His work when He sees the Father cease.   But in this case we should have simply ἕως (ix. 4), and not ἕως ἄρτι ; ἕως ἄρτι means nothing more nor less than *usque adhuc* (ii. 10, xvi. 24 ; 1 John ii. 9), limiting the *now* still more definitely than ἕως τοῦ νῦν (Lobeck, *ad Phryn.* pp. 19, 20). — κἀγὼ ἐργάζομαι] is not to be again supplemented by ἕως ἄρτι.   *I also* (do not rest, but) *work.*   The relation of the two sentences is not that of *imitation* (Grotius), or *example* (Ewald), but of *necessary equality* of will and procedure.   The *asyndeton* (instead of "*because my Father,*" etc.) makes the statement more striking.   See on 1 Cor. x. 17.

Ver. 18. Διὰ τοῦτο] because He said this, and ὅτι as in ver. 16.   "Apologiam ipsam in majus crimen vertunt," Bengel. — μᾶλλον] neither *potius* nor *amplius* (Bengel : " modo persequebantur, nunc amplius quaerunt occidere") ; but, as its position connects with it necessarily ἐζήτ., *magis*, "*they redoubled their endeavours.*"   It has a reference to ἐδίωκον in ver. 16, so far as this general expression includes the desire to kill.   Comp. for the ζητεῖν ἀποκτεῖναι, vii. 1, 19, 25, viii. 37, 40, xi. 53. — πατέρα ἴδιον, κ.τ.λ.] *patrem proprium.*   Comp. Rom. viii. 32.   They *rightly* interpreted ὁ πατήρ μου as signifying *peculiar* and personal fatherhood, and not what is true also

God rested on the seventh day after the six days of creation (against Ammon) ; but He affirms that since then He is ever active, even on the Sabbath-days, for man's redemption. Nor does He speak of the law concerning the Sabbath as not of divine institution (Baur), as of no obligation, or as abrogated ; but *He* as the *Son* stands *above* it, and is as little bound by it as the Father, who ever continues to work, even on the Sabbath. This against Hilgenfeld (*Lehrbegriff*, p. 81 ; *Evang.* p. 270; and in his *Zeitschrift* 1863, p. 218), who considers that, according to this Gospel, Jesus, passing by the O. T. representation of God, rises to the absolutely transcendental essence, exalted above all contact with the finite, and manifest only to the Son ; and that the evangelist, following the Gnostics, refers the history of the creation to the Demiurge, as distinct from the most high God.   This is not the "*eagle height*" of John's theology.

[1] ἕως ἄρτι carries our view of God's working, which began with the creation, *onward to the present moment*; the moment wherein Jesus has to defend Himself on account of Sabbath-breaking.   In conformity with this redemptive work of God the Father onwards until now, and which was interrupted by no rest, *He* also works.   The inference that herein is implied a divine *rest* at a *future* period, as Luthardt thinks,— who regards the day of Christ's resurrection as the then approaching Sabbath of God's redemptive work,—is quite remote from the text. Ἕως ἄρτι includes the survey of the entire past down to the moment then present, without any intimation of a change in the future, which, if intended, should appear in the *context*, as in xvi. 24.

with reference to others, "sed id misere pro blasphemia habuerunt," Bengel. Comp. x. 33. — ἴσον ἑαυτόν, κ.τ.λ.] not an explanation, nor exactly (B. Crusius) a proof of what precedes, which the words themselves of Jesus, ὁ πατήρ μου, supply ; but what Jesus says of *God's* relation to *Him* (πατέρα ἴδιον), declares at the same time, as to the other side of the relationship, what He makes *Himself out to be* in *His* relation to God. We must translate : " *in that He* (at the same time) *puts Himself on the same level with God,*" *i.e.* by that κἀγὼ ἐργάζομαι of ver. 17, wherein He, as the Son, claims for Himself equality of right and freedom with the Father. Comp. also Hofmann, *Schriftbeweis*, I. p. 133. The thought of claiming equality of *essence* (Phil. ii. 6), however, lies in the background as an indistinct notion in the minds of His opponents.

Ver. 19 ff. Jesus does not deny what the Jews attributed to Him as the capital offence of blasphemous presumption, namely, *that He made Himself equal with God ;* but He puts the whole matter in its true light, and this from a consideration of His whole present and future work, onward to ver. 30 ; whereupon, onwards to ver. 47, He gives vent to an earnest denunciation of the unbelief of the Jews in the divine witness to Himself.

Ver. 19. Οὐ δύναται] denies the possibility, from the point of view of an *inner* necessity, involved in the relationship of the Son to the Father : by virtue of this it is *impossible* for Him to act with an individual *self-assertion* independent of the Father, which He could then only do if He were not the *Son.*[1] In ἀφ' ἑαυτοῦ, as the subject of the reflexive is the *Son* in His relation to the *Father*, there does not lie an opposition between the human and divine wills (Beyschlag), nor an indistinct and onesided reference to the human element in Christ (de Wette) ; but it is *the whole theanthropic subject,*the *incarnate Logos*, in whom the *Aseietas agendi*, the self-determination of action independently of the Father, cannot find place ; because otherwise He must either be absolutely divine only, and therefore without the subordination involved in ·the economy of redemption (which is the case also with the πνεῦμα, xvi. 13), or absolutely human ; therefore there is here no contradiction with the prologue (Reuss ; comp. on the other side, Godet). — ἐὰν μή τι, κ.τ.λ.] refers simply to ποιεῖν οὐδέν, and not also to ἀφ' ἑαυτοῦ. See on Matt. xii. 4 ; Gal. ii. 16. — βλέπῃ τ. πατ. ποιοῦντα] a familiar description, borrowed from the attention which children give to the conduct of their father—of the inner and immediate intuition which the Son perpetually has of the Father's work, in the perfect consciousness of fellowship of life ·with Him. This relation, not merely of moral and religious, but of metaphysical and essential communion, is the necessary and immediate standard of the Son's working. See on ver. 20. — ἃ γὰρ ἂν ἐκεῖνος, κ.τ.λ.] Proof of the negative assertion by means of the *positive* relationship subsisting. — ὁμοίως] *similarly, proportionately,* qualifying ποιεῖ, indicating again the reciprocity or sameness of action already expressed by ταῦτα, and thus more strongly confirming the perfect equality of the relationship. It is, logically speaking, the *pariter* (Mark iv. 16 ; John xxi. 13 ; 1 Pet. iii. 1) of the *category mentioned.*

---

[1] Comp. Bengel, *in loc.*, and Fritzsche, *nova opusc.* p. 297 f.

Ver. 20. Moral necessity in God for the aforesaid ἃ γὰρ ἂν ἐκεῖνος, etc. Comp. iii. 35. — γάρ refers to the whole of what follows down to ποιεῖ, of which καὶ μείζονα, etc., gives the result. — φιλεῖ] "qui *amat*, nil *celat*," Bengel. The distinction between this and ἀγαπᾷ (which D., Origen, Chrysostom here read), *diligit*,[1] is to be retained also in John, though he uses both to denote the same relationship, but with varying definiteness of representation. Comp. iii. 35, xxi. 15. Φιλεῖν is always the proper *affection* of love.[2] But this love has its basis in the metaphysical and eternal relation of the Father to the Son, as His μονογενὴς υἱός (i. 14, 18), and does not first begin in time. Comp. Luthardt. — πάντα δείκνυσιν] *He shows Him all*, permits Him to see in immediate self-revelation all *that He Himself doeth*, that the Son also may do these things after the pattern of the Father. Description of the inner and essential *intimacy* of the Father with the Son, according to which, and by virtue of His love to the Son, He makes all His own working an object of intuition to the Son for His like working (comp. ver. 17),— the humanly conditioned continuation of what He had seen in His prehuman existence, iii. 11, vi. 46.[3] — καὶ μείζονα, κ.τ.λ.] a new sentence, and an advance in the discourse, the theme of all that follows down to ver. 30 : *and greater works than these* (the healings of the sick spoken of) *will He show Him ;* He will give Him His example to do them also. — ἵνα] the divine purpose of this,—not in the sense of ὥστε (Baeumlein). — ὑμεῖς] *ye unbelievers*. Jesus does not say πιστεύητε ; He means the *surprise of shame*, viz. at the sight[4] of His works.

Ver. 21. Jesus now specifies these μείζονα ἔργα, namely, the quickening of the dead, and judgment (vv. 21–30) ; ἔργα accordingly is a broader conception than miracle, which, however, is included in the category of the Messianic ἔργα. See especially ver. 36.

Ver. 21. He speaks of the operation of His power in judging and raising the dead, first *in an ethical sense* down to ver. 27, and then, vv. 28, 29, subjoins the *actual and universal* awakening of the dead as the completion of His entire life-giving and judicial work as the Messiah. Augustine anticipated this view (though illogically apprehending ver. 21 in a moral sense, and ver. 22 in a physical), and it is adopted among the older writers, especially by Rupertius, Calvin, Jansen, Calovius, Lampe, and more recently by Lücke, Tholuck, Olshausen, Maier, de Wette, Lange, Hilgenfeld, Lechler,[5] Weiss, Godet. *Others* have extended the ethical interpretation even as far as vv. 28, 29,[6] which, however, is forbidden by the language and

---

[1] See Tittmann, *Synon.* p. 50.

[2] Comp. xi. 3, 36, xvi. 27, xx. 2, *et al.*

[3] This intimate relationship is to be regarded as one of *uninterrupted continuity*, and not to be limited merely to occasional crises in the life of Jesus (Gess, *Pers. Chr.* p. 237), of which there is not the slightest indication in John's Gospel. Comp. i. 52. This very *continuous* consciousness depends upon the continuance of the *Logos* consciousness (viii. 29, 59, xvii. 5, xvi. 32),—a view which is to be maintained against

Weizsäcker, who introduces also *visions* (*evang. Gesch.* p. 435) in explanation of this passage, in the face of the known history of Jesus.

[4] For the astonishment connected *with* the θεᾶσθαι is implied in the context. See Nägelsbach, *z. Ilias*, p. 200, ed. 3.

[5] *Apost. Zeitalt.* p. 225 f.

[6] So Deysing in the *Bibl. Brem.* i. 6, Eckermann, Ammon, and many others ; recently, Schweizer, B. Crusius, Reuss.

contents of vv. 28, 29 ; see on vv. 28, 29. Further, when Luthardt[1] understands ζωοποιεῖν generally of the impartation of life, he takes *both* kinds of
quickening as the two *sides* of the life, which appears, however, irreconcilable
with the right understanding of οὓς θέλει, and with the distinct separation
between the present and the future (the latter from ver. 28 onwards). The
ζωοποιεῖν of the Messiah during His *temporal* working concerns the *morally*
dead, of whom He morally quickens whom He will ; but *at a future day*,
at the end of all things, He will call forth the *physically* dead from their
graves, etc., vv. 28, 29. The carrying out of the double meaning of ζωοποιεῖν
onwards to ver. 28 (for vv. 28, 29 even Luthardt himself takes as referring
only to the *final* future) leads to confusion and forced interpretation (see on
οἱ ἀκούσαντες, ver. 25). Further, most of the Fathers,[2] most of the older expositors,[3] and recently Schott in particular,[4] Kuinoel, Baumeister,[5] Weizel,[6]
Kaeuffer,[7] Baeumlein and Ewald, take the entire passage vv. 21–29 in a *literal* sense, as referring to the resurrection and the final judgment. Against
this it is decisive : (*a*) that ἵνα ὑμεῖς θαυμάζητε in ver. 20 represents the
hearers as continuous witnesses of the works referred to, and these works,
therefore, as successive developments which they will see along with others ;
(*b*) that οὓς θέλει is in keeping only with the ethical reference ; (*c*) that ἵνα
πάντες τιμῶσι, etc., ver. 23, expresses a continuing result, taking place in the
present (in the αἰών οὗτος), and as divinely intended ; (*d*) that in ver. 24, ἐκ
τοῦ θανάτου *cannot* be explained of physical death ; (*e*) that in ver. 25, καὶ
νῦν ἐστιν and οἱ ἀκούσαντες are compatible only with a reference to spiritual
awakening. To this may be added, (*f*) that Jesus, where He speaks (vv. 28,
29) of the literally dead, very distinctly marks out the resurrection of these
latter from that of the preceding as something greater and as still future,
and designates the deed not merely with great definiteness *as such* (πάντες
οἱ ἐν τοῖς μνημείοις), but also makes their ἀνάστασις ζωῆς conditional, not, as in
ver. 24, upon *faith*, but, probably seeing that they for the most part would
never have heard the gospel, upon *having done good*,—thus characteristically
distinguishing *this* quickening of the dead from that spoken of immediately
before.— ὥσπερ . . . ζωοποιεῖ] The awakening and reviving of the dead is
represented as the essential and peculiar business of the Father ;[8] accordingly
the *Present* tense is used, because the statement is *general*. Comp. Rom. iv.
17. Observe, however, that Jesus here speaks of the awakening of the dead,
which is peculiar to the *Father*, still without distinguishing between the
spiritual and literal dead ; this separation first appears in the following
reference to the *Son*. The awakening of *both* springs from the same divine
source and basis of life. — ἐγείρει and ζωοποιεῖ we might expect in reverse
order (as in Eph. ii. 5, 6) ; but the ζωοποιεῖν is the essential and controlling
fact, of which the *awakening* (ἐγείρειν) is popularly conceived as the beginning,

---

[1] Comp. Tholuck on vv. 21–23, and Hengstenberg on vv. 21–24, also Brückner on ver.
21.

[2] Tertullian, Chrysostom and his followers, Nonnus, and others.

[3] Erasmus, Beza, Grotius, Bengel, and
many others.

[4] *Opusc.* i. p. 197.

[5] *Würtemb. Stud.* II. 1.

[6] *Stud. u. Krit.* 1836, p. 636.

[7] *De ζωῆς αἰων not.* p. 115 ff.

[8] Deut. xxxii. 39 ; 1 Sam. ii. 6 ; Tobit xiii.
2 ; Wisd. xvi. 13.

and appearing thus merely as its immediate antecedent, does not recur in the apodosis. [See Note XXIII. p. 195.] — οὓς θέλει] for He will *not* quicken others because they *believe* not (ver. 24) ; this, and not an absolute decree (Calvin, Reuss), is the *moral* condition of His self-determination, just as also His κρίσις (ver. 22) is in like manner morally determined.   That this spiritual resurrection is *independent of the descent from Abraham*, is evident from the fact of its being spiritual ; but this must not be taken as actually *stated* in the οὓς θέλει.   Many, who take ζωοποιεῖ *literally*, resort to the historical accounts of the raising of individuals from the dead (Lazarus, etc.), for which few cases the οὓς θέλει is neither appropriate nor adequate. See, besides, ver. 25.   Ewald takes *God* as the subject of θέλει, which is neither logical (on account of the καί, which places the two subjects in the same line), nor possible according to the plain words, though it is evident that the Son acts only in the harmony of His will with that of the Father ; comp. ver. 30, vi. 40. — ζωοποιεῖ] ethically, of the spiritual quickening to the higher moral life, instead of that moral death in which they were held captive in their unconverted state of darkness and sin.[1]   Without this ζωοποίησις, their life would remain ethically a ζωὴ ἄβιος,[2] βίος ἀβίωτος.[3] The *Present*, for He does it *now*, and is *occupied* with this ζωοποιεῖν, that is, by means of his *word*, which is the life-giving call (vv. 24, 25). The *Future* follows in ver. 28.

Ver. 22 does not state the ground of the Son's call to bestow life (Luthardt, comp. Tholuck and Hengstenberg), but is a justification of the οὓς θέλει,—because the κρίσις refers only to those whom He will not raise to life,—in so far as it is implied that the *others*, whom the Son will *not* make alive, will experience in themselves the *judgment of rejection* (the anticipatory analogon of the decisive judgment at the second advent, ver. 29). It is given to no other than the *Son* to execute this final judgment. The κρίνει οὐδένα should have prevented the substitution of the idea of *separation* for that of *judgment* (comp. iii. 17, 18). — οὐδὲ γὰρ ὁ π.] *for not even the Father*, to whom, however, by universal acknowledgment, judgment belongs.[4] Consequently it depends only upon the *Son*, and the οὓς θέλει has its vindication.   Concerning οὐδέ, which is for the most part neglected by commentators, comp. vii. 5, viii. 42, xxi. 25.   The antithesis ἀλλὰ, κ.τ.λ., tells *how far*, though God is the world's Judge, the Father does not judge, etc. — κρίνει] *the judgment of condemnation* (iii. 17, 18, v. 24, 27, 29), whose sentence is the opposite of ζωοποιεῖν, the sentence of spiritual death. — τὴν κρίσιν πᾶσαν] *judgment altogether* (here also to be understood on its *condemnatory* side), therefore not only of the last act on the day of judgment (ver. 27), but of its *entirety* (see on xvi. 13), and consequently in its progress in time, whereby the οὓς θέλει is decided.

Ver. 23. The *divine purpose* which is to be attained in the relation of mankind to this judicial action of the Son. Observe the *Present Subjunctive.* — καθώς] *just as*, for in the Son, who judges, we have the appointed *representative* of the Father, and *thus far* (therefore always relatively, xiv. 23) He is to

[1] See on Luke xv. 24 ; Matt. iv. 16 ; Eph. v. 14 ; Rom. vi. 13 ; Isa. xxvi. 19.
[2] Jacobs, *ad Anthol.* VII. p. 152.
[3] Xen. *Mem.* iv. 8. 8.
[4] Weiss, *Lehrbegr.* p. 185, explains it as if it ran : οὐδὲ γὰρ κρίνει ὁ πατήρ, etc.

be honoured *as* the Father. Comp. what follows. How utterly opposed to this divine intention was the procedure of the Jews, ver. 18 ! But it is incorrect to take καθώς with Baeumlein, as *causal* (see on xiii. 34, xvii. 2), because the whole context turns upon *the equality* of the Father and the Son. — οὐ τιμᾷ τὸν πατέρα] *i.e.* by this very fact, that he does not honour the Son, who is the Sent of the Father.

Ver. 24. The οὓς θέλει ζωοποιεῖ now receives—and that with increasing solemnity of discourse—its more minute explanation, both as to the subjects whom it specifies (ὁ τὸν λόγον μου ἀκούων, κ.τ.λ.), and the ζωοποίησις itself (ἔχει ζωήν). — ἀκούων is simply *heareth*, but is closely connected with the following καὶ πιστεύων (comp. Matt. xiii. 19 ff.), and thereby receives its definite reference. For the opposite, see xii. 47. — ἔχει ζ. αἰ.] The ζωοποιεῖν is accomplished in him ; he *has* eternal life (iii. 15), *i.e.* the higher spiritual ζωή, which, upon his entrance into the Messiah's kingdom, reaches its consummation in glorious Messianic ζωή. He *has*, in that he is become a believer, *passed from* spiritual death (see on ver. 21) *into eternal life* (the ζωὴ κατ᾽ ἐξοχήν), and *cometh not into* (condemnatory, comp. iii. 18) *judgment*, because he has already attained unto that *life*.[1] The result of this is : θάνατον οὐ μὴ θεωρήσῃ, viii. 51. On the Perfect μεταβέβ., see iii. 18 ; 1 John iii. 14.

Ver. 25. Jesus re-affirms what He had already asserted in ver. 24, but in the more concrete form of allegorical expression. — καὶ νῦν ἐστιν] *i.e.* in its beginning, since Christ's entrance upon His life-giving ministry. Comp. iv. 23. The duration of this ὥρα, however, continues till the second advent ; already had it begun to be present, but, viewed in its completeness, it still belonged to the future. The expositors who take the words to denote the *literal* resurrection (see ver. 25, also Hengst.), refer καὶ νῦν ἐστιν to the *individual* instances of raising from the dead *which Jesus has wrought ;*[2] but this is as inappropriate in general as it is specially un-Johannean, for those individuals were not awaked to ζωή in the sense of the context, but only to the earthly life, which was still liable to death. Olshausen, who illogically explains ver. 25 as referring to the resurrection of the body, appeals to Matt. xxvii. 52, 53. — οἱ νεκροί] the *spiritually* dead ; Matt. viii. 22 ; Rev. iii. 1 ; and see on ver. 21. — τῆς φωνῆς] according to the context, *the resurrection summons* (ver. 28), which is here *really*, in the connection of the allegory, the morally life-giving *preaching* of Christ. The spiritually dead, *generally*, under the category οἱ νεκροί, *will hear* this voice, but all will not *awake* to its call ; only οἱ ἀκούσαντες, which therefore cannot be taken in the same sense as ἀκούσονται, but must signify : *those who will have given ear thereto.* Comp. viii. 43, 47. In Latin : "Mortui *audient* . . . *et qui audientes fuerint*," etc. It is the ἀκούειν καλοῦντος,[3] *al.*, ἀκούειν παραγγέλλοντος, and

---

[1] Melanchthon : "Postquam illuxit fides seu fiducia Christi in corde, qua agnoscimus nos vere a Deo recipi, exaudiri, regi, defendi, sequitur pax et laetitia, quae est inchoatio vitae aeternae et tegit peccata, quae adhuc in imbecillitate nostra haerent." Baur is wrong in concluding from such passages (comp. viii. 51, xi. 26) that our evangelist verges closely on the doctrine of the Gnostics, 2 Tim. ii. 18.

[2] John xi. ; Mark v. 41 ; Luke vii. 14 ; Matt. xi. 5.

[3] Plut. *Sert.* 11.

the like, ἀκούειν τοῦ προστάγματος.[1] If we understand the words of *bodily* awakening, οἱ ἀκούσαντες with the article is quite *inexplicable*. Chrysostom : φωνῆς ἀκούσαντες ἐπιτατττούσης ; Grotius : " simul atque audierint." All such renderings, as also the vague explanation of Hengstenberg,[2] would require ἀκούσαντες *merely without* the article ;[3] and ζήσουσιν would, in opposition to the entire context, signify "*to live*" generally, in an indifferent sense. Olshausen, indeed, supplements ἀκούσαντες—which, nevertheless, must of necessity refer to τῆς φωνῆς—by τὸν λόγον from ver. 24 : "they who in this life hear the word of God." It is just as impossible to hold, with Luthardt (so far as he would include the literal resurrection), that οἱ ἀκούσαντες refers to those "who hear the last call of Jesus differently from others, *i.e. joyfully receiving it*, and therefore attain to life." This is an *imported* meaning, for there is no such modal limitation *in the text ;* but οἱ ἀκούσαντες *alone*, in so far as it must differ from the general ἀκούσονται, can only designate those who *give ear*, and by this the literal resurrection is *excluded*. For *this* double meaning of ἀκούειν in one sentence, see Plat. *Legg.* p. 712 B : θεὸν . . . ἐπικαλώμεθα· ὁ δὲ ἀκούσειέ τε καὶ ἀκούσας (cum exaudiverit) . . . ἔλθοι, and also the proverbial expression ἀκούοντα μὴ ἀκούειν.

Vv. 26, 27. The life denoted by this ζήσουσιν, seeing the subjects of it were *dead*, must be something which is in process of being *imparted* to them,—a life which comes from the Son, the quickener. But He could not impart it if He had not in Himself a divine and independent fountain of life, like the Father, which the Father, the absolutely living One (vi. 57), gave Him when He *sent* Him into the world to accomplish His Messianic work ; comp. x. 36. The following ἔδωκεν (ver. 27) should itself have prevented the reference to the eternal generation.[4] Besides (therefore ver. 27), if only the ἀκούσαντες (comp. οὓς θέλει, ver. 21) are to live, and the other νεκροί not, the Son must have received from the Father the warrant and power of judging and of deciding who are to live and who not. But this power is given Him by the Father *because He is the Son of man ;* for in His *incarnation*, *i.e.* in the fact that the Son of *God* (incarnate) is a child of *man*,[5] consists the *essence* of His nature as Redeemer, and with this the *reason in the history of redemption* why the Father has equipped Him for the Messianic function of judgment. Had the Son of *God* not become a child of *man*, He could not have been the fulfiller of the Father's decree of redemption, nor been entrusted with judicial power. Luthardt[6] says incorrectly : "for God desired to judge the world by means of a *man*," a thought quite too vague for *this* passage, borrowed from Acts xvii. 31. Better de Wette, with whom Brückner concurs (comp. also Reuss) : "It denotes the *Logos* as a *human manifestation*,[7] and in this lies the reason why He judges, *for the hidden God could not be judge*." But this negative and refined definition of the reason given, "because He is

---

[1] Polyb. xi. 19. 5.

[2] The article is said to indicate the inseparable connection between *hearing* and *life*.

[3] See Eurip. *Hec.* 25, 26, and Pflugk thereon. But οἱ ἀκούσαντες *with* the article is : *quicunque audiverunt.*

[4] Augustine and many others, also Gess.

[5] Comp. Phil. ii. 7; Gal. iv. 4; Rom. i. 3, viii. 3.

[6] Comp. Hofmann, *Schriftbew.* II. 1, p. 78.

[7] Or the *relative humanity* of Him who is *God's Son*. The expression is therefore different from : "*because He is man.*"

the Son of man," is inappropriately read between the lines, since it savours
of Philonic speculation, and since the view of the Deity as a Judge was
current among the Jews. So, following Augustine, Luther, Castalio, Jansen,
and most others, B. Crusius (comp. also Wetstein, who adduces Heb. iv.
15) : "because executing judgment requires direct operation upon mankind."[1] *Others* :[2] "υἱὸς ἀνϑρ. is He who is *announced* in Dan. vii. and in the
book of Enoch as *the Messiah*" (see on Matt. viii. 20), where the thought
itself is variously set forth ; Lücke (so also Baeumlein) : "because He is the
Messiah, and judgment essentially belongs to the work of the Messiah"
(comp. Ewald). Tholuck comes nearest to the right sense : "because He is
become man, *i.e.* is the *Redeemer*, but with this redemption itself the κρίσις
also is given." Hengstenberg : "as a *reward for taking humanity upon
Him*." Against the whole explanation from Dan. vii. 13, however, to which
Beyschlag, *Christol.* p. 29, with his explanation of the *ideal* man (the personal standard of divine judgment), adheres, it is decisive that in the N. T.
throughout, wherever "Son of man" is used to designate the Messiah, both
words *have the article:* ὁ υἱὸς τοῦ ἀνϑρώπου :[3] υἱὸς ἀνϑρώπου without the article[4] occurs in Rev. i. 13, xiv. 14, but it does not denote the Messiah.
Thus the prophecy in Daniel does *not* enter into consideration here ; but
"*son of a human being*" is correlative to "*son of God*" (of the *Father*, vv. 25,
26), although it must frankly be acknowledged that the expression does not
necessarily presuppose *birth from a virgin.*[5] The Peshito, Armenian version,
Theophylact, Euthymius Zigabenus, Paulus, connect the words—rightly
taking υἱὸς ἀνϑρ. to mean *man*—with what follows : "*Marvel not that He is
a man.*" This is not in keeping with the context, while τοῦτο witnesses for
the ordinary connection. — ζωὴν ἔχειν ἐν ἑαυτῷ] *in Himself.* "Est emphasis
in hoc dicto : vitam habere in sese, i.e. alio modo quam creaturae, angeli
et homines," Melanchthon. Comp. i. 4, xiv. 6.[6] The words καὶ νῦν ἐστιν are

---

[1] Comp. also Baur in Hilgenfeld's *Zeitschr.
f. wiss. Theol.* 1860, p. 276 ff., and *N. T.
Theol.* p. 79 ff.; Holtzmann in the same,
1865, p. 234 f. Akin to this interpretation is
that of Weiss, p. 224 : "so far as He is a
son of man, and *can in human form bring
near to men the life-giving revelation of God.*"
Even thus, however, what is said to be the
point of the reason given has to be supplied. This holds also against Godet, who
confounds things that differ : "On one
side judgment must proceed from the
womb of humanity as an 'hommage à Dieu,'
and on the other it is entrusted by God's
love as a purification of humanity to Him
who voluntarily became man." Groos (in
the *Stud. u. Krit.* 1868, p. 260) substantially
agrees with Beyschlag.

[2] Grotius, Lampe, Kuinoel, Lücke, Olshausen, Maier, Baeumlein, Ewald, and most
others, now also Tholuck.

[3] In John i. 52, iii. 13, 14, vi. 27, 52, 62, viii.
28, xii. 23, 34, xiii. 31.

[4] Weizsäcker (*Unters. üb. d. evang. Gesch.*
p. 431) cuts away this objection by the statement, without proof, that υἱὸς ἀνϑρ. without the article belongs to the explanatory
exposition of the fourth Gospel. Baeumlein
and Beyschlag, to account for the absence
of the article, content themselves with saying that υἱὸς ἀνϑρ. is the predicate, and
therefore (comp. Holtzmann) the point
would turn on the meaning of the conception. But the *formal* and *unchanging*
title, ὁ υἱὸς τοῦ ἀνϑρ., would not agree with
that ; and, moreover, in this way the omission only of the first article, and not of the
second (τοῦ), would be explained ; υἱὸς
ἀνϑρώπου can only mean *son of a man.*
Comp. Barnabas, *Ep.* xii. (Dressel).

[5] He who is Son of *God* is son of a *man*—
the latter κατὰ σάρκα, i. 14 ; the former κατὰ
πνεῦμα ἁγιωσύνης, Rom. ix. 5, i. 3.

[6] Quite in opposition to the ἐν ἑαυτῷ,
Weizsäcker, in the *Jahrb. f. Deutsche Theol.*
1857, p. 179, understands the possession of

certainly decisive against Gess,[1] who ascribes the gift of life by the Father to the Son as referring only to His pre-existent glory and His state of exaltation, which he considers to have been " *suspended* " during His earthly life. The prayer at the grave of Lazarus only proves that Christ exercised the power of life, which was bestowed upon Him as His own, in accordance with the Father's will. See on ver. 21.

Vv. 28–30. *Marvel not at this* (comp. iii. 7), viz. at what I have asserted concerning my life-giving and judicial power ; *for*[2] the last and greatest stage of this my Messianic quickening work (not the work of the λόγος as the absolute ζωή, to whom Baur refers the whole passage, vv. 20 ff. ; see, on the contrary, Brückner) is yet to come, namely, the raising of the actually dead out of their graves, and the final judgment.[3] Against the interpretation of this verse (see on ver. 21) in a *figurative* sense (comp. Isa. xxvi. 19 ; Ex. xxxvii. 12 ; Dan. xii. 2), it is decisive that οἱ ἐν τοῖς μνημείοις would have to mean *merely* the spiritually dead, which would be quite out of keeping with οἱ τὰ ἀγαθὰ ποιήσαντες. Jesus Himself intimates by the words οἱ ἐν τοῖς μνημείοις that He here is passing from the spiritually dead, who thus far have been spoken of, to the *literally* dead. — ὅτι] *argumentum a majori ;* the wonder at the *less* disappears before the *greater*, which is declared to be that which is *one day* to be accomplished. We are not to supply, with Luthardt, the condition of a *believing* estimate of the latter, for the auditors were unbelieving and hostile ; but the far more wonderful fact that is told does away with the wonder which the lesser had aroused, transcends, and, as it were, overwhelms it. — ἔρχεται ὥρα] Observe that no καὶ νῦν ἐστιν, as in ver. 25, *could* be added here. — πάντεσ] Here it is as little said that all shall be raised *at the same time*, as in ver. 25 that all the spiritually dead shall be quickened simultaneously. The τάγματα, which Paul distinguishes at the resurrection, 1 Cor. xv. 23, 24, and which are in harmony with the teaching of Judaism and of Christ Himself regarding a twofold resurrection (Bertholdt, *Christol.* pp. 176 ff., 203 ff. ; and see on Luke xiv. 14), find room likewise in the ὥρα, which is capable of prophetic extension. — οἱ τὰ ἀγαθὰ ποιήσαντες, κ.τ.λ.] that is, the first resurrection, that of the *just*, who are regarded by Jesus in a purely ethical aspect, and apart from all national particularism. See on Luke xiv. 14, and comp. John vi. 39. It was far from His object here to dwell upon the necessity of His redemption being appropriated by faith on the part of the dead here spoken of ; He gives expression simply to the abstract moral normal condition (comp. Rom. ii. 7, 13 ; Matt. vii. 21). This necessity, however, whereby they must belong to the οἱ τοῦ Χριστοῦ (1 Cor. xv.

life as brought about "*by transference or communication from the Father.*" Chap. vi. 57 likewise indicates life as an *essential* possession, brought with Him (i. 4) from His pre-existent state in His mission from the Father, and according to the Father's will and appointment, Col. i. 19, ii. 10.

[1] *Pers. Chr.* p. 301.

[2] Ewald renders ὅτι *that :* "Marvel not *at this, that* (as I said in ver. 1) *an hour is coming,*" etc. But in ver. 25 the thought

and expression are different from our text.

[3] It is not right, as is already plain from the text and ver. 27, to say that in John the judgment is *always* represented as an *inner* fact (so even Holtzmann, *Judenth. u. Christenth.* p. 422). The saying, "The world's history is the world's judgment," only partially represents John's view ; in John the last *day* is not without the last *judgment*, and *this* last judgment is with him the *world*-judgment. See on iii. 18.

23 ; comp. Matt. xxv. 31 sqq.), implies the *descensus Christi ad inferos.* — εἰς ἀνάστ. ζωῆς] they will come forth (from their graves) *into a resurrection of life* (represented locally), *i.e.* to a resurrection, the necessary result of which[1] is *life*, life in the Messiah's kingdom.[2] — κρίςεως] to which *judgment* pertains, and judgment, according to the context, in a *condemnatory* sense (to eternal death in Gehenna) ; and accordingly ἀνάστασις ζωῆς does not exclude an act of judgment, which awards the ζωή. — As to the distinction between ποιεῖν and πράττειν, see on iii. 20, 21. Ver. 30 further adds the *guarantee of the rectitude* of this κρίσις, and this expressed in a *general* way, so that Jesus describes His judgment *generally ;* hence the *Present,* denoting *continuous* action, and the general introductory statement of ver. 19, οὐ δύναμαι, etc. — καθὼς ἀκούω] *i.e.* from God, who, by virtue of the continual communion and confidence subsisting between Him and Christ, always makes *His* judgment directly and consciously known to Him, in accordance with which Christ gives His verdict.   Christ's sentence is simply the declaration of God's judgment consequent upon the continuous self-revelation of God in His consciousness, whereby the ἀκούειν from the Father, which He possessed in His pre-existent state, is continued in time. — ὅτι οὐ ζητῶ, κ.τ.λ.] " I cannot therefore *deviate* from the *judging as I hear ;* and my judgment, seeing it is not that of an individual, but divine, *must* be just." — τοῦ πέμψ. με, κ.τ.λ.] as it consequently accords with this my dependence upon God.

Ver. 31. Justification of His witness to Himself from ver. 19 ff., intermingled with denunciation of Jewish unbelief (vv. 31–40), which Jesus continues down to ver. 47. — The *connection* is not that Jesus now passes on to the τιμή which is due to Him (ver. 23), and demands faith as its true form (Luthardt), for the conception of τιμή does not again become prominent ; but ἐπειδὴ τοιαῦτα περὶ ἑαυτοῦ μαρτυρήσας ἔγνω τοὺς Ἰουδαίους ἐνθυμουμένους ἀντιθεῖναι καὶ εἰπεῖν· ὅτι ἐὰν σὺ μαρτυρεῖς περὶ σεαυτοῦ, ἡ μαρτυρία σου οὐκ ἔστιν ἀληθής· οὐδεὶς γὰρ ἑαυτῷ μαρτυρῶν ἀξιόπιστος ἐν ἀνθρώποις δι' ὑποψίαν φιλαυτίας· προέλαβε καὶ εἶπεν ὃ ἔμελλον εἰπεῖν ἐκεῖνοι, Euthymius Zigabenus.   Comp. Chrysostom.   Thus at the same time is solved the seeming contradiction with viii. 14. — ἐγώ] emphatic : if there is only my *personal witness concerning myself,* and with this no attestation *from any other.* Comp. ἄλλος, ver. 32. — οὐκ ἔστιν ἀληθ.] *i.e. formally* speaking, according to the ordinary rule of law.[3] In reality, the relation is different in Christ's case, see viii. 13–16 ; but He does not insist upon this here, and we must not therefore understand His words, with Baeumlein, as if He said : εἰ ἐγὼ ἐμαρτύρουν . . . οὐκ ἂν ἦν ἀληθὴς ἡ μαρτυρία μου.   Chap. viii. 54, 55 also, and 1 Cor. iv. 15, xiii. 1, Gal. i. 8, are not conceived of in this way.

Ver. 32. *Another is He who bears witness of me.*   This is understood either of *John the Baptist*[4] or of *God.*[5]   The latter is the right reference ; for Jesus

---

[1] Comp. Winer, p. 177 [E. T. p. 188].

[2] Comp. 2 Macc. vii. 14 : ἀνάστασις εἰς ζωῆν ; Dan. xii. 2 ; Rom. v. 18 : δικαίωσις ζωῆς.

[3] Chetub. f. 23. 2 : " testibus de se ipsis non credunt," and see Wetstein.

[4] Chrysostom, Theophylact, Nonnus, Euthymius Zigabenus, Erasmus, Grotius,

Paulus, Baumgarten Crusius, de Wette, Ewald.

[5] Cyril, Augustine, Bede, Rupertius, Beza, Aretius, Cornelius à Lapide, Calovius, Bengel, Kuinoel, Lücke, Tholuck, Olshausen, Maier, Luthardt, Lange, Hengstenberg, Brückner, Baeumlein, Godet.

Himself, ver. 34, does not attach importance to John's witness, but rather lays claim, vv. 36, 37, only to the higher, the *divine* witness. — καὶ οἶδα ὅτι, κ.τ.λ.] not a *feeble* assurance concerning God (de Wette's objection), but all the weightier from its simplicity, to which the very *form* of the expression is adapted (ἡ μαρτυρία, ἣν μαρτυρεῖ περὶ ἐμοῦ), and, moreover, far *too* solemn for the *Baptist's* testimony.[1]

Vv. 33, 34. " *That* witness, whose testimony you have *yourselves* elicited, *John the Baptist*, I do not, since it is a human testimony, accept for myself ; I mention him for *your* salvation (not for *my* advantage), because ye have not appreciated him according to his high calling (ver. 35) ; the witness which *I* have is *greater*," etc. Ver. 36. — ὑμεῖς] *you, on your part.* — μεμαρτ. τῇ ἀληθ.] i. 19 ff. "'All that he said was testimony in favour of the truth ; for the state of the case (with reference particularly to what he said of the Messiah) was as he testified." — ἐγὼ δέ] *but I on my part.* — τὴν μαρτυρίαν] the witness in question, which is to tell for me. This I cannot receive *from any man.* [See Note XXIV. p. 195.] Jesus will not avail Himself of any human witness in this matter ; He puts it away from Him. Accordingly, λαμβ. τ. μαρτυρίαν, just as in iii. 11, 32, is to be taken of the *acceptance*, not indeed believing acceptance, but acceptance as *proof*, conformably with the context. Others, unnecessarily deviating from John's usage, "I borrow" (Lücke), "I *strive after*, or *lay hold of*" (B. Crusius, comp. Beza, Grotius), "I *snatch*" (de Wette). — ἵνα ὑμεῖς σωθῆτε] *for your advantage, that you on your part* (as contrasted with any personal interest) *may attain to salvation.* They should take to heart his recalling of the Baptist's testimony (ταῦτα λέγω), and thus be roused to faith, and become partakers of the Messiah's redemption ; " *vestra* res agitur," Bengel.

Ver. 35. What a manifestation he was, yet how lightly ye esteemed him ! — ἦν and ἠθελ. point to a manifestation already past. — ὁ λύχνος] not τὸ φῶς, i. 8, but less ; hence φῶς in the second clause is used only predicatively. The *article* denotes the *appointed* lamp which, according to O. T. promise, was to appear, and had appeared in John as the forerunner of the Messiah, whose vocation it was to inform the people of the Messianic salvation (Luke i. 76, 77). The reference to the man who lights the way for the approaching bridegroom (Luthardt) is too remote. Comp. rather the similar image, though not referred to here, of the mission of Elijah, Ecclus. xlviii. 1. The comparison with a lamp in similar references was very common (2 Sam. xxi. 17 ; Rev. xxi. 23 ; 2 Pet. i. 19).[2] — καιόμενος καὶ φαίνων] is not to be interpreted of two different properties (burning zeal and light-giving) ; in the nature of things they go together. A lamp *burns and shines ;* this it does of necessity, and thus it is represented. Comp. Luke xii. 35 ; Rev. iv. 5. — ὑμεῖς δέ, κ.τ.λ.] striking description of the frivolous worldliness which would gratify its own short-lived excitement and pleasure in this new and grand manifestation, instead of making use of it to obtain saving knowledge, and allowing its full solemnity to operate upon them. The Jews flocked in

---

[1] On μαρτυρίαν μαρτυρεῖν, comp. Isa. iii. 11, xii. 25 ; Plato, *Eryx.* p. 399 B ; Dem. 1131. 4.

[2] Comp. also Strabo, xiv. p. 642, where Alexander the rhetorician bears the surname ὁ Λύχνος.

great crowds to the Baptist (Matt. iii. 5, xi. 7 ff.), as to the messenger of the approaching glorious kingdomof the Messiah ; but instead of finding what they *desired* (ἠθελήσ.), they found all the severity of the spirit of Elijah calling to repentance, and how soon was the concourse over ! In like manner, the Athenians hoped to find a new and passing *divertissement* when the Apostle Paul came among them. " Johanne *utendum* erat, non *fruendum*," Bengel.— πρὸς ὥραν] τοῦ εὐκολίαν αὐτῶν δεικνύντος ἐστὶ καὶ ὅτι ταχέως αὐτοῦ ἀπεπήδησαν, Chrysostom. Comp. Gal. ii. 5 ; Philem. 15. The main feature of the perverted desire does not lie in πρὸς ὥραν, which more closely marks the ἀγαλλ. in its frivolity, so soon changing into satiety and disgust, but in ἀγαλλ. itself, instead of which μετάνοια should have been the object of their pursuit. — ἐν τῷ φωτὶ αὐτοῦ] *in, i.e.* encompassed by *his light*, the radiance which shone forth from him. Comp. 1 Pet. i. 6 ; and for χαίρειν ἐν, see on Phil. i. 18.

Ver. 36. Ἐγὼ δέ] Formal antithesis to ὑμεῖς in ver. 35, and referring back to the ἐγὼ δέ of ver. 34. — *I have my witness, which is greater* (not " the greater witness ;" see Kühner, II. § 493. 1) *than John.* τοῦ Ἰωάννου in the sense of τῆς τοῦ Ἰωάν., according to a well-known *comparatio compendiaria.* See on Matt. v. 20. On μείζω, *i.e.* " *of weightier evidence*," comp. Isoc. *Archid.* § 32 : μαρτυρίαν μείζω καὶ σαφεστέραν. — τὰ ἔργα] not *simply* the *miracles* strictly so called, but *the Messianic works generally*, the several acts of the Messiah's entire work, the ἔργον of Jesus (iv. 34, xvii. 4). Ἐργα are always *deeds*, not word and teachings (*word* and *work* are distinct conceptions, not only in Scripture, but elsewhere likewise) ; [2] but what the word of Jesus *effected*, spiritual quickening (ver. 20), separation, enlightenment, and so on, and in like manner the resurrection of the dead and judgment (vv. 28, 29), are included *in* the ἔργα, and constitute His ἔργον as a whole. When *miracles* properly so called are designated by the more general term ἔργα, it is indicated in the context, as in iii. 2, vii. 3, 21, and often. — ἔδωκε] *hath given*, expressing the divine appointment, and bestowment of power.[3] — ἵνα τελ. αὐτά] Intention of the Father in committing to Him the works : *He was to accomplish them* (comp. iv. 34, xvii. 4), not to leave them undone or only partially accomplished, but fully to carry out the entire task which the works divinely entrusted to Him involved for the attainment of the goal of Messianic salvation. — αὐτὰ τὰ ἔργα] *the very works*, emphatic repetition,[4] where, moreover, the homoeoteleuton (the five times recurring *a*) must not be regarded as a dissonance.[5] — ἃ ἐγὼ ποιῶ] ἐγώ with august self-consciousness. As to *how* they witness, see xiv. 11.

Ver. 37. From the works which testified that He was the Sent of God, He now passes to the *witness of the Sender Himself ;* therefore from the *indirect* divine testimony, presented in the works, to the *direct* testimony in the Scriptures. *And the Father. who hath sent me, hath Himself borne witness of*

---

[1] The reading adopted by Lachmann, μείζων (A. B. F. G. M, Δ., Cursives), is nothing else than an error of transcription.

[2] See, Lobeck, *Paralip.* pp. 64, 65 ; Ellendt, *Lex. Soph.* I. p. 672 ; Pflugk, *ad Eur. Hec.*

373.

[3] Comp. Homer, *Il.* ε. 428 : οὔ τοι, τέκνον ἐμόν, δέδοται πολεμήϊα ἔργα. Comp. ν. 727

[4] Kühner, II. § 632.

[5] Lobeck, *Paralip.* p. 53.

THE GOSPEL OF JOHN.

me. The subject, placed at the beginning of the sentence, the independence (immediateness) expressed by αὐτός, and the Perfect μεμαρτ., unite to
prove that there is no longer any reference here to the previous testimony,
that of the *works,* by which God had borne testimony.[1] Quite arbitrary,
and in opposition to the account of the baptism *given by John,* is the view
which *others* take, that the divine witness given in *the voice at the baptism,*
Matt. iii. 17 (but see rather John i. 33), is here meant.[2] While Ewald[3]
includes together both the baptism *and* the works, and Hengstenberg adds
to these two the witness of *Scripture,* others understand "*the immediate
divine witness in the believer's heart,* by means of which the indirect testimony
of the works is first apprehended "[4] the "drawing" of the Father, vi. 14,
comp. vi. 45, viii. 47, but without the slightest indication in the text that
an outward, perceptible, concrete, and objective witness is meant ; and
even in the face of the following connection (φωνὴν . . . εἶδος). The
only true interpretation in harmony with the context is that which takes it
to mean *the* witness which God Himself has given in His *word, in the Scriptures of the O. T.*[5] In the O. T. prophecies, God Himself has lifted up His
voice and revealed His form. — οὔτε φωνήν, κ.τ.λ.] Reproach of *want of susceptibility* for this testimony, all the *more emphatic* through the absence of
any antithetic particle. *Neither a voice of His have ye ever heard, nor a form
of His have ye ever seen.* With respect to what God has in the O. T. *spoken* as
a testimony to Christ (μεμαρτύρ. περὶ ἐμοῦ), or to His *manifesting* Himself
therein, for a like purpose, to spiritual contemplation (He has made known
his δόξα ; comp. μορφὴ θεοῦ, Phil. ii. 6),—to the one ye have been spiritually
deaf, to the other spiritually *blind.* As the first cannot, conformably with
the context, be taken to mean the revealing voice of God within, vouchsafed to the prophets (de Wette), so neither can the second refer merely to
the *Theophanies* (in particular, to the appearances of the *Angel* of the Lord,
Hengstenberg) and prophetic *visions,*[6] but to the entire *self-revelation of God
in the O. T. generally,* by virtue of which He lets Himself be seen by him
who has eyes to see ;—a general and broad interpretation, which corresponds with the general nature of the expression, and with its logical relation to μεμαρτ. π. ἐμοῦ. The Jews *could* not have heard the *voice at the baptism,* nor *could* they have seen the form of God as the Logos had seen it, i.
18, iii. 13 ; and for this reason neither the one meaning nor the other can
be found in the words (Ewald). Every interpretation, moreover, is incorrect which finds in them anything but a reproach, because Jesus speaks
in the second person, and continues to do so in ver. 38, where the tone of
censure is still obvious. We must therefore reject the explanation of
B. Crusius : "never hitherto has this immediate revelation of God taken

---

[1] Against Augustine, Grotius, Maldonatus, Olshausen, Baur, and most others.

[2] Chrysostom, Rupertius, Jansen, Bengel,
Lampe, Paulus, Godet.

[3] *Johann. Schr.* I. 216.

[4] De Wette, B. Crusius, Tholuck.

[5] Cyril, Nonnus, Theophylact, Euthymius
Zigabenus, Beda, Calvin, Kuinoel, Lücke,
Lange, Maier, Luthardt.

[6] Jesus could not reproach His opponents
with not having received prophetic revelations, such as Theophanies and Visions, for
these were marks of distinction bestowed
only on individuals. This also against
Weiss, *Lehrbegr.* pp. 104, 105.

place ;" and that of Tholuck : " ye have not received a still more direct
revelation than did Moses and his contemporaries (Num. xii. 8 ; Deut. iv.
15, v. 24), but ye have not accepted within you the witness of the revelation
in the word,"—an artificial connecting of ver. 37 with ver. 38, which the
words forbid. Paulus and Kuinoel (comp. Euthymius Zigabenus) likewise
erroneously say that " Jesus here *concedes*, in some degree, to the Jews what
they had themselves wished to urge *in objection*, viz. that they had heard no
divine voice, etc. Comp. Ebrard (in Olshausen), who imports the idea of
irony into the passage.

Ver. 38. After ver. 37 we must place only a comma. John might have
continued : οὔτε τὸν λόγον, κ.τ.λ. ; instead of which he attaches the negation
not to the particle, but to the verb (οὔτε . . . καί, see on iv. 11), and thus the
new thought comes in more independently : *And ye have not His word
abiding in you ;* ye lack an inner and permanent appropriation of it ; comp.
1 John ii. 14. The λόγος θεοῦ is not "the inner revelation of God in the
conscience" (Olshausen, Frommann), but, conformably with the context (vv.
37, 39), *what God has spoken in the O. T.,* and this according to its *purport.* Had they given ear to this as, what it is in truth, the word of God
(but they had no ear for God's voice, ver. 37), had they discerned therein
God's manifestation of Himself (but they had no eye for God's form, ver.
37), what God had spoken would have penetrated through the spiritual ear
and eye into the heart, and *become the abiding power in their inner life.* — ὅτι
ὃν ἀπέστειλεν, κ.τ.λ.] demonstration of the fact. He who rejects the *sent* of
God cannot have that *word* abiding in him, which witnesses to Him who is
sent (ver. 37). " Quomodo mandata regis discet qui legatum excludit ?"
Grotius. — τούτῳ ὑμεῖς] observe the emphatic conjunction of the words.

Vv. 39, 40 bring out to view the complete *perversity of this unbelief.*
"The Scriptures testify of me, as the Mediator of eternal life ; he, therefore,
who searches the Scriptures, because in them he thinks he has eternal life,
will by that witness be referred to me ; ye search the Scriptures, because,
etc., and yet refuse to follow me according to their guidance." How inconsistent and self-contradictory is this ! That ἐρευνᾶτε is *Indicative,*[1] and
not *Imperative,*[2] is thus clear from the context, in which the Imperative
would introduce a foreign element, especially out of keeping with the correlative καὶ οὐ θέλετε.[3] [See Note XXV. p. 196.] The *searching of the Scriptures* might certainly be attributed to the Jews, comp. vii. 52 (against B.
Crusius and Tholuck) ; but a special significance is wrongly attached to ἐρευνᾶτε (a study which penetrates into the subject itself, and attains a truly
inward possession of the word, Luthardt) ; and the contradiction of ver. 40,
which forms such a difficulty, is really nothing but the inconsistency which
Jesus wishes to *bring out to view.* — ὑμεῖς] emphatic, *for you, ye on your part,*

[1] Cyril, Erasmus, Casaubon, Beza, Ben-
gel, and many moderns, also Kuinoel,
Lücke, Olshausen, Klee, de Wette, Maier,
Hilgenfeld, Brückner, Godet.

[2] Chrysostom, Augustine, Theophylact,
Euthymius Zigabenus, Luther, Calvin, Aretius, Maldonatus, Cornelius à Lapide, Gro-

tius, Calovius, Wolf, Wetstein, Paulus, B.
Crusius, Tholuck, Hofmann, Luthardt,
Baeumlein, Ewald, Hengstenberg, arguing
from Isa. xxxiv. 16.

[3] Comp. also Lechler in the *Stud. u. Krit.*
1854, p. 795.

are the people who think this. Still there lies in δοκεῖτε neither blame,[1] nor (as Ewald maintains, though ver. 45 is different) a delicate sarcastic reference to their exaggerated and scholastic reverence for the letter of Scripture, but certainly a contrast to the actual ἔχειν, which Jesus *could* not affirm concerning them, because they did not believe in Him who was testified of in the Scriptures as the Mediator of eternal life.[2] Theoretically, they were right in their thinking (δοκεῖν), but practically they were wrong, because Christ remained hidden from them in the Scriptures. Comp. as to the thing itself, 2 Cor. iii. 15, 16 ; and on ἔχειν ζωὴν αἰ., iii. 15. — ἐν αὐταῖς] The possession of Messianic life is regarded as *contained* in the Scriptures, in so far as they contain that by which this possession is brought about, that which is not given *outside* the Scriptures, but only *in* them. — καὶ ἐκεῖναι, κ.τ.λ.] Prominence assigned to the identity of the subject, in order to bring out the contrast more fully : *and they*, those very Scriptures which ye search, *are they which*, etc. — καὶ οὐ θέλετε] καί does not mean *and yet*, but simply *and*. This simplicity is all the more *striking*, more striking and tragic even than the interrogative interpretation (Ewald). On ἐλθεῖν πρός με, denoting a believing adherence to Christ, comp. vi. 35. They stood aloof from Him, and this depended on their *will*, Matt. xxiii. 37. — ἵνα ζωὴν ἐχ.] " in order that that δοκεῖν of yours may become a reality."

Vv. 41–44. "I do not utter these reproaches against you from (disappointed) ambition, but because I have perceived what a want of all right feeling towards God lies at the root of your unbelief." — δόξαν παρὰ ἀνθρ.] These words go together, and stand emphatically at the beginning of the sentence, because there is presupposed the possibility of an accusation *on this very point*.[3] — οὐ λαμβ.] *i.e.* "I reject it," as in ver. 34. — ἔγνωκα ὑμάς] "*cognitos vos habeo ;* hoc radio penetrat corda auditorum," Bengel. — τ. ἀγάπ. τ. θεοῦ] If they *had love to God* in their hearts (this being the summary of their law !), they would have felt sympathy towards the Son, whom the Father (ver. 43) sent, and would have received and recognized Him. The *article* is *generic ;* what they lacked was *love to God.* — ἐν ἑαυτοῖς] *in your own hearts ;* it was an excellence *foreign* to them, of which *they themselves* were destitute—a mere theory, *existing outside the range of their inner life.* — Ver. 43. Actual result of this deficiency with reference to their relation towards Jesus, who had come in His Father's name, *i.e.* as His appointed representative, and consequently as the true Christ (comp. vii. 28, viii. 42), but who was unbelievingly despised by them, whereas, on the other hand, they would receive a false Messiah. — ἐν τῷ ὀνόματι τῷ ἰδίῳ] *in*

[1] According to Hilgenfeld, *Lehrbegr.* p. 213 (comp. his *Evang.* p. 272, and *Zeitschr.* 1863, p. 217), directed against the *delusion* of the Jews, that they possessed the perfect source of blessedness in the literal sense of the O. T. which proceeded from the Demiurge, and was intended by him. Even Rothe, in the *Stud. u. Krit.* 1860, p. 67, takes δοκεῖτε in the sense of a *delusion*, viz. that they possessed eternal *life* in a *book*.

Such explanations are opposed to the high veneration manifested by Jesus towards the Holy Scriptures, especially apparent in John, though here even Weiss, p. 106, approves of the interpretation of an *erroneous* δοκεῖν.

[2] Comp. Hofmann, *Schriftbeweis*, I. 671.

[3] Comp. Plato, *Phaedr.* p. 282 A ; see also 1 Thess. ii. 6.

his own name, i.e. in his own authority and self-representations, not as one commissioned of God (which He of course is *alleged* to be), consequently a *false Messiah ;* [1] ψευδώνυμος ἀνὴρ ἀντίθεος, Nonnus. He will be received, because he satisfies the opposite of the love of God, viz. *self*-love (by promising earthly glory, indulgence towards sin, etc.). For a definite prophecy of false Messiahs, see Matt. xxiv. 24. To suppose a special reference to *Barkochba* (Hilgenfeld), is arbitrarily to take for granted the uncritical assumption of the post-apostolic origin of this Gospel. According to Schudt [2] (in Bengel), sixty-four such deceivers have been counted since the time of Christ. — Ver. 44. The reproach of unbelief now rises to its highest point, for Jesus in a wrathful question denies to the Jews even the *ability* to believe. — ὑμεῖς] has a deeply emotional emphasis : How is it possible *for you* people to believe ? And the ground of this impossibility is : *because ye receive honour one of another* (δόξαν παρὰ ἀλλ. are taken together), because ye reciprocally give and take honour of yourselves. This ungodly desire of honour (comp. xii. 43 ; Matt. xxiii. 5 sqq.), and its necessarily accompanying indifference towards the true honour, which comes from God, must so utterly blight and estrange the heart from the divine element of life, that it is not even *capable* of faith. That divine δόξα is indeed the true *glory of Israel* (Luthardt), comp. Rom. ii. 29, but it is not here designated *as such,* as also the δόξαν παρὰ ἀλλ. λαμβ. does not appear as a designation of the "*spurious-Judaism*," which latter is in general a wider conception (Rom. ii. 17 ff.). — τὴν παρά, κ.τ.λ.] for it consists in this, that one knows himself to be recognized and esteemed of God. Comp. as to the thing itself, xii. 43 ; Rom. ii. 29, iii. 23. — παρὰ τοῦ μόνου θεοῦ] not "*from God alone,*" [3] but *from the only* (alone, single) *God.* Cf. xvii. 3 ; Rom. xvi. 26 ; 1 Tim. vi. 15. The adj. shows the exclusive *value* of this honour. — οὐ ζητεῖτε] The transition from the participle to the finite tense gives independence and impressiveness to the second clause.

Vv. 45–47. In concluding, Jesus sweeps away from under their feet the entire ground and foundation upon which they based their hope, by representing Moses, their supposed saviour, as really their *accuser,* seeing that their unbelief implied unbelief in Moses, and this latter unbelief made it impossible for them to believe in Jesus. This last completely annihilating stroke at the unbelievers is not only in itself, but also in its implied reference to the cause of the hostility of the Jews (ver. 15), "maxime aptus ad conclusionem," Bengel. — μὴ δοκεῖτε] as you might perhaps believe from my previous denunciation. — κατηγορήσω] not of the final judgment, [4] where certainly Christ is *Judge ;* but in general, Jesus, by virtue of His permanent intercourse with the Father, might *at any time* have accused them before Him. — ἔστιν ὁ κατηγ. ὑμ.] The emphatic ἔστιν : there *exists* your accuser

---

[1] This reference of the text to false Messiahs is not too narrow (Luthardt, Brückner), because ἐλθη corresponds to the ἐλήλυθα; and this, as the entire context shows, indicates that the appearance of the Messiah had taken place. This also tells against Tholuck's general reference to

false prophets. Many of the Fathers have taken the words to refer to *Antichrist.*

[2] *Jüdische Merkwürdigkeit,* vi. 27–30.

[3] Grotius, de Wette, Godet, and most others, from an erroneous reference to Matt. iv. 4, 10.

[4] Ewald and early writers.

Moses—he *as the representative of the law* (not of the whole of the O. T., as Ewald thinks); therefore not again the *future*, but the present participle used as a substantive, expressing *continuous* accusation. — ὑμεῖς] has tragic emphasis. — ἠλπίκατε] *ye have set your hope, and do hope ;* comp. iii. 18, and see on 2 Cor. i. 10. As a reward for their zeal for the law, and their obedience (Rom. ii. 17 ff., ix. 31 f.), the Jews hoped for the salvation of the Messianic kingdom, towards the attainment of which Moses was accordingly their patron and mediator.

Ver. 46. Proof that Moses was their accuser. Moses wrote of *Christ*, referring to Deut. xviii. 15, and generally to all the Messianic types (comp. iii. 14) and promises of the Pentateuch, and to its general Messianic import (Luke xxiv. 44 ; Rom. x. 5) ; in this, that they did not believe *Christ* (*i.e.* that He spoke the truth), is implied that they rejected the truth of what *Moses* had written concerning Him. This unbelief is the subject-matter of Moses' accusation. Well says Bengel : "Non juvit Judaeos illud : Credimus vera esse omnia, quae Moses scripsit. Fide *explicita* opus erat." — Ver. 47. δέ] Further conclusion from the unbelief with regard to Moses, pointed out in ver. 46. Thus the discourse ends with a question implying hopelessness. — The antithesis is not between γράμμασιν and ῥήμασι (as if the *writings* were easier of belief than the *words*), but between ἐκείνου and ἐμοῖς (faith in *him* being the necessary condition of faith in *Christ*) ; while the distinction of Moses having *written* (comp. ver. 46), and Christ *spoken*, simply presents the *historical* relation. Were the antithesis between γράμμ. and ῥήμ., these words would have taken the lead ; were it between *both*, in γράμ. and ῥήμ., *and at the same time* in ἐκείνου and ἐμοῖς likewise, this twofold relationship must have been shown, thus perhaps : τοῖς γράμμασι τοῖς ἐκείνου . . . τοῖς ῥήμασι τοῖς ἐμοῖς.

Note.—The discourse, vv. 19–47, so fully embodies in its entire progress and contents, allowing for the necessary Johannine colouring in the mode of representation, those essential doctrines which Jesus had to advocate in the face of the unbelieving Jews, and exhibits, in expression and practical application, so much that is characteristic, great, thoughtful, and striking, that even Strauss himself does not venture to deny that it came substantially from the Lord, though as to its form he attaches suspicious importance to certain resemblances with the first Epistle ; but such a suspicion is all the less weighty, the more we are warranted to regard the Johannine idiosyncrasy as developed and moulded by a vivid recollection of the Lord's words, and as under the guidance of His Spirit, which preserved and transfigured that recollection. The reasons which lead Weisse to see nothing in the discourse but synoptical matter, and B. Bauer to regard the whole as a reflection of the later consciousness of the church, while Gfrörer supposes a real discourse, artificially shaped by additions and formal alterations, consist so much of arbitrary judgments and erroneous explanations and assumptions, that sober criticism gains nothing by them, nor can the discourse which is attacked lose anything. Certainly we have in it "a genuine exposition of Johannine theology" (Hilgenfeld, *Evang.* p. 273), but in such a manner, that it is the theology of *Christ Himself*, the miracle of healing at Bethesda being historically the occasion of the utterance in this manner of its main elements. This miracle itself is indeed by Baur regarded as a fictitious pretext, invented for the delivery of the discourse, so much so that "every feature in it seems to have been intended for this purpose" (p. 159) ; and this in the face of the fact that no reference whatever is made (in ver. 19 ff.) to the point in connection with the miracle at which the Jews took offence, viz. the *breaking of the Sabbath* (ver. 16). Nothing whatever is specially said concerning *miracles* (for ἔργα denotes a far wider conception), but the whole discourse turns upon that *Messianic faith* in the person of Jesus which the Jews refused to entertain. The fundamental truths, on this occasion so triumphantly expressed, "were never taught by Him so distinctly and definitely as now, when the right opportunity presented itself, at the very time when, after the Baptist's removal, He came fully forth as the Messiah, and was called upon, quietly and comprehensively, to explain those highest of all relations, the explanation of which was previously demanded." Ewald, *Gesch. Chr.* p. 298 f. ; comp. his *Johann. Schr.* I. 206 ff. At this crisis of His great mission and work, the references of his discourse to the Baptist, and the apologetic appeal to his works of spiritual and literal resurrection and the divine witness of Scripture, connect themselves so necessarily with His historical position, that it cannot even remotely suffice to suppose, with Weizsäcker, p. 282, that the discourse was composed simply with an eye to the synoptical statements of Matt. xi.

Notes by American Editor.

XXIII. ἐγείρει καὶ ζωοποιεῖ. Ver. 21.

"The ἐγείρει stands first (unlike Eph. ii. 5, 6), because the reference is not to a making alive that which has not had life, but to an *awakening from death*— though not so as to require us, with Godet, to connect the object merely with ἐγείρειν and take the ζωοποιεῖν absolutely. In the closing clause, therefore, the ζωοπ. stands alone" (Weiss).

I conceive, however, that Meyer's reason for the *order* holds good, that while the ζωοποιεῖν expresses the whole essential fact, yet to the popular *conception* the " awakening " is its precedent condition.

XXIV. " *But I do not receive,*" etc. Ver. 34.

The Common Ver. is here insufficient, in omitting entirely the article with μαρτυρίαν (I do not receive testimony). The Rev. Ver. makes it, perhaps, unnecessarily prominent, and then, with its very emphatic and somewhat ungainly "howbeit," gives undue contrastive force to the following clause. The following seems to me a better and adequate rendering : " But *I* do not receive my testimony from a man ; yet I say these things" (*i.e.* I appeal to John as voucher for myself and for the truth) " that *ye* may be saved."—It is impossible often to distinguish in English between the stronger and the more slightly adversative Gr. particles δέ and ἀλλά. The rendering of the former fluctuates about equally between *and* and *but;* the latter is commonly given by *but* or *yet;* it is rarely so strongly adversative as our "howbeit."

XXV. Ἐρευνᾶτε τὰς γραφάς. Ver. 39.

Opinions fluctuate between the Ind. and Imper. constructions of ἐρευνᾶτε. Weiss follows Meyer (with perhaps the majority of interpreters, including the R. V.) in making it Ind., which, in connection with the following clause, seems at first view more probable. To me, however, the Imperative construction (held generally by the Greek interpreters) seems preferable : first, from the *position* of the verb, which favors the Imperative ; secondly, because it seems more natural that Jesus should have so appealed to the Jews ("*search* the Scriptures") than have declared them as doing that which was at this time probably true of but very few of them ; and thirdly, because of the following ὑμεῖς, which, following the Ind. ("Ye search the Scriptures because *ye* think," etc.) seems wholly unaccountable ; but, on the other hand, taking the verb as Imper. and the following clause as justifying His exhortation, seems entirely in order : "Search the Scriptures ; and I may well bid you do this, because *ye* deem that in these ye have eternal life. I may properly refer you to them, as being in your own judgment the arbiters of spiritual truth and destiny." Having assigned this justification of His referring them to their Scriptures, He then declares in two brief sentences the essential *reason* of the reference—their testimony to Him, and the Jewish inconsistency in nevertheless rejecting Him. Both the following καί's are pregnantly weighty. The first attaches itself to the preceding clause, "and (while this is the case) these are they," etc.; the second succeeds to this with nearly the force of *and yet*—perhaps a very emphatic *and*. Weiss explains the ὑμεῖς (against Meyer) by making it imply the Saviour's *dissent* from the Jewish opinion that they had in the Scriptures eternal life. But in this he is surely mistaken. The language does not apply to actual *individual posssesion*, but to the ideal character of the Scriptures. They were the fountain of eternal life. The Jewish estimate of their character was correct, and on this ground the Saviour presses home the obligation to examine them and accept their testimony. It is unwarrantable to force into His language a reference to their efficacy on the persons whom He was addressing.

CHAPTER VI.

Ver. 2. ἑώρων] Lachm. and Tisch. : ἐθεώρουν, after A. B. D. L. ℵ. Cursives, Cyr. The origin of this reading betrays itself through A., which has ἐθεώρων, judging from which ἑώρων must have been the original reading. The ἐθεώρ. was all the more easily received, however, because John invariably uses the Perfect only of ὁρᾶν.—After this Elz. has αὐτοῦ, against decisive testimonies.— Ver. 5. ἀγοράσομεν] Scholz, Lachm., Tisch., read ἀγοράσωμεν, in favour of which the great majority of the testimonies decide. — Ver. 9. ἕν] is wanting in B. D. L. ℵ. Cursives, Or. Cyr. Chrys. and some Verss. Rejected by Schulz after Gersd., bracketed by Lachm., deleted by Tisch. But how easily might it have been overlooked, because superfluous, and coming after the syllable ON !—For ὅ Lachm. and Tisch. read ὅς, following decisive witnesses ; transcribers were easily led to make changes according to the *grammatical* gender. — Ver. 11. After διέδωκε Elz. has τοῖς μαθηταῖς, οἱ δὲ μαθηταί, words which are wanting in A. B. L. ℵ.* Cursives, Fathers, and almost all Versions. An enlargement in imitation of Matt. xiv. 19 and parallels. — Ver. 15. Lachm. and Tisch. have rightly deleted αὐτόν after ποιήσ. ; an addition wanting in A. B. L. ℵ. Cursives, Or. Cyr. — Ver. 17. οὐκ] B. D. L. ℵ. Cursives, Versions (not Vulgate), and Fathers read οὔπω. So Lachm. and Tisch. A gloss introduced for the sake of more minute definition. — Ver. 22. ἰδών] Lachm reads εἶδον, after A. B. Chrys. Verss. (L. ιδον) ; D. ℵ. Verss. read οἴδεν. The finite tense was introduced to make the construction easier. — After ἕν Elz. Scholz have ἐκεῖνο εἰς ὃ ἐνέβησαν οἱ μαθηταὶ αὐτοῦ, against very important authorities. An explanatory addition, with many variations in detail. — πλοῖον] Elz. : πλοιάριον against decisive witnesses. Mechanical and careless (vv. 17, 21) repetition borrowed from what precedes. — Ver. 24. αὐτοί] Elz. καὶ αὐτοί, against decisive witnesses. — Ver. 36. με is bracketed by Lachm., deleted by Tisch. The authorities against it are insufficient (only A. ℵ. among the Codices), and it might easily have been left out after TE. — Ver. 39. After με Elz. has πατρός, the omission of which is over-whelmingly attested. An addition. — Ver. 40. τοῦ πατρός μου] So also Lachm. and Tisch. The Textus Receptus is τοῦ πέμψαντός με. Preponderance of testimony is in favour of the former ; the latter is a repetition from ver. 39, whence also, instead of γάρ, the Received reading δέ was inserted. — τῇ ἐσχ. ἡμ.] According to A. D. K. L., etc., ἐν τ. ἐσχ. ἡμ. is to be restored, as in ver. 39, where ἐν, indeed, is wanting in many witnesses ; but that it was the original reading is indicated by the reading αὐτόν (instead of αὐτό). In ver. 54, also, ἐν is sufficiently confirmed, and (against Tisch.) is to be in like manner restored. — Ver. 42. The second οὗτος has against it B. C. D. L. T. Cursives, Verss. Cyr. Chrys.; bracketed by Lachm. But it might easily have been overlooked as being unnecessary, and because the similar OTI follows.— Ver. 45. ἀκούσας] ἀκούων, which Griesbach received and Scholz adopted, has important authority, but this is outweighed by the testi-monies for the Received reading. It is nevertheless to be preferred ; for, con-sidering the following μαθών, the *Aorist* would easily occur to the transcribers who did not consider the difference of sense. οὖν before ὁ ἀκούων is to be struck out (with Lachm. and Tisch.) upon sufficient counter testimony, as being a connective addition. In vv. 51, 54, 57, 58, the form ζήσει is, upon strong evidence, to be uniformly restored. — Concerning the omission of the words, ἣν ἐγὼ δώσω in ver. 51, see the exegetical notes. — Ver. 55. For ἀληθῶς Lachm. and Tisch. have both times ἀληθής, which is strongly confirmed by B. C. K. L. T. Cursives, Versions (yet not the Vulgate), and Fathers (even Clement and Origen). The genuine ἀληθής, as seeming inappropriate, would be glossed and supplanted now by ἀληθῶς and now by ἀληθινή (already in Origen once). — Ver. 58. After πατέρες, Elz. Scholz have ὑμῶν τὸ μάννα, Lachm. simply τὸ μάννα, both against very important testimony. An enlargement. — Ver. 63. λελάληκα] Elz. λαλῶ, against decisive witnesses. Altered because the reference of the Perfect was not understood. Comp. xiv. 10. — Ver. 69. ὁ Χριστὸς ὁ υἱὸς τ. θεοῦ] The reading ὁ ἅγιος τ. θεοῦ is confirmed by B. C.* D. L. ℵ. Nonn. Cosm., and adopted by Griesb. Lachm. Tisch. The Received reading is from Matt. xvi. 16, whence also came the addition τοῦ ζῶντος in the Elz. — Ver. 71. Ἰσκαριώτην] Lachm. and Tisch. read Ἰσκαριώτου, after B. C. G. L. 33, and Verss. So, after the same witnesses in part, in xiii. 26. But as in xiv. 22 Ἰσκαριώτης occurs critically confirmed as the name of Judas himself (not of his father), and as the genitive might easily be introduced as explanatory of the name (ἀπὸ Καριώτου, as ℵ, and many Cursives actually read here), the Received reading is to be retained. Had John regarded the name as designating the *father* of Judas, it would not be apparent why he did not use the genitive in xiv. 22 also. See, besides, the exegetical notes.

Ver. 1. The *account of the Feeding* is the same with that given in Matt. xiv. 13 ff., Mark vi. 30 ff., Luke ix. 10 ff., and serves as the basis of the discourse which follows, though Schweizer denies that vv. 1–26 proceed from John. The discrepancies in matters of detail are immaterial, and bear witness to the independence of John's account. The author of this narrative, according to Baur, must have appropriated synoptical material for the purpose of his own exposition, and of elevating into a higher sphere the miracle itself, which in the Synoptics did not go beyond the supply of temporal needs. The *historical connection* with what precedes is not the same in John and in the Synoptics, and this must be simply acknowledged. To introduce more or less synoptical history into the the space implied in μετὰ ταῦτα (Ebrard, Lange, Lichtenstein, and many), is not requisite in John, and involves much uncertainty in detail, especially as Matthew does not agree with Mark and Luke ; for he puts the mission of the disciples earlier, and does not connect their return with the Miraculous Feeding. To interpolate their mission and return into John's narrative, inserting the former at chap. v. 1, and the latter at vi. 1, so that the disciples rejoin Jesus at Tiberias, is very hazardous ; for John gives no hint of it, and in their silence concerning it Matthew and John agree (against Wieseler and most expositors). According to Ewald, at a very early date, a section, "probably a whole sheet," between chap. v. and vi., was *altogether lost.* But there is no indication of this in the text, nor does it form a necessary condition of the succeeding portions of the narrative (as vii. 21). — μετὰ ταῦτα] after these transactions at the feast of Purim, chap. v. — ἀπῆλθεν] from Jerusalem ; whither ?

πέραν τ. θαλ., κ.τ.λ., tells us.[1] To suppose some place in *Galilee*, as the starting point of the ἀπῆλθεν,[2] — Capernaum, for example,—is, after v. 1, quite
arbitrary. Ἀπῆλθε πέραν, κ.τ.λ., rather implies : ἀπολιπὼν Ἱεροσόλυμα ἦλθε
πέραν, κ.τ.λ. Comp. x. 40, xviii. 1. — τῆς Τιβερ.] does not imply that He set
sail from Tiberias (Paulus), as the genitive of itself might indicate,[3] though
this use of it does not occur in the N. T. ; it is the chorographical genitive,[4]
more closely describing τῆς θαλάσσ. τῆς Γαλιλ. (comp. Vulg. and Beza :
"mare Galilaeae, *quod est Tiberiadis*"). Therefore "*on the other side of the
Galilaean lake of Tiberias*," thus denoting the southern half of the lake, on
the western shore of which lay the town built by Antipas, and called after
the emperor Tiberias. Comp. xxi. 1. In Pausan. v. 7. 3, the entire lake is
called λίμνη Τιβερίς. In Matthew and Mark we find the name θάλασσα τῆς
Γαλιλ. only ; in Luke v. 1 : λίμνη Γεννησαρέτ. Had John intended τῆς Τιβε-
ριάδος not as a more exact description of the locality, but only for the *sake of
foreign readers*,[5] it would have been sufficient to omit τῆς Γαλιλ. (comp. xxi.
1), which indeed is wanting in G. and a few other witnesses.

Vv. 2, 3. Ἠκολούθει] on this journey, continuously. — ἑώρων] *saw*, not *had
seen* (against Schweizer, B. Crusius), but *saw*. He performed them (ἐποίει)
upon the way. — ἐπὶ τ. ἀσθ.] *among the sick.*[6] — εἰς τὸ ὄρος] *upon the mountain
which was there.* See on Matt. v. 1. The mountain was certainly on the *other*
side of the lake, but we cannot determine the locality more nearly. The
mountain solitude does not contradict Matt. xiv. 13, nor does the *eastern* side
of the lake contradict Luke ix. 10 ff. (see *in loc.*).

Ver. 4. Ἐγγύς] *close at hand.* See on v. 1. Paulus wrongly renders it *not
long since past.* See, on the contrary, ii. 13, vii. 2, xi. 55. The statement
is intended as introductory to ver. 5, explaining how it happened (comp.
xi. 55) that Jesus, after He had withdrawn to the mountain, was again attended by a great multitude (ver. 5),—a thing which could not have happened had not the Passover been nigh. It was *another* crowd (not, as is *commonly* assumed, that named in ver. 2, which had followed Him in His progress towards the lake), composed of *pilgrims to the feast*, who therefore were
going the opposite way, from the neighbourhood of the lake *in the direction
of Jerusalem.* Thus ver. 4 is not a mere *chronological* note,[7] against which
the analogy of vii. 2 (with the οὖν following, ver. 3) is decisive ; nor does
it, as every more specific hint to that effect is wanting, refer by anticipation[8]
to the following discourse of Jesus concerning eating His flesh and blood as
the antitype of the Passover.[9] — ἡ ἑορτὴ τ. Ἰουδαίων] κατ. ἐξοχήν. There is no
intimation that Jesus Himself went up to this feast (Lücke). See rather
vii. 1.

---

[1] Thuc. i. 111. 2, ii. 67. 1 : πορευθῆναι πέραν
τοῦ Ἑλλησπόντου ; Plut. *Per.* 19 ; 1 Macc. ix.
34 ; and comp. ver. 17.

[2] Brückner, Luthardt, Hengstenberg, Godet, and earlier critics.

[3] Kühner, II. 160.

[4] Krüger, xlvii. 5. 5-7.

[5] Lücke, Godet, Ewald, and others.

[6] Dem. 574. 3 ; Plat. *Pol.* iii. p. 399 A ;
Bernhardy, p. 246.

[7] B. Crusius, Maier, Brückner, Ewald.

[8] Comp. also Godet : Jesus must have
been in the position " *d'un proscrit*," and
could not go to Jerusalem to the Passover ;
He therefore saw in the approaching
multitudes a sign from the Father, and
thought, " *Et moi aussi, je célébrerai une
pâque.*" This is pure invention.

[9] B. Bauer ; comp. Baur, p. 262, Luthardt,
Hengstenberg, and already Lampe.

Vv. 5, 6. According to the reading ἀγοράσωμεν, *whence are we to buy? de-liberative* conjunctive. The fact that Jesus thus takes the *initiative* (as *host*, Ewald thinks, but this is not enough), and takes action without the prompt-ing of any expressed need, however real, is not to be explained merely on the supposition that this is an abridgment (Lücke, Neander, Hengstenberg) of the synoptical account (Matt. xiv. 15) ; it is a *diversity*, which, however, does not destroy the fact that John was an eye-witness. It is purely arbi-trary on Baur's part to assume the design to be that of directing attention more directly to the spiritual purpose of the miracle, or, with Hilgenfeld, to regard all here as *composed* out of synoptical materials to prove the omnipo-tence of the Logos. The most simple and obvious course is to explain the representation given as flowing from the preponderating idea of the *Mes-siah's autonomy*.[1] See on Matt. xiv. 15. It is an analogous case when Jesus *Himself gave occasion to* and introduced the miracle at Bethesda, v. 6. It is a *supplement* to the narrative in the Synoptics, that Jesus discussed with *Philip* (i. 44) the question of bread. Why with *him ?* According to Ben-gel, because it fell to him to manage the *res alimentaria*, which is improb-able, for *Judas* was treasurer, xiii. 29. Judging from ver. 6, we might say it was because Philip had to be tested in his intellectual capaci-ties (xiv. 8 ff.), and convinced of his *inability to advise*. The πειράζειν does not signify the trial of *faith* (so usually, also Hengstenberg), but, as αὐτὸς γὰρ ᾔδει shows, was a *test whether he could here suggest any expedient ;* and the *answer* of the disciple (ver. 7) conveys only the impression that he knew of *none*. *This* consciousness, however, was intended also to prepare the disciple, who so closely resembled Thomas, and for whom the question, therefore, had an *educative* purpose, the more readily to feel, by the new and coming miracle, how the power of faith in the divine agency of his Lord transcended all calculations of the intellect. This was too important a matter for Jesus with respect to that disciple, to allow us to suppose that πειράζων αὐτόν is a mere notion of John's own, which had its origin among the transfiguring recollections of a later time (Ewald). Ἤδει τῶν μαθητῶν τοὺς μάλιστα δεομένους πλείονος διδασκαλίας, Theodore of Mopsuestia ; in which there is nothing to suggest our attributing to Philip a " *simplicité naïve*," Godet. — αὐτός] *Himself*, without having any need to resort to the advice of another.

Vv. 7–9. *For* 200 *denarii* (about 80 Rhenish Guldens, nearly £7) *we can-not get bread enough for them*, etc. This amount is not named as the *con-tents of the purse*, but generally as *a large sum*, which nevertheless was *inad-equate* for the need. Different in Mark vi. 37. — Vv. 8, 9. A special trait of originality. — εἰς ἐκ τ. μαθητ. αὐτοῦ] may seem strange, for Philip was him-self a disciple, and it is explained by Wassenbach as a *gloss*. It has, how-

---

[1] Amid such minor circumstances, the *idea* might certainly supplant the more exact *historical* recollection even in a John. We have no right, however, on that ac-count, to compare Jesus, according to John's representation, to a housewife, who, when she sees the guests coming in the distance, thinks in the first place of what she can set before them, as Hase (*Tübing. Schule*, p. 4) very inappropriately has done.

ever, this significance ; Philip had been specially asked, and after he had answered so helplessly, *another from the circle of the disciples,* viz. Andrew. directed a communication to the Lord, which, though made with a like consciousness of helplessness, was made the instrument for the further procedure of Jesus. — παιδάριον ἕν] who had these victuals for sale as a market boy, not a servant of the company, B. Crusius. It may be read *one single lad* (Matt. xi. 16), or even *one single young slave.*[1] Comp. the German *ein Bürschchen* (a lad), as also the manner in which παιδίον is used (Aristoph. *Ran.* 37 ; *Nub.* 131). In which of the two senses it stands here we cannot decide. In neither case can ἕν stand for τὶ, but ἕν, as well as the diminutive παιδίον, helps to *describe* the meagreness of the resource, the emphasis, however, being on the latter ; and hence ἕν *follows,* which is not to be taken as an argument against its genuineness (Gersd. p. 420 ; Lücke, and most others), though in *all* other places, when John uses εἰς with a substantive (vii. 21, viii. 41, x. 16, xi. 50, xviii. 14, xx. 7), the numeral has the emphasis, and *therefore* takes the lead. But here : "one single *lad,*" a mere boy, who can carry little enough ! — ἄρτους κριθίνους] comp. Xen. *Anab.* iv. 5. 31 ; Luc. *Macrob.* 5. *Barley bread* was eaten mainly by the poorer classes ; Judg. vii. 13, and Studer, *in loc. ;* Liv. xxvii. 13 ; Sen. *ep.* xviii. 8 ; see also Wetstein and Kypke, I. p. 368. — ὀψάριον] generally a small relish, but in particular used, as here (comp. xxi. 9, 13), of fish. It belongs to later Greek. See Wetstein. — εἰς τοσούτους] *for so many.* Comp. Xen. *Anab.* i. 1. 10 : εἰς δισχιλίους μισθόν.

Vv. 10–13. Οἱ ἄνδρες] They were *men* only who formally sat down to the meal, as may be explained from the subordinate position of the women and children ; but the feeding of these latter, whose presence we must assume from ver. 4, is not, as taking place indirectly, excluded. — τὸν ἀριθμόν] Accusative of closer definition.[2] — Ver. 11. εὐχαρ.] The grace before meat said by the host. See on Matt. xiv. 19. There is no indication that it contained a special petition ("that God would let this little portion feed so many," Luthardt, comp. Tholuck). — διέδωκε] He distributed the bread (by the disciples) collectively to those who were sitting ; and of the fishes as much as they desired.[3] — Ver. 12. It is not given as a *command* of Jesus in the synoptical account. As to the miracle itself,[4] and the methods of explaining it away, wholly or in part, see on Matt. xiv. 20, 21, note, and on

---

[1] See Lobeck, *ad Phryn.* p. 240 ; Schleusner, *Thes.* III. p. 160.

[2] See Lobeck, *Paralip.* p. 528.

[3] Luther's translation, "as much as *He would,*" rests upon an unsupported reading in Erasmus, edd. 1 and 2.

[4] By Ewald (*Gesch. Chr.* p. 442 sq. ed. 3) apprehended *ideally,* like the turning of the water into wine at Cana, as a *legend,* upon the formation of which great influence was excited by the holy feeling of higher satisfaction, which resulted from the participation in the bread of life partaken of by the disciples after Christ's resurrection. This

is incompatible with the personal recollection and testimony of John, whom Hase, indeed, supposes by some accident to have been absent from the scene. With equally laboured and mistaken logic, Schleiermacher (*L. J.* 234) endeavours to show that ver. 26 excludes this event from the category of σημεῖα. Weizsäcker leaves the fact, which is here the symbol of the blessing of Jesus, in perfect uncertainty; but the description by an eye-witness of the work effected in its miraculous character, which only leaves the *how* unexplained, does not admit of such an evasion.

Luke ix. 17, and observe besides on ver. 13, that according to John the twelve baskets were filled with fragments of *bread* only (otherwise in Mark vi. 43). — Luthardt, without sanction from the text, assumes a *typical* reference in the baskets to the twelve tribes of Israel. Jesus will have nothing wasted, and each apostle fills his travelling wallet with the surplus. John indicates nothing further, not even that the Lord wished to provide ἵνα μὴ δόξῃ φαντασία τις τὸ γενόμενον,[1] *that the occurrence might not seem a sort of illusion.*

Vv. 14, 15. Ὁ προφήτης, κ.τ.λ.] *the Prophet who* (according to the promise in Deut. xviii. 15) *cometh into the world, i.e.* the *Messiah.* — ἁρπάζειν] come and *carry him away by force,*[2] *i.e.* to Jerusalem, as the seat of the theocracy, whither they were journeying to the feast. — πάλιν] comp. ver. 3. He had come down from the mountain on account of the feeding, ver. 11. — αὐτὸς μόνος] as in xii. 24.[3] — The *enthusiasm* of the people, being of so *sensuous* a kind, does not contradict ver. 26.—The *solitude* which Jesus sought was, according to Matt. xiv. 23, Mark vi. 46, that of *prayer,* and this does not contradict John's account ; the two accounts *supplement* each other.

Vv. 16–21. Comp. Matt. xiv. 22 ff., Mark vi. 45 ff., which do not refer to a *different* walking on the sea (Chrysostom, Lücke). — ὡς δὲ ὀψία ἐγένετο] According to ver. 17, the time meant is *late in the evening, i.e.* the so-called second evening, as in Matt. xiv. 24, from the twelfth hour until the *darkness,* ver. 17. See on Matt. xiv. 15. — εἰς τὸ πλοῖον] *into the ship,* in which they had crossed over (ver. 1). In it they now return to the western side of the lake. So Luthardt rightly. But it does not follow that Jerusalem could not have been the place of departure in ver. 1 ; from ver. 1 we rather infer that they had travelled from Jerusalem to the western shore of the lake, and have crossed over from thence. — ἤρχοντο] They were *upon* their return journey, coming across, but the coming was not yet completed. Lampe and Paulus erroneously speak of their actual *arrival,* what follows being taken as *supplementary.* In Mark vi. 45 Bethsaida is named (on the western shore). An immaterial discrepancy. See on Matt. xiv. 22, 23. — καὶ σκοτία . . . διηγείρετο] describing how little they could have expected that Jesus would come after them. — Ver. 19. ὡς σταδίους . . . τριάκοντα] indicative of an eye-witness, and nearly agreeing with μέσον in Matt. xiv. 24, for the lake was forty stadia or one geographical mile wide.[4] — θεωροῦσι and ἐφοβήθ.] Correlatives ; discountenancing the naturalistic interpretation, which makes ἐπὶ τ. θαλ. mean not *on the sea,* but *towards the sea* (so Paulus, Gfrörer, and many, even B. Crusius ; but see, on the contrary, note on Matt. xiv. 25). — Ver. 21. ἤθελον, κ.τ.λ.] comp. i. 44 ; but observe the *Imperfect* here. After Jesus had reassured them by His call, *they wish to take Him into the ship, and straightway* (while entertaining this ἐθέλειν) *the ship is at the land, i.e.* by the wonder-working power of Jesus, both with respect to the distance from the shore, which was still far off, and the fury of the sea, which

---

[1] Euthymius Zigabenus, Erasmus, and several others.

[2] Acts viii. 39 ; 2 Cor. xii. 2 ; 1 Thess. iv. 17.

[3] See Toup. *ad Longin.* p. 526 ; Weisk. Heind. *ad Charm.* p. 62.

[4] Josephus, *Bell.* iii. 10. 7.

had just been raging, but was now suddenly calmed. The idea that Jesus, to whom the disciples had stretched out their hands, had just *come on board* the ship, introduces a foreign element (against Luthardt and Godet), for the sake of bringing the account into harmony with Matthew and Mark. The discrepancy with Matthew and Mark, according to whom Christ was actually received into the ship, must not be explained away, especially as in John a more wonderful point, peculiar to his account, is introduced by the καὶ εὐθέως, etc., which makes the actual reception *superfluous* (Hengstenberg, following Bengel, regards it as implied). [See Note XXVI. p. 226.] An unhappy attempt at harmonizing renders it, "*they willingly received Him,*" [1] which cannot be supported by a supposed contrast of previous unwillingness (Ebrard, Tholuck), but would be admissible only if the text represented the will *and* the deed as undoubtedly simultaneous. [2] John would in that case have written ἐθέλοντες οὖν ἔλαβον. — εἰς ἥν ὑπῆγον] to which they were intending by this journey to remove.—The miracle itself cannot be resolved into a natural occurrence, [3] nor be regarded as a story invented to serve Docetic views (Hilgenfeld) ; see on Matt. xiv. 24, 25. The latter opinion appears most erroneous, especially in the case of John, [4] not only generally because his Gospel, from i. 14 to its close, excludes all Docetism, but also because he only introduces, with all brevity, the narrative before us by way of transition to what follows, without laying emphasis upon the miraculous, and without adding any remark or comment, and consequently without any special doctrinal purpose ; and thus the attribution to the occurrence of any symbolical design, *e.g.* prophetically to shadow forth the meetings of the risen Lord with His disciples (Luthardt), or the restless sea of the world upon which Christ draws nigh to His people after long delay (Hengstenberg), is utterly remote from a true exegesis. Weizsäcker's narrowing of the event, moreover,—abstracting from the history its miraculous element,—into an intervention of the Lord to render help, does such violence to the text, and to the plain meaning of the evangelist, that the main substance of the narrative is explained away. But the purpose assigned to it by Baur, viz. to set forth the greedy importunity of the people, only to experience the cold hand of denial, and bring out the spiritual side of the miracle of the feeding, did not require for its realization this miraculous voyage.

Vv. 22–24. The complicated sentence (so rare in John ; comp. xiii. 1 ff., 1 John i. 1 ff.) here proceeds in such a manner that the ὁ ὄχλος standing, without further government, at the head as the subject of the whole, is resumed [5] in ver. 24 by ὅτε οὖν εἶδεν ὁ ὄχλος, while ver. 23 is a parenthesis, preparing the way for the passing over of the people in the following clause.

---

[1] Beza, Grotius, Kuinoel, Ammon, etc. ; see, on the contrary, Winer, p. 436 [E. T. p. 467] ; Buttmann, *N. T. Gk.* p. 321 [E. T. p. 375].

[2] See the passages given in Sturz, *Lex. Xen. ;* Ast, *Lex. Plat.* I. 596.

[3] Ewald probably comes to that conclusion, for he takes θεωροῦσι, ver. 19, to denote a *mere* vision (phantasmagoria ?),

and ἐφοβήθησαν to signify *disquietude of conscience :* "He finds them not pure in spirit."

[4] Who, moreover, in the deviations from Matthew and Mark, possesses the deciding authority (against Märcker, p. 14).

[5] On the usual resumptive οὖν, see Winer, p. 414 [E. T. 444] ; Baeumlein, *Partik.* p. 177.

The participial clause, ἰδὼν ὅτι . . . ἀπῆλθον, is subordinate to the ἑστηκὼς πέραν τ. θαλ., and explains why the people expected Jesus on the next day still on the east side of the lake. John's narrative therefore runs thus : " *The next day, the people who were on the other side of the lake, because* (on the previous evening, ver. 16 f.) *they had seen that no other ship was there save only the one, and that Jesus did not enter into the ship with His disciples, but that His disciples sailed away alone [but other ships came from Tiberias near to the place,* etc.],—*when now the people saw that Jesus was not there, nor His disciples,*[1] finding themselves mistaken in their expectation of meeting Him still on the eastern shore, *they themselves embarked in the ships,*" etc. [See Note XXVII. p. 227]. As to details, observe further, (1) that πέραν τ. θαλ. in ver. 22 indeed, means the *eastern side* of the lake in ver. 1, but in ver. 25 the *western ;* (2) that ἰδών is spoken with reference to the *previous* day, when the multitude had noticed the departure of the disciples in the evening, so that the conjecture of εἰδώς (Ewald) is unnecessary ; that, on the contrary, ὅτε οὖν εἶδεν. ver. 24, indicates that they became aware *to-day,*—a difference which is the point in the cumbrously constructed sentence that most easily misleads the reader ; (3) that the arrival of the ships from Tiberias, ver. 23, occurred while the people were still on the eastern shore, and gave them a convenient opportunity, when undeceived in their expectation, of looking for Jesus on the western shore ; (4) that αὐτοί, *ipsi,* indicates that, instead of waiting longer for Jesus to come to them, they *themselves* set out, and embraced the opportunity of seeking Jesus on the other side, by embarking in the ships, and sailing across to Capernaum, the well-known place of our Lord's abode ; (5) that the circumstantial character of the description throughout indicates the vivid communication of an eye-witness, which John had received, and does not permit our taking the transit of the people (which, however, must not be pressed as including the whole 5000) as invented to confirm the story of the walking on the sea (Strauss).

Vv. 25, 26.[2] Πέραν τ. θαλάσσ.] in the synagogue at Capernaum, ver. 59. But πέραν τ. θαλ. has importance *pragmatically,* as showing that it formed a subject of *amazement* to them to find Him already on the *western* shore. — πότε] *when?* for it must have been, at the earliest, *after* the arrival of the *disciples* (ver. 22) ; and in this lay the incomprehensible *how ?* no other boat having crossed, and the journey round by land being too far. They have a dim impression of something miraculous ; " quaestio de *tempore* includit quaestionem de *modo,*" Bengel. Jesus does not answer their question, nor gratify their curiosity, but immediately charges them with the unspiritual motive that prompted them to seek Him, in order to point them to higher spiritual food. For γέγονας, *venisti,* see on i. 15. — οὐχ . . . ἀλλ.] not "*non tam . . . quam*" (Kuinoel, etc.) ; the ὅτι εἴδετε σημ. is *absolutely* denied.[3] In

---

[1] *Jesus* was not there, because, though they did not think of His going away, He did not show Himself anywhere ; the *disciples* were not, because they could not have remained unobserved if they had come back again from the other side ; and such a return could not have taken place in the ἄλλοις πλοιαρίοις, for these latter came not from Capernaum, but from Tiberias.

[2] See, concerning all the occurrences, ver. 26 ff., Harless, *Luther. Zeitschrift,* 1867, p. 116 ff.

[3] Comp. Fritzsche, *ad Marc. Exc.* II. p 773.

the miraculous feeding they should have seen a divinely significant reference to the higher Messianic bread of life, and *this* ought to have led them to seek Jesus ; but it was only the material satisfaction derived from the miraculous feeding that brought them to Him, as they hoped that He would further satisfy their carnal Messianic notions. — σημεῖα] They had seen the outward miracle, the mere event itself, but not its spiritual significance,— that wherein the real essence of the σημεῖον, in the true conception of it, consisted. The *plural* is not intended to include the healings of the sick, ver. 2 (Bengel, Lücke, and most others), against which see ver. 4, but refers only to the feeding, as the antithesis ἀλλ᾽ ὅτι shows, and is to be taken *generically*, as the plural of *category*.

Ver. 27. "*Strive to obtain, not the food which perisheth, but the food which endureth unto life eternal.*" The *activity and labour* of acquiring implied in ἐργάζεσθαι, *laborando sibi comparare*,[1] consists, when applied to the everlasting food, in striving and struggling after it, without which effort Jesus does not bestow it. We must come believingly to Him, must follow Him, must deny ourselves, and so on. Then we receive from Him, in ever-increasing measure, divine *grace and truth*, by a spiritual appropriation of *Himself ;* and *this* is the abiding food, which forever quickens and feeds the inner man ; in substance not essentially different from the *water*, which forever quenches thirst (iv. 14).[2] Under this view, the thought conveyed in ἐργάζεσθαι, as thus contrasted with that of δώσει on the other side, cannot be regarded as strange (against de Wette) ; the two conceptions are necessary correlatives. Phil. ii. 12, 13. — τὴν ἀπολλυμ.] not merely in its power, but in its very nature ; it is digested and ceases to be (Matt. xv. 17 ; 1 Cor. vi. 13). On the contrast, τ. μένουσ. εἰς ζ. αἱ., comp. iv. 14, xii. 25. — ἐσφραγ.] *sealed, i.e.* authenticated (see on iii. 33), namely, as the appointed Giver of this food ; in what way ? see vv. 36–39. — ὁ θεός] emphatically added at the end to give greater prominence to the highest authority.

Vv. 28, 29. The people perceive that a *moral* requirement is signified by τὴν βρῶσιν τ. μένουσαν, etc. ; they do not understand *what,* but they think that Jesus means *works,* which God requires to be done.[3] Hence the question, "*What are we to do, to work the works required by God ?*" (which thou seemest to mean). Ἐργάζεσθαι ἔργα, "*to perform works,*" very common in the Greek (see on iii. 21) ; ἐργάζ. here, therefore, is not to be taken as in ver. 27. — Ver. 29. See Luthardt in the *Stud. u. Krit.* 1852, p. 333 ff. Instead of the many ἔργα θεοῦ which they, agreeably to their legal standing-point, had in view, Jesus mentions only one ἔργον, in which, however, all that God requires of them is contained—the work (the moral act) of *faith.* Of this one divinely appointed and all embracing work—the fundamental *virtue* required by God—the manifold ἔργα τοῦ θεοῦ are only different manifestations. — In the *purpose* expressed by τοῦτο . . . ἵνα there lies the idea : "This is the

[1] Comp. ἐργάζ. τὰ ἐπιτήδεια, Dem. 1358. 12 ; ἐργάζ. βρῶμα, Palaeph. xxi. 2 ; ἐργάζ. θησαυρούς, Theodot. *Prov.* xxi. 6 ; see especially Stephan. *Thes. Ed. Hase,* III. p. 1968.

[2] See on βρῶσις, iv. 32, also, and the οὐρά-

νιος τροφή in Philo, *de profug.* p. 749 ; *Allegor.* p. 92.

[3] ἔργα τ. θεοῦ, comp. Matt. vi. 33 ; Rev. ii. 26 ; Baruch ii. 9 ; Jer. xlviii. 10.

work which God wills, *ye must believe.*" [1] And this fundamental requirement repeatedly recurs in the following discourses, vv. 35, 36, 40, 47, etc.

Vv. 30, 31. Οὖν] *What doest thou, therefore, as a sign?* for they knew well enough that by ὃν ἀπέστ. ἐκεῖνος He meant *Himself*, and that, too, as Messiah. Hence also the emphatic σύ, *thou, on thy part.* The *question itself* does not imply that it is asked by those who had not seen the miraculous feeding the day before (Grotius), or by prominent Jews in the synagogue (Kuinoel, Klee). Moreover, this demand for a sign after the miracle of the feeding must not be regarded as contradictory and unhistorical,[2] nor as proof of the non-Johannine origin (Schweizer), or non-miraculous procedure (Schenkel), in the account of the feeding. For the questioners, in their ἀναίσθησις (Chrysostom), indicate at once (ver. 31), that having been miraculously fed with *earthly* food, they, in their desire for miracles, require something *higher* to warrant their putting the required faith in Him, and expect a sign from *heaven, heavenly* bread, such as God had given by Moses. Thus they explain their own question, which would be strange only if ver. 31 *did not immediately follow.* Their eagerness for Messianic miraculous attestation (vv. 14, 15) had *grown* during the night. This also against de Wette, who, with Weisse, concludes that this discourse was not originally connected with the miraculous feeding ; see, on the contrary, Brückner. — τί ἐργάζῃ] a pointed retorting of the *form* of the requirement given, vv. 27, 29. Not to be explained as if it were τί σὺ ἐργ. (de Wette), but what (as σημεῖον) dost thou *perform?* — γεγραμμ.] a free quotation of Ps. lxxviii. 24 ; comp. cv. 40, Ex. xvi. 4, where the subject of ἔδωκεν is God, but by the medium of *Moses*, this being taken for granted as known (ver. 32). The Jews regarded the *dispensing of the manna* as the greatest miracle (see Lampe). As they now regarded Moses as in general a type of Christ,[3] they also hoped in particular, "Redemtor prior descendere fecit pro iis manna ; sic et redemtor posterior descendere faciet manna."[4]

Vv. 32, 33. Jesus does not mean to deny the miraculous and heavenly origin of the manna in itself (Paulus), nor to argue polemically concerning the O. T. manna (Schenkel), but He denies its origin as heavenly in the higher *ideal sense* (comp. τὸν ἀληθινόν). The antithesis is not between the ἀήρ and the κυρίως οὐρανός,[5] but between the type and the antitype in its full realization. — ὑμῖν] *your nation.* — ἐκ τοῦ οὐρανοῦ] here and in the second half of the verse to be joined to δέδωκεν (and διδωσιν) : "It is not Moses who dispensed to you the bread from heaven, but it is my Father who dispenseth to you from heaven that bread which is the true bread." In ver. 31, too, ἐκ τοῦ οὐρανοῦ is to be joined with ἔδωκεν ; and observe also, that in Ex. xvi. 4 מִן הַשָּׁמַיִם belongs not to לֶחֶם, but to מַמְטִיר. The expression ἐκ τοῦ οὐρ. is taken from Ex. xvi. 4 ; for, if we follow Ps. lxxviii. 24, cv. 40 (where שמים is an attribute of *bread*), we should have ἄρτον οὐρανοῦ. Comp. Targ. Jonath. Deut. xxxiv. 6 : "Deus fecit descendere filiis Israel panem de coelo." —

[1] Comp. v. 50, xv. 8, 12, xvii. 3 ; 1 John iv. 17, v. 3. See on Phil. i. 9.

[2] Kern, B. Bauer, Weisse.

[3] Schoettgen, *Hor.* II. p. 475.

[4] *Midrash Coheleth*, f. 86. 4.

[5] Chrysostom, Euthymius Zigabenus, Grotius, and most others.

δίδωσιν] continuously ; for Jesus means Himself and His work. — τὸν ἀληθινόν] corresponding in reality to the idea. See on i. 9.[1] This defining word, placed emphatically at the end, explains at the same time the negative statement at the beginning of the verse. — Ver. 33. Proof that it is the *Father* who gives, etc. (ver. 32) ; *for* it is none other than the *bread which is being bestowed by God, that comes down from heaven and giveth life to the world.* The argument proceeds *ab effectu* (ὁ καταβ. . . . κόσμῳ) *ad causam* (ὁ ἄρτος τοῦ θεοῦ). — ὁ καταβαίνων, κ.τ.λ.] refers to ὁ ἄρτος, and states its *specific property*, both as to its origin and working, both being essentially connected ; it does not refer to *Jesus* (" *He* who cometh down," etc.), though, in the personal application of the general affirmation, Jesus, by the bread, *represents*, and must represent, Himself ; and hence the expression "*cometh down.*"[2] The direct reference to Jesus would anticipate the subsequent advance of the discourse (ver. 35), and would require ὁ καταβάς (ver. 41 ; comp. ver. 48). See on ver. 50. — ζωήν] *life.* Without this bread, humanity (ὁ κόσμος) is *dead* in the view of Jesus—dead spiritually (ver. 35) and eternally (vv. 39, 40).

Ver. 34 ff. Πάντοτε] emphatically takes the lead.—The request is like that in iv. 15, but here, too, without *irony*,[3] which would have implied unbelief in His power to give *such* bread. To explain the words as prompted by a dim *presentiment concerning the higher gift* (Lücke, B. Crusius, and most other expositors), is not in keeping with the stiffnecked antagonism of the Jews in the course of the following conversation. There is no trace of a further development of the supposed presentiment, nor of any approval and encouragement of it on the part of Jesus. The Jews, on the contrary, with their carnal minds, are quite indifferent whether anything supersensuous, and if so, what, is meant by that bread. They neither thought of an *outward glory*, which they ask for (Luthardt),—for they could only understand, from the words of Jesus, something analogous to the *manna*, though of a higher kind, perhaps " a magic food or means of life from heaven" (Tholuck),—nor had their thoughts risen to the *spiritual* nature of this mysterious bread. But, at any rate, they think that the higher manna, of which He speaks, would be a welcome gift to them, which they could always use. And they could easily suppose that He was capable of a still more miraculous distribution, who had even now so miraculously fed them with ordinary bread. Their unbelief (ver. 36) referred to Jesus Himself as that personal bread of life, to whom, indeed, as such, their carnal nature was closed. — Vv. 35, 36. Explanation and censure. — ἐγώ] with powerful emphasis. Comp. iv. 26. — ὁ ἄρτος τ. ζωῆς] ζωὴν διδοὺς τῷ κόσμῳ, ver. 33. Comp. ver. 68. — ὁ ἐρχόμ. πρός με] of a *believing* coming (v. 40) ; comp. vv. 47, 44, 45, 65. For ἐρχόμ. and πιστεύων, as also their correlatives οὐ μὴ πειν. and οὐ μὴ διψ., do not differ as antecedent and consequent (Weiss), but are only *formally* kept apart by means of the *parallelism*. This parallelism of the discourse, now become more excited, has caused the addition of the οὐ

---

[1] Ἐκεῖνος γὰρ ὁ ἄρτος τυπικὸς ἦν, προτυπῶν, φησὶν, ἐμέ τὸν αὐτοαλήθειαν ὄντα, Euthymius Zigabenus.

[2] Against Grotius, Dav. Schulz, Olshau-

sen, Fritzsche in his *Novis opusc.* p. 221, Godet, and others.

[3] Against Calvin, Bengel, Lampe.

μὴ διψήσῃ, which is out of keeping with the metaphor hitherto employed, and anticipates the subsequent turn which the discourse takes to the eating of the flesh and drinking of the blood. We must not imagine that this is intended to express a superiority to the manna as being able to satisfy *hunger* only (Lücke); for both οὐ μὴ πειν. and οὐ μὴ διψ. signify the *same* thing—the everlasting satisfaction of the higher spiritual need. Comp. Isa. xlix. 10. ἀλλ᾿ εἶπον ὑμῖν] *But I meant to say to you that,* etc. Notice, therefore, that ὅτι ἑωράκ., κ.τ.λ., does not refer to a *previous* declaration, as there is not such a one (Beza, Grotius, Bengel, Olshausen, B. Crusius, Luthardt, Hengsten-berg, Baeumlein, Godet, and most others : to ver. 26 ; Lücke, de Wette : to vv. 37–40 ; Euthymius Zigabenus : to an *unwritten* statement ; Ewald : to one in a supposed fragment, *now lost,* which preceded chap. vi. ; Brück-ner : to a reproof which runs through the whole Gospel); on the contrary, the statement is itself announced by εἶπον (*dictum velim*).[1] In like manner xi. 42. In classical Greek, very common in the Tragedians.[2] — καὶ ἑωράκ. με κ. οὐ πιστ.] *ye have also seen me* (not simply heard of me, but even are eye-witnesses of my Messianic activity), *and believe not.*[3]

Vv. 37 ff. Through this culpable *non-believing,* they were quite different from those whom the Father gave Him. How entirely different were all these latter ; and how blessed through me, according to the Father's will, is their lot ! — πᾶν] Neuter, of persons as in iii. 6, xviii. 2 ; 1 Cor. i. 27. It designates them as a "*totam quasi massam,*" Bengel. — ὁ δίδ. μοι ὁ πατ.] viz. by the efficacious influence of His grace (vv. 44, 45), whereby He inclines them to come, and draws them to me ; οὐ τὸ τυχὸν πρᾶγμα ἡ πίστις ἡ εἰς ἐμέ. ἀλλὰ τῆς ἄνωθεν δεῖται ῥοπῆς, Chrysostom. Moral self-determination (v. 40, vii. 17 ; Matt. xxiii. 37) may obey this influence (ver. 40), and may withstand it ; he who withstands it is *not* given Him by the Father, Phil. ii. 13 "There is implied here a *humble,* simple, hungering and thirsting soul," Luther. Explanations resting on dogmatic preconceptions are : of the absolute *election of grace* (Augustine, Beza, and most others[4]), of the natural *pietatis studium* (Grotius), and others. — πρὸς ἐμέ] afterwards πρός με. But ἐμέ is emphatic. The ἥξει is not *more* (*arrivera jusqu'à moi,* Godet) than ἐλεύσεται, as ver. 35 already shows ; comp. the following κ. τ. ἐρχόμενον, with which ἥξω is again resumed. — οὐ μὴ ἐκβάλω ἔξω] *I certainly will not cast*

---

[1] See, for this use of the word, Bern-hardy, p. 381 ; Kühner, II. § 443. 1.

[2] See especially Herm. *ad Viger.* p. 746.

[3] On the first καί, comp. ix. 37, and see generally Kühner, *ad Xen. Mem.* i. 3. 1 ; Baeumlein, *Partik.* p. 149 ff.

[4] See, on the contrary, Weiss, *Lehrbegr.* p. 142 ff.—Schleiermacher rationalizes the divine gift and drawing into a divine *arrangement of circumstances;* see *L. J.* p. 302 ff. Thus it would be resolved into the general government of the world. — According to Beyschlag, p. 162, there would be in this action of the Father, pre-paring the way for a cleaving to Christ (comp. vv. 44, 45), an opposition to the light-giving action of the Logos (vv. 4, 5, 9), if the Logos be a personality identical with the Son. But the difference in person be-tween the Father and the Son does not ex-clude the *harmonious* action of both for each other. Enlightening is not a monop-oly of the Son, excluding the Father ; but the Father draws men to the Son, and the Son is the way to the Father, Weiss has rightly rejected as unjohannean (p. 248 f.) the idea of a hidden God, as absolutely raised above the world, who has no im-mediate connection with the finite.

him out, *i.e.* will not exclude him from my kingdom on its establishment ; comp. vv. 39, 40, xv. 6 ; also Matt. viii. 12, xxii. 13. The negative expression is a loving *litotes ;* Nonnus adds : ἀλλὰ νόῳ χαίροντι δεδέξομαι. — Vv. 38, 39. "How could I cast them out, seeing that I am come only to fulfil the *divine* will ? and this requires of me, not the rejection of any one, but the blessed opposite." — οὐχ ἵνα, κ.τ.λ.] Comp. v. 30. — τοῦτο δὲ . . . πέμψ. με] impressive repetition of the same words. — πᾶν ὁ δέδωκε, κ.τ.λ.] *Nominative absolute*, unconnected with the following, and significantly put first.[1] Here the *Perfect* δέδωκε, because spoken from the standing-point of the *future.* — μὴ ἀπολ. ἐξ αὐτοῦ] sc. τι ; see Fritzsche, *Conject.* p. 36. The conception *of losing* (*i.e.* of letting fall down to eternal death ; see the contrastive ἀλλά, etc.) is correlative to that of the δέδωκέ μοι. Comp. xvii. 12. — ἀναστήσω, κ.τ.λ.] of the actual resurrection at the last day (comp. v. 29, xi. 24, xii. 48), which, as a matter of course, includes the transformation of those still living. The designation of the thing is *a potiori.* It is the *first* resurrection that is meant,[2] that to the *everlasting life of the Messianic kingdom.* See on v. 29. Bengel well says : "hic finis est, ultra quem periculum nullum." Comp. the recurrence of this blessed refrain, vv. 40, 44, 54, which, in the face of this solemn recurrence, Scholten regards as a gloss.

Ver. 40. Explanation, and consequently assigning of the reason for the statement of God's will, ver. 39 ; the words τοῦτο, etc., being an impressive *anaphora*, and τοῦ πατρός μου taking the place of τοῦ πέμψ. με, because Jesus wishes at the close still to describe Himself, with specific definiteness, as the *Son.* — ὁ θεωρ. τὸν υἱὸν κ. πιστ. εἰς αὐτ.] characterizes those meant by the ὁ δέδωκέ μοι. There is implied in θεωρ. the *attenta contemplatio* (τοῖς ὀφθαλμοῖς τῆς ψυχῆς, Euthymius Zigabenus), the *result* of which is faith. Observe the *carefully chosen* word.[3] The Jews have *seen* Him, and have *not* believed, ver. 36. One must *contemplate* Him, *and* believe. — ἔχῃ and ἀναστήσω are both dependent upon ἵνα. There is nothing decisive against the rendering of καὶ ἀναστ. independently (Vulgate, Luther, Luthardt, Hengstenberg), but the analogy of ver. 39 does not favour it. Observe the change of tenses. The believer is said to have eternal Messianic life already in its *temporal development* (see on iii. 15), but its perfect *completion*[4] at the last day through the resurrection ; therefore ἀναστήσω *after* the ἔχειν of the ζωὴ αἰών. — ἐγώ] from the consciousness of Messianic power. Comp. vv. 44, 54.

Vv. 41, 42. "*They murmured*, and this μετ᾽ ἀλλήλων, ver. 43, *against Him with reference to what He had said, viz. that,*" etc. Upon all the rest they reflect no further, but *this* assertion of Jesus impresses them all the more offensively, and among themselves they give expression half aloud to their *dissatisfaction.* This last thought is not contained in the word itself (comp.

---

[1] Comp. viii. 38, xv. 2, xvii. 2 ; and see on Matt. vii. 24, x. 14, 32, xii. 36 ; Buttmann, *N. T. Gr.* p. 325 [E. T. p. 379].

[2] See on Luke xiv. 14, xx. 34 ; Phil. iii. 11 ; 1 Cor. xv. 23.

[3] Tittmann, *Synon.* p. 121 ; Grotius, *in loc.*

[4] Nothing is further from John than the Gnostic opinion, 2 Tim. ii. 18, upon which, according to Baur, he is said very closely to border.

vii. 32, 12 ; according to Pollux, v. 89, it was also used of the cooing of
doves), but in the context (οἱ Ἰουδαῖοι). We are not therefore, with de Wette,
to think of it merely as a *whispering*. Comp. rather ver. 61 ; Matt. xx. 11 ;
Luke v. 30 ; 1 Cor. x. 10 ; Num. xi. 1, xiv. 27 ; Ecclus. x. 24 ; Judith v.
22.[1] — οἱ Ἰουδαῖοι] The opposition party among the Jews were therefore
among the ὄχλος (vv. 5, 22, 24). Even in the congregation of the synagogue
itself (ver. 59), though it included many followers of Jesus (ver. 60), there
may have been present members of the spiritual aristocracy (see on i. 19).
The assumption that the ὄχλος itself is here called οἱ Ἰουδαῖοι, on account of
its refusal to recognize Jesus,[2] is more far-fetched, for hitherto the ὄχλοσ
had shown itself sensuously eager indeed after miracles, but not hostile. —
ἐγώ εἰμι ὁ ἄρτος κ.τ.λ.] compiled from vv. 33, 35, 38. — οὗτος] on both occasions, contemptuously. — ἡμεῖς] we on our part. — οἴδαμεν τ. πατ. κ. τ. μητ.]
This human descent which they knew (comp. Matt. xiii. 55) seemed to them
in contradiction with that assertion, and to exclude the possibility of its
truth. Heb. vii. 3 (ἀπάτωρ ἀμήτωρ) does not apply here, because it is not a
question of the Messiahship of Jesus, but of His coming down from heaven.
— τὸν πατέρα κ. τὴν μητ.] The words, on the face of them, convey the impression that *both* were still alive ; the usual opinion that Joseph (whom subsequent tradition represents as already an old man at the time of his espousal
with Mary)[3] was already dead, cannot, to say the least, be certainly proved,[4]
though in John also he is entirely withdrawn from the history.

Vv. 43, 44. Jesus does not enter upon a *solution* of this difficulty, but admonishes them not to trouble themselves with it ; they should not dwell
upon such questions, but upon something far higher ; the " drawing" of
the Father is the condition of participating in His salvation. — The ἑλκύειν is
not simply a strengthening of the διδόναι in vv. 37, 38, but specifies the
method of it, an *inner drawing and leading to Christ through the working of
divine grace* (comp. LXX. Jer. xxxi. 3), which, however, does not *annul*
human freedom, but which, by means of the enlightening, animating, and
impelling influence, and of the instruction appropriated by the man, wins
him over. Comp. xii. 32. Ἑλκύειν (ver. 45) *includes* the Father's *teaching*
by His witness to Christ (Weiss), but this is not all that it comprehends ;
it denotes rather the whole of that divine influence whereby hearts are won
to the Son. In the consciousness of those who are thus won, this represents
itself as a holy *necessity*, to which they have yielded. Comp. Wisd. xix. 4,
where the opposite, the attraction of evil, appears as a necessity which draws
them along, yet without destroying freedom.[5] Augustine already compares
from the Latin the " *trahit sua quemque voluptas*" of Virgil. The word [6] *in
itself may* denote what *involves force*, and is involuntary,[7] which is *always* ex-

---

[1] Lobeck, *ad Phryn.* p. 358.

[2] De Wette, Tholuck, Baur, Brückner,
Hengstenberg, Godet, and most others.

[3] See Philo, *ad Cod. Apocr.* I. p. 361.

[4] Comp. also Keim, *Gesch. J.* I. 426.

[5] See Grimm, *Handb.* p. 292 f. Comp. also
the classical ἑλκομαι ἦτορ (Pind. *Nem.* iv. 56),
ἕλκει τὸ τῆς φύσεως βάρβαρον (Dem. 563, 14),

and the like.

[6] The Attics also prefer the Aorist form
of ἑλκύω to that of ἕλκω, but they form
the future ἕλξω rather than ἑλκύσω (xii. 32).
See Lobeck, *Paral.* p. 35 f.

[7] Acts xvi. 19 ; 3 Macc. iv. 7 ; 4 Macc.
xi. 9 ; Homer, *Il.* xi. 258 ; xxiv. 52, 417 ;
Soph. *O. C.* 932 ; Aristoph. *Eq.* 710 ; Plato,

pressed in σύρειν ;[1] but the context itself shows that this is *not* meant *here* (in the classics it may even stand for *invitare*).[2] Accordingly it is not, as Calvin judges, false and impious to say : "*non nisi volentes trahi ;*" and Beza's " Volumus, quia datum est, ut velimus," is true and pious only in the sense of Phil. ii. 13. Comp. Augustine : "non ut homines, quod fieri non potest, nolentes credant, sed ut volentes ex nolentibus fiant." — ὁ πέμψ. με] a specific relation with which the saving act of the ἑλκύειν essentially corresponds. — καὶ ἐγὼ ἀναστήσω, κ.τ.λ.] the same solemn promise which we have already, vv. 39, 40, but with the ἐγώ of Messianic authority and power, as in ver. 54.

Vv. 45, 46 serve more fully to explain ἑλκύειν. — ἐν τοῖς προφ.] *in volumine prophetarum*, Acts vii. 42, xiii. 40 ; Rom. ix. 24. The passage is Isa. liv. 13 (a free quotation from the LXX.), which treats of the divine and universal enlightenment of Israel in the time of the Messiah (comp. Joel iii. 1 ff. ; Jer. xxxi. 33, 34): "and they shall be wholly *taught of God.*" The main idea does not lie in πάντες, which, moreover, in the connection of the passage refers to all *believers*, but in διδακτοὶ θεοῦ,[3] which denotes the divine drawing viewed as *enlightening* and influencing. The διδακτὸν θεοῦ εἶναι is the *state* of him who hears and has learned of the Father ; see what follows. — πᾶς ὁ ἀκούων, κ.τ.λ.] The spurious οὖν rightly indicates the connection (against Olshausen) ; for it follows from that promise, that every one *who hears and is taught of the Father* comes to the Son, and no others ; because, were it not so, the community of believers would not be unmixedly the διδακτοὶ θεοῦ. Ἀκούειν παρὰ τοῦ πατρός is the spiritual perception of divine instruction ; the subject-matter of which, as the whole context clearly shows, is the Son and His work. The communication of this revelation is, however, *continuous* (hence ἀκούων), and the "having learned" is its *actual result*, by the attainment of which through personal exertion the ἔρχεται πρός με is conditioned. One hears and has learned of the Father ; in no other way is one in the condition which internally necessitates a believing union with the Son. Comp. Matt. xi. 25 ff. — Ver. 46. By this hearing and having learned of the Father, I do not mean an immediate and *intuitive* fellowship with Him, which, indeed, would render the coming to the Son unnecessary ; no ; no one save the *Son* only has had the *vision* of God (comp. i. 18, iii. 13, viii. 38) ; therefore all they who are διδακτοὶ θεοῦ have to find in the Son alone all further initiation into God's grace and truth. — οὐκ ὅτι] οὐκ ἐρῶ, ὅτι.[4] It serves to obviate a misunderstanding. — εἰ μή, κ.τ.λ.] *except He who is from God, He hath seen the Father* (that is, in His pre-existent state).[5] Comp.

Rep. iv. p. 539 B, and often ; see Ast, *Lex. Plat.* I. p. 682.

[1] Comp. Tittm. *Syn.* p. 56 ff.

[2] See Jacobs, *ad Anthol.* IX. 142.

[3] *A Deo edocti ;* as to the genitive, see on 1 Cor. ii. 13, and Kühner, II. § 516, *b.*

[4] See Hartung, II. 154 ; Buttmann, *N. T. Gr.* p. 318 ff. [E. T. p. 372].

[5] This clear and direct reference to His pre-human state in God (comp. vv. 41, 42),

and consequently the agreement of Christ's witness to Himself with the view taken by the evangelist, should not have been regarded as doubtful by Weizsäcker. The divine life which was manifested in Christ upon earth was the personal life of His pre-existent state, as the prologue teaches, otherwise John had not given the original sense of the declaration of the Lord regarding Himself (to which conclusion

Gal. i. 7. — ὁ ὢν παρὰ τ. θ.] for He is *come* from the Father, with whom He was (i. 1). See on i. 14, viii. 42, vii. 29, xvi. 27.

Vv. 47, 48. Jesus had given His answer to the murmurings of the Jews in vv. 43–46. He now returns to the subject which He had left, and first repeats in solemn asseveration what He had said in ver. 40 ; then He again brings forward the metaphor of the bread of life, which sets forth the same thought.

Vv. 49, 50. Οἱ πατέρες, κ.τ.λ.] "regeruntur Judaeis verba ipsorum ver. 31," Bengel. — ἀπέθανον . . . ἀποθάνῃ] a diversity in the reference which is full of meaning : loss of *earthly* life, loss of *eternal* life, whose development, already begun in time (see on iii. 15), the death of the body does not interrupt (xi. 25). — οὗτός ἐστιν ὁ ἄρτος, κ.τ.λ.] of *this* nature is the bread which cometh down from heaven : *one* (τὶς) *must eat thereof*, and (in consequence of this eating) *not die*. This representation is contained in οὗτος . . . ἵνα ; see on ver. 29. The expression, however, is not conditional (ἐάν τις), because the telic reference (ἵνα) does not belong to the last part merely. The *present participle* shows that Jesus does not mean by οὗτος His own concrete Personality, which is not named till ver. 51, but intends to set forth and exhibit the true bread from heaven generally, according to its real nature (comp. ver. 58).[1]

Ver. 51. Continuation of the exposition concerning the bread of life, which He is. "I am not only the life-giving bread (ὁ ἄρτος τ. ζωῆς, ver. 48); I am also the *living* bread ; he who eats thereof shall live forever," because the life of this bread is imparted to the partaker of it. Comp. v. 26, xiv. 19. Observe the threefold advance : (1) ὁ ἄρτοσ τ. ζωῆς, ver. 48, and ὁ ἄρτος ὁ ζῶν, ver. 51 ; (2) the continuous καταβαίνων, ver. 50, and the historically concrete καταβάς, ver. 51 ; (3) the negative μὴ ἀποθάνῃ, ver. 50, and the positive ζήσεται εἰς τὸν αἰῶνα, ver. 51. — καὶ ὁ ἄρτος δὲ ὃν ἐγὼ δώσω] Christ *is* the bread, and He will also *give* it (consequently give *Himself*) ; how *this* is to take place, He now explains. The advance lies in ὃν ἐγὼ δώσω ; hence also the καὶ δέ which carries on the discourse, and the emphatic repetition of the thought, ἣν ἐγὼ δώσω. Translate : "and *the* bread also *which I* (*I* on my part, ἐγώ) *will give* [instead now of saying : *is myself*, He expresses what He

Weizsäcker comes in the *Jahrb. f. D. Th.* 1862, p. 674), which, however, is inconceivable in so great and ever-recurring a leading point. It is the transcendent recollection in His temporal self-consciousness of that earlier divine condition, which makes itself known in such declarations (comp. iii. 11). See on viii. 38, xvii. 5. His certitude concerning the perfect revelation does not first begin witn the baptism, but stretches back with its roots into His pre-human existence. See, against Weizsäcker, Beyschlag also, p. 79 ff., who, however (comp. p. 97 f.), in referring it to the sinless birth, and further to the preexistent state of Jesus, *as the very image*

of God, is not just to the Johannean view in the prologue, and in the first epistle, as well as here, and in the analogous testimonies of Jesus regarding Himself. See on ver. 62. Beyschlag renders : "*because* He is of God, He has seen God *in His historical existence*." The far-fetched thought is here brought in, that only the pure in heart can see God. Comp. rather i. 18, iii. 13, 31, 32, viii. 26, 38. See, against this view of the continuous historical intimacy with God, Pfleiderer in Hilgenfeld's *Zeitschr.* 1866, p. 247 ff. ; Scholten, p. 116 ff.

[1] On τίς, *one*, comp. Dem. *Phil.* i. 8, and Bremi, p. 118 ; Ellendt, *Lex. Soph.* II. 883 ; Nägelsbach on the *Iliad*, p. 299, ed. 3.

means more definitely] *is my flesh*," etc.[1] It often introduces, as in this case, something specially important.[2] Observe, moreover, that what Christ promises to give is not *external to His own Person*.[3] — ἡ σάρξ μού ἐστιν] He promises to give His *flesh*, *i.e.* by His bloody *death*, to which He here, as already in ii. 19, and to Nicodemus, iii. 14, 15, prophetically points. Σάρξ is the *living* corporeal substance ; this His living corporeity Christ will *give, give up, that it may be slain* (ἣν ἐγὼ δώσω), in order that thereby, as by the offering of the propitiatory sacrifice,[4] He may be the means of procuring eternal life for mankind, *i.e.* ὑπὲρ (for the sake, on behalf of) τῆς τοῦ κόσμου ζωῆς ; comp. 1 John iv. 10, 14. But as the atoning efficacy which this giving up of His flesh has, must be inwardly *appropriated* by faith, Christ's σάρξ, according to the figure of the bread of life, inasmuch as He means to give it up to death, appears as the *bread* which He will give *to be partaken of* (ὃν ἐγὼ δώσω). In the repeated *give* there lies the voluntariness of the surrender (Euthymius Zigabenus). But observe the differing reference, that of the first δώσω to the giving up *for eating*, and that of the second to the giving up *to death*.[5] This eating is the *spiritual* manducatio,[6] the inward, real appropriation of Christ which, by means of an ever-continuing faith that brings about this appropriation, and makes our life the life of Christ within us (Gal. ii. 20 ; Eph. iii. 17), takes place with regard to all the benefits which Christ " carne sua pro nobis in mortem tradita et sanguine suo pro nobis effuso promeruit." *Forma Concordiae*, p. 744. On the idea of the life of Christ in believers, see on Phil. i. 8. On σάρξ, so far as it was put to death in Christ by His crucifixion, comp. 1 Pet. iii. 18 ; Eph. ii. 14 ; Col. i. 20 ff. ; Heb. x. 20. This explanation, which refers the words to Christ's *propitiatory death*, is

---

[1] Concerning καί ... δέ, *atque etiam*, καί being *and*, and δέ *on the other hand*, see in particular Krüger, and Kühner, *ad Xen. Mem.* i. 1. 3 ; Baeumlein, *Partik.* p. 149.

[2] See Bremi, *ad Dem. Ol.* II. p. 173.

[3] Against Kling in the *Stud. u. Krit.* 1836, p. 142 f.

[4] Not that by the death of Jesus the barrier of the independent individuality existing between the Logos and the human being is destroyed. See against this explanation (Köstlin, Reuss), so foreign to John, Weiss, *Lehrbegr.* p. 65 ff.

[5] The words ἣν ἐγὼ δώσω are wanting in B C D L T ℵ, a few cursives, several versions (following Vulg. It.), and Fathers (even Origen twice), and are rejected by Lachm., Ewald, Tisch., Baeumlein, Harless. The preponderance of testimony is certainly against them ; and in omitting them we should not, with Kling, take ἡ σάρξ μου as in apposition with ὁ ἄρτος (see, on the contrary, Rückert, *Abendm.* p. 259), but simply render it : " *the bread which I shall give is my flesh for the life of the world*" (the *former* is the *latter* for the life of the world). But this short pregnant mode of expression is so little like John, and the repetition of ἣν

ἐγὼ δώσω is so completely Johannean, that I feel compelled to retain the words as genuine, and to regard their omission as a very early error, occasioned by the occurrence of the same words a little before. Following ℵ, Tischendorf now reads, after κ. ὁ ἄρτ. δὲ ὃν ἐγὼ δώσω ὑπὲρ τῆς τοῦ κόσμου ζωῆς, ἡ σάρξ μου ἐστίν. This is manifestly an arrangement resorted to in order to assign to the words ὑπ. τ. τ. κ. ζωῆς the place which, in the absence of ἣν ἐγὼ δώσω, seemed to belong to them. Baeumlein supposes that ὑπ. τ. τ. κ. ζωῆς is an ancient gloss.

[6] Hence the expression " resurrection of the *flesh*" cannot be justified from John vi., as Delitzsch, *Psychol.* p. 460 [E. T. p. 541], supposes. If it cannot be justified by anything in St. Paul, which Delitzsch admits, it can least of all by anything in St. John. When, indeed, Delitzsch says (p. 339), " The flesh of Christ becomes in us a *tincture of immortality, which, in spite of corruption, sustains the essence of our flesh, in order one day at the resurrection to assimilate also His manifestation to itself,*" we can only oppose to such fancies, " *Ne ultra quod scriptum est.*"

that of Augustine, Luther, Melanchthon, Calvin, Beza, Aretius, Grotius, Calovius, Wetstein, Lampe, and most others, also of Kuinoel, Lücke, Tholuck, Ammon, Neander, J. Müller,[1] Lange, Ebrard,[2] Keim,[3] Weiss ; comp. also Ewald, Kahnis,[4] Godet.[5] Others, following Clement of Alexandria, Origen, Basil, have understood by "flesh" *the entire human manifestation of the Logos*, which He offered up for the world's salvation, *including* therein His death.[6] Not only is the future *will give* opposed to this view, but the drinking of the blood in ver. 53 still more distinctly points to Christ's death as *exclusively* meant ; because it is not apparent why Jesus, had He intended generally that collective dedication of Himself, should have used expressions to describe the appropriation of it, which necessarily and directly point to and presuppose His death. That general consecration was already affirmed in ἐγώ εἰμι ὁ ἄρτος, κ.τ.λ. ; the advance from *being* and *giving* now demands something else, a concrete act, viz. His atoning death and the shedding of His blood. This tells also against the profounder development of the self-communication of Jesus supposed to be meant here, and adopted by Hengstenberg and Hofmann,[7] following Luther ;[8] viz. that faith in the human nature of Jesus eats and drinks the life of God, or that His life-giving power is bound up in His flesh, *i.e.* in His actual human manifestation (Brückner). *Others*, again, have explained it *of the Lord's Supper;* viz. Chrysostom, Cyril, Theophylact, Euthymius Zigabenus, most of the Fathers (among the Latin Fathers, Cyprian, Hilary, perhaps also Augustine, etc.) and Catholic writers, also Klee and Maier, further, Calixtus too, strongly opposed by Calovius ; and among moderns, Scheibel, Olshausen, Kling,[9] Lindner, Köstlin, Delitzsch in Rudelbach's *Zeitschrift*, 1845, ii. p. 29 ; Kaeuffer,[10] Kahnis, *Abendm.* p. 104 ff. ; Luthardt ; Richter ;[11] further, while also calling in question the genuineness of the discourse, Bretschneider, Strauss, Weisse, Baur, Hilgenfeld, and many others. Thus, as iii. 5 refers to baptism, we have now, it is said, a reference to the second sacrament. This explanation [12] has already this against

---

[1] *Diss.* 1839.

[2] *Dogma v. Abendm.* I. p. 78 ff.

[3] *Jahrb. f. d. Theol.* 1859, p. 109 ff.

[4] *Dogmat.* I. p. 624.

[5] Who, however, attaches great importance to the corporeal side of the real fellowship of believers with Christ, by virtue of which they will become at the resurrection the reproduction of the glorified Christ, referring to Eph. v. 30. The eating and drinking alone are figurative, while the not merely spiritual, but also bodily appropriation, must, according to him, be taken literally. This, however, is not required by the ἀναστήσω αὐτόν, κ.τ.λ., ver. 54, which we already had in ver. 39, and is not even admissible by ver. 63.

[6] So in modern times, in particular, Paulus, D. Schulz, *Lehre vom Abendm.*, B. Crusius, Frommann, de Wette, Baeumlein ;

comp. Schleiermacher, *L. J.* p. 345, and Reuss.

[7] *Schriftbew.* II. 2, p. 245 ff.

[8] "Therefore one eats and drinks the Godhead in His human nature.—This flesh does not carnalize, but will deify thee, *i.e.* give the divine power, virtue, and work, and will take away sins," and so on (*Pred. Dom. Oculi*).

[9] *Stud. u. Krit.* 1836, p. 140 ff.

[10] *Sächs. Stud.* 1846, p. 70 ff.

[11] *Stud. u. Krit.* 1863, p. 250.

[12] A view which Luther decidedly opposed previous to the controversy regarding the Lord's Supper. In the heading or gloss he says : "This chapter does not speak of the sacrament of the bread and wine, but of spiritual eating, *i.e.* of the belief that Christ, both God and man, hath shed His blood for us."

it, that the eating and drinking is regarded as *continuous* (ver. 56); and, moreover, it can be maintained only by *surrendering the authenticity* of John. But if this be assumed, and the discourse be regarded as historical, Jesus could not Himself speak, as He speaks in this passage, of the Lord's Supper. Had this been His reference, He would have spoken inappropriately, and in terms which differ essentially from His own mode of expression at the institution of the holy meal, irrespectively of the fact that a discourse upon the *Lord's Supper* at this time would have been utterly incomprehensible to His hearers, especially to the Ἰουδαίοις who were addressed. Moreover, there nowhere occurs in the Gospels a hint given *beforehand* of the Supper which was to be instituted ; and therefore, that this institution was not now already in the thoughts of Jesus (as Godet, following Bengel and others, maintains), but was the product of the hour of the Supper itself, appears all the more likely, seeing how utterly groundless is the assumption based on ver. 4, that Jesus, in the feeding of the multitude, improvised a paschal feast. To this it must be added, that the promise of life which is attached to the eating and drinking could apply only to the case of those who worthily partake. We should therefore have to assume that the *reporter John* [1] *put* this discourse concerning the Lord's Supper *into the mouth of Christ ;* and against this it tells in general, that thus there would be on John's part a misconception, or rather an arbitrariness, which, granting the genuineness of the Gospel, cannot be attributed to this most trusted disciple and his vivid recollections ; and in particular, that the drinking of the blood, if it were, as in the Lord's Supper, a special and essential part, would not have been left unmentioned precisely at the end of the discourse, vv. 57, 58 ; and that, again, the evangelist would make Jesus speak of the Lord's Supper in terms which lie quite beyond the range of the N. T., and which belong to the mode of representation and language of the apostolic Fathers and still later times. [2] This is specially true of the word *flesh*, for which all passages in the N. T. referring to the Lord's Supper, [3] have *body ;* so that here accordingly there ought to have been stated the identity, not of the bread and the *flesh* (which Baur in particular urges), but of the bread and the *body ;* while with reference to the blood, the identical element (the *wine*) ought also to have been mentioned. Further, the passage thus taken would speak of the literal *"eating and drinking"* of the flesh and blood, which is a much later materializing of the N. T. κοινωνία in the Lord's Supper ; and lastly, the absolute necessity of this ordinance, [4] which ver. 53 ff. would thus assert, is not once mentioned thus directly by the Fathers of the first centuries ; while the N. T., and John in particular, make *faith* alone the absolutely necessary condition of salvation. Had John been

[1] See especially Kaeuffer, *l.c.* ; comp. also Weisse, B. Crusius, Köstlin, etc.

[2] See the passages in Kaeuffer, p. 77 ff. ; Rückert, p. 274 f. ; Hilgenfeld, *Evang.* p. 278. Hilgenfeld calls the passages in Justin, *Apol.* i. 66; Ignatius, *ad Smyrn.* 7. *ad Rom.* 7, an admirable commentary upon our text. They would, indeed, be so if our

evangelist himself were a post-apostolic writer belonging to the second century.

[3] Matt. xxvi. 26 ff. ; Mark xiv. 22 ff. ; Luke xxiv 24 ff. ; 1 Cor. xi. 23 ff.

[4] Its limitation to the *Contemtus* sacramenti (Richter) is a dogmatic subterfuge which has no foundation in the text.

speaking of the Lord's Supper, he must have spoken in harmony with the N. T. view and mode of expression, and must have made Jesus speak of it in the same way. But the discourse, *as it lies before us*, if taken as referring to the Lord's Supper, would be an unexampled and utterly inconceivable ὕστερον πρότερον ; and therefore even the assumption that at least the same *idea* which lay at the root of the Lord's Supper, and out of which it sprang, is here expressed,[1] is admissible only so far as the appropriation of Christ's life, brought about by faith in His death, which here is enjoined with such concrete vividness as absolutely necessary,[2] likewise constitutes the sacred and fundamental basis presupposed in the institution of the Supper, and forms the condition of its blessedness ; and therefore the *application* of the passage to the Lord's Supper (but at the same time to baptism and to the efficacy of the word) justly, nay necessarily, arises. Comp. the admirable remarks of Harless, p. 130 ff. — According to Rückert,[3] the discourse is not intended by Jesus to refer to the Supper, but is so intended by John, through whose erroneous and crude method of apprehension the readers are to be taught, whether they themselves have believed in an actual eating of the flesh and drinking of the blood, or whether this has been a stumbling-block to them. An interpretation this which is neither indicated by the text nor has any historical basis. — Upon the history of the interpretation of our text, see Lücke, ed. 2, App. 2 ; Lindner, *vom Abendm.* p. 241 ff. ; Tischendorf, *De Christo pane vitae*, 1839, p. 15 ff. ; Mack, *Quartalschr.* 1832, I. p. 52 ff. ; Kahnis, p. 114 ff. ; Rückert, p. 273 ff. The exposition which takes it to refer to faith in the atoning death forms the basis of Zwingle's doctrine of the Eucharist.[4]

Vv. 52, 53. The Jews rightly add φαγεῖν, borrowing it from the preceding context ; but the meaning and reference of the expression, which they certainly recognized as somehow to be taken figuratively, are to them so indistinct, that they fall into a dispute with each other ("non jam solum murmurabant uti ver. 41," Bengel) upon the question : "*How can this man give us his flesh* (τὴν σάρκα also without the αὐτοῦ, a gloss in Lachm.) *to eat ?*" Not as if they had *missed hearing* something (Luthardt : "the *futurity* expressed in ver. 51") : they have not *understood* the enigmatical statement. Instead now of explaining the *how* of their question, Jesus sets before them the absolute *necessity* of their partaking, and pushes to an extreme the seemingly paradoxical requirement; for He nows adds the *drinking of His blood*, in order thus to bring more prominently into view the reference to *His death*, and its life-giving power to be experienced by believing appropriation. — τοῦ υἱοῦ τ. ἀνθρ.] This prophetic and Messianic self-designation (i. 52, iii. 13, 14), which could now less easily escape the notice of His hearers than in ver. 27, serves as a still more solemn expression in place of μου, without,

---

[1] Olshausen, Kling, Lange, Tholuck, etc. ; comp. Kahnis, Keim, Luthardt, Hengstenberg, Ewald, Godet.

[2] "He makes it so that it could not be plainer, in order that they might not think that he was speaking of something else, or of anything that was not before their eyes ; but that He was speaking of Himself."—LUTHER.

[3] *Abendm.* p. 291 f.

[4] See Dieckhoff, *evangel. Abendmahlslehre*, I. p. 440.

however, affecting the meaning of the eating and drinking. — οὐκ ἔχετε ζωὴν ἐν ἑαυτ.] "*ye have have not life in yourselves*," "*life* is foreign to and remote from your own inner nature,"—*death* is the power that ye have in you, spiritual and eternal death ; life must first, by that eating and drinking, be inwardly united with your own selves. In that appropriation of the flesh and blood of Jesus, this life flows forth from *His* life (vv. 56, 57, v. 26) ; and it is attached to faith only, not to the use of any outward element (comp. Harless, p. 124).

Vv. 54, 55. He now more fully explains Himself, onwards to ver. 58, with regard to the saving efficacy of this spiritual eating and drinking : "*He who eateth my flesh*," etc. — ὁ τρώγων] Previously the word was φάγητε, but the change implies no special intention to use a stronger term (to chew, to crunch), as the repetition of πίνων shows.[1] — ζωὴν αἰών.] Fuller definition of the general ζωή which precedes ; it signifies the *eternal Messianic life*, but the development of this in time as *spiritual* life is included in the thought ; therefore ἔχει (iii. 15), and the result of the possession of this life : ἀναστήσω, κ.τ.λ. Comp. ver. 40. — Ver. 55. Proof of the assertion ἔχει . . . ἡμέρᾳ ; for if the flesh of Jesus were not *true* food (something *which in very deed has nourishing power*), etc., the effect named in ver. 54 could not ensue. It is self-evident that food for the *inner* man is meant ; but ἀληθής (see the critical notes) is not the same as ἀληθινή (this would mean *genuine* food, food that realizes its own ideal). It denotes the opposite of that which is merely apparent or so called, and therefore expresses the *actual fact* (1 John ii. 27 ; Acts xii. 9), which the Jews could not understand, since they asked πῶς δύναται, κ.τ.λ., ver. 52.

Vv. 56, 57. A statement parallel with what precedes, concerning him "who eats," etc., and explaining *how that comes to pass* which is said of him in ver. 54. — ἐν ἐμοὶ μένει κἀγὼ ἐν αὐτῷ] an expression distinctively Johannean of abiding, inner, and mutual fellowship (xv. 4 ff., xvii., 23 ; 1 John iii. 24, iv. 16), by virtue of which we live and move continually in Christ, and Christ works and rules in our minds, so that thus Christ's life is the centre and circumference, *i.e.* the all-determining power of our life. — Ver. 57. Consequence of this spiritual union : *life, i.e.* true imperishable life, as proceeding from the Father to the Son, so from the Son to believers. Observe (1) that the consequent clause does not begin with κἀγώ (Chrysostom and his followers); but, as ver. 56 requires, with κ. ὁ τρώγ. με, *so also he that eateth me ;* (2) that in the antecedent clause the emphasis is on ζῶν and ζῶ (therefore ἀπέστειλε does not introduce any strange or unnatural thought, as Rückert supposes), while in the consequent it is upon the *subject*, which accordingly is made prominent by κἀκεῖνος, *he also.* — ὁ ζῶν πατήρ] the living Father ; (comp. ver. 26), the Living One absolutely, in whose nature there is no element of death, but all is life. — κἀγὼ ζῶ διὰ τ. πατ.] *and I*—by virtue of my community of essence with the Father—*am alive because of the Father.* διὰ with the accus. does not denote the cause,[2] *per patrem ;* nor *for* the

[1] Comp. Dem. 402. 21 : τρώγειν καὶ πίνειν. Plut. *Mor.* p. 613 B ; Polyb. xxxii. 9. 9. Comp. also xiii. 18 ; Matt. xxiv. 38.

[2] Castalio, Beza, de Wette, Gess, Rückert, and several.

218   THE GOSPEL OF JOHN.

Father ;[1] but, according to the context, the *reason : because of* the Father, *i.e.*
because my Father is the Living One.[2] — ὁ τρώγων με] This sufficed to denote
the relation, and is in keeping with the transition to ver. 58 ; whereas, if
the discourse referred to the Lord's Supper, the eating and drinking of the
flesh and blood should again have been mentioned, as in vv. 53–56. Note
also that ὁ τρώγων με expresses a permanent, continuous relation, not one
taking place from time to time, as in the Lord's Supper. — ζήσει] in contrast
with spiritual and eternal death. — δι' ἐμέ] *on account of me*, because he thus
takes up *my* life into himself.

Vv. 58, 59. A concluding summary, repeating *the* figure from which the
whole discourse arose, ver. 32. — οὗτος] of *this* nature, as explained in vv.
32–57. Comp. ver. 50 ; not : "*this*, which gives life to him who partakes
of it" (Lücke) ; nor: *this, i.e. my flesh and blood*" (de Wette) ; what follows
requires in οὗτος the idea of *modality*. — οὐ καθώς, κ.τ.λ.] It is the bread
that came down from heaven, but not in *the same* way and manner that the
fathers did eat heavenly bread. It is quite *different* in the case of this
bread. — Ver. 59 is simply an historical observation, without any further
significance (Chrysostom : in order to impress us with the great *guilt* of the
people of Capernaum). That ταῦτα means simply the discourse from ver. 41
onwards, and that what precedes down to ver. 40 was not spoken in the
synagogue, but elsewhere, upon the first meeting with the people, vv. 24,
25 (Ewald), would need to have been more distinctly indicated. Taking
John's words as they stand, ἐν συναγωγῇ, etc., is a more definite (according
to Schenkel, indeed, mistaken) supplementary explanation of the vague
πέραν τ. θαλάσσης of ver. 25. — ἐν συναγωγῇ, without the Art. as in xviii. 20 :
in a synagogue ; then follows the still more detailed designation of the
locality, "*while teaching in Capernaum.*"

Ver. 60. Πολλοὶ οὖν] *Many therefore*, for in Capernaum He had many
adherents (μαθηταί is here used in the wider sense, not of the apostles ; see
ver. 67). — σκληρός] *hard, harsh*, the opposite of μαλακός ;[3] — in a moral sense,
Matt. xxv. 24 ; Ecclus. iii. 24 ; 3 Esdr. ii. 27 ;[4]—of *speeches*,[5] Gen. xlii. 7,
xxi. 11, Aq. ; Prov. xv. 1. It here denotes *what causes offence* (σκανδαλίζει,
ver. 61), does not comply with preconceived views, but is directly *antag-
onistic*, the relation in which the assurances and demands of Jesus from ver.
51 stood to the wishes and hopes of His disciples.[6] He had, indeed, from
ver. 51 onwards, required that they should eat His flesh (which was to be
slain), and drink His blood (which was to be shed), in order to have life.
By this—whether they rightly understood it or not—they felt sorely perplexed and wounded. The *bloody death*, which was certainly the condition

---

[1] Paulus, Lange.
[2] See on xv. 3 ; Plat. *Conv.* p. 203 E :
ἀναβιώσκεται διὰ τὴν τοῦ πατρὸς φύσιν; and
see Nägelsbach, *Ilias*, p. 39 ff. ed. 3.
[3] Plat. *Legg.* x. p. 892 B ; *Prot.* p. 331 D.
[4] Soph. *Oed. R.* 36, *Aj.* 1340 ; Plat. *Locr.* p.
104 C, and often.
[5] Comp. Soph. *Oed. C.* 778 : σκληρὰ μαλθα-
κῶς λέγων.

[6] Not as if they had understood the eating and drinking of the flesh and blood in
a literal and *material* sense (hence the expression " manducatio *Capernaitica*"), and
so nonsensical an affirmation had provoked
them (Augustine, Grotius, Lücke, Keim,
and many others). The speakers are μαθηταί ; but not even the Ἰουδαῖοι, ver. 52, so
grossly misunderstood Jesus.

of the eating and drinking, was an offence to them, just as in that lay the lasting offence of the Jews afterwards, xii. 34 ; 1 Cor. i. 23 ; Gal. v. 11 ; comp. also Matt. xvi. 21 ff. The explanation "*difficult to be understood*" (Chrysostom, Euthymius Zigabenus, Grotius, Olshausen) lies neither in the word nor in the context, for τίς δύναται, κ.τ.λ. affirms : "*it is a thing not to be borne, to listen to the discourse,*" such insuperable offence does it excite. Tholuck, following early writers, finds the offence to be that Jesus seemed *arrogant* in making life dependent upon participation in His flesh and blood. But it was not the *arrogant*, it was the lowly and suffering, Messiah that was a σκάνδαλον to the Jew. As little did the offence consist in the requirement that Christ "*would be all, and they were to be nothing*" (Hengstenberg), which, indeed, is only an abstract inference subsequently drawn from His discourse.

Vv. 61, 62. Ἐν ἑαυτῷ] *In Himself*, without communication ; αὐτόματος, Nonnus. — γογγύζ.] as in ver. 41. — περὶ τούτου] concerning this harshness of His discourse. — τοῦτο ὑμ. σκανδ.] Question of astonishment : *this*, namely, which you have found so hard in my discourse (Jesus *knew* what it was), *does this offend you?* Are you so mistaken in your opinion and feelings towards me ? . Comp. ver. 66. — ἐὰν οὖν θεωρῆτε, κ.τ.λ.] *if, then, ye behold,* etc. Aposiopesis, which, especially "in tam infausta re" (Dissen, *ad Dem. de cor.* p. 362), is entirely in place. See on Luke xix. 41 ; Acts xxiii. 9 ; Rom. ix. 22. The completion of it must be derived solely from the context, and therefore is not τί ἐρεῖτε or the like (Nonnus, Euthymius Zigabenus, Kuinoel, and many) ; but τοῦτο ὑμᾶς οὐ πολλῷ μᾶλλον σκανδαλίσει :[1] "*Will not this impending sight offend you still more?*" By ἀναβαίνειν ὅπου ἦν τὸ πρότερον Jesus indicates His *death ;* and, indeed, as *He*—in whom Daniel's prophecy of the Son of man was to be fulfilled (comp. xii. 23 ; Matt. xxvi. 24)—contemplated it in the consciousness of His heavenly origin and descent (iii. 13), of which He had already spoken in ver. 58,— His death, therefore, so far as it would be to Him, by means of the resurrection and ascension therewith connected, a return to the δόξα which He had before His incarnation. Comp. xvii. 5, and the ὑψωθῆναι ἐκ τῆς γῆς. xii. 32. To the spectators, who only saw the humiliating and shameful *outward spectacle* of His death, it served only to give the deepest *offence.* The concluding argument *a minori ad majus* which lies in οὖν, is like that in iii. 12. The interpretation of the ancient Church, which referred the words to *the corporeal ascension in and by itself,*[2] would require us of logical necessity to supply, not the supposed *increase* of offence (Baeumlein), but a question expressing *doubt* or *denial:* "would ye still take offence then ?" Comp. viii. 28. But this import of the aposiopesis, which also Ewald and Brückner adopt, though not explaining the words merely of the ascension, has the οὖν itself decidedly against it, instead of which ἀλλά would be logically required ; and the reference to the ascension as such, *as an event by itself,* is totally without analogy in the discourses of Jesus, and quite un-

[1] Comp. Winer, p. 558 [E. T. p. 600]; Fritzsche, *Conject.* pp. 22, 31.
[2] So also Olshausen, Lindner, Maier, Ebrard, Kahnis, p. 120, Hilgenfeld, Hofmann, Hengstenberg, Baeumlein, Godet, Harless.

Johannean.[1] So also the θεωρῆτε, in particular, is against this view ; for, with the *Present* participle ἀναβαίνοντα, it would describe the ascension *expressly* as a *visible* event (in answer to Luthardt's observations, who explains it of the ascension, but with Tholuck regards its visibility as a matter of indifference, so far as the present passage is concerned), though its *visible* occurrence is attested by no apostle, while in the non-apostolic accounts (Mark xvi. 19 ; Luke xxiv. 51 ; Acts i. 9) only the disciples in the *narrower* sense, the twelve, who are just those not meant by the " ye " in our text, are represented as the eye-witnesses. On the other hand, the opinion that there lies in θεωρ. only the *possibility* of those present being eye-witnesses (Kahnis, Hofmann)[2] is nothing more than a subtle evasion, unsupported by the ἐάν (comp. xii. 32, xiv. 3, xvi. 7), and no better than Hengstenberg's assertion (comp. Tholuck) : " those who were present at the ascension were the *representatives* of the collective body of the disciples." Parallel with ἀναβαίνειν is the designation of the death of Jesus as *a going to God*, vii. 33, xiii. 3, xiv. 12, 28, xvi. 5, 28, xvii. 11, 13. That He, in our passage, describes His death not in its humble and painful phase, but according to the essence of its triumphant consummation as present to His own consciousness, is therefore quite Johannean ; comp. also xvii. 5, xii. 23. The reference to *the gift of the Spirit*, the exaltation being intended as the *medium* of effecting this (Lange), is remote from the context, and is not indicated by any word in the sentence ; for nothing is spoken of but the *seeing with the eyes* the future *departure*. — Upon τὸ πρότερον, see on Gal. iv. 13. It refers to the period preceding His present form of being, when as to the divine part of His nature, *i.e.* as the Logos, He was in heaven ;[3] comp. xvii. 5, 24, viii. 58.

[1] Appeal is made, but unreasonably, not only to iii. 13, but likewise to xx. 17 (see especially Hofmann, *Schriftbew.* II. 1, 517, and Godet). Jesus there is speaking *after* His death, when that blessed *end* was still future, in reference to which *before* His death he was wont to describe that event as a departure and an ascension to the Father. There, accordingly, He could not avoid mentioning the ascension *alone*.

[2] " For they would certainly see Him die, but they would see Him ascend only if they remained His disciples," Hofmann. The former is as incorrect as the latter. For Jesus is speaking to His *Galilean* disciples, and, indeed, to His disciples in the *wider* sense (ver. 67), of whom therefore we cannot say that they would certainly be present at His death in Jerusalem ; while the witnesses of the ascension were not those who remained faithful to Him generally, but the *apostles*. According to Harless, Christ means to say that they must not think of His flesh and blood in His state of humiliation, but of both in His state of glory. But flesh and blood is the contra-

dictory of δόξα. The *glorified* body of Christ in the form of *flesh and blood* is inconceivable (1 Cor. xv. 49, 50).

[3] The meaning is not that " *we immediately substitute another subject*" (Beyschlag, *Christol.* p. 29) ; but, in harmony with the witness of Jesus regarding Himself elsewhere in John, we have given us a *more definite* mention of the state wherein the Son of man had His pre-existence in heaven. That He had this *as the Son of man*, as Beyschlag, p. 85, explains (understanding it of the eternal divine image, whose temporal realization Jesus, by an intuition given Him on earth, knew Himself to be), the text does not say ; it says : " the Son of man, *i.e.* the Messiah, will ascend up where He was before." There can be no doubt, if we will follow John, *in what form of existence* He previously was in heaven. Neither is there any doubt if we ask Paul, who speaks of the pre-existence of Jesus ἐν μορφῇ θεοῦ. See on Phil. ii. 6 ; comp. 2 Cor. viii. 8, 9. He does not there mean that He pre-existed *as Jesus*, but as the υἱὸς τ. θεοῦ. For the rest, comp. ver. 46, viii. 58, xvii. 5, i. 18. If it be true, as

Vv. 63, 64. Instead of appending to the foregoing protasis its mournful *apodosis* (see on ver. 62), Jesus at once discloses to His disciples with lively emotion (hence also the asyndeton) the *groundlessness of the offence that was taken. It is not His bodily form*, the approaching surrender of which for spiritual food (ver. 51) was so offensive [1] to them, *but His spirit that gives life; His corporeal nature was of no use* towards *giving life*. But it was precisely His *bodily* nature to which they ascribed all the value, and on which they built all their hope, instead of His life-giving Divine *Spirit, i.e.* the Holy Spirit given Him in all fulness by the Father (iii. 34), who works in believers the birth from above (iii. 6), and with it eternal life (comp. Rom. viii. 2 ; 2 Cor. iii. 6). Hence His death, through which His *flesh* as such would disappear, was to them so offensive a σκάνδαλον. Observe further, that He does not say τὸ πνεῦμά μου and ἡ σάρξ μου, but expresses the above thought in a *general* statement, the personal *application* of which is to be to Himself.[2] Note once again that ἡ σὰρξ οὐκ ὠφελεῖ οὐδέν does not contradict what was previously said of the life-giving participation in the flesh of Jesus ; for this can take place only by the appropriating of the *spirit* of Christ through faith, and apart from this it cannot take place at all. Rom. viii. 2, 6, 9, 11 ; 1 Cor. vi. 17. Comp. 1 John iii. 24. The flesh, therefore, which "profiteth nothing," is the flesh *without the Spirit;* the Spirit which "quickeneth" is the Spirit whose *dwelling-place* is the flesh, *i.e.* the corporeal manifestation of Christ, the corporeity which must be offered up in His atoning death (ver. 51), in order that believers might experience the full power of the quickening Spirit (vii. 39). When Harless, following Luther, understands indeed by the flesh which profiteth nothing, the σάρξ of Christ in His *humiliation*, but by the quickening Spirit, *"the spirit which perfectly controls the flesh of the glorified Son of man,"* he *imports* the essential point in his interpretation, and this in opposition to the N. T., in which the conception of σάρξ is utterly alien to the σῶμα τῆς δόξης of the Lord, Phil. iii. 21 ; see 1 Cor. xv. 44–50 ; so that the σῶμα πνευματικόν cannot possibly be regarded as flesh pervaded by spirit (comp. 2 Cor. iii. 18). In no form is *flesh* ever ascribed to the *exalted* Lord. The antithesis here is not between carnal flesh and glorified flesh, but simply between flesh and spirit. According to others, τὸ πνεῦμα is the human *soul*, which makes the *body* to have life (Beza, Fritzsche in his *Nov. Opusc.* p. 239). But ζωοποιοῦν must, according to the import of the preceding discourse, be taken in the *Messianic* sense. Others say : τὸ πνεῦμα is the spiritual *participation*, ἡ σάρξ the material ;[3] but thus again the peculiar element in the exposition, viz. the partaking of the *Lord's Supper*, is foisted in.[4] Others, interpolating in like

Keim says (*Geschichtl. Chr.* p. 102, ed. 3), that "not one particle of the self-consciousness of Jesus reaches back beyond His temporal existence," the fundamental Christological view not only of the fourth Gospel but of Paul also, is based upon a great illusion. As to the Synoptics, see on Matt. xi. 27, viii. 20.

[1] Godet, according to his rendering of ver. 62 : "which you will see to vanish at my ascension."

[2] Comp. Hofmann, II. 2, p. 252.

[3] Tertullian, Augustine, Rupertius, Calvin, Grotius, and most others ; also Olshausen, comp. Kling and Richter.

[4] Kahnis (*Abendm.* p. 122) has explained the passage in this sense seemingly in a manner most in keeping with the words:

manner, interpret τὸ πνεῦμα as the spiritual, and ἡ σάρξ as the unspiritual, sensuous *understanding;* [1] comp. Tholuck. Others differently still.[2] " Quantopere sit hic locus variis expositionibus exagitatus, vix credibile est," Beza. —τά ῥήματα ἂ ἐγώ, κ.τ.λ.] This does not mean that we are to hold to His *words* instead of to His corporeal *flesh* (Rückert, Keim), His words which remain as a compensation to us after His death (Lücke, de Wette, B. Crusius). It stands (seeing that σάρξ has already its full antithesis in what precedes) in close connection with the following ἀλλ' εἰσὶν ἐξ ὑμῶν τινὲς οἳ οὐ πιστ., and therefore a comma only is to be placed after ζωή ἐστιν. " *The words which I have spoken unto you*" (meaning the discourse in the synagogue just ended [3]), " so far from containing any real ground for σκάνδαλον, *are* rather *spirit and life, i.e.* containing and revealing the divine spirit in me, and the Messianic life brought about by me ; but the real guilt of the offence lies with *you, for among you are many who believe not.*" He, namely, who does not believe in Him as the true Messiah who secures by His death the life of the world, but expects Messianic salvation by His corporeal manifestation alone, as that which is not to die, but to triumph and reign—to him who is such a μαθητής of Jesus the discourse concerning feeding upon His flesh and blood can only be a stumbling-block and an offence. And of such τινές there were πολλοί, ver. 60. — ἐγώ and ἐξ ὑμῶν stand in emphatic antithesis. — πνεῦμά ἐστι καὶ ζωή ἐστιν] The two predicates are thus impressively kept apart, and the designation by the *substantive* is fuller and more exhaustive (comp. iii. 6 ; Rom. viii. 10) than would be that by the adjective.[4]— ᾔδει γάρ, κ.τ.λ.] an explanation added by John himself of the preceding words, ἀλλ' εἰσίν, κ.τ.λ., which imply a higher knowledge ; comp. ii. 24, 25. — οἳ οὐ πιστεύουσιν] result of their wavering ; for they are μαθηταί, who, from an imperfect and inconstant faith, have at last come to surrender faith altogether. They had been πρόσκαιροι (Matt. xiii. 21). Here we have οὐ with the relative, then μή with the participle accompanied by the article (iii. 18), both quite regular. — ἐξ ἀρχῆς] neither " from the *first beginning*" (Theophylact, Rupertius) ; nor "*before this discourse,* and not for the first time after the murmur-

---

" What imparts the power of everlasting life to them who fêed upon my flesh, is not the flesh as such, but the spirit which pervades it." According to this view, the glorified flesh of Christ, which is eaten in the Supper, would be described as the vehicle of the Holy Spirit, and the latter, not the flesh itself, as that which gives life. Comp. also Luthardt. But it is self-evident that the thought of glorified flesh has to be imported from without.

[1] Chrysostom, Theophylact, Euthymius Zigabenus, Mosheim, Lampe, Klee, Ammon, etc. So also Luther : " Ye must indeed have the Spirit likewise, or obtain a spiritual understanding, because it is too high and inconceivable for the flesh." See the striking remarks of Calovius against this interpretation.

[2] Wieseler, on *Gal.* p. 446, takes σάρξ in the sense of original sin ; sinful human nature can do nothing for man's salvation ; the Spirit of God produces this. But σάρξ must take its stricter definition *from the foregoing discourse,* and if it were intended as in iii. 6, οὐκ ὠφελεῖ οὐδέν would be far too little to say of it. This also tells against the similar interpretation of Hengstenberg : "The πνεῦμα is the Spirit represented through Christ, and incarnate in Him, and the σάρξ humanity destitute of the Spirit."

[3] The usual but arbitrarily general rendering brought with it the reading λαλῶ. Tholuck and Ebrard have the right reference. Comp. εἴρηκα, ver. 65.

[4] πνευματικὰ καὶ ζωηρά, Euthymius Zigabenus.

ing ; " [1] nor again *"from the beginning of the then existing acquaintance"* (Grotius, de Wette, B. Crusius, Maier, Hengstenberg, etc. ; comp. Tholuck, "from the very time of their call ") ; but, as the context shows (see especially καὶ τίς ἐστιν, κ.τ.λ.), *from the beginning, when He began to gather disciples around Him* (comp. i. 43, 48, ii. 24), consequently from the commencement of His Messianic ministry. Comp. xvi. 4, xv. 27. From His first coming forth in public, and onwards, He knew which of those who attached themselves to Him as μαθηταί did not believe, and in particular who should be His future betrayer. On this last point, see the note following ver. 70. Were we, with Lange and Weiss, to render : *"from the beginning of their unbelief,"* this would apply only to disciples in constant intercourse with Him, whom He always could observe with heart-searching eye,—a limitation, however, not justified by the text, which rather by the very example of Judas, as the sole unbeliever in the immediate circle of His disciples, indicates a range beyond that inner circle.

Ver. 65. See on vv. 37, 44. — διὰ τοῦτο] because many of you believe not ; and therefore, though there is in them the outward appearance of discipleship, they lack the inward divine preparation. — ἐκ τοῦ πατρ. μ.] *from my Father.* [2]

Vv. 66, 67. Ἐκ τούτου] not : *"from this time forwards,"* [3] for a *gradual* going away is not described ; but (so Nonnus, Luthardt) : *on this account,* because of these words of Jesus, ver. 61 ff., which so thoroughly undeceived them as regarded their earthly Messianic hopes. So also xix. 12. [4] — εἰς τὰ ὀπίσω] they went away, and went *back,* so that they no longer accompanied Him, but returned to the place whence they had come to Him. [5] — τοῖς δώδεκα] who and what they were, John takes for granted as well known. — μὴ καὶ ὑμεῖς, κ.τ.λ.] *ye too do not wish to go away?* Jesus knows His twelve too well (comp. xiii. 18) to put the question to them otherwise than with the presupposition of a *negative* answer (at the same time He knew that He must except one). But He wishes for their avowal, and therein lay His comfort. This rendering of the question with μή is no "pedanterie grammaticale" (Godet, who wrongly renders "*vous ne voulez pas?*"), but is alone linguistically correct. [6] According to Godet, the thought underlying the question is, "*If you wish, you can,*" which is a pure invention.

Vv. 68, 69. *Peter,* according to the position, for which the foundation is already laid in i. 43, makes the confession, and with a resolution how deep and conscious ! — ἀπελευσόμεθα] Future, *at any time.* "*Da nobis alterum Te,*" Augustine. — ῥήματα ζωῆς, κ.τ.λ.] Twofold reason for stedfastness : (1)

---

[1] Chrysostom, Maldonatus, Jansenius, Bengel, etc.

[2] See Bernhardy, p. 227 f ; comp. Plat. *Lys.* p. 104 B : τοῦτο δέ μοί πως ἐκ θεοῦ δέδοται. Soph. *Philoct.* 1301 : τὰς μὲν ἐκ θεῶν τύχας δοθείσας. Xen. *Anab.* i. 1. 6 ; *Hellen.* iii. 1. 6.

[3] So usually, also Lücke, de Wette, Hengstenberg.

[4] Xen. *Anab.* ii. 6. 4, iii. 3. 5, vii. 6. 13. Comp. ἐξ οὖ, *quapropter,* and see generally, concerning the ἐκ of cause or occasion, Matthiae, II. 1334; Ellendt, *Lex. Soph.* i. 551, who justly remarks : "His etiam subest *fontis,* unde aliquid exoriatur, notio."

[5] Comp. xviii. 6, xx. 14 ; 1 Macc. ix. 47 ; Prov. xxv. 9 ; Gen. xix. 17 ; Luke xvii. 31 ; Plato, *Phaedr.* p. 254 B ; *Menex.* p. 246 B ; Polyb. i. 51. 8.

[6] Baeumlein, *Partik.* p. 302 f.

ῥήματα . . . ἔχεις, and (2) καὶ ἡμεῖς, κ.τ.λ. Thou hast *words of everlasting life* (ζωὴν αἰώνιον προξενοῦντα, Euthymius Zigabenus ; more literally : "whose specific power it is to secure eternal life") ; an echo of ver. 63. The ῥήματα which proceed from the Teacher are represented as *belonging to Him*, a *possession* which He has at His disposal. Comp. 1 Cor. xiv. 26. — καὶ ἡμεῖς] *and we* for our part, as contrasted with those who had fallen away. — πεπιστ. κ. ἐγνώκ.] "*the faith and the knowledge to which we have attained, and which we possess, is that,*" etc. (Perfect). Conversely, xvii. 8 ; 1 John iv. 16. Practical conviction may precede (Phil. iii. 10) and follow (comp. viii. 32) the insight which is the product of reason. The former quite corresponds to the immediate and overpowering impressions by which the apostles had been won over to Jesus, chap. i. Both, therefore, are conformable with experience, and mutually include, and do not exclude, each other. — ὁ ἅγιος τοῦ θεοῦ (see the critical notes) : *He who is consecrated of God* to be the Messiah through the fulness of the Spirit and salvation vouchsafed Him. See on x. 36 ; 1 John ii. 20 ; comp. Mark i. 24 ; Luke iv. 34 ; Acts iv. 27 ; Rev. iii. 7. — The similar confession, Matt. xvi. 16, is so different in its occasion, connection, and circumstances, that the assumption that our passage is only another version of the synoptical account (Weisse and others) is unwarrantable. Who can take exception to the repetition of a confession (of which the apostles' hearts were so full) upon every occasion which presented itself ? But it is certainly, according to John (see already i. 42 ff., ii. 19), untenable to suppose that in our passage, according to the right reading (see the critical notes), we have *not yet a complete and unhesitating confession of the Messiah* (Ewald) ; or that the disciples had *only now* attained a full faith in Him (Weizsäcker). We should have to assume in the earlier passages of (chap. i.) a very awkward ὕστερον πρότερον on the part of the evangelist,—a view in which Holtzmann acquiesces.[1] [See Note XXVIIa., p. 228.]

Vv. 70, 71. Not a justification of the question in ver. 67, nor in general any utterance of reflection, but an outburst of grief at the sad catastrophe which He foresaw (ver. 64), in the face of that joyous confession which the fiery Peter thought himself warranted in giving in the name of them *all.*— The *question* extends only as far as ἐξελεξ. ; then comes with the simple καί the mournful contrast which damps the ardour of the confessing disciple. Comp. vii. 19.—Observe the *arrangement of the words*, ἐγώ and ἐξ ὑμῶν impressively taking the lead : *Have not I* (even *I*, and no other) *chosen you the twelve to myself ? And of you* (these *chosen by myself*) *one is a devil!* not *the* devil, but of *devilish kind and nature.* Comp. θεός, i. 1. In what an awful contrast the two stand to each other ! The addition of τοὺς δώδεκα to ὑμᾶς heightens the contrast, laying stress upon the great *significance* of the election, which nevertheless was to have in the case of one so contradictory a result. — διάβολος] not *an informer*,[2] not *an adversary* or *betrayer*,[3] but, in keeping with the deep emotion (comp. Matt. xvi. 23), and the invariable usage of the N. T. in all places where διάβ. is a substantive (in John viii. 44, xiii. 2 ; 1

---

[1] *Judenth. u. Christenth.* p. 376.
[2] Theophylact, de Wette, Baeumlein.
[3] Kuinoel, Lücke, B. Crusius, and earlier writers.

John iii. 8, 10) : *devil,* by which antagonism to Christ is set forth in its strongest manner, because in accordance with its demoniacal nature. That John would have written υἱός, or τέκνον διαβόλου (viii. 44 ; 1 John iii. 10), is an arbitrary objection, and does not adequately estimate the strength of the emotion, which the expression employed, never forgotten by John, fully does. — Ver. 71. ἔλεγε δὲ τόν, κ.τ.λ.] *He spoke of,* like ix. 19 ; Mark xiv. 71.[1] As to the name Ἰσκαρ.,[2] *man of Karioth,* see on Matt. x. 4. Observe the sad and solemn emphasis of the full name Ἰούδαν Σίμωνος Ἰσκαριώτην, as in xiii. 22. Ἰσκαριώτην itself is used quite as a *name,* as forming with Ἰούδ. Σίμωνος one expression. Bengel, therefore, without reason desiderates the article τόν before Ἰσκαρ., and prefers on that account the reading Ἰσκαριώτου (see the critical notes). — ἤμελλεν, κ.τ.λ.] *traditurus erat,* not as if he was already revolving it in his mind (see, on the contrary, xiii. 2), but suggesting the idea of *the divine destiny.*[3] Comp. vii. 39, xi. 51, xii. 4, 33, xviii. 32 ; Wisd. xviii. 4 : δι᾽ ὧν ἤμελλε . . . δίδοσθαι ; Judith x. 12. Kern has erroneously lowered the expression to the idea of *possibility.* — εἰς ὧν ὤ, κ.τ.λ.] *although he,* etc. Still ὤν is critically doubtful (omitted by Lachmann), and without it the tragic contrast is all the stronger.

Note 1.—With respect to the psychological difficulty of Jesus having chosen and retained Judas as an apostle, we may remark : 1. That we cannot get rid of the difficulty by saying that Jesus did not make or intend a definite election of disciples (Schleiermacher, *L. J.* p. 370 ff.), for this would be at variance with all the Gospels, and in particular with ver. 70. 2. Jesus cannot have received Judas into the company of the apostles with the foreknowledge that He was choosing His betrayer (Hengstenberg ; comp. Augustine in Ps. lv.: electi undecim *ad opus probationis,* electus unus *ad opus tentationis*) ; this would be psychologically and morally inconceivable. He must have had confidence that each one of the twelve, when He selected them according to the variety of their gifts, temperaments, characters, etc., would become under His influence an effective supporter of His work ; and, at any rate, the remark in ver. 64 is only a retrospective inference from the inconceivableness of so hideous an act in the case of one selected by the Lord Himself. The view in question also goes too far in this respect, that it attributes the crime not to the dangerous *disposition* of Judas, but to the knowledge of Christ from the outset, which would logically lead to the outrageous and inadmissible thought of Daub, that He *purposely* chose Judas, *in order that* he might betray Him. Comp. Neander, Lücke, Kern, Ullmann (*Sündlosigk.*), Tholuck, de Wette, Ewald, and many others. 3. Although the bent of the man, and his inclination towards an unhallowed development,— which, however, did not lead to a complete rupture until late (xiii. 2),—must have been known to Christ, the reader of all hearts, yet it may have been accompanied with the hope that this tendency might be overcome by the presence of some other apostolic qualification possessed by Judas, perhaps a very special gift for external administration (xii. 6, xiii. 28). 4. As it became gradually evident that this hope was

---

[1] See Stallb. *ad Plat. Rep.* p. 363 B.
[2] Not equivalent to אִישׁ שְׁקָרִים, *man of lies,* as Hengstenberg maintains, after Prov. xix. 5 ; the Greek form itself already forbids this.
[3] Ellendt, *Lex. Soph.* II. p. 72.

226 THE GOSPEL OF JOHN.

to be disappointed when the care of the money affairs became a special temptation to the unhappy man, it was the consciousness of the divine destiny
herein manifesting itself (vv. 70, 71 ; Acts iv. 28) which prevented Jesus from
dismissing Judas, and so disturbing the further progress of the divine purpose ; while on the part of the Lord, we must, in conformity with His calling,
suppose a continual moral influence bearing upon Judas, though this to the
last remained without effect, and turned out to his condemnation,—*a tragic
destiny* truly, whose details, finally, in the want of sufficient historical information concerning him before the commission of his bloody deed, are too far
withdrawn from our critical judgment to lend any support to the difficulties
arising from them as to the genuineness of vv. 70, 71 (Weisse, Strauss, B.
Bauer), or to warrant the assumption of any modification of the statement,
which John, in accordance with his later view, might have given to it (Lücke,
Ullmann, and others).

Note 2.—The aim of Jesus in the discourse vv. 26 ff. was to set before the
people, who came to Him under the influence of a carnal belief in His miracles, the duty of seeking a true and saving faith instead, which would secure
a deep living reception of and fellowship with Christ's personal life, and that
with a decision which, with an ever-advancing fulness, lays open this true
work of faith in the appropriation of Himself to the innermost depth and the
highest point of its contents and necessity. Baur's opinion, that the discourse
sets forth the critical process of the self-dissolution of a merely apparent faith,
so that the latter must acknowledge itself as unbelief, has no such confession
in the text to support it, especially as the ὄχλος and the Ἰουδαῖοι are not identical. See, besides, Brückner, p. 143 ff. Regarding the *difficulty of understanding* this discourse, which Strauss urges, it may partly be attributed to the Johannean idiosyncrasy in reproducing and elaborating his abundant recollections of
the words of Jesus. The difficulty, however, is partly exaggerated (see Hauff
in the *Stud. u. Krit.* 1846, p. 595 ff.) ; and partly it is overlooked that Jesus, in
all references to His death and its design, had to reckon on the light which
the *future* would impart to these utterances, and sowing, as He generally did,
for the future in the bosom of the present, He was obliged to give expression
to much that was mysterious, but which would furnish material for, and support to, the further development and purification of faith and knowledge.
The wisdom thus displayed in His teaching is justified by the *history*.

NOTES BY AMERICAN EDITOR.

XXVI. Ἤθελον οὖν λαβεῖν. Ver. 21.

Whether or not Jesus actually came on board the ship, John's language seems
to leave undecided. If it intends to affirm that he did *not*, we might expect
ἤθελον μὲν οὖν λαβεῖν . . . εὐθέως δὲ ἐγένετο (they wished indeed, therefore—
but immediately), or less classically ἤθελον οὖν λαβεῖν . . . ἀλλ' εὐθέως, or something similar. For the other view we might expect ἐθέλοντες, or ἄσμενοι οὖν
ἔλαβον, or the like. Still, the more natural inference from the entire passage
seems to be, even apart from the Synoptics, that he *was* taken into the ship, and
that in consequence of, or at least *upon* this reception, the ship came immediately
by miracle to its destination. The verb seems specially *chosen*. It is not ἐπεθύμουν,
or ἐβούλοντο (expressing mere *desire*), but ἤθελον, *willed, would*, which often makes

the willing and doing coincident : a usage that seems rather a favourite with John (John i. 44, vii. 17, viii. 44 ; Rev. ii. 21, all which passages imply the doing, and emphasize the willing). Thus, "they *willed to, would* receive him, and," as a consequence, "were immediately," etc. Buttmann admits the possibility of the construction, but objects that the ἐθέλοντες is inconsistent with ἐφοβήθησαν. But it is just as inconsistent, if they did not suceed, as if they did. De W. also declares it in itself admissible, but inconsistent with the context. It is difficult to see why : the following καί suggests and almost requires it.

Such being the state of the question in our Gospel, the Synoptical narrative, it should seem, must decide it. That declares positively that Jesus was received on board ; and this fact must have been an integral part of the narrative and of the current tradition. Matthew and Mark affirm the reception ; John does not expressly affirm, or clearly imply, the contrary. The affirmative view, then, is not " an unhappy attempt at harmonizing," but a legitimate application of the principle which explains the uncertain from the certain, and avoids forcing into reputable writers unnecessary discrepancies. Further, the different accounts supplement each other. The Synoptics record the incident with Peter, and the lulling of the wind ; John records the sudden coming of the ship to land.

XXVII. " *The next day, when the people,*" etc. Vv. 22–24.

The main difficulty of this somewhat cumbrous passage is occasioned, I think, by the substitution of εἶδεν or εἶδον of the leading uncials (א, A B) for the participle ἰδών of the Received text. True, εἶδεν (or εἶδον) gives a more regular construction, is at first view seemingly easier, and is, therefore, such a change as would commend itself to a superficial copyist. On the other hand, it obscures the thought, introducing as main objects of their seeing what would naturally be mentioned incidentally, and that as actually *seen* on the morrow which had occurred the day before. With Meyer, I think ἰδών to be decidedly preferable ; and though the consent of the three great uncials is weighty, yet they sometimes concur in readings admitted by all to be erroneous. The resumption (ver. 24) of ἰδών by ὅτε οὖν εἶδον, though apparently, is not really, difficult. The verb which would have been awkward above becomes now natural as it presents the added feature of the present situation; and the construction, seemingly so harsh, makes rather an elegant *anacolouthon*, by no means out of harmony with the easy carelessness of Greek construction, and is really among the many proofs which this Gospel furnishes of the freedom which the Apostle's Ephesian residence had given him in his use of the Greek language. The ἦν and εἰσῆλθεν of ver. 22 must with either reading (ἰδών or εἶδεν) be rendered as Plup. (which with the participle it very easily can be, and with the verb, possibly). To the rendering of the Revised Ver., " On the morrow they saw—that Jesus entered not with His disciples," etc., it is difficult to attach any intelligible meaning. They surely had seen it on the *day before*. We may render ἰδών either *seeing* or *having seen*, and render the following verbs accordingly. The passage will run about as follows : " On the morrow the multitude, who were standing on the other side of the sea, seeing that there was no other ship there except one, and that Jesus had not entered into the ship with His disciples, but that His disciples had gone away alone—but there came ships from Tiberias near to the place where they ate the

bread after the Lord had given thanks—when therefore the multitude saw
that Jesus was not there, nor His disciples, they themselves entered into the
ships, and came into Capernaum, seeking for Jesus."

We may add (after Weiss) that the fact of the multitude seeking for Jesus at
Capernaum harmonizes incidentally with the Synoptical statement that He
had made Capernaum His residence, and makes it probable (against Meyer) that
the ἀπῆλθεν (*He went away*) of vi. 1 has its point of departure not from Jerusalem, but from Capernaum, in connection with which the expression is far more
natural. From the starting point of Jerusalem the words "went away beyond
the sea of Galilee" seem unnatural and abrupt.

XXVIIa. " *Thou art the Holy One of God.*" Ver. 69.

Weiss (ed. Meyer) maintains that the usual opinion held by Meyer, Ewald,
etc., that this confession of Peter is a different one from that recorded by
Matt. xxi. 16, Mark viii. 29, is entirely untenable, and that in all probability
the two must be considered identical. No argument, he urges, can be drawn
against this identification from difference of place, for to the scene of this
confession John assigns no locality. There is no certainty, nor scarcely probability, that it was in Capernaum, where the previously recorded conversation
had taken place ; for the defection which followed that conversation he holds
(against Meyer) to have been gradual, and our Lord had in the mean time
probably left Capernaum, and may now have been in the neighbourhood of
Hermon. In *time*, too, the confessions substantially coincide, as they both follow
on the miraculous feeding and the demand of the Jews for a *sign ;* and in both
cases they are partly followed, partly preceded, by those open disclosures of
Christ's impending death which He had hitherto made only by obscure intimations. Whether there is ground for a confident decision on the point may be
doubtful. Certainly the *essence* of the two confessions is the same ; they agree
nearly enough in time and place ; while yet the different attending circumstances and the difference of colouring may well justify doubt. And if
Nathanael, so early as in John i., could make the declaration there recorded, it
could not surprise us if, at this later period, the ardent spirit of Peter should
prompt him to *more than one* such utterance as the Evangelists have recorded.

CHAPTER VII.

Ver. 1. μετὰ ταῦτα] B. C. D. G. K. L. X. ℵ. Cursives, Verss. Cyr. Chrys. have these words before περιεπ. So Scholz, Lachm. Tisch. Considering the preponderance of testimonies, this arrangement is to be preferred. Were it an alteration in imitation of iii. 12, v. 1, vi. 1, the καὶ deleted by Tisch. would be omitted to a greater extent, but it is wanting only in C.** D. ℵ. and a few Cursives and Versions. — Ver. 8. The first ταύτην is wanting in B. D. K. L. T. X. ℵ.** Cursives, Verss. Cyr. Chrys. Rejected by Schulz and Rink, deleted by Lachm. and Tisch. ; a mechanical addition, in imitation of what follows. — οὐκ] Elz. Lachm. read οὔπω, according to the preponderance of Codd. indeed (only D. K. M. ℵ. and three Cursives have οὐκ), but against the preponderance of Versions (even Vulg. It.), most of which have οὐκ. Of the Fathers, Epiph. Cyr. Chrys. Augustine, Jerome have οὐκ. Porphyry, in Jerome, c. *Pelag.* ii. 17, already found οὐκ, and inferred from it the accusation of vacillation. Just on account of this objection, οὔπω was introduced. — Ver. 9. αὐτοῖς] Tisch. αὐτός, following D.* K. L. T. X. ℵ. Cursives, Cyr. Augustine, and several Versions. Testimony preponderates in favour of the Received Text, and this all the more, that αὐτός might have been easily written on the margin as a gloss from ver. 10. — Ver. 12. After ἄλλοι, Elz. Lachm. have δέ, which has many important witness against it, and is an interpolation. — Ver. 15. Instead of καὶ ἐθαύμαζ. we must, with Lachm. and Tisch., read ἐθαύμ. οὖν, and still more decisively is ο ν confirmed after ἀπεκρ., ver. 16 (which Elz. has not). — Ver. 26. After ἐστιν Elz. has again ἀληθῶς, against decisive testimony. An interpolation (which displaced the first ἀληθ. in some witnesses) ; comp. iv. 42, vi. 14, vii. 40. — Ver. 31. The arrangement ἐκ τοῦ ὄχλου δὲ πολλοὶ ἐπ. is, with Lachm., to be preferred. Tisch., following D. ℵ., has πολλ. δὲ ἐπ. ἐκ τ. ὀ. — ὅτι] wanting indeed in B. D. L. T. U. X. ℵ. Cursives, Verss. Cyr., and deleted by Lachm. and Tisch. But it was greatly exposed to the danger of being overlooked between ON and O, as well as because it was unnecessary. — For μήτι we must, with Lachm. Tisch., following decisive testimonies, read μή. In like manner, τούτων after σημ. is, with Lachm. Tisch., to be deleted. An addition to explain the genitive ὧν. For ἐποίησεν, ποιεῖ (Tisch.) is too weakly attested. — Ver. 33. After οὖν Elz. has αὐτοῖς, against decisive testimony. — Ver. 39. πιστεύοντες] Lachm. πιστεύσαντες, upon too weak and (in part) doubtful authority. — After πνεῖμα, Elz. Scholz have ἅγιον, Lachm. δεδομένον (B. and a few Verss. and Fathers). Both additions are glosses ; instead of δεδομ. there occur also δοθέν or *acceptum*, or ἐπ' αὐτούς or ἐπ' αὐτοῖς. — Ver. 40. πολλοὶ οὖν ἐκ τ. ὀχλου] Lachm. Tisch.: ἐκ τοῦ ὄχλου οὖν, following B. D. L. T. X. ℵ. Verss. Origen] Rightly ; the Received reading is an interpretation. — τὸν λόγον] Lachm. Tisch.: τῶν λόγων τούτων, according to preponderating witnesses. The genitive and plural were certainly more strange to the transcribers. — Ver. 41. ἄλλοι δέ] Lachm. οἱ δέ, following B. L. T. X. Cursives, Verss. Origen, Cyril ; Tisch. also, following weighty witnesses (even D. E. ℵ.) : ἄλλοι. The original reading is οἱ δέ, instead of which

ἄλλοι was mechanically repeated from what precedes, sometimes with, sometimes without δέ. — Ver. 46. οὕτως ἐλάλ. ἄνθρ. ὡς οὗτος ὁ ἄνθρ.] Lachm. has
merely : ἐλάλ. οὕτως ἄνθρ., following B. L. T. two Cursives, Copt. Origen, Cyr.
Chrys. Aug. But how superfluous would have been the addition, and how
easily might their omission have occurred in looking from the first ἄνθρ. at
once to the second ! The *order*, however, ἐλάλ. οὕτως (Tisch.), is attested by
preponderating evidence. — Ver. 49. ἐπικατάρατοι] Lachm. Tisch. : ἐπάρατοι,
after B. T. ℵ. 1, 33, Or. Cyr. Chrys. Rightly ; the Received text is from the
familiar passage, Gal. iii. 10, 13. — Ver. 50. ὁ ἐλθ. νυκτὸς πρὸς αὐτ.] Lachm.:
ὁ ἐλθ. π. α. πρότερον (after B. L. T. ℵ. al.). Νυκτὸς is certainly an explanatory
addition (comp. xix. 39), which also has various positions in the Codd.; but
πρότερον is so decisively attested, and so necessary, that Lachmann's reading is
to be regarded as the original one, although the whole ὁ ἐλθ. . . . . αὐτόν is not
to be deleted, with Tisch. (so ℵ.*). — Ver. 52. ἐγήγερται] Lachm. Tisch. :
ἐγείρεται, following B. D. K. S. (in the margin) T. Γ. Δ. ℵ. Cursives, Vulg. It.
Syr. Goth. Aeth. Or. An early emendation of the historical error. Copt.
Sahid. have the *Future*. — Ver. 53, see on viii. 1.

Vv. 1, 2.[1] Μετὰ ταῦτα] after these transactions, chap. vi. — οὐ γὰρ ἤθελεν ἐν
τ. ᾽Ιουδ. περιπ.] whither He would already have gone for the approaching
Passover (vi. 4), but for this consideration (comp. v. 16, 18). We must
not assume from this, with B. Crusius, that John regards Judea as the
proper seat of the ministry of Jesus ; nor, with Schweizer, make use
of the passage to impugn the genuineness of vi. 1–26 ; nor, with Brückner, say that John here resumes the theme of the hostility of the Jews,
because this had not been dropped in what precedes (vi. 11, 52), where
so late as in vv. 60, 61 even, a division among the disciples is mentioned,
and does not immediately become prominent in what follows.—To this
sojourn in Galilee, to describe which was beyond the plan of John's Gospel,
most of the narrative in Matt. xiv. 34–xviii. belongs. It lasted from a
little before the Passover (vi. 4), which Jesus did not attend in Jerusalem,
onward to the next feast of Tabernacles (ver. 2) ; hence also the *Imperfects*.
— δέ] passing over to what, nevertheless, afterwards induced Him to go to
Jerusalem. — ἡ σκηνοπηγία] חַג הַסֻּכּוֹת, beginning on the 15th Tisri (in Octo-
ber), and observed with special sacredness and rejoicing.[2]

Ver. 3. The *brothers* (ii. 12 ; their names are given, Matt. xiii. 55, Mark
vi. 3) were still *unbelievers* (ver. 5), because biassed by the prevailing Messianic views ;[3] yet, allowing to themselves, because of the miracles, the possi-

---

[1] As to Baur's assaults on the historical
character of the contents of chap. vii., see
Hauff in the *Stud. u. Krit.* 1849, p. 124 ff.
According to Baur, the object of chap. vii.
is to show how the reasoning on which unbelief ventures to enter only becomes its
own logical refutation.

[2] Lev. xxiii. 33 ; Josephus, *Antt.* iii. 10. 4,
al.; Plutarch, *Symp.* iv. 6. 2 ; Ewald, *Alterth.*
p. 481 f. ; Keil, *Archaeol.* I. § 85.

[3] Hengstenberg is not deterred even by
this passage from recognizing in these

brothers of Jesus His *cousins* (the sons, he
thinks, of Cleopas and Mary ; but see on
xix. 25), and from maintaining, with all the
arbitrariness and violence of exegetical
impossibilities, that three of them, James,
Simon, and Judas, were apostles, in spite
of vv. 3, 5, 7 (comp. xv. 19). Against every
attempt to explain away the literal brothers and sisters of Jesus, see on Matt. i. 25,
xii. 46 ; 1 Cor. ix. 5 ; also Laurentius, *N. T.
Stud.* p. 153 ff. ; comp. Pressensé, *Jesus Chr.*
p. 287.

bility of His being the Messiah, they are anxious—partly, perhaps, for the sake of their own family—for the *decision* of the matter, which they thought might most appropriately take place at the great joyous feast of the nation, and which certainly must occur, if at all, in Jerusalem, the seat of the theocracy. A malicious and treacherous intention [1] is imputed to them without foundation. They are of cold Jewish natures, and the higher nature belonging to their Brother is as yet hidden from them. The light of faith seems not to have dawned upon them until after His resurrection, and by means of that event (1 Cor. xv. 7 ; Acts i. 14). This long-continued unbelief of His own earthly brothers (comp. Mark iii. 21) is important in estimating the genuineness of the accounts given in Matthew and Luke of the miraculous birth and early childhood of Jesus. — καὶ οἱ μαθηταί σου] This expression entirely corresponds with the position of the brothers as *outside* the fellowship of Jesus. It does not say, "thy disciples *there* also" (so *usually ;* even Baur, who takes it to refer to those who are first to be won over in Judea), for the word *there* does not occur, nor "thy disciples *collectively*," but simply, "thy disciples also." They would be gathered together from all parts at the feast in Jerusalem, and He should let Himself and His works be seen *by them also*. It does not, indeed, clearly appear from this that coldness began to be exhibited towards Him within the circle of His disciples (Weizsäcker), but rather perhaps that Jesus had gone about in Galilee and worked miracles very much in secret, without attracting observation, and not attended by any great following, but perhaps only by the trusted twelve, which silent manner of working He was perhaps led to adopt by the lying in wait of the Jews (ver. 1). Comp. ver. 4 : ἐν κρυπτῷ. According to B. Crusius, the brothers speak as if nothing miraculous had been done by Him in Galilee. Contrary to the narrative ; and therefore ἃ ποιεῖς cannot mean "what thou art *reported* to have done" (B. Crusius), but "*what thou doest*," *i.e.* during thy present sojourn in Galilee, although ἐν κρυπτῷ, ver. 4. According to Brückner (comp. Ebrard, and substantially also Godet), the brothers express themselves as if Jesus had made and retained no disciples in Galilee, and, indeed, with malicious and ironical allusion to the fact stated vi. 66, and to the report (iv. 1) which they did not believe. But, considering the long interval which elapsed between chap. vi. and vii. 2, such allusions, without more precise indication of them in the text, are not to be assumed. Luthardt attributes to the brothers the notion that in Galilee it was only the multitudes that followed Him, and that there was no such personal adherence to Him as had taken place in Judea (in consequence of His baptizing). But it is incredible that they should entertain a notion so obviously *erroneous*, because the events which they were continually witnessing in Galilee, as well as those which they witnessed in Judea on occasion of their journeys to the feast, must have been better known to them.

Ver. 4. "*For no one does anything in secret, and along with this seeks to be personally of bold and open disposition ; i.e.* no one withdraws himself with

---

[1] ἵνα ἀναιρεθῇ παρὰ τῶν ζητούντων ἀποκτεῖναι αὐτόν, Euthymius Zigabenus, also Luther.

his *works* into silence and seclusion, and yet strives frankly to assert his *personal* position (as thou must do if thou art the Messiah). The two things are, indeed, contradictory ! On ἐν παῤῥησ. comp. xi. 54 ; Wisd. v. 1 ; and Grimm, *Exeg. Handb.* p. 110 f. ; Eph. vi. 19 ; Phil. i. 20 ; Col. ii. 15. The word does not signify "*manifest*" or "*known*" (de Wette, Godet, and most others), but it means the opposite of a *shy* and *timid* nature which shrinks from playing the part of a fearless and frank character. [See Note XXVIII. p. 253.] — τί] is the simple *aliquid*, not *magnum quid* (Kuinoel and others) ; and καί does not stand for ὅς, making αὐτός superfluous (Grotius, Kuinoel), but is the simple "and," while αὐτός [1] is *ipse*, thus putting the *person* attributively over-against the *work* [2] and not merely resuming the subject (Lücke, Tholuck), as also it must not be taken in Matt. xii. 50. — As to εἶναι ἐν, *versari in*,[3] thus designating the adverbial predicate as *permanent*, see Buttmann, *N. T. Gr.* p. 284 [E. T. p. 330]. — εἰ ταῦτα ποιεῖς] answers to the τὰ ἔργα σου ἃ ποιεῖς, ver. 3, and to οὐδεὶς . . . ποιεῖ, ver. 4, and therefore, according to the context (comp. also the consequent clause, which corresponds with καὶ ζητεῖ αὐτός, κ.τ.λ.), refers to the *miracles* which Jesus did in Galilee. Ταῦτα has the emphasis : "If thou doest *these things, i.e. if thy work consists in such wonderful deeds* as thou art performing here in Galilee, do not foolishly confine thyself with such works within so narrow and obscure a range, but *present thyself openly before the world*, as thou must do in *Judea*, which during the feast is the *theatrum mundi*." Σεαυτόν, like the preceding αὐτός, gives prominence to His *person*, as opposed to His *work*. But the εἰ is not expressive of *doubt*,[4] as if we were to supply, if it be really *as we hear ;* comp. also Brückner, who considers that it is intended to intimate in a disagreeable manner that the fact was doubtful), it is *logical ;* the brothers *know* that His works are of an extraordinary kind, as was evident to them in Galilee ;[5] and they consider it *absurd* that He should withdraw Himself personally from the place whither all the world was flocking.

Vv. 5, 6. *For not even His brothers*, whom we might have expected to have been foremost, etc. ; otherwise they would not have urged Him to the test of a public appearance. They urged this upon Him all the more, because He had absented Himself from the previous Passover at Jerusalem,—a fact which could not have been unknown to them. — ἐπίστ. εἰς αὐτ.] in the ordinary sense ; they did not believe in Him *as the Messiah*. To take the words to mean only the *perfect self-surrender* of faith, which they had not yet attained to (Lange, Hengstenberg), is an inference necessitated by the mistaken notion that these brothers were *not* literally brothers.[6] Nonnus admir-

---

[1] The reading αὐτό (Lachm. following B. D.*) is only an error in transcription. Ebrard, who maintains its genuineness, yet marvellously renders : "*but* he strives, that it may take place openly." Καί, meaning "*but*," is said to be *Johannean ;* it is really neither Johannean nor Greek at all, but simply *wrong*. The frequent Greek use of it in John in the sense of "*and yet*" is something quite different ; see on ver. 29.

[2] Herm. *ad Vig.* p. 735 ; Fritzsche *ad Rom.* II. p. 75

[3] Bernhardy, p. 210.

[4] Euthymius Zigabenus : εἰ ταῦτα σημεῖα ποιεῖς καὶ οὐ φαντάζεις ; Lücke, de Wette, and most.

[5] ποιεῖς denotes a *permanent* course of action ; Bernhardy, p. 370.

[6] See on Matt. xii. 46 ; Acts i. 14 ; Mark iii. 31 ; 1 Cor. ix. 5.

ably says : ἀπειθέες οἰάπερ ἄλλοι, Χριστοῦ παμμεδέοντος ἀδελφειοί περ ἐόντες. See
ver. 7. — ὁ καιρὸς ὁ ἐμός] cannot mean the time *to make the journey to the feast;* [1]
the antithesis ὁ καιρὸς ὁ ὑμ. demands a deeper reference. It is, according to
the context, *the time to manifest myself to the world,* ver. 4, by which Jesus
certainly understood the divinely appointed yet still expécted moment of
public *decision* concerning Him (comp. ii. 4), which did come *historically* at
the very next Passover, but which He now felt in a general way was not
yet come. Thus the explanation of Chrysostom, Euthymius Zigabenus,
Lampe, and most others, who refer the words to the *time of His passion,* is
not wrong, only that this is not actually *expressed,* but was *historically the
fulfilment* of what is here said. The corresponding ὁ καιρὸς ὁ ὑμέτερος in like
manner means the time *for showing themselves openly to the world,* which the
brothers might do at *any time,* because they stood in no opposition to the
world (ver. 7, xv. 19).

Vv. 7, 8. Οὐ δύναται] "psychologically *it cannot,* because you are in perfect
accord with it." "One knave agrees with another, for one crow does not
scratch out the eye of another crow," Luther. [2] — ὁ κόσμος] not as in ver. 4,
but with a *moral* significance (the unbelieving world). Comp. here 1 John
v. 19. — ἐγὼ οὐκ ἀναβαίνω, κ.τ.λ.] not an *indefinite* answer, leaving the matter
spoken of *uncertain* (Hengstenberg), but, as the *Present* shows, a direct and
categorical refusal : I, for my part, *do not go up.* [See Note XXIX. p. 253.]
Afterward He *changed* (ver. 10) His intention *not* to go up to the feast, and
went up to it after all, though as secretly as possible. Porphyry's reproach
(in Jerome) of *inconstantia* is based upon a correct interpretation, but is not
in itself just ; for Jesus might *alter* His intention without being fickle, especially as the particular motive that prompted the change does not appear.
In the case of the Canaanitish woman also, Matt. xv. 26 ff., He changed His
intention. The result of this change was that once more, and for some
length of time before the last decision, He prosecuted His work by way of
refutation and instruction at the great capital of the theocracy. The attempt
to put into οὐκ the sense of οὔπω, or to find this sense in the context, is as
unnecessary as it is erroneous. Either the *Present* ἀναβ. has been emphasized,
and a νῦν introduced, [3] or ἀναβ. has been taken to denote [4] the *manner* of
travelling, viz. *with the caravan of pilgrims,* or the like ; or the meaning of
ἑορτήν has been narrowed, [5] as, besides Hofmann, *Weissag. u. Erf.* II. p. 113,
and Lange, [6] Ebrard's expedient of understanding the feast "*in the legally
prescribed sense*" does ; or οὐκ has been regarded as limited by the following
οὔπω (de Wette, Maier, and many), which is quite wrong, for οὔπω denies the

---

[1] Luther, Jansen, Cornelius à Lapide, and
most expositors.

[2] τὸ ὅμοιον τῷ ὁμοίῳ ἀνάγκη ἀεὶ φίλον εἶναι,
Plato, *Lys.* p. 214 B ; comp. *Gorg.* p. 510 B.

[3] Chrysostom, Bengel, Storr, Lücke, Olshausen, Tholuck.

[4] Comp. Bengel, Luthardt (who would
supply "*as ye think*"), Baumgarten, p. 228 ;
Baeumlein ; in like manner Godet, who
explains ἀναβαίνω, "I go not up *as King*

Messiah." As if one had only to foist in
such interpolations !

[5] Apol. : οὐ μετὰ ἱλαρότητος ; Cyril : οὐχ
οὕτως ἑορτάζων.

[6] See his *Leben Jesu,* II. 927 : He did not
actually visit the *feast,* but He went up in
the second half of the week of the feast, and
not before. Jesus never resorted to any
such subtleties.

fulfilment of the καιρός in the present generally (including the *whole* time of
the feast). So little does the true interpretation of the οὐκ justify the objection of modern criticism against the evangelist (B. Bauer : "Jesuitism ;"
Baur : " the seeming independence of Jesus is supposed thus to be preserved ;"
comp. also Hilgenfeld), that, on the contrary, it brings into view a
striking trait of originality in the history. — Observe in the second half of
the verse the simple and emphatic repetition of the same words, into which
ταύτην, however, is introduced (see the critical notes), because Jesus has in
view a visit to a future feast. Observe also the repetition of the reason
already given in ver. 6, in which, instead of πάρεστιν, occurs the weightier
πεπλήρωται.

Ver. 10. Ὡς δὲ ἀνέβ.] Aor. pluperfect.[1] — ὡς ἐν κρυπτῷ] *He went not openly,*[2]
but *so to speak secretly* (*incognito*), not in the company of a caravan of
pilgrims, or in any other way with outward observation, but so that His
journey to that feast is represented as made in secrecy, and consequently
quite differently from His last entry at the feast of the Passover.[3] The
context does not intimate whether Jesus took a different *road* (through
Samaria, for instance, as Hengstenberg with Wieseler, according to Luke
ix. 51 ff., supposes), de Wette, Krabbe, and early writers, but shows only
that He was without *companions* (except His disciples, ix. 2). Baur (also
Hilgenfeld finds in οὐ φαν., ἀλλ' ὡς ἐν κρυπτῷ, something *Docetic*, or at least[4]
bordering upon *Gnosticism* (besides viii. 59, x. 39, vi. 16), which it is easy
enough to find anywhere if *such* texts are supposed to be indications. See,
on the contrary, Brückner. — This journey finally takes Jesus away from
Galilee (*i.e.* until after His death), and *thus far* it is parallel with that in
Matt. xix. 1, but *only* thus far. In other respects it occurs in quite a different historical connection, and is undertaken with a different object (the
Passover). The journey, again mentioned in Luke ix. 51 ff., is *in other
respects quite different.* The assumption that Jesus returned to Galilee
between the feast of Tabernacles and the feast of the Dedication (Ammon,
Lange ; see on x. 22), is the result of a forced attempt at harmonizing,
which exceeds its limits in every attempt which it makes to reconcile the
Johannean and the synoptic accounts of the last journey from Galilee to
Judea.[5]

Vv. 11, 12. Οὖν] For He did not come with the Galilean travellers. — οἱ
Ἰουδαῖοι] not all the people (Hengstenberg, Baeumlein), but the opposing
hierarchy ; vi. 41, 52, vii. 13, 15. Their *search* is prompted by *malice,* not
by aimless curiosity (Luthardt) ; see vv. 1, 13. On ἐκεῖνος, which means the
well-known absent one, Luther well remarks : " Thus *contemptuously* can
they speak of the man, that they almost would not name Him." The *people's*
judgment of Him was a *divided* one, not frank and free, but timid, and
uttered half in a whisper (γογγυσμός, murmuring, ver. 32). — Observe the

[1] Winer, p. 258 [E. T. p. 541].
[2] φανερῶς ; comp. Xen. *Anab.* v. 4. 33 :
ἐμφανῶς, instead of which ἐν ὄχλῳ follows.
[3] On ὡς, comp. Bernhardy, p. 279 ; Ellendt,
Lex. Soph. II. p. 1004. Otherwise **in i. 14**

(against B. Crusius).
[4] *N. T. Theol.* p. 367.
[5] Comp. also Ewald, *Gesch. Chr.* p. 491,
ed. 3.

change of number : ἐν τοῖς ὄχλοις : *among the multitudes* (the *plural* here only in John) ; τὸν ὄχλον : *the people.* — ἀγαθός] *upright,* a man of honour, no demagogue, seeking to make the people believe falsely that He ·was the Messiah. Comp. Matt. xxvii. 63.

Ver. 13 is usually, after Augustine, only referred to the party who judged favourably.[1] The more arbitrarily, because this was first mentioned, and because the general expression ἐλάλει περὶ αὐτοῦ is quite against any such limitation ; οὐδείς onwards to αὐτοῦ can only be taken as corresponding to the γογγυσμὸς ἐν τοῖς ὄχλοις, ver. 12, which refers to *both* parties. *Both* mistrusted the hierarchy ; even those hostile in their judgment were afraid, so long as they had not given an *official* decision, that their verdict might be *reversed.* A trustworthy indication of an utterly jesuitical domination of the people. — διὰ τὸν φόβον] on account of the fear that *prevailed.*

Ver. 14. Τῆς ἑορτ. μεσ.] when the feast was half way *advanced,* ἤγουν τῇ τετάρτῃ ἡμέρᾳ (or nearly) : ἑπτὰ γὰρ ἡμέρας (yet see on ver. 37), ἑώρταζον αὐτήν, Euthymius Zigabenus. Jesus was already, before this, in the city (ver. 10), but in concealment ; now He goes up *into the temple.* The text does not say that He had only now *come into Jerusalem.* μεσοῦν (comp. Ex. xii. 29 ; Judith xii. 5 ; 3 Macc. v. 14) only here in the N. T., but very common in the classics. That the day was precisely the *Sabbath* of the feast[2] is uncertain, as μεσούσης is only an *approximate* expression. For the rest, the discourses which follow, and the discussions onward to chap. x., are not (with Weizsäcker) to be ranked as parallel with the synoptical accounts of proceedings in Jerusalem, but are wholly independent of them, and must be attributed to the vivid recollections of the evangelist himself regarding a time unnoticed by the Synoptics. Over and above this, we must, as an historical necessity, expect to find many points of resemblance in the several encounters of Jesus with His Jewish opponents.

Ver. 15. Οἱ Ἰουδαῖοι] as in vv. 11, 18. The teaching of Jesus produces a feeling of *astonishment* even in the hierarchy ; but how ? Not through the power of His truth, but because *He is learned without having studied.* And with a question *upon this point,* they engage in conversation with Him, without touching upon *what* He had taught. The *admission,* indeed, which is contained in their question, and that, too, face to face with the people, is only to be explained from the real impression produced upon their learned conceit, so that they ask not in the spirit of shrewd calculation, but from actual amazement. — γράμματα] not *the O. T. Scriptures* (Luther, Grotius, and many), but *literas,* (theological) *knowledge,* which, however, consisted in *scriptural erudition.* Jesus had doubtless exhibited this knowledge *in His discourse by His interpretations of Scripture.*[3] — μὴ μεμαθ.] *though he has not learned them,*[4] perhaps in a Rabbinical school as Paul did from Gamaliel.

---

[1] So also Lücke, de Wette, Ewald, Baeumlein ; not B. Crusius, Brückner, Tholuck, Hengstenberg, Godet.
[2] Harduin, Bengel, Kuinoel, Wieseler, *Synopse,* pp. 309, 329.
[3] Comp Acts xxvi. 24 ; Plato, *Apol.* p. 26

D : οἴει αὐτοὺς ἀπείρους γραμμάτων εἶναι, and the citations in Wetstein. Upon διδάσκειν γράμματα, used of teachers, see Dissen, *ad Dem. de cor.* p. 299.
[4] Buttmann, *N. T. Gk.* p. 301 [E. T. p. 350 f.].

The members of the Sanhedrim do not thus speak in conformity with the author's representation of the Logos (Scholten) ; they *know*, doubtless, from information obtained concerning the course of His life, that Jesus had not studied ; He was reckoned by them among the ἀγράμματοι and ἰδιῶται, Acts iv. 13.   This tells powerfully against all attempts, ancient and modern, to trace back the wisdom of Jesus to some school of human culture.   Well says Bengel : "non usus erat schola ; *character Messiae.*" This *autodidactic* character does not necessarily exclude the supposition that during His childhood and youth He made use of the ordinary popular, and in particular, of the synagogal instruction (Luke ii. 45).[1]

Ver. 16. Jesus at once solves for them the riddle.   "The contradictory relation : that of learning in the case of one who had been uninstructed, would be found in my teaching only if it were *mine*," etc. — ἡ ἐμή and οὐκ ἐ. ἐμή are used in different senses : "the teaching *which I give*," and "it is not *my possession*, but *God's ;*" how far, see ver. 17, comp. v. 19, 30. — τοῦ πέμψ. με] a carefully-chosen designation, because the Sender has communicated to His messenger, and continually communicates what He is to say in His name.[2] — οὐκ . . . ἀλλά] here also not : *non tam . . . quam*, but absolutely excluding human individuality. Comp. viii. 28, xiv. 24.

Ver. 17. *The condition of knowing this* is that *one be willing*—have it as the moral aim of his self-determination—*to do the will of God.*   He who is wanting in this, who lacks fundamentally the moral determination of his mind towards God, and to whom, therefore, Christ's teaching is something strange, for the recognition of which as divine there is in the ungodly bias of his will no point of contact or of sympathy ; this knowledge is to him a moral impossibility.   On the contrary, the bias towards the fulfilling of God's will is the subjective factor necessary to the recognition of divine doctrine as such ; for this doctrine produces the immediate conviction that it is certainly divine by virtue of the moral ὁμοιότης and ὁμοιοπάθεια of its nature with the man's own nature.[3]   See also on iii. 21 and xv. 19.   It is only in form, not in substance, that the τὴν ἀγάπην τ. θεοῦ ἔχειν ἐν ἑαυτῷ, v. 42, differs from the θέλειν τὸ θέλημα τ. θεοῦ ποιεῖν here, for this latter is the moral praxis of the love of God.   Accordingly, we certainly have in this passage the *testimonium internum*, but not in the ordinary theological sense, as a thing for those who already believe, but for those who do not yet believe, and to whom the divine teaching of the Lord presents itself for the first time. — The θέλῃ is not superfluous (Wolf, Loesner, and most), but is the very *nerve* of the relation ; note the "suavis harmonia" (Bengel) between θέλῃ and θέλημα.   The θέλημα αὐτοῦ, however, must not be limited either to a definite *form of the revelation* of it,[4] to any one particular *requirement* (that

[1] Comp. Schleiermacher, *L. J.* p. 120 f., and in particular Keim, *Gesch. J.* I. p. 427 ff.

[2] Bengel (in Wächter in the *Beitr. z. Beng. Schrifterklär.* 1865, p. 125).   "If we may speak after the manner of men, the heavenly Father gives him a *collegium privatissimum*, and that upon *no author.*"

This relation, however, does not justify such one-sided exaggerations as those of Delitzsch, *Jesus u. Hillel*, 1866.

[3] Comp. Aristotle, *Eth.* ix. 3, iii. 1 : τὸ ὅμοιον τοῦ ὁμοίου ἐφίεται.

[4] The O. T., Chrysostom, Euthymius Zigabenus, Bengel, Hengstenberg, Weiss, and most.

of faith in Christ),[1] which would contradict the fact that the axiom is stated without any limitation ; it must be taken in its full breadth and comprehensiveness—"that which God wills," whatever, how, and wherever this will may require. Also the natural moral law within (Rom. i. 20 ff., ii. 14, 15) is not excluded, though those who heard the words spoken must have referred the general statement to the revelation given to *them* in the law and the prophets. Finally, it is clear from vi. 44, 45, viii. 47, that willingness to do God's will must be attributed to the gift and drawing of the Father as its source. — περὶ τῆς διδ.] concerning the teaching now in question, ver. 16. — ἐγὼ ἀπ' ἐμαυτοῦ] *I of myself*, strongly marking the opposite of ἐκ τοῦ θεοῦ. Comp. v. 30. The classical expression πότερον . . . ἤ occurs only here in the N. T.

Ver. 18. Here is the *characteristic proof and token*, given almost in *syllogistic* form, that He *spoke not from Himself*. — τὴν δόξ. τ. ἰδ. ζητ.] that is, among others. Comp. v. 41. — ὁ δὲ ζητῶν, κ.τ.λ.] *minor premiss and* (οὗτος, κ.τ.λ.) *conclusion*, in which, instead of the *negative*, " He speaks not from Himself," we have the *positive*, "the same is true," etc. But this positive conclusion is *logically* correct, both in itself, because ἀφ' ἑαυτοῦ λαλεῖν is throughout the context regarded as something untrue and immoral (Grotius : " sua cogitata proferens, cum Dei mandatum prae se ferat"), and with reference to the hierarchy, and some of the people, who took Jesus to be a *deceiver*. Observe further, that ὁ δὲ ζητῶν, κ.τ.λ., is in the *form* of a *general* proposition, corresponding with the opposite proposition, ὁ ἀφ' ἑαυτοῦ λαλῶν, κ.τ.λ. ; but it is derived exclusively from the relation of *Jesus*, and is descriptive therefore of *no other than He*. — ἀδικία] *improbitas, immorality of nature*, a deeper contrast to ἀληθής than ψεῦδος, for which τινὲς in Euthymius Zigabenus, Grotius, Bengel, B. Crusius, Maier, and many take it,—a view which cannot be justified by the inexact LXX. translation of Job xxxvi. 4 (Ps. lii. 4 ; Theod. Mic. vi. 12). Ἀδικία is the inner (ἐν αὐτῷ) moral basis of the ψεῦδος. For the contrast between ἀλήθεια and ἀδικία, see Rom. i. 18, ii. 8 ; 1 Cor. xiii. 6 ; 2 Thess. ii. 12 ; see also on viii. 46. An allusion to the charge of breaking the Sabbath (Godet) is not indicated, and anticipates what follows, ver. 21.

Ver. 19. There is no ground for supposing that some unrecorded *words* on the part of the Jews (Kuinoel and many others), or some *act* (Olshausen), *intervened* between vv. 18 and 19. The chain of thought is this : Jesus in vv. 16–18 completely answered the question of the Jews, ver. 15. But now He Himself assumes the offensive, putting before them the real and malicious *ground* of all their assaults and oppression, namely, *their purpose to bring about His death ;* and He shows them *how utterly unjustifiable*, on their part, this purpose is. — The note of interrogation ought to be placed (so also Lachm. Tisch.) after the first τὸν νόμον ; and then the declaration of their contradictory behaviour is emphatically introduced by the simple καί. In like manner vi. 70. — οὐ Μωϋσῆς, κ.τ.λ.] The emphasis is upon Μωϋσ. as the great and highly esteemed authority, which had so strong a claim on their

---

[1] Augustine, Luther, Erasmus, Lampe, Ernesti, Storr, Tittmann, Weber, *Opusc.*, and most expositors ; comp. the saying of Augustine, right in itself, *intellectus est* merces *fidei*.

obedience. — τὸν νόμον] *without limitation ;* therefore neither the *command-ment forbidding murder* merely (Nonnus, Storr, Paulus), nor that *against Sabbath-breaking* simply (Kuinoel, Klee. So once Luther also, but in his Commentary he refers to Rom. viii. : "what the law could not do," etc., which, indeed, has no bearing here), which, according to Godet, Jesus must have already in view. — καὶ οὐδεὶς ὑμ. ποιεῖ τ. νόμον] so that you, all of you, are liable to the condemnation of the law ; and should, instead of seeking to destroy me as a law-breaker, confess yourselves to be guilty. — τί] *Why ? i.e. with what right ?* The emphasis cannot be upon the enclitic με (against Godet).

Ver. 20. This interruption, no notice of which, seemingly (but see on ver. 21), is taken by Jesus in His subsequent words, is a characteristic indication of the genuineness of the narrative. — ὁ ὄχλος] *the multitude* (not the same as the Ἰουδαῖοι, see ver. 12), unprejudiced, and unacquainted with the designs of the hierarchy, at least so far as they referred to the death of Christ, consisting for the most part, probably, of pilgrims to the feast. — δαιμόνιον] causing in thee such perverted and wicked suspicions. Comp. viii. 48, x. 20. An expression not of ill-will (Hengstenberg and early writers), but of *amazement,* that a man who taught so admirably should imagine what they deem to be a moral impossibility and a dark delusion. It must, they thought, be a fixed idea put into his mind by some daemon, a κακοδαιμονᾶν.

Vv. 21, 22. Ἀπεκρίθη] The reply of Jesus, not to the Ἰουδαῖοι (Ebrard), but to the ὄχλος (for it is in reality addressed to them, not in appearance merely, and through an inaccurate account of the matter on John's part, as Tholuck unnecessarily assumes), contains, indeed, no direct answer to the question, but is intended to make the people feel that *all* had a guilty part in the murderous designs against Him, and that none of them are excepted, because that one work which He had done among them was unacceptable to *them all,* and had excited their unrighteous wrath. Thus He deprives the people of that assurance of their own innocence which had prompted them to put the question to Him ; " ostendit se profundius eos nôsse et hoc radio eos penetrat," Bengel. — ἐν ἔργον] *i.e.* the healing on the Sabbath, v. 2 ff., the only miraculous work *which He had done in Jerusalem* (against Weisse [1]) (not, indeed, the only work at all, see ii. 23, comp. also x. 32, but the only one during the last visit), for the remembrance of which the fact of its being so striking an instance of Sabbath-breaking would suffice. — καὶ πάντες θαυμάζετε] πάντες is correlative with ἐν, " and ye *all* wonder" (Acts iii. 12), *i.e.* how I could have done it as a *Sabbath work* (v. 16) ; it is the object of your *universal astonishment ! An exclamation ;* taken as a question (Ewald), the expression of disapprobation which it contains would be less emphatic. To put into θαυμάζετε the idea of *alarm* (Chrysostom), of *blame* (Nonnus), of *displeasure* (Grotius), or the like, would be to anticipate ; the bitterness of tone does not appear till ver. 23. — διὰ τοῦτο] connected with θαυμάζετε by

---

[1] How does he make out the ἐν ἔργον ? It is the one miracle which Christ came to accomplish (Matt. xii. 28, xvi. 1 sqq. ; Luke xi. 29 ff.), described by Him metaphorically as a Sabbath healing ; this the evangelist has taken for a single miraculous act. See *Evangelienfr.* p. 249.

Theophylact, and most moderns ;[1] but Syr. Goth. Codd. It., Cyril, Chrysostom, Nonnus, Euthymius Zigabenus, Luther, Castalio, Erasmus, Aretius, Grotius, Cornelius à Lapide, Jansen, Bengel, Wetstein, and several others, also Luthardt, and most of the Codices, with true perception, place the words at the beginning of ver. 22 (so also Elzevir); for, joined with θαυμάζετε, they are cumbrous and superfluous,[2] and contrary to John's method elsewhere of beginning, not ending, with διὰ τοῦτο.[3] Only we must not take them either as *superfluous* (Euthymius Zigabenus) or as *elliptical:* "therefore *hear*," or "*know*;"[4] the former is inadmissible, the latter is neither Johannean nor in keeping with what follows, which does not contain a declaration, but a deduction of a logical kind. We ought rather, with Bengel ("*propterea*, hoc mox declaratur per οὐχ ὅτι, *nempe non quia*") and Luthardt, following Cyril, to regard them as standing in connection with the following οὐχ ὅτι. With this anticipatory διὰ τοῦτο, Jesus begins to diminish the astonishment which His healing on the Sabbath had awakened, showing it to be *unreasonable*, and this by the *analogy of circumcision*, which is performed also on the Sabbath. Instead of simply saying, "*because it comes from the fathers*," He puts the main statement, already introduced by διὰ τοῦτο, and so important in the argument, both *negatively* and *positively*, and says, "*Therefore* Moses gave you circumcision, *not because it originated with Moses, but (because it originated) with the fathers*, and so ye circumcise" (καί consecutive), etc.; that is, this οὐχ ὅτι, on to πατέρων, serves to show that circumcision, though divinely commanded by Moses in the law, and thus given to the Jews as a ritualistic observance, was not Mosaic in its origin, but was an *old patriarchal* institution dating back even from Abraham. The basis of its historic claim to validity lies in the fact that the law of circumcision *precedes* the law of the Sabbath, and consequently the enjoined rest of the Sabbath must *give way* to circumcision.[5] Even the Rabbins had this axiom : "*Circumcisio pellit sabbatum*," and based it upon the fact that it was "*traditio patrum*." See Wetstein on ver. 23. The anger of the people on account of the *healing* on the Sabbath rested on a false *estimate* of the Sabbath ; comp. Matt. xii. 5. From this explanation it is at the same time clear that οὐχ ὅτι . . . πατέρων is not of the nature of a parenthesis (so usually, also Lachmann). Of those

[1] Also Lücke, Tholuck, Olshausen, de Wette, B. Crusius, Maier, Lange, Lachmann, Hengstenberg, Ewald, Baeumlein, Ebrard, Godet ; among earlier expositors, Beza, Casaubon, Homberg, Maldonatus, Wolf, Mill, Kypke, etc. ; see on Mark vi. 6.

[2] This accounts for the omission of διὰ τοῦτο in ℵ*. Tisch. deletes it, and with ℵ* reads ὁ Μωϋσ. (with the article).

[3] V. 16, 18, vi. 65, viii. 47, x. 17, *al. ;* see Schulz on *Griesbach*, p. 543.

[4] Grotius, Jansen, also Winer, p. 58 [E. T. p. 59].

[5] The patriarchal period was indeed that of *promise*, but this is not *made prominent*

here, and we cannot therefore say with Luthardt : "Jesus puts the law and the promise over against one another, like Paul in Gal. iii. 17." There is no hint of this in the text. Judging from the text, there rather lies in οὐχ ὅτι, κ.τ.λ., the proof that, in the case of a collision between the two laws, that of circumcision and that of the Sabbath, the former must have the precedence, because, though enjoined by *Moses*, it already had a *patriarchal* origin, and on account of this older sanctity it must suffer no infringement through the law of the Sabbath. Nonnus well describes the argumentation by the words ἀρχεγόνῳ τινὶ θεσμῷ.

who so regard it, some rightly recognize in the words the authority of circumcision as *outweighing* that of the Sabbath ; while others, against the context, infer from them its *lesser sanctity* as being a traditional institution (Paulus, B. Crusius, Ewald, Godet). Others, again, take them as an (objectless) *correction* (de Wette, Baeumlein), or as an *historical* observation (equally superfluous) of Jesus (Tholuck, Hengstenberg, and earlier expositors) or of John (Lücke, cf. Ebrard). Above all, it would have been very strange and paltry to suppose (with Hengstenberg) that Jesus by this remark was endeavouring, with reference to ver. 15, to do away with the *appearance of ignorance.* — Μωϋσῆς] Lev. xii. 3. — οὐχ ὅτι] not as in vi. 46, but as in xii. 6. — ἐκ τοῦ Μωϋσέως] Instead of saying ἐξ αὐτοῦ, Jesus repeats the *name*, thus giving more emphasis to the thought. See Kühner, *ad Xen. Mem.* i. 6. 1, *ad Anab.* i. 6. 11. — ἐκ τῶν πατέρων] Gen. xvii. 10, xxi. 4 ; Acts vii. 8 ; Rom. iv. 11. — ἐν Σαββ.] if it be the eighth day. Comp. the Rabbinical quotations in Lightfoot. Being emphatic, it takes the lead.

Ver. 23. Περιτομήν] *Circumcision*, without the article, but placed emphatically first, corresponding with ὅλον ἄνθρωπον in the apodosis. — ἵνα μὴ λυθῇ, κ.τ.λ.] in order *that so the law of Moses be not broken* (by the postponement of the rite), seeing that it prescribes circumcision upon the eighth day. Jansen, Bengel, Semler, Paulus, Kuinoel, Klee, Baeumlein, wrongly render ἵνα μή " *without,*" and take ὁ νόμ. Μωϋσ. to mean the *law of the Sabbath.* — ἐμοὶ χολᾶτε] towards me how unjust ! Χολᾶν, denoting *bitter*, violent anger (only here in the N. T.)[1] — ὅτι ὅλον ἄνθρ. ὑγ. ἐπ. ἐν σαββ.] The emphasis of the antithesis is on ὅλον ἄνθρ., in contrast with the *single member* in the case of circumcision. We must not, therefore, with Kling,[2] find here the antithesis between *wounding* and *making whole;* nor, with B. Crusius, that between an act for the *sake of the law*, on account of which circumcision was performed, and one for the sake of the *man himself;* similarly Grotius. In ὑγ. ἐποίησα, further, there must necessarily be expressed an analogy with what is done in circumcision, which is therefore equally regarded as a *cure* and a *healing*, not with reference to the subsequent *healing of the wound* (Cyril, Lampe), for περιτ. is circumcision itself, not its healing ; nor with reference to the supposed *medical object* of circumcision,[3] no trace of which was contained either in the law or in the religious ideas of the people ; but with reference to the *purification* and sanctification wrought upon the member by the removal of the foreskin.[4] In this theocratic sense, a single *member* was made *whole* by circumcision ; but Christ, by healing the paralytic, had made *an entire man* whole, *i.e. the whole body* of a man. The argument in justification, accordingly, is one *a minori ad majus;* if it was right not to omit the lesser work on the Sabbath, how much more the greater and more

[1] Comp. 3 Macc. iii. 1 ; Artemid. i. 4 ; Beck, *Anecd.* p. 116.

[2] *Stud. u. Krit.* 1836, p. 157 f.,

[3] Rosenmüller, Kuinoel, Lücke, Lange ; comp. Philo, *de Circumcis.* II. 210 f. ; see, on the contrary, Keil, *Archaeol.* I. 309 f.

[4] Comp. Bammidbar, R. xii. f. 203. 2: "praeputium est vitium in corpore." With this view, which regards the foreskin as impure,—a view which does not appear till a late date (Ewald, *Alterth.* p. 129 f.),—corresponds the idea of the circumcision of the *heart*, which we find in Lev. xxvi. 41, Deut. x. 16, xxx. 6, and often in the prophets and the N. T., Rom. ii. 29, Col. ii. 11, Acts vii. 51.

important! To take ὅλον ἄνθρ., with Euthymius Zigabenus 2, Beza, Cornelius à Lapide, Bengel, and Olshausen, as signifying body *and soul*, in contrast with the σάρξ, on which circumcision was performed, is alien to the connection, which shows that the Sabbath question had to do only with the *bodily* healing, and to the account of the miracle itself, according to which Jesus only *warned* the man who had been made whole, v. 14.

Ver. 24. This closing admonition is *general*, applicable to every case that might arise, but drawn by way of deduction from the special one in point. *According to the outward appearance*, that act was certainly, in the Jewish judgment, a breach of the Sabbath ; but *the righteous judgment* was that to which Jesus had now conducted them.[1] It does not here mean *visage*, as in xi. 44, and as Hengstenberg makes it, who introduces the contrast between *Christ* " without form or comeliness," and the shining countenance of *Moses*.[2]

Vv. 25–27. Οὖν] in consequence of this bold vindication. These Ἱεροσο-λυμῖται, as distinct from the uninitiated ὄχλος of ver. 20, as inhabitants of the Holy City, have better knowledge of the mind of the hierarchical opposition ; they wonder that the Sanhedrim should let Him speak so boldly and freely, and they ask, "*The rulers have not perchance really ascertained, have they, that this,*" etc. ? This, however, is only a momentary thought which strikes them, and they at once answer it themselves. — πόθεν ἐστίν] does not denote the *birthplace*, which was known both in the case of Jesus (ver. 41) and of the Messiah (ver. 42), but the *descent ;* not, indeed, the *more remote*, which in the case of the Messiah was undoubted as being *Davidic*, but (comp. vi. 42) the *nearer* — father, mother, family (Matt. xiii. 55).[3] — ὁ δὲ Χρι.] is in antithesis with τοῦτον, and it therefore takes the lead. The popular belief that the immediate ancestry of the Messiah would be unknown when He came, cannot further be historically proved, but is credible, partly from the belief in His divine origin,[4] and partly from the obscurity into which the Davidic family had sunk, and was supported, probably, by the import of many O. T. passages, such as Isa. liii. 2, 8, Mic. v. 2, and perhaps also by the sudden appearance of the Son of man related in Dan. vii. (Tholuck), and is strongly confirmed by the description in the book of Enoch of the heavenly Messiah appearing from heaven (Ewald). The passages which Lücke and de Wette quote from Justin[5] are inapplicable, as they do not speak of an unknown *descent* of the Messiah, but intimate that, previous to His anointing by Elijah, His Messiahship was unknown to Himself and others. The beginning of Marcion's Gospel (see Philo, p. 403), and the Rabbinical passages in Lightfoot and Wetstein, are equally inapplicable.

Vv. 28, 29. The statement in ver. 27, which showed how utterly Christ's higher nature and work were misunderstood by these people in consequence of the entirely outward character of their judgments, roused the emotion of

---

[1] Upon ὄψις *id quod sub visum cadit, res in conspicuo posita*, see Lobeck, *Paralip.* p. 512.

[2] On κρίνειν κρίσιν δικαίαν, comp. Tobit iii. 2 ; Susannah 53 ; Zech. vii. 9.

[3] Comp. xix. 9 ; Homer, *Od.* ρ. 373 : αὐτὸν δ᾽ οὐ σάφα οἶδα, πόθεν γένος εὔχεται εἶναι ; Soph. *Trach.* 1006 ; Eur. *Rhes.* 702 ; Heliod. iv. 16, vii. 14.

[4] Bertholdt, *Christol.* p. 86.

[5] *c. Tryph.* pp. 226, 268, 336, ed. Col.

THE GOSPEL OF JOHN.

Jesus, so that He raised His voice, *crying aloud*,[1] and thus uttered the solemn conclusion of this colloquy, while He taught in the temple, and said : κἀμὲ οἴδατε, κ.τ.λ. The ἐν τῷ ἱερῷ διδάσκων is in itself unneeded (see ver. 14), but serves the *more vividly to describe* the solemn moment of the ἔκραξεν, and is an indication of the *original genuineness* of the narrative. — κἀμὲ οἴδατε, κ.τ.λ.] *i.e.*, "*ye know not only my person, but ye also know my origin.*" As the people really had this knowledge (vi. 42), and as the divine mission of Jesus was independent of His human nature and origin, while He himself denies only their knowledge of His divine mission (see what follows ; comp. viii. 19), there is nothing in the connection to sanction an *interrogatory* interpretation,[2] nor an *ironical* one,[3] nor the paraphrase : "Ye *think* that ye know" (Hengstenberg). Least of all can we read it as a *reproach*, that they knew His *divine* nature and origin, yet maliciously*concealed it.*[4] No ; Jesus *allows* that they have that outward knowledge of Him which they had avowed in ver. 27, but He further—in the words καὶ ἀπ' ἐμαυτοῦ, κ.τ.λ.—sets before them the *higher* relationship, which is here the main point, and which was *unknown* to them. — καὶ ἀπ' ἐμ. οὐκ ἐλήλ.] *and*—though ye think that, on account of this knowledge of yours, ye must conclude that I am not the Messiah, but have come by self-appointment merely—*of myself* (αὐτοκέλευστος, Nonnus) *am I not come ;* comp. viii. 42. This καί, which must not be regarded as the same with the two preceding, as if it stood for καὶ ὅτι (Baeumlein), often in John connects, like *atque*, a *contrasted* thought, *and yet.*[5] We may pronounce the *and* with emphasis, and imagine a pause after it.[6]— ἀλλ' ἔστιν ἀληθινός] *but it is a real one who hath sent me, whom ye* (ye people !) *know not.*[7] Ἀληθινός is not *verax*,[8] but, according to the invariable usage of John (see on i. 9), a real, genuine one, in whom *the idea is realized.* The substantive belonging to this adjective is not πατήρ, which Grotius gets out of πόθεν ; but, according to the immediate context, it is to be taken from ὁ πέμψας με, namely πέμπων, *a real sender*, a sender *in the highest and fullest sense.*[9] We cannot take ἀληθ. by itself as *absolutely* denoting the *true essential* God (Olshausen, Lange, Hengstenberg ; comp. Kling : "one who whose essence and action is pure truth"), because ἀληθινός in the Johannean sense is not an independent conception, but receives its definite meaning from the substantive of which it is predicated. — Ver. 29. *I* (antithesis to ὑμεῖς) *know*

---

[1] ἔκραξεν, comp. i. 15, vii. 37, xii. 44, Rom. ix. 27 ; κράζειν never means anything but *to cry out ; "clamores*, quos edidit, magnas habuere causas," Bengel.

[2] Grotius, Lampe, Semler, Storr, Paulus, Kuinoel, Luthardt, Ewald.

[3] Luther, Calvin, Beza, and many others ; likewise Lücke, Tholuck, Olshausen, B. Crusius, Lange, and Godet who considers the words "*légèrement ironique*," and that they have "*certainement* [?] *une tournure interrogative.*"

[4] Chrysostom, Nonnus, Theophylact, Euthymius Zigabenus, Maldonatus, and most.

[5] See Hartung, *Partikell.* I. 147.

[6] Comp. Stallbaum, *ad Plat. Apol.* p. 29 B ; Wolf, *ad Leptin.* p. 238.

[7] Of course in *a relative* sense, as in iv. 22. If they had possessed the true and full knowledge of God, they would then have recognized the Interpreter of God, and not have rejected Him for such a reason as that in ver. 27. Comp. viii. 54, 55 ; Matt. xi. 27.

[8] Chrysostom, Euthymius Zigabenus, Luther, Stolz, Kuinoel, Klee, B. Crusius, Ewald, and most.

[9] Comp. Matthiae, p. 1533 ; Kühner, II. 602.

Him, for I am from Him, have come forth from Him (as in vi. 46) ; *and* no other than *He* (from whom I am) *hath sent me.* This weighty, and therefore independent κἀκεῖνός με ἀπέστ., not to be taken as dependent upon ὅτι, comprehends the full explanation of the πόθεν εἰμί in its higher sense, which was not known to the Ἱεροσολυμίταις, and, with the ἐγὼ οἶδα . . . εἰμί, bears the seal of immediate certainty. Comp. viii. 14.

Ver. 30. Οὖν] Because He had so decidedly asserted His divine origin and mission, which His adversaries regarded as blasphemy (comp. v. 18).— The *subject* of ἐζήτουν is Ἰουδαῖοι, the hierarchy, as is self-evident from the words and from the contrasted statement of ver. 31. — καί] as in ver. 28. — ὅτι οὔπω, κ.τ.λ.] *because the hour appointed for Him* (by God—the hour when He was to fall under the power of His enemies) *was not yet come ;* comp. viii. 20. The reason here assigned is that higher religious apprehension of the history, which does not, however, contradict or exclude the immediate historical cause, viz. that through fear—not of conscience (Hengstenberg, Godet), but of the party who were favourably inclined to Christ, ver. 31— they dared not yet lay hands on Him. But John knows that the threads upon which the outward history of Jesus runs, and by which it is guided, unite in the counsels of God. Comp. Luthardt, I. 160.

Ver. 31. According to the reading ἐκ τοῦ ὄχλου δὲ πολλοί (see the critical notes), ὄχλος stands emphatically opposed to the subjects of ἐζήτουν in ver. 30. Δέ after three words, on account of their close connection ; see Klotz, *ad Devar.* p. 378 ; Ellendt, *Lex. Soph.* I. 397. — ἐπίστ. εἰς αὐτ.] not only as a *prophet* (Tholuck), or as one *sent of God* (Grotius), but conformably with the fixed sense of the absolute expression (comp. ver. 5), *as the Messiah.* What follows does not contradict this, but rather sustains their avowal that they see realized in Jesus their Ideal-Miraculous of the promised Messiah ; and, accordingly, ὁ Χριστὸς ὅταν ἔλθῃ does not imply any doubt on *their* part as to the Messiahship of Jesus, but refers to the doubt of the *opposite party.* Comp. Euthymius Zigabenus 2 : θῶμεν, ἕτερον εἶναι τὸν Χριστόν, ὡς οἱ ἄρχοντες λέγουσιν, etc. — ὅτι] might be regarded as *giving the reason* for their faith (Nonnus : μὴ γὰρ Χριστός, κ.τ.λ.), but more simply as *recitative.* — μή] *"he will not do more signs, will he?* = *will he do more signs?* To the one miracle wrought in Jerusalem (ver. 21) they added the numerous Galilean miracles, which they, being in part perhaps pilgrims to the feast from Galilee, had seen and heard.

Vv. 32–34. The Pharisees present hear how favourable are the murmured remarks of the people concerning Jesus, and they straightway obtain an edict of the Sanhedrim (οἱ Φαρισ. κ. οἱ ἀρχιερ.,—οἱ Φαρισ. *first,* for they had been the first to moot the matter ; otherwise in ver. 45), appointing officers to lay hands on Him. The Sanhedrim must have been immediately assembled. Thus rapidly did the ἐζήτουν of ver. 30 ripen into an actual decree of the council. The thing does not escape the notice of Jesus ; He naturally recognizes in the officers seeking Him, who were only waiting for a suitable opportunity to arrest Him, their designs against Him ; and He therefore (οὖν) says what we have in vv. 33, 34 in clear and calm foresight of the nearness of His death,—a death which He describes as a going away to God

(comp. on vi. 62). — μεθ᾽ ὑμῶν] Jesus speaks to the whole assembly, but has
here the hierarchy chiefly in his eye ; comp. ver. 35. — πρὸς τὸν πέμψαντά με]
These words are, with Paulus, to be regarded not as original, but as a
Johannean addition ; because, according to vv. 35, 36, Jesus cannot have
definitely indicated the *goal* of His going away, but must have left it enigmatical, as perhaps in viii. 22 ; comp. xiii. 33. Had He said πρ. τ. πέμψ.,
His enemies could not have failed, after vv. 16, 17, 28, 29, to recognize the
words as referring to God, and could not have thought of an unknown ποῦ
(against Lücke, de Wette, Godet), There is no room even for the *pretence*
"that they acted as if they *could* not understand the words of Jesus," after
so clear a statement as πρὸς τ. πέμψ. με (against Luthardt). — ζητήσετέ με,
κ.τ.λ.] not of a *hostile* seeking, against which is xiii. 33 ; nor the seeking of
the *penitent* (Augustine, Beza, Jansen, and most), which would not harmonize (against Olshausen) with the absolute denial of any finding, unless
we brought in the doctrine of a peremptory limitation of grace, which has
no foundation in Holy Scripture (also not in Heb. xii. 17 ; see Lünemann,
in loc.), and which could only refer to individuals ; but a *seeking for help and
deliverance.*[1] This refers to the time of the divine judgments in the destruction of Jerusalem (Luke xx. 16 ff., xix. 43, *al.*), which were to ensue as the
result of their rejection of Jesus. Then, Jesus would say, the tables will
be turned ; after they had persecuted and killed Him who now was present,
they then would anxiously long, but in vain, for Him, the absent One,[2] as
the wonder-working helper, who alone could save them from the dire calam-
ity. Comp. Prov. i. 28. The prophecy of misfortune involved in ζητήσετέ
με, κ.τ.λ. is not expressly declared ; but it lies in the thought of *retribution*
which the words contain, — like an enigma which history was to solve ;
comp. viii. 21. Theodoret, Heracleon (?), Maldonatus, Grotius, Lücke,
de Wette, take the whole simply as descriptive of *entire separation*, so that
nothing more is said than : *Christum de terris sublatum iri, ita ut inter viros
reperiri non possit*," Maldonatus. The poetical passages, Ps. x. 15, xxxvii.
10, Isa. xli. 12, are appealed to. But even in these the seeking and finding
is not a mere figure of speech ; and here such a weakening of the signification is all the more inadmissible, because it is not *annihilation*, as in those
passages, which is here depicted, and because the following words, καὶ ὅπου
εἰμὶ ἐγώ, κ.τ.λ., describe a *longing* which was not to be satisfied. Luke xvii.
22 is analogous. — καὶ ὅπου εἰμί, κ.τ.λ.] still more clearly describes the tragic
οὐχ εὑρήσ. : "and where *I* (then) am, thither *ye* cannot come," *i.e.* in order
to find me as a deliverer, or to flee to me. Rightly says Euthymius Ziagabenus : δηλοῖ δὲ τὴν ἐπὶ τοῦ οὐρανοῦ ἐν δεξιᾷ τοῦ πατρὸς καθέδραν. The εἰμι (*I go*),
not found in the N. T., is not the reading here.[3] Comp. xiv. 3, xvii. 24.

---

[1] Chrysostom, Theophylact, Euthymius
Zigabenus, Erasmus, Calvin, Aretius,
Hengstenberg; comp. Luthardt, Ewald,
Brückner.

[2] They would long for Him in His own
person, for *Jesus* the rejected one, and not
for the *Messiah generally* (Flacius, Lampe,
Kuinoel, Neander. Ebrard), whom they had

rejected in the person of Jesus (comp.
also Tholuck and Godet),—an explanation
which would empty the words of all their
tragic nerve and force.

[3] Against Nonnus, H. Stephens, Casaubon, Pearson, Bengel, Wakefield, Michaelis,
and most.

Vv. 35, 36. An insolent and scornful conjecture, which they themselves, however, do not deem probable (therefore the question is asked with μή), regarding the meaning of words to them so utterly enigmatical. The bolder mode of teaching adopted by Jesus, His universalistic declarations, His partial non-observance of the law of the Sabbath, would lead them, perhaps, to associate with the unintelligible statement a mocking thought like this, and all the more because much interest was felt among the heathen, partly of an earnest kind, and partly (comp. St. Paul in Athens) arising from curiosity merely, regarding the oriental religions, especially Judaism.[1] — πρὸς ἑαυτούς] the same as πρὸς ἀλλήλους, yet so that the conversation was confined to one party among the people, to the exclusion of the others.[2] — οὗτος] contemptuously, *this man!* — ὅτι] not to be arbitrarily supplemented by a supposed λέγων put before it, or in some other way ;[3] but the simple *because :* " Where will this man go, because, or seeing, that *we* are not (according to his words) to find him ?" It states the *reason* why the ποῦ is *unknown*. — εἰς τ. διασπ. τ. Ἑλλ.] *to the dispersion among the Greeks.*[4] The *subjects* of the διασπορά are the *Jews*,[5] who lived beyond Palestine dispersed *among the heathen*, and these latter are denoted by the genitive τῶν Ἑλλήν. Comp. 1 Pet. i. 1, and Steiger and Huther thereon. Differently in 2 Macc. i. 27 ; LXX. Ps. cxlvi. 2. The *abstract* διασπορά is simply the sum-total of the concretes, like περιτομή and other words. See 2 Macc. i. 27. Ἕλληνες in the N. T. invariably means the *heathen*, Gentiles, not the Hellenists (Grecian Jews), so also in xii. 20 ; it is wrong, therefore, to understand τῶν Ἑλλήν. of *the latter*, and take these words as the subject of the διασπορά (Scaliger, Lightfoot, Hammond, B. Crusius, Ammon), and render διδάσκ. τ. Ἑλλ. : "teach the *Hellenists*." The thought is rather : " Will Jesus go to the Jews scattered among the Gentiles, to unite there with the *Gentiles*, and become their teacher ?" This was really the course of the subsequent labours of the apostles. — Ver. 36. τίς ἐστιν] Their scornful conjecture does not even satisfy themselves ; for that they should *seek Him*, and *not be able to come to Him*— they know not what the assertion can mean (τίς ἐστιν, κ.τ.λ.).

Ver. 37. As the *eighth* day (the 22d Tisri) was reckoned along with the seven feast days proper, according to Lev. xxiii. 35, 36, 39, Num. xxix. 35, Neh. viii. 18, as also according to *Succah*, f. 48. 1, the *last* day of the feast is the *eighth*, it is clear that John meant *this* day, and not the *seventh*,[6] especially as in later times it was usual to speak of the *eight* days' feast of Tabernacles.[7] In keeping with this is the very free translation ἐξόδιον (*termination of the feast*), which the LXX. give for the name of the eighth day, עֲצֶרֶת (Lev. xxiii. 36 ; Num. xxix. 35 ; Neh. viii. 18), *i.e.* "*assembly.*"[8] — τῇ μεγάλῃ] *the*

---

[1] See Ewald, *Gesch. Chr.* p. 110 f. ed. 3.

[2] See Kühner, *ad Xen. Mem.* ii. 6. 20.

[3] Buttmann, *N. T. Gr.* p. 305 [E. T. p. 358].

[4] Comp. Winer, p. 176 [E. T. p. 187] ; and upon the thing referred to, Schneckenburger, *N. T. Zeitgesch.* p. 94 ff.

[5] Not the *heathen*, as if ἡ διασπ. τ. Ἑλλ. were the same as *Dispersi Graeci* (Chrysostom and his followers, Rupertius, Maldon-

atus, Hengstenberg, and most). Against this Beza well says : " Vix conveniret ipsis indigenis populis nomen διασπορᾶς."

[6] Theophylact, Buxtorf, Bengel, Reland, Paulus, Ammon.

[7] 2 Macc. x. 6 ; Josephus, *Antt.* iii. 10. 4 ; *Gem. Eruvin.* 40. 2 ; *Midr. Cohel.* 118. 3.

[8] Comp. Ewald, *Alterth.* p. 481.

(pre-eminently) *great*, solemn.   Comp. xix. 31.   The superlative is implied
in the attribute thus given to this day above the other feast days.   Wherein
consisted the special distinction attaching to this day ?   It was simply the
great closing day of the feast, appointed for the solemn return from the
booths into the temple,[1] and, according to Lev. xxiii. 35, 36, was kept holy
as a Sabbath.   The explanation of ἐξόδιον in Philo,[2] as denoting the end of
the yearly feasts collectively, has as little to do with the matter (for τῇ μεγάλῃ
has reference only to the feast of Tabernacles) as has the designation יוֹם טוֹב
in the Tr. *Succah*, for this means nothing more than "*feast day.*"   This day
had, indeed, according to Tr. *Succah*,[3] special services, sacrifices, songs, yet
no more was required than to honour it "sicut reliquos dies festi."   Its
μεγαλότης consisted just in this, that it brought the great feast as a whole to
a sacred termination. — The *express designation* of the day as τῇ μεγάλῃ is in
keeping with the solemn coming forth of Jesus with the great word of invitation and promise, vv. 37, 38.   The solemnity of this coming forth is also
intimated in εἱστήκει (*He stood there*) and in ἔκραξε (see on ver. 28). — ἐάν τις
διψᾷ, κ.τ.λ.] denoting spiritual need[4] and spiritual satisfaction, as in iv. 15,
in the conversation with the Samaritan woman, and in vi. 35 ; Matt. v. 6.
We are not told what led Jesus here to *this metaphorical* expression.   There
needed nothing special to prompt Him to do so, least of all at a feast so
joyous, according to Plutarch, *Symp.* iv. 6. 2, even so bacchanalian in its
banquetings.   A reason for the expression has been usually found in the
daily *libations* which were offered on the seven feast days (but also on the
eighth, according to R. Juda, in *Succah* iv. 9), at the time of the morning
sacrifice, when a priest fetched water in a golden pitcher containing three
logs from the spring of Siloam, and poured this, together with wine, on
the west side of the altar into two perforated vessels, amidst hymns of praise
and music.[5]   Some reference to this libation may be supposed, because it was
one of the *peculiarities* of the feast, even on the hypothesis that it did *not*
take place upon the eighth day, whether springing from the old idea of
libations with water ;[6] or, according to the Rabbis (so also Hengstenberg),
from Isa. xii. 3, a passage which contains the words sung by the people
during the libation.   But any connection of the words of Jesus with this
libation is doubtful, because He speaks of *drinking*, and this is the *essential*
element of His declaration.   Godet arbitrarily interpolates : "He compares
Himself with the *water from the rock in the wilderness*, and represents Himself
as *this true* rock" (comp. 1 Cor. x. 4).

Ver. 38. The πίνειν is brought about by faith ; hence the continued
statement *: ὁ πιστεύων, κ.τ.λ. — καθὼς εἶπεν ἡ γρ.*] is simply the formula of
quotation, and cannot belong to ὁ πιστεύων εἰς ἐμέ, as if denoting a faith
conformable to Scripture ;[7] ὁ πιστ., on the contrary, is the nominative absolute

---

[1] **Ewald**, *Alterth.* p. 481.
[2] *de Septenario*, II. p. 298.
[3] See Lightfoot, p. 1032 f.
[4] **Luther**: "a heartfelt longing, yea, a
troubled, sad, awakened, stricken conscience, a despairing, trembling heart, that

would know how it can be with God."
[5] See Dachs, *Succah*, p. 368.
[6] 1 Sam. vii. 6 ; Hom. *Od.* μ. 362, *al.*, so de
Wette.
[7] Chrysostom, Theophylact, **Euthymius**
Zigabenus, Calovius, and most.

(see on vi. 39), and καθὼς εἶπεν, κ.τ.λ., belongs to the following ποταμοί, etc., the words which are described as a *declaration of Scripture*. There is no exactly corresponding passage, indeed, in Scripture ; it is simply a free quotation harmonizing in thought with parts of various passages, especially Isa. xliv. 3, lv. 1, lviii. 11.[1] Godet refers to the account of the rock in the wilderness, Ex. xvii. 6, Num. xx. 11 ; but this answers neither to the thing itself (for the subject is the person drinking) nor to the words. To think in particular of those passages which make mention of a stream flowing from the temple mount, the believer being represented as a living temple (Olshausen), is a gloss unwarranted by the context, and presents an inappropriate comparison (κοιλίας). This last is also in answer to Gieseler,[2] whom Lange[3] follows. To imagine some *apocryphal* or lost canonical saying,[4] or, with Ewald, a fragment of Proverbs no longer extant, or of some similar book, is bold and unnecessary, considering the freedom with which passages of Scripture are quoted and combined, and the absence of any other certain trace in the discourses of Jesus of extra-canonical quotations, or of canonical quotations not now found in the O. T. ; although, indeed, the characteristic ἐκ τῆς κοιλίας αὐτοῦ itself occurs in none of the above-named places, which is certainly surprising, and not to be explained by an inappropriate reference to Cant. vii. 3 (Hengstenberg). But the expression, *" out of his body,"* considering the connection of the metaphor, is very natural ; the water which he drinks becomes in his body a spring from which streams of living water flow, *i.e. the divine grace and truth which the believer has received out of Christ's fulness into his inner life, does not remain shut up within, but will communicate itself in abundant measure as a life-giving stream to others,* and thus the new divine life overflows from one individual on to others. As represented in the metaphor, these ποταμοί take their rise from the water which has been drunk, and is *in* the κοιλία, and flow forth from it in an *oral* effusion ;[5] for the effect referred to takes place in an outward direction *by* an inspired *oral* communication of one's own experience of God's grace and truth.[6] The mutual and inspired intercourse of Christians from Pentecost downwards, the speaking in psalms and hymns and spiritual songs, the mutual edification in Christian assemblies by means of the charismata even to the speaking with tongues, the entire work of the apostles, of a Stephen and so on, furnish an abundant historical commentary upon this text. It is clear, accordingly, that κοιλία does not, as is *usually* supposed, denote the *inner* man, man's *heart*,[7] but must be left in its literal meaning *" belly,"* in conformity with the *metaphor* which determines the expression.[8] The flowing forth of the water, moreover, is not to be un-

---

[1] Comp. also Ezek. xlvii. 1, 12, Zech. xiii. 1, xiv. 8; Joel iii. 1, 23 ; but not Cant. iv. 12, 15.

[2] *Stud. u. Krit.* 1829, p. 138 f.

[3] *L. J.* II. p. 945.

[4] Whiston, Semler, Paulus; comp. also Weizsäcker, p. 518 ; Bleek, p. 234, and in the *Stud. u. Krit.* 1853, p. 331.

[5] Comp. ἐρεύξομαι, Matt. xiii. 35.

[6] πιστεύομεν, διὸ καὶ λαλοῦμεν, 2 Cor. iv. 13.

[7] Prov. xx. 27 ; Ecclus. xix. 12, li. 21 ; LXX. Ps. xl. 9, following A. ; comp. the Latin *viscera*.

[8] Already Chrysostom and his followers took κοιλίας as equivalent to καρδίας ; a confounding of the metaphor with its import. Hofmann's objection (*Schriftbew.* II. 2, p. 13), "that the water here meant

derstood as something operating upon the *subject himself* only (B. Crusius : "his whole soul, from its very depth, shall have a continual quickening and satisfaction," comp. Maier), but, as shown by ἐκ τ. κοιλ., as describing an efficacy *in an outward direction*, and therefore is not the same as the kindred utterance, chap. iv. 14. If we join ὁ πιστ. εἰς ἐμέ with πινέτω, αὐτοῦ must refer to Christ ; and this is the meaning that we get : "He that thirsteth, let him come to me ; and he that believeth in me, let him drink of me : for to me refers what the Scripture hath said concerning a river which shall flow forth from Jehovah in the time of the Messiah."[1] But against this it is decisive, first, that he who believes on Jesus *has* already *drunk* of Him (vi. 35), and the call to come and drink must apply not to the believer, but to the thirsty ; and secondly, that the expression ἐκ τῆς κοιλίας αὐτοῦ would be unnecessary and unmeaning, if it referred to Jesus, and not to *him* who has performed the πινέτω.[2] — ὕδωρ ζῶν, as in iv. 10 ; ζῶντος δέ, ἤγουν ἀεὶ ἐνεργοῦντος ἀεικνήτου, Euthymius Zigabenus.—Observe further the ποταμοί emphatically taking the lead and standing apart ; "not in spoonfuls, nor with a pipe and tap, but in full streams," Luther.

Ver. 39. Not an interpolated gloss (Scholten), but an observation by John in explanation of this saying. He shows that Jesus meant that the outward effect of which He spoke, the flowing forth, was not at once to occur, but was to commence upon the *reception of the Spirit after His glorification.* *He*,—evidently, and, according to the οὗ ἔμελλον, undoubtedly meaning the *Holy* Spirit,—He it was who would cause the streams of living water to flow forth from them. John's explanation, as proceeding from inmost experience, is *correct*, because the principle of Christian activity in the church, especially in its outward workings, is none other than the Holy Spirit Himself ; and He was not given until after the Ascension, when through Him the believers spoke with tongues and prophesied, the apostles preached, and so on. Such overflowings of faith's power in its outward working did not previously take place. The objection urged against the accuracy of John's explanation, that ῥεύσουσιν is a relative future only, and does not refer to that outpouring of the Spirit which was first to take place at a future time (de Wette), disappears if we consider the *strong* expression ποταμοί, κ.τ.λ., ver. 38, to which John gives due weight, inasmuch as he

does not go into the belly at all," rests solely upon the same confusion of the figure with its meaning. According to the figure, it comes into the κοιλία because it is *drunk*, and this drinking is in like manner *figurative*. When Hofmann finds indicated in the word even a *springing place* of the Holy Spirit *within the body*, he cannot get rid of the idea of something within the *body* as being implied in κοιλία, because the text itself presents this figure as being in harmony with that of the *drinking ;* unless, indeed, the concrete expression is to give way to an exegetical prudery foreign to the text itself, and is to

be blotted out at pleasure. κοιλία in *no* passage of the N. T. means anything else than *body, belly.*—Strangely out of keeping with the unity of the figure, Lange, following Bengel (comp. also Weizsäcker), now finds in κοιλία an allusion to the *belly of the golden pitcher* (see on ver. 37), and Godet to the *inner hollow of the rock* whence the water flowed, so that ἐκ τ. κοιλ. αὐτοῦ corresponds with מִפֶּנּוּ, Ex. xvii. 6. So inventive is the longing after types !

[1] So Hahn, *Theol. d. N. T.* I. p. 229 f., and Gess, *Pers. Chr.* p. 166.

[2] Nonnus, διὰ γαστρὸς ἐκείνου.

takes it to refer not simply to the power of one's own individual faith upon
others, so far as that was possible previous to the outpouring of the Spirit,
but to something far greater and mightier—to those *streams* of new life which
flowed forth from the lips of believers, and which were originated and
drawn forth by the *Holy Ghost.* The strength and importance of the expression (ποταμοί, κ.τ.λ.) thus renders it unnecessary to supply ποτέ or
the like after ῥεύσουσιν (in answer to Lücke) ; and when Lücke calls John's
explanation *epexegetically* right, but *exegetically* incorrect, he overlooks the fact
that John does not take *the living water itself* to be the Holy Ghost, but simply
says, regarding Christ's *declaration as a whole*, that Jesus meant it of the Holy
Spirit, leaving it to the Christian consciousness to think of the Spirit as the
Agens, the divine charismatic *motive power* of the streams of living water. —
It remains to be remarked that the libation at the feast of Tabernacles was interpreted by the Rabbis as a symbol of the outpouring of the Spirit (see Lightfoot) ; but this is scarcely to be connected with the words of Jesus and
their interpretation, as it is by no means certain that there is any reference in
the words to that libation ; see on ver. 37. — οὔπω γὰρ ἦν πνεῦμα] *nondum enim
aderat* (i. 9), furnishing the reason for the οὗ ἔμελλον λαμβάνειν as the statement of what was still *future.* [See Note XXX. p. 254.] The ἦν, " *He was
present* " (upon earth), is appropriately explained by δεδομένον (Lachmann ; see
on Acts xix. 2) ; Jesus alone possessed Him in His entire fulness (iii. 34).
The absolute expression οὔπω ἦν is not, therefore (with Hengst. and Brückner),
to be weakened, as if it were relative (referring to an increase which put
out of consideration all former outpourings), but, " at the time when Christ
preached He *promised* the Holy Spirit, and therefore the Holy Spirit was *not
yet there,*" Luther.[1] For the rest, the statement does not conflict with the
action of the Spirit in the O. T.,[2] or upon the prophets in particular ;[3] for here
the Spirit is spoken of as the principle of the *specifically Christian* life. In
this *characteristic definiteness,* wherein He is distinctively the πνεῦμα Χριστοῦ, the
πν. τῆς ἐπαγγελίας (Eph. i. 13), τῆς υἱοθεσίας (Rom. viii. 15), τῆς χάριτος (Heb. x.
29), the ἀρραβὼν τῆς κληρονομίας (Eph. i. 14), the Spirit of Him who raised Jesus
from the dead (Rom. viii. 11), and according to promise was to be *given* after
Christ's *exaltation* (Acts ii. 33), He was not yet present ; just as also, according to i. 17, grace and truth first *came into existence* through Christ. The
reason of the οὔπω ἦν is : " *because Jesus was not yet glorified.*" He must
through death return to *heaven,* and begin His *heavenly* rule, in order, as
σύνθρονος with the Father, and Lord over all (xvii. 5 ; 1 Cor. xv. 25), as
Lord also of the Spirit (2 Cor. iii. 18), to *send* the Spirit from heaven, xvi.
7. This *sending* was the condition of the subsequent εἶναι (adesse). " The
outpouring of the Spirit was the proof that He had entered upon His supra-
mundane state ; "[4] and so also the office of the Spirit to glorify Christ (xvi.
14) presupposes, as the condition of its operation, the commencement of
the δόξα of Christ. Till then believers were dependent upon the *personal*

[1] Comp. Flacius, *Clav.* II. p. 326 : " *sc. pro-
palam datus.* Videtur negari substantia,
cum tamen *accidens* negetur." See also
Calvin.

[2] Ps. li. 13 ; 1 Sam. xvi. 12, 13.
[3] 2 Pet. i. 21 ; Acts xxviii. 25, i. 16.
[4] Hofmann, *Schriftbeweis,* I. p. 196.

manifestation of Jesus ; He was the possessor of that Spirit who, though given in His fulness to Christ Himself (iii. 34), and though operating through Him in His people (iii. 6, vi. 63 ; Luke ix. 55), was not, until after Christ's return to glory (Eph. iv. 7, 8), to be given to the faithful as the Paraclete and representative of Christ for the carrying on of His work. See chap. xiv.-xvi. Chap. xx. 21, 22 does not contradict this ; see *in loc.* The thought of an identity [1] of the glorified Christ with the Holy Spirit might easily present itself here. [2] But we must not, with de Wette, seek for the reason of the statement in the *receptivity of the disciples,* who did not attain to a pure and independent development of the germ of spirit within them until the departure of Jesus ; the text is against this. As little can we regard the *flesh* of Christ as a *limitation* of the Spirit (Luthardt), or introduce the *atonement wrought through His death* as an intervening event ; [3] because the point lies in the *glorifying* of Christ, [4] not in His previous death, nor in the subjective preparation secured by faith. This also tells against Baeumlein, who understands here not the Holy Spirit objectively, but the Spirit *formed* in believers by Him, which τὸ πνεῦμα never *denotes,* and as shown by λαυβάνειν, *cannot* be the meaning here.

Vv. 40–43. Ἐκ τοῦ ὄχλου οὖν ἀκούσαντες τῶν λόγων τούτων (see the critical notes), κ.τ.λ. Now, at the close of all Christ's discourses delivered at the feast (vv. 14–39), these verses set before us the various impressions which they produced upon the people with reference to their estimate of Christ's person. " *From among the people, many, after they had heard these words, now said,*" etc. With ἐκ τοῦ ὄχλου we must supply τινές, as in xvi. 17. [5] By ὁ προφήτης, as in i. 21, is meant the prophet promised Deut. xviii. 15, not as being himself the Messiah, but a *prophet* preceding Him, a more minute description of whom is not given. — μὴ γὰρ ἐκ τ. Γαλ., κ.τ.λ.] " *Why, does the Messiah come out of Galilee?*" Γάρ refers to the assertion of the ἄλλοι, and assigns the reason for the *contradiction* of it which οἱ δὲ ἔλεγον indicates. [6] [See Note XXXI. p. 254.] Christ's birth at *Bethlehem* was unknown to the multitude. John, however, records all the various opinions in a purely objective manner ; and we must not suppose, from the absence of any correction on his part, that the birth at Bethlehem was unknown *to the evangelist himself.* [7] Baur (p. 169) employs this passage and ver. 52 in order to deny to the author any *historical* purpose in the composition of his work. This would be to conclude too much, for every reader could of himself and from his own knowl-

[1] Tholuck: "*the Spirit communicated to the faithful, as the Son of man Himself glorified into Spirit.*" Phil. iii. 21 itself speaks decisively enough against such a view. Wörner, *Verhältn. d. Geistes,* p. 57, speaks in a similar way of "the elevation of Christ's flesh into the form of the Spirit itself," etc. Baur, on the contrary, *N. T. Theol.* p. 385, says: "Not until His death was the Spirit, *hitherto identical* with Him, separated from His person in order that it might operate as an independent principle."

[2] See on 2 Cor. iii. 17 ; and likewise Gess, *Pers. Chr.* p. 155.
[3] Messner, *Lehre d. Ap.* p. 342 ; Hengstenberg and early writers.
[4] Comp. Godet and Weiss, *Lehrbegr.* p. 286 f.
[5] Buttmann, *N. T. Gr.* p. 138 [E. T. p. 159] ; Xen. *Mem.* iv. 5. 22 ; and Bornem. *in loc.*
[6] See Hartung, *Partikell.* I. 475 ; Baeumlein, *Partik.* p. 73.
[7] De Wette, Weisse, Keim ; comp. Scholten.

edge supply the correction. — ἡ γραφή] Mic. v. 1 ; Isa. xi. 1 ; Jer. xxiii. 5.
— ὅπου ἦν Δ.] *where David was.* He was born at Bethlehem, and passed
his youth there as a shepherd, 1 Sam. xvi. — *A division therefore* (ἑκάστου
μέρους φιλονεικοῦντος, Euthymius Zigabenus) *took place among the people concerning Him.*[1]

Ver. 44. Ἐξ αὐτῶν] Those, of course, who adopted the opinion last named.
The contest had aroused them. Τινές, standing first and apart, has a special emphasis. " *Some* there were among the people, who were disposed,"
etc. — ἀλλ’ οὐδείς, κ.τ.λ.] according to ver. 30, through divine prevention.[2]
On ἐπιβάλλ. τ. χεῖρ., see on Acts xii. 1. — According to de Wette (see also
Luthardt), the meaning should be that they would have supported the
timid officers, or would have acted for them. A gloss ; according to John,
they were inclined to an *act of popular justice,* independently of the officers, but it was not carried into effect.

Vv. 45, 46. Οὖν] *therefore,* seeing that no one, not even they themselves,
had ventured to lay hands on Jesus. — οἱ ὑπηρέται] In accordance with the
orders they had received (ver. 32), they had kept close to Jesus, in order
to apprehend Him. But the divine power and majesty of His words, which
doubtless hindered the τινές in ver. 44 from laying hands on Him, made it
morally impossible for the officers of justice to carry out their orders, or even
to find any pretext or justification for so doing ; they were *overpowered.*
Schleiermacher, therefore, was wrong in inferring that they had received
no *official* orders to take Him. — τοὺς ἀρχιερ. κ. Φαρ.] by the non-repetition
of the article, construed as *one category, i.e.* as the Sanhedrim, who must be
supposed to have been assembled in session. When first mentioned, ver.
32, both divisions are distinguished with logical emphasis.[3] — ἐκεῖνοι] the
ἀρχιερ. κ. Φαρισ. ; of the nearest subject, though remote to the writer.[4] — Ver.
46. There is a solemnity in the words ὡς οὗτος ὁ ἄνθρ., in themselves unnecessary. "It is a *weighty* statement, a *strong* word, that they thus *meekly*
use," Luther. " Character veritatis etiam idiotas convincentis prae dominis
eorum," Bengel. It is evident that Jesus must have said *more* after ver. 32
than John has recorded.

Vv. 47–49. The answer comes from the *Pharisees* in the Sanhedrim, as from
that section of the council who were most zealous in watching over the interests of orthodoxy and the hierarchy. — μὴ καὶ ὑμεῖς] *are ye also*—officers
of sacred justice, who should act only in strict loyalty to your superiors.
Hence the following questions : " *Have any of the Sanhedrim believed in him,
or of the Pharisees ?*" The latter are specially named as the class of *orthodox
and most respected theologians,* who were supposed to be patterns of orthodoxy, apart from the fact that some of them were members of the Sanhedrim. — ἀλλά] *but,* breaking off, and passing suddenly to the following
counter exclamation.[5] — ὁ ὄχλος οὗτος] *this multitude,* uttered with the

---

[1] Comp. ix. 16, x. 19 ; 1 Cor. i. 10; Acts
xiv. 4, xxiii. 7 ; Herod. vii. 219: καὶ σφεῶν
ἐσχίζοντο αἱ γνῶμαι. Xen. *Sympos.* iv. 59 ;
Herod. vi. 109 ; Eur. *Hec.* 119; and Pflugk,
in loc.

[2] ἐπεχόμενος ἀοράτως, Euthymius Ziga-

benus.

[3] See Dissen, *ad Dem. de cor.* p. 373 f.

[4] Winer, p. 148 [E. T. p. 157], and Ast, *ad
Plat. Polit.* p. 417 ; *Lex. Plat.* pp. 658, 659.

[5] Baeumlein, *Partik.* p. 15 ; Ellendt, *Lex.
Soph.* I. p. 78.

greatest scorn. The people adhering to Jesus, "this *mob*," as they regard them, are before their eyes. It is evident, further, that the speakers do *not* include their own official servants in the ὄχλος, but, on the other hand, prudently separate them with their knowledge from the ὄχλος. — ὁ μὴ γινώσκ. τ. νόμον] because they regarded such a transgressor of the law as the Prophet, or the Messiah, vv. 40, 41. — ἐπάρατοί εἰσι] *they are cursed*, the divine wrath is upon them ! The *plural* is justified by the collective ὁ ὄχλος, comp. ver. 44. The exclamation is to be regarded merely as a blindly passionate utterance [1] (Ewald) ; as a haughty outbreak of the *rabies theologica*, and by no means a *decree* (Kuinoel and others), as if the Sanhedrim had now *come to a resolution*, or at least had immediately, in keeping with the informal words, put *in regular form* (Luthardt) what is mentioned in ix. 22. Such an excommunication of the ὄχλος *en masse* would have been *preposterous*. Upon the unbounded scorn entertained by Jewish pride of learning towards the unlettered multitude (עַם הָאָרֶץ), see Wetstein and Lampe *in loc.*[2] — ἐπάρατος] (see the critical notes), not elsewhere in the N. T., nor in the LXX. and Apocrypha ; it is, however, classical.

Vv. 50, 51. The Pharisees in the Sanhedrim had expressed themselves as decisively and angrily against Jesus, as if His guilt had already been established. But *Nicodemus*, who had secretly been inclined towards Jesus since his interview with Him by night, now raises a protest, in which he calmly, plainly, and rightly points the excited doctors to the law itself.[3] — πρὸς αὐτούς] to the Pharisees, ver. 47. — ὁ ἐλθὼν . . . αὐτῶν] *who had before come to Jesus, although he was one of them (i.e.* of the Pharisees), iii. 1. — μὴ ὁ νόμος, κ.τ.λ.] The emphasis is on ὁ νόμος : "surely, our *law* does not judge ? " etc. They had just denied that the people knew the *law*, and yet they were themselves acting contrary to the *law*. — τὸν ἄνθρ.] *the man ;* the article denotes the person referred to in the given case ; see on ii. 25. We are not to supply ὁ κρίτης to ἀκούσῃ (Deut. i. 16, 17) and γνῷ, for the identity of the subject is essential to the thought ; but the *law itself* is regarded and personified as (through the judge) examining and discerning the facts of the case.[4] — τί ποιεῖ] *what he doeth*, what the nature of his conduct is.

Ver. 52. *Thou art not surely* (like Jesus) *also from Galilee*, so that thy sympathy with Him is that of *a fellow-countryman ?* — ὅτι προφήτης, κ.τ.λ. *a prophet ;* not : "no *very distinguished prophet*, nor any *great number* of prophets" (Hengstenberg) ; nor again : " a prophet has not appeared in Galilee *in the person of Jesus*" (Godet) ; but the appearance of any prophet out of Galilee is, *in a general way*, denied *as a matter of history ;* hence also the *Perfect*. The plain words can have no other meaning. To Godet's altogether groundless objection, that John must in this case have written οὐδεὶς προφ., the reference to iv. 44 is itself a sufficient answer. Inconsiderate zeal led the members of the Sanhedrim into historical *error ;* for, apart from the

---

[1] Not of an *argumentative* character, as if they had inferred their disobedience from their unacquaintance with the law (Ewald). Their frame of mind was not so reflective.

[2] Gfrörer in the *Tüb. Zeitschr.* 1838, I.

p. 130, and *Jahrb. d. Heils*, I. p. 240 f.

[3] See Ex. xxiii. 1 ; Deut. i. 16, 17 ; xix. 15.

[4] For a like personification, see Plato, *de Rep.* vii. p. 538 D. Comp. νόμος πάντων βασιλεύς from Pindar in Herod. iii. 38.

unknown birthplaces of many prophets, *Jonah* at least, according to 2 Kings xiv. 25, was of Galilee.[1] This error cannot be removed by any expedient either critical[2] or exegetical ; yet it furnishes no argument against the genuineness of the Gospel (Bretschneider), for it needed no correction since it did not *apply* to Jesus, who was *not* from Galilee. This also tells against Baur, p. 169. The *argument* in ὅτι προφ., κ.τ.λ., is from the general to the particular (" *to say nothing of the Messiah !*"), and is a conclusion from a negative induction.

Ver. 53. Belonging to the spurious section concerning the adulteress. " *And every one went* "—every one, that is, of those assembled in the temple —*to his own house ;* relating the end of the scene described in ver. 37 f. Chap. viii. 1 is against the view which understands it of the members of the *Sanhedrim*, who separated without attaining their object (against Grotius, Lampe, etc., also Maier and Lange). Chap. viii. 2 forbids our taking it as referring to the *pilgrims at the feast* returning to their homes (Paulus).

XXVIII. παῤῥησίᾳ. Ver. 3.

" Παῤῥησίᾳ can hardly denote here the frank and bold, in contrast with the timid and shrinking, nature, with which the ζητεῖ (*seeks for*, as something *outward*), does not harmonize. It marks rather the *publicity* of his position (Lck. : " *in ore hominum versari*)" (Weiss). Weiss, therefore, renders: " for no man withdraws himself with his works into silence and seclusion, and yet endeavours to maintain for his person a position of publicity (as thou must do, if thou art the Messiah)."

XXIX. " *I go not up to this feast.*" Ver. 8.

Weiss disapproves Meyer's view that Christ " *changed* his intention," alleging that in this case Porphyry's charge of inconstancy would hardly have been entirely undeserved." It was, he says, " rather from the divine intimation which came to Him, bidding Him no longer shun the conflict which at vv. 6, 7 He still wished to avoid. The signal came to Him as at ii. 4, but in this case sooner than He expected. And it now bade Him go to Jerusalem, not to bring on the final crisis, but that, under the divine protection, He might yet once and for a longer time resume His work in the way of instruction and refutation, at the great seat of the Theocracy. . . . John recounts [this incident regarding

---

[1] Not *Elijah* also, whose Thisbe lay in Gilead (see Thenius on 1 Kings xvii. 1; Fritzsche on Tobit i. 2; Kurtz, in *Herzog's Encykl.* III. p. 754). It is very doubtful, further, whether the Elkosh, whence *Nahum* came, was in Galilee or anywhere in Palestine, and not rather in Assyria (Michaelis, Eichhorn, Ewald, and most). Hosea came from the northern kingdom of Israel (Samaria) ; see Hos. vii. 1, 5.

[2] By giving preference, namely, to the

reading ἐγείρεται, according to which only the *present* appearance of a prophet in Galilee is denied (so also Tiele, *Spec. contin. annotationem in loc. nonnull. ev. Joh.*, Amsterdam 1853). This ἐγείρεται would have its support and meaning only in the experience of history, because προφήτης, without the article, is quite general, and cannot mean the Messiah. This also in answer to Baeumlein.

Christ's brethren], to prove how Jesus had not Himself sought the inevitable conflict in Jerusalem, and had even wished to shun it ; and to point to the reader that if He who could of Himself do nothing (ver. 19) now still went to the feast, it could only be at the special will and summons of God, who, therefore, brought Him off unharmed and victorious from the perils and conflicts to which the visit subjected him."

XXX. " *The Spirit was not yet (present).*" Ver. 39.

" The absolute expression οὔπω ἦν is not to be weakened into a *relative* absence, as compared with subsequent higher manifestations ; or by appended modifying clauses (as 'in abiding and controlling agency,' de W. ; or '*dwelling* in humanity,' Godet). Nor is it exegetically defensible to refer the statement (with Meyer) to the Spirit in His specifically New Test. form, or to the Spirit in His characteristic definiteness, as a principle of the Christian life. Certainly we are to understand in it no denial of the existence of the Spirit in Christ (comp. i. 32, iii. 34), or of his agency in the Old Test. ; for it is with *design* that the expression is not simply τὸ πνεῦμα. The single and sole denial is, that of such a Spirit as believers were to receive for the possible realization of the phenomena depicted ver. 38, there was as yet any presence whatever" (Weiss.)

XXXI. Γάρ, *elliptical ; why ?* Ver. 40.

"Γάρ refers to the assertion of the ἄλλοι, and assigns the reason for the contradiction of it which the οἱ δὲ ἔλεγον, *others said*, indicates."

This elliptical use of γάρ is frequent in the classics. It is here ignored in the Common Version, and its force is fairly given in the Revision by *what ?* Perhaps *why* would represent it somewhat more exactly, being a little less emphatic. Γάρ and *why* are nearly equivalent, as they represent the same ellipsis. Thus in English, "Why do you say that ? Does the Messiah come out of Galilee ?" Elliptically, "Why, does the Messiah come out of Galilee ?" So in Greek, Διὰ τί τοῦτο λέγεις ; or something similar) μὴ γὰρ ὁ Χριστός κ.τ.λ. Elliptically : Μὴ γὰρ ὁ Χριστός, κ.τ.λ. ; The English indicates the preceding denial by retaining the *why*, the Greek by retaining the γάρ. The combination μὴ γάρ (the interrogative μή indicating a negative answer, being very frequent with John) is among the elegances which, with all its simplicity, yet characterize our Gospel.

CHAPTER VIII.

The section treating of the woman taken in adultery, vv. 1–11, together with vii. 53, is a document by some unknown author belonging to the apostolic age, which, after circulating in various forms of text, was inserted in John's Gospel, probably by the second, or, at latest, by the third century (the *Constitutt. Apost.* ii. 24. 4, already disclose its presence in the canon), the remark in vii. 53 being added to connect it with what precedes. That the interpolation of this very ancient fragment of gospel history was derived from the *Evang. sec. Hebraeos* cannot, as several of the early critics think (comp. also Lücke and Bleek), be proved from Papias, in Euseb. *H. E.* 3. 39 ; for in the words ἐκτέθειται (Papias) δὲ καὶ ἄλλην ἱστορίαν περὶ γυναικὸς ἐπὶ πολλαῖς ἁμαρτίαις διαβληθείσης ἐπὶ τοῦ κυρίου, ἣν τὸ καθ' Ἑβραίους εὐαγγέλιον περιέχει, the general expression ἐπὶ πολλαῖς ἁμαρτίαις and the mere word διαβληθ. are not favourable to that identity between the two which Rufinus already assumed. It is, however, only its high antiquity, and the very early insertion of the section in the Johannean text, which explain the fact that it is found in most Codices of the Itala, in the Vulgate, and other versions ; that Jerome, *adv. Pelag.* ii. 17, could vouch for its existence " *in multis et Graecis et Latinis Codd.* ;" and that, finally, upwards of a hundred Codices still extant, including D. F. G. H. K. U., contain it. Its *internal character*, moreover, speaks in favour of its having originated in the early Christian age ; for, although it is, indeed, quite alien to the Johannean style of thought and expression, and hence not for a moment to be referred to an oral Johannean source (Luthardt), it is entirely in keeping with the tone of the synoptical Gospels, and does not betray the slightest trace of being a later invention to favour either a dogmatic or ecclesiastical purpose. Comp. Calvin : " Nihil apostolico spiritu indignum continet." The occurrence related bears, moreover, so strong a stamp of originality, and is so evidently not compiled in imitation of any other of the Gospel narratives, that it cannot be regarded as a later legendary story, especially as its *internal truthfulness* will be vindicated in the course of the exposition itself, in opposition to the manifold doubts that have been raised against it. *But the narrative does not proceed from John.* [See Note XXXII. p. 294.] Of this we are assured by the remarkable and manifestly interpolated link, vii. 53, which connects it with what precedes ; by the strange interruption with which it breaks up the unity of the account continued in viii. 14 ff. ; by its tone and character, so closely resembling that of the synoptic history, to which, in particular, belongs the propounding of a question of law, in order to tempt Christ,—a thing which does not occur in John ; by the going out of Jesus to the Mount of Olives, and His return to the temple, by which we are transported to the Lord's *last* sojourn in Jerusalem (Luke xxi.) ; by the entire absence of the Johannean οὖν, and in its stead the constant recurrence of δέ ; and, lastly, by the non Johannean expressions ὄρθρου, πᾶς ὁ λαός, καθίσας ἐδίδασκεν αὐτούς, οἱ γραμματ. κ. οἱ Φαρισ., ἐπιμένειν, ἀναμάρτητος, καταλείπεσθαι and κατακρίνειν, πλήν

256   THE GOSPEL OF JOHN.

also, in ver. 10 (Elz.). With these various internal reasons many very weighty
external arguments are conjoined, which show that the section was by no
means received into all copies of John's Gospel ; but, on the contrary,
from the third and fourth centuries was tacitly or expressly excluded from
the canonical text. For Origen, Apollinarius, Theodore of Mopsuestia, Cyril,
Chrysostom, Nonnus, Theophylact, Tertullian, and other *Fathers* (except Jerome, Ambrose, Augustine, Sedulius, Leo, Chrysologus, Cassiodorus), as well
as the Catenae, are altogether silent about this section ; Euthymius Zigabenus,
however, has it, and explains it, indeed, but passes this judgment upon it :
Χρὴ δὲ γινώσκειν, ὅτι τὰ ἐντεῦθεν (vii. 53) ἄχρι τοῦ· πάλιν οὖν ἐλάλησεν, κ.τ.λ.
(viii. 12) παρὰ τοῖς ἀκριβέσιν ἀντιγράφοις ἢ οὐχ εὕρηται, ἢ ὠβέλισται. Διὸ φαίνονται
παρέγγραπτα καὶ προσθήκη· καὶ τούτου τεκμήριον, τὸ μηδὲ τὸν Χρυσόστομον ὅλως
μνημονεῦσαι αὐτῶν. Of the versions, the Syr. (in Codd., also of the Nestorians,
and in the first edd.), Syr. p. Copt. (in most mss.) Ar. Sahid. Arm. Goth. Verc.
Brix. have not the section. It is also wanting in very old and important
Codices, viz. A. B. C. L. T. X. Δ. ℵ., of which, however, A. and C. are here defective (but according to Tisch., C. never had it ; see his edition of Codex C.,
Proleg. p. 31), while L. and Δ. leave an empty space ; other Codices mark it as
suspicious by asterisks or an obelus, or expressly so describe it in Scholia (see
especially Scholz and Tisch.). Beyond a doubt, this apocryphal interpolation
would have seemed less surprising to early criticism had it found a place, not
in John's Gospel, but in one of the Synoptics. *But wherefore just here ?* If we
decline to attribute this enigma to some accidental, unknown cause and thus
to leave it unsolved, then its position here may be accounted for in this way :
that as an abortive plan of the Sanhedrim against Jesus had just before been
narrated, it appeared to be an appropriate place for relating a new, though
again unsuccessful, attempt to trip Him ; and *this* particular narrative may
have been inserted, all the more, because the saying about judging and not
judging, in ver. 15, might find in it an historical explanation ; while, perhaps,
an old uncritical tradition, that John was the author of the fragment, may
have removed all difficulty. But even on this view the attempts of criticism
to correct the text very soon appear. For the Codd. i. 19, 20 *et al.*, transfer
the section as a doubtful appendix to the end of the Gospel ; others (13, 69,
124, 346) insert it after Luke xxi. 38. where, especially considering vv. 1 and
2, it would appropriately fit in with the historical connection ; and possibly
also it might have had a place in one of the sources made use of by Luke.
How *various the recensions* were in which it was circulated, is proved by the remarkable number of various readings, which for the most part bear the impress, not of chance or arbitrariness, but of varying originality. D., in
particular, presents a peculiar form of text ; the section in it runs thus : Ἰησ.
δὲ ἐπ. εἰς τ. ὄρ. τ. ἐλ. Ὄρθρ. δὲ π. παραγίνεται εἰς τ. ἱερ. κ. π. ὁ λ. ἦρχ. πρὸς αὐτ.
Ἀγ. δὲ οἱ γρ. κ. οἱ Φ. ἐπὶ ἁμαρτία γυν. εἰλημμένην, κ. στ. αὐτ. ἐν μ. λ. αὐτῷ ἐκπειράζον-
τες αὐτὸν οἱ ἱερεῖς, ἵνα ἔχωσι κατηγορίαν αὐτοῦ· διδ., αὔτ. ἡ γ. κατείληπται ἐπ. μοιχ.
Μωϋσῆς δὲ ἐν τ. νόμῳ ἐκέλευσε τὰς τοιαύτ. λιθάζειν· σὺ δὲ νῦν τί λέγεις ; Ὁ δὲ Ἰησ.
κ. κ. τ. δ. κατέγραφεν εἰς τ. γ. Ὡς δὲ ἐπ. ἐρωτ., ἀνέκυψε καὶ εἶπεν αὐτοῖς· ὁ ἀν ὑμ
πρ. ἐπ' αὐτὴν βαλλέτω λίθον. Κ. π. κατακύψας τῷ δακτύλῳ κατέγραφεν εἰς τ. γ.
Ἕκαστος δὲ τῶν Ἰουδαίων ἐξήρχετο, ἀρξάμενος ἀπὸ τῶν πρεσβυτέρων, ὥστε πάντας
ἐξελθεῖν, κ. κατελ. μόν. κ. ἡ γυνὴ ἐν μ. οὖσα. Ἀνακ. δὲ ὁ Ἰησ. εἰπ. τῇ γυναικί· ποῦ
εἰσιν ; οὐδείς σε κατεκρ. ; Κἀκείνη εἶπεν αὐτῷ· οὐδείς, κύρ. Ὁ δὲ εἶπεν· οὐδὲ ἐγ. σ. κ.
Ὕπαγε, ἀπὸ · ϡ νῦν μηκέτι ἁμάρτανε. — The Johannean authorship was *denied* by

Erasmus, Calvin (?), Beza, Grotius, Wetstein, Semler, Morus, Haenlein, Wegscheider, Paulus, Tittmann (*Melet.* p. 318 ff.), Knapp, Seyffarth, Lücke,
Credner, Tholuck, Olshausen, Krabbe, B. Crusius, Bleek, Weisse, Lücke,
de Wette, Guericke, Reuss, Brückner, Luthardt, Ewald, Baeumlein, Hengstenberg (who regards the section as a forgery made for a particular purpose),
Schenkel, Godet, Scholten, and most critics ; Lachmann and Tischendorf also
have removed the section from the text. Bretschneider, p. 72 ff., attributing it
to the Pseudo-Johannes, endeavours to establish its spuriousness, and so uses
it as an argument against the genuineness of the Gospel ; Strauss and Bauer
deal with it in the same way, while Hitzig (on *John Mark*, p. 205 ff.) regards
the evangelist Mark as the author, in whose Gospel it is said to have stood
after xii. 17 (according to Holtzmann, in the *primary* Mark). Its authenticity,
on the contrary, was *defended* in early times especially by Augustine (*de conjug.
adult.* 2. 7),[1] whose subjective judgment is, that the story had been rejected by
persons of weak faith, or by enemies of the true faith, who feared " peccandi
impunitatem dari mulieribus suis ;"—in modern times by Mill, Whitby,
Fabricius, Wolf, Lampe, Bengel, Heumann, Michaelis, Storr, Dettmers (*Vin-
diciae authentiae textus Gr. peric. Joh.* vii. 53 ff., Francof. ad Viadr. p. 1, 1793) ;
Stäudlin (in two *Dissert.*, Gott. 1806). Hug (*de conjugii Christ. vinculo indis-
solub.*, Frib. 1816, p. 22 ff.) ; Kuinoel, Möller (*neue Ansichten*, p. 313 ff.) ; Scholz
(*Erklär. der Evang.* p. 396 ff., and *N. T.* I. p. 383) ; Klee and many others, in
particular, also Maier, i. p. 24 f. ; Ebrard, Horne, *Introduction to the Textual
Criticism of the N. T.*, ed. Tregelles, p. 465 ; Hilgenfeld, *Evang.* p. 284 ff., and
again in his *Zeitschrift*, 1863, p. 317, Lange. Schulthess, in Winer and Engelhardt *krit. Journ.* v. 3, pp. 257–317, declares himself in favour of the genuineness of a text purified by the free use of various readings. — Ver. 14. ἢ ποῦ
ὑπάγω] Elz. Lachm. : καὶ ποῦ ὑπ. But B. D. K. T. U. X. Λ. Curss. and many
Vss. have ἤ ; and καί might easily have been repeated from what precedes,
while there was nothing to occasion the change of καί into ἤ. — Ver. 16. ἀληθής]
Lachm. and Tisch. : ἀληθινή, after B. D. L. T. X. 33. Or. Rightly ; ἀληθής was
introduced from the context (vv. 14, 17). — Ver. 20. After ἐλάλησεν Elz. has ὁ
Ἰησοῦς, against decisive witnesses. — Ver. 26. λέγω] Lachm. Tisch. ; λαλῶ, following important witnesses ; but from vv. 25, 28. — Ver. 28. ὁ πατήρ] Elz. Scholz :
ὁ πατήρ μου. But μου is wanting in D. L. T. X. א. 13, 69, 122, al. Slav. Vulg. It.
Eus. Cyr. Hilar. Faustin., and is a later addition, intended to mark the
peculiar relation of the ὁ πατήρ. — Ver. 29. After μόνον Elz. Scholz have ὁ πατήρ.
A gloss which 253, 259 have inserted *before* μόνον. — Ver .34. τῆς ἁμαρτίας] wanting
only in D. Cant. Ver. Clem. Faustin., witnesses which are too weak to justify
our condemning it as a gloss. It was left out on account of the following
general expression ὁ δὲ δοῦλος. — Ver. 38. ἃ ἠκούσατε παρὰ τοῦ πατρὸς ὑμῶν] Elz.
Scholz : ὃ ἑωράκατε παρὰ τῷ πατρὶ ὑμῶν. But B. C. D. K. X. א. Curss. Or. have
ἅ ; B. C. K. L. X. א.** Curss. and some Vss. and Fathers, even Or., read
ἠκούσατε and τοῦ πατρός. The received text, of which Tisch. has inconsistently
retained ἑωράκ., is a mechanical imitation of the first half of the verse. The
pronouns μου and ὑμῶν must, with Lachm. and Tisch., following very important
witnesses, be deleted as clumsy additions inserted for the purpose of marking

[1] Nikon, in the 13th century, attributed the omission to solicitude lest the contents should have an injurious effect upon the multitude. See Cotelerius, *Patr. Apost.* i. 235.

the distinction. Finally, ἄ also in the first half has almost entirely the same witnesses in its favour as the second ἄ, so that with Lachm. and Tisch. we must read ἄ in both places. — Ver. 39. ἧτε] B. D. L. ℵ. Vulg. Codd. It. Or. Aug. : ἐστε. So Griesb. Lachm. Tisch. ; rightly defended by Buttmann in the *Stud. u. Krit.* 1858, p. 474 ff. The seemingly illogical relation of the protasis and apodosis caused ἐστε to be changed into ἧτε, and ἐποιεῖτε into ποιεῖτε (Vulg. Or. Aug.). — After ἐποιεῖτε, Elz. Lachm. have ἄν, which is wanting in important witnesses, and is an unnecessary grammatical addition. — Ver. 51. τὸν λόγ. τὸν ἐμόν] Lachm. Tisch. : τὸν ἐμὸν λόγον, which is preponderatingly attested, and therefore to be adopted. — Ver. 52. Instead of γεύσηται Elz. has γεύσεται, against conclusive testimony. — Ver. 53. After σεαυτόν Elz. has σύ, which the best Codd. unanimously exclude. — Ver. 54. δοξάζω] Lachm. Tisch. : δοξάσω, after B. C.* D. ℵ. Curs. Cant. Verc. Corb. Rd. Colb. Or. Chrys. Ambr. Rightly ; the present (comp. the following δοξάζων) would involuntarily present itself to the copyists. — For ἡμῶν (so also Tisch.) Elz. has ὑμῶν (as also Lachm.). The testimonies are divided between the two ; but ἡμῶν might easily have been changed into ὑμῶν, after the preceding ὑμεῖς, through not observing the direct construction. — Ver. 57. The reading τεσσαράκοντα, which Chrysostom has, and Euthymius Zigabenus found in mss., is still in Λ. and three Curs., but is nothing save an historical *retouche.* — Ver. 59. After ἱεροῦ Elz. Scholz have : διελθὼν διὰ μέσου αὐτῶν, καὶ παρῆγεν οὕτως, words which are wanting in B. D. ℵ.* Vulg. It. al. Or. Cyr. Arnob. An addition after Luke iv. 30, whence also ἐπορεύετο has been interpolated after αὐτῶν in several witnesses.

Vv. 1–3. Ἐπορ.] *down from the temple.* — εἰς τ. ὄρ. τ. ἐλ.] where He passed the night ; comp. Luke xxi. 37. Displays the synoptic stamp in its circumstantiality of description and in the use of words ; instead of ὄρθρου (Luke xxiv. 1), John uses πρωΐ (xviii. 28, xx. 1 ; comp. πρωΐα, xxi. 4) ; for πᾶς ὁ λαός John uses ὁ ὄχλος and οἱ ὄχλοι ; καθίσας ἐδίδ. αὐτ. is synoptical ; on ἐδίδασκεν, however, *without mention of the topic,* comp. vii. 14 ; the γραμματεῖς never appear in John ; nor does he anywhere name the Mount of Olives. — The crowd of people, *after the conclusion of the feast,* would not be surprising, considering the great sensation which Jesus had caused at the feast. — The expression "*Scribes* and *Pharisees*" is the designation in the *synoptic* narrative for His regular opponents, answering to the Johannean οἱ Ἰουδαῖοι. They do not appear here as *Zealots* (Wetstein, Kuinoel, Staeudlin), whose character would not correspond either with their questioning of Jesus or with their subsequent slinking away ; nor even as a *Deputation from the Sanhedrim,* which certainly would not have condescended to this, and whose delegates would not have dared to let the woman slip. It is rather a *non-official tentative attack,* like several that are narrated by the Synoptics ; the woman has just been taken in the very act ; has, as a preliminary step, been handed over to the Scribes and Pharisees for further proceedings ; has not yet, however, been brought before the Sanhedrim, but is first made use of by them for this attempt against Jesus.

Vv. 4, 5. Observe especially here and in vv. 5, 6 the thoroughly *synoptical* diffuseness of the account. — κατειλήφθη] with the augment of εἴληφα, see Winer, p. 60 [E. T. p. 72]. On the expression, comp. κατείληπτο μοιχός, Arrian.

Epict. 2. 4. — ἐπ' αὐτοφώρῳ] *in the very act.* Herod. 6. 72, 137 ; Plato, *Pol.* 2, p. 359 C ; Xen. *Symp.* 3. 13 ; Dem. 378. 12 ; Soph. *Ant.* 51 ; Eur. *Ion.* 1214. Comp. Philo, p. 785 A : μοιχεῖαι αὐτόφωροι. On λαμβάνειν ἐπί, of taking in adultery, see Toup. *Opp. Crit.* I. p. 101. — The *adulterer*, who in like manner was liable to death (Lev. xx. 10 ; Deut. xxii. 24), may have *fled.* — λιθοβολ- εῖσθαι] This word cannot be called un-Johannean (in John x. 31 ff. λιθάζειν is used) because of its being taken from Deut. *l.c.* According to Deut. xxii. 23, 24 the law expressly appoints *stoning* for the particular case, when a *betrothed maiden* allows herself to be seduced by a man in the city, where she could have summoned help. The woman here taken must therefore necessarily be regarded as *such an one,* 'because the λιθοβολεῖσθαι is *expressly referred to a command contained in the Mosaic law.* From Deut. *l.c.*, where the betrothed, in reference to the seducer, is termed אֵשֶׁת רֵעֵהוּ, it is clear that the crime in question was regarded as a *modified* form of *adultery,* as it is also called εἶδος μοιχείας by Philo, *de legg. special.* ii. p. 311. The rarity of such a case as this made it all the more a fit topic for a tempting question in casuistry. Accordingly, τὰς τοιαύτας is to be understood as denoting the class of adulteresses of this *particular kind,* to whom refers that law of Moses appointing the punishment of stoning : *"adulteresses of this kind."* That Moses, in Deut. *l.c.*, does not use the expression נאף (Lücke's objection) is immaterial, because he has not this word at all in the connection, nor even in the other cases, but designates the thing in another way. *Usually* the woman is regarded as a *married* woman ; and as in Lev. xx. 10 and Deut. xxii. 22, not stoning specifically, but *death* generally is the punishment adjudged to adulteresses of this class, some either infer the internal false- hood of the whole story (Wetstein, Semler, Morus, Paulus, Lücke, de Wette, Baur, and many others ; comp. also Hengstenberg and Godet), or assume that the punishment of death, which is not more precisely defined by the law ("to die the death"), must mean stoning (Michaelis, *Mos.* R. § 262 ; Tholuck, B. Crusius, Ebrard, Keil, *Archæol.* § 153, 1 ; Ewald, Brückner hesitatingly, Luthardt, Baeumlein). As to the last view, judging from the text in Deut. *l.c.*, and also according to Rabbinical tradition, it is certainly an unsafe assumption ; comp. Saalschütz, *Mos. R.* p. 571. Here, however, where the λιθοβολεῖσθαι is distinctly cited as a positive provision of the law, we have neither reason nor right to assume a reference to any other precept save that in which stoning is expressly named as the punishment, viz. Deut. xxii. 24 (LXX. : λιθοβολήσονται ἐν λίθοις), with which also the Talmud agrees, *Sanhedr.* f. 51, 2 : "Filia Israelitae, si adultera, cum nupta, strangulanda,[1] cum *desponsata, lapidanda.*" The supposition of Grotius, that the severer punishment of stoning for adultery was introduced after the time of Ezekiel, cannot be proved by Ezek. xvi. 38, 40 ; Sus. 45 ; the Μωϋσῆς ἐνετείλατο more- over, is decidedly against all such suppositions.

Ver. 6. Πειράζοντες αὐτόν] denoting, not a good-natured questioning

---

[1] According to the Talmudic rule : "Om- nis mors, cujus et mentio in lege sim- pliciter, non alia est quam strangulatio," *Sanhedr. l.c.* The incorrectness of this rule (Michaelis, *l.c.*) is a matter of no con- sequence, so far as the present passage is concerned.

(Olshausen), but, agreeably to the standing *synoptical* representation of the relation of those men to Jesus, and in keeping with what immediately follows, *malicious tempting.* The *insidious* feature of the plan consisted in this: " If He decides *with* Moses *for* the stoning, He will be accused before the Roman authorities ; for, according to the Roman criminal law, adultery was not punishable with death, and stoning in particular was generally repudiated by the Romans (see Staeudlin and Hug). But if He decides *against* Moses and *against* stoning, He will then be prosecuted before the Sanhedrim as an opposer of the law." That they expected and wished for the *former* result, is shown by the *prejudicial* way in which they introduce the question, by quoting the express punishment prescribed by Moses.[1] Their plan here is similar in design to that of the question touching the tribute money in Matt. xxii. It is objected that the Romans in the provinces did not administer justice strictly in accordance with their own laws ; but amid the general immorality of the times they certainly did not conform to the rigour of the Mosaic punishment for adultery ; and how easy would it have been before the Roman magistrates to give a revolutionary aspect to the hoped-for decision of Jesus in favour of Moses, even if He had in some way reserved the competency of the Roman authorities ! If it be said that Jesus needed only to declare Himself in favour of execution, and not exactly for *stoning*, it is overlooked that here was the *very* case for which *stoning* was expressly appointed. If it be urged, lastly, that when Jesus was required to assume the position of a judge, He needed only to *refer* His questioners to the *Sanhedrim*, and to tell them to take the woman *thither* (Ebrard), that would have amounted to a *declining* to answer, which would, indeed, have been the surest way of escape from the dilemma, but inappropriate enough to the intellectual temperament of Jesus in such cases. *Other explanations* of $\pi\epsilon\iota\rho\acute{a}\zeta\epsilon\iota\nu$—(1) They would either have accused him to the Romans *imminutae majestatis*, because they then possessed the jus vitae et necis, or to the Jews *imminutae libertatis* (Grotius), and as a false Messiah (Godet). But that prerogative of the Romans was not infringed by the pronouncing of a sentence of *condemnation ;* it was still reserved to them through their having to confirm and carry out the sentence. Accordingly, B. Crusius gives this turn to the question : " Would Jesus decide for the popular *execution* of the law . . . or would He peradventure even take upon Himself to pass such a judgment" (so, substantially, Hitzig also on *Joh. Markus*, p. 205 ff., and Luthardt), where (with Wetstein and Schulthess) the law of the Zealots is called in by way of help ? But in that case the interrogators, who intended to make use of a negative answer against Him as an overturning of the law, and an affirmative reply as an interference with the functions of the authorities, would then have put *no question at all* relating to the thing which they really wanted (*i.e.* the execution, and that immediate and tumultuous). (2) As the punishment of death for adultery had at that time already fallen into disuse, the drift of their question was

---

[1] Observe also, in reference to this, the οὖν in ver. 5, which logically paves the way for an answer in agreement with Moses.

simply *whether or not legal proceedings should be instituted at all* (Ebrard, following Michaelis). The words themselves, and the design expressed in the κατηγορεῖν, which could not take place before the *people*, but before the competent judges, as in Matt. xii. 10, are quite opposed to this explanation. (3) Dieck, in the *Stud. u. Krit.* 1832, p. 791, says : As the punishment of death for adultery presupposes *liberty of divorcement*, and as Jesus had Himself *repudiated* divorce, He would, by pronouncing *in favour of* that punishment, have contradicted Himself ; while, by pronouncing *against* it, He would have appeared as a despiser of the law. But apart from the improbability of any such logical calculation on the part of His questioners as to the first alternative,—a calculation which is indicated by nothing in the text,—the ἵνα ἐχ. κατηγ. αὐτ. is decisive against this explanation ; for a want of logical consistency would have furnished no *ground for accusation*.[1] (4) The same argument tells against Augustine, Erasmus, Luther, Calvin, Aretius, Jansen, Cornelius à Lapide, Baumgarten, and many other expositors : according to whom an *affirmative* reply would have been *inconsistent with the general mildness* of His teaching ; a *negative* answer would have been a decision against Moses. (5) Euthymius Zigabenus, Bengel, and many others, Neander also, Tholuck, Baeumlein, Hengstenberg (who sees here an unhistorical mingling of law and gospel), are nearer the mark in regarding the plan of attack as based upon the assumption, which they regarded as certain, that in accordance with His usual gentleness He would give a *negative* answer : γινώσκοντες γὰρ αὐτὸν ἐλεήμονα κ. συμπαθῆ, προσεδόκων, ὅτι φείσεται αὐτῆς, καὶ λοιπὸν ἕξουσι κατηγορίαν κατ᾽ αὐτοῦ, ὡς παρανόμως φειδομένου τῆς ἀπὸ τοῦ νόμου λιθαζομένης, Euthymius Zigabenus. But this explanation also must be rejected, partly even on *à priori* grounds, because an ensnaring casuistic question may naturally be supposed to involve a *dilemma ;* partly and mainly because in this case the introduction of the question by ἐν δὲ τῷ νόμῳ would have been a very unwise method of preparing the way for a *negative* answer. This latter argument tells against Ewald, who holds that Christ, by the acquittal which they deemed it probable He would pronounce, would have offended against the Mosaic law ; while by condemning, He would have violated as well the milder practice then in vogue as His own more gentle principles. Lücke, de Wette, Brückner, Baur,[2] and many other expositors

---

[1] What they really wished was to *accuse* Him, on the ground of the answer He would give. Hilgenfeld therefore is in error when he thinks they sought to force Him to give a decisive utterance as the *obligation of the Mosaic law*. By an affirmative reply (he says) Christ would have recognized this obligation, and by His non-observance of the law (v. 18, vii. 23) He would have been self-condemned ; by a negative answer He would have been guilty of an express rejection of the law. Viewing the matter thus, they could not, indeed, have *accused* Him on account of His answer if affirmative ; they could only have charged Him with logical inconsistency. This tells substantially also against Lange's view, viz. that they wished to see whether He would venture, in the strength of His Messianic authority, to set up a new law. If in this case He had decided *in favour of* Moses, they could not have *accused* Him (to the Sanhedrim).

[2] According to Baur (p. 170 sq.), there is nothing historical whatever in the story; it has a purely ideal import. The main idea he holds to be the consciousness of one's own sinfulness breaking the power of every sin, in opposition to the accusation brought against Jesus by the Pharisees, that He associated with sinners, and thus was so ready to forgive.

renounce the attempt to give any satisfactory solution of the difficulty. — τᾷ δακτύλῳ ἔγραφεν εἰς τ. γῆν] as a sign that He was not considering their question, ὅπερ εἰώθασι πολλάκις ποιεῖν οἱ μὴ θέλοντες ἀποκρίνεσθαι πρὸς τοὺς ἐρωτῶντας ἄκαιρα καὶ ἀνάξια. Γνοὺς γὰρ αὐτῶν τὴν μηχανήν, προσεποιεῖτο γράφειν εἰς τ. γῆν, καὶ μὴ προσέχειν οἷς ἔλεγον, Euthymius Zigabenus. For instances of behaviour like this on the part of one who turns away from those around him, and becomes absorbed in himself, giving himself up to his own thoughts or imaginings, see from Greek writers Aristoph. *Acharn.* 31, and Schol. Diog. Laert. 2. 127, and from the Rabbins, in Wetstein. Isa. xvii. 13 does not here serve for elucidation. *What* Jesus wrote is not a subject even of inquiry ; nor are we to ask whether, by the act, He was symbolizing any, and if so what, *answer* (Michaelis : the answer " *as it is written*"). There is much marvellous conjecture among the older expositors. See Wolf and Lampe, also Fabricius, *Cod. Apocr.* p. 315, who thinks that Jesus wrote the answer given in ver. 7 (after Bede ; comp. also Ewald, *Gesch. Chr.* p. 480, ed. 3, and Godet). Suffice it to say, the strange manner in which Jesus silently declines to give a decisive reply (acting, no doubt, according to His principle of not interfering with the sphere of the magistracy (here a matter of criminal law), Matt. xxii. ; Luke xii. 13, 14),[1] bears the stamp of genuineness and not of invention, though Hengstenberg deems this procedure unworthy of Jesus ; the tempters *deserved* the *contempt* which this implied, ver. 9.—Observe in ἔγραφεν the descriptive imperfect. The reader *sees* Him writing with His finger. The additions in some Codd. καὶ προσποιούμενος, and (more strongly attested) μὴ προσποιούμ., are glosses of different kinds, meaning " *though He only pretended* (*simulans*) to write ;" and, " *without troubling Himself about them*" (*dissimulans*, Ev. 32 adds αὐτούς). See Matthaei, ed. min. *in loc.*

Ver. 7. ʼΑναμάρτητος] *faultless*, here only in the N. T., very often in the Classics. Whether it means freedom from the possibility of fault (of error or sin), as in Plato, *Pol.* I. p. 339 B, or freedom from *actual* sin (comp. γυνὴ ἀναμάρτητος, Herod. v. 39),—whether, again, it is to be understood *generally* (2 Macc. viii. 4), or with reference to any *definite category* or *species* of ἀμαρτία (2 Macc. xii. 42 ; Deut. xxix. 19), is a matter which can be decided by the *context* alone. Here it must signify actual freedom from the sin, not indeed of *adultery* specially, for Jesus could not presuppose this of the hierarchy as a whole, even with all its corruption of morals. but probably of *unchastity*, simply because a woman who was a sinner of *this* category was here in question, and stood before the eyes of them all as the living opposite of ἀναμάρτητος. Comp. ἁμαρτωλός, Luke vii. 37 ; ἁμαρτάνειν, Jacobs, *ad Anthol.*

---

[1] According to Luthardt, to show that the malice of the question *did not deserve an answer.* But the numerous testing questions proposed to Him, according to the Synoptics, by His opponents, were all of them malicious ; yet Jesus did not refuse to reply to them. According to Lange's fancy, Jesus assumed the gesture of *a calm majesty*, which, in its *playful ease*, refused to be disturbed by any *street scandal.* Melanchthon well says: " Initio, cum accusatur mulier, nihil respondit Christus, *tanquam in aliam rem intentus, videlicet prorsus a sese rejiciens hanc quaestionem pertinentem ad cognitionem magistratus politici.* Postea, cum urgetur, respondet non de muliere, sed de ipsorum peccatis, qui ipsam accusabant."

x. p. 111 ; in chap. v. 14, also, a special kind of sinning is intended by
μηκέτι ἁμάρτανε ; and the same command, in ver. 11, addressed to the *adulteress*, authenticates the sense in which ἀναμάρτητος is used. The men tempting Him knew how to avoid, in outward appearance rather than in reality,
the unchastity which they condemned. Taking the words to mean *freedom
from sin generally*,[1] we make Jesus propose an impracticable condition in the
given case, quite unfitted to disarm His opponents through their own consciences ; for it would have been a purely ideal condition, a standard impossible to man. If we take ἀναμάρτητος, however, in the concrete sense
above explained, the condition named becomes quite appropriate to baffle
the purpose of the tempting questioners ; for the prescription of the Mosaic
law is, on the one hand, fully recognized ;[2] while, on the other, its fulfilment is made dependent on a condition which would effectually banish
from the mind of His questioners, into whose consciences Jesus was looking,
all thought of making His answer a ground of accusation to the authorities.
—Observe, further, how the general moral maxim to be deduced from the
text condemns generally in the Christian community, viewed as it ought to
exist conformably to its ideal, the personal condemnation of the sins of
others (comp. Matt. vii. 1 ; Gal. vi. 5), and puts in its place brotherly admonition, conciliation, forgiveness—in a word, love, as the πλήρωσις of the
law. — τὸν λίθον] *the stone* which He would cast at her in obedience to the
law. — ἐπ’ αὐτῇ] *upon her*.[3] — βαλέτω] not mere permission, but *command*, and
therefore all the more telling. The place of stoning must be conceived
as lying outside the city (Lev. xxiv. 14 ; Acts vii. 56). We must further
observe that Jesus does not say *the first stone*, but let the *first* (i.e. *of you,
ὑμῶν*) *cast the stone*, which does not exclude that casting of the first, which
was obligatory on the *witnesses* (Deut. xvii. 7 ; Acts vii. 58).

Vv. 8, 9. Πάλιν, κ.τ.λ.] To indicate that He has nothing further to do
with the case. According to Jerome[4] and Euthymius Zigabenus, "in
order to give space to the questioners to take themselves away ;" but this
is not in keeping with ver. 6. — ἐξήρχοντο] *descriptive* imperfect. — εἰς καθ’
εἰς] Mark xiv. 19. — ἕως τ. ἐσχάτ.] is to be connected with εἰς καθ’ εἰς, ἀρξ.
ἀπὸ τ. πρεσβ. being an intervening clause. See on Matt. xx. 8.—The πρεσ-
βύτεροι are the *elders in years*, not the *elders of the people ;* for there would be
no apparent reason why the latter should be the first who should have
chosen to go away ; besides, the elders of the people are not named along
with the others in ver. 3. Those *more advanced in years*, on the other hand,
were also *thoughtful* and *prudent* enough to go away first, instead of stop-
ping to compromise themselves further. — ἕως τῶν ἐσχάτ.] attested as genuine
by preponderating evidence. It does not refer to *rank, the least* (so most
modern expositors, also Lücke, B. Crusius, de Wette, Maier, Lange),

---

[1] Baur, who draws from the passage
an erroneous doctrinal meaning, Luthardt,
Ewald, Hengstenberg, Godet, following
early expositors.

[2] The section cannot therefore be used,
as Mittermayer uses it (*d. Todesstr.* 1862), as

a testimony of Jesus against capital punishment.

[3] See Berhardy, p. 249 ; Ellendt, *Lex. Soph.*
i. p. 467.

[4] According to whom Christ wrote the
sins of His accusers and of all mortals !

which the context does not sanction ; the context (see εἰς καθ᾽ εἷς) leads us rather to render it *unto the last*, viz. *who went out*, i.e. until all were gone. The feature that the eldest (who probably stood nearest to Jesus) were the first to go out, is characteristic and original ; but that the going away took place in the order of rank, is a meaning imported into the words by the expositors. After ἀκούσ. the received text has καὶ ὑπὸ τῆς συνειδήσεως ἐλεγχόμενοι, a gloss opposed to very important witnesses ; but as to the matter of fact, right enough. — μόνος ὁ Ἰησ., κ.τ.λ.] Augustine well says : "Relicta sunt duo, *miseria et misericordia.*" But it does not exclude the presence of the disciples and the crowds of lookers-on at a distance.

Vv. 10, 11. Οἱ κατήγ.] who have accused thee to me, as if I were to be judge. — οὐδείς] is emphatic : Has *no one* condemned thee ? Has no one declared that thou art to be stoned ? Were it not so, they would not have left the woman to go free, and all of them gone away. The κατέκρινεν here designates the *sententia damnatoria*, not as a *judicial sentence* (for the γραμματεῖς and Pharisees had come merely as *asking a question* concerning a matter of *law or right*), but simply as the judgment of an *individual*. — οὐδὲ ἐγώ σε κατακρ. : *I also do not condemn thee.* This is not the declaration of *the forgiveness of sin*, as in Matt. ix. 2, Luke vii. 48, and cannot therefore justly be urged against the historical genuineness of the narrative (see, in particular, Hengstenberg) ; nor is it a mere declinature of *judicial competency*, which would be out of keeping with the preceding question, and with the admonition that follows : on the contrary, it is a *refusal to condemn*, spoken in the consciousness of His *Messianic calling*, according to which He had *not come to condemn*, but to seek and save the lost (iii. 17, xii. 46 ; Matt. xviii. 11) ; not to cast out sinners ; "not to quench the smoking flax," etc. He accordingly does in this case what by His office He is called to do, namely, to awaken and give room for repentance [1] in the sinner, instead of condemning ; for He dismisses her with the admonition μηκέτι ἁμάρτανε. Augustine well says : "Ergo et Dominus damnavit, sed peccatum, non hominem." How striking the force of the negative *declaration* and the positive *admonition !*

Ver. 12. The interpolated section, vii. 53–viii. 11, being deleted, we must look for some connection with vii. 52. This may be found simply as follows. As the Sanhedrim had not been able to carry out their design of apprehending Jesus, and had, moreover, become divided among themselves (as is recorded in vii. 45–52), He was able, in consequence of this miscarriage in their plans against Him (οὖν), to come forth afresh and address the assembled people in the temple (αὐτοῖς, comp. ver. 20). This renewed coming forward to address them is not, however, to be placed on the last day of the feast, but is so definitely marked off by ver. 20 as a special act, and so clearly distinguished from the preceding, that it must be assigned to one of the *following* days ; just as in ver. 21 the similar transition and the recurring πάλιν introduce again a new discourse spoken on another day. Others take a

---

[1] In connection with the marriage law, it is clear from this passage that, in the case of adultery, repentance on the part of the guilty party makes the continuance of the marriage allowable.

different view, putting the discourses in vv. 12–20, and even that also in
ver. 21 ff., on the day named in chap. vii. 37 ; but against this is not only
the πάλιν of ver. 12 and ver. 21, but the οὖν, which in both places bears an
evident reference to some preceding *historical* observation. Though Lücke's
difficulty, that a single day would be too short for so many discourses and
replies, can have no weight, there is yet no sufficient ground for de Wette's
supposition, that John did not know how to hold securely the thread of the
history. — *I am the light of the world,* i.e. (comp. on i. 4) *the possessor and
bearer of the divine truth of salvation* (τ. φ. τῆς ζωῆς), *from whom this saving
truth goes forth to all mankind* (κόσμος), who without Christ are dark and
dead.   The light is not *identical* with the salvation (Hengstenberg), but salvation is the necessary *emanation* therefrom ; *without* the light there is *no*
salvation. So also Isa. xlix. 6 ; comp. xlii. 6. To regard the figure which
Christ here employs, in witnessing to Himself, as suggested by some outward object—for example, by the two colossal golden candlesticks which
were lighted at the feast of Tabernacles (but certainly only on the first day ;
see Succah v. 2) in the forecourt of the women, where also was the γαζοφυλάκιον, ver. 20, on either side of the altar of burnt-offering (Wetstein, Paulus,
Olshausen),—is a precarious supposition, as the feast was now over ; at the
most, we can only associate the words with the *sight* of the candelabra, as
Hug and Lange do—the latter intermingling further references to spiritual
darkness from the history of the adulteress. But the figure, corresponding
as it essentially does with the thing signified, had been given long before,
and was quite a familiar one in the prophetic view of the idea of the Messiah
(Isa. ix. 1, xlii. 6 ; Mal. iv. 2). Comp. also Matt. iv. 15, 16 ; Luke ii. 32 ;
and the Rabbinical references in Lightfoot, p. 1041.   There is really no
need to suppose any special suggesting cause, not even the reading of Isa.
xlii. ; for though the Scriptures were read in the synagogues, we have no
proof that they were read in the temple.   To find also a reference to the
pillar of fire in the wilderness (Godet), according to which the ὁ ἀκολουθῶν,
κ.τ.λ., has reference to Israel's wanderings, is quite arbitrary ; no better,
indeed, than the reference of vii. 37 to the rock in the wilderness. — οὐ μὴ
περιπατήσει] The strongly attested, though not decisively confirmed, subjunctive περιπατήσῃ (so Lachmann, Tischendorf) would be the *most usual*
word in the N. T. after οὐ μή, and might therefore all the more easily have
displaced the future, which could hardly have been introduced through the
following ἕξει, seeing that the latter word has no connection with οὐ μή. Upon
οὐ μή, with the more definitely assuring *future,* see on Matt. xxvi. 35 ; Mark
xiv. 31. — ἕξει τὸ φῶς τ. ζωῆς] As the antithesis of the divine ἀλήθεια, the
σκοτία, is the causative element of death, so is the light the cause of life, *i.e.*
of the true eternal *Messianic* life, not only in its consummation after the
Parousia, but already in its temporal development (comp. iii. 15).   ἕξει, *it
will not be wanting to him, he will be in possession of it,* for it necessarily communicates itself to him direct from its personal source, which he follows in
virtue of his fellowship with Christ ("lux enim *praeferri* solet," Grotius).
The ἀκολουθεῖν takes place through *faith ;* but in the believer, who as such
walks no more in darkness (xii. 46 ; Eph. v. 8 ; Col. i. 13), Christ Him-

self lives (the Johannean "I in you," and the Pauline Gal. ii. 20 ; see on vi.
51), and therefore he has that light of life which proceeds from Christ as a
real and inward possession (Nonnus, ὁμόφοιτον ἐν αὐτῷ) ; he is υἱὸς φωτός (xii.
36), and himself "light in the Lord" (Eph. v. 8).   This explanation, not
merely the *having Christ with him* (Weiss), is required by the context ;
because ἕξει, κ.τ.λ., is the *result* of the ἀκολουθεῖν, and therefore of faith
(comp. iii. 15, 36, v. 24, vi. 47), and accordingly τῆς ζωῆς is added.

Vv. 13, 14.   This great declaration the Pharisees present (οἱ Φαρισ.) cannot leave unchallenged ; they, however, cleverly enough, while avoiding
dealing with its real substance, bring against it a *formal* objection ; comp.
v. 31.   Jesus replies, that the rule of law referred to does not apply to *His*
witness regarding Himself, as He testified concerning Himself, not in His
own human individuality, but in the conscious certainty of His having been
sent from, and being about to return to, heaven—a relation which is, of
course, unknown to His opponents, who therefore reject His testimony.
The refutation lies in the fact that God is able, without any departure from
truth, to testify concerning Himself. — κἂν ἐγώ μαρτ., κ.τ.λ.] not : *if also
I* (Lücke), nor : *although I*, etc. (B. Crusius), for both would require ἐὰν
καί ; but : *even if*, i.e. *even in case* (*adeo tum, si*), if I for my part (ἐγώ), etc.[1]
— ποῦ ὑπάγω] through death, vii. 33. — ἔρχομαι] ἦλθον was previously used of
the historical point of the past ; here, however, the *Praes.*, in using which
Jesus means His *continuous coming forward* as the ambassador of God.
Comp. iii. 31.   The latter represents it more as a matter of the *present*. — ἤ]
not again καί, because the two points are conceived, not as before *copula-
tively*, but *alternatively* ("whether I speak of the one *or* the other, you do
not know it").[2]   The latter is more *expressive*, because it is disjunctive.

Vv. 14, 16.   The course of thought repeated with some minuteness
(Tholuck), but similarly to vii. 24.   The rejection of His testimony by the
Pharisees in ver. 13, was an act of *judgment* on their part which, unacquainted as they were with His higher position as an ambassador of God, had
been determined merely by *His outward sensuous appearance*, by His *servant's*
form,[3] as to which He seemed to them to be an ordinary man.   This Jesus
tells them, and adds, how very differently He proceeds in this respect.[4]
Κρίνειν receives through the context the *condemnatory* sense, and κατὰ τὴν
σάρκα is not to be understood of the *subjective* norm (Chrysostom : ἀπὸ ἀνθρω-
πίνης διανοίας . . . ἀδίκως : de Wette : in a carnal, selfish manner ; comp.
B. Crusius), but of the *objective* norm.[5] — ἐγὼ οὐ κρίνω οὐδένα] *I condemn no
one*.   There is no need, however, for supplying in thought κατὰ τ. σάρκα, as
even Augustine proposed, and after Cyril's example many modern writers
(also Kuinoel, Paulus) ; to the same thing comes Lücke's supplement : *as*

---

[1] See Klotz, *ad Devar.* p. 519 ; Stallb. *ad
Plat. Apol.* p. 32 A ; Baeumlein, *Partik.*
p. 151.

[2] Comp. 1 Cor. xi. 27.

[3] εἰσορόωντες ἐμὴν βροτοειδέα μορφήν, Nonnus.

[4] Hilgenfeld, *Evang.* p. 286, ought there-

fore not to have concluded that the words,
"I judge no man," presuppose the history
of the woman taken in adultery.

[5] Comp. κατ' ὄψιν, vii. 24 ; Euth. Zigabenus,
πρὸς μόνον τὸ φαινόμενον βλέποντες, καὶ μηδὲν
ὑψηλότερον καὶ πνευματικὸν ἐννοοῦντες. Comp.
2 Cor. v. 16.

you do. This is decidedly to be rejected, partly for the general reason that the proper *point* would have to be supplied in thought, and partly because, in ver. 16, καὶ ἐὰν κρίνω cannot be taken otherwise than absolutely, and *without* supplement. For these reasons *every* kind of supplement must be rejected, whether by the insertion of νῦν, which would point to the future judgment,[1] or of μόνος (Storr, Godet), as though John had written αὐτὸς ἐγώ. Jesus rather gives utterance to *His maxim* in the consciousness of having come, not *to judge*, but to save and bless (comp. on ver. 11), which is what He carried out *principaliter ;* but this principle was, *that He refrained from all condemnation of others*, knowing as He did that κρίνειν was neither the end (Brückner) nor the sphere of His life (Hengstenberg). This principle, however, did not exclude *necessary cases of an opposite kind ;* and of such cases ver. 16 supplies the necessary explanation. Luther aptly remarks : "He herewith clothes Himself with His *office ;*" but an antithesis to *teaching* (Calvin, Beza) is foreign to the verse ; and the interpretation : I have no *pleasure* in judging (de Wette), imports into the words what they do not contain.[2] — Ver. 16. καὶ ἐὰν κρίνω δὲ ἐγώ] καὶ δέ here and in ver. 17, *atque etiam*, see on vi. 51. The thought is : *and even if a κρίνειν on my part should take place*, etc. Notwithstanding His maxim, not to judge, such cases had actually occurred in the exercise of His vocation, and, indeed, just for the purpose of attaining its higher object—as was, moreover, inevitable with His antagonism to sin and the κόσμος. Comp. Luther : "If thou wilt not have our Lord God, then keep the devil ; and the office which otherwise is not set for judgment, but for help and consolation, is compelled to assume the function of condemnation." Luthardt : " *But my witness becomes a judgment through unbelief.*" This, however, is not in the passage ; and Jesus was often enough forced into actual, direct judging, ver. 26. — δέ] occupies the fourth place, because the preceding words are connected with each other, as in ver. 17, vi. 51 ; 1 'John i. 3 ; Matt. x. 18, *al.*—According to the reading ἀληθινή (see the critical notes), the meaning of the second clause is : my judgment is a *genuine* one, *answering to the idea*, as it *ought* to be— not equivalent to ἀληθής (B. Crusius). Comp. on vii. 28. Reason : *For it is not* (like an ordinary human personality, restricted to myself) *I alone* (who judge), *but I and the Father that hath sent me* (are the κρίνοντες), which fellowship[3] naturally excludes everything that could prevent the κρίσις from being ἀληθινή. Comp. v. 30.

Vv. 17, 18. After the *first* reason in answer to the Pharisaic rejection of His self-witness (namely, that He gave it in the consciousness of His divine mission, ver. 14), and after administering a reproof to His antagonists, in connection therewith, for their judging (vv. 15, 16), there follows a *second* reason, namely, *that His witness to Himself is no violation of the Jewish law,*

---

[1] Augustine, Chrysostom, Euth. Zigabenus, Erasmus, etc.

[2] Among the meanings imported into the passage may be reckoned Lange's fanciful notion (*L. J.* II. p. 958) that Jesus can never regard the *real essence* of man as worthy of rejection (but merely the caricature which man has made of his own nature by sin). Where is there anything in the passage about the real essence of man ?

[3] ὅπερ ἐγὼ κρίνω, τοῦτο καὶ ὁ πατήρ, Euth. Zigabenus.

but has more than the amount of truth thereby required. — καὶ . . . δέ] *atque etiam,* as above in ver. 16. — τῷ ὑμετ.] emphatically, from the point of view of His opponents (comp. x. 34, xv. 25), who took their stand thereon, and regarded Jesus as a *law-breaker,* and even in ver. 13 had had in view a well-known prescription of the law.   The words of Christ are therefore no doubt anti-Judaic, but not in themselves antinomian,[1] or belonging to a later Christian point of view ;[2] nor must they be taken to mean : for Christ and believers the law exists no longer,[3] though, no doubt, they expressed His consciousness of being exalted above the Jewish law as it then was, and in the strange and hostile form in which it met Him.   Keim[4] is therefore mistaken in saying : "In *this* way neither could *Jesus* speak nor *John* write—not even *Paul.*" See v. 45–47, vii. 19, 22 f., v. 39, x. 35, xix. 36. — The passage itself from the law is quoted with considerable freedom (Deut. xvii. 6, xix. 15), ἀνθρώπων being uttered with intentional emphasis, as Jesus draws a conclusion *a minori ad majus.*   If the law demands two *human* witnesses, in my witness there is still more ; for the witnesses whose declaration is contained therein are (1) my own individuality ; and (2) the Father who has sent me ; as His representative and interpreter, therefore, I testify, so that *my* witness is also *His.*   That which took place, as to substance, in the living and inseparable unity of the divine-human consciousness, to wit, *His* witnessing, and *God's* witnessing, Jesus discriminates here only *formally,* for the sake of being able to apply the passage of the law in question, from which He argues κατ' ἀνθρωπον ; but not incorrectly (Schenkel) : hence, also, there is no need for supplying in thought to ἐγώ : "*As a human knower of myself, as an honest man*" (Paulus), and the like ; or even, "*as the Son of God*" (Olshausen, who also brings in the Holy Ghost).

Ver. 19. The question of the Pharisees, who only pretend not to understand what Jesus means by the words ὁ πέμψας με πατήρ, between which and ver. 27 there is no inconsistency, is *frivolous mockery.*   "Where is, then, this second witness, thy Father ?"   He has no actual existence !   He ought, surely, to be here on the spot, if, as thou hast said, He were a witness with thee on thy behalf !   To regard their question as the expression of a *veritable material understanding* on their part, that He referred to a *physical father,*[5] some also having found in it a blasphemous allusion to bastardy (Cyril, Ammon), is irreconcilable with the circumstance that Jesus had already so frequently and unmistakably pointed to *God* as His Father ; the questioners themselves also betray their dissimulation by the word ποῦ ; they do not ask τίς.   Totally different is the relation of the question put by Philip in xiv. 8. — The *reply* of Jesus unveils to them with clear composure whence it arose that they put so wicked a question.   To take the words οὔτε ἐμέ as far as μου as a *question* is less appropriate (Ewald), as it is scarcely

---

[1] Schweizer, Baur, Reuss.
[2] De Wette, B. Crusius, Tholuck.
[3] Messner, *Lehre der Apostel.* p. 345.
[4] See his *Geschichtlich. Christ.* p. 14, ed. 3. Note, on the contrary, that it is John himself who stands *higher* than Paul. But not

even the Johannean Jesus has broken with the law, or treated it as antiquated. See especially vv. 45–47. *His* relation to the law is also that of *fulfilment.*

[5] Augustine, Bede, etc. ; de Wette, Olshausen, Brückner, and, doubtfully, Lücke.

likely that Jesus was *taken by surprise*. The εἰ ἐμὲ ᾔδειτε, etc., rests on the fact that the Father reveals Himself in Him. Comp. xiv. 9, xvi. 3.

Ver. 20. Ταῦτα τὰ ῥήματα] Vv. 12, 13. Godet arbitrarily imports into the text "*words so important.*" Comp. vi. 50. — ἐν τῷ γαζοφυλ.] *At the treasury.* On ἐν, as denoting immediate neighbourhood, see Kühner, *ad Xen. Anab.* iv. 8. 22 ; Ast, *Lex. Plat.* I. p. 700 ; Winer, p. 360 [E. T. p. 385], who, however, is of opinion—though it cannot be substantiated—that the *place itself where* the treasury stood was called γαζοφυλ.; so also Tholuck, Brückner. Respecting the γαζοφυλάκιον, which consisted of thirteen brazen chests destined to receive the taxes and charitable offerings in the temple, see on Mark xii. 41. In a place so much frequented in the forecourt of the women did Jesus thus speak,—and no one laid hands on Him. — καὶ οὐδείς, etc.] Historical refrain, constituting a kind of triumphal (comp. vii. 30) close to the delivery of this discourse.

Ver. 21. A *new* scene here opens, as in ver. 12, and is therefore, after the analogy of ver. 12, to be placed in one of the *following* days (so also Ewald ; and in opposition to Origen and the *common* supposition). — The connecting word, with which the further discussion on this occasion (it is different in ver.12) takes its rise, is a word of grave *threatening*, more severely punitive than even vii. 34.—οὖν] As no one had laid hands on Him, comp. ver. 12.— πάλιν, as in ver. 12, indicating the delivery of a *second discourse*, not a repetition of vii. 34. — αὐτοῖς] to the Jews who were present in the temple, vv. 20, 22. — ζητήσετέ με] namely, as a deliverer from the misfortunes that are coming upon you, as in vii. 34. But instead of the clause there added, καὶ οὐχ εὑρήσετε, here we have the far more tragical and positive declaration, κ. ἐν τ. ἁμαρτ. ὑμ. ἀποθ. and (not reconciled and sanctified, but) *in your sin* (still laden with it and your unatoned guilt, ix. 34 ; 1 Cor. xv. 17) *ye shall die*, namely, in the universal misfortunes amid which you will lose your lives. Accordingly, ἐν is the state *wherein*, and not the cause *whereby* (Hengstenberg) they die. The text does not require us to understand *eternal* death, although that is the *consequence* of dying in this state. Ἐν τῇ ἁμαρτίᾳ ὑμῶν, however, is to be taken in a *collective* sense (see ver. 24, i. 29, ix. 41), and not as *merely* referring to the sin of *unbelief;* though being itself sin (xvi. 9), it is the ground of the non-extinction and increase of their sin. Between ζητήσετέ με, finally, and the dying in sin, there is no contradiction ; for the seeking in question is not the seeking of *faith*, but that seeking of *desperation* whose object is merely deliverance from *external* afflictions. The *futility* of that search, so fearfully expressed by the words καὶ—ἀποθαν., is further explained by ὅπου ἐγὼ ὑπάγω, etc., for they cannot ascend into *heaven*, in order to find Jesus as a deliverer, and to bring Him down (to this view xiii. 33 is not opposed). Accordingly, these words are to be taken quite as in vii. 34, not as referring to *hell* into which they would come through death ; for Jesus speaks, not of their condition *after*, but *up to*, their death.

Ver. 22. It did not escape the notice of the Jews that in using ὑπάγω He meant a *voluntary* departure. But that *they* should not be able to come whither *He* goeth away, excites in them, not fear and concern on His account (Ewald), but *impious mockery ;* and they ask : He will not perchance

kill himself, in that he saith, etc. ? In this case, indeed, we shall not be
able to reach him ! The emphasis rests on ἀποκτενεῖ, as the *mode* in which
they scornfully conceive the ὑπάγειν to take place. — *Gehenna* being the ὅπου
which would follow on such a departure (Joseph. *Bell.* iii. 8. 5, and see
Wetstein and Ewald, *Alterth.* p. 232). The scorn (which Hengstenberg
also groundlessly denies) is similar to that in vii. 35, only much more malicious.

Vv. 23, 24. Without further noticing their venomous scorn, Jesus simply
holds up before them, with firm and elevated calmness, *their own low nature*,
which made them capable of thus mocking Him, because they did not understand Him, the heavenly One. — ἐκ τῶν κάτω] *from the lower regions*, i.e.
ἐκ τῆς γῆς (comp. Acts ii. 19), the opposite of τὰ ἄνω, *the heavenly* regions ;
ἄνω being used of *heavenly* relations in solemn discourse (Col. iii. 1, 2 ; Gal.
iv. 26 ; Phil. iii. 14) ; comp. on ἄνωθεν, iii. 31. Ἐκ designates *derivation ;*
you spring from the earth, I from the heaven. To understand κάτω as denoting the *lower world* (Origen, Nonnus, Lange), a meaning which Godet
also considers as *included* in it, would correspond, indeed, to the current
classical usage, but is opposed by the parallel of the second half of the
verse. — οὐκ εἰμὶ ἐκ τ. κόσμου τούτου] *I do not spring from this* (pre-Messianic,
comp. αἰὼν οὗτος) *world ;* negative expression of His supramundane, heavenly
derivation.[1] Comp. xviii. 36. Both halves of the verse contain the same
thought ; and the clauses ἐκ τῶν κάτω ἐστέ and ἐκ τοῦ κόσμου τούτου ἐστέ imply,
in their pregnant meaning, that those men are also of *such a character and
disposition* as correspond to their low extraction, without higher wisdom
and divine life. Comp. iii. 31. Therefore had Jesus said to them—He
refers them again to His words in ver. 24—they would die in their sins ;
and now He adds the reason : ἐὰν γάρ, etc. ; for only *faith* can help to the
higher divine life in time and eternity (i. 12, iii. 15 f., vi. 40 ff., xvii. 3,
al.), those who are ἐκ τῶν κάτω and ἐκ τοῦ κόσμου τούτου, and as such, are born
flesh of flesh.—Notice, that in this repetition of the minatory words the emphasis, which in ver. 20 rested on ἐν τ. ἁμ. ὑμ., is laid on ἀποθαν. ; and that
thus prominence is given to the *perishing itself*, which could be averted
only by conversion to faith. — ὅτι ἐγώ εἰμι] namely, *the Messiah*, the great
name which every one understood without explanation, which concentrated
in itself the highest hopes of all Israel on the basis of the old prophecies,
and which was the *most present thought* both to Jesus and the Jews, especially
in all their discussions—to Jesus, in the form, " I am the Messiah ;" to the
Jews, in the form of either, " Is *He* the Messiah ?" or, " *This* is not the
Messiah, but another, who is yet to come." Comp. ver. 28, xiii. 19.   In
opposition to the notion of there being another, Jesus uses the emphatic
ἐγώ. The non-mention of the name, which was taken for granted (it had

---

[1] Not merely of the heavenly *direction of
His spirit* (Weizsäcker), which must be
taken for granted in the Christ who springs
from above (comp. iii. 31). Wherever Christ
speaks of His heavenly descent, He speaks
in the consciousness of having had a pre-
human, supra-mundane existence (in the
consciousness of the Logos), xvii. 5, and
lays claim to a transcendent relation of His
essential nature. Comp. Weiss, *Lehrbegr.*
p. 215 f. Nonnus : ξεῖνος ἔφυν κόσμοιο.

been *mentioned* in iv. 25, 26), confers on it a quiet *majesty* that makes an irresistible impression on the minds of the hearers while Christ gives utterance to the brief words, ὅτι ἐγώ εἰμι. As God comprehended the sum of the Old Testament faith in הוּא אֲנִי,[1] so Christ that of the New Testament in ὅτι ἐγώ εἰμι.[2] The definite *confession* of this faith is given in xvi. 3, vi. 68, 69 ; 1 John iv. 2.

Ver. 25. The Jews understand the ὅτι ἐγώ εἰμι well enough, but refuse to recognize it, and therefore ask pertly and contemptuously : σὺ τίς εἶ ; *tu quis es?* σύ being emphasized to express disdain ; comp. Acts xix. 15. Jesus replies with a *counter-question of surprise* at so great obduracy on their part ; but then at once after ver. 26 discontinues any further utterance regarding them, His opponents. His counter-question is : τὴν ἀρχὴν ὅ, τι καὶ λαλῶ ὑμῖν ? *What I from the very beginning also say to you?* namely, do you ask that ? Who I am (to wit, the Messiah, vv. 24, 29), that is, the very thing which, from the very beginning, since I have been among you, and have spoken to you, has formed the matter of my discourse ;[3] and can you still ask about that, as though you had not yet heard it from me ? They ought to have *known* long ago, and to have *recognized*, what they just now *asked* with their wicked question σὺ τίς εἶ. This view is not complicated, as Winer objects, but corresponds simply to the words and to the situation. On ἀρχήν as used frequently in an adverbial sense, both among the Greeks and by the LXX., with and without the article, to denote time, *ab initio, from the very beginning*, see Schweighaüser, *Lex. Herod.* I. p. 104 f. ; Lennep *ad Phalar.* p. 82 ff. It *precedes* the relative, because it is the *point* which makes the obduracy of the Jews so very perceptible.[4] — ὅ, τι] interrogatively, in relation to a question with τίς immediately preceding,—as frequently in the Classics, so that some such words as *thou askest* must be supplied in thought.[5] — καί] *also*, expresses the *corresponding* relation (Baeumlein, *Partik.* p. 152), in this case, of *speech* to *being :* what from the very beginning, as *I am* it, so also, I *say* it to you. — λαλῶ] *speak*, not : *say*. Comp. on vv. 26, 43 ; and see on Rom. iii. 19. He does not use λελάληκα, because it is a *continuous* speaking ; the sound of it is, in fact, still ringing in their ears from. vv. 23, 24. — The passage is also taken *interrogatively* by Matthaei, Lachmann, Tischendorf, and Lücke. The latter [6] renders : *Why,*

---

[1] Deut. xxxii. 39 ; Isa. xli. 13, xliii. 10.

[2] Comp. Hofmann, *Schriftbew.* I. p. 63 f.

[3] According to John, at His very first appearance in the temple, ii. 19.

[4] Comp. iv. 18 ; Buttmann, *Neut. Gram.* p. 333 d. [E. T. p. 389].

[5] See Kühner, II. § 837, note 1 ; Bernhardy p. 443 ; Krüger, § 51. 17. 3.

[6] So, without doubt, Chrysostom also, who gives as the meaning : τοῦ ὅλως ἀκούειν τῶν λόγων τῶν παρ' ἐμοῦ ἀνάξιοί ἐστε, μήτι γε καὶ μαθεῖν ὅστις ἐγώ εἰμι. Comp. Cyril and Theophylact, also Euth. Zigabenus. Matthaei explains the words in exact accordance with Lücke : " *Cur vero omnino*

vobiscum loquor? cur frustra vobiscum disputo?" See *ed. min.* I. p. 575. With this also is in substantial agreement the view of Ewald, who, however, regards the words rather as the expression of righteous indignation than as a question : " *That I should, indeed, speak to you at all!*" It would be more correct to say : " *That I should at all even* (still) *speak to you!*" But how greatly is the *at all* thus in the way ! Ὅτι, too, would then need a supplement, which is not furnished by the text. Besides, the following words, especially if introduced without an ἀλλά or μέντοι (indicating that Jesus had collected Himself again, and

indeed, do I still speak to you at all? With this view, it is true, τὴν ἀρχήν is quite compatible ; for it is confessedly often used in the Classics for *ab initio*, in the sense of *omnino*,[1] though only in *negative* propositions, or such whose signification really amounts to a negation,[2] which latter, however, might be the case here ;[3] it is also allowable to take ὅ, τι in the sense of *why*.[4] But the *thought itself* has so little meaning in it, and is so little natural, expressing, besides, a *reflection*, which is at the bottom so empty, and, at the same time, through τὴν ἀρχήν, so expanded and destitute of feeling, that we should scarcely expect it at the lips of the Johannean Jesus, especially in circumstances so lively and significant as the present. Further thus understood, the saying would have no connection whatever with what follows, and the logical connection assumed by Lücke would require the insertion of some such words as περὶ ἐμοῦ. The words would thus likewise stand in no relation to the question σὺ τίς εἶ, whereas John's general manner would lead us to expect an answer which had reference in some significant way or other to the *question* which had been put. The following are *non-interrogative views :—* (1) *" What I have already said to you at the beginning, that am I!"* So Tholuck after Castalio, Beza, Vatablus, Maldonatus, Clericus, Heumann, and several others ; also B. Crusius. Jesus would thus be announcing that He had already, from the very beginning in His discourses, made known His higher personality. The Praes. λαλῶ, as expressing that which still continues to be in the present, would not be opposed to this view ; but it does not harmonize with the arrangement of the words ; and logically, at all events, καί ought to stand before τὴν ἀρχήν (comp. Syriac). (2) *"From the very first (before all things), I am what I also speak to you."* So de Wette ; comp. Luther ("I am your preacher ; if you first believe that, you will then learn what I am, and not otherwise"), Melanchthon, Aretius, and several ; also Maier, who, however, takes τὴν ἀρχήν incorrectly as *thoroughly (nothing else)*.[5] On this view Jesus, instead of answering directly : " I am the Messiah," would have said that He was to be known above all things from His discourses.[6] But τὴν ἀρχήν

---

suppressed His indignation), would not be appropriate. In the *Theol. Quartalschr.* 1855, p. 592 ff., Nirschl renders : " To what purpose shall I speak further to you of the origin, *i.e.* of God, and my own derivation from Him?" But on this view Christ ought, at the very least, to have said τὴν ἀρχήν μου.

[1] Raphel, *Herod. in loc.;* Hermann, *ad Viger.* p. 723 ; Ellendt, *Lex. Soph.* I. p. 237 ; Breitenbach, *ad Xen. Oec.* ii. 12.

[2] See especially Lennep, *l.c.* and p. 94 ; Brückner on the passage.

[3] As in Plat. *Demod.* p. 381 D ; Philo, *de Abr.* p. 366 C.

[4] See on Mark ix. 11 ; Buttmann, *neut. Gram.* p. 218 [E. T. p. 253].

[5] Comp. Winer, p. 432 [E. T. p. 464], who gives as the meaning : *" I am entirely that*

which *I represent myself as being in my discourses."* So also Godet : " Absolument ce que je vous dis ; ni plus ni moins que ce que renferme ma parole." But τ. ἀρχήν is used in the sense of *completely, entirely,* only in connection with negations (usually, too, *without* the article) : *not at all, not in the least;* " cum negatione praefracte negando servit," Ellendt, *Lex. Soph. l.c.*

[6] Under this head belongs also the view taken by Grotius (which is substantially adopted by Lange) : " *Primum* (in the first instance) *hoc sum, quod et dico vobis,* hoc ipsum quod me hoc ipso tempore esse dixi, *i.e.* lux mundi." As though we read ; πρῶτον μὲν ὅ, τι καὶ λέγω ὑμῖν. In the same way as Grotius, has Calov. also explained it, taking, however, τὴν ἀρχήν in the sense of *omnino, plane* (consequently like Winer).

does not mean "*above all things*," either in Xen. *Cyr.* i. 2, 3 (τὴν ἀρχὴν μὴ τοιοῦτοι, *at the very outset not such, i.e.* not such *at all, omnino non tales*), or in Herod. i. 9, where also, as frequently in Herodotus, it denotes *omnino*.[1] And how entirely without any reference would be the words *ante omnia* (surely some sort of *posterius* would need to be supplied in thought). Brückner has rightly, therefore, rejected the "*above all things*" in de Wette's rendering, though regarding it otherwise as the correct one, and keeping to the interpretation "*from the very first*" in its *temporal* sense. One cannot, however, see what is really intended by the words "*from the very first*, I am, etc.," especially as placed in such an emphatic position at the commencement of the clause. For Jesus had neither occasion nor ground for giving the assurance that He *had been* from His earliest appearance, and still *was*, such as He declared Himself to be in His discourses, and thus perchance had not since become different. (3) "*Undoubtedly* (nothing else) *am I what I also say to you*." So Kuinoel ;—a view which assigns an incorrect meaning to τὴν ἀρχήν, and confounds λαλῶ with λέγω ; objections which affect also the similar interpretation of Ebrard : "*I am altogether that which I also say to you* (that I am He)." (4) "*At the very outset I uttered of myself what I also declare to you, or what I also now say*." So Starck, *Not. sel.* p. 106 ; Bretschneider. But the supplying of λελάληκα from the following λαλῶ[2] would be suggested only if we read ὅ, τι καὶ νῦν λαλῶ ὑμῖν. (5) Fritzsche,[3] whom Hengstenberg follows, takes the view : "*Sum a rerum primordiis* (i. 1) *ea natura quam me esse vobis etiam profiteor*." Jesus would thus have designated Himself as the *primal Logos*. Quite unintelligibly for His hearers, who had no occasion for taking τὴν ἀρχήν in the absolute sense, as though reminded of the angel of the Lord in Mal. iii. and Zech. xi., nor for understanding ὅ, τι κ. λ. ὑμ. as Fritzsche does ; at all events, as far as the latter is concerned, λέγω ought to have been used instead of λαλῶ. (6) Some connect τὴν ἀρχήν with πολλὰ ἔχω, etc., ver. 26, and after λαλῶ ὑμῖν place merely a comma. So already Codd., Nonnus, Scaliger, Clarius, Knatchbull, Raphel, Bengel, and, more recently, Olshausen, Hofmann, *Schriftbew.* I. p. 65, II. p. 178, and Baeumlein. In taking the words thus, ὅ, τι is either written ὅτι, *because*, with Scaliger and Raphel (so also Bengel : "*principio, quum etiam loquor vobis* [Dativus commodi : '*ut credatis et salvemini* '] *multa habeo de vobis loqui*, etc."[4]), or is taken as a pronoun, *id quod*. In the latter way, Olshausen explains it, following Clarius : "*In the first place, as I also plainly say to you, I have much to blame and punish in you ;* I

---

[1] Comp. Wolf, *Dem. Lept.* p. 278.

[2] Comp. Dissen, *Dem. de Cor.* p. 359.

[3] *Lit. Bl. z. allg. Kirchenz.* 1843, p. 513, and *de conform. Lachmann*, p. 53.

[4] Comp. Hofmann : "At first, namely for the present, because this is the time, when He speaks to them, He has much to speak and to judge about them in words." Τὴν ἀρχήν is alleged to be used in opposition to a τὸ τέλος, *i.e.* to a time when that which He now *speaks* will be proved by *deeds*, ver. 28. In this way meaning and connection are imported into the passage, and yet the καί (with an appeal to Hartung, *Partik.* I. p. 129) is completely neglected, or rather transferred from the relative to the principal clause. How the passages adduced by Hartung may be explained without any transference, see in Klotz, *ad Devar.* p. 635 ff. In particular, there is no ground for supposing the existence of a *trajection* of the καί in the N. T. Hofmann explains, as though John had written : τὴν ἀρχήν, ὅτι νῦν λαλῶ ὑμῖν, καὶ πολλὰ ἔχω, etc.

am therefore your serious *admonisher*." Baeumlein, however, renders : "*I have undoubtedly—as I also do—much to speak and to judge concerning you.*" But on this view of the words Jesus would have given no answer at all to the question σὺ τίς εἶ ; according to Olshausen, τὴν ἀρχήν would have to be transformed into πρῶτον, *in the first place ;* and the middle clause, according to Olshausen and Baeumlein, would give a quite superfluous sense ; while, according to the view of Bengel and Hofmann, it would be forced and unnatural. (7) Exegetically impossible is the interpretation of Augustine : "*Principium* (the very beginning of all things) *me credite, quia* (ὅτι) *et loquor vobis,* i.e. *quia humilis propter vos factus ad ista verba descendi ;*" comp. Gothic, Ambrose, Bede, Ruperti, and several others. Calvin rightly rejects this interpretation, but himself gives one that is impossible. (8) Obscure, and far-fetched, is Luthardt's view (ὅτι, *that :* "*from the beginning am I, that I may also speak to you*"), that Jesus describes the act of His speaking, the existence of His word, as His presence for the Jews ; that from His first appearance He who was then present as the Word of God on the earth had been always used to give Himself a presence for men in the Word. If, according to this view, as it would seem, τὴν ἀρχὴν ὅτι denotes : "*from the beginning it is my manner, that,*" this cannot possibly be in the simple εἰμί, which has to be supplied in thought ; besides, how much is forced into the mere λαλῶ ὑμῖν ! [See Note XXXIII. p. 295.]

Ver. 26. The question in ver. 25 was a *reproach*. To this (not to ver. 24, as Godet maintains) refers the word πολλά, which is placed with full emphasis at the beginning of the verse ; the antithetical ἀλλ', however, and the excluding word ταῦτα, inform us that He does *not* say the *many things* which He has to speak and judge of them (and which He has in readiness, in store) ; but only that which He has heard from Him who sent Him. Comp. xvi. 12 ; 2 John 12. Similarly Euth. Zigabenus, after Chrysostom and B. Crusius. After the question in ver. 25, we must imagine a reproving *pause*. To be paraphrased : "I have very much to speak concerning you, and especially to blame ; but I refrain therefrom, and restrict myself to my immediate task, which is to utter forth to the world *that* which I have heard from God the True, who has sent me (namely, what I heard during my existence with God, before my mission ; comp. on ver. 28 [1])—in other words, to the communication of divine truth to the world." For divergent views of the course of thought, see Schott, *Opusc.* I. p. 94 ff. After the example of older writers, Lücke and de Wette take the view that Jesus meant to say : But, however much I have to judge concerning you, my judgment is still true ; for I speak to the world only what I have heard from my Father, who is true." Comp. also Tholuck. In this way, however, the antithesis has to be *artificially formed*, whilst the *expressed* antithesis between that which Jesus *has* to speak (ἔχω λαλεῖν) and that which He actually *says* (λέγω) is neglected. This is in answer to Ewald also, who imports into ἀλλ' the meaning : " Yet I will not therefore be afraid, like a man ;" and against Hengst., who, after

---

[1] So also vv. 38, 40. Not as Beyschlag maintains : immediately before my public appearance. Comp. on vi. 46.

πολλὰ . . . κρίνειν, supplies in thought : "This is the reason why you will not accept my utterances in relation to my person." — κἀγώ] and I, for my part, in contrast to God ; the word is connected with ταῦτα, etc. — ταῦτα] this and nothing else. As to the main point, Chrysostom aptly says : τὰ πρὸς σωτηρίαν, οὐ τὰ πρὸς ἐλεγχον. — εἰς τ. κόσμ.] See on Mark i. 39.[1] Not again λαλῶ (Lachmann, Tischendorf), but λέγω, because the notion has become by antithesis more definite : what He has heard, that it is which He says ; He has something else to say to the world than to speak of the worthlessness of His opponents. The former He does; the latter, much occasion as He has for doing it, He leaves undone.

Ver. 27. Ὠ τῆς ἀγνοίας ! οὐ διέλιπεν αὐτοῖς περὶ αὐτοῦ διαλεγόμενος, καὶ οὐκ ἐγίνωσκον, Chrysostom ; and Euth. Zigabenus calls them φρενοβλαβεῖς. But the surprising, nay more, the very improbable element (de Wette) which has been found in this non-understanding, disappears when it is remembered that at ver. 21 a new section of the discourse commenced, and that we are not obliged to suppose that precisely the same hearers were present in both cases (vv. 16, 17). The less, therefore, is it allowable to convert non-understanding into the idea of non-recognition (Lücke) ; or to regard it as equivalent to obduracy (Tholuck, Brückner) ; or to explain ὅτι as in which sense (Hofmann, l.c. p. 180) ; or with Luthardt, to press αὐτοῖς, and to give as the meaning of the simple words : "that in bearing witness to Himself He bears witness to them that the God who sends Him is the Father;" or with Ebrard, to find in ἔλεγεν : "that it is his vocation" to proclaim to them ; or, with Hengstenberg, to understand ἔγνωσαν, etc., of the true knowledge, namely, of the deity of Christ. For such interpretations as these there is no foundation in the passage ; it simply denotes : they knew not (comp. ver. 28) that in these words (ὁ πέμψας με, etc.) He spoke to them of the Father.[2]

Vv. 28, 29. Οὖν] not merely "continuing the narration" (de Wette), but : therefore, in reference to this non-understanding, as is confirmed by the words τότε γνώσεσθε, which refer to οὐκ ἔγνωσαν in ver. 27, and, indeed, considered as to its matter, logically correct, seeing that if the Jews had recognized the Messiahship of Jesus, they would also have understood what He said to them of His Father. — ὅταν ὑψώσητε, etc.] when ye shall have lifted up, namely, upon the cross. Comp. on iii. 14, vi. 62. The crucifixion is treated as an act of the Jews, who brought it about, as also in Acts iii. 14 f. — τότε γνώσ.] Comp. xii. 32, vi. 62. Then will the result follow, which till then you reject, that you will know, etc. Reason : because the death of Jesus is the condition of His glory, and of the mighty manifestations thereof (the outpouring of the Spirit ; miraculous works of the apostles; building up of the Church ; punishment of the Jews ; second coming to judgment). Then shall your eyes be opened, which will take place partly with your own will, and still in time (as in Acts ii. 36 ff., iv. 4, vi. 7 ; Rom. xi. 11 ff.) ; partly against your will, and too late (comp. on Matt. xxiii. 39 ; Luke

[1] Comp. Soph. El. 596: κήρυσσέ μ' εἰς ἅπαντας.
[2] On λέγειν, with the accus. in the sense of λαλ. περί, see Stallbaum, ad Plat. Apolog. p. 23 A ; Phaed. p. 79 C. Comp. on i. 15.

xiii. 34 f.). Bengel aptly remarks : "cognoscetis *ex re*, quod nunc ex verbo
non creditis." — καὶ ἀπ' ἐμαυτοῦ, etc.] still dependent on ὅτι, and, indeed, as
far as μετ' ἐμοῦ ἐστιν ; so that to the universal ποιῶ, the special λαλῶ *and* the
general μετ' ἐμοῦ ἐστιν (is my helper and support) *together* correspond. Hence
there is no brevity of discourse requiring to be completed by supplying in
thought λαλῶ to ποιῶ, and ποιῶ along with λαλῶ.[1] Nonnus already took the
correct view (he begins ver. 29 with ὅττι καί, etc.); and the objection[2] that
οὐκ ἀφῆκε, etc. would then stand too disconnected, has no force, since it is
precisely in John that the asyndetic continuation of a discourse is very common, and, in fact, would also be the case here if καί ὁ πέμψ. etc. were not
dependent on ὅτι. — ταῦτα] is arbitrarily and without precedent (Matt. ix. 33
cannot be adduced as one) explained as equivalent to οὕτως, from a commingling of two notions. By the demonstrative ταῦτα Jesus means *His doctrine* generally (comp. ver. 26), *with whose presentation He was now occupied.*
But of this He discoursed in harmony with the instructions received from
the Father, *i.e.* in harmony with the instructions derived from His direct
intuition of divine truth with the Father prior to His incarnation. Comp.
ver. 38, i. 18, iii. 13, vi. 46, vii. 16 f. — οὐκ ἀφῆκε, etc.] Independent corrob-
oration of the last thought, negatively expressed on account of His apparent abandonment in the face of many and powerful enemies. The *Praet.*
refers to *the experience felt in every case, during the course of His entire ministry, until now* (comp. afterwards πάντοτε), not to the *point of time when He
was sent ;* the reason afterwards assigned would not be appropriate to this
latter reference. Comp. also xvi. 32. — ὅτι ἐγώ, etc.] *because I,* etc. Reason
assigned for the οὐκ ἀφῆκε, etc. How could He ever leave me alone, as I am
He who, etc. ? (ἐγώ with emphasis). Comp. xv. 10. Olshausen regards οὐκ
ἀφῆκε, etc. as the expression of *equality of essence,* and ὅτι as assigning the
ground of His knowledge. The former idea is erroneous, as the meaning of
οὐκ ἀφῆκε, etc. is identical with that of μετ' ἐμοῦ ἐστιν ; and the latter would
be an inadequate reason, because it relates merely to moral agreement.

Vv. 30–32. The opening of a new section in the discourse, but not first
on the following day (Godet), which must then have been indicated as in
vv. 12, 21. — Notice the separation of the persons in question. The πολλοί
are many among His *hearers in general ;* among these *many* there were also
Jewish hierarchs, and because He knew how fleeting and impure was their
momentary faith,[3] Jesus addresses to *them* the words in vv. 31, 32, which at
once had the effect of converting them into opponents ; hence there is no
inconsistency in His treatment of His hearers. — πεπιστ. αὐτῷ] previously
ἐπίστ. εἰς αὐτόν. The latter was the consequence of their having believed
Him, i.e. His words. — ἐὰν ὑμεῖς, etc.] if *you on your part,* etc. ; for they
were mixed up with the unbelieving crowd, and by means of ὑμεῖς are selected from it as *the* persons to whom the admonition and promise are addressed. They are to *abide* in the word of Jesus, as in the permanent ele-

[1] De Wette, after Bengel.
[2] Lücke, de Wette, and others.
[3] Mere *susceptibility* to salvation is not
termed *Faith* by John, as Messner (*Lehre*

der *Ap.* p. 349) assumes in reference to
this passage. Also not in vi. 69, or 1 John
iv. 16.

ment of their inner and outer life. For another form of the conception, see ver. 38, xv. 7, xii. 47. Comp. 2 John 9. — ἀληθῶς] really, not merely in appearance, after being momentarily carried away. — γνώσεσθε τ. ἀλήθ.] for divine *truth* is the *substance* of the λόγος of Christ, Christ Himself is its possessor and vehicle ; and the *knowledge* of it commences when a man believes, inasmuch as the knowledge is the inwardly experienced, living, and moral *intelligence* of faith (xvii. 17 ; 1 John i. 3 ff.). — ἐλευθερ.] from the slavery, *i.e.* from the determining power, of sin. See ver. 34 ; Rom. vi. 18 ff. "Ea libertas est, quae pectus purum et firmum gestitat" (Ennius, fr. 340). Divine truth is conceived as the *causa medians* of that regeneration and sanctification which makes him morally free who is justified by faith. Comp. Rom. viii. 2 ; Jas. i. 20, ii. 12.

Ver. 33. Ἀπεκρίθησαν] No others can be the subject, but the πεπιστευκότες αὐτῷ Ἰουδαῖοι, ver. 31. So correctly, Melanchthon ("offensi resiliunt"), Maldonatus, Bengel, Olshausen, Kling, B. Crusius, Hilgenfeld, Lange, Ewald, and several others, after Chrysostom, who aptly observes : κατέπεσεν εὐθέως αὐτῶν ἡ διάνοια· τοῦτο δὲ γέγονεν ἀπὸ τοῦ πρὸς τὰ κοσμικὰ ἐπτοῆσθαι. John himself has precluded us from supposing any other to be intended, by expressly referring (ver. 31) to those Jews among the *many* (ver. 30) who had believed, and emphatically marking them as the persons who conduct the following conversation. To them the last word of Jesus proved at once a stone of stumbling. Hence we must not suppose that *Jews* are referred to who had remained unbelieving and hostile,[1] and different from those who were mentioned in ver. 31 (ἀπεκρ. *they*, indef.) ; nor do the words ζητεῖτέ με ἀποκτ. in ver. 37 necessitate this supposition, inasmuch as those πεπιστευκότες might have at once veered round and returned again to the ranks of the opposition, owing to the offence given to their national pride by the words in ver. 32. There is no warrant therefore for saying with Luthardt that the reply came *primarily* from *opponents*, but that some of those who *believed* chimed in from want of understanding. The text speaks *exclusively* of πεπιστευκότες. — σπέρμα Ἀβρ. ἐσμ.] to which, as being destined to become a blessing to, and have dominion over, the world,[2] a state of bondage is something completely foreign. As every Hebrew servant was a son of Abraham, this major premiss of their argument shows that they had in view, not their *individual* or civil (Grotius, Lücke, Godet), but their *national* liberty. At the same time, in their passion they leave out of consideration the Egyptian and Babylonian history of their nation, and look solely at the present generation, which the Romans had, in accordance with their prudent policy, left in possession of the semblance of political independence (Joseph. *Bell.* vi. 6. 2). This, according to circumstances, as in the present case, they were able to class at all events in the category of *non-bondage.* Hence there is no need even for the distinction between dominion *de facto* and *de jure*, the latter of which the Jews deny (Lange, Tholuck). Selden had already distinguished between *servitus extrinseca* and *intrinseca* (*the latter* of which would be denied by the Jews).

[1] As do Augustine, Calvin, Lampe, Kuinoel, de Wette, Tholuck, Lücke, Maier, Hengstenberg.

[2] Comp. Gen. xxii. 17 f., xvii. 16.

278 THE GOSPEL OF JOHN.

On the passionate pride taken by the Jews in their freedom, and the ruinous consequences it brought upon them, see Lightfoot, p. 1045. According to Luthardt, they protest against *spiritual* dependence, not indeed as regards the disposition (B. Crusius), but *as regards their religious position*, in virtue of which all other nations are dependent on them, the privileged people of God, for their attainment of redemption. But the coarser misunderstanding of *national* freedom is more in keeping with other misapprehensions of the more spiritual meaning of Jesus found in John (comp. Nicodemus, the Woman of Samaria, the discourse about the Bread of Life) ; and what was likely to be more readily suggested to the proud minds of these sons of Abraham than the thought of the κληρονομία τοῦ κόσμου (comp. Rom. iv. 13), which in their imaginations excluded every sort of national bondage ? Because they were Abraham's seed, they felt themselves as αἷμα φέροντες ἀδέσποτον (Nonnus).

Ver. 34. Δείκνυσιν (and that with solemn asseveration), ὅτι δουλείαν ἐνέφηνεν ἀνωτέρω τὴν ἐξ ἁμαρτίας, οὐ τὴν ἐκ δυναστείας ἀνθρώπου, Euth. Ziagabenus. — ὁ ποιῶν] instead of keeping himself free from it. — δοῦλος] as to His moral personality or *Ego*, comp. as to the figure and subject-matter, Rom. vi. 17 ff., vii. 14 ff.[1]

Vv. 35, 36. But what prospect is there before the slave of sin ? Exclusion from the kingdom of the Messiah! This threat Jesus clothes in the *general principle* of civil life, that *a slave has no permanent place in the house ;* he must allow himself to be sold, exchanged, or cast out. Comp. Gen. xxi. 10 ; Gal. iv. 30. The application intended to be made of this general principle is this : "The servant of sin does not remain eternally in the theocracy, but is cast out of the midst of the people of God at the establishment of the kingdom of Messiah." There is nothing to indicate that *the slave* is intended to refer to *Ishmael* as a type of the bastard sons of Abraham, and *the son* to *Isaac* as a type of Christ ;[2] such a view rather is out of accord with this general expression in its Present tense form, which simply marks an universally existing legal relation between the different positions of the *slave* and the *Son* of the house. — εἰς τὸν αἰῶνα] *for ever*, an expression to be understood in harmony with the *relation which has been figuratively represented*. After αἰῶνα a full stop should be inserted, with Lachmann and Kling, because ἐὰν οὖν, etc., is a consequence deduced simply from ὁ υἱὸς μ. εἰς τ. αἰ., not from what precedes, and because ὁ υἱός, etc., begins a new section in the logical progress of the discourse. The course of thought is this : (1) Whoever commits sin is the bondsman of sin, and is excluded from the Messianic people of God. (2) Quite different from the lot of the bondsman, who must quit the house, is that of the Son (the Master of the house) ; hence it is this latter who procures for you actual freedom. — ὁ υἱὸς μένει εἰς τ. αἰῶνα] namely, ἐν τῇ οἰκίᾳ,—also a general proposition or principle, but with an intentional *application* of the general expression ὁ υἱός to *Christ*, who, as the Son of *God*, retains for ever His

[1] Analogous examples from the Classics in Wetstein ; from Philo in *Loesner*, p. 149.
[2] Ebrard.

position and power in the house of God, *i.e.* in the theocracy ; [1] comp. Heb. iii. 5, 6. From this μένει εἰς τ. αἰῶνα it *follows* (οὖν) that if He frees from the state of a bondsman, a *real* and not merely an apparent freedom commences, seeing that, on account of the perpetual continuance of His domestic rights in the theocracy, the emancipation effected by Him must have a real and finally valid result. This would not necessarily be the case if He remained merely for a time in the house ; for as both His right and ἐξουσία would then lack certainty and permanence, so the freedom He procured would lack the guarantee of reality. This line of argumentation presupposes, moreover, that the *Father* does not Himself directly act in the theocracy ; He has entrusted to the *Son* the power and control. — The reference of the slave to *Moses* [2] is foreign and opposed to the text, see ver. 34. Grotius, however, aptly remarks : "tribuitur hic *filio* quod modo *veritati*, quia eam profert filius. — ὄντως] *in reality ;* every other freedom is mere appearance (comp. ver. 33), not corresponding to its true nature ; no other is ἡ παντελὴς καὶ ἀπὸ πασῶν ἀρχῶν ἐλευθερία,[3] which alone is that gained through Christ, 1 Cor. iii. 22 ; Rom. viii. 35, 36 ; 2 Cor. vi. 4, 5.

Ver. 37. Now also He denies that they are *children of Abraham*, although hitherto they had boastfully relied on the fact as the premiss of their freedom, ver. 33. — ἀλλὰ ζητεῖτε] How opposed to a true, spiritual descent from Abraham ! But the reproach had its *justification*, because these Jews had already turned round again, and the death of Jesus was the goal of the hierarchical opposition. — οὐ χωρεῖ ἐν ὑμῖν] *has no progress in you,* in your heart. This view of the meaning, which is philologically correct,[4] thoroughly applies to the persons concerned ; because whilst the word of Christ had penetrated their heart and made them for the time believers (vv. 30, 31), it had had no further development, it had made no *advance ;* on the contrary, they had, after believing for a moment, again gone back. Hence, also, it is not allowable to take ἐν ὑμῖν as equivalent to *inter vos* (Lücke, Hengst). *Others* interpret : *It finds no place in you.*[5] Without any warrant from usage.[6] *Others* again render : It finds no *entrance* into you ; so that ἐν ὑμῖν would be used pregnantly, indicating the persistence that follows upon movement.[7]

---

[1] If the *man* who is morally free be supposed to be the object of the intended application of ὁ υἱός—the man, namely, who "holds not merely an historical relation to God, but one that is essential, because ethically conditioned" (Luthardt, comp. de Wette)—we should have to take the second ὁ υἱός in the *sensu eminenti* (of *Christ*). The text, however, especially as ver. 36 is connected with ver. 35 by οὖν, offers no ground for this distinction, Hence, also, it is wrong to apply ὁ υἱός in ver. 35 to those who are liberated by Christ *along with* Christ (Hengstenberg). These first come under consideration in ver. 36.

[2] Euth. Zigabenus, after Chrysostom.

[3] Plat. *Legg.* iii. p. 698 A.

[4] Plat. *Legg.* iii. p. 684 E ; *Eryx.* p. 398 B ; ᾗ ἔμελλεν ὁ λόγος χωρήσεσθαι αὐτῷ ; Herod.

iii. 42, v. 89 ; Xen. *Oec.* i. 11 ; Polyb. 28. 15, 12, 10. 15, 4 ; Aristoph. *Pax,* 472 ; *Ran.* 472 ; 2 Macc. iii. 40.

[5] Vulgate : non *capit* in vobis ; so Origen? Chrysostom, Theophylact, Erasmus, Castalio, Beza, Aretius, Maldonatus, Corn. à Lapide, Jansen, and several others ; also B. Crusius, Ewald, and Baeumlein.

[6] Arist. *H. A.* ix. 40, is not relevant ; χωρεῖ there is impersonal, and the words mean : *if there is no advance* in their work.—The sense : *It has no place in you,* ought to have been expressed τὸν λόγον οὐ χωρεῖτε ἐν ὑμῖν. Comp. xxi. 25, and see on 2 Cor. vii. 2. [But see Alciphr. Epp. iii. 7 (cited by Field, Ot. Norv. iii. p. 67), where ἐχώρησε means *had place, room.*—K.]

[7] So Nonnus, Grotius, Kuinoel, de Wette, Maier, Tholuck, Luthardt.

The expression would have to be referred back to the meaning—*move forward, stretch forward* (Wisdom vii. 23; 2 Pet. iii. 9, and frequently in classical writers). But this explanation is neither indicated by the text (for the words are not εἰς ὑμᾶς), nor is it even appropriate to the sense, seeing that the word of Christ had actually stirred those men to momentary faith. But this explanation is forced on those who refuse to regard the πεπιστευκότες in ver. 31 as those who answer in ver. 33.

Ver. 38. That my word has thus failed to produce any effect in you, is due to the fundamentally different origin of my discourse on the one hand, and of your doings on the other. — ἑώρακα π. τ. πατρί] by which Jesus means the intuition of the divine truth which He derived from His *prehuman* state (comp. on ver. 28), not from His intercourse with God in time (Godet, Beyschlag), as though this latter were involved in the parallel καὶ ὑμεῖς, whereas the *difference* in the analogous relation is betrayed by the very difference of expression (ἠκούσατε and παρὰ τοῦ πατρός). — καὶ ὑμεῖς οὖν] *you also therefore*, following my example of dependence on the Father. There is a stinging irony in the word οὖν. — ἠκούσατε] *i.e.* what your father has commanded you. Note the distinction between the Perf. and Aor. *Who* their father is, Jesus leaves as yet unsaid ; He means, however, the *devil*, whose children, *ethically* considered, they are ; whereas He is the Son of God in the essential, metaphysical sense. — ποιεῖτε] *habitual* doing (vii. 51), including, but not exclusively referring to, their wish to kill Him (ver. 37). It is *indicative*, and no longer imperative (Hengstenberg, after Matt. xxiii. 32) than in ver. 41.

Vv. 39, 40. The Jews observe that He means another father than Abraham. — Jesus proves to them from their non-Abrahamic mode of action that they are no children of Abraham. — τέκνα and ἔργα are correlates ; the former is used in an *ethical* sense, so that here (comp. ver. 37) a distinction is drawn, as in Rom. ix. 8, between the fleshly σπέρμα and the moral τέκνα. —In the reading ἐστε (see the critical notes) there is a change in the view of the relationship, as in Luke xvii. 5 f. See remarks on the passage. On the non-employment of ἄν, see Buttmann in *Studien u. Kritiken* for 1858, p. 485, and his *Neutest. Gramm.* p. 195 [E. T. p. 224]. — νῦν δέ] but as it is, but as the case stands, *nunc autem.* — ἄνθρωπον in reference to παρὰ τ. θεοῦ. The λελάληκα following in the *first* person is regular.[1] — τοῦτο] viz. seeking to take the life of a man who speaks the truth which he has heard of God— *this Abraham did not do !*[2] The words are far from referring to Abraham's conduct towards the angel of the Lord, Gen. xviii. (Hengstenberg, after Lampe) ; nor is such a reference involved in ver. 56. — παρὰ τοῦ θεοῦ] when I was in my prehuman state, παρὰ τῷ πατρί μου, ver. 38. To this view ἄνθρωπον is not opposed (Beyschlag), for Jesus must needs describe Himself in this general human manner, if there were to be congruity between the category of His self-description and *the example of Abraham.*

Ver. 41. *You do what your father practices,*—result of vv. 39, 40, though

[1] See Buttm. *Neut. Gramm.* p. 241 [E. T. p. 396].

[2] The expression is a *Litotes* (" From the like of this the God-fearing spirit of the patriarch was far removed"), but all the more fitted to put them to shame.

still without specifying *who* this father is. "Paulatim procedit castigatio" (Grotius).—As the Jews are not to look upon Abraham as their father, they imagine that some other human father must be meant. In this case, however, they would be bastards, born of fornication (the fornication of Sarah with another man) ; and they would have two fathers, an actual one (from whom they descend ἐκ πορνείας) and a putative one (Abraham). But inasmuch as their descent is certainly not an adulterous one,[1] and still Abraham is not to be regarded as their father, there remains in opposition to the assertion of Jesus, so they think, only *God* as the one Father; to whom, therefore, they assign this position : " *We are not born of fornication,*" as thou seemest to assume, in that thou refusest to allow that Abraham is our father ; *one father only* (not two, as is the case with such as are born of adultery) *have we,* and that *God,* if our descent from Abraham is not to be taken into consideration. For God was not merely the creator (Mal. ii. 10) and *theocratic* Father of the people (Isa. lxiii. 16, lxiv. 8); but His Fatherhood was further and specially grounded in the power of His promise made at the conception of Isaac (Rom. iv. 19 ; Gal. iv. 23). The supposition that they implicitly drew a contrast between themselves and *Ishmael* (Euth. Zigabenus, who thinks that there is an allusion to the birth of Jesus, Ruperti, Wetstein, Tittmann) is erroneous, inasmuch as Ishmael was not born ἐκ πορνείας. We must reject also the common explanation of the passage as a denial of the charge of *idolatry ;*[2] "our filial relationship to God has not been polluted by idolatry,"[3] as opposed to the context, since the starting-point is not the idea of a superhuman Father, nor are the Jews reproached at all with idolatry ; but the charge is brought against them, that Abraham is not their father. Hence also the supposition of an antithesis to a combined Jewish *and heathen* descent,[4] such as was the case with the *Samaritans* (Paulus), is inadmissible. Ewald also takes the same simple and correct view ;[5] comp. Erasmus, *Paraphr.* Bengel, however, aptly char-

---

[1] 'Εκ πορνείας implies one mother, but several fathers. Who is the one mother, follows from the denial of the paternity of *Abraham,* consequently *Sarah,* the ancestress of the theocratic people. Hence the inadmissibility of Luthardt's explanation based on the idea, "Israel is Jehovah's spouse ;" according to which the thought of the Jews would have been : they were not sprung from a marriage covenant of Israel with another, so that Jehovah would thus be merely nominally their father, in reality, however, another ; and they would thus have several fathers. Moreover, a *marriage* covenant between Israel and another would be a contradiction, this other must needs also be conceived as a true *God,* consequently as a *strange* God, a notion which Luthardt justly rejects. It is surprising how B. Crusius could adduce Deut. xxiii. 2 for the purpose of representing the Jews as affirming their theocratic

equality of birth.

[2] Hos. i. 2, ii. 4 ; Ezek. xx. 30 ; Isa. lvii. 3.

[3] De Wette ; comp. Grotius, Lampe, Kuinoel, Lücke, Tholuck, Lange, Hengstenberg, Baeumlein, and several others.

[4] Theodore of Mopsuestia, Theophylact, Godet.

[5] Although characterized by Ebrard as *absurd.* He regards ἐκ πορνείας οὐ γεγ. as merely a "*caricatured form*" of the accusation that they are not Abraham's children, and in this way, of course, gets rid of the need of *explaining* the words. He then takes ἕνα πατέρα ἔχομεν in the sense of *we and thou have one common Father,* which is incompatible with the word ἡμεῖς, which also belongs to ἔχομεν, and is, besides, altogether opposed to the context ; for the entire dialogue is constituted by the *antithesis* of *we* and *thou, I* and *ye.* Ebrard's view is an unfortunate evasion of a *desperate* kind.

acterizes the entire objection raised by the Jews as a "novus importunitatis Judaicae paroxysmus." — ἡμεῖς] spoken with the emphasis of pride.

Ver. 42 f. God is not your Father, else would ye *love* me, because ye would be of like descent with me.[1] This ἠγαπᾶτε ἂν ἐμέ would be "the ethical test" (Luthardt) of the like paternity ; the fact of its *non-existence*, although it *might have existed*, is evidence to the contrary. — ἐγώ] spoken with a feeling of divine assurance. — ἐξῆλθον] the *proceeding forth from that essential pre-human* fellowship with God, which was His as the *Son* of God, and which took place through the incarnation (xiii. 3, xvi. 27, 28, 30, xvii. 8). The idea of a mere *sending* would not be in harmony with the context, the proper subject of which is the *Fatherhood* of God ; comp. vi. 62, xvii. 5. — καὶ ἥκω] Result of the ἐξῆλθον : and am here, it belongs, along with the rest, also to ἐκ. τ. θεοῦ. — οὐδὲ γὰρ ἀπ' ἐμαυτοῦ, etc.] Confirmation of ἐκ τ. θεοῦ, etc. ; *for neither of my own self-determination*, etc. If Jesus, namely, had not manifested Himself as proceeding from God, He might have come either from a third person, or, at all events, ἀφ' ἑαυτοῦ ; on the contrary, not even (οὐδέ) was this latter the case. — Ver. 43. After having shown them that they were the children neither of Abraham nor of God, before positively declaring *whose* children they actually are, He discloses to them the ground of their not understanding His discourse ; for everything that they had advanced from ver. 33 onwards had been in fact such a non-understanding. The form of expression here used, namely, *question* and *answer* (ὅτι *because ;* comp. Rom. ix. 32 ; 2 Cor. xi. 11), is an outflow of the growing excitement.[2] De Wette (comp. Luther, Beza, Calvin) takes ὅτι as equivalent to εἰς ἐκεῖνο ὅτι (see on ii. 18) : "I say this with reference to the circumstance that." Illogical, as the clauses must then have stood in the reverse order (διατί οὐ δύνασθε . . . ὅτι τὴν λαλιάν, etc.), because the words οὐ γινώσκετε denote the relation which is *clear* from what has preceded. — In the question and in the answer, that on which the emphasis rests is thrown *to the end*. His discourse was *unintelligible* to them, because its substance, to wit, His *word*, was inaccessible to their apprehension, because they had no ears for it. For the cause of this ethical οὐ δύνασθε, see ver. 47. λαλιά, which in classical Greek denoted *talk, chatter* (see on iv. 42), signifies in later writers,[3] and in the LXX. and Apocrypha, also *Discourse, Sermo*,[4] without any contemptuous meaning.[5] So here ; and, indeed, thus differing from ὁ λόγος, that whilst this last mentioned term denotes the doctrinal substance expressed by the λαλιά,—the *doctrine*, the *substance* of that which is delivered,[6]

---

[1] ἑνὸς γεγαῶτα τοκῆος ἀρραγέος φιλίης ἀλύτῳ ξυνώσατε θεσμῷ, Nonnus.

[2] Dissen, *ad Dem. de Cor*. p. 186, 347.

[3] *E.g.* Polyb. 32. 9, 4 ; Joseph *Bell.* ii. 8. 5.

[4] On λάλιος in bonam partem, see Jacobs, *ad Anthol.* vi. p. 99, vii. p. 140.

[5] Comp. Matt. xxvi. 73.

[6] Comp. Weizsäcker in *d. Jahrb. für deutsche Theol.* 1857, p. 196 f. But in the Gospel it is always the verbum *vocale*, and it should not be confounded with the λόγος of the prologue, which is the verbum *substantiale ;* hence, also, it furnishes no evidence of a deviation from the doctrine of the Logos. The consciousness Jesus possessed of speaking, keeping, doing, etc., the λόγος of God, rested on His consciousness of His *being* that which is denoted by the Logos of the prologue. Now this consciousness is not the abstract divine, but that of the *theanthropic* Ego, corresponding to the ὁ λόγος σὰρξ ἐγένετο.

—λαλιά denotes the *utterance itself*, by which expression is given to the doctrine.[1]

Ver. 44. After the negative statement in vv. 42, 43 comes now the positive : *Ye* (ὑμεῖς, with decided emphasis—*ye* people, who deem yourselves children of God !) *are children of the devil,*[2] in the sense, namely, of *ethical genesis* (comp. 1 John iii. 8, 12), which is further explained from ἐκεῖνος onward. The expression must therefore not be regarded as teaching an *original* difference in the natures of men (Hilgenfeld, comp. on iii. 6). — ἐκ τοῦ πατρ. τ. διαβ.] *of the father who is the devil*, not of *your* father, etc. (de Wette, Lücke), which is inappropriate after the emphatic ὑμεῖς, or ought to have been specially marked as emphatic (ὑμεῖς ἐκ τοῦ ὑμῶν πατρός, etc.). Nonnus well indicates the qualitative character of the expression : ὑμεῖς δῆτα τέκνα δυσαντέος ἐστὲ τοκῆος. Hilgenfeld's view, which is adopted by Volkmar : " Ye descend *from the father of the devil,*" which father is the (Gnostic) God of the Jews, is not only generally unbibical, but thoroughly un-Johannine, and here opposed to the context. John could have written simply ἐκ τοῦ διαβ., if the connection had not required that prominence should be given to the idea of *father.* But in the entire connection there is nothing that would call for a possible father of the *devil ;* the question is solely of the devil himself, as the father of *those* Jews. Erroneously also Grotius, who explains the passage as though it ran,—τοῦ πατρ. τῶν διαβόλων. — καὶ τὰς ἐπιθυμίας, etc.] The *conscious will* of the child of the devil is to accomplish that after which its father, whose organ it is, lusts. This is rooted in the similarity of their moral nature. The *desire* to *kill* is not exclusively referred to, though, as even the plural ἐπιθυμίας shows, it is included. — ἐκεῖνος, etc.] for *murder* and *lying* were precisely the two devilish lusts which they were minded to carry out against *Jesus.*— ἀνθρωποκτόνος ἦν ἀπ' ἀρχῆς] *from the beginning* of the human race. This more exact determination of the meaning is derivable from ἀνθρωποκτόνος, inasmuch as it was through his seduction that the *fall* was brought about, in whose train death entered into the world (Rom. v. 12). [See Note XXXIIIa. p. 296.] So Origen, Chrysostom, Augustine, Theophylact, and the majority of commentators ; also Kuinoel, Schleiermacher, Tholuck, Olshausen, Klee, Maier, Lange (referring it, however, after the example of Euth. Zigabenus, also to *Cain*), Luthardt, Ewald, Godet, Hofmann,[3] Müller,[4] Lechler,[5] Hahn,[6] Messner,[7] Philippi.[8] This view is alone ap-

---

[1] Comp. xii. 48 : ὁ λόγος ὃν ἐλάλησα ; Phil. i. 14 ; Heb. xii. 7.

[2] In his *Leben Jesu* (p. 338 ff.), Schleiermacher groundlessly advances the opinion that Jesus had here no intention of teaching any doctrine regarding the devil, but wished merely to add force to His reproach by referring to the generally-adopted interpretation of the narrative of the fall. On the contrary, by His reproach, he not merely *lays down* the doctrine, but also further intentionally and explicitly *expounds* it, especially by assigning the ground, ὅτι οὐκ ἔστιν, etc. Baur (still in his *Neut. Theol.*

p. 393) deduces from this passage that, according to John, Jesus had little sympathy for the Jews. He is speaking, however, not at all against the *Jews in general*, but merely against the *party that was hostile* to Him.

[3] *Schriftbeweis*, I. pp. 418, 478.

[4] *Lehre v. d. Sünde*, II. p. 544 f. ed. 5.

[5] *Stud u. Kritik.* 1854, p. 814 f.

[6] *Theol. d. N. T.* I. p. 355.

[7] *Lehre d. Apostel*, p. 332.

[8] *Glaubenslehre*, III. p. 272 ; see especially Hengstenberg on the passage, and his *Christol.* I. p. 8 ff. ; Weiss, *Lehrbegr.* p. 133 f.

propriate to the expression ἀπ᾽ ἀρχῆς, which the design of the context requires to be taken exactly,[1] as it must also be understood in 1 John iii. 8.[2]   *Others* refer to *Cain's murder of his brother*,[3] which is not, however, rendered necessary by 1 John iii. 12, and would, without any warrant, exclude an earlier commencement ; would be opposed to the national and New Testament view[4] of the fall and the connection of the present passage ; and would finally lack any allusion to Gen. iv. ; while on the contrary, the antithesis between truth and falsehood, which follows afterwards, points unmistakably to Gen. iii.   Finally, inasmuch as ἀπ᾽ ἀρχῆς must signify some definite historical starting-point, it is incorrect, with B Crusius, to deny a reference either to the fall or to Cain's murder of his brother, and to take ἀνθρωποκτ. ἀπ᾽ ἀρχῆς as simply a *general* designation.—Brückner also treats the reference to a definite fact as unnecessary. — ἦν] that is, during the entire past, ἀπ᾽ ἀρχῆς onwards. — κ. ἐν τῇ ἀληθ. οὐχ ἕστηκεν] does not refer to the *fall* of the devil,[5] as Augustine, Nonnus, and most Catholics maintain,[6] as though εἱστήκει (Vulg. : *stetit*) had been employed, but is his constant *characteristic :*[7] *and he does not abide in the truth*, ἐμμένει, ἀναπαύεται, Euth. Zigabenus.   The *truth* is the domain in which *he has not his footing ;* to him it is a foreign, heterogeneous sphere of life : the truth is the opposite of the lie, both in formal and material significance.   The *lie* is the sphere in which he holds his place ; in it he is in the element proper and peculiar to him ; in it he has his life's standing. — ὅτι οὐκ ἔστιν ἀληθ. ἐν αὐτῷ] the inner ground of the preceding statement.   The determining cause of this inner ground, however, is expressed by the words ἐν αὐτῷ, which are emphatically placed at the end. As truth is not found *in him*, as it is lacking to *his inner essence and life*, it cannot possibly constitute the sphere of his objective life.   Without truth in the inward parts—truth regarded, namely, as a subjective qualification, temper, tendency—that is, without truth in the character, a man must necessarily be foreign to, and far from, the domain of objective truth, and cannot have his life and activity therein.   Without truth in the inward parts, a man deals in life with lies, deception, cunning, and all ἀδικία.   Note that

---

Compare the corresponding parallels, Wisd. ii. 24 ; Apoc. xii. 9, xx. 2 ; also Ev. Nicod. 23, where the devil is termed ἡ τοῦ θανάτου ἀρχή, ἡ ῥίζα τῆς ἁμαρτίας ; see also Grimm on Wisd. i. 1.

[1] מֵן בְּרֵאשִׁית, Lightfoot, p. 1045.

[2] Comp. Joseph. *Antiq.* I. 1, 4.

[3] Cyril, Nitzsch in the *Berl. theol. Zeitschr.* III. p. 52 ff., Schulthess, Lücke, Kling, de Wette, Reuss, *Beitr.* p. 53, Hilgenfeld, Baeumlein, Grimm.

[4] See on 2 Cor. xi. 3.

[5] 2 Pet. ii. 4 ; Jude 6.

[6] Comp. also Martensen's *Dogmatics*, § 105. Delitzsch, too (see *Psychol.* p. 62), explains the passage as though εἱστήκει were used : the devil, instead of "*taking* his stand in the truth," revolted, as the god of the world, selfishly against God ; for which reason the world has been " degraded and

materialized" by God to a תֹּהוּ וָבֹהוּ, תֹּהוּ וָבֹהוּ, etc. In this way a *new creation* of the world is made out of the creation in Gen. i., and out of the *first* act in the history of the world, a *second.*

[7] At the same time, we do not mean herewith to *deny* to John the idea of a *fall* of the devil, or, in other words, to represent him as believing the devil to have been *originally* evil.   The passage under consideration treats merely of the evil constitution of the devil *as it is*, without giving any hint as to its origin.   This in answer to Frommann, p. 330, Reuss, and Hilgenfeld. In relation to the doctrine of the *fall* of the devil *nothing* is here taught.   Comp. Hofmann, *Schriftbeweis*, passim ; Hahn, *Theol. d. N. T.* I. p. 319.   Such a fall is, however, necessarily presupposed by this passage.

ἀλήθ. is used first *with*, and then *without*, the article. — ἐκ τῶν ἰδίων] *out of that which is his own*, which constitutes the proper ground or essence of his inner man,—out of that which is most peculiarly his ethical nature. Comp. Matt. xii. 34. —κ. ὁ πατὴρ αὐτοῦ] namely, *of the liar ;* he, *generically* considered, to wit, the liar as such *in general*, is the devil's child. The characterization of the devil thus aptly concludes with a declaration which at the same time confirms the reproach, ὑμεῖς ἐκ τ. πατρὸς τοῦ διαβ. ἐστέ. The less to be approved, therefore, is the *common* explanation of αὐτοῦ, as standing for τοῦ ψεύδους, which is to be derived from ψεύστης (*mendacii auctor*, after Gen. iii. 4 f.) ; although, linguistically considered, it is in itself admissible.[1] The correct view has been taken also by B. Crusius, Luthardt, Tholuck, Hengstenberg, and as early as Bengel. The old heretical explanation, "*as his father*,"[2] or, "*also his father*, referring αὐτοῦ to the *devil*, and ὁ πατήρ to the *demiurge*, whose lie is the pretending to be the most high God,[3] must be rejected ; for, on the one hand, John should at the very least, to avoid being completely misunderstood, have written ὅτι αὐτὸς ψ. ἐ. κ. ὁ. π. ἀ ;[4] while, on the other hand, he did not in the remotest degree entertain the monstrous, wholly unbiblical notion of a *father of the devil.* Nor would a father of *this kind* at all harmonize with the context. Even a writer as early as Photius, *Quaest. Amphiloch.* 88, takes the opposite view ; as also Ewald, *Jahrb.* V. p. 198 f. It was in the highest degree unnecessary that Lachmann,[5] to avoid referring αὐτοῦ to the devil, should approve the reading *qui*, or ὃς ἄν, instead of ὅταν, which is supported by the feeblest evidence : " qui loquitur mendacium, ex propriis loquitur, quia patrem quoque mendacem habet." [See Note XXXIV. p. 296.]

Ver. 45. *Because I, on the contrary, speak the truth, ye believe me not.* — ἐγὼ δέ] for the sake of strong emphasis, in opposition to the devil, placed at the beginning ; and the causative ὅτι, a thoroughly tragical *because*, has its ground in the alien character of the relation between that which Jesus speaks and their devilish nature, to which latter a lie alone corresponds. Euth. Ziagbenus aptly remarks : εἰ μὲν ἔλεγον ψεῦδος, ἐπιστεύσατέ μοι ἄν, ὡς τὸ ἴδιον τοῦ πατρὸς ὑμῶν λέγοντι. To take the sentence as a *question* (Ewald) would weaken its tragical force.

Ver. 46. Groundlessness of this unbelief. Εἰ μή, διότι τὴν ἀλήθειαν λέγω, ἀπιστεῖτέ μοι, εἴπατε, τίς ἐξ ὑμῶν ἐλέγχει με περὶ ἁμαρτίας ὑπ' ἐμοῦ γενομένης, ἵνα δόξητε δι' ἐκείνην ἀπιστεῖν ; Euth. Zigabenus. Ἁμαρτία, *fault*, is not to be taken in the intellectual sense, as *untruth, error*,[6] but, as employed without exception in the N. T., as equivalent to *sin.* Jesus boldly urges against His opponents His unassailable moral purity—and how lofty a position of superiority does He thus assume above the saints of the Old Testament !—the fact that against Him can be brought ἁμαρτίας ὄνειδος οὐδέν,[7] as a guarantee that

---

[1] Winer, p. 181 f. [E. T. p. 145] ; Buttmann, p. 93 [E. T. p. 106].

[2] Hence, also, the readings ὡς and καθὼς καί, instead of καί, which, though early in date, are supported by feeble testimony.

[3] Hilgenfeld, Volkmar.

[4] Comp. Nonnus : ψεύστης αὐτὸς ἔφυ, ψευδήμονος ἐκ γενετῆρος.

[5] *Praef.* II. p. 7.

[6] Origen, Cyril, Melanchthon, Calvin, Beza, Bengel, Kypke, Tittmann, Kuinoel, Klee, and others.

[7] Soph. *O. C.* 971.

He speaks the truth ; justly too, for according to ver. 44 ἀλήθεια must be regarded as the opposite of ψεῦδος, whereas a lie falls undei the category of ἁμαρτία (comp. ἀδικία, vii. 18). The conclusion is from the genus to the species ; hence also it is inadmissible to take ἁμαρτία in the special sense of "*fraus*" ("qua divinam veritatem in mendacium converterim")[1] "*wicked deception*" (B. Crusius), "*sin of word*,"[2] "*false doctrine*,"[3] and so forth. Even in classical usage ἁμαρτία, in and by itself, would denote neither *error* nor *deception*, but only acquire this specific meaning through an addition more precisely determining its force.[4] Considered in itself it denotes *fault, perversity*, the opposite of ὀρθότης.[5] Remark further, in connection with this important passage : (1) The argument is based, not upon the position that "*the sinless one is the purest and surest organ of the knowledge and communication of the truth*" (Lücke) ; or that "*the knowledge of the truth is grounded in the purity of the will*" (de Wette, comp. Ullmann) ; for this would presuppose in the consciousness in which the words are spoken, to wit, in the consciousness of Jesus, a knowledge of the truth obtained *mediately*, or, at all events, acquired first in His *human* state ; whereas, on the contrary, especially according to John's view, the knowledge of the truth possessed by Jesus was an intuitive one, one possessed by Him in His *pre-human* state, and preserved and continued during His human state by means of the constant intercourse between Himself and God. The reasoning proceeds rather in this way : Am I really without *sin*,—and none of you is able to convict me of the contrary,—then am I also without ψεῦδος ; but am I without ψεῦδος, then do I speak the *truth*, and you, on your part (ὑμεῖς), have no reason for not believing me. This reasoning, however, is abbreviated, in that Jesus passes at once from the denial of the possibility of charging Him with ἁμαρτία, to the positive, special contrary which follows therefrom,—leaving out the middle link, that consequently no ψεῦδος can be attributed to Him,—and then continues : εἰ ἀλήθ. λέγω.[6] *Further*, (2) the proof of the sinlessness of Jesus furnished by this passage is purely *subjective*, so far as it rests on the decided expression of His own moral consciousness in the presence of His enemies ; but, at the same time, it is as such all the more striking in that the confirmation of His own testimony (comp. xiv. 30) is added to the testimony of *others*, and to the *necessity* of His sinlessness for the work of redemption and for the function of judge. This self-witness of Jesus, on the one hand, bears on itself the seal of immediate truth (otherwise, namely, Jesus would have been chargeable with a καυχᾶσθαι of self-righteousness or self-deception, which is inconceivable in Him) ; whilst, on the other hand, it is saved from the weakness attaching to other self-witnessings, both by the whole evangelical history, and by the

[1] Ch. F. Fritzsche in Fritzsch. *Opusc.* p. 99.

[2] Hofmann, *Schriftbew.* II. 1, p. 33 f.

[3] Melanchthon, Calvin.

[4] Polyb. 16. 20, 6, is, without reason, adduced by Tholuck against this view. In the passage referred to, ἁμαρτίαι are *faults, goings wrong* in general. The sentence is a general maxim.

[5] Plat. *Legg.* i. p. 627 D, ii. p. 668 C. Comp. δόξης ἁμαρτία, Thuc. i. 32. 4 ; νόμων ἁμαρτία, Plat. *Legg.* i. p. 627 D ; γνώμης ἁμάρτημα, Thuc. ii. 65. 7.

[6] Lachmann and Tischendorf correctly without δέ.

fact of the work of reconciliation. (3) The sinlessness itself, to which Jesus here lays claim, is in so far *relative*, as it is not absolutely divine, but both is and must be *divine-human*, and was based on the human development of the Son of God.[1] He was actually *tempted*, and *might have* sinned ; this abstract possibility, however, never became a reality. On the contrary, at every moment of His life it was raised into a practical impossibility.[2] Thus He *learned* obedience (Heb. v. 8). Hence the sinlessness of Jesus, being the result of a normal development which, at every stage of His earthly existence, was in perfect conformity with the God-united ground of His inner life (comp. Luke ii. 40, 52), must always be regarded as conditioned, so far as the human manifestation of Jesus is concerned, by the entrance of the Logos into the relation of growth ; whilst the unconditioned correlate thereto, namely, *perfection*, and accordingly *absolute* moral goodness—goodness which is absolutely complete and above temptation at the very outset— belongs alone, nay, belongs *necessarily* to God. In this way the apparent contradiction between this passage and Mark x. 18 may be resolved. For the rest, the notion of sin as a necessary transitional point in human development is shown to be groundless by the historic fact of the sinlessness of Jesus.[3]

Ver. 47. Answer to the question in ver. 46,—a syllogism whose minor premiss, however, needs not to be supplied in thought (de Wette : "Now I speak the words of God "), seeing that it is contained in (ὑμεῖς) ἐκ τοῦ θεοῦ οὐκ ἐστέ. That *Jesus* speaks the words of God is here *taken for granted*. The major premiss is grounded on the necessary sympathy between *God* and him who *springs from God ;* he who *hears* the words of God, that is, *as such*, he has an *ear* for them. The words, ἐκ τοῦ θεοῦ εἶναι, in the sense of being spiritually constituted by God, do not refer to Christian regeneration and to sonship,—for this begins through faith,—but merely to a preliminary stage thereof, to wit, the state of the man whom God draws to Christ by the operation of His grace (vi. 44), and who is thus prepared for His divine preaching, and is given to Him as His (vi. 37). Compare xvii. 6. — διὰ τοῦτο—ὅτι] as in v. 16, 18. See on x. 17. — Note in connection with ver. 47, compared with ver. 44, that the moral dualism which is characteristic, not merely of John's Gospel, but of the gospel generally, here so far reveals its metaphysical basis, that it is traced back to the genetic relation, either to the devil or to God—two opposed states of dependence, which give rise to the most opposite moral conditions, with their respective unsusceptibility or susceptibility to divine truth. The assertion by Jesus of this dualism was not grounded on historical reflection and a conclusion *ab effectu ad causam*, but on the immediate *certitude* which belonged to Him as *knowing the heart* of man. At the same time, it is incorrect to suppose that He as-

---

[1] Comp. Gess, *Pers. Chr.* p. 212. At the same time, the sinless development · of Jesus is not to be subsumed under the conception of *sanctification.* See also Dorner's *Sinless Perfection of Jesus*, and the striking remarks of Keim, *Geschichtl. Chr.*

p. 109 ff., ed. 3, also p. 189 f.

[2] Any moral stain in Christ would have been a negation of His consciousness of being the Redeemer and Judge.

[3] See Ernesti, *Ursprung der Sünde*, I. p. 187 ff.

sumes the existence of two classes of human nature differing radically from each other at the very outset.[1] On the contrary, the moral self-determination by which a man surrenders himself either to the one or the other principle, is no more excluded than the personal guilt attaching to the children of the devil (vv. 24, 34); though their freedom is the more completely lost, the more completely their hearts become hardened (ver. 43). The problem of the *metaphysical relation* between human freedom and the superhuman power referred to, remains, however, necessarily unsolved, and, indeed, not merely in this passage, but in the whole of the New Testament (even in Rom. ix.–xi.); comp. also 1 John iii. 12, iv. 4. But the freedom itself, in face of that power, and the moral imputation and responsibility remain intact, comp. iii. 19–21.

Vv. 48, 49. In ver. 42 ff. Jesus had denied that His opponents were sons of God, and had stamped them as children of the devil. This procedure they regard only as a confirmation of the accusation which they bring against Him (λέγομεν) of being a *Samaritan*, *i.e.* an heretical antagonist of the pure people of God (for in this light did they view that despised people of mixed race), and *possessed with a devil* (vii. 20). So *paradoxical*, not merely presumptuous (as Luthardt explains Σαμαρ.), and so *crazed* did the discourse of Jesus appear to them. No reference whatever was intended to iv. 5 ff. (Brückner, Ewald). On καλῶς, *aptly*, comp. iv. 17, xii. 13. — Ver. 49. ἐγὼ δαιμόν. οὐκ ἔχω, etc.] The emphatic ἐγώ does not contain a retort by which the demoniacal element would be ascribed to His opponents,[2]—a reference which would require to be indicated by arranging the words οὐκ ἐγὼ δαιμ. ἔχω,—but stands simply in opposition to the following καὶ ὑμεῖς. With quiet earnestness, leaving unnoticed the reproach of being a Samaritan, Jesus replies : I for my part am not *possessed*, but *honour* (by discourses which you consider demoniacal, but by which I in reality preserve and promote the glory of God) *my Father ;* and you, on your part, what is it that you do ? You *dishonour me !* Thus does He unveil to them the *unrighteousness* of their abusive language.

Vv. 50, 51. *I, however*, in contrast to this unrighteousness by which you wound my honour, *seek not the honour which belongs to me*—ἔστιν ὁ ζητ. κ. κρίνων, *there is one* (comp. v. 45) *who seeks it* ("qui me honore afficere velit," Grotius), *and pronounces judgment*, that is, *as a matter of fact*, between me and my revilers. The expression καὶ κρίνων includes a reference, on the one hand, to the *glorification of Jesus*, by which He was to be justified (xvi. 10 ; comp. the διό, Phil. ii. 9); and, on the other, as regards His *opponents*, a hint at their just *punishment* (with eternal death, ver. 51). Hence He adds in ver. 51 a solemn assurance concerning *that which is necessary to the obtaining of eternal life, instead of this* punitive κρίσις, to wit, the keeping of His word ; thus deciding that the exclusion of His opponents from eternal life was inevitable as long as they did not return to repentance ; but also pointing out the only way to salvation which was still remaining open to them. Quite arbitrarily some have treated ver. 51 as not forming part of His dis-

[1] Baur, Hilgenfeld.   [2] Cyril, Lücke.

course to His enemies.[1] After a pause, Jesus turns again to those who believed on Him, in the sense of ver. 31. Lücke maintains, indeed, that the discourse is addressed to His opponents, but regards it rather as the conclusion of the line of thought begun at ver. 31 f. than a direct continuation of ver. 50. The connection with ver. 50 is in this way likewise surrendered. The discourse is a direct continuation of the import of καὶ κρίνων, for the result of this κρίνειν to the opponents of Jesus is *death.* — ἐάν τις, etc.] Note the emphasis which is given to the pronoun by the arrangement of the words τὸν ἐμὸν λόγον. It is the word of *Christ,* whose keeping has so great an effect. τηρεῖν is not merely keeping in the heart,[2] but, as always, when united with τὸν λόγον, τὰς ἐντολάς, etc., keeping by *fulfilling* them (ver. 55, xiv. 15, 21, 23 f., xv. 20, xvii. 6). This fulfilment includes even the faith itself demanded by Jesus (iii. 36 ; comp. the conception of ὑπακοὴ πίστεως), as also the accomplishment of all the duties of life which He enjoins as the fruit and test of faith. — θάνατον οὐ μὴ θεωρ. εἰς τ. αἰ.] not : *he will not die for ever,*[3] but : *he will never die,* i.e. he will live eternally.[4] *Death* is here the antithesis to the *Messianic* life, which the believer *possesses* even in its temporal development, and which he will never *lose.* — On θεωρ. comp. Ps. lxxxix. 44 ; Luke ii. 25 ; see also on iii. 36. The article is not necessary to θάνατος.[5]

Vv. 52, 53. The Jews understood Him to speak of *natural* death, and thus found a confirmation of their charge that He was mad in consequence of being possessed with a devil. It is in their view a senseless self-exaltation for Jesus to ascribe to His word, and therefore to Himself, greater power of life than was possessed by Abraham and the prophets, who had not been able to escape death. — νῦν ἐγνώκ.] " antea cum dubitatione aliqua locuti erant," in ver. 48, Bengel. — γεύσηται] a different and *stronger* designation, not intentionally selected, but the result of excitement.[6] The image employed, probably not derived from a death-*cup,*—a supposition which is not favoured by the very common use of the expression in other connections,—serves to set forth to the senses the πικρότης, the *bitterness* of experiencing death.[7] The kind of experience denoted by γεύεσθαι is always specified in the context. — Ver. 53. *Surely thou art not greater* (furnished with greater power against death), and so forth ; σύ is emphatic. Comp. iv. 12. — ὅστις] *quippe qui, who in sooth ;* assigning the ground. — τίνα σεαυτ. ποιεῖς] *What sort of one dost thou make thyself?* (v. 18, x. 33, xix. 7), " quem te venditas ?" (Grotius), that thy word should produce such an effect ?

Vv. 54, 55. Justification against the charge of self-exaltation contained in the words τίνα σεαυτ. ποιεῖς. Jesus gives this justification a *general* form, and then proceeds to make a *special* declaration regarding *Abraham,* which

[1] Calvin and De Wette.
[2] Tholuck.
[3] Kaeuffer, de ζωῆς αἰων., not. p. 114.
[4] Comp. ver. 52, xi. 25 ff., v. 25, vi. 50.
[5] xi. 4, and very frequently in the N. T. ; see Ellendt, *Lex. Soph.* II. p. 234.
[6] Comp. on the expression Matt. xvi. 28, and the Rabbis as quoted by Schoettgen and

Wetstein; Leon. Alex. 41 : γεύεσθαι ἀστόργου θανάτου.
[7] Comp. the classical expressions, γεύεσθαι πένθους, Eur. *Alc.* 1072 ; μόχθων, Soph. *Trach.* 1091 ; κακῶν, Luc. *Nigr.* 28 ; πόνων, Pind. *Nem.* 6. 41 ; πενίης, Maced. 3 ; ὀϊστοῦ, Hom. *Od.* φ, 98, χειρῶν ν, 181.

makes it clear that He is really greater than Abraham. — ἐγὼ—ἐμαυτόν] emphatic designation of self (comp. v. 30, 31, vii. 17) ; δοξάσω, however, is not the *future* [see the critical notes] (although ἐάν with the indicative is not absolutely to be condemned ; see on Luke xix. 40 ; Matt. xviii. 19), but, according to *regular* usage, the *Conj. Aor.: in case I shall have glorified myself.* — ἐστιν ὁ πατήρ μου, etc.] *My Father is the one who glorifies me,* He is my glorifier. The Partic. Praes. with the article has a *substantival* force, and denotes *habitual, continuous* doing ; hence it refers not merely to a particular mode and act of δοξάζειν exclusively, but to its whole course (in the works wrought, in the divine testimonies, and in His final glorification). — ὃν ὑμεῖς λέγετε, etc.] On the construction see x. 36. Comp. on v. 27, ix. 19 ; Acts xxi. 29. Jesus unfolds to them why this activity of God, by which He is honoured, is hidden from them ; notwithstanding, namely, their theocratic fancy, " *it is our God,*" they have not known God.[1] Jesus, on the contrary, is certain that He knows Him,[2] and keeps His word. — ὅμοιος ὑμῶν ψεύστης] *a liar like unto you.* " *Mendax est qui vel affirmat neganda vel negat arffimanda,*" Bengel. The charge points back to ver. 44.[3] — ἀλλά] *but,* far from being such a liar. — τὸν λόγ. αὐτ. τηρῶ] exactly as in ver. 51. The entire life and work of Christ were in truth one continuous *surrender* to the *counsel* of God, and *obedience* (Phil. ii. 8 ; Rom. v. 19 ; Heb. v. 8) to the divine will, whose injunctions He constantly discerned in His fellowship with the Father, iv. 34. Comp. as to the subject-matter, ver. 29.

Ver. 56. Εἶτα κατασκευάζει καὶ ὅτι μείζων ἐστὶ τοῦ ᾿Αβρ., Euth. Zigabenus, and, indeed, in such a manner, that He, at the same time, puts the hostile children of Abraham to shame. — ὁ πατὴρ ὑμῶν] with a reproving glance back to ver. 39. — ἠγαλλιάσατο, ἵνα ἴδῃ] *he exulted to see ;* the *object* of his exultation is conceived as the *goal* to whose attainment the joyous movement of the heart is directed. He rejoiced in the *anticipation* of seeing my day, *i.e. of witnessing the day of my appearance on earth.*[4] As to its *historical date,*

[1] Not because they held another divine being, their own national god, to be the highest (Hilgenfeld) ; but because they had formed false conceptions of the one true God, who had manifested Himself in the Old Test., and had not understood His highest revelation in Christ, in consequence of their blindness and hardness of heart. Comp. ver. 19, and see Weiss, *Lehrbegr.* p. 60 f. In Hilgenfeld's view, indeed, John teaches that the Jewish religion, as to its substance, was the work of the *Demiurge,* and it was only without his knowledge that the Logos hid in it the germs of the highest religion ! By the same exegesis by which this doctrine is derived from John, one might very easily show it to be taught by Paul, especially in the sharp antagonism he assumes between νόμος and χάρις,—if one desired, *i.e.* if one were willing to bring down this apostle to the period of transition from the Valentinian to the Marcionite Gnosis.

[2] *Regarding Himself,* Jesus does not say

ἔγνωκα (although considered in itself He *might* have said it, comp. xvii. 25), because He here speaks in the consciousness of His *immediate, essential* knowledge of the Father. — According to Ewald, the words, "*It is our God,*" contain an allusion to well-known songs and prayers which were constantly repeated. But the frequent occurrence of "*our God*" in the O. T. is quite sufficient to explain their import.

[3] ὅμοιος with the Gen. as in Theophr. *H. pl.* ix. 11, also Xen. *Anab.* iv. 1. 17 ; see Bornemann, *ad h. l.*

[4] ἡμέρα ἡ ἐμή expressly denotes (hence not τὰς ἡμέρας τὰς ἐμάς, comp. Luke xvii. 22) *the exact, particular day of the appearance of Christ* on earth, *i.e.* the day of *His birth* (Job iii. 1 ; Diog. L. 4. 41), from the Johannine point of view, the day on which the ὁ λόγος σὰρξ ἐγένετο was accomplished. This was the great epoch in the history of redemption which Abraham was to behold.

ἠγαλλιάσατο does not refer to an event in the *paradisaical* life of Abraham ; but, as Abraham was the recipient of the Messianic promise, which designated the Messiah as His own σπέρμα, but himself, as the founder and vehicle of the entire redemptive Messianic development for all nations, the allusion is to the time in his *earthly* life *when the promise was made to him.* His *faith* in this promise (Gen. xv. 6) and the certainty of the Messianic future, whose development was to proceed from him, with which he was thus inspired, could not but fill him with joy and exultation ; hence, also, there is no need for an express testimony to the ἠγαλλ. in Genesis (the supposed reference to the *laughing* mentioned in Gen. xvii. 17 which was already interpreted by Philo to denote great joy and exultation, and which Hofmann also has again revived in his *Weissag. und Erfüll.* II. p. 13, is inadmissible, on a correct explanation of the passage). So much, however, is presupposed, namely, that Abraham recognized the *Messianic* character of the divine promise; and *this* we are justified in presupposing in him who was the chosen recipient of divine revelations. For inventions of the Rabbis regarding revelations of future events asserted, on the ground of Gen. xvii. 17, to have been made to Abraham, see Fabric. *Cod. Pseudepigr.* I. p. 423 ff. The *seeing* of the day (the experimental perception of it through the *living to see it,* Luke xvii. 22 ;[1] to which (ἵνα) the exultation of Abraham was directed, was, for the soul of the patriarch, a moment of the *indefinite future.* And this seeing was *realized,* not during his earthly life, but in his *paradisaical* state,[2] when he, the ancestor of the Messiah and of the nation, learnt that the Messianic age had dawned on the earth in the birth of Jesus as the Messiah. In like manner the advent of Jesus on the earth was made known to Moses and Elijah (Matt. xviii. 4), which fact, however, does not justify us in supposing that reference is here made to occurrences similar to the transfiguration (Ewald). In Paradise Abraham saw the day of Christ, as indeed, he there maintained in general a relation to the states and experiences of his people (Luke xvi. 25 ff.). This was the object of the καὶ εἶδε καὶ ἐχάρη ; it is impossible, however, to determine exactly the form under which the εἶδε was vouchsafed to him, though it ought not to be explained with B. Crusius as *mere anticipation.* We must rest contented with the idea of *divine information.* The apocryphal romance, *Testamentum Levi,* p. 586 f. (which tells us that the Messiah Himself opens the gates of Paradise, feeds the saints from the tree of life, etc., and then adds : τότε ἀγαλλιάσεται Ἀβραὰμ καὶ Ἰσαὰκ κ. Ἰακὼβ κἀγὼ χαρήσομαι καὶ πάντες οἱ ἅγιοι ἐνδύσονται εὐφροσύνην), merely supplies a general confirmation of the thought that Abraham, in the intermediate state of happiness, received with joy the news of the advent of Messiah. Supposing, however, that the relation between promise (ἠγαλλιάσατο, ἵνα ἴδῃ, etc.) and fulfilment (καὶ εἶδε κ. ἐχάρη), expressed in the two clauses of the verse, do require the beholding of the day of Christ to be a *real beholding,* and the day of Christ itself to be the day of His *actual appearance,* i.e. the day of the *incarnation* of the promised One on earth, it is

---

[1] Polyb. x. 4. 7 ; Soph. *O. R.* 831, 1528 ; and see Wetstein and Kypke on the passage.
[2] Comp. Lampe, Lücke, Tholuck, de Wette, Maier, Luthardt, Lechler in the *Stud. u. Krit.* 1854, p. 817, Lange, Baeumlein, Ebrard, Godet.

THE GOSPEL OF JOHN.

not allowable to understand by it, either, with Raphelius and Hengstenberg, the appearance of the angel of the Lord (Gen. xviii.) *i.e.* of the Logos, to Abraham ; or, with Luther, "*the vision of faith with the heart*," at the announcement made in Gen. xxii. 18 ;[1] or, with Olshausen, a *prophetic* vision of the δόξα of Christ (comp. xii. 41) ; or, with Chrysostom, Theophylact, Euth. Zigabenus, Erasmus, and most of the older commentators, also Hofmann, the beholding of an event which merely *prefigured* the day of Christ, a *typical* beholding, whether the *birth* of Isaac be regarded as the event in question,[2] or the offering up of Isaac as a sacrifice, prefiguring the atoning sacrifice and resurrection of Christ (Chrysostom, Grotius, and many others). According to Linder,[3] the day of Christ denotes nothing but the time of *the birth of Isaac*, which was promised in Gen. xviii. 10, so that Christ would thus appear to have represented Himself as one of the angels of the grove of Mamre,[4] and, by the expression ἡμέρα ἡ ἐμή, to have denoted a time of *special, actual revelation.* Taken thus, however, the day in question would be only *mediately* the day of Christ ; whereas, according to the connection and the express designation τὴν ἡμέραν τὴν ἐμήν, Christ Himself must be the *immediate subject of the day*, as the one whose appearance constitutes the day emphatically *His*—His κατ᾽ ἐξοχήν, analogously to the day of His second advent ;[5] hence, also, the plural had not to be employed (in answer to Linder's objection). — καὶ ἐχάρη] appropriately interchanged for ἠγαλλ., the latter corresponding to the first outburst of emotion at the unexpected proclamation.

Ver. 57. The Jews, referring κ. εἶδε κ. ἐχάρη to the earthly life of Abraham, imagine the assertion of Jesus to imply that He had lived in the days of the patriarch, and professed to have been personally acquainted with him ! How absurd is this ! — πεντήκοντα] Placed first to indicate emphasis, corresponding to the position afterwards assigned to the word Ἀβρ. *Fifty* years are specified as the period when a man *attains his full growth :*[6] thou hast not yet passed the full age of manhood ! Consequently, neither the reading τεσσαράκοντα is to be preferred (Ebrard), nor need we conclude either that Jesus was above forty years of age (the Presbyters of Asia Minor in Iren. II. 22. 5) ; or that He was taken to be so old ;[7] or that He *looked* so old (Lampe, Heumann, Paulus) ; or that they confounded " the *intensity of the devotion of His soul*" as it showed itself in His person, with the traces of *age.*[8]   In the act of instituting a comparison with the *two thousand years* that had elapsed since Abraham's day, they could not well care about determining very precisely the age of Christ.   In answer to E. v. Bunsen,[9] who seeks to establish

[1] Comp. Melanchthon, Calvin, and Calovius ; Bengel also : " Vidit diem Christi, qui in semine, quod stellarum instar futurum erat, sidus maximum est et fulgidissimum."

[2] Hofmann ; see also his *Schriftbew.* II. 2, p. 304 f.

[3] *Stud. und Krit.* 1859, p. 518 f., 1867, p. 507 f.

[4] Comp. Hengstenberg.

[5] Luke xvii. 24 ; 1 Cor. i. 8, v. 5 ; 2 Cor. i. 14 ; Phil. i. 6, ii. 16 ; 1 Thess. v. 2 ; 2 Thess. ii. 2.

[6] Comp. Num. iv. 3, 39, viii. 24 f. ; Lightfoot, p. 1046 f.

[7] διὰ τὴν πολυπειρίαν αὐτοῦ Euth. Zigabenus.

[8] Lange, *Life of Jesus.*

[9] *The Hidden Wisdom of Christ, etc.,* Lond. 1865, II. p. 461 ff.

the correctness of the statement in Irenaeus, see Rösch in *Die Jahrb. für deutsche Theol.* 1866, p. 4 f. Without the slightest reason, Bunsen finds in the forty-six years of chap. iv. 2, the *age of Christ.* But also Keim is not opposed to the idea of Christ being forty years of age.[1]

Ver. 58. Not a continuation of the discourse in ver. 56, so that Jesus would thus not have given any answer to the question of the Jews (B. Crusius) ; but, as the contents themselves, and the solemn ἀμὴν ἀμὴν λ. ὑμ. shows, an *answer* to ver. 57. This reply asserts even more than the Jews had asked, namely, πρίν, etc., *before Abraham became*, or was born (not : *was*, as Tholuck, de Wette, Ewald, and others translate),[2] *I am ; older* than Abraham's origin is my existence. As Abraham had not pre-existed, but *came into existence*[3] (by birth), therefore γενέσθαι is used ; whereas εἰμί denotes *being per se*, which belonged to Jesus, so far as He existed before time, as to His divine nature, without having previously come into being. [See Note XXXV. p. 297.] Comp. I. 1. 6 ; and see even Chrysostom. The *Praesens* denotes that which *continues from the past, i.e.* here : that which *continues* from before time (i. 1, xvii. 5).[4] Ἐγώ εἰμι must neither be taken as *ideal* being (de Wette), nor as being Messiah (Scholten), and transferred into the *counsel of God* (Sam. Crellius, Grotius, Paulus, B. Crusius), which is forbidden even by the use of the *Praesens ;* nor may we, with Beyschlag, conceive the being as that of the real *image of God*,—a thought which, after ver. 57, is neither suggested by the context, nor would occur to Christ's hearers without some more precise indication ; nor, lastly, is the utterance to be regarded merely as a *momentary* vision, as in a state of *prophetic elevation* (Weizsäcker), inasmuch as it corresponds essentially to the permanent consciousness which Jesus had of His personal (the condition, in the present connection, of His having seen Abraham) pre-existence, and which everywhere manifests itself in the Gospel of John. Comp. on xvii. 5, vi. 46, 62. The thought is not an intuitive *conclusion* backwards, but a *glance* backward, of the consciousness of Jesus.[5] Only noteworthy in a historical point of view is the perverse explanation of Faustus Socinus, which from him passed over into the Socinian confession of faith :[6] "Before Abraham becomes Abraham, *i.e.* the father of many nations, I am it, namely, the Messiah, the Light of the world." He thus admonishes the Jews to believe on Him while they have an opportunity, before grace is taken from them and transferred to the heathen, in which way Abraham will become the father of many nations.

Ver. 59. The last assertion of Jesus strikes the Jews as *blasphemous ;* they therefore set themselves, in the spirit of zealotry, to inflict punishment (comp. x. 31). A stoning in the temple is mentioned also by Joseph, *Antt.* xvii. 9. 3. The *stones* were probably building stones lying in the fore-court. See Lightfoot, p. 1048. —ἐκρύβη κ. ἐξῆλθεν] *He hid Himself* (probably *in the crowd*), *and*

---

[1] *Gesch. Jes.* I. p. 469 ; comp. his *Geschichtl. Chr.* p. 235.

[2] Also the English Authorized Version.

[3] This view, "*factus est*," forms a more significant correlate to εἰμί than if γενέσθαι were taken as equivalent to *nasci*, which

in itself would be also correct (Gal. iv. 4 ; and see especially Raphelius on the passage).

[4] Comp. LXX.; Ps. xc. 2 ; also Jer. i. 5.

[5] Against Beyschlag.

[6] See *Catech. Racov.*, ed. Oeder, p. 144 f.

went out (whilst thus hidden).[1] The word ἐκρύβη explains *how* He was able
to go out, and therefore (how very different from this is Luke iv. 30 !) *precludes* the notion of anything *miraculous*,[2]—a notion which gave rise to the
addition in the *Text. Rec.* (see the critical observations), which Ewald
defends. Baur, who likewise defends the *Text. Rec.* (p. 384 ff.), finds here
also a *docetic disappearance* (comp. on vii. 10 f.) ; if, however, such was
John's meaning, he selected the most unsuitable possible terms to express it
in writing ἐκρύβη (comp. on the contrary, Luke xxiv. 31 : ἄφαντος ἐγένετο ἀπ'
αὐτῶν) and ἐξῆλθεν ἐκ τοῦ ἱεροῦ. The "*providential protection of God*" (Tholuck)
is a matter of course, but is not expressed.—There is no exegetical ground
for supposing that the simple close of the narrative is designed to *prefigure*
the death of Christ, which, being accomplished under the appearance of
legality, released the Lord from the judgment of Israel, so that He left the
old Israel as the school of Satan, and, on the other hand, gathered around
Him the true Israel (Luthardt). Note how the breach between Jesus and
the Jews gradually approached the extremity, and "how admirable also
in the details, is the delineation of the ever-increasing intensification of the
crisis."[3]

NOTES BY AMERICAN EDITOR.

XXXII. *The woman taken in adultery.* Ver. 53 ; chap. viii. ver. 11.

In the face of all the evidence, internal and external, it seems impossible to
vindicate for this remarkable passage a right to its time-honoured place here,
although the internal testimonies seem to me far from convincing. The exchange of John's favourite οὖν for δέ is, indeed, striking, yet hardly decisive
on the point of style. Taking a few passages at random, we find in ch. ii. 1
12 δέ four times, and no οὖν ; in the whole chapter, δέ 7 times, οὖν 3. In ch. v.
1–13, δέ 5 times, οὖν 2 ; ch. vi. 1–13, δέ 6 times, οὖν 4 ; ch. vii. 1–13, δέ 4
times, οὖν 3. Neither πᾶς ὁ λαός (in its place here), nor ὀρθροῖ, nor γραμματεῖς
καὶ φαρισαῖοι, nor κατακρίνω, would of themselves awaken serious suspicion. The
peculiar situation suggests its peculiar words. Nor, what is generally urged as
the strongest internal reason against the passage, does the interruption of the
narrative seem violent enough to be decisive. It unites itself naturally and
even gracefully with what precedes, and the αὐτοῖς of viii. 12 finds its antecedent
as easily in πᾶς ὁ λαός of ver. 2 (who, of course, are not among the con-
science-smitten retreaters, and especially as they may have consisted largely
of his yesterday's auditors), as to any assumed antecedent in ch. vii. In any
case, the connection is somewhat loose.

Still, uniting the internal with the external difficulties, the numerous vari-
eties of reading (always suspicious) and the absence of the passage from so many
mss., versions, and Fathers, the case is strong against it—only, however, against
its genuineness *here*. That it is, if not Johannean, at least Apostolic, and de-

---

[1] Hengstenberg reverses the logical relation : καὶ ἐξῆλθε stands, he says, for ἐξελθών,
and describes *the manner in which* He hid
Himself,—a purely arbitrary statement,
and if ἐξελθών had been used, it would
have *preceded* the ἐκρύβη (*egressus*), as in

the case of ἀπελθών, xii. 36.

[2] ἀόρατος αὐτοῖς κατέστη τῇ ἐξουσίᾳ τῆς θεότητος, Euth. Zigabenus ; comp. Grotius,
Wolf, Bengel, Luthardt, Hilgenfeld, and
even Augustine.

[3] Ewald, *Gesch. Chr.* p. 477, ed. 3.

scribes a real and most remarkable incident in the life of our Lord, cannot be well doubted ; there is none in the record of our Saviour's life that is more completely lifted above any conception which belonged to the men of his time, and more completely beyond the probability of fabrication. In the Lord's answer to His accusers, by his ready escaping from the snares laid for Him, and that subtle appeal to their consciences, which, by placing the lustful feeling on a virtual equality with the outward act (as Matt. v. 28 ff.), dissolved the accusation and dispersed the accusers ; and in His subsequent treatment of the woman, His separating His mission, on the one hand, from human civil tribunals, and His assertion of His divine relation as not here to condemn and punish, but to pity and save, it proves itself worthy of a place—however it got there—in the heart of the most spiritual of the Gospels. It is urged by some that it is allied rather to the Synoptic than to the Johannean spirit. It seems to me otherwise, and that an unerring instinct caught it, if it was found floating round, and fixed it in that Gospel which pre-eminently presents the deeper and, if we may so say, the diviner aspects of the Saviour.

XXXIII. Τὴν ἀρχὴν ὅ,τι καὶ λαλῶ ὑμῖν. Ver. 25.

This exceedingly difficult passage is variously interpreted. To the rendering of the Comm. Ver. there are three grammatical objections. Τὴν ἀρχήν should be, according to Johannean usage, ἀπ' ἀρχῆς· ὅ,τι indef. or indirect interrog. should be the simple relative (ὅ, what, that which), and λαλῶ should be the perf. λελάληκα or λαλῶν εἴρηκα. (So Field in Otium Norv. p. 66.) To Meyer's construction, [Do you ask me] what I say to you from the beginning [that I am] ? the same objections (urged by Weiss) are in part applicable : τὴν ἀρχήν should be ἀπ' ἀρχῆς ; καί is without significance ; λαλῶ should be λελάληκα, and the question stands in no clear connection with what precedes or follows. The use of ὅ, τι (indirect interrog.) is, indeed, strictly grammatical. Weiss adopts as the only fitting explanation that of the ancient interpreters (Chrys., Theoph., Euthym. Zigab.), which takes it as a question of displeasure : " Why do I even speak to you at all ?" Thus καί and the pres. λαλῶ (as also λαλῶ for λέγω) become strictly in place. Τὴν ἀρχήν, placed emphatically at the head, has a well-known classical use (equivalent to the Latin omnino), at the outset, at all, in sentences actually or, like this, virtually negative. The ὅ,τι, standing for the direct interrog. τί, is, indeed, scarcely classical, but is found in the Sept., and has some analogous classical uses. It did not stumble the early Greek interpreters. Meyer's objection to this (which Weiss calls trivial) seems to me, however, weighty, and the question quite unnatural in the mouth of our Lord at this stage of the conversation. Some bring out the same meaning by taking ὅτι as that, and reading the sentence as an exclamation, "That I even speak to you at all !" It seems questionable, after all, whether the rendering of the Comm. Ver. (retained by the Revisers) is not, with all its strict grammatical objections, as best fitting the connection, the most probable. If it be objected to this that our Lord had not *from the beginning* declared His divine origin and sonship, we must regard the objection as only seemingly valid. Explicitly, indeed, He had not, perhaps (though see John i. 50), but *implicitly* He had perpetually declared it. Every sentence of the Sermon on the Mount involves a virtual assertion of His Messianic character and Divine Sonship. Besides, Field's objection, that λαλῶ should be λελάληκα, does not seem serious. Our Lord may regard His teaching as a *continuous* whole, and the τὴν ἀρχὴν λαλῶ may be elliptical for τὴν ἀρ. λελάληκα καὶ ἔτι λαλῶ.

XXXIIIa. " *He was a murderer from the beginning.*" Ver. 44.

Rightly has Meyer, with many able expositors, explained this, not of that special and outward act of homicide which so speedily followed the Fall, exhibiting in ghastly form the malignity of its generating principle, but of the one primal murder which involved all the rest. Sin in the person of the devil ; the devil, as the embodied principle of evil, *murdered* the race ; implanted in the heart of humanity a seed which was to bear, in innumerable forms, the fruit of death.

The thought is the same as that uttered by Paul in Rom. vii. 8–11, where, with characteristic vigor and vivacity, he portrays, as in his personal experience, the great catastrophe of humanity ; shows the impotence of sin without the vantage-ground of law, and its promptness to avail itself of this— the prohibition to taste the fruit under penalty of death—to seduce and slay its victims. Apart from the law the man *lived*, had in him no element of death ; with its innocent coming, the seducer springs into life, and the victim of his machinations *dies*, morally and physically. The devil thus commenced his recorded career on our planet with lying and murder. He charged with falsehood Him whom he knew to be absolute truth, and by this seduced man into a transgression whose threatened penalty, however vague might be his conception of it, he knew enough of its utterer to know would be certainly executed, and in its nature inconceivably disastrous. The Jews, says Christ, imitate their moral father in these so marked attributes.

XXXIV. " *When he speaketh a lie,*" etc. Ver. 44.

Opinions differ as to whether ὁ πατὴρ αὐτοῦ should be rendered "the father of him," *i.e.* of the liar, or "the father of *it*," the abstract, ψεῦδος, being developed out of the preceding ψεύστης. Meyer prefers the former ; Weiss goes back to the latter, more common construction. Either would be admissible if the article were wanting, so that πατήρ could be taken predicatively, though even then πατὴρ τοῦ ψεύστου or τῶν ψευστῶν, in the one case, and πατὴρ τοῦ ψεύδους or πατὴρ τούτου in the other, would be much easier and more natural. With the reading ὁ πατήρ, the two constructions are about equally difficult, and both, it seems to me, unsanctioned by any law of good Greek usage. There is no competent Greek scholar who would not, but for considerations outside of grammatical laws, render, either " because he is a liar and his father [is one] "; or, much better, " because his father also is a liar." But we thus seem to be thrown back upon the unscriptural and monstrous doctrine of a father of the devil or demiurge, asserting rival claims to those of God. To escape this dilemma we must look back to find, if possible, a different subject for λαλῇ : one which shall refer it not to the devil, but to his child, the human liar. This may be done by either one of two different ways. The first, by a critical emendation of the text, reading, with an authority cited by Lachmann, but almost conjecturally ὃς ἂν for ὅταν : " whoever speaketh a lie, speaketh from what belongs to him ; because his father also is a liar." The other by grammatical interpretation (as suggested, I think, first by Middleton on the Greek Article), assuming viz. an indefinite subject (τὶς), and referring it to the subject naturally in the reader's mind : " When one speaketh a lie, he speaketh," etc. Of these the former seems very easy and intrinsically probable ; yet as it has no good MS. authority in its favour, we are perhaps hardly at liberty to adopt it on conjecture, however plausible. The other—the assumption of τὶς—is not specially harsh, and though not to be unnecessarily resorted to, yet accords with the very free way in which the Greek generally treats the subject of the verb, as 2 Cor. x. 10, " For his letters φησί, says one, are weighty." Perhaps 2 Cor. iii. 16, " But when one may turn (ἐπιστρέψῃ τις) unto the Lord ;" see Arist. de Rhet. lib. I. v. 17 for the freedom with which the subject of the verb is treated, and of which examples might be multiplied indefinitely. If any objection may lie against this construction, it does not approach in harshness to that which makes ὁ πατὴρ αὐτοῦ a predicate in the sense ordinarily assigned to it. Besides this, the *meaning* seems much more appropriate. To say of a *man*—who has been charged with being a child of the devil—that when he utters falsehood he speaks out of what properly *belongs* to him, because his father is a liar, is a natural and emphatic expansion of the previously implied idea. But to say of the devil that when he utters a lie he speaks from what belongs to him, because he is a liar, is little more than an identical proposition, and turns aside to apply to Satan the illustrative expression which would be naturally applied to his human votaries with whom the Lord is directly dealing. Besides, the conjunctive construction ὅταν λαλῇ, *when he may be speaking*, favors the reference to a *human* personage whom we do not assume always and everywhere to utter falsehood, rather than to the great original Liar, of whom the language would naturally be ὅτε λαλεῖ, "when he *speaketh*" (as he always and necessarily does). Besides, the ordinary construction almost requires αὐτός, and the clause would naturally read ὅτι καὶ αὐτός ἐστι ψεύστης καὶ πατὴρ τούτου (or τοῦ ψεύδους).

Towards the construction here advocated, modern English scholarship seems rapidly tending. The Revised Version gives it a place in the margin. Canon Westcott, in the Speaker's Commentary, declares in its favor, and Profs. Milligan and Moulton (of Aberdeen and Cambridge universities) in Schaff's Popular Commentary. Prof. Watkins, in Ellicott's Comm. for English Readers, contemptuously rejects it, but in a way that proves him to understand but imperfectly the problem, charging it with reviving the old heresy which gives a father to the devil, and thus " opposed to the context, the teaching of the Gospel," and " the whole tenor of biblical truth." It is in truth simply a question of linguistic and rhetorical propriety, and not at all of theology. Our construction avoids serious and, I think, insuperable grammatical difficulties, puts into the Lord's mouth a much more pertinent statement, and when finally admitted will make one of the most important recent advances in N. T. philology.

XXXV. " Before Abraham was." Ver. 59.

The R. V. here translates γενέσθαι *was* in the text, but places *was born*, as its Greek equivalent, in the margin. I do not see why the true force of the Greek (as Meyer, Weiss, etc. against Thol., de W., Ew.), should not be given in the text. Admitting the reality of the distinction, much is surely gained in rhetorical force by putting the two words into juxtaposition, the *was* and the *was born* (became, came into being), the timeless *being* of the Son against the historical *becoming* of Abraham.

CHAPTER IX.

Ver. 4. ἐμέ] B. D. L. א.* Copt. Sahid. Aeth. Arr. Cant. Cyr. Nonn. read ἡμᾶς. Instead of the following με, L. א.* Copt. Aeth. Arr. Cyr. also have ἡμᾶς. Had the saying been changed into a general proposition, and had ἐμέ therefore been altered into ἡμᾶς, then, instead of με, ἡμᾶς must necessarily have been used *in all cases alike.* ἡμᾶς, which Tisch. also adopts, appears to be the original reading (instead of ἐμέ). It was changed into ἐμέ, because the plur. appeared inappropriate, and on account of the following με ; this latter, on the other hand, was assimilated to ἡμᾶς in L., etc. — Ver. 6. After ἐπέχρισε, Lachm. and Tisch. read αὐτοῦ ; so A. B. C.** L. א. Cursives, to which also D. must be added with αὐτῷ. On the other hand, the τοῦ τυφλοῦ that follows is wanting in B. L. א. Cursives (D. has αὐτοῦ). It is put in bracké́ts by Lachm., deleted by Tisch. We ought to read : ἐπέχρ. αὐτοῦ τὸν πηλ. ἐπὶ τ. ὀφθ. τοῦ τυφλοῦ. Αὐτοῦ was referred to the blind man ; in that case, however, either this αὐτοῦ itself must be deemed out of place (on account of the following τοῦ τυφλοῦ), or τοῦ τυφλοῦ must be omitted. — Ver. 7. νίψαι] bracketed by Lachm., wanting only in A.* and the Codd. of the It. A copyist's omission after ver. 11 ; hence, also, A** has supplied καὶ νίψαι after Σιλ. — Ver. 8. προσαίτης] Elz. : τυφλός, in opposition to decisive authorities. A correction. — Ver. 11. εἰς τὸν Σιλωάμ] Elz., Scholz : εἰς τὴν κολυμβήθραν τοῦ Σιλωάμ, in opposition to very weighty testimonies. Repetition from ver. 7. — Ver. 14. ὅτε] B. L. X. א. 33, Codd. It. Cyr. : ἐν ᾗ ἡμέρᾳ. So Lachm. and Tisch. Correctly : the redundant expression was easily supplanted by the word ὅτε, which readily suggested itself. — Ver. 16. Lachm. and Tisch. : οὐκ ἐστιν οὗτος παρὰ θεοῦ ὁ ἀνθρ., after B. D. L. X. א. 33, 157. The position in the Elz. (οὗτ. ὁ ἄνθρ. οὐκ ἐ. π. τ. θ.) is a transposition to make the reading easier. — Ver. 17. After λέγουσιν weighty witnesses require the insertion of οὖν, which Lachm. and Tisch. have adopted. Lachmann's insertion of οὖν, however, after ἀπεκρ. in ver. 20, is supported solely by B. א., whereas A. and other uncials and Cursives have δέ. Both seem to be additions ; as also the following αὐτοῖς, which is wanting in B. L. X. א. Cursives, Verss. Cyr. — Ver. 25. καὶ εἶπεν] to be deleted, as is done by Lachm. and Tisch. A mechanical addition opposed by weighty witnesses. — Ver. 26. The preponderance of evidence is in favour of δέ in place of οὖν (Lachm.) ; πάλιν, however, with Lachm. and Tisch., after B. D. א.* Verss. Nonn. Aug., is to be deleted, as an addition which would readily suggest itself. — Ver. 28. After ἐλοιδ. Elz., following Cursives, Vulg. Codd. It., inserts οὖν ; instead of which B. א.* Sahid. Cyr. Ambr. read καὶ ἐλ., and D. L. א.** Verss. οἱ δὲ ἐλ. Various modes of es-tablishing the connection. — Ver. 30. The reading ἐν γὰρ τοῦτο (approved by Rinck) is only found in X. Λ. and Cursives, and is on that ground alone to be rejected ; at the same time, it bears witness, also, to the fact of the original position of γάρ being immediately after ἐν (Tisch. : ἐν τούτῳ γάρ, with B. L. א. Cursives, Cyr. Chrys.). The reading ἐν τούτῳ οὖν found in D. may be explained from the circumstance that the relation of γάρ presented a difficulty. Instead of θαυμ. we must, with Tisch., read τὸ θαυμ., as in B. L. אּ. Cursives, Cyr. Chrys. How easily might the superfluous τό be suppressed! — Ver. 35. τοῦ θεοῦ] B. D. אּ. Aeth. : τοῦ ἀνθρώπου, because Jesus was accustomed thus to designate Himself. — Ver. 36. καὶ τίς ἐστι] Elz. Lachm. do not read καί ; the evidence for it, however, is very weighty, and it may easily have been passed over by clumsy copyists. — Ver. 41. ἡ οὖν ἁμαρτ.] οὖν, bracketed by Lachm. and deleted by Tisch., is wanting in decisive witnesses. A connective addition ; superfluous, and weakening the force.

Ver. 1 f. The direct connection, by means of καί, with the preceding words ἐξῆλθεν ἐκ τ. ἱεροῦ, and the correlation with it of παράγων, makes it impossible, without arbitrariness, to take any view but this,—that the healing of the blind man, instead of not being determinable with chronological exactness (Hengstenberg), must rather be placed soon after Jesus had left the temple, while He was still on His way, and on the very same day, the record of whose scenes commences with viii. 21. This day was a Sabbath (ver. 14) ; not, however, the one mentioned in vii. 37 (Olshausen), but a later one, see on viii. 12. The objection that the calmness which marks the transaction, and the presence of the disciples, are not in keeping with the scene which had occurred shortly before (viii. 59), and that therefore another day ought to be assumed,[1] has little force ; for the calmness of the bearing of Jesus is anything but a psychological riddle, and the disciples might easily have gathered round Him again. — παράγων] in passing by, namely, the place where the blind beggar was (probably in the neighbourhood of the temple, Acts iii. 2). Comp. on Matt. ix. 9, and Mark ii. 14. — τυφλὸν ἐκ γενετῆς.] So much the greater was the miracle ; comp. Acts iii. 2, xiv. 8. The supposition, based on ver. 5, that this blind man represents the κόσμος, to which Jesus, having been spurned by the Jews, now turns (Luthardt), is the less warrantable, as the stress in that verse is laid on φῶς, and not on τοῦ κόσμου (comp. even viii. 12). This healing of the blind is not intended to have a figurative import, though it is afterwards used (ver. 39 ff.) as a figurative representation of a great idea. — τίς ἥμαρτεν, etc.] The notion of the disciples is not, that neither the one nor the other could be the case ;[2] but, as the positive mode of putting the dilemma shows, that either the one or the other must be the case. See Baeumlein, Partic. p. 132. They were still possessed by the popular idea[3] that special misfortunes are the punishment of special sins ; against which view Jesus, here and in Luke xiii. 9 ff., decidedly declares Himself. Now, as the man was born blind, either it must have been the guilt of his parents, which he was expiating,— a belief which, in accordance with Ex. xx. 5, was very prevalent,[4] and existed even among the Greeks,[5]—or he himself must have sinned even while in the womb of his mother. The latter alternative was grounded in the popular notion that even an embryo experiences emotions (comp. Luke i. 41,

[1] De Wette and others.
[2] Euth. Zigabenus, Ebrard, comp. also Hengst.
[3] Comp. on Matt. ix. 2, also the book of Job, and Acts xxviii. 4.
[4] Lightfoot, p. 1048.
[5] Maetzner in Lycurg. in Leocr. p. 217.

43), especially evil emotions, and that the latter predominate.[1] The explanation of the question from the belief (which is also not to be presupposed
in Matt. xiv. 2) in the *transmigration of souls*[2] is as inadmissible as the assumption of a belief in the *pre-existence of souls*.[3] For apart from the uncertainty
of the fact whether the doctrine of the transmigration of souls was entertained by the Jews in the days of Christ (see Tholuck on the passage, and
Delitzsch, *Psychol.* p. 463 f. [E. T. p. 545 f.]), those two doctrines could
not have been known among the people, and therefore must not be assumed
to have been held by the disciples, although it is true that the pre-existence
of souls, both of good and bad, is an unquestionable article of doctrine in
Wisd. viii. 19 f., as also with Philo and the Essenes, with the Rabbins, and
in the Cabbala.[4] It is quite out of place, however, to. refer to the *heathen*
view of the pre-existence of souls.[5] Tholuck's suggestion, finally, that the
thought, though obscurely conceived, is, that the blind man, through being
born blind, is marked out as a sinner in virtue of an *anticipation* of punishment, both contradicts the words, and is altogether destitute of biblical support. In Luthardt's view, the disciples, in accordance with Ex. xx. 5, regarded the second of the two supposed cases as alone possible, but mentioned
the first as a possibility, in order that *Christ* might solve the riddle which
they were unable to solve. Similarly Baeumlein and Delitzsch, who looks
upon the question as the mere expression of perplexity resulting from a
false premiss. It is an arbitrary procedure, however, to ascribe such a difference to two cases regarding which a question is asked in *precisely the
same form*, or to treat the possibility in the one case as assumed merely in
appearance. The disciples considered *both* cases *possible*, and wished to
know which of them was *real*. But at the same time they deemed a *third*
case out of the question, and this was the error in the dilemma which they
put forth,—an error which Jesus (ver. 3) lays bare and corrects by setting
before them the *Tertium datur.* — ἵνα τυφλ. γενν.] The retributive result, in
accordance with the teleological connection of the divine destiny. That the
man was *born* blind might have been previously known to those who asked
the question ; or the man himself might just have informed them of the
fact, for the purpose of adding force to his request for alms (ver. 8).

Ver. 3. Οὐ παντελῶς ἀναμαρτήτους αὐτούς φησιν, ἀλλ' ὅσον εἰς τὸ τυφλωθῆναι αὐτόν,
Euth. Zigabenus. — ἀλλ'] sc. τυφλὸς ἐγεννήθη. — τὰ ἔργα τοῦ θεοῦ] *the works of
God*, i.e. *what God works*, should be manifested in Him. The expression
must be left in this general form (it first acquires its more exact force in ver.
4) ; it denotes the entire *category* of which such miraculous healings were a
particular *species ;* hence the works of God were set forth and brought to
light in this concrete case, to wit, in the man (ἐν αὐτῷ) who experienced the
divine miraculous power. In the connection of the divine decree, however,
from which everything accidental, everything independent of the divine

---

[1] See Sanhedr. f. 91. 2 ; Beresh. Rabba, f.
38. 1, b. ; Lightfoot, comp. Wetstein.

[2] Calvin, Beza, Drusius, Aretius, Grotius,
Hammond, Clericus, and several others.

[3] Cyril, de Wette, Brückner.

[4] See Grimm on *Wisdom* of Solomon in
the *Exeget. Handb.* p. 177 f.; Bruch, *Lehre v.
d. Prae-existenz d. Seel.* p. 22.

[5] Isidorus and Severus in *Corder. Cat.*

plan, is excluded, this φανέρωσις must stand in the relation of a *purpose* towards the sufferings which, in this particular concrete case, are miraculously removed. Hence ἵνα φανερ., etc., is a thought which contains the true nature of the *Theodicy* for all sufferings. According to Weiss,[1] the ἔργα θ. are *spiritual* operations, namely, the *enlightenment of the world*, symbolically set forth by this healing of the blind. This, however, anticipates the doctrinal *application* which Jesus Himself makes of the work which He wrought (ver. 39).

Ver. 4. By the participative ἡμᾶς (see the critical observations), Jesus includes the disciples with Himself as helpers and continuers of the Messianic activity. The further progress of the discourse is indicated by the *pronoun* which, for the sake of emphasis, is placed at the *beginning of the sentence;* the *subject* is thus specified through whose activity the φανέρωσις mentioned in ver. 3 is to be accomplished. " It is *we* who are destined by God to work His works as long as we live, and until death puts an end to our activity." There is no hint whatever in the text that Jesus wished to meet the scruples of the disciples on account of the healing which He was about to perform *on the Sabbath* (Kuinoel) ; indeed, as far as the disciples were concerned, to whom Sabbath healings by Jesus were nothing new, there was no ground for such a procedure. — τοῦ πέμψ. με] Jesus does not again say ἡμᾶς ;[2] for *His* mission involved also that of the disciples, and it was He who commissioned the disciples (xiii. 20, xx. 21). — ἕως] *so long as*, denoting contemporaneous duration, very frequently so in the classics subsequent to Homer, with the praes. or imperf.[3]—*Day* and *Night* are images, not of *tempus opportunum* and *importunum*, nor also of αἰὼν οὗτος and μέλλων ;[4] but (for Jesus was thinking of His speedy departure out of the world, ver. 5) of *life* and *death.*[5] The latter puts an end to the activity of every one on earth (even to that of Christ in His human manifestation). By the different use made of the same image in xi. 9 f., we are not justified in regarding it as including the period of the *passion* (Hengstenberg). Moreover, Christ was still working whilst He hung on the *cross.* Olshausen's view is wrong : ἡμέρα denotes the *time of grace*, which was then specially conditioned by the presence of Christ, the Light of the world ; with His removal *darkness* assumed its sway. Against this view the general and unlimited form of the expression ὅτι οὐδεὶς δύναται ἐργάζεσθαι (which Olshausen arbitrarily restricts by adding " for a time," and " in spiritual matters") is in itself a decisive objection ; not to mention that Jesus regarded His death, not as the beginning of spiritual darkness, but as the very condition of greater enlightenment by the Spirit (xvii. 7, xv. 26, xiv. 26, *al.*). With Olshausen agrees substantially B. Crusius ; comp. also Grotius, Bengel, and several others. Luthardt also refers day and night to the *world*, whose day-time coincided with the presence of Christ in the world, and whose night began when he departed

[1] *Lehrbegr.* p. 201.

[2] Which Ewald prefers in opposition to his own translation. But see the critical note.

[3] See Blomfield, *Gloss. ad Aesch. Pers.* 434.

[4] Chrysostom, Theophylact, Euth. Zigabenus, Ruperti, and others.

[5] Comp. Hom. *Il.* ε. 310, λ. 356 ; Aesch. *Sept.* 385 ; *Pers.* 841 ; Plat. *Apol.* p. 40 D, and Stallbaum thereon ; *Hor. Od.* 1. 28. 15.

out of the world ; as soon as He should leave the world, no other could occupy His place in the accomplishment of redemption ; from that time onward, there would be no longer a redemptive history, but merely an appropriation of redemption. But apart from the hair-splitting character of the distinction thus drawn, the grounds adduced against Olshausen hold substantially good against this explanation also, especially that ἐργάζεσθαι— which here has no determining object, as in the previous case—and οὐδείς are quite general ; and accordingly, ἔρχεται νὺξ—ἐργάζεσθαι must be regarded as a commonplace. Godet finds in νύξ the thought of the *evening rest*, which Christ was to enjoy in His *heavenly* state. This is erroneous, however, because it is not *evening* but *night* that is mentioned, and because δύναται would then be inappropriate.

Ver. 5. A more precise description of His earthly vocation, characteristically expressed in relation to the sight which was to be bestowed on the blind man. Ὅταν, however, is neither *quamdiu* (so usually) nor *quandoquidem* (so Lücke and Fritzsche, *ad Marc.* p. 86),—which latter usage is foreign to the N. T., and is only apparently found in passages such as Thuc. 1. 141. 5, 142. 1,—but : *When* (*quando*, at the time in which) *I am in the world, I am the Light of the world.* It expresses the necessary *contemporaneousness* of the two relations. He cannot be in the world, says Christ, without at the same time enlightening the world. *Thus*, also, did it behove Him to show Himself in the case of this blind man. φῶς is employed, it is true, in a spiritual sense, as in i. 5 ff., viii. 12, but also with a significant reference to the sight which was to be restored to the blind man. In healing him, that enlightening activity of Jesus by which those who did not see were to be made to see (see ver. 39), is set forth in a transaction which, though primarily sensuous, was also suggestive of spiritual enlightenment (ver. 37 f.). In itself the first clause of the verse—ὅταν . . . ὦ—might have been dispensed with viii. 12); its utterance, however, in connection with ver. 4, was occasioned by the consciousness that He was soon to depart from the world, and that after His departure the present mode and action of the φῶς εἶναι, which were bound up with His corporeal earthly career, must come to an end. Then Christ would work through the Paraclete and through the vehicles of the Paraclete, as the Light of the world.

Ver. 6 f. For what reason Jesus anointed the eyes of the blind man with clay John does not inform us ; but this does not justify us in leaving the question unanswered (Brückner). The procedure was certainly not adopted for the purpose of *defying the hierarchy* (Ewald) because it was the Sabbath, according to which view it would have had nothing to do with the healing itself. At the same time, it was equally far from being of a *medicinal* nature ; for often as spittle was applied in the case of diseases of the eye (see Wetstein and Lightfoot), the means employed would bear no proportion to the rapidity with which the cure took place, especially considering that the man was *born* blind ; the same remark applies also to Mark vii. 32 and viii. 23. To treat the anointing with the clay as merely a *means of awakening faith* (comp. Lücke), or as a *test* of faith (Calvin), and, consequently, as having a purely *psychological* effect, is to represent the entire procedure as adopted solely with an eye to *appearances*, to making an impression on the blind man. On this view, therefore, the ointment of clay had in itself nothing to do with the cure performed, which is scarcely reconcilable with the truthfulness and dignity of Jesus. Regard for this rather compels the assumption that the ointment was the *real medium* of the cure, and formed an essential part of the act ; and that, accordingly, the spittle was the *continens of the objective healing virtue*, by means of which it came into, and remained actively in contact with, the organism. Comp. Tholuck and Olshausen, who characterize the spittle as the *conductor* of the healing virtue ; so Lange, who, however, conjoins with it the psychological action referred to above ; and also Nonnus, though he draws a very arbitrary distinction, terming the spittle λυσίπονον, and the πηλός, φαεσφόρον. There is nothing against this mode of viewing the matter, in the fact that Jesus used a medium in so few of His miracles of healing, and in so many others employed no medium at all (as [See Note XXXVa., p. 314] in the case of the blind men of Jericho, Matt. xx. 20 ff. ; Mark x. 46 ff.) ; for He must Himself have known when it was necessary and when not, though no clearer insight into the causal connection between the means and the result is vouchsafed to us. We have no authority for attributing to John a view of miracles which regarded them as *mysteries*, and which prevailed at a later date ;[1] for with his christology he, least of all, would find occasion for its adoption ; besides, that the procedure followed in the case of this miracle was unique, and thus its speciality was carefully substantiated by the judicial investigation which grew out of the occurrence. According to Baur (comp. Ewald, as above), the miracle was performed in this circumstantial way in order that it might wear the appearance of a work done on the *Sabbath ;* the supposition, however, is incorrect, if for no other reason, because the healing by itself, apart altogether from the circumstances attending it, was a breaking of the Sabbath. Baur, indeed, regards the whole narrative, notwithstanding the remarkable circumstantiality and naïve liveliness which mark it, as an *invention ;* so also Strauss, Weisse, comp. the note after ver. 41. In harmony with his view of the figurative design of the entire healing, Luthardt (comp. also Godet) interprets the anointing with clay to mean : "He must become blind who wishes to receive sight" (the sending to the pool of Siloam being intended to typify the ἔρχεσθαι πρὸς αὐτόν, iii. 20 f.). But interpretations of this sort have no warrant in the text, and furnish at the same time unintentional support to the unhistorical view of those who treat the narrative as the *mere* vehicle of an idea,—a remark which holds good against Hengstenberg, who, like Erasmus[2] and others, regards πηλός, after Gen. ii. 7, as the symbol of *creative* influence, although in this case we have only to do with an *opening* of the eyes (vv. 10, 14), and that by means of a subsequent washing away of the πηλός. — καὶ ἐπέχρισεν αὐτοῦ τ. πηλὸν ἐπὶ τ. ὀφθ. τ. τυφλοῦ]

[1] De Wette, comp. B. Crusius.

[2] Erasmus, *Paraphr.:* "paternum videlicet ac suum verius opificium referens, quo primum hominem ex argilla humore macerata finxerat. Ejusdem autem erat auctoris restituere quod perierat, qui condiderat quod non erat." So substantially, also. Theophylact, Euth. Zigabenus, Beza, and several others. Comp. also Iren. 5. 15.

According to this reading (see the critical note), αὐτοῦ must be referred to the *spittle* of Jesus ; He rubbed the *ointment made* of it and the clay on the eyes of the blind man.[1] — εἰς τὴν κολυμβ.] not dependent on ὑπαγε,[2] which is not connected with νίψαι even by a καί,[3] but : *Into the pool of Siloam*, so that the πηλός is washed away *into the pool* by the process of cleansing which takes place on the edge of the basin.[4] — On the *Pool Siloam* (Fountain, Isa. viii. 6 ; Luke xiii. 4 ; Pool, Neh. iii. 15) and its doubtful situation,—which, however, Robinson,[5] following Josephus, re discovered at the entrance of the Tyropoeum Valley, on the south-east side of Zion.[6] The expression κολυμβ. τοῦ Σιλ. denotes the pool formed by the *fountain* Siloam (ὁ Σιλ., Luke xiii. 4 ; Isa. viii. 6).—*The washing in the pool of Siloam* is no more to be regarded as a medicinal prescription than the application of the πηλός (the Rabbinical traces of a healing virtue of the water relate to the digestive organs, see Schoettgen), but was required by Jesus for the purpose of allowing the clay the necessary time for producing its effect, and, at the same time, this *particular* water, the pool of Siloam, was mentioned as being *nearest* to the scene of the action (in the vicinity of the temple, viii. 59, ix. 1), and as certainly also *well known* to the blind man. According to Lange,[7] the intention of Jesus, in prescribing the sacred fountain of the temple, was to set manifestly forth the *co-operation of Jehovah* in this repeated Sabbath act. But neither John nor the discussion that follows in ver. 13 ff.— in the course of which, indeed, the pool is not once mentioned—betrays the slightest trace of this supposed mystery. This also in answer to the meaning imported by Godet into the text, that Siloam is represented as the type of all the blessings of which Christ is the reality, so that, in the form of an action, Christ says, " *Ce que Siloé est typiquement, je le suis en réalité.*" This does not at all harmonize with the narrative ; in fact, on such a view, the confused notion would result, that the true Siloam sent the blind man to the typical Siloam in order to the completion of his cure,—that the *Antitype*, in other words, sent him to the *Type!* — ἀπεσταλμένος] The name שִׁילוֹחַ (which even the LXX. and Josephus give in Greek as Σιλωάμ) denotes originally *missio* (*sc.* aquarum), *i.e.* outflow ; but John, adopting a typical etymology, renders it directly שָׁלוּחַ, *missus*, which in itself was grammatically allowable, either after the analogy of לִוֹּי. (see Hitzig on Isa. viii. 6), so that the word would be a strengthened particip. Kal with a passive signification, or, in virtue of the resolution of the dagesh forte in the particip. Piel into *yod*.[8] He thus finds, in the name of pool, a noteworthy typical reference, not indeed to Christ, the messenger of God, the true Siloam,[9] but to the cir-

---

[1] Note the näive, attractive *circumstantiality* which is characteristic of the entire narrative.

[2] Comp. on Matt. ii. 23.

[3] Against Lücke and Winer.

[4] Comp. on the pregnancy of this mode of expression, Kühner, *ad Xen. Anab.* ii. 2. 10 ; Winer, p. 387 [E. T. p. 415].

[5] II. p. 142 ff.

[6] See Tobler, *d. Siloahquelle u. d. Oelberg*,

1852, p. 1 ff. ; Rödiger in *Gesen. Thes.* III. p. 1416 ; Leyrer in *Herzog's Encykl.* XIV. p. 371 ff.

[7] *L. J.* p. 635.

[8] See Tholuck, *Beiträge zur Spracherklär.* p. 120 ff. ; Ewald, *Lehrb. d. Hebr. Spr.* § 156 a.

[9] As Theophylact, Erasmus, Beza, Calvin, Corn. à Lapide, and many other earlier commentators, also Schweizer, Ebrard,

cumstance that the blind man was *sent* to this pool by Christ.   The pool of שלוח has the "*nomen et omen*" of this *sending away*.   The context naturally suggests nothing further than this.[1]   It is arbitrary with Wassenberg and Kuinoel to pronounce the entire parenthesis spurious (it is absent only in Syr. and Pers. p.), a view to which Lücke also inclined, out of regard for John.   But why should a fondness for typical etymologies have been foreign to John ?   Comp. the much more peculiar example of Paul in Gal. iv. 25.   Such things leave the pneumatic character of the evangelist unaffected. — ἀπῆλθεν] which he, being well acquainted with the neighbourhood, was able to do without any one to take him by the hand, τυφλῷ ποδί (Eur. *Hec.* 1050), as, indeed, many blind men are able in like manner to find their way about alone. — ἦλθε] namely, to his dwelling, as is indicated by the words οἱ οὖν γείτονες which follow.   Jesus did not meet him again till ver. 35.

Vv. 8-12. Καὶ οἱ θεωροῦντες, etc.] *And they who before had seen him that he was a beggar,* the previous eye-witnesses of his being a beggar.   The καί gives the force of universality : *and in general ;* the partic. *praes.* has the force of the *imperfect.* — ὁ καθήμ. κ. προσαιτ.] *who is accustomed to sit there and beg.* They had known him for a long while as occupied in no other way than in begging. — The peculiarly vivid and detailed character of what follows renders it probable that John derived his information from the lips of the man himself after he had become a believer. — Ver. 11. ἄνθρωπος λεγόμ. Ἰησοῦς] "nescierat caecus celebritatem Jesu," is the opinion of Bengel and others. But he must surely have learnt something more regarding his deliverer than His mere name.   The quondam blind man conducts himself rather throughout the whole affair in a very impartial and judicious manner, and for the present keeps to the *simple matter of fact*, without as yet venturing on a further judgment. — ἀνέβλεψα] may signify, *I looked up.*[2]   So Lücke ; but this meaning is inadmissible on account of vv. 15, 18, which require *I recovered my sight, visum recepi.*[3]   As regards the man *born* blind, indeed, the expression is inexact, but rests on the general notion that even one born blind has the natural power of sight, though he has been deprived of its use from his very birth, and that he *recovers* it through the healing.[4] — That the man is able to give, at all events, the *name* of his benefactor, is intelligible enough from the inquiries which he would naturally institute after he

Luthardt, Hilgenfeld, Lange, Hengstenberg, Brückner, Godet maintain.

[1] Not to the fact that in ἀπεσταλμ., which should denote "*freely flowing, streaming,*" a deliverance from certain evils was found, as Ewald supposes.   It is quite a mistake to suppose any allusion to the *water of baptism* (Calovius, after Ambrose, Jerome, and others) ; as also to identify the name with שלה in Gen. xlix.6 (Grotius).   The simple and correct view is taken also by Bengel, de Wette, and several others ; by Baeumlein with hesitation.   Nonnus aptly remarks : ὕδωρ στελλομένοιο προώνυμον ἐκ σέο πομπῆς. Comp. Euth. Zigabenus : διὰ τὸν ἀπεσταλμένον ἐκεῖ τότε τυφλόν.

[2] Mark xvi. 4 ; 2 Macc. vii. 25 ; Plat. *Pol.* vii. p. 515 C ; Ax. p. 370 C ; Xen. *Cyr.* vi. 4. 9.

[3] Comp. Matt. xi. 5 ; Tob. xiv. 2 ; Plat. *Phaedr.* p. 243 B.

[4] Comp. Grotius : "Nec male *recipere* quis dicitur, quod communiter tributum humanae naturae ipsi abfuit." In Pausanias, also (Messen. iv. p. 240), we read of one who was born blind and received sight, ἀνέβλεψε. Comp. Evang. Nicod. 6, where the man born blind who there speaks says : ἐπέθηκε τὰς χεῖρας ἐπὶ τ. ὀφθαλμούς μου, κ α ὶ ἀ ν έ β λ ε ψ α π α ρ α χ ρ ῆ μ α.

had been healed. But the circumstance that while at the outset he expresses
no opinion regarding the person of Jesus (see previously on ἀνθρ. λεγ. Ιησ.),
he notwithstanding afterwards declares Him to be a *Prophet* (ver. 17), and
One sent of God (ver. 33), though he was first brought by Jesus Himself to
believe in Him as the *Messiah* in vv. 35 ff., is entirely in keeping with the
gradual nature of the development through which he passed. Such a gradation is, indeed, natural and necessary in some cases, whereas others differently constituted are at once carried to the goal by the force of the first impression. This in opposition to Baur's supposition. that the narrator *designedly* so framed his account that the miracle should be viewed as an ἔργον
θεοῦ *primarily in its pure objectivity.* — εἰς τὸν Σιλωάμ] here the name of the
pool ; hence the Rec. has εἰς τ. κολυμβ. τ. Σιλ.,—a correct gloss.

Ver. 13 f. Ἄγουσιν] These belong still to the persons designated in ver.
8. They act thus because the healing had taken place *on the Sabbath* (ver.
14), the violation of which they, in their servile dependence, believed it to
be their duty not to conceal from the guardians of the law who ruled over
the people. It does not, however, follow, from the fact that there were no
sittings of the courts on the Sabbath, that the man was not brought on the
day of the healing (so Lücke and several others suppose), but that by πρὸς
τοὺς Φαρισ. is meant neither the *Sanhedrim*,[1] nor a *synagogal court*,[2] of which,
moreover, the text contains no notice.[3] Especially must it be remembered
that in John the Sanhedrim is never simply designated οἱ Φαρισαῖοι (not even
vii. 47), but always οἱ ἀρχιερεῖς κ. οἱ Φαρισ., or (vii. 32) in the reverse order.
The *Pharisees as a corporate body* are meant, and a number of them might
easily have come together at one of their houses to form a kind of sitting.
— τόν ποτε τυφλ.] A more precise designation of αὐτόν.[4] — Ver. 14 assigns the
reason *why* they bring him. — τὸν πηλόν] the clay in question.

Vv. 15, 16. Πάλιν] Glancing back at the same question asked by *others*
(hence καὶ οἱ Φαρ.) in ver. 10. — πηλόν, etc.] *clay He laid on mine eyes* (μου
ἐπὶ τ. ὀφθ.), etc. Comp. on xi. 32. Note how the man only states what he
himself felt ; hence there is no mention of the spittle. Compare already
ver. 11. — ὅτι τὸ σάββ. οὐ τηρεῖ] A Rabbinical precept specially forbids the
anointing of the eyes with spittle on the Sabbath.[5] Even if this were not
yet in existence or recognized as binding, still the general principle was admitted that healing should take place on the Sabbath solely in case of
danger to life.[6] — ἀλλοι] who judged more candidly and conscientiously.
Grotius well remarks :, "Qui nondum occaluerant." They conclude from
the *miraculous* element in the healing, so far as it implied a special *divine*
help, which would not be vouchsafed to a *sinner* who disregarded God's
commands, that there must be something peculiar in this action performed
on the Sabbath, rendering it unfair to pass the judgment in question on its
performer without further consideration. — The *Hyperbaton* in the position,

---

[1] Tholuck, Baeumlein.
[2] Lücke, Lange. Of such subordinate courts with twenty-three members there were two in Jerusalem. See Saalschütz, *Mos. R.* p. 601.
[3] Comp. vii. 45, xi. 47.
[4] See Buttmann, *Neut. Gr.* p. 342 [E. T. p. 400].
[5] Maimonides Schabb. 21.
[6] Schoettgen and Wetstein ad Matt. xii. 9.

οὐκ ἔστιν οὗτος παρὰ θεοῦ ὁ ἄνθρ., serves to lay stronger emphasis first on οὗτος, and then on παρὰ θεοῦ.¹ — σχίσμα] comp. vii. 43.

Ver. 17. As there was such a difference of views among those who were assembled, they feel it to be of importance to ascertain the opinion of the man who had been healed. It might lead to further light being thrown on the affair. The *subject* of λέγουσιν is οἱ Φαρισ., neither the *hostile* among them merely (Apollinarius and many others), nor the *well-wishers* alone (Chrysostom and his followers). — πάλιν] a *repetition* of the question after ver. 15. — ὅτι] εἰς ἐκεῖνο, ὅτι ; see on ii. 18. Theodore of Mopsuestia well remarks : ὑπὲρ ὤν. — προφήτης] who had shown Himself to be such by this miracle. Comp. iii. 2, iv. 19, vi. 14, *al.* Thus the faith of the man became clear and confirmed by the controversy of the Pharisees. And he makes *confession* of what he up to this time believes.

Ver. 18. Observe that the mere verb is not again employed, nor even οἱ Φαρισαῖοι, but οἱ Ἰουδαῖοι, *i.e.* the hostile hierarchical party among the assembled Pharisees, which now carries on further proceedings. Comp. ver. 22. — οὐκ ἐπίστ. placed emphatically at the beginning. — οὖν] as the healed man had declared Him to be a prophet. They now suspected the existence of a fraudulent understanding between the two. — ἕως ὅτου] *till they called*, etc. Then first, after these had come and made their declaration, were they unable any longer to call the cure in question (vv. 26, 34). — αὐτοῦ τοῦ ἀναβλέψ.] *of the very man who had recovered his sight*, concerning whom his own parents must surely know best.

Vv. 19–21. To the two questions put in ver. 19 exactly corresponding answers are returned in vv. 20, 21 ; the second, however, twice *nesciendo*. — ὃν ὑμεῖς λέγετε] opposed to the personal unbelief of the questioners ; ὅν as in vi. 71. — πῶς] how does it happen that ? — οὖν] as it is alleged that he was born blind. — Ver. 20. πῶς δὲ ἄρτι βλέπει, ἀγνοεῖν λέγουσι, φοβούμενοι τοὺς Ἰουδαίους. Ἔξω κινδύνου καθιστῶντες ἑαυτούς, ἐπὶ τὸν τεθεραπευμένον παραπέμπουσι τὴν ἐρώτησιν, ὡς ἀξιοπιστότερον αὐτῶν ἐν τῷ τοιούτῳ ζητήματι, Euth. Zigabenus. — ἡμεῖς] opposed to the αὐτός . . . αὐτόν . . . αὐτός, afterwards thrice repeated, and asyndetically, with passionate emphasis. ἡλικίαν ἔχει] *he himself is of full age.*² — αὐτὸς περὶ αὐτοῦ] he will *himself* speak *concerning himself.*³

Ver. 22. Ἤδη γὰρ συνετέθ.] *for*—so great cause had they for that fear—*the Jews had already agreed*, had already come to an understanding with each other ; *conspiraverant*, Vulgate.⁴ The context does not justify the assumption of a *decree of the Sanhedrim* to that effect. The hope, however, was cherished of being able without difficulty to convert the arrangement in question into a decree of the Sanhedrim ; and the parents of the blind man might easily have come to know of this. We can readily understand that they should prefer exposing their son rather than themselves to this danger,

¹ Comp. in general Bernhardy, p. 460.
² Comp. Herod. 3. 36, 7. 18 ; Thuc. 8. 75 ; Polyb. 9. 23. 9, *al.* See Kypke, I. p. 387 ; Loesner, p. 150.
³ αὐτοῦ with the Spir. lenis. Buttm.

Neut. Gr. p. 97 f. [E. T. p. 112].
⁴ Comp. Luke xxii. 5 ; Acts xxiii. 20 ; Thuc. 4. 19 ; 1 Macc. ix. 70 ; Ast, *Lex. Plat.* III. p. 340.

since they must have been certain that he would not refuse to make for the sake of his benefactor the dangerous confession. — ἵνα] *that which* they had agreed on is conceived as the *intention* of their agreement.[1] — ἀποσυνάγ. γέν.] Exclusion from the fellowship of the synagogue, and in connection therewith from the common intercourse of life, was probably at this time the sole form of excommunication. See on Luke vi. 22.

Vv. 24, 25. Δὸς δόξαν τ. θεῷ] "Speciosa praefatio," Bengel ; for they expect a declaration prejudicial to Jesus, such as the man had hitherto refused to make, and therefore employ this sacred and binding requirement to declare the truth, by which God would be honoured, inasmuch as to speak the truth was to show reverence to Him.[2] — ἡμεῖς οἴδαμεν, etc.] This assertion of hierarchical authority (ἡμεῖς with emphasis) was intended to overawe the man, and give a bias to his judgment. In vain. With cautious reticence he prudently refers them simply to what had actually happened ; this alone was known to him ;[3] but not *whether*, etc. — τυφλὸς ὤν] *being blind*, namely, in his natural state, from birth. Comp. iii. 13.

Vv. 26, 27. As they are unable to attain their end, they return to the question as to the *How?* (comp. ver. 15) in order conclusively to establish the fact in the course of this second examination of the man. He, however, with his straightforward, honest mind,[4] becomes irritated, and even embittered, at this repeated interrogation. — καὶ οὐκ ἠκούσατε] is taken as a declaration : *and ye did not listen thereto* (taken heed). It corresponds better, however, with the naïve character of the man, and with the liveliness of his irritation, as also with the succeeding ἀκούειν, which denotes simply "*hear*," to take the clause as a *question: And did you not hear it?* — τί] *why*, as you surely must have heard it. — μὴ καὶ ὑμεῖς] *surely not you also?* like others. To the θέλειν, etc., would correspond the effort to be convinced of the reality of the miracle that had been performed. Chrysostom, Bengel, and several others consider that καί indicates *that the blind man confessed himself to be* one of His disciples, or that it was his intention to become one. His development, however, had not yet advanced so far. See vv. 35, 36. But that his benefactor had *disciples* about Him (ver. 2), he must certainly have learnt from others.

Vv. 28, 29. Ἐλοιδόρ.] as preliminary to the following words. Passionate outburst in an unrighteous cause. — σὺ εἶ μαθ. ἐκ. They had been unable to get out of him any declaration *against* Jesus, and regarded his behaviour, therefore, as a taking part with Christ. Bengel aptly remarks on ἐκείνου : "Hoc vocabulo *removent* Jesum a sese." Comp. on vii. 11. — Ver. 29. ἡμεῖς] once again with proud emphasis. — Μωϋσῇ] has the emphasis in opposition to τοῦτον. which is thus *the more contemptuous* in meaning (vi. 42, and often). — πόθεν ἐστίν] *i.e.* by whom he is sent. Comp. viii. 14.

Vv. 30–33. The passionateness of the Jews now *emboldens the man to make a further confession* (ver. 17). — ἐν γὰρ τούτῳ τὸ (see the critical notes) θαυμ.

---

[1] Comp. ἀξιοῦν ἵνα in Dem. *de Cor.* 155 (see Dissen on the passage), and Nägelsbach on the *Iliad*, p. 62, ed. 3.

[2] Comp. Josh. vii. 19 ; Esr. x. 11 ; 3 Esr.

ix. 8.

[3] Comp. Soph. *O. C.* 1103 : οὐκ οἶδα πλὴν ἕν.

[4] ἀνὴρ ἀδόνητος, Nonnus.

ἐστιν] *Why, herein* (in this state of the case) *is the marvel, that ye know not from whence He is, and* (that) *He hath opened mine eyes.* The *force* of the θαυμαστόν lies in καὶ ἀνέῳξε, etc., in virtue of the *groundless nature* of that ignorance to which actual testimony was thus borne ; see vv. 31–33. Concerning a man who has done that, ye ought surely to know, etc. γάρ, "respicit ad ea, quae alter antea dixerat, et continet cum affirmatione conclusionem, quae ex rebus ita comparatis facienda sit," Klotz, *ad Devar.* p. 242. Comp. on 1 Cor. xi. 22. It is often thus used, especially when "miratio rei aut aliorum incredulitatis ad significatur." [1] Comp. Xen. *Mem.* iv. 2. 6. — ὑμεῖς] *Ye people,* who ought to know this best. — Ver. 31. The man now *proves* to them, onward to ver. 33, how clearly it is evident from the act of Jesus that He is no sinner (ver. 16), but a pious man, nay, a man sent of God. He begins his proof with a major premiss, which he postulates as universally conceded and known, [2] and which rests on the idea that miracles are answers to prayer. [3] A sufficient reason for not assuming that Jesus actually pronounced a prayer aloud in performing the miracle (as Ewald thinks), is the silence of John, who would scarcely have omitted this detail from a narrative so minute as this. Ver. 32. Minor premiss ; then in ver. 33, conclusion, both in popular form. — οὐδέν] effect *nothing*—is restricted by the connection to miraculous deeds such as the one here recorded.

Ver. 34. Thou wert born with thy whole nature laden with sin, so that *nothing* in thee is pure from sins ; but thou art *entirely,* through and through, a born reprobate. [4] They entertain the same prejudice regarding sinfulness before birth (not of the parents) to which the disciples had previously given expression (ver. 2), and make here a spiteful application of it. Comp. on ὅλος xiii. 10. The notion of "*heightened original sin*" [5] is not appropriate to the connection, as the inference from being born blind implies sins committed before birth.—Note the contemptuous emphasis of the σύ . . . σύ. — διδάσκ. ἡμ.] The emphasis rests here, not on διδάσκ., but on ἡμᾶς : dost thou comport thyself as our *teacher ?* — ἐξέβαλ. αὐτ. ἔξω] not designating *excommunication,* [6] as no sitting of the Sanhedrim had taken place ; and, besides, how indefinite a mode of designating the matter would it be ! although ἐκβάλλειν is frequently used by Thucydides, Xenophon, and others to denote *exile.* Comp. also 3 John, ver. 10. As the context suggests nothing else, and as there is not a hint of a sentence of excommunication, which might perhaps have been pronounced a few days later in the synagogue (Ewald), we must simply explain : *they cast him out.* Significant enough as the final result of the hostile and passionate discussion. [7] The remark of Maldonatus is correct : "ex loco, in quo erant." [8]

Vv. 35, 36. The inner connection is formed, not by the thought that

---

[1] Ellendt, *Lex. Soph.* I. p. 332.

[2] οἴδαμεν, Job xxvii. 9, xxxv. 13; Ps. lxvi. 18, cix. 7; Prov. xv. 29; Isa. i. 15.

[3] Comp. xi. 41 ff. ; Mark vii. 34.

[4] Nonnus : σύγγονος ἀμπλακίησιν ἐμαιώθης ὅλος ἀνήρ.

[5] Hengstenberg, after Ps. li. 7.

[6] Olshausen, de Wette, Tholuck, Baeumlein, and many older commentators.

[7] Comp. Chrysostom, Nonnus, and Theophylact, who, however, transfers the scene to the *temple.*

[8] Comp. Bengel, *Dem.* 1366. 11 ; Acts vii. 58.

Jesus, when He had heard, etc., *wished to confer on the man rich compensation ;*[1] but, as the question σὺ πιστεύεις, etc., shows (thou believest on the Son of God ? which presupposes an *affirmative* reply), Jesus heard of his being cast out, inferred from this that the man had confessed Him to be the Messiah, and therefore asked when He met him, etc. The conclusion which Jesus arrived at was substantially correct ; for he who had been born blind had confessed regarding Him that He was παρὰ θεοῦ, although the man did not yet consciously associate with this more general predicate a *definite refer-ence to the Messiah.* Lücke finds in πιστεύεις merely the *inclination* to be-lieve ; were this, however, its force, we must have had θέλεις πιστεύειν, or some similar *mode of expression.* Like πιστεύω in ver. 38, πιστεύεις here also denotes *actual* faith, namely, in the *manifested Messiah.* — The words τὸν υἱὸν τ. θεοῦ[2] must be taken, not in their metaphysical,[3] but simply in their theocratic signification (comp. i. 50), as the man who had been born blind, to whose notions Jesus had to accommodate Himself, could and did only understand this at the time. That Jesus, however, *on His side,* and *for Himself,* entertained the higher view, must be taken for granted. — Ver. 36. Surprised by this question, and quickly taking it as a point of connection, the man puts a counter-question, which was designed to show that he is *un-able* as yet to believe in the Messiah, though *ready* to do so as soon as he shall know him. With regard to καὶ τίς ἐστι, comp. xiv. 22, and on Mark x. 26. — ἵνα] Design of the inquiry, as in i. 22.

Vv. 37, 38. Καὶ . . . καί] *thou hast actually seen Him, and,* etc. Comp. on vi. 36. The substantial meaning of the second clause is : *and hearest Him speak with thee ;* but it has a more concrete and lively turn. — ἑώρακας] refers to the *present* interview, not to a former one ; for he had not *seen* Jesus whilst the act of healing was being performed, and he had not re-turned to Him from Siloam (see on ver. 7). The use of the *perf.* as the present, of completed action (thou hast a view of Him), need not surprise.[4] — ἐκεῖνός ἐστιν] ἐκεῖνος is not predicate ;[5] but, as John's very favourite man-ner is, *subject,* demonstratively comprehending the foregoing participial des-ignation of the same, as in i. 18, 33, v. 11. Comp. 2 Cor. x. 18. So also in the Classics, although they more frequently use οὗτος in this way.[6] The connection alone, then, shows whether the person intended is some one else, or, as in this case, and in xix. 35, the *speaker himself,* who presents himself *objectively* as a *third person,* and thus introduces himself to the person addressed with special emphasis. At the same time, the force of ἐκεῖνος is not thus transformed into that of *idem* or *ipse.*[7] — κύριε] "jam augustiore

---

[1] Chrysostom and several others.

[2] τ. υἱὸν τοῦ ἀνθρώπου (see the critical notes) Jesus could not have expected the blind man to understand, as included in this question.

[3] Olshausen, Ebrard.

[4] Bernhardy, p. 378.

[5] Hilgenfeld in his *Zeitschrift,* 1859, p. 416.

[6] See Krüger on Thuc. 2. 15. 4.

[7] In relation to the erroneous assertion

that ἐκεῖνος in xix. 35 betrays an author different from the Apostle John (see on the passage), the Johannine use of the word was discussed at length by Steitz in *d. Stud. u. Krit.* 1859, p. 497 ff. ; Buttmann in the same journal for 1860, p. 505 ff. ; and then again by Steitz in the *Stud. u. Krit.* for 1861, p. 368 ff. These controversial discussions (see, finally, Steitz in Hilgen-feld's *Zeitschr.* 1862, p. 264 ff.) were in so

sensu ita dicit, quam dixerat," ver. 36, Bengel. — προσεκίνησεν αὐτῷ] John uses προσκυνεῖν solely of *divine* worship, iv. 20 ff., xii. 20. The man was seized by the feeling—as yet indeed vague and indistinct—of the *divine δόξα*, the bearer of which, the Messiah, the object of his newly awakened faith and confession, stands before him. The higher conception of ὁ υἱὸς τ. θεοῦ has struck him.

Ver. 39. An *Oxymoron*, to which Jesus (comp. 1 Cor. i. 18 ff.), seeing at His feet the man born blind, and now endued not only with bodily, but also with spiritual sight, gives utterance with profound emotion, addressing Himself, moreover, not to any one particular person (hence εἶπεν without the addition of a person, comp. i. 29, 36), but to those around Him in general. From among these the Pharisees then (ver. 40) come forward to reply. The compact, pregnant sentence is uttered irrespectively of the man who had been blind, who also in a higher sense appears in ver. 36 as still μὴ βλέπων, and in ver. 38 as βλέπων. — εἰς κρῖμα] *telically*, *i.e.* to this end, as is clear from the more exact explanation ἵνα, etc., that follows. This κρῖμα [1] is an *end*, though not the *ultimate end*, of the appearance of Jesus. He came to bring about, as a matter of fact, *a judicial decision ;* He came, namely, in order that, by means of His agency, *those who see not might see*, *i.e.* in order that those who are conscious of the lack of divine truth (comp. the *poor in spirit* in Matt. v. 3) may be illumined thereby, and *they who see may become blind* (not merely : *appareant* caeci, as Grotius and several others explain), *i.e.* those who fancy themselves to be in possession of divine truth,[2] might not become participators therein ; but (comp. Isa. vi. 9 f.) be closed, blinded, and hardened against it (like the self-conceited Pharisees). The point of the saying lies in this : that οἱ μὴ βλέποντες is *subjective*, and βλέπωσι *objective ;* whereas οἱ βλέποντες is *subjective*, and τυφλοὶ γένωνται *objective*.[3] — κρῖμα is neither merely *separation*,[4] nor equivalent to κατάκρισις ;[5] but what Christ here says regarding Himself is a *matter of fact*, a retributive

far unnecessary, as the use of ἐκεῖνος in John does not deviate from the genuine Greek usage ; and as the context of xix. 35 shows, as clearly as that of the present passage that the *person who speaks* is pointed to, being presented objectively as though he were a third person.

[1] On this accentuation of κρῖμα, see Lobeck, *Paral.* p. 418 ; comp. however, Lipsius, *grammat. Unters.* I. p. 40. — The word itself is used by John only in this place. It denotes, not the *trial* which is *held*, the judicial *procedure* (κρίσις), but its result, the judicial *sentence* which is pronounced, the *decision* of the court, what is judicially measured out, etc. Hence κρῖμα λαμβάνειν, βαστάζειν, etc.

[2] Comp. Luke xi. 52 ; Matt. xi. 25 ; Rom. ii. 19 ; 1 Cor. i. 21, iii. 18.

[3] It is true, indeed, that the μὴ βλέποντες are *susceptible*, and the βλέποντες *unsusceptible ;* but this was not determined by the

consideration that the former believed without seeing, whilst the latter refused to believe, notwithstanding all they had seen of Jesus (see Baur, p. 179) ; on the contrary, the susceptibility of the one and the unsusceptibility of the other were rooted in their inner relation to Christ, which is necessarily moral, and the result of free self-determination. Indeed, against the view now controverted, ver. 41 alone is decisive, apart even from the mysterious designation of the matter by a circumstance occurring in connection with it. Comp. Delitzsch, *Psych.* p. 162.—On μὴ βλέπειν, *to be blind*, comp. Soph. *O. C.* 73 ; *O. R.* 302 ; see also Xen. *Mem.* i. 3. 4. On τυφλός in the figurative sense, see Soph. *O. R.* 371.

[4] Castalio, Corn. à Lapide, Kuinoel, de Wette, and several others.

[5] Ammonius, Euth. Zigabenus, Olshausen.

312 THE GOSPEL OF JOHN.

judicial arrangement, affecting both sides according to the position they take up relatively to Him. Hence there is no contradiction with iii. 17, viii. 15, xii. 47.[1] If, with Godet, we understand οἱ μὴ βλέποντες and οἱ βλέ-ποντες of those who have not and those who have the knowledge of the Jewish law, we must refer βλέπωσι and τυφλοί to the *divine* truth which Christ reveals. A twofold relation is thus introduced, to which the words λέγετε ὅτι βλέπομεν, ver. 41, are also opposed.

Ver. 40. *Pharisees* were no doubt in His company, whose object was to mark all the more carefully His further behaviour after the performance of the miracle, not apostate disciples of Jesus,[2] or adherents of a Pharisaic spirit (Lange). See x. 6, 21. They imagine that, in conformity with the opinion which Jesus entertains regarding them, He must needs reckon them among the μὴ βλέποντες ; and they fail altogether to perceive that, according to the sense in which He used the expression,—which, however, they do not understand,—He must include them among the βλέποντες. That they, the wise men of the nation, should be μὴ βλέποντες or τυφλοί (comp. Matt. xv. 14), seems to them, in their conceit, so astonishing and singular, that they ask : *We also are surely not blind ?* The Pharisees did not understand Jesus to be speaking of *physical* blindness,[3] because otherwise they would certainly *not* have put such a question.

Ver. 41. Alas ! virtually replies Jesus, Ye are not blind. *Were ye blind* (as I intended the μὴ βλέποντες in ver. 39), that is, people who are conscious of being destitute of the true knowledge,[4] *then ye would be without sin, i.e.* your unbelief in me would not be sinful, just because it would involve no resistance to divine truth, but would simply imply that ye had not yet attained to it, a result for which ye were not to blame. *But now ye assert that ye see* (profess to be possessors of divine truth) ; the consequence whereof is, that *your sin remaineth* (is not removed),[5] *i.e.* that your unbelief in me not only is sinful, but this your sin *continues to exist, remains unde-stroyed,*[6] because your conceit is a perpetual ground for rejecting me, so that you cannot attain to faith and the forgiveness of sin. " Dicendo *videmus,* medicum non quaeritis," Augustine. " Si diceretis : *caeci sumus,* visum peteretis et peccatum jam desiisset," Bengel. According to Lücke,[7] whom J. Müller follows,[8] the meaning is : " Were you blind, *i.e.* without the *capability* of knowledge, there would be no sin (guilt) in your unbelief ; you would then be *unable* to believe with knowledge. But so long as you say, notwithstanding all your blindness, We see, and therefore do not put away your conceited self-deception, so long your unbelief cannot depart, but must remain." Against this view are the following objections : 1. Τυφλοί, because answering to μὴ βλέποντες in ver. 39, cannot denote *incapacity*

[1] Comp. also Weiss, *Lehrbegr.* p. 186 f.
[2] Chrysostom, Euth. Zigabenus.
[3] Chrysostom, Theophylact, Euth. Zigabenus, and others.
[4] Not, *physically blind,* as Nonnus, Theophylact, Euth. Zigabenus, and several others here, as well as in ver. 40, after the example of Chrysostom, wrongly under-stand.
[5] Not, " *The sin remains yours*" (Ewald). Comp. xv. 16.
[6] ἀνεξάλειπτος μένει, Theodoret, · Heracleon.
[7] So substantially Baeumlein.
[8] *Lehre v. d. Sünde,* I. p. 286, ed. 5.

for knowledge ; 2. The antithesis λέγετε ὅτι βλέπ. suggests for τυφλοί, not the objective, but the subjective meaning ; 3. Ἁμαρτία is thus taken in different senses in the two halves.   Other far-fetched meanings are : *Were you blind*, like the *multitude* which you regard as blind, *perhaps* you would have no sin, etc. ; [1] or (Hengst.), if ye suffered merely from the simple blindness of the human race, which is blind from birth, ye would have no sin of decisive significance, no unpardonable sin ; as though there were the slightest reference to anything of the kind !   Substantially correct are Erasmus, Beza, Grotius, and several others ; comp. Luthardt and Ebrard ; still οὐκ ἂν εἴχ. ἁμ. ought not to be transposed into, "*then would your sin forgive you.*" The explanation of Godet is a natural consequence of his interpretation of ver. 39, but founders on the words λέγετε ὅτι βλέπομεν.[2] [See Note XXXVI. p. 314.]

OBSERVATION.—The absence from the Synoptics of the miracle performed on the man who was born blind finds its explanation simply in the circumstance that it did not take place in the (Galilean) sphere of the synoptic narrative, and ought not to have been made the ground of an attack on its historical credibility, as was done by Strauss (who compares the healing of Naaman in 2 Kings v. 10) ; by Weisse (who derives the narrative, by means of a misunderstanding, from ver. 39) ; and by Baur (who regards this story as the intensified expression of the healings of the blind recorded by the synoptists, p. 245 f.) ; whilst Gfrörer, on the contrary, content with asserting the presence of unhistorical additions, comes to a conclusion disadvantageous to the synoptists.—— According to Baur (p. 176 ff.), the narrative of the miracle was definitely and intentionally shaped, so as to *set forth faith in its pure objectivity*, the susceptibility to the divine as it is affected by the pure impression of the divine element in the ἔργα θεοῦ, even when it is not yet aware who is the subject of these ἔργα. "It clings to the thing itself ; and the thing itself is so immediately divine, that in the thing, without knowing it, one has also the person." In such wise are arbitrary, and not even relevant (see Brückner), abstractions from history converted into the *ground* of history.   Ammon makes the occurrence a natural healing of an *inflammation of the eyes !* a counterpart to the converse travesty of some of the Fathers, who express the opinion that the *blind man lacked eyes altogether*, and that Jesus formed them out of the πηλός, as God at first formed man from the earth ; [3] comp. on ver. 6 f.

---

[1] Ewald, as though besides ἂν John had written also τάχα or ἴσως.

[2] " *S'ils appartenaient à la multitude ignorante, leur incrédulité à l'égard de Jésus pourrait n'être qu'une affaire d'entraînement* (it would be merely a sin against the Son of man) ; *mais éclairés, comme ils le sont, par la connaissance de la parole de Dieu, c'est sciemment, qu'ils rejettent le Messie*" (this is a sin against the Holy Ghost). In this case, however, Jesus must have said : νῦν δὲ βλέπετε, not νῦν δὲ λέγετε ὅτι βλέπομεν, which Godet, it is true, regards merely as an allusion to the question in ver. 40 ; while in reality it is the key to the correct understanding of the entire passage.

[3] See especially Irenaeus, Theodore of Mopsuestia, and Nonnus.

XXXVa. " Made clay from the spittle." Ver. 6.

Weiss holds Meyer entirely correct in declaring it incompatible with the truthfulness and dignity of Jesus that there should have been in the application of the
spittle *no real* influence upon the result.   Whether, with Meyer, we regard the
spittle as *containing*, or, with Thol. and Ols., as *conducting* the healing virtue,
which reached and wrought effectually on the organism, he would leave undecided.   It is only certain, he holds, that the divine agency which restored sight
to the blind man did not *depend* upon the natural qualities of the spittle, but
miraculously enhanced them.   He rejects Meyer's inference that the fact that
Jesus did not elsewhere in his miracles employ like outward means, proves that
he alone knew where there was a *necessity* of any such outward accessories. He
rejects it on the ground that any *necessity* involved in the case is incompatible
with the miraculous character of the event.   This seems eminently just, and it
is extraordinary how any can associate with a miracle, wrought by omnipotence,
the necessity of any special form of intermediate agency.   To me, moreover,
both Meyer and Weiss seem wrong in considering any merely accompanying
outward, and perhaps symbolical act, as inconsistent with the Saviour's truthfulness and dignity.   It surely may be proper by some external word or act,
accompanying, though not directly aiding the miracle, to connect it manifestly
with the person of the agent, and make an impression on the senses and the
minds of men.   Such, in the O. T. miracles, was Elisha's smiting the waters of
the Jordan with the mantle of Elijah, Moses' stretching out his rod over the Red
Sea, and smiting the rock for water in the desert.   Such in reality was our
Lord's bidding the man with the withered hand *stretch out his hand*, not in aid,
but as symbol of the healing ; his sending Peter to the sea to obtain the stater
from the mouth of the fish, and his breaking the five loaves to feed more than
five thousand persons.   Such was the carrying of handkerchiefs to the sick
from the persons of the Apostles.   It seems perfectly consonant with his constant course in nature that the Great Miracle-worker should partially disguise,
partially reveal, the exercise of his power under some outward act which seems
consonant with, while it can have no real bearing on, the result.   It seems a
natural way for the Infinite Spirit to deal with finite beings at once sensuous
and spiritual.   What the special accessories shall be may vary according to the
pleasure of the Worker, and the circumstances of the case.   The *scene* of this
particular restoration, occurring in Jerusalem, the theocratic centre, and on the
Sabbath, with its certain exposure to the hostile scrutiny and judgment of the
chief men of the nation, with whom the Lord's relations were becoming those
of more pronounced enmity, may naturally have led Him to make the accessories of this miracle unusually prominent and striking.   Much more than
would the utterance of any mere words, it prevents the miracle from being
" done in a corner."   It almost flings the Lord's challenge and defiance into
the face of the theocratic rulers.

XXXVI. " If ye were blind." Ver. 41.

" If ye were blind, ye would not have sin ; but as it is (νῦν δέ) ye say, We
see : your sin remaineth."   If ye were in a mental condition answering to that
of the physically blind, ye would not have sin.   As the physically blind is not

to blame for not seeing physical light and the objects which it reveals, so if ye had no *capacity* of moral vision, ye would be without blame for not discerning spiritual truth. But as the case stands, ye *say* that ye see : ye claim to have the power of vision. Ye renounce the plea of spiritual incapacity, and yet refuse to *exercise* the power of seeing and recognizing the truth, and must be treated as those who have the faculty of vision and whose blindness is *wilful.* Your sin, therefore, *remaineth.* The term is used, I think, in a judicial sense. Your sin is not taken away by any plea of ignorance which might be urged in your favour. It *stands.* Meyer and nearly all the commentators take it in various modifications of *irremovable,* I think wrongly.

The difficulty in the passage lies partly, at least, in the fact that the cases of physical and moral blindness are analogous indeed, but not parallel. There *is* no such moral blindness as to exempt completely from moral responsibility. Every one has *some* light, and he who possesses a little, being yet conscious *how* little it is, is the Saviour's $\mu\dot{\eta}\ \beta\lambda\dot{\epsilon}\pi\omega\nu$: while he who, possessing perhaps much more, yet fancies that he possesses all, and rejects the larger and diviner light, is the $\beta\lambda\dot{\epsilon}\pi\omega\nu$ who, in this rejection, becomes blind.

CHAPTER X.

Ver. 3. καλεῖ] A. B. D. L. X. ℵ. Curss. Cyr. : φωνεῖ. Recommended by Griesb., accepted by Lachm. and Tisch. Correct ; the following κατ' ὄνομα was the occasion of writing the more definite word alongside, whence it was then introduced into the text. — Ver. 4. τὰ ἴδια πρόβατα] Lachm. and Tisch. : τὰ ἴδια πάντα, after B. D. L. X. ℵ.** Cursives, Copt. Sahid. Cyr. Lucif. Cant. πάντα, after the preceding occurrence of the word, passed mechanically óver into πρόβατα. — Ver 5. ἀκολουθήσωσιν] Lachm. and Tisch. : ἀκολουθήσουσιν, after preponderating testimony ; the Indicat. was displaced by the usual conjunct. — Ver. 8. πάντες] is omitted in D. Cant. Ver. Foss. Didym., and πρὸ ἐμοῦ is absent from E. F. G. M. S. U. Δ. ℵ.* Cursives, Verss. the Fathers. The omission of πάντες is to be explained from its being superfluous ; and that of πρὸ ἐμοῦ, which Tisch. has deleted, from the Gnostic and Manichaean misuse of the passage in opposition to the Old Testament. — The place of πρὸ ἐμοῦ after ἦλθον is decisively attested (Elz., Scholz. : before ἦλθον). — Instead of τίθησιν, ver. 11, δίδωσιν (Tisch.) is too feebly attested. So also δίδωμι, ver. 15. — Ver. 12. τὰ πρόβατα after σκορπ. is wanting in B. D. L. ℵ. Cursives, Verss. Lucif. ; bracketed by Lachm. and suppressed by Tisch. But why should it have been added ? Appearing as it would altogether superfluous, it might easily be passed over. — Ver. 13. ὁ δὲ μισθωτ. φεύγει] wanting in B. D. L. ℵ. Cursives, Verss. Lucif. ; bracketed by Lachm., rejected even by Rinck, and deleted by Tisch. But how easily might the eye of a copyist pass at once from ὁ δὲ μισθ. to ὅτι μισθ., so that ὁ δὲ μισθ. φεύγει was omitted. This explanation is suggested further by A.,* which omits μισθ. φεύγει ὅτι. — Ver. 14. γινώσκομαι ὑπὸ τῶν ἐμῶν] B. D. L. ℵ., most of the Verss. Cyr. Epiph. Nonn. : γινώσκουσίν με τὰ ἐμά. Recommended by Griesbach, accepted by Lachm. and Tisch. This active turn is a transformation in harmony with the following verse, in which also there is no passive expression. — Ver. 16. The position δεῖ με (Lachm. and Tisch.) is strongly supported, but would easily suggest itself as the more usual instead of με δεῖ. — γενήσεται] B. D. L. X. and some Verss. : γενήσονται. Mechanically introduced after the preceding plural form. — Ver. 18. αἴρει] Tisch. : ἦρεν, only after B. ℵ.* — Ver. 26. Instead of οὐ γάρ we must read, with Tisch., ὅτι οὐκ, after B. D. L. X. ℵ. Curss. Or. Cyr. Chrys. — καθὼς εἶπον ὑμῖν] wanting in B. K. L. M.* ℵ. Curss. Verss. and Fathers. Bracketed by Lachm. The apparent incongruity caused the omission. — Ver. 29. ὃς δέδωκε] D. : ὁ δεδωκώς. A stylistic alteration. B. L. ℵ.* Copt. Sahid. Vulg: It. Goth. Tert. Hil. : ὃ δέδωκεν. A. B. X. It. Vulg. read μεῖζον afterwards. The latter is to be regarded as original, and because the neuter was not understood relatively to ὁ πατήρ as the source of the alteration, ὁ δέδωκεν. — Ver. 33. λέγοιτες] is, with Lachm. and Tisch., after preponderating testimony, to be deleted. — Ver. 38. πιστεύητε] Tisch. : πιστεύετε, after inadequate evidence for this irregularity, especially as πιστεύετε precedes and follows ; for instead of the following πιστεύσατε, decisive evidence renders it necessary, with Tisch., to read πιστεύετε.— ἵνα γνῶτε καὶ πιστεύσητε] Lachm. and Tisch. :

ἴνα γνῶτε κ. γινώσκητε, after B. L. X. Curss. Copt. Sahid. Arm. Aeth. and some Fathers. Correctly ; not being understood after γνῶτε, γινώσκ. was altered into πιστεύσ. — αὐτῷ] B. D. L. X. ℵ. Curss. and most of the Verss., also Or. Athan. and others, have τῷ πατρί. Recommended by Griesbach, accepted by Lachm. and Tisch. With such decided witnesses in its favour, justly ; for the emphasis lying in the repetition of the word mighty easily escape the copyists. — Ver. 42. ἐκεῖ] Decisive evidence assigns it its place after αὐτόν. So also Lachm. and Tisch.

Ver. 1.[1] The new chapter should have begun with ix. 35 ; for x. 1–21 constitute *one* act with ix. 35–41, as is evident both from the circumstance that x. 1 ff. follow immediately without the slightest indication of a change having taken place, and also from ver. 6 (comp. ix. 41). The parable is therefore still addressed to the Pharisees of chap. ix. ; as ver. 21 also shows by the reference which it contains to the healing of the blind man. — ἀμὴν ἀμήν, etc.] After the punitive words of ix. 41, Jesus now, with solemn earnestness, and through the medium of a parable, unveils to them how their hostile relation to Him, in rejecting Him, while at the same time regarding themselves as the leaders of the people of God, necessarily made them the corrupters of the nation. His discourse proceeds, however, without any objection or contradiction being raised by His opponents ; for they did not understand the figure, ver. 6 ; many also fail to understand the explanation, and despise the speaker as crazy (ver. 20) ; whilst others, again, yield to the impression made by the penetrating truth of His words (ver. 21). It happened, accordingly, that Jesus was able to carry out the beautiful allegory (ver. 6) in all its detail, without interruption, as it were in one breath ; and had therefore, at its close, nothing further to do than to let the words spoken produce their natural impression. Their primary effect was a division among His hearers (ver. 19), in accordance with ix. 39 ; such as had already showed itself in ix. 16. — ὁ μὴ εἰσερχόμενος, etc.] The flocks of sheep spent the night in a fold (αὐλή, גְּרֵרָה) surrounded by a wall, at whose gate an under-shepherd (ὁ θυρωρός, ver. 3) kept watch during the night. See especially Bochart, *Hieroz.* I. p. 482, ed. Rosenm. Opposed to the εἰσερχόμ. διὰ τ. θύρας (the emphasis lies on the last word) is the ἀναβαίνων ἀλλαχόθεν, *who gets up* (on to the wall, for the purpose of coming into the αὐλή, over it) *from elsewhere, i.e.* from another direction than that indicated by the gate. There is only *one* door. On ἀλλαχόθεν; which is equivalent to the old classical ἀλλοθεν, see.[2] — κλέπτ. κ. λῃστής] *Thief and robber ;* a climactic strengthening of the idea ;[3] the individual features, however, of the soul-destroying, selfish procedure thus indicated[4] are not to be dissevered. — For the *explanation of the figure* we must note,—(1) The αὐλὴ τῶν προβάτων is the *community of the people of God*, whose members are the πρόβατα,[5] conceived in their totality as the future community of the Messianic kingdom

[1] On the parable, see Fritzsche in *Fritzschior. Opusc.* p. 1 ff. ; Voretzsch, *Diss. de John* x. 1-18, Altenb. 1838.

[2] Ael. *H. A.* 7. 10 ; *V. H.* 6. 2 ; 4 Macc. i. 7.

[3] Bornemann, *Scholia in Lucam*, p. xxx. ; Lobeck, *Paralip.* p. 60 f.

[4] Ezek. xxxiv. 8 ; Mal. ii. 8 ; Jer. xxiii. 1.

[5] Comp. Ps. xxiii. lxxvii. 21, xcv. 7, c. 3.

(xxi. 16 f.) ;[1] thus *ideally in their theocratic destination*. It is correct, indeed, as to substance, to assume a reference to the *predestinated* (Augustine, Lampe) (though not in the Augustinian sense) ; but in form it introduces something foreign to the context.   (2) The θύρα is not to be left without its proper signification ;[2] nor to be taken as denoting in general the *legitimus ordo*, the *divine calling*, the *approach ordained by God*, and the like ;[3] but *Christ Himself* is the door ; indeed, He Himself in ver. 7 expressly thus interprets this point, because His hearers had failed to understand it.[4]   The true leaders of the theocratic people can enter on their vocation in no other way than *through Him ; He* must qualify and commission them ; *He* must be the mediator of their relation to the sheep.   Quite a different position was taken up by the Pharisees ; independently of Him, and in an unbelieving and hostile spirit towards Him, they arrogated to themselves the position of the leaders of the people of God.   It is thoroughly arbitrary to assume that Jesus did not here intend by the figure of the door to denote Himself, notwithstanding the distinct declaration contained in ver. 9.   Chrysostom, Ammonius, Theophylact, Euth. Zigabenus, and several others, have perversely interpreted the door of *the Holy Scriptures*.   "Ipse textus addit imagini interpretationem qua contenti simus," Melanchthon.

Vv. 2, 3. Ποιμήν] *Shepherd*, without the article *qualitatively ;* it characterizes such a one, not specially as the *owner* (the antithesis to the hireling first appears in ver. 12), but in general, in contrast to the *robber*. — ὁ θυρωρὸς ἀνοίγει] belongs to the *description* of the legitimate mode of entering, and is not intended to have any special explanation ; for which reason also no further notice is taken of it in vv. 7, 8.   It must not, therefore, be explained either of *God ;*[5] or of the *Holy Spirit*, Acts xiii. 2 ;[6] or of *Christ ;*[7] or of *Moses ;*[8] or of *John the Baptist.*[9]   He enters into the fold, *and the sheep hear His voice* (His call, His address, His appeal) ; they *listen* to it as to the voice which is *known* to them (comp. ver. 4).   Comp. the shepherd's cry to his flock, "σίττα," in *Theocr.* iv. 46, viii. 69. — τὰ πρόβατα] are the sheep in the fold generally.   It was common for several flocks to pass the night in one fold ; and their shepherds, because they come every morning to lead out the individual flocks, are known to *all* the sheep in the fold.   On the contrary, τὰ ἴδια πρόβατα are the sheep which *belong to the special flock* of him who has entered ;[10] these he calls κατ' ὄνομα, *i.e.* not merely *by name*

---

[1] Comp. Matt. xxv. 32.

[2] Lücke, de Wette.

[3] Maldonatus, Tholuck, Luthardt, Brückner, Hengstenberg, Godet, and others.

[4] Comp. Ignat. *ad Philad.* 9, where Christ is termed θύρα τοῦ πατρός ; also Herm. *Past.* 3 ; *Sim.* 9. 12.

[5] Calvin, Maldonatus, Bengel, Tholuck, Ewald, Hengstenberg, following vi. 44 f.

[6] Theodoret, Heracleon, Ruperti, Aretius, Corn. à Lapide, and others, also Lange.

[7] Cyril, Augustine.

[8] Chrysostom, Theodore of Mopsuestia, Euth. Zigabenus, Luther, following Deut.

xviii. 15.

[9] Godet, after i. 7.

[10] Into the beautiful general figure of τὰ πρόβατα, the word ἴδια introduces a special, individual element, which makes it all the richer and more telling.   It has been incorrectly maintained (by Bengel, Luthardt, Hengstenberg, and others), that although ἴδια is first associated with πρόβατα when it occurs for the second time, the πρόβατα which hear must necessarily be the same as those which are afterwards described as τὰ ἴδια πρόβατα.   These latter are no doubt *among* the πρόβατα which hear ; but it is

ὀνομαστί,[1] but distributively — *by their names, each by its name.*[2] To give to the individual animals of their flock a *name* was not an unusual custom among the shepherds of ancient times.[3] In Lange's view [4] the ἴδια πρόβ. are the *favourite sheep* (image of the elect), the bell-wethers, which are followed by the whole flock (τὰ πρόβατα, ver. 4). Erroneously ; for, on the one hand, ἴδια alone would not sufficiently support this notion (comp. ver. 12) ; and on the other, ἔμπροσθεν πορεύεται and ἀκολουθεῖ, ver. 4, are so completely correlate, that αὐτῶν and τὰ πρόβατα must necessarily be the same : at all events, αὐτοῖς must otherwise have been used instead of αὐτῷ, ver. 4. — ἐξάγει] to pasture, vv. 9, 10. Looking back to ix. 34, 22, Godet imports into the words the idea of separation from the old theocracy, which is devoted to ruin.[5] Such a thought is contained neither in the words [6] nor in the context.

Ver. 4. *And when he has brought out all his own sheep* (those belonging to *his* flock), and so forth. He leaves none behind (πάντα, see the critical note). ἐκβάλῃ pictures forth the *manner* of the ἐξάγειν. He *lays hold on* the sheep which he has called to him, and brings them out to the door. — The idea, which is symbolically set forth in vv. 3 and 4, is that of the living, loving *fellowship* which subsists between the leaders of the people of God, whom Christ has appointed, and Christ Himself, for the satisfaction of the spiritual needs of the Church, both in general and in particular.

Ver. 5. Ἀλλοτρίῳ δέ, etc.] *But a stranger,* who does not belong to them as their shepherd. It is not exclusively the ἀναβαίνοντες ἀλλαχ. of ver. 1 who are here intended, but *every other one* in general who is not their shepherd. The fellowship referred to in vv. 3 and 4 is portrayed according to its *exclusive* nature. — οὐ μὴ ἀκολουθήσουσιν] *future* (see the critical note), as in viii. 12. It is not *prophetical* (Lampe : of the "cathedra Mosis plane deserenda," comp. Luthardt), but describes what *will be the result* of the intervention of a stranger. The sheep will certainly not follow, but flee from him.

Vv. 6, 7. Παροιμία] Every species of discourse that deviates from the common course (οἶμος) ; hence in the classical writers especially—*proverb.*[7] It denotes here, as corresponding to the Hebrew מָשָׁל, if we define the conception more· exactly, not· parable (because it is not a history), but *allegory.*[8] — The *Pharisees* do not understand the meaning of what He thus allegorically delivered to them, and therefore (οὖν, ver. 7) Jesus sees Himself compelled to begin again (πάλιν), and to explain to them, first of all, the *main point* on which the understanding of the whole depended, namely,

---

only τὰ ἴδια that the shepherd calls by name, and so forth. Thus the particular Church belongs to the Universal.

[1] That would be merely ὄνομα, or ὀνόματι, or ἐπ' ὀνόματος, Polyb. 5. 35. 2, 11. 15. 1.

[2] ἐκ τῆς εἰς ἕκαστον ἄκρας φροντίδος, Euth. Zigabenus.

[3] See *Interpp. ad Theocr.* 5. 101 ; Pricaeus on the passage.

[4] *Leben Jesu,* II. p. 955.

[5] Similarly even Luther : " It denotes the Christian freedom from the law and judgment."

[6] *Pollux,* i. 250.

[7] Plat. *Soph.* p. 261 B ; Soph. *Aj.* 649 ; *Ael. N. H.* 12. 22 ; Lucian, *Nigr.* 1. 37 ; comp. 2 Pet. ii. 22.

[8] See Wilke, *Rhetor.* p. 109. Suidas : ἡ παροιμία ἐστὶ λόγος ἀπόκρυφος δι' ἑτέρου προδήλου σημαινόμενος,

how the *door* in ver. 1 is to be understood. It is incorrect, therefore, with most recent commentators (also Hengstenberg and Godet), to say that we have a second parable with a different turn ; if Christ had not intended even in ver. 1 to describe Himself as the door, He would only have confused His hearers in ver. 7, instead of enlightening them. — ἐγώ] with great emphasis. — τῶν προβάτων] *to the sheep*, as is required by ver. 1 ; not, *through which the sheep enter into the fold*,[1] so that Jesus characterizes Himself as the *tutorem ac nutritorem* of the sheep (Fritzsche). Christ, however, is the door *to the sheep*, so far as the true spiritual leaders of the people of God receive *through Him* the qualification and appointment to their vocation. See on ver. 1.

Ver. 8. See Ewald, *Jahrb.* ix. p. 40 ff. The actual antithesis to the ἐγώ εἰμι ἡ θύρα is formed by the many who had come forward to be the teachers and leaders of the people of God, without connecting their working with Christ. He describes them from the point of view of the *time* at which they came forward : *before me ;* they came forward *before* Christ had appeared as the door to the sheep ; they had developed their power and activity since the time of the second temple, in a way that gradually grew more and more pernicious, and they formed now the party of *hierarchical, specially Pharisaical, antagonists of Christ.* The members of *this hierarchical caste* are intended ; the expression used by Christ, however, is popular, and not to be pressed as hard and unhistorical (Hase) ; the use of the present εἰσί, moreover, gives it a living relation to the leaders of the people, as they *then* actually were before his eyes. On the other hand, passages like vii. 19, v. 39, 45, iv. 22, exclude any possible reference to Moses and the prophets. Hence we may not, with Hilgenfeld, regard the language as " harshly *anti-Judaistic,*" or under cover of the Gnostic dualism, refer it to the entire Old Testament past, *i.e.* to *all* the pre-Christian leaders of the people of God. Nor may we in any way set aside the temporal meaning of πρό, whether explaining, with Calovius : *in advance of me* (antequam mitterentur) ; or, with Brückner (after Stier) : *before* they have sought and found me as the door ; or, with Wolf, converting it into χωρίς,—a view which comes substantially to that of Olshausen ("without connection with the Logos") ; or, with Tittmann and Schleusner, taking it for ὑπέρ, *loco,* and with Lange importing into this view, " *instead of me,*" the notion of *absolute pre-eminence,* as though the one who precedes would thrust completely aside him who is thus thrown into the background. πρό, in the sense of *instead,* is foreign to the New Testament, and rare in Greek writers. But when ἦλθον, with a view to the removal of everything objectionable, is taken *pregnantly,* making it express an *arbitrary* or *unauthorized*[2] coming forward,[3] we import into the word a meaning which in itself, indeed, is a matter of course, but must have been distinctly expressed (as in ver. 43), if it were to be *emphatic.*[4] This also

---

[1] Chrysostom, Euth. Zigabenus, Wolf, Lampe, Fritzsche, Ebrard, Hengstenberg, Baeumlein, Godet, and others.

[2] Nonnus takes it in the sense of *creeping in secretly :* πάντες ὅσοι πάρος ἦλθον ὑποκλέπτοντι πεδίλῳ.

[3] Hieronymus, Augustine, Isidore, Heracleon, Euth. Zigabenus, Luther, Melanchthon, Jansen, and several others ; also Luthardt, Ebrard.

[4] In ἦλθον by itself, so far as it precedes πρὸ ἐμοῦ, it is impossible to find, as Luthardt

against B. Crusius, who lays the stress on the purpose of the ἦλθον ("in order to give the people a new time"). The explanation, finally, of *false Messiahs*,[1] is unhistorical, as their coming began after Christ's day ; a circumstance indeed on which B. Bauer grounds against John a charge of anachronism. De Wette considers the discourse out of harmony with the wisdom and gentleness of Jesus. But the worthless men, to whose entire class He alludes, stood actually in His presence, and had surely done enough to call forth His severity and wrath. — κλέπται εἰσὶ κ. λησταί] namely, of the sheep, ver. 1. Comp. the wolves in sheep's clothing. Instead of πάντες ὅσοι, ἅπαντες ὅσοι would have been still stronger.[2] — ἀλλά]. The want of success which attends this predatory (soul-destroying) procedure. — οὐκ ἤκουσαν] *did not listen to them.* For *their* adherents did not belong to the true people of God (τὰ πρόβατα).

Ver. 9. Ἐγώ εἰμι ἡ θύρα] τῷ διπλασιασμῷ τοῦ ῥητοῦ βεβαιοῖ τὸν λόγον, Euth. Zigabenus. — δι' ἐμοῦ] emphatically occupying the front place, excluding every other mediation. — εἰσέλθῃ] namely, to the sheep in the fold. Comp. vv. 1, 7. The subject is therefore a *shepherd* (τὶς), who goes in to the sheep through the door. *Others*, on the contrary,[3] regard the *sheep* as the subject, and the θύρα as the door *for* the sheep. But there is no ground for such a change of figure, since both the *word* εἰσέρχεσθαι after vv. 1 and 2, and the singular and masculine τὶς, can refer only to the *shepherd*, and any other entrance than *through the door* is for the sheep inconceivable ; so that the emphatic δι' ἐμοῦ, so far as the ἐγώ is the *door*, would be without any possible antithesis. — σωθήσεται] is not (with Luthardt and older comm. after 1 Tim. iv. 16) to be understood directly of the *attainment of the Messianic redemption* (compare especially 1 Cor. iii. 15), which would be foreign to the context (see what follows) ; but means : *he will be delivered*, *i.e.* he will be set free from all dangers by the *protecting* door ;—in its deeper significance the figure undoubtedly involves safety from the *Messianic* ἀπώλεια, and the guarantee of future *eternal* redemption. This happy σωθήσεται is then followed by *unrestrained* and *blessed service*, which is graphically set forth by the words εἰσελ. κ. ἐξελ., as in Num. xxvii. 17, as an unhindered entering in and going out of the fold, at the head of the flock, whilst engaged in the daily duty of tending it ; and by νομὴν εὑρήσει, as the finding of pasture for the flock.[4] That this νομή, in the interpretation of the allegory, is ψυχῆς νομή,[5] which works for the eternal life of those who are fed through the evangelical grace and truth which they appropriate (comp. ver. 10), needs no illustrating.

---

does, the thought "on his own responsibility," or "so that he places Christ after himself." ἦλθον denotes neither more nor less than the simple *venerunt ;* as in ver. 10. ἐγὼ ἦλθον is equal to the simple *ego veni ;* the emphasis rests primarily on πάντες ὅσοι, *omnes quotquot*, and then on πρὸ ἐμοῦ, which is placed at the end.

[1] Chrysostom, Cyril, Theodore of Mopsuestia, Euth. Zigabenus, Theophylact, Grotius, Maldonatus, Hammond, Tittmann, Schleusner, Klee, Weizsäcker, and several others.

[2] Strabo, p. 18, 1. 11, Isocr. *Loch.* 12.

[3] Chrysostom, Euth. Zigabenus, Maldonatus, Bengel, and several others ; also Fritzsche, Tholuck, de Wette, B. Crusius, Maier, Baeumlein, Hengstenberg, Godet, etc.

[4] ποιμνίων νομάς, Soph. *O. R.* 760 ; compare Plat. *Legg.* iii. p. 679 A : νομῆς γὰρ οὐκ ἦν σπάνις.

[5] Plat. *Phaedr.* p. 248 B.

322 THE GOSPEL OF JOHN.

Ver. 10. The opposite of such a one as entered δι' ἐμοῦ, is the *thief* to whom allusion was made in ver. 1 ; when he comes to the sheep, he has only selfish and destructive ends in view.[1] — ἐγὼ ἦλθον, etc.] Quite otherwise *I!* *I have come* (to the sheep), etc. By this new antithesis, in which Christ contrasts *Himself*, and not again the shepherd appointed through Him, with the thief, the way is prepared for a transition to another use of the figure which represents Him no longer as the door.[2] Compare the promise in Ex. xxxiv. 23 ; xxxvii. 24, in contrast to the false shepherds in Ezek. xxxiv. 2 ff. — ἵνα ζωὴν ἔχωσι]. The opposite of θύσῃ κ. ἀπολ.; the sheep are not to be slaughtered and perish, but to have *life;* and as required by the figure, the *Messianic* life in its temporal development and eternal perfection. — καὶ περισσὸν ἐχ.] *and have it abundantly* (overflowingly), *i.e.* in the *figure:* rich fulness of nourishment (comp. Ps. xxiii) ; as to the thing, abundance of spiritual possessions (grace and truth, i. 14, 17), in which the life consists. Incorrectly Vulgate, Chrysostom, Euth. Zigabenus, Grotius, and many others, compare also Ewald, who interpret the passage as though περισσότερον were used, *more than* ζωή, viz.—*the kingdom of heaven;* or, according to Ewald, "Joy, and besides, constantly increasing blessing." The *repetition* of ἔχωσιν gives the second point a more independent position than if καί alone had been used.[3]

Ver. 11. Ἐγώ] Repeated again with lively emphasis. It is no other. — ὁ ποιμὴν ὁ καλός] *the good*, the excellent *shepherd*, conceived absolutely as He ought to be : hence the article and the emphatic position of the adjective. In Christ is realized the ideal of the shepherd, as it lives in the Old Testament.[4] With the conception of καλός compare the Attic καλὸς κἀγαθός,[5] and the contrary : πονηρός, κακός, ἄδικος. — In the following specification of the things in which the good shepherd proves himself to correspond to his idea, ὁ ποιμ. ὁ καλός is solemnly repeated. — τιθέναι τ. ψυχήν] As to substance, though not as to the meaning of the words, equivalent to δοῦναι τ. ψ. (Matt. xx. 28). It is a *Johannean* expression,[6] without corresponding examples in the classics ;[7] and must be explained, neither from the simple שׂוּם, Isa. liii. 10,[8] nor from שׂוּם נֶפֶשׁ בְּכַף,[9] where בכף is *essential;* but from the idea of the sacrificial death as a ransom that has been paid.[10] Its import accordingly is : *to pay down* one's *soul, impendere,* in harmony with the use of τιθέναι in the classics, according to which it denotes *to pay.*[11] Compare Nonnus : καὶ ψυχῆς ἰδίης οὐ φείδεται, ἀλλὰ ἐθήσει λύτρον ἑῶν ὀίων. — ὑπέρ] *for the good of,* in order to turn aside destruction from them by his own self-sacrifice. Compare xi. 50 f. It is less in harmony with this specific point of view, from which the sacrifice of the life of Jesus is regarded throughout the entire

[1] Comp. *Dem.* 782. 9: ἅ φησι φυλάττειν πρόβατα, αὐτὸς κατεσθίων.
[2] From ver. 11 onward, but as the true *Shepherd Himself* (Matt. xxvi. 31; Heb. xiii. 20; 1 Pet. ii. 23.
[3] Comp. ver. 18; Xen. *Anab.* i. 10. 3: καὶ ταύτην ἔσωσαν καὶ ἄλλα — ἔσωσαν.
[4] Ps. xxiii. ; Isa. xl. 11 ; Ezek. xxxiv.; Jer. xxiii.; Zech. xi. ; also Mic. v. 3.
[5] Also Tob. vii. 7 ; 2 Macc. xv. 12.
[6] xiii. 37 f., xv. 13 ; 1 John iii. 16.
[7] Against Kypke, I. p. 388.
[8] Hengstenberg.
[9] Judg. xii. 3; 1 Sam. xix. 5.
[10] Matt. xx. 28 ; 1 Tim. ii. 6.
[11] So frequently in Demosthenes and others ; see Reiske, *Ind. Dem.* p. 495, ed. Schaef. ; Dissen, *ad Dem. de Cor.* p 271.

New Testament, to take τιθέναι, with de Wette, Ebrard, God‑t, as denoting merely *lay down* (as in xiii. 4) ; or to assume the idea which is foreign to the passage, "*to offer as a prize for competition*" (Ewald).

Ver. 12 f. In opposition to the idea of the good shepherd, we have here that of the *hireling*. The term μισθωτός must not be taken to refer to the conduct of the *Pharisees* in their leadership of the people (Baeumlein and older writers, also my own view previously), as these hierarchs are included in the characteristic designation of *Thieves* and *Robbers* (vv. 8, 2), with which the description of the hireling, who is *cowardly*, and *careth not* for the sheep, would not harmonize. Nor can it be directed against the mode in which the *legitimate priesthood* lead the people, as Godet thinks ; for the priesthood consisted to a large extent of Pharisees, and formed with these latter, as far as antagonism to Christ was concerned, one great party (vii. 32, 45 ; xi. 47, 57 ; xviii. 3). The expression ὁ μισθωτός rather represents those leading teachers of the people of God, *who, instead of being ready to sacrifice their lives for the community, flee from danger, and forsake, from indifference and disregard, their charge.* Under the figure of the μισθωτός, there rise to the view of Christ the many cross-forsaking teachers, who would arise even in the apostolic age (Gal. vi. 12 ; Phil. iii. 18), and to whom the Apostle Paul forms the most brilliant historical contrast. The question by whom the μισθωτός is *hired*, leads beyond the purpose of the allegory, which sets forth, in contrast to the good shepherd, a shepherd who, influenced solely by *self*-interest, takes charge of a flock, which is *not his own property*. — καὶ οὐκ ὢν ποιμήν] is closely connected with ὁ μισθ. δέ : *but he who is a hireling* (hired for wage) *and is not a shepherd,*—shepherd in the sense of being *owner* of the sheep which he leads out to pasture ; hence the words οὗ οὐκ εἰσί, etc., are added for the purpose of more emphatically expressing the meaning. Note that Christ possesses a Church (flock) even before His death ; partly, according to the old theocratic *idea*, namely, that of the old people of God as His ἴδιοι, i. 11 ; partly *in reality*, namely, the totality of those who believed on Him, whom the Father has given Him (vi. 37) ; partly *proleptically* (ver. 16) ; though, as far as He is concerned, they are first *purchased* (compare Acts xx. 28 ; Titus ii. 14) by Him through His death, after which event began the extension of His shepherd's functions to all, by the drawing of His Holy Spirit (xii. 32). — There is no justification for interpreting the *wolf* specially, either of the *devil*,[1] or of heretics, after Acts xx. 20.[2] It is a general image of every sort of *power, opposed to the Messiah*, and bent on destroying the kingdom of God, which may make its appearance ; this power, however, as such, has its causal and ruling principle in the devil, xii. 31 ; xiv. 30 ; Matt. x. 16. — ἁρπάζει αὐτὰ κ. σκορπίζει τὰ πρόβ.] *he snatches them* (namely, the individuals on which he falls), *and scatters the sheep, i.e.* the mass of them, the flock ; hence the word πρόβατα is neither superfluous nor harsh (de Wette). — ὅτι μισθωτ. ἐστι] nothing else. This and what follows supplies the ethical key to the behaviour described. — Notice

[1] Euth. Zigabenus, Aretius, Olshausen, and several others ; admitted even by Chrysostom.

[2] Augustine, Jansen, and several others.

further, that while in verse 12 we read ὁ μισθ. δέ, here we have ὁ δὲ μισθ.; because the antithesis of the hireling was first *brought forward* in ver. 12, and greater emphasis was secured by the immediate connection of μισθ. with ὁ.[1]

Ver. 14 f. After the description of the hireling, there now follows again that of the *opposite*,—the characterization of Himself as the good shepherd, first specifying His intimate *acquaintance* with His sheep, and then repeating His readiness to *sacrifice Himself* on their behalf. The latter point constitutes the *refrain* of the characterization (vv. 17, 18), being here concretely expressed (it is different in ver. 11, where it was predicated of the good shepherd *in abstracto*). — καθὼς γινώσκει με, etc.] The *nature and mode*, the holy nature of that reciprocal acquaintanceship. Compare xiv. 20, xv. 10, xvii. 8, 21. As between God and Christ, so also between Christ and His people, the reciprocal knowledge is a knowledge growing out of the most intimate fellowship of love and life,—that fellowship which directly involves γινώσκειν ; comp. on Matt. vii. 23. — τίθημι] *I lay down ;* near and certain future. The clause κ. τ. ψ. is not dependent on καθώς.

Ver. 16. The repeated mention of His sacrificial death, by which the union of Jews and heathen into one community of believers was to be effected (see on Eph. ii. 14), raises His look to the future when He (as the good Shepherd *lifted up on high*,[2] shall be the guide also of the *heathen*, who have become believers, and whom he now *prophetically* terms His sheep.[3] But the thought that He does not need the faith of the Jews (Hengstenberg after Ruperti) is arbitrarily forced into the passage as an intervening link of logical connection. The *Jews outside of Palestine*[4] are not intended, as they form part of the fold of the *Jewish* theocracy, to which the words ἐκ τῆς αὐλῆς ταύτης refer, and within which Jesus Himself lived and spake ; hence also the demonstrative ταύτης. — ἔχω] He is their *owner*.[5] "Hoc verbum habet magnam potestatem," Bengel. — ἃ οὐκ ἔστιν ἐκ τῆς αὐλῆς ταύτης] *which are not from this fold,* which are not derived from it. This expression, however, does not imply that Jesus conceived the heathen *as also in an αὐλή* ;[6] for the emphasis rests not on ταύτης, but on τῆς αὐλῆς, and the characteristic feature of the heathen is the *dispersion* (vii. 35, xi. 52) ;[7] while the thought of a divine

---

[1] Comp. Klotz, *ad Devar.* p. 378.

[2] Compare Heb. xiii. 20 ; 1 Pet. ii. 25.

[3] The relation of ver. 16 to what precedes corresponds entirely to the New Testament idea, that salvation proceeds from the Jews to the heathen (comp. iv. 22, xi. 52). This advantage of the Jews is also to be recognized as acknowledged by John, to whom we are not to ascribe the idea of a perfect equality of the two (Lücke, B. Crusius ; comp. also Messner, *Lehre der Ap.* p. 355). The heathen who are to be gained are, however, even before they are recipients of salvation, τέκνα τ. θεοῦ, and Christ *has* them as His sheep, according to the ideal view of the *future*, as an *actuality so far as it is certainly fixed in the counsel of*

God (comp. Rom. xi. 28). It is therefore incorrect to explain the mode of expression from the fellowship with God realized through *conscience* (Luthardt) ; because, to be a child of God and an adherent of Christ presupposes *regeneration*. For this, however, they are destined by the divine election of grace, and fitted and prepared by the prevenient divine drawing. Compare xi. 52, xii. 32, and prophetic utterances, such as Mic. iv. 2 ; Isa. xlix. 1 ff., lii. 13 ff., liii. 10 ff.

[4] Paulus.

[5] Comp. Acts xviii. 10.

[6] In answer to de Wette.

[7] Correctly Bengel : "*alias oves dicit*, non *aliud ovile ;* erant enim dispersae in mundo."

leading of the heathen [1] does not correspond at all to the figure of an αὐλή, of which the conception of theocratic fellowship constitutes an essential feature. Compare the figure of the olive tree in Rom. xi. 17 ; Eph. ii. 12 ; Matt. viii. 11. — δεῖ] according to the divine decree. — ἀγαγεῖν] neither *adducere, fetch ;* [2] nor συναγαγεῖν, *assemble,* xi. 52 ; [3] but *lead,* as shepherd, who precedes the sheep, and whom they follow, ver. 4. Bengel's remark is appropriate : " Non opus est illis *solum* mutare ;" for the shepherd who leads also the heathen is the *exalted* Christ, πάντων κύριος, Acts x. 36. — καὶ γενήσεται, etc.] *and will become,* inasmuch as I lead, beside my sheep out of the Jewish αὐλή, those other sheep of mine, also, *one flock* (consisting of the two parts, ἀμφοτέρωθεν, Nonnus), one *shepherd.* This is the happy issue ; by the asyndetic collocation, the conception of unity (μία, εἷς) is made to appear with more marked prominence. Comp. 1 Cor. x. 17 ; Eph. iv. 5. On εἷς ποιμήν, observe in reference to γενήσεται : "de jure Jesus semper unicus *est* pastor ; de jure et *facto* igitur unus *fiet,*" Bengel. The *fulfilment* of His declaration, which began with the conversion of the heathen by the apostles, is still advancing, and will be completed only with the realization of what is spoken of in Rom. xi. 25 f. The *Stoic* dream of the union of all men ὥσπερ ἀγέλης συννόμα νόμῳ κοινῷ συντρεφομένης [4] has been dispelled ; the *idea,* however, considered in itself, goes on realizing itself in Christ till the judgment day.

Vv. 17, 18. Christ's portraiture of himself as the Good Shepherd is finished. He now further bears testimony to that which filled His heart, while setting forth this great vocation, which was only to be fulfilled by dying and rising again, namely, *the love of His Father,* which rests upon Him just because of that which He has declared concerning Himself as the good shepherd.— διὰ τοῦτο . . . ὅτι] is to be taken as in all the passages where it occurs in John : [5] *therefore—because, namely,* διὰ τοῦτο referring to what had *preceded,* and ὅτι introducing a more precise explication of διὰ τοῦτο. The sense consequently is : *therefore,* because of this my relationship as Shepherd, of which I have spoken down to ver. 16, *my Father loves me, because, namely, I* (ἐγώ ; no other does so or can do so) *lay down my life, in order to take it again.* Note in particular : (1) The explanation ὅτι . . . μου is pragmatically correct, because it is precisely a readiness to sacrifice His life which is the main characteristic of the good shepherd (vv. 11, 15). (2) ἵνα πάλ. λάβω αὐτήν does not belong to ἀγαπ., but expresses the *intention* or *design* of τίθ. τ. ψ. μου (not merely its *result,* as Theodore of Mopsuestia, Euth. Zigabenus, Grotius, and many suppose ; or its *condition,* as Calvin, de Wette, and several others maintain) ; for the ground of the love of God lies not merely in the sacrifice considered by itself, but in the fact that the Good Shepherd, when He gives up His life, is resolved to take it again, in order that He may continue to fulfil His pastoral office till the final goal is reached, when all mankind shall constitute His flock. Indeed, only on the condition of His taking His life again, could He fulfil the office of Shepherd unto the final completion contem-

---

[1] Acts xiv. 17, xvii. 27.
[2] Vulgate, Luther, Beza, and many others ; also Tholuck, Luthardt, Hengstenberg, Godet.
[3] Nonnus, Euth. Zigabenus, Theophylact, Casaubon.
[4] Plut. *de fort. Alex.* 6.
[5] V. 16, 18, viii. 47, xii. 18, 39 ; 1 John iii. 1.

plated in the divine decree, and referred to in ver. 16.   For this reason, also, ἵνα cannot be regarded as introducing the *divine* intention (Tholuck), because the ground of the Father's love must lie in the volition of *Jesus*,—which volition, it is true, corresponds to the Father's will, though this is not here expressly declared, but first in ver. 18. — Ver. 18. It must be, however, not an *unwilling*, but a *voluntary* self-sacrifice, if it is to form the ground of the love of the Father to Him ; hence the words οὐδεὶς . . . ἀπ' ἐμαυτοῦ (*mea ipsius sponte*).   Nor must He proceed to effect this voluntary sacrifice of His own authority ; but must *receive a warrant thereto*, as also for that which He had in view in so doing, viz. the resumption of His life ; hence the words :[1] ἐξουσίαν . . . λαβεῖν αὐτήν.   Nay, more ; even *this very thing* which He purposed to do, namely, the surrender and resumption of His life, must have come to Him as a *commission* from God ; hence the expression : ταύτην τ. ἐντολὴν . . . πατρός μου, in which ταύτην (*this and not something different*) is emphatic, and τὴν ἐντολήν is correlate to the idea of ἐξουσία, as this latter is grounded in the divine *mandate*.   Notice further : (1) The ἐξουσία, the power *conferred* (so also in xix. 10 f., not *power* generally), lies in the relation of subordination to God, of whom the Son is the *commissioned representative*, and to whom He submits Himself voluntarily, *i.e.* from no compulsion exerted by a power outside of Himself, but with self-determined obedience to the Father.[2] Equality of nature[3] is the condition of this moral harmony.   (2) The view which pervades the New Testament, that Christ did not raise Himself from the dead, but was raised by the Father, is not affected by this passage, inasmuch as the *taking* again of His life, for which the theanthropic Christ had received authorization, implies the *giving* again of the life, to wit, the re-awakening activity of the Father.   This giving again on the part of God, by which Christ becomes ζωοποιηθεὶς πνεύματι (see 1 Pet. iii. 19, and Huther on the passage), and that ἐξουσία, which Christ receives from God, are the two factors of the resurrection—the former being the causa *efficiens*, whilst the latter, the ἐξουσία of Christ, is the causa *apprehendens*.[4] — (3) ταύτην τὴν ἐντολ. embraces the aforementioned twofold ἐξουσία ; justly so, inasmuch as the authorization to die and to rise again was only formally divided according to its two aspects.   Chrysostom and several others erroneously refer ταύτην to the dying alone.

Vv. 19–21. Πάλιν] see ix. 16. — ἐν τοῖς Ἰουδαίοις.] These words refer to the *Pharisees* (ix. 40) who, in keeping with their relationship to Jesus (against de Wette), are designated according to the *class* to which they belonged (as the Jewish hierarchical opposition).   The majority of them clung to the hostile judgment (compare viii. 48), which they had contemptuously expressed ; some of them, however, felt themselves impressed, and denied the assertion of the rest.   Comp. ix. 16. — τί αὐτοῦ ἀκούετε] *i.e.* of what use is it to you to listen to His discourses ? — καὶ μαίνεται] in conse-

---

[1] [ἐξουσίαν, *right, privilege, permission* ; not, as in the Eng. Version, *power*. It is a privilege accorded to Him by His Father.— K.]

[2] xiv. 30 f. ; Matt. xxvi. 53.

[3] Olshausen.

[4] Compare *Constitutiones Apostol.* 5. 7. 8 : ἑαυτὸν προστάγματι τοῦ πατρὸς διὰ τριῶν ἡμερῶν ἀνεγείρας.

quence of being possessed by a demon. — μὴ δαιμόνιον, etc.] *surely a demon cannot*, etc. ; a confirmation of that denial from the miracle which had given rise to the entire discussion. We see from this that these ἄλλοι belonged to the more unprejudiced and conscientious class which had given expression to its feelings in ix. 16. At the same time, the conclusion must not be drawn that they would have refused to recognize any demoniacal miracles (if in themselves beneficent)—Matt. xii. 24 is opposed to this view ; but they believed it impossible to attribute a miracle of so *great* a kind to a *demon*, who must have been working through the medium of Jesus. Note, moreover, that also here they do not get further than a *negative* judgment.

Vv. 22, 23. A new section ; the proceedings at *the feast of the Dedication of the Temple.* — As there is not the least hint of a return journey to Galilee or Perea, and as vv. 26 ff. point back to the discourse concerning the Good Shepherd, we must needs suppose that Jesus remained in Jerusalem and the neighbourhood between the feast of Tabernacles and the feast of Dedication (about two months), and did not labour outside of Judea ; He first leaves Judea in ver. 40.[1] The insertion here of a journey to Galilee or Perea[2] is dictated by harmonistic assumptions and clumsy combinations (suggested especially by the narrative of the journey in Luke ix. 51 ff.), and not by the requirements of exegesis ; for πάλιν in ver. 40 cannot be reckoned among such requirements. — τὰ ἐγκαίνια] *the feast of Renewal*, founded by Judas Maccabaeus, to commemorate the purification and consecration anew of the temple after its desecration by Antiochus Epiphanes, celebrated for eight days every year, from the 25th Kislev onward (the middle of December), and especially distinguished by the illumination of the houses ; hence also termed τὰ φῶτα. See 1 Macc. iv. 50 ff. ; 2 Macc. i. 18, x. 6 ff. ; Joseph. *Antiq.* xii. 7. 7. From this festival (הֲנֻכָּה) sprang the Christian Church Dedication Festival, and its name ἐγκαίνια. See Augusti, *Denkw.* III. p. 316. — ἐν Ἱερουσ.] The celebration was not restricted to Jerusalem, but was universal (see Lightfoot, p. 1063 f.) ; the words ἐν Ἱερουσ. are added because Jesus was still there. — κ. χειμὼν ἦν] a remark added for the sake of John's Gentile Christian readers, for whom the statement that it was *winter* when the festival occurred, would be sufficient to explain why Jesus walked about in Solomon's porch and not in the open air ; hence the explanation, *stormy weather* (Matt. xvi. 3, so Er. Schmid, Clericus, Lampe, Semler, Kuinoel, Lange), is not in harmony with the context. — The στοὰ Σολομῶνος (comp. Acts iii. 11) was a portico on the eastern side of the temple buildings,[3] which, according to Josephus, was a relic from Solomon's days which had remained intact in the destruction of the temple by Nebuchadnezzar. The mention of this particular part of the temple is one of the traces of the writer having been himself an eye-witness ; events like this no doubt impressed themselves on the memory so as never to be forgotten

---

[1] Compare also Wieseler, p. 318; Ewald, *Gesch. Christi*, p. 471.

[2] As recently proposed, especially by Ebrard, Neander, Lange *L. J.* II. p. 1004 f.,

Riggenbach, Luthardt, Godet.

[3] Hence denominated στ. ἀνατολική by Josephus in his *Antt.* xx. 9. 7.

(comp. viii. 20). Any *reason* for Jesus being in the porch, beyond the one given in the words καὶ χειμὼν ἦν,[1] must be rejected as arbitrary, since John himself gives no hint regarding it.

Ver. 24. Οἱ Ἰουδαῖοι] Here too the standing party of opposition. — ἐκύκλωσαν] *encircled* Him. The word graphically sets forth the urgency and obtrusiveness of the Jews ; but neither implies that Jesus had been deserted by His followers (Lange), nor represents the Ἰουδαῖοι as pushing in *between* Him and His disciples, and *so* enclosing Him in their midst (Godet). — ἔλεγον αὐτῷ] "This speak they out of a false heart, with a view to accusing and destroying Him," Luther. According to Hengstenberg, they really vacillated between an inclination and disinclination to believe. But see vv. 26, 31. They desire an *express* and thoroughly *direct* declaration, though not as if making a last attempt to induce Jesus to take up the *rôle* of a political Messiah (Lange). — τ. ψυχ. ἡμ. αἴρεις] αἴρειν not in the sense of *take away* ;[2] but in that of *lift up*. It denotes to *excite* the soul, which, according to the connection, may be due to very different mental influences ;[3] in this case, by *strained expectation*, which thou causest us. The explanation : ἀναρτᾷς μεταξὺ πίστεως κ. ἀπιστίας,[4] is an approximation to the *sense*, but is not the precise signification of the *words*. — εἰ σὺ εἰ, etc.] *if thou*, and so forth, as in Luke xxii. 67.

Vv. 25, 26. Jesus had not only *told* them (on many occasions, if not always so directly as, for example, to the woman of Samaria, or the man born blind) that He was the Messiah, but had also testified to the fact by His Messianic *works* (v. 36). But they do not believe. The actual *proof* of their unbelief is first subjoined in the second clause : *for ye belong not to my sheep ;* otherwise ye would stand in a totally different relation to me than that of unbelief ; ye would hear my voice, and know me, and follow me, vv. 4, 14, 27. — ἐγὼ . . . ὑμεῖς] Reproachful antithesis. — καθὼς εἶπον ὑμῖν] belong, as also Lachmann and Tischendorf punctuate, to *what precedes* (comp. i. 33) ; but not in such a way as to involve merely a retrospective reference to the figure of the πρόβατα (Fritzsche : "ut similitudine utar, quam supra posui"), which would render this repulse very meaningless ; but in such a way as to recall to their recollection the *negative declaration itself* as having been already uttered. It is true, indeed, that He had not given *direct* expression to the words ὅτι οὐκ ἐστέ, etc. in the preceding allegory ; *indirectly*, however, He had done so, namely, by a description of His sheep, which necessarily involved the *denial* that the Ἰουδαῖοι belonged to them. That this is the force of καθ᾽ εἶπ. ὑμ., He Himself declares by the exhibition of the relation of His sheep that follows. We are precluded from regarding it as an introduction to *what follows,*[5] which would require a comma before καθὼς, and a colon after ὑμῖν, by the circum-

---

[1] Luthardt, after Thiersch, *Apost. Zeitalter*, p. 73 : for "the purpose of expressing in a *figurative* way the *unity of the Old and New Covenants*."

[2] Nonnus : ὑποκλέπτεις φρένα ; Elsner : *enecas*.

[3] Eur. *Ion*. 928 ; *Hec.* 69 ; Aesch. *Sept* 198 :

Soph. *O. R.* 914 ; Prov. xix. 18 ; Philo, *de Monarch.* I. p. 218 ; Joseph. *Antt.* iii. 2. 3 ; iii. 5. 1.

[4] Euth. Zigabenus, and many others.

[5] Curss., Cant., Corb., Arr., Euth. Zigabenus, Tholuck, Godet.

stance that Jesus nowhere else quotes and (in the form of a summary) *repeats* a longer discourse of His own. In keeping with the style of the Gospels, only a brief, sententious saying, such as xiii. 33, would be fitted for such self-quotation. In this case, however, the quotation would embrace at least vv. 27 and 28.—The circumstance that Jesus should refer to this allegory about two months after the date of vv. 1–21, which has been erroneously used as an argument against the originality of the discourse (Strauss, Baur), may be simply accounted for by the assumption that during the interval He had had no further discussions with His hierarchical opponents,—a supposition which is justified by its accounting for the silence observed by John relatively to that period. The presupposition involved in the words καθὼς εἶπον ὑμῖν, that Jesus here has in the main the same persons before Him as during the delivery of His discourse regarding the shepherd, has nothing against it ; and there is no necessity even for the assumption that John and Jesus conceived the discourses to be directed against the Ἰουδαῖοι as a *whole* (Brückner).

Vv. 27, 28. Description of the relation of the *sheep* to Him (comp. vv. 4, 14), which brings clearly to view that the Ἰουδαῖοι cannot belong to them. Notice in ver. 27 the *climactic parallelism* of the two halves of the verse as far as δίδωμι αὐτοῖς (ver. 28), after which, commencing with καὶ οὐ μὴ ἀπόλ., etc., the discourse goes on to express in a double form the inseparableness of the blessed relationship. On the emphatic polysyndeton, compare vv. 3, 12. — τὰ πρόβ. τὰ ἐμά] the sheep which belong to *me*. — ζωὴν αἰών.] also conceived already in its temporal development, iii. 15, v. 24, and repeatedly.— καὶ οὐ μὴ ἀπόλ.] The negation belongs to the verb ; this declaration : "they shall certainly not perish," will be accomplished in eternity. The lost sheep, *i.e.* the sheep which has been separated, and wandered away from the flock (Matt. x. 6 ; Luke xv. 4), typifies him who is separated from the protection and gracious leading of Christ, and has fallen into unbelief. Compare the following καὶ οὐχ ἁρπάσει, etc., where this protection and gracious leading is set forth with still more concrete tenderness by the words ἐκ τῆς χειρός μου. His hand protects, bears, cherishes, leads them. Liberty and the *possibility of apostasy* are not thus excluded (in answer to Augustine and the teaching of the Reformed Church) ; he who has fallen away is no longer a πρόβατον, but on the part of Christ everything is promised by which preserving grace is secured, and this is the ground of the *Certitudo salutis.*

Vv. 29, 30. Explanation of the assertion just made, οὐχ ἁρπάσει, etc. If in *my* hand, they are also in the hand of my *Father*, who is greater than all, so that an ἁρπάζειν, etc. is *impossible ;* I am one with Him. — ὃς δέδωκέ μοι] sc. αὐτά. On the import of the words, compare on vi. 37. In characterizing God as the *giver of the sheep*, Jesus enables us to see how fully He is *justified* in appealing, as He here does, to the Father. — μεῖζον (see the critical note) : *something greater*, a greater potence. On the neuter here employed, compare Matt. xii. 6 (Lachmann).[1] — πάντων] Masculine. Compare

---

[1] See Bernhardy, p. 335 ; Kühner II. p. 45 ; Dissen *ad Dem. de Cor.* p. 396 (πονηρὸν ὁ συκοφάντης).

τίς, ver. 28, and οὐδείς, ver. 29. Without any limitation : *all* besides God. — καὶ οὐδεὶς δύναται, etc.] Necessary consequence of the μεῖζον πάντων, but not setting aside the possibility of losing the grace by one's *own fault*, vi. 66. — ἐκ τ. χειρ. τοῦ πατρ. μου]. This expression, τοῦ πατρ. μ., is due to the presupposition, flowing out of ὃς δεδωκέ μοι, that God did not let the sheep out of His hand, *i.e.* out of His protection and guidance, when He gave them to Christ. But this continued *divine* protection is really nothing else than the protection of *Christ*, so far, that is, as the Father is in the Son and works in Him (see vv. 37, 38) ; hence the latter, as the organ and vehicle of the divine activity in carrying out the Messianic work, is not separated from God, is not a second some one outside and alongside of God ; but, by the very nature of the fellowship referred to, *one with God*.[1] Compare on ἐν ἐσμεν, 1 Cor. iii. 8. *God's* hand is therefore *His* hand in the accomplishment of the work, during the performance of which He administers and carries into execution the power, love, etc. of God. The unity, therefore, is one of *dynamic* fellowship, *i.e.* a unity of action for the realization of the divine decree of redemption ; according to which, the Father is in the Son, and moves in Him, so that the Father acts in the things which are done by the Son, and yet is greater than the Son (xiv. 28), because He has commissioned, consecrated, and sent Him. The *Arian* idea of *ethical agreement* is insufficient ; the reasoning would miss its mark unless unity of *power* be understood (on which Chrysostom, Euth. Zigabenus, and many others, also Lücke, justly lay emphasis). The *orthodox* interpretation, which makes it denote *unity of essence* (Nonnus : ἐν γένος ἐσμέν ; Augustine : *unum*, delivers us from Charybdis, that is, from Arius, and *sumus* from Scylla, that is, from Sabellius), specially defended by Hengstenberg, though rejected even by Calvin as a misuse of the passage, goes beyond the argumentation ; although, in view of the metaphysical character of the relation of the Son to the Father, clearly taught elsewhere, and especially, in John, the Homoousia, as the essential foundation, must be regarded as presupposed in the fellowship here denoted by ἐν ἐσμεν.

Vv. 31, 32. The Jews understood the expression in ver. 30 to refer to *essential unity*, and in their tumultuous and angry excitement would even stone (Lev. xxiv. 10 f.) the *blasphemer ;* the overawing impression, however, produced by Christ's reply was powerful enough to restrain them. — ἐβάσ-τασαν] *sustulerunt* (Vulgate), ἀνηέρταζον (Nonnus) *they lifted up stones*, with the intention of throwing them at Him. The word is more characteristic than αἴρειν in viii. 59, though on account of πάλιν the two must have the same import ; hence the interpretation : *they fetched* (Hengstenberg, Godet, and others), is less exact.[2] — πάλιν] viii. 59. — καλὰ ἔργα] not specially : works of *love* (Kuinoel, B. Crusius), but in general : *praeclara opera, distinguished* works.[3] — ἔδειξα ὑμῖν] *have I showed you*, v. 20. Comp. ii. 18 ; Ps. lxxviii.

---

[1] Compare Weiss, *Lehrbegr.* p. 205 f.

[2] Compare Hom. *Od.* λ. 594 ; Soph. *Aj.* 814 ; Polyb. 15. 26. 3.

[3] Jesus was the more able thus to designate His acts, because He characterized them as works of *God* performed through Him. The explanation of Luthardt says too little : " Works with which no fault can be found."

11.[1] — ἐκ τοῦ πατρός μου] *from my Father*, who is in me, and from whom, therefore, they go out through me. Compare vv. 37, 38. — διὰ ποῖον, etc.] *propter quale*, etc. Not without the irony of profound indignation (comp. 2 Cor. xii. 13) does Jesus ask, What, then, is the *character* of that one of His works, on account of which they are about to stone Him?[2] Not as though He did not *know why* they were intending to stone Him, but doubtless in the consciousness of having actually shown Himself by His works to be something totally different from a blasphemer. — περὶ βλασφημ. καὶ ὅτι] *for blasphemy, and, indeed, because.* The reproach : "thou makest thyself God" (comp. v. 18), *i.e.* a divine being (i. 1), was a consequence of the mistaken view taken of ver. 30, which they had interpreted of essential unity. Καί connects with the general charge a more exact definition of that on which it was based.

Vv. 34–38. Jesus *justifies* Himself from the reproach of blasphemy by defending His assertion that He was the Son of God—the words of ver. 30 which had excited the opposition amounted to this—from the *Scriptures* (vv. 34–36) ; He then sets forth the unity affirmed in ver. 30 as credibly attested by His *works* (vv. 37, 38).

Vv. 34–36. In Ps. lxxxii. 6, unrighteous *authorities of the theocratic people* —not *angels* (Bleek), nor yet heathen princes (de Wette, Hitzig)—whose approaching destruction, in contrast with their high *dignity*, is intended to stand out, are called *gods*, agreeably to the old sacred view of rulers as the representatives of God, which was entertained in the theocratic nation. Compare Ex. xxi. 6, xxii. 8, 28. From this, Jesus draws the conclusion *a minori ad majus*, that He might call Himself *God's Son* without blasphemy. He is surely far more exalted than they (ὃν ὁ πατὴρ ἡγίασε, etc.) ; and nevertheless had designated Himself, not θεός, as though wishing to make a God of Himself, but merely υἱὸς τ. θεοῦ.[3] — ἐν τῷ νόμῳ] Spoken of the Old Testament generally, of which the law was the fundamental and authoritative portion. Comp. xii. 34, xv. 25 ; Rom. iii. 19 ; 1 Cor. xiv. 21. — ὑμῶν] as in viii. 17. — ἐκείνους] whom ? Jesus takes for granted as known. — εἶπε] namely, ὁ νόμος (compare afterwards ἡ γραφή), not *God* (Hengstenberg). — πρὸς οὕς] *to whom*, not *adversus quos* (Heinsius, Stolz), which does not follow from the context. There is nothing to warrant the supposition that the *prophets* are also referred to (Olshausen). — ὁ λόγος τοῦ θεοῦ] Neither the λόγος ἄσαρκος (Cyril), nor the *revelations* of God (Olshausen, comp. Godet). but the *saying of God just mentioned: ἐγὼ εἶπα*, etc. This saying belongs, not to the time when the Psalm was written, but to that earlier period (the period of the *induction* of the authorities into their office, comp. Ps. ii. 7), to which God, the speaker, points back. — καὶ οὐ δύναται, etc.] This clause,

[1] Plat. *Crat.* p. 430 E : τὸ δεῖξαι λέγω εἰς τὴν τῶν ὀφθαλμῶν αἴσθησιν καταστῆσαι.
[2] λιθάζετε, see Bernhardy, p. 370 ; Buttm. *Neut. Gr.* p. 178 [E. T. p. 205].
[3] Hengstenberg incorrectly remarks: "He *accepts* the charge, 'Thou makest thyself God.'" On the contrary, He does not enter on it at all, but simply justifies the predicate, "*Son* of God," which He had assumed for Himself. But Beyschlag also is wrong when he says (p. 106): "That which Jesus here affirms concerning Himself (ὃν ὁ πατὴρ ἡγίασε, etc.) might equally have been affirmed by every prophet." On such a view, no regard would be paid to the relation of πατήρ and υἱός.

though containing only an auxiliary thought, and not a main point of the argumentation (Godet), has been without reason treated as a parenthesis ; whereas both in point of structure and sense it is dependent on εἰ : *and it is impossible,* etc. So also Ewald, Godet, Hengstenberg. — λυθῆναι] The Scripture (consequently, also, that saying of the Psalms) cannot be *loosened, i.e. cannot be deprived of its validity.*[1] The *auctoritas normativa et judicialis* of the Scriptures must remain unbroken. Note, in connection herewith, the idea of the *unity* of the Scriptures as such, as also the presupposition of their *theopneustia.* — ὃν ὁ πατὴρ ἡγ. etc.] That is surely something still greater than that address of the λόγος τ. θεοῦ to authorities when they were installed in their offices. In this question, which is placed in the apodosis, and which expresses surprise, the object, which is correlate to the ἐκείνους of ver. 35, is very emphatically placed at the commencement ; and ὑμεῖς (*you people*) is placed over against the inviolable authority of the Scripture. — ἡγίασε *hath consecrated,* a higher analogue of the consecration to the office of prophet (Jer. i. 5 ; Sir. xlv. 4, xlix. 7), denoting the divine consecration to the office of *Messiah,* who is the ἅγιος τοῦ θεοῦ (vi. 69 ; Luke iv. 34). This consecration took place on His being sent from heaven, and immediately before His departure (hence ἡγίασε καὶ ἀπέστ.), in that the father not merely "*set apart*" the Son to the work (as though the word ἐξελέξατο had been used ; Hofmann, *Schriftbew.* I. p. 86 ; comp. Euth. Zigabenus, Hengstenberg, and Brückner), but also conferred on Him the Messianic ἐντολή and ἐξουσία, with the fulness of the Spirit appertaining to them (iii. 34), and the power of life (v. 26), and the πλήρωμα of grace and truth (i. 14). — ὅτι βλασφημεῖς] The reply which, in view of ὃν, etc., we should have expected to be in the oblique construction (βλασφημεῖν or ὅτι βλασφημεῖ, comp. ix. 19), passes over with the increasing vivacity of the discourse into the direct construction.[2] — ὅτι εἶπον] *because I said.* He had set it *indirectly* in vv. 29, 30.

Vv. 37–39. Your unbelief, which lies at the foundation of the judgment ὅτι βλασφημεῖς, would then be justifiable, if I did not, etc. In the other case, however, you ought to believe, if not me, at all events my works, in order that you, etc. — εἰ οὐ ποιῶ] if I leave them undone.[3] — τὰ ἔργα τοῦ πατρ. μ.] which my Father works ; compare on ix. 3, xiv. 10, also ver. 23. — μὴ πιστ. μοι] not merely permissive, but an actual *command,* as in the case of the following πιστεύετε (see the critical note). The alternative is *decided :* they *ought* not to believe Him if, etc. — ἐμοί] My person in and by itself, apart from the actual testimony borne to it by the ἔργα. — *To believe the works,* is to hold for true the testimony which is contained in them (v. 36). The *object* of faith is that which Jesus declares concerning Himself, and what, in agreement therewith (comp. xiv. 11), the works prove concerning Him. According to the reading ἵνα γνῶτε κ. γινώσκητε (see the critical note), which Hengstenberg, notwithstanding, rejects as giving an intolerable meaning, Jesus describes this as the end to be attained by His prescription : *in order*

---

[1] Comp. Matt. v. 19 ; John v. 18, vii. 23 ; Herod. 3, 82 ; Plat. *Phaedr.* p. 256 D ; *Gorg.* p. 509 A ; Dem. 31. 12, 700, 13.

[2] Compare viii. 54, and see Buttm. *Neut.*

Gr. p. 234 [E. T. p. 272].

[3] Comp. Buttm. *Neut. Gr.* p. 297 [E. T. p. 346] ; Baeumlein, *Partik.* p. 278.

that ye may attain to knowledge, and may (permanently) *know*, etc.—distinguishing between the *act* and the *state* of knowledge.[1]— ὅτι ἐν ἐμοὶ ὁ πατ. κἀγὼ ἐν αὐτῷ] *This* now is the *unity* which He meant in ver. 30 ; not *essential* unity (old orthodox explanation of the περιχώρησις essentialis patris in filio et filii in patre, see Calovius), although it is metaphysically the fundamental condition, but *dynamic* unity : the Father lives and moves in Christ, who is His active organ, and again Christ is in the Father, so far as Christ in God is the power which determines the execution of the divine ἔργον. The thought that Christ has in God "the ground of His existence and working" (de Wette), lies far remote from the words κἀγὼ ἐν αὐτῷ, because the relation of the clauses of the proposition must be *equal*. But this relation is nothing else than that of inner, active, *reciprocal fellowship*. In accordance therewith, the Father is in the Son, as in the executor of His work, as the Son is also in the Father, because Christ is the regulative and determining *agens et movens* of the work of redemption in the Father. Comp. the many Pauline passages which represent all the divine redemptive activity as taking place *in Christ; e.g.* Rom. viii. 39 ; Eph. i. 3 ff. — Ver. 39. οὖν] In consequence of this defence, which averted the threatened tumultuous stoning, for which the Jews had begun to prepare themselves. The supposition that πιάσαι denotes laying hold of *with a view to carrying out the stoning*, is opposed by the πάλιν, which refers back to vii. 30, 32, 44 (against Calvin, Luthardt, Hengstenberg). — καὶ ἐξῆλθεν, etc.] And yet they were unable to carry their plan into execution ; *He escaped out of their hands*, which are conceived as already stretched out after Him. *How* this deliverance was effected must be left undetermined (Kuinoel : by the arrival of His adherents ; Hengstenberg : by the indecision of His enemies) : of any miraculous element (*e.g.* becoming invisible) in His escape, although assumed by many early commentators, and still by B. Crusius and Luthardt, John gives no hint. Comp. on viii. 59. Euth. Zigabenus : ἀναχωρεῖ διὰ τὸν θυμὸν τῶν φθονερῶν, ἐνδιδοὺς αὐτῷ λωφῆσαι καὶ λῆξαι τῇ ἀπουσίᾳ αὐτοῦ.

Vv. 40–42. Πάλιν.] i. 28. — πέραν τ. Ἰορδ.] He went away from Jerusalem, *beyond the Jordan* (as in vi. 1, xviii. 1) *to Perea*, and, indeed, to the place, etc. Instead of allowing themselves to be won over to faith and redemption, the Ἰουδαῖοι had grown ever more hardened and decided in their hostility, till it had reached the extreme ; the Lord then finally gives them up, and knowing that His hour was near, though not yet fully come, He withdraws for a calm and undisturbed, although brief, season of activity to *Perea*, where He was safer from the hierarchs (comp. xi. 54) ; and in the place *where John was when he baptized for the first time* (namely, i. 28 ; later, in Salim, iii. 23), there could be as little lack of susceptible hearts as of quiet, elevating, and sacred memories for Himself. —ἔμεινεν ἐκεῖ] How long, we cannot precisely ascertain, as He spent also some time in Ephraim before the feast of the Passover (xi. 54 f.). In any case, however, the ἔμεινεν ἐκεῖ lasted but for a very short period, as is evident also from the word νῦν in xi. 8. — καὶ πολλοί, etc.] "Fructus posthumus officii Johannis," Bengel. —

---

[1] Compare ἐπιμεληθῆναι καὶ ἐπιμελεῖσθαι, Plat. *Legg.* viii. p. 849 B.

ἔλεγον] not αὐτῷ, but a bearing of testimony in general. — Ἰωάννης μέν, etc.] Logically we should expect μέν after σημεῖον ; but even classical writers frequently disregard logical precision in their mode of placing μέν and δέ.[1] — σημεῖον ἐποίησεν οὐδέν] A characteristic feature of the history of John, which in this respect also has remained free from fanciful additions ; the people, however, referred to the circumstance in view of the σημεῖα which *Jesus* had wrought, as they had been informed, elsewhere, and probably here also, before their own eyes. In this way we may also account for μέν not occupying its strictly logical position.—The repetition of Ἰωάννης in ver. 42 belongs to the simplicity of the style, which is here faithfully reflected, and is in harmony with the feeling of reverence entertained by the people for the holy man whose memory still lived among them. — ἀληθῆ ἦν] As was actually shown by the works of Jesus. In this way, their experience of the truth of the testimony of John became the ground of faith in Christ. What a contrast to the experiences which Jesus had just had to pass through among the Ἰουδαῖοι ! The ray of light thus vouchsafed to Him in the place where He first commenced His labours, is here set forth in all historical simplicity. Baur, however,[2] maintains that the people are merely represented as speaking these words in order that the entire preceding description of the life and works of Jesus may be surveyed from the point of view of the *miracles*. John himself gives a comprehensive retrospect, but in the right place, namely, at the close of the active ministry of Jesus in xii. 37 ff., and in how different a manner ! — ἐκεῖ (see the critical note), emphatically closes the verse.

[1] See Kühner, *ad Xen. Mem.* i. 6. 11; Baeumlein, *Partik.* p. 168.

[2] p. 182 f., and *Theol. Jahrb.* 1854, p. 280 f.

CHAPTER XI.

Ver. 12. οἱ μαθηταὶ αὐτοῦ] A. 44 have merely αὐτῷ. D. K. II. א. Curss. Verss.: αὐτῷ οἱ μαθηταί (so Lachm. and Tisch.). B. C.* L. X. Copt.: οἱ μαθ. αὐτῷ. The simple αὐτῷ is the original reading ; οἱ μαθ. was written in the margin ; then was introduced into the text partly before and partly after αὐτῷ ; and in the former position brought about the partial change of αὐτῷ into αὐτοῦ. — **Ver. 17.** ἐλθών. . . εὗρεν] Lachm. : ἦ᾽θεν . . . καὶ εὗρεν, solely after C.* D. Partly before (so Lachm. in the margin), partly after ἡμέρας (so Elzev. and Lachm.), stands ἤδη, which, however, is altogether omitted (so Tisch.) by A.* D. Curss. Verss.: τέσσ. ἤδη ἡμ. must be regarded as the original reading (B. C.*). The word ἤδη, beginning and ending with H, was easily passed over, as standing immediately before ἡμέρας, which also begins with H, and was then restored in the wrong place. — **Ver. 19.** Instead of καὶ πολλοί, we must, with decisive testimonies, read πολλοὶ δέ with Lachm. and Tisch. — αὐτῶν] after ἀδελφοῦ must, with Tisch., after B. D. L. א., be deleted as a usual addition. — **Ver. 21.** ὁ ἀδελφ. μου οὐκ ἂν ἐτεθνήκει] Lachm. and Tisch., after decisive witnesses, read οὐκ ἂν ἀπέθανεν ὁ ἀδ. μου. If ἐτεθνήκει had been the original reading, it would have been found as a various reading also in ver. 32 ; it is a clumsy interpretation. — **Ver 22.** ἀλλά] is wanting in B. C.* X. א. Curss. Verss. Chrys. Bracketed by Lachm., deleted by Tisch. An antithetical interpolation. — Ver. 29. ἐγείρεται] B. C.* D. L. א. Curss. Verss.: ἠγέρθη. So Lachm. A mechanical transposition into the historical tense, with which the reading ἤρχετο (instead of ἔρχεται) in the same Codd., except D., is also connected. — **Ver. 30.** After ἦν Lachm. and Tisch. have ἔτι (B. C. X. א. Curss. Verss.). An addition more precisely determining the meaning, which other witnesses place *before* ἦν. — **Ver. 31.** λέγοντες] B. C.* D. L. X. א. Curss. Verss. : δόξαντες, which, as an unusual expression, must with Tisch. be received into the text on the authority of these decisive witnesses. — **Ver. 32.** The position of αὐτοῦ *before* εἰς τ. πόδ. (Elz. and Lachm. place it *after*) has the decision of the Codd. in its favour. — εἰς] B. C.* D. L. X. א. Curss. : πρός. So Tisch., and the witnesses are decidedly in its favour. — **Ver. 39.** Instead of τετελευτηκότος, Elz. has τεθνηκότος, in opposition to decisive testimonies. A gloss. — **Ver. 40.** The future form ὄψῃ has decisive evidence in its favour (Lachm. and Tisch.). — **Ver. 41.** After λίθον Elz. places οὗ ἦν ὁ τεθνηκὼς κείμενος, in opposition to decisive testimony. Other witnesses have other explanatory additions. — **Ver. 45.** ἅ] Lachm. has ὅ, after A.** B. C. D. Curss. Verss. (in ver. 46, also, the ὅ is adopted by Lachm., although the evidence in its favour is weaker). The one act, which is meant, would easily suggest the singular. — After ἐποίησεν Elz. inserts ὁ ᾽Ιησοῦς. An unusual addition, opposed to overwhelming evidence. — **Ver. 50.** διαλογίζεσθε] A. B. D. L. א. Curss. Or. Cyr. Chrys. : λογίζεσθε. Recommended by Griesbach ; adopted by Lachm. and Tisch., and correctly too ; διαλογίζεσθαι was more familiar to the copyists from the other Gospels. — **Ver. 57.** δὲ καί] Lachm. and Tisch. have deleted καί on the authority of decisive witnesses. — Instead of ἐντολήν, B. J. M. א. Curss.

Or. (twice) have ἐντολάς, which, with Tisch., is to be adopted.   The Recepta is
a correction.

Ver. 1 f.[1] This stay of Jesus in retirement, however, is terminated by the
sickness of Lazarus (δέ). — Simplicity in the style of the narrative : *But
there was a certain one sick,* (namely) *Lazarus of Bethany, of the town,* etc. :
ἀπό (vii. 42 ; Matt. ii. 1, xxvii. 57) and ἐκ denote the same relation
(i. 46 f.), that of *derivation ;* hence it is the less allowable to regard the two
sisters and the brother as *Galileans,* and Mary as the Magdalene (Hengstenberg).[2] That Lazarus *lived* also in Bethany, and was lying ill there, is plain
from the course of the narrative.   For change of preposition, without any
change of relation, comp. i. 45 ; Rom. iii. 30 ; 2 Cor. iii. 11 ; Gal. ii. 16 ;
Eph. i. 7 ; Philem. 5.[3]—This Bethany, situated on the eastern slope of the
Mount of Olives, and, according to ver. 18, about three-quarters of an hour's
walk from Jerusalem (see on Matt. xxi. 17), was characteristically and specially known in the evangelical tradition from the two sisters who lived
there ; hence its more exact designation by the words ἐκ τῆς κώμης Μαρίας,
etc.,[4] for the sake of distinguishing it from the Bethany mentioned in i. 28
(see critical note on i. 28).[5] — ἦν δὲ Μαρία, etc.] Not to be put in a parenthesis.
A more exact description of *this* Mary,[6]—who, however, must not be identified with the woman who was a sinner, mentioned in Luke vii., as is done
still by Hengstenberg (see on Luke vii. 36, 37 f.)—from the account of the
anointing (Matt. xxvi. 6 ff. ; Mark xiv. 3 ff.), which John presupposes, in a
general way, as already *known,* although he himself afterwards takes occasion to narrate it in xii. 1 ff.   So important and significant did it appear to
him, although tradition had not preserved it in its pure original form
(not even in Matthew and Mark). — ἧς ὁ ἀδελφός, etc.] Thus, to refer to Lazarus as the brother of *Mary,* was perfectly natural to the narrative, and after
ver. 1 is clear in itself.   Entirely baseless is Hengstenberg's remark : the
relation of Lazarus to the *unmarried* Mary was more intimate than to the
married Martha, who had been the wife of Simon the leper, Matt. xxvi. 6
(which is a pure invention).   See in general, against the erroneous combinations of Hengstenberg regarding the personal relations of the two sisters
and Lazarus, Strauss, *Die Halben und die Ganzen,* p. 79 ff.

Vv. 3, 4. Merely the *message* that the beloved one is sick.   The *request*

[1] On the whole section relating to the
raising of Lazarus, see Gumlich in the *Stud.
u. Kritiken,* 1862, pp. 65 ff., 248 ff.

[2] In the *Constitt. Apost.* 3. 6. 2, also, Mary
Magdalene is expressly *distinguished* from
the sister of Lazarus.

[3] Kühner, II. p. 219.

[4] This genitive, presupposing, as it does,
the nominative form Μαρία, is opposed to
the adoption in John of the Hebrew form
Μαριάμ, which, in the various passages
where the name occurs, is supported by
very varying testimony, in some cases by
very strong, in other passages, however, by
no evidence at all.

[5] For the legends about Lazarus, see especially Thilo, *Cod. Apocry.* p. 711 ; Fabric.
Cod. Apocr. III. pp. 475, 509.

[6] On account of her predominant importance, and from being so well known, Mary
is mentioned *first* in ver. 1.   Had she been
the *elder* sister (Ewald), there would be no
apparent reason why Martha should be
mentioned first in vv. 5, 19, and 20.   Comp.
also Luke x. 38, where Martha appears as
mistress of the house.—Lazarus seems to
have been younger than the sisters, and to
have held a subordinate place in the household, xii. 2.

lay in the message itself, and the addition ὃν φιλεῖς supplied the motive for
it fulfilment. — εἶπεν] spoken generally, and not addressed to any definite
person, but in the hearing of those present, the messenger and the disciples.
Sufficient for the moment as a preparation both for the sisters and the disciples. — οὐκ ἐστι πρὸς θάνατον] πρός refers to destination (comp. afterwards
ὑπέρ) : *it is not to have death for its result,* which, however, does not mean,
as the antithesis shows : it is not *deadly,* he will not die of it. The idea of
death is used with a *pregnancy* of meaning, and the words signify : he shall
not fall a prey to death, as death is wont to be, with *no reawakening.*[1]
Comp. Matt. ix. 24. That Jesus certainly knew, by His higher knowledge, that the death of Lazarus was *certain* and *near at hand,* though
the death must be conceived as not having yet actually taken place (see on
ver. 17), is confirmed by ver. 14 ;—for the assumption of a second message
(Paulus, Neander, Schweizer) is purely arbitrary. With this significant
declaration, Jesus designed to supply to the sisters something fitted, when
the death of their brother took place, to stimulate the hope to which Martha
gives actual expression in ver. 22. There is no warrant for introducing a
reference to the spiritual and eternal life of the resurrection (Gumlich). —
ὑπὲρ τῆς δόξ. τ. θ.] *i.e.* for the *furtherance* of the honour of God. Comp. ix.
3. The emphatic and more definite explanation of the expression is given
in ἵνα δοξασθῇ, etc.—words which, containing the intention of God, state
the *kind* and *manner* of the ὑπὲρ τ. δόξ. τ. θ., so far, namely, as the glorification of the *Son* of God involves the honour of *God Himself,* who works
through Him (comp. v. 23, x. 30, 38). It is in these words, and not in
ver. 25 (Baur), that the doctrinal design of the narrative is contained.
Comp. vv. 40, 42.

Ver. 5 is not an elucidation of ver. 3 (de Wette), seeing that ver. 4 inter-
venes ; nor is it a preparation for ver. 6 (B. Crusius : " although He loved
them all, He nevertheless remained ") ; but explains the motive impelling
Him to open to them the consolatory prospect referred to in ver. 4 :
" Felix familia," Bengel. — ἠγάπα] An expression chosen with delicate
tenderness (the more sensuous φιλεῖν is not again used as in ver. 3), because
the *sisters* are also mentioned.[2] Martha is named *first,* as being the mistress
of the house, and the eldest (ver. 19 f.). Compare the preceding note.
Arbitrarily Hengst. : " Mary is not required to be separated from Lazarus,
because she was most deeply affected by his death."

Vv. 6, 7. Οὖν] Resumption of the narrative after the observation in ver.
5. — After ver. 6 a colon only ought to be placed, for the course of the narrative is this : " When therefore He heard that he was sick, He remained
then, indeed, etc. ; (but) *afterwards,*" etc. — μέν] logically is quite correct
after τότε : *then,* indeed (*tum quidem*), *when* He heard, He did not immediately go away, but remained still two days. [See Note XXXVII. p. 360.]
There is no corresponding δέ after ἔπειτα, as one would naturally expect,[3]

---

[1] θάνατος γὰρ κυρίως ὁ μέχρι τῆς κοινῆς ἀνασ-
τάσεως, Euth. Zigabenus.

[2] Comp. Xen. *Mem.* ii. 7. 12 ; Tittmann,
Synon. p. 53 ; and Wetstein.

[3] [But in the classics ἔπειτα sometimes
takes the place of δέ as the antithetic correlative of μέν. With πρῶτον μέν this is constant.—K.]

because the adversative relation, which was in view at first, has given way
to one of simple succession.[1] — ἔπειτα μετὰ τοῦτο] deinde postea (Cic. p. Mil.
24), as in the Classics also (comp. Plat. Phaedr. p. 258 E : ἔπειτα λέγει δὴ
μετὰ τοῦτο) synonymous adverbial expressions are frequently conjoined.[2]—
The question why Jesus did not leave at once for Bethany is not solved by the
assumption, that He designed to test the faith of the parties concerned
(Olshausen ; Gumlich also mixes this reason up with his otherwise correct
view), which would, in opposition to ver. 5, have amounted to a harsh and
arbitrary delaying on His part ; nor is it explained by the similar notion,
that the message of ver. 4 was meant first to produce its effect (Ebrard), as
though there had not been without that time enough for this ; just as little
is it accounted for by the supposition that important business connected
with His work in Peraea still detained Him,[3] for John gives not the slightest hint of such a reason, and it is a purely à priori assumption. It is to be
explained by a reference back to ver. 4, according to which Jesus was conscious of its being the divine will that the miracle should be performed precisely under the circumstances and at the time at which it actually was performed, and no otherwise (comp. ii. 4), for the glory of God. The divine
δεῖ, of which He was conscious, decided Him, and that, under a moral
necessity, lest He should act ὑπὲρ μοῖραν, to remain still ; the same δεῖ again
impelled Him at once to depart, when, in virtue of His immediate knowledge, He became aware of the death of His friend. Comp. on ver. 17. All
the more groundless was it to make use of the delay of Jesus as an argument
against the historical truth of the narrative (Bretschneider, Strauss, Weisse,
Gfrörer, Baur, Hilgenfeld), according to which Jesus intentionally allowed
Lazarus to die, in order that He might be able to raise him up again (Baur,
p. 193). — εἰς τὴν Ἰουδαίαν] for they were in Peraea, x. 40. The more definite goal, Bethany, is not at first mentioned ; but is specified afterwards, vv.
11, 15. The less reason, therefore, is there for finding a special design in
the use of the words εἰς τ. Ἰουδ. (Luthardt : " into the land of unbelief and
hostility"), a meaning which Godet and Gumlich import also into πάλιν.

Ver. 8. The question breathes solicitude for the safety and life of the
beloved Master. — νῦν] just now, refers to the recent events which, though
past, seemed still to form part of the present, x. 31. Hence the use of the
imperfect ; see Kühner, II. p. 385. — πάλιν] emphatically at the beginning.
— ὑπάγεις] Present, as in x. 32.

Vv. 9, 10. The sense of the allegorical answer is this : " The time
appointed to me of God for working is not yet elapsed ; as long as it lasts, no
one can do anything to me ; but when it shall have come to an end, I shall fall
into the hands of my enemies, like him who walketh in the night, and who
stumbleth, because he is without light." In this way Jesus sets aside the
anxiety of His disciples, on the one hand, by directing their attention to the

---

[1] Comp. Klotz, ad Devar. p. 539 ; Stallbaum, ad Plat. Phaed. p 89 A ; Baeumlein,
Partic. p. 163.

[2] Kühner, II. p. 615 ; Fritzsche, ad Marc.
p. 22. Comp. τότε ἔπειτα, which occurs frequently as early as in Homer ; Nägelsbach

on the Ilias, p. 149, ed. 3.

[The adverbs are scarcely synonymous.
ἔπειτα, then, afterwards : δή, vivacious, in
sooth, you see.—K.]

[3] Lücke, Krabbe, Neander, Tholuck,
Lange, Baumgarten.

fact that, as His time is not yet expired, He is *safe* from the apprehended dangers ; and, on the other, by reminding them (ver. 10) that He must make *use* of the time apportioned to Him, before it come to an end.[1] So substantially Apollinaris (διδάσκει ὁ κύριος ὅτι πρὸ τοῦ καιροῦ τοῦ πάθους οὐκ ἂν ὑπὸ Ἰουδαίων πάθοι· καὶ διδάσκει τοῦτο διὰ παραβολῆς, ἡμέρας μὲν καιρὸν ὀνομάζων τὸν πρὸ τοῦ πάθους, τὸν δὲ τοῦ πάθους νύκτα), Ruperti (only partially), Jansen, Maldonatus, Corn. à Lapide, Wolf, Heumann, and several others ; also Maier and B. Crusius ; comp. Ewald and Hengstenberg. On individual points, note further : (1) δώδεκα is placed emphatically at the beginning, signifying that the day referred to is *still running on*, and that anxiety is still premature (not : *only* twelve hours ; Bengel correctly remarks : "jam multa erat hora, sed tamen adhuc erat dies"). The supposition that Jesus spoke the words early in the morning, at sunrise (Godet, Gumlich), is as arbitrary as it is unnecessary. (2) τὸ φῶς τ. κόσμ. is the *sunlight*, so designated in harmony with the elevated tone which marks the entire saying ; the words ὅτι . . . βλέπει belong merely to the *coloring* of the picture, and are not intended to be specially *interpreted* (for example, of the guidance of the divine will, as Godet thinks, following older commentators). (3) Applying the figure to Jesus, *night* (ver. 10) commenced with the ἐλήλυθεν ἡ ὥρα, xvii. 1 (comp. xii. 27) ; the *day* with its twelve hours was then over for Him, and, according to the divine decree, the *stumbling* in His path which, with the close of the twelfth hour, had become dark, must now follow,[2] in that He fell into the hands of His enemies ; till then, however, οὔπω ἐληλύθει ἡ ὥρα αὐτοῦ, vii. 30, viii. 20. (4) The expression ὅτι τὸ φῶς οὐκ ἔστιν ἐν αὐτῷ, which is also a detail not intended for interpretation, is not equivalent to : *he has not*, etc. (Ewald ; it is also inadmissible to take this view of Ps. xc. 10), but is an outflow of the notion that, in the case of a man walking in the night, it is dark *in him*, *i.e. his representation* of his surroundings is dark and without light, so that he cannot discover his whereabouts *in his consciousness* of that which is round about him. Grotius : " in *oculis* ejus ;" but the expression ἐν αὐτῷ suggests the inner intuition and representation. (5) Substantially the same, and decisive for the view which the disciples would take, are the thought and figure in ix. 3 f. ; hence also here neither is *day* to be taken as an image of *tempus opportunum*,[3] nor νύξ of *tempus importunum ;* nor is it any more allowable to say, with Gumlich and Brückner (comp. Melanchthon, Beza, and Calvin), that φῶς τοῦ κ. τ. is *God*, who shows the Son the way, so that this latter thus walks *in the day*, and His person and work remain unendangered (οὐ προσκόπτει[4]) ; similarly Baeum-

---

[1] Not, as Godet interprets : that He *dare not lengthen* the working time appointed to Him by the divine will, that He may not venture to *add to it as it were a thirteenth hour*. Such a thought was totally foreign to the minds of the disciples in giving their warning. All that they desired was, that He should not *shorten* His life by exposing Himself to the threatening danger of death.

[2] The idea set forth is therefore not " the

wish to be active *beyond the ordained goal and limit of life*," which would, indeed, be absurd (Tholuck's objection) ; but to be removed from activity *on the attainment of the ordained goal of life*. When the twelfth hour has passed, *night* falls on the wanderer, and he stumbles.

[3] Morus, Rosenmüller, Paulus, Kuinoel.

[4] Ver. 10. τὸ φῶς οὐκ ἔστιν ἐν αὐτῷ is then explained by Brückner, after Matt. vi. 22 f.,

lein ; Lücke, on the other hand, rightly refers τῆς ἡμέρας to the "*day's work*" of Christ, which has its *definite limit* (its twelve hours) ; but then he explains ἐν τῇ ἡμέρᾳ of fulfiling the *duties of his calling* (comp. Melanchthon), which is always the way of safety, and takes νύξ as an image of *unfaithfulness to one's calling*, which leads to destruction. In this way, however, *two* totally *different* meanings are assigned to the figurative term ἡμέρα, the second of which is the more decidedly to be rejected, as the mention of twelve hours is evidence that the *temporal* explanation alone is correct. For this reason, further, we must reject not only the view taken by de Wette, who regards the day as the image of "*upright, innocent, clear action,*" the twelve hours, as the *ways and means* of action, and the night as the *lack of prudence and singlemindedness ;* but also that of Luthardt : "He who keeps within the limits of his calling will not strike against anything, will not make false steps, for the light of the world, *i.e.* the will of God, gives him light ; he, however, who passes beyond the limits of his calling will go wrong in his doings, seeing that he is guided, not by God's will, but by his own pleasure." Tholuck also diverges from the consistent carrying out of the temporal view ; for, though understanding the twelve hours of the day of the fixed *time* of the vocation, he afterwards introduces the calling itself : "Whoso abides not by his calling will come to damage." Comp. Schweizer, p. 106 ; also Lange, who combines several very different views. According to Chrysostom, Theophylact, and Euth. Zigabenus, the walking in the day denotes either a *blameless walk*, in which a man has no need to be afraid ; or *fellowship with Christ* (so also Erasmus : "quamdiu vobis luceo, nihil est periculi ; veniet nox, quando a me semoti conturbabimini." [1] Vatablus, Clarius, Lampe, Neander). Both are incorrect, for the simple reason that the disciples had expressed concern, not for *themselves*, but for *Christ*, by their question in ver. 8 (Chrysostom and his followers arbitrarily remark that they had been more in anxiety, ὑπὲρ ἑαυτῶν) ; and because the former of these views would furnish no explanation of the *mention of the hours*, which is just the key to the figure. This objection holds good also against Hilgenfeld,[2] who brings out as the meaning of Jesus : He has the light absolutely in Himself, and for him, therefore, no dark point can exist in His earthly course. On this view, moreover, ver. 10 remains without explanation. Olshausen, adopting the second view of Chrysostom, is prepared to accept an inadmissible double meaning of ἡμέρα ;—partly in His brotherly relationship to men, Jesus regards Himself as accomplishing His ordained *day's work ;* but again, in His higher dignity, as the *spiritual enlightener*, in whose brightness the disciples would have nothing to fear.[3] Comp. Bengel, who thinks

to mean that the eye, which has received the light, becomes itself a lamp, and so the whole man is illumined. But how could Jesus expect the disciples to understand so far-fetched an illusion? If such had been His meaning, He must have used, in agreement with Matt. vi. 23, some such words as : ὅτι τὸ φῶς τὸ ἐν αὐτῷ σκότος ἐστίν.

[1] So in the *Paraphr.* But in the *Annotat.*

he takes substantially our view : "Dies habet suas horas, nec is nostro arbitrio fit previor aut longior ; et ego tempus habeo praescriptum, quo debeam redimendi orbis negotium peragere, id Judaeorum malitia non potest anticipari : proinde nihil est, quod mihi timeatis."

[2] *Lehrbegr.* p. 263.

[3] Ebrard adopts Olshausen's view in the

that τὸ φῶς τ. κόσμ. τούτου signifies the "providentia *Patris* respectu *Jesu,* et providentia *Christi* respectu *fidelium.*

Vv. 11–13. Καὶ μετὰ τοῦτο λέγει] This representation separates the two discourses, between which a pause is to be conceived as intervening.—The *death* of Lazarus, which has just taken place, and become the occasion of the determination to leave at once (ver. 7 ; see on ver. 17), Jesus designates (comp. Matt. ix. 24), in view of his resurrection, by the word κεκοίμ., *has fallen asleep*, the event having become known to Him by *immediate knowledge* (spiritual far-seeing). Hence also the *definiteness* of His statement, to which the addition of the words ὁ φίλος ἡμ. communicates a touch of painful sensibility, while the ἡμῶν (*our*) claims also the loving sympathy of His disciples. — ἐξυπνίσω] *awaken out of sleep ;* a late Greek word, rejected by the Atticists.[1] — The *misunderstanding* of His disciples, who thought of the sleep which follows after a crisis has been passed through (see examples of the same thing in Pricaeus ; comp. also Sir. xxxi. 2, and Fritzsche's remarks thereon), loses its apparent improbability (against Strauss, de Wette, Reuss) when we refer back to ver. 4, the words of which they had naturally understood, not in the sense intended by *Jesus*, that He would raise him up from the *dead*, but, after the analogy of ix. 3, as signifying that He purposed to come and miraculously heal him. The journey thereby involved, however, they did not desire (ver. 8) ; the expression κεκοίμηται accordingly corresponded to their wishes ; hence the conclusion at once drawn, that he must be on the way to recovery, and the effort, by calling attention to this fact, to make the journey appear unnecessary. The very earnestness of their desire, caused them to overlook the *significant* nature of the words ἵνα ἐξυπνίσω αὐτόν, and to fail to see that it would have been absurd thus to speak of one who was *really* asleep. Such a mistake on their part is psychologically intelligible enough.[2] The notion that ver. 4 had led them to believe that Jesus had already *healed at a distance* (Ebrard, Hengst.), and that, *in consequence*, they necessarily understood sleep to refer to recovery, is incompatible with the fact that the words of ver. 4 do not at all suggest such a healing (how different in iv. 50 !) ; and that if they had thought of such a healing having taken place, they would have grounded their σωθήσεται on this, and not on the fact of *sleeping ;* they would hence have dissuaded from this journey as unnecessary in a very *different* way. According to Bengel (and Luthardt), the disciples believed, "somnum ab Jesu immissum esse Lazaro ut eveniret quod praedixerat ipse ver. 4." But there is no ex-

following more definite shape : "The day has its determinate measured duration. If a man use the day as *day, i.e.* the time for working given him by God *as a time of working,* he needs to be in no fear that his working will bring him mischief, for the light of the mundane sun illumines him. But he who walks *as though it were night, i.e. without working the will of God,* would procure for himself eternal mischief, because he would not have in him the light (in the absolute sense, i. 5)." In this way the es-

sential elements are read into the passage ; and what a strange difference in the conceptions found in the same expressions ! How could the disciples have possibly understood their Master !

[1] Lobeck *ad Phryn.* p. 224. Comp. Acts xvi. 27.

[2] "Discipuli *omni modo* quaerunt Dominum ab isto itinere avocare," Grotius ; "*libenter* hanc fugiendi periculi occasionem *arripiunt*," Calvin.

egetical support for this view, not even in the use of the first person singular πορεύομαι, which finds its very natural explanation in the connection
with ἐξυπνίσω (the case is different with ἀγωμεν, ver. 7), without that supposition (against Luthardt).

Ver. 14 f. Παῤῥησίᾳ] *i.e.* without the help of figurative hints as in ver. 11.
Comp. x. 24, xvi. 25. — Λάζ. ἀπέθ.] Now a declaration of the *simple occurrence ;* hence there is no addition to the word Λάζ. as in ver. 11. — δι' ὑμᾶς]
is immediately explained by the words ἵνα πιστεύς. ; for every new *advance*
in faith is, in respect to degree, a *coming to believe,* comp. ii. 11. The words
ὅτι οὐκ ἤμ. ἐκεῖ are to be taken together with χαίρω. If Jesus had been there,
He would not have permitted His friend to die (against Paulus), but have
saved him even on the sickbed ; in this case the far greater σημεῖον of His
δόξα, the raising him from the dead, would not have taken place, and the
faith of the disciples would therefore not have had the benefit of it, though,
just on the eve of the death of their Lord, it stood greatly in need of being
increased. Bengel aptly remarks : "cum decoro divino pulchre congruit,
quod praesente vitae duce nemo unquam legitur mortuus." — ἵνα] indicates
the telic direction, or *intention* of the emotion (not merely hope, de Wette).
Comp. viii. 56. Remark that Jesus rejoices not at the sorrowful event *in
itself,* but *at the circumstance* that He was not there, in consequence of which
it assumed a salutary relation to the disciples. — ἀλλ'] Abrupt transition.[1]
And the summons is now brief and measured.

Ver. 16. *Thomas* (תְּאֹמָא = תְּאֹם), after the Greek translation of his name
(*twin*), was called among the Gentile Christians *Didymus.* That *Jesus* gave
him this name for the purpose of signifying that his nature was one which
halted, and was divided between the old and the new man, is an invention
of Hengstenberg's, which he even goes so far as to base on Gen. xxv. 23 f.—
Notwithstanding what had been said in ver. 9, Thomas looked upon the
return of Jesus as leading to His death ; with His ardent temperament,
he at once expresses what is in His mind, but with the immediate
resignation and courage of love,[2] since their business was to obey the
clearly and definitely declared will of the Lord (differently in xiv. 5, xx.
24). There is no ground for charging him here with "inconsideratus
zelus" (Calvin) ; nay, "Fear and Unbelief" (Chrysostom, Euth. Zigab.) ;
dualism of Belief and Unbelief (Hengstenberg), and the like. — μετ' αὐτοῦ]
refers to Jesus,[3] not to Lazarus (Grotius, Ewald). — συμμαθητής occurs in the
New Testament only here.[4]

Ver. 17. Ἐλθών] into the neighbourhood of Bethany, see ver. 30. That
Jesus went by the direct road, may, in view of this object, be taken for
granted ; to insert here events from the Synoptic Gospels for harmonistic
purposes, only causes confusion. — εὗρεν] namely, by inquiry. — τέσσαρασ]
As we must assume that Lazarus did not die before the day on which the

[1] Herm. *ad Vig.* p. 812; Baeuml. *Partic.* p. 15.
[2] Soph. *Fragm.* 690. Dind : θανόντι κείνῳ συνθανεῖν ἔρως μ' ἔχει. Eur. *Suppl.* 1009 ff.
[3] This reference follows in accordance with the context from ver. 8 and from καὶ ἡμεῖς, in which the καί points to Jesus. On the thought, comp. Matt. xxvi. 35 and parallels.
[4] But see Plat. *Euthyd.* p. 272 c.

words of vv. 7 ff. were spoken, whilst Jesus was made at once and directly aware of the departure of His friend, then, if the Lord, as is probable, commenced the journey on the same day, and if Lazarus, agreeably to the Jewish custom, was buried on the day of his death, two full days and parts of two other days (the first and fourth) must have been spent in travelling to Bethany. No material objection can be urged against this supposition, since we do not know how far northwards in Perea Jesus was sojourning when He received the message announcing the illness. The *usual* opinion— still entertained by Luthardt, Ebrard, Gumlich, Hengstenberg, Godet—is, that Lazarus died and was buried on the very day on which Jesus received the message. In this case Jesus must have remained that day and the two following in Peraea, and begun the journey on the fourth day (a journey which some suppose to have occupied merely ten or eleven hours, or even a shorter time),[1] and completed it on the same (Ebrard) or on the following day. On this supposition, however, Jesus would either not have known of the death of His friend before the third day, which would be quite opposed to the character and language (vv. 4, 6) of the narrative ; or else He would know of it as soon as it happened, and therefore at the time of the arrival of the messenger, which would alone accord with the tone of the entire history. In this latter case, the two days' postponement of His departure, which, notwithstanding He had resolved on, would be unnatural and aimless, and the words of ver. 4, which treat the sickness of Lazarus as still continuing, would have been inappropriate. Correctly, therefore, have Bengel (on ver. 11 with the comparison of iv. 52) and Ewald fixed the death of Lazarus as contemporaneous with vv. 7, 8, so that the occurrence of the death and the knowledge of it possessed by Jesus determined His leaving at once. They would then have arrived at Bethany on the fourth day (comp. on i. 28).

Ver. 18. This observation explains the fact mentioned in the following verse, that so many of the Ἰουδαῖοι (from the neighbouring capital) were present. — ἦν] The use of the *praet.* does not of itself necessarily imply that Bethany had ceased to exist at the time when the writer wrote, but might be explained (as it usually is) from the general connection with the past events narrated.[2] Still, as John is the only one of the evangelists who thus uses the *praet.* (see besides xviii. 1, xix. 41), and as he wrote a considerable time after the destruction of Jerusalem, it is more natural to suppose that Jerusalem and the surrounding region were conceived by him as lying waste, and Bethany as *no longer existing.* — ἀπὸ σταδίων δεκαπ.] *fifteen stadia off, i.e.* about three-eighths of a geographical mile. On this mode of describing the distance (Apoc. xiv. 20) see Buttm. *Neut. Gr.* p. 133 [E. T. p. 153]. Compare also xii. 1, and on Acts x. 30. A stadium = 589⅓ feet Rhenish (606¾ feet English) measure.

Ver. 19. Ἐκ τῶν Ἰουδαίων] is generally taken as equivalent to Ἱεροσολυμιτῶν, but altogether without ground. Wherever John uses the term "*the Jews,*"

---

[1] But see van der Velde, *Reise durch Syr. u. Pal.* II. p. 245 ff. The actual road was undoubtedly considerably longer than the distance in a straight line.

[2] See on Acts xvii. 21 ; Krüger on *Xen. Anab.* i. 4. 9 ; Breitenbach, *ad Xen. Hier.* 9. 4.

unless it be in the purely *national* sense (as in ii. 6, ii. 13, iii. 1, iv. 9, and frequently), to distinguish them as a *nation* from other nations, he constantly means the *Jewish opposition* to Jesus. See on i. 19. So also here.[1] On them, however, the miracle produced the noteworthy deep impression which will be recorded in vv. 45, 46. The Lazarus family, which, without doubt, was a highly respected one, must—and might it not have been so, notwithstanding its friendship with Jesus?—have had many acquaintances, perhaps also relatives, among these Jews. — πρὸς τὰς περὶ M. κ. M.] is not quite identical in force with πρὸς τὴν M. κ. M.,[2] but designates *the two sisters with their surroundings* (Bernhardy, p. 263 ; Kühner, *ad Xen. Mem.* ii. 4. 2 ; comp. Acts xiii. 13). The words might denote the sisters alone, according to later Greek usage (see Valckenaer, *Schol. ad Act.* xiii. 13 ; Lehrs *Quaest. Ep.* p. 28 ff.) ; but this usage is quite foreign to the New Testament, and in the present connection, the expression employed has its special *decorum*, they being *men* who had come. It implies, moreover, that the household was one of a *higher* class. —ἵνα παραμ. αὐτ.] The expression of sympathy and consolation, which was connected with definite formalities, lasted usually seven days.[3]

Ver. 20. Martha, now also discharging her duties as hostess, and in consequence coming more into contact with others from without, is first informed of the coming of Jesus (*how* must be left undecided), and with judicious haste goes at once to meet Him, without exciting attention by communicating the fact to her sister. — ἐκαθέζετο] The manifestations of sympathy were received *sitting*.[4]—Note the different nature of the two sisters, as in Luke x. 38 ff.

Vv. 21, 22. Εἰ ἦς ὧδε] Not a reproach, but a lament : *Hadst Thou been here*, and stayed not in the distant Peraea. — καὶ νῦν] Without ἀλλά (see the critical note) the expression simply connects past and present : *and now*, when he is dead. She then gives expression *indirectly* (" ob voti magnitudinem," Grotius) to her *confidence*, which had quickly arisen in consequence of the arrival of Jesus, that by His prayer He would be able to raise the dead one to life. Having the confidence, she expresses the *wish*. We can understand from ver. 4 why, now that the *healing* could no longer be effected, she should think of a *resurrection ;* for with her faith in Jesus, and her knowledge of His wonderful works, she must have felt sure that the declaration of ver. 4 would be fulfilled in some way or other. The less, therefore, may we adopt Calvin's judgment : " magis *affectui suo indulget*, quam se contineat sub fidei regula."— The *position of the words* αἰτήσῃ τὸν θεόν, δώσει ὁ θεός is emphatic ; and the emphasis is heightened by the repetition of ὁ θεός.[5] This word αἰτεῖσθαι, *to beg for oneself*, is not elsewhere used of *Jesus* praying to God (but ἐρωτᾶν, παρακαλεῖν, προσεύχεσθαι, δεῖσθαι) ; it corresponds to the intensity of Martha's *emotion*, which would lead her to choose the more concrete, more human expression (comp. Matt. vii. 9 ; John xv. 16, *al.*). Thus

---

[1] Compare Brückner, Gumlich, Godet.
[2] So Lachmann after B. C. L. X. א.
[3] 1 Sam. xxxi. 13 ; 1 Chron. x. 12 ; Judith xvi. 23. See Lightfoot, p. 1070 ff.

[4] See Geier, *de Luctu Hebraeorum*, p. 211 ff. Comp. Dougt. *Anal. ad Ez.* viii. 14.
[5] Comp. *Xen. Mem.* i. 3. 2 : εὔχετο δὲ πρὸς τοὺς θεοὺς . . . ὡς τοὺς θεοὺς κάλλιστα εἰδότας.

naïvely, as to *form*, does she speak in the excitement of her feeling ; for the idea of the superhuman relation of Jesus to God had not as yet presented itself in any way to her mind.   But as to *substance* she was right ; see vv. 41, 42.

Vv. 23, 24. Jesus understood her, and promises ἀναστήσεται ὁ ἀδ. σου !
He meant [1] to carry out the purpose stated in ver. 11, but *expressed* Himself ambiguously—no doubt intentionally—in order to lead the faith of Martha away from her merely personal interest, and to raise it rather to the higher general domain of the one thing that is needful.   His words might as easily denote a raising up to be accomplished at once, as the resurrection at the last day.   Martha ventures to take it only as a consolatory word of promise relatively to Lazarus' participation in this *latter* resurrection ; she had previously dared to hope for so much, that she was not now able to interpret so indefinite a reply in her own favour.   Accordingly, her response expresses that resignation of disappointed expectation, which would now so naturally present itself to her mind ; an answer full of submission, and not one of " as it were further inquiry." [2]

Vv. 25, 26. Jesus connects with her answer that which He intended to say, as fitted to draw her faith from her own interest to *His person : I*, no other than I, *am the resurrection and the life*, *i.e.* the personal *power* of both, the one who raises again, and who makes alive.   Comp. xiv. 6 ; Col. iii. 4. The ζωή *after* the ἀνάστασις is its positive *result* (not its *ground*, as Luthardt and Ewald think), the *eternal* life, which, however, also presupposes the happy state of ζωή in Hades, in Paradise (Luke xvi. 22, xxiii. 43).   In the course of what follows, Jesus tells who it is that *experiences* Him as this power of resurrection and life, [3] namely, ὁ πιστεύων εἰς ἐμέ.   The thought is in both clauses the same ; they form a parallelism with a positive and negative declaration concerning the same subject, which, however, in the second clause, is described not merely by πιστεύων again, but by ζῶν καὶ πιστεύων, because this was the only way of making the significant antithetical reciprocal relationship complete.   With a view to this end, *dying* denotes in the first clause physical death, whereas in the second clause it is used in the higher sense ; whereas, *vice versâ*, *life* is spoken of in the first clause in the higher sense, in the second in its physical sense.   *Whoso believeth in me, even if he shall have died* (physically), *will live* (be a partaker of life *uninterruptedly*, as, prior to the resurrection, in Paradise, so, by means of the resurrection, *eternally*) ; *and every one who lives* (is still alive in time) *and believes in me, will assuredly not die for ever*, *i.e.* he will not lose his life in eternity; viii. 51,—a promise which, though not excluding physical death in itself, does

---

[1] That is, He meant the *raising of Lazarus*, which *actually* afterwards took place, and which was the fulfilment of the ἐξυπνίζειν ; παλίνορσος ἐγείρεται, Nonnus. Quite in opposition to the progress and connection of the narrative, with its beautiful significance, is Hengstenberg's remark : " Jesus means *specially* the resurrection at *the last day*, and along with this, also, *His trans-*

ference to Paradise."   The soul of the deceased must already have *been* in Paradise, Luke xxiii. 43.

[2] De Wette, compare Calvin.

[3] It is not merely ζωή that is carried out in what follows (Luthardt) ; for the life which Jesus ascribes to the believer, even in death, finds its completion precisely in the resurrection.

exclude it as the negation of the true and eternal ζωή, vi. 50. Compare Rom. viii. 10. In accordance herewith, ζῶν neither can nor may be taken in the *spiritual* sense (Calvin and Olshausen) : to apply κἂν ἀποθ., however, to Lazarus, and ζῶν to the sisters,[1] is inadmissible, simply because Lazarus was to be raised again solely to *temporal* life. Both are to be left in their generality.—On πᾶς Bengel remarks ingeniously : "hoc versu 25 non adhibitum ad majora sermonem profert," and on πιστ. τοῦτο : "applicatio . . . per improvisam interrogationem valde pungens."

Vv. 27, 28. Martha's answer *affirms* the question, and gives the *reason* for the affirmation ; for to Messiah alone could and must we be indebted for that which is mentioned in ver. 25 f.[2] — ἐγώ] with the emphasis of conscious assurance. — πεπίστευκα] I have convinced myself, and believe. Comp. vi. 69. — ὁ Χριστός, ὁ υἱὸς τοῦ θεοῦ] The second predicate, although conceived by Martha still in the popular theocratic sense, and not yet understood in its *essentially* divine import (comp. on i. 50), satisfactorily expresses her faith in the divinely-conferred ἐξουσία of her friend, and is correlative to the ὁ εἰς τ. κόσμ. ἐρχόμενος, and to be connected with it. The *present* ἐρχόμενος is employed because she looks for the advent of the Messiah as close at hand. Compare on Matt. xi. 3 ; Luke ii. 25, 38. — Ver. 28. That Martha called her sister *at the bidding of Jesus*, is clear from καὶ φωνεῖ σε ; and any doubt as to whether He actually commissioned her to do so is baseless.[3] — λάθρα] not openly, that is, *whispering* these words to her *secretly*, so that the Ἰουδαῖοι in ver. 31 who were present—these men so hostilely disposed towards the beloved Teacher—might not observe *what* she should say to her, in order that they might not disturb the further consolation and elevation which she now, with the faith in her heart that she had just so decidedly expressed, expected for her sister and herself from Jesus. — ὁ διδάσκ.] This designation, which had probably been customary in the family, was sufficiently intelligible to her sister ; she did *not need* to mention His name, nor does she *mention* it, for the sake of secrecy. Compare Mark xiv. 14.

Vv. 30, 31. He had remained *outside the place*, not, however, because of the proximity of the grave (He did not even know where it was, ver. 34, against Hengstenberg and others), but doubtless because Martha had informed Him of the presence of the many Ἰουδαῖοι,—which it was so natural for Martha to do, that Luthardt should not have called it in question. He did not desire their presence while He said to Mary what He intended to say, for which reason also He had her called *secretly*. His intention, however, was not realized, for the Jews thought that when Mary went away so hastily she had gone to the grave,[4] and followed after her, in order not to leave her alone in her sorrow without words of sympathy and consolation. On εἰς τ. μνημ. comp. ver. 38, xx. 1.

---

[1] Euth. Zigabenus, Theophylact.

[2] The simple and full affirmation of what was asked is contained therefore in ναί, κύριε, and ἐγὼ πεπίστευκα is not a *Confiteor* freely formed by Martha in response to the question (Godet, after Lange) ; on the contrary, her *Confiteor* is *contained* in the words ναί, κύριε, and the further words πεπίστευκα, etc., express the holy *foundation* on which her ναί rested in her heart.

[3] Brückner, compare Tholuck ; Hengstenberg, after Chrysostom.

[4] On this custom see Geier, *de Luctu Hebr* VII. 26, and Wetstein.

Ver. 32. Ἔπεσεν, etc.] Not so Martha, ver. 21. Mary's feelings were of an intenser and stronger kind. — αὐτοῦ πρὸς τ. πόδας] *at His feet* (πρός, Mark v. 22, vii. 25). So afterwards, μου ὁ ἀδελφός, *my brother* had not died, as in xiii. 6, and very often in the New Testament and in the classics.[1] — εἰ ἦς ὧδε, etc.] like Martha in ver. 21, but without adding anything beyond her tears. This thought had unquestionably been the oft-repeated refrain of their mutual communications on the subject of their sorrow.—No further conversation takes place, because the Ἰουδαῖοι by coming with her disturbed them, vv. 31, 33 ; according to Luthardt, because Jesus wished a *deed* to take the place of *words ;* but of this there is no hint in the text.

Vv. 33, 34. — Τοὺς συνελθ. αὐτῇ Ἰουδ.] *The Jews who had come with her* (see on Mark xiv. 53). Note the emphatic κλαίουσαν . . . κλαίοντας. — ἐνεβριμήσατο τῷ πνεύματι] Alone correct are the renderings of the Vulgate : *infremuit* spiritu ; of the Gothic : *inrauhtida* ahmin ; and of Luther : er *ergimmete* im Geiste, *He was angered* in the spirit. On τῷ πνεύματι, comp. xiii. 21 ; Mark viii. 12 ; Acts xvii. 16. The words βριμάομαι and ἐμβριμάομαι are never used otherwise than of hot *anger* in the Classics, the Septuagint, and the New Testament (Matt. ix. 30 ; Mark i. 43, xiv. 5), save where they denote snorting or growling proper.[2] For this reason the explanation of sharp *pain* (so also Grotius, Lücke, Tholuck, who thinks the word denotes a painful, sympathetic, and shuddering movement, not expressed in sounds, B. Crusius, Maier, and several ; compare already Nonnus) must be rejected at the very outset, as opposed to the usage of the word. The same applies also to Ewald's notion[3] that it is simply a somewhat stronger term for στενάζειν or ἀναστενάζειν (Mark vii. 34 ; comp. viii. 12). But at *what* was He *angered?* This is not expressed by τῷ πνεύματι (against this supposition ἐν ἑαυτῷ in ver. 38 is sufficiently decisive), as though He were angry at being affected as He was (τῷ πάθει). This view, which quite misconceives the humanity of Jesus, is taken by Origen, Chrysostom, Theophylact, Euth. Zigabenus, and several others.[4] Nor was His anger enkindled at *death as the wages of sin ;*[5]

[1] See Kühner, § 627 A 4 ; Stallbaum, *ad Plat. Rep.* p. 518 C.

[2] Aeschyl. *Sept.* 461 ; Lucian, *Necyom.* 20. See Gumlich, p. 265 f.

[3] " As though compelled to gather up all the deepest powers of love and compassion, first, in deepest emotion, repeatedly sighing and weeping," *Gesch. Christi,* p. 486. Somewhat differently in the *Johann. Schr.* I. p. 322 : " Like an old hero of the primeval age, like a Jacob, who, gathering together the deepest forces of his spirit, prepares for the combat, and in the midst of the struggle weeps aloud." Melanchthon has a similar idea.

[4] To much the same effect is Cyril's view, who takes τῷ πνεύματι to mean the *Holy* Spirit, and to be used *instrumentally :* τῇ δυνάμει τοῦ ἁγίου πνεύματος, Jesus was angered at the human compassion which He had felt.

Hilgenfeld, in his *Lehrbegr.* p. 260, *Evang.* p. 296 (comp. Köstlin, p. 139), has recently modified this view as follows : a genuinely human feeling threatened to tear away the human person joined with the Logos from His fellowship with the Logos, and the displeasure of the Logos was therefore only able to express itself inwardly, to vent itself on the humanity. See, on the contrary, Weiss, *Lehrbegr.* p. 257. Interpretations like these spring from a soil which lies altogether outside the domain of exegesis. More simply, but also doing violence to the moral nature of the human compassion felt by Jesus, is the view taken by Merz (in *die Würtemb. Stud.* 1844, 2) : He became angry with Himself because He felt as if His heart would break.

[5] Augustine, Corn. à Lapide, Olshausen, Gumlich.

nor at the *power of death* (Melanchthon, Ebrard),[1] the dread foe of the human race (Hengstenberg); nor at the *unbelief* of the Jews (Erasmus, Scholten) as well as of the sisters (Lampe, Kuinoel, Wichelhaus ;[2] nor, finally, at the fact *that He had not been able to avert this melancholy occurrence* (de Wette). The last-mentioned notion is appropriate neither to the idea, nor to the degree of anger, nor to ver. 4 ; and all these references are *forced* into the text. Brückner's opinion : the anger is that of the Redeemer misunderstood by His enemies, and not understood by His friends, is also an importation ; so also Godet's forced expedient : Jesus was *indignant* that, in performing this His greatest miracle, to which He found Himself pressed by the sobbings of those who were present, *He should be pronouncing His own death-sentence ; Satan* purposed making it the signal of His condemnation, and some even of those who were weeping were destined to become *His accusers.* Of all which nothing is either found or hinted at in the passage. The reference lying in the context was overlooked in consequence of the word Ἰουδαῖοι not being taken in the sense in which it is constantly used by John, namely, as the designation of the hostile party. It must be remembered that, in ver. 38 also, this inward wrath of the Lord was aroused by the behaviour of the Jews noticed in ver. 37. He was angered, then, at the *Jews,* when He saw them lamenting with the deeply-feeling Mary, and professing by their cries (of condolence) to share her feelings, while at the same time aware of their bitter hostility to Him who was the beloved friend both of those who mourned and of him whom they mourned, nor is ver. 45 inconsistent therewith. The moving cause of His wrath therefore lay solely in that which the text states (ὡς εἶδεν . . . κλαίοντας); the separative expression : αὐτὴν κλαίουσαν . . . Ἰουδαίους κλαίοντας, sets forth the contrast presented by the procedure of the two, while going on together before Him. Alongside of the lamentation of Mary, He could not but see that the weeping of the *Jews* was *hypocritical,* and this excited His strong moral indignation and wrath. John has simply expressed this indignation by the right term, without, as Lange thinks, combining in ἐνεβριμήσ. the most varied emotions of the mind, as in a " *divine thunderstorm of the spirit.*" By the addition of τῷ πνεύματι the indignation experienced by Jesus is defined as having been *felt in the depths of His moral self-consciousness.* During this experience, also, the πνεῦμα of Jesus was a πνεῦμα ἁγιωσύνης ; see on Rom. i. 4. John might also have written τῇ ψυχῇ (see on xii. 27); but τῷ πνεύματι is more characteristic. — καὶ ἐτάραξεν ἑαυτόν] not equivalent to ἐταράχθη τῷ πνεύματι, xiii. 21 ; nor even denoting, " *He allowed* Himself to be troubled (agitated), *surrendered Himself to the agitation*" (de Wette); but, as the active with the reflective pronoun necessarily requires, *He agitated Himself,* so that the *outward manifes-*

---

[1] So also Luthardt (who is followed by Weber in his v. *Zorne Gottes,* p. 24): " He was angered at death and him who has the power of death, His antagonist, that he had done such a thing to Him, that he had thus penetrated into His innermost circle, and had thus, as it were, thrown out threatenings against Himself." Comp. Kahnis, *Dogmatik,* I. p. 504, " at the *unnaturalness* of death."

[2] *Komm üb. d. Leidensgesch.* p. 66 f.

tation, the bodily shuddering, during the internal movement of indignation, is designated by the words, and not the emotion itself.[1] Euth. Zigabenus remarks, in the main correctly : διέσεισε· συμβαίνει γὰρ τινάσσεσθαι τὰ ἀνώτερα μέρη τῶν οὕτως ἐμβριμωμένων. The use of the reflective expression has no dogmatic basis (Augustine, Bengel, and several ; also Brückner and Ebrard suppose that it was designed to exclude the notion of the *passivity* of the emotion), but is simply due to its being more descriptive and picturesque. The reader is made to *see* how Jesus, in His inner indignation, *shakes Himself and shudders*. — ποῦ τεθείκ. αὐτόν ;] This question He puts to Mary and Martha, and it is they who answer it. Having experienced the stirrings of indignation, without any further delay, gathering Himself up for action, He now asks that which it was in the first instance *necessary* for Him to know. The assumption made by Hengstenberg,[2] that He already *knew* that which He asked, is due solely to exegetical assumptions, and reduces the question to a mere formality.

Ver. 35. 'Εδάκρ. ὁ 'Ι.] He weeps,[3] while on His way to the sepulchre, with those who were weeping. Mark the eloquent, deeply-moving *simplicity* which characterizes the narrative ; and remark as to the subject-matter, how, before accomplishing His work, Jesus gives full vent to the *sorrow* which He felt for His friend, and for the suffering inflicted on the sisters. It is also worthy of notice, that δακρύειν is here used, and not again κλαίειν,— His lamenting is a *shedding of tears* in quiet anguish, not a weeping with loud lamentation, not a κλαυθμός as over Jerusalem, Luke xix. 41. It is a delicate discrimination of expressions, unforced, and true. According to Baur, indeed, tears for a dead man, whose grave was being approached in the certainty of his being raised to life again, could not be the expression of a true, genuinely human sympathy. As though such sympathy could measure itself by any merely reflective standard, and as if the death of His friend, the grief of those who surrounded Him, and the wailings of the sisters, were not sufficient, *of themselves*, to arouse His loving sympathy to tears ! It is precisely a genuine human emotion, which neither could nor should resist the painful impression produced by such a moment. But they obliterate the delicate character of this trait with their hard dogmatic hand, who make the tears shed by Christ refer to " the *misery of the human race* pictured forth in Lazarus" (Hengstenberg, comp. Gumlich).

Vv. 36, 37. The 'Ιουδαῖοι express themselves variously : those who were better disposed say, How must He have *loved* Lazarus whilst alive (*imper.*), if He thus weeps for him now that he is dead ! Those who were maliciously and wickedly disposed treat His tears as a welcome proof, not of His want of love (Luthardt), but of His *inability*, apart from which He must surely have been able to heal Lazarus of his *sickness*, even as He had healed the blind man of his blindness ! In this way they at the same time threw doubt on the reality of the healing of the blind man (for they regard it as the

---

[1] As Hengstenberg maintains ("Jesus stirs Himself up to energetic struggle," etc.) ; compare also Godet.

[2] So also Gumlich, after Augustine, Eras-mus, Jansen, and others.

[3] [Incept. Aor.; He began to weep : burst into tears.—K.]

majus in their conclusion *ad minus*), and suppose, moreover, that Jesus did not come sooner to Bethany because He was unable to save Lazarus ; for the conclusion drawn by them implies that He had received information concerning the sickness. The *malicious* import of the question in ver. 37 has been correctly recognized by Chrysostom, Nonnus (ἀντιάχησαν), Theophylact, Euth. Zigabenus, Erasmus, Calvin, Bengel, and most of the older commentators, as also by Luthardt, Lange, and Godet ; some recent writers, however, as Lücke, de Wette, Tholuck, Maier, Brückner, Ewald, Gumlich, Hengstenberg, groundlessly reject this view, notwithstanding that the following words, πάλιν ἐμβριμ., rightly interpreted, find their explanation in these expressions of His opponents.—The circumstance of their appealing to the *healing of the blind man*, instead of to the *awakenings from the dead*, recorded by the Synoptics, is no argument against the reality of the latter miracles (Strauss) ; nor even is this appeal less appropriate (de Wette), but it was, on the contrary, naturally suggested by their *own most recent experience ;* it was also thoroughly appropriate, inasmuch as they were thinking, not of a raising from the dead, but simply of a *healing* of Lazarus, which was to have been effected by Jesus. — ἵνα] the thought is : be active, *in order that.* Comp. on Col. iv. 16. — καὶ οὗτος] like the blind man whom He healed. For the *healing* (the opposite of μὴ ἀποθάνῃ) is the point of comparison.

Ver. 38. This πονηρία (Chrysostom) of the τινές stirred afresh, in the midst of His pain, His deep, though quiet, indignation ; in this case, however, it was less noticeable, not being attended with the ταράσσειν ἑαυτόν of ver. 33. — εἰς τὸ μνημεῖον] *to the grave* (not *into*, see what follows ; comp. ver. 31). The sepulchral vaults were entered either by a perpendicular opening with steps, or by an horizontal one ; they were closed either by a large stone, or by a door. They exist in great numbers, down to the present day.[1] The grave of Lazarus would have been of the first kind if ἐπέκειτο ἐπ' αὐτῷ be rendered : *it lay upon it ;* the one at present shown as the grave of Lazarus, though probably without sufficient reason,[2] is such. But ἐπέκ. ἐπ' αὐτ. may also mean : *it lay against it, before it ;* [3] and then the reference would be to a grave with an horizontal entrance. No decision can be arrived at. The description of the grave would seem to imply that Lazarus was a man of some position.

Vv. 39, 40. While Jesus called upon those present to take away the stone (which was done, as related in ver. 41), Mary waited in silent resignation. On Martha, however, with her mobile practical tendency, the command of Jesus, which implied a desire to *see* Lazarus, produced a *terrifying* effect. Her sisterly heart (hence ἡ ἀδελφὴ τοῦ τετελ.) shudders at the thought, and rises up against it, and she wishes not to see the corpse of her beloved brother, already passing over into a state of putrefaction, exposed to the gaze of those who were present ;—from the fact of his having already lain four days, she *concludes*, with good reason, that he must already have begun to stink. For her earlier idea of a possible resurrection (ver. 22), which,

---

[1] Robinson, II. p. 175 ff., and his more recent *Researches*, p. 327 ff. ; Tobler, *Golgotha*, p. 251 ff.

[2] See Robinson, II. p. 310.

[3] Comp. Hom. *Od.* 6. 19 : θύραι δ' ἐπέκειντο.

moreover, had been entertained only for a time, had passed over, owing to the expressions of the Lord in vv. 23–26, into faith in Christ, as the *Resurrection* and the Life in general, through whom the dear departed one also liveth (ver. 26). Accordingly, it is incorrect to suppose that her wish was to call the attention of Jesus to the magnitude of the work to be performed by Him, with a view to calling forth a new confirmation of His promise (Hengstenberg) ; on the contrary, far removed from such reflections, she now *no longer at all expects the reawakening of the corpse,* and that, too, not from unbelief, but because the higher direction which her faith had received through Christ's words had taught her resignation. — The *embalming* of the body (its fumigation, embrocation, and envelopment in spices, as also its anointing, xii. 7) can *not* have taken place ; otherwise Martha could not have come to the conclusion which she expresses. This omission may have been due to some cause unknown to us ; but the supposition that the sisters still *intended* carrying out the embalming is inadmissible owing to the ἤδη ὄζει. — τεταρταῖος] *of the fourth day* (comp. on ver. 17), that is, one buried for that time.[1]— The gentle reproof contained in ver. 40 refers to vv. 23 ff., and is justified ; for that which He had said regarding the glory of God in ver. 4 was to be realized through the *resurrection* promised in ver. 23—promised in the sense present to Christ's mind. At the same time, the performance of the miracle was itself dependent on the fulfilment of the condition ἐὰν πιστεύσ. (which had been required also in vv. 25 f.) ; to *unbelieving* sisters He could no more have restored the dead brother than to an unbelieving Jairus his child (Luke viii. 50), or to the widow of Nain her son, if her attitude towards His compassion and His injunction μὴ κλαῖε (Luke vii. 13) had been one of unbelief.

Vv. 41, 42. Jesus *knows* that His prayer, that God would suffer Him to raise Lazarus to life,—a prayer which He had previously offered up in stillness, perhaps only in the inarticulate yearnings of His heart,—has been heard, and He *thanks* God for hearing it. Petition and thanksgiving are not to be conceived as blended in one ;[2] nor is the latter to be regarded as *anticipatory* (Hengstenberg), as though He *offered* thanks in the certain anticipation of the hearing of His *prayer* (Ewald, comp. Godet). Not that He offers thanks because the hearing of His prayer was unexpected and unhoped for (εἶπον) ; no, He for His part (ἐγώ) knew, even while He was asking God in stillness, that God always heard Him ;[3] but because of the people standing by, etc. — Some have stumbled at ver. 42, and looked on it either as *spurious*,[4] or as a *reflection of the evangelist* who puts this "show-prayer" (Weisse), or even "sham-prayer" (Baur), into the mouth of Christ for the purpose of supplying an argument for the story (de Wette ; see, on the other hand, Brückner), or for the divinity of Christ (Strauss, Scholten).

[1] See Wetstein. Comp. Xen. *Anab.* vi. 4. 9: ἤδη γὰρ ἦσαν πεμπταῖοι (dead) ; Diog. Laert. 7. 184.
[2] Merz in *die Wurtemburg. Stud.* 1844, 2, p. 65 ; Tholuck.
[3] Correct reason for this : πάντοτε θέλεις ἃ θέλω (Euth. Zigabenus) ; but also conversely, πάντοτε θέλω ἃ θέλεις ; see v. 30, xii. 27.
[4] Dieffenbach in Bertholdt's *Krit. Journ.* vol. i. p. 8.

But it is precisely He who is most intimate with the Father, who may indulge in reflection even in prayer, if His reflections relate to God, and *are* prayer. The opposite judgment applies an arbitrary standard to the subject. Moreover, if it had been *his own* reflection, John would probably have said: διὰ τοὺς Ἰουδαίους instead of διὰ τ. ὄχλον. Comp. ver. 45. — εἶπον] as in vi. 36 : *I will have said it,* namely the εὐχαριστῶ σοι, etc. To refer to ver. 4 (Ewald) is inadmissible even on account of διὰ τ. ὄχλον alone. — σύ] Thou and no other. They shall be convinced of it by learning from my thanksgiving that *my* working takes place in *Thy* strength, in the full certainty of a victory of *Thy* sending.

Vv. 43–46. *With a loud voice, He cried out ;* this was the mighty medium through which He caused His miraculous power to operate. — The expression δεῦρο ἔξω (*hither out! huc foras!* without verb,)[1] includes in itself the resurrection-call, but does not imply that the act of reawakening has been already performed (Origen). Nonnus correctly remarks : ἄπνοον ἐψύχωσε δέμας νεκυοσσόος ἠχώ. Jesus did not here call out ἐγείρου or ἐγέρθητι (as in the case of the daughter of Jairus, and of the son of the widow of Nain, Luke viii. 54, vii. 15), because the words δεῦρο ἔξω seemed the most natural to employ in the case of a dead man already lying *in the tomb.* — δέδεμ. τ. πόδ. κ. τ. χεῖρ. κειρίαις] By Basil (θαύμαζε θαῦμα ἐν θαύματι), Chrysostom, Euth. Zigabenus, Augustine, Ruperti, Aretius, Lightfoot, Lampe, and several others, this is regarded as a *new miracle,* to which is reckoned, besides, even the covering up of the countenance. An arbitrary disfiguration of the fact to the point of introducing apocryphal elements. It is not necessary, with the purpose of escaping from this view, that the Aor. ἐξῆλθε should be understood *de conatu* (Kuinoel) ; nor to assume that each limb was enwrapped *by itself,* as was the custom in *Egypt* (Olshausen, de Wette, B. Crusius, Maier) ; but the winding-sheet in which the corpse was wound from head to foot (Matt. xxvi. 59), thus embracing the entire body,[2] might, especially as it had to hold no spices (ver. 39), be slack and loose enough to render it possible, after it had been loosened by his movements, for the awakened man to come forth. He was not completely freed from the grave-clothes, till the command λύσατε αὐτόν had been given. — κειρία] *Girdle, bandage ;* in the N. T. it occurs only here, but see Prov. vii. 16.[3] — καὶ ἡ ὄψις αὐτοῦ σουδ. περιεδ.] *special* mention is here added of the last part of the complete death-dress in which he issued forth from the tomb, not, however, in the participial form.[4] *His face was bound about with a napkin.*[5] — λέγει αὐτοῖς] to those who were present in general, as in ver. 39. *Let him go away* (comp. xviii. 8). With strength so completely restored had he risen again. But any further excitement was now to be avoided.

OBSERVATION. — *On the history of the resurrection of Lazarus, which constitutes the culminating point* of the miraculous activity of our Lord, we have to remark :

---

[1] Comp. Hom. *Od.* ϑ. 192 ; Plat. *Pol.* iv. p. 445 D, v. p. 477 ; D. Stallb. *ad Plat. Apol.* p. 24 C.

[2] See Jahn, *Arch.* I. 2, p. 424.

[3] Aristoph. *Av.* 817 ; Plut. *Alc.* 16.

[4] Kühner, II. p. 423.

[5] On περιεδ. comp. Job xii. 8 ; Plut. *Mor.* p. 825 E.

(1) the assumption of a merely *apparent death*[1] is decidedly opposed, both to the character of Jesus Himself, and to the style and purpose of the narrative, which is distinguished for its thoughtful tenderness, certainty, and truthfulness. (2) To reduce the account to a strange *misunderstanding*, which either makes a conversation between Christ and the two sisters, on the occasion of the death of Lazarus, regarding the resurrection, originate the story of the miracle,[2] or (with Gfrörer[3]) confounds the latter with the account of the awakening of the (only apparently dead) youth of *Nain*, — Nain being thus an abridgment of the name *Bethany*, — or which converts, in the tradition prevailing at Ephesus, the Lazarus of the parable in Luke xvi. into a Lazarus raised from the dead by Jesus (Schenkel), is an arbitrary and violent procedure, simply incompatible with the genuineness of the Gospels. (3) The complete *annihilation* of the history into a *myth* (Strauss) is a consequence of assumptions which, in connection with so detailed and unique a narrative as this,[4] reach the very acme of boldness and arbitrariness, in order to demonstrate by misrepresentation of individual features the existence of internal improbabilities, and the want of external evidence for the credibility of the narrative. (4) The *subjective theory* of the occurrence, which makes it to be a form created[5] by the writer himself for the purpose of setting forth the idea of the δόξα of Christ (Baur, p. 191 ff.), which claims adequate recognition only when it demonstrates its death-denying power (comp. Keim, *Gesch. J. I.* p. 132), makes out of the miracle of the history a miraculous production of the second century, a creation of the idea in a time which bore within itself the conditions for productions of quite a different kind. That very *artistic* style of representation which, in the account of this last and greatest miracle, is most strikingly prominent, is only comprehensible from the personal, profound, and sympathizing recollection which had preserved and cherished, even in its finest traits, the truth and reality of the event with peculiar vivacity, fidelity, and inspiration. No narrative of the N. T. bears so completely the stamp of being the opposite of a later invention. But in none, again, was the glow of the hope of the Messianic fulfilment so immediately operative to preserve and animate each feature of the reminiscence. This also in answer to Weizsäcker, p. 528, who leaves it undecided how far the *allegorical* point of the narrative assumed by him—the setting forth, namely, of the doctrine that believers have everlasting life—is attached to *actual facts*. But in this way, with ideal assumptions, even the best attested history would fall into the dead condition of *à priori* doubt. And what an incredible height of art in the allegorical construction of history must we ascribe to the composer!

---

[1] Paulus, Gabler in his *Journ. für auserl. theol. Lit.* III. p. 235 ff. ; Ammon, *Leben Jesu*, III. p. 128 ; Kern in the *Tüb. Zeitschr.* 1839, I. p. 182 ; Schweizer, p. 153 ff.

[2] Weisse, II. p. 260 ff.

[3] *Heiligth. und Wahrh.* p. 311 ff.

[4] Ewald, *Gesch. Chr.* p. 484. "No narrative of this apostle is pervaded by so intense a glow and rapid liveliness of description as this, in which he undertakes to set forth, in one great picture, the trembling of Jesus for the life of His friend, the attendant struggle with the darkness of the world, and the calmness and joy of victory, prominent over all, and undisturbed from first to last ; while between these press in the still higher tones of the consciousness of His Messianic glory and of its confirmation in power."

[5] This subjective picture would seem, according to Baur, p. 247, an intensification of the (two) synoptical raisings from the dead (comp. Scholten) : "the superlative to the lower degrees, on which the Synoptics remain." The name Lazarus is significantly taken from the parable, Luke xvi. The substantial contents of the narrative are in ver. 25, and all else unsubstantial form.

Yet Holtzmann also [1] appears to think only of an allegory ("living hieroglyph"). (5) It appears, indeed, surprising *that the Synoptics are silent concerning the raising of Lazarus,* an event in itself so powerful to produce conviction,[2] and so influential in its operation on the last development of the life of Jesus. Yet this is not inexplicable (Brückner), but is connected with the entire distinguishing peculiarity of John ; and the *argumentum e silentio* employed against *the latter* must—the genuineness of the Gospel being granted—rather turn against the Synoptics if their silence were conceivable only as the consequence of their want of acquaintance with the history (Lücke, de Wette, Baur). But this silence is intelligible, not on the supposition of tender considerateness towards the family at Bethany,[3] in which—even setting aside the fact that Luke also wrote only a few years earlier than John, and not before the destruction of Jerusalem—there is suggested something altogether arbitrary,[4] and in unexampled contradiction to the feeling and spirit of that early Christian time. Just as little is it to be explained from the fact that the deep and mysterious character of the history placed it in the class of what belonged to the special mission of that evangelist who had been in most confidential relations with Jesus (Hengstenberg),[5]—a view which is not to be adopted, for the reason that the synoptical raisings from the dead also are not less profound and mysterious, as lies, indeed, in the *facts themselves.* Rather is that silence of the Synoptics only comprehensible when we consider that they so limit the circle of their narratives that, before they open, with the entrance of Christ into Jerusalem (Matt. xxi. and parall.)—and thus with the so-called Passion-week, the scene of the last development—they have introduced nothing of the Lord's ministry in the metropolis and its immediate neighbourhood ; but up to that point confine themselves absolutely to his proceedings in Galilee, and generally to those quite remote from Jerusalem (the geographically nearest miraculous work being the healing of the blind men at Jericho, Matt. xx. 29 ff.). This, as their Gospels actually prove, is the *allotted province* to which the older evangelistic historical writings confined their task and performance, and this included the Galilean raisings from the dead, but excluded that of Lazarus. John, on the other hand, conversely, choosing from the different classes of miracles, selected out of the raisings from the dead not a Galilean one, but that which lay beyond that older theatre of the Saviour's history, and was most closely connected with

[1] *Judenth. u. Christenth.* p. 657.

[2] It is well known what Spinoza himself (according to Bayle, *Dict.*) is said to have confessed : "that could he have persuaded himself of the truth of the raising of Lazarus, he would have rent in pieces his whole system, and would have embraced without repugnance the ordinary faith of Christians."

[3] Epiphanius, Grotius, Wetstein on xii. 10, Herder, Schulthess, Olshausen, Baeumlein, Godet ; so also with pictorial fancifulness, Lange, *L. J.* II. 2, p. 1133 f.

[4] It would have certainly sufficed, instead of passing over the entire history in silence, simply not to have mentioned the *names*, as in the case of Peter's smiting with the sword. And is it supposed, then, that when

the synoptists wrote (thirty years and more after the Lazarus incident), the resolution to put him to death, xii. 10, was still to be feared ! Is it known that at so late a period Lazarus and his sisters were still alive ?

[5] So also Philippi, *der Eingang des Joh. Ev.* 1866, p. 11 f. He thinks that *Matthew* related nothing of that which was reserved for *John ;* that he *knew* that *the latter* also would write his Gospel. A classified distribution of the material of this kind is in itself very improbable in view of the spirit of the apostolic time, even irrespective of the fact that the first Gospel, in its present form, cannot have proceeded from the hands of the apostle.

its great final period. He has thus certainly supplied—as in general by his notices from the Judean ministry of the Lord—an essential deficiency in the older evangelical narrative. The acquaintance of the Synoptics, which is not to be doubted, with the raising of Lazarus, makes their silence regarding it appear not inexcusable (Baur's objection), but simply a consequence of that limitation which the older evangelical history had prescribed to itself, so as neither to contain any mention of the stay of Jesus in Bethany at that time, nor of His subsequent sojourn in Ephraim, but to make the Messianic entrance of Jesus to proceed from Jericho onwards, excluding any lodging in the family of Bethany ; comp. on Matt. xxi. 1, note. (6) The fact that in the accusation and condemnation of Jesus no use was made of this miracle, either against or for Him (employed by Strauss, and especially by Weisse), cannot be evidence against its historical character, since the Jews were prudent enough to give a *political* colour to their accusation, and since the disciples *could* not appear in favour of Jesus, and He Himself *would* not enter upon a more minute defence of Himself ; while Pilate, as judge, even if he had heard of the act, and had interested himself about it, yet was not warranted to introduce it into the examination, because it was not brought forward either in confirmation or refutation of the charge. Moreover, had the evangelist recorded this history merely as an introduction to the entry which follows, etc. (Keim), he could less properly have left the further development without any reference to it. (7) The impossibility of an actual awakening from the dead is relative, not absolute (as Jesus' own resurrection shows), and can yield no *à priori* counter-proof—even setting aside the fact that the ἤδη ὄζει rests on an inference only, however probable—where, as here, the worker is the bearer of the *divine life*. He certainly ascribes the result to *God;* but this applies to all His miracles, which were indeed ἔργα τοῦ πατρός, and Christ was the Accomplisher through the power of God. Hence Schleiermacher's proposal (*L. J.* p. 233) to put Christ— with the exception of the firm persuasion, that that which He prayed for will also be done by God—*outside the realm of miracle,* erroneously puts aside the question. It is *Christ* who raised Lazarus, ver. 11, but therein also exhibited an ἔργον ἐκ τοῦ πατρός, x. 33.

Vv. 45, 46. This occurrence makes an overwhelming impression upon the party adverse to Jesus, upon the ᾽Ιουδαῖοι. Many from the ᾽Ιουδαίοις — those, namely, who had come to Mary, and had seen the act of Jesus—believed on Him. A certain number, however, of them (of these who had become be-lievers) went away (from the scene of the miracle) to the Pharisees, and said to them, etc., but with *well-meaning* intent, in order to put them in posses-sion of a correct account of the act, and to bear witness to them of the miracle (comp. Origen). The *ordinary* understanding of the passage finds here *two sections among the ᾽Ιουδαῖοι who had come to Mary ;* many of them had become *believers,* but certain of them remained *unbelieving,* and the latter had denounced Jesus to the Pharisees with evil intent (as a juggler, thinks Euth. Zigabenus ; as a sacrilegious person, who had disinterred the corpse, thought Theophylact ; as a *dangerous person,* think most commentators), or communicated the fact, simply with the view of obtaining a judgment upon it (Luthardt). The error of this interpretation lies in not observing that John has not written τῶν ἐλθόντων (which is the reading of D,) but οἱ

356 THE GOSPEL OF JOHN.

ἐλθόντες, κ.τ.λ., so that ἐκ τῶν Ἰουδαίων is said *generally* of the Ἰουδαῖοι *in general*, and οἱ ἐλθόντες (*ii*, *qui*, etc.) *more closely defines* the πολλοί ; instead of τινές, however, ver. 46, there now remain no *others*, none who had *not* become believers, since ἀπῆλθον indicates that they went *away from the place* to the Pharisees, while in the preceding only the Jews *who came to Mary* are mentioned. Lachmann and Tischendorf have rightly placed a comma after Ἰουδ. — πρὸς τὴν Μαρίαν] for the same reason as in ver. 1 she was named *first*, —here she is briefly named *alone*. Hengstenberg strangely imports into the words an antithesis to those who had come only for *Simon's* sake. See on vv. 1, 2.

Vv. 47, 48. Now, since Jesus had, even according to the testimony of His earlier opponents, even raised a dead man, the matter becomes too serious for the Pharisees to permit them to look on any longer without taking a decisive step. The *chief priests* (with whom they have accordingly communicated) and *they themselves* summon a *sitting of the council*, *i.e.* a sitting of the Sanhedrin. On συνάγ. συνέδρ. comp. Diod. Sic. ii. 25. Not to be translated : they assembled *the Sanhedrin*. In that case, as everywhere, where this is expressed by συνέδρ., the article must have been used. — τί ποιοῦμεν] *what are we do?* The *Indic.* is used ;[1] for that something must *now definitively* be done, was undoubted. Comp. Acts iv. 15, 16. — ὅτι] the simple *because*, as statement of the *ground* of the question. — οὗτος ὁ ἄνθρ.] contemptuously. — οὕτω] without interposing. — καὶ ἐλεύσονται, κ.τ.λ.] so they fear, in keeping with the *political* view of the Messiah. Comp. vi. 15. And they *really* fear it (against Strauss, Weisse, who here see an invention); they do not merely delude themselves with it (Luthardt) ; nor do they wish to give to their proper motive (envy, Matt. xxvii. 18) only another colour (Calvin, Hengstenberg). Now, when they saw the last outbreak before their eyes, their calculation must necessarily be shaped according to the *popular conception* of the Messiah, and according to the effects which this notion would produce upon the mass (uproar, etc.). — ἀροῦσιν] they will *take away* (*tollent*, Vulgate), not equivalent to ἀπολέσουσιν,[2] which is less appropriate to the egoistic sense, which is concerned about the withdrawal of their *own power*. Nonnus well remarks : ἀφαρπάξουσι. — ἡμῶν] correlative to Ῥωμαῖοι, placed first *with the emphasis of egoism*, though not as genit. of separation (*away from us*), since such a construction with αἴρω is only poetical ;[3] but : the place and nation *belonging to us*. — τὸν τόπον] is to be defined solely from the emphatic ἡμῶν ; *our place*, *i.e.* the holy *city*,[4] the residence of the Sanhedrin and of the entire hierarchy. Hence neither : *the country* (so most commentators, as Luther : "country and people"), nor : the *temple*.[5] The latter is sustained neither by Acts vi. 13, nor by passages like 3 Esdr. viii. 78 ; 2 Macc. v. 19 ; Matt. xxiii. 38. The Sanhedrists apprehend that the Romans, who had, indeed, acquiesced in great

---

[1] See Stallbaum, *ad Plat. Symp.* p. 176 A.
[2] Euth. Zigabenus, Beza, Grotius, Lücke, de Wette, Tholuck, Hengstenberg, and others.
[3] Kühner, II. p. 160.

[4] Chrysostom, Grotius, Ewald, Baeumlein, Godet.
[5] Maldonatus, Lücke, de Wette, Maier, B. Crusius, Hengstenberg.

part hitherto in the hierarchical constitution of the Jews, and the spiritually political sway of the Sanhedrin, would enter Jerusalem, and remove the city as well as the people [1] from the rule of the Sanhedrin, because it knew so badly how to maintain order.

Vv. 49, 50. Caiaphas, however, solves this question of helplessness, censuring his colleagues on account of the latter, since the means to be adopted had been clearly put into their hands by circumstances. — εἰς τις] *unus quidam*. [2] This one alone was a man of counsel. — Καϊάφας] see on Matt. xxvi. 3 ; Luke iii. 2. — τοῦ ἐνιαυτοῦ ἐκείνου] He was high priest *of that year.* The previous and following time is left out of consideration, not, however, negatived, but simply *that remarkable and fatal year* is brought into prominence. Comp. xviii. 13. The supposition of an annual *change* in the office cannot be ascribed [3] even to a Pseudo-John, considering his manifest acquaintance elsewhere with Jewish affairs ; but to appeal *to the fact* that the high priests were frequently changed in those times, and that actually before Caiaphas several were only a year in office, Josephus [4] (Hengstenberg), is least of all applicable in the case of Caiaphas, who was already in office, A.D. 25. Again, the assumption of an alternative holding of the office by *Annas* and Caiaphas, in virtue of a *private* agreement (comp. on Luke, *loc. cit. ;* so Baur, ascribing this view to the Pseudo-John, and Maier [5]), is as purely arbitrary (see Bleek, p. 257) as the pretended allusion to the change of *Asiarchs* (Gfrörer). — ὑμεῖς] *you*, people. — οὐκ οἴδατε οὐδέν] that you can still ask : τί ποιοῦμεν. — οὐδὲ λογίζ.] (see critical notes) : *nor do ye consider that*, etc. The proud, discourteous style of this address evinces *passionate feeling* generally, not exactly the manner [6] of *Sadduceeism* (Hengstenberg, Godet) ; from Acts v. 17 it is by no means clear that Caiaphas was a Sadducee. — ἡμῖν] for us Sanhedrists. — Ἰn συμφέρει ἵνα, as in xvi. 7, the conception of divine destination is expressed : that it is of advantage to us *that one man must die*, etc. — ὑπέρ] *in commodum*, in order that the people may be preserved from the destruction which threatens them, ver. 48. — ἀπόληται] through their subjugation, and the overthrow of the national independent existence. — Observe the interchange of ἔθνος (the people as a *nation*) and λαός (the people as a political, here theocratic, *community*). — The principle itself, which regarded in itself may be moral and noble, is expressed in the feeling of the most ungodly and selfish policy. For similar expressions, see Schoettgen and Wetstein. To refer the scene to a legend afterwards current among the Christians (Weizsäcker), is opposed to the earnest narrative of the evangelist.

Vv. 51, 52. Observation of John, that Caiaphas did not speak this out of his own self-determination, but with these portentous words—in virtue of the high priest's office which he held in that year—involuntarily delivered

---

[1] ἔθνος, Luke, xxiii. 2 ; Acts x. 22, *et al.*

[2] Comp. Mark xiv. 47, 51, *et al. ;* Bernhardy, p. 442.

[3] Against Bretschneider, Strauss, Schenkel, Scholten.

[4] *Antt.* xviii. 2. 2.

[5] Here, too, belongs the supposition of Ebrard (apud Olshausen), that the two alternated with each other in the offering of the annual sacrifice of atonement. And that John means to say that in that year this function fell to Caiaphas. But he does *not say* so.

[6] Josephus, *Bell.* ii. 8. 14.

a *prophecy*.[1]—The high priest passed in the old Israelitish time for the bearer of the divine oracle, for the organ of the revelation of the divine decisions,[2] which were imparted to him through the interrogation of the Urim and Thummim (Ex. xxviii. 30 ; Num. xxvii. 21). This mode of inquiry disappeared, indeed, at a later time,[3] as the high-priestly dignity in general fell gradually from its glory ; yet, there is still found in the prophetic age the belief in the high priest's prophetical gift (Hos. iii. 4), as also in Josephus,[4] the idea of the old high-priesthood as the bearer of the oracle distinctly appears, and Philo[5] sets forth at least the *true* priest as prophet, and thus idealizes the relation. Accordingly—as closely connected with that venerable and not yet extinct recollection, and with still surviving esteem for the high priestly office—it was a natural and obvious course for John, after pious reflection on those remarkable words which were most appropriate to the sacrificial death of Jesus, to find in them a disclosure of the divine decree,—expressed without self-knowledge and will, —and that by no means with a "sacred irony" (Ebrard). Here, too, the extraordinary *year* in which the speaker was invested with the sacred office, carries with it the determination of the judgment ; since, if at any time, it was assuredly in this very year, in which God purposed the fulfilment of His holy counsel through the atoning death of His Son, that a revelation through the high-priestly organ appeared conceivable. ἀρχιερ. ὤν certainly bears the main emphasis : but τοῦ ἐνιαυτ. ἐκ. is again significantly added to it (not, as de Wette thinks, "mechanically, as it were"), as in ver. 49.[6] For Rabbinical passages on *unconscious* prophecies, see in Schoettgen, p. 349. The notion of prophecy, however, is different from that of the בַּת־קוֹל (against de Wette) ; comp. on xii. 27, 28. The latter is a *heavenly voice* of revelation. — ὅτι] not : *that*, according to which what follows would directly state the *contents* of προεφήτ., but : he gave utterance to a prophecy *in reference to the fact that*.[7] For what follows goes *beyond* that which the words of Caiaphas express. — ὑπὲρ τοῦ ἔθνους] Caiaphas had said : ὑπὲρ τοῦ λαοῦ ; but John turns to the *negative* part of ver. 50 (κ. μὴ ὅλ. τὸ ἔθνος ἀπόλ.), because he wishes to set the Gentiles over against the Jews, and this separation is *national*.[8] *For the benefit of* the nation Christ was to die ; for through His atoning death the Jews, for whom, in *the first instance*, the Messianic salvation was designed, iv. 22, were to become partakers through

---

[1] Here there is the conception of an *unconscious* prophecy, so far as that which Caiaphas spoke in another sense must yet, according to divine direction, *typically* set forth the substance and object of the redemptive death. See Düsterdieck, *De rei propheticae naturâ ethicâ*, Göttingen 1852, p. 76.

[2] See generally Ewald, *Alterth.* p. 385 ; Keil, *Arch.* I. p. 182.

[3] Josephus, *Antt.* iii. 8. 9.

[4] *Antt.* vi. 6. 3.

[5] *de Creat. Princ.* II. p. 367.

[6] According to Tholuck, τ. ἐνιαυτοῦ ἐκ.

should be understood in the sense that the high priest himself was bound to explain that in this year a greater and more general collective sacrifice was to be offered than that offered by him once a year on behalf of the people (Heb. ix. 7). But how can this lie in τ. ἐνιαυτοῦ ἐκ.? Especially as ἀρχιερεύς, κ.τ.λ., would seem only to make the προεφήτ. explicable, but expresses nothing as to the relation of the high-priestly *sacrifice*. This also against Luthardt's similar interpretation, I. p. 87.

[7] ii. 18, ix. 17, *et al.*

[8] Comp. Luke vii. 5 ; John xviii. 35.

faith in the eternal saving deliverance. But the object of His death extended still further than the Jews ; not for the benefit of the *nation* alone, but *in order also to bring together into one the scattered children of God.* These are the *Gentiles*, who believe on Him, and thereby are partakers of the atonement, children of God (i. 12). The expression is *prophetic*, and, just as in x. 16, *proleptic*,[1] according to the N. T. *predestinarian* point of view,[2] from which they appear as those who, in order to further their entrance into the filial state, are drawn by God (vi. 44), are given by the Father to the Son (vi. 37), and endowed with the inward preparation (vi. 65), Euth. Zigabenus rightly remarks : τέκνα μὲν οὖν τοῦ θεοῦ τὰ ἔθνη ὠνόμασεν ὡς μέλλοντα γενέσθαι. This likewise in answer to Hilgenfeld,[3] according to whom the Gentiles, as *natural* children of God, who do not first *become* so through Christianity, must be meant (but see i. 12, iii. 3, 6, *et al.*). A *filial state towards God out of* Christ is opposed to the N. T., not only as Hilgenfeld puts it, from a Gnostic, dualistic point of view, but also, as Luthardt conceives it,[4] referring the essence of it only to the *desire* after Christ (Tholuck, Weiss, Godet, to the *susceptibility*). This is only the *preliminary step* to the filial state. The *gathering into one*, i.e. *to a unity*, to an undivided community, is not intended in a *local* sense ; but, amid their local dispersion, they were to become united in a higher sense, in virtue of a faith, etc., through the κοινωνία τοῦ ἁγίου πνεύματος, as *one communion* ἐν Χριστῷ. Chrysostom aptly remarks : ἐν σῶμα ἐποίησεν· ὁ ἐν Ῥώμῃ καθήμενος τοὺς Ἰνδοὺς μέλος εἶναι νομίζει ἑαυτοῦ. The uniting with the believing *Jews*[5] is not spoken of here, but in x. 16 ; here only the Christian *folding together* of the scattered *Gentiles themselves.*[6]

Vv. 53, 54. Οὖν] In consequence of this word of Caiaphas, which prevailed. — ἵνα] They held deliberations with one another, *in order*, etc., Matt. xxvi. 4. — παῤῥησ.] frankly and freely, vii. 4. — ἐν τοῖς Ἰουδαίοις] He withdrew Himself—since those deliberations of the high council, whether through Nicodemus or otherwise, had become known to Him (οὖν)—from intercourse with His Jewish adversaries, and betook Himself to the sequestered village of *Ephraim*, according to Eusebius 8 miles, according to Jerome 20 miles[7] N.E. from Jerusalem, in Judea ; according to Josephus,[8] in the neighbourhood of Bethel, comp. 2 Chron. xiii. 20 (according to the Keri). It can hardly be the present village of *Taiyibeh*,[9] considering its more westerly situation. Hengstenberg identifies it on insufficient grounds with Baal Hazor, 2 Sam. xiii. 23 ; and Vaihinger, in Herzog's *Encycl.*, with עָפְרָה, Josh. xviii. 22. The mention of the *desert* is not opposed to the north-easterly situation of Ephraim, as Ebrard thinks ; for the desert of Judea (*i.e.* ἡ ἔρημος κατ᾽ ἐξοχήν) extended as far as the region of Jericho. — εἰς τ. χώραν,

---

[1] Calvin well remarks : " Filios ergo Dei, etiam antequam vocentur, ab electione aestimat, qui fide tandem et sibi et aliis manifestari incipiunt."

[2] Rom. ix. 24 ff., xv. 27 ; Gal. iii. 14 ; Eph. 1. 9 ff. ; Rom. viii. 29, 30, xi. 25, 26, xvi. 25, 26 ; Eph. iii. 4 ff. ; Col. i. 27 ; Acts xiii. 48, xviii. 10.

[3] *Lehrbegr.* p. 153. *Evang.* p. 297.

[4] Comp. also Messner, *Lehre der Ap.* p. 330 f.

[5] The ποιεῖν τὰ ἀμφότερα ἕν. Eph. ii. 14.

[6] For the *expression* συνάγειν (and the like) εἰς ἕν, comp. Plat. *Phileb.* p. 378 C ; Eur. *Or.* 1640. *Phoen.* 465.

[7] So also Ritter, XV. p. 465, XVI. p. 531 ff.

[8] *Bell.* iv. 9. 9.

[9] See Robinson, II. p. 337 f.

κ.τ.λ.] He departed *into the country* (as opposed to Jerusalem, the capital city) ; then a more precise defining of the place to which He withdrew, namely, *the neighbourhood of the desert ;* and, finally, definite mention of the place, *a town named Ephraim.*[1]

Ver. 55. Ἦν δὲ ἐγγ. τ. πάσχα τ. 'I.] Comp. ii. 13, vi. 4. — ἐκ τῆς χώρας] as in ver. 45,—thus : *out of the country* (as opposed to Jerusalem), not : *out of that district* (Grotius, Bengel, Olshausen). — ἵνα ἁγνίσ. ἑαυτ.] refers to the legal usages of self-purification, which varied greatly according to the degrees of the Levitical uncleannesses (washings, sacrifices, etc.). These, in compliance with the general principle of appearing before God pure,[2] were completed before the beginning of the feast, in order to obtain from the priest the declaration of ceremonial cleanness.[3] Pilgrims accordingly set out according to their needs, in good time *before* the feast ; see Lightfoot, p. 1078, and Lampe.

Ver. 56. The people, owing to the sensation which Jesus had in so many ways already aroused, and the edict of their spiritual superiors against Him (ver. 57), have taken a lively interest in the question, whether He will venture, as heretofore, to come to the feast. Their anxious *question* is a *double question ; What think you ?* (do you think) *that He certainly will not come?* Since He has not performed the pilgrimage with any of them, and is not yet present, His coming is strongly *doubted of* among them. Lücke : what do you think (in reference to this), *that* He will not, etc. But on that view His not coming would be already presupposed as *certain*, which would be premature. To understand the words in the sense that He *is not come* [4] is grammatically incorrect. The passages quoted by Hartung [5] do not apply here.[6] — The inquiry is interchanged *in the court of the temple*, because it was there that His appearance was to be looked for ; while ἑστηκότες vividly represents the groups as standing together.

Ver. 57. With the explanatory δέ (καί is spurious) the particular circumstance is now added, *on account of which* men so greatly doubted of His coming. — δεδώκεισαν] comes first with emphasis. Already had the directions of the rulers in question been given. — ἵνα] *object*, and with this contents of the ἐντολαί, the issuing of which we are to think of as the fruit of the sitting, ver. 47 ff., and of the further deliberations, ver. 53.

NOTES BY AMERICAN EDITOR.

XXXVII. *"When therefore he heard,"* etc. Ver. 6.

The rendering of this verse is not quite happy, either in the Common or the Revised Version, owing to the failure to give the force of the μέν with τότε. The Common Ver. says, " He abode two days still," apparently mistranslating

---

[1] On χώρα, comp. Plat. *Legg.* v. p. 745 C, vii. p. 817 A ; Mark i. 5 ; Acts xxvi. 20 ; 3 Macc. iii. 1.

[2] Gen. xxxv. 2 ; Ex. xix. 10, 11.

[3] Num. ix. 10 ; 2 Chron. xxx. 17, 18, *et al.* Comp. xviii. 28.

[4] Erasmus, Castalio, Paulus, and several others ; not the Vulgate.

[5] *Partikell.* II. p. 156.

[6] Tholuck (who otherwise follows our interpretation) incorrectly adduces Polyp. iii. 111. 1. In that passage μή stands with the perf. quite as in Gal. iv. 11. See Ellendt, *Lex. Soph.* II. p. 412.

τότε by "still." The Revision renders τότε correctly, but neglects μέν, and both seem to imply that *because* He heard he was sick He lingered two days in the same place. The original gives a distinctly different conception. "When He heard that he was sick, at that time, indeed, He remained two days in the place in which He was ; then, after this, He saith," etc. The concessive μέν shows that, though naturally He would have immediately gone, yet *then*—for reasons afterwards given or implied—He yet lingered two days. The matter is correctly explained by Meyer.

CHAPTER XII.

Ver. 1. ὁ τεθνηκώς] is wanting in B. L. X. ℵ. Verss. Bracketed by Lachm.,
deleted by Tisch. But those testimonies are here the less decisive, since the
word before ὃν ἐγ. ἐκ. νεκρ. ὁ 'I. appeared entirely superfluous, and hence was
easily dropped. For its addition there was no reason. — Ver. 2. ἀνακ. σὺν αὐτῷ]
Elz. : συνανακ. αὐτῷ, against decisive testimonies. — Ver. 4. Instead of 'Ιούδ.
Σίμ. 'Ισκαρ., Tisch. has merely 'Ιούδας ὁ 'Ισκαρ., and that before εἷς, according
to B. L. ℵ. Cursives, Verss., where, however, the position before εἷς is not so
strongly supported. Σίμωνος was, after vi. 71, xiii. 2, 26, readily added. — Ver.
6. εἶχεν καί] B. D. L. Q. ℵ. Cursives, Copt. Vulg. Or. : ἔχων. A correction of
the style. — Ver. 7. εἷς τ. ἡμέρ. τ. ἐνταφ. μ. τετήρ.] Lachm. and Tisch. : ἵνα εἷς τ.
ἡμέρ. τ. ἐνταφ. μου τηρήσῃ, after decisive testimonies. Not being understood,
the words were altered according to the thought in the parallel passages, especially Mark xiv. 8. — Ver. 8 is entirely wanting in D., and, had the counter
testimony been stronger, would have been liable to the suspicion of having
been interpolated from Matt. xxvi. 11, Mark xiv. 7, if it stood *before* ἄφες, κ.τ.λ.,
and occupied the characteristic position of words as in the Synoptics (πάντοτε
first). — Ver. 13. ἔκραζον] Lachm. and Tisch., ἐκραύγαζον, after preponderating
evidence. The *Rec.* is from Matt. and Mark. — Ver. 15. θύγατερ] θυγατηρ (Lachm.,
Tisch.) is so decisively supported, that the vocative—which of itself might
easily find its way into the text—must be traced to the LXX., Zech. ix. 9. —
Ver. 17. ὅτι] The witnesses are much divided between ὅτι and ὅτε (Tisch.) ; but
the latter (A. B. Q. ℵ.) is the more strongly attested. Nevertheless ὅτι, which
Lachm. also has, is to be preferred ; it was changed into ὅτε, because mechanically referred to the preceding ὁ ὢν μετ' αὐτοῦ. — Ver. 22. καὶ πάλιν] Lachm.
and Tisch. : ἔρχεται, and then before λέγουσιν : καί, according to A. B. L. Cursives, Codd. d. It. Aeth. Rightly. The more closely defining κ. πάλιν was
added to the repeated ἔρχεται (so ℵ.) ; and as this had at a later time displaced
the verb, the καί before λέγουσιν also disappeared, as a disturbing element. Had
the verb been written as a gloss, ἔρχονται would have been found. — Ver. 25.
Instead of ἀπολίσει, read with Tisch. ἀπολλύει, according to B. L. ℵ., etc. The
future was introduced through the parallelism. — Ver. 26. ἐάν τις] Elz. : καὶ ἐάν
τις, against such weighty testimony, that καί was already rightly deleted by
Griesb. — Ver. 30. The position of ἡ φωνὴ αὕτη (Lachm., Tisch.) is decisively
accredited. — Ver. 31. The first τοῦτον is wanting in witnesses of too weak
authority to cause its rejection (Griesb.). — Ver. 35. ἐν ὑμῖν] Elz. : μεθ' ὑμῶν,
against preponderating testimonies. An interpretation. — Vv. 35, 36. Instead
of ἕως, Lachm. and Tisch. have both times ὡς, after decisive testimony. The
first ἕως arose through the final letter of the preceding περιπατεῖτε, and the
more readily, as a reminiscence of ix. 4 suggested itself. The second ἕως then
followed of itself, but has, besides, some other testimonies (including ℵ.) than
the first. — Ver. 40. ἐπιστραφ.] Lachm. and Tisch. : στραφ., according to B. D.
ℵ. 33. The compound form is from the LXX., Isa. vi. 10 (hence also many

witnesses have ἐπιστρέψωσιν). On the other hand, ἰάσομαι (so Lachm. and Tisch.) instead of ἰάσωμαι is so decisively supported by almost all the Uncials, that it is not to be traced to the LXX., but the conjunctive is to be regarded as an attempt to conform to what precedes. — Ver. 41. ὅτε] Lachm. and Tisch., after decisive testimony : ὅτι, which, not being understood, was altered. — Ver. 47. καὶ μὴ πιστεύσῃ] Lachm. and Tisch. : κ. μ. φυλάξῃ, according to preponderating testimonies, and rightly ; for πιστ. has manifestly arisen from the preceding (vv. 44, 46). The omission of the μή in D. and Codd. of the It. is to be explained from the apparent paradox.

Vv. 1, 2. Οὖν] is the simply *resumptive* particle by which the narrative *returns* to *Jesus*, whom it had quitted at xi. 55. To assume a sequence from xi. 57, so that He is supposed to go to Bethany, either on account of His safety, or of its nearness to Jerusalem (Luthardt : "so consciously and freely He went to meet death"), and in order to put to shame the thought mentioned in xi. 55–57 (Hengstenberg), as though δέ or ἀλλά were expressed, —is not supported by any indication in the text. — πρὸ ἐξ. ἡμ. τοῦ π.] *six days before the Passover.* Comp. Amos i. 1.[1] Analogously in designations of *space*, as in xi. 18. It is no Latinism. As regards the *reckoning* of the six days, it is to be observed that, since the 14th Nisan, on the evening of which the paschal meal was kept, was wont to be counted as already belonging entirely to the feast (see on Matt. xxvi. 17), and hence also had been already called ἡμέρα τοῦ πάσχα (see Introd. § 2), the 13th Nisan is most naturally assumed to be the *first* day before the Passover ; consequently the *sixth* day will be the 8th Nisan, *i.e.* (since the 14th Nisan, on which Jesus, according to John, died, was a *Friday*) the *Saturday* before Easter. So also Ebrard, Godet, and Ewald,[2] who, however, elsewhere,[3] without any sufficient grounds, finds the previous evening probable, making John at once name the full day of the sojourn, with which Godet also substantially agrees. But according to the *Synoptics*—because they make the 14th Nisan a Thursday—it would have been the *Friday* before Easter.[4] Against the above assumption of the *Saturday* as the day of arrival, the law of the Sabbath day's journey (see on Matt. xxiv. 20) is no objection,[5] since it is not clear *from what place* Jesus started on that day ; He may have arrived from a place that lay *very near* at hand. Others, reckoning the 14th Nisan as the first day before Easter, regard the 9th Nisan as the day of arrival.[6] Others, again, including in their calculation even the 15th Nisan, arrive at the result of the 10th

[1] Frequently thus in Plutarch, Appian, Josephus. See Kypke, I. p. 393 f.

[2] *Gesch. Chr.* p. 511.

[3] *Johann. Schr.* I. p. 329.

[4] As also Wieseler, Hengstenberg, and others assume, who (see on xviii. 28) regard the account of John, in respect to the day of Jesus' death, as agreeing with that of the Synoptics.

[5] Against Grotius, Tholuck, Wieseler, and several others.

[6] This must therefore, according to the calculation which gave Saturday for the 8th Nisan, have been the *Sunday* (Hase, de Wette). But if we hold that John does not fix the day of death differently from the Synoptics, we get as the result the *Saturday* (Wichelhaus and several others), reckoning backwards from Thursday the 14th Nisan inclusive. Further, the 9th Nisan is expressly fixed as the day of arrival in Bethany by Theophylact, and recently by Lücke and several others.

Nisan (Monday) ; so Hilgenfeld, Baur, Scholten, who find a twofold objection to the historical truth of the Gospel, in the day of the month for the
selection of the paschal lamb (Ex. xii. 3), and the day of the week which
opened the Christian Easter week, and from this chronology demonstrate
the secondary relation of our evangelist to the Synoptics.   Yet Baeumlein
also reckons in this way. — ἦλθεν εἰς Βηθανίαν] according to the Harmonists
(including Hengstenberg and Godet), making a circuit by Jericho, which
is as inappropriate to the Johannean as to the synoptical account (see on
Matt. xxi. 1).   The return by Jericho is not reconcilable with the notice in
xi. 54, where He, in fact, by the healing of the blind men, and by the visit
to Zacchaeus, awakened so much attention. — ὅπου ἦν Λάζαρος, κ.τ.λ.] added,
on account of the great importance of the matter, without any further special
purpose, yet with emphatic circumstantiality. — ἐποίησαν] the family of
Bethany, namely, xi. 1. 2, which is clear from the following κ. ἡ Μ. διηκ.[1]
On this and the other variations from the narrative of Matt. xxvi. 6 ff.,
Mark xiv. 3 ff., which, however, do not set aside the identity of the occurrence (different from Luke vii. 3 ff.), see on Matt. xxvi. 6 ff.   The peculiarity of John's account is founded on the fact of the writer's being an eye-
witness ; but is referred by Baur, p. 256 ff., to an eclectic and arbitrary
treatment, dependent on an ideal point of view ; comp. also Hilgenfeld. —
ὁ δὲ Λάζαρος εἰς ἦν, κ.τ.λ.] appears, indeed, a matter of course (hence Baeumlein and others believe Simon the leper to be indicated as the entertainer) ;
but the *complete restoration* of him who had been raised from the dead is so
weighty a consideration with John,· that he further specially brings him
forward as the present table companion of his Restorer.   This also in answer
to Marcker, *Passim.* p. 17.

Vv. 3, 4. To explain the *great quantity* of the ointment (12 ounces) as
the outcome of the superabundance of her love (Olshausen), is arbitrary.
Mary did not anoint *with* the whole pound, but with a *portion* of it (comp.
on ver. 7).   On πιστικός,[2] *genuine, unadulterated*, see on Mark xiv. 3. — πο-
λυτίμου] belongs to μύρου, as πολυτελ., Mark xiv. 3.—τοὺς πόδας αὐτοῦ] repeated,
on account of the correlation with ταῖς θριξὶν αὐτῆς, in order to make promi-

---

[1] That this meal is to be placed still on
the same day, therefore Saturday, at the
usual time of the evening repast, appears
from the fact that the ἐπαύριον does not follow before ver. 12 (against Wichelhaus, p.
153 f.).   The Sabbath is not opposed to this,
since the preparations which had possibly
been necessary for the meal might already
have been made on the preceding day, if
the family—which is a supposition sufficiently obvious—knew that Jesus was coming.—But the supposition that the meal was
a *solemn banquet*, where Godet, following
Bengel, introduces a company of the inhabitants of Bethany as the subject of ἐποίησαν,
finds no support in the text, where, besides
Jesus and the disciples, only the members
of the family (no other participators) are
named, and has the *serving* of Martha
against it, which only bespeaks the usual
domestic entertainment, although the gratitude and respect of the family had more
richly set forth the meal expressly given *to
Him*, to which the description δεῖπνον ποιεῖν
(Mark vi. 21) with the dative points.

[2] If John adopted this word from Mark,
—which, considering the rareness of its occurrence, is probable, and may have been
done quite involuntarily,—this shows no
literary dependence, and does not justify
the suspicion that he also drew the subject-
matter from this source (Hilgenfeld).
Should πιστικός be the adjective of a proper
name (Pistic), all objection would disappear
of itself.   Comp. on Mark xiv. 3, note 2,
Goth. also has *pistikeinis*.

nent the greatness of the love ; with her *hairs*, His *feet.* - - ἐκ τῆς ὀσμῆς] ἐκ *causal.*[1] — εἰς ἐκ τ. μαθ. ἀ.] the rest did not agree with him ; but it was *Judas*, etc. — ὁ μέλλων, κ.τ.λ.] This utterance stood in truth already in psychological connection with this *destiny ;* see on vi. 71.

Vv. 5, 6. Τριακοσίων] Mark xiv. 5 sets forth the climax in the tradition by ἐπάνω τριακ. The mention of the *price* itself (about 120 Rhenish guldens, or about £10) is certainly original, not the indefinite πολλοῦ of Matt. xxvi. 9. — πτωχοῖς] without the article : to *poor people.* — κ. τ. γλωσσ. εἶχε κ. τ. β. ἐβάστ.] gives historical definiteness to the general κλέπτης ἦν. He had the chest, the cash-box,[2] in his keeping, and bore away that which was thrown into it, *i.e.* he *purloined* it. This closer defining of the sense of βαστάζειν, *auferre*,[3] is yielded by the *context*.[4] The article does not signify that he had taken away *all* the deposits (objection of Lücke and several others), but refers to the *individual cases* which we are to suppose, in which deposits were removed by him. The explanation *portabat*[5] yields a meaning which is quite tautological, and a matter of course. The βαλλόμενα were gifts of friends and adherents of Jesus for the purchase of the necessities of life and for charitable uses. Comp. Luke viii. 3 ; John xiii. 29. That the disciples had acquired earnings by the labour of their hands, and had deposited such earnings in the bag, nay, that even Jesus Himself had done so (Mark vi. 3),—of this there exists no trace during the period of His ministry. — The question, why Jesus had not taken away the custody of the chest from the dishonest disciple (which indeed, according to Schenkel, he probably did not hold), is not answered by saying that He would remove from him every pretext for treason,[6] or that He did not desire violently to interfere with the development of his sins (Hengst.) ; for neither would harmonize with the educative love of the Lord. Just as little, again, is it explained by suggesting that Judas carried on his thefts *unobserved*, until perhaps shortly before the death of Jesus (Lücke), which would be incompatible with the higher knowledge of the Lord, ii. 25 ; comp. vi. 64, 71. The question stands rather in the closest connection with another—how Jesus could adopt Judas at all as a disciple ; and here we must go back solely to a *divine destination*, Acts i. 16, ii. 23. Comp. the note after vi. 70, 71. That the custody of the chest had been entrusted to Judas only by *agreement of the disciples among one another* (Godet), is an assumption which quite arbitrarily evades the point, while it would by no means have excluded the competency of *Jesus* to interfere.

Vv. 7, 8. According to the *Recepta*, Jesus says : " She has fulfilled a

---

[1] Comp. Matt. xxiii. 25 ; Rev. viii. 5 ; Plat. *Phaedr.* p. 235 C ; *Dem.* 581. 26, *et al.*

[2] See as regards γλωσσόκ..2 Chron. xxiv. 8 ; Lobeck, *ad Phryn.* p. 98 f.

[3] xx. 15 ; Matt. vii. 17 ; Polyp. i. 48. 2, *et al.*

[4] See Krebs, *Obss.* p. 153. So Origen, Codd. of the It. Nonnus, Theophylact, Cornelius à Lapide, Kypke, Krebs, and several others, including Maier, Grimm ; comp. Lange, who, however, explains : *he laid hold of.* But βαστάζειν denotes to *lay hold of*

only in the sense of ψηλαφᾶν (Suidas). See Reisig, *ad Soph. O. C.* 1101 ; Ellendt, *Lex. Soph.* I. p. 299. And in this sense only in the tragic poets.

[5] Vulgate, Luther, Beza, and many others, including Lücke, de Wette, B. Crusius, Luthardt, Ebrard, Wichelhaus, Baeumlein, Godet, Hengstenberg, Ewald ; Tholuck doubtful.

[6] Ammonius, Chrysostom, Theophylact, Euth. Zigabenus, and several others.

higher purpose with the spikenard ointment (αὐτό); *in order to embalm me with it to-day* (as though I were already dead), *has she* (not given it out for the poor, but) *reserved it.*" Comp. on Matt. xxvi. 12. But according to the correct reading (see the critical notes): "Let her alone, *that she may not give away to the poor this ointment, of which she has just used a portion for the anointing of my feet, but preserve it for the day of my embalment.*" Nonnus aptly remarks : ὄφρα φυλάξη σώματος ἡμετέρου κειμήλιον, εἰσόκεν ἔλθη ἡμετέρων κτερέων ἐπιτύμβιος ὥρη. Comp. also Baeumlein. According to this view, the ἡμέρα τοῦ ἐνταφ. is the *actual, impending* day of embalment, in opposition to which, according to the *Recepta*, the present day of the anointing of the feet would be represented *proleptically* as that of the anointing of the corpse. [See Note XXXVIII., p. 383.] The thought of the *Recepta* is that of the Synoptics ; the Johannean carries with it the air of originality, and, comparing the *significance* of the two, the Johannean is more in harmony with the fact that Mary anointed *the feet merely*, and by no means resembles a faulty correction (Hengst., Godet). The circumstance that the corpse of Jesus was not afterwards actually anointed (Mark xvi. 1), can, in view of an utterance so rich and deep in feeling, afford no ground for deserting the simple meaning of the words. — τηρεῖν is to be explained, agreeably to the context (comp. ii. 10), as an antithesis to ἐπράθη, ver. 5, but not by the quite arbitrary assumption that the ointment had remained over from the burial of Lazarus (Kuinoel and several others); but to understand τηρήσῃ of the past ; that she *may have preserved* it (B. Crusius, Ebrard) is grammatically wrong.[1] According to Ewald, τηρεῖν is to be understood, as elsewhere, of festal usages (ix. 16): " *Let her so observe this on the day of my burial,*" so that Jesus would have that day already regarded as equivalent to the day of His burial, when such a loving custom was suitable. But as regards τηρεῖν, see what precedes ; instead of the indefinite αὐτό, *it*, however, τοῦτο was at least to have been expected. — Ver. 8. Reason of the statement introduced with ἵνα, κ.τ.λ. — μεθ᾽ ἑαυτῶν] in your own neighbourhood, so that you have sufficiently immediate opportunity to give alms to such. For the rest, see on Matt. xxvi. 11.

Vv. 9–11. Οὖν] since Jesus thus tarries in the neighbourhood. The lively intercourse among the pilgrims to the feast tended the more to spread the information. — ἐκ τῶν Ἰουδαίων] here again (comp. xi. 19), not generally of the *inhabitants of Jerusalem* (so *usually*), but, according to the standing usage in John, of the *Jewish opposition.* They came, *not for Jesus' sake alone*, to observe Him further, but *in order also to see Lazarus*, and to be convinced of His actual and continued restoration to life. Since, however, *many* of the Ἰουδαῖοι went forth (from Jerusalem) for the sake of Lazarus, and became *believers* in Jesus, the chief priests (*i.e.* not indeed the Sanhedrim as such in general, but rather that part of it which composed its hierarchical head) took counsel to put Lazarus also to death. We have here, accord-

---

[1] The modification of this rendering in Lüthardt : " Leave her in peace as regards the fact that she has kept the ointment for me with the design (even though unconscious) of preserving it for the representation, beforehand, of the day of my embalment," is a grammatical impossibility. Similarly, however, Bengel.

ingly, the opposite results, that the sight of Lazarus subdues many of the hitherto adverse party to faith (comp. already xi. 45); and on the other hand, that the extreme Right of the hierarchy resolves the more energetically to counterwork this. — ἦλθον] Still on Saturday evening and Sunday. The procession *of people* took place then on Sunday (ver. 12). — ἐβουλ. δέ] Simple continuation of the narrative ; hence, neither is δέ to be understood as *namely*, nor ἐβουλ. as *pluperfect* (Tholuck). — οἱ ἀρχιερ.] It was indeed for the interest of the *hierarchy* (not exactly for that of the *Sadducees*, Acts v. 17, as Lampe thought, since the chief priests are here adduced *as such* generally, not in their possible *sectarian* tendency) to remove out of the way the living witness also on whom the miracle had been wrought, not merely the miracle-worker Himself. The tyrannical power, in this way, proceeds consistently, in order, as it imagines, to put away even the recollection of the affair. "Praeceps est malitia et semper ultra rapit," Grotius. — ὑπῆγον] not : *they fell away*,[1] which, without closer definition, does not lie in the word, but rather : *they took themselves off, they removed to a distance ;* so great an attractive power did the matter possess for them, and then *followed* the falling away. The separation in the position of the words : πολλοὶ . . . τῶν Ἰου-δαίων, brings both points emphatically out.

Vv. 12, 13. Τῇ ἐπαύρ.] after the day designated in ver. 1, consequently Sunday (*Palm* Sunday), not : after the deliberation mentioned in vv. 10, 11 (Ebrard and Olshausen, *Leidensgesch.* p. 36). — ὄχλ. πολ. κ.τ.λ.] Unprejudiced pilgrims to the feast, therefore, not again Ἰουδαῖοι. — ἀκούσαντες] perhaps from the Ἰουδαῖοι in ver. 11 who had returned as believers. — τὰ βαΐα τ. φ.] as a symbol of joy. The article τῶν (not τά) contains the element of definiteness ; the branches of the palm-trees *standing on the spot*.[2] The *expression :* the *palm branches of the palms*, is similar to οἰκοδεσπότης τῆς οἰκίας, and the like.[3] The *thing itself* has in other respects nothing to do with an analogy to the *Lulab* at the feast of Tabernacles (Lev. xxiii. 40). Comp. however, 1 Macc. xiii. 51. — ὑπάντησιν αὐτῷ] see Buttmann, *Neut. Gr.* p. 156 [E. T. p. 320]. — ὡσαννά, κ.τ.λ.] See on Matt. xxi. 9. — βασιλεὺς τ. Ἰ.] *without* the article :[4] *the King of Israel who comes in the name of the Lord.*

Vv. 14, 15. Εὑρὼν δέ, κ.τ.λ.] The more detailed circumstances, how he had obtained the young ass (ὀνάριον), are passed over by John ; hence he is not in contradiction with the Synoptics (Matt. xxi. 2 ff. parall.). — καθώς ἐστι γεγρ.] Zech. ix. 9. See on Matt. xxi. 5. John cites very freely from memory ; hence the omission of the other prophetic predicates (even of the πραΰς in Matt.), because he has in his eye simply the point of the *riding in upon the young ass*, as a Messianic σημεῖον excluding all doubt. All the more fitted to tranquillize, then (μὴ φοβοῦ), in ever more peaceful array, without horse and chariot, is the coming of the King of Zion. Instead of μὴ φοβοῦ, John might also have said χαῖρε σφόδρα LXX.) ; but there floated before him, in his citation from memory, simply the opposition to that terror by which otherwise a royal entrance may be accompanied. "*The Church's figure of*

---

[1] Cornelius à Lapide, Lampe, Paulus.
[2] On βαΐον comp. 1 Macc. xiii. 51; Symm. *Cant.* i. 8; Sturz, *Dial. Al.* p. 88,
[3] Lobeck, *Paralip.* p. 536 f.
[4] Lachmann has it ; Tischendorf, καὶ ὁ.

the cross" (Hengst.) did not yet lie on this ass's foal, otherwise John would
not have passed over the עֲיִי of the passage, nor have found the emphasis in
μὴ φοβοῦ.

Ver. 16. Observation by John. Comp. ii. 22, xx. 9. *But this* which
here took place, namely, that Jesus mounted a young ass which He had
obtained, *His disciples at first* (when it took place) *did not understand*, so
far, namely, as the connection of the matter with the prediction of the
prophet remained still hidden from them ; *when, however, Jesus was glorified,
they remembered* (under the illumination of the Spirit, vii. 39, xiv. 26) *that this*,
this riding on the young ass did not accidentally occur, but *that it was written of Him, and* that *they* (the disciples) *did this*, nothing other than this
which had been written of Him, *to Him*, on the occasion of that entrance, —
in bringing, namely, the ass to Him, whereby they became the instruments
of the fulfilment of prophecy. In this ἐποίησαν αὐτῷ there is the echo from
John's recollection of the way and manner of the εὑρὼν ὀνάριον as known
from the Synoptics. To take ἐποίησαν generally : *they* (indef.) *did*, and to
refer it to ver. 13,[1] is incorrect, since the first two ταῦτα can only point to vv.
14, 15. — On ἐπ' αὐτῷ see Bernhardy, p. 249. Winer, p. 367 [E. T. p. 393].

Vv. 17, 18. Οὖν] Leading back again after the intermediate observation
of ver. 16 to the story, and this so as to state how it was *the raising of Lazarus* which so greatly excited both the people who thronged with Jesus from
Bethany to Jerusalem (the Ἰουδαῖοι who had become believers, vv. 9, 11, and
others, certainly including many inhabitants of Bethany itself), and the
multitude which came to meet them from Jerusalem (ver. 12). — ἐμαρτ.
κ.τ.λ. ὅτι][2] for they had, in truth, *themselves seen* the reanimated man ; had
also, perhaps, themselves witnessed in part the process of the miracle, or at
least heard of it from eye-witnesses, and could accordingly *testify* to His
resurrection. — ἐφώνησεν . . . νεκρῶν] The echo of their triumphant words.
— διὰ τοῦτο . . . ὅτι] *On this account* (on account of this raising from the
dead), namely, *because ;* see on x. 17. — ὑπήντησεν] not pluperfect in sense,
but : *they went to meet* (as already stated above, vv. 12, 13). — ὁ ὄχλος] The
article points to ver. 12. — ἤκουσαν] namely, previously, in Jerusalem. —
τοῦτο] with emphasis ; hence also the separation in the order of the words.

NOTE.—While we necessarily recognize the main difference between the Synoptics and John, namely, that according to the former, the journey of Christ to Jerusalem is made from *Jericho,* where He had remained for the night at the house
of Zacchaeus, and the stay in Bethany is excluded (see on Matt. xxi. 1, note),
the Messianic entry is yet *one and the same* event in all four evangelists. Against
the assumption of *two distinct entries,*[3] which makes one entry from Jericho, and
another one or two days later, from Bethany, the very nature of the transaction is
decisive, of which a repetition, and that so early, could have hardly failed to

---

[1] De Wette, Ewald, and older commentators.
[2] With the reading ὅτε (see critical notes),
ἐμαρτ would have to be taken absolutely :
the people bore witness, who, viz. were with
Him at the raising of Lazarus. Comp. Lu-

ther, Erasmus, and many others. Thus the
ὄχλος would be the same as in xi. 42, which,
however, is not appropriate to ver. 12 and
ver. 18, and would only tend to confuse.
[3] Paulus, Schleiermacher, *üb. d. Schriften
des Luk.* p. 243 ff., and *L. J.* p. 407 ff.

degenerate into an organized procession. Only in its occurring once, and being brought about accidentally, as it were, by the circumstances, does it retain a moral agreement with the mind of Jesus. With this view, too, all four accounts conform, and they all show not merely by their silence respecting a second procession, but also by the manner in which they represent the one, that they are entirely ignorant of any repetition. Such a repetition, especially one so uniform in character, is as improbable in itself, as opposed to the natural development of the history of Jesus, which here especially, when the last bloody crisis is prepared for by the entry of the Messianic King, must preserve its divine *decorum*, and finds its just measure in the simple fulfilment of the prophetic prediction.

Ver. 19. Contrast to the triumph ; the despairing self-confession of *the Pharisaic adversaries*, not as Chrysostom, in spite of the article in οἱ Φαρισ., explained of the quiet *friends* of Jesus among the Pharisees. — πρὸς ἑαυτούς] *to one another ;* but ἀλλήλ. is not employed, because the utterance is to appear as *limited to the particular circle.* Comp. on vii. 35. — θεωρεῖτε, κ.τ.λ.] *You perceive that we profit nothing,* namely, by our previous cautious, expectant, feeble procedure. "Approbant Caiaphae consilium," Bengel. — ὁ κόσμος] designation, indicative of their despair, of the *great multitude.* Comp. עוֹלָם in the Rabbins. See Wetstein. — In ἀπῆλθεν (is *gone off* or *away*) is contained, by means of the pragmatic connection with ὀπίσω αὐτοῦ, the representation of the falling away from the legitimate hierarchical power. Comp. ὑπῆγον, ver. 11.

Ver. 20. The *Hellenes* are, as in vii. 35, not Greek *Jews, Hellenists,*[1] but *Gentiles,*— proselytes, however, as is shown by what follows (note especially the pres. part. ἀναβαιν. : who *were wont* to go up), and that of the *gate,* like the Aethiopian chamberlain, Acts viii. 27, not *pure* Gentiles.[2] — *Where* did the scene take place ? Probably in the court of the temple, with which locality, at least, the entry just related, and the connected transactions, onwards to ver. 36, best correspond. According to Baur (comp. also Scholten), the whole affair is to be referred simply to the *idea of the author,* who makes Jesus, under the ascendency of Jewish unbelief, to be glorified by believing heathendom. This idea is that of the history itself. Bengel rightly observes : "Praeludium regni Dei a Judaeis ad gentes transituri."

Vv. 21, 22. The Messianic hope, which they as proselytes share, draws their hearts to Him whose Messiahship has just found so open and general a recognition. They wish to *see* Jesus, that is, to be introduced to Him, in order to make His nearer personal acquaintance, and this it is which they *modestly* express. For *mere* seeing, as in Luke xix. 3, any intervention of a third party (as Brückner now also recognizes) would not have been required. — Whether they came to Philip *accidentally,* or because the latter was *known* to them (perhaps they were from Galilee), remains undetermined. To presuppose in Philip, on account of his Greek name, a *Greek education* (Hengst.), is arbitrary. — κύριε] not without the tender of honour, which they naturally

---

[1] Calvin, Semler, B. Crusius, Ewald.
[2] Chrysostom, Theophylact, Euth. Ziga-
benus, Salmasius, Selden, and several others, including Paulus, Klee, Schweizer.

paid even to the disciple of a Master so admired, who truly appeared to be the very Messiah.—That Philip first communicates the proposal to Andrew, who was possibly in more confidential relations with Christ (Mark xiii. 3), and who was on terms of intimacy with him by the fact of the same birth-place (i. 45), and that *with* him he carries out their wish, rests on the circumstance that he was himself too timid to be the means of bringing about an interview between the Holy One of God—whose immediate destination he knew to be for Israel—and *Gentiles*. His was a circumspect nature, prone to scruples (vi. 5 ff., xiv. 8, 9). "Cum sodali, audet," Bengel. Note the stamp of *originality* which appears in such side-touches. — In the reading ἔρχεται 'Ανδρ. κ. Φ. καὶ λέγουσι τῷ 'Ι. (see critical notes), observe (1) the lively mode of representation in the repetition of ἔρχεται ; (2) the change from the singular to the plural of the verb, which occurs also in the classics.[1]

Ver. 23. The proposal of the Gentiles, which had been brought to Him, awakens in Jesus, with peculiar force and depth, the thought of His approaching *death ;* for through His *death* was His salvation in truth to be conveyed to the Gentiles (x. 16, 17).—Accordingly, this wish of the Gentiles must appear to Him as already commencing that which was to be effected by His death. Hence His *answer to those two disciples* (not to the Ἕλληνες, Ebrard), which is pervaded by a full presentiment of the crisis at hand, and at the close, ver. 27, resolves itself into a prayer of deep emotion, but, by means thereof, into complete surrender to the Father. This answer is consequently neither *inappropriate* (de Wette), nor contains an indirect *refusal* of the request of the Greeks.[2] Nor is the *granting* of it to be conceived as having previously taken place, and *been passed over in silence* by John,[3] as shown by the naturally succeeding ἀπεκρ. αὐτοῖς,—nor as *indirectly conceded* by the fact that the Apostles brought it before Jesus, and that He commenced speaking (Luthardt), which involves the improbability that Jesus was on the point of addressing Himself to these Heathen (whom Ewald supposes present), but that their *admission*, which was to have followed this outburst of emotion, was prevented by the voice from heaven which broke in and changed the scene.[4] The theory that in v. 23 ff. the synoptical accounts of the transfiguration, and of the conflict of soul in Gethsemane, are either fused into a historical mixture (Strauss), or formed into an ideal combination (Baur), proceeds from presuppositions, which make it possible to adduce even Gal. ii. 9 as a witness against John xii. 20 (see against this, Bleek, p. 250 ff.), as Baur has done. — ἐλήλυθεν] Placed first with emphasis. — ἵνα]

---

[1] Xen. *Anab.* ii. 4. 16, and Kühner *in loc.*

[2] Ewald, Hengstenberg, Godet.

[3] Tholuck, B. Crusius, and older commentators.

[4] According to Ewald, *Gesch. Chr.* p. 527, Jesus would, in *granting* the request, be exposed to a *temptation*, and have done something at this last development out of keeping with His previous ministry, which would have awakened disquiet, furnished a new embarrassment to the hierarchs, etc. But we may also conversely pass the judgment that Jesus, on the very threshold of His death, could not have designed to refuse an actual manifestation of His universal destination, which He, moreover, had expressed in x. 16,—offered so accidentally, as it were,—especially since the conversion of the Gentiles to the Messiah was grounded in prophecy. To yield to the prayer was, further, by no means a full concession to the petitioners.

Comp. xiii. 1, xvi. 2, 32. The hour is conceived of absolutely (in the consciousness of Jesus the present *hora fatalis κατ' ἐξοχήν*), and that which is to take place in it, as the divine indication of its arrival. — δοξασθῇ] through *death*, as the necessary passage to the heavenly glory.[1]

Ver. 24. My death, however, is *necessary* to the successful and victorious development of my work, as the wheat-corn must fall into the earth and die, in order to bring forth much fruit. The *solemn assurance* (ἀμήν, ἀμήν, κ.τ.λ.) is in keeping with the difficulty of getting the disciples to accept the idea of His death. — ἀποθάνῃ] For the *vital principle* in the corn, the *germ*, forces itself out ; thus the corn is *dead*, and become a prey to dissolution, comp. 1 Cor. xv. 36. — αὐτὸς μόνος] *by itself alone*, vi. 15.[2] The life of the corn which has not fallen into the earth remains limited and bound to itself, without the possibility of a communication and unfolding of life outwards issuing from it, such as only follows in the case of *that* corn which dies in the earth through the bursting forth of the living germ, and in this way of death produces much fruit. Thus, also, with Christ ; it is through His death that there first comes upon all peoples and times the rich blessing which is destined for the world. Comp. ver. 32.

Ver. 25. As it is my vocation, so also is it that of those who are mine, to surrender the temporal, in order to gain the eternal life. Comp. Matt. x. 39 ; Luke ix. 24, xvii. 33.—The ψυχή is in each instance the *soul*, as αὐτήν also is be taken in like manner in each instance. This is clear from its being distinguished from ζωή. *He who loves his soul*, will not let it go (ὁ φιλοψυχῶν ἐν καιρῷ μαρτυρίου, Euth. Zigabenus), *loses it* (see critical notes)— *i.e.* causes it to fall into the death of everlasting condemnation ; *and he who hates his soul in this world* (gives it up with joy, as something which is a hindrance to eternal salvation, and in so far must be hated) *will preserve it for everlasting life*, keep it to himself as a possession in the everlasting Messianic life. Note the correlatives : φιλῶν and μισῶν, ἀπολέσει and φυλάξει (comp. xvii. 12), ἐν τῷ κόσμῳ τούτῳ (in the pre-Messianic world), and εἰς ζωὴν αἰώνιον. — On μισεῖν, whose meaning is not to be altered, but to be understood relatively, in opposition to φιλοψυχία, comp. Luke xiv. 26. "Amor, *ut* pereat; odium *ne* pereat ; si male amaveris, tunc odisti ; si bene oderis, tunc amasti," Augustine.

Ver. 26. Requirement and promise, in accordance with that which was expressed generally in ver. 25. —*follow*] on the way of my life-surrender ; comp. Matt. x. 38, xvi. 24. — ὅπου εἰμὶ ἐγώ] comp. xiv. 3, xvii. 24. The pres. tense represents the fut. as present : *where I am, there will also my servant be*, namely, after I have raised him up (vi. 39, 40, 44, 54) in the Parousia. Comp. xiv. 3, xvii. 24. That following after me will lead him into blessed fellowship with me in my kingdom. Comp. Rom. viii. 17 ; 2 Tim. ii. 11, 12. For the counterpart, see vii. 34. According to Luthardt,[3] the being *on the same way* is meant, consequently the contents of that requirement are simply turned into a promise. A feeble tautology, especially after ver. 25

---

[1] Comp. xvii. 5, vi. 62 ; 1 Pet. i. 11.
[2] Ast, *Lex. Plat.* I. p. 314.
[3] Comp. Euth. Zigabenus 1.

(εἰς ζωὴν αἰώνιον). — ἐάν τις ἐμ. διακ. κ.τ.λ.] Parallel with the preceding, further designating, particularly and specifically, the promised happiness, and that in the light of the divine *recompense* contained in it. This thought is expressed by the conjunction of διακονῇ and τιμήσει, which verbs have the emphasis (it is different previously, when ἐμοί . . . ἐμοί bore the emphasis) ; he who *serves* me, him will the Father *honour*, actually, through the glory in the everlasting life, comp. Rom. ii. 10, viii. 17. The διακονεῖν, however, is here to be understood with the previously enjoined quality of following Christ.

Vv. 27, 28. The realization of His sufferings and death, with which His discourse from ver. 23 was filled, shakes Him suddenly with apprehension and momentary wavering, springing from the human sensibility, which natur-ally struggles against that heaviest suffering, which He must yet undergo. To define this specially as the feeling *of the divine anger* (Beza, Calvin, Calovius, Hengstenberg, and many others), which He has certainly appeased by His death, rests on the supposition, which is nowhere justified, that, ac-cording to the *object* of the death,[1] *its severity* also is measured in the con-sciousness. Bengel well says : " *concurrebat horror mortis et ardor obedien-tiae.*" The Lord is thus moved to *pray ;* but He is for the moment uncertain for *what* (τί εἴπω), ἀπορούμενος ὑπὸ τῆς ἀγωνίας, Euth. Zigabenus. *First,* a momentary fear of the sufferings of death (comp. on Luke xii. 50) obtains the upper hand, in virtue of that human weakness, in which even He, the Son of God, because He had become man, had His share (Heb. iv.15, v. 7, 8), and He prays : *Father, save me from this hour*, spare me this death-suf-fering which is awaiting me, quite as in Matt. xxvi. 39, so that He thus not merely " cries for support through it, and for a shortening of it" (Ebrard). But immediately this wish, resulting from natural dread of suffering and death,[2] yields to the victorious consciousness of His great destiny ; He gives expression to the latter (ἀλλὰ διὰ τοῦτο, κ.τ.λ.), and now prays : *Father, glorify Thy name ; i.e.*, through the suffering of death appointed to me, let the glory of Thy name (of Thy being in its self-presentation, comp. on Matt. vi. 9) be manifested. The fulfilment of this prayer was brought about in this way, that by means of the death of Jesus (and of His consequent δόξα) the divine decree of salvation was fulfilled, then everywhere made known through the gospel, in virtue of the Holy Spirit (xiv. 16 ff.), and obedience to the faith established to the honour of the Father, which is the last aim of the work of Christ, Phil. ii. 11. — ἡ ψυχή μου] not as a designation of *in-dividual* grief (Olshausen), but as the seat of the affections generally. He might also have said τὸ πνεῦμά μου (comp. xi. 33, 38), but would then have meant the deeper basis of life, to which the impressions of the ψυχή, which is united with the σάρξ, are conveyed. Comp. on Luke i. 46, 47. — πάτερ, σῶσόν με, κ.τ.λ.] The hour of suffering is regarded as present, *as though He were already at that hour. To take the words *interrogatively :* shall I say :

[1] i. 29, iii. 14, x. 11, 12 ; Matt. xx. 28 ; Rom. viii. 3, iii. 25 ; 2 Cor. v. 21, *et al.*
[2] Which in itself is not only not immoral, but the absence of which would even lower the moral greatness and the worth of His sacrifice. Comp. Dorner, *Jesu Sündlose Vollkommenh.* p. 6.

save me ? etc.[1] yieldes the rsult of an actual prayer interwoven into a reflective monologue, and is therefore less suitable to a frame of mind so deeply
moved. — ἀλλά] objecting, like our *but no!*[2] — διὰ τοῦτο] *wherefore*, is contained in the following prayer, πάτερ, δόξασον, κ.τ.λ. Consequently : *therefore, in order that* through my suffering of death *Thy name may be glorified.*
The completion : *in order that the world might be redeemed* (Olshausen and
older commentators), is not supplied by the context ; *to undergo this suffering*[3] is tautological ; and Lampe : *to be saved*, is inappropriate. The τοῦτο is
here *preparative* ; let only διὰ τοῦτο . . . ταύτην be enclosed within dashes,
and the sense is made clearly to appear : *but no—therefore I came to this
hour—Father, glorify*, etc. Jesus might have said : ἀλλά, πάτερ, δόξασον σου
τὸ ὄνομα, διὰ τοῦτο γὰρ ἦλθον ἐ. τ. ὥ. τ. But the deeply emotional language
throbs more unconnectedly, and as it were by starts. — The *repetition* of
πάτερ corresponds to the thrill of filial affection. — σου stands emphatically,
in the first place, in antithesis to the reference which the previous prayer of
Jesus contained to Himself. On the subject-matter, comp. Matt. xxvi. 39.
— οὖν] corresponding to this petition. — φωνὴ ἐκ τ. οὑρ.] The voice which
came from heaven : *I have glorified it* (in Thy mission and Thy whole previous work), *and shall again* (through Thine impending departure by means
of death to the δόξα) *glorify it*,[4] is not to be regarded as actual, natural
thunder (according to the O. T. view conceived of as the voice of the Lord,
as in Ps. xxix., Job xxxvii. 4, and frequently), in which only the *subjective
disposition*, the so-attuned *inner ear* of Jesus (and of the disciples), distinguished the words καὶ ἐδόξασα, κ.τ.λ. ; while others, less susceptible to this
divine symbolism of nature, believed only in a general way, that in the
thunder an angel had spoken with Jesus ; while others again, unsusceptible,
understood the natural occurrence simply and solely as such, and took it for
nothing further than what it objectively was. So substantially, not merely
Paulus, Kuinoel, Lücke, Ammon, de Wette, Maier, Baeumlein, and several
others, but also Hengstenberg.[5] Several have here had recourse to the
later Jewish view of *Bath-Kol* (by which, however, only real literal voices,
not natural phenomena, without speech, were understood ; see Lübkert in
the *Stud. u. Krit.* 1835, 3), as well as to the Gentile interpretations of
thunder as the voice of the gods (see Wetstein). Against this entire view,

[1] So Chrysostom, Theophylact, Jansen,
Grotius, Lampe, and many others, includ-
ing Lachmann, Tholuck, Kling, Schweizer,
Maier, Lange, Ewald, Godet.

[2] See Hartung, *Partikell.* I. p. 36 ; Baeumlein, *Partik.* p. 13 f.

[3] Grotius, de Wette, Luthardt, Lange,
Ebrard, Godet ; comp. Hengstenberg : "in
order that my soul may be shaken."

[4] The reference of ἐδόξασα to the *O. T.
revelation*, which is now declared to be
closed (Lange, *L. J.* II. p. 1208), is without
any foundation in the context.

[5] See, in answer to him, some appropriate
observations in Engelhardt, in the *Luth.*

Zeitschr. 1865, p. 209 ff. He, however, refers the δοξάσω to the fact that the Son, even
in His sufferings, will allow the will of God
entirely to prevail with Him. The glorifying of God, however, by means of the
death of Jesus, which was certainly the
culminating point of His obedience to the
Father, reaches further, namely (see especially xvii. 1, 2) to God's honour through the
Lord's attainment of exaltation throughout
the whole world by means of His death. As
ἐδόξασα refers to His munus *propheticum*, so
δοξάσω to the fact that He attains to the
munus *regium* through the fulfilment of the
munus *sacerdotale*.

it is decisive that John Himself, the ear-witness, describes a φωνὴ ἐκ τοῦ οὐρανοῦ, which was an objective occurrence ; that he repeats its express words ; that, to understand the first half of these words referring to the past, as the product of a merely subjective perception, is without any support in the prayer of Jesus ; that, further, Jesus Himself, ver. 30, gives His confirmation to the occurrence of an actual voice ; that, finally, the ἄλλοι also, ver. 29, must have heard a *speech.* Hence we must abide by the interpretation that a *voice actually issued from heaven,* which John relates, and Jesus confirms as an objective occurrence. It is a voice which came miraculously from God (as was the case, according to the Synoptics, at the baptism and the transfiguration), yet as regards its intelligibility conditioned by the subjective disposition and receptivity of the hearers,[1] which sounded with a *tone as of thunder,* so that the definite words which resounded in this form of sound remained unintelligible to the unsusceptible, who simply heard that majestic kind of sound, but not its contents, and said : βροντὴν γεγονέναι ; whereas others, more susceptible, certainly understood this much, that the thunder-like voice was a *speech,* but not what it said, and thought an angel (comp. Acts xxiii. 9) had spoken in this thunder-voice to Jesus. This opinion of theirs, however, does not justify us in regarding the divine word which was spoken as also actually communicated by angelic ministry (Hofmann), since the utterance of the ἄλλοι is not adduced as at all the true account, and since, moreover, the heavenly voice, according to the text, appears simply as the *answer of the Father.*

Vv. 30, 31. Ἀπεκρίθη] not to the *disciples* (Tholuck), but, according to ver. 29, with reference to these two expressions of opinion from the *people.* He leaves their opinions, as to what and whose the voice was, unnoticed, but recognizes in their hearts the more dangerous error, that they do not put the voice (this thunder or this angelic speech, according to their supposition) in any relation to themselves. — δι' ἐμέ] to assure me that my prayer has been heard ; "*novi* patris animum in me," Erasmus. — δι' ὑμᾶς] in relation to you to overcome unbelief, and to strengthen faith. Comp. xi. 42. — νῦν κρίσις, κ.τ.λ.] Not an interpretation of the voice (Hengstenberg), but also not without reference to δι' ὑμᾶς (Engelhardt), which is too weighty an element. Rather : how the crisis of this time presses for the use of that δι' ὑμᾶς ! — νῦν . . . νῦν] with triumphant certainty of victory, treating the near future as present ; *now, now* is it gone so far ! He speaks " quasi certamine defunctus," Calvin. — κρίσις] Now is *judgment, i.e.* judicial (according to the context : condemnatory) decision passed *upon this world, i.e.* on the men of the αἰὼν οὗτος who reject faith. This judgment is an *actual one ;* for in the victory of the Messianic work of salvation, which was to be brought about by the death of Jesus, and His exaltation to the heavenly glory connected therewith,[2] the κόσμος was to be set forth in the entire sin-

[1] So also Tholuck, Olshausen, Kling, Luthardt, Hofmann, *Schriftbew.* I. p. 391 f., Lange, Ebrard, Godet, following the old commentators.
[2] There lies in it, accordingly, no opposition to the belief in the last judgment (against Hilgenfeld, *Lehrbegr.* p. 274), as has been supposed from a misinterpretation also of iii. 19, 20, in spite of the repeated mention of the last day, and in spite of v.

fulness and impotence of its hostility towards Christ, and thereby in fact judged.¹ Comp. xvi. 9, 10, 33. This victory the *ruler* of this world in particular (τ. κόσμ. τ. solemnly repeated), the *devil*, was to submit to :² His dominion must have an end, because the death of Jesus effected the reconciliation of humanity, by which reconciliation all were to be drawn away from the devil by becoming believers, and placed under the spiritual power of the Christ exalted to glory, ver. 32, Rom. v. 12 ff.; Phil. ii. 9–11. He is called the ἄρχων τοῦ κόσμου τούτου, as the ruler of the *unbelieving*, Christ-opposing humanity (comp. 2 Cor. iv. 4 ; Eph. ii. 2, vi. 12), as in the writings of Rabbins, he, as ruler of the *Gentiles*, in opposition to God and His people, bears this standing name (שר העולם).³ *Here* he is so called, because precisely the judgment of his *dominium*, the *world*, was declared. — ἐκβληθήσεται ἔξω] The necessarily approaching removal of the power of the devil through the death and the exaltation of Jesus is vividly represented as a *casting out from his empire*, namely from the κόσμος οὗτος. Only this supplement is yielded by the context, not τῆς ἀρχῆς (Euth. Zigabenus, Beza), nor τοῦ δικαστηρίου (Theophylact), nor out of the kingdom of God (Ewald), and least of all τοῦ οὐρανοῦ.⁴ The indefinite rendering : he is *repulsed*,⁵ or to be *removed from the presence of the judge* (Hofmann, *Schriftbew.* I. p. 449), is excluded by the appended ἔξω. —Note further, that the victory here announced over this world and over the reign of the devil was indeed decided, and commenced with the death and the exaltation of Christ, but is in a state of continuous development onward to its consummation at the last day (comp. Rev. xx. 10) ; hence the passages of the N. T. on the continuing power and influence of the devil (2 Cor. iv. 4 ; Eph. ii. 2, vi. 12 ; Rom. xvi. 20 ; 1 Pet. v. 8, and many others) do not stand in contradiction to the present passage. Comp. Col. ii. 15.

Vv. 32, 33. And I shall establish my own dominion in place of the devil's rule. —κἀγώ] with victorious emphasis, in opposition to the devil. — ἐὰν ὑψωθῶ ἐκ τ. γῆς] so that I shall be no more upon the earth. Comp. on ὑψόω

27, against which here the very absence of the article should have been a warning. Again, what is subsequently said of the *devil* (as also the passages xiv. 30, 31, xvi. 11) is not to be explained from the Gnostic idea, that the devil, through his having contrived the death of Christ, but having after His death recognized Him as the Son of God, had been *cheated*, and so forfeited his right (Hilgenfeld). Of such Gnostic fancies the N. T. knows nothing. The conquest of the devil is necessarily given along with the *atoning* effect of the death of Jesus, and through the operation of the Spirit of the *exalted one* it is in process of completion until the Parousia.

¹ As hereafter the devil is the subject which is cast out, so here the κόσμος is the *subject which is judged.* This in answer to Bengel : "judicium *de mundo, quis posthac jure sit obtenturus mundum.*" Grotius ex-

plains κρίσις simply of the *vindicatio in libertatem ;* humanity is to be freed from its unjust possessor ; consequently as regards the material contents, substantially as Bengel, comp. also Beza.

² Schleiermacher, indeed (*L. J.* p. 343), interprets the ἄρχ. τ. κ. τ. of "*the public power*" in its conflict with the activity of Jesus. In reference to the declarations of Jesus regarding the devil, it is most markedly apparent with what difficulty Schleiermacher subordinated himself to exegetical tests.

³ See Lightfoot and Schoettgen, also in Eisenmenger, *Entdeckt. Judenthum*, I. p. 647 ff.

⁴ Luke x. 18; Rev. xii. 8, so Olshausen ; hence the reading κάτω.

⁵ De Wette ; comp. Plat. *Menex.* p. 243 B ; Soph. *Oed. R.* 386.

ἐκ, Ps. ix. 14. Probably Jesus (differently in iii. 14) used the verb רוּם
(comp. Syr.): אם הרמתי מן הארץ. This exaltation from earth into heaven
to the Father (vii. 33 ; Acts ii. 33, vi. 31) was to be brought about by the
death of the cross; and this *manner* of His death, Jesus, in the opinion of
John, indicated (xviii. 32, xxi. 19) by the word ὑψωθῶ (comp. iii. 14, viii.
28). Thus, according to John, the designation of the return from earth to
heaven, which Jesus gives by ὑψωθῶ ἐκ τ. γ., is not merely a representation of
His *death*, so far as this exalts him to the Father, but an announcement of the
manner of the death (comp. xviii. 32, xxi. 19), through which He will end
His earthly life, since He was to die *exalted on the cross.* But this interpretation of John's does not justify us in at once understanding ὑψ. ἐκ τ. γ.
of the *crucifixion* (so the Fathers, and most older commentators, including
Kling, Frommann, Hengstenberg), which is forbidden by ἐκ τῆς γῆς, nor in
finding therein [1] a "*sermo anceps*" (Beza and several others including
Luthardt, Ebrard, Godet, comp. Engelhardt), since by the very force of ἐκ
τ. γ. the double sense is *excluded.* It belongs to the freedom of mystic
exposition linking itself to a single word (comp. ix. 7), as it was sufficiently
suggested, especially here, by the recollection of the ὑψωθῆναι already
employed in iii. 14, and is thus as justifiable in itself in the sense of its
time as it is wanting in authority for the historical understanding. To this
mystical interpretation is opposed, indeed, the expression ἐκ τῆς γῆς (comp.
Isa. liii. 8) ; but John was sufficiently faithful in his account not to omit
this ἐκ τ. γῆς for the sake of his interpretation of ὑψωθῶ, and simply adhered
to this ὑψ., and disregarded the connection.[2] — On ἐάν, comp. on xiv. 3. —
πάντας ἑλκ. πρὸς ἐμαυτ.] *all*, i.e. not merely adherents of all *nations*, or all
elected ones and the like, but *all men*, so that thus none remain belonging to
the ἄρχων τοῦ κόσμου τούτου. But *to the latter*, the devil, stands opposed not
the mere πρὸς ἐμέ, but, *to myself*, to my own communion. Comp. xiv. 3 ;
ἐμαυτόν never stands for the simple ἐμέ, also not in xiv. 21 (against Tholuck).
The *drawing* takes place by means of the Holy Spirit, who, given by the
exalted Lord (vii. 39, xvi. 7), and taking His own place (xiv. 18, 19), wins
men for Christ in virtue of faith, and, by means of internal moral compulsion, places them in the fellowship of love, of obedience, and of the true
and everlasting life with Him. Comp. vi. 44, where this is said of the
Father. The *fulfilment* of this promise is world-historical, and continually
in process of realization (Rom. x. 18), until finally the great goal will be
reached, when all will be drawn to the Son, and form *one* flock under *one*
shepherd (x. 16). In this sense πάντας is to be left without any arbitrary
limitation (Luthardt's limitation is baseless : all, *namely, those whom He
draws to Himself*). For the manner in which *Paul* recognized the way and
manner of the last consummation of the promise thus made, see Rom. xi. 25,
26.

Ver. 34. The people—rightly understanding ἐὰν ὑψ. ἐκ τ. γῆς, ver. 32, of
an exaltation to take place by the way of *death*—gather thence, that in ac-

---

[1] "His suspension on the *cross* appears to Him the *magnificently ironical emblem* of His elevation on the *throne*," Godet. An iron-ical touch would here be very strange.

[2] Scholten sets aside the whole comment as an *interpolation.*

cordance therewith no everlasting duration of life (μένει, see on xxi. 22) is destined for Him on the earth, and do not find this reconcilable with that which *they* on their part (ἡμεῖς) had heard out of the Scripture (νόμος, as in x. 34 (of the Messiah (ἠκούσ., namely, by reading, comp. Gal. iv. 21). They reflect on the scriptural doctrine (comp. also the older book of Enoch) of the everlasting kingdom of the Messiah, which they apprehend as an earthly kingdom, and especially on passages like Ps. cx. 4, Isa. ix. 5, 7, and particularly Dan. vii. 13, 14. — From the latter passage, not from ver. 23, where He does not speak to the people, they put into the mouth of Christ the words τὸν υἱὸν τοῦ ἀνθρ., as He had designated Himself so frequently by this Messianic appellation, in order at once to make manifest that He, although He so terms Himself, yet on account of the contradictory token of the ὑψωθῆναι ἐκ τ. γῆς which He ascribes to Himself, cannot be the Danielian Son of man, He who was so characterized in the Scripture ; *the* Son of man, by which name *He* is wont to designate Himself, must in truth be quite another person. — οὗτος] this strange Son of man, who is in opposition to the Scripture, over whom that ὑψωθῆναι is said to be impending.[1] That the speakers, however, were unacquainted with the appellation ὁ υἱὸς τοῦ ἀνθρ. for Jesus (Brückner) is, after the first half of the verse, not to be assumed.

Vv. 35, 36. Jesus does not enter upon the question raised, but directs the questioners to that one point which concerns them, with the intensity and seriousness of one who is on the point of taking His departure. To follow this one direction must indeed of itself free them from all those doubts and questions. — ἐν ὑμῖν] *among you.* — περιπ. ὡς τὸ φῶς ἔχετε] On the reading ὡς, see the critical notes. *Walk as you have the light, i.e.* in conformity with the fact that you have among you the possessor and bearer of the divine truth (comp. on viii. 12) ; be not slothful, but spiritually active, and awake in the enjoyment of this relation, just as one does not rest and lie still when he has the bright light of day, but walks in order to attain the end in view before the darkness breaks in (see what follows). On ὡς as assigning the motive (*in the measure that*), comp. generally on xiii. 34, and here especially on Gal. vi. 10. Ellendt aptly says, *Lex. Soph.* II. p. 1008 : "nec tamen causam per se spectatam, sed quam quis, qualis sit, indicat." The signification *quamdiu* (Baeumlein) is not borne by ὡς, not even in Soph. *Aj.* 1117,[2] *Phil.* 635. 1330. — ἵνα μὴ σκοτία, κ.τ.λ.] *in order that—* which would smite you as a penal destiny in retribution of your μὴ περιπατεῖν —*darkness* (the element opposed to the divine truth of salvation, which still at present shines upon you) *may not seize you,* like a hostile power. Comp. Rom. i. 21 : ἐσκοτίσθη ἡ ἀσύνετος αὐτῶν καρδία. On καταλάβῃ, comp. 1 Thess. v. 4 ; also in the classics very frequently of danger, misfortune, and the like, which befall any one.[3] — καὶ ὁ περιπ., κ.τ.λ.] and how dangerous were

---

[1] The inquiry has in it something pert, saucy, as if they said : "A fine 'Son of man' art thou, who art not to remain for ever in life, but, as thou dost express it, art to be exalted !" To the Danielian Son of man an everlasting kingdom is given, Dan.

vii. 14. This also in answer to Hofmann, *Schriftbew.* II. 1, p. 79.

[2] See Schneidewin *in loc.*

[3] Arrian, *Alex.* i. 5. 17 : εἰ νὺξ καταλήψεται αὐτούς.

this condition ! This is brought home in a saying from ordinary life ;
comp. xi. 9, ix. 4. — ποῦ ὑπάγει] *whither he is departing*, iii. 8. Thus the
ἐσκοτισμένος goes away, without knowing the unhappy end, into everlasting
destruction ; comp. 1 John ii. 11. For the opposite of *this* ποῦ ὑπάγει, see
viii. 14, 21, xvi. 5, *et al.* — ὡς τ. φῶς ἐχετε] Repeated and placed first with
great emphasis. — πιστεύετε εἰς τ. φῶς, ἵνα, κ.τ.λ.] More minute designation
of that which was previously intended by the figurative περιπατεῖτε. — υἱοὶ
τοῦ φωτ.] Enlightened persons. See on Luke xvi. 8 ; Eph. v. 8. — γένησθε]
not *be*, but *become*. Faith is the condition and the beginning of it ; comp.
i. 12. — ἐκρύβη ἀπ᾽ αὐτῶν] The situation in viii. 59 is different. He now,
according to the account of John, withdraws from them into concealment,
probably to Bethany, in order to spend these last days of life, before the
arrival of His hour, in the quiet confidential circle, not as a warning,
"summi judicii occultationis Domini" (Lampe, Luthardt), which is not indicated, and is all the more without support, that the last discourse was
not condemnatory, but only hortatory.

Ver. 37. At the close of the public ministry of Jesus there now follows a
general consideration of its results in respect to faith in Him, as far as ver.
50. — τοσαῦτα] not *so great*,[1] but *so many*,[2] vi. 9, xiv. 9, xxi. 11. Comp. the
admissions of the Jews themselves, vii. 31, xi. 47. The *multitude* of the
miracles, *i.e.* the *so-often-repeated* miraculous demonstration of His Messianic
glory, must have convinced them (comp. xx. 30), had they not been blinded
and hardened by a divine destiny. The *reference*, however, of τοσαῦτα is
not : so many *as have hitherto been related*, for our Gospel contains the few-
est miraculous narratives,—but it lies in the general recognition of their
great multitude. Comp. xiv. 9 ; 1 Cor. xiv. 10 ; Heb. iv. 7. — ἔμπροσθ.
αὐτ.] *before their eyes*. — οὐκ ἐπίστ. εἰς αὐτ.] summary statement.

Ver. 38. Ἵνα] *in order that*, according to divine determination, the
prophecy might be fulfilled. This "*in order that*" contains the definite
assumption that the prophet Isaiah predicted what, according to divine
destiny, was to come to pass ; thus, then, the historical fulfilment stood in
necessary relation of final cause to the prediction. Comp. on Matt. i. 22.
— ὃν εἶπε] similar pleonasms, which, however, as here, may denote an
emphatic circumstantiality, are found also in the Greek writers.[3] The passage is Isa. liii. 1, closely following the LXX. The lament of the prophet
over the unbelief of *his* time towards *his* preaching (and that of his fellows,
ἡμῶν), and towards the mighty working of God announced *by him*, has, according to the Messianic character of the whole grand oracle, its reference
and fulfilment in the unbelief of the Jews towards *Jesus ;* so that in the sense
of this fulfilment, the speaking subject (addressing God, κύριε, comp. Matt.
xxvii. 46), which Isaiah introduces, is *Jesus*, not the *evangelist* and those of
like mind with him (Luthardt). — τῇ ἀκοῇ ἡμ.] *to that heard from us, i.e.* to
the message which they receive from us (comp. on Rom. x. 16), not : which
we receive (comp. Sir. xliii. 24), namely, actually in Christ (Luthardt), as

---

[1] Lücke, de Wette, and several others.
[2] Comp. on the distinction between the
two notions, the phrase current in the clas-

sics, τοσαῦτά τε καὶ τοιαῦτα, Heindorf, *ad
Plat. Gorg.* p. 456 C.
[3] Xen. *Cyr.* viii. 2. 14, *Anab.* i. 9. 11.

Hengstenberg also understands it of that which we have received through revelation (comp. Euth. Zigabenus).[1] The *plural*, however, *ἡμῶν*, comprises God and Christ in the fulfilment. — *ὁ βραχίων κυρ.*] Plastic expression for the *power* of God,[2] and that according to the Messianic conception ; in the *miraculous signs of Christ*—in which the unbelieving do not recognize the *brachium Dei.* "In se exsertum est, sed cæci non viderunt illud," Bengel. But to understand *Christ Himself*[3] is required neither by the original text nor here by the connection.

Vv. 39, 40. *Διὰ τοῦτο . . . ὅτι*] as always in John (see on x. 17) : *therefore,* referring to what *precedes,* on account of this destiny contained in ver. 38— *namely, because,* so that thus with *ὅτι* the reason is still more minutely set forth. Ebrard foists in an entirely foreign course of thought, because Israel has not *willed* to believe, therefore has she not *been able* to believe. Contrary to this Johannean use of *διὰ τοῦτο . . . ὅτι*, Theophylact, Beza, Jansen, Lampe, and several others, including Lücke, Tholuck, Olshausen, Maier, B. Crusius, Luthardt, take *διὰ τοῦτο* as *preparative.* — *οὐκ ἠδύναντο*] not : *nolebant,*[4] but—thus solving the enigma of that tragic unbelief—*they could not,* an *impossibility* which had its foundation in the divine judgment of obduracy. "Hic subsistit evangelista, quis ultra nitatur ?" Bengel. On the relation of this inability, referred back to the determination of God, to moral freedom and responsibility, see on Rom. ix.–xi. — *τετύφλωκεν*] The passage is Isa. vi. 9, 10, departing freely from the original and from the LXX. In the original the *prophet* is said, at the command of *God*, to undertake the blinding, etc., that is, the intellectual and moral hardening ("*harden* the heart," etc.). Thus what God then *will allow* to be done is represented by John in his free manner of citation as *done by God Himself*, to which the recollection of the rendering of the passage given by the LXX. ("the heart has *become hardened*," etc.) might easily lead. The subject is thus neither *Christ* (Grotius, Calovius, and several others, including Lange and Ebrard), nor the *devil* (Hilgenfeld, Scholten), but, as the reader would understand as a matter of course, and as also the entire context shows (for the necessity in the divine fate is the leading idea), *God.* Christ first appears as subject in *ἰάσομαι.* — *πεπώρ.*] *has hardened.*[4] — *καὶ στραφῶσι*] *and* (not) *turn,* return to me. — *ἰάσομαι*] Future, dependent on *ἵνα μή.* See on Matt. xiii. 15. The moral corruption is viewed as *sickness,* which is *healed* by faith (vv. 37, 39). Comp. Matt. ix. 12 ; 1 Pet. ii. 24. The healing *subject,* however, cannot, as in Matt. xiii. 15, Acts xxviii. 27, be *God* (so *usually*), precisely because this is the subject of *τετύφλωκεν, κ.τ.λ.*, but it must be *Christ ;* in *His* mouth, according to the Johannean view of the prophecy from the standpoint of its fulfilment, Isaiah puts not merely the utterance in ver. 38, but also the words *τετύφλωκεν . . . ἰάσομαι αὐτούς,*

---

[1] Comp. on the genitive, Plat. *Phaedr.* p. 274 C ; Pausan. viii. 41. 6 ; Pind. *Pyth.* i. 162.

[2] Comp. Luke i. 51 ; Acts xiii. 17 ; Wisd. v. 16, xi. 21 ; Bar. ii. 11 ; Isa. li. 5, lii. 10.

[3] Augustine, Photius, Euth. Zigabenus, Beda, Ruperti, Zeger, Jansen, Maldonatus, Calovius, and several others.

[4] Chrysostom, Theophylact, Euth. Zigabenus, Wolf.

[5] See Athenaeus, 12, p. 549 B ; Mark vi. 52, viii. 17 ; Rom. xi. 7 ; 2 Cor. iii. 14.

and thus makes Him say : God has blinded the people, etc., that they should not see, etc., and should not turn to Him (Christ), and He (Christ) should heal them. Nonnus aptly says : Ὀφθαλμοὺς ἀλάωσεν ἐμῶν ἐπιμάρτυρας ἔργων . . . μὴ κραδίῃ νοέωσι . . . καί μοι ὑποστρέψωσι, νοοβλαβέας δὲ σαώσω ἄνδρας ἀλιτραίνοντας ἐμῷ παιήονι μίθῳ. Thus the 1st person ἰάσομαι is not an instance of "*negligence*," [1] but of *consistency*.

Ver. 41. Ὅτι] (see the critical notes) : *because He saw His glory, and* (in consequence of this view) *spoke of Him*. This was the *occasion* that moved him, and it led to his speaking what is contained in ver. 40. — αὐτοῦ] refers to *Christ*, the subject of ἰάσομαι, ver. 40, and the chief person in the whole subject under contemplation (ver. 37). According to Isa. vi. 1 ff., the prophet, indeed, beheld *God's* glory, *God* sitting upon His throne, attended by seraphim, etc. ; but in the O. T. theophanies, it is precisely Christ who is present as the *Logos*,[2] and their glory is His. See on i. 1. Of course the glory of Christ *before* the incarnation is intended, the μορφὴ θεοῦ (Phil. ii. 6), in which He was. — καὶ ἐλαλ. περὶ αὐτοῦ] still dependent on ὅτι ; ἐλάλησε has the emphasis as the correlate of εἶδε.

Vv. 42, 43. Ὅμως μέντοι] *yet, notwithstanding*.[3] It limits the judgment on the unbelief of the Jews, which had previously been expressed in general terms. — καὶ ἐκ τ. ἀρχ.] *even of the Sanhedrists* (in secret, vii. 48). — διὰ τοὺς Φαρισ.] the most hostile and dreaded party opposed to Jesus in and outside the Sanhedrim. — ἀποσυνάγ.] comp. ix. 22. — τὴν δόξ. τ. ἀνθρ.] *the honour coming from men*. Comp. v. 44. — τὴν δόξ. τοῦ θεοῦ] *the honour which God imparts*. Comp. Rom. iii. 23. They preferred the *honour of men* (*potius*, see on iii. 19) rather than to stand in honour with *God*. Theirs was thus not yet the faith strengthened for a free confession, which Jesus demands (Matt. x. 32), with the setting aside of temporal interests ; Augustine calls it *ingressus fidei*. Where subsequently the right *advance* followed, the un-hesitating *confession* also was forthcoming, as in the cases of Nicodemus and of Joseph of Arimathaea. But the case of *Gamaliel* is not applicable here (Godet) ; he did *not* get so far as faith. — On ἤπερ, as strengthening the negative force of the ἤ (comp. 2 Macc. xiv. 42), see Kühner, II. sec. 747, note 4.

Vv. 44, 45. The closing observations on Jewish unbelief, vv. 37–43, are ended. Over against this unbelief, together with that faith which stood in fear of men, vv. 42, 43, John now gives further, vv. 44–50, an energetic *summing up*, a condensed *summary* of that which Jesus has hitherto clearly and openly preached concerning His personal dignity and the divinity of

[1] Tholuck, comp. his *A. T. im N. T.* p. 35 f. ed. 6.

[2] From which a conclusion can as little be drawn against the personality of the Logos (Beyschlag, p. 166 f.), as from the angelic theophanies against the personality of the angel or angels concerned (not even in Rev. v. 6). That the idea of angels in the N. T. wavers between personality and personification is not correct. Observe also, that the self-revelation of the devil does not set aside the personality of the man who is the bearer of it (as Judas). Further, the αὐτοῦ, implying the identity of Christ with the Logos, here shows clearly enough that the latter is viewed as personal. Comp. also Pfleiderer, in Hilgenfeld, *Zeitschr.* 1866, p. 258.

[3] Herod. i. 189 ; Plat. *Crit.* p. 54 D, *Men.* p. 92 E ; comp. the strengthened ὅμως γε μέντοι, Klotz, *ad Devar.* p. 343 ; Baeumlein, *Partik.* p. 172 f.

His teaching, in condemnation of such conduct (" *Jesus, on the other hand, cried and said*," etc.), by which the reprehensible nature of that unbelief and half-belief comes clearly into view. So substantially Bengel, Michaelis, Morus, Kuinoel, Lücke, Tholuck, Olshausen, Maier, Schweizer, B. Crusius, Reuss, Baur,[1] Lange, Brückner, Weizsäcker,[2] Ebrard, Baeumlein, Ewald, Godet. Ver. 36 is decisive, for the correctness of this interpretation, according to which Jesus has departed from the public scene of action without any announcement of His reappearance ; and it is confirmed partly by the nature of the following discourse, which contains mere echoes of earlier utterances ; partly by the fact that throughout the whole discourse there are no addressed persons present ; partly by the aorists, ἐλάλησα, vv. 48, 49, pointing to the concluded past. This is not in opposition to ἔκραξε καὶ εἶπεν,[3] since these words (comp. vii. 28, 37, i. 15) do not of themselves more closely define the point of time which is intended. Hence we are neither to assume, with de Wette, that with John the recollection of the discourses of Jesus shaped itself " under his hand " into a discourse, genuine indeed, but never delivered in such language (what unconsciousness and passivity he is thereby charged with ! and see, in opposition, Brückner); nor are we to say, with Chrysostom and all the older commentators, also Kling and Hengstenberg, that Jesus here for once did publicly so speak (ἐνδόντος τοῖς Ἰουδαίοις τοῦ θυμοῦ, πάλιν ἀνεφάνη κ. διδάσκει, Euth. Zigabenus), in accordance with which some resort to the explanation, in contradiction with the text, that He spoke what follows *in ipso discessu*, ver. 36 (Lampe). But when Luthardt, following Besser,[4] assumes that Christ spoke these words *in the presence of* the disciples, and with reference to the Jews, there is opposed to this not only the fact, in general, that John indicates nothing of the kind, but also that ἔκραξε is not appropriate to the circle of disciples, but to a scene of publicity. *Crying aloud He exclaimed*, whereby all His hearers were made sensible enough of the importance of the address, and the excuse of ignorance was cut off from them. — ὁ πιστ. εἰς ἐμέ, κ.τ.λ.] An utterance which John has not in the previous discourses. Comp., however, as to the thing, v. 36 ff., vii. 29, viii. 19, 42, x. 38. — οὐ . . . ἀλλ'] simply negativing. The object of faith is *not* the personality of Jesus in itself,—that human appearance which was set forth in Him, as if He had come in His own name (v. 43),—but *God*, so far as the latter reveals Himself in Him as His ambassador, by means of His words and deeds. Comp. vii. 16 ; Mark ix. 37. Similarly : *He who beholds me*, etc., ver. 45. Comp. i. 14, xiv. 9. Yet in *this* connection the negation (οὐ θεωρεῖ ἐμέ) is not expressed, although it *might* have been expressed ; but what had to be affirmed was, that the beholding of Christ was *at the same time* the beholding of His sender. In

---

[1] Baur, however, finds in this recapitulatory discourse only a new proof, that with John historical narration is a *mere form* of his method of representation. Comp. also Hilgenfeld.

[2] Yet the ideas (against Weizsäcker, in the *Jahrb. f. Deutsche Theol.* 1857, p. 167 f.) contained in this speech are not different from those of the prologue. The *form* is different, but not the *matter ;* and the prologue contains *more*.

[3] Against Kling, de Wette, Hengstenberg ; also Strauss in advocacy of the non-originality of the Johannean discourses.

[4] *Zeitschr. f. Luth. Theol.* 1852, p. 617 ff.

His working and administration, the believing eye beholds that of the *Sender ;* in the glory of the *Son,* that of the *Father,* i. 14 ; Heb. i. 3.

Ver. 46. Comp. viii. 12, ix. 5, xii. 35, 36. — *ἐγώ*] *I,* no other, *I am the light,* as possessor and communicator of the divine truth of salvation, *come into the world,* etc. — *μὴ μείνῃ*] as he is, in a state of unbelief, but that he may be enlightened. Comp. ver. 36, i. 4 ff.

Vv. 47, 48. Comp. iii. 17, 18, v. 45 ff., viii. 15 ff. — *If any one shall have heard the words from me,* does not denote hearing in the sense of *believing* (Lücke), but a hearing which is in itself indifferent (Matt. vii. 26 ; Mark iv. 15, 16, xviii. 20) ; and by the *κ. μὴ φυλάξῃ* which follows (see the critical notes), that very faith which follows hearing is *denied.* *φυλάσσειν,* namely, denotes not indeed the mere *holding fast, guarding* (ver. 25), but, as throughout, where doctrines, precepts, and the like are spoken of (see especially Luke xi. 28, xviii. 21 ; Rom. ii. 26), the keeping by actual *fulfilment.* But this takes place simply by *faith,* which Christ demands for His *ῥήματα :* *with faith* the *φυλάσσειν comes into action ;* [1] the *refusal of faith* is the *rejection of Christ,* [2] and *non-adoption of His words,* ver. 48, is the opposite of that *φυλάσσειν* so far as its essence is just the *ὑπακοὴ τῆς πίστεως.* — On *ἀκούειν* with a double genitive as in Luke vi. 47, Acts xxii. 1, comp. xviii. 37. [3] — *ἐγὼ οὐ κρίνω αὐτόν*] *I,* in my person, *am not his judge,* which is meant *generally,* not exclusively of the *last* judgment, but in a *condemnatory* sense, as opposed to *σώζειν,* as in iii. 17. — Ver. 48. *ἔχει*] Placed first with great emphasis : he *has his judge ;* he *stands already under his trial.* But this judge, says Christ, is not Himself, as an individual personally considered in and by Himself, but His spoken *word ;* this, and nothing else, will be (and with this arises before the mind all the terror of the *final* decision) the determining rule of the *last* judgment. It is *Christ,* indeed, who holds the judgment (v. 22, 27), but as the bearer and executor of His *word,* which constitutes the divine power of the judgment. Comp. vii. 51, where the *law* judges and takes cognizance. How decisively does the present passage declare against the attempt of Scholten, Hilgenfeld, Reuss, and others, to explain away the last judgment out of John ! Comp. vv. 28, 29 ; 1 John iv. 17.

Vv. 49, 50. Comp. vii. 16, v. 30. — *ὅτι*] gives the reason for the expression in vv. 47, 48 : for how plainly *divine* is this my word ! — *ἐξ ἐμαυτοῦ*] *αὐτοκέλευστος,* Nonnus. — *αὐτός*] *ipse.* — *ἐντολ. ἔδ.*] He has *given* (laid upon) me *a charge, what I should say, and what I should speak.* The former designates the doctrine in its *contents,* the latter the *publication* of it through the *delivery* which makes it known. Comp. on viii. 43 ; Rom. iii. 19. [4] — *ἡ ἐντολὴ αὐτοῦ*] namely the commission which has just previously been more minutely designated. This is, because it is in truth the outflow and channel of the divine redemptive will, *eternal life* (alike in its temporal development and eternal consummation) ; it *is* this, however (comp. vi. 33,

---

[1] Hence the *Recepta κ. μὴ πιστεύσῃ* is a correct gloss.

[2] *ἀθετεῖν,* here only in John, but comp. Luke x. 16 ; 1 Thess. iv. 8.

[3] Buttmann, *N. T. Gr.* p. 145 [E. T. p. 167].

[4] For similar accumulations of the verbs of speaking in Greek writers, see Dissen, *ad Dem. de Cor.* p. 187 ; Lobeck, *Paral.* p. 61.

xvii. 17 ; comp. xi. 25, xiv. 6), not as the mere *means*, but as, in its fulfilment, the efficient *power* of life in virtue of the grace and truth which are
received by believers out of the fulness of Jesus, i. 14, 16. — οὖν] Since that
ἐντολή is of so great efficacy, how could I speak that which *I* speak otherwise than as the *Father* has said it to me (at my inauguration) ? Observe
the correlation of ἐγώ and ὁ πατήρ, as well as the measured simple solemnity
of this closing address.

NOTE BY AMERICAN EDITOR.

XXXVIII. Ἄφες αὐτήν, ἵνα κ.τ.λ. Ver. 7.

The rendering of the Rev. Ver., which is substantially that of Meyer,
" Suffer her to keep it against the day of my burying," seems to have little
pertinence against the murmuring of the thievish disciple (which was not directed against any supposed future use of the money, but only against its present alleged waste), nor very intelligible in itself, as that part of it which had
been used *could* not be so preserved (and this was probably a large part of
it), and of a *remaining portion* of it the text says nothing. If τετήρηκεν, therefore, is to be decisively rejected, the rendering of the margin of the Rev. Ver.
seems the only right one, which gives to ἄφες αὐτήν its ordinary N. T. meaning,
and assumes a not unallowable ellipsis with ἵνα. " Let her alone : *it was that*
she might keep it against the day of my burial," of which the present anointing is regarded as a type, and this the more naturally as that real embalming was
so close at hand. To him who is not afraid to find coincidences in the Gospels,
Matt. xxvi. 12 is corroborative of this view. The words "that she might keep it"
are not probably used of her having kept it over from the entombment of Lazarus, but refer to the suggestion made by Judas of its being given to the poor.
She has not applied it to any such purpose, however intrinsically good ; under
higher influence it has been kept for even a more sacred purpose, my figurative
burial.

CHAPTER XIII.

Ver. 1. ἐλήλυθεν] Lachm. and Tisch. : ἦλθεν, according to preponderating evidence. The perfect arose from xii. 23. — Ver. 2. γενομένου] B. L. X. ℵ. Cant. Or. : γινομένου (but Or. has once γενομ.). So Tisch. The aorist was introduced through the non-observance of the point of time, as being the more current form in the narrative. — Ἰούδα Σίμ. Ἰσκ., ἵνα αὐτὸν παραδῷν] B. L. M. X. ℵ. Copt. Arm. Vulg. Codd. It. Or. : ἵνα παραδῷ αὐτὸν Ἰούδας Σίμωνος Ἰσκαριώτης. So Lachm. on the margin, and Tisch. (both, however, reading παραδοῖ, according to B. D.* ℵ. only). This reading, considering the important witnesses by which it is attested, is the more to be preferred, as it was very early misunderstood, because it was supposed that the seduction of Judas by the devil was here related (so already Origen). The *Recepta* is an alteration in consequence of this misunderstanding. The conjunctive form παραδοῖ, however, remains generally doubtful in the N. T. — Ver. 3. ὁ Ἰησοῦς] is wanting in B. D. L. X. Cursives, Vulg. It. Or. Bracketed by Lachm., omitted by Tisch. It was mechanically repeated from ver. 1. — Ver. 10. The position of the words οὐκ ἔχει χρείαν is decisively attested. — Instead of ἤ, important witnesses have εἰ μή (so Lachm.), which, however, is an attempt at explanation or correction. Tisch. has deleted ἢ τ. πόδας, but only after ℵ. Or. one Cod. of It. and Vulg. mss. An old omission, occasioned by the following καθαρ. ὅλος. — Ver. 12. ἀναπεσών] Lachm. : καὶ ἀναπ. according to A. L. Verss. Chrys. In favour of καί, witness also B. C.* ℵ. Or., which have καὶ ἀνέπεσεν (so Tisch.). The καί before ἔλαβ. is omitted by Lachm. after A. L. Verss. Since καί before ἀναπ. is in any case decisively accredited ; since, further, the witnesses for ἀνέπεσεν are more important than for ἀναπεσών ; and since, had ἀναπεσών been the original reading, it would not have been resolved into καὶ ἀνέπεσεν, but into ἀνέπεσεν καί, —we must read with Tisch. καὶ ἀνέπεσεν, so that the apodosis first begins with εἶπεν. This was not observed, and it was made to commence either after πόδας αὐτῶν (thus arose the reading in Lachm.), or after ἱμάτ. αὐτοῦ (hence the *Recepta*). — Ver. 22. οὖν] is wanting in B. C. and certain Verss. ; deleted by Tisch. Was easily passed over after the last syllable of ἔβλεπον. — Ver. 23. ἐκ τῶν (Elz.: τῶν) is decisively attested. — Ver. 24. πυθέσθαι, τίς ἂν εἴη] B. C. L. X. 33. Aeth. Ver. Rd. Vulg. Or. : καὶ λέγει αὐτῷ· εἰπὲ τίς ἐστιν. So Lachm. and Tisch. Rightly : the *Recepta* is added, as a gloss, after what John does in ver. 25. ℵ. has the gloss *alongside* of the original reading in the text. — Ver. 25. ἐπιπεσών] B. C.* K. L. X. Π.* ℵ.** Cursives, Or. : ἀναπεσών (so Lachm.). But ἐπιπίπτειν does not occur elsewhere in John ; and how readily would the familiar expression of lying *at table* suggest itself to mechanical copyists ! — Instead of οὖν, Elz. and Lachm. have δέ. Witnesses are much divided. Originally, no particle at all appears to have been found ; so B. C. Or. Griesb. — After ἐκεῖνος, important witnesses (including B. C. L.) have οὕτως, which, however, although defended by Ewald, very readily arose from οὗτος, which was added to ἐκεῖνος in explanation, as it still found in K. S. U. Λ. — Ver. 26. βάψας τὸ ψωμίον ἐπιδώσω] Tisch. : βάψω τ. ψ. καὶ δώσω αὐτῷ, after B. C. L. Copt. Aeth. Or. But ἐπιδιδόναι, which is not elsewhere found in John, does not betray the hand of an interpreter, and therefore the reading of Tisch. is rather to be considered as the usual resolution of the participle, with neglect of the compound.—Instead of βάψας, as above, Lachm. has ἐμβάψ., following A. D. K. Π. Theodoret. Although these witnesses form the preponderance among those which read the participle, yet ἐμβάψ. might be very readily introduced from the parallels, Matt. xxvi. 23, Mark xiv. 20 ; and for the originality of the simple form, the weighty witnesses (B. C. L. etc.) which have βάψω (not ἐμβαψω) are accordingly all the more to be taken into account. Therefore, too, below, instead of καὶ ἐμβάψας (so also Lachm.), with B. C. L. X. א. 33. Or. Cyr., βάψας οὖν (so Tisch.) ought to be read (D. has καὶ βάψας). — After ψωμίον, Tisch. has, moreover, λαμβάνει καί, following B. C. L. M. X. א.** Aeth. Or. Rightly : it was, through misapprehension, omitted as irrelevant. — Instead of Ἰσκαριώτη, Lachm. should consistently, following B. C. L. M. X. א. Cursives, Codd. It. Or., here also (see on vi. 71) have read Ἰσκαριώτου (as Tisch. has). — Ver. 30. Instead of εὐθέως ἐξῆλθ. read with Lachm. and Tisch. ἐξῆλθ. εὐθύς. — Ver. 31. After ὅτε, Elz. Lachm. and Tisch. have οὖν ; rightly, since B. C. D. L. X. א. Cursives, Verss. Or. Cyr., turn the scale in favour of οὖν, while the omission (Griesb. Scholz) was the more readily suggested, as there was an inclination to begin the new sentence with ἦν δὲ νύξ. — Ver. 32. εἰ ὁ θ. ἐδοξ. ἐν αὐτῷ] is rejected by Scholz as " inepta iteratio," and bracketed by Lachm. The words are wanting in B. C.* D. L. X. Π. א.* Cursives, Verss. Tert. Ambr. But the very repetition and the *homoeoteleuton* would so readily occasion the omission, that these adverse witnesses cannot overthrow the reading. — Ver. 33. The order ἐγὼ ὑπάγω (Lachm. Tisch.) is too decisively attested to admit of its being derived from viii. 21. — Ver. 36. The order ἀκολ. δὲ ὕστερον (without μοι) is to be adopted, with Lachm. and Tisch ; so also in ver. 38, ἀποκρίνεται (instead of ἀπεκρίθη). — Ver. 38. The form φωνήσῃ (Lachm. Tisch.) is decisively accredited ; and instead of ἀπαρνήσῃ, ἀρνήσῃ is, with Lachm. and Tisch., following B. D. L. X. 1. Or., to be read, in place of which the compound was introduced from Matt. xxvi. 34 and the parallel passages.

Vv. 1–5. On the construction [See Note XXXIX. p. 402], observe : (1) vv. 1–5 are not to be taken together as a single period ; [1] as Paul also [2] defines the connection : " *He arises before the Passover feast at the meal then taking place*," which latter would more nearly define πρὸ τ. ἑορτ. τ. π. This constructing the whole together is inadmissible, because εἰς τέλος ἠγάπ. αὐτούς, being connected with πρὸ δὲ ἑορτ. τ. π., completes regularly the construction of ver. 1, and with καὶ δείπνου γιν. a new period begins ; consequently (this also in answer to Knapp, Lücke, Ebrard, and several others) εἰδώς, ver. 3, cannot be the resumption of εἰδώς, ver. 1. Rightly Lachmann and Tischendorf close ver. 1 with a *full stop*.[3] (2) We may not join πρὸ τῆς ἑορτ. τ. πάσχα with εἰδώς,[4] because the expression states too vaguely and indefinitely the point of time in which the definite consciousness of His hour entered the

---

[1] Griesbach, Matthaei, Schulz, Scholz, Bleek, Ebrard, and several others.
[2] *Stud. u. Krit.* 1866, p. 362 ff., 1867, p. 524 ff.
[3] Comp. Hengst. Godet, Ewald.

[4] Kling, Luthardt, Riggenbach, Graf in the *Stud. u. Krit.* 1867, p. 741 ff.; before him also Baeumlein in the *Stud. u. Krit.* 1846, p. 397.

mind of Jesus ; the definite day before the feast would be *designated* as such (perhaps by πρὸ μιᾶς ἡμέρας τοῦ πάσχα, comp. xii. 1 ; Plut. *Sull.* 37). But that πρὸ τῆς ἑορτῆς—comp. with xii. 1—must denote this very *day before* the feast, namely, the 14th Nisan,[1] is an altogether arbitrary assumption. Just as incorrect is it (3) to refer it to ἀγαπήσας,[2] so that the love entertained *before the feast* stands over against the love entertained *until the end*,—which assumption is extorted simply by an attempt at harmonizing, is opposed to the order of the words (ἀγαπήσας . . . κόσμῳ must in that case have stood *before* εἰδώς, κ.τ.λ.), and—through the *division* which is then made to appear of the love of Jesus (the love *before* the feast, and the love *from* the feast *onwards*)—is in contradiction with John's more reflective and spiritual manner ; while it leaves, moreover, the participial clause εἰδὼς . . . πατέρα without appropriate significance. The simple literal mode of connection is rather : *Before the feast, Jesus gave, since He knew, etc., to His own the closing proof of love. While, then, a meal is being observed, as the devil already, etc.,* He arises from the meal, although *He knows that the Father, etc.* There is thus nothing to place in a parenthesis.

Ver. 1. Πρὸ δὲ τ. ἑορτ. τ. πάσχα] πρό is *emphasized* by the intervening δέ. Jesus had arrived at Bethany six days before the Passover, on the following day (xii. 1, 12) had entered Jerusalem, and then, xii. 36, withdrawn Himself into concealment. But *before* the paschal feast began,[3] there followed the closing manifestation of love before His death, which John intends to relate. *How long* before the feast, our passage does not state ; but it is clear from ver. 29, xviii. 28, xix. 14, 31, that it was not on the 14th Nisan, as the harmonists have frequently maintained (see, however, on xviii. 28), but[4] *on the 13th Nisan,* Thursday evening, at the Supper. On the 14th Nisan, in the evening, the festival commenced with the *paschal* meal, after Jesus had been crucified on the afternoon of the same day. Such is the view of John ; see on xviii. 28. — εἰδώς, κ.τ.λ.] Not, "*although* He knew" (this is unpsychological, Hengstenberg), but *because* He knew. He gives expression to that which inwardly drew and impelled Him to display towards His own a further and a last token of love ; He *knew*, indeed, *that for Him the hour was come, that he should go*, etc. (ἵνα comp. xii. 23). On μεταβῇ, comp. v. 24 ; 1 John iii. 14. — ἀγαπήσας, κ.τ.λ.] is regarded by interpreters as co-ordinated with εἰδώς, κ.τ.λ., according to the well-known usage, which rests on a logical basis, of the *asyndetic* connection of several participles ;[5] so that the meaning would be : *As He had* (ever) *loved His own*, so also at the very last He gave them a true proof of love. But opposed to this is the absence of

[1] Hofmann, *Schriftbew.* II. 2, p. 295, Lange, Baeumlein, and several others, including Paul and Hengstenberg.

[2] Wieseler, Tholuck, see in opposition Ewald, *Jahrb.* IX. p. 208.

[3] Rightly has Rückert observed. *Abendm.* p. 26, that by πρὸ δὲ τῆς ἑορτῆς the possibility of thinking of a point of time within the Passover, and thus even of the paschal meal, is precluded for the reader who has

advanced so far. Incorrectly, Riggenbach, *Zeugn. f. d. Ev. Joh.* p. 72 : there hangs over the present passage "*a certain darkness.*" Certainly, if we set out from a harmonistic point of view. With such, rather is it entirely irreconcilable.

[4] See also Isenberg, *d Todestag des Herrn*, 1868, p. 7 ff.

[5] Voigtler, *ad Luc. D. M.* xii. p. 67 ff. ; Kühner, *ad Xen. Anab.* i. 1. 7.

an ἀεί, which Nonnus supplies, or of ἀπ' ἀρχῆς, or πάλαι or the like, along with ἀγαπήσας, whereby a correlation with εἰς τέλος would have been established.   In addition to this, the clause τοὺς ἐν τῷ κόσμῳ, not in itself indispensable, but expressive of sorrow, is manifestly added in reference to the preceding ἐκ τοῦ κόσμου τ., and thus betrays the connection of ἀγαπήσας . . . κόσμῳ with the final clause ἵνα μεταβῇ, κ.τ.λ.   Hence : " in order to pass to the Father, after He should have (not had) loved," etc. [See Note XL. p. 403.]   This, "after He should have loved," etc., is a testimony which His conscience yielded Him with that εἰδώς, κ.τ.λ. — τοὺς ἰδίους] This relationship —the N. T. fulfilment of the old theocratic, i. 11—had its fullest representation in the circle of apostles, so that the apostles were pre-eminently the ἴδιοι of Jesus. — εἰς τέλος ἠγάπ. αὐτούς] to be connected with πρὸ δὲ τῆς ἑορτ. τ. π. : at last (εἰς τέλος is emphatic) He loved them, i.e. showed them the last proof of love before His death.[1]   How, the καὶ δείπνου, κ.τ.λ., which immediately follows, expresses, namely, by means of the washing of the feet, hence it cannot be understood of the whole work of love in suffering (Graf). εἰς τέλος denotes at the end, finally, at last.[2]   So also 1 Thess. ii. 16.   It may also denote fully, in the highest degree ;[3] but this yields here an inappropriate gradation, as though Jesus now exercised His love to the utmost (in answer to Godet).   It was the like love with the preceding ἀγαπήσας, only the last proof before departure ; for His hour was come. — On ἠγάπησεν, of actually manifested love, comp. ver. 34 ; 1 John iv. 10, 19 ; Eph. ii. 4, v. 2, 25.

NOTE.—From the present passage—since πρὸ τῆς ἑορτῆς gives the chronological measure for the following supper, and with this for the whole history of the passion—already appears the irreconcilable difference between John and the Synoptics in respect of the day of Jesus' death.   See details on xviii. 28. Even if πρὸ τῆς ἑορτ. were connected with εἰδώς, this statement of time would be historically explicable only from the fact that Jesus, conformably to the certainty which entered His mind before the feast —" my hour is come"—did what follows not at the feast, i.e. after the beginning of the feast on the evening of the 14th Nisan, but just before the feast (i.e. at least on the evening of the 13th Nisan), in the consciousness that now His time was fulfilled, satisfying His love for the last time.   Luthardt incorrectly concludes that, if Jesus knew already before the feast, etc., He must have died at the feast.   Of such an antithesis the text contains not the slightest indication.   Rather, if Jesus knew before the feast, etc., and acted in this consciousness, we are not at liberty to move forward the δείπνον, and that which is connected with it, to the feast. The matter lies simply thus : If the supper were that of the 14th Nisan, then John could not say πρὸ τῆς ἑορτῆς, but only either πρὸ τοῦ δείπνου τοῦ πάσχα (which sense is imported by Hengstenberg) ; or, on the other hand, like the Synoptics, τῇ πρώτῃ τῶν ἀζύμων (Matt. xxvi. 17), or τ. πρώτῃ τῆς ἑορτῆς.   The 15th Nisan was already ἡ ἐπαύριον τοῦ πάσχα (LXX. Num. xxxiii. 3 : מִמָּחֳרַת הַפֶּסַח,

---

[1] Ebrard's inconsiderate objection (on Olshausen, p. 337) against my connection of εἰς τέλ. ἠγάπ. with πρὸ τ. ἑορτῆς, since εἰς τέλ. ἠγάπ. is the last performance of love, will probably be found by him to fall of itself to the ground.

[2] Luke xviii. 5 (see commentary in loc.); Hdt. iii. 40 ; Xen. Oec. xvii. 1b ; Soph. Phil. 407 (and Hermann's note).

[3] Pflugk, ad Eur. Hec. 817; Schweighäuser, Lex. Polyb. p. 616 ; Grimm on 2 Macc. viii. 29.

comp. Josh. v. 11) ; but the 14th was פֶּסַח לַיהֹוָה, Num. xviii. 16, *et al.*, ἡ ἡμέρα
τοῦ πάσχα. Comp. *Introd.* § 2.

Vv. 2–5. And (*et quidem*) this εἰς τέλος ἠγάπησεν αὐτούς He fulfilled at the
supper by the washing of the feet. — δεῖπνον γινομ.] Note the *present*, standing in relation to the present ἐγείρεται, ver. 4 (see critical notes). *Whilst it
is becoming supper-time*, i.e. *whilst supper-time is on the point of being kept.*[1]
They had already *reclined* for the purpose, vv. 4, 12. According to the
Recepta, γενομ., the meal was not yet over (Luther and several others, including Klee and Hofmann, p. 207, who explains as though μετὰ τὸ δεῖπνον were
expressed), but already in progress,—supper had *begun*. This itself was,
according to ver. 1, not the *paschal supper*, but (hence also without the
article [2]) an ordinary evening meal on the 13th Nisan (in opposition to the
synoptical account) in Jerusalem (not in Bethany, see on xiv. 31), the *last*
repast of Jesus before His death, at which He founded the Lord's Supper
(xiii. 21 ff., 38, xviii. 1). The *institution of the Supper* John leaves unmentioned—not as being unacquainted with it (Strauss), or seeing in it
no ecclesiastical rite (Scholten), but because it was universally known (1
Cor. xi.), and the practice itself was in daily use (Acts ii. 46). Rather, therefore, than repeat the familiar account, he selected from the abundance of
that last night what, besides this, he found most in harmony with his
peculiar object, the making known the *glory* of the λόγος in the flesh,—in the
washing of the feet, χάρις, in the discourses, χάρις and ἀλήθεια. According
to Schenkel, John desired by his silence to preclude the notions of a *magical*
effect resulting from the Lord's Supper, and the later *controversies* concerning it. But such a purpose would have required the very opposite procedure, viz. distinct *instruction*. Baur assumes, p. 264, that the evangelist
has dated back the significance of the Supper to the second Passover, chap.
vi., because he did not wish to allow the last meal of Jesus to pass for
the same as that in the Synoptics, namely, a paschal meal. Comp. also
Scholten, p. 289 ff. But for this purpose such an inversion of the synoptical
material was not at all necessary. He could have mentioned the institution
of the Supper at the last meal in such a way that this would still *not* have
been a paschal meal. — τοῦ διαβόλου ἤδη, κ.τ.λ.] cannot serve merely as a *prelude* to the *subsequent* and more frequent mention of the relation of Jesus to
the traitor (vv. 10, 18, 21, 26, 27, 30), as Godet maintains, which would be
but a formal purpose, and not in harmony with the tragic emphasis of the
language. Nor is it intended to make us sensible of the *forbearance* of
Jesus, who Himself washed the feet of *Judas*,[3] nor in general, the mere *short-*

---

[1] [Or rather, perhaps, *while a supper is taking place.*—K.]
[2] Certainly it is often indifferent whether
the article stands with δεῖπνον or not, but
here it *must* have stood, had it been intended to indicate that solemn meal of the 14th
Nisan, the venerable *meal of the feast*. In
xxi. 20 the article had to be expressed, because it *points backwards*. This in answer

to Tholuck. Hofmann, Lange, and Paul also get over too readily the want of the article ; and even Graf imports the meaning,
which is incompatible with the absence of
the article : "After the principal part of
the supper, the eating of the paschal lamb,
was over."
[3] Otherwise special prominence must have
been given in what follows to the washing

ness of the interval (ἤδη) ere the final tragedy, which he yet devoted to such a work of love (this, indeed, was already contained in εἰδώς, κ.τ.λ.), but—to which the ἤδη points—the *undisturbed clear elevation* of this His might of love over the impending outbreak of the tragic devilish treachery, which could not even now, immediately before its occurrence, confuse His mind. According to the reading Ἰούδας Σίμ. Ἰσκαριώτης (see the critical notes), we must explain : *the devil having already formed the design that Judas should deliver Him up.* The καρδία is not that of *Judas* (Luthardt, Baeumlein), as in the *Recepta*, but of the *devil* (comp. Vulgate) ; as in the classics βάλλειν or βάλλεσθαι εἰς νοῦν, εἰς θυμόν, ἐν φρεσίν, frequently denotes *in animum inducere, statuere, deliberare.*[1] [See Note XLI. p. 403.] Current as was this mode of speech, we cannot be surprised, in an anthropomorphic representation of the devil, at the mention of his *heart* (in answer to Lücke, Godet, and others), in which he has his ἐπιθυμίας (viii. 44), μεθοδείας (Eph. vi. 11), νοήματα (2 Cor. ii. 11), etc. As the heart of *God* may be spoken of (Acts xiii. 22), so also the heart of the *devil.* — Ἰούδας Σίμ. Ἰσκαρ.] The full name, and at the close, contains a shuddering emphasis. — The participial clause is not to be placed in a parenthesis ; it is co-ordinated with δείπνου γινομ. — εἰδώς, κ.τ.λ.] *Although He knew* (ὅμως εἰς ἄκραν συγκατέβη ταπείνωσιν, Euth. Zigabenus). The consciousness of His divine elevation rested, while on this threshold of death, in the fact that now, being on the point of entering, by stepping over this threshold, upon His glorification, the *Messianic fulness of power*, which had formerly been bestowed upon Him on the occasion of His mission (Matt. xi. 27), which extended over all things, and was limited by nothing, was given into His hands for complete exercise (comp. on xvii. 2, Matt. xxviii. 18) ; and that *God*, as He was the source of His coming (comp. on viii. 42), so is the goal of His present departure. — On πάντα δέδωκεν αὐτῷ comp. 1 Cor. xv. 25 ; Eph. ii. 22 ; Phil. ii. 9–11, *et al.* — Ver. 4. ἐγείρεται, κ.τ.λ.] Note how the *whole representation regards things as present ;* to the historic present correspond the present and perfect participles γινομ., βεβληκ., εἰδώς, vv. 2, 3. On τίθ. τὰ ἱμάτ. comp. Plut. *Alc.* 8. — The *washing of the feet* was wont to take place *before the beginning* of the meal, by the ministry of *slaves ;*[2] it was not, however, always observed ; see on Luke vii. 44. Hence we cannot argue, from the omission of it up to this point at this meal (for the guests had already reclined at table), either *against* (Wichelhaus) or *in favour of* (Lange : the host was bound to eat *with his family*) the supposition that the meal was the Passover meal.—Any *peculiar cause* for the extraordinary procedure of Jesus is not intimated by John ; and to introduce one from the dispute among the disciples about rank, mentioned in Luke xxii. 24 ff. (so, following the older commentators, Ebrard, Hengstenberg, Godet, with various representations of the scenic associations ; also Baur, who, however, regards the narrative only as the exposition, given in a historical form, of Matt. xx. 26, 27, and Luke xxii. 26, 27, 28, after Strauss had maintained it to be a mythical rendering of a synoptical discourse on humility), is arbitrary in

of *his* feet. Euth. Zigabenus, comp. Chrysostom, Calvin, and several others.

[1] See Wetstein *in loc.;* Kypke, II. p. 399 ;

Ellendt, *Lex. Soph.* I. p. 294.

[2] See Dougt. *Anal.* II. p. 50 ; Stuck. *Antt. conviv.* p. 217.

itself, since John, fully as he introduces his narrative in vv. 1, 2, gives not
even the slightest indication of it, while it is appropriate neither to the
position nor to the validity of the account of Luke (see on Luke xxii. 24).
The symbolical act of departing love must, especially since Jesus had already
reclined at table, have been the outcome of the moment, arising from His
own urgent consideration of that which was needful for the disciples and
for His work.[1] — διέζωσεν. ἑαυτ.] indicating the *personal performance* more
than the means (comp. xxi. 18). He is, in truth, entirely a *servant*, πάντα
μετὰ πάσης προθυμίας αὐτουργήσας (Euth. Zigabenus). — βάλλει ὕδωρ] *He pours
water.*[2] — εἰς τ. νιπτ.] into the wash basin standing by. Nihil ministerii
omittit," Grotius. — ἤρξατο] for the act *commenced* was *interrupted* when
Peter's turn came, and not till after ver. 10 was it continued and finished.
John employs the ἤρξατο, so common in the other evangelists, here only in this
minute description. — ᾧ] *with which*,[3] or instead of ὅ, by attraction (Rev. i.
13, xv. 6), as in xvii. 5, 11.

Vv. 6 – 9. Ἔρχεται οὖν] So that He thus made a commencement with
another disciple, not with *Peter himself* (so Augustine, Beda, Nonnus,
Rupertius, Cornelius à Lapide, Maldonatus, Jansen, and other Catholics in
the Romish interest ; but also Baumgarten-Crusius, Ewald, Hengstenberg).
With *whom* (Chrysostom and Euth. Zigabenus point to Judas Iscariot,
whom, however, Nonnus makes to be last) is left altogether undetermined.
— σύ μου, κ.τ.λ.] ἐκπλαγεὶς εἶπε τοῦτο καὶ σφόδρα εὐλαβηθείς, Euth. Zigabenus.
The emphasis lies primarily upon σύ ; but not secondarily on μου, as if ἐμοῦ
were used, but on τ. πόδας : Dost *Thou* wash my *feet?* The present
νίπτεις, like λιθάζετε, x. 32, and ποιεῖς, ver. 27. — Ver. 7. Note the antithesis
of ἐγὼ . . . σύ. What *He* did was not the external work of washing (so *Peter*
took it), but that which this washing signified in the *mind* of Jesus, namely,
the *token* of the morally purifying, ministering love. — μετὰ ταῦτα] namely,
through the instruction, vv. 13–17. To refer this to the *later apostolic enlightenment and experience*[4] is not justified by the text (comp. γινώσκετε. ver.
12), and would have been expressed, as in ver. 36, by the antithesis of νῦν
and ὕστερον. — Ver. 8. Peter, instead of now complying, as became him,
refuses with definite and vehement decision. But Jesus puts before him a
threat connected with the necessity of this feet-washing, which could only
have its ground and justification in the *higher moral* meaning of which the
act was to be the quiet symbolic language. Thus He intends what He now
says not of the external performance as such in and by itself, *but* of the
ethical contents which it is symbolically to set forth, after He had already
indicated, ver. 7, *that* something higher lay in this act. It is precisely John
who has apprehended and reported in the most faithful and delicate manner
how Jesus knew to employ the sensuous as a foil to the spiritual, and thus
to ascend, first enigmatically, then more clearly, and ever higher, towards
the very highest. He says : *If I shall not have washed thee, thou hast no part*

[1] Comp. Ewald, *Gesch. Chr.* p. 542.   p. 443 B.
[2] Comp. Planudius in Bachmann, *Anal.* 2.   [4] Chrysostom, Grotius, Tholuck, Hengs-
p. 90, 18.   tenberg, Ewald, and several others.
[3] Hom. *Il.* x. 77, *Od.* xviii. 66 ; Athen. x.

with me. By this He undoubtedly means the *feet-washing* which He intended to perform (τοὺς πόδας σου was to be understood as a matter of course, according to the connection,—against Hofmann, II. 2, p. 323), yet still under the *ethical* sense, which it was to set forth symbolically, and impress in a way not to be forgotten. Washing is the time-consecrated image of moral purification. Hence the thought of Jesus divested of this symbolical wrapping is : *If I shall not have purified thee,* just as I now would wash thy feet, *from the sinful nature still adhering to thee, thou hast no share with me* (in the eternal possession of salvation). Hengstenberg's view, who here takes the washing as the symbol of the *forgiveness of sins* (according to Ps. li. 4), is opposed to vv. 12 ff. — Peter, as ver. 9 shows, did not yet understand the higher meaning of the Lord's words ; he could but take His answer in the external sense that immediately offered itself (*if, in disobedience to me, thou dost not suffer thyself to be washed by me, thou hast,* etc.). The thought, however, of being a man separated, by further resistance, from Jesus and His salvation, was sufficiently overpowering for His ardent love to make him offer forthwith not merely His feet, but also the remaining unclothed parts of His body, His hands and His head, to be washed ; καὶ ἐν τῇ παραιτήσει καὶ ἐν τῇ συγχωρήσει σφοδρότερος, ἑκάτερα γὰρ ἐξ ἀγάπης, Cyril. — εἰς τὸν αἰῶνα] *while eternity lasts,* spoken passionately. Comp. 1 Cor. viii. 13. — μέρος ἔχειν μετά τινος] denotes the *participation in the same relation, in the like situation with any one,* Matt. xxiv. 51, Luke xii. 46, after the Hebrew חֵלֶק אֶת (Deut. xii. 12), and חֵלֶק עַם (Deut. x. 9, xiv. 27 ; Ps. l. 18). The expression in the classics would be οὐκ ἔχεις or μετέχεις μέρος μου. It is the denial of the συγκληρονόμον εἶναι Χριστοῦ, and thus the threatening of exclusion from the ζωή and δόξα of the Lord.

Vv. 10, 11. Jesus corrects the disciple by proceeding to speak of the washing in question according to its intended spiritual significance, that he may thus lead the disciple, who had misunderstood Him, to the true comprehension of the matter. According to the mere verbal sense, He says : "*He who has bathed needs nothing further than to wash his feet* (which have been soiled again by the road) ; *rather is he* (except as to this necessary cleansing of the feet) *clean in his entire body.*" But this statement, derived from experience of the sensuous province of life, serves as a symbolical veiling of the ethical thought which Jesus desires to set forth : "*He who has already experienced moral purification in general and on the whole* in fellowship with me, like him who has cleansed his whole body in the bath, *requires only to be freed from the sinful defilement in individual things which has been again contracted in the intercourse of life ;* as one who has bathed only requires again the washing of his feet, *but in other respects he is clean as to his whole moral personality.*" This necessity of *individual purification* demanding *daily penitence,* which Jesus here sets forth in the λελουμένος by τοὺς πόδας νίψασθαι, how manifest it became in the very case of Peter ! *E.g.,* after he denied his Lord, and after the hypocrisy exhibited at Antioch. Gal. ii. To illustrate the *entire* spiritual *purification* [1] by ὁ λελου-

---

[1] Calvin well remarks : "Non quod omni ex parte puri sint, ut nulla in illis macula

μένος, however, suggested itself so very naturally through the very feet-washing, which was just about to be undertaken as its correlate, that an allusion to *baptism*[1] (with Olshausen, B. Crusius, Ewald, Hengstenberg, Godet), perhaps after 1 Cor. vi. 11, cannot be made good, while we need not even assume a reference to the by no means universal custom of bathing before meals. The *word* is to be thought of as the *purifying* element represented in ὁ λελουμένος ; as also in the simile of the vine, which is analogous in regard to the matter of fact depicted, the καθαροί ἐστε, xv. 3, is referred back only to the *word* of Christ as the ground thereof. But the notion of ethical *purification* must, in the connection of the entire symbolism of the passage, be also strictly and firmly maintained in οὐ χρείαν . . . νίψασθαι ; so that the latter is not, as Linder[2] thinks, intended to suggest that the clean man even may undergo the feet-washing,—not, however, for the object of purification, but *as a token of love or humble subjection.* — καὶ ὑμεῖς καθαροί ἐστε] Hereby Jesus now makes the *application to Peter and his fellow-disciples* of what was previously said in the form of a general proposition : "*Ye also are clean*," as I, namely, have just expressed it of the λελουμένος ; you also have attained in your living fellowship with me through my word to this moral purity of your entire personality ; *but*—so He subjoins with deep grief, having Judas Iscariot in view—*but not all!* One there is amongst you who has frustrated in his own case the purifying influence of this union with me ! Had Peter hitherto not yet seized the symbolical significance of the discourse of Jesus, yet now, on this application καὶ ὑμεῖς, κ.τ.λ., and on this tragical addition ἀλλ᾽ οὐχὶ πάντες, its meaning must have dawned upon his understanding. — ἤ] gives a comparative reference to the absolute expression οὐκ ἔχει χρ. : has no need (*further*) *than.*[3] — τὸν παραδιδ. αὐτόν] *His betrayer*, Matt. xxvi. 48 ; John xviii. 2. — Further, what has been said of an *anti-Petrine aim* in this passage, in spite of i. 43, vi. 68, 69 (Strauss, Schwegler, Baur, Hilgenfeld), by which the desire for an Ebionitic lavation of the whole body has actually been ascribed to Peter (Hilgenfeld), is purely imaginary.

Vv. 12, 13. Γινώσκετε, κ.τ.λ.] *know ye*, etc. ; ἐρωτᾷ ἀγνοοῦντας, ἵνα διεγείρῃ εἰς προσοχήν, Euth. Zigabenus. Comp. Dissen, *ad Dem. de Cor.* p. 186. — τί] namely, according to the spiritual contents whose symbolical representation was the act that was presented to the senses. — Ver. 13. *Ye call me Teacher and Lord.* It was in this way that the pupils of the Rabbins addressed their teachers, רבי and מר ; and so also did the disciples address *Jesus* as the *Messiah*, whose pupils (Matt. xxiii. 8) and δοῦλοι (ver. 16) they were. Comp. on ὁ διδάσκ., xi. 28.[4] φωνεῖν does not signify *to name ;* but in the *article* lies the σύ that is present to the mind in uttering the words.[5]

---

amplius haereat, sed quoniam praecipua sui parte mundati sunt, dum scilicet ablatum est regnum peccato ut justitia Dei superior sit."

[1] Theodore of Mopsuestia, Augustine, Ruperti, Erasmus, Jansen, Zeger, Cornelius à Lapide, Schoettgen, Wetstein, and many others.

[2] *Stud. u. Krit.* 1867, p. 512 ff.

[3] Comp. Xen. *Mem.* iv. 3. 9 ; Herod. vi. 52 : οὐ δυναμένους δὲ γνῶναι ἢ καὶ πρὸ τούτου (*better* than even formerly); Soph. *Trach.* 1016 ; Winer, p. 473 [E. T. p. 508].

[4] On the nominativus *tituli*, see Buttmann, *N. T. Gramm.* p. 132 [E. T. p. 151].

[5] Krüger, § 45. 2. 6.

Vv. 14, 15. It is not the act itself, but its moral essence, which, after His example, He enjoins upon them to exercise. This moral essence, however, consists not in lowly and ministering love *generally*, in which Jesus, by washing the feet of His disciples, desired to give them an example, but, as ver. 10 proves, in *the* ministering love which, in all self-denial and humility, *is active for the moral purification and cleansing of others.* As Jesus had just set forth *this* ministering love by His own example, when He, although their Lord and Master, performed on the persons of His disciples the servile duty of washing their feet,—as an emblem, however, of the efficacy of His love to purify them spiritually,—so ought they to wash one another's feet ; *i.e. with the same self-denying love to be reciprocally serviceable to one another with a view to moral purification.* The understanding of the injunction ὀφείλετε, κ.τ.λ., in the *proper* sense was not that of the apostolical age, but arose at a later time, and was followed (first in the fourth century, comp. Ambrose, *de sacram.* iii. 1 ; Augustine *ad Januar. ep.* 119) by the introduction of the washing of the feet of the baptized on Maundy Thursday, and other symbolical feet-washings (later also amongst the Mennonites and in the community of Brothers). 1 Tim. v. 10 contains the non-ritualistic reference to hospitality. The feet-washing by the *Pope* on Maundy Thursday is a result of the pretension to represent Christ, and as such, also, was strongly condemned by the Reformers. Justly, however, the church has not adopted the feet-washing into the number of the *sacraments ;* for it is not the practice itself, but the spiritual action which it symbolizes, that Jesus enjoined upon the disciples. And it is solely to this moral meaning that the promise in ver. 17 is attached ; and hence the essential marks of the specific sacramental idea, corresponding to the essence of baptism and of the Supper—sacramental institution, promise, and collative force—are wanting to it. This in answer to Böhmer,[1] who designates it an offence against Holy Scripture, that the Protestant church has not recognized the feet-washing as a sacrament, which, outside the Greek church,[2] it was explained to be by Bernard of Clairvaux (" Sacramentum *remissionis peccatorum quotidianorum*"), without any permanent result. Baeumlein also favours the maintenance of the practice as a legacy of Christ. But its *essence* is preserved, where the *love,* from which the practice flowed, abides. Nonnus aptly designates the καθὼς ἐγώ, κ.τ.λ. as ἰσοφυὲς μίμημα. The practice itself, moreover, cannot in truth be carried out either everywhere, or at all times, or by all, or on all. — ἐγὼ . . . καὶ ὑμεῖς] Argumentum a *majori* ad *minus.* The majus implied in ἐγώ is further, by the subjoined ὁ κύριος κ. ὁ διδάσκ., brought home with special force, and therefore, also, the principal point, ὁ κύριος (comp. ver. 16), is here *thrown back.* — ὑπόδειγμα] Later term, instead of the old παράδειγμα.[3] — ἵνα, κ.τ.λ.] Design in setting the example : that, as *I* have done to you ("in *genere* actus," Grotius), you also may do, namely, in ministering to one another in self-denying love for the removal of all sinful contamination, as I, for my part,

---

[1] *Stud. u. Krit.* 1850, p. 829 ff.
[2] In which it has been preserved as a custom in monasteries.
[3] Lobeck, *ad Phryn.* p. 12.

have just now figuratively fulfilled in your case, in the symbol of the feet-washing, this ministering love directed to your moral purification.

Vv. 16, 17. Truly you, the lesser (ἀπόστολος : *commissioned*), may not dispense with the performance of that which I, the greater, have here performed. Comp. xv. 20 ; Matt. x. 24 ; Luke vi. 40. — ταῦτα] That which I have herein (vv. 13–16) set forth to you by my ὑπόδειγμα, by means of the feet-washing, and have made an obligation. — εἰ expresses the general, and ἐάν the particular, additional condition.[1] The εἰ makes a *definite* supposition[2] (οἴδατε δὲ αὐτὰ παρ' ἐμοῦ μαθόντες, Euth. Zigabenus) ; ἐάν is *in case* you, etc. The knowing is objectively granted, the doing subjectively conditioned. — μακαρ.] said in reference to the happiness of the present and future *Messianic life.* Comp. on xix. 29.

Vv. 18, 19. Οὐ περὶ πάντ. ὑμῶν λέγω] Namely, this that ye μακάριοί ἐστε, κ.τ.λ. "Est inter vos, qui non erit beatus neque faciet ea," Augustine. Unnecessarily and inappropriately, Tholuck refers back to ver. 10. — ἐγώ] *I for my part*, opposed to the *divine* determination (ἀλλ' ἵνα, κ.τ.λ.), which required however, the selection of apostles so to take place that the traitor entered into the number of the chosen. In a very arbitrary manner Tholuck gives the *pregnant* meaning to ἐξελεξ. : whom I *peculiarly* have chosen. — οἶδα] I know of what *character* they are, so that I do not therefore deceive myself, if I do not say of you all, etc. — ἀλλ'] is *ordinarily* taken as the antithesis of οὐ περὶ π. ὑμ. λ., and is supplemented by τοῦτο γέγονεν (namely, that I cannot affirm, ver. 17, of you all) ; while *others* connect it with ὁ τρώγων, κ.τ.λ., thus taking ἵνα ἡ γρ. κλ. as an intermediate clause.[3] The former view is unauthorized by the context, which suggests a τοῦτο γέγονεν just as little as in 1 Cor. ii. 9 ; the latter does not correspond to the importance in the connection of this declaration of purpose. The only supplement *in accordance with the text* is (comp. ix. 3, i. 8) : ἐξελεξάμην αὐτούς : *But I made the choice in obedience to the divine destiny, in accordance with which the Scripture* (that which stands written, comp. xix. 37 ; Mark xii. 10 ; Luke iv. 21) *could not but be fulfilled*, etc. Comp. vi. 70, 71. The passage, freely cited from the original, is Ps. xli. 40, where the theocratic sufferer (*who* is unknown ; not *David*, whom the superscription names) makes an utterance which, according to divine determination, was to find its Messianic historical fulfilment in the treason of Judas. — ὁ τρώγ. μετ' ἐμοῦ τ. ἄρτ.] Deviating from the original (אוֹכֵל לַחְמָי), and from the LXX., yet without substantial alteration of the sense (*intimacy of table-companionship*, which, according to Hellenic views also, aggravated the detestable character of the crime,[4] and involuntarily suggesting itself, since Judas actually *ate with Jesus* (τρώγ., vi. 56–58). — ἐπῆρεν] *has lifted up*. Note the *preterite ;* Judas, so near to an act of treason, is like him who has already lifted up his heel, in order to administer a kick to another. To explain the figure from a crafty tripping up

---

[1] Comp. on the twofold *protasis*, Stallbaum, *ad Plat. Phaed.* p. 67 E, *Apol.* p. 20 C ; Klotz, *ad Devar.* p. 512 ; Ellendt, *Lex. Soph.* I. p. 493.

[2] [Mere *condition*, without implying doubt.—K.]

[3] Semler, Kuinoel; admitted also by Lücke.

[4] See Pflugk, *ad Eur. Hec.* 793.

of the foot in wrestling ($\pi\tau\epsilon\rho\nu\iota\zeta\epsilon\iota\nu$), is less appropriate both to the words and to the facts (Jesus was not *overreached*). — Ver. 19. $\dot{\alpha}\pi'\,\dot{\alpha}\rho\tau\iota$] not *now*, but as always in the N. T. (i. 52, xiv. 7 ; Matt. xxiii. 39, xxvi. 29, 64 ; Rev. xiv. 13) : *from this time forward*. Previously, He has not yet *definitely* disclosed it. — $\pi\iota\sigma\tau\epsilon\acute{\nu}\sigma\eta\tau\epsilon,\,\kappa.\tau.\lambda.$] Ye may believe that I am He (the Messiah), and that no other is to be expected ; see on viii. 24. How easily might the disciples have come to vacillate in their faith through the success of the treason of Judas, if He had not foreseen and foretold it as lying in the ordered plan of the divine destiny ! Comp. xiv. 29. But through the predictive declaration, what might have become ground of *doubt* becomes ground for *faith*.

Ver. 20. And for the furtherance and confirmation of this your fidelity in the faith, which, in spite of the treason arising from your midst, must not vacillate, I say to you, that ye may confidently go forward to meet your calling as my ambassadors (xx. 21). The *high and blessed position* of my ambassadors remains so unimpaired, that whoever accepts *them* accepts *me*, etc. And the more, that Jesus must apprehend a disheartening impression from the treason on the rest of the disciples, the more earnestly ($\dot{\alpha}\mu\acute{\eta}\nu,\,\dot{\alpha}\mu\grave{\eta}\nu$ $\lambda\acute{\epsilon}\gamma\omega\,\dot{\nu}\mu.$) does He introduce this encouragement. Comp. Calvin : Christ would " *offendiculo mederi ;*" and Grotius : " ostendit ministeria ipsis injuncta *non caritura suis solatiis.*" The contrast of the treason to the dignity of the apostolic circle (Hilgenfeld) He certainly does not mean to assert, so self-evident was this contrast. Nor do the words serve to confirm the $\pi\iota\sigma\tau\epsilon\acute{\nu}\sigma.$, $\ddot{o}\tau\iota\,\dot{\epsilon}\gamma\acute{\omega}\,\epsilon\dot{\iota}\mu\iota$ (Ebrard), to which the first half of the verse is not appropriate, in which, indeed, Godet, without justification, would give to the simple $\dot{\epsilon}\acute{\alpha}\nu$ $\tau\iota\nu\alpha$ the limiting sense : He among you, who is *really* my ambassador. Further : to join ver. 20 with vv. 16, 17 [1] is an arbitrary construction, which Kuinoel aggravates by explaining the words as a *gloss* from Matt. x. 40, added to ver. 16, and which subsequently entered the text in the wrong place, as Lücke also has revived the suspicion of a gloss (from Luke ix. 48). The lack of connection, employed by Strauss as an argument against the originality, is external, and not in the sequence of the *thought ;* and besides, the emotion and agitation of Jesus are here to be considered. The manifest identity of the saying with that of Matt. x. 40, forbids our explaining it in an essentially different sense (Luthardt explains of the sending of those needing the ministry of love to the disciples). But to bring in here the dispute about rank, which Luke xxii. 24 ff. places *after* the supper (Baeumlein), is groundless, and useless in the way of explanation.

NOTE.—The story of the feet-washing, vv. 1-20,—rejected by Bretschneider, Fritzsche, and Strauss as a mythical invention, and recognized by Weisse as genuine only in individual portions,—has been justly defended by Schweizer, p. 164 ff., in conformity with its stamp of truth and originality, which throughout indicates the eye-witness ; in opposition to which, Baur can only recognize a free formation out of synoptical material (see on vv. 2-5) in behalf of the idea, as also Hilgenfeld, comp. Scholten. The non-mention of the oc-

---

[1] Lampe, Storr, Klee, Maier, Hengstenberg, comp. Brückner.

currence in the Synoptics is explained from the fact that with them the situation is quite different, and the main point is the institution of the Supper.

Vv. 21, 22. The thought of Jesus recurs in deep excitement and agitation —owing to which, probably, an interrupting pause occurred—back to the traitor ;[1] it constrains Him now to testify with the most straightforward definiteness what He knows, but at which He had previously only hinted : *One of you will betray me!* Comp. Matt. xxvi. 21, 22, in comparison with whose representation that of John is to be preferred. — τῷ πνεύματι] *in His Spirit* (xi. 33), not : through the *divine* Spirit (Hilgenfeld). — ἔβλεπον οὖν, κ.τ.λ.] "perculsi rei atrocitate vix credibili animis probis minimeque suspicacibus," Grotius. Judas may likewise have *dissembled*.

Vv. 23, 24. There was, however, reclining at table, one of the disciples, etc., so that ἦν belongs to ἐν τῷ κόλπῳ (Luke xvi. 23). The custom was to lie with the left arm supported on the cushion, and the feet stretched out behind, so that the right hand remained free for eating. The one who lay next reached, with the back of his head, to the *sinus* of the girdle[2] of the first, and had the feet of the first at his back ; in like manner, the third in the κόλπος of the second.[3] — ὃν ἠγάπ. ὁ 'Ι.] κατ' ἐξοχήν. Comp. xix. 26, xx. 2, xxi. 7, 20. It explains the fact that he was Jesus' *nearest* table-companion. And here, out of the recollection of that sacred, and by him never to be forgotten moment, there *first* breaks from his lips this nameless, and yet so expressive *designation* of himself. It is arbitrary, however, to take this as a *circumlocution* for his name ;[4] such a view is precluded by the circumstance that ὃν ἠγ. ὁ κύριος is never employed (but always ὁ 'Ιησοῦς). — According to the reading κ. λέγει αὐτῷ· εἰπὲ τίς ἐστιν (see critical notes), Peter supposes, with his characteristic hasty temperament, that John, as the confidant of Jesus, would know whom the latter meant.[5] The λέγει is uttered in a *whisper*, as implied also in the vividly portraying νεύει. Should εἰπέ be taken as : "say *to Jesus*" (Ewald), either περὶ οὗ λέγει would be omitted, or λέγεις would take the place of λέγει.

Vv. 25, 26. Graphic representation. Raising himself from the κόλπος of Jesus to His breast, nearer to His ear, he draws close to Him, and asks (in a whisper). — ἐγώ] *I, for my part.* — τὸ ψωμ.] which he meanwhile took into His hand. — ἐπιδώσω] *shall give, present to.* The morsel is a piece of bread or meat, which Jesus dips into a broth on the table (not into the *Charoseth*, see on Matt. xxvi. 23, since the meal, according to John, was not the

---

[1] The course of thought assumed by Godet is pure invention : " If the true apostle carries within Himself God (ver. 20), the traitor carries in himself Satan" (ver. 25).

[2] κόλπος, Luke vi. 38 ; Plin. *ep.* iv. 22.

[3] See Lightfoot, p. 1095 f.

[4] Gotthold, Bengel, Hengstenberg, Godet.

[5] In this and other individual traits (xviii. 15, 16, xix. 26, 27, xx. 2, 3, xxi. 3, 4, xviii. 10, xiii. 8, xxi. 15, 16) the design has been discovered to make Peter appear in a less advantageous light than John, or to make him appear so generally,—which would be in keeping with the anti-Judaic tendency of the author. See especially Baur, p. 320 ff. Comp. Hilgenfeld, *Evang.* p. 335 ; Spaeth in *Hilgenf. Zeitschr.* 1868, p. 182 f. But if the author had actually entertained this design, it would have been an easy thing for him—since he is said to have disposed of the historical material in so altogether free a manner—to have satisfied it in dogmatic points (which would be principally concerned), and yet more easy, at least in i. 43, and vi. 68, 69, to have remained silent. Comp. on vv. 10, 11.

paschal meal).— The closing words of ver. 26 have a certain tragic solemnity.[1] By the designation of the traitor, it was not the curiosity of
John, but his own *love*, which Jesus satisfied, and this by means of a token
not of *apparent*, but of *real* and sorrowful goodwill towards Judas, in whom
even now conscience might be awakened and touched through a token at
the same time, such as most naturally suggested itself at table to the Lord as
the head of the family, expressive of forbearance towards the traitor. This
in answer to Weisse, who psychologically mishandles the entire representation as a fiction derived from ver. 18, and finds the true occurrence only in
Mark, while Strauss gives the relative preference to Luke (xxii. 21).

Vv. 27, 28. Καὶ μετὰ τὸ ψωμ.] *and after the morsel, i.e.* after Jesus had
given him the morsel, ver. 26. So frequently also in the classics a single
word only is used with μετά, which thus in the context represents an
entire clause.[2] — τότε] *then, at that moment*, intentionally bringing into
relief the horribly tragic moment. — εἰσῆλθεν, κ.τ.λ.] so that he was thus
from henceforward a man *possessed* by the devil, Mark v. 12, 13, ix. 25 ;
Luke viii. 30 ; Matt. xii. 45. The expression (comp. Luke xxii. 3) forbids
a *figurative* interpretation (that Judas completely hardened himself after
this discovery was understood by him to have been made), found already in
Theodore of Mopsuestia. The complete hardening, in consequence of which
he *could* no more retrace his steps, was simply the immediate consequence of
this possession by the devil. But against a magical causal connection, as it
were, of the entrance of the devil along with the morsel, Cyril already justly
declared himself. The representation rather is, that now, just when Judas
had taken the morsel without inward compunction, he was given up by
Christ, and being laid open to the unhindered entrance of the devil (καθά-
περ τινὰ πύλην τὴν τοῦ φυλάττοντος ἐρήμην, Cyril), experiences this entrance.
John did not *see* this (in the external bearing of Judas, as Godet supposes) ;
but it is with him a *psychological certainty*. — ὃ ποιεῖς, ποίησον τάχιον] *What
thou purposest to do,*[3] *do more quickly*. In the *comparative* lies the notion :
hasten it. So very frequently in Homer θᾶσσον.[4] The imperative, however,
is not *permissive* (Grotius, Kuinoel, and several others) ; but Jesus *actually
wishes* to surmount *as soon as possible* the last crisis (His ὥρα), now determined
for Him in the divine destiny. The resigned, characteristic decision of
mind brooks no delay. To suggest the intention, on the part of Jesus, *to be
rid of the oppressive proximity of the traitor*,[5] is to anticipate what follows.

Vv. 28, 29. Οὐδείς] Even John not excepted (against Bengel, Kuinoel,
Lange, Hengstenberg, Godet), from whom the thought was remote, that
now already was the treason to be accomplished. — πρὸς τί] *for behoof of
what.* — Ver. 29. γάρ] Proof, by way of example, of this non-comprehension.
Some of the disciples had taken those words as an order, *to hasten a matter*

---

[1] To this belongs also the circumstantial
λαμβάνει καί and ψωμ. (see critical notes).
Jesus has put the morsel into the broth
(βάψας), and then *takes* it, etc.

[2] See Ast, *ad Plat. Leg.* p. 273 f., *Lex. Plat.*
II. p. 311 ; Jacobs, *ad Anthol.* XIII. p. 82.

[3] Comp. ver. 6 ; Winer, p. 249 [E. T. p. 243].

[4] See Duncan, *Lex. ed. Rost,* p. 524, and
generally Nägelsbach, *Anm. z. Ilias,* p. 21,
314, ed. 3 ; on the graecism of τάχιον, Lobeck, *ad Phryn.* p. 77.

[5] Ambrose : " ut a consortio suo recede-
ret," comp. Lücke, B. Crusius, Tholuck.

of business known to Judas, the bearer of the chest. They had therefore two more definite suppositions between which they wavered, both produced by a helpless state of mind, but not irrational, since it is not said that they thought of instantaneous attention to the command, nor in the night. — εἰς τ. ἑορτ.] belongs to ὧν χρ. ἔχ. There was therefore as yet *no* matter needful for the feast purchased. This, following as it does the statement of time already adduced in ver. 1, presupposes that the present meal was not the *festal* meal, for the latter belonged to the *feast itself*, which, according to ver. 1, was still *impending*.[1] — τοῖς πτωχοῖς] placed first as the other subject referred to in this second supposition. Comp. Gal. ii. 10. This giving to the poor is likewise thought of as designed for the approaching *celebration*, because they attempted thus to explain the *present* direction to the purveyor. —In the transition into the indirect form of speech, ἤ, κ.τ.λ. must be completed ; *or that He said that to him, in order that he*, etc.

Vv. 30, 31. Λαβὼν οὖν] connecting with ver. 27. With ἐξῆλθεν εὐθύς begins the fulfilment of the command of Christ, given in ver. 27. How erroneous therefore is Hengstenberg's statement, in spite of the εὐθύς : he went away only at the close of the meal ! Before the ἐξῆλθεν the supper, in sooth, is to have had its place, and Judas to have taken part in it ! — ἦν δὲ νύξ] The meal had begun in the evening, and—when we consider also the time consumed in the feet-washing—had already advanced into the night. This conclusion of the narrative respecting Judas presents, unsought, something *full of horror*, and which precisely in this most simple brevity of expression takes profoundest hold of the imagination. Comp. Luke xxii. 53. With ὅτε οὖν ἐξῆλθε begins a fresh break in the narrative. To omit οὖν (see critical notes), and to connect these words with ἦν δὲ νύξ,[2] has against it, apart from the critically certified οὖν, the considerations that the following λέγει would stand very abruptly,[3] ὅτε ἐξῆλθε itself would be very superfluous, and the deeper emphasis of the bare ἦν δὲ νύξ at the close would be lost.

Vv. 31, 32. Νῦν ἐδοξάσθη, κ.τ.λ.] The traitor is gone, and now the heart of the Lord, which has become freer and more at ease, pours itself forth as in an anticipated triumph. In view, namely, of the near and certain end, He sees in His death, as though He had already undergone it, *His life-work as accomplished*, and Himself thereby *glorified*, and in this *His* glorification the glory *of God*, who completes His work in the work of the Son. The δόξα intended by Jesus is, therefore, not that which is contained for Him in the feet-washing and in the departure of Judas, which would not correspond to the sublime and· victorious nature of this moment (against Godet). But neither, again, is it the *heavenly* glory (Luthardt) ; for to this the future δοξάσει, ver. 32, first refers, and this change of tense possesses a

---

[1] Against Wieseler, pp. 366, 381, Tholuck, Lange, Luthardt, Baeumlein, Hengstenberg, Paul in the *Stud. u. Krit.* 1866, p. 366 f., and several others). See also Bleek, p. 129 f. : Rückert, *Abendm.* p. 27 f. ; Hilgenfeld, *Paschastr.* p. 147 ; Isenberg, p. 10 f.

[2] Chrysostom, Theophylact, Euth. Ziga-

benus, and others, including Bengel, Paulus, Ewald.

[3] Ewald supposes that "by an old mistake" ὅτε οὖν ἐξῆλθεν had dropped out before λέγει. But such is the reading of Cyril only.

determinative force. Rather does the ἐδοξάσθη denote the *actual δόξα*, which lies in the fact, and of which the manifestation has begun, *that now at length His earthly work of salvation is brought to a state of completion*, the task appointed to the Son by the Father is *discharged*. It is the glory of *His death*, the splendour of His τετέλεσται, which, as already arrived, He contemplates, feels, expresses. — ἐν αὐτῷ] *in Him*, in His person, so far as it has been glorified. — Ver. 32 has a *climactic* relation to ver. 31, passing from the δόξα, which He has on the threshold of *death*, to the heavenly glory, which from this time God will secure to Him (hence the future δοξάσει). — εἰ ὁ θεὸς ἐδοξ. ἐν ἑαυτῷ] Solemn repetition, in order to subjoin a further thought. — ἐν ἑαυτῷ] To be referred to the subject, not, with Ewald, to Christ : *in Himself*, corresponding. as recompense, to the ἐν αὐτῷ. He will be so glorified by God, that His heavenly glory will be *contained in God's own peculiar* glory ; His glory will be none other than the divine glory itself, completed in God Himself (comp. Col. iii. 3) through the return into the fellowship of God out of which He had come forth, and had become man. Comp. xvii. 4, 5. — The first καί, ver. 32, is the *also* of the corresponding relation (on the other hand, again) ; and the second : *and that.*[1] On the idea of the *recompense*, comp. xvii. 4, 5 ; Phil. ii. 9. — εὐθύς] *straightway ;* for how immediately near is this blessed goal towards which my death is the departure !

Ver. 33. The εὐθύς changes—when He glances at His loved ones, whom He is to leave behind—His mood, which but now was that of victory, again into one of softness and emotion. Here, in the first place, the tender τεκνία (comp. xxi. 5) with all the intensity of departing love. — μικρόν] Accusat. neut.[2] — ζητήσετε] the seeking of *faith* and *love* in distress, in temptation, etc. — καὶ καθώς, κ.τ.λ.] *and* as I have said, . . . say I now *also to you*.[3] — τ. Ἰουδ.] to these, however, with a penal reference, vii. 34, viii. 21, 24, and with the threatening addition, κ. οὐχ εὑρήσετε. And for the disciples the οὐ δύνασθε ἐλθεῖν is intended only of the *temporal* impossibility. See xiv. 2, 3. — ἄρτι] emphatically at the end, as in vv. 7, 37, xvi. 12. He could no longer spare them the announcement.

Ver. 34. *Commandment* now of the departing Lord for those who, according to ver. 33, are to be left behind, which He calls a *new* one, *i.e.* one not yet given either in the Decalogue or otherwise, in order the more deeply to impress it upon them as the specific rule of their conduct. The *novelty* lies not in the commandment of love in itself (for see Lev. xix. 18, comp. Matt. v. 43 ff., xix. 19, xxii. 37, 38), nor yet in the *higher degree* of love found in καθὼς ἠγάπ. ὑμ., so that the requirement would be, that one should love one's neighbour not merely ὡς ἑαυτόν, but ὑπὲρ ἑαυτόν,[4] since καθώς does not indicate the degree or the type (see below,) and since, moreover, the O. T. ὡς ἑαυτόν does not exclude, but includes the self-sacrifice of

---

[1] Hartung, *Partikell.* I. p. 145.

[2] Comp. xiv. 16, xvi. 19 ; Heb. x. 37 ; LXX. Job xxxvi. 2 ; Sap. xv. 8, *et al.*

[3] Luther incorrectly begins a new sentence with καὶ ὑμῖν (" and I say to you now : a new commandment," etc.). Ebrard's

rendering is also quite erroneous.

[4] Cyril, Theodore of Mopsuestia, Theophylact, Euth. Zigabenus, and many, including especially Knapp, *Scr. var. arg.* p. 369 ff.

love. The novelty lies rather in the *motive power* of the love, which must be the love *of Christ*, which one has *experienced*. Comp. 1 John iii. 16. Thereby the commandment, in itself old, receives the new definiteness,[1] the definiteness of loving ἐν Χριστῷ, and therewith the new moral absolute character and contents, and is given forth with this specifically N. T. definition, founded on faith in Christ, a *new* commandment. Comp. Luthardt, Ebrard, Brückner ; also Baeumlein, Hengstenberg, and Godet, who, however, take along with this the *circle* of Christian love (ἀλλήλους) as a point of novelty. Grotius treats this in a similar way to these last-named commentators, when he, as also Kölbing,[2] regards *Christian brotherly love*, in its distinction from the general love of one's neighbours, as the *new* commandment which is prescribed. Nevertheless, this distinction rests simply upon the fact that Christian brotherly love must be mutually determined and sustained *by the personal experience of the love of Christ*, or else it is destitute of its peculiarly Christian character ; hence it is always *this* point alone which forms the substantial contents and the distinguishing feature of the *new* commandment as such, of which none could be more intensely and truly conscious than John himself, especially while he wrote the καινήν and the καθὼς ἠγάπησα ὑμᾶς. Opposed to the sense of the word are the interpretations : a commandment which contains all laws of the N. T., in opposition to the many laws of the O. T. (Luther); praeceptum *illustre*,[3] mandatum *ultimum* = Testament (Heumann); further : ὁπλοτέρην ἐν ἅπασιν, a *youngest* commandment (Nonnus) ; further : a commandment *that never grows old*, with ever youthful freshness, as though ἀεὶ καινήν were expressed (Olshausen [4]) ; further, a *renewed* commandment,[5] or even one that *renews* the old man (Augustine); further : a commandment *unexpected* by you (Semler, on the presumption of the dispute about precedence which has just taken place, Luke xxii. 24 ff.). According to de Wette, καινήν refers to the fact, that in the commandment lies the *principle of the new life brought by Christ*. Thus, therefore, καινὴ ἐντολή would be here a new moral *principle* (comp. Gal. vi. 2), opposed to the O. T. principle of righteousness. That this *is* the new ἐντολή (comp. already Melanchthon) is, however, not *expressed* by these simple words. Against the sense, finally, and without any indication in the text, is Lange's view : a new διαθήκη which is the *institution of the Supper* which Christ here founded. This, besides, is opposed to the obvious parallel passages, 1 John ii. 8. — ἵνα ἀγαπ. ἀλλ.] The contents of the commandment are set forth as the *purpose* of the ἐντ. καιν. διδ. ὑμ. — καθὼς ἠγάπ. ὑμ.] is to be separated only by a comma from ἀλλήλ., containing the *agens*[6] of the ἀγαπ. ἀλλ., and then, by means of ἵνα καὶ ὑμεῖς, κ.τ.λ., the ethical purpose of the ἠγάπ. ὑμ. which belongs here is added ; the emphasis, however, lies on ἀγαπᾶτε, ὑμᾶς, καὶ ὑμεῖς. Hence : that ye may *love*

---

[1] αὐτὸς αὐτὴν ἐποίησε καινὴν τῷ τρόπῳ, Chrysostom.

[2] In the *Stud. u. Krit.* 1845, p. 685 ff.

[3] Hackspan, Hammond, Wolf.

[4] So also Calovius, who, however, mingles together many other interpretations of various kinds.

[5] Calvin, Jansen, Maldonatus, Schoett-

gen, Raphel, and already Irenaeus.

[6] This *agens* can be the love evinced by Christ only on the ground of *faith;* hence John fully accords with the Pauline view of faith, *which is operative through love*, but does not (against Baur, *N. T. Theol.* p. 397) place love immediately in the position which faith holds with Paul.

one another, in conformity with the fact that I have loved *you*, and, indeed, have loved you with the design that *you also*, on your part, etc. But that here καθώς does not express the *degree*, but the corresponding relation, which constrains to the ἀγαπ. ἀλλ., appears with logical necessity from the subjoined clause denoting purpose ἵνα καὶ ὑμεῖς κ.τ.λ. (without an οὕτως, which Ewald interpolates in his explanation). It is similar to our *wie denn* (as then),[1] *stating the ground*, as ὡς also is very frequently used in the classics.[2] To take the sentence καθὼς . . . ἀλλήλους as a parallel to the preceding ἵνα ἀγαπ. ἀλλ., whereby καθὼς ἠγ. ὑμ. is emphatically placed first (so many commentators, from Beza to Hengstenberg and Godet), would cause no difficulty in the case of Paul, but does not correspond to the simple style of John elsewhere. — ἠγάπησα] Aorist ; for Jesus sees Himself already at the end of the work of His loving self-devotion. Comp. ver. 1. Finally, ver. 34 is not to be explained of Christ's imparting a new *legislation*, in opposition to the Mosaic.[3] He, indeed, does *not* say νόμον καινόν. The ἐντολὴ καινή belongs rather to His πλήρωσις of the law (Matt. v. 17), especially in respect of Lev. xix. 18, and does not exclude, but includes, the other moral precepts of the law.[4]

Ver. 35. Ἐν τούτῳ] *in this*, with ἐάν following ; comp. 1 John ii. 3. — ἐμοί] not dative, but *mei, my*, with emphasis, as in xv. 8, comp. xviii. 36. — How greatly love was really the *Gnorisma* of the Christians (1 John iii. 10 ff.), see *e.g.* Tertullian, *Apol.* 39.

Vv. 36–38. The words spoken in ver. 33 are still in Peter's mind ; he has not understood them, but can the less therefore get quit of them, and hence asks : ποῦ ὑπάγεις ; Jesus does not directly answer this, but points him to the personal experience of a later future, in which he (in the path of martyrdom) will follow after Him (comp. xxi. 18, 19), which at present is not possible. The latter statement surprises the fiery disciple, since he feels that he is ready to sacrifice his very life for Him. Jesus then quenches this fire, ver. 38. οὐ δύνασαι] not meant of *moral* ability (against Tholuck, Hengstenberg), as Peter took it, but of *objective* possibility as in ver. 33. The disciple also has " his hour," and Peter had first a great calling before him, xxi. 15 ff. ; Matt. xvi. 18. — τ. ψυχ. θήσω] See on x. 11. In the zeal of love he mistakes the measure of his moral strength. — On the discrepancy, that Matthew and Mark place the prediction of the denial on the way to Gethsemane (Luke xxii. 23 agrees substantially with John), see on Luke xxii. 31. The declaration of ver. 38 itself is certainly more original in John and Matt. xxvi. 34, Luke xxii. 34 (without δίς), than in Mark xiv. 30.

NOTE.—The question, to what place in John's narrative the celebration of the Supper belongs, is not to be more precisely determined on the ground of Matt. xxvi. 23–25 (against Luke xxii. 21), than that the Supper finds its place, not before the departure of Judas,[5] consequently *after* ver. 30. Nothing more

---

[1] Comp. on xii. 35 ; 1 Cor. i. 6 ; Eph. i. 4 ; Matt. vi. 12.
[2] Klotz, *ad Devar.* p. 766 ; Ast, *Lex. Plat.* iii. p. 584.
[3] Hilgenfeld, comp. above Luther
[4] Comp. in Paul love as the fulfilment of

the law ; see also Weiss, *Joh. Lehrbegr.* p. 166.

[5] That Judas did not join in celebrating the Supper (Beza and several others), has been recently (also by Kahnis, not by Hofmann, and Hengstenberg, who places the

definite can be said (Paulus, B. Crusius, Kahnis, place it immediately after ver.
30, against which, however, is the reading οὖν before ἐξῆλθε in ver. 30 ; Lücke,
Maier, and several others, between vv. 33 and 34, opposed to which is the
question of Peter, ver. 36, which looks back to ver. 33 ; Neander, Ammon, and
Ebrard, after ver. 32 ; Tholuck, in ver. 34 ; Lange, indeed, says : the ἐντολὴ
καινή, ver. 34, is the ordainment of the Supper itself ; Olshausen after ver. 38),
since the entire arrangement of John in these chapters leaves the Supper completely out of consideration, and, what is to be particularly noted here in ver.
30, xiv. 1 ff., is so inseparably connected together, that, in reality, there remains nowhere in his narrative an opening for its insertion.   This betrays, indeed, the free concatenation of the discourses on the part of John,
but not his non-acquaintance with the institution (Strauss), and cannot justify the extreme assumptions, that it is to be placed, in spite of the periodic
structure of vv. 1–4, already before the feet-washing (Sieffert. Godet), or first
after xiv. 31 (Kern).   So also Bengel, Wichelhaus, and Röpe, in so far as they
make Jesus, in xiv. 31, to be setting out for the Paschal Supper to Jerusalem.
See on xiv. 31.   According to Schenkel, the feet-washing does *not* fall within
the last hours of Jesus, but at an earlier period, whereby, to be sure, all difficulty would be removed.

NOTES BY AMERICAN EDITOR.

XXXIX. " *Before the feast of the Passover.*"   Ver. 1.

Weiss agrees with Meyer in connecting the πρὸ τῆς ἑορτῆς neither with εἰδώς
(as too vague and indefinite to mark the point of time at which the consciousness of the arrival of His hour came to Jesus, and too weighty in its position
to belong to a mere incidental statement), still less with ἀγαπήσας (as giving this
an entirely unnatural limitation), nor again with ἐγείρεται, ver. 4 (assuming an
unneeded and unindicated grammatical or logical parenthesis, and most harshly
resuming in ver. 3 the εἰδώς of ver. 1), but with ἠγάπησεν, which thus regularly
completes the period.   Still, as to the *fact*, it belongs virtually to the following
verses, which give the *contents* of ἠγάπησεν.   It seems to me that this combination, "Before the feast of the Passover He loved, (gave a proof of His love"
aor.), is sufficiently natural.   The *loved*, (aor. gave a proof of His love), which
Meyer confines to the foot-washing, Weiss justly, as it would seem, extends
over the entire scene of the Last Supper from chap. 13 to 17, including not
only the foot-washing, which was an act rather of condescension and the incul-
cation of loving condescension than strictly of love, and really applies pre-eminently to those tender and loving discourses which follow.   It does not include
the crucifixion, because that was a display of love, not primarily to His disciples,
but to the world.   The first verse Weiss thus regards as a sort of superscription

celebration before ἐξῆλθεν, ver. 30) almost
universally recognized, although formerly
(even already in the Fathers) the opposite
view preponderated, and, owing to a dogmatic interest, was supported in the Lutheran Church against the Reformed, on
account of the participation of the unworthy. See Wichelhaus, *Komm. zur Leidens-*
gesch. p. 256 f.   In quite a different interest
has Schenkel maintained that Jesus did
not exclude the traitor from the solemnity ;
that He, in fact, desired thereby to remove
even the pretext "*for its again being made
an ordinance,*" and that without preparation or antecedent confession He granted
an unconditional *freedom of participation.*

to the whole section, chap. 13-17. Yet it seems doubtful whether the words
πρὸ δὲ τῆς ἑορ. τ. πάσχα do not rather stand at the head of the whole, without
any determinate grammatical connection, simply as marking another stage to
which Jesus has now arrived, that namely which introduces the eventful scenes
of the Passover. The main question, however, is, What is the *time* indicated by
this πρὸ τῆς ἑορτῆς? Meyer is certainly right in saying that it does not indicate
how long before the Passover, and this must be determined by the connection.
Now if it refers to the day or the night before the slaying of the paschal lamb,
then it brings John into irreconcilable contradiction with the Synoptical
Gospels, all of which place the Last Supper by universal consent on the evening
of the 14th Nisan, after the slaying of the paschal lamb, and make the feast
identical in time and in fact with the Paschal Supper. If John *intended* to fix
a date which should be in distinct opposition to this current and well-known
date, it seems inconceivable that He should have done it by a statement so
entirely vague and indeterminate. It is his habit, perhaps beyond that of
either of his fellow-Evangelists, to give in his history definite designations of
time (i. 29, 35, 43, ii. 1, iv. 43), and just before, in chap. xii. 1, without any
apparently important cause, he has given us one of these definite dates (six days
before the feast of the Passover); and now, when a very serious point of chronology was involved, and He was going consciously to correct a widely diffused
error of the Synoptists in regard to the time of the Lord's Supper, that he should
have satisfied himself with this vague and indefinite language seems incredible.
How easy to have said "one day before the feast," etc. ; and had he *meant* this,
how naturally would he have said so ! Even with the Synoptists, the supper *introduced* the Passover festival, *stood at its head*, and the part in John which
constituted the foot-washing might have actually anticipated even the paschal
δεῖπνον, and been merely preliminary and preparatory to it. I cannot but think
with many, that this phrase is intended to be no exact designation of time ;
that John puts it loosely at the head of the section, as marking the commencement of the Passover feast, and that he is not conscious of any intention to cross
the track of the fixed evangelical tradition on this point. With anything like
a polemical purpose or consciousness, his language would surely have been more
precise.

XL. Ver. 1.

In this verse Weiss also, rightly I think, rejects Meyer's construction of
ἀγαπήσας ("that he might depart out of this world to the Father after having
loved—given a proof of love—to his own") as artificial, and not corresponding to the evident correlation of ἀγαπήσας—ἠγάπησεν. Nor is ἀγαπήσας co-ordinated with εἰδώς (by familiar asyndeton, *knowing, having loved*, for *knowing and
having loved*), but it is a part of the *apodosis* or after clause of the sentence,
εἰδώς supplying the place of the *protasis*, as appears by resolving it into *since
he knew* ("since he knew that his hour, etc., having loved his own, he loved
them").—εἰς τέλος not *unto the end*, but either *at the last, finally*, or (better, *in the
highest degree, pre-eminently*.) So Weiss.

XLI. " *The devil having put it into the heart*," etc. Ver. 2.

Weiss justly, I think, rejects Meyer's construction which makes " the
heart" here the heart of the devil, on the ground that even admitting that we
might speak of the *heart* of the devil, it should be in a connection which clearly

THE GOSPEL OF JOHN.

requires or justifies such a usage. But in the first place the active voice is strongly against such a construction. It should be clearly βάλλεσθαι, not βάλλειν, and
βάλλειν εἰς καρδίαν for Satan's own heart would seem quite inadmissible. Again,
it is unnatural that the devil, whose hate and hellish purpose never slumbered,
should be represented as having *just now* put into his own heart the evil purpose. It is much more natural to refer it to that of Judas : "the purposing of
the *man* can be fixed to a definite point, but not so naturally that of the
devil." Judas having recently, no doubt, conceived the plot, nothing is more
natural than to ascribe its origin to the devil. The harshness of the construction is amply compensated by its bringing out with great emphasis the name
of the traitor : " The devil having already (or now) put it into the heart that
Judas Iscariot son of Simon should deliver him up." Such *trajections* are by
no means unfamiliar to the Greek.

CHAPTER XIV.

Before πορεύομαι, ver. 2, ὅτι (Lachm. Tisch.) is decisively attested. Its omission is therefore to be explained from the fact that it was taken for the recitative ὅτι, as which it appeared superfluous, since the recitative ὅτι is so frequently passed over in the Codd. — Ver. 3. καί before ἑτοιμ. is wanting in A. E. G. H. K. Δ. Curss., some Verss., Phot. Deleted by Matth. and Lachm. D. M. Curss. Syr. Cant. Theophyl. Euth. : ἑτοιμάσαι. This mechanical repetition from what precedes was the cause of the omission of the καί, which, however, is still very strongly attested by B. C. L. N. U. X. Λ. ℵ. Vulg. It. and important witnesses. — Ver. 4. οἴδατε, καὶ τ. ὁδὸν οἴδατε] B. C.* L. Q. X. ℵ. 157, Copt. Aeth. Pers. p. Verc. have merely οἴδατε τ. ὁδόν. So Tisch., whilst Lachm. only brackets the καί and the second οἴδατε. The Recepta is an explanatory expansion ; against it ver. 5 also witnesses. — Ver. 5. δυνάμεθα τ. ὁδὸν εἰδέναι] Lachm. and Tisch. : οἴδαμεν τὴν ὁδόν, according to B. C.* D. Codd. It. Cyr. Tert., among which, however, a few (including D.) have τ. ὁδ. οἴδ. The Recepta is an explanatory expansion. — Ver. 7. ἐγνώκειτε ἄν] B. C.* L. Q. X. Curss. Cyr. Ath. : ἂν ᾔδειτε, or (X.) ᾔδ. ἄν. From viii. 19. — Ver. 9. τοσοῦτον χρόνον] Lachm. Tisch. : τοσούτῳ χρόνῳ, according to D. L. Q. ℵ. Cyr. The accusative is an unnecessary gloss. — Ver. 10. αὐτὸς ποιεῖ τὰ ἔργα] Tisch. : ποιεῖ τὰ ἔργα αὐτοῦ, according to B. D. ℵ. Rightly. The αὐτός, added in explanation, dislodged the αὐτοῦ, and that in such a way that it took its place (L. X.) in some instances, in others was placed before the verb. — Ver. 11. After ἐμοί Elz. has ἐστίν. A supplementary addition against decisive testimony. — μοι at the end is rejected by Schulz, deleted by Tisch. It suggests the suspicion of being a mechanical repetition ; besides, the omitting witnesses (amongst them Codd. D. L. ℵ. 33) are sufficiently strong. — Ver. 12. μου] is, according to preponderating evidence, with Lachm. and Tisch., to be deleted. — Ver. 14 is entirely wanting in X. Λ. Curss., some Verss. Chrys. Nonnus ; witnesses, however, which are too weak to permit us, with Rinck, to condemn it, especially since, on account of the similar beginning in vv. 14 and 16, and considering its superfluous character, it might very easily be passed over. — Ver. 15. τηρήσατε] Tisch. : τηρήσετε, according to B. L. ℵ. (?) Curss. Euseb. But the future readily arose from the entire context. — Ver. 16. μένῃ] B. L. Q. X. ℵ. Codd. It. Goth. Copt. Syr. and several Fathers have ᾖ. So Lachm. (but, with B., after αἰῶνα) and Tisch. Rightly ; μένῃ is a more closely-defining gloss from ver. 17. — Ver. 17. ἔσται] Lachm. : ἐστίν, according to B. D.* Curss. Verss. Lucif. According as MENEI was taken as present (E. G. K. M. U. X. Λ.) or as future (Vulg.), ἐστίν or ἔσται may be written after it ; hence it is only the preponderance of witnesses which decides, and this is in favour of the future. — Ver. 20. Since the first ὑμεῖς stands in some of the witnesses after, in some before, γνώσ. (so, only bracketed in Lachm.), while in some it is entirely wanting (A. Verss. Fathers), it must be regarded as an addition. — Ver. 22. Instead of καὶ τί, Elz. and Lachm. have merely τί, in accordance with preponderating evidence. But καί (which ℵ. also has) might be readily passed over by clumsy copyists, especially, too, as the preceding κύριε might occasion its being overlooked. -- Ver. 23. ποιήσομεν] Lachm. and Tisch. : ποιησόμεθα, in accordance with important witnesses (D. also with ἐλεύσομαι κ. ποιήσομαι declares for the middle voice). Rightly ; the middle, which John uses nowhere else, was unfamiliar to the copyists. — Ver. 28. ἠγαπᾶτε] D.* H. L. and a few Curss. : ἀγαπᾶτε, to which Buttmann, in the *Stud. u. Krit.* 1858, p. 481 f., gives the preference. Too weakly attested ; and how easily would a stumbling-block be found in the imperf., as denying love to the disciples !—Between ὅτι and πορεύομαι Elz. has εἶπον, against decisive witnesses. An interpolation in conformity with the preceding.

Ver. 1.[1] From Peter Jesus now turns, with consolatory address in reference to His near departure, to the disciples generally ; hence D. and a few Verss. prefix καὶ εἶπεν τοῖς μαθηταῖς αὐτοῦ (so also Luther, following Erasmus). But the cause of the address itself is fully explained in John's narrative by the situation, and by no means requires the reference, arbitrarily assumed by Hengstenberg, to Luke xxii. 35–38. The whole of the following farewell discourses, down to xvii. 26, must have grown out of the profoundest recollections of the apostle, which, in a thoroughly genial manner, are vividly recalled, and further expanded. It accords with the entire peculiarity of the Johannean narrative of the last Supper, that the Synoptics offer no parallels *to these* farewell discourses. Hence it is not satisfactory, and is not in keeping with the necessary personal recollection of John, to regard him as taking his start from certain *primary words of earlier gospels*, which he, like an artist of powerful genius, has transfigured by the freest, but, at the same time, most appropriate and enchanting transformation (Ewald). — μὴ ταρασσ.] by anxiety and apprehension. Comp. xii. 27. It points to what He had spoken in the preceding chapters of His *departure*, not (with Chrysostom, Theodore of Mopsuestia, Theophylact, Euth. Zigabenus, and many) to *Peter's denial*, after the prediction of which the rest of the disciples also might have become anxious about their constancy. This is erroneous, because the following discourse bears no relation to it.— πιστεύετε, κ.τ.λ.] By these words Jesus exhorts them not to faith generally (which they certainly had), but to that confident *assurance* by which the μὴ ταράσσεσθαι was conditioned : *trust in God, and trust in me.* To take, in *both* cases, πιστεύετε as *imperatives*[2] appears most in conformity with the preceding imperative and the direct character of the address.[3] [See Note XLII. p. 425.] Others : the first πιστ. is indicative, and the second imperative : *ye believe on God, believe*

[1] Luther's exposition of chap. xiv., xv., xvi. belongs to the year 1538. He terms these discourses "the best and most consoling sermons that the Lord Christ delivered on earth," and "a treasure and jewel, not to be purchased with the world's goods." — Luther's book (which originated in sermons, which Casp. and Cruciger took down) is among his most spirited and lively writings. How highly he himself esteemed it, see in Matthesius, *eilfte Pred.* (ed. Nürnb. 1592, p. 119a).

[2] Cyril., Gothic, Nonnus, Theophylact, Euth. Zigab., Bengel, and several others, including most moderns, from Lücke to Hengst. and Godet.

[3] So also Ebrard, who, however, in conformity with a supposed Hebraism (see on Eph. iv. 26), finds the inappropriate meaning : "*Believe on God, so ye believe on me.*" Thus the emotional address becomes a reflection. Olshausen arrives at the same sense, taking the first πιστ as imperative, the second as indicative.

therefore on me.[1] Luther, who regards the first sentence as hypothetical (in itself admissible),[2] in his translation takes πιστεύετε, in *both* cases, as *indicatives*. According to any rendering, however, the inseparable coherence of the two elements of faith (God in Christ manifest and near) is to be noted. Comp. Rom. v. 2.

Vv. 2, 3 serve to *arouse* the πιστεύειν demanded in ver. 1, to which *a prospect so blessed* lies open. *In the house of my Father are many places of sojourn*, many shall find their abiding-place (μονή only here and in ver. 23 in the N. T. ; frequent in the classics, comp. also 1 Macc. vii. 38), so that such therefore is not wanting to you also ; *but if this were not the case I would have told you* ("ademissem vobis spem inanem," Grotius). After εἶπον ἂν ὑμῖν a full stop must be placed, and with ὅτι (see critical notes) πορεύομαι a new sentence begins.[3] But the Fathers of the church, Erasmus, Luther, Castalio, Wolf, Maldonatus, Bengel, and many others, including Hofmann,[4] and Ebrard, refer εἶπον ἂν ὑμῖν to what follows : if it were not so, *then I would have said to you: I go*, etc. Against this ver. 3 is decisive, according to which Jesus actually says that He is going away, and is preparing a place.[5] Others take it *as a question*, where, however, we are not, on account of the aorist εἶπον, to explain . *would I indeed say to you: I go*, etc.?[6] But : would I indeed *have said* to you, etc. ? In this way there would either be intended an earlier saying *not preserved in the Gospel* (Ewald),[7] possibly with the stamp of a gloss on it (Weizsäcker), or a reference to the earlier sayings regarding the passage into the heavenly world (Lange). But for the latter explanation the language in the present passage is too definite and peculiar ; while the former amounts simply to an hypothesis which is neither necessary nor capable of support on other grounds.—The οἰκία τοῦ πατρός is not *heaven generally*, but the peculiar *dwelling-place* of the divine δόξα *in* heaven, the place of His glorious throne,[8] viewed, after the analogy of the temple in Jerusalem, this earthly οἶκος τοῦ πατρός (ii. 16), as a heavenly sanctuary (Isa. lvii. 15). [See Note XLIII. p. 426.] Comp. Heb. ix. — πολλαί] ἱκαναὶ δέξασθαι καὶ ἡμᾶς, Euth. Zigabenus. The conception of *different degrees* of blessedness (Augus-

---

[1] Vulgate, Erasmus, Luther in his *Exposition*, Castalio, Beza, Calvin, Aretius, Maldonatus, Grotius, and several others.

[2] Bernhardy, p. 385 ; Pflugk, *ad Eur. Med.* 386, comp. on i. 51.

[3] So, first Valla, then Beza, Calvin, Casaubon, Aretius, Grotius, Jansen, and many others, including Kuinoel, Lücke, Tholuck, Olshausen, B. Crusius, de Wette (who terms the assertion "somewhat *naïve*." But it has rather its full weight in the faith presupposed in the disciples, that He cannot leave them uninstructed on any essential point of their hope ; comp. Köstlin, *Lehrbegr.* p. 163), Maier, Hengstenberg, Godet, Lachmann, Tischendorf.

[4] *Schriftbew.* II. 2, p. 464.

[5] This reason is valid, whether we read now in ver. 3 καὶ ἑτοιμάσω, or with Lachmann merely ἑτοιμάσω : Hofmann follows

the latter, and connects therewith, as well as with ἐάν, artificial and laboured departures from the simple sense of the words. Ebrard also adopts a forced and artificial view, according to which ἑτοιμάσαι is said to be *objective : bring about your presence ;* but ἑτοιμάσω (without καί) must *point to the making accessible for the disciples*. How could a listener hit upon this difference of idea in the same word ?

[6] Mosheim, Ernesti, Beck in the *Stud. u. Krit.* 1831, p. 130 ff.

[7] He would also place εἰ δὲ μὴ . . . τόπον ὑμῖν within a parenthesis, and finds here either a saying out of a now unknown gospel, or rather out of the fragment supposed to have been lost before chap. vi.

[8] Ps. ii. 4, xxxiii. 13, 14 : Isa. lxiii. 15, *et al.*

tine and several others) lies entirely remote from the meaning here ; for *many* the house of God is *destined and established*, and that already ἀπὸ κατα-βολῆς κόσμου, Matt. xxv. 34. — ὅτι πορεύομαι, κ.τ.λ.] *for I go*, etc., assigns the reason of the assurance : ἐν τῇ οἰκίᾳ . . . πολλαί εἰσιν, so that εἰ δὲ μή, εἶπον ἂν ὑμῖν is to be regarded as logically inserted. The πορεύομαι ἑτοιμάσαι, κ.τ.λ., however, is an actual proof of the existence of the μοναὶ πολλαί in the heavenly house of God (not of the εἶπον ἂν ὑμῖν, as Luthardt thinks, placing only a colon after ὑμῖν), because otherwise Jesus could not go away with the design of getting prepared for them in those μοναί a place on which they are thereafter to enter, a place for them. This ἑτοιμάζειν τόπον presupposes μονὰς πολλάς, in which the dwelling-place to be provided must exist. The idea is, further (comp. the idea of the πρόδρομος, Heb. vi. 20), that He having attained by His death to the fellowship of the divine δόξα, purposes to prepare the way for their future συνδοξασθῆναι with God (comp. xvii. 24) ; but " therefore He speaks with them in the simplest possible, as it were, child-like fashion, according to their thoughts, as is necessary to attract and allure simple people," Luther. — Ver. 3. Καὶ ἐὰν . . . τόπον] Emphatic repetition of the consolatory words, with which is united the still more consolatory promise : *I will come again, and will* (then) *receive you to myself.* Jesus says, καὶ ἐάν, not κ. ὅταν, for He does not mention the *point of time* of His return, but what *consequences* (namely, the πάλιν ἔρχομαι, κ.τ.λ.) will be connected with this departure of His, and preparation of a place of which He had just given them assurance. The πορεύεσθαι κ. ἑτοιμ, κ.τ.λ., is the conditioning fact which, if it shall take place, has the πάλιν ἔρχεσθαι, κ.τ.λ., as its happy consequence. Comp. xii. 32. The nearness or remoteness of the appearance of this result remains undefined by ἐάν. Comp. Düsterdieck on 1 John ii. 28, where the reading ὅταν is an alteration proceeding from clumsy copyists.—By πάλιν ἔρχομαι Jesus means, and that not indefinitely, or verging towards a merely spiritual import (de Wette), but distinctly and clearly, His *Parousia* at the last day (vi. 39, 40, xi. 24), and not His *resurrection* (Ebrard), to which the following κ. παραλ., κ.τ.λ., is not appropriate. That in John (comp. 1 John ii. 28), and in Jesus, according to John (comp. xxi. 22, v. 28, 29), as in the whole apostolic church, existed the conception of the Parousia as near at hand,[1] although in the Gospel, on account of its spiritual character, it comes less into the foreground, see in Kaeuffer, *de ζωῆς αἰων, not.* p. 131 f., comp. also Frommann, p. 479 f. ; Lechler,[2] Wittichen,[3] and Weiss.[4] On this His glorious return He will receive the disciples into His personal fellowship (as raised from the dead or transformed respectively), and that as partakers of His divine δόξα in the heavenly sanctuary which has descended with Him to the earth, in which a place will be already prepared for them. He comes in the glory of His Father, and they enter into fellowship with

[1] However decidedly this is still denied by Scholten, who finds in John only *a spiritual* coming, in the sense. namely, that the *Spirit* of Jesus *remains*. According to Keim (*Geschichtl. Chr.* p. 45, ed. 3), the fourth Gospel has, " in sufficiently modern fashion, relegated the future kingdom to heaven," and " broken off the head " of the expectation of the Parousia. But the head is exactly in the present passage.

[2] *Apost. und Nachapost. Zeit.* p. 224 ff.
[3] *Jahrb. f. D. Th.* 1862, p. 357 f.
[4] *Lehrbegr.* p. 181.

Him in this δόξα in the Messianic kingdom.[1] The explanation of a coming, only regarded as such more or less *improperly*, in order to receive the disciples by a blessed death into heaven,[2] is opposed to the words (comp. xxi. 22) and to the mode of expression elsewhere employed in the N. T. respecting the coming of Christ, since death does indeed translate the apostles and martyrs to Christ ;[3] but it is nowhere said of Christ that He *comes* (in order to be personally present at their dying bed (as Hengstenberg, indeed, thinks) and *brings* them to Himself. Except in the Paraclete, Christ first *comes* in His glory at the Parousia. But the understanding of the words here (acc. to vv. 18 ff.) only of the *spiritual* return of Christ to His own, and their *reception into the full sacred fellowship of the Spirit* of the glorified Christ," [4] is ruled out by the fact that Jesus himself has in advance (ver. 2) required their reference to His actual return, and to local fellowship with Him (in vv. 18 ff. the entire *context* is different). — πρὸς ἐμαυτόν] spoken in the consciousness of the great value which the love of the disciples placed on *fellowship with his own person.* Only with *Himself* have faith and love the final object of hope, and their blessed reward [5] in the Father's house.

Vv. 4, 5. In order now to lead the disciples to that which, on their side, in respect of the promise contained in ver. 3, was the main practical matter, He says, arousing inquiry : *And whither I go . . . ye know the way* (so, according to the amended reading, see critical notes) which leads thither, namely, to the Father. And the disciples, had they already been more susceptible to the communications of the Lord respecting His higher Messianic destiny, must have known Him—this way,—since Christ had already so frequently set Himself forth as the only Mediator of salvation, as in chap. vi., x. 1 ff., xi. 25, *et al.* He means, that is, not the way to *suffering and death*, which He Himself is about to tread, [6] but the way designated in ver. 6 (*He Himself is that way!*) along which every one is directed who would attain to that glorious fellowship with the Father. — ὅπου ἐγὼ ὑπάγω is an anacoluthon, with the emphasis of the certainty of the near and blessed completion, and ἐγώ has the accent of self-conscious and unique pre-eminence.—Thomas, as in xx. 25, speaks the language of sober, hesitating intelligence, not of dejection at the approaching suffering of the Lord, as Ebrard thinks. He seeks *information ;* ᾤετο γὰρ αἰσθητὸν εἶναί τινα τόπον, ὅπου

---

[1] Comp. Origen and several others, including Calvin, Lampe, Luthardt, Hofmann, *Schriftbew.* I. p. 194, Hilgenfeld, Brückner, Ewald.

[2] Grotius, Kuinoel, B. Crusius, Reuss, Tholuck, Lange, Hengstenberg, and several others.

[3] 2 Cor. v. 8 ; Phil. i. 23 ; Acts vii. 59 ; see on Phil. i. 26, note.

[4] Lücke, Neander, Godet, comp. Olshausen, Ebrard.

[5] It is incorrect to maintain that in John the notion of *reward* is entirely wanting (so Weiss in the *Deutsch. Zeitschr.* 1853, pp. 325, 338, and in his *Petr. Lehrbegr.* p. 55 f.). As

Christ seeks in prayer eternal glory for Himself as a reward, xvii. 4, 5, so He assigns it to the disciples also as a reward. See xvii. 24, xii. 25, 26, xi. 26. Here applies also the promise of ἰδεῖν τὴν βασιλ. τοῦ θεοῦ, iii. 3, 5, and the resurrection at the last day, v. 28, 29, vi. 40, 54. Comp. 1 John iii. 2, 3, where the future transfiguration and union with Christ is expressly designated as the object of ἐλπίς, as well as John viii., where even the expression μισθὸν πλήρη is employed, and is to be understood of eternal blessedness (see Düsterdieck, II. p. 505).

[6] Luther, Jansen, Grotius, Wetstein, also Tholuck and Luthardt.

ὑπάγει, καὶ ὁδὸν ὁμοίως τοιαύτην, Euth. Zigabenus. The *heavenly* ποῦ, however distinctly Jesus had already designated it, Thomas did not yet know clearly how to combine with his circle of Messianic ideas ; but he desired to *arrive at clearness.* That Thomas is here cited without the name Δίδυμος, which is added in xi. 16, xx. 24, xxi. 2, is accidental, and without the design which Hengstenberg imports (that he does not speak here according to his *individual spiritual* character). — πῶς, κ.τ.λ.] " Quodsi ignoretur, quae sit *meta,* non potest via *sub ratione viae* concipi," Grotius.

Ver. 6. *I* (no other than I) *am the way,* on which men must go, in order to come to the Father in His heavenly house, vv. 2, 3, *and the truth, and the life.* But since no one, without going the prescribed *way,* without having appropriated to himself the *truth,* and without bearing in himself the life, can come to that goal, οὐδείς, κ.τ.λ., is thus the exponent to all *three* particulars, not merely to the first. The three terms lay down the proposition that no other than Christ is the Mediator of eternal salvation with God in the Messianic kingdom, under three several characteristic aspects which are co-ordinated, yet in such a way that the advance is made from the general to the particular. The characteristic of the mediation of salvation, in the first point, is designated with reference not to matter (as in ἡ ἀλήθεια and ἡ ζωή), but to *form,* in so far, namely, as the mediation of salvation itself is therein expressed in a specific *figure* (comp. x. 9). On individual points, note : (1) Christ is the *Way,* not because He ὑπέδειξε τὴν ὁδόν (Cyril., Melanchthon, and many others, departing from both the expression and the figure, and failing to observe the relation of things), but because in His personal manifestation the mediation of salvation is objectively given, absolutely the sole mediation for all men, but which has to be made use of subjectively, that is, by faith on Him, like the man who is aiming at a goal, and for that purpose must take and pursue the given way which is the means of its attainment. (2) Christ is the *Truth,* because He is the self-revelation of God which has been manifested (vv. 7, 9), the Light that is come into the world, without the appropriation of which salvation is not obtained. (3) He is the *Life* (Col. iii. 4), because He is the Principle and Source of eternal life (in its temporal development and future consummation) ; so that whoever has not received Him into himself by faith (vi. 50, 51, xi. 25, 26), has become a prey to spiritual and eternal death.[1] These three points are not to be separated according to time (Luther : beginning, middle, end ; so also Calvin), but Christ is all three *at once,*—in that He is the one, He is also the second and the third,—although this cannot justify an arbitrary fusion of the three predicates (as would be the Augustinian *vera via vitae*). — οὐδεὶς ἔρχεται, κ.τ.λ.] the Johannean *sola fide.* Note how ver. 6 is the *summary of the most perfect self-confession* of the Son regarding Himself and His work.

Ver. 7. *Had you known me* (for they had indeed not known that He was the Way), *you would also have known the Father* (of their non-acquaintance

[1] Comp. Ignatius, *ad Trall.* 9 : οὗ χωρὶς τὸ ἀληθινὸν ζῆν οὐκ ἔχομεν ; *ad Eph.* 3 : Χριστὸς τὸ ἀδιάκριτον ἡμῶν ζῆν.

with whom their οὐκ οἴδαμεν, ποῦ ὑπάγεις, ver. 5, had testified).—The emphasis changes (otherwise in viii. 19) ; it lies in the protasis on ἐγνώκ., not on the enclitic με ; in the apodosis on τ. πατ. μου. — καὶ ἀπ᾿ ἄρτι, κ.τ.λ.] and—which I can nevertheless now add—*from henceforward* (after I have told you in ver. 6 so definitely and fully what *I* am) *you know Him, and have* (in me, ver. 9) *beheld Him*. This view of the meaning, which flows immediately out of the context, vv. 6 and 9, the point of which is the idea of the adequate self-revelation of God in Christ, entirely excludes any interpretation of the two verbs in a future sense,[1] and the reference to a future *terminus a quo*,[2] which is wont to be assumed as the time of the communication of the Spirit, nay, even a mentally supplied "*I hope*" (de Wette), with ἀπάρτι. The reference of ἀπάρτι to the whole time of their fellowship with Christ since their conversion (Hengstenberg), is, even grammatically, impossible. See on xiii. 19, i. 52. In that case only νῦν could stand. Godet's remark is also incorrect : "*at the point* at which my teaching has now arrived," as if ἄρτι merely were expressed. — On καί, which, without altering its meaning, significantly subjoins an adversative clause (*and . . . i.e.* and nevertheless), see on vii. 28.

Vv. 8, 9. *Philip*, like Thomas in a certain hesitation, corresponding to his want of apprehension, has not yet understood the ἑωράκατε αὐτόν ; instead of seeing it fulfilled in the manifestation of Jesus Himself, it excites in him the wish that the Lord would effect a *Theophany*, perhaps such as Moses once beheld (Ex. xxiv. 9, 10), or desired to see (Ex. xxxiii. 18), or the prophets had predicted for the inauguration of the Messianic kingdom (Mal. iii. 1 ff.). — ἀρκεῖ ἡμῖν] and then *are we contented ;* then we see the measure of the revelation of the Father, given to us by Thee, fulfilled to such a degree that we do not covet a further until the last glorious appearance.—On the dative of duration of time, τοσούτῳ χρόνῳ (see critical notes).[3] καὶ οὐκ ἐγν. με] *And thou hast not known me ?* A question of melancholy surprise, and hence also in loving emotion, He addresses him *by name*. Had Philip *known* Jesus, he would have said to himself, that in Him the highest revelation of God was manifested, and the wish to behold a Theophany must have remained foreign to his mind. Hence : *He who has seen me has seen the Father ;* for He reveals Himself in me, I am ἀθηήτοιο τοκῆος συμφυὲς ἔνθεον εἶδος ἔχων βροτοειδέι μορφῇ, Nonnus. The proposition is to be left in *objective generality*, and ἑωρ. is not to be limited to *believing* seeing.[4] *Every one* has, if he has seen Christ, seen the Father *objectively ;* but only he who has *known* Christ for that which He is, *subjectively* also, "according to the sight of the Spirit and of faith," Luther. Comp. i. 14, v. 37.

Vv. 10, 11. This language of thine amounts indeed to this : as though thou didst not believe that, etc. —ὅτι ἐγὼ ἐν τ. πατρί, κ.τ.λ.] On this mutual fellowship, which "virtutis potius quam essentiae elogium est" (Calvin), see on x. 38. Comp. xvii. 21. Here the ἐγὼ ἐν τ. πατ. stands *first*, because

---

[1] Chrysostom, Kuinoel, and many others.

[2] Chrysostom, Lücke, Ewald, and several others.

[3] Comp. Buttmann, *N. T. Gram.* p. 161

[E. T. p. 186].

[4] Luther, Lücke, de Wette, and many others.

the matter in question is the way which the knowledge has to take *from the Son to the Father.* — τὰ ῥήματα . . . τὰ ἔργα αὐτοῦ] (see critical notes) : the proof of this union of mine with the Father is, *that I do not speak from myself;* but the proof *for that* (for this ἀπ' ἐμαυτοῦ οὐ λαλῶ) is, that the Father *does His works through me.* The δέ is therefore *continuative (autem),* not antithetical. Further, we must neither say that the ῥήματα are to be reckoned along with the ἔργα, nor that τὰ ἔργα signifies the *business of teaching* (Nösselt) ; but, from the fact that the Messianic *works* (see on v. 36) are the works of the *Father,* it is inferred, with necessary dialectic certainty, from whom also the *discourses* of Jesus proceed ; if the former are divine, the latter must be adequately related to them. The first proposition is often arbitrarily supplemented from the second, and *vice versá.*[1] This, however, does not agree with the Greek mode of allowing, in antithetic propositions, one clause to be completed from the other,[2] and would here run counter to the *context,* since Jesus, ver. 11, desires to have deduced from the ἔργα that which He had brought into light by τὰ ῥήματα . . . λαλῶ. Hence we are not to escape the difficulty either by the assumption of an "incongruity in the antithetic propositions" (Tholuck), or, with Lange, pronounce that the words belong *pre-eminently* to the Son, the works *pre-eminently* to the Father, which is not contained in the expressions, and would be an un-Johannean *halving* of the thought (v. 19, viii. 28, xii. 49) ; nor are we to assume, with Ewald, that *a lesser significance* is to be ascribed to the works in opposition to the words. — ὁ ἐν ἐμοὶ μένων] expressing the ὁ ἐν ἐμ. ὢν as *enduring* (he who does not depart from me). According to the reading ποιεῖ τ. ἔργα αὐτοῦ (see critical notes), the works of Jesus are set forth as the works *of God,* which the Father performs, that is, in virtue of His immanence in the Son, making them to operate in an outward direction. — Ver. 11. From Philip, Jesus now turns to the disciples collectively, and that *with an exhortation* to the faith, in reference to which He had been obliged to *question* Philip in a manner implying doubt. — πιστεύετέ μοι] namely, without anything further, in addition to my personal assurance. — ὅτι] not *because* (Bengel), but *that,* as in ver. 10. — διὰ τὰ ἔργα αὐτά] *On account of the works themselves (in and of themselves),* irrespective of my oral testimony, believe me in this. The works are the actual proofs of that fellowship, v. 19, 20, x. 37, 38.

Vv. 12, 13. Truly, on the compliance with this πιστεύετέ μοι there awaits a ministry like my own, yea, and still greater. What encouragement to fidelity in the faith ! Schott, *Opusc.* p. 177, imports the meaning : "neque *ad ea tantum* provoco, quae me ipsum hucusque vidistis perficientem, *imo,*" etc. Comp. also Luthardt, according to whom Jesus proceeds to a still further *demonstration of his fellowship with God.* — ὁ πιστ. εἰς ἐμέ] intended not universally, but for (comp. vv. 11, 13) the *disciples.* On εἰς ἐμέ, Bengel aptly remarks : "qui *Christo* de se loquenti (see πιστ. μοι, ver. 11), *in Chris-*

---

[1] The words which I speak to you, I speak not of myself ; and the works which I do, I do not of myself, but the Father who is in me. He teaches me the words, and does the works — de Wette, comp. Bengel.

[2] Kühner, II. p. 608 f. ; Bernhardy, p. 455.

tum credit." — κἀκεῖνος] *he also,* in comparison, emphatically repeating the subject.[1] — καί] heightening the effect : *and besides, indeed.*[2] — μείζονα τούτων] *greater than these,* ἃ ἐγὼ ποιῶ, comp. v. 20, and on the thought, Matt. xxi. 21, 22. It is not, however, to be referred to *single separate* miracles, which are reported by the apostles ; Ruperti names the healing power of Peter's shadow, Acts v., and the speaking in foreign tongues, which latter Grotius also has in view ; Bengel appeals to Acts v. 15, xix. 12 ; Mark xvi. 17 ff. A measuring of miracles of this kind by their magnitude is entirely foreign to the N. T. Rather in μείζονα τούτων is the notion of ἔργα *expanded,* so that its predominant signification is not that of miraculous deeds in the narrower sense (as in ἃ ἐγὼ ποιῶ), but in a broader sense, the world-subduing *apostolic work* in general, produced by the Holy Spirit (xvi. 18 ff.) in the diffusion of the gospel, with its light and life, amongst all peoples, in the conquest of Judaism and paganism by the word of the cross, etc. The history of the apostles, and especially the work of Paul, is the commentary thereon. These were ἔργα of a greater kind than the miracles proper which Jesus wrought,[3] and which also, categorically, those of the apostles resembled. — ὅτι, κ.τ.λ.] *assigns the reasons* of the preceding assurance, τὰ ἔργα ἃ ἐγὼ ποιῶ . . . μείζ. τούτ. ποιήσει (not merely the μείζονα, for which limitation no reason presents itself), and this statement of reason continues to the end of ver. 13, so that καὶ ὅ, τι ἂν still depends on ὅτι. Since He is going *to the Father,* and thus, elevated to the position of heavenly rule, will do all that they shall *ask* in His name, there can be no doubt that the assurance of those ἔργα will be justified. So, substantially, Grotius, Lücke, Olshausen, de Wette, Ewald, Godet, comp. already Cyril. Considering the internal coherence, and the immediately continuative καί, ver. 13, it is incompetent to separate ver. 13, as if it were independent, from ver. 12, whereby ὅτι ἐγὼ πρὸς τ. π. πορ. is taken either merely in *the* sense : ὑμῶν λοιπόν ἐστι τὸ θαυμα- τουργεῖν, ἐγὼ γὰρ ἀπέρχομαι ;[4] or more correctly, because really assigning a reason, with Luther : "for through the power that I shall have at the right hand of the Father, . . . I will work in you," etc.[5] — ἐγώ] In opposition to the πιστεύοντες, who continue their activity on earth. — ἐν τῷ ὀνόματί μου] Comp. xv. 16, xvi. 23. The prayerful request to God (for it is to *God* that the absolute αἰτήσητε refers, comp. xv. 16) is made in the *name of Jesus,* if this name, Jesus Christ, as the full substance of the saving faith and confession of him who prays, is in his consciousness the *element in which* the prayerful activity lives and moves, so that thus that Name, embracing the whole revela- tion of redemption, is that which specifically measures and defines the dispo- sition, feeling, object, and contents of prayer. The express *use* of the name of Jesus therein is no specific token ; the question is of the *spirit* and *mind* of

[1] Xen. *Mem.* i. 2. 24.
[2] See Hartung, *Partikell.* I. p. 145 f.
[3] "For He assumed only a small corner for Himself, a little time for His preaching and working of miracles ; but the apostles and their successors went through the whole world," etc.—Luther.
[4] ["*Yours* is henceforth the province of

working miracles ; for *I* go away."—K.] Chrysostom, so Theophylact, Euth. Ziga- benus, Erasmus, Wolf, Kuinoel, Ebrard, and several others.
[5] Comp. Calvin and several others, in- cluding B. Crusius, Luthardt, Hengsten- berg.

him who prays. The apostolic mode of expression is analogous : to be, have, say, do, anything, etc., ἐν Χριστῷ, ἐν κυρίῳ.[1] The renderings : *invocato meo nomine* (in connection with which reference is irrelevantly made to Acts iii. 6;[2] *me agnoscentes mediatorem* (Melanchthon) ; *ut mea causa faciat* (Grotius) ; *per meritum meum* (Calovius and several others) ; *in my mind, in my affairs* (de Wette), and the like, are partly opposed to the words, partly too narrow, and comprised in the foregoing explanation. But if we proposed to interpret, with Godet : *in my stead*, that is, *in such a way as though I myself were the subject that prays through you*,[3] the first person ποιήσω would be inappropriate to a *self*-hearing ; and essential prayers like those for the forgiveness of sin would be excluded. — τοῦτο ποιήσω] nothing else. This definite and unlimited promise rests upon the fact that the petition of him who prays in the name of Jesus is in harmony with the will of Christ and of God, but in every case subordinates itself in the consciousness of him who prays to the restriction : not my, but Thy will ! hence also the *denial* of a particular petition is the *fulfilment* of prayer, only in another way. Comp. 2 Cor. xii. 8, 9.—That Christ asserts the *doing of himself* (xv. 16, and xvi. 23 of the Father), lies in the consciousness of His unity with God, according to which He, even in His exalted condition, is in the Father, and the Father is in Him. Hence, if, through the fulfilment of these petitions, the Son must be glorified, the *Father* is glorified in the Son ; wherefore Jesus adds, as the *final aim* of the τοῦτο ποιήσω : ἵνα δοξασθῇ ὁ πατ. ἐν τῷ υἱῷ. Comp. xiii. 31. The *honour of the Father* is ever the last object of all that is attained in the affairs of the Son, xii. 28, xi. 4 ; Phil. ii. 11 ; Rom. xvi. 25 ff. ; Gal. i. 5 ; Eph. iii. 21. Note the emphatic collocation ὁ πατὴρ ἐν τῷ υἱῷ, where, however, the main stress lies upon ὁ πατήρ.

Ver. 14. Τὸ αὐτὸ λέγει βεβαιῶν μάλιστα τὸν λόγον, Euth. Zigabenus. But this is done to make it specially prominent that *He* is the active subject. Bengel well remarks : "ἐγώ hoc jam indicat gloriam."

Ver. 15. A new exhortation—to keep His commandments in proof of their love to Him—in order, ver. 14, to attach thereto a new promise. But exhortation and promise are thus necessarily connected, as in vv. 11, 12 ff. Hence the latter not without the former. Comp. ver. 21. — Note the emphatic τὰς ἐμάς : which you have *from me ;* they are not those of the O. T., but the completion of these. Comp. on xiii. 34.

Vv. 16, 17. The καί is in both instances *consecutive*. On the succession of thoughts, see ver. 21. — ἐγώ] Emphatically introducing, after what He had required of the *disciples*, what *He on His part* will do as the Mediator of the divine love. The ἐρωτήσω does not conflict with xvi. 26, 27, where there is a different relation of time. ἐρωτᾶν is in John the standing word in the mouth of Jesus, when He addresses the Father in prayer, xvi. 26, xvii. 9, 15, 20.

---

[1] Comp. on Col. iii. 17, and see also Hofmann, *Schriftbew.* II. 2, p. 357, and generally Gess, *d. Gebet im Nam. Jesu*, 1861.

[2] Chrysostom, Nonnus, Theophylact, Euth. Zigabenus, Maldonatus, and several others.

[3] So also Weiss, *Lehrbegr.* p. 272, who regards the *works* only as the object of prayer. But for this the expression is too general ; just as general, xvi. 23 ff. The works are *subsumed* under the general statement.

But there is no difference of meaning from αἰτεῖν, see 1 John v. 16. — ἄλλον παράκλητον] *another Advocate* (instead of myself), another, who will as counsellor assist you. The word is found in the N. T. only in John (xiv. 26, xvi. 7, 1 John ii. 1,) and the signification given holds good in Dem. 343. 10, Diog. Laert. iv. 50, Dion. Hal. xi. 37, and passages from Philo in *Locsner*, p. 496 f., both in the proper judicial sense (*Advocate*), and also in general as here.[1] With this agrees also the Talmudic פְּרַקְלִיט.[2] Rightly, after Tertullian and Augustine, Melanchthon, Calvin, Beza, Grotius, Wolf, Lampe, and several others, have most of the moderns so interpreted it.[3] See also Hahn, *Theol. d. N. T.* I. p. 225. The equally ancient explanation : *Comforter*,[4] rests on a confusion, inadmissible on account of its passive form, with παρακλήτωρ (LXX. Job xvi. 2) in Aquila and Theodction, Job xvi. 2.[5] Equally incorrect is the rendering *Teacher* in Theodore of Mopsuestia, Ernesti,[6] Luthardt, Hofmann.[7] — Observe on ἄλλον, that in 1 John ii. 1 *Christ Himself* might also be designated as παράκλητος, without implying any difference of doctrine (Baur, Schwegler, Hilgenfeld). Nonnus aptly says : Χριστῷ σίγγονον ἄλλον. — ἵνα ᾖ μεθʼ ὑμ. εἰς τ. αἰῶνα] *in order that He* may ; not as I now, again be taken from you, but *be with you* (*i.e.* may stand at your side protecting, helping, strengthening you against all hostile powers ; comp. Matt. xxviii. 20) *for ever*. Comp. 2 John 2. In the Paraclete, however, Christ Himself is present with His own (Matt. xxviii. 20) ; for in the mission of the Spirit, who is the Spirit of Christ (Rom. viii. 9 ; Gal. iv. 6), the self-communication of the exalted Christ takes place (Rom. viii. 10 ; Gal. ii. 20), without, however, the Paraclete ceasing to be an ἄλλος, another—although dependent on the Son—subject than He ;[8] the obscure idea that the Paraclete is "*the Christ transfigured to Spirit*" (Tholuck) is un-Johannean and unbiblical generally. Comp. on 2 Cor. iii. 17. See also, against the blending of the idea of the Logos with that of the Spirit, in Reuss ; Godet, II. p. 480. — τὸ πνεῦμα τῆς ἀληθείας] *the Spirit of Truth, i.e.* the Holy Spirit, who is Possessor, Bearer, and Administrator of the divine ἀλήθεια. He is the divine principle of revelation, by whose agency in human hearts the redemptive truth

---

[1] So also Philo, *de opif. m.* p. 4 E, and Letter of the Church of Vienne in Eusebius, v. 2.

[2] See Buxtorf, *Lex. Talm.* p. 1843, and generally Wetstein *in loc. ;* Düsterdieck on 1 John ii. 1, p. 147 ff.

[3] See especially Knapp, I. p. 115 ff.

[4] Origen, Chrysostom, Theophylact, Euth. Zigabenus, Jerome, Erasmus, Castalio, Luther, Maldonatus, Jansen, Lightfoot, and several others, including van Hengel, *Annott.* p. 40 ff.

[5] Certainly it is obvious that the interpreter could not be responsible for this confusion which is opposed to the language; but *for this* he is responsible, that he should not thrust it upon John, if another use of the word, grammatically *correct*, is undoubtedly before us. This in answer to

Hofmann's too readily adopted observation in his *Schriftbew.* II. 2, p. 16.—Luther has correctly explained the word itself by *advocate*, but inconsistently translated it *Comforter*. The Vulgate has *paracletum*, the Codd. of It. in some cases the same, in others *advocatum*. Goth. has *paraklêtu*.— Were the word not *Advocatus*, but the active form, it must have been, not παράκλητος, but παρακλητικός (Plato, *Rep.* p. 521 D). Comp. ἐπικλητικός, ἀνακλητικός, and others. — The usual designation of counsel in the Greek writers is, moreover, σύνδικος or συνήγορος. On παράκλητος, comp. Hermann, *Staatsalterth.* § 142. 16.

[6] *Opusc.* p. 215.

[7] *Schriftbew.* II. 2, p. 17.

[8] Comp. Wörner, *d. Verhältn. d. Geistes zum Sohne,* p. 93.

given by God in Christ, *i.e.* the truth κατ᾽ ἐξοχήν, is transformed into knowledge, made to be vitally appropriated, and brought to powerful moral expression. Nonnus : ἀτρεκίης ὀχετηγόν. Comp. xv. 26, xvi. 13. The opposite : τὸ πνεῦμα τῆς πλάνης, 1 John iv. 6. — ὁ κόσμος] *The unbelieving*, as opposed to Christ and His work. These are unsusceptible to the Spirit, because the capacity of inward vision (of experimental perception) of the Spirit is wanting to them ; He is to them something unknown and foreign, so that they have no subjective point of attachment for receiving Him. Comp. 1 Cor. ii. 14. — ὑμεῖς δέ, κ.τ.λ.] The presents γινώσκετε and μένει [1] are as little to be taken *as future* as the presents in the first clause of the verse. They denote the *characteristic* relation of the disciples to the Spirit without reference to definite time. They are *absolute* presents : *but you know Him, since He has His abiding amongst you* (not far from you, but in your midst, in the Christian community), *and* (the discourse now first enters the point of view of definite time) *will be in you* (in your own hearts). This being the specific character of His relationship to you, how should He be an unknown Something to you ? Let the gradation be observed : παρ᾽ ὑμῖν . . . ἐν ὑμῖν. On the latter, Nonnus : ὁμόστολον ἔσται ὑμῖν, πάντας ἔχον νοερὸν δόμον. — Note, generally, the Trinitarian relation here and ver. 26, and particularly [2] the definitely expressed *personality* of the Paraclete.[3] But in passages, again, like i. 33, xx. 22, the *presupposition* of the *personality*, whose life and powers are communicated, is by no means excluded.

Ver. 18. Development of the consolatory element in this promised communication of the Spirit, onwards to ver. 21. — οὐκ ἀφήσω ὑμ. ὀρφ.] *I will not leave you behind, as those who* (after my departure) *are to be orphans.*[4] The expression itself (comp. τεκνία, xiii. 33) is that of the πατρικὴ εὐσπλαγχνία (Euth. Zigabenus). — ἔρχομαι πρὸς ὑμᾶς] Without connecting particle (γάρ) in the intensity of emotional affection. That Jesus means by this *coming*, *i.e.* in the connection, *coming again* (see on iv. 16), not the final historical *Parousia*,[5] is shown by the whole following context (quite otherwise, ver. 3). See, especially, ver. 19, where it is *not the world*, but the *disciples* who are to see Him, which is as little appropriate to the Parousia as the ἔτι μικρόν ;[6] vv. 20, 21, where *spiritual* fellowship is spoken of, the knowledge of which cannot begin with the Parousia ; and ver. 23, where μονὴν παρ᾽ αὐτῷ ποιησ. is not in harmony with the idea of the Parousia, since in this the disciples take up their abode with *God* (ver. 3, comp. 2 Cor. v. 8), not God with *them*, which takes place through the communication of the *Spirit*. Most of the older expositors refer to the *Resurrection* of Christ, and to the new *union with the Risen One.*[7] But vv. 20, 21, 23, xvi. 16, 22, 23, all point to a higher

---

[1] Not *manebit*, with the Vulgate, and μενεῖ with Ewald.

[2] Against B. Crusius and Tholuck.

[3] See Köstlin, p. 109 ; Hofmann, I. p. 192 f. ; Melanchthon, *in loc.*

[4] Ver. 27 ; Mark xii. 19 ; Tob. xi. 2 ; Sir. vi. 2. 1 ; Macc. xii. 41 ; *Soph. Aj.* 491 ; *Phil.* 484.

[5] Augustine, Beda, Maldonatus, Paulus,

Luthardt, Hofmann.

[6] Without ground, 1 John ii. 18, Rev. xxii. 7, 12, are appealed to for the setting aside of this shortness of time. How much later were these passages written than our ἔτι μικρόν was spoken !

[7] So Chrysostom, Theophylact, Euth. Zigabenus, Ruperti, Erasmus, Grotius, and many others, and again Kaeuffer, Hilgen-

spiritual fellowship,[1] as the οὐκ ἀφ. ὑμ. ὀρφ. also already presupposes a new *abiding* union. Justly, therefore, have most of the moderns [2] understood the *spiritual* coming of Christ through the *Paraclete*, in whom He Himself, only in another form of existence, came to the disciples. It is not yet, indeed, the *consummation* of the reunion which takes place at the Parousia : till that time the state of orphanage relatively continues : the church seeks its Lord (xiii. 33) and waits for Him ; and believers have to regard themselves as ἐκδη-μοῦντες ἀπὸ τοῦ κυρίου (2 Cor. v. 6), whose life in Him with God is not yet revealed (Col. iii. 1–4) (in answer to Luthardt). *Others* explain it *in a twofold sense*, alike of Christ's Resurrection, and His spiritual return. So Luther, Beza, Lampe, Bengel, Kuinoel, de Wette, Brückner, Lange, Ebrard ; in which de Wette (as also Hengst.), assigns the first place to the spiritual return. But the *bodily* ἔρχεσθαι is not indicated *at all* (as, in contrast with the mission of the Paraclete, would have been done by an added ἐγὼ αὐτός), and the entire promise of the Paraclete, of which the present passage is an integral part, transports to a time in which the Resurrection of Christ has long passed. And in general the maintenance of a double sense can be justified only by the demands of the connection.

OBSERVATION.—That Jesus, according to John, does not speak *at all* in express terms of His resurrection, but only in allusions like ii. 19, x. 17, 18, is in entire harmony with the spiritual character of the Gospel, according to which the return of the Paraclete was the principal thing on which the hopes of the disciples had to fix themselves. From death to the δόξα, out of which Jesus had to send the Spirit, the resurrection formed only the transition. But that He also cannot have in reality predicted His resurrection with such definiteness as it is related in the Synoptics, is clear from the whole behaviour of the disciples before and after the occurrence of the resurrection, so that in this point also the preference belongs to the Johannean account. See on Matt. xvi. 21.

Ver. 19. Ἔτι μικρ.] *sc.* ἐστι. Comp. xiii. 33, xvi. 16 ; Heb. x. 37 ; Hos. i. 4 ; Ps. xxxvii. 10. — οὐκέτι θεωρεῖ] Corporeally. Comp. also Acts x. 41. — θεωρεῖτε] But you, whilst the world no more beholds me, *do behold me*, although corporeally I am no more present, through the experience of my spiritual presence ; [3] you behold me *spiritually*, in that you experience my presence and my communion with you, in the communication of myself, and in my working upon you by means of the Paraclete. The *terminus a quo* of the present tenses, which represent the near future as present, is, indeed, not

feld, Weiss, and, with a spiritualizing view of the resurrection, Ewald.

[1] Which historically took its beginning, not with the appearances of the Risen One, so enigmatic to the disciples themselves, removed and estranged from the old confidential relations, but first with the outpouring of the Spirit. *Thence*forward Christ lived in them, and His heart beat in them, and out of them He spake.

[2] Lücke, Tholuck, Olshausen, B. Crusius, Frommann, Köstlin, Reuss, Maier, Baeumlein, Godet, Scholten, but also already Calvin and several others.

[3] Not : through the *being caught away to me at the Parouisa* (Luthardt). The οὐκέτι θεωρεῖ and the θεωρεῖτε must certainly be *contemporaneous*. Invisible for the *world* (comp. vii. 33, 34), Christ is beheld by *His own*.

418 THE GOSPEL OF JOHN.

quite the same in θεωρεῖ and θεωρεῖτε, since the ὁ κόσμος με οὐκέτι θεωρεῖ already begins with the death of Jesus, but the ὑμεῖς δὲ θεωρ. με first after His return to the Father ; this distinction, however, disappears before the Johannean view of the death of Jesus as a departure to God. — ὅτι ἐγὼ ζῶ, κ. ὑμ. ζήσεσθε] Not : *because I live, you also will live* (Nonnus, Beza, Godet), but, corresponding to the progress of the discourse (comp. ver. 17), a statement of the reason of what precedes : *because I live, and ye shall live.* [Note XLIV. p. 426.] Note the change from the present to the future, and that ζῶ and ζήσεσθε cannot without arbitrariness be taken as essentially different in idea, but that ζῶ manifestly, since it exists without interruption (present), denotes *the higher life of Christ independent of death*, of Christ, who, by His departure to the Father, becomes a partaker of the heavenly *glory*. Christ *lives*, for He is, indeed, Himself the Possessor and bearer of the true ζωή (comp. v. 26). Death, which translates Him into the glory of the Father, by no means breaks off this true and higher life of His (although His life ἐν σαρκί ceases), but is only the medium of the consummation and transfiguration of this His living into the everlasting heavenly ζωή and δόξα (comp. Col. iii. 3, 4). Out of *this* consciousness the Lord here utters the words : ἐγὼ ζῶ. And He adds thereto : καὶ ὑμεῖς ζήσεσθε : *and you shall live, i.e.* you shall be partakers (in its temporal development on to its glorious consummation) of the same higher life, liable to no death (xi. 26), under the life-giving (vi. 33) influence of the Spirit. "Stat enim illud fixum, nullam fore *ejus* vitam *membris* mortuis," Calvin. Thus the life is in both essentially *alike*, only with the difference, that it is original in Jesus, and with his approaching departure is already at its glorious consummation ; but in the case of the disciples, being imparted by Christ in the Holy Spirit, who is the πνεῦμα τῆς ζωῆς (Rom. viii. 2), it is first to be unfolded within (before the Parousia, as the living fellowship with the exalted Christ), in order to become, at the Parousia through the resurrection (Rom. viii. 11) and relative transformation (1 Cor. xv. 51, 52), the participation in His glory. Comp. the idea of the συζῆν τῷ Χριστῷ in Paul, Rom. vi. 8 ; 2 Cor. vii. 3 ; 2 Tim. ii. 11. The ground of the *proof* (ὅτι) lies simply in this, that the above twofold ζῆν is the necessary condition of the promised θεωρεῖτέ με. If the higher ζωή belonged only to Christ, and not also thereafter (through the working of the Spirit) to the disciples, there could be no mention of a beholding of the Lord on the part of the disciples. The *paritas rationis* for the mutual relation would be wanting, and thereby the disciples would lose the capacity (the eye, as it were) to see Christ. But thus *the living behold the Living One.* The reference to the resurrection of Jesus has led to interpretations like that of Grotius (comp. Euth. Zigabenus) : you shall see me *actually alive* ("non spectrum") and *remaining in life* amidst the impending dangers ; or (so Theophylact, comp. Kuinoel) : I shall, as having risen, be *alive*, and you shall be as *newly made alive* for *joy!* or : *I rise again*, and you shall (at the last day) *arise* (so Augustine). Again the interpretation of ζήσεσθε in Weiss [1] of the new life, which arises in the disciples through the reappearance of the Risen One, who

---

[1] *Lehrbegr.* p. 70.

is recognized by them (as in the case of Thomas, xx. 28), is a forced expedient, proceeding from an erroneous assumption, inappropriate to ἐν ἐκείνῃ τῇ ἡμέρᾳ, ver. 20, which is definite and valid for all disciples, and to the intimate reciprocal confidence of vv. 20, 21 ; whence Weiss again, adding violence to violence, explains ver. 21 of the further unfolding of the new communion begun with the appearances of the Risen One (p. 276). Understood of the resurrection, the simplest explanation would be that of Kaeuffer, p. 136 : "quae instat fortunae vicissitudo nec me nec vos poterit pessumdare !" but the thought becomes trivial, and the change of the tense meaningless. But if, according to the above, both ζῶ and ζήσεσθε must embrace time and eternity, then de Wette has incorrectly limited ζήσεσθε to the *life of faith* with its joyous victory over death and the fear of death. Luthardt, on the other hand, erroneously restricts it to the *life of transfiguration* after the Parousia, on the ground that ἐγὼ ζῶ can only denote the glorified life,—an unsupported assumption, since the expression is not ἐγὼ ζήσομαι.

Vv. 20, 21. *On that day ;* [1] in the *historical* fulfilment this was the day of Pentecost. Not : *at that time* (de Wette), or, as Hengstenberg changes it : in the *period of time*, beginning with the day of the *resurrection* (comp. Weiss) ; for a definite fact, marked off in point of time, is treated of, and this is the advent of Christ in the Paraclete. Comp. xvi. 23. — γνώσεσθε, κ.τ.λ.] This dynamic immanence of Christ in the Father (see on x. 38), which exists even in His state of exaltation (Col. iii. 3), like the analogous reciprocal relation between Him and the disciples, by which they live and move in Him and He in them (Gal. ii. 20), was to become for them a matter of experimental acquaintance through the Spirit. — Ver. 21. General moral condition of this promised γνώσεσθε. Comp. ver. 15. — ὁ ἔχων, κ.τ.λ.] Augustine : "qui habet in memoria et servat in vita." The ἔχειν, however, is rather the internal *possession* of the commandments, obtained by faith, the appropriated living presence of them in the believing consciousness, as the consequence of the ἀκούειν. Comp. v. 38. — ἐκεῖνός ἐστιν] with great and exclusive emphasis. — In ἀγαπηθήσ. and ἀγαπήσω lies the peculiar mutual love. — καὶ ἐγὼ ἀγαπ.] ὡς ἀμφοτέρων τὰ αὐτὰ θελόντων κ. ἀποδεχομένων, Euth. Zigabenus. — ἐμφανίσω αὐτῷ ἐμαυτόν] corresponds to the γνώσεσθε, which was to commence through this very *causing of Himself to appear* in virtue of the communication of the Spirit. [2] The expression is such, that it sets forth the relation of the self-demonstration of the Lord *to His individual loving ones*, not His manifestation at the *Parousia*, which certainly will be glorious and universal (in answer to Luthardt). Those who explain it of the resurrection of Christ understand the appearances of the Risen One to be referred to, 1 Cor. xv. [3]

Ver. 22. *Judas* (Thaddaeus or Lebbaeus, Matt. x. 3 ; not, however, a brother of the Lord, Acts i. 13, 14, but son of one James, Luke vi. 16)[4] ex-

---

[1] Luthardt, according to his view of the entire passage, must understand the day of the *Parousia*, whereby he assigns to γνώσεσθε the moment of the *completed* knowledge.

[2] On ἐμφαν., comp. Ex. xxxiii. 13, 18 ; Sap. i. 2 ; Matt. xxvii. 53.

[3] Grotius, Hilgenfeld, and many others.

[4] Nonnus correctly remarks : υἱὸς Ἰακώβοιο, κ. οὐ θρασὺς Ἰσκαριώτης.

pects a *bodily* appearance of Christ in Messianic glory, has in this view misunderstood Jesus, and is therefore surprised that He has spoken of His ἐμφα-
νίζειν ἑαυτόν as having reference only to the man who loves Him, and not
also to the world of the unbelieving, on whom the Messiah when He appeared
was in truth to execute judgment. — τί γέγονεν] *What has come to pass*, in
respect to the fact that, etc.? What occurrence has determined Thee, etc.? [1]
The foregoing καί as in ix. 36. — The addition οὐχ ὁ 'Ισκαρ. was indeed, after
xiii. 30, quite superfluous, but is to be explained as an involuntary outflow
of the deep loathing felt toward the traitor of like name. The latter is not
to be thought of as *again present* (Bengel).

Vv. 23, 24. Jesus repeats—and that was sufficient for the removal of such
a misunderstanding—substantially, yet now at once placing love as the
principal matter in the immediate foreground, the condition to which His
self-revelation, ver. 22, is attached, by more closely defining it in its divine
and blessed mode of existence ; and shows from this, and from the antithesis added in ver. 24, that the κόσμος—this κόσμος which hates Him and is
disobedient to Him—is quite incapable of receiving that self-revelation.
The more precise explanation, πρὸς αὐτ. ἐλευσόμ. κ. μονὴν παρ' αὐτῷ ποιησόμεθα,
is intended to make this very incapacity still more distinctly and deeply
felt. At the foundation of the expression lies the theocratic idea, realized in
this spiritual fellowship, of the dwelling of God amongst His people, [2] with
which also the later representation of the dwelling of the Shekinah with the
pious [3] is connected. *This* representation, however, is not to be assumed
here, since Jesus means an *invisible* presence. In the plural of *communion*,
ἐλευσόμεθα is the clear expression of the theanthropic consciousness, x. 30. —
On the genuinely Greek expression μονὴν ποιεῖν, see Kypke, I. p. 404. The
Middle (see critical notes) : *we will make to ourselves.* — παρ' αὐτῷ] The *unio
mystica*, into which God and Christ thus enter with man through the Paraclete, [4] is presented in the sensuous form of the taking up an abode *with Him*
(comp. vv. 17, 25), *i.e. in His dwelling* (comp. i. 40, Acts xxi. 8, *et al.*),
under His roof. They come, like wanderers from their heavenly home (ver.
2), and *lodge with Him*, "will be daily His guests, yea, house and table companions," Luther. — The λόγοι, *discourses*, are the individual parts of the
collective λόγος, and the ἐντολαί are its *preceptive* parts, and form, therefore,
a more special conception than the λόγοι. — καὶ ὁ λόγος ὃν ἀκούετε, κ.τ.λ.] *and*
—from this you may infer how unfitted such a man is to experience that
visitation—*the word which ye hear* (now, still !), etc. Comp. vii. 16, viii. 28,
xii. 49, 50, iii. 34. He therefore rejects God Himself. The second person
(ἀκούετε) is individualizing (not to be limited to what was said in vv. 23, 24,
as Godet takes it), and makes the expression at the close of this portion of
the address more lively.

Vv. 25, 26. We are to suppose a pause before ver. 25 ; Jesus looks back

---

[1] See Kypke, I. p. 403 f.

[2] Ex. xxv. 8, xxix. 45 ; Lev. xxvi. 11, 12 ;
Ezek. xxxvii. 26 ff.

[3] Danz in Meuschen, *N. T. ex Talm. ill.* p.
701 ff.

[4] Not : "in the divine elevation above
space and time" (Weiss, *Lehrbegr.* p. 276),
which introduces here a speculative idea
remote from the meaning.

upon all that He has hitherto said to them at His farewell supper, and of
which so much still remained to them enigmatical, and continues : " *These
things have I spoken to you, whilst I* (still) *tarry with you ; but the Paraclete*
who, after my impending separation from you, will have come to you from
the Father, He will further instruct you," etc. — ἐν τῷ ὀνόμ. μου] Specific
limitation of the act of sending.   God sends the Spirit *in the name of Jesus*,
i.e. so that what the name Jesus Christ comprises in itself, forms the *sphere
in which* the divine thought, counsel, and will lives, and is active in the
fending.   Comp. on ver. 13.   The name of Jesus is the only name which
includes in itself the eternal salvation of men (Acts iv. 12) ; but God intends
and designs, in the mission of the Spirit—of which the *causa meritoria* lies
in this name, and its actual manifestation is connected with the glorification of Jesus (viii. 39)—nothing else than this Name, the complete saving
knowledge of which, its confession, influence, glorification, etc., is to be
brought about and advanced through the mission of the Spirit, as in general,
all that He has done in the carrying out of His redemptive counsel, He has
done ἐν Χριστῷ, Eph. i. 3 ff.   The notion : *at my request* (comp. Godet :
" in meam gratiam"), is not contained in the words, although, according to
ver. 14, the prayer of Jesus *precedes* (in answer to Lücke, de Wette, Ebrard,
Godet, and several others).   Better, but only an approximation, and wanting in precision, is the interpretation of B. Crusius : in my *affair*, and of
Melanchthon and several others : *propter me.*   The rendering, *in my stead*,[1]
is not appropriate, since, according to it, the Spirit would not appear as the
Representative of Christ (comp. v. 43), but *God*, as *in Christ's stead*, executing the *mission*—which would be absurd.   It should in that case run :
ὁ ἐλεύσεται παρὰ τοῦ πατρὸς ἐν τῷ ὀνόματί μου, comp. xvi. 7. — In the ministry
of the Spirit ὑμᾶς διδάξει πάντα is the general feature : *He will not leave you
uninstructed respecting any portion of the divine truth* (comp. xvi. 13) : to
this the particular is then joined : καὶ ὑπομνήσει, κ.τ.λ. : *and* (and especially)
will He bring to your recollection, etc.   To the first belong also new portions
of doctrine, not yet delivered by Jesus (see on xvi. 12), also disclosures of
the future (xvi. 13).   On ὑπομνήσει, κ.τ.λ., comp. *e.g.* ii. 22, xii. 16.   ἃ εἶπον
ὑμῖν might also be referred to διδάξει πάντα,[2] but xvi. 12, 13 justifies the
ordinary reference, which also logically at once suggests itself, merely to the
second πάντα, and nevertheless excludes the misuse of the present passage
in favour of Catholic *tradition* (see on xvi. 12), as well as of the revelations
of *fanaticism.*   Of the actual fulfilment of the entire promise, the apostolic
discourses and letters supply the full proof. — εἶπον] Not merely now, but
generally, as the context, by the first πάντα, demands.

Ver. 27.   "These are last words, as of one who is about to go away and
says good-night, or gives his blessing," Luther. — εἰρήνην ἀφίημι ὑμῖν] The
whole position of affairs, as Jesus is on the point of concluding these His
last discourses (ver. 31), as well as the characteristic word εἰρήνη, introduced
without further preface, justifies the ordinary assumption that here there is

---

[1] Euth. Zigabenus and others, including
Tholuck, Baeumlein, Ewald, Weiss.

[2] Luther, Melanchthon, Grotius, Calovius,
and others.

an allusion to the Oriental greetings at partings and dismissals, in which שָׁלוֹם (*i.e.* not specially : *Peace of soul,* but generally : *Prosperity*) was wished.   Comp. 1 Sam. i. 17, xx. 42, xxix. 5 ; Mark v. 34 ; Luke vii. 50, viii. 48 ; Acts xvi. 36 ; Jas. ii. 16 ; also the Syrian *pacem dedit,* in the sense of *valedixit* in Assem. Bibl. I. p. 376 ; and finally, the epistolary farewell-greeting, Eph. vi. 23 ; 1 Pet. v. 14 ; 3 John 15.   That which men were wont to *wish* at departure, namely, *prosperity,* Jesus is conscious of *leaving behind,* and of *giving* to His disciples, and that in the best and highest sense, namely, *the entire prosperity of His redemptive work,* '' fore ejus benedictione semper felices" (Calvin), in which, however, the *peace of reconciliation with God* (Rom. v. 1), as the first essential element, is also included.   To assume (with Lücke) in the expression a reference, at the same time, to the O. T. peace-assuring and encouraging address שָׁלוֹם לָכֶם (Gen. xliii. 23 ; Judg. vi. 23, *et al.*), is less in harmony with the *departing* scene, and the *remote* μὴ ταρασσέσθω, κ.τ.λ., *as well as with the expression* of this consolatory address. — εἰρ. τ. ἐμὴν δίδ. ὑμ.] More precise designation of what has preceded.   It is *His,* the *peculiar* prosperity proceeding *from Him,* which He *gives* to them as His bequest.   Thus speaks He to His own, who, on the threshold of death, is leaving hereditary possessions : '' I *leave behind,* I *give,*" in the consciousness that this will be accomplished *by His death.*   So also Jesus, whose δίδωμι is to be understood neither as *promitto* (Kuinoel), nor even to be conceived as first taking place through the Paraclete (who rather brings about only the *appropriation* of the salvation given in the death of Jesus).— *Not as the world gives, give I* TO YOU !   Nothing is to be supplied.   *My* giving to *you* is of *quite another kind* than the giving of the (unbelieving) *world ; its* giving bestows treasure, pleasure, honour, and the like, is therefore unsatisfying, bringing no permanent good, no genuine prosperity, etc.[1]   Quite out of relation to the profound seriousness of the moment, and therefore irrelevant, is the reference to the usual empty formulas of salutation (Grotius, Kling, Godet). — μὴ ταρασσέσθω, κ.τ.λ.] '' Thus does He conclude exactly as He first (ver. 1) began this discourse," Luther.   The short asyndetic (supply in thought οὖν) sentences correspond to the deep emotion. — δειλιάω (Diod. xx. 78) here only in the N. T., frequently in the LXX., which, on the other hand, has not the classical (δοκιμώτερον, Thomas Magister) ἀποδειλιάω.

Ver. 28. Instead of being terrified and alarmed, you should *rejoice,* that I, etc.   ἠκούσατε, κ.τ.λ. (ver. 18) prepares for this. — εἰ ἠγαπ. με] intended by Jesus to be understood in its ideal sense, of true, complete love, which consists simply and solely in entire self-surrender to Him, so that all other interests are subordinated to it. — ὅτι ὁ πατήρ μου μείζων μου ἐστί] Statement of the reason for the joy which they would have felt (ἐχάρητε) : *since my Father is greater,* as generally, so particularly, more powerful (comp. ver. 12, viii. 53, x. 29 ; 1 John iv. 4) *than I;* since I, consequently, through my departure to Him, shall be elevated in the higher fellowship with Him, *to*

---

[1] Hengstenberg introduces quite groundlessly a reference to the θλῖψις which the world gives, according to xvi. 33.

far greater power and efficiency for my aims, for victory over the world, etc.
Comp. Melanchthon. In *this* gain, which is awaiting me, how should not
he rejoice who loves me ? *Others* find the motive to joy indicated by Christ
in the *glory and blessedness* which awaits Him with the Father.[1] But thus
the motive would lie only in the departure to the Father generally (with
which the attainment of the δόξα was necessarily associated), not to the Father's superior *greatness*, irrespectively of the fact, that on this view the
reference which Jesus would be giving to the love of the disciples would
contain something selfish. *Others* make the occasion of joy lie in the
more powerful *protection* which the μείζων πατήρ would assure to the disciples,
beyond what He, during His presence on earth, was able to do.[2] But this does
not apply to the condition of love to *the person of Jesus*, which this explanation transforms rather into love towards His *work*. *Others*, as Luther, Beza,
Grotius, Bengel, Lampe, mingle together in the determination of the cause
of joy, the interest of Christ *and* of the disciples ; comp. Calvin : "quia
haec ultima est meta, ad quam tendere vos oportet." — The μειζονότης of the
Father (formerly the point of controversy with the Arians, see Suicer, *Thes.*
II. p. 1368) does not rest in the pre-eminence of the *unbegotten* over the *begotten*,[3] for which special expedient the text offers no occasion whatever, nor
again in the temporal *humiliation* of Christ,[4] since God is also greater than
the *exalted* Christ,[5] as He was also greater than the pre-existent Logos (i. 1–
3) ; but in the *absolute monotheism of Jesus* (xvii. 3) and of the whole N. T.
(see on Rom. ix. 5), according to which the Son, although of divine essence,[6]
and ὁμοούσιος with the Father,[7] nevertheless was, and is, and remains *subordinated* to the Father, the immutably Highest One, since the Son, as Organ,
as Commissioner of the Father, as Intercessor with Him, etc., has received
His whole power, even in the kingly office, from the Father (xvii. 5), and,
after the complete accomplishment of the work committed to Him, will re-
store it to the Father (1 Cor. xv. 28). The remark of Hengstenberg is
incorrect : Only such a pre-eminence of greatness on the part of the Father
can be intended, as came to an end with the departure of Christ to the
Father.

Ver. 29. *And now*, even now, when my departure is approaching, *I have
said it to you*, namely, ὅτι πορεύομαι πρὸς τ. π., ver. 28, not what was said in
ver. 26, as Lücke thinks. — ὅταν γένηται] *cum factum fuerit*, namely, through
my death ; comp. xiii. 19. — πιστεύσητε] Not absolutely, so as simply to express what is more precisely defined in xiii. 19 by ὅτι ἐγώ εἰμι ; but : *that*

[1] So Cyril (τὴν ἰδίαν δόξαν ἀναληψόμενος),
and several, including Tholuck, Olshausen,
Kling, Köstlin, Maier, Hilgenfeld, Hengstenberg, Baeumlein, comp. Godet.

[2] Theophylact, Euth. Zigabenus, and several others, including Kuinoel, Lücke, de
Wette.

[3] Athanasius, Faustinus, Gregory Nazian-
zus, Hilarius, Euth. Zigabenus, and many
others, including again Olshausen.

[4] Cyril, Augustine, Ammonius, Luther,
Melanchthon, Calvin, Beza, Aretius, and

many others, including de Wette, Tholuck,
and Luthardt.

[5] See ver. 16, ἐρωτήσω, xvii. 5 ; 1 Cor. xv.
27, 28 ; Phil. ii. 9–11 ; 1 Cor. iii. 23, xi. 3, and
generally throughout the N. T.

[6] This forms the previous assumption of
the declaration, which otherwise would be
without meaning and relevancy. Comp. on
x. 30. In truth, from the mouth of an ordinary human being it would be an utterance of folly.

[7] I. 1 ; Phil. ii. 6 ; Col. i. 15 18, *et al.*

you may believe it, namely, that I have gone to the Father. Comp. πιστεύετέ μοι, ver. 11. The point for the departing Lord was, that when His approaching death should take place, the disciples should have the true believing apprehension of it, namely, as His departure to the Father.

Ver. 30. Οὐκέτι πολλά, κ.τ.λ.] " Quasi dicat : temporis angustiae abripiunt verda," Grotius. — *For the prince of the world* (see on xii. 31) *is coming* (is already drawing near). Jesus sees the devil himself in the organs and executors of his design (xiii. 2, 27, vi. 70 ; Luke iv. 13). — τοῦ κόσμου] is here emphatically placed first in antithesis to ἐν ἐμοί. — καὶ ἐν ἐμοὶ οὐκ ἔχει οὐδέν] *and in me* (antithesis of the κόσμος, xvii. 16) *he possesses nothing*, namely, as pertaining to his dominion, which more minute statement flows from the conception of the ἄρχων ; hence neither ποιεῖν (Kuinoel), nor μέρος (Nonnus), nor " of which he could *accuse* me before God " (Ewald), is to be supplied ; nor again is the simple sense of the words to be transformed into "he has no *claim* on me" (Tholuck, Hofmann, and several others) ; comp. Luther : "cause and right." In any case, Christ expresses the full *moral freedom* with which He subjects Himself to death (x. 18). The *sinlessness*, which Cyril, Augustine (" in me non habet quicquam, *nullum omnino scilicet peccatum*"), Euth. Zigabenus, Cornelius à Lapide, and many others, including Olshausen, here find expressed, certainly lies at the foundation as a necessary causal *condition*, since only provided that Jesus were sinless, could the devil have in Him nothing that was his, but is not directly *expressed*. That He has already overcome the world (xvi. 33) is not the reason (Lücke), but the consequence of His freedom from the prince of the world. — The καί is not : *but* (Ebrard, Godet) ; for the antithesis first follows with ἀλλά. Therefore : he comes, and is powerless over me (wherefore I needed not to surrender myself to him), *but, nevertheless, that*, etc., ver. 31.

Ver. 31. *That the world may know*, etc. (as far as οὕτω ποιῶ), *rise* (from table), *let us go hence !* In order to bring the world to the knowledge of my love and my obedience to the Father (" ut mundus desinat mundus esse et patris in me beneplacitum agnoscat salutariter," Bengel), let us away from here, and go to meet the diabolical power, before which I must now fall according to God's counsel ! The apodosis does not begin so early as καὶ καθώς (Grotius, Kuinoel, Paulus), in which case καί would mean *also*, and a reflection less appropriate to the mood of deep emotion would result. If a full point be placed after ποιῶ,[1] which, however, renders the sentence heavy, and makes what follows to stand too abruptly, then after ἀλλ' a simple ἔρχεται would have to be supplied. Comp. xv. 25. — After the summons ἐγείρεσθε, κ.τ.λ., we are to think of the company at table as having risen. But Jesus, so full of that which, in view of the separation ever drawing nearer, He desired to impress on the heart of the disciples, and enchained by His love for them, takes up the word anew, and standing, continues to address chap. xv. and xvi. to the risen disciples, and then follows the prayer of chap. xvii., after which follows the actual departure, xviii. 1. This view[2] appears to be correct from this, that John, without any indica-

---

[1] Bengel, Lachmann, Tischendorf, Ewald.   [2] Knapp, Lücke, Tholuck, Olshausen,

tion of a change of place, connects xv. 1 immediately with xiv. 31 ; while, that the following discourses, and especially the prayer, were uttered *on the way*,[1] is neither in any way indicated, nor reconcilable with xviii. 1, nor psychologically probable. A pure importation, further, is the opinion of Chrysostom, Theophylact, Euth. Zigabenus, Erasmus, and several others, that Christ, xiv. 31, went with the disciples to a more secluded and safer place, where He (" sur la pente couverte de vignes, qui descend dans la vallée du Cédron," Godet) delivered chap. xv., xvi., xvii. ; so also is Bengel's harmonistic device, which Wichelhaus has adopted, that the local-ity of the discourse from xiii. 31 [2] to xiv. 31 had been outside the city, but that now He set forth to go to Jerusalem for the passover.[3] Others, while de Wette abides by the hypothesis of an *hiatus* between chap. xiv. and xv., the reason of which remains unknown, have sought to make use of the ἐγείρεσθε, ἄγωμεν, Matt. xxvi. 46, Mark xiv. 42, in spite of the quite different historical connection in Matthew and Mark, in order to charge the author with a clumsy attempt to interweave that reminiscence in his narrative (Strauss, Scholten) ; in opposition to which Weisse, with equal arbitrariness and injustice, accuses the supposed editor of the Gospel with having placed in juxtaposition, without any link of connection, two Johannean composi-tions, of which the one closed with xiv. 31, and the other began with xv. 1. Baur and Hilgenfeld, indeed, make the synoptic words, divested of their more definite historical justification, stand here only as a sign of *pause*. The Johannean words, and those in the Synoptics uttered in Gethsemane, have *nothing* to do with one another ; but the apparent incongruity with the present passage speaks, in fact, in favour of the personal testimony of the reporter, before whose eyes the whole scene vividly presented itself. Comp. Bleek's *Beitr.* p. 239.

NOTES BY AMERICAN EDITOR.

XLII. " *Believe in God.*" Ver. 1.

With Meyer also Weiss concurs (along with many others) in rendering the two verbs here both in the imperative, against our Received Version, which the Revi-sion follows. That the imperative construction of both is the true one seems to me almost certain. It suits better the turn of thought indicated and introduced by the preceding imperative (μὴ ταρασσέσθω), and harmonizes with the direct and simple manner in which the Saviour would be likely to address the disciples. They did, indeed, believe in God, as they also believed in Him, but their faith in both would well admit, as it also required, a deepening into that fuller and practical trust to which the Lord exhorts them. Dr. Schaff well says (Lange

Klee, Winer, Luthardt, Ewald, Brückner, Bleek, following the older expositors, also Gerhard, Calovius, and Maldonatus.
[1] Ammonius, Hilarius, Beza, Luther, Are-tius, Grotius, Wetstein, Lampe, Rosenmül-ler, Lange, Ebrard.
[2] Bengel on xiii. 31 : "λέγει : dicit postri-die, nempe mane, feria V."

[3] So also again Röpe, *d. Mahl des Fuss-wasch.*, Hamb. 1856, p. 25 f., who, following Bynaeus, assumes that in ἐγείρεσθε, κ.τ.λ. is contained the setting forth from Bethany for Jerusalem, and that chap. xv.-xvii. were then spoken at the paschal meal on the 14th Nisan, in reference to the institution of the Supper.

in loco) : Reading "πιστευετε both times imperatively agrees best with the preceding imperative, and with the fresh, direct, hortatory character of the address. The other interpretations introduce a reflective tone. Our Lord exhorts and encourages the disciples to dismiss all trouble from their hearts, to exercise full trust and confidence (πιστεύετε emphatically first and last) in God, who has in reserve for them many mansions in heaven, and consequently also to trust in Christ, who is one with the Father, and is going to prepare a place for them : faith in God and faith in Christ are inseparable (hence εἰς ἐμέ is placed before the second πιστεύετε), and the glorification of the Son is the glorification of the Father in the Son . . . There is here no *addition* of faith in Christ to faith in God (as Olshausen objects), nor a transfer of our trust from its proper object to another, but simply the concentration of our trust in the unseen God—who out of Christ is a mere abstraction—upon the incarnate Son, in whom this trust becomes real and effective."

XLIII. "*In my Father's house.*" Ver. 2.

According to Meyer this is not heaven in general, " but the peculiar dwelling-place of the divine glory in heaven." Weiss dissents, maintaining that "heaven is *eo ipso* the dwelling-place of God," and that Meyer's distinction is unfounded and arbitrary.

XLIV. "*Because I live and ye shall live.*" Ver. 19.

So Meyer and his German editor Weiss agree, along with many others, against the common rendering (retained by the revisers), "Because I live, ye shall live also." The two renderings are grammatically equally possible. They object to the latter rendering that it does not assign any logical reason for the θεωρεῖτέ με which it apparently conditions. Still it may indirectly, though not directly, assign such a reason. The thought might run : "In the life which I live, triumphing over my impending death, ye shall have a moral and spiritual life, culminating finally in a spiritual and glorified corporeal life, in both of which you shall thus have that union with and *vision* of me which the world in its moral deadness will be unable to attain."

Still, Meyer's construction I think more probable : "Because I live and ye shall live," thus giving the double condition under which the beholding of Him is possible. "The world beholdeth me no more" (evidently a *bodily* beholding). I completely vanish from its gaze. "But ye behold me," because I survive death. My life will not be buried in the grave. This is one condition of their beholding Him. The other condition is that *they* also will live. But here the meaning of *live* obviously changes. *His* life is the divine-human, theanthropic life, over which death has no power. The life of the disciples is not their continued existence : this they will share with the morally dead world. It is the spiritual life which the Spirit of the living Christ will impart to them, by which they will behold Him both corporeally—even for this the carnal world is utterly unprepared — and spiritually through moral communion. So, substantially, Weiss. But it is difficult to believe that this exhausts the Saviour's meaning. His starting point is indeed on the earth. The disciples, after His resurrection, will have a vision of Him of which the world will be incapable. Yet the thought surely goes beyond that. He *lives* (the Present, ζῶ, because His life is at bottom changeless and eternal) a life which not only survives His death, but runs through the endless future. They too will live *here* in a spiritual life, which gives them here the vision and partial communion of their Lord, but by and by also in a glorified resurrection-body, in which their life will be consummated and their *beholding* of Him attain perfection. Such, with Meyer and partially against Weiss, I believe to be the thought.

CHAPTER XV.

Ver. 4. Tisch. has the forms μένῃ and μένητε ; similarly, ver. 6, μένῃ. Lachm. also has the latter and μένητε, ver. 4. Considering the divided state of the evidence (A. B. ℵ. in particular agree in favor of μεν.), no decision can be come to. — Ver. 6. τὸ πῦρ] Elz. Lachm. have merely πῦρ, against preponderating testimony. In the passage of similar meaning, Matt. iii. 10, vii. 19, Luke iii. 9, there is likewise no article found, which, consequently, was more readily omitted than added. — Ver. 7. αἰτήσεσθε] A. B. D. L. M. X. Curss. Verss. Chrys.: αἰτήσασθε. Recommended by Griesb., adopted by Lachm. and Tisch. This preponderant attestation, the reference of the word to the fut., and the immediate proximity of the future tense, decide in favour of the genuineness of the aorist. — Ver. 8. γενήσεσθε] Rinck and Lachm.: γένησθε. The witnesses are greatly divided. But the conjunctive is a correction after φέρητε. — Ver. 11. μείνῃ] A. B. D. Curss. It. Vulg. et al.: ᾖ. Recommended by Griesb., adopted by Lachm. Rightly ; after the previous frequent recurrence of the verb μένω, μείνῃ very readily and involuntarily arose here out of the last syllable of ΥΜΙΝ and the following ᾖ. — Ver. 13. The deletion of τις (Tisch.) is too weakly supported. It came to be passed over as superfluous. — Ver. 14. ὅσα] D. L. X. ℵ. : ἅ. So Lachm. Tisch. The singular ὅ is found in B. Codd. of It. Goth. Aeth. Cypr. Lucif. The witnesses alone are decisive, and that for the plural, more precisely for ἅ. — Ver. 15. The order λέγω ὑμᾶς (Lachm. Tisch.) is accredited by preponderating evidence. — Ver. 21. ὑμῖν] Lachm. and Tisch.: εἰς ὑμᾶς, after B. D.* L. ℵ.** 1, 33, Verss. Chrys. Rightly ; the more current and customary dative flowed of itself from the copyists' pens, as it was also added in xvi. 3. — Ver. 22. εἶχον] Here and in ver. 24 Lachm. and Tisch. have the Alexandrine form εἴχοσαν, according to B. L. Π.** ℵ. 1, 33, Or. Cyr. Not to be adopted, since this form appears certain only in Rom. iii. 13, in a citation from the O. T. (ἐδολιοῦσαν), while here the evidence is not sufficiently strong (not found even in A.). Buttmann, in the Stud. u. Krit. 1858, p. 491 f., supposes that εἴχοσαν arose from the original εἶχον ἄν. Yet of ἄν no further trace is found in the critical witnesses, and its (rhetorical) omission (see Buttmann, l.c. p. 489) is quite free from doubt. — Ver. 24. πεποίηκεν] A. B. D. J. K. L. X. Π. ℵ. Curss. Chrys.: ἐποίησεν. So Lachm. Tisch. The testimony in favour of this reading is decisive.

Ver. 1. Since the image is introduced altogether without any suggesting object, it is natural to assume some external occasion for it, which John has not related.[1] That which most obviously suggests itself is the *look at the cup of wine* (comp. Matt. xxvi. 29 : τὸ γέννημα τοῦ ἀμπέλου), which pre-

---

[1] Almost throughout the entire chapter (as far as ver. 18) the particles of connection between the individual utterances are wanting, and this is in keeping with deeply stirred and intense emotion.

cisely at *this* supper had assumed so great significance.[1] [See Note XLI. p. 403.] Had Jesus spoken what follows on the way (see on xiv. 31), or even, as G. Hier. Rosenmüller[2] supposed, in the temple, then in the former case the walk through vineyards (comp. especially Lange, who assumes the existence of garden-fires by night, and Godet), and in the latter case the golden vine at the gate of the temple,[3] might be supposed to present a suitable occasion. It is more arbitrary to suppose (Knapp, Tholuck) a vine whose tendrils had crept into the room (comp. Ps. cxxviii. 3), or : that there was at full moon a view of the vineyards from the room (Storr), or of the golden vine of the temple (Lampe). Most arbitrary of all is the supposition that John may have placed the similitude, in itself genuine, here in the wrong place (de Wette). If the thought of the cup at the meal just concluded did not so spontaneously suggest itself, it would be safer, with Lücke and B. Crusius, to assume *no* external occasion at all, since the figure itself was so frequent in the O. T. ;[4] and therefore (comp. Matt. xxi. 33 ff.) the disciples who were standing around Him could immediately, and of themselves, see Jesus set forth under this venerable figure.[5] — ἡ ἀληθινή] *genuine, real, i.e.* containing the reality of the idea, [See Note XLVI. p. 441] which is figuratively set forth in the natural vine (comp. on i. 9, vi. 35), not in antithesis to the *unfruitful* vine, *i.e.* the degenerate people of Israel (Ebrard, Hengstenberg), which is here remote, since the Lord is designating *Himself* as ἄμπελος, not His ἐκκλησία (this regarded as in antithesis to the Jewish). Christ is the *Vine* in relation to His *believing ones* (the branches), whose organic connection with Him is the constant, fruitful, and most inward fellowship of life. Quite similar as to the thing is the Pauline figure of the head and the members.[6] The *vine-dresser*[7] is *God ;* for He has sent Christ, and established the fellowship of believers with Him (vi. 37, *et al.*), and tends it in virtue of His working through Christ's word, and (after His departure) through the power of the Holy Spirit.

Ver. 2. As on the natural vine there are fruitful and unfruitful branches, *i.e. tendrils,*[8] so there are in the fellowship of Christ such as evince their faith by deed as faith's fruit, and those with whom this is not the case. — The latter, who are not, with Hengstenberg, to be taken for *the unbelieving Jews* (as is already clear from ἐν ἐμοί and from ver. 5), but for the *lip-Christians* and those who say Lord ! Lord ! (comp. those who believe without love, 1 Cor. xiii.), God separates from the fellowship of Christ, which act is conceived from the point of view of divine retribution (comp. the thing, according to another figure, viii. 35) ; the former He causes to experience His purging influence, in order that their life of faith may increase in moral activity and efficiency. This purification is effected by the aid, indeed, though not exclusively, of conflict and suffering. — πᾶν κλῆμα

[1] Comp. Grotius and Nösselt, *Opusc.* II. p. 25 ff., also Ewald.

[2] In F. E. Rosenmüller, *Repert.* I. p. 167 ff.

[3] Joseph. *Antt.* xv. 11. 3, *Bell.* v. 5. 4.

[4] Isa. v. 1 ff. ; Jer. ii. 21 ; Ezek. xv. 1 ff., xix. 10 ff. ; Ps. lxxx. 9 ff. ; comp. also Lightfoot and Wetstein.

[5] Luthardt and Lichtenstein, following Hofmann, also Ebrard.

[6] Eph. v. 30 ; Col. ii. 19.

[7] γεωργός, Matt. xxi. 23, *et al. ;* Aelian, *N. A.* vii. 28 ; Aristaen. i. 3.

[8] Plat. *Rep.* p. 353 A ; Pollux, vii. 145.

ἐν ἐμοί] Nominat. absol. as in i. 12, vi. 39, xvii. 2, with weighty emphasis. — αἴρει] *takes it away* with the pruning-knife. It forms with καθαίρει a "suavis rhythmus," Bengel. — τὸ κάρπ. φέρ.] *which bears fruit;* but previously μὴ φέρ. : *if* it does not bear. — καθαίρ.] He *cleanses, prunes.* Figure of the *moral* καθαρισμός,—continually necessary even for the approved Christian,—through the working of divine grace, xiii. 10. — For a *political* view of the community under the figure of the vine, see in Aesch. *adv. Ctesiph.* 166 ; Beck.[1]

Ver. 3. Application of the second half of ver. 2 to the *disciples*, in so far as they belong to the κλήματα ; as a preparation for the exhortation in ver. 4. " Already are *ye* clean" (such purified κλήματα); already there has taken place *in your case*, that which I have just said. The ἤδη ὑμεῖς glances at the multitude of those who were yet to become καθαροί *in the future*. That their purity *originally* is intended, not excluding the necessary continuance and practical further development of the relation (comp. xiii. 10), is understood as a matter of course, and see ver. 4. The *mundi* cease not to be *mundandi*. — διὰ τ. λόγου] διά, as vi. 57 of the *ground;* hence : *on account of* the word, *i.e.* because the word ("provided it be received and apprehended in faith," Luther, comp. Acts xv. 9) is the power of God (Rom. i. 16), in virtue of which it effects its καθαίρει, ver. 2 ; Jas. i. 18 ; 1 Pet. i. 23.[2] The *word*, however, is the *whole* word, the entire doctrine which Jesus has delivered to them (comp. on viii. 43), not the utterance in xiii. 10 (Hilgenfeld, Ebrard).

Ver. 4. To this purity, however, must be added the continuous *faithful persistence* in my living fellowship. — ἐν ἐμοί] here : *on* (not *in*) *me*, συμπεφυῶτες ἐμοί (Nonnus), as is required by what follows, hanging on me as the branches hang on the vine, ver. 2. [See Note XLVII. p. 441.] Euth. Zigabenus aptly remarks : συγκολλώμενοί μοι βεβαιώτερον διὰ πίστεως ἀδιστάκτου καὶ σχέσεως ἀρρήκτου. — κἀγὼ ἐν ὑμῖν] to the fulfilment of the requirement[3] is attached the promise : *and I will abide on you*—συνὼν τῇ δυνάμει, Euth. Zigabenus—with the whole power of spiritual life, which I impart to my faithful ones ; I will not separate myself from you, like the vine, which does not loosen itself from its branches. On μενῶ as a supplement, see Bornemann in the *Sächs. Stud.* 1846, p. 56. The harsher mode of completing the sense : *and cause that I abide on you* (Grotius, Bengel), is not demanded by ver. 5, where ὁ μένων . . . αὐτῷ is the *fulfilled* μείνατε . . . ὑμῖν. — ἐὰν μὴ μείνῃ, κ.τ.λ.] *If it shall not have abided*, etc., refers merely to οὐ δύναται καρπὸν φέρειν (as in v. 19), and is so far a more exact definition of the ἀφ᾽ ἑαυτοῦ, " *vi aliqua propria*, quam habeat extra vitem," Grotius. — οὕτως οὐδὲ ὑμεῖς] *so neither you*, namely δύνασθε καρπ. φέρειν ἀφ᾽ ἑαυτῶν, *i.e.* ποιεῖν τι χωρὶς ἐμοῦ, ver. 5. Bengel well remarks : " Hic locus egregie declarat discrimen naturae et gratiae," but also the *possibility of losing* the latter.

Ver. 5. Abide *on me*, I say, for *I* am the vine, *ye* the branches ; thus then only *from me* (not ἀφ᾽ ἑαυτῶν, ver. 4) can you derive the living power for bearing fruit. And you must *abide* on me, as I on you : *so* (οὗτος : *he*, no

---

[1] ἀμπελουργοῦσί τινες τὴν πόλιν, ἀνατετμήκασί τινες τὰ κλήματα τὰ τοῦ δήμου.

[2] Comp. Fritzsche, *ad Rom.* II. p. 162, I.

p. 197 ; Nägelsbach, *z. Ilias*, p. 39 f., ed. 3.

[3] Comp. Weiss, *Lehrbegr.* p. 74.

other than *he*) will you bring forth *much* fruit. In this way, by means of
ἐγώ . . . κλήματα the preceding ἐν ἐμοί, and by means of ὁ μένων, κ.τ.λ., the
preceding μείνητε is confirmed and brought into relief. Hence also the emphatic position of ἐγώ and μένων. — κἀγὼ ἐν αὐτῷ] Instead of καὶ ἐν ᾧ ἐγὼ μένω,
this clause—not relative, but appending itself in an easy and lively manner
—is introduced.[1]—χωρὶς ἐμοῦ] χωρισθέντες ἀπ᾿ ἐμοῦ, out of living fellowship
with me. [See Note XLVIII. p. 441.] Comp. Eph. ii. 12; Tittmann, *Synon.*
p. 94. Antithetic to ἐν ἐμοὶ μένειν. — ποιεῖν οὐδέν] *effect nothing*, bring about
nothing, passing from the figure into the literal mode of presentation. The
reference is to *the Christian life in general*, not merely to that of the apostles,
since the disciples are addressed, not especially in respect of their narrower
vocation, but generally as κλήματα of Christ, which standing they have in
common with all believers. The utter incapacity for Christian efficiency
without the maintenance of the living connection with Christ is here decidedly and emphatically expressed ; on this subject, however, Augustine, and
with him ecclesiastical orthodoxy, has frequently drawn inferences too wide
in favour of the doctrine of moral inability generally (see especially Calovius) ; since it is only the ability for the specifically *Christian* ποιεῖν τι (the
καρπὸν φέρειν) which is denied to him who is χωρὶς Χριστοῦ. For this *higher*
moral activity, which, indeed, is the only *true* one, he is unable (iii. 6),
and in this sense it may be said with Augustine, that Christ thus spoke, "*ut
responderet futuro Pelagio ;*" where, however, a natural moral volition and
ability of a lower grade in and of itself[2] is not denied, nor its measure and
power more exactly defined than tò this effect, that it cannot attain to
Christian morality, to which rather the ethical power of the living fellowship with Christ here depicted, consequently the new birth, is indispensable.
Luther well says : "that He speaks not here of the natural or worldly being
and life, but of fruits of the gospel." And in *so far* "nos penitus privat
omni virtute, nisi quam suppeditat ipse nobis," Calvin.

Ver. 6. Νῦν λέγει καὶ τὸν κίνδυνον τοῦ μὴ ἐν αὐ, ῷ μένοντος, Euth. Zigabenus ;
and how terrible in its tragic simplicity ! — ἐὰν μή τις] *nisi quis manserit.*[3] —
ἐβλήθη ἔξω, κ.τ.λ.] The representation is highly vivid and pictorial. Jesus
places Himself *at the point of time of the execution of the last judgment*, when
those who have fallen away from Him are gathered together and cast into
the fire, after they have been *previously* already cast out of His church,
and become withered (having completely lost the higher true ζωή). Hence
the graphic lively change of tense : *In case any one shall not have abided on
me ; he has been cast out like the branch, and is withered* (already *before* the
judgment), *and* (now what *takes place at the last day itself*) *they gather them
together*, etc. The aorists therefore neither denote what is wont to be
(Grotius), nor do they stand for futures (Kuinoel, B. Crusius, and older expositors), nor are they to be explained, "par la *répétition de l'acte* aussi
longtemps que dure l'opération de la taille" (Godet) ; nor are they designed,
as in Matt. xviii. 15, to express that which is at once done or appointed to

---

[1] See on this classic idiom, Bernhardy, p. 304 ; Nagelsbach, *z. Ilias*, p. 6, ed. 3; Butt-mann, *N. T. Gr.* p. 327 f. [E. T. p. 382].

[2] Comp. Rom. ii. 14, 15, vii. 14 ff.

[3] See Baeumlein, *Partik.* p. 289. Comp. iii. 3, 5.

be done with the non-abiding.[1] To the latter interpretation is opposed the circumstance that, in point of fact, the being cast out and being withered cannot be appointed or effected immediately at and with the falling away, but that conversion and re-adoption must remain open (comp. ἡ πρόσληψις, Rom. xi. 15), if ἐὰν μή τις, κ.τ.λ. is not to have in view the time of the judgment at the last day. The ἐβλήθη, κ.τ.λ. appears as a definite result and as a completed *act of the past*,[2] and that, as the further pictoral description, κ. συνάγουσιν, κ.τ.λ., shows, from the standpoint *of the last day* (comp. also Heb. vi. 8, x. 27), and further in such a way that it is accomplished between the beginning of the falling away and the last day on which the gathering together and burning is now performed.[3] — ὡς τὸ κλῆμα] *as the branch*, which has not remained on the vine, but has been broken off or cut off, and cast out of the vineyard. But the vineyard represents the fellowship of the Messianic people of God, out of which he who has fallen away from Christ has been thrust. Hence ἔξω refers to the *vineyard*, so far as this is the *church*. Outside it, the life of the man who has fallen away, which he had derived from Christ, has completely perished and is dead. This is expressed by ἐξηράνθη, by which the man is identified with the withered branch, which is his image. Euth. Zigabenus well remarks : ἀπώλεσεν ἣν εἶχεν ἐκ τῆς ῥίζης ἰκμάδα χάριτος. — καὶ συνάγ. αὐτὰ, κ.τ.λ.] Jesus now represents as present what is done with these cast-out and withered branches at the last day. The *polysyndeton* (comp. x. 3, 12 ; Matt. vii. 27, *et al.*) and the simply solemn expression has much in it that seizes the imagination. The subject of συνάγ. and βάλλ. is understood of itself ; in the *figure* it is the servants of the γεωργός, as to the thing, the αἰθέριοι δρηστῆρες (Nonnus), the *angels*, are intended (Matt. xiii. 41). — εἰς τὸ πῦρ (see critical notes) : *into the fire*, already burning for this purpose, by which, in the interpretation of the figure, *Gehenna* is intended,[4] not also the fire of the divine anger generally (Hengstenberg). —καὶ καίεται] *and they burn!* The simple form (οὐ μὴν κατακαίονται Euth. Zigabenus) as in Matt. xiii. 40. "Magna vi positum eximia cum majestate," Bengel.

Ver. 7. After thus deterring from non-abiding, in ver. 6, now again an inducement to abiding. But the *figure* now ceases, and barely still leaves in what follows some slight allusions (vv. 8, 16).— ἐὰν μείν. ἐν ἐμοί] Still in the sense of the figure, as the branches on the vine ; but with καὶ τὰ ῥήμ. μ. ἐν ὑμῖν (*in animis vestris*), expressing the necessary consequence of a man's abiding on Jesus, the language at once becomes *proper*, no longer figurative. —ὃ ἐὰν θέλ.] stands first with emphasis ; but such an one wills and prays simply and solely in the name of Jesus (xiv. 13, 14), and cannot do otherwise.

---

[1] So most expositors, including Lücke, Winer, Tholuck, de Wette, Luthardt, Weiss, Hengstenberg ; comp. Hermann, *de emend. Grammat.* p. 192 f. ; Buttmann, *N. T. Gram.* p. 172 [E. T. p. 199].

[2] Hence the aorist, instead of which the perfect was not required, as Luthardt objects. The ἤδη κέκριται of iii. 18 is conceived

of differently.

[3] The reading μένῃ (see critical notes) would not essentially alter the sense ; it expresses : *nisi quis manet, i.e.* until the judgment.

[4] Matt. xiii. 42, xxv. 41, iii. 10, vii. 19, v. 22, *et al.*

Ver. 8. A further carrying out of this incitement to abiding on Him, and that by bringing out the great importance, rich in its results, of this granting of prayer, which is attached to the abiding required. — ἐν τούτῳ] *Herein*, to this a *forward* reference is generally given, so that ἵνα, κ.τ.λ. is the contents of τοῦτο. But thus understood, since ἵνα is not equivalent to ὅτι, this ἵνα would express, that in the *obligation* (you *ought*, ver. 12, comp. on vi. 29), or in the *destination* to bear much fruit, the δόξα of the Father is given. This is inadmissible, as it is rather in the actual fruit-bearing itself that that δόξα must lie, and hence ὅτι must have been employed. To distinguish ἵνα, however, merely by supplying "as I hope" (Lücke) from ὅτι, does not satisfy the telic nature of the word.[1] Hence (and not otherwise in 1 John iv. 17) ἐν τούτῳ, as in iv. 37, xvi. 30, is to be taken as a *retrospective* reference (so also Lange), and that not to the μένειν in itself, but to the immediately preceding ὃ ἐὰν θέλητε αἰτήσασθε κ. γενήσ. ὑμῖν, *so far*, namely, as it takes place in him who abides in Christ. *In this granting of prayer allotted to the μένειν ἐν ἐμοί*, says Jesus, a twofold result—and this a high incentive to that μένειν—is given, namely, (1) when what you ask falls to your lot, then in this result *my Father has been glorified*,[2] *that you*—for that is God's *design* in this His δοξάζεσθαι—*may bear much fruit* (which is just to be the actual further course of that granting of prayer, comp. ver. 16) ; and (2) *you will*, in virtue of the fulfilment of all your prayers, *become*, in a truly proper and specific sense, *my disciples*, who belong to no other (note the emphatic possessive ἐμοί, as in xiii. 35), since this hearing of prayer is the holy characteristic simply and solely of *my* disciples (xiv. 13, 14). — The future γενήσεσθε *may* depend on ἵνα (comp. on ἰάσομαι, xiii. 40, see also on 1 Cor. ix. 18 ; Eph. vi. 3), as Ewald connects it ; independently, however, of ἵνα, and therefore connected with ἐν τούτῳ, the words convey more weight in the independence appropriate to their distinctive contents. The Lord, however, does not say ἔσεσθε, but He sees the full *development* of His discipledom beginning with the ἐν τούτῳ.

Vv. 9, 10. But as *disciples* of Christ, they are the object of His *love ;* hence, to the general exhortation to abide on *Him*, is added now the particular one to abide in His *love*, which is done by keeping His commandments, according to the archetype of *His* harmonious moral relation to the *Father*. — *As the Father has loved me, I have also loved you* (aorists, because Jesus, at the boundary of His life, stands and looks back, xiii. 1, 34) : *abide* (keep yourselves continually) in my love.[3] To extend the protasis to ὑμᾶς, and begin the apodosis with μείνατε (Maldonatus, Grotius, Rosenmüller, Olshausen, and several others), is opposed by the fact that between καθὼς ἠγάπ. με ὁ π. and μείνατε, κ.τ.λ. no correlation exists ; for the ἀγάπη ἡ ἐμή is not love *to me*,[4] but : *my* love *to you*, as is clear from ἠγάπησα ὑμᾶς and from the analogy of

---

[1] Cyril already rightly recognized that ἵνα cannot be an explanation of ἐν τούτῳ, but only a statement of the purpose of ἐδοξ. ὁ πατ. μ. But quite irrelevantly he referred ἐδοξ. ὁ πατ. μ. to the *mission of the Son.*

[2] ἔλλαχε τιμήν, Nonnus.

[3] Instead of μείνατε, Ewald conjectures μείνητε, which he still makes depend on ἵνα, ver. 8 ; but this is unsuitable, since καθώς appears without καί.

[4] Maldonatus, Grotius, Nösselt, Kuinoel, Baeumlein, and several others.

434   THE GOSPEL OF JOHN.

ἡ χαρὰ ἡ ἐμή, ver. 11 ;¹ comp. vv. 12, 13.   Olshausen mingles the two
together, the active and passive love. — ἐν τῇ ἀγάπῃ μου] = ἐν τῇ ἀγάπῃ τῇ ἐμῇ.
But the latter purposely lays emphasis on the thought that it was nothing less
than *His* love, that love so great and holy, as He had just expressed by καθὼς
ἠγάπ., κ.τ.λ., in which they were to abide. — τετήρηκα] Self-witness in the
retrospect which He takes of His whole ministry on the threshold of its accomplishment. — κ. μένω αὐτοῦ ἐν τ. ἀγάπῃ] Consequence of τετήρηκα.   The
prominent position of αὐτοῦ corresponds to the consciousness of the happiness
and the dignity of abiding in the love which His *Father* bears to him (x.
17, xvii. 24).   The present includes continuance also for the future ; hence
it is not, with Ewald, to be accented μενῶ.

   Ver. 11. Conclusion of the section vv. 1–10 (ταῦτα). [See Note XLIX. p.
441.] — ἵνα ἡ χαρά, κ.τ.λ.] Note the juxtaposition of ἡ ἐμή and ἐν ὑμῖν ; that
my joy may be *in you*, *i.e.* that the same joy which *I* have may be *yours*.
The holy joyous tone of soul is intended, the conscious moral courage of
joy, which rises victorious over all suffering, as Christ, in virtue of His
fellowship with the Father and of His obedience towards Him, must and
did possess it (comp. xvii. 13), and as it so often finds utterance with
Paul in the spirit of Christ.²   Yet ἡ ἐμή is not : the joy *produced by me*
(Calvin, de Wette), or of which I have opened to you the spring (Tholuck),
which is forcing a meaning on the simple possessive expression (comp. iii.
29, xvii. 13 ; 2 Cor. ii. 3), and does not satisfy the significant juxtaposition
of ἡ ἐμή and ἐν ὑμῖν (comp. 2 Cor. ii. 3 : ὅτι ἡ ἐμὴ χαρὰ πάντων ὑμῶν ἐστιν).
The explanations : *mea de vobis laetitia* (corresponding to χαίρειν ἐν),³ or
even : *gaudium vestrum de me*,⁴ are to be rejected because the correct reading is ᾖ (see critical notes).   Luthardt : that *my* joy may have its *cause and
object* in *you* (not in anything else).   This is grammatically correct (ἐν of
causal foundation) : the πληρωθῇ, however, which is subsequently said of the
joy of the disciples, presupposes that in the first clause the joy of the *disciples themselves*, the *consummation* of which is intended, is already indicated ;
πληρωθῇ otherwise would remain without corresponding correlation.   Had
the object been merely to express the *reciprocity* of the joy, we should
necessarily have expected in the second half simply : καὶ ἡ χαρὰ ὑμῶν ἐν ἐμοί.
See, in answer to Luthardt, also Hofmann.⁵ — If *Christ's* joy is in His own,
their joy will be thereby *completed* (comp. iii. 29), developed to its full
measure in contents, purity, strength, victoriousness, etc.⁶   Hence : κ. ἡ
χαρὰ ὑμ. πληρωθῇ.

   Vv. 12, 13. Now, for the purpose of furnishing a more exact guide to this
joy, is given the *precept of reciprocal love, founded on the love of Christ* (xiii.
34), which is the collective conception of the ἐντολαί, ver. 10, Jesus' *pecul-*

¹ That ἡ ἀγάπη ἡ ἐμή may denote love *to
me*, should not have been called in question,
as being contrary to the genius of the language. Comp. φιλία τῇ σῃ, Xen. *Anab.* vii.
7. 29 ; Thucyd. i. 137. 4 : διὰ τὴν σὴν φιλίαν,
Rom. xi. 31.
   ² 1 Cor. vii. 30 ; 2 Cor. xiii. 11 ; Phil. ii. 17,
18, iv. 4 ; Rom. xiv. 17 ; Gal. v. 22.

³ So Augustine, Schoettgen, Lampe, Kuinoel, Ebrard, Hengstenberg, and several
others.
   ⁴ Euth. Zigabenus, Grotius, Nösselt, Klee,
and several others.
   ⁵ *Schriftbew.* II. 2. p. 325 f.
   ⁶ Comp. xvi. 24 ; 1 John i. 4 ; 2 John 12.

iar, specific precept (ἡ ἐμή). — ἵνα] *you should* (see on vi. 29). — Ver. 13 *char-acterizes* the καθὼς ἠγάπ. ὑμᾶς. *A greater love than this* (just designated by καθὼς ἠγάπ. ὑμᾶς) *no one cherishes ;* it is the *greatest* love which any one can have, such as, according to the divine purpose, shall impel to this (ἵνα), *that* (after my example) *one* (indefinite) *should give up his life for the advantage of his friends.* For a like readiness to self-sacrifice the *greatness* of my love shall be the motive, 1 John iii. 16. The *ordinary* interpretation which takes ἵνα as *expository of ταύτης* [See Note L. p. 441], does not correspond to the idea of purpose in ἵνα, and the attempts to preserve this conception (*e.g.* de Wette : in ἀγάπῃ there lies a law, a will, comp. Luthardt, Lange ; Godet : the culminating point of loving effort lies therein) are unsatisfactory and forced expedients.[1] — The difference between the present passage and Rom. v. 6 ff. (ὑπὲρ ἀσεβῶν) does not rest upon the thing itself, but only on the different point of view, which in Romans is general, and here is limited, in the special connection, to the circle of friends, without excepting the friends from the general category of sinners. To *designate* them, however, by that quality, was not relevant in this place. Against the weakening of the idea of φίλων : "those who are actually objects of His love" (Ebrard), ver. 14 should have been a sufficient guard.

Ver. 14. " *For his friends,*" Jesus had just said. There was a presumption implied in this, that He also would die for His *friends* (Euth. Ziga-benus briefly and correctly points out the sequence of thought by supplying at the end of ver. 13 : καθὼς ἐγὼ ποιῶ νῦν). And who are these ? *The disciples* (ὑμεῖς), if they do what He commands them.—The conception of the φίλοι is that of the loving confidential companionship with Himself, to which Christ has raised them ; see ver. 15. Later on, He designates them even as His *brethren*, xx. 17.

Ver. 15. The *dignity*, however, which lies in this designation "friends," was to become known to them. — οὐκέτι] *No longer*, as before (xii. 26, xiii. 13 ff.). No contradiction to ver. 20, where Jesus does not anew give them the *name* of δοῦλοι, but only *reminds* them of an earlier saying ; nor with Luke xii. 4, where He *has* already called them friends, which, however, is also not excluded by the present passage, since here rather the previous designation is only indicated *a potiori*, and the new is intended *in a pregnant* sense, which does not do away with the objective and abiding relation of the disciples, to be δοῦλοι of Christ, and their profound consciousness of this their relation,[2] as generally Christians are at once δοῦλοι and ἀπελεύθεροι κυρίου (1 Cor. vii. 22), at once δοῦλοι and yet His brothers (Rom. viii. 29), at once δοῦλοι and yet His συγκληρονόμοι (Rom. viii. 16). — αὐτοῦ ὁ κύρ.] Although he is *his* lord. — τι ποιεῖ] Not : what he *intends to do* (Grotius, Kuinoel, and several others), which is not appropriate in the application to Jesus, whose work was in full process of accomplishment, nay, was so near to its earthly consummation, but the *action itself*, while it is going on. The slave, although he sees it externally, *is not acquainted with it*, does not know the proper

[1] On τιθέναι τ. ψυχ., see on x. 11; on τίς, corresponding to the universal one (*man*, Ger.), *any one*, see Nägelsbach, z. *Ilias*, p. 299, ed. 3.

[2] Acts iv. 29; Rom. i. 1; Gal. i. 10; Phil. i. 1, *et al.*

nature of the action of his master,[1] because the latter has not taken him
into his confidence in respect of the quality, the object, the means, the motives, and thoughts, etc. ; "servus tractatur ut ὄργανον," Bengel. — εἴρηκα]
Ver. 14. — πάντα ἃ ἤκουσα, κ.τ.λ.] does not refer to all the *doctrinal* teaching,
nor again is it elucidated from the quite general saying, viii. 26 (Tholuck) ;
and just as little does it require the arbitrary and more exact limitation to
that which is necessary to salvation (Calvin), to the principles (de Wette), to
that designed for communication (Lücke, Olshausen), which thus seeks
to avoid the apparent contradiction with xvi. 12 ; but[2] it alludes to that
which the Father has laid upon Him *to do*, as appears from the context by
the correlation with ὅτι ὁ δοῦλος οὐκ οἶδε, κ.τ.λ. He has made known to the
disciples the whole *saving will* of God, the *accomplishment* of which had been
entrusted to Him on His being sent from His pre-existent state into the
world ; but this by no means excludes instructions standing in connection,
which they could not bear at the present time, xvi. 12.

Ver. 16. Along with this dignity, however, of being Jesus' friends, they
were not to forget their *dependence* on Him, and their destiny therewith
appointed. — ἐξελέξασθε . . . ἐξελεξάμην] as Master . . . as disciples, which
is understood of itself from the historical relation, and is also to be gathered
from the word chosen (vi. 70, xiii. 18 ; Acts i. 2). Each of them was a
σκεῦος ἐκλογῆς of Christ (Acts ix. 15) ; in each the initiative of this peculiar
relation lay not on his but on Christ's side. Hence not to be taken merely
in a general sense of the selection for the fellowship of love.[3] — ἔθηκα ὑμᾶς]
have appointed you, as my *disciples*, consequence of the ἐξελεξάμην. The "*do-
tation spirituelle*" (Godet) goes beyond the meaning of the word, although it
was historically connected with it (Mark iii. 14, 15). Comp. on τιθέναι,
instituere, appoint (not merely *destine*, as Ebrard thinks), 1 Cor. xii. 28 ; 1
Tim. i. 12 ; 2 Tim. i. 11 ; Heb. i. 2 ; Acts xx. 28, *et al.*[4] The rendering
of Chrysostom, Theophylact, Euth. Zigabenus, is incorrect : I have *planted*
you.[5] The figure of the vine has in truth been dropped, and finds only an
echo in the καρπὸν φέρειν, which, however, must not be extended to ἔθηκα,
since the disciples appear not as planted, but as *branches*, which have grown
and *remain* on the vine. Quite arbitrarily, Bengel and Olshausen see here a
new figure of a *fruit-tree.* — ἵνα ὑμεῖς ὑπάγ.] *that you* on your side may *go away*,
etc., is by Chrysostom, Theophylact, Euth. Zigabenus, in consequence of
their interpretation of ἔθηκα, erroneously explained by ἵνα ἐκτείνησθε αὐξανόμενοι.
Nor does it merely denote "*independent and living* action ;"[6] comp. Luther :
"that you sit not still without fruit or work"), or "*continual movement*"
(Hengstenberg), with which sufficient justice is not done to the peculiarity of
this point, which, in truth, belonged in the most proper sense to the disciples'
calling. According to Ebrard, it would even be simply an auxiliary verb,

---

[1] Comp. Xen. *ep.* i. 3.

[2] This, at the same time, in answer to
Beyschlag, p. 101, who considers a reference
here to the pre-existent state as *absurd*.
Comp. also against the same, Johansson, *de
Chr. praeexistentia,* p. 14.

[3] Euth. Zigabenus, Luther, and several

others, including Luthardt, Lange.

[4] Hom. *Od.* xv. 253, *Il.* vi. 300 ; Dem. 322.
11, *et al.* .

[5] Xen. *Oec.* xix. 7, 9.

[6] De Wette, Lücke, Baumgarten-Crusius,
Luthardt, Godet.

like *ire* with the supine. It signifies rather the *execution of the ἀποστολή*, in which they were to *go away* into all the world, etc. Comp. Luke x. 3 ; Matt. xxviii. 19. — μένῃ] comp. iv. 36. The results of their ministry are not to go backward and be brought to naught, but are to be continuous and enduring even into the *αἰὼν μέλλων*.— The *second ἵνα* is *co-ordinated* with the first. See on vv. 7, 8. It is in truth precisely the granting of prayer here designated which brings about the fruit and its duration in all given cases. Comp. the prayers of Paul, as in Col. i. 9 ff. ; Eph. iii. 14 ff. — ἐν τῷ ὀνόμ. μ.] See on xiv. 13.

Ver. 17. At the close (comp. ver. 11) of this section, vv. 12–16, Jesus refers once more to its main point, *reciprocal love*. — ταῦτα] *points backwards*. as in ver. 11, namely, to what is contained in vv. 12–16, so far as the contents are of a *preceptive* nature. And *that which* is therein enjoined by Jesus on the disciples has for its object (ἵνα), etc., as He had in truth required this duty at the very beginning of the section. The remainder of the section (vv. 14–16) was indeed not directly of a preceptive nature, but in support and furtherance of what had been enjoined.

Vv. 18, 19. But now your *relation to the world!* as far as ver. 27. — In your fellowship, *love;* from without, on the part of the unbelieving, *hatred* toward you ! Consolation for you : γινώσκετε (imperat.) ὅτι ἐμὲ πρῶτον ὑμῶν (i. 15), μεμίσηκεν. Comp. 1 Pet. iv. 12, 13. This hatred is a *community of destiny with me*. A further consolation : this hate is the proof that you no longer belong to the *world*, but to *me* through my selection of you (ver. 16) ; therein exists the *reason* for it. How must that fact tend to elate you ! Comp. 1 John iii. 13, iv. 5. —The fivefold repetition of κόσμος is solemn. Comp. iii. 17. — τὸ ἴδιον] "*Suum* dicitur pro *vos*, atque sic notatur *interesse* mundi," Bengel. Comp. vii. 7. They have become a *foreign* element to the world, and therewith the object of its *antipathy;* χαίρει γὰρ τῷ ὁμοίῳ τὸ ὅμοιον, Euth. Zigabenus.[1]

Ver. 20. A recalling of xiii. 16, presupposing, however, a different application than in that passage—namely, a slave has no better lot to claim than his lord (comp. Matt. x. 24, 25).—*If they have persecuted me, they will also persecute you; if they have kept my word, they will also keep yours*. Which of these two cases will in general occur, Jesus leaves to the decision of the disciples themselves, since they in truth knew from experience how it had gone with Him. To take the second clause *ironically*,[2] is appropriate neither to the seriousness of the first, nor to the tone of the whole passage. Olshausen holds incorrectly (comp. B. Crusius, Maier, Godet), "if *many*, etc.," where, in the first half, according to Godet, we should have to think of the *mass* of the people. But the variation of the subjects is a pure importation. Finally, when Bengel and other older expositors (in Wolf) interpret τηρεῖν as *watch*, this is quite opposed to the Johannean usage of τὸν λόγ. τηρεῖν (viii. 51, xiv. 23, 24, and frequently), comp. ver. 10, and it would be too weak a conception after the first half of the verse. Irrespectively of this,

[1] Comp. Plat. *Lys.* p. 214 B ; τὸ ὅμοιον τῷ ὁμοίῳ ἀνάγκη ἀεὶ φίλον εἶναι.

[2] "Quasi dicat : non est, quod hoc speretis," Grotius, Lampe.

usage would not stand in the way of such rendering, Gen. iii. 15 (according to the usual reading).[1]

Ver. 21. 'Αλλά] antithesis of *consolation* against this state of persecution [See Note LI. p. 441] : ταῦτα πάντα π. εἰς ὑμ., however, presupposes that the second of the cases supposed in ver. 20 is *not* the actual one. The *consolation* lies in διὰ τὸ ὄνομά μου : *because my name is your confession.* " The name of Christ from your mouth will be to them nothing but poison and death," Luther. Comp. Acts iv. 17, ix. 14, xxvii. 9. This thought : it is for the sake of Christ's name that I suffer (Acts ix. 16), was to exalt the persecuted,[2] and did exalt them (Acts v. 41, xxi. 13, *et al.*), and they boasted of these sufferings,[3] which constituted their holy pride (Gal. vi. 17) and their joy (Phil. ii. 17, 18). Comp. Matt. x. 22, xxiv. 9, v. 11. According to *others*,[4] ὅτι οὐκ οἴδασι, κ.τ.λ., has the emphasis. But in that case the thought διὰ τὸ ὄνομά μου is arbitrarily thrust back, and rendered unnecessary, although throughout the whole of the following discussion the reference of the persecutions *to Christ* is the prominent and controlling point (see especially vv. 25–27). Hence ὅτι οὐκ οἴδασι, κ.τ.λ., is to be taken as subordinated to διὰ τὸ ὄνομά μου, as giving, that is, its explanation. Had they possessed the true acquaintance with God, they would, because God has sent Christ, have also known Christ (comp. Luke xxiii. 34), and would not for His name's sake have persecuted His disciples.

Vv. 22–24. *Sinfulness*, not of this non-acquaintance with God (Ebrard, Ewald, Godet), but, as vv. 23–25 show, of this hatred of the name of Jesus, in respect of which they are inexcusable, since He has *come* and *spoken to them* (vv. 22, 23), and done before their eyes His *Messianic works* (miracles), ver. 24. — ἁμαρτ. οὐκ εἶχον] For their hatred of my name would then be *excusable*, because, without my appearance and discourses, the true knowledge of Him who sent me—and the non-acquaintance with whom is in truth the ground of their hatred (ver. 21)—would have remained inaccessible to them. My appearance and discourses ought to have opened their eyes, and brought them to the knowledge of Him who sent me ; but since this has not taken place, their hatred against me, which flows from their non-acquaintance with Him who sent me, is *inexcusable ;* it is the hatred of hardened blindness before God's revelation of Himself in my advent and discourses. — The weight of the protasis lies in ἦλθον and ἐλάλ. αὐτοῖς *together* (not merely in the latter) ; ἦλθον is the Messianic ἔρχεσθαι, correlative to the preceding τ. πέμψαντά με. The ἁμαρτία, however, referable to the μισεῖν,[5] must not be referred merely to *unbelief,* which reference does not correspond to the con-

---

[1] Dem. 317 ult., 1252. 8 ; Soph. *O. R.* 808 ; Arist. *Vesp.* 364 ; Thuc. iv. 108. 1, vii. 80. 1 ; Lys. iii. 34.

[2] πρὸς τιμὴν μὲν ὑμῖν τοῦτο ποιοῦσιν, Ammonius.

[3] Rom. v. 3 ; 2 Cor. xi. 23 ff., xii. 10, 11 ; 1 Pet. iv. 12 ff.

[4] Including Lücke, de Wette, Hengstenberg.

[5] Hence, too, on the question as to the salvation of the heathen, to whom Christ has not been preached, nothing is to be gathered from the present passage ; and one may now, with Augustine, decide in favour of *mitiores poenas* for them, or, in confirmation of their condemnation, propose, with Melanchthon, to extend the words of Christ to the *protevangelium* in paradise, and bring in at the same time the natural moral, law, Rom. ii.

text in vv. 19, 21, 23–25.[1] The words ἁμαρτ. οὐκ ἔχειν, ix. 41, were spoken of *unbelief.* — The non-occurrence of ἄν with εἶχον is as in viii. 39. — νῦν δέ] *But as it is,* since I *have appeared and have spoken to them.* [See Note LII. p. 442.] — πρόφασιν οὐκ ἔχουσι, κ.τ.λ.] In that supposed case they would have *no sin,* so far, namely, as their hatred would be only an excusable *peccatum igno-rantiae;* but as the matter stands, they have no *pretext* in respect of their sin (to which they are subject through their hatred) ; they can allege noth-ing by way of *escape.* πρόφασιν ἔχειν, to have *evasions, exculpations,* only here in N. T., very frequent in the classics.[2] Euth. Zigabenus well remarks : ἀποστερεῖ τοὺς Ἰουδαίους ἀπάσης συγγνώμης ἐθελοκακοῦντας. — Ver. 23. And how exceedingly great is this sin ! Comp. v. 23. — Ver. 24, parallel to ver. 22, as there from the discourses, which the unbelieving have heard, so here similarly from that which they have *seen,* revealing their guilt. — οὐδεὶς ἄλλος] that is, in their nature and appearance *divine* works, v. 36, ix. 3, 4, x. 37, xiv. 10, *et al.* — νῦν δὲ καὶ ἑωράκασι, κ.τ.λ.] *But as it is* (νῦν δέ, as in ver. 22), *they have actually seen* (as vi. 36), and *yet hated both me and my Father.* Not merely μεμισ., but also ἑωράκ., is connected with καὶ ἐμέ, κ.τ.λ. ; *in the works* they have seen Christ (x. 25) and the Father (xiv. 10) ; for both have revealed themselves in them, which, indeed, the unbelieving have seen only as an external sensuous occurrence, not with the inward un-derstanding, giving significance to the outward σημεῖα ; not with the eye of spiritual knowledge and inward being, vi. 26.

Ver. 25. Yet this hatred against me stands in connection with the divine destiny,[3] according to which the word of Scripture must be fulfilled by their hatred : *they have hated me groundlessly.* The passage is Ps. lxix. 4, or xxxv. 19, where the theocratic sufferer (David?) utters that saying which has reached its antitypical Messianic destination in the hatred of the un-believing against Christ (comp. on xiii. 18). The passage Ps. cix. 3, which Hengstenberg further adduces, does not correspond so literally, as neither does Ps. cxix. 161 (Ewald). — ἀλλ'] *sc.*μεμισήκασίν με. as the ground-thought of what precedes. [See Note LIII. p. 442.] — δωρεάν] חִנָּם, *immerito,* according to the LXX., but opposed to the Greek signification *(gratis).*[4]— The *irony* which de Wette discovers in ἐν τῷ νόμῳ αὐτῶν : "they comply faithfully with what stands in their law," is an erroneous assumption, since ἵνα πληρ. is the usual formula for the fulfilment of *prophecies,* and since νόμος here, as in x. 34, stands in a wider sense, while αὐτῶν is to be taken as τῷ ὑμετέρῳ, viii. 17 (see *in loc.*), comp. ὑμῶν, x. 34. Bengel well says : "*in lege eorum,* quam assidue terunt et jactant."

Vv. 26, 27. Over against this hatred of the world, Jesus further appeals confidently, and in the certainty of His future justification, to the *testimony* which the *Paraclete,* and also the *disciples themselves,* will bear regarding

<hr>

[1] In answer to Bengel, Luthardt, Lange, Hengstenberg, and several others.

[2] Dem. 526. 15 ; Plat. *Pol.* v. p. 469 C ; Xen. *Cyr.* iii. 1. 27. Antithesis : ἀφελεῖν πρόφασιν, Dem. 26. 2, 635. 24.

[3] Which, as a matter of course, and ac-cording to vv. 22–24, does not do away with responsibility. Comp. Weiss, *Lehrbegr.* p. 151.

[4] Comp. 1 Sam. xix. 5 ; Ps. xxxiv. 7 (where Symmachus has ἀναιτίως); Sir. xx. 21, xxix. 6, 7.

Him. The *Paraclete* was to give testimony of Christ *through the disciples*, in speaking forth from them (Matt. x. 20 ; Mark xiii. 11). But the testimony of the disciples to Christ was at the same time also *their own*, since it expressed their own experiences with Christ from the beginning onwards, i. 14 ; 1 John i. 1 ; Acts i. 21, 22. Both were, in so far as they, filled and enlightened by the divine *Spirit*, delivered *His* instructions (xiv. 26), and what *they themselves* had heard and seen of Jesus, *both* consequently ἐν πνεύματι, *one* witness ; it is, however, separated into its two actual factors (comp. Acts i. 8 ; Rom. viii. 16, ix. 1), and they are kept apart. — ὃν ἐγὼ πέμψω ὑμ. παρὰ τοῦ πατρ.] How ? see xiv. 16. As ἐγώ is used with the weight of authority, so also has the determining expression : τὸ πνεῦμα τ. ἀληθ. (see on xiv. 17), with its added ὁ π. τ. πατρ. ἐκπορ., in emphatic confirmation of the above παρὰ τοῦ πατρός, the pragmatic weight of demonstrating the *truth* and *validity* of the Spirit's testimony, which thus goes back to the *Father*. But the general term ἐκπορ. which is without definite limitation of time, refers not to the immanent relation of subsistence (*actus hypostaticus*), but, in accordance with the connection, to the efficacious outward communication [1] from the Father, through which, in every recurring case, the Spirit is received. "Itaque hujusmodi testimonia nec a Graecis (against the *filioque*) nec contra Graecos (against the διὰ τοῦ υἱοῦ ἐκ τοῦ πατρός) . . . satis apposite sunt citata," Beza. For its dogmatic use in the interest of the Greek Church, see already in Theodore of Mopsuestia. Recently, Hilgenfeld especially has laid great stress on the hypostatic reference, in support of the doctrine of a Gnostic emanation. — ἐκεῖνος] opposed to the Christ-hating world. — περὶ ἐμοῦ] of my Person, my work, etc. Comp. 1 John v.6. — καὶ ὑμεῖς δέ] *atque vos etiam.* Comp. on vi. 51, viii. 17. — μαρτυρεῖτε] *ye also are witnesses, since ye from the beginning* (of my Messianic activity) *are with me* (consequently *are able* to bear witness of me from your experience). Jesus does not say μαρτυρήσετε, because the disciples *were* already the witnesses which they *were to be* in future. They were, as the witnesses, *already forthcoming.* ἐστέ denotes that which still continues from the commencement up to the present moment. Comp. 1 John iii. 8. μαρτυρ. taken as *imperative* would make the command appear too abrupt ; considering its importance, a more definite unfolding of it was to be expected, which, however, is not missed, if the words are only a part of the *promise* to bear witness.[2] An echo of this word of Christ regarding the united testimony of the Spirit and the apostles is found in Acts v. 32, also in Acts xv. 28.

---

[1] The Spirit *goes out* if He *is sent*, xiv. 16, 26 ; Gal. iv. 6. Comp. the figurative expression of the *outpouring.* See also Hofmann, *Schriftbew.* I. p. 203 f.

[2] In answer to B. Crusius and Hofmann *Schriftbew.* II. 2, p. 19.

NOTES BY AMERICAN EDITOR.

XLV. "*I am the true vine.*" Ver. 1.

Weiss considers Meyer's reference of the probable introduction of this metaphor to the wine cup of the supper, as well as all the other modes of accounting
for it, to be entirely without foundation. The familiarity of the figure in
the O. T. abundantly explains it.

XLVI. "*The true vine.*" Ver. 1.

The genuine ($\dot{a}\lambda\eta\theta\iota\nu\dot{\eta}$) vine, that which corresponds to the idea. According
to Weiss, this genuine, archetypal vine is not here opposed to the *natural* vine,
which Meyer makes figuratively but imperfectly represent it. Rather, according to Weiss, *Israel* is the *typical* representation of this idea, while Jesus with
His church stands in contrast (not with the unfruitful vine, the degenerate Israel,
but) with the imperfect realization of the genuine theocracy in Israel. Thus
Christ puts Himself with His church over against the imperfect Jewish church.

XLVII. "*Abide in me.*" Ver. 4.

According to Weiss : "*in* me, not *on* me" (as Meyer), "inasmuch as the
direction is in part independent of the image of the vine and branches, and
partly also the branches root themselves *in* the vine-stalk, and only as the result
of this are suspended from it.''

XLVIII. "*Without me.*" Ver. 5.

"Not (as Meyer) $\chi\omega\rho\iota\sigma\theta\acute{\epsilon}\nu\tau\epsilon\varsigma$ $\dot{\epsilon}\mu o\tilde{\upsilon}$, separated from vital communion with me.
It corresponds not to the $\dot{\epsilon}\nu$ $\dot{\epsilon}\mu o\grave{\iota}$ $\mu\acute{\epsilon}\nu\epsilon\iota\nu$, but to the $\dot{\epsilon}\gamma\grave{\omega}$ $\dot{\epsilon}\nu$ $a\dot{\upsilon}\tau\tilde{\wp}$, as the new feature, in the repetition : *without me as Him who is and works in you*" (Weiss).

XLIX. $\tau a\tilde{\upsilon}\tau a$. Ver. 11.

"$\tau a\tilde{\upsilon}\tau a$ refers not (with Meyer, Lücke, etc.) to all from 1 to 10, but to v. 9 and
foll. (de W., God.) as the clause of purpose, rightly taken, clearly implies"
(Weiss).

L. $\tau a\dot{\upsilon}\tau\eta\varsigma$. Ver. 13.

"$\tau a\dot{\upsilon}\tau\eta\varsigma$ here does not refer back to the love expressed by the$\kappa a\theta\grave{\omega}\varsigma$ $\dot{\eta}\gamma\dot{a}\pi\eta\sigma a$
$\dot{\upsilon}\mu\tilde{a}\sigma$,but forward to the clause introduced by $\iota\nu a$. Meyer explains the $\iota\nu a$ of the
divine purpose in the fact of the transcendent greatness of His love, viz. that
one must yield up His life. But the negative clause $\mu\epsilon\acute{\iota}\zeta o\nu a$ $\dot{a}\gamma\dot{a}\pi\eta\nu$ $o\dot{\upsilon}\delta\epsilon\grave{\iota}\varsigma$ $\dot{\epsilon}\chi\epsilon\iota$ is
by no means equivalent to the positive statement which Meyer substitutes for
it : the $\tau\iota\varsigma$ corresponding to $o\dot{\upsilon}\delta\epsilon\acute{\iota}\varsigma$ is not *every one ;* and the context declares
not *why* we must have the greatest love, but wherein the greatest love consists.
All efforts to preserve the *telic* force of $\iota\nu a$ are unsuccessful" (Weiss).

LI. $\dot{a}\lambda\lambda\dot{a}$, *but.* Ver. 21.

"$\dot{a}\lambda\lambda\dot{a}$ introduces not the *contrast of the consolation*, against this state of persecution, but shows, in contrast with the previous supposition, that they will per-

secute the disciples for their own sakes, which is the deepest ground of their persecution" (Weiss).

LII. Vv. 22, 23.

Observe the twice recurring logical νῦν δέ, so frequent in the N. T., *but as it is, as the case stands.* The uniform English rendering *now* is unidiomatic and often obscure or misleading (Luke xix. 42 ; 1 Cor. xv. 20).

LIII. ἀλλ' ἵνα πληρωθῇ.   Ver. 25.

Meyer and Weiss (Weiss hesitatingly) supply the ellipsis with μεμισήκασίν με. Better, I think, τοῦτο γέγονεν, or some general expression like the Eng. Ver., *this cometh to pass.*   See i. 8, and especially xiii. 18.

CHAPTER XVI.

Ver. 3. After ποιήσ. Elz. has ὑμῖν, against decisive testimony. — Ver. 4. ἡ
ὥρα] Lachm.: ἡ ὥρα αὐτῶν, according to A. B., a few Cursives, Syr.; also L.,
Cursives, Vulg. It. Arr. Cypr. Aug., who, however, omit the αὐτῶν that follows.
This betrays an already ancient variation in the position of the once original
αὐτῶν, which, placed *before* μνημον., was readily drawn to ὥρα, and then
also again restored *after* μνημον. D. 68, Arm. have *no* αὐτῶν at all, which is explained from its original position *after* μνημον., in which it appeared superfluous. — Ver. 7. ἐὰν γὰρ ἐγώ] ἐγώ, which is wanting in Elz. Tisch., has important testimony against (B. D. L ℵ.) and for it (A. E. G. H. K. M. U. Δ. Λ.). It
was, however, because unnecessary, and also as not standing in opposition, more
readily passed over than added. — Ver. 13. εἰς πᾶσαν τὴν ἀλήθειαν] Lachm.: εἰς
τὴν ἀλήθ. πᾶσαν (A. B. Y. Or. Eus.) ; Tisch. : ἐν τῇ ἀληθείᾳ πάσῃ (D. L. ℵ.
Cursives, Verss. Fathers). The reading of Lachm. has stronger attestation, and
is, in respect of the position of the words, supported by the reading of Tisch.,
which latter may have arisen through a comparison of the construction of ὁδηγ.
with ἐν in the LXX. (Ps. lxxxvi. 10, cxix. 35, *et al. ;* Sap. ix. 11, x. 17). — Ver. 15.
λαμβάνει] Elz. : λήψεται, against decisive testimony ; from ver. 14. — Ver. 16.
οὐ] B. D. L. Λ. ℵ. Curss. Verss. (including Vulg. It.) Or. *et al.* : οὐκέτι. Recommended by Griesb., adopted by Lachm. and Tisch. An interpretation in conformity with ver. 10 and xiv. 19. — ὅτι ὑπάγω πρὸς τ. πατ.] is wanting in B. D.
L. Copt. Sahid. Cant. Ver. Verc. Corb. Bracketed by Lachm., deleted by
Tisch. An addition from ver. 17, whence also the ἐγώ in Elz. after ὅτι,—which
ἐγώ, however, is in ver. 17, with Lachm. and Tisch., to be deleted, in conformity with A. B. L. M. Λ. ℵ. Curss. Verss., since it is supported by only very
weak testimony in the above addition in ver. 16. — Ver. 19. After ἔγνω, Elz.
Lachm. have οὖν. A connective addition, instead of which δέ is also found. —
Ver. 20. The second δέ has been justly deleted by Lachm. and Tisch. in conformity with B. D. Λ. ℵ. 1, It. Copt. Arm. Syr. Goth. Cypr. It was added in
mechanical repetition of the antithesis. — Ver. 22. The order νῦν μὲν οὖν λύπ. ἔχ.
is, with Tisch., to be preferred on preponderating testimony. But instead of
ἔχετε, read with Lachm. ἕξετε, after A. D. L. Curss. Verss. Fathers ; the present
was mechanically introduced after ἔχει, ver. 21, and on occasion of the νῦν. —
αἴρει] Lachm. : ἀρεῖ, according to B. D.* Γ. Vulg. Codd. It. Cypr. Hil. Explanatory alteration in accordance with the preceding futures. — Ver. 23. ὅτι
ὅσα ἄν] Many variations. As original appears the reading in A., ὅ τι ἄν (so
Lachm. in the margin), in connection with which copyists were induced,
through the preceding λέγω ὑμῖν, to take OTI (differently from xiv. 13) recita-
tively, which thus led to the readings ἄν τι (so Lachm. and Tisch., comp. xx.
23), ἐάν τι, ὅσα ἄν, and thus the ὅτι, which had now become superfluous, disappeared in many copies (not ℵ., which has ὅτι ὅ ἄν). — ἐν τῷ ὀνόμ. μου] is placed
by Tisch. after δώσει ὑμῖν, in conformity with B. C.* L. X. Y. Δ. ℵ. Sahid. Or.
Cyr. Rightly ; the ordinary position after πατέρα is determined by xiv. 13, xv.

16, and appeared to be required by ver. 24. — Ver. 25. Before ἔρχεται, Elz. and Lachm. (the latter in brackets) have ἀλλ', contrary to important testimony. A connective addition. — Instead of ἀναγγελῶ, ἀπαγγελῶ is, with Lachm. and Tisch., to be adopted on decisive testimony. The former flowed from vv. 13, 14, 15. — Ver. 27. θεοῦ] B. C.* D. L. X. ℵ.** Verss. Cyr. Did. : πατρός. A gloss by way of more precise definition (Verss. have : a deo patre). — Ver. 28. παρά] Lachm. and Tisch. : ἐκ, which is sufficiently attested by B. C.* L. X. Copt. Epiph. Hil. (in D. is wanting ἐξῆλθον . . . πατρός), and, in conformity with what immediately precedes, was dislodged by παρά. — Ver. 29. παῤῥησ.] Lachm. and Tisch. : ἐν παῤῥησ., in conformity with B. C. D. ℵ. Rightly ; ἐν, because unnecessary, after ver. 25, came to be dropped, and the more readily after NYN. — Ver. 32. νῦν] is, in conformity with decisive testimony, with Lachm. and Tisch., to be deleted. — Ver. 33. ἔχετε] So also Tisch. But Elz. Lachm. : ἕξετε only, after D. Verss. (including Vulg. It.) and Fathers. The present is so decisively attested, that the future appears to be simply a closer defining of the meaning (comp. ver. 22).

Ver. 1. Ταῦτα λελάλ. ὑμῖν] As the same expression, xv. 11, pointed back to the preceding section, vv. 1–10, and then ταῦτα ἐντέλλομαι ὑμῖν, ver. 17, to vv. 11–16, so here ταῦτα λελ. ὑμ. refers to xv. 18–27, so that the substantial contents of this section are intended, namely, *that which had been said of the hatred of the world*. — ἵνα μὴ σκανδαλ.] Comp. Matt. xiii. 21, xxiv. 10, xi. 6. Prepared beforehand, and armed by Christ's communications, they were not to be made to stumble at Him, but were to oppose to the hatred of the world all the greater efficiency and constancy of faith.

Vv. 2, 3. Of the ταῦτα, ver. 1, He now gives certain concrete manifestations, which might tend to their becoming offended. — ἀποσυναγ.] See on ix. 22, xii. 42. — ἀλλ'] At, i.e. *nay, yet more !* it introduces the antithesis of a *yet far heavier, of a bloody* fate. Comp. on 2 Cor. vii. 11. To take ἀποσυναγ. ποιήσ. ὑμ. interrogatively (Ewald), is unnecessarily artificial. — ἵνα] *That which* will take place in the ὥρα is conceived as the *object of its coming :* there is coming an hour, in order that, etc. Comp. on xii. 23. — πᾶς ὁ ἀποκτ., κ.τ.λ.] that *every one, who shall have put you to death, may think that he offers a sacrificial service to God* (namely, through the shedding of your blood). On λατρεία, *cultus*,[1] here with προσφέρειν, the standing word for sacrifices (see Matt. v. 23, viii. 4 ; Acts vii. 32 ; Heb. v. 1 ; Schleusner, *Thes.* IV. p. 504), in the special relation of *sacrificial* divine service, comp. Rom. xiii. 1 ; Heb. ix. 1, 6. The maxim of Jewish fanaticism is well known (and how often was the pagan enmity against the apostles no better !) : " Omnis effundens sanguinem improborum, aequalis est illi, qui sacrificium facit."[2] On this δοκεῖν, comp. Saul's example, Acts xxvi. 9 ; Gal. i. 13, 14. — On ver. 3, comp. xv. 21. Jesus once more recalls with *profound sadness* this tragic *source* of such conduct, the inexcusableness of which, however, He had already decisively brought to light (xv. 22 ff.). The supposed purpose of making the adversaries *contemptible* in the eyes of the disciples (Calvin, Hengstenberg) must have been indicated had it existed.

---

[1] Plat. *Apol.* p. 23 C, *Phaedr.* p. 224 E ; Rom. ix. 4.   [2] *Bammidbar Rabba*, f. 329. 1.

Ver. 4. Ἀλλά] *But : breaks off* the enumeration.[1] Jesus will not go further into details, and recurs to the thought in ver. 1. The explanation : "although it is not to be expected otherwise, I have nevertheless foretold it to you" (Lücke, de Wette), is the less agreeable to the text, since ταῦτα λελάλ. had just been already said, and that without any antithetic reference of the kind. The explanations of Tholuck and Lange, again, are far-fetched : "but so little would I terrify (?) you by this, that I have only (?) said it to you," etc. — ταῦτα] What was said in vv. 2, 3. — αὐτῶν, ὅτι ἐγὼ εἶπ. ὑμ.] Attraction.[2] — ἐγώ] with weighty emphasis : *I*, the Person, with whom your faith is concerned. Comp. ver. 1, ἵνα μὴ σκανδαλ. — ἐξ ἀρχῆς] xv. 27. The question, how this declaration of Jesus may be reconciled with the announcements found in the Synoptics, even from the time of the Sermon on the Mount, of predestined sufferings,[3] is not solved by saying that here φοβερώτερα ἐκείνων[4] are announced ;[5] or that Christ spoke at an earlier period *minus aperte et parcius* (Bengel, comp. Grotius), and in much more *general* terms (Ebrard), but now more expressly set forth *in its principles* the character of the world's attitude towards the disciples (Tholuck, comp. Lange) ; or, that He has now stated more definitely the *cause* of the hatred (Lampe) ; or, that He utters it here as a *parting word* (Luthardt) ; or even: that at an earlier period, because the thoughts of the disciples had not yet dwelt upon it, it was "*for them as good as not said*" (Hengstenberg). The difference lies clearly before us, and is simply to be recognized ;[6] to be explained, however, from the fact that in the Synoptics the more general and less definite allusions of the earlier time appear with the more definite form and stamp of later utterances. The living recollection of John must here also preponderate as against the Synoptics, so that his relation to theirs here is that of a corrector. — ὅτι μεθ' ὑμῶν ἤμην] It would have been unnecessary in the time of my personal association with you, since it is not till after my departure that your persecution (up to that time the hatred of the world affected *Himself*) is to commence. "Because you have me with you, they cannot well but leave you in peace, and can do nothing to you, *they must have done it to me previously*, but now it will begin," etc., Luther.[7] As yet they had suffered *no* persecution ; hence the thought, "I could console you,"[8] is not to be introduced. The interpretation also : "now first, when I promise you the Spirit, can I thus openly speak to you" (Bengel, Tholuck), is not in harmony with the words.

Vv. 5, 6. *Now, however*, this my *being with you* is past ! *Now I go away to Him who has sent me, and* in what a mood of mind are you at the prospect of this my impending departure ! *None of you asks me : whither dost Thou go away ?* [See Note LIV. p. 457] *but because I have spoken this to you*, namely, that after my departure such sufferings shall befall you, *grief has filled your*

---

[1] Baeumlein, *Partik.* p. 15.
[2] See Winer, p. 581 f. [E. T. p. 625 ff.].
[3] Matt. v. 10 ff. ; Luke vi. 22 ff. ; Matt. x. 16 ff. ; Lucke xii. 4 ff. ; Matt. xxi. 12 ff., xxiv. 9.
[4] Euth. Zigabenus, comp. also Chrysos-tom.
[5] See, on the contrary, Matt. x. 16–18, 28.
[6] Comp. also Godet.
[7] Comp. Chrysostom, Euth. Zigabenus, Grotius.
[8] Lücke, de Wette, and older expositors.

heart, so that you have become quite dumb from sorrow, and blunted to the higher interest which lies in my going home to Him who sent me. According to de Wette and Lücke, there would seem a *want of exactness in the entire presentation,* resting on the fact that ver. 6 does not stand before καὶ οὐδείς. The incorrectness of this assumption, in itself quite unnecessary, lies in this, that the first proposition of ver. 5 is thus completed : "But now at my departure I could not keep silence concerning it," by which the 6th verse is anticipated. According to Kuinoel and Olshausen, a full point should be placed after πέμψ. με, and a *pause* is to be assumed, in which Jesus in vain awaited a question, so that He continued subsequently *with an interrogation:* "Nullusne vestrum me amplius interrogat, quo abiturus sim ?" But the assumption of pauses (others, including de Wette, make the pause after ver. 5) is, when the correlation of the conjunctions is so definitely progressive, unwarranted. — The fact that already in xiii. 36 the question had been put by Peter ποῦ ὑπάγεις (comp. the question of Thomas, xiv. 5), does not stand in contradiction with the present passage ; but Jesus censures simply the degree of distress, which they had *now* reached, in which *none* among them fixed his eye on the *goal of the departing One,* and could come to a question for more definite information respecting it. — ἡ λύπη] simply, *in abstracto: sadness.*

Ver. 7. *Nevertheless,* how should you raise yourselves above this sorrow ! How is my departure your own gain ! Through it in truth will the Paraclete be imparted to you as a support against the hatred of the world. [See Note LV. p. 457] — ἐγώ] in the consciousness of the personal guarantee. – ἵνα ἐγὼ ἀπέλθω] ἐγώ in contradistinction to the Paraclete, who is to come in His place (xiv. 16) ; ἵνα implies the *divine* necessity, as in xi. 50. On the dependence of the mission of the Paraclete upon the departure of Jesus, see on vii. 39.

Ver. 8.[1] The threefold ministry of the Paraclete towards the unbelieving Jews and Gentiles. *Thus* will He be your advocate against the κόσμος ! — ἐλέγξει] *convict,* namely, through His testimony of me, xv. 26. This *convicting,* of which the apostles were to be the bearers in their office, is the activity which *convinces* the person concerned (*arguendi ratio exprobans*), which reveals to him his unrighteousness, and puts him to shame,[2] and the consequence of which may be in the different subjects either conversion (1 Cor. xiv. 24), or hardening and condemnation (Acts xxiv. 25 ; Rom. xi. 7 ff.). To apprehend it only of the latter side of the matter (Erasmus and many others, including de Wette, Brückner, and especially Wetzel, following the Fathers), is not justified by περὶ κρίσεως, since the κρίσις is intended, not of the world, but of the devil, and stands opposed to the Johannean view of the deliverance of the world through Christ ; the unbelieving world (ver. 9) is to be convicted of the *sin* of unbelief ; and this, to him who is not hardened, is the way to faith (comp. xvii. 20, 21), and therewith to separation from the world. Godet well designates the threefold ἔλεγξις as the

---

[1] See Wetzel, *üb. d. Elenchus des Parakl.* John xvi. 8–13, in the *Zeitschr. f. Luth. Theol.* 1856, p. 624 ff.

[2] iii. 20, viii. 9, 46 ; 1 Cor. xiv. 24 ; Tit. i. 9 ; Matt. xviii. 15 ; Luke iii. 19, *et al.*

moral victory of the Spirit through the preaching of the apostles. As the
first prominent example, see the discourse of Peter, Acts ii., with its consequences. — περὶ ἁμαρτίας, κ.τ.λ.] The objective contents of the ἐλεγξις set
forth separately in three parts (themata). See, respecting the individual
points, on vv. 9–11.

Ver. 9. First part : *in reference to sin* He will convince them. The more
exact defining, *as to how far* He will convince them περὶ ἁμαρτίας ; *so far as
they, namely* (ὅτι, equivalent to εἰς ἐκεῖνο ὅτι, ii. 18, ix. 17, xi. 51), *do not
believe on me,* which He will reveal to them *as sin,* and will bring them to a
consciousness of guilt : ὅτι ἁμαρτάνουσι μὴ πιστεύοντες ἐτι, Euth. Zigabenus.
Following Calvin (comp. already Apollinarius, Ammonius, and also Luther),
de Wette and Brückner (comp. also Ebrard) interpret not of the conviction
of sin, so far as the *unbelief* of the world will be brought to its consciousness *as sin,* but of *sin generally* ("qualis *in se sit hominum natura,*" Calvin),
of the condition under the wrath of God, in which the world, as opposed
to the ever-increasing multitude of believers, who are victorious through the
power of truth, appears involved, *because it does not believe,* for faith is the
bond between the sinful world and God. Comp. Lange, who understands
the rejection of Christ as the essential manifestation of all sin, as also Wetzel and Godet ; which, however, does not correspond to the simplicity of
the words.[1] On the ἐλεγξις of the world περὶ ἁμαρτ., and that with regard
to its converting power, comp. 1 Cor. xiv. 24, 25. Tholuck makes out of
the simple ἁμαρτίας the *guilt* of sin, and that the *unpardonable* (ix. 41). —
Note further that ὅτι is the exponent, not of ἁμαρτίας, but of ἐλέγξει
περὶ ἁμ.

Ver. 10. The second particular : *in reference to righteousness,* thus to the
opposite of ἁμαρτία. As, however, in ἁμαρτίας the subject of the ἐλεγξις is the
world itself, so the subject of δικαιοσύνη is *Christ ;* hence the more exact statement : *in that I go to my Father, and you see me no more ;* δικαίου γὰρ γνώρισμα
τὸ πορεύεσθαι πρὸς τὸν θεὸν κ. συνεῖναι αὐτῷ, Euth. Zigabenus; *righteousness,* since
it thus, in virtue of the context, is necessarily an attribute of *Christ,* denotes
His *guiltlessness and holy moral* perfection. The unbelieving held Him to
be a *sinner* (comp. ix. 24), and put Him to death as such (xviii. 30) ; He was,
however, the *righteous one* (1 John ii. 1, 29, iii. 7 ; comp. Acts iii. 14, vii.
52 ; 1 Pet. iii. 18), and was proved to be such by the testimony of the Paraclete, by whose power the apostles preached the exaltation of Christ to the
Father (comp. Acts ii. 33 ff.), and thus convicting the world as guilty περὶ
δικαιοσύνης, the opposite of which the unbelieving assumed in Christ, and
thought to be confirmed by the *offence* of His cross. So substantially
Chrysostom and his successors, Beza, Maldonatus, Bengel, Morus, Tittmann,
and others, as Lücke, Klee, Olshausen, de Wette, B. Crusius, Maier, Godet,
Baeumlein. Since, after the analogy of the triple division, *Christ* must be
the subject of *righteousness,* we on this ground must at once reject not only the

[1] The sense would be this : in reference
to sin He will convince them that *unbelief
is the true essence of sin.* How easy would
it have been for Jesus to have actually *said*
this! for example, by : περὶ ἁμαρτίας, ὅτι ἡ
ἁμαρτία ἐστὶν ἡ ἀπιστία. And such an expression of the thought assumed would have
been quite Johannean.

interpretation of Grotius of the compensatory *justice of God*,[1] and that of the Socinians and Kuinoel, *quod jus et fas est* (Matt. xii. 15), but also that of Augustine, Erasmus, Luther,[2] Melanchthon, Calvin, Calovius, Jansen, Lampe, Storr, Hengstenberg, and others, who understand the *righteousness of man through faith* in the Pauline sense,[3] which also de Wette (with the modification that it is its victorious power in the world which is spoken of) inappropriately mixes up with the other interpretation. The form given by Luthardt to the interpretation of Augustine, etc., that the passage does not indeed express that Christ has by His departure *acquired* righteousness, but rather has *rendered* righteousness through faith in Himself as unseen, *possible*, is likewise opposed by the fact that Christ would not be the subject of δικαιοσύνη ; and the thought, moreover, is both artificial and inappropriate, since faith in Christ cannot be conditioned by His invisibility, although faith must exist in spite of His invisibility (xx. 29). The thought is rather : "The fact that I go the Father, and shall then be removed from your eyes, will serve to the Spirit in His ἐλεγξις of the world as demonstration that I am δίκαιος."[4] And thus the by no means idle, but tender and sympathetic expression, κ. οὐκέτι θεωρεῖτέ με, as denoting the translation into the invisible world, is an outflow of the thoughtful and feeling *interest* of Jesus in the approaching *pain of separation which the disciples* were to experience, to whom this grief, in view of the higher object of that ἐλεγξις of the world, could not be spared. A reference to the *scorn of the world* to be expected on the removal of Jesus, as if He were thereby to be manifested an impostor,[5] is remote from the connection. De Wette's remark is incorrect : that κ. ὑμεῖς θεωρεῖτέ με was rather to be expected. *That* must have been expected if, with Tholuck, it had to be explained of the *moral purity* (= ζωή) only to be found in Christ, the revelation of which was completed by the spiritual communication of the exalted One, who now may be contemplated *spiritually* instead of bodily. But thus all essential points would be read between the lines.

Ver. 11. If the Paraclete by means of His testimony convinces the world of its sin of unbelief, and of Christ's righteousness, than the *third* ἐλεγξις

---

[1] "Deum aequum esse rectorem, ut qui me extra omnem injuriae contactum in suae majestatis consortium receperit." Comp. also Ewald, *Jahrb.* VIII. p. 199, and *Johann. Schr.* I. p. 381.

[2] " For Christians should know no other righteousness, as the ground of their standing in the sight of God ... than this departure of Christ to the Father, which is nothing else than that He has taken our sins on His neck," etc.

[3] Here also Ebrard's view comes in, who, indeed, considers the Pauline sense of δικαιοσύνη to be remote, but explains it : of the righteousness, *which the world should have and has not*, since it has cast out the Lord, and compelled Him to go to the Father, and to hold intercourse with His

own only in an invisible manner. This interpretation is incorrect, for the reason that, in accordance with it, the ἐλεγξις περὶ δικαιοσύνης would substantially coincide with the ἐλεγξις περὶ ἁμαρτίας. Moreover, the *rejection* of Christ and His invisible *intercourse* with His society is an *imported* meaning.

[4] What Wetzel finds over and above this in the words : that in Christ " *all righteousness rests, and from Him again all righteousness proceeds*," is indeed a correct dogmatic deduction from the present passage, but is not contained in the words themselves as their meaning.

[5] Linder, in the *Stud. u. Krit.* 1867, p. 514 ff.

cannot be wanting, which must refer to *him*, who rules the unbelieving world, and is the original enemy of Christ and His kingdom, to the *devil*. He is *judged*, i.e. *actually condemned*, by the fact that Christ has accomplished His world-redeeming work, whereby in truth every one who becomes a believer is withdrawn from the sway of the devil, so that his cause in and with the fulfilment of the redemptive work is objectively a *lost* one. Comp. on xii. 30, 31. *Of this* the Paraclete will rebukingly convict the world, dependent on the dominion of the devil, in order that the world, in acknowledgment of the sinfulness of its unbelief (ver. 9), and of the holy righteousness of the Christ rejected by it (ver. 10), may turn its back in penitence on the prince of the world, over whom already sentence has been pronounced (ver. 10). Thus, through the apostolic preaching is accomplished on the κόσμος the *officium Spiritus s. elenchticum.*

NOTE.—The three more precise statements with ὅτι (vv. 9–11) express the relations from the standpoint of the *presence of the speaker*. Hence, in ver. 9, the present πιστεύουσιν (which was altered at a very early period—so Vulg. and It. —into ἐπίστευσαν) ; hence also in ver. 10 the *present* ὑπάγω and the *second* person θεωρεῖτε, because Jesus is speaking to the *disciples*, and it is in fact His departure from *them* which is filling His mind, which lively directness of style de Wette unjustly criticises as surprisingly inappropriate ; hence, finally, in ver. 11 the *perfect* κέκριται, because Jesus sees Himself at the end of His work, and therewith the actual condemnation of Satan already completed and secured. Comp. ver. 33.

Ver. 12. Jesus breaks off, and states the reason. — πολλά] Much, that belongs to the entirety of the divine ἀλήθεια (ver. 13). That He means only *further developments* (Luther, Melanchthon, and many others, including Lücke, de Wette), is not to be deduced (see *in loc.*) from xv. 15, comp. xiv. 26. Nevertheless, the portions of doctrine themselves, which may belong to the πολλά, although they are in general to be sought for in the letters and discourses of the apostles, cannot be completely determined ; but neither are they, with Grotius (comp. Beza), to be limited to the " cognitio corum, quae *ad ecclesias constituendas* pertinent" (spirituality of the kingdom of Christ, abolition of the law, apostolic decrees), because we are not fully acquainted with the instructions of Jesus to His disciples. In general, it is certain that information respecting the further development of His work, and particularly matters of knowledge which, as history attests, still necessitated special revelation, as the immediate calling of the Gentiles, Acts x., and eschatological disclosures like 1 Cor. xv. 51, Rom. xi. 25, 1 Thess. iv. 15 ff., form *part* of their contents. The non-apostolical Apocalypse (against Hengstenberg and others), as likewise the ἀποκαλύψεις granted to Christian prophets in the N. T., are here, where Jesus is concerned with the circle of *apostles*, left out of consideration. Augustine, however, is already correct generally : " cum Christus ipse ea tacuerit, quis nostrum dicat : illa vel illa sunt ?"˗ Since, however, we cannot demonstrate that even the oral instruction of the *apostles* was completely deposited in their writings (especially as undoubted epistles are lost, while very few of the original apostles left behind them any

writing), *Tradition* in and of itself (*in thesi*) cannot be rejected, although its
reality in regard to given cases (*in hypothesi*) can never be proved, and it must
therefore remain generally without normative validity.¹ In opposition to tradition, Luther limited the *many things*, in entire contradiction of the context,
to the *sufferings* that were to be endured. — ἐχω]I have in readiness, viii. 6 ; 2
John 12 ; 3 John 13. — βαστάζειν] That which is too *heavy*, for the spiritual
strength, for understanding, temper, strength of will, cannot be *borne*.² On
the thing : 2 Cor. iii. 2. Note, further, Bengel's appropriate remark, to
the effect that the Romish traditions can least be borne by those who have
the Spirit. — ἀρτι] at the end, as in xiii. 33.

Ver. 13. Τὸ πν. τ. ἀλ.] See on xiv. 17. — ὁδηγ. ὑμ. εἰς τ. ἀλ. πᾶσαν] *He will
be to you a guide into all the truth.* Comp. ver. 23 ; πᾶσαν, in its position
after τ. ἀλ. (see critical notes), does not belong to the verb, as if it expressed
the *complete introduction* (Lücke), but describes, as in v. 22, divine truth in its
entirety, according to its collective contents.³ As to the thought, πᾶσαν τὴν
ἀλήθειαν, Mark v. 33,⁴ would not be different ; but the present construction
makes ἀλήθεια *more prominent.* — οὐ γάρ, κ.τ.λ.] Reason, from the origin and
compass of His communications. — ἀφ' ἑαυτοῦ] αὐτοκέλευστος, ἀνήκοος, Nonnus.
This negative statement is, indeed, the denial of anything conceived of
after a human manner, which is absolutely out of the question,⁵ but serves
completely to set forth the unity of the Spirit's teaching with that of the
Lord.⁶ Comp. v. 19. — ὅσα ἂν ἀκούσῃ] *All, whatsoever He shall have heard
from God,* so that He will withhold from you nothing of that which has
been divinely heard by Him.⁷ The Spirit, however, hears from God not externally as a Subject separated from God, but (comp. 1 Cor. ii. 11) through
an *interna* acceptio ; for He is in God, and proceeds from Him, xv. 26.
That the hearing from *God*, not from *Christ*,⁸ is meant, is to be assumed on
account of the *absolute* ἀκούσῃ, and ver. 15 renders it certain. On ἀκούσῃ
itself, comp. also Luther : Faith must make its way universally over all
creatures, and not cleave to thoughts of listening to bodily preaching, but
lay hold of a preaching, word, and hearing *in essence.*" — τὰ ἐρχόμενα] So
that you, through the revelation of the Spirit, will also become acquainted
with the *future*,⁹ the knowledge of which belongs to the whole ἀλήθεια (particularly the eschatological developments).¹⁰ Finally, τὰ ἐρχόμενα belongs
also to that denoted by ὅσα ἂν ἀκούσῃ, and is related to it as species to genus,

---

¹ Comp. on 1 Cor. xi. 34.
² Comp. Kypke, I. p. 404 f.
³ Comp. v. 22: τ. κρίσιν πᾶσαν, Plat.
Theaet. p. 147 E, τὸν ἀριθμὸν πάντα δίχα διελά-
βομεν ; Krüger, § 50. 11. 11.
⁴ Krüger on *Thuc.* vi. 87. 1.
⁵ "Spiritus enim, qui a semet ipso loquitur, non spiritus veritatis, sed spiritus est
mendacii," Ruperti ; comp. already Ignatius, *ad Eph. interpol.* 9.
⁶ "Consequently He sets, for the Holy
Spirit Himself, a goal and measure of His
preaching, that He shall preach nothing
new nor different from that which Christ
and His word is, so that we may have a

certain mark of truth and touchstone, to
judge of false spirits," Luther.
⁷ When Godet says, on ver. 13: " *The
word in* xiv. 26 *included the formula of the
inspiration of our Gospels ; ver.* 13 *gives that
of the inspiration of the Epistles and of the
Apocalypse,*" the simple addition must be
made, "*in so far as* and *to the extent in
which* these writings are actually *apostolic.*"
⁸ Olshausen, Kling, B. Crusius, Luthardt,
Hengstenberg, Godet : from both.
⁹ ἁ δ' ἐρχομένα μοῖρα, Soph. *Trach.* 846.
¹⁰ Comp. Isa. xli. 22, 23, xliv. 7, xlv. 11 :
τὰ ἐπερχόμενα.

so that καί *brings into relief* from that which is general, something further
that is particular.

Vv. 14, 15. For *me*, with a view to glorify *me* (ἐμέ, with emphasis), will
the Paraclete, as is said in ver. 13, operate, for the advancement of *my* glory
among men, since He will announce to you nothing else than what is *mine*,
what in the identity of its substance is *my* truth, of which *I* am the
possessor and disposer.[1] Justly do I designate the *divine* truth, which He
is to announce, as *my* property, since all that the *Father* has, *i.e.* according
to the context, *the whole truth possessed by the Father* (Col. ii. 3), belongs
properly *to me*, as to the Son, who was in intuitive fellowship with the
Father (i. 18), went forth from the Father (viii. 42), was consecrated (x.
36) and sent for the accomplishment of His work, and, moreover, continually lives and moves in the Father, and the Father in Him. Comp. xvii. 10.
Calvin, in opposition to the *ontological* interpretation, well observes, that
Christ speaks : " de *injuncto sibi erga nos efficio.*" Note further, the emphatic, all-embracing πάντα ὅσα, κ.τ.λ., as major premiss in the argument from
the universal to the particular ; hence all the less is ver. 14 to be referred,
with Grotius and Hengstenberg, merely to the announcement of what is
future. — λαμβάνει] Conceived as a *constant* relation.

Ver. 16. *Soon*, after a *short* separation, will this arrival of the Paraclete,
and in it our spiritual reunion, take place. Comp. xiv. 19. — κ. ὄψεσθέ με] As
in xiv. 18, 19, not to be referred to the *resurrection*[2] [See Note LVI. p. 457],
nor to the *Parousia*,[3] but to the *spiritual* vision of Christ in the ministry of
the Paraclete, which they experience, and that without any double meaning.
See on xiv. 18. — Were ὅτι ὑπάγω πρὸς τ. πατ. genuine (but see the critical
notes), it would assign the reason for the promise ὄψεσθέ με, since the seeing
again here intended is *conditioned* by the departure to the Father (ver. 7).

Vv. 17, 18. Jesus makes a pause ; some of His disciples (ἐκ τ. μαθ. αὐτ. sc.
τινές, as in vii. 40) express (in a whisper) to one another, how enigmatic
this language, ver. 16, is to them. They indicate, accordingly (ver. 18), the
μικρόν that was mentioned as the point of unintelligibility : " what shall
this be, what does He mean by μικρόν ? " Note τοῦτο placed first with emphasis,
as well as the article with μικρόν, pointing backwards. — καὶ ὅτι ὑπάγω πρ. τ.
πατ.] ὅτι is recitative. Since the words in ver. 16 are not genuine, we must
assume that the disciples place what Jesus said in ver. 10, in connection
with these enigmatic words, ver. 16, and *here* include along with it the
point *there* expressed in their seeing Him no more :—ὑπάγω πρ. τ. πατ. —
in order to receive an explanation regarding it, probably feeling that this

---

[1] Every claim that anything belongs to
what Christ terms τὰ ἐμοῦ must necessarily,
according to the *analogia fidei*, be measured
by His and His disciples' extant *word ;*
hence the present passage, in like manner,
as ver. 13, excludes all the pretended claims
of fanaticism.

[2] As Lange, Ebrard, Hengstenberg, Ewald,
Weiss still maintain, in spite of ver. 23,
comp. with Acts i. 5, 6.

[3] The πάλιν μικρόν, which decidedly opposes this interpretation, because it is entirely unrelated to the first μικρόν, leads
Luthardt to the supposition that the return
of Christ is here promised to the disciples
in such a way, that they were to see in the
transitory return of the *risen one* a pledge
of the future *Parousia*. But of this Jesus
certainly says nothing, either here or in
what follows.

explanation must necessarily serve for the clearing up of the obscure words before them.

Ver. 19. Jesus observes what they would ask (comp. vi. 6), and extracts from them (as one who knows the heart, ii. 25 ; see subsequently ver. 30) the inquiry, not, however, setting aside the point, which they had also introduced from His earlier discourse (ὑπάγω πρ. τ. π.) but deferring it till the solemn conclusion of His instruction, ver. 28.

Vv. 20–22. He gives no explanation of the meaning, but depicts the *alternation of sorrow and joy*, which the not seeing and seeing again will bring with them. In this way they might, with the correct *apprehension* and *hope*, advance towards the approaching development. — κλαύσετε κ. θρηνήσ. ὑμεῖς] *ὑμεῖς* with peculiar emphasis, moved to the end, and placed immediately before ὁ δὲ κόσμ. The mourning and lamentation, this loud outburst of the λύπη of the disciples over the death of Jesus (not : " over the church of Christ given up to death," Luthardt), becomes yet more tragic through the contrast of the joy of the world. — εἰς χαρὰν γενήσεται] *will be turned into joy*, namely, when that ὄψεσθέ με takes place. — Ver. 21. ἡ γυνή] *the woman ;* the article is *generic*, comp. ὁ δοῦλος, xv. 15. — ὅταν τίκτῃ] *when she is bringing forth.* — ἡ ὥρα αὐτῆς] her hour of distress, ὥρα βαρυώδινος, Nonnus. Comp. afterwards τῆς θλίψεως, which denotes the distress during the occurrence of birth. — ἄνθρωπος] *a man*. In this lies a *self-consciousness* of maternal joy. — εἰς τὸν κόσμ.] born and therewith come *into the world* (i. 9, xviii. 37). An appeal to the Rabbinical בּוֹא בְּעוֹלָם is not required. — The picture of the *woman bringing forth*, to set forth the sorrow which issues in joy, is also frequent in the O. T. (Isa. xxi. 3, xxvi. 17, lxvi. 7 ; Hos. xiii. 13 ; Mic. iv. 9, 10). Its importance in the present passage Jesus Himself states, ver. 22, definitely and clearly, and in regard to it no further exposition is to be attempted. In accordance with this view, the grief and the joy of the *disciples* is the *sole* thing depicted, not also the passing of Christ through death to life (Brückner), as the birth of the new fellowship for the disciples, and the like. There is much arbitrary interpretation in Chrysostom, Apollinaris, Theophylact, Euth. Zigabenus, Ruperti, and several others, including Olshausen, according to whom the *death of Christ* is said to appear as the *sorrowful birth-act of humanity*, out of which the God-man comes forth, glorified to the eternal joy of the whole ; even in de Wette the living Christ is subjectively a child of the spiritual productivity of the disciples. Similarly Tholuck, also Lange, in conformity with his explanation of Christ's *resurrection*, understanding this as involving the birth of the new humanity out of the birth-sorrow of the theocracy ; comp. Ebrard, who finds depicted the resurrection of the Lord as the birth of the church, which is begotten and suckled from His heavenly life. And further, since the *Parousia* is not referred to, and the *you*, ver. 22, are the *disciples*, we must not, with Luthardt, explain it of the *passing of the church into the state of glorification* at the future coming of Christ (Rev. xxi. 4), so that the church is to be thought of as " bringing forth in its death-throes the new state of things. — Ver. 22. According to the amended reading (see the critical notes) : *you also will thus* (corresponding to this παρουσία) *now indeed* (over my death, which is immedi-

ately impending) *have sorrow ; but again I shall see you*, etc. That here
Christ does not again say ὄψεσθέ με, as in ver. 19, is only a change in the
correlate designation of the same fact (Godet's explanation is an artificial
refinement), which, expressed in vv. 19 and 22 under both its aspects,
is, by means of vv. 23 and 25, obviously designated, neither as the *Parousia*,[1] nor as the return by the *resurrection*, or at least as taking its beginning from this (see on xiv. 18), but as the *communication of the Paraclete*.
The exalted Christ, returning to them in the Holy Ghost, *sees them again*.
— αἴρει] represents the certain future as present. Climax of the representation. Then your joy will be *incapable of being taken from you*, on account
of the renewed fellowship, like this fellowship itself (Matt. xxviii. 20).

Vv. 23, 24. Happy result of this spiritual reunion in reference to the disciples' official relationship : *illumination—granting of prayer.* — ἐν ἐκείνῃ τ.
ἡμ.] On the day that I shall again be seen by you (spiritually), not : "If
the disciples shall spiritually have given birth in themselves to the living
Christ" (de Wette) ; not : on the never-ending day which is to begin with
Easter in their souls (Lange), to which the interpretations of Ebrard and
Hengstenberg also substantially amount, comp. Brückner.— ἐμὲ οὐκ ἐρωτ.
οὐδέν] Because, the enlightenment through the *Paraclete* will secure you so
high a sufficiency of divine knowledge, that you would have no need to
question *me* (note the emphatic ἐμέ) about anything (as hitherto has been
the case so frequently and so recently, ver. 19). The discourse of Peter,
Acts ii. 14 ff., is a living testimony of this divine certainty here promised,
which took the place of the want of understanding.[2] Chrysostom, Grotius,
and several others, including Weizsäcker and Weiss, incorrectly take ἐρωτ.
to mean *pray*. Comp. vv. 19, 30.— ἀμὴν ἀμήν, κ.τ.λ.] The further good to
be promised is introduced with emphatic asseveration in the consciousness
of its great importance. — In adopting the reading δώσει ὑμῖν ἐν τῷ ὀνόμ. μου
(see the critical notes), we must explain : He will give it you, *in virtue of
my name*, by its power as the *determining motive*,[3] because you have not
prayed otherwise than in my name (see on xiv. 13). The interpretation :
in my stead (Weiss), yields a paradoxical idea, and has opposed to it ver.
24. — ἕως ἄρτι, κ.τ.λ.] Because, that is, the higher illumination was wanting
to you, which belongs thereto, and which will be imparted to you through
the medium of the Paraclete only after my departure. You are wanting up
to this time in the spiritual ripeness and maturity of age for such praying,
as the highest grade of prayer that may be heard. This reason appears in

---

[1] In interpreting it of the *Parousia*, the
assumption is forced on one, that with
ἀμήν, ἀμήν λέγω, κ.τ.λ., a new section of the
discourse commences, which refers to the
intermediate time until the Parousia. See
especially Luthardt and Lechler, p. 225.
This is certainly opposed, and decisively,
by the ἐν ἐκείνῃ τ. ἡμέρᾳ, ver. 26, which is
solemnly repeated, and points back to ver.
23. And the above assumption is, in and
of itself, entirely arbitrary. Comp. the

ἀμήν, κ.τ.λ., ver. 20. In interpreting it of
the *Resurrection*, Ebrard sees himself necessitated to give to οὐκ ἐρωτήσ. οὐδέν the limitation : *in the sense of* ver. 19. A pure importation.

[2] Scholten's view is a misunderstanding
of an enthusiastic kind, to the effect that
this saying overthrows the entire Protestant principle of Scripture.

[3] Winer, p. 362 [E. T. p. 390].

454 THE GOSPEL OF JOHN.

harmony with the text from the reciprocal relation of ἐν ἐκείνῃ τ. ἡμέρᾳ and ἕως ἄρτι, if we note that by ἐμὲ οὐκ ἐρωτ. οὐδέν that very divine clearness and certainty is expressed, which is still wanting to them ἕως ἄρτι. The reason, therefore, is not to be determined in this wise, that Christ had not yet been glorified (Luthardt), and had accordingly not yet become to the disciples that which He was to become.[1] — ἵνα] Divinely ordained object of the λήψεσθε. — ἡ χαρὰ ὑμ.] Ver. 22. It is to be *filled up*, *i.e.* to be complete, that nothing may be wanting to it. Comp. xv. 11. There is thus *fulfilled* in the disciples, after their reception of the Spirit through the granting of their prayers, the consolatory picture of the bearing woman in her joy after the sorrow she has surmounted. Luthardt also transposes vv. 23, 24 into the time *before* the last future ; but necessitated to this, he should *not* have referred ver. 16 ff. to the Parousia.

Ver. 25. Ταῦτα] that, namely, after which the disciples, in vv. 17, 18, had asked, and what He Himself, ver. 20 ff., had more fully carried out ; that, consequently, which had been spoken of His departure and of His being seen again, and its circumstances and consequences. He has uttered this in improper, allegorical expressions (ἐν παροιμ., comp. on x. 6, and on the generic plur., Mark xii. 1), proportioned to their capacity of comprehension ; but when the hour of the fulfilment of the promise of the Paraclete shall have arrived, He will then, and that through the Paraclete, no longer speak to them under such sensuous veils of thought, but without circumlocution, and directly, frankly and freely (παρρησίᾳ, adverbial instrumental dative, as in xi. 14), give them tidings of the Father. In answer to Luthardt, who refers ταῦτα to all that was previously said, including the discourse on the vine (comp. also Godet), xvi. 1 is decisive, and the fact that before ver. 19 the *disciples* have spoken.

Vv. 26, 27. Ἐν ἐκ. τ. ἡμ. ἐν τῷ ὀν. μ. αἰτήσ.] Because enlightened by the Paraclete. Comp. ver. 24. Bengel's remark is apt : "Cognitio parit orationem," and that, the prayer to be heard in the name of Jesus.[2] — καὶ οὐ λέγω, κ.τ.λ.] *and I say not*, etc. ; I should therewith promise something for that coming time that may be dispensed with. For on my part (ἐγώ) an intercession on your behalf in order to the hearing of these your prayers will not at all be needed, because, that is, they are precisely prayers *in my name* (see on xiv. 14). The opposite meaning is deduced by Aretius, Grotius, Wolf, Rosenmüller, Kuinoel : that οὐ λέγω ὑμ. means : *I will not mention at all*, so that the intercession is thus designated as a matter of course. Against this the following αὐτὸς γάρ, κ.τ.λ., is decisive. There is no contradiction, however, with xiv. 16, xvii. 9, since in these places the intercession of Christ belongs to the time *prior* to the communication of the Paraclete. — αὐτός] *ipse*, from the proper divine impulse of love, without the need of my intercessory mediation. — φιλεῖ] "*amat vos*, adeoque vos exaudit," Bengel. The present tense represents the future as present. They have then the

[1] Hofmann, *Schriftbew.* II. 2, p. 358, comp. Hengstenberg.
[2] "For thou comest not in thine own name, work, or merit, but on this, that it is announced to thee by the Holy Spirit what God's will and command is, which He has performed through Christ," Luther.

πνεῦμα υἱοθεσίας, Rom. viii. 15 ; Gal. iv. 6 ; along with which, however, the intercession intended in 1 John ii. 1, Heb. vii. 25, Rom. viii. 34, on the part of the exalted Jesus, is not excluded. This intercession is not required in order to the hearing of prayer, if it is made in virtue of the Spirit in the name of Jesus, but rather generally in order to the continued efficacy of the atonement on behalf of believers. — The reason of that αὐτὸς . . . φιλεῖ ὑμᾶς is : ὅτι ὑμεῖς, κ.τ.λ. : "for He will not thus remove Himself out of the midst, that they should pray without and exclusive of Him," Luther. Note ὑμεῖς ἐμέ : because *ye* are they who have loved *me*. πεφιλ. is *placed first* as the correlate of φιλεῖ ; and with logical correctness, since faith, in this definiteness of development (ὅτι . . . ἐξῆλθον), could in its progress gradually unfold itself only in their loving union with Christ, through the exercise and experience of this love. On the *perfects*, as the presents of the completed act, Bengel says, and rightly : "amore et fide prehensum habetis." Hofmann[1] incorrectly explains them from the standpoint of the Parousia, from which a glance is taken backwards to the love that has been borne to the close. The entire promise has nothing to do with the Parousia ; see on vv. 16, 22, xiv. 18. — ἐξῆλθον] See on viii. 42.

Ver. 28. With ἐξῆλθον, solemnly, and with still more definite precision by means of ἐκ τοῦ πατρός, a fresh confirmation of these fundamental contents of faith is commenced, and the return to the Father is subjoined,— and with this a conclusion is made with the same thought,—now, however, through the intervening explanatory clauses, brought nearer to the understanding of the disciples—from which the whole discussion, vv. 16, 17, took its rise. A simple and grand summary of His entire personal life.

Vv. 29, 30. The disciples, aroused, nay, astonished (ἴδε), by the clearness of the last great declaration, now find the teachings contained in vv. 20–28 so opened to their understanding, and thereby the enigmatical character of vv. 16, 17 so solved, that they judge, even *now*, that in this instruction just communicated He speaks so openly and clearly, so entirely without allegorical disguise, that He is *at the present time* doing for them (not merely a *prelude* thereof, as Hengstenberg tones down the meaning) that, for the attainment of which He had in ver. 25 pointed them to a *future* hour. But as He, by this teaching in vv. 20–28, had anticipated (ver. 19) the *questions* which they, according to vv. 16, 17, had upon their heart, they are also in this respect so surprised, that they at the same time feel certain that He knows all things, and needs not first to be inquired of, since He replies unasked to the questions on which information was desired ; hence the *future* things promised by Him in the words ἐν ἐκείνῃ to οὐδέν, ver. 23, may likewise already exist as *present*, on account of His unlimited knowledge. "Exultant ergo ante tempus perinde acsi quis nummo uno aureo divitem se putaret" (Calvin) ; but however incomplete their understanding was as yet, it was sufficient for them to experience a deep and vivid impression therefrom, and to lead up to the expression of the decided confession of faith, ἐν τούτῳ πιστεύομεν, κ.τ.λ. Augustine exaggerates when he says : "Illi usque

---

[1] *Schriftbew.* II. 1, p. 543.

adeo non intelligunt, ut nec saltem se non intelligere intelligant. Parvuli enim erant." Schweizer has very arbitrarily declared ver. 30 to be spurious ; but Lange maintains that the disciples regarded a ray of light from the Spirit, which they now received as the beginning of an uninterrupted holiday of the Spirit. This is by no means to be established by ἐν τούτῳ, κ.τ.λ. — Ver. 29. νῦν] *Now*, what thou first didst promise as *future*, ver. 25. — Ver. 30. νῦν] What we, according to thy declaration, ver. 23, should first become aware of *at a future time*. The obvious retrospective reference, given in the words themselves that are employed, of ver. 29 to ver. 25, and of ver. 30 to ver. 23, is neither to be concealed nor denied. — ἵνα] as in ii. 25. — ἐν τούτῳ] *propter hoc*, Acts xxiv. 16. Comp. ἐν ᾧ, *quoniam* (Fritzsche, *ad Rom*. II. p. 93). ἐν denotes causal dependence (Bernhardy, p. 211). Not now commences their faith, that (ὅτι) Christ came forth from God (see ver. 27), nor do they now first believe it *because* of His omniscience ; but for their *existing* faith in His divine origin they recognize in this discovered omniscience a new and peculiar *ground of certainty ;* comp. on ii. 11. Lange erroneously explains ὅτι as *because ;* " in this our faith is rooted, *because* Thou," etc. The procession of Christ from His pre-human existence with God was indeed not the *ground* of faith (this were His words and works, xiv. 10, 11, x. 38), but the grand *subject* of faith (ver. 27, xvii. 8, xx. 31). Comp. 1 John iv. 2, 3 ; 2 John 7. According to Ewald, ἐν τούτῳ would express that *in which* they believe, namely, in the fact *that* (ὅτι), etc. But John never designates the object of faith by ἐν (Mark i. 15) ; he would probably have written τοῦτο πιστ. (xi. 26).

Vv. 31, 32. Since ἄρτι must bear the emphasis, and since Jesus could not and would not doubt of [1] the faith of the disciples *at this moment*, ἄρτι πιστ. is not to be taken *interrogatively* [2] (according to the analogy of i. 51, xiii. 38, xx. 29), but *concessively :* " *Now, just now*, ye believe, but how soon will ye become vacillating !" [3] The faith itself did not pass away (hence there is no contradiction to ver. 27, comp. Luke xxii. 32), but it did not stand the test of self-denial and of heroism. This must first appear in the school of conflict and experience. — καὶ ἐλήλυθεν] so immediately at hand is it. — ἵνα] See on ver. 2. — εἰς τὰ ἴδια] *into His own, i.e.* His own place of residence. [4] Opposite of the κοινωνία, which is thus rent asunder. [5] On the prediction itself comp. Matt. xxvi. 31, and on its fulfilment xxvi. 56. — καί] The emphatic *and* . . ., which (with a pause to be supplied in thought) unexpectedly introduces the contrast. See on vii. 28. — οὐκ εἰμὶ μόνος, κ.τ.λ.] The calm,

---

[1] " He will not punish them nor discountenance them, as those who are as yet weak and without understanding, but answers them in the most friendly manner, as though He should say : " Ye are good pious children, you may probably imagine that you understand and believe, and it is indeed true that you now believe, as you in truth acknowledge from the heart that He went forth from God (which is ever the true faith), but ye know not how it will go, and how weak your faith is," etc., Luther.

[2] With Euth. Zigabenus, Calvin, Wetstein, and several others, including Kuinoel, Olshausen, de Wette, B. Crusius, Tischendorf, Hengstenberg, Ewald.

[3] οἱ λέγοντες πιστεύειν φεύξεσθε μικρὸν ὕστερον, κινηθείσης ὑμῶν ὑπὸ τοῦ φόβου τῆς πίστεως, Apollinaris.

[4] xix. 27 ; Plat. *Pol.* 8, p. 543 B.

[5] ἀπόσσυτος ἄλλος ἀπ' ἄλλου, Nonnus, comp. Plat. *Gorg.* p. 502 E : ἕνεκα τοῦ ἰδίου τοῦ αὐτῶν ὀλιγωροῦντες τοῦ κοινοῦ.

clear self-consciousness, elevated above all human desertion, of the Father's protection, comp. viii. 29. The *momentary* feeling which appears in Matt. xxvii. 46 is not in conflict with this.

Ver. 33. "This is the last word given, and struck into their hand by way of good-night. But He concludes very forcibly with that for which he has made the entire discourse," Luther. — ταῦτα] pointing back, at the close of the whole discourses again resumed from xiv. 31, to chap. xv. 16. — ἐν ἐμοὶ εἰρήνην . . . ἐν τῷ κόσμῳ θλῖψιν] exact correlates : *in me* (living and moving), *i.e.* in vital fellowship with me : *Peace*, rest of soul, peace of heart (comp. xiv. 27) ; *in the world, i.e.* in your intercourse with the unbelieving ; *affliction* (xvi. 21, and see xv. 18 ff.). — ἐγώ] Luther aptly remarks : "He does not say : "Be comforted, *you* have overcome the world ; but this is your consolation, that *I, I* have overcome the world ; *my* victory is your salvation." And upon *this* victor rests the imperishability of the church. — νενίκ τ. κόσμ.] The Perf. declares the victory immediately impending, which is to be gained through His glorification by means of death, already completed. Prolepsis of the certain conqueror on the boundary of His work. Comp. xii. 31, xiii. 31. But if *He* has overcome the anti-Messianic power of the world, how could *His own*, in spite of all affliction, become disheartened, as though He would give up His work, which was to be continued through them, and suffer His victory to fall to the ground ? Comp. rather 1 John v. 4, 5, iv. 4. Therefore *take away*. *Paul* especially is a living commentary on this θαρσεῖν. See *e.g.* Rom. viii. 37 ; 2 Cor. ii. 14, iv. 7 ff., vi. 4 ff., xii. 9, his discourse before Felix and Festus, etc. Comp. Luther's triumphant exposition.

NOTES BY AMERICAN EDITOR.

LIV. Ver. 5.

Νῦν δέ is not here, as often in John and elsewhere, logical, *but as it is ;* but strictly temporal, *but now. — And none of you asketh me.* Generally taken as implying some censure, because they are not more ready to question him. Weiss holds that, because of the clear declarations already made, there was no room for further questioning, and the Saviour's only meaning can be : You have no need of questioning ; you know, each of you, whither I go.

LV. " *It is expedient for you.*" Ver. 7.

Meyer: because the Spirit assures to them aid against the hating world. Weiss: on account of His agency in the world, which Christ proceeds, in the following words, to unfold. Better still, perhaps, on account of the Spirit's entire ministry, both in the disciples and in the world, which makes His coming more than a compensation for the personal presence of Christ.

LVI. " *And yet a little while, and ye shall see me.*" Ver. 16.

Meyer makes this renewed vision refer, not to Christ's reappearance in the resurrection or in the Parousia, but to the spiritual vision of Christ in the ministry of the Paraclete. Weiss dissents, and maintains (with Lange, Ebr.

Hengst. Ew.) that it can refer only to his bodily reappearance after the resurrection. So again in ver. 20, according to Weiss the sorrow and mourning
of the disciples over the death of Jesus are turned into joy on His reappearance ;
while Meyer refers the change to the coming of the Paraclete. Granting Weiss's
rendering mainly correct, it should not, I think, be too closely pressed ; the
whole series of events hangs together, from the wailing of the disciples at the
crucifixion, passing over into the ultimate glory of the Parousia, and the corresponding change from exultation to sorrow in the emotions of the world.

CHAPTER XVII.

Ver. 1. ἐπῆρε] B. C.* D. L. X. ℵ. Curss. Or. Cyr. : ἐπάρας without the following καί. So Lachm. Tisch. A frequently-occurring improvement of the style.
In like manner is the reading τελειώσας, ver. 4, instead of ἐτελείωσα to be regarded. — ἵνα καί] καί is condemned by decisive witnesses. — Ver. 3. γινώσκωσι]
Tisch. : γινώσκουσιν, following A. D. G. L. Y. Δ. Λ. An error in transcription,
instead of which Lachm., following B. C. E. ℵ., has rightly retained the conjunctive. — Ver. 4. Between the forms δέδωκα and ἔδωκα, the Codd. in this chap.
vacillate in various ways. — Ver. 7. ἐστίν] Tisch. : εἰσίν, according to preponderant evidence. The *Recepta* is an attempted improvement. — Ver. 11. Instead
of ᾧ Elz. has οὕς, against decisive witnesses. The too weakly attested reading
ὅ (D.* U. X.), which is a resolution of the attraction, testifies also in favour of
ᾧ. — Ver. 12. ἐν τῷ κόσμῳ] after αὐτῶν, is wanting in the majority of witnesses ;
deleted by Lachm. and Tisch. An addition after ver. 11. — Instead of οὕς,
Tisch. has ᾧ, according to B. C.* L. Mechanical repetition from ver. 11. —
Ver. 16. The position of οὐκ εἰμί after ἐγώ (Lachm. Tisch.) is decisively attested.
— Ver. 17. After ἀλήθεια the Edd., except Lachm., have σου, which must be
deleted on the decisive testimony of A. B. C.* D. L. 1, Vulg. It. Goth. Sahid.
Cyr. Did. Ambr. Aug. A more definite exegetical definition in accordance
with what follows. Bengel aptly remarks in his *Appar.*: "persaepe *veritas*
apud Joh . . . nunquam additur *Dei.*" — Ver. 19. The order ὦσιν καὶ αὐτοί
(Lachm. Tisch.) is decisively attested. — Ver. 20. Instead of πιστευόντων Elz.
has πιστευσόντων, contrary to decisive testimonies. — Ver. 21. ἐν ἡμῖν ἓν ὦσιν] B.
C.* D. Codd. of It. Sahid. Arm. Ath. Hil. Vig. Tisch. have merely ἐν ἡμῖν ὦσιν.
Lachm. has ἓν in brackets. This ἓν is a glossematic addition. — Ver. 23. καὶ
ἵνα] B. C. D. L. X. Curss. Verss. Fathers have merely ἵνα. καί is rightly deleted
by Lachm. and Tisch. An interpolation irrelevant to the connection, made
without attending to the construction of ver. 21. — Ver. 24. οὕς] B. D. ℵ. Copt.
Goth. Vulg. ms. : ὅ. So Tisch. Considering the weighty attestation, and that
οὕς very readily suggested itself as an improvement, ὅ must be regarded as the
original reading. Comp. on ver. 11.

[See Note LVII. p. 476.] Vv. 1, 2.[1] The parting discourses to the disciples are finished, and that with the words, giving assurance of victory, ἐγὼ
νενίκ. τ. κόσμ. But now, before Jesus goes forth into the fatal night, as He
casts a parting glance on His disciples, who are standing there ready to
depart (xiv. 31), and on the whole future of His work, now to be completed for the earth, His communion with the Father impels Him to *prayer*.
He prays aloud (ver. 13) and long, on His own behalf (vv. 1–5), on behalf of
His disciples (vv. 6–19), and on behalf of those who are to become believers
at a later time (vv. 20 ff.), with all the depth, intensity, clearness, and re-

---

[1] Luther's exposition of chap. xvii. belongs to the year 1534.

pose of the moral need and the childlike devotion of the Fulfiller. Because He, by this prayer, prepares Himself for the high-priestly act of the atoning self-sacrifice (see especially ver. 19), it is justly termed the *precatio summi sacerdotis* (Chytraeus), an appellation which is arbitrarily explained by Hengstenberg from the Aaronic blessing (Lev. ix. 22 ; Num. vi. 22 ff.). Luther aptly says : "that He might fully discharge His office as our sole high priest." — ταῦτα ἐλάλησεν . . . καὶ . . . καί] Not negligence of style (de Wette), but solemn circumstantiality. — εἰς τ. οὐρ.] does not establish the point that Jesus spoke *in the open air* (see on xiv. 31 ; so Ruperti, Grotius, Ebrard, Hengstenberg, and many others), nor necessitates the suggestion (Gerhard) that through the window of the room the heavens were accessible to view, but the eye of one who prays is *on all occasions* raised toward heaven. Comp. Acts vii. 55. — ἡ ὥρα] *The hour* κατ' ἐξοχήν, *i.e.* the hour of my death, as that of my passage to Thee, xiii. 1, xii. 23. [See Note LVIII. p. 476]. — δόξασον . . . δοξάσῃ] The former through His *elevation into the heavenly glory* (comp. ver. 5), the latter through the *revelation of the glory of God*, so far, that is, as the victory of the gospel in the world, and the entire continuance and consummation of the divine work of redemption was conjoined with the heavenly glorification and ministry of Christ. To refer δόξασον to the *earthly, moral* glorification of Christ in the recognition of His Person and cause,[1] or to the *communication of the true God-consciousness to humanity* (Baur), is opposed to the context, which involves Christ's glorification through His death, always in John the *personal heavenly* glorification. Note further σου τὸν υἱόν and ὁ υἱός σου ; the emphasis of the σου, which is moved to the first place, is related to the prayer as *assigning a reason for it ;* it is in truth *Thy* Son whom Thou art to glorify. — Ver. 2 presents to the Father the *definite motive* for the fulfilment of that which was prayed for, and that in such a manner that καθὼς . . . σαρκός corresponds to the preceding δόξασόν σου τὸν υἱόν, and ἵνα πᾶν, κ.τ.λ., which contains the purpose of ἐδωκας αὐτῷ ἐξουσ. π. σ., is correlative to ἵνα ὁ υἱός σ. δοξ. σε.[2] — καθὼς denotes the motive contained in the relation of *fitness, in the measure that, according as.* Comp. on xiii. 34. — *Full power over all men* has the Father given to the Son on His mission (xiii. 3), for He has endowed Him as the sole Redeemer and Saviour with power for the execution of the decree of salvation, which extends to all ; none is exempted from His Messianic authority. But this ἐξουσία He cannot carry out without returning to the heavenly glory, whence He must carry on and complete His work. By πάσης σαρκός, however, the *whole of humanity*—and that in its imperfection (see on Acts ii. 17), conditioned by the very fact of the σάρξ, iii. 6, by which it is destitute of eternal life—is, with a certain solemnity of the O. T. type (כל בשר), designated. The expression is not elsewhere found in John, but it corresponds

---

[1] Didymus, Nösselt, Kuinoel, de Wette, Reuss.

[2] Ewald begins a new sentence with καθώς, which is completed in ver. 4, so that ver. 3 is a parenthesis: "*Even as Thou gavest to Him full power . . . I glorified Thee* *upon the earth.*" But the *periodic* form which thus arises is less in harmony with the manner of this prayer ; and the change of persons in vv. 2 and 4 betrays the want of mutual connection.

exactly to this elevated mood of prayer. — ἵνα πᾶν, κ.τ.λ.] Not a mere statement of the contents and compass of the ἐξουσία (Ebrard) : no, in the attainment of the blessed *design* of that fulness of power (comp. v. 26, 27)
lies precisely that glorification of the Father, ver. 1.   Not all, however,
without distinction, can receive eternal life through Christ, but (comp. ver.
6) those whom the Father has *given* to the Son (through the attraction by
grace, vi. 37, 39, 44, 65) are such, designated from the side of the *divine*
efficiency, the same who, *on their side*, are the *believing* (i. 12, iii. 15, *et al.*),
not " the spiritual supramundane natures" whom Hilgenfeld here discovers.
Comp. besides, on vi. 37, 39. — αὐτοῖς] to be referred to the subjects of the
absolute,[1] collective πᾶν (Bremi, *ad Isocr.* I. Exc. X.).   Note further the
weighty parallel arrangement δέδωκας αὐτῷ, δώσῃ αὐτοῖς.[2]   Not *future* conjunctive (Bengel, Baeumlein), but a corrupt form of the aorist.

Ver. 3. The continuative δέ adduces, in the connection, a more precise
definition [3] of ζωὴ αἰώνιος (not a transposition of its idea, as Weiss holds),
and that with a retrospective glance to the glorification of the Father in ver.
1.   On ἐστίν, comp. on Rom. xiv. 17 ; John iii. 19. — *In this consists eternal
life, that they should* recognize (ἵνα, comp. on vi. 29) *Thee as the only true
God* (as Him to whom alone belongs the reality of the idea of God, comp. 1
Cor. viii. 4), *and Thy sent one Jesus as Messiah*.   This knowledge of God
here desired (which is hence the believing, living, practical knowledge,
καθὼς δεῖ γνῶναι, 1 Cor. viii. 2), *is* the ζωὴ αἰώνιος, in that it is its essential
subjective principle, unfolding this ζωή out of itself, its continual, ever self-
developing germ and impulse (comp. Sap. xv. 1, 3), even now in the temporal evolution of eternal life, and still yet after the establishment of the
kingdom, in which faith, hope, and love abide (1 Cor. xiii.) ; the fundamental
essence *of which* is in truth nothing else than that knowledge, which in the
future αἰών will be the perfected knowledge (1 Cor. xiii. 12), comp. 1 John
iii. 2.   The *contents* of the knowledge are stated *with the precision of a Confession*,—a summary of faith in opposition [4] to the *polytheistic* [5] and *Jewish*
κόσμος, which latter rejected *Jesus* as Messiah, although in Him assuredly
was given the very highest revelation of the only true God.   It is in the
third person, however, that the praying Jesus speaks of Himself from ver. 1
forwards, placing Himself in an objective relation towards the Father during the first intensity of this solemn mood, and first at ver. 4 continuing
the prayer with the familiar ἐγώ ; nay, He mentions His *name* in ver. 3,
because in His designation of Himself through the third person, it here *specifically* suggested itself, in correspondence to the *confessional* thought. —

[1] Buttmann, *N. T. Gr.* p. 325 [E. T. pp. 379, 380].

[2] On the form δώσῃ, see Buttmann, *N. T. Gr.* p. 31 [E. T. p. 36].

[3] No formal *definition*. See the apposite observations of Riehm in the *Stud. u. Krit.* 1864, p. 539 f.

[4] An antithesis which might present itself naturally and unsought to the world-em-bracing glance of the praying Jesus, on the

boundary line of His work, which includes entire humanity. But He had also thought further of the ἐξουσία πάσης σαρκός, which was given to Him. This likewise in opposition to Weiss, *Lehrbegr.* p. 56, who considers the antithesis foreign to the con-nection.

[5] τ. μόνον ἀληθ. θεόν, comp. v. 44; Deut. vi. 4 ; 1 Cor. viii. 5 ; 1 Thess. i. 9.

THE GOSPEL OF JOHN.

Χριστόν] is an appellative predicate : *as Messiah*, comp. ix. 22. To connect it as a proper name with Ἰησ. (*Jesus Christ*, comp. i. 17), to ascribe to the evangelist an offence against historical decorum,[1] and to see in this a proof of a later reproduction (comp. Tholuck and Weizsäcker, p. 286 ; also Scholten, p. 238), would be to accuse the writer, especially in the report of such a prayer, of a surprising want of consideration. Luthardt also takes Χριστόν as a proper name, which he thinks was here, in this extraordinary moment, used for the first time by Jesus, and thereby at the same time determined the use of the word by the apostles (Acts ii. 38). So also Godet, comp. Ebrard. But Jesus prayed in Hebrew, and doubtless said יֵשׁוּעַ הַמָּשִׁיחַ, from which expression a proper name could by no means be recognized. The predicative view of τ. μόν. ἀλ. θεόν and of Χριστόν is also justly held by Ewald. [See Note LIX. p. 476.] — Although τ. μόνον ἀληθ. θεόν refers solely to the *Father*, the true divine nature *of Christ* is not thereby excluded (against the Arians and Socinians, who misused this passage), all the less so as this, in accordance with His (Logos) relationship as dependent on the Godhead of the Father, forms the previous assumption in ὃν ἀπέστειλας, as is certain from the entire connection of the Johannean Christology, and from ver. 5.[2] Hence it was unnecessary,—nay, even a perversion of the passage, and running counter to the strict monotheism of John, when Augustine, Ambrose, Hilary, Beda, Thomas, Aretius, and several others explained it as if the language were : *ut te et quem misisti Jesum Christum cognoscant solum verum Deum.* Only One, the *Father*, can absolutely be termed the μόνος ἀληθ. θεός (comp. ὁ ὢν ἐπὶ πάντων θεός, Rom. ix. 5), not at the same time Christ (who is not even in 1 John v. 20 the ἀληθινὸς θεός), since His divine entity stands in the relation of *genetic* subsistence to the Father, i. 18, although He, in unity with the Father, works as His commissioner, x. 30, and is His representative, xiv. 9, 10.

Vv. 4, 5. Once more the prayer of ver. 1, δόξασόν σου τὸν υἱόν, but stating a different reason for it (" ostendit, non iniquum se petere," Grotius), and setting forth the δόξα more definitely. — ἐγώ σε ἐδόξ. ἐπὶ τ. γ.] *By what*, is expressed by the following parallel proposition, which is subjoined with asyndetic liveliness. The Messianic work glorified *God*, to whose highest revelation, and therewith to His knowledge, praise, and honour it bore reference. Comp. ver. 6. — The *aorists* ἐδόξ. and ἐτελεί. are employed, because Jesus stands at the goal of His earthly activity, where He already includes in this account the fact which puts a close to His earthly work, the fact of His death, as already accomplished. Christ is not passive in His sufferings ; His obedientia *passiva* is *active*, the highest point of His activity. — καὶ νῦν] *And now*, when I take leave of this my earthly ministry. — In what follows note the correlation of με σύ with ἐγώ σε, in which the thought of *recompense* (comp. διό, Phil. ii. 9) is expressed. The emphasis lies on ἐγώ and σύ, hence after με no comma should stand. — παρὰ σεαυτῷ] so that I may be united with *Thyself* in heavenly fellowship (Col. iii. 3), corresponding to ἐπὶ τ. γῆς. Comp. on xiii. 32. — The δόξα, which Jesus possessed before the creation of

---

[1] Bretschneider, Lücke, de Wette.   [2] Comp. Wetstein, and Gess, *Pers. Chr.* p. 162.

the world, and thus in eternity before time was (εἶχον, which is to be understood *realiter*, not with the Socinians, Grotius, Wetstein, Nösselt, Löffler,
Eckermann, Stolz, Gabler, comp. B. Crusius, Schleiermacher, *L. J.* p. 286
f., Scholten, *ideally* of the *destinatio* divina), was the divine glory, *i.e.* the
essentially glorious manifestation of the entire divine perfection and blessedness, the μορφὴ θεοῦ (Phil. ii. 6) in His pre-existent state (John i. 1), of which,
He divested Himself when He became man, and the resumption of which
in the consciousness of its once enjoyed possession,[1] He now asks in prayer
from God.   That Christ contemplated Himself as the eternal archetype of
humanity in His pre-historical unity with the proper personal life of God,
and attributed to Himself in *this* sense the premundane glory (Beyschlag, p.
87 f.), is contradicted by the expression εἶχον παρὰ σοί, which so separates
the possessor of the glory from the divine subject as to place it *alongside* of
that subject ; and contradicted also by the prayer for the *restored* glory ;
for the essence of this is the σύνθρονον εἶναι θεοῦ, which must therefore have
been also that of the earlier glory.   Comp. on vi. 62. — For the fulfilment of
this prayer : Phil. ii. 9 ; 1 Tim. iii. 16 ; Heb. i. 8, 13 ; Acts ii. 34 ; 1 Pet. iii.
22, *et al.*   The δόξα, however, which His believing ones beheld in Him in
His *earthly working* (i. 14), was not the heavenly majesty in its Godlike,
absolute existence and manifestation,—that He had as λόγος ἄσαρκος, and
obtained it again in theanthropic completeness after His ascension,—but
His *temporal* theanthropic glory, the glory of God present in earthly and
bodily limitation, which He had in the state of κένωσις, and made known
through grace and truth, as well as through His entire ministry.[2]

Vv. 6–8. Hitherto Jesus has prayed *on behalf of Himself*.   But now He introduces His *intercession on behalf of His disciples*, which begins with ver. 9,
by representing them as *worthy* of this intercession. — σου] With emphasis,
as opposed to τοῖς ἀνθρώπ., in the deep feeling of the holiness and greatness
of the task discharged. — What the *name of God* comprises in itself and
expresses (see on Matt. vi. 9), was previously made known to the disciples
only in so far as it brought with it its O. T. imagery ; but the specific disclosures respecting God and His counsel of salvation resting in Christ, and
His entire redemptive relation to men, which Christ had given them by virtue of His prophetic office (the *Christian* contents, therefore, of the divine
name), entitled Him to pray ; ἐφανέρωσά σου τ. ὄν., κ.τ.λ.   Comp. Col. i. 26,
27.   A reference to the *Jewish practice of keeping secret* the name of *Jehovah*
(Hilgenfeld) lies entirely remote from the meaning. — οὓς δέδωκ. μοι ἐκ τ.
κόσμου] Necessary limitation of τοῖς ἀνθρώποις (hence not to be connected
with σοὶ ἦσαν) ; *whom Thou hast given to me out of the world* (separated from

---

[1] Not merely in a momentary anticipation, in which it appeared before the eye of His spirit (Weizsäcker). Comp. on viii. 58. It is a perversion of the exegetically clear and certain relation when Weizsäcker finds in such passages, instead of the self-consciousness of Jesus reaching back into His pre-human state, only "the culminating point of an advancing self-knowledge." But

that here, and in ver. 25, different modes of apprehending the person of Christ are intimated (Weizsäcker in the *Jahrb. f. D. Th.* 1862, p. 645 ff.), cannot be established on exegetical grounds. See on ver. 25.

[2] Comp. on i. 14 ; see also Liebner, *Christol.* I. p. 323 f.

out of the unbelieving, xv. 19), that is, the *disciples* (see vv. 8, 11), as objects of the divine counsel of salvation. God has *given* them through the attraction of His grace ; see on vi. 37. — σοί] *Possessive* pronoun, as in ver. 9 ; they *belonged to Thee*, were *Thine*, "per fidem V. T.," Bengel.[1] Therefore not in the sense of predestination (Beza, Calvin), but of *motive*, from which God, to whom they indeed already inwardly belonged, has drawn them to Christ. God knows His own. The non-ethical conception of *property in general* (Cyril. : ἴδια γὰρ πάντα θεῷ), or, "as Thy *creatures*" (Hengstenberg), yields no special ground of reason. — καὶ τὸν λόγον σου τετήρ.] and with what result gavest Thou them to me ! On τ. λόγον σου, comp. vii. 16, xii. 48, 49, and on τετηρ., they have *kept* Thy word (by faith and deed), viii. 51, xiv. 23. — νῦν ἐγνωκαν, κ.τ.λ.] Progress in the picturing of this result, which is *now* advanced so far, that they have recognized (and do recognize, *Perfect*) all that the Father has communicated to Christ as that which it is, as proceeding from God. *All which Thou hast given to me* points not merely to the *doctrine* (de Wette), but to the *entire ministry* of Jesus (Luthardt), for which He has received from the Father a commission, direction, power, result, etc. Comp. ver. 4, xii. 49, v. 36. A more definite limitation is arbitrary, because not demanded by what follows, which rather establishes the general expression (ver. 7) by the particular (τὰ ῥήματα). — Ver. 8 gives the causative (ὅτι *because*) information *how they attained to the knowledge of ver.* 7,[2] namely, (1) *on the part of Jesus*, in that He communicated to them *the words given Him by God, i.e.* that which He, as Interpreter of God, had to announce (nothing else) ; and (2) *on their part* (αὐτοί), in that they have adopted this,[3] and have actually known it (vii. 26). *Thus* with them that ἐγνωσαν of ver. 7 *has come to completion*. — καὶ αὐτοί] is only to be separated by a comma from what precedes, and is connected with ὅτι. The καὶ ἐπίστευσαν, κ.τ.λ., parallel to ἐγνωσαν ἀληθῶς, κ.τ.λ., adding *faith* to knowledge (see on vi. 69), and the above ἐξῆλθον (comp. on viii. 42), leading back to the Fatherly *behest*, whereby it is accomplished, *completes* the expression of the *happy result* attained in the case of the disciples. Note, further, the historical *aorists* ἐλαβ. and ἐπίστ. in their difference of sense from the perfects.

Ver. 9. *I* pray *for them!* Both in ἐγώ and in περὶ αὐτῶν there lies a *motive* element in reference to God. That which lies in περὶ αὐτῶν is then further made specially prominent, first negatively (οὐ π. τ. κόσμ. ἐρ.), and then positively (ἀλλὰ περὶ, κ.τ.λ.). — οὐ περὶ τοῦ κόσμου] has no *dogmatic* weight, and is therefore not to be explained in the sense of the condemnation of the world (Melanchthon), or of absolute predestination,[4] or of the *negation of*

---

[1] Comp. i. 37, 42, 46, 48, and generally viii. 47, vi. 37, 44.

[2] Ewald begins with ὅτι (*because*), a protasis, the apodosis of which (*I therefore beg*) follows in ver. 9, in such a manner, however, that from οὐ περὶ τοῦ κόσμου to ἔρχομαι, ver. 11, a parenthesis is introduced, and then first with πάτερ ἅγιε comes the supplication conveyed by ἐρωτῶ. But this compli- cated arrangement is neither necessary nor appropriate to the clear and peaceful flow of the language of this prayer as it stands.

[3] *i.e.* They have not rejected the ῥήματα, but have allowed them to influence themselves. This is the necessary pre-condition of knowledge and of faith. Comp. Weiss, *Lehrbegr.* p. 28.

[4] Calvin, Jansen, Lampe.

such intercession in general (Hengstenberg), but refers simply and solely to
this present intercession, which relates not to those who are strangers to
God, but to His own, whom He has given to Jesus,—and should all the
more *move* Him to fulfil the prayer. Prayer for the unbelieving has been
enjoined by Jesus Himself (Matt. v. 44), and has been offered by Himself
upon the cross (Luke xxiii. 34), and for them did He die, comp. also ver.
20 ; but here He has only the disciples in view, and lays them, by the antithesis οὐ περὶ τ. κόσμου, the more earnestly on the Father's heart. Luther
well says : "At other times one should pray for the world, that it may be
converted." Comp. ver. 21. — ὅτι σοί εἰσι] Ground of the intercession : *because
they*—although given to me—*are Thine*, belonging to Thee as my believing
ones, since they *were* Thine (ver. 6) already, before Thou gavest them
to me.

Ver. 10. Καὶ τὰ ἐμὰ πάντα . . . ἐμά] is parenthetic (on καί *parentheticum*,
see Fritzsche, *ad Rom.* I. 13, p. 35), and καὶ δεδόξ. ἐν αὐτοῖς is still in connection with ὅτι, ver. 9, containing a second ground of the intercession. — As
regards the above parenthesis [See Note LX. p. 476], as Jesus prayed ὅτι σοί
εἰσι, ver. 9, His glance extended itself from this concrete relation to the
category, to the *general reciprocal community of property*, which, in matters
relating to His work, exists between Him, the Son and plenipotentiary of
the Father, and the Father. Both have the same work, the same aim, the
same means, the same power, the same grace and truth, etc., in common ;
neither has and works separate from the other, and for Himself ; God in
Christ, and He in God. Comp. on xvi. 15. Luther aptly remarks : "It
were not so much if He simply said : All that is mine is Thine ; for that
every one can say . . . it is much greater that He inverts the relation, and
says : All that is Thine is mine ; this no creature can say in reference to
God." — δεδόξ. ἐν αὐτ.] *I am glorified in them*, in their person and activity,
in so far as they are bearers and furtherers of my glory and knowledge
upon earth, so precious and important, then, that I pray for them. What
is already begun, and is certainly to be further accomplished in the near
future, Jesus views, speaking in the *perfect* with prophetic anticipation, as
completed and actually existing,[1] and ἐν denotes the relation resting on,
contained in them, as in xiii. 31, 32, xiv. 13.

Ver. 11. Before He now gives expression to the special supplication
itself (πάτερ ἅγιε, τήρησον, κ.τ.λ.), He first brings forward the peculiar *ground
of need*, connecting in profound emotion its individual members unperiod-
ically by καί. — οὐκέτι εἰμί, κ.τ.λ.] Thus He speaks, "nunc quasi provincia
sua defunctus," Calvin. — καὶ οὗτοι, κ.τ.λ.] "hos relinquam in tantis flucti-
bus," Grotius. — ἅγιε] As in ver. 25, δίκαιε, so here ἅγιε is added *significantly ;* for to guarantee that which Jesus would now pray (τήρησον, κ.τ.λ.)
is in harmony with the *holiness* of His Father, which has been revealed to
Him in entire fulness, a holiness which is the absolute antithesis of the ungodly nature of the profane world.[2] Placed by their calling in this unholy

[1] Kühner, II. p. 72.
[2] According to Diestel in the *Jahrb. f. Deutsche Theol.* 1859, p. 45, God is here con- ceived of as ἅγιος τοῦ Χριστοῦ, which is the completion of the N. T. ἅγιος τοῦ Ἰσραήλ. But of this there is neither any indication in

κόσμος, they shall be guarded by the holy God so as to abide faithfully in
His name. In harmony with this antithesis of the holiness of God to the
nature of the world, stands the petition, "hallowed be Thy name," at the
head of the Lord's Prayer. Comp. also 1 John ii. 20 ; Heb. xii. 10 ; 1 Pet.
i. 16 ; Rev. vi. 10. Thus the Father discharges the obligation lying on
Himself, if He keeps the disciples of the Son in His name. — ἐν τῷ ὀνόμ. σ.]
Specific *sphere*, in which they are to remain through being so kept ; the
name of the Father is made known to them (vv. 6, 26), and with a happy
result (vv. 6–8) ; thus are they to persevere *in His* living *acquaintance* and
believing confession, not to depart out of this holy element of their life. —
ᾧ δέδωκ. μοι] ᾧ by attraction, instead of ὅ, which, however, does not stand
instead of οὕς,[1] but : God has given His name to Christ, and that not in the
sense of the *divine nature* entering into manifestation, as Hengstenberg here
brings in from Ex. xxiii. 21, but rather in the sense of ver. 6, *for revelation
to the disciples ;* He has for such a purpose delivered His name to Him as
the object of a holy commission. In conformity with this, the Lord prays
that God would *keep* them in this His name, *in order that* they, in virtue of
the one common faith and confession resting on the name of God, *may be
one* (in the spiritual fellowship, of like mind and love, comp. vv. 22, 23),
in conformity with the archetype[2] of the ethical unity of the Father and
the Son (comp. the Pauline εἰς θεὸς κ. πατὴρ πάντων, κ.τ.λ., Eph. iv. 6).
Hence ἵνα expresses the object of τήρησον, κ.τ.λ., not of δέδωκ. μοι.

Vv. 12, 13. A more definite outpouring of heart concerning ver. 11. —
ὅτε ἤμην, κ.τ.λ.] As in ver. 11, οὐκέτι εἰμὶ ἐν τ. κόσμῳ, Jesus speaks as though
He had already departed out of the world. "Jam in exitu mundi pedem
irrevocabilem posuerat," Ruperti on ver. 11. — ἐγώ] That which *Thou* mayest
now do, ver. 11. — οὓς δέδωκ. μοι ἐφύλ., κ.τ.λ.] Not a parenthesis, but a further
expression of the τήρησις just described, in which a sorrowful but telically
clear and conscious mention of Judas obtrudes itself. — ἐφύλαξα] Through
the φυλάσσειν (*custodire*) is the τηρεῖν (*conservare*) accomplished.[3] The disciples were handed over to Him for *protection and guardianship, ut eos salvos
tueretur.* This He has accomplished, and *none of them has fallen into destruction* (*i.e.* into eternal destruction through apostasy, which leads to the
loss of ζωή), *except him who belongs to destruction* (Matt. xxiii. 15), *i.e.* who is
destined to destruction. Comp. vi. 64, 70. Jesus does not like to *name* Judas,
who forms this tragical *exception* (εἰ μή is not equivalent to ἀλλά, as Scholten
thinks), but his destruction—and therein the purity of the consciousness of
Jesus in the matter is expressed—is *nothing accidental*, capable of being
averted, but is prophesied in the Scripture as a divine destiny, and *must
take place in fulfilment thereof.* On account of xiii. 18, it is without
warrant to think of another saying of Scripture than, with Luther, Lücke,
and several others, of Ps. xli. 10 (Kuinoel refers it to the prophecies of the

the context, nor do we find at all the idea
of God as of the ἅγιος τοῦ Χριστοῦ expressed.
Hengstenberg refers too exclusively to the
power of the holy God.

[1] Bengel, comp. Ewald and Godet, who

would *read* ὅ, see the critical notes.

[2] Bengel : "Illa unitas est ex natura, haec
ex gratia ; igitur illi haec similis est, non
aequalis."

[3] Comp. Sap. x. 5 ; Dem. 317. ult.

death of Jesus generally ; Lange,[1] to Isa. lvii. 12, 13 ; Euth. Zigabenus,
Calovius, and many to Ps. cix. 8, which passage, however, has its reference
in Acts i. 20). The designation of *Antichrist* by ὁ υἱὸς τ. ἀπωλ., 2 Thess.
ii. 3, is parallel in point of *form*. In the *Evang. Nikod.* 20 (see Thilo on
the passage, p. 708), the *devil* is so called.—Ver. 13. *But now I come to Thee,
and* since I can no longer guard them personally as hitherto, *I speak this*
(this prayer for Thy protection, ver. 11) *in the world* ("jam ante discessum
meum," Bengel), *that they*, as witnesses and objects of this my intercession,
knowing themselves assured of Thy protection, *may bear my joy* (as in xv.
11, not xiv. 27) *fulfilled in themselves.* On this expression of prayer regarding the influence which the *listening to* prayer should have upon the *listeners*,
comp. xi. 42. Luther well says : "that they, through the word, apprehended by the ears, and retained in the heart, may be consoled, and be
able cheerfully to presume thereon, and to say : See, this has my Lord
Christ said, so affectionately and cordially has He prayed for me," etc.

Vv. 14, 15. The intercession addresses itself to a *particular, definite* point
of the τήρησις prayed for, namely, ἐκ τοῦ πονηροῦ, ver. 15, and this is introduced, ver. 14, from the side of their *necessities.* — ἐγώ] antithesis : ὁ κόσμος.
— ἐμίσ. αὐτούς] *has conceived a hatred against them.*[2] This hatred Luther
terms "the true court colours of Christians that they bear on earth."
Further, see on xv. 18, 19. — The more precise defining of τήρησις follows in
ver. 15 negatively and positively. They are *not* ("for I have still more to
accomplish by their means," Luther) *to be taken out of the* unbelieving *world*
which hates them (which would take place by death, as now in the case of
Jesus Himself, ver. 11), but *they are to be kept* by God, so that they ever
come forth, morally uninjured, *from the encompassing power of Satan*, the
Prince of the world. ἐκ τ. πονηροῦ is not, with Luther, Calvin, and many
others, including Olshausen, B. Crusius, Hengstenberg, Godet, to be taken
as *neuter*, but comp. 1 John ii. 13 ff., iii. 12, v. 18, 19, iv. 4 ; Matt. vi. 13 ;
2 Thess. iii. 3 ; comp. on τηρεῖν ἐκ, Rev. iii. 10, also φυλάσσειν ἐξ ἐπιβουλῆς in
Themist. 181. 19 (Dindorf). Nonnus : δαίμονος ἀρχεκάκοιο δυσαντήτων ἀπὸ
θεσμῶν.

Vv. 16, 17. From the *keeping* hitherto prayed for, the intercession advances
to the positive consecrating, ver. 17 ; and this part of it also is *introduced* in
ver. 16, and that by an emphatic resumption of what was said in ver. 14 on
the side of the *condition fitted* for the ἁγιάζειν. — ἁγίασον αὐτοὺς ἐν τῇ ἀληθ.]
The disciples were *in the truth*, for since they had believingly accepted the
word of God given to them by Christ, and had kept it (vv. 6, 12), the divine
truth, the expression of which that word is, was the *element of life*, in which
they, taken from the world and given to Christ, were found. Now He prays
that God would not merely keep them (which He has previously prayed for),
but yet further : He would *provide them with a holy consecration* (comp. on
x. 36) in this their sphere of life, whereby is meant not indeed the translation
into "the true position of being" (Luthardt), but the equipment with divine
illumination, power, courage, joyfulness, love, inspiration, etc., for their

----

[1] *L. J.* II. p. 1412.   [2] Aor., see Lobeck, *ad Phryn.* p. 197 ; Kühner, *ad Xen. Mem.* i. 1. 18.

official activity (ver. 18) which should ensue, and did ensue, through the
Holy Spirit, xiv. 17, xv. 26, xvi. 7 ff. Comp. on ἐν, Sir. xlv. 4. Ordinarily
it is taken *instrumentally*, in virtue of, by means of,[1] but in arbitrary neglect
of the analogy of the correlate τηρεῖν ἐν, vv. 11, 12 ; whilst de Wette, B.
Crusius, Baeumlein, just as arbitrarily here again mix up also the notion of
τηρεῖν ; "so that they *remain* in the truth," whereby the *climactic* relation of
τηρεῖν and ἁγιάζειν is misapprehended. When, with Luther, ("*make truly
holy*") ἐν τ. ἀληθ. is taken as equivalent to ἀληθῶς, of *complete* sanctification
in contrast with their hitherto *defective* condition (Hengstenberg), against
the view is decisive, not indeed the article,[2] but rather the following ὁ
λόγος, κ.τ.λ. The reading ἐν τ. ἀλ. σου correctly, though in the way of a gloss,
defines the idea. — ὁ λόγος ὁ σὸς ἀλήθ. ἐστι] a supporting of the prayer, in
which ὁ σός has peculiar weight ; *Thy word* (xiv. 24, xii. 49, vii. 16), the
word of no other, *is truth*. How shouldst Thou, then, not grant the ἁγιάζειν
prayed for ? That ἀλήθ. is *without the article*, does not rest upon the fact that
it is a predicate, but upon the conception that the *essence* of the λόγος is truth,
so that ἀλήθ. is *abstract*, not a noun appellative. Comp. iv. 24, 1 John iv. 16.

Vv. 18, 19. In support of the prayer for the *consecrating* of the disciples,
there now follow further two *motives for its being granted*, deduced, (1) from
the mission of the disciples into the world, on which account they need consecration ; and (2) from Christ's own personal consecration for the purpose of
their ἁγιασμός, which purpose God will not be willing to leave unattained. —
καθὼς ἐμέ, κ.τ.λ.] Placed first with pragmatic weight ; for as He could not
execute His mission without the divine consecration (x. 36), so neither could
they who were sent by Him. — κἀγώ] Not instead of οὕτως ἐγώ (de Wette),
but simply : *I also* have sent. Comp. xv. 9, xx. 21, *et al.* — ἀπέστειλα] The
mission was indeed not yet objectively a fact (xx. 21 ; Matt. xxviii. 19),
but already conceived in its idea in the appointment and instruction for
the apostolic office (Matt. x. 5 ff.). Comp. on iv. 38. — Ver. 19. Note the
emphatic *correlation* of αὐτῶν . . . ἐγὼ ἐμαυτόν . . . καὶ αὐτοί. — The ἁγιάζω
ἐμαυτόν, not including in it *the whole life* of the Lord (Calvin, Hengstenberg,
Godet), but now, when the hour is come, to be carried out, is the *actual consecration, which Christ, in offering Himself through His death as a sacrifice to
God accomplishes on Himself*,[3] so that ἁγιάζω is substantially equivalent to
προσφέρω σοὶ θυσίαν (Chrysostom), comp. 4 Macc. xvii. 19, ἁγιάζειν, הִקְדִּישׁ, is
a sacred word for *sacrifices* in the O. T.[4] Christ is at once the Priest and
the Sacrifice (Ep. to the Heb.) ; and *for*[5] *the disciples* He performs this sacrifice,—although it is offered for all,[6]—so far as it has, in respect of the disci-

---

[1] Chrysostom, Nonnus, Theophylact, Calvin, and many others, including Lücke,
Tholuck, Godet.

[2] Comp. Xen. *Anab.* vi. 2. 10.

[3] Comp. generally, Ritschl in the *Jahrb.
f. D. Theol.* 1863, p. 240 f.

[4] See Ex. xiii. 2 ; Deut. xv. 19 ff. ; 2 Sam.
viii. 11 ; Esr. v. 52 ; Rom. xv. 16 ; comp. also
Soph. *Oed. Col.* 1491 ; Dion. H. vii. 2.

[5] ὑπέρ, *in commodum*, xv. 13.

[6] Even this solemn ὑπέρ (vi. 51, x. 11, xi.
50, xv. 13, xviii. 14 ; 1 John iii. 16) should
have prevented ἁγιάζω ἐμ. from being understood in the *ethical* sense of the *ripening to
moral perfection* through faithful, loving
obedience towards the Father (so Wörner,
Verhältn. d. Geistes z. Sohne Gottes, p. 41 f.)
Simply correct is Euth. Zigabenus, ἐγὼ
ἑκουσίως θυσιάζω ἐμαυτόν.

ples, the *special purpose: that they also may be consecrated in truth,* namely, in virtue of the *reception of the Paraclete* (πνευματικῷ πυρὶ γυῖα λελουμένοι, Nonnus), which reception was conditioned by the *death* of Jesus, xvi. 7. The καί has its logical justification in the idea of *consecration* common to both clauses, although its *special* sense is different in each ; for the *disciples* are, through the sacrifice of Jesus, to be consecrated to God *in the sense of holy purity, endowment, and equipment* for their calling. On the other hand, the self-consecration of Christ is *sacrificial,*—the former, however, like the latter, the consecration in the service of God and of His kingdom. Comp. on the self-consecration of Christ, who yields Himself voluntarily to be a sacrifice (x. 18, xv. 13), Eph. v. 2 : παρέδωκεν ἑαυτὸν ὑπὲρ ἡμῶν προσφοράν, κ.τ.λ. ; *that* is the idea of the present passage, not that He renounced the mortal *flesh,* and entered fully into the divine mode of existence and fellowship (Luthardt). See also Heb. ix. 14. — ἐν ἀληθείᾳ] Modal definition of ἡγιασμένοι : *truly* consecrated, Matt. xxii. 16 ; 2 Cor. vii. 14 ; Col. i. 6 ; 1 John iii. 18 ; 2 John 1 ; 3 John 1.[1] In the classics the mere dative and ἐπ' ἀληθείας are frequent. The *true* consecration is not exactly an antithesis in the *Jewish sanctimonia ceremonialis* (Godet and older expositors), to which nothing in the context leads, but simply sets forth *the eminent character of the relation generally.* As contrasted with every other ἀγιότης in human relations, that wrought through the Paraclete is the *true* consecration. Comp. Luther : "against all worldly and human holiness." So substantially,[2] Chrysostom, Euth. Zigabenus, Beza, Calvin, Bengel, and several others, including Hengstenberg, Godet. The interpretation which has recently, after Erasmus, Bucer, and several others, become current,[3] that ἐν ἀληθ. is not different from ἐν τῇ ἀληθείᾳ, ver. 17, is erroneous, because the article is wanting which here, in the retrospective reference to the truth already defined with the article, was absolutely necessary ; for of an antithesis " to the state of being in which the disciples would find themselves outside of this" (Luthardt), the text suggests nothing, even leaving out of sight the fact that a *state of sanctification* in such an opposite condition would be inconceivable. Without any ground, appeal is made, in respect of the absence of the article, to i. 14, iv. 24, where truth is expressed as a general conception (comp. viii. 44) (Sir. xxxvii. 15 ; Tob. iii. 5 ; 2 Tim. ii. 25, iii. 7), and to 3 John 3,[4] where ἐν ἀληθ. must be taken as equivalent to ἀληθῶς,[5] and consequently as in the present passage and as in 3 John 1.

---

[1] See on 2 Cor. *loc. cit. ;* LXX. 2 Reg. xix. 17 (where, however, ἐν is doubtful) ; Sir. vii. 20 ; Pind. *Ol.* vii. 126.

[2] In so far as they understand ἐν ἀληθ. of the *true* ἁγιάζεσθαι, in which, however, they find an antithesis to the *typical* holiness of the O. T. sacrifice, as *e. g.* Euth. Zigabenus : ἵνα καὶ αὐτοὶ ὦσι τεθυμένοι ἐν ἀληθινῇ θυσίᾳ· ἡ γὰρ νομικὴ θυσία τύπος ἦν, οὐκ ἀλήθεια. Comp. Theophylact ; also Holtzmann, *Judenth. u. Christenth.* p. 421.

[3] Lücke, Tholuck (?), Olshausen, de Wette, B. Crusius, Luthardt, Lange, Brückner, Ewald.

[4] Ver. 4 is, with Lachm. and Tisch., to be read ἐν τῇ ἀληθ.

[5] The passage means : "I rejoiced when brethren came and gave witness for Thy *truth (i.e.* for Thy morally true Christian constitution of life), as Thou *truly (in deed)* walkest." καθώς, κ.τ.λ., that is, not forming a part of that testimony of the brethren, gives to this testimony the confirmation of John himself. As the brothers have testified for Gaius, so he *actually* walks. This John *knows,* and the brethren have told

Vv. 20, 21. In His prayer for the *disciples* for their preservation and sanctification (vv. 11–19), Jesus now also includes *all who* [1] shall *believe on Him* [2] *through the apostles' word* (διὰ τοῦ κηρύγματος αὐτῶν, Euth. Zigabenus). The *purpose* for which He also includes these : *that all* (all my believing ones, the apostles and the others) *may be one* (ethically, in likeness of disposition, of love, of endeavour, etc., on the ground of faith, comp. Eph. iv. 3 ff. ; Rom. xv. 5, 6; Acts iv. 32). — This ethical unity of all believers, to be specifically Christian, [3] must *correspond* as to its original type (καθώς) *to the reciprocal fellowship between the Father and the Son* (according to which the Father lives and moves in the Son, and the Son in the Father, comp. x. 38, xiv. 10, 11, xv. 5), the *object* of which, in reference to believers collectively, is, *that in them also the Father and the Son may be the element in which they* (in virtue of the *unio mystica* brought about through the Spirit, 1 John i. 3, iv. 13 ; 1 Pet. i. 4) *live and move* (ἵνα κ. αὐτοὶ ἐν ἡμῖν ὦσιν).—This ethical unity of all believers in fellowship with the Father and the Son, however (comp. xiii. 35), *shall serve to the unbelieving world as an actual proof and ground of conviction that Christ*, the grand central point and support of this unity, *is* none other than *the sent of God.* " That is the *fruit* which must follow through and from such unity, namely, that Christ's word shall further break forth and be received in the world as God's word, wherein stands an almighty, divine, unconquerable power and eternal treasure of all grace and blessedness," Luther, in opposition to which, Calvin (as also Scholten) gets into confusion by introducing the doctrine of predestination, making of πιστεύειν a *reluctant agnoscere.* Thus the *third* ἵνα is *subordinated* to the first, as introducing its *further* aim : the *second*, however, because defining specifically the aim of καθώς, κ.τ.λ., is related to the first *explicatively.*

Vv. 22, 23. What He on His part (ἐγώ) has done in order to bring about this unity of His believing ones and its object—a newly introduced and great thought of the power of His kingdom—not still dependent on ὅτι (Ewald). — τὴν δόξαν] The *heavenly* glory. [See Note LXI. p. 476.] Comp. 1, 5, 24. This, once already possessed by Him before the incarnation, the Father has *given* to Him, not yet, indeed, *objectively*, but as a secure possession of the *immediate future ;* He has *obtained* it from God, *assigned* as a property, and the actual taking-possession is now for Him close at hand. In like manner has *He given* this, His δόξα, in which the eternal ζωή, vv. 2, 3, is consummated, to His *believing ones* (αὐτοῖς), who will enter on the real possession at the Parousia, where they συνδοξάζονται (Rom. viii. 17), after that they, up to that time, *had been saved in hope* (Rom. viii. 24). Comp. on Rom. viii. 30. They *are* in Christ already His joint heirs, and the Spirit which they are to receive will be to them the ἀρραβὼν τῆς κληρονομίας (Eph. i. 14 ; 2 Cor. i. 22, v. 5) ; but the actual entrance on the inheritance is accomplished

---

him nothing new by that testimony, however greatly he has rejoiced in the fact of receiving such a testimony concerning his Gaius. Therefore he adds, with loving recognition, *as thou truly walkest.* That testimony therefore only corresponds to the reality.

[1] Comp. Rom. x. 14.

[2] πιστευόντων, regarding the future as present.

[3] " Non vult concordiam coetus humani, ut est concors civitas Spartana contra Athenienses," Melanchthon.

at the Parousia (xiv. 2, 3 ; Rom. viii. 11 ; Col. iii. 4). Yet this relation does not justify us in interpreting διδόναι as *destinare* (Gabler, B. Crusius), or at least δέδωκα as *constitui dare* (Grotius), while the explanations also which take δόξα of the *glory of the apostolic office* in teaching and working miracles,[1] or of the *inner glory of the Christian life*,[2] of the *life of Christ in believers*, in accordance with Gal. ii. 20 (Hengstenberg), of *sonship* (Bengel),[3] of *love* (Calovius, Maldonatus), of *grace and truth*, i. 14,[4] are opposed to the context.[5] See immediately, ver. 24. — ἵνα ὦσιν ἐν, κ.τ.λ.] For what a strong bond of unity must lie in the sure warrant of fellowship in eternal δόξα ! Comp. Eph. iv. 4. — ἐγὼ ἐν αὐτοῖς κ. σὺ ἐν ἐμοί] Not out of connection with the construction (de Wette), since it fits into it ; nor again beginning a new proposition, and to be completed by εἰμί,[6] since thus the discourse on the δόξα would be, in opposition to the context (see ver. 24), interrupted ; but an *appositional separation from* ἡμεῖς, from which it is therefore, with Lachmann and Tischendorf, to be divided only by a comma. In ἡμεῖς is contained : ἐγὼ καὶ σύ, and both are pragmatically, *i.e.* in demonstration of the specific internal relation of the ἓν εἶναι of believers to the oneness of the Father and the Son, thus expounded : *I* moving *in them, and Thou in me.* In accordance with this appositional, more minute definition, the ἵνα ὦσιν ἐν is again taken up with liveliness and weight (" see how His mouth overflows with the same words," Luther), and that in the expression containing the *highest degree of intensity :* ἵνα ὦσι τετελειωμένοι εἰς ἕν, that they may be *completed* to one (to one unity), be united in *complete degree.* εἰς in the sense of the *result*.[7] — ἵνα γινώσκῃ ὁ κόσμος, κ.τ.λ.] Parallel to ἵνα ὁ κόσμος πιστεύσῃ, ver. 21, adding to faith the *knowledge* connected therewith (conversely, ver. 8), and then completing the expression of the happy result to be attained by the designation of the highest *divine love*, of which the believer is conscious in that knowledge. We are not even remotely to think of the "*forced conviction of rebels*" (Godet) ; against this vv. 2, 3 already declare, and here the entire context. Note rather how the glance of the praying Jesus, vv. 21–23, rises to the highest goal of His work on earth, when, namely, the κόσμος shall have come to believe, and Christ Himself shall have become in fact ὁ σωτὴρ τοῦ κόσμου (iv. 42, comp. x. 16). This at the same time against the supposition of *metaphysical dualism* in Hilgenfeld. — κ. ἠγάπησας, κ.τ.λ.] *and hast loved them* (as a matter of fact, through this sending of me) *as Thou hast loved me*, therefore with the same Fatherly love which I have experienced from Thee. Comp. iii. 16 ; Eph. i. 6 ; Rom. v. 5, viii. 32.

Ver. 24. What He has already bestowed on them, but as yet as a posses-

---

[1] Chrysostom, Theophylact, and, but with intermixture of other elements, Euth. Zigabenus, Erasmus, Vatablus, Grotius, and several others, including Paulus and Klee.

[2] Olshausen, comp. Gess, p. 244.

[3] Comp. Godet, who refers to Rom. vii. 29.

[4] Luthardt, Ebrard, a part also of Tholuck's and Brückner's interpretation.

[5] The δόξα is explained away also by

Weizsäcker in the *Jahrb. f. Deutsche Theol.* 1857, p. 181. It is said to be substantially the same as the λόγος, ver. 14.

[6] Augustine, Theophylact, Euth. Zigabenus, Beda, Beza, Bengel, and several others, including Luthardt.

[7] Comp. passages like Plato, *Phileb.* p. 18 B : τελευτᾶν τε ἐκ πάντων εἰς ἕν ; Dem. p. 368. 14 : εἰς ἓν ψήφισμα ταῦτα πάντα συνεσκεύασαν.

sion of hope (ver. 22), He *wills* (θέλω) that they may also partake of in reality.
He does not merely *wish* it,[1] but the Son prays in the consciousness of the
authority bestowed on Him by the Father according to ver. 2, for the communication of eternal life to His own.   This consciousness is that of the most
intimate confidence and clearest accord with the Father.   Previously He
had said ἐρωτῶ ; "nunc *incrementum* sumit oratio," Bengel.   The idea of
the *final* will, however (Godet), is not to be introduced here. — The relative
defining clause is placed first emphatically, because justifying the θέλω in its
contents.   This is *neuter* (ὅ, see the critical notes), by which the persons
(ἐκεῖνοι, *i.e.* the disciples and all believers, ver. 20) are designated *in abstracto*,
according to their category (comp. ver. 2, vi. 37), and the force of δέδωκάς
μοι, which is a motive cause to the granting of the prayer, becomes more
prominent *in and of itself*. — ἵνα] *Purpose* of θέλω (they *should*, etc.), and
with this its *contents ;* see on Luke vi. 31. — ὅπου εἰμὶ ἐγώ, κἀκεῖνοι, κ.τ.λ.]
shall be realized at the *Parousia*.[2] See on xiv. 3, also on ἀναστήσω αὐτό, κ.τ.λ.,
vi. 39. — θεωρῶσι] *may behold*, experimentally, and with *personal participation*, as συνδοξασθέντες, Rom. viii. 17, 29, and συμβασιλεύοντες, 2 Tim. ii. 12.
The opposite : behold eternal death, viii. 51.[3] Against the interpretation that the
beholding of the glory of Christ *in itself* (its reflection, as it were) constitutes
blessedness,[4] ver. 22 testifies, although it is also essentially included in it,
1 John iii. 2 ; Heb. xii. 14. — ἥν ἐδωκάς μοι, ὅτι, κ.τ.λ.] Further added, in
childlike feeling of gratitude, to τὴν ἐμήν, and that *proleptically* (comp. εἰμί),
because the Lord is on the point of entering into this glory (ver. 1), as if He
had already received it (comp. ver. 22) : *which Thou gavest me, because*
(motive of the ἐδωκ.) *Thou lovedst me before the foundation of the world* (πρὸ
κατ. κ. not belonging to ἐδωκ. μ., as Paulus and B. Crusius think).   The δόξα
of Christ, as the λόγος ἄσαρκος (ver. 5), was, according to the mode of view
and expression of the N. T., not one *imparted* to Him from love, but in virtue of the ontologically Trinitarian relation to the Father,[5] that which per-
tained with metaphysical necessity to the Son in the unity of the divine
nature, the μορφὴ θεοῦ, which He as θεὸς λόγος, i. 1, *had*, being from eternity
eternally with the Father (ver. 5) ; whereas the glory *here* intended is in His
exaltation after the completion of His work, since it concerned His entire
person, including its human side, that *given* to Him by the Father from love
(Phil. ii. 9), from *that* love, however, which did not originate in time, but
was cherished by the Father toward the Son before the foundation of the
world.   The δόξα possessed by Jesus before His incarnation, to which for
the most part (as still Luthardt, Ebrard, Hengstenberg) reference is wrongly

[1] Against Beza, Calvin, B. Crusius, Tholuck, Ewald.
[2] The intermediate state denoted in Phil.
i. 23 (see *in loc.*) is not meant (Hengstenberg),
nor *a part* of the meaning (Godet), but as
what follows shows, the *completed fellowship of glory*. Comp. 1 John iii. 2.
[3] Baur thus explains away the historical
sense: "They behold this glory, see it in
reality before them, if in them, through the
communication of the true God conscious-

ness, and of the eternal life thereby conditioned, through which they have become
one with Jesus and the Father, just as He
is one with the Father, the divine principle
(*to this*, according to Baur, δέδωκα, ver. 22.
refers) has realized itself as that which it
is in itself."
[4] Olshausen, comp. Chrysostom and Euth.
Zigabenus.
[5] Comp. J. Müller, *Von der Sünde*, II. p.
183 f.

made, whereby, according to ver. 5, ἔδωκας would have to be conceived of as brought about through the generation of the μονογενής, was the *purely divine ;* that given to Him through His exaltation is indeed the same, into which He now again has entered, but, because it is the glory of the λόγος ἔνσαρκος, *theanthropic* in eternal perfection (Phil. ii. 9). Comp. on ver. 5, i. 14. *Nowhere* in the N. T. is the *premundane* δόξα of the Son, designated as *given* to Him (Phil. ii. 6 ; Col. i. 15 ; 2 Cor. viii. 9), although this would be imaginable in and of itself as an eternal self-communication of Fatherly love.[1] Further, it is strangely incorrect that the δόξα, which the Father has *given* to the Son, has been explained here differently from that in ver. 22. — The *love* of the Father to the Son before the foundation of the world implies the *personal pre-existence* of the latter with God, but is not reconcilable with the idea of the pre-temporal *ideal* existence which He has had in God, as the archetype of humanity. This in answer to Beyschlag, p. 87, who considers the relation as analogous to the eternal election of grace, Eph. i. 4, Rom. viii. 29 ; which is not appropriate, since the election of grace concerns those as yet *not in existence*, namely, *future* believers, whom God προέγνω as future. The Son, however, whom He loved, must personally exist with the Father, since it was in Christ that the motive already lay for the election of grace (see on Eph. i. 4). Comp. also on ver. 5. To suppose that God, according to the present passage, had loved *His own ideal of humanity* before the foundation of the world, the idea consequently of His own thought, is an idea without any analogy in the N. T., and we thereby arrive at an anthropopathic *self-love*, as men form to themselves an ideal, and are glad to attain it.

Vv. 25, 26. Conclusion of the prayer : Appeal to the *righteousness* of God, for, after that which Jesus here states of Himself and of the disciples in opposition to the world, it becomes the righteous Father not to leave ungranted what Jesus has just declared, ver. 24, to be His will (θέλω, ἵνα, κ.τ.λ.). Otherwise the final recompense would fail to come, which the divine *righteousness* (1 John i. 9) has to give to those who are so raised, as expressed in ver. 25, above the world ; the work of divine *holiness*, ver. 11, would remain without its closing *judicial consummation and revelation.* — καὶ ὁ κόσμος, κ.τ.λ.] The apparent inappropriateness of the καί, from which also its omission in D. Vulg. *et al.*, is to be explained, is not removed by placing, with Grotius and Lachmann, only a comma after ver. 24, and allowing καὶ ὁ κόσμος σε οὐκ ἔγνω to run with what precedes, since this thought does not fit into this logical connection, and the address πάτερ δίκαιε, according to the analogy of ver. 11, leads us to recognize the *introductory* sentence of a prayer. According to Bengel and Ebrard, καὶ . . . καί, *et . . . et*, correspond to one another, which, however, is allowed neither by the antithetic character of the conceptions, nor the manifest reference of the second καί to ἐγὼ δέ. Following Heumann, de Wette, Lücke, Tholuck

---

[1] Comp. Brückner and Ebrard. Euth. Zigabenus : τὴν δόξαν τῆς θεότητος, ἣν δέδωκάς μοι, οὐχ ὡς ἐλάττονι ἢ ὑστερογενεῖ, ἀλλ' ὡς αἴτιος, εἴτουν ὡς γεννήσας με. But in the N. T. this mode of presentation is unsupported ; in ver. 26, to which Johansson appeals, ἔδωκεν in truth refers first to the time of the sending into the world.

make καί correspond to the following δέ, so that two simultaneously occurring but contrasted relations [1] would be indicated : " whilst the world knew Thee not, yet I knew Thee." Not to be justified on grammatical grounds ; for τέ . . . δέ,[2] but never καί . . . δέ, is thus employed, and the passages of that kind adduced by Lücke from Plato[3] are not in point ; in other passages [4] καί is the simply connective *and*, without reference to the subsequent δέ. The καί in the present passage is rather the *and* serving to link on an *antithetic* relation (*and notwithstanding*), and is particularly frequent in John, see on vii. 28. Had Jesus said : πάτερ, δίκαιος εἶ, καὶ ὁ κόσμος, κ.τ.λ., then καί would have been free from any difficulty. Nevertheless, the connection and its expression are the same. Christ is, in the address πάτερ δίκαιε, absorbed in the thought of the *justice* of God now invoked by Him, the thought, therefore, of this self-revelation of God, which was so easily to be recognized (Rom. i. 18 ff.), in spite of which the world, in its blinded security, has not known Him (comp. Rom. i. 28), and gives expression to this latter thought in painfully excited emotion (Chrysostom : δυσχεραίνων), immediately connecting it by καί with the address. After πάτ. δίκαιε we may suppose a pause, a break in the thought : *Righteous Father*—(yea, such Thou art !) *and* (and yet) *the world knew Thee not!* [5] Luthardt also, with Brückner's concurrence, takes καί as *and yet*, but so that it stands in opposition to the revelation of God through Christ previously (see ver. 22) stated. Too indefinite, and leaving without reason the characteristic πάτερ δίκαιε out of reference. — ἔγνω] namely, from Thy displays in my words and deeds ; ἔγνων, on the other hand (Nonnus : σύμφυτος ἔγνων), refers to the immediate knowledge which the Son had in His earthly life of the Father moving in Him, and revealing Himself through Him. Comp. viii. 54, 55. Not without reason does Jesus introduce His ἐγὼ δέ σε ἔγνων between the κόσμος and the disciples, because He wills that the disciples should be where He is (ver. 24), which, however, presupposes a relative relation of equality between Him and them, as over against the world. — οὗτοι] Glancing at the disciples. — ὅτι σύ με ἀπέστ.] The specific element, the central point of the knowledge of God, of which the discourse treats ; δείκνυσιν ἐνταῦθα, μηδένα εἰδότα θεόν, ἀλλ᾽ ἢ μόνον τοὺς τὸν υἱὸν ἐπεγνωκότας, Chrysostom. Comp. vv. 8, 23, xvi. 27, *et al.* — Ver. 26. Whereby this ἔγνωσαν has been effected (comp. ver. 7), and will be completely effected (γνωρίσω, through the Paraclete : καὶ . . . καί, *both* . . . *and also*), *that* (purpose of the γνωρίσω) *the love with which Thou hast loved me* (comp. ver. 24) *may be in*

---

[1] Hence also the reading : εἰ καὶ ὁ κ. σ. οὐκ ἔγνω, ἀλλ᾽ ἐγώ, κ.τ.λ., which is found not merely in Hippolytus, but also in the *Constitt. Ap.* 8. 1. 1.

[2] Kühner, II. p. 418; Hartung, *Partikell.* I. p. 92 f. ; Klotz, *ad Devar.* p. 741 f.

[3] *Menex.* p. 235 E (where καὶ ἄλλους means *also* others, and *Eryx.* p. 393 E (where καὶ ἐλάχιστα is *only also* the least.

[4] As Soph. *Ant.* 428.

[5] This interpretation is followed also by Hengstenberg. But Ewald places καὶ ὁ

κόσμος to γνωρίσω, ver. 26, in a parenthesis, and then takes ἵνα ἡ ἀγάπη, κ.τ.λ., still as the contents of θέλω, ver. 24. How broken thus becomes the calm, clear flow of the prayer ! According to Baeumlein, the parallel clauses would properly be καὶ ἐγὼ σὲ ἔγνων καὶ οὗτοι ἔγνωσαν ; but there is thus interpolated before the first clause a contrasted clause, which properly should have μέν, so that then the main thought follows with δέ. Alike arbitrary, but yet more contorted, is the arrangement of Godet.

them, i.e. may rule in their hearts,[1] *and* with this—for Christ, communicating himself through the Spirit, is the supporter of the divine life in believers,[2] —*I in them.* On ἀγάπην ἀγαπᾶν, see on Eph. ii. 4. So rich in promise and elevating with the simply grand " *and I in them*," dies away the word of prayer, and in the whole ministry and experience of the apostles was it fulfilled. As nothing could separate them from the love of God in Christ (Rom. viii. 39), Christ thus remained in them through the Spirit, and they have conquered far and wide through Him who loved them.

NOTE.—The *originality* of the high-priestly prayer stands upon the same footing with that of the longer discourses of Jesus generally in the Evangelist John. The substance of the contents is original, but the reproduction and vivid remodelling, such as could not come forth from the Johannean individuality, with which the recollection had grown up, otherwise than with quite a Johannean stamp. Along with this, however, in reference to contents and form, considering the peculiarly profound impression which the prayer of this solemn moment must necessarily have made upon the spirit and memory of that very disciple, a superior degree of fidelity of recollection and power of rendering must be assumed. How often may these last solemn words have stirred the soul of John ! To this corresponds also the self consciousness, as childlike as it is simple and clear in its elevation, the victorious rest and peace of this prayer, which is the noblest and purest pearl of devotion in the whole N. T. " For plain and simple as it sounds, so deep, rich, and wide it is, that none can fathom it," Luther. Spener never ventured to preach upon it, because he felt that its true understanding exceeded the ordinary measure of faith ; but he caused it to be read to him three times on the evening before his death, see his *Lebensbeschr.* by Canstein, p. 145 ff. The contrary view, that it is a later idealizing fiction of a dogmatic and metaphysical kind (Bretschneider, Strauss, Weisse, Baur, Scholten), is indeed a necessary link in the chain of controversy on the originality of the Johannean history generally, but all the more untenable, the more unattainable, the depth, tenderness, intensity, and loftiness here sustained from beginning to end, must have been for a later inventor. But to deny the inward truth and splendour of the prayer (see especially Weisse, II. p. 294), is a matter evincing a critically corrupt taste and judgment. The *conflict of soul in Gethsemane*, so soon after this prayer which speaks of overcoming the world and of peace, is, considering the pure humanity of Jesus (which was not forced into stoical indifference), psychologically too conceivable, not, indeed, as a voluntary undergoing in his own person of all the terrors of death coming from a world's sin (Hengstenberg), but rather from the change of feelings and dispositions in the contemplation of death, and of *such* a death, to be made to pass as an historical contradiction to chap. xvii. See on Matt., note after xxvi. 46. John himself relates nothing of the crisis of this final agony ; but this is connected with the general character of his selection from the

---

[1] Comp. Rom. v. 5. Bengel aptly remarks : "*ut cor ipsorum theatrum sit et palaestra hujus amoris*," namely, διὰ πνεύματος ἁγίου, Rom. *l.c.* According to Hengstenberg (comp. also Weiss, p. 80), Jesus merely intends to say : " that Thou mayest love them with the love with which Thou hast loved me." But this does not suit the expression ἐν αὐτοῖς ᾖ, either in itself or in the parallel relation to κἀγὼ ἐν αὐτοῖς. An inward efficacious presence must be thereby intended.

[2] xiv. 20 ff. ; Rom. viii. 10; Gal. ii. 20; Eph. iii. 17.

evangelical material, and he might be determined in this matter particularly by the account already given of the similar fact, xii..23 ff., which *he only* adduces, while the conflict in the garden was already a common property of scriptural tradition (comp. also Heb. v. 7), which he as little needed to repeat as the institution of the Lord's Supper and many other things. That this final agony had not for John the importance and historic reality which it had for the Synoptics, is, considering the free selection which he has made out of the rich material of his recollection, a hasty conclusion.[1] The historic reality of the Gospel facts, if nothing essential is otherwise opposed to them, is not affected by the silence of John.

NOTES BY AMERICAN EDITOR.

LVII. Vv. 1–8.

Meyer regards the prayer of Jesus for His glorification as extending from ver. 1 to 5 ; Weiss, with Lücke, de Wette, and Ebrard, regards it as extending to ver. 8, thus including the backward glance over the completion of His earthly work, upon which the prayer for His glorification rests.

LVIII. "The hour." Ver. 1.

According to Meyer, the hour of His death (but as a transition to His Father). Weiss : not properly the hour of His death, but the hour upon which open the words now following, and in which His glorification finds its allotted place.

LIX. "Thee the only true God . . . Jesus Christ." Ver. 4.

Meyer takes these as predicative : "thee as the only true God, and Jesus as Christ." Weiss, more correctly, I think, as apposition (as Eng. Ver.).

LX. "And all mine are thine, and thine are mine." Ver. 10.

This clause should, with Meyer, be placed in parenthesis ; it is an incidental expansion of the idea into universality. As it stands, the Eng. Ver. (including the Rev.) obscures or misrepresents the meaning of the following αὐτοῖς, which certainly refers only to the disciples.—Observe the remarkable τὰ σὰ ἐμά, *all that is thine is mine*—irreconcilable, it would seem, with anything but essential Deity.

LXI. "And the glory which thou hast given me I have given them." Ver. 22.

Meyer refers this to "the heavenly glory" given in promise and anticipation to all His people. Weiss thinks that the perf. δέδωκα, *have given*, precludes it from being applied to the πάντες of ver. 21, and that therefore its only proper reference, as Christ's revelation of His glory in His own works of power cannot be well called a *giving* (διδόναι), is to that wonder-working power which He has bestowed upon His disciples. Meyer's view seems right.

[1] In answer to Baur, in the *Theol. Jahrb.* 1854, p. 224.

CHAPTER XVIII.

Ver. 1. The *Recepta* τῶν κέδρων has the preponderance of testimony, Griesb. Scholz, Lachm., following A. S. Δ. Verss. Hier. Ambr. have τοῦ κεδρῶν ; Tisch., following D. ℵ. 2 Cod. of It. Sah. Copt. : τοῦ κέδρου. The reading τοῦ κεδρῶν is to be preferred, since we cannot suppose that John somehow connected the name קִדְרוֹן with κέδρος or κέδρον, as was done in 2 Sam. xv. 23 and 1 Kings xv. 13, LXX. — Ver. 4. ἐξελθὼν εἶπεν] B. C.* D. Curss. Verss. Or. Syr. Chrys. Aug. : ἐξῆλθεν καὶ λέγει. So Lachm. and Tisch. Rightly ; the *Recepta* is an alteration after ver. 1, which was made, because what was intended by ἐξῆλθεν was not distinguished from that expressed by it in ver. 1. — Ver. 6. ὅτι] which, though deleted by Lachm. and Tisch., has very important witnesses for and against it ; yet how readily would it come to be omitted after ver. 5 ! — Ver. 10. ὠτίον] Tisch. : ὠτάριον, after B. C.* L. X. ℵ., which (comp. also on Mark xiv. 47) is the more to be preferred, that the better known ὠτίον is found in Matt. — Ver. 11. After μάχαιρ. Elz. has σου., against decisive witnesses, from Matt. xxvi. 52. — Ver. 13. αὐτόν] has against it witnesses of such importance, that Lachm. has bracketed, Tisch. deleted it. But, unnecessary in itself, how readily might it be passed over after the similar final sound of the preceding word ! — Ver. 14. ἀπολέσθαι] Lachm. Tisch. ; ἀποθανεῖν. The witnesses are very much divided. ἀποθ. is from xi. 50. — Ver. 15. ἄλλος] Elz. Griesb. Scholz, Tisch. : ὁ ἄλλος. The article is wanting in A. B. D. ℵ. Curss., but retains, notwithstanding, a great weight of testimony, and might readily come to be omitted, since it appeared to have no reference here. — Ver. 20. Instead of the first ἐλάλησα, λελάληκα (Lachm. Tisch.) is so decisively attested, that the Aor. appears to have been introduced in conformity with the following aorists. — The article before συναγ. is decidedly condemned by the evidence (against Elz). — Instead of the second πάντοτε, Griesb. Lachm. Tisch. have πάντες, which is to be preferred, on account of preponderant testimony, and because πάντοτε might readily be mechanically repeated from the preceding πάντοτε ; πάντοθεν (Elz.) rests on conjecture (Beza) and Curss. — Ver. 21. ἐπερωτ. ; ἐπερῶτ.] The simple forms (Lachm. Tisch.) are preponderantly attested. The compound forms were readily introduced through the concurrence of the two E's (μΕΕρωτ.), in recollection of ver. 7. — Ver. 22. Read with Lachm. Tisch., according to B. ℵ. It. Vulg. Cyr. εἰς παρεστ. τῶν ὑπ. Various transpositions in the Codd. — Ver. 24. After ἀπέστ., Elz. Lachm. Tisch. have οὖν, which has important witnesses for and against it. Since, however, other Codd. read δέ, and several Verss. express καί, any particle is to be regarded as a later connective addition. — The same various connective particles are found inserted in Codd. and Verss., after ἠρνήσατο, ver. 25. — Ver. 28. πρωΐ] Elz. Scholz : πρωΐα, against decisive testimony. But how readily might the quite unnecessary ἵνα disappear ! — Ver. 29. After Πιλάτος Lachm. and Tisch. have ἔξω (B. C.* L. X. ℵ. Curss. Verss.), which other witnesses first place after αὐτούς. This different position, and the importance of the omitting witnesses, show it to be an interpolation, with a view to greater definiteness of designation. — κατά] is deleted by Tisch., according to B. א.* alone. Being unnecessary, it was passed over. — Ver. 34. αὐτῷ after ἀπεκρ. in Elz. is decisively condemned by the witnesses.— Ver. 37. ἐγώ. 'Εγώ] The omission of one ἐγώ (Lachm. has bracketed the second, Tisch. has deleted the first) is not sufficiently justified by B. D. L. Y. א. Curss. Verss. Fathers, since the omission was so readily suggested in copying, if the weight of the repeated ἐγώ was not observed.

Vv. 1, 2. 'Εξῆλθε] from *Jerusalem*, where the meal, xiii. 2, had been held. The ἀγωμεν ἐντεῦθεν, xvi. 31, was now first carried out ; see *in loc.* : πέραν τοῦ χειμ. then expresses : *whither* He went ; see on vi. 1. — τοῦ Κεδρών] Genit. of apposition.[1] It is a torrent dry in summer [2] (קִדְרוֹן, *i.e. niger, black stream*), flowing eastward from the city through the valley of the same name.[3] As to the name, comp. the very frequent Greek name of rivers, Μέλας.[4] — κῆπος] According to Matt. xxvi. 36, a garden of the landed estate of Gethsemane. The owner must be conceived as being friendly to Jesus. — ὅτι πολλάκις, κ.τ.λ.] points back to earlier festal visits, and is a more exact statement of detail, of which John has many in the history of the passion. We see from the contents that Jesus offered Himself with conscious freedom to the final crisis. Comp. ver. 4. — *Typological* references (Luthardt, after older expositors : to *David*, who, when betrayed by Ahithophel, had gone the same way, 2 Sam. xv. 23 ; Lampe, Hengstenberg, following the Fathers : to *Adam*, who in the garden incurred the penalty of death) are without any indication in the text.

Ver. 3. The σπεῖρα is the *Roman cohort*,[5] designated by the article as the *well-known* band, namely, because serving as the garrison of the fort Antonia, distinguished by what follows from the company of *officers of justice* appointed on the part of the Sanhedrim, and not to be explained of the *Levitical temple-watch*.[6] That Judas arrived with the *whole* σπεῖρα is, as being disproportionate to the immediate object (against Hengstenberg), not probable ; but a *division*, ordered for the present service, especially as the chiliarch himself was there (ver. 12), *represented* the cohort.[7] Of this co-operation of the Roman military, for which the Sanhedrim had made requisition, the Synoptics say nothing, although Hengstenberg takes pains to find indications of it in their narrative. John's account is *more complete*. — φανῶν κ. λαμπ.] with *torches* and *lamps* (the latter in lanterns ; Matt. xxv. 1 ff.).[8] Extreme precau-

---

[1] 2 Pet. ii. 6, comp. πόλις 'Αθηνῶν and the like.

[2] χείμαρρος, Hom. *Il.* xi. 493 ; Soph. *Ant.* 708 ; Plat. *Legg.* v. p. 736 A ; Joseph. *Antt.* viii. i. 5.

[3] See Robinson, II. p. 31 ff. ; Ritter, *Erdk.* XV. 1, p. 598 ff.

[4] Herod. vii. 58. 198 ; Strabo, viii. p. 386, *et al.*

[5] See Matt. xxvii. 27 ; Acts xxi. 31 ; Polyb. xi. 23, i. 6, xxiv. 3 ff. ; Valckenaer, *Schol.* I. p. 458 f.

[6] Michaelis, Kuinoel, Gurlitt, *Lect. in N. T. Spec.* IV. 1805, B. Crusius, Baeumlein.

[7] This is quite sufficient for the inexact-

ness of popular information. We have hence neither to understand a *manipulus* (*i.e.* the third part of the cohort), for which an appeal is erroneously made to Polyb. xi. 23. 1, nor, generally, a *band*, a detachment of soldiers (2 Macc. vii. 23, xii. 22 ; Judith xiv. 11). Not the latter, because it is *Roman* military that is spoken of ; not the former, because although Polybius elsewhere employs σπεῖρα as equivalent to *manipulus* (see Schweighäuser, *Lex.* p. 559), yet a whole maniple (some 200 men) would here be too many.

[8] Comp. Dion. H. xi. 40.

tion renders this preparation conceivable even at the time of full moon. The *arms* are, as a matter of course, carried by the soldiers, not by the ὑπηρέται, and are mentioned as helping to complete the picture. — The καί's are not *accumulated* (Luthardt), not one of them is unnecessary.

Vv. 4, 5. This advance of Judas occasioned (οὖν) Jesus to come forth, since He knew all that was about to come upon Him, and at the same time was far removed from any intention of withdrawing Himself from His destiny, of which He was fully and clearly conscious. — ἔρχεσθαι, of *destinies*, happy (Matt. x. 13) and unhappy (Matt. xxiii. 35),[1] in the classics more frequently with the dative,[2] than with ἐπί. — ἐξῆλθεν (see the critical notes) : *from the garden*, ver. 1, Nonnus : κῆπον ἐάσας. The context yields no other meaning, and ver. 26 is not opposed to it. Hence not : from the *garden-house*,[3] or from the *depth* of the garden,[4] or from the *circle of disciples*.[5] — εἱστήκει δὲ καὶ 'Ιούδας, κ.τ.λ.] *Tragic* feature in the *descriptive picture* of this scene, without any further special purpose in view. Tholuck arbitrarily remarks : John wished to indicate the *effrontery* of Judas ; and Hengstenberg : he wished to guard against the false opinion that the ἐγώ εἰμι was intended to convey to the officers something unknown to them. *This* he could surely have *expressed* in few words. — The *kiss* of Judas (Matt. xxvi. 47 ff.), instead of which John gives the above personal statement (as Strauss indeed thinks : for the *glorification* of Jesus), is not thereby excluded, is too characteristic and too well attested to be ascribed to tradition, and cannot have followed (Ewald) the question of Jesus (ver. 4), but, inasmuch as the immediate effect of the ἐγώ εἰμι did not permit of the interruption of the kiss, must have *preceded*, so that immediately on the coming forth of Jesus from the garden, Judas stepped forward, kissed Him, and then again fell back to the band. Accordingly, John, after the one factor of the betrayal, namely the *kiss*, had been already generally disseminated in tradition, brings into prominence the other also, the *personal statement* ; hence this latter is not to be ascribed merely to the *Johannean* Jesus (Hilgenfeld, Scholten).

Ver. 6. *They gave way,—drew back* (see on vi. 66), *and fell to the earth*, (χαμαί = χαμᾶζε, very frequently in the classics also); this was regarded, first by Oeder,[6] and recently by most expositors,[7] as a *natural* consequence of terror and of sudden awe, in support of which reference is made to the (weaker) analogies from the history of M. Antonius,[8] of Marius,[9] and even of Coligny ; while Brückner conceives of the effect at least as "scarcely purely human." Lange, in like manner, deduces it from terror of conscience, and finds the miracle only in the fact that it was not unexpected by the Lord, and not undesigned by Him. But, presumptively, the very falling to the ground, and the designating those who fell generally and without exception, thus including with the rest the Roman soldiers, justifies the ancient com-

[1] Aesch. *Pers.* 436, 439 ; Ellendt, *Lex. Soph.* I. p. 686 f.
[2] Thuc. viii. 96. 1.
[3] Rosenmüller, Ewald.
[4] Tholuck, Maier, de Wette, Luthardt.
[5] Schweizer, Lange, Hengstenberg.

[6] *Miscell. sacr.* p. 503 ff.
[7] Including Lücke, Tholuck, Olshausen, de Wette, B. Crusius, Ewald, Baeumlein.
[8] Val. Max. viii. 9. 2.
[9] Velleius Paterc. ii. 19. 3.

mentators, followed by Strauss (who, however, with Scholten, views the matter as unhistorical), Ebrard, Maier, Luthardt, Hengstenberg, Godet, in regarding it as a *miraculous* result of the *power of Christ* (Nonnus : οἰστρηθέν-τες ἀτευχέϊ λαίλαπι φωνῆς). Christ wished, before His surrender, to make known His might over His foes, and thus show the voluntariness of His surrender. He *could* remain free, but He is *willing* to surrender Himself, because He knows His hour is come, xvii. 1.

Vv. 8, 9. Jesus guarded against the seizure at the same time of the disciples. That *hands had* already *been laid on them,*[1] the text does not say. He should and would suffer *alone.* — ἵνα πληρ. κ.τ.λ.] Divinely-determined *object* of ἀπεκρίθη, in reference to the words εἰ οὖν, κ.τ.λ. John discovers in the saying, xvii. 12 (the quoting of which, without verbal exactness, should be noted as an instance of the free mode of citation in the N. T.), a prophetic reference to the preservation of the disciples from being taken prisoners along with Him, *in so far, that is,* as the Lord, in virtue of this protection, *brought none of them into destruction,* namely, through the apostasy to which any captured with him would have been exposed. This prophetic reference (against Schweizer's and Scholten's severe judgment) is justified by the fact that Jesus, in xvii. 12, delivers a *closing* avowal of His acting on the disciples' behalf ; consequently, that which is still further to be done on their behalf must be conformable to that declaration, and appear as the fulfilment, as the actual completion of what was therein expressed.

Vv. 10, 11. Comp. Matt. xxvi. 51 ff., and parall. — οὖν] In consequence of this danger, which he now saw for Jesus. On its position between Σίμ. and Πέτρ., comp. xxi. 7.—Only John here *names* Peter, and also *Malchus.*[2] Personal considerations, which may have kept the names so far away from the earliest tradition, that they are not adduced even by Luke, could now no longer have influence. — δοῦλον] *slave,* therefore none of the officials of the court of justice, ver. 3, but also not the guide of the temple-watch (Ewald). The slave had accompanied the rest, and had pressed forward. — τὸ ὠτάριον] not *purposely* (Hengstenberg), but the blow which was aimed at the head *missed.* — *Cast the sword into the sheath !* certainly more original than the calmer and more circumstantial words in Matt.[3] In the classics, κολεός.[4] — τὸ ποτήρ.] Comp. Matt. xx. 22, xxvi. 39. The suffering of death which He must now, in accordance with God's clearly recognized will and purpose (iii. 14, 15, vi. 51), approach, is the cup to be drunk, which the Father has already *given* to Him (into His hand) δέδωκε. — αὐτό, as in xv. 2.

Vv. 12–14. Οὖν] Since no further attempt at resistance dared be made. In the complete statement : *the cohort and the tribune,*[5] *and the servants,* any special design (Luthardt : the previous occurrence, ver. 6, had for its result that now *all* helped, in order to secure Him) is not to be supposed, since ἡ σπεῖρα, κ.τ.λ., is the subject not merely of συνέλαβον and ἐδησαν, but also of ἀπήγαγον. Tholuck's remark, however, is erroneous : that the soldiers had

---

[1] Bengel, B. Crusius, and several others.
[2] A name of frequent occurrence ; see Wetstein. In *Phot. Bibl.* cod. 78, a Sophist is so called. Hengstenberg gives artificial

interpretations.
[3] On θήκη, *sheath,* see Poll. x. 144.
[4] Comp. Hom. *Od.* x. 333 ; κολεῷ μὲν ἄορ θέο.
[5] ὁ χιλίαρχος τῆς σπείρης, Acts xxi. 31.

now first again (?) united with the Jewish watch. — συνέλαβον, κ.τ.λ.] A
non-essential variation from Matt. xxvi. 50, where the capture takes place
before the attempt at defence made on Peter's part. For ἐδησαν, see on Matt.
xxvii. 2.—On *Annas*, see on Luke iii. 1, 2. To him, which circumstance
the Synoptics pass over, Jesus was *first* (πρῶτον) brought, before He was conducted to the actual high priest, Caiaphas (ver. 24). An extra-judicial *preliminary examination* had first to be gone through. And *Annas* had been
selected for this purpose because he was *father-in-law* of the actual high
priest (ἦν γὰρ πενθερός, κ.τ.λ.) ; thus they believed it to be most certain that
he would so act in advance [1] as to serve the ends of his son-in-law, who then
had to conduct the proper judicial process in the Sanhedrim. Ewald's
assumption,[2] that Annas was at that time invested with the office of *superior
judicial examiner* (אבי בית דין), does not correspond to the fundamental
statement of John, which merely adduces the relation of *father-in-law ;* and
therefore, also, we are not to say with Wieseler and others (see also Lichtenstein, p. 418 f.), that Annas was president, Caiaphas vice-president of the
Sanhedrin ; or that the former still passed as the proper and legitimate
high priest (Lange) ; or even that John conceived of an *annual exchange of
office* between Annas and Caiaphas.[3] Quite arbitrarily, further, do others
suppose : the house of Annas lay *near to the gate* (Augustine, Grotius, and
many), or : Jesus was led, as *in triumph*, first to Annas (Chrysostom, Theophylact, and several others). — Ver. 14 points back to xi. 50, on account
of the prophetic nature of the saying, which had now come so near its fulfilment. Hence also the significant τοῦ ἐνιαυτοῦ ἐκείνου is repeated.

Ver. 15. Ἠκολούθει] correlative to the ἀπήγαγον, κ.τ.λ., ver. 13, and the
imperfect is *descriptive*. — ὁ ἀλλ. μαθ.] *The other disciple known* to the reader,
whom I do not name. *Self*-designation ; not a citizen of Jerusalem (Grotius), not Judas Iscariot (Heumann), not some unknown person (Augustine,
Calovius, Calvin, Gurlitt). Only the first rendering corresponds to the
article, and to John's peculiar manner. A tendency to elevate John above
Peter is here as little to be found as in xx. 2, 3 (Weizsäcker would conclude
from this passage that a *scholar* of John was the writer) ; it is a simple reproduction of the contents of the history. — γνωστός] *whence* and *how* is undetermined. Nonnus : ἰχθυβόλου παρὰ τέχνης ; Ewald : because he was *related*
to the priestly stock (see *Introd.* § 1) ; Hengstenberg : from earlier religious necessities. γνωστός does not mean *related*. — τῷ ἀρχιερεῖ, and then τοῦ
ἀρχιερέως, cannot, after ἀπήγ. αὐτ. πρὸς Ἄνναν, ver. 13, and ἠκολούθει, κ.τ.λ.,
ver. 15, refer to *Caiaphas*, but, as Ewald also assumes, though Baeumlein
groundlessly disputes it, only to *Annas*, as *the* high priest (he had *been* so,
and still enjoyed the *title*, see Luke iii. 2 ; Acts iv. 5), to whom Jesus was
brought. The remark on the *acting* ἀρχιερ. Caiaphas (ὃς ἦν, vv. 13, 14) was
only an *intermediate observation*, which the reference demanded by the course
of the history of ἀρχιερ. to Annas cannot alter. Accordingly, both the following denial of Peter (vv. 16–18) and the examination (vv. 19–21) and

---

[1] Comp. Steinmeyer, *Leidensgesch.* p. 115 f.   [3] Scholten ; comp. on xi. 49.
[2] *Gesch. Chr.* p. 562.

the maltreatment (vv. 22, 23), took place in the dwelling of Annas. Of the synoptic examination before Caiaphas, John gives no account, and only briefly indicates in ver. 24 that Jesus was sent away to Caiaphas ; a step which followed after the examination before Annas, presupposing as well known the trial before Caiaphas, which took place after this sending away. On the second and third denials, which are likewise to be placed in the court of Annas, see on ver. 25. This exegetical result, according to which John does not give any account of the hearing in the presence of Caiaphas,[1] but indicates as the locality of the three denials the court of Annas (see on Matt., note after xxvi. 75), is opposed to the older and modern system of harmonizing,[2] according to which, if one common court be not assigned to the dwellings of the two high priests (so again Hengstenberg in particular ; comp. on ver. 24), the leading away to Caiaphas is already presupposed in ver. 15, and then ver. 24 is disposed of with forced arbitrariness, partly on critical, partly on exegetical grounds ; see on ver. 24. The above exegetical conclusion is confirmed even on harmonistic principles, namely, from the side of the examination, by the fact that vv. 19–21 present no resemblance at all to the Synoptic examination before Caiaphas, as also that there is no trace in John of *judicial* proceedings before the Sanhedrim. Further, we are not to conclude, from the silence of the Synoptics as to the examination before Annas, that they knew nothing of it (Schweizer) ; but because it was no *judicial* examination, it might easily fall into the background in the circle of tradition followed by them. On the other side, the credibility of John (against Weisse) must turn the scale as well in favour of the historical character of the above examination as of the occurrence of the three denials in the court of *Annas*, without granting that the Synoptic and Johannean denials are to be counted together as so many different ones, beyond the number of three (Paulus). But when Baur takes the account of the examination in Annas' presence to proceed from the *design* of strengthening the testimony of the unbelief of the Jews by the condemnatory judgment of the *two* high priests, and [3] of bringing into prominence the surrender of Jesus by the

---

[1] Considering that this examination was well known from the older Gospels, of which he was fully aware, it was quite sufficient for him to *recall the recollection* of it simply by the observation inserted in ver. 24 — a proof of his independence of the Synoptics. Others have sought to explain the silence of John on the examination before Caiaphas differently, but in a more arbitrary manner, as *e.g.* Schweizer : that after ver. 14 this examination appeared to the apostle as a mere formality, not worth consideration. But as the *judicial* process proper, it was nevertheless the *principal* examination. According to Brückner, John has directed his principal aim to the denial of Peter and to the proceedings before Pilate. But this needed not, nevertheless, to have led him to be entirely silent on the examination before Caiaphas. Accord-

ing to Schenkel, Jesus, according to the present Gospel, underwent *no examination* at all before Caiaphas. But why then does John relate that Jesus was led away to Caiaphas? According to Scholten, John has kept silence regarding the examination before the latter in order not to cause Jesus to make the confession that He was the (Jewish) Messiah, Matt. xxvi. 64. As if this would have required the omission of the whole history ! And the confession of Jesus, Matt. xxvi. 64, is sublime enough even for John.

[2] Cyril, Erasmus, Luther, Beza, Calvin, Grotius, Wolf, Bengel, and many others, including Lücke, Tholuck, Klee, de Wette, Maier, Baeumlein ; also Brandes, *Annas u. Pilat.*, Lemgo 1860. See in opposition, Weiss in the *Lit. Bl. d. allg. K. Z.* 1860, Nr. 39.

[3] *Theol. Jahrb.* 1854, p. 285.

Jewish authority into the hands of the Roman, as brought about by *both* high priests, this is opposed by the fact, setting aside the entirely incidental manner in which Caiaphas is mentioned, ver. 24, and the arbitrary character of such inventions generally, that John as little mentions a *sentence* delivered by Annas as by Caiaphas, which nevertheless suggested itself so naturally in ver. 24, and the place of which xi. 50 by no means supplies, as respects Caiaphas.

Vv. 16–18. *Peter*, who had no acquaintance in the house, had not been admitted into the court (αὐλή, ver. 15), but stood, after John had gone in with the procession, *outside at the door ;* [1] hence John obtains, by means of the portress (Joseph. *Antt.* vii. 2. 1 ; Acts xii. 13), permission to introduce him. The εἰσήγαγε refers to *John ;* by Erasmus, Grotius, Ewald, and several others, it is referred to the *portress*, but in that way would give an unnecessary change of subject. The portress at the gate within the court asks of Peter, when admitted : " *Thou art not also, (art thou)* etc. ? The καί carries the presumption that *John*, whom she had nevertheless also admitted for acquaintance' sake, was a disciple of Jesus ; the *negative* question rests on the feeling that probably she ought not otherwise to have admitted him. [See Note LXII. p. 496.] — τοῦ ἀνθρ. τούτου] contemptuously, not compassionately.[2] — After the denial, Peter, whom, notwithstanding, his love to the Lord still detains at least in the open place, finds himself among the slaves (of Annas) and the officers of justice (the soldiers, ver. 3, appear to have gone with Jesus into the building as an escort), with whom he stands at the fire of coals in the court, and warms himself. Holding aloof, he would have been assailed. *John*, probably by help of his acquaintanceship, pressed with others *into the interior of the house*, not exactly into the audience-chamber.

Vv. 19–21. Οὖν] Again connecting the narrative with vv. 13, 14, after the episode of Peter. — περὶ τ. μαθητ. αὐτ. κ. π. τ. διδαχ. αὐτοῦ] Annas [3] then put general questions, in keeping with a private hearing of the kind, but well planned, so as to connect something further according to the eventual reply. —Jesus, as far as possible, not to inculpate His disciples (vv. 8, 9), replies, in the first instance (and further questioning was broken off, ver. 22), only to the second point of the interrogation, and that by putting it aside as something entirely objectless, appealing to the publicity of His life. — ἐγὼ παρρησίᾳ, κ.τ.λ.] *I*, on my part, *have frankly and freely* (comp. vii. 4, xi. 54) *spoken to the world ;* παρρησ. is to be taken *subjectively, without reserve*, not : *openly*, which it does not mean, and which is contained only in τῷ κόσμῳ. The κόσμος is the *whole public*, as in vii. 4, xii. 19. — ἐν συναγ. κ. ἐν τ. ἱερῷ] *in synagogue* (see on vi. 59) and *in the temple*. He appeals to His work of teaching not merely in *Jerusalem*, but as He has *always* carried it on, though He does not mean by πάντοτε to deny His public discourses in other places

---

[1] It was the street door of the court, the αὐλεία θύρα (see Dorvill, *ad Char.* p. 31, Amst. ; Dissen, *ad Pind. Nem.* i. 19, p. 361).

[2] Chrysostom, Theophylact, and several others.

[3] Not Caiaphas. Hengstenberg imagines the situation : " Annas presides, as it were (?), at the examination, but Caiaphas might not hand over to him the properly judicial function." So also Godet.

(in the open air, etc.), but only to express that He never, in the course of His teaching, withdrew Himself from synagogues and from the temple. — ὅπου πάντες, κ.τ.λ.] refers to the *temple.* — καὶ ἐν κρυπτῷ ἐλάλ. οὐδέν] By which, of course, the private instructions given to His disciples (comp. also Matt. x. 27) are not denied, since it is the ministry of the *teacher of the people* that is here in question ; and besides, those private instructions do not fall under the category of *that which is secret.* — τί με ἐρωτ.] For *what object* dost thou ask me ? με does not bear the emphasis ; otherwise ἐμέ would have been used. — The *second* τί, *quid,* depends on ἐρώτησον. — ἐρώτ. τ. ἀκηκ.] "Hoc jubet lex, a testibus incipi," Grotius. — οὗτοι] The ἀκηκοότες, not pointing to John and Peter (Ewald).

Vv. 22, 23. ῥάπισμα] *blow on the face, box on the ear* (so usually), or *stroke with a rod* (Beza, Bengel, Godet). [See Note LXIII. p. 497.] Comp. on Matt. ii. 67. The former, because the blow was wont to be the chastisement for an impudent speech (comp. Acts xxiii. 2), is the more probable, and δέρεις is not opposed to it (2 Cor. xi. 20). That which here one of the officers of justice, who stood in waiting (see the critical notes), takes upon himself for the honour of his master ("fortis percussor et mollis adulator," Rupert.), can hardly be conceived as taking place in an orderly sitting of the San- hedrim before the acting high priest (in Acts xxiii. 2 it is done *at the com- mand* of the latter), but rather at an extra-judicial sitting. — οὕτως] So un- becomingly.[1] — Ver. 23. Important for the ethical idea expressed in Matt. v. 39.[2] Comp. the note on Matt. v. 41. — μαρτύρησον] *bear witness.* He must, in truth, have been an ear-witness.

Ver. 24. By the incident vv. 22, 23, the conversation of Annas with Jesus was broken off, and the former *now sent Him bound* (as He was since ver. 12) *to Caiaphas,*—therefore now for the first time, not already before ver. 15. In order to place the scene of the denials in Caiaphas' presence, it has been discovered, although John gives not the slightest indication of it, that Annas and Caiaphas inhabited *one house with a court in common.*[3] In order, also, to assign the hearing of 19–21 to Caiaphas, some have taken *critical liberties,* and placed ver. 24 after ver. 14 (so Cyril, who, however, also reads it, consequently, a second time in the present passage, which Beza admits),[4] or have moved it back so as to follow ver. 13 (a few unimportant critical witnesses, approved by Rinck) ; some also have employed *exegetical violence.* Ver. 24, that is, was regarded either as a *supplemental historical statement to prevent misunderstanding ;*[5] or the emphasis has been laid

---

[1] Fritzsche, *ad Marc.* p. 150 f. ; Bremi, *ad Lys. et Aesch.* p. 124, 355) ; comp. on 1 Cor. v. 3.

[2] Luther : "This thou shouldest therefore understand, that there is a great difference between these two ; to turn the cheek to the one, and with words to rebuke him who strikes us. Christ must suffer, but never- theless the word is put in His mouth, that He should speak and rebuke what is wrong. Therefore, I must separate the *mouth* and the *hand* from one another."

[3] Euth. Zigabenus, Casaubon, Ebrard, Lange, Lichtenstein, Riggenbach,Hengsten- berg, Godet.

[4] Comp. Luther, who, after ver. 14, com- ments : "Here should stand the 24th verse. It has been misplaced by the copyist in the turning over of the leaf, as frequently hap- pens."

[5] So Erasmus, Castalio, Calvin, Vatablus, Calovius, Cornelius à Lapide, Jansen, and several others, including Lücke, Tholuck, Krabbe, de Wette, Maier, Baeumlein.

on δεδεμένον, to which word Grotius ascribed a force explanatory of the following denial, but Bengel one explanatory of the previous maltreatment.
These exegetical attempts coincide in this, that ἀπέστειλεν is understood in a
pluperfect sense (*miserat*), and is regarded as *supplying an omission.*[1] The
aorist, in order to adduce this as a supplemental addition, would rather be :
Annas *sent* Him.   But when the *Aor.* actually stands, making a *supplemental
statement*, the context itself incontestably shows it,[2] as in Matt. xiv. 3, 4
(not Matt. xvi. 5, xxvi. 48, xxvii. 27, nor John i. 24, 28, vi. 59).   Here,
however, this is certainly not the case (see rather the progress of the history,
vv. 13, 24, 28), and it is only a harmonistic purpose which has compelled the
interpretation, which is least of all justified in the case of John.   John had
the pluperfect at command just as much as the aorist, and by the choice of the
latter in the sense of the former he would, since the reader has nothing in
the context to set him right, have expressed himself so as greatly to mis-
lead, while, by the whole supplemental observations, he would have given to
the narrative, which has flowed on from ver. 15 down to the present point,
the stamp of the greatest clumsiness.   The expedients of Grotius and Bengel
are, however, the more inappropriate, the more manifest it is that δεδεμένον
simply looks back to ver. 12, ἐδησαν αὐτόν.   The sole historical sequence
that is true to the words is given already by Chrysostom : εἶτα, μηδὲ οὑτὼς
εὑρίσκοντές τι πλέον, πέμπουσιν αὐτὸν δεδεμένον πρὸς Καιάφαν.

Vv. 25–27. When Jesus was sent to Caiaphas, Peter was still on the spot
mentioned in ver. 18, standing and warming himself.   There follow his
second and third denials, which, therefore, according to the brief and accu-
rate narrative of John, who relates the denials generally with more precision, took place likewise in the court of *Annas.*   The text gives no indication that Peter followed Jesus into the house of Caiaphas.[3]   For the agreement of Luke with John in the *locality* of the denials, but not in the more
minute determination of time, see on Luke xxii. 54–62. — εἶπον] Those
standing there with him, ver. 18. — The individual, ver. 26, assails him
with his own eye-witness. — ἐγώ) I, for my part. — ἐν τῷ κήπῳ] *sc.* ὄντα.
The slave *outside* the garden (for, see on ver. 4) has been able, over the fence
or through the door of the garden, to see Peter *in the garden* with Jesus.
When the blow with the sword was struck, he cannot (in the confusion of
the seizure of Jesus) have had his eye upon him, otherwise he would have
certainly reproached him with *this* act. — ἀλέκτωρ] *a cock*. See on Matt.
xxvi. 74.   The *contrition* of Peter, John does not here relate in his concise
account ; but all the more thoughtfully and touchingly does this universally known psychological fact receive historical expression in the appendix,
chap. xxi.[4]

Ver. 28. Εἰς τὸ πραιτώριον] *into the praetorium*, where the procurator dwelt,

---

[1] So also Brandes, *Annas u. Pilat.* p. 18 f.,
who adduces many unsuitable passages in
proof.
[2] The pluperfect usage of the aorist in
relative clauses, Kühner, II. p. 79 ; Winer,
p. 258 [E. T. p. 275], is not relevant here.

[3] Comp. Olshausen, Baur, Bleek.
[4] Which, indeed (see Scholten, p. 382), is
alleged to be a *mistake* of the appendix,
the writer of which did not see through the
(anti-Petrine) tendency of the Gospel.

whether it was the palace of Herod (so usually), or, more probably, a building in the tower of Antonia (so Ewald). Comp. on Matt. xxvii. 27 ; Mark xv. 16. — πρωΐ] *i.e.* in the fourth watch of the night (see on Matt. xiv. 25), therefore toward daybreak. Pilate might expect them so early, since he had in fact ordered the σπεῖρα, ver. 3, on duty. — αὐτοί] They *themselves* did not go in, but caused *Jesus* only to be brought in by the soldiers, ver. 3. — ἵνα μὴ μιανθῶσιν, ἀλλ' ἵνα φάγ. τὸ πάσχα] Emphatic repetition of ἵνα, comp. Rev. ix. 5.[1] The entrance into the pagan house, not purified from the corrupt leaven, would have made them levitically impure (μιαίνω, the solemn word of profanation),[2] and have thereby prevented them from eating the Passover on the legal day (they would have been bound, according to the analogy of Num. ix. 6 ff., to defer it till the 14th of the following month). [See Note LXIV. p. 497.] Since φαγεῖν τὸ πάσχα throughout the N. T.[3] denotes nothing else than *to eat the paschal meal*, as אָכַל הַפֶּסַח, 2 Chron. xxx. 18, comp. 3 Esr. i. 6, 12, vii. 12, it is thus clear that on the day, in the early part of which Jesus was brought to the procurator, the paschal lamb *had not yet been eaten*, but *was to be* eaten, and that consequently Jesus was crucified on the day *before the feast*.[1] This result of the Johannean account is undoubtedly confirmed by xiii. 1, according to which πρὸ τῆς ἑορτῆς gives the authoritative standard for the whole history of the passion, and that in such wise that the Jewish Passover feast was necessarily still *future* when Jesus held His last meal with the disciples, with which latter, then, the seizure, condemnation, and execution stood in unbroken connection ; further, by xiii. 29, according to which the Johannean last supper cannot have been the paschal meal ; finally, by xix. 14 and 31 (see on those passages), while, moreover, the view that the murdered Jesus was the antitype of the slaughtered paschal lamb (xix. 36), is appropriate only to that day as the day of His death, on which the paschal lamb was slaughtered, *i.e.* on the 14th Nisan.[4] Since, however, according alike to the Synoptics and to John (xix. 31), Jesus died on the *Friday*, after He had, on the evening preceding, held His last meal (John xiii.), there results the variation that, with the *Synoptics* the feast begins on *Thursday evening*, and Jesus holds the actual Jewish *paschal meal*, but is crucified on the *first feast-day* (Friday) ; while with John the feast begins on *Friday* evening, the last supper of Jesus (Thursday evening) is an *ordinary meal*,[5] and His death follows on the *day before* the feast (Friday). According to the *Synoptics*, the Friday of the death of Jesus was thus the 15th Nisan ; but according to John, the 14th Nisan. We can scarcely conceive a more indubitable result of exegesis, recognized also by Lücke, ed. 2 and 3, Neander, Krabbe, Theile, Sieffert, Usteri, Ideler, Bleek, de Wette, Brückner, Ebrard[6] (not in Olshausen, *Leidensgesch.*, p. 43 f.),

---

[1] Xen. *Mem.* i. 2. 48.

[2] Plat. *Legg.* ix. p. 868 A ; *Tim.* p. 69 D : Soph. *Ant.* 1031, LXX. in Schleusner, III. p 559.

[3] Matt. xxvi. 17 ; Mark xiv. 12, 14; Luke xxii. 11, 15 ; comp. ἐτοιμάζειν τὸ πάσχα, Matt. xxvi. 19 ; Mark xiv. 16 ; Luke xxii. 8 ; θύειν τὸ πάσχα, 1 Cor. v. 7 ; Luke xxii. 7 ; Mark

xiv. 12 ; see also Ex. xii. 21 ; 2 Chron. xxxv. 13.

[4] Tertullian, *adv. Jud.* 8 : " Passio perfecta est die azymorum, quo agnum occiderent ad vesperam a Mose fuerat praeceptum."

[5] See Winer, *Progr. : δεῖπνον, de quo Joh.* xiii., etc., Leips. 1847.

[6] *Krit. de Evang. Gesch.*, ed. 2.

Ewald, Baur, Hilgenfeld, Hase, Weisse, Rückert,[1] Steitz, J. Müller, Koessing (Catholic),[2] Kahnis,[3] Pressensé, Keim, and several others. Nevertheless, harmonistic attempts have been made as far as possible to prove the agreement, *either* of the Synoptics with John (so mostly the older harmonists) ;[4] recently, especially Movers,[5] Maier,[6] Weitzel, Isenberg,[7] and several others), *or* of John with the Synoptics (so most later harmonists).[8] Attempts of the first kind break down at once before this consideration, that in the Synoptics the last meal is the *regular*[9] *and legal one of the* 14*th* Nisan, with the Passover lamb, slaughtered of necessity on the *self-same* day between the two evenings in the forecourt,[10] but not a paschal meal *anticipated* by Jesus contrary to the law (abrogating, in fact, the legal appointment, see Weitzel), as Grotius, Hammond, Clericus, and several others thought, also Kahnis,[11] Godet,[12] who appeals specially again to Matt. xxvi. 17, 18, Märcker,[13] who thinks the non-legal character of the meal is *passed over in silence* by the Synoptics. *Those* attempts, however, which identify John's account with that of the Synoptics,[14] Lightfoot, p. 1121 ff., Reland, Bengel,

[1] *Abendm.* p. 28 ff.

[2] *De Suprema Chr. coena*, 1858, p. 57 ff.

[3] *Dogm.* I. p. 417.

[4] See Weitzel, *Passahfeier*, p. 305 f.

[5] *Zeitschrift f. Phil. u. Kathol. Theol.*, 1833, vii. p. 58 ff., viii. p. 62 ff.

[6] *Aechth. d. Ev. Joh.*, 1854, p. 429 ff.

[7] *D. Todestag des Herrn*, 1868, p. 31 ff.

[8] Chrysostom gives a choice between the two attempts at reconciliation. *Either* John means by τὸ πάσχα : τὴν ἑορτὴν τὴν πᾶσαν ; *or*, Christ anticipated the celebration on the day before the Passover of the Jews, τηρῶν τὴν ἑαυτοῦ σφαγὴν τῇ παρασκευῇ, on which the O. T. paschal meal was solemnized. In this way Chrysostom already writes the programme for the whole of the later investigations on this point down to the present day. For the history of the controversy, see in Wichelhaus, *Kommentar über d. Leidensgesch.* p. 191 ff.

[9] The view which became current at the time of the Reformation and afterwards among the older theologians, especially through Casaubon's and Scaliger's influence, that the Jews *had postponed* the Passover *for a day*, was entirely baseless, but found all the more ready acceptance because there remained thereby time in full accordance with the law for the observance of the paschal meal on the part of Jesus. According to this view, which has again been recently supported by Philippi (*Glaubensl.* I. p. 266 f., ed. 2), the Jews, in order not to be bound for two days running to the strictness of the Sabbath observance, transferred the first feast-day, which at that time fell on the Friday, to the Sabbath ; whereas Christ abided faithfully by the legal term ; the synoptical account goes

by this legal determination, but the Johannean by the former arbitrary one. From ἔδει, Luke xxii. 7, no inference whatever can be drawn in favour of this harmonistic expedient, which is without any historical support. Serno (*d. Tag. d. letzten Passahmahls*, Berl. 1859) has sought, in a peculiar way, to confirm the correctness of both accounts by the doubling of the feast days during the *diaspora*. According to this, it may have come about that for the Galileans in Jerusalem that was the first day of the Passover, which for the Jerusalemites was but the day before the feast. In this way the twofold representation was stamped on the page of history. Against this it is decisive that the Galileans did not belong to the *diaspora*. See, moreover, Weiss, in the *Lit. Bl. d. allg. K. Z.* 1860, Nr. 42 ; Wieseler and Reuter's *Repert.* 1860, p. 132 ff. ; Ewald, *Jahrb.* XI. p. 253 f. On the above doubling of the feast-days, see Ideler, *Handbuch d. Chronol.* I. p. 513 ff. According to Isenberg, *l.c.*, "many thousand strangers," in order not to break in upon the Sabbath with the preparation for the Passover meal, held this meal already on the 13th Nisan. So also did Jesus, in order to institute the Lord's Supper as the fulfilment of the Passover feast, and to die as the Antitype of the Passover lamb. The above supposition, however, is unhistorical. A paschal lamb on the 13th Nisan is to the Jewish consciousness an impossibility.

[10] Comp. Lightfoot, p. 470 f., 651.

[11] *Abendm.* p. 14, Krafft, p. 130.

[12] p. 629 ff.

[13] *Uebereinst. d. Matth. und Joh.* p. 20 ff.

[14] Bynaeus, *de morte J. Ch.* III. p. 13 ff.

and several others ; latterly, especially Tholuck, Guericke, Olshausen, B. Crusius, Hengstenberg,[1] Wieseler,[2] Luthardt, Wichelhaus, Hofmann,[3] Lichtenstein and Friedlieb,[4] Lange, Riggenbach, von Gumpach, Röpe,[5] Ebrard on Olshausen, Baeumlein, Langen,[6] are rendered void by the correct explanation of xiii. 1, 29, xix. 14, 31, and, in respect of the present passage, by the following observations : (*a*) τὸ πάσχα cannot be understood of the sacrificial food of the feast to the exclusion of the lamb, particularly not of the *Chagigah* (חֲגִיגָה, the freewill passover offerings, consisting of small cattle and oxen, according to Deut. xvi. 2, on which sacrificial meals were held ; see Lightfoot), as is here assumed by the current harmonists,[7] since rather by φαγεῖν is the Passover lamb constantly designated,[8] also in Josephus and in the Talmud (אכל הפסח), and consequently no reader could attach any other meaning to it ; [9] in Deut. xvi. 2, 3, however, פסח does not mean " as a passover," [10] but likewise nothing else than *agnus paschalis*, from which, then, צאן וּבָקָר are distinguished as other sacrifices and sacrificial animals (comp. vv. 6, 7), whereby with עליו, ver. 3, we are referred back to the *whole* of the eating at the feast. 2 Chron. xxxv. 7-9 also (comp. rather vv. 11 and 13) contributes as little to prove the assumed reference of πάσχα to the Passover sacrifices generally, as Ex. xii. 48 for the view that to *eat* the Passover signifies the celebration of the feast in general ; since, certainly, in the passage in question, the general ποιῆσαι τὸ π. (*prepare*) is by no means equivalent to the special ἔδεται ἀπ᾽ αὐτοῦ.[11] (*b*) The objection, that entering the Gentile house would only have produced pollution *for the same day* (טְבוּל יוֹם),[12] which might be removed by washing before evening, and there-

---

[1] *In loc.*, and in the *Evang. K.-Zeit.* 1838, Nr. 98 ff.

[2] *Synopse*, p. 333 ff., and in Herzog's *Encyklop.* XXI. p. 550 ff.

[3] *Zeitschr. f. Prot .u. Kirche*, 1853, p. 260 ff.

[4] *Gesch. d. Lebens J. Chr.* p. 140 ff.

[5] *D. Mahl. d. Fusswaschens*, Hamb. 1856.

[6] *Letzte Lebenstage Jesu*, 1864, p. 136.

[7] Although the eating of the *Chagigah* was not necessarily restricted to the 15th Nisan, but might take place well enough on any of the following Passover feast-days ; hence a *religious obligation* as regards the 15th Nisan by no means lay in the way of their entering the Gentile house, *so that they might be able to eat the Chagigah*. But the partaking of the *paschal lamb* was restricted to its definite day, the 14th Nisan.

[8] Comp. generally Gesenius, *Thes.* II. p. 1115.

[9] Paul also, in the *Stud. u. Krit.* 1866, p. 367 ff., and 1867, p. 535 ff., explains it of the eating of the Passover lamb, but thinks that they had not been able to accomplish the eating on the evening that preceded the πρωί, and now " at the first gray of morning" desired to make up for that which was omitted in the urgency of their haste. What an irregular-

ity against the law (Lev. xxiii. 5, Deut. xvi. 7 ; Saalschütz, *M. R.* p. 407 f.) and usage is thus imagined, without the slightest indication in the text ! And the thought of such a completely exceptional early eating could not be entertained by the Jews, moreover, for this reason, that they must indeed stand by, and did stand by their delinquent, could not leave him as he was, and go thence, in order to eat the neglected Passover.— Aberle, in the *Tüb. Quartalschr.* 1863, p. 537 ff., admits indeed the difference of John's representation from that of the Synoptics, but thinks the Johannean day of death of Jesus appears through their account (in itself correct), and that they intentionally expressed themselves in an ambiguous manner (incorrect). See against Aberle, Hilgenfeld in his *Zeitschr.* 1865, p. 94 ff.

[10] Hengstenberg, comp. Schultz on Deut. p. 471.

[11] 2 Chron. xxx. 22, where the eating of the feast sacrifices generally (המויעד) is spoken of, proves nothing whatever for the special expression : " eat the Passover," rather is *distinguished* from it.

[12] Judith xii. 7-9 proves nothing in this respect for our passage (against Hengstenberg), where the evening bath of Judith

fore before the beginning of the new day, so that the Jews would have still
been able to eat the Passover lamb, which was not to be partaken of till
evening,[1] cannot be proved from Maimonides.[2] In view, rather, of the great
sacredness of the Passover feast (comp. xi. 55), this must be regarded
as invalidated by the present passage (at all events *in reference to the
time of Jesus*), irrespectively of the fact that such a pollution would
have been a hindrance to the personal *slaughtering* of the lamb, and
certainly by the hierarchs, 2 Chron. xxx. 17, 18.   (*c*) On the whole of
the inadmissible plea, which has been raised from the history of the Easter
controversies against the fact, that John places the death of Jesus on the
14th Nisan, see *Introd.* § 2. (*d*) It has even been asserted, in order to make
the account of John apply to the synoptic determination of time, that the
time of the Passover meal was not the evening of the 14th Nisan at all, but
the evening of the 13th Nisan (consequently the beginning of the 14th) ; so,
after Frisch, recently Rauch,[3] who understands our φαγεῖν τ. πάσχα of the
eating of the ἄζυμα. But the evening of the 14th (consequently the beginning of the 15th) stands so unassailably firm on the foundation of the law,
according to Jewish tradition, and according to Josephus,[4] that the above
attempt is simply to be noted as a piece of history, as also that of Schneckenburger,[5] which is based on the error that xix. 14 is the παρασκευή for the
Feast of Sheaves. (*e*) Had John conceived the last Supper to be the Passover
meal, there would certainly not have been wanting in the farewell discourses
significant references to the Passover ;[6] they are, however, entirely wanting,
and, moreover, the general designation of the Supper itself, δείπνου γινομένου,
xxii. 2 (comp. xii. 2), agrees therewith, to remove from the mind of the unprejudiced reader the thought of the festival meal. — If, however, the difference between John and the Synoptics is incapable of being adjusted, the
question then arises, *On which side historical accuracy lies?* Those who dispute the authenticity of the Gospel could not be in doubt on this point.
But it is otherwise from the standpoint of this authenticity, and that not of
mediate, second-hand authenticity (assuming which, Weizsäcker gives the
preference to the synoptic account), but of that which is immediate and
apostolical. If, that is to say, in the case of irreconcilable departures from
the synoptic tradition, the first rank is in general, *a priori*, to be conceded to
John, as the sole direct witness, whose Gospel has been preserved unaltered ;
if the representation also by the Apostle Paul of Christ as the Passover Lamb
applies only to the Johannean designation of the day of His death (see on 1
Cor. v. 7) ; and if, along with this, Paul's account of the institution of the

---

falls at most (comp. Grotius) under the
point of view of Mark vii. 4, where there is
no question of any eating of a holy, festal
character.

[1] See especially Hengstenberg, Wieseler,
and Wichelhaus, following Bynaeus and
Lightfoot.

[2] *Pesach.* iii. 1, vi. 1.

[3] *Stud. u. Krit.* 1832, p. 537 ff.

[4] See de Wette in the *Stud. u. Krit.* 1834,

4 ; Lücke, II. p. 728 ff.

[5] *Beitr.* p. 4 ff.

[6] This circumstance is also decisive
against the invention of an *anticipated*
Passover. For precisely at a Passover
feast of so *exceptional* a character the Passover ideas which furnished its motive
would not have been kept at a distance by
John, but would have been brought by him
into the foreground.

Lord's Supper does not run counter (in answer to Keim) to this Johannean
date ; if, further, even the statement of the Judaism which was outside the
church, that Jesus was executed *vespera paschatis* (ערב הפסח), *i.e.* on the
14th Nisan, supports the account of John,[1] where the fabulous element in the
Talmudic narration of the *circumstances* attending the execution does not
affect the simple date of *time;* if the conducting of a criminal trial[2] and
execution on the first feast-day, even after the most recent attempts to show
their admissibility,[3] is at least highly improbable,[4] and is opposed by Acts
xii. 31 ff., and in the case before us would be regarded as an exception from
the rule,[5] in fact, imprudent and irreconcilable with the great danger which
was well known to the Sanhedrim (Matt. xxvi. 5) ; if, generally, the 15th
Nisan, with its Sabbatic character, and as the legal day of the festive
gathering in the temple, is altogether unsuitable to all the undertakings,
processions, and parades which were set on foot by the hierarchs and by the
people on the day of Jesus' death, as well as to the taking down from the
cross and the burial ; if, on the other hand, the custom of setting at liberty
a prisoner (ver. 39) most naturally corresponds to the idea, and therewith to
the day of the paschal lamb, to the idea and to the day of *forgiveness ;* if,
finally, even in the Synoptics themselves, traces still exist of the true historical relation, according to which the day of Jesus' death must have been no
first day of the feast, but a day of traffic and labour,[6] as, moreover, the
opinion of the Sanhedrim, Matt. xxvi. 5, Mark xiv. 1 : μὴ ἐν τῇ ἑορτῇ ! corresponds to the Johannean account, and to the haste with which, according to
the latter, the affair was despatched, actually still before the feast,—then
all these points are so many reasons, the collective weight of which is
decisive *in favour of John*,[7] without the further necessity of making an uncertain appeal to the present calendar of the feast, according to which the
15th Nisan may not fall on a Friday,[8] and to the prohibition, Ex. xii. 22,
against quitting house and town after the Passover meal.[9] — The question
how the correct relation of time in the synoptic tradition *could be altered by a
day*, withdraws itself from any solution that is demonstrable from history.
Most naturally, however, the institution of the Lord's Supper suggests the
point of connection, both by the references, which Jesus Himself in His dis-

[1] See *Sanhedr.* 6. 2 f., 43. 1, in Lightfoot,
ad Act. i. 3.

[2] This difficulty drives Hilgenfeld (*Paschastr. d. alten Kirche*, p. 154, also in his
Zeitschr. 1863, p. 338 ff.), after the precedent
of Jost, *Gesch. d. Judenth.* I. p. 407 ff., to the
desperate assumption that no actual criminal proceedings took place at all. Neither
in Matt. xxvi. 3, nor xxvi. 57, and xxvii. 1, is
an actual Synedrium intended, but only
councils summoned by the high priest.

[3] See especially Wieseler, p. 361 ff.

[4] See Bleek, p. 139 ff. ; Ewald, *Alterth.* p.
415.

[5] Among the Greeks also, an execution
on a feast day was regarded as a profanation and pollution, and was, if it exception-

ally took place, as in the case of Phocion
(Plutarch, *Phoc.* 37), a great scandal ; see
Hermann, *Gottesd. Alterth.* § 43. 12.

[6] Matt. xxvi. 59, 60 ; Mark xv. 21, 42, 46 ;
Luke xxiii. 26, 54, 56.

[7] Here the appeal urged by Movers to *Tr.
Sanhedr.* f. 63. 1, is by no means required,
according to which the members of the
Sanhedrim might not eat anything on the
day on which they had pronounced a sentence of death. On 'this showing, they absolutely *could* not have had the design of
eating the *Chagigah.*

[8] See against his application to *that* period, Wieseler, p. 437 f.

[9] See on Matt. xxvi. 30, and Wetstein on
Mark xiv. 26.

courses connected therewith gave to the Supper in its bearing on the Passover meal, by the idea of which He was moved (Luke xxii. 15), as also by the view of the Supper as the antitypical Passover meal, which view must necessarily have been developed from the apostolic apprehension of Christ as the Paschal Lamb (xix. 36 ; 1 Cor. v. 7), so far as He in the Supper had given Himself to be partaken of, Himself the perfected Passover Lamb, which He, simply by His death, was on the point of becoming. Thus the day of institution of the Supper became, in the antitypical mode of regarding it, an *ideal* 14th Nisan, and in the tradition, in virtue of the reflective operation of the idea upon it, gradually became an *actual* one, and consequently the preparation which was firmly established as the day of death, became, instead of the preparation of the Passover (14th Nisan) as John has again fixed it, the preparation of the Sabbath,[1] this Sabbath, however, regarded, not as the first day of the feast, as in John, consequently not as the 15th Nisan, but as the second day of the feast (16th Nisan). — Nor is the deviation of John from the Synoptics to be made a reason for doubting the genuineness of the former. For it is wholly improbable that a late inventor, who nevertheless sought apostolic authority, would have run the risk of entering into conflict with the prevailing tradition in so extremely important a determination, and, in subservience to the idea of Christ as the perfected Passover Lamb,[2] to date back by a day the execution of Christ. Were the Johannean history, in so far substantially unhistorical, a production resulting from the idea of the Passover lamb, then certainly this idea would itself stand forth with far more of purpose and expression than it does (especially, for instance, in the farewell discourses), and would have been indicated, not merely on the occasion of the wound in the side, xix. 36, by one individual ; in that case one might believe oneself justified, with Weisse,[3] in laying to the charge of the writer of the Gospel that he had, in conformity with certain presuppositions, in part put together for Himself the sequence of events in an *accidental* and arbitrary manner.

Vv. 29, 30. In the prudent, concessive spirit of Roman policy towards the Jews in the matter of religion, Pilate[4] comes forth to them, and demands

---

[1] Moreover, the *Passover* meal, on the Friday evening, could by no means have been deranged by the dawning of the Sabbath. For the slaying and roasting of the lamb took place *before* the dawn of the Sabbath, and the pilgrims were wont to arrive early enough in Jerusalem (comp. xi. 55). The burning of the remains of the lamb was not, however, prevented by the Sabbath (Schoettgen, *Hor.* I. p. 121), and generally the rule held good : "Si quis unum praeceptum observat, ille ab observatione alterius praecepti liber est," Sohar, *Deut. princ.* f. 107, c. 427. This also in answer to Isenberg, *l.c.* Besides, the paschal lamb was a *sacrifice*, the arrangements connected with which the Sabbath consequently did not prevent, even if the 14th Nisan itself was a

Sabbath.

[2] See especially Baur, p. 272 ff., and in the *Theol. Jahrb.* 1854, p. 267 f. ; Hilgenfeld, *Pascha streit d. alten K.* p. 221 ff. ; Schenkel, p. 362 f. ; Keim, *Gesch. J. I.* p. 132 ; Scholten, p. 282 ff.

[3] *Evangelienfrage*, p. 130.

[4] The whole behaviour of Pilate in all the following proceedings is depicted with such psychological truth, that the opinion that his interest in Jesus was ascribed to him only by the evangelist (Strauss, Baur, Schenkel), can appear only as the consequence of presuppositions, which lie quite outside the history. Note particularly how just his *suspicion* against the *Jews*, owing to their personal behaviour, must have been from the first ; and how, on the other hand,

first of all, *in accordance with regular procedure*, a *definite accusation*, although he knew it, ver. 33 ; "sed se scire dissimulabat," Ruperti. But the hierarchical insolence, in its evil conscience, demands of him, contrary to all forms of legal procedure, to assume the *delivering-up* of the prisoner *itself* as a warrant of crime. *Him* who is not a misdoer, they reply, *they would not have delivered up to the procurator.* They had in truth themselves sufficient power to punish, although not extending to execution. If, therefore, the offence exceeds this power of theirs to punish, requiring a surrender to the procurator, this surrender is sufficient proof that the person is a criminal. The *kind and manner* of the crime (Tholuck : politico-criminal offence) is not yet defined by their words. The idea : " one hand washes the other" (Lange), lies entirely remote. — κατὰ τοῦ ἀνθρ. τούτου] is, further, uttered with *indifference;* not, "against such a pious and renowned a man," Luther.

Ver. 31. Since they bring forward no definite charge, Pilate refers them to their own tribunal (the Sanhedrim). As he, without such an accusation, from which must arise his competency to act, *could* take no other course than at once refer the matter to the regular Jewish authority, he also *incurred no danger* in taking that course ; because if the κρίνειν, *i.e.* the judicial procedure against Jesus, should terminate in assigning the punishment of death, they must still come back to him, while it was at the same time a *prudent* course (φθόνον ὀξὺ νοήσας, Nonnus) ; because if they did not wish to withdraw with their business unfinished, they would, it might be presumed, be under the necessity of laying aside their insolence, and of still coming out with an accusation. If κρίνειν, which, according to this view, is by no means of doubtful signification (Hengstenberg), be understood as meaning to *condemn*, or even to *execute* (Lücke, de Wette, who, as already Calvin and several others, finds therein a *sneer*), which, however, it does not in itself denote, and which sense it cannot acquire by means of the following ἀποκτεῖναι, something of a very *anticipatory* and relatively *impertinent character* is put in the procurator's mouth. — ὑμεῖς] With emphasis. — The *answer* of the Jews rests on the thought that this κρίνειν was, on their part, already an accomplished fact, and led up to the sentence for execution, which they, however, were not competent to *carry out.* They therefore understood the ·κρίνειν not as *equivalent to ἀποκτεῖναι*, but regarded the latter as the established *result* of the former. Any *limitation*, however, of ἡμῖν οὐκ ἔξεστιν, κ.τ.λ. to the *punishment of the cross*,[1] or to the *feast day*,[2] or to *political crimes*,[3] is imported into the words ; the Jews had, since the domination of the Romans (according to the Talmud, forty years before the destruction of Jerusalem[4]), lost the *just vitae et necis* generally ; they could, indeed, sentence to death, but the confirmation and execution belonged to the superior Roman authority.[5] The

owing to Jesus' personal bearing, his *sympathy* for Him must have developed and increased, so that in the mind of the procurator strength of character and of conscience alone was wanting, to prevent him, after perverted measures and concessions, from yielding ignominiously at last. See also Steinmeyer, *Leidensgesch.* p. 143 ff.

[1] Chrysostom, Theophylact, Euth. Zigabenus, Calovius, and others.
[2] Semler and Kuinoel.
[3] Krebs.
[4] See Lightfoot, p. 455, 1133 ff.
[5] See generally Iken, *Diss.* II. p. 517 ff. ; Friedlieb, *Archäol.* p. 96 f.

stoning of Stephen, as also at a later period that of James, the Lord's brother, was a *tumultuary* act.[2]

Ver. 32. The aim ordained in the divine purpose, why the Jews, in consequence of having lost the right of life and death, were obliged to answer "ἡμῖν οὐκ ἔξεστιν, κ.τ.λ." Otherwise, Jesus, as a false prophet and blasphemer of God, would have been *stoned* (like Stephen, and comp. viii. 59, x. 31), but would not have been visited with the Roman punishment of *crucifixion*, namely, as one guilty of high treason, as He, with His pretensions as Messiah, could not but appear to be before the Roman courts ; and the word of Jesus, xii. 32, would have remained unfulfilled.

Vv. 33, 34. Pilate does not, indeed, enter at present into further discussion with the Jews, but, because he quite perceived that they had set their minds on the punishment of death, he returns into the praetorium, into which Jesus, ver. 28, was led, and causes Him to be summoned before him, in order personally to examine him (taking a sufficiently inconsistent course), instead of simply persisting in his refusal on account of the want of a definite ground of accusation, and waiting for some further step on the part of the Jews. His question : *Thou art the king of the Jews?* which has an air of contemptuous unbelief (he does not ask, for example, σὺ λέγεις, κ.τ.λ., or the like), is explained, even without a κατηγορία on the part of the Jews, from the fact that the arrest, because made with the help of the σπεῖρα, ver. 3, could not have taken place without previous intimation to and approval by Pilate, who must therefore have been acquainted with its reason. We need not, therefore, with Ewald, assume the presentment of a written accusation, or, as is ordinarily done, infer that the Jews, even after ver. 31, came forward with the κατηγορία. This agrees with Luke xxiii. 2, but is not indicated by a single word in John, who could not have passed over, as a matter of course, so essential a point, which would yet have required but the briefest allusion. By his counter-question, ver. 34, Jesus does not desire, as Olshausen, Neander, Godet, Ewald, and several others suppose, to gather the more exact *sense* of the question,—whether, namely, it is intended in a Jewish and theocratic or in a Roman and political sense (for such a separation of the ideas concerning the Messiah was neither to be presumed in Pilate, nor to be suggested by this question of Jesus),—but He simply claims the *right to know the author* of the accusation contained in the words of Pilate ; to know whether Pilate put to Him the above question at his own instance, and without foreign prompting, or at the instigation of others. That the latter was the case, He indeed knew ; the ἄλλοι stood, in fact, before the door ; but Pilate should speak out and set forth clearly the *status causae.* It was this which Jesus could demand, and with the intrepidity of innocence did demand, without exactly intending to evoke a *movement of conscience* (Hengstenberg), which He could not at this point expect in the cold man of the world ; or to call his attention to the *suspicious source* of the accusation (Luthardt, Tholuck, Brückner), to which the wholly impartial ἄλλοι is not appropriate.

---

[1] Josephus, *Antt.* **xx. 9. 1).**   [2] Comp. also Keil, *Archäol.* II. p. 259.

Vv. 35, 36. The answer of the procurator, irritated and haughty, gives in μήτι . . . εἰμι an indirect denial of the first question, and with this an affirmation of the second. — μήτι ἐγὼ Ἰουδαῖός εἰμι] Ἐγώ with proud emphasis : you do not surely suppose that *I*, I your procurator, am a *Jew ?* How should *I* of myself think of trying thee as a *Jew*, and as *king of the Jews ?* The emphasis of ἐγώ Nonnus denotes by : μὴ γὰρ Ἰουδαῖος κἀγὼ πέλον ; The *opposite* of this : *Thine own nation* (τὸ ἔθνος τὸ σόν), *and especially* (καί) *the high priests,* have delivered thee to me ; what hast thou done ? No further ceremony ! — Jesus now *confesses* His kingship, [1] but, in the first instance, only *negatively* (positively : ver. 37) : " The kingdom which is *mine* springs not (like other kingdoms) from this *world* (which endures only until the establishment of my kingdom) ; if the kingdom which is *mine* proceeded from this *world*, the servants whom *I* (οἱ ἐμοί) have would assuredly fight that I should not be delivered (as was done, xix. 16) to the Jews (the hierarchical opposition) ; but as it is (since they do not fight for me), *my* kingdom is not from *thence*" (ἐντεῦθεν = ἐκ τοῦ κόσμ. τούτου). — Note in this *Demonstratio ad oculos* the solemn repetition of ἐκ τοῦ κόσμου τ. and of ἡ βασιλεία ἡ ἐμή, as well as that ἐντεῦθεν, *from here, hence*, is expressed *deictically*, as a vivid opposition to that which is *coelitus*, and, finally, that in ἐκ τοῦ κόσμου τούτου, not τούτου, which might also have been omitted, but κόσμου bears the emphasis. The ὑπηρέται οἱ ἐμοί are not the servants whom He *would* have in the case supposed, [2] but He *has* His servants, they are His *disciples and adherents* (not the *angels*, as Luthardt thinks), xii. 26 ; 1 Cor. iv. 1 ; 2 Cor. vi. 4, xi. 23 ; 1 Tim. iv. 6; but these also not from this world (xvii. 16) ; they also do not *fight*, etc. [See Note LXV. p. 501.] Note how also the designation of His own by ὑπηρέται expresses his *kingly* consciousness.

Ver. 37. A βασιλεία Jesus had actually ascribed to Himself in ver. 36, which Pilate certainly did not expect ; hence he asks, in surprise and not without a flash of haughty scorn : *Nonne igitur rex tu es ?* since thou, that is, speakest of thy βασιλεία. [3] [See Note LXVI. p. 501.] The sentence is an inference, but asking (*is it not then true, that thou art a king ?*) whether the questioned person agrees. — ὅτι] Confirmation of the assertion expressed by σὺ λέγεις (comp. Matt. xxvi. 25). — ἐγώ] Corresponding to the contemptuously emphasized σύ at the end of Pilate's question, emphasized with noble self-consciousness, and still more emphatically brought into prominence by the ἐγώ, which immediately begins the next sentence ("*potens* anadiplosis," Bengel) ; the repetition of εἰς τοῦτο twice also adds weight. — γεγένν. and ἐλήλ. εἰς τ. κόσμ.] with Grotius, Lücke, and de Wette, designate as the *birth* and the *official appearance ;* a separation which is not justified by the Johannean ἔρχεσθαι εἰς τ. κόσμ., in which the birth is substantially included (iii. 17, ix. 39, xi. 27, xii. 47, xvi. 28, i. 9), and which here renewedly describes it in relation to its specific higher nature, as the *entrance of*

---

[1] This confession must, according to Schenkel, have probably been spoken on another occasion. Groundless supposition. Comp. 1 Tim. vi. 13, and Huther *in loc.*

[2] Lücke, Tholuck, Hengstenberg, and several others.

[3] On οὐκοῦν, not elsewhere found in the N. T., see Kühner, *ad Xen. Mem. Exc.* III. p. 517 ff. ; Baeumlein. *Partik.* p. 198.

the sent of God into the world, so that the divine ἀποστέλλειν εἰς τὸν κόσμον (iii. 17, x. 36, xvii. 18) is correlative.[1] The *coming into the world* is related to the conception of *being born*, as the leaving of the world (xvi. 28) and going to the Father to the conception of *dying*. — ἵνα μαρτυρ. τῇ ἀληθ.] He was to bear *testimony* on behalf of the divine truth, for He had seen and heard it with God. Comp. iii. 11, 32, i. 17, 18. — ὁ ὢν ἐκ τ. ἀληθ.] *Genetic* designation (comp. on Gal. iii. 7) of the adherents of His kingdom ; their origin is the divine truth, *i.e.* their entire spiritual nature is so constituted, that divine truth exercises its formative influence upon them. These are the souls drawn by the Father (vi. 44 ff.), and given to Christ as His own. Comp. viii. 47. Bengel correctly observes : " *Esse ex veritate* praecedit, *audire* sequitur." — ἀκούει μου τ. φωνῆς] *heareth my voice, i.e.* (otherwise, xii. 47), he gives ear to that which I speak, follows my call, command, etc. With this Jesus has declared Himself regarding His kingdom, to the effect partly that He is a king, and with what definition He is so, partly as to his subjects. He has thus *completely* answered the question, and has in no way, as Hengstenberg thinks, *omitted* to answer it as too difficult for Pilate's comprehension, and expressed Himself instead concerning His *prophetic* office. The πᾶς ὁ ὤν, κ.τ.λ. marks an *essential* characteristic of His kingdom ; and any special purpose of the language, with reference to Pilate (an appeal to his religious consciousness, Chrysostom, Olshausen, Neander ; an explanation of the fewness of Christ's adherents, Calvin ; a reminder for Pilate, how he would have to lay hold upon salvation), lies remote from the sense, equally remote with an appeal " a caecitate *Pilati* ad captum *fidelium* " (Bengel), or from the *judge* to the *man* (Hengstenberg).

Ver. 38. Pilate, now fully convinced that he has before him an innocent and harmless enthusiast, asks, with that air of contemptuous *depreciation* which belongs to the material understanding in regard to the abstract and supersensuous sphere, *What is truth?* A *non ens*, a *phantom*, he thus conceives it to be, with which *He* would found a kingdom ; and weary of the matter, and abruptly breaking it off, he goes straightway forth to the Jews, and declares to them that he finds no guilt in Jesus,[2] from which definite declaration we see that by the above question he does not mean at all to designate the matter merely as not coming within his jurisdiction (Steinmeyer). Something of good-nature lies in this conduct, but it is the weak and shallow good-nature of the man of the world who is indifferent towards higher things ; nothing of the disconsolate tone of the searcher for truth (Olshausen). Against the view of Chrysostom, Theodorus Heracl., Euth. Zigabenus, Aretius, and several others, however, that Pilate had *actually* become desirous to *be acquainted with the truth* (Nonnus even thinks : καὶ

---

[1] Calovius aptly says : Christ was so born, " ut quum antea fuerit apud patrem, in tempore nascendo in mundum venerit, a patre in mundum missus." Contrary to the words and the contex is Scholten's view, that γεγένν. denotes the premundane procession from God.

[2] Here we are to think of the sending away of Jesus to Herodes Antipas. See on Luke, note after xxiii. 12. But how could the fourth evangelist have omitted this episode, had he been a *Gentile Christian*, and designed to concentrate the guilt of the death of Jesus as much as possible on the Ἰουδαῖοι? This in answer to Baur and Schenkel.

Πιλᾶτος θάμβησε) ; it is decisive that he immediately turns his back and goes
out. — *Whence did John learn of this conversation of Pilate with Jesus ?* He can
hardly have been himself an ear-witness of it.[1] But whether we assume
that Pilate communicated it to his own circles and that hence it reached
John, or that some actual ear-witness reported it to John, the matter creates
no difficulty (against Scholten). In no case have we the right to ascribe the
account merely to the *invention* of John (Strauss), and with Baur, for example, to find in the declarations of Pilate that he "finds no guilt in Jesus,"
only the *aim of the evangelist* to roll the guilt as far as possible off from Pilate
upon the Jews, which purpose also the question, What is truth ? is intended to serve, into which Baur foists the sense : how can one *make a
crime* out of the truth ?

Vv. 39, 40. Instead of steadfastly protecting the innocence of Jesus, he
seeks, unwisely enough, in order not to be unpopular, a circuitous way, by
which he practically surrenders the innocent one. — ἵνα, κ.τ.λ.] A custom
exists amongst you : *I am to release to you*, etc. On the thing itself, see
on Matt. xxvii. 15. — ἐν τῷ πάσχα] Pilate could thus express himself as well
on the 14th (against Hengstenberg), as on the 15th Nisan, but the releasing
itself corresponds most naturally to the sacred significance of the 14th.
Comp. on ver. 28. Moreover, it is in itself more probable that the statement of the time of this customary release as one that was legally stationary
is expressed also in the *strict* sense of τὸ πάσχα (Lev. xxiii. 5 ; Num. xxviii.
16). — βούλεσθε . . . ἀπολύσω] *Do you wish that I release?* Deliberative conjunctive. Comp. on Matt. xiii. 28.[2] — τὸν βασιλ. τ. Ἰουδ.] Unwise and
scornful bitterness. Hengstenberg imagines a serious view of the Messianic
idea to which certainly Pilate was wholly unequal. — πάλιν] presupposes a
general clamour already raised in vv. 30 and 31. — Βαραββ.] See on Matt.
xxvii. 16. — ἦν δὲ ὁ Β. λῃστής] Tragical addition. The designation by
λῃστής does not exclude the statement in Mark xv. 7 ; Luke xxiii. 19.[3] According to Matt. xxvii. 17, Pilate offered a *choice* between Barabbas and
Jesus ; Mark and Luke agree with John.

Notes by American Editor.

LXII. "*Art thou also one of the disciples?*" etc. Ver. 17.

"The negative question," says Meyer, "rests on the feeling that probably she
ought not otherwise to have admitted him." It is difficult to see how the
negative form of the question could express any such idea. It seems to be
simply the expression of the portress' modesty, at least of manner, in putting
in a negative form what she believed to be the fact. She believed Peter to be
one of Jesus' disciples, but instead of saying, "Art thou not one?" she said,
"Thou art not one, art thou?" (See John iv. 29.)

---

[1] So Steinmeyer, *Leidensgesch.* p. 143.   [3] λῃσταὶ φονεύουσι, Soph *O. R.* 719.
[2] Kühner, II. § 464.

LXIII. Ῥάπισμα. Ver. 22.

Blow on the face with the hand, or *stroke with a rod.* So the Revised Version gives the two alternative readings in the text and the margin. Mr. Frederick Field (in his *Otium Norvicense*) seems to show satisfactorily that its meaning in later Greek is confined to *a blow with the hand.* He cites Phrynichus, who forbids the use of ῥάπισμα for *a blow on the cheek with the open hand* as not Attic, showing that it *was so used* in his time. Field quotes many passages for ῥαπίζω and ῥάπισμα (Isa. i. 6 ; Hos. xi. 5 ; Matt. v. 39 ; Jos. Ant. vii. 15. 4, comp. with 1 Kings xxii. 24). Ῥαπίζω having come to be used for *strike with the palm,* instead of *strike with a rod* (ῥαβδίζω), gradually lost that earlier signification, and came to have *only* its later meaning.

LXIV. "*That they might eat the Passover.*" Ver. 28.

Meyer and Weiss hold confidently (with many others) the opinion that John contradicts the Synoptists as to the time of the Lord's last supper with His disciples. The Synoptical Gospels, it is universally agreed, place the last supper on the evening of the 14th Nisan, the regular time of the paschal meal, and make the crucifixion to occur on Friday, the 15th Nisan, the first day of the Passover festival. John, they maintain, on the other hand, places the last supper on the 13th, anticipating by a day the regular Passover celebration, and places the crucifixion still on Friday, but on the 14th, the day *preceding* the Passover. Affirming this contradiction, Meyer affirms likewise the superior credibility of John, and pronounces the Synoptists in error. It is indeed inconceivable that John should have been mistaken on so capital a point as to whether our Lord's last meal with His disciples coincided with or antedated the regular paschal feast, and the date which he unquestionably gives, it should seem, must be accepted. But it is equally inconceivable that the other Evangelists, one an Apostle and like John present at the supper, the other two, companions and friends of the Apostles, and thoroughly versed in the Gospel history, could have been mistaken on this point, and united in connecting a miracle (which His instructions to the disciples, one of them John himself, regarding the *place* of the feast clearly involved) with an event that did not occur on the evening they assign to it, and that evening the most sacred in the Jewish calendar. A mistake on this point shakes the whole fabric of their historical credibility. As between any two *ordinary* evenings, a difference of recollection (apart from inspiration) would be easily enough supposable. But as between the evening of the Passover festival and *any* preceding evening (no matter how near), a mistake is wholly inexplicable. With the Synoptists the accompanying circumstances are given in minute detail. The disciples come to Jesus and volunteer the question (Matt. xxvi. 17) where he will have them make the preparations for the Passover. He sends Peter and John with minute instructions, involving miraculous prevision ; and when they are assembled at the appointed time and place he says, "With desire have I desired to eat this Passover with you before I suffer (Luke)." And yet this was not the Passover at all ! The miracle, if it occurred, is misplaced, and the Lord's weighty and tender words were either not at all or mistakenly uttered ! We cannot set aside such a narrative without the most irrefragable evidence. Do we have such evidence in our Gospel? So maintain **Meyer and** not a few others ; but to very many the counter evidence seems wholly insufficient. Admitting that our Gospel of itself *seems* to intimate an evening before the paschal meal, yet when brought into comparison with these full and clear statements of the other Gospels, have we reason to suppose that it is intended to contradict them ?

The intimations mainly relied on are four. One of them, the πρὸ τῆς ἑορτῆς of xiii. 1, we have already considered. It is certainly too vague to be regarded as decisive, and if unsupported would probably never have been relied upon by any one for the point which it is adduced to sustain. It would seem almost certain that when John came to the account of the last supper, if he did not mean merely to *supplement* the Synoptical record—if he meant to fix a date which both ran counter to the unanimous testimony of that record, and, in so doing, changed the very character of the meal, showing it to be no Passover supper at all—he would not in the first place pass in utter silence the Synoptical account, as if taking for granted its correctness, and then give his counter date under the vague phrase πρὸ τῆσ ἑορτῆς, which *might* connect itself with εἰδώς, denoting the time of His becoming aware of His approaching departure, or might be taken as nearly equivalent to προεόρτιον, marking rather the initial part of the feast, and which in any case marks no definite period before it. Its terms would be fulfilled even if the foot-washing were a ceremony prior and introductory to the paschal feast, rather than an integral part of it. At all events this vague phrase, we may safely say, is not the only direct means which the Evangelist would employ for correcting an important error pervading all the Synoptics, and running like an intricate thread through all their various narratives, so that if they erred they, we must say, erred deliberately—an error affecting alike the date and the character of the feast, and requiring a more effectual extirpation than this mere πρὸ τῆς ἑορτῆς.

2. But it is said, xiii. 29, that when Judas went out from the supper the disciples thought that Jesus had said to him, " Buy things which we have need of for the Passover," or that he might give something to the poor ; and this it is supposed on the ground that the Passover had not yet been slain, and the preparations were yet to be made. But if this was on the evening of the day preceding the Passover meal, then there was no such haste required. There were yet twenty-four hours before the paschal meal, during which the purchases might be made, and there would be no need of sending one of the band out from this sacred occasion for such a service. Besides, the idea that Judas might have gone out for Passover purchases was with the disciples a mere uncertain conjecture : he *might* have gone out simply to give something to the poor. But if this was the evening of the paschal celebration, then for some of the numerous provisions of the following day (as for the *chagigah*), some haste might be required, at all events enough to originate such a conjecture on the part of the disciples. On the whole, this scene appears quite as compatible—probably considerably more compatible—with the occurrence of the meal on the Passover evening than on the evening preceding.

3. But another argument is drawn from the name given to the crucifixion day of παρασκευὴ τοῦ πάσχα (xix. 14), *the preparation of the Passover*, from which it is inferred that it was not the first day of the Passover, but the day before it. But as on the Passover, as on the other festivals, the preparation of food was allowed, there was no occasion of a day of preparation for it, and if there was one it would not be likely to occupy more than a small part of the day. On

the other hand, the law strictly forbidding the kindling of fire and all preparation of food on the weekly Sabbath, the preceding Friday was naturally, and indeed almost necessarily, devoted in part to preparation for it, and hence at last went by the name of "the preparation." Thus Matt. xxvii. 62 the Sabbath is spoken of as "the morrow which follows upon the preparation (μετὰ τὴν παρασκευήν);" and so in John it is repeatedly (xix. 31, 42) called the "preparation," and "the preparation of the Jews," evidently not with reference to the Passover, but to the coming Sabbath. There is therefore no good reason for taking it in ver. 14 in any different sense. It was the regular "preparation" day, but as occurring during the Passover, and thus having a double sacredness, John calls it the Preparation of the Passover, or the "Passover-preparation," such being a very easy and familiar use of the gen. in Greek. There seems to be no necessity for supposing this a day of "double preparation," but its occurring in the Passover gave it peculiar significance, just as the following Sabbath (Saturday) was a great or high day (xix. 3), not because it was the first day of the Passover, but because it was the Sabbath in the Passover, or the Passover Sabbath, and hence doubly consecrated. The fact, then, of this Sabbath being a "great day" does not, as has been alleged, prove it to have been the first day of the Passover. The last day of the feast of the Tabernacles is called, "that great day" (vii. 37), though having in itself nothing specially sacred.

4. But the passage most relied upon to prove John's difference from the other Evangelists on this point is xviii. 18. "The priests did not enter the Praetorium that they might not be defiled, but might eat the Passover." This certainly looks at first view as if the paschal supper was yet to be eaten, and as if therefore the Lord's supper of the preceding evening must have anticipated the regular Passover. Indeed it seems doubtful if, but for this passage, any serious suspicion of a discrepancy between John and the Synoptics would ever have arisen. Yet it seems remarkable that the only passage on which the correction of so important an error was to rest, and by which it could really have been suggested, should have come in in a way so purely incidental. To explain it without involving the alleged discrepancy, we may adopt either one of two ways. We may either take φαγεῖν τὸ πάσχα in the general sense of celebrating the Passover—a meaning which it has not elsewhere in the N. T. (being used exclusively of eating the paschal supper)—but which there is no special reason why it may not have, and which once at least its corresponding Heb. term has 2 Chron. xxx. 22 ("for seven days they ate the Passover"), while τὸ πάσχα often denotes the entire Passover festival; or, retaining the stricter meaning of φαγεῖν, it may refer to the feast of chagigah, eaten especially during the first day of the Passover, and from which the priests therefore would not exclude themselves by the pollution of entering the Gentile's house. This explanation is the more probable as this defilement was of a nature that would have terminated with the day, and they would therefore have been able at evening to partake the paschal supper, if this were the day before the Passover. Some scholars have preferred the explanation, that the priests, wholly absorbed on the preceding evening and night in the seizure and trial of Jesus, had foregone the paschal supper at the regular time, and were now looking forward to a later celebration of it. This explanation seems by no means impossible, but I think either of the others to be preferred as simpler.

It has been urged also that such a public act as the trial, condemnation, and execution of Jesus would not have been performed on a festival day, or upon the Sabbath. To this we may reply : 1. that the execution took place under Roman authority, and with the whole affair the Roman power was mixed ; 2. that we are but very imperfectly acquainted with the extent of the licenses or restrictions connected with festival days, and many things were permitted on them which were not allowed on the Sabbath ; 3. that in the Jew's hatred of Jesus they might easily deem themselves justified, and even doing God service, in transcending ordinary usages for the sake of destroying so heinous an offender, and that as matter of fact they did repeatedly endeavour to seize upon Him on festival days, as, at John xii. 32, 37, this was done by the assembled Sanhedrim ; and on another occasion (Matt. xxvi. 3–5) the objection was not any scruples of conscience, but the fear of an uproar among the people. But the most decisive reply of all is that the Synoptists, about whose date of the crucifixion there is no doubt, do not hesitate to connect all these public acts with that day. They must assuredly have been competent judges as to the usages of their time.

I shall not dwell upon the intimations of ecclesiastical tradition in connection with the later celebration of the Lord's supper, but merely remark that they furnish nothing unfavourable to the view here advocated. It remains but to say a word in regard to Meyer's explanation of the way in which the strange discrepancy originated. It was forsooth so strongly impressed upon the minds of the church that the last supper *ought* to have been held upon the Passover evening, that at length it came to be believed that it *was* so held, and it passed, in the Synoptic Gospels, from the sphere of imagination into the sphere of history ! Nothing, it would seem, could be well conceived more preposterous ; and if a chain of logic is not stronger than its weakest link, it surely will not take long for the whole chain to fall to pieces. The Evangelists, or their authorities, came to *imagine* that the last supper occurred on the Passover evening, and in harmony with this to which this belongs *invented* the whole series of circumstances which were to accompany it. They make the disciples come voluntarily to Jesus (Matt. xxvi. 17) and say, "Where wilt thou that we prepare the Passover?'' They make the Lord, in reply, send Peter and *John* (Luke xxii. 8), saying, " Go and prepare for us the Passover, that we may eat.'' They make the Lord exercise His divine prescience in giving the directions. They make Him utter the intensity of desire with which He had desired to eat this Passover with them (Luke xxii. 15). And the whole of this was an illusion !

One word finally on the *anticlimax* of the Jewish people's sacrificing (in the ordering of Providence) the *real* antitypal paschal lamb, and then sitting down on the evening after to partake of that typical meal whose significance and whose office had now been done away forever. In the Synoptical account it seems much more naturally ordered--the typical sacrifice on the preceding evening, and on the next day the efficacious sacrifice which forever supersedes it.

LXIVa. " *If my kingdom were of this world, then would my servants contend . . . but as it is, my kingdom is not of this world.*" Ver. 36.

Meyer and Weiss, with many, understand "my servants" as those whom Jesus actually has, not as those whom He would have in the case supposed. But in the supposed case the conditions of the problem would be essentially different, and the servants whom he would then have would not be the outwardly in-significant following that now wait on the spiritual Monarch, and whom it seems absurd to conceive of as arraying themselves against his powerful worldly enemies. I think, therefore, the other view more probable, and the statement a general one, that were he a secular monarch he would employ secular means of defending himself, and vindicating his claims. True, the Greek verb employed, ἀγωνίζομαι, contend, struggle, is somewhat more favourable to Meyer's view than that of our version, fight (as if it were μάχομαι). His small band of followers might more easily be conceived as struggling for their Master, than making a strictly armed resistance. Ἀγωνίζομαι is a much more general word, and is often used where there is strictly no fighting in the case. Thus, 2 Tim. i. 7, "I have fought the good fight," implies no proper fighting at all. It is contending in the games, striving with competitors for a prize, not fighting with enemies for conquest or victory.

LXV. Νῦν δέ, " But as it (since they do not fight for me) my kingdom is not of this world." Ver. 36.

Meyer (and after him Weiss) inverts the reasoning involved in the νῦν δέ. It is not, " If my kingdom were of this world my servants would contend ; but they do not contend, and therefore my kingdom is not," etc. It is rather, " If my kingdom were of this world, my servants would contend ; but now, but as it is, it is not of this world (and therefore they do not contend)." Such is the uniform use of this νῦν δέ both in the New Test. and in the classics (in the latter more generally in the form of νυνὶ δέ, in the N. T. almost invariably νῦν δέ). Thus John xv. 22 : " If I had not come and spoken to them, they had not had sin ; but as it is (I have come and spoken to them, and therefore) they have no cloak for their sin." See John iv. 41 ; 1 Cor. xii. 19 ; Luke xix. 42.

LXVI. " Art thou a king ? " Ver. 37.

Erroneously, I think, Meyer and Weiss agree in rendering " Art thou not, therefore, a king ?" which would require οὔκουν, not οὐκοῦν. The latter, I think, with Winer and Buttmann can here be rendered only, "Art thou, therefore, a king ?" The negative force seems to have dropped out from οὐκοῦν, from its having been first used in an affirmation (it is not, therefore), and then as a question, in which what was before denied categorically (it is not, therefore) is denied interroga-tively (is it, therefore? No). The meaning " Art thou not then a king ?" seems an unnatural reply to a declaration of Jesus in which He had virtually affirmed His kingship. Pilate in surprise naturally asks, " Art thou then a king ?" and this is the regularly established use of οὐκοῦν (with accent on οὖν) in distinction from οὔκουν, with accent on οὐκ.

CHAPTER XIX.

Ver. 3. καὶ ἔλεγον] B. L. U. X. Λ. Π. ℵ. Curss., most Verss. Cyr. Nom. Aug. : καὶ ἤρχοντο πρὸς αὐτὸν καὶ ἔλεγον. Rightly adopted by Lachm. and Tisch. The *Recepta* originated in a mechanical way, just as readily through an erroneous transition from the first αὐτόν to the second, as through the ·apparently unnecessary, indeed unsuitable, character which ἤρχ. πρ. αὐτ. might possess.— ἐδίδουν] Lachm. and Tisch. : ἐδίδοσαν. But see on xv. 22. — **Ver. 4.** Elz. Scholz : ἐξῆλθεν οὖν. Lachm. : καὶ ἐξῆλθεν. The witnesses are very much divided, but there is preponderant testimony in favour of καὶ ἐξῆλθ. (A. B. K. L. X. Π. Curss. Syr. Aeth. Cyr.). Nevertheless, considering the frequency of such insertions, the omission of the particle (Griesb. Tisch.) is sufficiently justified by D. Γ. ℵ. Curss. Verss. — ἐν αὐτ. οὐδ. αἰτ. εὑρ.] Very many variations, amongst which the simple αἰτ. οὐχ εὑρ. would, with Tisch., be preferable, if it were not that it has only ℵ.* in its favour. — **Ver. 6.** αὐτόν] is omitted after the second σταύρ. in Elz. Tisch., but has the preponderance of testimony in its favour, for amongst the Uncials only B. L. omit it. Nevertheless, the addition was so easily suggested of itself, and through Luke xxiii. 21, Mark xv. 13, John xix. 15, that it is to be regarded as a supplement. — **Ver. 7.** ἡμῶν] is wanting in B. D. L. Δ. ℵ. Vulg. It. Or. Hil. Aug. Deleted by Lachm. and Tisch. But how easily might its omission have been caused, partly by the preceding syllable MON, partly by its being apparently superfluous ! — **Ver. 10.** After λέγει, Elz. Lachm. have οὖν, which, indeed, is wanting only in A. ℵ. Curss. Syr. Perss. Copt. Arm. Slav. Cyr. (deleted by Tisch.) ; considering, however, the appropriateness of the connection which it expresses, it would hardly have been omitted had it been genuine. The copyists can scarcely have felt that there was anything cumbrous (in answer to Lücke, de Wette) in the expression. — **Ver. 11.** εἶχες] A. D. L. X. Y. Λ. Π. ℵ. Curss. : ἔχεις. Defended by Buttmann in the *Stud. u. Krit.* 1858, p. 485 ff., adopted by Tisch. An old copyist's mistake, which is supported by none of the Verss. except Copt., and by none of the Fathers, which, however, crept in readily enough after the shortly preceding ἔχω. — **Ver. 12.** ἔκραζον] Lachm. Tisch. : ἐκραύγαζον, according to important witnesses, indeed, but derived from vv. 6, 18, 40, whence B. D. Curss. have directly repeated ἐκραύγασαν. — **Ver. 13.** τοῦτον τὸν λόγον] The genit. plur., and that either τούτων τῶν λόγων, or, more strongly still, τῶν λόγων τούτων, is so decisively attested, that the latter, with Lachm. and Tisch., is to be adopted. The *Recepta* is derived from ver. 8. — **Ver. 14.** Instead of δέ after ὥρα, Lachm. and Tisch. have ἦν, on decisive testimony ; δέ is a stylistic correction. — ἕκτη] D. L. X. Δ. ℵ.** Curss. Chronic. alex. (the latter appealing to the ἀκριβῆ ἀντίγραφα, nay, even to the ἰδιόχειρον of John !) Nonn. Sev. ant. (appealing to Euseb.) Ammon. Theophyl. : τρίτη. An old harmonistic alteration in conformity with Mark xv. 25 (comp. Matt. xxvii. 45 ; Mark xv. 33 ; Luke xxiii. 44). — **Vv. 16, 17.** Instead of ἤγαγον. Elz. has ἀπήγαγον, against decisive testimony. But B. L. X. Curss. Codd. N. Copt. Cyr. entirely omit καὶ ἤγαγον. So Lachm. and Tisch.

But if the continuation had here been supplied from the parallel passages, not ἤγαγον, but ἀπήγαγον (comp. Matt. xxvii. 31 ; Luke xxiii. 26), would have the preponderance of testimony. Καὶ ἤγαγον, however, might easily have disappeared in the course of transcription, owing to a transition having been at once made from the first καί to the second. — τὸν σταυρ. αὐτοῦ] Lachm. : αὐτῷ τ. στ. (B. X.); Tisch. : ἑαυτῷ τ. στ. (L. א. Or.). The latter, in favour of which D. also testifies with ἑαυτοῦ, is to be preferred. The reflexive pronoun was frequently neglected. The *Recepta* is an alteration in conformity with the most current mode of expression. — Ver. 20. The order of the words Ἑβρ., Ῥωμ., Ἑλλ. (so Tisch., according to B. L. X. א. Curss. Copt. Sah. Aeth. Cyr.) has probability, considering the standpoint of Pilate, in its favour. — Vv. 26, 27. Instead of ἰδού, we should, in conformity with important testimony, read both times with Lachm. and Tisch. ἴδε, frequent in John (he has ἰδού only in iv. 35, xvi. 32, and from the LXX. xii. 15), though we are not to assume any difference of meaning between the two forms. — Ver. 29. οὖν] is wanting in A. B. L. X. Codd. It., whilst a few other witnesses (including א.) have δέ. Rightly deleted by Lachm. Tisch. — οἱ δὲ πλῆσ. σπόγγ. ὀξ καί] Lachm. : σπόγγ. οὖν μεστὸν τοῦ ὄξους, according to B. L. X. א. Curss. Verss. Cyr. Hilar. So also Tisch., but without τοῦ, which X. א. do not contain. The *Recepta* is shaped in conformity with Matt. xxvii. 48, Mark xv. 36, where οἱ δέ was readily suggested as an insertion on account of the change of persons. — Ver. 31. Instead of ἐκείνου, Elz. has ἐκείνῃ, against decisive testimony. — Ver. 35. καὶ ὑμεῖς] Elz. has merely ὑμεῖς. But καί is so strongly attested, and might be so readily omitted as being without reference, that it must be preserved. — Ver. 40. ἐν ὀθον.] The mere ὀθον. (Elz. Lachm.) is very strongly attested (B. K. L. X. Y. II. א.), but the superfluous ἐν might readily be passed over, comp. xii. 44, especially as the preponderance of parallel passages presents the mere dative.

Vv. 1-3. Οὖν] After the miscarriage of this attempt at deliverance, Pilate will at least make *the* further trial whether the *compassion* of the Jews may not be awakened. Hence he causes to be inflicted on Jesus the *scourging*, to which in any case, if He were to be crucified, He must be subjected ; and hopes, in the folly of his moral vacillation, by means of such maltreatment, although inflicted without sentence and legality, to satisfy the Jews, and avert something worse. Comp. on Matt. xxvii. 26. With a like purpose in view, he also gives Him up to the contumelious treatment of the soldiers, who deck Him out as *king* (xviii. 39) with a crown of thorns (see on Matt. xxvii. 29) and a purple mantle (comp. on Matt. xxvii. 28 ; Mark xv. 17). — Ἔλαβεν] shows the simple style of the narrative. — κ. ἤρχ. πρ. αὐτ.] See the critical notes. It is a *pictorial* trait. He stands arrayed before them ; *they go up to Him* and do obeisance to Him ! — ῥαπίσματα] As in xviii. 22. Codd. of It. add *in faciem*.

Vv. 4, 5. Πάλιν] For, according to xviii. 40, Pilate has returned into the praetorium, and has caused Jesus to be scourged, ver. 1. The scourging was certainly carried out so that the Jews could see it. The prisoner, scourged and arrayed in the caricature of a king, he causes to be led forth with him. — ὑμῖν] *Vobis ;* what follows gives the more exact explanation of this reference. — ἵνα γνῶτε, κ.τ.λ.] For had he found Him guilty, he would certainly not make the repeated attempt, implied in this leading forth and presentation of Jesus to them, to change the mind of the Jews, but would dispose of the matter by ordering execution. — Ver. 5. ἐξῆλθεν . . . ἱμάτιον is not a *parenthesis*, but the narrative, according to which Jesus comes forth *in the train of Pilate*, proceeds without interruption, in such a manner, however, that with λέγει (Pilate) the subject suddenly changes.[1] — φορῶν] not φέρων ; for the kingly attire is now to the close of the proceedings His permanent garb.[2] — The short significant *ecce homo !* behold the man, whose case we are treating ! has its eloquent commentary in the entire *manifestation of suffering* in which the ill-treated and derided one was set forth. *This suffering* form cannot be the usurper of a throne ! The words are gently and compassionately spoken, and ought to excite compassion ;[3] in ver. 14 he first says with bitterness : ἴδε ὁ βασιλεὺς ὑμῶν.

Vv. 6–8. Of the presence of the *people* (who perhaps kept *silence*, Lücke thinks ; comp. Luthardt, according to whom the high priests desired to forestall any possible expressions of compassion on the part of the people) the text says nothing ; the Ἰουδαῖοι, xviii. 31, 38, were pre-eminently the ἀρχιερεῖς of the present passage. — ὅτε οὖν εἶδον] The spectacle, instead of calming their bitterness, goads them on. — λάβετε αὐτὸν ὑμεῖς, κ.τ.λ.] A *paradox*, amounting to a peevish and irritated refusal, since the Jews did not possess the *right* of execution, and crucifixion was certainly not a *Jewish* capital punishment. Crucify him yourselves, if you will have him crucified ! —Now, however, they introduce the authority of their law, according to which Jesus (as being a blasphemer, namely, of God, Lev. xxiv. 16 ; Matt. xxvi. 63, 64) must die. They thus prudently give to their demand another legal basis, to be respected by the procurator in conformity with Roman policy, and to the accusation the corresponding religious sanction. An admission, however, that their political suspicion of Jesus had only been a pretext (Steinmeyer), is not contained in this ; it is only another turn given to the charge. — ἡμεῖς] With haughty emphasis, opposed to the preceding ἐγὼ . . . αἰτίαν. On ὅτι υἱόν, κ.τ.λ., comp. v. 18, x. 33. — μᾶλλον ἐφοβ.] *His fear only became the greater* (μᾶλλ., see v. 18), namely, of suffering Jesus to be executed. To the previous *fear of conscience* was now, in truth, added the fear of the *vengeance of a God*, namely, of Jehovah, the God of the Jews, in case the assertion mentioned should turn out to be true. He explained to himself the υἱὸς θεοῦ after the analogy of pagan *heroes*, like the centurion, Matt. xxvii. 54. That he was moved by the idea of the unity of God (Hengstenberg) has nothing to support it ; nay, viewed in the light of the wanton words, xviii. 38, very improbable.

Vv. 9, 10. He therefore took Jesus again away with him into the praetorium for a private audience. — πόθεν] asks after His *origin*, but not in the sense of the place of birth (Paulus), but in the sense occasioned by υἱὸν θεοῦ, ver. 7, in order to obtain a declaration from Jesus *on this point*, whether He were of human or divine origin. Comp. on viii. 14 ; Matt. xxi. 25. — ἀπόκρ. οὐκ ἔδωκ. αὐτῷ] Both this observation, as well as the peculiarity of Pilate's

---

[1] See Heindorf, *ad Plat. Euthyd.* p. 275 B ; Kühner, *ad Xen. Mem.* ii. 1. 8.

[2] Lobeck, *ad Phryn.* p. 585.

[3] Comp. already Chrysostom.

question, betraying a certain timidity, πόθεν εἶ σύ (how entirely different is his question, xviii. 33 ; while here he *shrinks* from asking directly), has the stamp of originality. Jesus is *silent ;* for what He would have had to say would only have been misunderstood by Pilate, or not understood at all (xvii. 25 ; Matt. vii. 6). Moreover, He had already in truth sufficiently indicated His heavenly origin, xviii. 36, 37, had Pilate only possessed susceptibility for the truth. But as it was, he was unworthy of further discussion, and in the silence of Jesus are seen precisely the self-assurance and majesty of the Son of God. Luthardt explains it *from the assumption* that Jesus will not give Pilate occasion to release Him from motives of fear, and thereby to interfere with the will of God. But on that supposition He must also have withheld the great and bold words, ver. 11. A resolute opposition on the part of the sceptical man of the world to the desire of the Jews, Jesus assuredly neither hoped nor feared. — Ver. 10. Καὶ φοβεῖται καὶ φοβεῖ, Euth. Zigabenus. — ἐμοὶ οὐ λαλεῖς ;] ἐμοί bears the emphasis of mortified power, which then also attempts alike to *terrify* and to *entice.* To mention *at first* the σταυρῶσαί σε, and *then,* not before, the ἀπολῦσαί σε, corresponded to the state of the procedure. But A. B. E. ℵ. Lachm. Tisch. have the converse order, which would meanwhile more readily suggest itself to the mechanical copyist. The repeated ἐξουσ. ἐχω is *weighty.*

Ver. 11. With a clear and holy defiance, to defend against this assertion of personal power at least the supremacy of His Father, Jesus now speaks His *last* word to Pilate. He points the latter, with his ἐξουσία which he has thus asserted in his σταυρῶσαί σε, to the supreme authority which has invested him with that ἐξουσία, but at the same time, with conciliatory mildness, deduces from it a standard to diminish the guilt of the judge. The saying breathes *truth and grace.* — οὐκ εἶχες] *Thou wouldst not have.*[1] "Indicativus imperfecti sine ἄν h. l. in firmissima asseveratione longe est aptissimus."[2] — δεδομένον] Namely, the ἐξουσιάζειν κατ᾽ ἐμοῦ.[3] Not : the definite act of condemnation (Steinmeyer). — ἀνωθεν] *i.e. from God,* iii. 3, 31. This even the *heathen* could understand. Had Jesus said ἐκ τοῦ πατρός μου, he would not have understood it. Pilate stands before Jesus with the ἐξουσία to destroy Him ; but he has this power from *God,* and he would not possess it if God had not appointed him for the fulfilment of His destiny concerning Jesus. For this reason, however (διὰ τοῦτο), that is, because he here acts not in independent self-determination, but as the divinely-ordained

---

[1] Buttmann, on account of the absence of ἄν, would interpret the reading εἶχες as follows : " *Thou hadst, i.e.* when thou didst receive the accusation against me ... no power over me, unless it *was given* to thee by God for that purpose." See *Stud. u. Krit.* 1858, p. 501. But irrespective of the dragging in, in this forced manner, of this exacter definition of time in εἶχες, it is in truth precisely the *undoubted* possession of the ἐξουσία which forms the presupposition of the διὰ τοῦτο κ.τ.λ. that follows. With the reading ἔχεις, which Buttmann

prefers, he explains : " *thou hast* no power over me, if it *had not been given* thee from above," p. 494. But why in that case should the *pluperf.* ἦν δεδομένον stand ? Instead of ἦν, ἐστί must have been used, in conformity with the sense.

[2] Kühner, *ad Xen. Anab.* vii. 6. 21. See also Stallbaum, *ad Plat. Sympos.* p. 190 C ; Bremi, *ad Lys. Exc.* IV. p. 438 ff. ; Winer, p. 286 [E. T. p. 305].

[3] See Kühner, II. sec. 421 ; Bernhardy, p. 335.

506

organ of the procedure which is pending against Him, he is not indeed free
from sin, since he condemns Jesus contrary to his own conviction of His innocence ; but greater is the guilt of him who delivered Jesus into Pilate's
hands, since that divinely-bestowed ἐξουσία is wanting to the latter.   The
logical connection of the διὰ τοῦτο rests on the fact that the παραδιδούς μ σοι
is the *high priest*, to whom, consequently, *no* power is given by God over Him,
the *Messiah*, who in truth is higher than the high priest ; to *Pilate*, on the
other hand, the *Roman* potentate, this power is lent, because, as bearer of
the highest magisterial authority, he derives his warrant from God (comp.
Rom. xiii. 1), to decide concerning every one who is brought before his
court, and therefore also concerning the Messiah, who has been accused and
delivered up as a pretender to a crown.   This power Pilate possessed simply
as a *Roman* potentate ; hence this point of view does not *confuse* the matter
(Luthardt), but makes it *clear*.   As δεδομ. is not to be transmuted into the
notion of *permission* (Chrysostom), so also there is nothing to be found in
διὰ τοῦτο which is not yielded by the immediate context.   Hence we are not
to understand with Euth. Zigabenus (comp. Theophylact) : διότι ἐξουσίαν
ἔχεις καὶ οὐκ ἀπολύεις με, so that the lesser degree of guilt rests on the weakness and timidity of Pilate (comp. Luther) ; nor with Grotius : [1] because thou
canst not know so well as the Jews (to whom ὁ παραδ. is referred) who I am ;
nor with Lampe : because the Jews have received no such power from God,
have rather *assumed* it to themselves (Luthardt) ; but solely in harmony
with the context : *because thou hast the disposal of me, not from thy proper
sovereignty, but from having been divinely empowered thereto.* — ὁ παραδιδούς]
he who delivers me up to thee ; the affair is still *in actu*, those who deliver Him
up stand without ; hence the *pres.*   The expression itself, however, cannot,
as elsewhere in John,[2] denote *Judas*, who here lies entirely remote from
the comparison, especially since σοι is used with it, nor (with most interpreters) be understood collectively of the *Jews*.   It is rather the chief of the
Jews, *the high priest Caiaphas*, who is meant,[3] who ought to have recognized
the Messiah, and not to have assumed to himself any power over Him. —
μείζονα] compares the sin of the παραδιδούς with that *of Pilate*, not with itself
so as to designate its guilt as *aggravated* by the misuse of the ἐξουσία of
Pilate.[4]   The guilt which belonged to the παραδιδούς in and by himself, was
in truth not aggravated by the delivering over *into the hands of the regular
magistracy*, which was rather the orderly mode of procedure.[5]

Ver. 12. Ἐκ τούτου] Not : *from this time forward* (so usually) ; for ἐζήτει,

[1] Comp. Bengel, Baeumlein, and already
Ruperti.

[2] xviii. 2, xiii. 2, xi. 21, xii. 4, vi. 64, 71 ;
comp. Mark xiv. 21.

[3] So also Bengel, and now Ewald ; comp.
Luthardt, Baumgarten, p. 388, Hengst.

[4] Calvin, Wetstein, Godet, also Baur.
Baur in the *Theol. Jahrb.* 1854, p. 283 :
"Since thou hast in my case the magisterial power over life and death, those who
surrender me to thee, incur by their action,
in itself immoral, all the greater guilt, if

they abuse the magisterial authority given
to thee for their own objects.

[5] According to Steinmeyer, p. 156, Jesus
would say : "Thy power, on the other
hand, to release me, is already as good as
wrested from thee on the part of the
παραδιδ. μέ σοι ; but on that very account
thy sin is the less." But this interpretation
of διὰ τοῦτο is in truth altogether untextual,
as the entire conception to which it would
refer is foreign to the connexion.

κ.τ.λ., is a particular act, which is immediately answered by the Jews with loud outcries ; but : *on this ground*, as vi. 66, occasioned by this speech of Jesus.[1] — ἐζήτει, κ.τ.λ., *he sought* to release Him.[2] In what this attempt, which, though made, yet remained unaccomplished (hence imperf.), may more definitely have consisted, John does not say, and therefore it was, probably, only in his making renewed representations. That which is usually supplied, as though μᾶλλον, as in v. 18, were expressed therewith : he sought *still more*, he sought *most earnestly* ("previously he appears to John rather to have played with the matter," Lücke), and the like, is capriciously imported, as also the rendering : now *he demanded peremptorily*, etc. (Steinmeyer). — With ἐὰν τοῦτον, κ.τ.λ., the Jews cunningly enough again return to and fasten upon the political side of the accusation, ὡς οὐ παροπτέον τῷ Πιλάτῳ διὰ τὸν ἀπὸ τοῦ Καίσαρος φόβον, Euth. Zigabenus. How greatly must he, who in so many features of his administration had anything but clean hands,[3] have desired to avoid an accusation before Tiberius, so suspicious and jealous of his authority ![4] — φίλος τοῦ Καίσ.] Not in the *titular* sense of *amicus Caesaris*, as high officials bore this title,[5] in which, however, the sense of *confidant* (counsellor) of Caesar exists ; but *faithful to the emperor*, friendly to him, and devoted to his interests.[6] — He who makes himself a *king*, by the fact, that is, of *declaring* himself to be such (comp. x. 33), thereby *declares himself* (ἀντιλέγει) *against the emperor.* Accordingly, ἀντιλέγει has not the more general meaning : he *opposes* ;[7] but the emphasis lies upon the correlates βασιλέα and Καίσαρι.

Ver. 13. These speeches penetrate the mind of Pilate, dismayed at the thought of Rome and the emperor. He will now, formally and solemnly, deliver the final sentence, which must be done, not *in the* praetorium, but *outside* in the open air ;[8] he therefore causes Jesus to be brought out, and *seats himself*, taking his place *on the judicial seat, at the place which is called Lithostroton,but in Hebrew, Gabbatha.* — ἐπὶ τοῦ βήματος] Modal defining of ἐκάθ. εἰς τόπον. — Since τόπος here denotes a definite and distinguished place, the article is as little required as with πόλις, ἀγρός, and the like in such cases.[9] —The place where the tribunal stood, before the praetorium in Jerusalem, bore the *Greek* name, derived from its *Mosaic floor*,[10] of Λιθόστρωτον, *i.e. stone-strown*, but in the *Aramaic* dialect that of גבתא, arising from its *elevated position ;* two *different* names, therefore, derived from different *properties*[11] of the same place. The place is mentioned neither in Josephus nor in the Rabbins. The name Γαββ. is not to be derived from גִּבְעָה, *hill*

[1] So also Luthardt and Lange.
[2] x. 30 ; Luke v. 18, xiii. 24, xix. 3 ; Acts xxvii. 30, *et al.*
[3] Josephus, *Antt.* xviii. 3. 1 ff. ; Philo, *de legat. ad Caj.* p. 1033.
[4] Suetonius, *Tib.* 58 ; Tacitus, *Ann.* iii. 38. Comp. Hausrath, *Christl. Zeitgesch.* I. p. 312 ff.
[5] See Wetstein ; Grimm on 1 Macc. ii. 18.
[6] Xen. *Anab.* iii. 2. 5.
[7] Grotius, de Wette, Maier.

[8] See Josephus, *Bell.* ii. 9. 3, ii. 14. 8.
[9] Comp. Matt. xxvii. 33 ; Kühner, II. p. 129.
[10] See Wetstein and Krebs, p. 158 f.
[11] Ewald attempts to refer Γαββαθᾶ also back to the signification of λιθόστρωτον by assuming a root גבע, but in the signification of קבע (Aram. : *insert*). Too bold an hypothesis. In the LXX. λιθοστρ. (Cant. iii. 10 ; 2 Chron. vii. 3 ; Esth. i. 7) corresponds to the Hebr. רצף.

508 THE GOSPEL OF JOHN.

(Hengstenberg), against which would be the double β,[1] but from גַב, *ridge, hump*.[2]

Ver. 14. Day and hour of the decisive moment, after which the narrative then proceeds with καὶ λέγει, κ.τ.λ., without the necessity of placing ἦν δὲ . . . ἕκτη in a parenthesis (rather, with Lachm. and Tisch., between two points). — παρασκ. τοῦ πάσχα] That the παρασκευή may not be understood of the weekly one, referable to the *Sabbath*,[3] but may be referred to the *Passover* feast-day, *of which* it was the preparation-day, John expressly subjoins τοῦ πάσχα. It was certainly a *Friday*, consequently *also* a preparation-day before the Sabbath ; but it is not *this* reference which is here to be remarked, but the reference to the *paschal feast* beginning on the evening of the day, the first feast day of which fell, according to John, on the Sabbath. The expression corresponds to the Heb. עֶרֶב הַפֶּסַח, not indeed verbally (for παρασκευή = עֲרוּבְתָא), but as to the thing. Those expositors who do not recognize the deviation of John from the Synoptics in respect of the day of Jesus' death (see on xviii. 28), explain it as : the *Friday in the Passover week*.[4] But it is in the later ecclesiastical language that παρασκ. first denotes directly Friday,[5] as frequently also in the *Constitt. ap.*, and that in virtue of the reference to be therewith supplied to the Sabbath ; which, however, *cannot* be here supplied, since *another* genitival reference is expressly given. An appeal is erroneously made to the analogy of Ignat. *Phil.* 13. *interpol.*, where it is said that one should not fast on the Sunday or Sabbath, πλὴν ἑνὸς σαββάτου τοῦ πάσχα ; for (1) σάββατον in and of itself is a *complete* designation of a day ; (2) σάββ. τοῦ πάσχα here denotes by no means the Sabbath in the Easter-tide, but the *Sabbath of the Easter-day, i.e.* the Saturday which precedes Easter-day, Easter-Saturday. And the more decidedly is this harmonistic and forced solution to be rejected, since the remaining statements of time in John place the death of Jesus *before* the first feast-day ;[6] and since John, if he had had the first feast-day before him as the day of death, would not have designated the latter (subtle evasions in Hengstenberg), with such a want of distinctness and definiteness, as "the Friday in Passover" (which in truth might have also been any other of the seven feast-days), especially here, where he proceeds with a precision that states even the *hour*.[7] Against Schneckenburger, *Beitr.* p. 1 ff., who, by referring παρασκ. to the *feast of harvest*, likewise brings out the 15th Nisan as the day of death, but makes it a Wednesday, see Wieseler, p. 338 f. — ἕκτη] According to the Jewish reckoning of hours, therefore twelve o'clock at noon,—again a deviation from the Synoptics, according to whom (see Mark xv. 25, with which also Matt. xxvii. 45, Luke xxiii. 44 agree) Jesus is *crucified* as early as *nine* o'clock in the morning, which variation in fixing so important a date includes much

---

[1] Comp. Γαβαθᾶ, Josephus, *Antt.* v. 1. 29, vi. 4. 2.

[2] See generally Fritzsche, *Verdienste Tholuck's*, p. 102 ; Tholuck, *Beitr.* p. 119 ff.

[3] Vv. 31, 42 ; Luke xxiii. 54 ; Mark xv. 42 ; Matt. xxvii. 62 ; Josephus, *Antt.* xvi. 6. 2, *et al.*

[4] See especially Wieseler, p. 336 f. ;

Wichelhaus, p. 209 f., and Hengstenberg *in loc.*, also Riggenbach.

[5] See Suicer, *Thesaur.*

[6] See on xiii. 1, xviii. 28.

[7] Comp. further Bleek, *Beitr.* p. 114 f. ; Rückert, *Abendm.* p. 31 ff. ; Hilgenfeld, *Paschastr.* p. 149 f., and in his *Zeitschr.* 1867, p. 190.

too large a space of time to allow us to resolve it into a mere indefiniteness in the statement of the hour, and, with Godet, following Lange, to say lightly : "the apostles had no watch in hand," especially as according to Matt. and Luke the darkening of the earth is expressly ascribed to the sixth hour. Since, however, with Hofmann,[1] with whom Lichtenstein agrees, we cannot divide the words : ἦν δὲ παρασκευή, τοῦ πάσχα ὥρα ἦν ὡς ἕκτη, *but it was preparation-day, it was about the sixth hour of the paschal feast* (reckoned, namely, from midnight forwards), which forced and artificial explanation would absolutely set aside παρασκευή, in spite of τοῦ πάσχα therewith expressed, and would yield an unexampled mode of computation of hours, namely, of the *feast*, not of the *day* (against i. 40, iv. 6, 52) ; since, further, the reading in our present passage is, both externally and internally, certain, and the already ancient assumption of a copyist's mistake[2] is purely arbitrary ; since, further, as generally in John (comp. on i. 40, iv. 6, 52), the assumption is groundless,[3] that he is reckoning according to the *Roman* enumeration of hours ;[4] since, finally, the *quarter of a day* beginning with this hour cannot be made out of the third *hour* of Mark,[5] and just as little (Hengstenberg, comp. Godet) can the sixth hour of John (comp. iv. 6) be taken into consideration only as the *time of day* in question ;[6]—the variation must be left as it is, and the preference must be given to the disciple who stood under the cross. Nor is the Johannean statement of the hour in itself improbable, since the various proceedings in and near the praetorium, in which also the sending to Herod, (Luke xxiii. 7 ff., is to be included (see on xviii. 38), may probably have extended from πρωΐ, xviii. 28, until noon (in answer to Brückner) ; while the execution, on the adjacent place of execution, quickly followed the judicial sentence, and without any intermediate occurrence, and the death of Jesus must have taken place unusually early, not to take into account the space which ὡσεί leaves open.[7] For the way, however, in which even this statement of time is deduced from the representation of the paschal lamb as

[1] In the *Zeitschr. f. Prot. u. Kirche*, 1853, Oct. p. 260 ff., and *Schriftbew.* II. 2, p. 204 f.

[2] Eusebius, Beza, ed. 5, Bengel; according to Ammonius, Severinus, τινὲς in Theophylact, Petavius : an interchange of the numeral signs γ and ϛ.

[3] In fact, it is precisely in the present passage that the *inadmissibility* of the Roman enumeration of hours is shown. For if Jesus was brought πρωΐ, xviii. 28, to the praetorium, it is impossible that after all the transactions which here took place, including the scourging, mocking, and also the sending to Herod (who questioned Him ἐν λόγοις ἱκανοῖς, Luke xxiii. 9, and derided Him), the case can have been matured for sentence as early as six o'clock in the morning, that is, at the end of about two, or at most three hours.

[4] Rettig, Tholuck, Olshausen, Krabbe, Hug, Maier, Ewald, Isenberg ; substantially so Wieseler, p. 414, who calls to his aid the first feast-day, Ex. xii. 29, which begins precisely at midnight.

[5] Calvin, Grotius, Jansen, Wetstein, and others, comp. Krafft, p. 147 ; see in opposition, Mark xv. 33, 34.

[6] On this theory Hengstenberg forms the certainly very simple example : the combination of the statements of Mark and John yields the result, that the sentence of condemnation and the leading away falls *in the middle*, between the third and sixth hour, therefore *about* 10.30 o'clock. Were this *correct*, the statements *of both* evangelists would be *incorrect*, and we should avoid Scylla to fall into Charybdis.—Godet only renews the idle subterfuge that in Mark xv. 25 the crucifixion is reckoned *from the scourging forwards*.

[7] Comp. Marcus Gnost. in Irenaeus, *Haer.* i. 14. 6: τὴν ἕκτην ὥραν, ἐν ᾗ προσηλώθη τῷ ξύλῳ.

an attempt to bring out the בֵּין הָעַרְבִּים, Ex. xii. 6 ; Lev. xxiii. 5 ; Num.
ix. 3), see, in Weisse, *Evangelienfrage*, p. 131. — ἴδε ὁ βασιλ. ἱμῶν !] Pilate is
indeed determined, on ascending his judicial seat, to overcome his sentiment of right ; but, notwithstanding, in this decisive moment, with his
moral weakness between the twofold fear of the Son of God and of the
Caesar, he still, before actually yielding, makes the *bitter* remark against
the Jews : *see, there is your king !* imprudently, ineffectually, but at least
satisfying in some degree the irony of the situation, into the stress of which
he sees himself brought.

Vv. 15, 16. The bitterness is still further embittered.   To the impetuous
clamour which demands crucifixion, the question of Pilate : *your king* shall
I crucify ? is only the feeble echo of ἴδε ὁ βασ. ἱμ., whereupon, with the
decisive οὐκ ἔχομεν βασιλέα, κ.τ.λ.,—decisive, though treacherously denying
the claim of the Hierarchy,—the again awakened fear of the emperor at
last completely disarms the procurator, so that now thus (τότε οὖν) comes
out the tragic and ignominious result of his judicial action.[1] — αὐτοῖς] *to
the chief priests*, ver. 15.   To these Jesus was *given over*, and that as a matter
of fact, not merely by the *sentence* of itself (Hengstenberg), that He might
be crucified under their direction by Roman soldiers.[2]   Comp. viii. 28 ;
Acts ii. 23, iii. 15.   παρέδ. does not signify to *yield* to their desire (Grotius,
B. Crusius, Baeumlein).—On crucifixion in general, see on Matt. xxvii. 35.

Vv. 17, 18. The *subject* of παρέλαβον, which is correlative to παρέδωκεν,
ver. 16, and of ἤγαγον, is necessarily, according to ver. 16, the ἀρχιερεῖς, not
the soldiers (de Wette, B. Crusius, Hengstenberg, Baeumlein, and older expositors).   The former are the persons [3] who act, which does not exclude
the service and co-operation of the soldiers (ver. 23). — βαστ. ἑαυτῷ τὸν σταυρ.
(see critical notes) : *bearing for Himself the cross*.[4]   See on Matt. xxvi. 32.
and Charit. iv. 2 ; and on *Golgotha*, on Matt. xxvii. 33. — ἐντεῦθ. κ. ἐντεῦθ.]
Comp. LXX. Dan. xii. 5.[5]   On the thing itself, comp. Luke xxiii. 33.
John gives peculiar prominence to the circumstance, adding further, μέσον
δὲ τ. Ἰησ.   Whether, and how far, the Jews thus acted *intentionally*, is undetermined.   Perhaps they scornfully assign to their "king" the *place of
honour !*   That Pilate desired thereby to deride them, in allusion to 1 Kings
xxii. 19 (B. Crusius, Brückner, Lange), we are not to suppose, since the
subject of ἐσταύρ. is the Jews, under whose direction the crucifixion of the
principal person takes place, and, at the same time, the two subordinate
persons are put to death along with Him.   Pilate first appears, ver. 19.
Of special *divine conceptions* in the intermediate position assigned to the
cross of Christ (see Steinmeyer, p. 176), John gives no indication.

Vv. 19, 20. Ἔγραψε] Not a supplemental statement : *he had written* (de

---

[1] Χριστὸν ἐκὼν ἀέκων ἀδίκῳ παρέδωκεν ὀλέθρῳ,
Nonnus.
[2] Ver. 23, comp. Matt. xxvii. 26, 27.
[3] By which also the fact is confirmed that
John had not in his mind the first feast-
day, which certainly possessed the authority of the Sabbath.
[4] The assistance of Simon in this, John,

who here gives only a *compendious* account,
has passed over as a subordinate circumstance, not, as Scholten thinks, in conformity with the idea that the Son of God
needed no human help.
[5] ἔνθεν καὶ ἔνθεν, Herod. iv. 175; Soph.
Aj. 725 ; Xen. *Cyr.* vi. 3, 3 ; 1 Macc. vi. 38,
ix. 45 ; 3 Macc. ii. 22, not Rev. xxii. 2.

Wette, Tholuck), but : *he wrote* (caused to be written), while the crucifixion took place without ; and when it had taken place, he caused the τίτλος (solemn Roman expression for a public inscription, particularly for the tablets, naming the criminal and his offence, see Lipsius, *de cruce,* p. 101, and Wetstein), to be placed on the cross. He himself was not present at the crucifixion, Mark xv. 43, 44. — ὁ βασιλ. τῶν Ἰουδ.] Consistent bitterness in the designation of Jesus. Ver. 20. τῶν Ἰουδαίων] of the hierarchic party. — ἐγγὺς ἦν, κ.τ.λ.] See on Matt. xxvii. 33. — καὶ ἦν γεγραμμ., κ.τ.λ.] No longer dependent on ὅτι, since τῶν Ἰουδαίων, ver. 20, unlike ver. 19, is not to be taken in a general sense. It rather attaches to the first point, which explains the proposal of the ἀρχιερεῖς, ver. 21, to Pilate (τοῦτον . . . Ἰουδαίων, ver. 20), a second circumstance assigning its *reason,* namely : *it* (that which ran on the τίτλος) *was written in three languages,* so that it could be read by everybody, including foreigners. For an inscription, even in *four* languages, on the tomb of Gordian, see in Jul. Capitolin. 24.

Vv. 21, 22. The Jewish opponents of Christ have, with hierarchic tact, deciphered the resentful bitterness in the τίτλος, hence the chief priests among them suggest to Pilate, etc. The expression οἱ ἀρχιερ. τ. Ἰουδ. does not stand in contrast to the βασιλεὺς τ. Ἰουδ. (Hengstenberg, Godet), but the high *clerus* of the opposition desired not to see the ancient sacred designation of Messiah profaned. — μὴ γράφε] The writing, because still capable of being altered, is conceived as not yet concluded. — ὃ γέγραφα, γέγραφα] Formal way of designating that with what is written the matter is unalterably to rest. Analogous formulae from the Rabbins, see in Lightfoot. Comp. also 1 Macc. xiii. 38 ; ὅσα ἑστήκαμεν . . . ἕστηκε. Now, too late, he who was previously so weak in character stands firm. In this subordinate point at least he will have his own opinion, and not expose his weakness.

Vv. 23, 24. Οὖν] again connects the history, after the intermediate narrative respecting the superscription, with ver. 18. — ἐσταύρωσαν] For they were the *executioners* of the crucifixion. — τὰ ἱμάτ. αὐτοῦ] *His garments,* with the exception, however, of the χιτών, which is afterwards specially mentioned, the shirt-like under-garment. The account of John is more exact and complete than that of the Synoptics (Matt. xxvii. 35 ; Mark xv. 24 ; Luke xxiii. 34). — τέσσαρα] There were accordingly four soldiers, the ordinary τετράδιον στρα τιωτῶν (Acts xii. 4). — ἐκ τῶν ἄνωθεν ὑφαντὸς δι᾽ ὅλου] *From the top* (where the button-hole was, ἀπ᾽ αὐχένος, Nonnus) *woven quite through, throughout,* so that thus the garment was a single texture, woven from above entirely throughout, without seam, similar to the priestly vestment in Joseph. *Antt.* iii. 7. 4.[1] — ἵνα ἡ γραφή, κ.τ.λ.] This casting of lots for the χιτών, after the division of the ἱμάτια, was not an accidental occurrence, but was in connection with the divine determination for the fulfilment of Scripture, which says, etc. The passage is Ps. xxii. 19, closely following the LXX. The suffering of the theocratic sufferer, in this psalm, is the prophetic type of the suffering of the Messiah. " *They have divided my gar-*

---

[1] See Braun, *de vestitu Hebr.* p. 342 ff. ; Rosenmüller, *Morgenl.* V. p. 273 f. On the adverbial δι᾽ ὅλου, comp. Asclep. 16 ; Nicand. 1 ; Plut. Mor. p. 695 f. ; Bernhardy, p. 235 ; also δι᾽ ὅλων, Plat. *Soph.* p. 253 C.

ments with one another (ἑαυτ. = ἀλλήλους, comp. Luke xxii. 17), *and cast lots over my raiment,*"—this complaint of the Psalmist, who sees himself as being already subjected to the death of a criminal, and the division of his garments among his executioners therewith connected, has found its Messianic fulfilment in the corresponding treatment of Christ, in so far as *lots* have also been cast over *His* raiment (in reality, over His under-garment). In this fulfilment the χιτών *was* that portion of His clothing on which the ἐπὶ τὸν ἱματισμόν μου ἔβαλον κλῆρον was historically carried out ; but we are not, for this reason, to say that John *took* τὸν ἱματισμόν as equivalent to τ. χιτῶνα (Lücke, de Wette.) — οἱ μὲν οὖν στρατ. τ. ἐποί] Simple (reminding one of Herod., Xen., and others) concluding formula for this scene of the *soldiers*' proceedings. On μὲν οὖν, see on Luke iii. 18. — ταῦτα] That related in vv. 23, 24. A *secret* allusion,[1] in these closing words (Hengstenberg, Godet), is arbitrarily forced upon them.

Vv. 25–27. Another narrative, selected by John, and peculiar to him, as elevated and striking in its contents as it is simple and tender in form, and all the more unjustly relegated to the inventions made (Strauss, Baur, Schenkel) in the interest of John, although in the Synoptics (Matt. xxvii. 56 ; Mark xv. 40) the women mentioned stand *at a distance*, which standing at a distance is to be placed *after* the present scene, not *before*, as Lücke and Olshausen, in opposition to the synoptical account, are of opinion. — ἡ μήτηρ αὐτοῦ . . . Μαγδαληνή] Are only *three* women here named (*usual* opinion), so that Μαρία ἡ τοῦ Κλωπᾶ is in apposition to ἡ ἀδελφή, κ.τ.λ. ; or are there *four*,[2] so that Μαρία ἡ τοῦ Κλωπᾶ is to be taken by itself, and the women are brought forward in *two pairs* ? The Syr. already interpreted in the latter mode, and hence inserted a καί before Μαρία (as also Aeth. and Pers.) ; so also have Lachm. (ed. *min.*, not in the large edition) and Tisch. interpunctuated (without a comma after Κλωπᾶ). As it is highly improbable of itself, and established by no instance, that two sisters bore the same name,—as, further, it is in keeping with the peculiarity of John not to mention his *own* name, if he also does not mention his *mother*,[3] or even his brother James, by name (see on i. 42), and as, according to Matt. xxvii. 56, Mark xv. 40, Salome was also among the above-named women, Wieseler's view, which is absolutely not opposed by any well-founded doubts,[4] is to

---

[1] Hengstenberg : " But the occupation itself stands under a secret direction, and *sacred irony passes over irony to the side of profane irony.*" Here Scholten coincides with Hengstenberg, supplying : " who knew nothing of the O. T. etc."

[2] Wieseler in the *Stud. u. Krit.* 1840, p. 648 ff., Lücke, Lange, Ewald, Laurent, *Neut. Stud.* p. 170 f.

[3] He does, indeed, name in xxi. 2 his *father*. But the latter appears so without participation in the evangelical history, that he might appear to John's mind in his Christian relation, especially in the late period of the composition of the appendix, chap. xxi., more foreign and remote, and

that consequently a hesitation might not exist in reference to naming him, as there did in the case of the mother, founded on a delicate and more spiritual consideration. — Scholten changes the mother into an *allegorical* person, in whom the *Church* is represented, to care for which was to be incumbent on John, not on Peter. So substantially also Späth in Hilgenfeld, *Zeitschr.* 1868, p. 187.

[4] Insufficient objections in Luthardt, Brückner, Baeumlein, Weizsäcker, and others. According to Euth. Zigabenus, Ebrard, Hengstenberg, and several others, ἀδελφή would signify *sister-in-law.*

be deemed not "a mere *learned refinement*" (Hengstenberg), but *correct*, so that thus the unnamed ἡ ἀδελφὴ τῆς μητρὸς αὐτοῦ is Salome, the mother of John. — ἡ τοῦ Κλωπᾶ] *The wife of Klopas*, according to Matt. xxvii. 56, Mark xv. 40, Luke xxiv. 10, mother of the younger James, hence *Klopas* is to be taken as *Alphaeus*, הלפי, Matt. x. 3. According to Ewald, on the other hand, the *mother* of *Kleopas*, Luke xxiv. 18, and according to Beza : the *wife* of this Kleopas. — Μαγδαλ.] See on Matt. xxvii. 56. — That Jesus enjoins on *John* to care for Mary, although the latter had several sons of her own, is not sufficiently explained by the unbelief of the brothers (vii. 5), for His speedy triumph over this (Acts i. 14) could not be hidden from Him (ii. 24, 25) ; but it presupposes the certainty in His mind that generally to *no other's* hand could this dear legacy¹ be so well entrusted. That Mary had no other sons (see in opposition to this vii. 3, and on Matt. i. 25) is, indeed, still inferred by Hengstenberg. For γύναι, comp. on ii. 4. — The words to the disciple, *behold thy mother*, meet no stumbling-block in the fact that he had his own actual mother, nay, that she herself was also present (see on ver. 25), but leave his relation to the latter untouched, and form with the ἴδε ὁ υἱός σου a parallelism, which expresses the filial care and protection which Mary, on the one hand, was to *expect* from John ; which John, on the other hand, was to *exercise* towards Mary. — καὶ ἀπ᾽ ἐκείνης τῆς ὥρας, κ.τ.λ.] Not to be regarded as a parenthesis ; to be taken with strict literality, that John *forthwith*, after Jesus had accomplished His end upon the cross, entered on his charge. Whether and where he possessed a property of his own is matter of conjecture. If he received Mary into his *dwelling*, into his *family circle*, formed by Salome, and perhaps by his brother, εἰς τὰ ἴδια (comp. xvi. 32), is the correct expression. Ewald well remarks on such traits of individual significance in the Gospel of John : "it was for him at a late period of life a sweet reward to call up reminiscences of all that was most vivid, but for the readers it is also, without his will, a token that only he could have written all this." If, indeed, the designation of the disciple *beloved* by Jesus as a *self*-designation were a *vanity* (Scholten), nay, an arrogant and scornful self-*exaltation* (Weisse), then it could *not* have been he who wrote all this. But the consciousness of pre-eminent love on the part of the Lord, true, clear, and still glowing with all intensity and strength, in the heart of the old man, is inconceivable without the deepest humility, and this humility, which has long since ceased to have anything in common with the feeling evinced in Mark x. 35 ff., Luke ix. 54, has precisely in that most simple of all expressions, ὃν ἠγάπα, its most correspondent expression and its necessary and sacred justification, which is as little to be passed over in silence, or to be denied, as is the consciousness of Paul, 1 Cor. xv. 10.

Ver. 28. Μετὰ τοῦτο] Not indefinitely *later*, but *after this scene* with Mary

¹ This noblest blossom of dying piety is violently removed into a sphere foreign to it, if it is transported into *dogmatic* ground, as Steinmeyer, p. 200, does. According to him, the death of the *Atoner for all men*, as such, has completely cut asunder the tie that hitherto existed ; by *this* death Jesus departed out of every naturally-conditioned individual fellowship, and like Melchizedek must also appear as ἀμήτωρ. Of such a meaning, John gives not the slightest indication.

514 THE GOSPEL OF JOHN.

and John. — εἰδώς, κ.τ.λ.] *as He was aware* (xiii. 1) *that* his death was already at hand, that with this all was now accomplished for fulfilling the predictions of Scripture regarding His earthly work, He now still desires, at this gaol of accomplishment, a refreshment, and says : *I thirst.* Accordingly, ἵνα τελ. ἡ γραφή is to be referred to πάντα ἤδη τετέλ.[1] And this, because πάντα ἤδη τετέλ. allows no fulfilment of Scripture still *remaining behind,* and thus *excludes* the connection of ἵνα τελ. ἡ γρ. with λέγει ; because τελειώθη is *selected* simply for the sake of its reference to τετέλ. (it is the πλήρωσις of Scripture, *to which now nothing more is wanting*) ; and because John never makes the clause of purpose, " that the Scripture might be fulfilled," *precede* the clause of fulfilment, and even where a single definite fact is the fulfilling element, always actually *adduces* the passage of Scripture in question (xvii. 12 is a retrospective indication of a passage already before *adduced*). We must abandon, therefore, the *ordinary* interpretation,[2] which refers ἵνα τελ., κ.τ.λ. to λέγει· διψῶ, as containing the scriptural ground of the *thirst,* to which Jesus gave expression, and of the *drinking of the vinegar* which was given to Him, and finds in Ps. lxix. 22 the passage intended ; where, moreover, the vinegar is the gift of scorn and malice, while *here* simply the *quenching of thirst* immediately before death is in question, with no ulterior purpose. — πάντα ἤδη τετέλ.] τουτέστιν ὅτι οὐδὲν λείπει τῇ οἰκονομίᾳ, Chrysostom ; ἤδη (*already*) points to the very *early* occurrence of His death (Nonnus : θοῶς).

Vv. 29, 30. Ἔκειτο] as in ii. 6. The vessel was in readiness for the purpose of quenching the thirst of those crucified (who had always to suffer much therefrom), with sponge and stalk of hyssop, which were to serve for handing it up. — ὄξους] *vinegar, i.e.* small sour wine (from the skins of grapes already pressed), which served as a drink for labourers and soldiers.[3] Of the bitter *stupefying drink,* which Jesus had disdained to receive,[4] John says nothing. On the drink tendered to him, Luke xxiii. 36, see *in loc.* — The *subject* of σπόγγον, κ.τ.λ. is not named ; yet there can be no doubt about who are meant, the *soldiers.* — ἰσσώπῳ] *More exactly* than in Matt. xxvii. 48, and since the hyssop grows stalks from 1 to 1½ feet high,[5] such an one was fully sufficient to reach to the mouth of Jesus on the not lofty[6] cross.[7] — αὐτοῦ τῷ στόματι] *to His mouth.* That the stalk was precisely of *hyssop,* is accidental ; as hyssop of *scorning,* in opposition to the hyssop of *reconciliation,* Ps. li. (Hengstenberg), it is not to be thought of, since the tender of the drink in the present passage is certainly not an act of scorn. Moreover,

[1] Cyril (?), Bengel, Michaelis, Semler, Thalem., van Hengel (*Annot.* p. 62 ff.), Paulus, Tholuck, Hofmann, (*Weissag. u.Erf.* II. p. 146. On the other hand, Hofmann, in the *Schriftbew.* II. 1, p. 314, has altered his views, and connects ἵνα τελ. ἡ γρ. with λέγει), Luthardt, Lange, Baeumlein, Scholten, Steinmeyer.

[2] Chrysostom, Theophylact, Euth. Zigabenus, Ruperti, and many others, including Lücke, de Wette, Brückner, Strauss, B. Crusius, Baur, Ewald, Hengstenberg, Godet.

[3] Wetstein on Matt. xxvii. 34 ; Hermann, *Privatalterth.* § 26. 10.

[4] Matt. xxvii. 34, 35 ; Mark xv. 23, 24.

[5] Bochart, *Hieroz.* I. 2. 50 ; Celsius, *Hierobot.* I. p. 407 f.

[6] Salmasius, *de cruce,* p. 284.

[7] Least of all with a *dogmatic* background, although Steinmeyer assumes that διψῶ is a *request to His enemies,* and thereby illustrates the *love,* which completed the act of *atonement.* This request, he thinks, only the dying *Mediator* could have made.

it is precisely such non-essential special statements as these which have flowed from the most vivid recollection of an eye-witness. — τετέλεσται] Quite as in ver. 28, to be referred to the *work* of Jesus. Comp. xvii. 4. It is *by Him* brought to completion with this *act of the last death-suffering.* Further, Bengel aptly remarks : " hoc verbum in corde Jesu erat, ver. 28, nunc ore profertur." — παρέδ. τὸ πν.] *He gave over* (to God) *His spirit,* characteristic designation of dying, in conformity with that which dying *was* in *Jesus*' case. It is the *actual* surrender of His self-conscious Ego on the decease of the body ; the *verbal* surrender, Luke xxiii. 46,[1] appears, since John has, instead of it, the simply grand concluding word τετέλεσται, to belong to the enlarging representations of tradition, but would, after the bowing of the head, be no longer suitable, and hence have to be assumed as following τετέλεσται. — Note further, that the εἶναι εἰς τ. κόλπον τοῦ πατρός of i. 18 did not now take place, but through and after the ascension (xx. 17).

Ver. 31. Οὖν] *Therefore,* since Jesus was already dead. Their object was already attained ; so now the Sabbath also should still have its rights. " Magnifici honoratores Dei, cum in conscientia mala reposuissent sanguinem justi," Ruperti. — ἵνα μὴ μείνῃ, κ.τ.λ.] Contrary to the Roman custom, of leaving the corpse to putrefy on the cross (comp. on Matt. xxvii. 58), on the part of the Jews, the injunction has to be applied respecting the removal of the *hanged person,* Deut. xxi. 22, 23,[2] especially in the present case where with sunset the Sabbath began, and *this* a *great* Sabbath, and therewith a wish was expressed to see the crucified ones removed and interred in the interval before the beginning of the holy day. — παρασκευή] Because it was the *day of preparation,* namely, τοῦ σαββάτου, for the Sabbath. *This* reference of παρασκ. necessarily follows from ἐν τῷ σαββάτῳ. But the parenthesis ἦν γὰρ μεγάλη, κ.τ.λ. indicates why they wished not to have the Sabbath, especially *on that occasion,* desecrated by the bodies remaining on the cross ; because *great, i.e.* pre-eminently holy (comp. vii. 37 ; Isa. i. 13), was the day of that Sabbath, because, that is, it was (not merely generally a Sabbath in the Passover feast time, but) at the same time the *first day of Passover* the 15th Nisan. It was thus a Sabbath *with twofold authority,* since the first feast-day also had the character of a Sabbath (Lev. xxiii. 7–15). With a Quartodeciman usage of speech (Hilgenfeld) the designation of the Sabbath in the present passage has nothing to do.[3] As the *second* feast-day, however, which is the day that results from the attempts at harmonizing (see on xviii. 28), it could only be termed μεγάλη, for the reason that on this day, *i.e.* the 16th Nisan, the *feast of Sheaves* took place, Lev. xxiii. 10 ff. (see especially Wieseler, p. 385 f., 344). But how could John have presupposed, in his readers, without any indication, a reference to *this?* These could explain to themselves the μεγαλότης of that Sabbath only from ver. 14, from

---

[1] Of the seven words on the cross, only Matt. xxvii. 46, according to Schenkel's too rash conclusion, is to be considered as altogether beyond doubt. Mark also has only this one (xv. 34), Luke has three (xxiii. 34,

43, 46), and John likewise three (xix. 26, 27, 28, 30).

[2] Comp. Joseph. *Bell.* iv. 5. 2.

[3] See Steitz in the *Jahrb. f. Deutsche Theol.* 1861, p. 113 ff.

the fact, namely, that the παρασκευὴ τοῦ σαββάτου of which John speaks was at the same time, according to ver. 14, παρασκευὴ τοῦ πάσχα. — ἵνα κατεαγῶσιν κ.τ.λ.] For two were, indeed, still living, and also with respect to Jesus they had at least no certainty that He was actually dead. On the apparent contradiction with Mark xv. 44, see on ver. 38. The *crushing of the legs* with clubs (*crucifragium*, σκελοκοπία) was to accelerate death (as John also manifestly views it, comp. ver. 33), and that in a barbarous manner, in order to take nothing from the severity of the punishment.[1] It also appears as a punishment by itself.[2] The addition of a *finishing blow*, by which (therefore not by the crucifragium in itself) death was brought about, cannot be shown, least of all, from ver. 34, against Michaelis, Semler, Kuinoel, Hug.[3]

Vv. 32, 33. To assume, on account of Mark xv. 39 (comp. Matt. xxvii. 54), that these soldiers were *others* (sent out by Pilate) than those who had crucified Jesus,[4] is indicated by nothing in the text, where rather οἱ στρατιῶται are those already *known*. The ἦλθον is only *pictorial*, and the *centurion* does not come into consideration with John. — Since they came to Jesus last, we must suppose that two each began on the two sides of the three crosses.

Ver. 34. The soldiers, *when they saw*, etc. The death of Jesus, in keeping with their attitude of indifference in the matter, had therefore been unobserved by them (in answer to Hengstenberg); they now omitted the leg-breaking in His case, as aimless in the case of one already dead. *But one pierced Him with a lance in the side.* Wherefore ? Not in order to *ascertain whether* He was actually dead ; for, according to the context, the thrust took the place of breaking the legs. Hence it must be assumed, according to the analogy of the latter, that the object of the thrust was *to make* quite *sure* of the death of Jesus, *i.e.* in case He should not yet be altogether dead, to put Him completely to death. — αὐτοῦ τ. πλευράν] *His side*. *Which ?* is not clear ; but the *left*, if he who dealt the thrust stood before the cross, was was most naturally at hand. — ἔνυξε] Neither the word itself (since νύσσειν ordinarily denotes *violent* thrusting or stabbing ; especially frequent in Homer,[5] nor the person of the rude soldier, nor the weapon (*lance*, belonging to the heavy armour, Eph. vi. 11), nor the purpose of the thrust, nor the palpable nature of the opening of the wound, to be assumed, according to xx. 27, nor ἐξεκέντησαν, ver. 37, admit the interpretation, which is implied in the interest of an apparent death, of a superficial *scratch* (Paulus) — αἷμα κ. ὕδωρ] is, considering the difference and significance of the two substances, certainly not to be taken as a *hendiadys* ("a reddish lymph, Paulus[6]).

---

[1] See Lactantius, *Instit. div.* iv. 26; Lipsius, *de cruce*, ii. 14.

[2] Suetonius, *Aug.* 67 ; Seneca, *de ira*, iii. 32 ; and see generally Wetstein, also Lipsius, *ad Plaut. Asin.* ii. 4. 68.

[3] On the aorist form with syllabic augment from κατάγνυμι, see Winer, p. 68 [E. T. p. 70].

[4] Storr, Kuinoel, Olshausen, Maier, Lange.

[5] See Duncan, ed. Rost, p. 796.

[6] To this conclusion Hofmann also (*Weissag. u. Erfüll.* II. p. 148 f.) again involuntarily returned, understanding *undecomposed*, still *flowing* blood, as a sign that the body of Jesus was exempt from corruption. See, in opposition, also Luthardt. But Hofmann, in his *Schriftbew.* II. 1, p. 490, has renounced the above interpretation, and now has represented the matter thus : the bleeding away of the dead one had been so com-

Whether the blood and water issued forth *contemporaneously* or *after one another*, does not appear from the words. In the *natural* [1] mode of regarding this twofold issue, it is thought *either* (1) that Jesus was *not* yet *dead*, but simply *died* in consequence of the thrust, which pierced the pericardium with its watery lymph, and at the same time the chamber of the heart, from which the blood welled, [2] to which, however, the mode of viewing it of the entire apostolical church is opposed, which was certain, and has the personal testimonies of Christ Himself to the fact, that in His *crucifixion itself* the putting to death was accomplished. *Or* (2) it is assumed that the blood had been *decomposed* in the corpse (Hase, Krabbe, and several others), so that *serum*, bloody water, and *placenta*, clots of blood, separately issued forth ; which separate outflow, however, of the constituent parts of blood cannot, in the case of a fresh body that had been healthy, be anatomically established. Or (3) the *heart* is considered, just as the Gruners suppose, as having been pierced through, though the death of Jesus is assumed to have already *previously* taken place, [3] as also Ewald, [4] the death of Jesus was a *sudden breaking of the heart*), holds to be most probable. Not substantially different is the view of the English physician William Stroud, [5] comp. Tholuck, who, besides the cavity of the heart, brings into consideration also the two bags of the diaphragm, with the fact of their fluidity in corpses. This mode of regarding the matter renders unnecessary the entirely arbitrary theory of Ebrard, p. 563 ff., of *extravasations* and *sugillations* which the thrust occasioned, [6] and would be quite satisfactory if John had desired to give an account generally of a natural, physiological effect of the lancethrust. But apart from the fact that he adduces nothing which would

plete, that at last not blood, but water flowed, and this was to the apostle a proof that Jesus' corpse remained exempt from corruption, which begins with the decomposition of the blood. Comp. also Baumgarten, p. 423 f., and Godet. But so physiological an observation and conclusion is not to be adopted without some more precise indication ; and of the *complete* bleeding away on which, *finally*, water flowed, the text says nothing, but speaks simply and solely of blood and water, which issued forth.

[1] In a natural way, but in a higher sense, Lange, II. p. 1614 f., explains the phenomenon from the process of *change* through which the body of Christ was passing. A precarious expedient, in which not only is the possibility of a clear representation wanting, but also the essential and necessary point of the reality of the *death*, as of the condition of separation from the body, is endangered, and instead of the *death*, the beginning of another modality of corporeal *life* is conceived ; while, generally also, the process of this assumed change must have been passed through in a very

material way. Besides, the body of the Risen One had not yet been transformed (He still eats, still drinks, etc.), though *altered* and become more spiritual, but the *transformation* first begins at the *ascension* (comp. 1 Cor. xv. 51-53). A possible *preparation* for this transformation from the moment of death onwards is beyond the scope of any more exact representation, and very precipitate is the conclusion that this preparation must also have announced itself by some sign in the wounded body.

[2] So the two physicians Gruner in the *Commentat. de Jesu Chr. morte vera non simulata*, etc., Halle 1805.

[3] Beza, Calvin, Grotius, Wetstein, and several others.

[4] *Gesch. Chr.* p. 584.

[5] *A Treatise on the physical cause of the death of Christ*, London 1847.

[6] They originated, he thinks, through the distension of the muscles, and from them the water issued ; but in penetrating deeper the lance also touched places of fluid blood. — But in this way not αἷμα καὶ ὕδωρ, but ὕδωρ καὶ αἷμα would have issued forth.

allow us to think in ὕδωρ not of actual *water*, but of *lymph* (ἰχώρ), he desires
to set forth the phenomenon manifestly as something entirely *unexpected*
(note also the εὐθύς), *extraordinary, marvellous.* Only thus is his solemn
asseveration in ver. 35, and the power of conviction for the Messiahship of
Jesus, which he finds in the truth of the ἐξῆλθεν, κ.τ.λ., to be comprehended.
To him it was not a *subsidiary circumstance,*[1] which convinced the *soldier who
gave the thrust* of the *death* of the Crucified One, but a *miraculous* σημεῖον,
which further set forth that the corpse was that of the divine *Messiah,*[2] of
whose specific calling and work, blood and water are the speaking *symbols,*
in so far, that is, as He has by blood brought the redemptive work to completion, and by means *of water* (*i.e.* by means of the birth from above, which
takes place through baptism, iii. 5) has appropriated it; a significance which
Tholuck also esteems probable in the mind of the Evangelist. Comp. also
Steinmeyer, who, however, ascribes to the water only the *subordinate* purpose, to place the blood under the point of view of the definite (purifying)
operation. Luther : " our redemption lies hidden in the miraculous work."
Comp. 1 John v. 6, where, however, τὸ ὕδωρ, agreeably to the standard of
the *historical* point of view (ἐλθών) stands first.[3] We must abide by this
exegetical conclusion[4] (comp. Hengstenberg on ver. 37), and must renounce
the demonstration of natural connection not less than in other miraculous
phenomena of the evangelical history.[5] The *figurative* interpretation or
explaining away of the fact itself (Baur, p. 217 ff. : by reference to vii. 38,
39 : it is the representation, contemplated in a spiritual manner by the
writer, of the idea that with the death of Jesus there immediately begins
the fulness of spiritual life, which was to proceed from Him on behalf of
the world) is only possible on the assumption that neither *John* nor He gave
an *historical* account, as further Baur (see p. 272 ff.), whom Scholten follows,
refers the entire narrative of the omission to break the legs, and of the side-
thrust, simply to the dogmatic purpose of representing Jesus as the true
Paschal lamb, and thereby the turning-point at which the O. T. economy of

[1] Ebrard, comp. Lücke on ver. 35, and Baeumlein.

[2] τρανῶς διδάσκον, ὅτι ὑπὲρ ἄνθρωπον ὁ νυγείς, Euth. Zigabenus.

[3] See also Weiss, *Lehrbegr.* p. 255.

[4] Fathers and artists have decked it out in monstrous colours, *e.g.* Nonnus, διδύμαις λιβάδεσσιν, first blood, then θέσκελον ὕδωρ flowed ; Prudentius. *Enchir.* 42 : *both* sides were pierced ; from *one* blood, from the *other* water flowed. See also Thilo, *ad Cod. Apocr.* p. 587 f. In the two substances the two sacraments were symbolically seen, as Augustine, Chrysostom, and many others ; Tertullian, Euth. Zigabenus, and several others saw therein the baptism of water and the baptism of blood. Comp. Cornelius à Lapide *in loc. Baptism* and the *Lord's Supper* have also recently been found set forth in several ways in water and blood.

See particularly Weisse, II. p. 326 f. In this way historic truth is of course given up. Hilgenfeld, *Evang.* p. 317 : " The redemp-tive death is the condition of the Christian sacrament generally, which here in its two-fold form figuratively flows forth from the body of the crucified One." This, he thinks, naturally suggested itself to John, since ac-cording to his representation Jesus was the true paschal sacrifice, the recognition of which in the *Gentile world* is brought into view by the lance-thrust of the *Roman* soldier. Other arbitrary explanations in Strauss.

[5] The symbolic signification in regard to the true *expiatio*, and the true *lavacrum*, is also assumed by Calvin ; but he disputes the supernatural element in the fact : " *naturale* enim est, dum *coagulatur sanguis*, omisso rubore fieri *aquae similem.*"

religion ceased to exist, and the new began, the essence of which is con-templated in the outflowing blood and water.[1]

Ver. 35. After μαρτυρία a comma only should be placed, and nothing should be put within a parenthesis, neither καὶ ἀληθινὴ . . . λέγει (van Hengel), nor κ. ἀληθινὴ . . . οἶδεν (Schulz), since the discourse progresses simply and without interruption by καί. — ὁ ἑωρακ.] placed first with great emphasis ; the correlate κἀκεῖνος has subsequently the like emphasis. *He who has seen it*, not heard only from others, but himself has been an *eye-witness*, *has testified it* (herewith, ver. 34), namely, this outflow of blood and water. *This* was indeed the apparently so incredible thing, not also the omission of the leg-breaking. In the third person, in which John here speaks *of himself* while passing over His name, commentators have found betrayed the difference of the writer and the witness.[2] Yet this is simply a misapprehension, discountenanced by the κἀκεῖνος οἶδεν, κ.τ.λ., of the circumstantially solemn style that corresponds to the extraordinary importance which John attributes to the phenomenon. The ἐκεῖνος, that is to say, is the *speaking subject himself* presented objectively, identical therefore with the ἑωρακώς, which clearly appears from the context by the pres. λέγει, and the final clause ἵνα κ. ὑμ. πιστ., especially also by the correlation of καὶ ὑμεῖς with the subject. Comp. on ix. 37. Hence we are by no means to assume that the *secretary* of the apostle speaks of him by ἐκεῖνος as of a third person,[3] but *the apostle himself* presents himself objectively as the *ille*, like a third person ; he may at the same time have employed another as amanuensis (which does not follow even from chap. xxi.)or not ; comp. xxi. 24. — ἀληθινή] placed with emphasis at the head of the clause (αὐτοῦ has then the next em-phasis) ; not, however, equivalent to ἀληθής, as is usually assumed, contrary to the constant usage of John (and the attribute of ἀλήθεια follows subse-quently), but : a *genuine* testimony is *his* witness, which corresponds in reality to the idea of a μαρτυρία—namely, for the very reason that he himself has seen what he testifies. Comp. on viii. 16. — ἵνα] Neither to be taken as dependent on ὁ ἑωρ. μεμαρτ. (Lücke), nor as independently : "and therefore should," etc. (de Wette), but, as the position of the words requires, stating the purpose of λέγει : he knows that he says the truth—says *that you also* (his readers) *may believe*, as he himself has believed through that miraculous appearance, namely, *on Jesus the Son of God*. As frequently in John (comp. on ii. 11), πιστεύειν is also here not the *entrance* into faith, but *a higher and stronger degree of faith*, which one experiences, the πιστεύειν in a new and exalted potency. Comp. xxi. 31. Others, as Baeumlein, still have incor-rectly referred πιστ. merely to what was last mentioned as object, whereby in truth the comparison with John himself, which lies in καὶ ὑμεῖς, would not be at all appropriate, because John has *seen* (not merely believed) what took place. The *solemn absolute* πιστεύειν, with its destination of purpose, makes the assumption of special designs, which have been ascribed to John in his testimony of the outflow of blood and water, appear unwarranted,

[1] See in opposition to Baur : Grimm in the *Stud. u. Krit.* 1847, p. 181 ff., and 1849, p. 285 ff.

[2] Weisse, Schweizer, Köstlin, Hilgenfeld, Tobler, Weizsäcker.

[3] Ewald, *Jahrb.* 10, p. 88.

namely, that he desired to prove the actual death of Jesus,[1] especially in opposition to *docetic* error.[2] Doubts of a naturalistic and docetic kind might rather have derived support than been precluded by the enigmatic outflow, which excited the derision of Celsus, in Or. ii. 36. The Valentinians maintained : ἐξεκέντησαν δὲ τὸ φαινόμενον, ὃ ἦν σὰρξ τοῦ ψυχικοῦ.[3]

Vv. 36, 37. Not without scriptural ground do I say : ἵνα κ. ὑμεῖς πιστεύσητε ; *for that is accomplished*, which I have just testified, vv. 33, 34, concerning the lance-thrust, which took the place of the omitted leg-breaking, in the connection of the divine determination *for the fulfilment of the scriptural saying* (γραφή as in xiii. 18) : *a bone of Him shall not be broken* (Ex. xii. 46 ; Num. ix. 12).[4] To John as to Paul (1 Cor. v. 7) Christ is the *antitype of the paschal lamb* intended in the historical sense of that passage, in which Baur and Hilgenfeld of course find the *formative* factor of the history. Ps. xxxiv. 21 (Grotius, Brückner), because the passage speaks of the protection *of life*, cannot here be thought of.—The second passage of Scripture, to which, moreover, the reader himself is left to supply the same telic connection, which was previously expressed by ἵνα ἡ γρ. πληρ., contains the O. T. prediction of the *lance-thrust* which has been narrated, so far as it concerned precisely the *Messiah : they will look on Him whom they have pierced*,—an expression of the future, repentant, believing recognition of and longing for Him who previously was so hostilely murdered. The subject of the two verbs is the *Jews* (not the *Gentiles*), whose work the entire crucifixion generally (comp. Acts ii. 23, 36), and thus indirectly the ἐκκέντησις also is. The passage is Zech. xii. 10, where the language is used of a martyr, who at a later time is repentantly mourned for. The citation is freely made from the original (so also Rev. i. 7), not from the LXX., who take דָּקְרוּ improperly : κατωρχήσαντο, *have insulted*.[5] John also follows the reading אֵלַי,[6] which Ewald also prefers. — εἰς ὅν] Attraction = εἰς ἐκεῖνον ὅν, comp. vi. 29. To make εἰς ὅν dependent on ἐξεκέντ[7] corresponds neither to the original, nor to the Greek construction, according to which not ἐκκεντεῖν εἰς τινα, but ἐκκ. τινα is said.[8] It always denotes *pierce, stab*. So also here. Jesus was not indeed killed by the lance-thrust, but this thrust formed, as its conclusion,

---

[1] Beza, Grotius, and many others.

[2] Hammond, Paulus, Olshausen, Ammonius, Maier, and several others.

[3] *Exc ex Theod.* 62.

[4] As regards its essential substance quite undestroyed, not like a profane dish of roast meat with bones broken in pieces, was the paschal lamb to be prepared as a sacrifice to God (Ewald, *Alterth.* p. 467 f. ; Knobel on Lev. i. 7). Any peculiar *symbolical* destination in this prescription (Bähr and Keil : to set forth the unity of those who eat) cannot be established, not even by a retrospective conclusion from 1 Cor. x. 17.

[5] Aquinas, Theodotus, and Symmachus have also ἐξεκέντησαν, and rightly.

[6] Not אֵלָי ; Umbreit's observation in the *Stud. u. Krit.* 1849, p. 104, that the passage of Zech. has a *Johannean* element for the idea of the Messiah, because God identifies Himself with the Messiah, applies only to the reading אֵלַי, which further Hofmann, *Weissag. u. Erf.* II. p. 152 f., has sought, in a very tortuous way, to unite with the following accus. אֵת אֲשֶׁר ; he is followed by Luthardt : "They will longingly look up to me, after Him (*i.e.* expect, *entreat* of me *Him*) whom they," etc.

[7] Luther, after the Vulgate : "they will see *into whom they have pierced ;*" Baur : "that they have, namely, pierced *into Him* from whose side blood and water flowed."

[8] Rev. i. 7 ; Judg. ix. 54 ; 1 Chron. x. 4 ; Isa. xiv. 19 ; 2 Macc. xii. 6 ; Polyb. v. 56. 12, xv. 33. 4, xxv. 8. 6.

a part of the whole act of putting to death, and formed, therefore, the Messianic fulfilment of the prophetic word.[1] The LXX. have ἐπιβλέψονται πρός. The *time of the fulfilment* of this prophetic ὄψονται, κ.τ.λ., is, as also in the original, that of the beginning of *repentance and conversion ;* comp. viii. 28, xii. 32 ; not the day of *judgment,*[2] to which ὄψονται, with the *mere* accus., as in Rev. i. 7, not with εἰς, would be appropriate. — A word of Scripture, speaking *specially of the outflow of blood and water*, does not, indeed, stand at the command of John ; but if the facts themselves, with which this outflow was connected, namely, the negative one of the non-breaking of the legs (ver. 36), and the positive one of the lance-thrust (ver. 37), are predicted, so also in the miraculous σημεῖον, by which the thrust was accompanied, is justly, and on the ground of Scripture (γάρ, ver. 36), to be found a special awakening of faith (ver. 35).—Schweizer, without reason, considers vv. 35–37 as spurious.

Vv. 38, 39. Μετὰ ταῦτα] Vv. 32–34. The request of Joseph of Arimathaea (see on Matt. xxvii. 57), that he might *take away* (ἄρῃ) the corpse, does not conflict with ver. 31. For let it be noted that the expression in ver. 31 is *passive*, not stating the subject who takes away. The Jews, who make the request, presume that it would be·the soldiers. Pilate had granted the request in ver. 31, and had charged the soldiers with its execution, consequently with the breaking of the legs, and removal. The breaking of the leg they have in fact executed on the two who were crucified with Him, and omit it in the case of Jesus ; and as *Joseph* requests from the procurator that he may take away the body of Jesus, and obtains permission, the order for removal given to the soldiers was now recalled in reference to Jesus, and they had to remove only the other two. It is, however, very conceivable that Joseph had still *time*, after vv. 32, 34, for his request, since the soldiers after the crucifragium must certainly await the complete decease of the shattered bodies, because it was permitted to remove only bodies actually dead from the cross. Thus there is neither here, and in ver. 31, a contradiction with Mark xv. 44 (Strauss) ; nor does μετὰ ταῦτα form, as de Wette finds, " a great and hitherto unnoticed difficulty ; " nor are we, with Lücke, to understand ἄρῃ and ἦρε of the *fetching away* of the bodies (which the *soldiers* had removed), which involves a groundless departure from the sense given in ver. 31, and an unauthorized variation, from Luke xxiii. 58 ; Mark xv. 46. — τὸ πρῶτον] *The first time,*[3] iii. 2. Comp. x. 40. It does not exactly presuppose a subsequent still more frequent coming (in vii. 50 also there is only a retrospective reference to what is related in chap. iii.), but may also be said simply with reference to the *present public* coming to the *dead person*, so that only the *death* of Jesus had overcome the previous fear of men on the part of Nicodemus. *Myrrh-resin* and *aloe-wood,* these fragrant materials (Ps. xlv. 9) were placed in a pulverized condition between the bandages (ver. 40); but the *surprising quantity* (comp. xii. 3) is

---

[1] On ὁράω εἰς, *look upon*, in the sense of regard, desire, hope, etc., comp. Xen. *Cyr.* iv. 1. 20 ; Soph. *El.* 913 ; Stanley, *ad Aesch. Sept.* 109. Just so ἀποβλέπειν εἰς or πρός :

Kühner, *ad Xen. Mem.* iv. 2. 2.

[2] Euth. Zigabenus, Grotius, and several others, comp. already Barnab. 7.

[3] [Rather, *at the first.*— K.]

here explained from the fact that extraordinary reverence in its sorrowful excitement does not easily satisfy itself ; we may also assume that a portion of the spices was designed for the *couch* of the body in the grave, 2 Chron. xvi. 14.

Vv. 40–42. 'Ἐν ὀθονίοις] *In bandages,* so that He was enveloped therein.[1] — καθὼς ἔθος, κ.τ.λ.] The custom of the Egyptians,[2] *e.g.*, was different ; amongst them the practice was to take out the brain and the intestines, or at least to deposit the body in nitre for seventy days. — ἐν τῷ τόπῳ] *in the district,* in the place. On ἐτέθη, used of the interment of bodies, comp. Stallbaum, *ad Plat. Rep.* p. 469 B. — The garden with the new grave, which as yet had been used for no other burial (and thereby worthy of the Messiah, comp. Luke xxiii. 53, xix. 30 ; Mark xi. 2), must have belonged to a proprietor, who permitted, or himself put it to this use. According to Matt. xxvii. 60, it belonged to Joseph himself ; but see *in loc.* — διὰ τὴν παρασκ.] Thus, on account of the haste, which the nearness of the commencing Sabbath enjoined. Retrospect of ver. 31. — On the relation of the Johannean account of the ἐνταφιασμός of Jesus to Matt. xxvii. 59, and parallel[3] passages, see on Matt.

NOTE BY AMERICAN EDITOR.

LXVI*a.* " *For this reason, he who delivereth thee to me hath greater sin.*" **Ver. 11.**

Not " *the* greater sin" (as in the Rec. Ver.), which suggests, though it does not require, a comparison of the person's sin not with that of another, but with his own under other circumstances. Here the former is the only right idea. The sin of the Jewish priest Jesus declares to be greater than that of Pilate ;—for the one who delivers Him up is here not Judas, but the high priest, Caiaphas. Meyer explains the difference in their guilt on the ground that while the Roman is an officer of government, one of the divinely ordained powers that be, to whom therefore it properly falls to sit in judgment upon Jesus, whom he knows merely as a common man, the high-priest, though also divinely ordained, has no rightful authority over Jesus, who, as Messiah, is his superior. This seems far-fetched and unsatisfactory. Rather, I think, Jesus recognizing Pilate as a duly authorized, and so to speak divinely commissioned magistrate, and thus standing on a level with the Jewish high-priest, and both being persons who would properly have cognizance of his case, the difference lies in the *manner* in which they execute their respective functions. In this the advantage lies decidedly with the Roman. He acts but passively and reluctantly in the matter. He simply *receives* for trial one whom the Jewish ruler has delivered over to him. His conduct, though criminal, is far less criminal than that of the hierarchical zealot who has taken the initiative, who has thrown into unwilling hands, and given over for trial and condemnation, one whom he knew, or ought to know, to be innocent of crime.

---

[1] Plato, *Legg.* ix. p. 882 B ; *Pol.* viii. p. 567 C ; Judith xvi. 8.

[2] Herod. ii. 86 ff.

[3] According to Krenkel, in Hilgenfeld, *Zeitschr.* 1865, p. 438 ff., implying a denial of the apostolical origin of our Gospel, Nicodemus is identical with Joseph of Arimathaea, and the ἐνταφιασμός in the present passage is unhistorical.

CHAPTER XX.

Ver. 11. τῷ μνημείῳ instead of the *Recepta* τὸ μνημεῖον, is decisively attested. — ἔξω] stands in B. O. X. Δ. ℵ.** 1, 33, Verss. Fathers *before* κλαίουσα, but is wanting in A. ℵ.* Verss. Lachm. It is to be placed before κλαίουσα ; so also Tisch. Being unnecessary in itself, it came to be readily passed over, considering the like final vowel of τῷ μνημείῳ ἔξω, and partially again restored in the wrong place. — Ver. 14. ταῦτα] Elz. : καὶ ταῦτα, against decisive witnesses (of which L. has ταῦτα δέ). — Ver. 16. Ἑβραϊστί] is wanting in Elz., and bracketed by Lachm., but so strongly attested, that it was far more probably passed over as superfluous and self-intelligible, than added to the text. — Ver. 17. μου] after the first πατέρα is wanting in B. D. ℵ. Codd. It. Or. (twice as against thrice) Chrys. Epiph. Deleted by Tisch., bracketed by Lachm. Was more readily added from the surrounding context than omitted, hence the omitting witnesses are strong enough for its deletion. — Ver. 18. ἀπαγγέλλουσα] Lachm. and Tisch. : ἀγγέλλουσα, according to A. B. J. X. ℵ. Codd. It. Since other important witnesses have ἀναγγέλλ., and copyists were not conversant with the simple form (it is not elsewhere found in the N. T.), ἀγγέλλ. is to be preferred. — Ver. 19. συνηγμένοι] after μαθ. is by Lachm. and Tisch. deleted, on decisive testimonies. A more exactly defining gloss. — Ver. 21. ὁ Ἰησοῦς] is omitted by Tisch., and, considering the frequency of the addition on sufficient testimonies, justly. — Ver. 23. ἀφίενται] Lachm. : ἀφέωνται. The weight of testimony is very much divided ; ἀφέωνται, however, was the more readily introduced for the sake of uniformity with κεκράτ., the more familiar it was to copyists from the Synoptics. — Ver. 25. Instead of the second τύπον, Lachm. and Tisch. have τόπον. So A. J. Curss. Vulg. Codd. It. Syr. Pers. Or. Hil. Ambr. Aug. Correctly ; τύπον was mechanically repeated, while the design of the different words was left unnoticed. — Vv. 28, 29. Before ἀπεκρ., Elz. has καί : before Θωμᾶς : ὁ : and before πεπίστ., Θωμᾶ. Merely additions contrary to decisive witnesses, as also αὐτοῦ also after μαθητ., ver. 30, is, on important testimonies, to be, with Lachm. and Tisch., deleted.

Vv. 1, 2. On the designation of the first day of the week by μία τῶν σαββ., as well as on the irreconcilable deviation of John,[1] who ("*for brevity's* sake !" Hengstenberg, indeed, thinks) makes only Mary Magdalene go to the grave, from the Synoptics, see on Matt. xxviii. 1. Of a *hastening beforehand* on the part of Mary, in advance of the remaining women (Luthardt, Lange, Ewald), there is no trace in the text. But when Luthardt even is of opinion that John, from the point of view of placing over against the consummation of

---

[1] In no section of the evangelical history have harmonists, with their artificial mosaic work, been compelled to expend more labour, and with less success, than in the section on the resurrection. The adjust- ment of the differences between John and the Synoptics, as also between the latter amongst themselves, is impossible, but the grand fact itself and the chief traits of the history stand all the more firmly.

Jesus Himself the perfecting of the disciples' faith, *could* not well have mentioned the other women (*why* not ?), this would be a very doubtful compliment to the historical truth of the apostle ; and equally doubtful, if he left other women without mention only *for the reason* that he heard the *first intelligence* from the mouth of the Magdalene (Tholuck). The reason, borrowed from οἴδαμεν, for the supposed plurality of the women is abundantly outweighed by οἶδα, ver. 13. — σκοτίας ἔτι οὔσης] Consequently not after sunrise, Mark xvi. 2. See *in loc.* "Ostenditur mulieris sedulitas," Grotius. — εἰς τ. μνῆμ.] *to the grave ;* comp. xi. 31, 38. — ἐκ τοῦ μνῆμ.] The stone had *filled* the opening of the grave outwards. — καὶ πρὸς, κ.τ.λ.] From the repetition of πρός, Bengel infers : "non una fuisse utrumque discipulum." [1] — ὃν ἐφίλει] Comp. xi. 3, of Lazarus. Elsewhere of John : ὃν ἠγάπα, xix. 26, xxi. 7, 20. With ἐφίλει the recollection speaks with more feeling. — οἴδαμεν] The plur. does not presuppose that Mary had gone *not alone* to the grave, which is opposed to the account of John, but in her excitement she includes *also the disciples,* with whom she was speaking, and generally *those also who stood nearer to the Crucified One,* along with herself, although they as yet knew nothing of the removal itself. She speaks with a certain self-forgetfulness, from the consciousness of *fellowship,* in opposition to *the* parties to whom she attributes the ἦραν. Note, further, how the possibility of His having arisen remains as yet entirely remote from her mind. Not a word of any angelic communication,[2] etc., which some, of course, seek prudently to cover by an intention on John's part to be *concise* (see especially Hengstenberg). — The harmonists, who make Mary to have only *hastened on before* the rest of the women, must lead them to Peter and John by *another* way than that which she followed. But surely it would have been most natural for her, in the first instance, to run to meet her companions who were following her, with the marvellous news, which, however, with Ewald, who makes the plur. οἴδαμεν indicate this, could only be read between the lines.

Vv. 3, 4. Note the alternation of aorists and pictorial imperfects ; comp. iv. 30. — Luke xxiv. 12 mentions only Peter ; but comp. also Luke xxiv. 23. See *in loc.* The more rapid running of John, and then, again, the greater boldness of Peter, vv. 5, 6, are individual traits so characteristically original, that here (comp. on xviii. 15) it is highly inappropriate to charge the writer with an intention to place John before Peter (Strauss), or with the endeavour at least not to allow John, as opposed to Peter, to stand in the background (Baur).[3] — τάχιον τοῦ Π.] Love impelled both, and gave wings to their steps ; but the *youthful* John *ran more quickly forwards* [4] *than Peter,* whose *consciousness of guilt* (Lampe, Luthardt), especially *after* his bitter repentance, hardly restrained his running, as little as it withheld him, ver. 6, from stepping *before* John. Euth. Zigabenus is simply correct : ὡς ἀκμαιότερος τὸν τόνον τοῦ σώματος.

---

[1] But comp. ver. 3, and see, generally, Buttmann, *Neut. Gr.* p. 293 f. [E. T. p. 340 ff.] ; comp. also Kühner, *ad Xen. Mem.* i. 2. 52, i. 3. 3.

[2] Matt. xxviii. 2 ; Mark xvi. 5 ; Luke xxiv.

4 ff., xxiv. 23.

[3] This also in answer to Späth in Hilgenfeld, *Zeitschr.* 1868, p. 189 f.

[4] προεδρ., comp. Xen. *Anab.* iv. 7. 10.

Vv. 5–8. *John* is withheld by natural terror (not dread of pollution, as Wetstein, Ammon, and several others think) from going in at once ; the bolder and older *Peter*, however, goes in, and then, encouraged by his example and presence, John also enters. — Note how earnestly the fourth Gospel also states the fact of the *empty* grave, which is by no means veiled in the darkness of a twilight investigation, and of the reports of the women (Weizsäcker). — βλέπει, *he sees ;* on the other hand, ver. 6, θεωρεῖ, *he contemplates.*[1] — τὰ ὀθόνια] The handkerchief (ver. 7) must consequently have so lain, that it did not meet the eye of John, when he, standing before the grave, bent down (παρακύψας), *i.e.* bowed his head forward through the low entrance in order to see within.[2] Observe, further, that τὰ ὀθόν. here in ver. 6 is *placed first* (otherwise in ver. 5) in contrast with τὸ σουδάριον. — τὸ σουδάρ.] xi. 44 ; Luke xix. 20. — χωρίς] used adverbially (*separatim*) only here in the N. T. ; very frequent in the Greek writers. — εἰς ἕνα τόπον] belongs to ἐντετυλιγμ. : *wrapped up*[3] *in one place apart,* so that it was not, therefore, lying along with the bandages, but apart in a particular place, and was not spread out, but folded together. In so *orderly* a manner, not in precipitate confusion, did that take place which had been here done. In ἕνα is implied that the ὀθόνια and the handkerchief occupied *two* places. How thoroughly does this whole pictorial representation, comp. with Luke xxiv. 12, reveal the eye-witness ! — εἶδε] Namely, the state of matters in the grave just related. — ἐπίστευσεν] that Jesus was *risen.* Comp. ver. 25. This, the grand object of the history, taken as a matter of course, and, from these unmistakable *indicia,* now bringing conviction to the disciples, and see ver. 9. Hence neither generally : he believed *on Jesus as the Christ,* as in xix. 35,[4] nor merely : he believed *that which Mary,* ver. 2, *had said.*[5] The articles left behind in the grave and laid aside, as related, in so orderly a manner, testified, in truth, precisely *against a removal* of the corpse.[6] The *singular* only satisfies the never-to-be-forgotten *personal* experience of that moment, but does not exclude the contemporaneous faith of Peter also (in answer to Hilgenfeld and others), as is, moreover, unmistakable from the following plur. ᾔδεισαν, although even Hengstenberg makes Peter, in conformity with Luke xxiv. 12, remain standing only in *amazement* (in which Godet also substantially follows him), but of which John says never a word.

Vv. 9, 10. Γάρ] Had they already possessed this understanding of Scripture at that time, the inspection made in the empty grave would not have been needed, that there might be faith in the accomplishment of the resurrection. — ὅτι] εἰς ἐκεῖνο, ὅτι. See on ii. 18, ix. 17, xi. 51, xvi. 9. — δεῖ] Divine necessity. Comp. Luke xxiv. 26, 44, ix. 22. This knowledge of Scripture (comp. 1 Cor. xv. 4) first arose in their minds by means of the Risen One Himself,[7] and subsequently in completeness through the outpour-

---

[1] See Tittmann, *Synon.* p. 111 f., 120 f.

[2] Luke xxiv. 12; Sir. xxi. 23, xiv. 23 ; Lucian, *Paras.* 42, *et al.,* Aristoph., Theocr., Plutarch, etc.

[3] Aristoph. *Plut.* 692 ; Nub. 983.

[4] Hengstenberg, Godet.

[5] Erasmus, Luther, Aretius, Jansen,

Clarius, Grotius, Bengel, Ebrard, Baeumlein, and several others, following Augustine and Theophylact.

[6] See Chrysostom, Euth. Zigabenus, Nonnus.

[7] Luke xxiv. 27, 46 ff.; Acts i. 3.

ing of the Spirit (Acts ii. 24 ff.). Moreover, the personal previous declarations of Christ concerning His resurrection first became clear to them *ex eventu* (ii. 21, 22); hence they are not indeed to be called in question, but they (comp. x. 17, 18) cannot have been so definitive in their purport as in the Synoptics (see on Matt. xvi. 21). — οὖν] Since they had now convinced themselves of the fact of the resurrection, they must now await further events. — πρὸς ἑαυτούς] *home*, πρὸς τὴν ἑαυτῶν καταγωγήν, Euth. Zigabenus. Comp. Luke xxiv. 12 and Kypke thereon, also Wetstein on the present passage.

Vv. 11–13. Mary has followed to the grave the two disciples who ran before, but does not again meet them, (they must have gone back another way), and now stands weeping at the grave, and that without, for she dares not go further. Yet she bends down in the midst of her weeping, involuntarily impelled by her grief, forward into the grave (see on ver. 5), and beholds two angels, etc. On the question of these : τί κλαίεις, Ammonius correctly observes : ἐρωτῶσι δέ, οὐχ ἵνα μάθωσι, ἀλλ' ἵνα παύσηται. — *Appearances of angels*, whom Schleiermacher indeed was here able to regard as persons commissioned by Joseph of Arimathaea,[1] are certainly, according to Scripture, not to be relegated into the mere *subjective* sphere ; but they communicate with and render themselves visible and audible simply and solely *to him* for whom they are real, while they are not perceptible by others (comp. xii. 29); wherefore we are not even to ask where the angels may have been in the grave during the presence of Peter and John (Griesbach thought : in the side passages of the grave). — ἐν λευκοῖς] Neut. : *in white*. That ἱμάτια are meant is a matter of course.[2] Clothed in *white*, the pure heavenly appearances, in keeping with their nature of light, represent themselves to mortal gaze.[3] — ὅτι ἦραν] *Because* they, etc. As yet the deep feeling of grief allows no place for any other thought. Of a message from angels, already received before this, there is no trace in John. The refrain of her deeply sorrowful feeling : *they have taken away my Lord*, etc., as in ver. 2, was still unaltered and the same.—On the *number and position* of these angels the text offers no indications, which, accordingly, only run out into arbitrary invention and fancy, as *e.g.* in Luthardt : there were *two* in antithesis to the two jointly-crucified ones ; they had *seated* themselves because they had no occasion to contend ; seated themselves *at the head and at the feet*, because the body from head to feet was under the protection of the Father and His servants.

Vv. 14, 15. Her conversation with the angels is interrupted, as she turns round and—sees Jesus standing by, but unrecognized by her. — ἐστράφη εἰς τ. ὀπίσω] Whether accidentally only, or as seeking after her Lord, or because she heard the rustle of some one present, is not clear. Unauthorized, however, is the view of the scene adopted by Chrysostom, Theophylact, and Euth. Zigabenus, that the angels, on the sudden appearance of Jesus, had expressed their astonishment by their mien and gestures, by

---

[1] *L. J.* p. 471.
[2] See Winer, p. 550 [E. T. p. 591] ; Wetstein *in loc.*
[3] Comp. Ewald, *ad Apoc.* p. 126 f.

which Mary's attention had been aroused. — καὶ οὐκ ᾔδει, κ.τ.λ.] The un-familiar clothing, her own troubled and weeping look, and, along with this, the entire remoteness from her mind of the thought of the accom-plished resurrection—all this may have contributed to the non-recognition. The essential cause, however, is to be found in the mysterious alteration of the corporeity and of the appearance of Jesus, which manifests itself from His resurrection onwards, so that He comes and disappears in a marvellous way, the identity of His person is doubted and again recognized, etc. See on Matt. xxviii. 17. That John imagined a *withholding* of her vision, as in Luke xxiv. 16,[1] is in nowise indicated. Again, the ἐν ἑτέρᾳ μορφῇ, Mark xvi. 12, does not apply here. — ὁ κηπουρός] Naturally, since this unknown person was *in the garden,* and already so early. Quite unnecessary, however, is the trivial assumption that He had on the *clothing of the gardener,*[2] or : He was clothed with the *loin-cloth,* a piece of raiment used for field and garden labour, in which He had been crucified (altogether without evidence, comp. on xxi. 18).[3] — κύριε] Address out of her deeply prostrate and helpless grief. — σύ] With emphasis, in retrospect of ver. 13. — αὐτόν] She presumes that the supposed gardener has heard her words just spoken to the angels. — κἀγὼ αὐτ. ἀρῶ] in order to inter Him elsewhere. Her overflowing love, in the midst of her grief, does not weigh her strength. "She forgets every-thing, her feminine habits and person," etc., Luther.

Ver. 16. Jesus now calls her *by name.* Nothing more. By the *voice,* and by *this* voice, which utters aloud her *name,* she was to recognize Him. — στραφεῖσα] She had therefore, after ver. 14, again turned towards the grave. — ῥαββουνί] See on Mark x. 51. — The Ἑβραϊστί is, indeed, matter of course, and in itself is superfluous ; but in this circumstantiality there lies a certain solemnity in the delineation of the impressive moment. Note how, on the mention of her name, there follows nothing further on her side also, except that she utters the expressive *Rabboni!* More she *cannot* in the press of her joyful surprise. Thus took place the ἐφάνη πρῶτον Μαρίᾳ τῇ Μαγδ., Mark xvi. 9.

Vv. 17, 18. Mary sees : it is the Lord. But affected and transported in the highest degree by His miraculous appearance, she knows not : is it He *bodily,* actually come forth out of the grave,—again become corporeally alive and risen ? Or is it, on the other hand, His glorified *spirit, which has been* already *raised up to God,* and which again has descended to appear to her, so that He has only the bodily form, not the corporeal substance ? Therefore, to have the certainty which her love-filled heart needed in this moment of sudden, profoundest emotion, she would *take hold of, handle* Him, in order by feeling to obtain the conviction which the eye alone, in presence of this marvellous happiness, could not give her. This, however, Jesus prevents : *touch me not !* and gazing into her soul, gives her, by His own assurance, the certainty which she seeks, adding, as a reason for that repulse : *for I am not yet ascended to the Father,* therefore, as yet, no glori-

[1] Calvin, Grotius, comp. already Ammo-nius.

[2] Kuinoel, Paulus, Olshausen, and several others.

[3] Hug's invention in the *Freib. Zeitschr.* VII. p. 162 ff., followed by Tholuck.

fied spirit who has again come down from heaven whither he had ascended.[1] [See Note LXVII. p. 537.] She would touch the Lord, as Thomas did subsequently, not, however, from unbelief, but because her faith strives after a definiteness with which her love cannot dispense. Only this interpretation, which is followed also by Baeumlein, strictly corresponds to the words generally, especially also to the γάρ, which assigns a reason, and imports no scenic accompaniments into the incident which are not in the passage ; for ἅπτου leaves the reader to suppose nothing else that Mary desired to do, save simply the mere ἅπτεσθαι, therefore no embracing and the like. But scenic accompaniments are imported, and go far beyond the simple ἅπτου, if it is assumed that Mary *clasped the knees of Jesus*,[2] and desired, as *supplex*, to manifest her προσκίνησις to Him, as to a Being already glorified and returned from God,[3] or as *venerabunda*.[4] This could not be expected to be gathered by the reader from the mere *noli me tangere ;* John must, in that case, have said, μὴ ἅπτου μου γονάτων, or μὴ γουνπέτει με, or μὴ προσκίνησόν μοι, or the like, or have previously *related* what Mary desired,[5] to which it may be added, that Jesus elsewhere does not refuse the προσκίνησις ; comp. especially Matt. xxviii. 9. He does not, indeed, according to Luke xxiv. 39, repel even the handling, but invites thereto ; but in that instance, irrespective of the doubtfulness of the account, in a historical point of view, it should be noted (1) that Jesus, in Luke, *loc. cit.* (comp. John xx. 24 ff.), has to do with the direct doubt of His disciples in the reality of His bodily appearance, which doubt he must expressly censure ; (2) that in the present passage, a *woman*, and one belonging to the *narrower circle of His loving fellowship*, is alone with Him, to whom He might be disposed, from considerations of sacred *decorum*, not to permit the ἅπτεσθαι desired in the midst of overflowing excitement. How entirely different was the situation with the sinning woman, Luke vii. 37 (in answer to Brückner's objection) ! Along with the correct interpretation of ἅπτεσθαι, in itself, others have missed the further determining of the sense of the expression, either in this way : Jesus forbade the handling, because His wounds still pained Him (Paulus) ! or : because His new, even corporeally glorified life was still so delicate, that He was bound to keep at a distance from anything that would disturb it (so Olshausen, following Schleiermacher, *Festpred.* V. p. 303) ; or : because He was still bodiless, and only after His return to the Father was again to

---

[1] In οὔπω γάρ, κ.τ.λ., is expressed, therefore, not "the dread of permitting a contract, and that which was thereby intended, before the ascension to the Father should be accomplished" (Brückner) ; but Jesus means thereby to say that Mary with her ἅπτεσθαι already presupposed in Him a condition which had not yet commenced, because it must have been preceded by His ascension to the Father.

[2] Comp. the frequent ἅπτεσθαι γούνων in Homer, *Od. a.* 512, *o.* 76, *φ.* 65, *ω.* 357, *et al.*

[3] My first edition.

[4] So Lücke, Maier, Lange, Hilgenfeld,

comp. Ewald.

[5] This also in answer to Baur, who thinks that Jesus was precisely on the point of ascending (see on ver. 18), and therefore did not wish to allow Himself to be detained by Mary *falling at His feet.* Comp. Köstlin, p. 190 ; Kinkel in the *Stud. u. Krit.* 1841, p. 597 ff. — Among the ancient interpreters I find the strict verbal rendering of ἅπτεσθαι most fully preserved in Nonnus, who even refers it only to the clothing : Mary had approached her right hand to His garment ; then Jesus says : ἐμῶν μὴ ψαῦε χιτώνων.

obtain a body (Weisse).   There is thus introduced what is certainly not contained in the words (Paulus), what is a thoroughly imaginary supposition
(Paulus, Olshausen), and what is in complete contradiction to the N. T. idea
of the risen Christ (Weisse).   Others take the language as an *urging to hasten on
with that which is immediately necessary ;* [1] she is not to detain herself with the
ἅπτεσθαι, since she can see and touch Him still at a later period ; [2] by which,
however, an arbitrarily adopted sense, and one not in keeping with the subsequent ἀναβαίνω, κ.τ.λ., would be introduced into the confirmatory clause,
nay, the prospect opened up, in reference to the future *tangere*, would be
inappropriate.   *Others,* that Jesus *demands a greater proffer of honour ;* for
as His body has already become divine, the ordinary touching of feet and
mode of intercourse is no longer applicable (Chrysostom, Theodore of
Mopsuestia, Theophylact, Euth. Zigabenus, Erasmus, Jansen, and several
others).   How inept in itself, and illogical in reference to the following
οὔπω γάρ, κ.τ.λ. !   Others : it was a *refusal of the enjoyment now sought in
His appearance,* which as yet is untimely, and is to take place not "terrestri
contactu," but *spirituali,* [3] by which, however, the proper contents, constituting the essence of the supposed sense, is arbitrarily read between the
lines.   Others still differently, as *e.g.* Ammon : Jesus desired to spare Mary
the touch of one levitically unclean ! and Hilgenfeld, *Evang.* p. 318 : the
refusal of the reverential touch was made by Jesus, for the reason that He
was not yet the man again united with the Logos, but at present only the
Man raised again from His grave. [4]   Both interpretations are entirely foreign

[1] At this conclusion Hofmann also arrives, *Schriftbew.* II. 1, p. 524 : Mary is not, in her joy at again having Jesus, to *approach and hang upon Him*, as if He had appeared *in order to remain*, but was to carry to the disciples the joyful message, etc. But even with this turn the words do not apply, and the thought, especially that He had appeared not *to remain*, would be so enigmatically expressed by οὔπω γάρ, κ.τ.λ., that it could only be discovered by the way, in nowise indicated, of an indirect conclusion. That ἅπτεσθαι may denote *attach oneself, fasten oneself on* (comp. Godet : "s'attacher à"), is well known ; but just as frequently, and in the N. T. *throughout*, it means *take hold of, touch, handle*, also in 1 Cor. vii. 1 ; 1 John v. 18.

[2] So, with a different explanation in other respects of ἅπτεσθαι itself, Beza, Vatablus, Calovius, Cornelius à Lapide, Bengel, and several others.

[3] Melanchthon, Calvin, Aretius, Grotius, and several others ; substantially also, but under various modifications, Neander, de Wette, Tholuck, Luthardt, Lange, Baumgarten, Hengstenberg, Godet.   Melanchthon : "Reprehenditur mulier, quod desiderio humano expetit complexum Christi et somniat eum revixisse ut rursus inter amicos vivat ut antea . . . ; nondum scit,

fide praesentiam invisibilis Christi deinceps agnoscendam esse."   So substantially also Luther.   According to Luthardt, Mary would grasp, seize, hold Jesus fast, in order to enjoy His fellowship and satisfy her love. This Jesus denies to her, because at present it was not yet time for that ; abiding fellowship as hitherto will first again commence when He shall have ascended, consequently shall have returned in the Paracelete ; it will not then be brought about corporeally, but the fellowship will be in the Spirit. According to Baumgarten, a renewed *bodily* fellowship is promised to Mary, but completely freed from sin, and sanctified by Christ's blood. According to Hengstenberg, Mary would *embrace* Jesus in the opinion that now the wall of separation between Him and her has fallen ; but the Lord repels her, for as yet His glorification is not completed, the wall of separation still in part subsists, etc. Godet : "It is not yet the moment for thee *to attach thyself to me, as if I were already restored to you.* For I am not as yet arrived at the state in which I shall be able to contract with my disciples the superior relation which I have promised to you ;" thus substantially like Luthardt.

[4] In his *Zeitschr.* 1868, p. 436, Hilgenfeld modifies his interpretation to the extent that

530 THE GOSPEL OF JOHN.

to the meaning. Scholten's view (p. 172) is also an impossibility, as if Jesus had said οὔπω μὲν γάρ, κ.τ.λ., as one already glorified. *Conjectures* even have been attempted ; Vogel : μὴ σὺ πτόον, Gersdorf and Schulthess : μου ἅπτου, or σύ μου ἅπτου. — πρὸς τοὺς ἀδελφ. μου] *This* designation of the *disciples* as His beloved associates in the filial relation to God, to His now fulfilled earthly work (comp. πρὸς τ. πατέρα, κ.τ.λ.), is not at all intended to serve the purpose of tranquillizing them on account of their flight (Bengel, Luthardt, comp. Luther). Of this the text contains no indication, all the less that the expression is found only in the address to *Mary*, but not as *to be communicated to the disciples.*. Rather has the designation its reference to *Mary herself,* who is to gather from it, that the loving fellowship of the Lord with His own, far removed from being dissolved by the new conditions of this miraculous manifestation, rather continues, indeed, now first (comp. xv. 15) has its completion. Note the like expression in Matt. xxviii. 10, where, however (see *in loc.*)., the pointing *to Galilee* is an essential variation in the tradition ; against which Luthardt, without reason, objects that Matt. xxviii. 10 refers to the promise, xxvi. 32. Certainly ; but this promise already has, as its historical presupposition, the appearance of the Lord before the disciples, which was to be expected in *Galilee,* as this is, xxviii. 16 ff., in fact set forth as the first and only one in Matthew. — ἀναβαίνω, κ.τ.λ.] *The near and certain future.* To announce this *consequence* of His resurrection to the disciples, must be all the more on His heart, since He so frequently designates His death as His departure to the Father, and had associated with it the personal hope of the disciples. This was not to be changed by His resurrection ; that was only the passage from death to the heavenly glory. As to the *mode and way* of the ascension ἀναβ. contains *nothing.* The added κ. πατέρα ἱμῶν and κ. θεὸν ἱμῶν was, however, intended to confirm the hope of the disciples in respect of their own συνδο-ξασθῆναι, since in truth, in virtue of their fellowship with Christ, the Father of Christ was also become *their* Father, the God of Christ (to whom Christ solely belongs and serves, comp. Matt. xxvii. 47, and see, in detail, on Eph. i. 17) also *their* God (comp. on Rom. i. 8) ; this is now, after the execution of the redemptive work, entirely accomplished, and will one day have also the fellowship-in δόξα as its final result, comp. Rom. viii. 17, 29. Note in πρὸς τὸν πατέρα, κ.τ.λ., that the article does not recur, but embraces all in the unity of the Person. To understand the pres. ἀναβ., however, of that which ensues *forthwith and immediately,* and in the following way [1] that already the appearance that follows is to be placed *after the ascension* (comp. Ewald, who understands the pres. of the ascension as already *impending*), is decisively opposed by the fact of the later appearance, vv. 26, 27, unless we surrender this as actual history, or, with Kinkel, resort to the extravagant notion of *many* ascensions.

Jesus, as the Risen One, did not as yet desire to be the object of *the* reverence *which belonged to Him as Lord of the Church* (Phil.-ii. 10). This was then first to begin, when, after His ascension, He should appear before His believing ones as Dispenser of the Spirit (vi. 62, 63). But even thus the points to be understood are quite too far-fetched.

[1] Baur, p. 222 ff., and *Neutest. Theol.* p. 381, Hilgenfeld, and others.

Vv. 19, 20. Comp. Luke xxiv. 36 ff., where, however, handling and eating is already added from tradition. The account in Mark xvi. 14 is different. Schweizer's reasons against the Johannean origin of vv. 19–29 amount to this, that, according to John, the resurrection of Jesus was no external one on *this side* of the grave, and that consequently the appearances could only be visionary. Against this ii. 21, 22, x. 17, 18 are decisive, as well as the faith and the testimony of the entire apostolic Church. — τ. θυρῶν κεκλεισμ.] can all the less be without essential significance, since it is repeated in ver. 26 also, and that without διὰ τὸν φόβον τ. 'Ιουδ.]. It points to a *miraculous* appearance, which did not require open doors, and which took place while they were closed. The *how* does not and cannot appear ; in any case, however, the ἄφαντος ἐγένετο, Luke xxiv. 31, is the correlate of this immediate appearance in the closed place ; and the constitution of His body, changed, brought nearer to the glorified state, although not immaterial, is the condition for such a liberation of the Risen One from the limitations of space that apply to ordinary corporeity. Euth. Zigabenus : ὡς λεπτοῦ ἤδη καὶ κούφου καὶ ἀκηράτου γενομένου τοῦ σώματος αὐτοῦ. More minute information concerning this change withdraws itself from more definite judgment ; hence, also the passage can offer no proof of the Lutheran doctrine of ubiquity, especially as the body of Jesus is not yet that which is glorified in δόξα. According to B. Crusius, and already Beza and several others,[1] the doors must have suddenly *opened* of themselves. But in this way precisely the *essential* point would be passed over in silence. According to Baeumlein, nothing further is expressed than that the disciples were assembled *in a closed room.*[2] But how easily would John have known how *actually to express* this ! *As* he has expressed himself, τ. θυρῶν κεκλεισμ. is the definite *relation, under which* the ἤλθεν, κ.τ.λ. took place, although it is not said that He passed διὰ τ. θυρ. κεκλ., as many Fathers, Calovius and others, represent the matter. — εἰς τὸ μέσον] *into the midst*, after ἔστη, as in Herod. iii. 130, and frequently. Comp. on ver. 7, xxi. 3. — εἰρήνη ὑμῖν] The usual greeting on entrance : *Peace to you !* This first greeting of the risen Lord in the circle of disciples still resounded deeply and vividly enough in the heart of the aged John to lead him to relate it (in answer to Tholuck) ; there is therefore no reason for importing the wish for the peace of *reconciliation* (comp. εἰρήνη ἡ ἐμή, xiv. 27). — ἔδειξεν αὐτοῖς, κ.τ.λ.] In proof of the corporeal identity of His Person ; for on the hands and on the side they must see the *wounds*. This was sufficient ; it was not also required to exhibit the *feet*. Variation from Luke xxiv. 40, where the feet are shown instead of the side, the piercing of which is not related by the Synoptics. Altogether groundlessly then is the present passage employed against the nailing of the feet (see generally on Matt. xxvii. 35) ; equally groundless also is the opinion that the *flesh* of Christ was only

---

[1] Comp. also Thenius, *Evangel. der Evangelien*, p. 45.

[2] Schleiermacher, *L. J.* p. 474, does not make the *room* at all, but only the *house* to be closed, and says there "may also have been somebody who had been appointed to open." Schenkel, to whom the Risen One is " *the Spirit of the Church*," can, of course, only allow the entrance through closed doors to pass as an *emblem*. Scholten, who considers the appearances of the Risen One to be *ecstatic contemplations of the glorified One*, employs the closed doors also for this purpose.

the already laid-aside earthly envelope of the Logos (Baur).   Comp. on i.
14. — οὖν] In consequence of this evidence of identity.   Terror and doubt,
certainly the first impression of miraculous appearance, now gave way to
joy.   And from out their joyful thoughts comes the utterance of John : ἰδόντες τὸν κύριον.

Vv. 21, 22. Οὖν] For now, after the joyful recognition, He could carry
out that which He had in view in this His appearance.   Hence He began
once again, repeated His greeting, and then pursued His further address.
The repetition of εἰρήνη ὑμῖν is not a *taking leave*, as Kuinoel, Lücke, B.
Crusius, and several others, without any indication in the text, still think,
which brings out a strange and sudden change from greeting to departure,
but emphatic and elevated *repetition of the greeting*, after the preliminary
act of self-demonstration, ver. 20, had intervened.   Hengstenberg makes an
arbitrary separation : the first εἰρ.ὑμῖν refers to the *disciples*, the second to the
apostles as such. — καθὼς ἀπέσταλκε, κ.τ.λ.] Comp. xvii. 18.   Now, however,
and in fact designated a second time, according to its connection with the
proper divine delegation, the mission of the disciples is formally and solemnly ratified, and how significantly at the very first meeting after the resurrection, to be witnesses of which was the fundamental task of the
apostles ! [1] — ἐνεφύσησε] To interpret it merely as a *symbol* of the impartation of
the Holy Spirit, under the relationship of breath and spirit (comp. Ezek.
xxxvii. 5 ff. ; Gen. ii. 7),[2] neither satisfies the preceding πέμπω ὑμᾶς, nor
the following λάβετε, κ.τ.λ. ; for, in connection with both, the breathing
on the disciples could only be taken as *medium (medians) of the impartation*
of the Spirit, *i.e.* as *vehicle for the reception*, which was to take place *by
means of* the breathing, especially as λάβετε (mark the imperat. and the aor.)
cannot merely *promise* a reception belonging to the *future*,[3] but expresses
a reception *actually present*.   So substantially Origen, Cyril, Melanchthon,
Calvin, Calovius, and several others, including Tholuck, Lange, Brückner
(in answer to de Wette's symbolical interpretation), Hengstenberg, Godet,
Ewald, and several others ; while Baur considers the whole occurrence as
being already the fulfilment of the promise of the Paraclete,[4] which is thus
an anticipation, and inapplicable to the idea of the *sending* of the Paraclete.
The later and full outpouring of the Spirit on the day of Pentecost, by
which Christ returned in the Paraclete, remains untouched thereby ; moreover, we are not to understand merely the in-breathing of a χάρις δεκτική for
the later reception of the Spirit (Euth. Zigabenus).   An actual *first fruits of the
Holy Spirit* is imparted to the disciples on account of a special aim belonging to their mission.   Bengel well says : "arrha pentecostes."   It belongs
to the peculiarities of the miraculous intermediate condition, in which Jesus

---

[1] Acts i. 22, ii. 32, iv. 2, *et al.*
[2] Augustine, *De trin.* iv. 29, and many
others: " demonstratio per congruam sig-
nificationem."
[3] Chrysostom, Theodore of Mopsuestia,
Grotius, Kuinoel, Neander, Baeumlein, and
several others.
[4] Comp. Hilgenfeld in his *Zeitschr.* 1868,

p. 438, according to whom here, as in ver.
17 the ascension, the feast of Pentecost
should be taken up into the history of the
Resurrection.   The originally apostolic
idea of apostles is, so soon as Paul is called
by the *Risen One*, " *adjusted* " according to
the Pauline conception.

at that time was, that He, the Bearer of the Spirit (iii. 34), could already impart such a special *first fruits*, while the full and proper *outpouring*, the fulfilment of the Messianic *baptism* of the Spirit, remained attached to His exaltation, vii. 39, xvi. 7. The *article* needed as little to stand with πνεῦμα ἁγ. as in i. 33, vii. 39 ; Acts i. 2, 5, and many other passages. This in answer to Luthardt, who lays the emphasis on ἁγιον ; it was a *holy* spirit which the disciples received, something, that is, different from the Spirit of God, which dwells in man by nature ; the breath of Jesus' mouth was now *holy* spirit,[1] but this is not yet the spirit of the world-mighty Jesus ; it is not as yet τὸ πνεῦμα ἁγιον, but nevertheless already the basis of it, and stands intermediately between the word of Jesus on earth and the Spirit of Pentecost. Such a sacred intermediate thing, which is *holy* spirit and yet not *the* Holy Spirit, the new living breath of the Lord, but yet only *of like kind* to the Spirit of God (Hofmann), cannot be established from the N. T., in which rather πνεῦμα ἁγιον with and without the article is ever the Holy Spirit in the ordinary Biblical dogmatic sense. Comp. on Rom. viii. 4 ; Gal. v. 16. The conceivableness of the above intermediate Spirit may therefore remain undetermined ; it lies outside of Scripture. — αὐτοῖς] belongs to ἐνεφύσησε. Comp. Job iv. 21.

Ver. 23. The peculiar authority of the apostolical office, for the exercise of which they were fitted and empowered by this impartation of the Spirit. It was therefore an individual and specific charismatic endowment, the bestowal of which the Lord knew must be connected with His personal presence, and was not to be deferred until after His ascension,[2] namely, that of the valid remission of sins, and of the opposite, that of moral disciplinary power, consisting in the authority not only to receive into and expel from the church,[3] but also to exercise pardoning or penal discipline on their *fellow-members*. The apostles exercised both prerogatives, and it is without reason to understand only the former, since both belonged essentially to the *mission* (πέμπω, ver. 21) of the apostles. The promise, Matt. xvi. 19, xviii. 18, is similar, but not equivalent. The apostolic power of the keys in the sense of the Church is contained directly in the present passage, in Matt. only indirectly. It had its *regulator* in the *Holy Spirit*, who separated its exercise from all human arbitrariness, so that the apostles were therein *organs of the Spirit*. This was the divine guarantee, as the consecration of moral certainty through the illumination and sanctification of the judgment

[1] Comp. also Hofmann, *Schriftbew.* II. 1, p. 522 f.; Gess, *Pers. Chr.* p. 251 ; Weiss, *Lehrbegr.* p. 289.

[2] Hence the objection : "they required at present no such impartation" (Hofmann), is precipitate. They made *use* of it first at a future time, but the *bestowal* was still to take place face to face, in this last sacred fellowship, in which a quite peculiar distinction and consecration was given for this gift.

[3] This in answer to de Wette and several others, including Ahrens (*Amt d. Schlüssel,*

1864, p. 31), who explains it of the reception or non-reception *to baptism*, and to the forgiveness of sins therewith connected. So also Steitz in the *Stud. u. Krit.* 1866, p. 480. But baptism is here, without any indication of the text, imported from the institution, which is non-relevant here, in Matt. xxviii. 18 ff. On the apostolic penal discipline, in virtue of the κρατεῖν τὰς ἁμαρτίας, on church members, comp. the apostolic handing over to Satan, and see on 1 Cor. v. 5.

in the performance of its acts.[1] — ἀφίενται] *They are remitted*, that is, by God.
— κρατῆτε] He abides by the figure ; opposite of loosing : *hold fast*.[2] — κεκράτ.]
They are held fast, by God.   Here the perf. ; for the κρατεῖν is on the part
of God no *commencing* act (such is the ἀφιέναι). — That upon Thomas, who was
at that time absent (ver. 24), the same full authority under the impartation
of the Spirit was further particularly and supplementarily (after ver. 29),
bestowed, is, indeed, not related, but must be assumed, in accordance with
the necessity which was involved in the equality of his position. — The
objections of Luthardt against our interpretation of this verse are unimportant, since in reality the eleven are thought of as assembled together
(vv. 19, 24) ; and since the assertion, that *all* charismatic endowments date
only from Pentecost, is devoid of proof, and is overthrown precisely by the
present passage ; comp. also already Luke ix. 55.   Calovius well says : "ut
antea jam acceperant Spiritum ratione sanctificationis, ita nunc accipiunt
ratione ministerii evangelici."   The full outpouring with its miraculous gifts,
but for the collective church, then follows at Pentecost.

Vv. 24, 25. Θωμᾶς . . . Δίδυμος] See on xi. 16. — οὐκ ἦν μετ' αὐτῶν, εἰκὸς
γάρ, αὐτὸν μετὰ τὸ διασκορπισθῆναι τοὺς μαθητὰς . . . μήπω συνελθεῖν αὐτοῖς, Euth.
Zigabenus.   There may also have been another reason, and conjectures
(Luthardt : melancholy led him to be solitary, similarly Lange) are fruitless.
— Thomas shows himself, ver. 25 (comp. on xiv. 5), in a *critical tendency of
mind*, in which he does not recognize the statement of eye-witnesses as a
sufficient ground of faith.   From this, however, we perceive how completely remote from his mind lay the *expectation* of the resurrection.   In the
fact that he wished to feel only the wounds of the *hands* and of the *side*, some
have found a reason against the *nailing of the feet* to the cross (so still Lücke
and de Wette).   Erroneously ; the above requirement was sufficient for
him ; in feeling the wounds on the feet, he would have required something
which would have been too much, and not consistent with decorum.   Comp.
on Matt. xxvii. 35. — τύπον is then interchanged with τόπον (see critical
notes), as correlative to *seeing* and *feeling*.   Comp. Grotius : "τύπος *videtur*,
τόπος *impletur*." — βάλω τὴν χεῖρά μου, κ.τ.λ.] is regarded as a proof of the
peculiar *greatness* of the wound.   But he would lay his hand in truth not in
the *wound*, but in the *side*, in order, that is, there to touch with his fingers the
wound on the mere skin, but which, at the same time, must have been even
then considerable. enough. — Note, further, the *circumstantiality* in the
words of Thomas, on which is stamped an almost defiant reliance in his unbelief, not melancholy dejection (Ebrard).

Vv. 26, 27. "Interjectis ergo diebus nulla fuerat apparitio," Bengel.
This appearance is contained *only* in John. — πάλιν ἦσαν ἔσω] points back to
the same locality as in ver. 19.   Wetstein, Olshausen erroneously transfer
the appearance to *Galilee*.   They were again *within*, namely, in the *house*
known from ver. 19 (comp. Kypke, I. p. 412) and again from a like self-
intelligible reason as in ver. 19, *with closed doors*.   Is·it, that they were gathered

---

[1] On ἄν instead of ἐάν, see Hermann, *ad Viger*. pp. 812, 822 ; frequent in Greek prose.   [2] Polyb. *i.* *x.* 8 ; Acts ii. 24.

together *for the celebration of the resurrection-day* (Luthardt, Lange), and that Jesus desired by His appearance to sanction this solemnity (Hengstenberg), is without any indication. The direction, ver. 27, presupposes an *immediate knowledge* of what is related in ver. 25, which in John least of all required to be indicated (in answer to Lücke, who, as also Schleiermacher, supposes a communication of the disciples to Jesus). — Bengel, moreover, well remarks : " Si Pharisaeus ita dixisset : *nisi videro*, etc., nil impetrasset ; sed discipulo pridem probato nil non datur." — φέρε . . . καὶ ἰδε] The wounds in the hand he is to feel *and see ;* the wound in the side, under the garments, only to *feel*. Observe the similarity in circumstantiality and mode of expression of the words of Jesus with the expression of the disciple in ver. 25. — καὶ μὴ γίνου ἄπιστος, ἀλλὰ πιστ.] Not : *be*, but : *become* not unbelieving, etc. Through his doubt of the actual occurrence of the resurrection Thomas was *in danger of becoming* an unbeliever (in Jesus generally), and in contradistinction to this his vacillating faith he was, through having convinced himself of the resurrection, *to become* a believer.

Vv. 28, 29. The doubts of Thomas, whose faith did not now require actual contact (hence also merely ἑώρακας, ver. 29), are converted into a straightforward and devoted confession ; comp. xi. 16. — ὁ κύριός μου κ. ὁ θεός μου] is taken by Theodore of Mopsuestia [1] as an exclamation of astonishment directed *to God*. So recently, in accordance with the Socinians,[2] especially Paulus. Decisively opposed to this view is εἶπεν αὐτῷ, as well as the necessary reference of ὁ κύρ. μου to Christ. It is a confessionary *invocation of Christ* in the highest joyful surprise, in which Thomas gives the fullest expression of profound emotion to his faith, which had been mightily elevated by the conviction of the reality of the resurrection, in the divine nature of his Lord. For the doctrinal *conception*, the vehement *emotion* certainly seems in itself scarcely calculated to produce this exclamation, which Ewald even terms *extravagant ;* but this is outweighed (1) partly by the account of John himself, who could find in this exclamation only an echo of his own θεὸς ἦν ὁ λόγος, and of the attestations of Jesus to His own divine nature ; (2) and chiefly by the approval of the Lord which follows. Erasmus aptly says : " *Agnovit* Christus utique *repulsurus*, si falso dictus fuisset Deus." Note further (1) the *climax* of the two expressions ; (2) how the amazed disciple keeps them apart from one another with a solemn emphasis by repeating the article [3] and the μου. This μου, again, is the outflow "ex vivo et serio fidei sensu," Calvin. — Ver. 29. The ὁ κύριός μ. κ. ὁ θεός μου was the complete and highest *confession of Messianic faith*, by the rendering of which, therefore, the above μὴ γίνου . . . πιστός was already fulfilled. But it was the consequence of his *having seen* the Risen One, which should not have been required, considering the sufficient ground of conviction which lay in the assurance of his fellow-disciples as eye-witnesses. Hence the loving *reproof* (not *eulogy*, which Paulus devises, but also not a confirmation of the *contents* of Thomas' confession, as Luthardt assumes, which is

---

[1] "quasi pro miraculo facto Deum collaudat," ed. Fritzsche, p. 41.

[2] See against these Calovius.

[3] See Dissen, *ad Dem. de Cor. p.* 374.

implied only in μακάριοι, κ.τ.λ.) for him who has attained in this *sensuous* way to decisive faith, and the *ascription of blessedness* to those who, without such a sensuous conviction, have become believers,—which is to be left as a *general* truth, and not referred to the *other disciples*, since it is *expressed* in a general way, and, in accordance with the supersensuous and moral nature of faith, is universally *valid*. In detail, note further : (1) to read πεπίστευκας *interrogatively* (with Griesbach, Scholz, Lachmann, Ewald) makes the element of *reproof* in the words, indicated by the emphatic (comp. i. 51) precedence of ὅτι ἑώρ. με, appear with more vivid prominence ; (2) the perf. is : *thou hast become believing and believest now ;* the aor. participles ἰδόντες and πιστεύσ. do not denote *wont* (Lücke), which usage is never found in the N. T., and would here yield no suitable meaning, but those who, regarded from the point of time of the μακαριότης predicated of them, *have* not seen, and yet have believed ; they have *become* believers without *having* first seen. (3) The point of time of the μακαριότης is, in correspondence with the general proposition, the *universal present*, and the μακαριότης itself is the happiness which they enjoy through the already present, and one day the eternal, possession of the Messianic ζωή. (4) The μακαριότης is not denied to Thomas, but for his warning the *rule* is adduced, to which he also ought to have subjected himself, and the *danger* is pointed out to him in which one is placed who demands sight as a way to faith, as he has done. (5) The antithesis in the present passage is, therefore, not that of faith on account of that which has externally *taken place*, and of faith *certain in itself of its contents* (Baur, comp. Scholten), but of faith (in a thing that has taken place) with and without a personal and special perception of it by the senses. (6) How significant is the declaration μακάριοι, κ.τ.λ., standing at the close of the Johannean Gospel ! The entire subsequent historical development of the church rests in truth upon the faith which has not seen. Comp. 1 Pet. i. 8.

Vv. 30, 31. Conclusion of the entire book (not merely of the *main portion* of it, as Hengstenberg maintains) ; for chap. xxi. is a supplement. — πολλὰ μὲν οὖν] *Multa quidem igitur.*[1] — καὶ ἄλλα] On the well-known καί after πολλά (*et quidem alia*), see Baeumlein, *Partik.* p. 146. Comp. Acts xxv. 7. — σημεῖα] *miraculous signs,* by which He has proved Himself to be the Messiah, the Son of God (ver. 31). Comp. xii. 37. To this corresponds in general also the conclusion of the appendix, xxi. 25.[2] Justly might John, looking back upon his now finished βιβλίον, adduce as its contents from the beginning of his history down to this conclusion, *a potiori*, the σημεῖα which Christ had wrought, since these form the distinguishing characteristic in the working of Jesus (comp. x. 41), and the historical basis, with which the rest of the contents (particularly the discourses) are connected. Others have taken σημεῖα in exclusive, or at least, like Schleiermacher, pre-eminent reference to the *resurrection: documenta resurrectionis* (comp. Acts i. 3).[3]

---

[1] It serves as a concluding summary, so as to prepare the way for a thought introduced by δέ. Comp. Baeumlein, *Partik.* p. 178. See Klotz, *ad Devar.* p. 663.

[2] Correctly so, by way of suggestion, Euth. Zigabenus, further Calvin, Jansen,

Wolf, Bengel, Lampe, Tholuck, de Wette, Frommann, Maier, B. Crusius, Luthardt, Hilgenfeld, Hengstenberg, Godet, Baeumlein, Scholten, and several others.

[3] So Chrysostom, Theophylact, Euth. Zigabenus, Ruperti, Luther, Beza, Calovi-

But to this corresponds neither the general and absolute σημεῖα in itself, nor the predicate πολλὰ κ. ἄλλα, since Christ, after His resurrection, both in accordance with the accounts in the Gospels, and also with that of 1 Cor. xv., certainly appeared only a few times ; nor, finally, ἐποίησεν and ἐν τῷ βιβλ. τούτῳ, which latter shows that John (for ἐνώπ. τ. μαθητ., moreover, does not point to another writer, against Weizsäcker) has in view the contents *of his entire Gospel.* — ἐνώπ. τ. μαθ.] So that thus still many more σημεῖα might have been related, as by an eye-witness, by John, who, in truth, belonged to the μαθηταί ; hence this addition is not to be employed as a ground for the interpretation by Chrysostom, etc., of σημεῖα, because, that is to say, Jesus before His death performed His signs in the sight of the *people,* etc. (comp. xii. 37). — ταῦτα δέ] sc. τὰ σημεῖα, namely, those recorded in this book, this selection which composes its contents. — ἵνα πιστεύσ.] refers to the readers, for whom the Gospel was designed. "*Scopus* evangelii," Bengel.[1] Of the *conversion of the Gentiles* (Hilgenfeld) to the faith, there is no mention. — ὁ υἱὸς τ. θεοῦ] in the Johannean sense. Without being *this,* He would not be the promised *Messiah.* — πιστεύοντες] *in your believing.* Thus, then, the ζωὴν ἔχειν is conceived of as a possession already beginning with faith ; faith, however, as a subjective *principle* of life, quite as with Paul, although the latter more sharply separates from one another, as conceptions, justification, and life.[2] — ἐν τῷ ὀνόμ. αὐτοῦ] belongs to ζωὴν ἔχ. *In the name of Jesus,* as the object of faith (i. 12), the possession of life is causally founded. — Baur, in accordance with false presuppositions, holds vv. 30, 31 to be *spurious,* because the previously related appearances (which, according to Baur, took place from out of *heaven*) must in themselves so bring to a close the appearance of the Risen One, that we cannot think of further appearances of this kind (πολλὰ κ. ἄλλα).

Note by American Editor.

LXVII. Μή μου ἅπτου. Ver. 17.

The first question, in this disputed passage, is of the meaning of ἅπτου, whether it is simply equivalent to θιγγάνω, *touch,* or has its more full and proper meaning of *fasten oneself upon, hold on to, cling.* Both the present tense and the connection seem to me to point to the latter. For simply touch we should naturally have the aor. ἅψαι, and merely to *touch* the Lord would surely not be forbidden to Mary.

As to the reason for the prohibition, omitting several of those invented by German ingenuity, we may mention three or four which have been alleged. First, the *incidental* reasons, as (1) That our Lord was on His way to His ascension and could not be detained, for which certainly there seems no sufficient ground. The arguments for repeated ascensions, one immediate, are by no means convincing. (2) That Mary would not delay in her execution of His message to the

---

us, Maldonatus, Semler, and several others, including Kuinoel, Lücke, Olshausen, Lange, Baur, Ewald, and several others.

[1] Comp. *Introd.* § 5. See also, as regards πιστεύσ., on xix. 35.

[2] Comp. Schmid, *Bibl. Theol.* II. p. 391

Apostles—which, however, seems hardly an adequate reason for such a demand —besides which, Christ does not give *this* as the real reason. (3) That the language is a familiar hyperbole for "I do not go immediately," as we say "I am not yet gone," which may relieve Mary from the anxious endeavour, by her clasp, to detain Him. I may mention (4) the quasi *indecorum* which Meyer finds in His receiving the touch (for He holds it as no more) of a woman, which I think, with Weiss, nearly fanciful.

The real or *essential* reason for the repelling of the clasp is given not very intelligibly by Meyer, as " *I am not yet ascended to my Father*, therefore, as yet no glorified spirit who has again come down from heaven, whither He had ascended." More satisfactorily, perhaps, Meyer says in his note, " Jesus intimates that Mary's ἅπτεσθαι presupposes in Him a condition which has not yet commenced, because it must have been preceded by His ascension to His Father!"

Better, I think, Weiss : " The prohibition lies simply in this, that He, although His ascension is not yet accomplished, is on the eve of ascending, and thus His appearance cannot have the purpose to renew His earlier intercourse with His friends."

To the same effect Luthardt : " It is not the one who has already ascended who is standing before her ; and accordingly it is not yet the time of which He had spoken, when He declared that He would go away to the Father, and then come to them. The time has not yet dawned at which their fellowship with Him is to come to the goal of its completion. . . . The time directly at hand is for the disciples as little as for Mary, a time of external sensible fellowship ; it is the time of the departure and distance of Jesus in which they can be sure of Him only by belief."

The single article with ἀναβαίνω πρὸς τόν, etc. makes the clause equivalent to " Him who is my Father and your Father and my God and your God," at once putting them and Him in a common relation to God, and yet by not saying " *our Father and our God* " (τὸν πατέρα ἡμῶν κ. τὸν Θεὸν ἡμῶν), keeping them distinctly separate.

CHAPTER XXI.

Ver. 3. Instead of ἐνέβησαν, Elz. has ἀνέβησαν, against decisive testimony. —
After πλοῖον, Elz. Griesb. Scholz have : εὐθύς, which is condemned by decisive
testimony. — Ver. 4. γενομ.] Tisch. : γινομ., which is to be preferred, since to
the witnesses C.* E. L., A. B. with γεινομ. are to be added ; though with the
copyists γενομ. was more current. — εἰς] Lachm. Tisch. : ἐπί. The Codd. are
very much divided ; ἐπί came to be more readily added as a gloss than εἰς.
Comp. Matt. xiii. 2, 48 ; Acts xxi. 5. — Ver. 6. ἴσχυσαν] Tisch. : ἴσχυον, according to preponderant testimonies. The aorist form was involuntarily suggested
from the surrounding context (ἔβαλον, ἑλκῦσαι). — Ver. 11. ἐπὶ τῆς γῆς] Lachm.
Tisch. : εἰς τὴν γῆν, according to A. B. C. L. ℵ., etc. Nevertheless, the Recepta
is to be retained. Ἐπὶ τὴν γ. (so D. Curss.) was written as a gloss in some instances,—in others, after ver. 9, εἰς τ. γ. was written. — In vv. 15, 16, 17, as in
i. 43, instead of Ἰωνᾶ, we are to read : Ἰωάννου. — Ver. 17. πρόβατά] A. B. C. :
προβάτια. Rightly adopted by Tisch. The Recepta is a repetition from ver. 16.
Tisch. has, indeed, even already in ver. 16, προβάτια, but only according to B.
C., so that the testimony of A. appears only for ver. 17. — Ver. 22. Read with
Lachm. Tisch., μοι ἀκολούθει. — Ver. 25 is wanting in ℵ.*, is explained in
Scholia as an addition, and has in detail the variations ἃ (Lachm. Tisch.) instead
of ὅσα ; Χριστὸς Ἰησοῦς (D.), in one Cod. of It. with the addition : quae non
scripta in hoc libro ; οὐδ' (Lachm. Tisch.) instead of οὐδέ ; χωρήσειν (Tisch. ac-
cording to B. C.* ℵ.** Or.) ; at the conclusion ἀμήν (Elz.).

Chap. xx. 30, 31, bears so obviously the stamp of a formal conclusion worthy
of an apostle, while chap. xxi., moreover, begins in a manner so completely unexpected, that this chap. can appear only as a supplement. The question is,
however,[1] whether this supplement proceeds from John or not. This question first
became a subject of investigation from the time of Grotius, who saw in the
chapter a supplement of the Ephesian church, composed after the apostle's death
by the bishop (perhaps by John the Presbyter). Since all witnesses contain
the chapter, a judgment can only be pronounced from internal grounds. These,
however, decide only against ver. 25, which contains an exaggeration so surprising, unapostolical, and in such absolute contradiction to the Johannean simplicity, intelligence, and delicacy, that it is impossible that it can have proceeded from the pen of the apostle, but must appear probably as a later, although
very ancient, form of conclusion, an apocryphal and inharmonious echo of xx.
30. The omission[2] of ver. 25 in ℵ*, and its suspicious character in the Scholia,

[1] See generally Hoelemann, der Epilog des Evang. Joh., in his Bibelstudien, II. p. 61 ff.
[2] According to the usual statement, ver. 25 should also be wanting in Cod. 63. This, however, Tisch. (Wann wurden unsere Evangelien verf. p. 127, ed. 4) declares to be an error. On ver. 25 in ℵ. Tisch. passes this judgment : the copyist of this Cod. did not find the verse in his copy, and therefore did not add it ; but the words are supplied, "ab eo qui eadem aetate totum librum re-censebat ac passim ex alio exemplari corri-gebat atque augebat," Cod. ℵ. ed. Lips. p. LIX.

rests upon a correct critical feeling. On such feeling, however, also rests the fact that this omission and suspicion have not likewise affected ver. 24, which contains absolutely nothing that John could not have written, but rather forms a worthy conclusion to the entire supplement of chap. xxi., and does not by οἴδαμεν betray the work of a strange hand (see the exegetical notes). The grounds, moreover, brought forward against the authenticity of vv. 1–23 are untenable. For (1) it by no means follows from ver. 23, that at the time of the composition the apostle was already dead (Weizsäcker, Keim, and others), since the speech there mentioned required precisely the correct historical explanation *for the eventuality* of his still *future* death. Comp. Ewald, *Jahrb.* III. p. 172. (2) The advent of Christ, mentioned in vv. 22, 23, is without any reason declared to be non-Johannean. See on xiv. 3. Just as little is (3) the self-designation, ver. 20, un-Johannean ; it corresponds rather just as well to the importance which the recollection, therein expressed, of the never-to-be-forgotten moment must have had for John, in and of itself, as also to the connection into which it is interwoven. See on ver. 20. Further, (4) the individual expressions[1] which are designated as non-Johannean (as *e.g.* ver. 3, ἔρχεσθαι σύν instead of ἀκολουθεῖν ; ver. 4, πρωΐας γινομ. instead of πρωΐ ; ver. 12, τολμᾶν and ἐξετάζειν ; ver. 18, φέρειν instead of ἄγειν) are, taken together, phenomena so unessential, nay, having for the most part in the sense of the context so natural a foundation, that they, especially in consideration of the later time of the composition of the supplement, leave behind them no serious difficulty whatever, and are far outweighed by the otherwise completely Johannean stamp, which the composition bears in itself, in the language, in the mode of presentation, and in the individual features which betray the eye-witness (how entirely different is the section concerning the adulteress !). For, in particular, (5) the alleged want of Johannean clearness and demonstrativeness is removed partly by correct exposition, partly in the question as to the genuineness, rendered ineffective by the fact that John, even in the earlier part of the Gospel, does not always narrate with *equal* clearness and perspicuity. (6) It is not correct to say that with the spurious conclusion the entire chapter also falls to the ground,[2] since the non-Johannean conclusion may have been added to the Johannean chapter, especially as, on the assumption of the genuineness of ver. 24, the appendix itself did not go forth without a conclusion from the hand of the apostle. In accordance with all that has been advanced, the view is justified, *that John by way of authentic historical explanation of the legend in ver. 23, some time after finishing his Gospel, which he had closed with* xx. 31, *wrote chap.* xxi. 1–24,[3] *as a complement of the book, and that this appendix, simply because its Johannean origin was immediately certain and recognized, already at a very early period, whilst the Gospel had not yet issued forth from the narrower circle of its first readers* (*Einl.* sec. 5), *had become an inseparable part of the Gospel ; but that simply owing to the fact that now the entire book was without a principal con-*

---

[1] For a minute discussion of the peculiarities of language in chap. xxi., and their variation from the Gospel, see in Tiele, *Annotatio in locos nonnull. ev. Joh. ad vindicand. huj. ev. authent.*, Amst. 1853, p. 115 ff. In answer to Scholten, who believes he has found most linguistic deviations, see Hilgenfeld in his *Zeitschr.* 1868, p. 441 ff.

[2] Much more correct would it be to say :

the chap. *partially* betrays, in so striking a manner, the Johannean delicacy and originality (pre-eminently vv. 15–17), that with this the *whole* stands as a production of the apostle.

[3] Vv. 1–14 hardly have an object unknown to us (Brückner), since they are in simple objective historical connection with what follows.

clusion, the apocryphal conclusion, ver. 25, *exaggerating the original conclusion,* xx. 31, *came to be added.* This addition of ver. 25 must have been made at a very early date, because only a few isolated traces of the spuriousness of ver. 25 have been preserved, which, however, by the evidence of א.* go back to a very ancient time ; while, on the other hand, in reference to vv. 1–24, not the faintest echo of a critical tradition is found which would have testified against their genuineness. Tisch. also designates only ver. 25 as spurious. — The apostolic origin of the chapter was *controverted,* in connection with very various theories, especially its derivation from the author of the Gospel, after Grotius, by Clericus, Hammond, Semler, Paulus, Gurlitt,[1] Lücke, Schott, de Wette, Credner, Wieseler[2] (John the Presbyter wrote the chap. after the death of the apostle), Schweizer, Bleek, Schwegler, Zeller, Baur (because it is not in keeping with the main idea of the whole), Köstlin, Keim, Scholten, and several others ; Brückner has doubts. In opposition to Baur's school, according to which it would seem designed, along with the entire chap., for the purpose of exalting the apostle of Asia Minor over Peter, see especially Bleek. — The Johannean origin, or at least the derivation from the writer of the Gospel, is defended, but in such a way that recently vv. 24, 25 have been for the most part rejected by Calovius, Rich. Simon, Mill, Wetstein, Lampe, Michaelis, Krause,[3] Beck,[4] Eichhorn, Kuinoel, Hug, Wegscheider,[5] Handschke,[6] Erdmann,[7] Weber,[8] Guerike, Redding (*Disput.* Groning. 1833), Frommann, Tholuck, Olshausen, Klee, Maier, B. Crusius (not decidedly),[9] Luthardt, Lange, Laurillard (*Disp. L. B.* 1853), Ebrard (on Olshausen), Hengstenberg, Godet; Hoelemann, Schleiermacher (at least in respect of the contents). According to Ewald,[10] a friend of the apostle (probably a presbyter at Ephesus), of whose hand, probably also of whose art, John availed himself in the composition of the Gospel, wrote the appendix for himself alone at a later date, without desiring in the slightest degree to conceal that it was by a different person. In his *Johann. Schriften,* I. p. 54 ff., Ewald ascribes the composition to the same circle of friends, in which the Gospel may have remained perhaps for ten years before its publication ; that the apostle himself, however, permitted the publication with this appendix (inclusive also of vv. 24, 25) before his death. Similarly Baeumlein. — Very superficially and peremptorily does Hengstenberg designate the entire view that chap. xxi. is a supplement, as leading to a view of the accidental nature of the authorship, which is unworthy of the apostle, and in conflict with the character of the Gospel. Hilgenfeld assigns the chap., *with inclusion of vv.* 24, 25, to the evan· gelist, who, however, was not the apostle. Comp. also Bretschneider, p. 182.

Vv. 1, 2. Μετὰ ταῦτα] Referring, in conformity with the nature of a supplement, to the *last* narrative *before* the conclusion in xx. 30, 31. — ἐφανέρωσεν ἑαυτόν] Comp. the passive expression, Mark xvi. 12, 14 ; the reflexive form of construction, however, is decidedly Johannean, see vii. 4. It presup-

---

[1] *Lection. im N. T. Spec.* III. Hamb. 1805. Bertholdt, Seyffarth (*Beitr. zur Specialcharakt. der Joh. Schriften,* Lpz. 1823, p. 271 ff.

[2] *Diss.* 1839.

[3] *Diss. Viteb.* 1793.

[4] Lips. 1795.

[5] *Einl. in d. Ev. Joh.*

[6] *De αὐθεντίᾳ* c. 21 *ev. Joh. e sola orat. indole dijud.,* Lips. 1818.

[7] *Bemerk. üb. Joh.,* Rostock, 1821.

[8] *Authentia . . . argumentor. intern. usu vindic.,* Hal. 1823.

[9] He, as also Lange, Hengstenberg, Hoelemann, ascribes also vv. 24, 25 to the apostle, in opposition to which Luthardt regards 24, 25 as a testimony added from the Ephesian church. *Stud. u. Krit.* 1849, p. 601 ff.

[10] *L.c.,* comp. also *Jahrb.* X. p. 87.

poses a *state of concealment*, from which He now again (πάλιν points back to ver. 14, to the two preceding appearances, xx. 19, 26) came forth and *made Himself manifest* to His disciples, brought Himself into view,—not a *spiritual* existence (de Wette), not "a sphere of *invisibility*, in which He moves by Himself" (Luthardt, comp. Tholuck), but rather a wonderfully altered existence, no longer belonging to ordinary intercourse, brought nearer to a state of glorification, yet still material, διὰ τὸ λοιπὸν ἀφθαρτον εἶναι τὸ σῶμα καὶ ἀκήρατον, Chrysostom. — ἐπὶ τῆς θαλ.] *on the lake*, because the shore is *over* the lake.[1] It belongs to ἐφαν. — ἐφανέρωσε δὲ οὕτως] *sc.* ἑαυτόν, not, as Hengstenberg borrows from ii. 11, τὴν δόξαν αὐτοῦ. Further, an *iteration* of this kind, in simple, continuous narration, is not elsewhere found in John. But he may here have purposely written in so diffuse a manner as a set-off to the distortions of actual fact in tradition (comp. ver. 23). — Of the seven disciples, ver. 2, the two last remain unnamed. Hence they are probably (vi. 60, vii. 3, viii. 31, xviii. 19) to be deemed disciples in the wider sense, with which ver. 1 does not conflict (in answer to Hengstenberg, who conjectures Andrew and Philip), since the two unnamed are simply subordinate persons. That of the disciples in the narrower sense the sons of Zebedee are mentioned *last*, accords with the composition of the narrative by John himself. Not any deeper or emblematic significance is to be sought as lying behind the succession of the names, or behind the number seven. Another author would probably have placed the sons of Zebedee immediately after Peter. — ὁ ἀπὸ Κανᾶ τ. Γαλ.] added, without any special design, in this supplement of late composition. According to Hengstenberg, the representative of the first miracle (chap. ii.) could not but be indicated, which is pure invention. — οἱ τοῦ Ζεβεδαίου] does not occur elsewhere in John ; but, at the same time, it is only here that the occasion presents itself to him to mention in a series of names himself [2] *and his brother* along with others. — On the tradition recorded by Luke, which is altogether irreconcilable with Galilean appearances of the Risen One, unless upon arbitrary harmonistic assumptions (such as even Luthardt entertains), see on Luke xxiv. 50. Acts i. 4 does not, however, necessarily presuppose, in reference to the appearances, that none took place in Galilee. Matthew, on the other hand, excludes the appearances which took place before the disciples *at Jerusalem*, which are related by John xx. See on Matt. xxviii. 10. Harmonistic expedients also in Hengstenberg and Godet.

Vv. 3, 4. Ἐρχόμ. κ. ἡμεῖς σὺν σοί] John has not employed ἀκολουθεῖν, nor said ἄγωμεν κ. ἡμεῖς (xi. 16), because he has *thought* just what was said. — The *circumstantiality* is not un-Johannean (Lücke), but comp. *e.g.* i. 39, 40, ix. 1–12. In particular, moreover, the ὑπάγω ἁλιεύειν is only the simple language of familiar association, in which neither a "*brusque tone*," nor "an *internal impulse*, a *presentiment*" (Godet), is to be recognized. The disciples desire again to pursue their earthly employments, "*quod privatos homines decebat*," Calvin. —ἐξῆλθον] from the place indicated in ver. 2, prob-

---

[1] Comp. on Matt. xiv. 25 ; Xen. *Anab.* iv. 3. 28 : ἐπὶ τοῦ ποταμοῦ, and passages from Herodotus in Schweighäuser's *Lex.* p. 245.

[2] Hence Nathanael cannot be John (Späth) ; comp. on i. 46.

ably Capernaum, out to the lake, ver. 1. — By *night* fishing was productive.[1]
But *they caught nothing.* How entirely different was it afterwards, when
they cast out *at the bidding of the Lord!* — ἐστη] Expressing the sudden appearance. Comp. xx. 19, 26. — εἰς τ. αἰγ.] Comp. xx. 19, 26. — οὐ μέντοι,
κ.τ.λ.] To be explained from the entirely altered condition and appearance of
the Risen One. Chrysostom assigns the reason to the will of Jesus : οὐκ εὐθέως
ἑαυτὸν δείκνυσιν, comp. also Luthardt and Hengstenberg, of which John, however, gives no indication. Comp. rather on xx. 14.

Vv. 5, 6. Παιδία] Not un-Johannean (1 John ii. 14, 18), although in xiii.
33 τεκνία is used. — μή τι προσφάγ. ἐχετε] The emphasis lies, as frequently, on
the concluding word : *you are not, I suppose,* (already) *in possession of something to eat?* The question presupposes the opinion of the questioner, that
they had probably as yet taken nothing, as well as the thought that in the
opposite case He need not step in. That, however, He designates exactly
fishes by προσφάγιον, is grounded on the fact that He intends to take a *breakfast* with the disciples on the fishes, after which He inquires.[2] — The disciples simply answer : *no;* they have therefore taken Him for an entire
stranger, who perhaps wishes to buy fishes for breakfast. The παιδία, intended
by Jesus in the sense of fatherly love, they may have *regarded,* in the mouth
of the unknown, as a friendly designation of the *state of service* (Nonnus :
παῖδες ἁλὸς δρηστῆρες ; Euth. Zigabenus : τοὺς ἐργατικούς). Comp. on vi. 6.
— εἰς τὰ δεξιὰ μ.] They had the net then in the lake, on quite another side
of the boat. — οὐκέτι] *no longer,* as previously, when it was empty and light.
Observe the pictorial imperf. ἰσχυον (see the critical notes). — ἑλκῦσαι] *draw,*
draw up the submerged net. On the other hand, σύροντες, ver. 8 : *tugging,
dragging forth.*[3] — ἀπό] *on account of.*[4] — To regard the above fruitless toils
(on the *left,* it is thought), and this abundant taking on the *right,* as a figure
of the apostolic ministry, in relation first to the *Jews* and then to the *Gentiles,*
is too special, and not even accordant with history (Gal. ii. 9 ; Acts xxii.
20, *et al.,* comp. Luthardt), without prejudice, however, to the symbolism of
the draught of fishes in itself ; see note after ver. 14.

Ver. 7. Πάλιν τὰ ἰδιώματα τῶν οἰκείων ἐπιδείκνυνται τρόπων οἱ μαθηταὶ Πέτρος
καὶ Ἰωάννης. Ὁ μὲν γὰρ θερμότερος, ὁ δὲ ὑψηλότερος ἦν· καὶ ὁ μὲν ὀξύτερος ἦν, ὁ δὲ
διορατικώτερος. Διὰ τοῦτο ὁ μὲν Ἰωάννης πρῶτος ἐπέγνω τὸν Ἰησοῦν· ὁ δὲ Πέτρος
πρῶτος ἦλθε πρὸς αὐτόν, Chrysostom. Comp. xx. 3 ff. — τὸν ἐπενδύτην διεζώσατο]
He had laid aside the ἐπενδύτης, and was in so far unclothed, which, however,
does not prevent his having on the shirt, χιτωνίσκος, according to the well-
known usage of γυμνός,[6] *nudus,* and עָרוֹם.[7] In order, however, not to appear

---

[1] Comp. on Luke v. 5 ; Aristot. *H. A.* viii.
19.

[2] On προσφάγ. itself, which is, like the
Attic ὄψον, used especially of fishes (comp.
προσφάγημα, Moeris, p. 204. 24; προσόψημα,
Athen. iv. p. 162 C, vii. p. 276 E) see Sturz,
Dial. Al. p. 191 ; Fischer, *de vitiis, Lex.* p.
697 f.

[3] See Tittmann, *Synon.* p. 57 f.

[4] See Bernhardy, p. 224.

[5] Grotius, Weitzel, Hengstenberg, Godet,
Hilgenfeld, and several others.

[6] This also in opposition to Godet, according to whom Peter was *quite naked.* This
would have been disgraceful even amongst
barbarians. See Krüger on Thuc. i. 6. 4.

[7] See Perizonius, *ad Ael. V. H.* vi. 11 ;
Cuper. *Obss.* i. 7, p. 39, *Interpp. zu Jes.* xxx
2; Grotius *in loc.*

unbecomingly in his mere shirt before Jesus, he girded around him the
ἐπενδύτης, *overgarment*, *i.e.* he drew it on, and gathered it with a girdle
on his body. Hengstenberg says incorrectly : he had the ἐπενδύτ. on, and
only girded himself *in the same* (accus. of closer definition), in order to be
able to swim the better.   The middle with accus. of a *garment* always
denotes to *gird oneself therewith* (Lucian, *Somm.* 6, *de conscrib. hist.* 3). Comp.
περιζώννυσθαι, Rev. i. 13.   The ἐπενδύτης is not equivalent to χιτών,[1] but an
overwrap, an *overcoat.*   *Any* garment drawn over may be so called ;[2] it was,
however, according to Nonnus and Theophylact, in the case of fishermen,
and according to the Talmud, which has even appropriated to itself the
word אפונדתא, in the case of workmen generally, a linen article of clothing
(possibly a short frock or *blouse*) which, according to the Talmud, was
worn, provided with pockets, over the shirt (according to Theophylact,
also over other articles of clothing).   See especially Drusius *in loc.*   According to Euth. Zigabenus, it reached to the knees, and was without sleeves. —
γυμνός] He had, in point of fact, no other clothing on except the mere shirt ;[3]
for precisely διὰ τὴν γύμνωσιν[4] he quickly put on the ἐπενδύτης, which had been
laid aside during his work. — He reached the land *swimming*, not *walking*,
on the water (Grotius and several others), which is a fanciful addition.
The ἐβαλεν ἑαυτόν graphically represents the *rapid self-decision.*

Vv. 8, 9. Τῷ πλοίαρ.] *in the little boat*, on board of which they remained ;
local dative.   Comp. Herod. v. 99 : ἀπικέατο εἰκοσι νηυσί.   See generally
Becker, *Homer. Blätter*, p. 208 f. — The γάρ in the parenthesis states the
reason why they did not quit the vessel ; they could in this way also quickly
enough reach the shore, which was very near (200 cubits = ½ stadium, 300
feet).[5] — On the form πηχῶν instead of the Attic πηχέων, see Lobeck, *ad Phryn.*
p. 245 f.   On ἀπό, see on xi. 18. — τὸ δίκτυον τῶν ἰχθ.] *the net, which was filled
with the fishes* (ver. 6).[6] — Ver. 6. βλέπουσιν, κ.τ.λ.] John relates simply what
they *saw* on landing, namely, a *fire of coals lying there, and food lying thereon*
(*i.e.* a *mess of fish*, see on vii. 9 ; the singul. not of a *single* fish, as Beza,
Hengstenberg, Godet, and others think, but *collectively*, as also ἄρτον,[7] *and
bread.*   That this preparation for the breakfast to be given was made by
Jesus, would be understood by the reader as matter of course (see vv. 12, 13).
But how He brought together the materials, and who kindled the fire,
cannot be determined ; He might, before He called to the disciples, have
Himself, or by other hands, made the preparations.   Hence the narrative
yields no *miracle* (bringing forth out of nothing, thought Chrysostom,
Theophylact, Euth. Zigabenus, Grotius, Calovius, Maldonatus, and several
others ; but Nicephorus, Jansen, Luthardt : the *angels* had provided Him
therewith ; finally, Hengstenberg, Godet : without more precisely defining
the marvellous *How*), nor even the *appearance* of such (Lücke).   But

---

[1] Fischer, Kuinoel, Bretschneider.

[2] See the LXX. in Schleusner, *Thes.* II. p.
436 ; Soph. *fragm.* in Pollux, vii. 45 ; Dind.
391, comp. ἐπένδυμα in Plut. *Alex.* 32.

[3] Comp. Dem. 583. 21 : γυμνὸν ἐν τῷ
χιτωνίσκῳ.

[4] Theodoret, Heracleus.

[5] See Wurm, *de ponder*, etc., p. 195 ; Hermann, *Privatalterth.* § 46. 7.

[6] Comp. on this genit., Nägelsbach, *z.
Ilias*, p. 31, ed. 3.

[7] Comp. Polyb. xxxiv. 8. 6 : τὸ θαλάττιον
ὄψον.

wherefore did Jesus make this *preparation ?* Because the disciples were to eat *with Him* the early meal, with which He designed to connect so significant a transaction as that related in vv. 15 ff. ; *He* willed to be the *giver of the meal.* Much that is irrelevant in the older expositors. According to Luthardt, the design is to depict how Jesus, without requiring their aid, knows how to feed the disciples from His own resources. But to what purpose any such further representation, when He had long ago miraculously fed thousands before the eyes of the disciples ?

Vv. 10, 11. 'Ενέγκατε, κ.τ.λ.] for the completion, in accordance with their needs, of the dish of fish already found upon the fire of coals. That the eating of Jesus and of the disciples was no material, but a *spiritual* one (the enjoyment which Jesus has from the labors of His apostles), is a fiction of Hengstenberg's. — According to ver. 11, Peter alone draws the full net to land, which, of course, since it hung on the vessel, that lay on the shore, was easier than to draw it up out of the water into the boat. ver. 6. According to Hengstenberg, he is, indeed, named only as being the chief person, because he had been the *instrument of the spiritual fishing.* The statement of the *number* of the fishes is as little an *apocryphal* trait as the statement of the number of those who were miraculously fed, vi. 10, and the less, since it is not a *round* number which is named. The μεγάλων *heightens* the miracle. — καὶ τοσούτων ὄντων, κ.τ.λ.] Regarded by John as *incomprehensible,* and as effected by *Christ ;* by Strauss, as manifestly *legendary,* as well as the number of the fishes, which, however, might surely well be to the minds of the disciples, in this *miraculous* experience, important enough, and such as never to be forgotten. On the allegorical interpretations of the number 153, see note after ver. 14.

Vv. 12, 13. 'Άριστον is, as little as in Matt. xxii. 4, Luke xi. 38, the *principal meal,* which, in spite of ver. 4, Hengstenberg suggests in the interest of allegorical interpretation, but *breakfast.* — ἐτόλμα] *dared,* presumed. Although, that is, it had been possible for them, in respect of the external appearance, to doubt whether He was the Lord, they were nevertheless convinced of His identity, and hence dared not to ask Him : Who art thou ? Reverential awe (comp. already iv. 27), in presence of the marvellous appearance of the Risen One, deprived them of the courage to do so. According to Augustine, Beda, Jansen, and several others, they dared not *doubt,* which however, is not expressed. Chrysostom aptly remarks : οὐκέτι γὰρ τὴν αὐτὴν παρρησίαν εἶχον· . . . τὴν δὲ μορφὴν ἀλλοιοτέραν ὁρῶντες καὶ πολλῆς ἐκπλήξεως γέμουσαν, σφόδρα ἦσαν καταπεπληγμένοι, καὶ ἐβούλοντο τι περὶ αὐτῆς ἐρωτᾶν· ἀλλὰ τὸ δέος καὶ τὸ εἰδέναι αὐτούς, ὅτι οὐχ ἕτερός τις ἦν, ἀλλ' αὐτός, ἐπεῖχον τὴν ἐρώτησιν. — ἐξετάσαι] *to explore* [1] *sciscitari ;* strong expression from the point of view from which the respectful timidity of the *disciples* regarded the daring nature of the question. — εἰδότες] Constructio κατὰ σύνεσιν.[2] — Ver. 13. ἔρχεται] The δεῦτε, ver. 12, has summoned the disciples to the place of the meal where the fire of coals was ; Jesus Himself, who had therefore

[1] Matt. ii. 8, x. 11; Sir. xi. 7, xiii. 11, frequent in the classics.   [2] See Kühner, II. § 419a ; Krüger, § 58. 4. 5.

stood at some distance therefrom, now steps forward, in order to distribute the breakfast. — τὸν ἄρτον] points back to ver. 9, but τὸ ὀψάριον to vv. 9 and 10 : the bread lying there, etc. Both are again *collective*. It is not merely *one* loaf and *one* fish which Jesus distributes, as Hengstenberg, for the purpose of symbolically interpreting it of a heavenly reward of toil, assumes ; see ver. 10. — A *thanksgiving* before the δίδωσιν is not related, not as though Jesus omitted τὰ ἀνθρώπινα (Euth. Zigabenus) ; nor as though He did not desire positively to offer Himself to their recognition (Lange, in opposition to ver. 12); nor, again, as though the meal was to be a *silent* [1] one (Luthardt, who adds : "for such is the table fellowship of Jesus and His own in the present aeon") ; nor, again, because the meal represented future blessings (Hengstenberg),—but because here it is not a question of any proper meal, as in Luke xxiv. 20, but rather only of a *breakfast*, of a morning meal, partaken of only while standing (there is no mention, moreover, of a lying down), which also was not to have, like that early meal of Paul, Acts xxvii. 35, a character of solemnity. It was not this breakfast in itself, which Christ prepared for the disciples, but that which preceded (the draught of fishes) and succeeded (vv. 15 ff.), that was the *object* for which the Risen One here appeared.

Ver. 14. Τοῦτο ἤδη τρίτον] *This already for the third time.* See on 2 Cor. xiii. 1. — ἤδη presupposes, on the one hand, that, according to John, *until now* any other appearances before the disciples had *not* taken place, with the exception of the three related (xx. 19 ff., 26 ff., xxi. 1 ff.) ; but, on the other hand, that at a *later* date several other appearances occurred. Since he, moreover, refers his τρίτον only to the appearances that were made to the *circle* of disciples (not to individual persons), a wider scope is thereby given to harmonists ; in no case, however, can they succeed in reconciling the three appearances with the statements of *Paul*, 1 Cor. xv. 5 ff., especially as there εἶτα and ἔπειτα (in opposition to Wieseler) denote *chronological* sequence. The Apostle Paul is charged, on the supposition that his account is to be understood in an internal way, with a great arbitrariness, when it is asserted that the *three* appearances related by John are comprised in εἶτα τοῖς δώδεκα in Paul (Luthardt, Lange). Not even can ὤφθη Κηφᾷ in Paul be reconciled with John. To John, however, must be accorded the preference over the tradition followed by Paul, so far as the latter does not agree with the former.

NOTE.—To the *draught of fishes*, to contest the historical truth of which, in a manner which evinced arbitrariness, and in part even malice, the similarity of the earlier history, Luke v. 2 ff., afforded a welcome opportunity (Strauss, Weisse, Schenkel, and several others), a symbolical destination has, since the most ancient times (Chrysostom and his followers, Cyril, Augustine, and many others), been ascribed, and in general justly, since the word of Jesus, Matt. iv.

---

[1] That the meal passed *generally in entire silence*, as also Hengstenberg suggests, as little appears from the text as that Jesus did not Himself partake of it (Hengstenberg). In favour of a symbolical interpretation of details, a gloomy and monstrous character is given to the incident. But the text breaks off with the distribution of the bread and of the mess of fish, and it says *nothing* of the *progress* of the breakfast.

19, parall., gives, naturally enough, the psychological solution why He, as the Risen One, performs, precisely in *this* fashion, a miraculous work in the presence of His disciples. The tradition in which, from the above word, the draught of fishes, Luke v., took shape (see on Luke v. 1 ff.), has, although pushing backward the later occurrence, nevertheless apprehended with right feeling the idea which it contained. The disciples themselves could not but find in the words of that first call, Matt. *loc. cit.*, the key to the symbolical significance of the miraculous fact, in which that word, which Jesus had spoken at the beginning, was now, on the boundary of their earthly intercourse with Him, and before the restoration (a renewed calling, as it were) of Peter, set forth and sealed as a fact with the highest appropriateness. Only in the interpretation of this symbolism, we have no right to go beyond Matt. iv. 14, and read in it more than the *rich blessing of the apostolical office*, of which the *men fishers* of Jesus were to be the possessors. To go further, and, with Augustine, expound all the individual features of the history allegorically,[1] is groundless and arbitrary, and without any definable limits. Especially unauthorized is an interpretation of the fish meal that refers it to the heavenly supper,[2] " which the Lord prepares for His own with Abraham, Isaac, and Jacob in the kingdom of God,"[3] since that supper of the kingdom does not concern the apostles *as such*, and foreign elements would mix themselves with the reference. The meal of our passage is only an ἄριστον, a breakfast, serving merely as an occasion for the appearance, and for the draught of fishes, as well as for the further scene with Peter. In a manner which serves as a special warning have the allegorical tendencies of the Fathers, in respect of the number of fishes, displayed themselves. Thus, Severus, Ammonius, Theophylact (also τι ἐς in Euth. Zigabenus) see depicted in the 100 fishes the Gentiles, in the 50 the Jews, and in the 3 the Trinity. Jerome, followed by Köstlin[4] and Hilgenfeld, recognizes in the 153 fishes, in spite of the fact that they were *large* ones only, *all genera piscium*, and thereby the *universality* of the apostolic activity,[5] which Ruperti even derives from the text by an arithmetical analysis[6] of the number ; whilst Hengstenberg, on the other hand (after Grotius), finds the key in the 153,600 strangers,[7] making John count a fish for every thousand (with which the surplus of 600 falls away) ! — That John *says nothing* regarding the symbolical purpose of the draught of fishes, is sufficiently explained from the fact that *Jesus Himself* does not expressly declare it, but allows the thing to speak for itself its silent symbolical language, as He also has not Himself interpreted the symbolism of the withered fig-tree (Matt. xxi. 21).

[1] So recently, especially Weitzel in the *Stud. u. Krit.* 1849, p. 618 f., Luthardt, Lange, Hengstenberg.

[2] Even the *Lord's Supper* was found by Augustine to be signified, and he went so far as to say : " *piscis assus Christus est passus.*"

[3] Olshausen, after Augustine.

[4] *Theol. Jahrb.* 185 1, p. 195.

[5] Hilgenfeld in his *Zeitschr.* 1868, p. 446 : " The copious draught . . ., *i.e.*, the *spiritual harvest from the Gentile world*, is now added to the provision of fish and bread already lying ready, I think, for the feeding of the *Jewish* people (comp. John vi. 12)." The

fundamental thought is, he thinks, in x. 16.

[6] Recently *enigmatic numeration* has been attempted in the case of these fishes, so that according to the Hebrew numerical letters 118 + 35 = יונה ן שמיען is = Σίμων 'Ιωνᾶ. See *Theol. Jahrb.* 1854, p. 135 ; on the other hand : Ewald, *Jahrb.* vi. p. 161. Volkmar also (*Mos. Prophetie*, p. 61 f.) gives the enigmatic solution of the number as " *Simeon Bar Jona Kepha.*"—Calvin already correctly observes : " quantum ad piscium numerum spectat, non est sublime aliquod in eo quaerendum mysterium."

[7] 2 Chron. ii. 17.

Vv. 15–17. The *thrice-repeated* question : "ut illi occasionem praeberet, triplicis abnegationis maculam triplici professione eluendi," Wetstein, which Hengstenberg arbitrarily denies. — Σίμων Ἰωάννου] Thrice the same complete mention of the name with a certain *solemnity of deeply-moved affection.* In the use of the name *Simon Joh.* in itself, we are not to recognize—since certainly it is not at all susceptible of proof, that Jesus elsewhere addressed the apostle by the name Peter or Cephas—another and special purpose as in view, either a reminiscence of the lost confidence (de Wette), or of the human condition of the apostolical calling (Luthardt), or a replacement into his natural condition for the purpose of an exaltation to the new dignity (Hengstenberg). The name of Peter is not *refused* to him (Hoelemann). — ἀγαπ.] He does not ask after his *faith ;* for this had not become wavering, but the *love* proceeding from the faith had not been sufficiently strong. [See Note LXVIII. p. 555] — τούτων] ἢ οὗτοι, than these my other disciples. They are still *present ;* comp. on ver. 20. Peter had *given expression,* in his whole behaviour down to his fall, to so pre-eminent a love for Jesus (bear in mind vi. 68, the washing of the feet, the sword-stroke, and xiii. 37), and in virtue of the distinction, of which Jesus had deemed him worthy (i. 43), as well as by his post at the head of the apostles (comp. on Matt. xvi. 18), into which he was not now first introduced (Hengst.), so pre-eminent a love was to be *expected* from him, that there is sufficient occasion for the πλεῖον τούτων without requiring a special reference to Matt. xxvi. 33 (from which, in comparison with John xiii. 37, a conclusion has been drawn adverse to the Johannean authorship). — *Peter in his answer* substitutes for the ἀγαπ. (*diligis*) of the question, the expression of *personal heart emotion,* φιλῶ, *amo* [See Note LXIX. p. 556] (comp. xi. 3, 5, xx. 2), by which he gives the most direct satisfaction to his inmost feeling ; appeals, in so doing, in the consciousness of the want of personal warranty, to the Lord's knowledge of the heart, but leaves the πλεῖον τούτων unanswered, because his fall has made him humble, for which reason Jesus also, in tender forbearance, omits that πλεῖον τούτων in the questions that follow—vivid originality of the narrative, marked by such delicacy of feeling. — βόσκε τὰ ἀρνία μου] Restoration to the previous standing, which the rest of the apostles did not require, therefore containing the primacy of Peter only in so far as it already previously existed ; see on Matt. xvi. 18. — ἀρνία] Expression of tender emotion : *little lambs,* without obliterating the diminutive signification also in Rev. v. 6 ; Isa. xl. 11, Aq. The discourse becomes firmer in ver. 16, where πρόβατα, and again, more emotional, in ver. 17, where προβάτια, *little sheep* (see the critical notes), is found. By all three words, the ἀρχιποίμην [1] means His *believing ones* in general (1 Pet. v. 4), without making a separation between beginners and those who are matured,[2] or even be-

---

[1] To apply the sense of the thrice-uttered behest so differently : duty of individuals ; care for the whole ; bringing in of individuals for the whole (Luthardt),—is a separation of the idea which cannot be proved by the change of the words, and is entirely out of keeping with the mood of emotional feeling. In each of the three expressions lies the *whole* duty of the shepherd. "Quam vocum vim optime se intellexisse Petrus demonstrat, 1 Pet. v. 2," Grotius.

[2] Euth. Zigabenus, Wetstein, Lange, and several others.

tween laity and clergy.[1] Maldonatus aptly remarks : the distinction is *non in re, sed in voce*, where, notwithstanding, he, with other Catholic expositors, erroneously lays emphasis on the fact that precisely to Peter was the *whole* flock entrusted ; the latter shared, in truth, with *all* the apostles, the same office of tending the entire flock. — πάλιν δεύτερον] See on Matt. xxvi. 42. — ποίμαινε] More universal, and more expressive of *carefully ruling* activity in general[2] than βόσκε, in which rather the special reference of *nourishing* protective activity is brought out.[3] The latter, therefore, corresponds to the diminutive designations. — In His third question, ver. 17, Jesus takes up the φιλῶ σε of Peter, and cuts, by means of the thus altered question, still more deeply into his heart. Peter was troubled about this, that Jesus in this third question appeared to throw doubt even upon his φιλεῖν. Hence now his more earnest answer, with an appeal to his Lord's *unlimited knowledge of the heart:* σὺ πάντα οἶδας, κ.τ.λ., which popular and deeply emotional expression is not to be interpreted of absolute omniscience (Baur), but according to the standard of xvi. 30, ii. 25, iv. 19, vi. 64, i. 49 f.

Ver. 18. With the thrice-uttered βόσκε τὰ προβάτιά μου Peter is again installed in his vocation, and with solemn earnestness (ἀμήν, ἀμήν, κ.τ.λ.) Jesus now immediately connects the prediction of *what he will one day have to endure* in this vocation. The prediction is clothed in a *symbolic* form. Comp. Acts xxi. 11. — ὅτε ἦς νεώτερος] than now. Peter, who had been already for a considerable time married (Matt. viii. 14), was at that time of middle age. In the contrast of past youth and coming old age (γηράσῃς) the *present* condition certainly remains without being characterized ; but this, in the vivid delineation of the prophetic picture, must not be pressed. Every expression of prophetic mould is otherwise subject to its "obliquity" (against de Wette). But the objection of the want of a simplicity worthy of Jesus (de Wette) is, considering the entire concrete and illustrative form of the prophecy, perfectly unjust. Note, moreover, that ὅτε ἦς νεώτερος . . . ἤθελες is not designed with the rest for symbolical *interpretation* (as referring perhaps to his self-willedness before his conversation, Euth. Zigabenus, Luthardt, or in the earlier time of youth, Lange ; to the autonomic energy in his calling, Hengst.), but serves only as a plastic preparation for the prediction (ὅταν δὲ γηράσῃς) from which, as a background, the predictive figure stands out more vividly. — ἐκτενεῖς τὰς χεῖρ. σου] Feebly stretching them out to the power of strangers, and therewith surrendering thyself to it. Then will *another* (undefined subject of the hostile power) *gird thee*, i.e. *surround thee with fetters, as with a girdle*, bind thy body around with bonds, *and convey thee away, whither thou wilt not*, namely, to the *place of execution* (comp. Mark xv. 22) ; for with ὅπου οὐ θέλεις : τῆς φύσεως λέγει τὸ συμπαθὲς καὶ τῆς σαρκὸς τὴν ἀνάγκην, καὶ ὅτι ἄκουσα ἀποῤῥήγνυται τοῦ σώματος ἡ ψυχή, Chrysostom. Note further, that as with the three clauses of the first half of the verse there is a complete correspondence formed by means of the

---

[1] Eusebius, Emiss, Bellarmine.
[2] Acts xx. 28 ; 1 Pet. v. 2 ; Rev. ii. 27, vii. 17, and see Dissen, *ad Pind. Ol.* x. 9.
[3] Hom. *Od.* μ. 97, ξ. 102, *et al.* ; comp. βοσκή,

and βόσκημα, *victus*, and the compounds like γηροβοσκεῖν, *et al.;* see also Philo, *deter. insid. pot.* I. p. 197 ; Ellendt, *Lex. Soph.* I. p 312 f.

three clauses of the second, namely (1) by ὅταν δὲ γηρ. ; (2) by ἄλλος σε ζώσει ; and (3) by οἴσει ὅπου οὐ θέλεις, the words ἐκτενεῖς τὰς χεῖράς σου form no independent point, but only serve for the illustration of the second, graphically describing the surrender into the power of the ἄλλος, who will perform the ζώσει (not the *joy* at being bound with fetters, Weitzel).   Erroneously, then, do the Fathers, and most later expositors,[1] make ἐκτεν. τ. χεῖρ. σ. the characteristic point of the prediction, and interpret it of the *stretching out on the transverse beam of the cross.*   In this case unless (with Hengst.) we volatilize ἄλλος σε ζώσει into the mere general idea of passivity, we must refer the ζώσει to the *binding to the cross* before the nailing,[2] or (with Brückner and Ewald) to the girding *with the loin cloth* (which can by no means be historically proved by *Ev. Nicod.* 10).[3]   It is decisive *against* the entire explanation, referring it to the crucifixion, that οἴσει ὅπου οὐ θέλεις, not *before* but *after* the stretching out of the hands and girding,[4] would be wholly incongruous, and we must then understand it of the *bearing* to the cross by the executioner's assistants,[5] in which, however, in spite of this very special interpretation, we again give up the reference of the *stretching out of the hands* to the crucifixion, and leave only the above doubtful binding of the girdle round the loins as a specific mark of crucifixion.   *Others* (so especially Gurlitt and Paulus) have found nothing more than the prediction of the actual *weakness of old age,* and therewith made of the saying so weightily introduced a mere nullity.   Olshausen refers to youth and old age in the *spiritual life;*[6] Peter, that is to say, will in his old age be in manifold ways hindered, persecuted, and compelled against his will to be active here and there, of which experiences his cross is the culminating point.   In a similar manner Tholuck : the apostle is given to understand how he, who had been governed in the earlier period of his life more by self-will, will come more and more under a higher power, and will submit himself at last even with resignation to the martyr-death destined by God.   Comp. Lange, and even Bleek, p. 235 f., who by the ἄλλος actually understands Jesus ; a mistaken view also in Mayerhoff.[7]   All such spiritual allusions fall to the ground in virtue of ver. 19, as also ὅπου οὐ θέλεις is not appropriate to the supposed representation of complete surrender, which should rather have required perhaps ὅπου ἄρτι οὐ θέλεις.   Unsuitable also would be ὅταν γηράσῃς, since in truth that spiritual maturity of the apostle could not first be a subject of expectation in his old age.   Beza is correct : "Christus in genere praedicat Petri mortem *violentam* fore."   Nonnus : Ὀψὲ δὲ γηράσκων τανύσειις

---

[1] Including Tholuck, Maier, de Wette, Brückner, Hilgenfeld, Hengstenberg, Baeumlein.

[2] Tert. *Scorp.* 15.

[3] See Thilo, *ad Cod. Apocr.* I. p. 582 f.

[4] A resource has indeed been sought with Casaubon by referring ἐκτ. τ. χεῖρ. σ. to the circumstance that before the crucifixion took place the cruciarii were carried about " collo furcae inserto et manibus dispessis et ad furcae cornua deligatis," Wetstein. But the *girding,* as it necessarily points to

binding round the body, would be an *inappropriate* figure of the attaching the *hands.* —Logical subtleties cannot succeed in putting right the incongruity above alluded to, although Brückner has made the attempt.

[5] Ewald, comp. Bengel.

[6] Comp. Euth. Zigabenus : to the life of Peter under the law, in which he has acted with self-will, the full maturity of the ἡλικία πνευματική is opposed, in which he will stretch out his hands for crucifixion, etc.

[7] *Petr. Schr.* p. 87.

σέο χεῖρας ἀνάγκῃ· | καί σε περισφίγξουσιν ἀφειδέες ἀνέρες ἄλλοι, | εἰς τινα χῶρον ἀγοντες, ὃν οὐ σέο θυμὸς ἀνώγει. Beyond this we cannot go without arbitrariness. Comp. also Luthardt and Godet.

Ver. 19. A comment, quite of Johannean stamp, on the remarkable utterance. Comp. xviii. 32, also xii. 33. — ποίῳ θανάτῳ] *i.e.* by what *manner* of death, namely, by the death of *martyrdom*, for which Peter, *bound round with fetters*, was conveyed to the *place of execution*. John, who wrote long after the death of Peter, presupposes the details as *well known*, as also Clem. *Cor.* I. 5. Peter was *crucified*, as tradition, from the time of Tertullian,[1] and Origen in Eusebius, credibly relates ; the reader had therefore to take this special element of the ποιότης of the execution from history, as the fulfilment of the less definite word of prophecy, *in addition to*, but not to *derive* it *from*, the words of Christ themselves. — δοξάσει τ. θεόν] For such a death tended to *the glorifying of God*, in whose service he suffered for the revelation of His counsel and for the victory of His work (comp. xvii. 4, 6) ; hence δοξάζειν τ. θεόν became "magnificus martyrii titulus," Grotius.[2] — ἀκολούθει μοι] [See Note LXX. p. 556.] On the *announcement* of the martyrdom which is destined for Peter in his old age, there now follows, after a pause, the *summons* thereto, and that in the significant form : *follow me!* Comp. xiii. 36 ; Matt. x. 38, xvi. 24. This, then, refers, according to the context, to the following of Christ in the like death that He had died, *i.e.* in the *death of martyrdom*, which Peter is to *undergo*. Luther : "give thyself willingly to death." Too special is the interpretation which refers it to the death of the *cross*, since this was not expressly characterized in ver. 18.[3] In opposition to the context (see also ver. 22), others, after Chrysostom and Theophylact, have referred it to the *appointment to be oecumenical bishop*. The reference to the guidance of the church is by no means to be *connected* with that to the death of martyrdom,[4] since ἀκολ. is the opposite of μένειν, ver. 22. *Others* divest the words of all significance : Jesus had something particular to speak of with Peter, and hence summoned him *to go with Him*. So Kuinoel, Paulus, and even Tholuck and Schleiermacher, while Grotius, Bengel, Luthardt, Lange, Hengstenberg, Brückner, Baeumlein, Godet blend together the proper and symbolical meaning.

Vv. 20, 21. From ἀκολουθοῦντα—which here, as belonging to the *narrative*, is, as a matter of course, not to be taken in the significant sense of the ἀκολούθει belonging to the language of Jesus, ver. 19—it results that Jesus, during the preceding conversation with Peter (not now first, as assumed by Luthardt, in accordance with ἀκολούθει μοι, ver. 19, which is to be left purely in its higher sense), has gone away with him a little distance from the disciples. Peter, engaged in walking with Jesus, *turns round*[5] *and sees that John is following them.* — ὃν ἠγάπα ὁ Ἰησοῦς] Not to be connected with ἀκολουθ. ("he knew that Jesus loved his company," Ewald, *loc. cit.*), but comp. xiii.

---

[1] *Scorp.* 15, " Tunc Petrus ab altero cingitur, cum cruci adstringitur," *de praescr.* 35.

[2] See Suicer, *Thes.* I. p. 949. Comp. also Phil. i. 20 ; 1 Pet. iv. 16 ; Acts v. 41.

[3] Against Euth. Zigabenus and many others.

[4] Ewald, *Jahrb.* III. p. 171.

[5] ἐπιστραφείς, comp. Matt. ix. 22.

23. — ὃς καὶ ἀνέπεσεν, κ.τ.λ.] Retrospect of the special circumstance, xiii. 25 ; hence, however, not : who also *lay at table*, etc. (Hengstenberg and others), but : who also *laid* himself *down* (with the head) at the well-known Supper (ἐν τῷ δείπνῳ) *on the breast of Jesus.* 'Ος . . . παραδ. σε is not to be placed *in a parenthesis*, since ver. 21 begins a new sentence. The subjoining of this observation is not intended to state the reason for John, as the confidant of Jesus following Him ; [1] but to prepare the way for the following question of petty jealousy, in which lies the point of the further narrative, while it indicates the consideration which determines Peter to put this question, *whether possibly a destiny of suffering might not in like manner be contemplated for the disciple so pre-eminently beloved and distinguished by Jesus, this* ἐπιστήθιος of the Lord. According to Chrysostom, Theophylact, and Euth. Zigabenus (similarly Olshausen), its purpose is to remind the reader how *far bolder* than at the Last Supper Peter has now become after his restoration. But the subsequent question neither presupposes any special boldness (comp. on ver. 22), nor, considering the peculiar situation of the Last Supper, was a *want* of boldness the reason why Peter did not himself put the question, xiii. 25. The καί after ὃς expresses the relation corresponding to ὃν ἠγάπα.[2] — οὗτος δὲ τί] *sc.* ἔσται.[3] Nonnus : καὶ τί τελέσσει οὗτος ἐμὸς συνάεθλος ; *but what will become of this man* if the result is to be such *for me ?* Will the issue be otherwise with him ? οὐκ ἀκολουθήσει σοι ; οὐ τὴν αὐτὴν ἡμῖν ὁδὸν τοῦ θανάτου βαδιεῖται ; Euth. Zigabenus. The rendering : *but what is this man to do ?* Shall he now be with us (Paulus and several others), a part of the false explanation of ἀκολούθει μοι, ver. 19. On the neut. τί, comp. Acts xii. 18.[4]

Ver. 22. Jesus gives, in virtue of His personal sovereignty over the life and death of His own (comp. Rom. xiv. 9), to the *unwarranted* question, put by Peter, too, not merely out of curiosity, but even from a certain *jealousy* (Chrysostom, Erasmus, Wetstein, and several others conceive : out of particular *love* to John),[5] the answer : that it does not at all concern him, if He have possibly allotted to John a more distant and happier goal, and leads him, who had again so soon turned away his gaze from himself, immediately back to the task of ἀκολούθει μοι imposed upon him, ver. 19. — μένειν] Opposite of the ἀκολουθεῖν, to be fulfilled by the death of martyrdom ; hence : *be preserved in life.*[6] Olshausen (and so substantially even Ewald) arbitrarily adds, after Augustine, the sense : "to tarry in quiet and peaceful life."[7] — ἕως ἔρχομαι] By this Jesus means, as the solemn and absolute

[1] Bengel, Luthardt, Lange, Godet.
[2] Baeumlein, *Partik.* p. 152.
[3] See Buttmann, *Neut. Gr.* p. 338 [E. T. p. 394].
[4] Xen. *Hell.* ii. 3. 17 ; ἔσοιτο ἡ πολιτεία ; Stallbaum, *ad Plat. Rep.* p. 332 E.
[5] Comp. Luthardt : "only loving interest for his comrade," to which, however, the reproving τί πρὸς σέ, ver. 22, does not apply.
[6] Comp. xii. 34 ; Phil. i. 25 ; 1 Cor. xv. 6 ; Kypke, I. p. 415 f.
[7] Comp. Godet, who, strangely enough, finds here an allusion *to the fact* that John

remained at rest in the boat, and with his comrades (except Peter) towed the full net to land, where Jesus was. This allusion again includes the other, that John, in the history of the development of the founding of the church, received "*a calm and collected part.*" And with this Godet finally connects : At the great gospel draught of fishes in the Gentile world, where Peter at the beginning stood foremost," *John was present thereat until the end of the first century, a type of the whole history of the church, and here begins the mystery—perhaps he is associat-*

ἔρχομαι itself renders undoubted, His final historical *Parousia*, which He, according to the apprehension of all evangelists and apostles, has promised will take place even before the passing away of the generation (see note 3 after Matt. xxiv.), not the destruction of Jerusalem, which, moreover, John far outlived (τινὲς in Theophylact, Wetstein, Lange, and several others, including Luthardt, who sees in this destruction the *beginning* of the Parousia, in opposition to the view of the N. T. generally, and to ver. 23); not the world-historical conflict between Christ and Rome, which began under Domitian (Hengstenberg) ; not the removing by a gentle death;[1] not the leading out from Galilee (where John in the meanwhile was to remain) to the scene of apostolic activity (Theophylact) ; not the apocalyptic coming in the visions of John's revelation (Ebrard); not the coming at any place, where John is to *wait* (Paulus) ! See rather xiv. 3 ; 1 John ii. 28, iii. 2. On ἕως ἔρχομαι (as 1 Tim. iv. 13), *as long as until* I come, see Buttmann, *Neut. Gr.* p. 199 [E. T. p. 231]. In σύ μοι ἀκολ., σύ bears the emphasis, in contrast with the other disciples.

Ver. 23. Hence there went forth (comp. Matt. ix. 26), in consequence of this answer of Jesus, the following legend[2] among the brethren (Christians): *that disciple does not die* (but remains in life until the Parousia, whereupon he experiences, not death, but change, 1 Thess. iv. 17 ; 1 Cor. xv. 51, 52). —The legend, which correctly took ἔρχομαι in the solemn sense of *Maranatha* (1 Cor. xvi. 22), would with reason have inferred its οὐκ ἀποθνήσκει from the word of Christ, had the latter run categorically : θέλω αὐτὸν μένειν ἕως ἔρχ. In the manner, however, in which Jesus expressed Himself, a *categorical judgment* was derived from the *conditional* sentence, and consequently the case supposed by Jesus, the occurrence of which is to be left to the decision of experience (ἐάν, not εἰ), was proclaimed as an actually existing relation. This John shows to be an overstepping of the words of Jesus, and hence his observation intimates that, on the ground of that saying, it was at once without reason asserted : this disciple dies not,—that rather the possible occurrence of the case supposed by ἐὰν θέλω must be left over to the experience of the future, without asserting by way of anticipation either the οὐκ ἀποθνήσκει or the opposite. Considering the expected nearness of the Parousia, it is conceivable enough how John himself does not absolutely declare the saying, which was in circulation about him, to be incorrect, and does not contradict it (it *might* in truth be verified through the impending Parousia), but only refers to its conditional character ("leaves it therefore to hang in doubt," Luther), and places it merely in its historical light, with verbally exact repetition of its source. According to others,[3] John would indicate that there is yet *another* coming of Jesus than that which is to take place at the close of history. But this other the expositors

ed with it in an incomprehensible manner until the end of the present economy, until the vessel touches the shore of eternity." Thus, if we depart from the clear and certain sense of the words, we fall into the habit of *phantasy*, so that we no longer *expound*, but invent and *create*.

[1] Olshausen, Lange, Ewald, after the older expositors, as Ruperti, Clarius, Zeger, Grotius, and several others.

[2] Which therefore did not originate from the Apocalypse (Baur, Hilgenfeld).

[3] See especially Heumann, B. Crusius, Hengstenberg.

have here invented, see on ver. 22.—After the death of the apostle, the legend was further expanded, to the effect that he slumbered in the grave, and by his breath moved the earth.[1]

Ver. 24. *Conclusion by John* to this his supplement, vv. 1–23, which he makes known as his work, and the contents of which he maintains to be *true.* To his *book* he had given the conclusion, xx. 31 ; all the less should the apostolic legitimation be wanting to the *appendix* added by him at a later time. — περὶ τούτων and ταῦτα refer to the supplementary narrative in vv. 1–23. — Observe the change of participles, *pres.* μαρτυρῶν (for his *witness, i.e.* his eye- and ear-witness, still continued a living one in an oral form) and *aor.* γράψας.[2]— οἴδαμεν] Not οἶδα μέν ;[3] but John, as he has avoided throughout in the Gospel, in accordance with his delicate peculiarity, the self-designation by *I,* here speaks *out of the consciousness of fellowship with his readers at that time,* none of whom the aged apostle justly presupposed would doubt the truth of his testimony. With this *good apostolical confidence* he utters his οἴδαμεν. He *might* have written, as in xix. 35, οἶδεν (Beza so conjectured). But his book up to this appendix, chap. xxi., had belonged in truth already for a considerable time to the narrower circle of his first readers ; they could not therefore but know from it how truly he had testified concerning all that he had written ; all the more could he now, when by way of supplement he further added the appendix, conceive what was to be said concerning the truth of the contents in the above form of fellowship, and as he *conceived* it, so he *says* it ; as he is in so doing certain of the concurrence of his readers (comp. 3 John 12) with his own consciousness, so he *writes* it. According to this, no satisfactory reason is apparent for recognizing in οἴδαμεν a composer *different* from the γράψας (Bleek, Baeumlein), and conceiving of *the Ephesian presbyters or friends of the apostle* as the subject, whether the chapter be now ascribed to them (or to an individual among them),[4] or only vv. 24, 25,[5] or again merely ver. 24, ver. 25 being rejected (Tischendorf).

Ver. 25. *Apocryphal conclusion* to the entire Gospel (see the critical notes) after the Johannean appendix, vv. 1–24, had been added. — ὅσα] ἅ, which Lachmann, Tischendorf, after B. C.* X. ℵ. Or. read, would give the relative limitation simply as to *matter (quae* fecit) ; but ὅσα gives it *quantitatively (quotquot* fecit), as, frequently also in the classics, ὅσος follows after πολύς. The ἐποίησεν (without σημεῖα, xx. 31) designates the working of Jesus in its entire universality, but as that which took place on *earth,* not also the *Logos* activity from the beginning of the world, as, in spite of the name ὁ Ἰησοῦς, comp. xx. 30, Hoelemann, p. 79 ff., assumes, who sees in ver. 25 the completion of the symmetry of the gospel in keeping with the prologue. The

---

[1] See *Introd.* § 1, and generally Ittig, *sel. capita hist. eccl.* sec. I. p. 441 ff.

[2] Note also how the witness is *identical* with the γράψας, so that John himself expressly announces himself as the composer of the appendix, and consequently also of the whole Gospel, with which the assumption that the Gospel proceeds from the apostle *through a second hand,* stands in contradiction.

[3] Chrysostom, Theophylact.

[4] Grotius, Lücke, Ewald, Bleek, and others.

[5] Tholuck, Luthardt, Godet, and others.

[6] Hom. *Il.* xxii. 380 ; Xen. *Hell.* iii. 4. 3.

pre-human activity of the Logos might be an object of speculation, as i. 1 ff., but not the subject of histories, written in detail (καθ' ἕν) : not the theme of a Gospel. Hence the composer of ver. 25, moreover, has throughout indicated nothing which points back further than to the activity of the Incarnate One,[1] and not even has he written ὁ Χριστός, or ὁ κύριος, or ὁ υἱὸς τοῦ Θεοῦ, but ὁ Ἰησοῦς. — ἅτινα] quippe quae, utpote quae. The relative is likewise qualitative,[2] namely, in respect of the great multitude ; hence not the simple ἅ. — καθ' ἕν] one by one, point by point.[3] — οὐδὲ αὐτὸν τ. κόσμ.] ne ipsum quidem mundum, much less a space in it. — οἶμαι] Placed in John's mouth by the composer of the concluding verse. — χωρῆσαι] to contain (comp. ii. 6 ; Mark ii. 2). The infin. aor. after οἶμαι without ἄν, a pure Greek idiom,[4] expresses what is believed with certainty and decision.[5] — τὰ γραφόμενα] the books, which, if the supposed case occurs, are being written. The world is too small, then thinks the writer, to include these books within it, not, as Luthardt suggests, to embrace the fulness of such testimonies, to which he inaptly (since in sooth it is books that are spoken of) adds : "for only an absolute external circumference is in keeping with the absolute contents of the Person and of the life of Christ." Hengstenberg also applies the expression of external dimension to the "internal overflowing greatness ;" comp. Godet ; the object of the history is greater than the world, etc. ; Ebrard extraordinarily : there would be for the books no room in literature. In opposition to the context, Jerome, Augustine, Ruperti (who says : the world is "et ad quaerendum fastidiosus et ad intelligendum obtusus"), Calovius, Bengel, and several others have explained it of the capacitas non loci, sed intellectus (comp. on Matt. xix. 11). — Not only is the absurd and tasteless exaggeration in ver. 25 un-Johannean (unsuccessfully defended by Weitzel,[6] and softened down by Ewald, with a reference also to Coh. xii. 12), bearing the Apocryphal stamp,[7] but also the periodic mode of expression, so at variance with the Johannean simplicity, as well as the first person (οἶμαι), in which John in the Gospel never speaks ; moreover, nowhere else does he use οἴεσθαι, which, however, is also found only once in Paul (Phil. i. 17). The variations are (see the critical notes) of no importance for a critical judgment.

NOTES BY AMERICAN EDITOR.

LXVIII. "He does not ask after his faith." Ver. 15.

The distinction here made seems unfounded. Both the faith and love of Peter had been in temporary abeyance. Both the Lord knew to be equally genuine and deep ; both had alike faltered under the ordeal. He naturally

---

[1] For that καθ' ἕν should point back to i. 3, and τὸν κόσμον to i. 10, is without any internal justification, and could be discovered by no reader.

[2] Kühner, II. § 781, 4, 5, and ad Xen. Mem. ii. 1. 30.

[3] Bernhardy, p. 240 ; Ast, Lex. Plat. I. p. 939 f.

[4] Lobeck, ad Phryn. p. 751 ff.

[5] See Bernhardy, p. 383, and on the distinction of the infin. pres. (Pflugk, ad Eur Hec. 283) and future, Kühner, II. p. 80 f.

[6] Loc. cit. p 632 ff.

[7] Comp. similar hyperboles in Fabricius, ad Cod. Apocr. I. p. 321 f., and Wetstein in loc.

expresses the quality which is the deepest element and essential mainspring of
the character, and in which it properly expresses itself.   Faith is but a special
modification of the vital, all-controlling quality of love.

LXIX. " *Lovest thou me ?*"   Ver. 15.

Whether the ordinary distinction between ἀγαπᾶν and φιλεῖν is observed in
these questions and answers has been matter of much doubt.   According to
their usual classical distinction, the Lord in the first two questions asks Peter
not so much after his personal affection as after that love of *moral choice* which
affects less immediately his relations toward Himself than his fitness for his
apostolic work.   Peter replies in each case by the assertion of that *personal affection* which had been apparently most immediately involved in his denial :
in this he had turned his back directly on the person.   In the third question
Jesus changes the verb, and as if satisfied of his love of moral choice, lets the
interrogation turn on his personal attachment.   It scarcely seems that the
change in verbs can have been without a purpose.   The Lord means, I think,
to draw from Peter his assurance of his love under both its forms ; while Peter,
feeling that each form of affection virtually includes the other, chooses in his
reply, and adheres to, the term which expresses most fully that consciousness
of personal love to which his denial had done so gross wrong, and to which
his ardent nature cannot refrain from giving utterance.

LXX. " *Follow me.*"   Ver. 19.

Weiss dissents from Meyer in his interpretation of this " follow me," by referring it, as he conceives according to the demands of the context, to a literal
temporary following of Jesus as He steps aside from the group of the apostles.
This would seem, indeed, at first view indicated by the immediately following
ἀκολουθοῦντα (ver. 20) of John, which *must* be so taken, and which seems at first
to be a mere echo of the preceding ἀκολούθει addressed to Peter.   Yet this influence is more than counterbalanced by the emphatically recurring σύ μοι ἀκολούθει (ver. 22), which *must* in the connection be taken in the deeper moral sense
of following Jesus in His life and to and in His death.   But this seems very certainly a repetition and echo of the first ἀκολούθει, and cannot be taken in a different sense.   If the one is clear, so is the other.   Both manifestly refer to a figurative and moral following.   The occurrence of the ἀκολουθοῦντα applied to
John (ver. 20) is accidental, and without reference to the ἀκολουθεῖν and
μένειν of the next verse.   It would seem, indeed, that Jesus accompanied His
injunction to Peter with a physical movement, stepping a little aside from the
company, which after the Oriental style may have had a symbolical significance (as the *scourge* of John ii. 15 ; the *binding*, Acts xxi. 11.)

The "follow me" thus interpreted has peculiar significance, and even dramatic force and beauty.   Some two or three years earlier, by this very sea,
quite possibly near this very spot, the Lord had addressed to Peter words of
the same import (δεῦτε ὀπίσω μου, *come after me*), which Peter and his companions unhesitatingly obeyed.   That now, after the experiences of these wonderful intervening years, he should again, after a like miracle (Luke v. 4–8), such
as had then resulted in their following Him (ἠκολούθησαν αὐτῷ, ver. 12), and after
this triple test of questioning, and the prophetic announcement of the tragic

issue of his discipleship — that now, when Peter could to much better judge (though still but inadequately) what the following involved, the Lord should solemnly and finally, in the very spot where the disciple had made his first surrender and consecration, lay upon him the command to follow him—seems singularly appropriate, and an eminently fitting close of the Lord's and the disciple's earthly companionship.